D1470125

The Bristol and Gloucestershire Archaeological Society
Gloucestershire Record Series

Hon. General Editor
Dr J D Hodsdon FSA

Volume 34

Managing Poverty: Cheltenham Settlement Examinations and Removal Orders
1831–52

MANAGING POVERTY:
CHELTENHAM SETTLEMENT EXAMINATIONS AND REMOVAL ORDERS, 1831–52

Edited by John Simpson

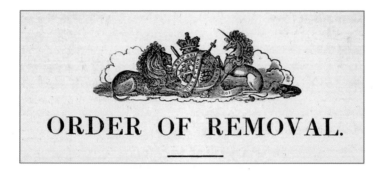

The Bristol and Gloucestershire Archaeological Society

2020

The Bristol and Gloucestershire Archaeological Society
Gloucestershire Record Series

© The Bristol and Gloucestershire Archaeological Society 2020

ISBN 978-0-900197-99-4

British Library Cataloguing in Publication Data
A catalogue entry for this book is available from the British Library

Produced for the Society
by 4word Ltd, Bristol
Printed in Great Britain

CONTENTS

d. The gender and age of examinants
e. Former occupations of paupers
f. Levels of literacy
g. Family structures

ILLUSTRATIONS, FIGURES AND TABLES

Illustrations

Figures

Tables

ACKNOWLEDGEMENTS

The first acknowledgement should go to Irvine Gray (1903–92), then Gloucestershire's County Archivist, whose edition of the Cheltenham Settlement Examinations from 1815 to 1826 was published as long ago as 1969, by the then Records Section of the Bristol and Gloucestershire Archaeological Society. That production – a slim octavo volume of 137 pages – was the Society's first foray into publishing stand-alone editions of record holdings other than parish records, breaking new ground and, as intended, bringing to wider notice the wealth of untapped material in the Gloucestershire Archives. Gray's edition, while much consulted by local historians, left unexplored the several registers covering the 1830s and 40s. These were decades when Cheltenham, arguably passing its prime as a spa venue, was much affected by national economic factors, and having to manage their societal consequences – poverty, misfortune and displacement. Here was a story waiting to be documented and told.

I am very grateful, therefore, to Dr James Hodsdon, General Editor of this series, for inviting me to consider editing the documents, in order to make them more easily available to a growing audience of researchers fascinated by local and social history. After some preliminary investigations, we agreed that the edition should consist of a full transcription of the material (except for standard introductory or pro-forma text), and that it should also include short commentaries on the lives of the individual paupers examined. I am also grateful to the Society for allowing me a small research grant to obtain birth, marriage, and death certificates for around 50 people, to supplement evidence from other sources. In addition, I have discussed the Cheltenham project at various stages with Keith Snell, Professor of Rural and Cultural History at the University of Leicester and doyen of English settlement studies, who was kind enough to encourage the venture and to comment on the final text.

The Gloucestershire Archives are owed a debt of thanks for allowing me to publish this material and to reproduce short sections here as illustrations. The Archive staff have been unfailingly courteous and timely in making the settlement examinations and other related documents available to me whenever I needed them. I am particularly grateful to Ann Attwood, Collections Care Development Officer at the Archives, for providing a detailed bibliographical description of the various register volumes.

I am grateful to The Cheltenham Trust and Cheltenham Borough Council for kindly allowing me to reproduce two images from their collection, and to

Cheltenham Borough Council, the Gloucestershire Archives, and Cheltenham Local History Society for jointly permitting me to reproduce part of the Cheltenham Old Town Survey of 1855-7. I should also like to thank Nick Chivers and Knight Frank for allowing me to reproduce a map of Cheltenham house prices in 2016, created by the Residential Research team based at their London offices.

Many other people have listened to me talking about the settlement registers, with varying degrees of interest: in particular, I have learnt much from Dr Steven Blake, long-time Cheltenham historian and former Curator of the Wilson, who has also supplied illustrative material for the volume. The staff of the Cheltenham Local and Family History Library, and in particular Christopher Rainey and Rebecca Sillence, have been unfailingly generous to me of their expertise. I should apologise in advance, as there will be times when I have occasionally and inadvertently followed the wrong trail in the genealogical research involved in compiling the commentaries in this volume: I have tried to triangulate evidence, but there will be times when this technique has failed and for this I take responsibility. Finally, I would like to thank the members of the Pittville History Works group for their support and encouragement over the five years or so over which the transcription and research for this volume were conducted.

John Simpson

Cheltenham

1 June 2020

ABBREVIATIONS; MONETARY UNITS

Standard abbreviations have been used for counties, days of the week and months of the year. Initials are used in commentaries for the name of examinants. 1Q, etc: the first (or subsequent) quarter of the year. Otherwise, abbreviations have been kept to a minimum in editorial text.

See Bibliography (p. xii) for a list and description of Gloucestershire Archive manuscript reference numbers cited.

Pre-decimal currency referred to in the text includes the following:

	Pre-decimal value	*Decimal equivalent*
sixpence	six pennies: 6*d*	2½ *p*
shilling	twelve pennies: 1*s* or 1/-	5 *p*
half-(a-)crown	two shillings and sixpence: 2*s* 6*d* or 2/6	12½ *p*
crown	five shillings: 5*s* or 5/-	25*p*
sovereign (sov)	one pound; 20 shillings: £1	£1
guinea (gn)	one pound and one shilling;	£1 5*p*
	21 shillings: £1 1s	

SELECT BIBLIOGRAPHY

Manuscript records in Gloucestershire Archives
PS/CH/RA2/1: Register of settlement examinations, Cheltenham Petty Sessions area. 1815–1826
PS/CH/RA2/2: Register of settlement examinations, Cheltenham Petty Sessions area. 1832–1840
PS/CH/RA2/3: Register of settlement examinations, Cheltenham parish. 1831–1837
PS/CH/RA2/4: Register of removal orders (incorporating examinations), Cheltenham parish. 1835–1838
PS/CH/RA2/5: Register of settlement examinations, Cheltenham parish. 1838–1843
PS/CH/RA2/6: Register of removal orders and examinations, Cheltenham parish. 1841–1843
PS/CH/RA2/7: Register of examinations, Cheltenham parish. 1843–1848
PS/CH/RA2/8: Register of examinations and removal orders, Cheltenham parish. 1846–1852

D4178/1: Cheltenham parish overseers' accounts, 1830–48
P78/1/OV/2/4: Overseers' accounts, arranged under separate headings (eg "Permanent" and "Occasional Relief", "Removals" etc), with index, 1829–35
P78/1/OV/2/7–19: Six-monthly statements of the numbers and names of paupers receiving indoor or outdoor relief, with number of days relief given, and the reasons, 1849–64
P78/1/OV/3/5: Miscellaneous settlement records: Disputed cases, 1720–1845
G/CH/9d/1 Cheltenham Poor Law Union – Non-settled Poor Ledger, 1845–48
G/CH/60/1–10: Cheltenham Workhouse: Admission & Discharge Books, 1835–55

Manuscript records and databases consulted online
Ancestry: www.ancestry.co.uk (subscription)
British Newspaper Archive: www.britishnewspaperarchive.co.uk (subscription)
FamilySearch: www.familysearch.org
Find My Past: www.findmypast.co.uk (subscription)
FreeBMD: www.freebmd.org.uk
FreeREG: www.freereg.org.uk
Justis: www.justis.com (subscription)
National Census of England and Wales: (National Archives) HO107 (1841, 1851), RG9 (1861), RG10 (1871), RG11 (1881), RG12 (1891) (Ancestry, Find My Past)

Printed books and articles
Adams, William Edwin, *Memoirs of a Social Atom,* 2 v. (London, 1903)
Apfel, William and Dunkley, Peter, 'English rural society and the New Poor Law: Bedfordshire, 1834–47', *Social History* 10:1 (1985), pp. 37–68.
Archbold, John Frederick, *The Poor Law, comprising the Whole of the Law of Settlement, and all the Authorities upon the Subject of the Poor Law generally, brought down to Hilary Term, 1856, with Forms* (London, ed. 8, 1856)
Davies, Henry, *A View of Cheltenham in its Past and Present State : being the Fourth Edition of the Stranger's Guide* (Cheltenham, ed. 4, [1843])
[Davies, Henry], *The Visitor's Hand Book for Cheltenham* (Cheltenham, 1840)

Dunkley, Peter, 'Whig and Paupers', *Journal of British Studies*, 20:2 (Spring, 1981), pp. 124–49

Goding, John, *Norman's History of Cheltenham* (London and Cheltenham, rev. ed., 1863)

Gray, Irvine (ed.), *Cheltenham Settlement Examinations, 1815–1826* (Bristol and Gloucestershire Archaeological Society, Records Section, v. 7, 1969)

Hart, Gwen, *A History of Cheltenham* (Leicester, 1965)

Hodsdon, James, *An Historical Gazetteer of Cheltenham* (Bristol and Gloucestershire Archaeological Society, Gloucestershire Record Series 9, 1997)

Jones, Anthea, *Cheltenham: a New History* (Lancaster, 2010)

King, S., 'It is impossible for our vestry to judge his case into perfection from here': managing the distance dimensions of poor relief, 1800–40', *Rural History*, 16:2 (2005), pp. 161–189

Lumley, William Golden, *The General Orders issued by the Poor Law Commissioners in 1841, 1842, and since the Passing of the 7 & 8 Vict. c. 101* [Poor Law Amendment Act 1843] (London, 1845)

Powell, John, *Hard Times in Herefordshire: the Effects of the Workhouse and the New Poor Law* (Almeley, 2008)

Pye, Henry James, *Summary of the Duties of a Justice of the Peace Out of Sessions* (London, ed. 4, 1827)

Rose, Lionel, *'Rogues and Vagabonds': Vagrant Underlife in Britain 1815–1985* (Routledge & Kegan Paul, 1988)

Rowe, George, *Illustrated Cheltenham Guide* (Cheltenham, [1845])

Seal, Christine, *Poor Relief and Welfare: a comparative study of the Belper and Cheltenham Poor Law Unions, 1780 to 1914* (University of Leicester, doctoral thesis [https://lra.le.ac.uk/bitstream/2381/8331/1/2009sealcvphd.pdf]: 2009)

Smith, Leonard, *Cure, Comfort and Safe Custody* (London and New York, 1999)

Snell, K. D. M., *Annals of the Labouring Poor: Social Change and Agrarian England, 1660–1900* (Cambridge, 1985)

Snell, K. D. M., *Parish and Belonging: Community, Identity and Welfare in England and Wales, 1700–1950* (Cambridge, 2006)

Sutton, Alan (ed.), *The Complete Diary of a Cotswold Parson: the diaries of the Revd. Francis Edward Witts, 1783–1854: in 10 volumes* (Stroud, 2008–18)

Tate, William Edward, *The Parish Chest: a Study of the Records of Parochial Administration in England* (Cambridge, 1946)

Taylor, J. S., *Poverty, Migration, and Settlement in the Industrial Revolution: Sojourners' Narratives* (Palo Alto, Calif., 1989)

Official reports

Census of England & Wales for the Year 1861: General Report (London, 1863)

Census of Great Britain, 1851: Population Tables: I. Numbers of Inhabitants: Report, and Summary Tables (London, 1852)

Edward Cresy, *Report to the General Board of Health on a Preliminary Inquiry into the Sewerage, Drainage, and Supply of Water, and the Sanitary Condition of the Inhabitants of the Town of Cheltenham, in the County of Gloucester* (London, 1849)

Eighth Annual Report of the Poor Law Commissioners with Appendices (London, 1842)

Report from the Select Committee on the Poor Laws (London, 1817)

Thirteenth Annual Report of the Poor Law Commissioners with Appendices (London, 1847)

CHELTENHAM SETTLEMENT EXAMINATIONS AND REMOVAL ORDERS 1831–52

1. BACKGROUND AND SCOPE

The rapid growth of Cheltenham as a favoured resort for the well-to-do in the late eighteenth and early nineteenth centuries brought great changes to the town. What had been a modest market town for much of its early history suddenly had to re-imagine itself. The population of Cheltenham parish increased by over 170% between 1801 and 1811, and although the pace of population growth reduced gradually over the following three decades as the boom started to fade, by 1841 it was still ranked thirtieth of the 74 principal cities and towns in England and Wales, when ranked by population size.[1]

Cheltenham's boom brought many people of substantial means to the town, either as permanent residents or as seasonal or short-stay visitors. The town became a destination of choice not just for residents from elsewhere in Britain, attracted by its reputation for health, elegant society, and refined entertainment, but also for many returning to Britain flushed by the benefits of military, administrative, and mercantile careers abroad. The town increasingly boasted grand Regency architecture and, in due course, schools which educated the Empire's children.

But there is always an underside to any period of rapid change. As the town grew, it needed a constant influx of people to service its newfound growth: domestic servants, builders and other craftspeople, wheel-chairmen, laundresses, apprentices, and others. Without a solid local industrial base, these service industries were subject to seasonal variations in demand, boom-and-bust, any slowdown in economic growth. Many people, often from agricultural areas where work was hard and scarce, and pay was low, saw the opportunities that seemed to present themselves in towns like Cheltenham, and decided to follow the growing trend away from rural life into the towns.

This volume looks at the experience of some 1,400 people and their dependants (around 3,530 people in all) who came to Cheltenham over a 20-year period from the early 1830s, in search of work, opportunity, or just survival, and who found themselves subject to a settlement examination. They were not the wealthy fallen on hard times, but people, for the most part, who started with little and for whom life got worse. Each one of them reached a crisis of their life in Cheltenham, when as paupers they had to beg for parish relief, often at a time when the parish

---

[1] Source: *Abstracts of the Answers and Returns: Enumeration. Part II England and Wales* in *British Parliamentary Papers* (1843) XXII. (CP 496) vol. 1. The parish of Cheltenham's population size rose by 921% between 1801 (3,076) and 1841 (31,411), the second-largest increase of the 74 chief cities and towns listed in the Government report.

authorities, the local community, and the government, were unsympathetic to their plight. In the late eighteenth and early nineteenth century, as Gwen Hart notes, Cheltenham "waged a constant war against the numerous poor who came into the town from other places and tried to acquire a settlement and so qualify for Poor Law benefits from the Cheltenham rates".[2]

The process described in these settlement examinations reveals the parish authorities deciding, in the light of the existing Poor Laws, whether they were required to help these paupers in need, or whether they could remove them from Cheltenham to their legal parish of settlement. Settlement examinations were highly likely to result in the removal of a pauper and his or her dependants from the parish, but it is also instructive to discover from associated records that many of them returned to Cheltenham after their removal, either no longer in need of parish relief, or supported in Cheltenham by their home parish, or once again to find themselves before the magistrates to be removed yet again. The individual stories of these paupers' lives, and the statistics extracted from their examinations and associated research, paint a broad picture of the lives of the paupers and of the social contract maintained between the authorities and the poor in Cheltenham at the time.

2. A SURVEY OF EDITORIAL METHODOLOGIES

Irvine Gray's *Cheltenham Settlement Examinations 1815–1826*, published in 1969 as part of the Record Series of the Bristol and Gloucestershire Archaeological Society, was a pioneering work of its day. Gray was responding to an earlier call by Sir Frank Stenton to historians of the British Records Society to make settlement examinations and similar records more readily available. Gray, then Gloucestershire's County Archivist, quoted William Tate's *Parish Chest* to the effect that such records provided what were "virtually autobiographies of persons in a class of which other biographical records are rarely found", and this has indeed proved to be the case.[3]

Cheltenham is fortunate, and unusual, in that the settlement examinations and removal orders relating to the early nineteenth century produced by the Office of the Clerk to the Magistrates are preserved in the Gloucestershire Archives in Gloucester in a set of eight folio registers, dating from 1815 to 1852. Elsewhere, most records of this type from the period are often preserved haphazardly as individual, unbound sheets.

These records shed much light on both the procedures adopted by the parochial administration in handling pauper cases, but they also illuminate the lives of a

---

[2] Hart, p. 279.
[3] Tate, p. 201.

subset of the people who received parish relief. Settlement records address only a subset of the pauper population, because they do not relate to the broad spectrum of the poor receiving parish relief within or outside a workhouse, but specifically to those paupers whom the local Overseers of the Poor regarded as likely to "belong" to other parishes, both inside and beyond Gloucestershire, to which they might be removed by due process, which would in turn potentially reduce the amount of poor rate to which the citizens of Cheltenham were subject.[4] Their experiences therefore additionally offer researchers considerable insights into the movement of the poor between parishes.

Since Gray's time, many more records have become publicly available, most recently online. Historical researchers, often particularly interested in the broad sweep of history, have been joined by family historians focusing on specific families, typically able to devote considerable time to uncovering detailed information about their forebears. The emergence of online genealogical databases, such as those of Ancestry and Find My Past, and databases of historical newspapers, including the *British Library Newspapers, Parts I and II: 1800–1900*, and the *British Newspaper Archive*, have revolutionised access to material that was previously hidden behind indexes and calendars and in library stacks, often involving lengthy journeys around the country on missions to County Record Offices, which often proved fruitless.

This volume provides transcripts of the manuscript text held in six of the eight comprehensive settlement and removal registers relating to Cheltenham held in the Gloucestershire County Archives.[5] Irvine Gray's volume published abstracts of all entries in the first register, with its settlement examinations from 1815 until 1826: these examinations related both to paupers who were, at the time of their examination, resident either in Cheltenham Parish or in any of the other parishes under the jurisdiction of the Cheltenham Petty Sessions, "then comprising the Hundreds of Cheltenham and Cleeve, plus the parish of Prestbury" (and so included paupers resident in Cheltenham, Charlton Kings, Leckhampton, and numerous other local parishes).[6] Cross-references to Gray's volume are given here, when the pauper's life and misfortunes span both sets of examinations. The second register contains records relating to the Petty Sessions area excluding Cheltenham, principally from 1832 until 1840, and so is not included in this collection.

The six volumes included here consist of three registers containing settlement examinations, and three containing the removal orders which might be prepared as a result of settlement examinations. All six registers relate specifically to

---

[4] As early as 1601, the Poor Relief Act (43 Eliz. c. 2, s.12) permitted Justices of the Peace to "rate every Parish to a weekly Sum" towards a Poor rate.
[5] Gloucestershire Archives (GA): PS/CH/RA/3-8.
[6] Gray, p. xviii.

Cheltenham Parish. The three settlement registers contained the "office" or "draft copy" of each examination, written up by one of the magistrates' clerks. The other three volumes contain removal orders. If a pauper was adjudged by the magistrates to be settled outside Cheltenham Parish, then a removal order would be drawn up in duplicate, on printed pro-formas. One copy would be retained by the Clerk to the Magistrates, and bound into a removal order register, and another would be delivered with the pauper to the Overseers and Churchwardens of the parish to which the pauper was removed. Until 1848, the removal orders included a copy of the settlement examination. After this date, and as a result of a provision of the County Law Procedure Act (11 & 12 Vict. c.31: enacted 22 July), these examinations were no longer included as part of removal orders (a fuller description of the registers can be found in section 9), as they were increasingly found to provide matter for trivial dispute between parishes over responsibility for a particular pauper. The 1,405 documents in this edition include 900 settlement examinations and 505 removal orders (many of which contain the related settlement examinations).

Editions of settlement records published since Gray's volume fall generally into three categories: indexes, abstracts, and transcriptions (some of which are now available online).[7] Although indexes and abstracts are very helpful to researchers as an initial point of entry to the records, they serve only limited purposes. It is often necessary to consult the original documentation to reverify the information and to extract further details. Because of the fragility of many of these records, record offices increasingly prefer researchers to consult secondary versions unless there is an absolute necessity to consult original documentation. Full transcriptions do not entirely remove the need to consult original works, of course, but they can significantly reduce the necessity to do this.

In addition, indexes and abstracts cannot convey the nuances of statement and interpretation that a full transcription allows. These settlement examinations ostensibly present the evidence given by paupers, but in every case the evidence is filtered by the Magistrates' Office to ensure that the documents are legally

---

[7] Examples include: (abstracts) *Settlement examinations 1728–1830 Rochford, Essex: (preserved at the Southend-on-Sea Branch of Essex Record Office)*: abstracted & edited by Jack H. Baxter (Benfleet: Essex Society for Family History (Essex settlement series; 1): 1985) and *St Botolph Aldgate 1742–1868 (including St Botolph Aldgate Within & St Botolph Aldgate Without)*: abstracted and indexed by Cliff Webb (West Surrey Family History Society: City of London settlement examinations; v. 1): 2007; (indexes) *Mitcham, Surrey: indexes to settlement examinations 1737-1772 (SRO ref. LA5/5): (and) 1814–1825 (SRO ref. LA5/5/56)* [microform]. East Surrey Family History Society. (Cheam: East Surrey Family History Society, 1: 1987) and *A Complete index of settlement certificates and examinations in Mansfield, 1726–1842: including a register of settlement certificates taken in and given out from the parish chest of St Peter and St Pauls Church Mansfield* (Mansfield: Mansfield and District Family History Society, 1994); (transcriptions) *Marlborough records. Volume 3 Marlborough Poor Law Union: settlement examinations and removals*: transcribed and edited by Jean Cole (Devizes: Wiltshire Family History Society, 2005) and *St Martin in the Fields Settlement Examinations, 1725-93* (http://www.londonlives.org/static/SMDSSET.jsp).

watertight and unlikely to be disputed by the receiving parish. Their tone is a mixture of simple reported statement and official legalese: a pauper would not have stated, for example, that "he believes his father is legally settled his said father having formerly rented a house at Deptford aforesaid" or that she had "not gained a Settlement by servitude or otherwise in her own right", though the information would have derived from statements made by them to the magistrates.[8] Minute differences of terminology between examinations reveal aspects of a case that would be obscured by abstracting or indexing alone. For more information on the editorial conventions adopted in this volume, see section 10.

The modern benefit system is centrally administered, and is not explicitly activated by "destitution", but it is frequently enlightening to investigate the similarities and differences between the early Victorian system and the system in operation today, especially in relation to the treatment of migrant workers (now typically from abroad rather than from neighbouring parishes) and asylum-seekers, and the implementation of a "universal" benefit, minimum wage, and housing and hardship allowances. The EU Settlement scheme, proposed in 2019, allows foreign nationals to remain living in Britain if they can demonstrate five years' residency, mirroring the Poor Removal Act (9 & 10 Vict. c. 66) of 1846, which offered incomers to a parish immunity from removal if they could demonstrate five years' residency within the parish. Regular changes to the modern benefit system show that it too addresses a constantly changing status quo, and so requires budgetary amendments as often as did the Victorian system, and is also frequently subject to appeals and claims of injustice.

3. THE POOR LAWS: HISTORICAL AND LOCAL CONTEXTS

A. AN OUTLINE TIMELINE FOR THE POOR LAWS

It had been necessary for the national government to intervene actively in the management of the country's poor since the dissolution of the monasteries in the 1530s, with the disappearance of many of the religious foundations which had previously provided a large measure of informal poor relief. The first concerted legislation to manage the poor dates from this era.

The earliest national Poor Laws, such as the Poor Relief Act of 1601 (43 Eliz. c.2), were at pains to point out that care for the poor was not, first and foremost, a national or a parochial responsibility, but a family duty. It was found, however, that families, often hard-pressed themselves, often did not take up their responsibility, or that individual paupers had no family to whom they could turn. In the light of this, Parliament increasingly found it necessary to legislate for the

---

[8] William Davis, wife Eliza and daughter Eliza (**31058SE:** Apr 1831); Martha Wood (**33009SE:** 7 Feb 1833).

provision of the poor, and this relief was typically centred around the parish, and by the early nineteenth century particularly the local magistracy, vestry, and overseers.

The laws of settlement and removal, whereby paupers would be relieved by their town or village of last legal settlement, and could be summarily removed there from another parish, took some years to evolve: the concept was enshrined in the Poor Relief Act of 1662 (14 Cha. 2 c.12), and the criteria conferring settlement were subject to extensive revision from that point onwards. Perhaps most significantly, the Poor Removal Act of 1795 (35 Geo. 3 c.101) stated that paupers could only be removed from one parish to another if they became an actual "charge" on the parish, by receiving relief. Previously, paupers could also be dispatched elsewhere if they were only "likely" to become chargeable.

In the south of England, this last change (which theoretically gave the unsettled poor more stability) dates from much the same time as a local system for addressing low agricultural wages, known as the "Speenhamland system", named after a village in Berkshire where it was first introduced.[9] The Speenhamland system allowed parish authorities to supplement low agricultural wages, and was another measure which attempted to promote stability amongst the working population. But such measures were unpopular with rate-payers, who had to foot the bill through the poor rate, and the Poor Law was furthermore increasingly seen as driving a wedge between those with (subsidised) work and the resultant dispossessed poor.

By the early nineteenth century, there were new pressures on parochial authorities, from extensive migration, poor housing and sanitation, and hence disease. Soldiers returning from the Napoleonic wars in the Spanish Peninsula and northern Europe, without work and often with no settled home, joined fortune-hunters, rogues, the destitute, and others making their way to larger towns and cities, and the opportunities they presented.[10] From the 1820s thousands of Scots and especially Irish came into England, dispossessed by famine or clearances in their own countries. Cholera struck Britain in the first of a series of waves in 1832, adding to migration and a sense of national confusion.[11] Cheltenham remained largely free of the disease, but it affected Gloucester and many other towns badly.[12]

The most significant legislative change affecting the poor during the period covered by these settlement examinations, and the first major reassessment of Poor Law policy since the Elizabethan age, was the Poor Law Amendment Act (the

---

[9] Snell, pp. 108-9.
[10] See Snell, pp. 315-15, 330-1.
[11] Davies 1843, App. p. 211, on "The escape of Cheltenham from the Cholera" in 1832.
[12] Hart, pp. 283-4.

"New Poor Law": 4 & 5 Will. 4 c.76), introduced after considerable discussion by Earl Grey's Whig government and enacted "against a background of serious disturbance amongst some of the labouring classes and extreme anxiety amongst the property classes".[13] The Act received royal assent on 14 August 1834 and drew the management of the poor back ultimately under the control of central government, by establishing Poor Law Commissioners for England and Wales. Furthermore, instead of allowing each parish to determine its own poor provision, the Act facilitated the establishment of Poor Law Unions, binding together groups of parishes within an area.[14]

Cheltenham Union Workhouse, Swindon Road, seen from the north of the site, with the chapel in the centre, flanked by the Women's Day Room (left) and by the Kitchen and Men's Day Room (right). Seen shortly before its demolition and replacement by the St Paul's Medical Centre (photograph by Steven Blake, 1978; reproduced with permission)

The effect of the Poor Law Amendment Act was considerable, and was played out over the following two decades covered by these registers. Amongst other things, its provisions revised the criteria by which place of settlement was decided, and promoted the workhouse as a deterrent rather than a safety net for people who had

---

[13] Powell, p. 187.

[14] Cheltenham became the administrative (though unusually not the geographical) centre of the Cheltenham Poor Law Union, established in November 1835. The constituent parishes of the Cheltenham Union were Badgeworth, Charlton Kings, Cheltenham, Coberley, Cowley, Great Witcombe, Leckhampton, Prestbury, Shurdington, Staverton, Swindon, Uckington, Up Hatherley. Note that the parish referred to as "Swindon" in the examination texts is Swindon (Village), adjacent to Cheltenham, unless stated to be "Swindon, Wiltshire".

fallen into extreme poverty. Out-relief (the provision of relief to paupers outside the workhouse) was frowned upon by the new Act. As Christine Seal explains: "relief was only to be provided in the workhouse for able-bodied men and destitution was the criterion for relief. The 1834 Act brought a change in the equal treatment of men and women. Under the new law, able-bodied men, and women with bastards, were discriminated against by the denial of out-door relief and admittance to the workhouse as the only means of assistance".[15]

B. MIGRATION FROM IRELAND AND SCOTLAND

The first pages of these settlement examinations are dominated by removals to Ireland and Scotland. It might be argued that the registers were initially kept to record evidence of this problem, though these immigrant examinations are very cursory. The examinations, for 123 Irish and Scots migrants in all (77 men and 46 women, with their dependants), are only found in the years 1831 to 1837, which raises questions about the context and management of immigration at the time as it affected Cheltenham.

Although the Great Famine in Ireland occurred in 1845–7, there were extensive food shortages throughout the 1820s and 1830s which, combined with pressure from many self-interested landowners and by Government inaction in Westminster, caused many poor Irish to seek better lives elsewhere, especially in mainland Britain and in North America.[16] In the winter of 1830 the *Cheltenham Chronicle*, along with many other local newspapers, carried a brief news item stating the disturbing fact that "There are 6000 paupers in the north parish of Cork, who rise in the morning without knowing where to procure breakfast or dinner!"[17] The previous news story in the *Chronicle* had told of a terrible "hurricane" in Galway, which left "the whole coast [...] strewed with wrecks". Similar problems were faced by the Scottish poor, where crofters and cottagers were dispossessed as a result of the Highland Clearances, and poverty was exacerbated by a moribund economy and lack of food.

The influx of Irish and Scots caused disruption on both a local and a national level, and the Irish Question was never far from the columns of the daily press. Resolutions, such as they were, were generally economic and practical, rather than humanitarian. The *Cheltenham Chronicle* was keen to report the situation in 1830:

> IRISH PAUPERS. - For several weeks past this town has been so numerously infested by beggars from the sister island, that no less than *nine* were passed back to their native country by the Magistrates on Tuesday. We understand it is the intention of our

---

[15] Seal, p. 5.
[16] For similar issues in Herefordshire, see Powell, p. 179.
[17] *Cheltenham Chronicle* (1830), 2 December p. 2.

parochial authorities to continue this practice, as the only remedy to a rapidly increasing evil.[18]

The heaviest footfall of Irish and Scots immigrants in the relevant examinations included in this volume (66 in all) occurs in the first year of the sequence, 1831. Years 1832–3 have a much-decreased number of immigrant examinations (18, 13), whilst 1834–7 show a further reduced count (9, 3, 4, 10). After 1837, there are no immigrant examinations. The problem had not gone away, but it was no longer handled at the parish level.

The country had been wrestling with how to manage and pay for the removal of Irish and Scots paupers. Individual parishes such as Cheltenham, on the migrant route from the docks and harbours of Bristol, Newport, Chepstow and elsewhere to London (and back again), did not want to shoulder the expense of removal, which in each case which might run to several pounds.

If individual parishes could not bear the expense of these removals, and Westminster did not regard it as a national charge, then the solution settled upon was that removals should be paid for from the County Rate (rather than the Parish Rate), lifting the immediate burden from individual parishes. The legislation enabling this was the Poor Removal Act of 1833 (3 and 4 William IV c.40), which stated that:

> the Charge and Expence [shall be repaid] to such complaining Parish, Township, or other Place maintaining its own Poor, out of the County Rate raised and levied in the County, City, Borough, Town Corporate, Division, or Liberty in which such Parish shall be situate.

Historians have noted a marked drop in the number of Irish and Scots migrants after this act, as happened in Cheltenham. Migrant records largely disappear from the registers of the local overseers, and the counties had to consider whether it made economic sense to fund the quite substantial cost of removal, or to capitulate and distribute relief. On 3 January 1837, for instance, the Cheltenham Overseers noted a repayment received from the County Treasurer "for removal of Irish Paupers" of £40 11s 1d.[19] From 1837, although the problem of Irish and Scots immigration continued for another decade and more, the day-to-day business of conducting removal examinations was no longer recorded in the Cheltenham settlement examinations registers.

---

[18] *Cheltenham Chronicle* (1830), 29 April p. 3. Ironically, the previous news item covered a far more acceptable immigration: "The Cheltenham Season. – The influx of visitors (including numerous families of the highest respectability,) during the past week, has been unusually great, and a considerable number of the principal lodging houses have been engaged for the whole of the summer".

[19] Cheltenham Overseers' Accounts, 3 January 1837 in Gloucestershire Archives D4178.

4. SETTLEMENT EXAMINATIONS IN CHELTENHAM

A. ANNUAL VARIATION IN THE NUMBER OF SETTLEMENT EXAMINATIONS
Cheltenham was in earlier years known for its "mild" implementation of the legislation referring to paupers; after the Poor Law Amendment Act of 1834, with Whigs in government and running the Magistrates' Office, one might expect a parochial administration sympathetic to the new legislation.[20] But to what extent did this mean that those subject to removal were treated harshly, for the benefit of rate-payers and the resident paupers of Cheltenham?

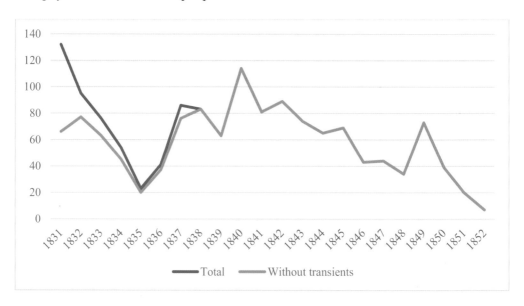

Fig. 1: Incidence of Cheltenham settlement examinations and removal orders 1831–52

The chart above shows the number of settlement examinations conducted each year from 1831 until 1852, as recorded in the registers. The figures exclude the heavy incidence of Scots and Irish immigrants entering Cheltenham in the early and mid-1830s. The evidence reveals an average of just over 58 settlement examinations conducted in Cheltenham parish each year over the period, but with significant variation. From an "average" number of settlement examinations in 1831, and a rise towards 80 in 1832, the figure then (perhaps surprisingly) declined in the years immediately before and after the Poor Law Amendment Act of 1834 (heralded by the establishment of a Royal Commission on the Poor Laws in 1832). These statistics are not always easy to interpret, as one might expect the

---

[20] Seal, p. 32. See also Hart, pp. 284-5: "It is easy to detect that undercurrent of party feeling which ran through every aspect of public affairs in Cheltenham at this time", and Snell, pp. 106, "in general the old Poor law's treatment of the elderly was largely benevolent and sympathetic in operation", and Apfel and Dunkley, pp. 37–68.

authorities to intensify their examinations at this point. Perhaps there are gaps in the record, or was this another example of Cheltenham's "mild" application of the law? Perhaps the non-settled poor (if they could) consciously avoided claiming relief for fear of its consequences.

The incidence of examinations then rose to a peak in 1840, as the Magistrates' Office apparently applied the provisions of the Act with some rigour, seeking to protect the poor-rate payers in the borough from further expense.[21] Nationally, poor rates declined for several years after the introduction of the Poor Law Amendment Act (though Cheltenham's poor rate was always considerably below the national average).[22] After 1840 there was a general relaxation in the severity by which the Act was applied (and the Cheltenham poor rate increases). In addition, Cheltenham perhaps gradually became a less attractive centre of recourse to the poor as the popularity of the spa began to ebb.

In 1847, the Poor Law Commission was replaced by the Poor Law Board, in an attempt by central government to adjust the implementation of the Poor Law Amendment Act, especially after abuses widely reported in the Andover workhouse in Hampshire and elsewhere. John Powell, writing of conditions in the adjacent county of Herefordshire, with its largely agricultural workforce, and in reference to the problems at Andover in Hampshire, states that "in July, 1847 after a reign of 13 years, the Poor Law Commission finally expired, hounded to death by public opinion – by the outrage felt by ordinary people against a dictatorial junta whose powers to oppress the starving poor had been used with heartless, doctrinal severity". [23] Nevertheless, Cheltenham experienced an increase in settlement examinations in the following few years, as the new authority found its feet. By the early 1850s, it is not clear that all examinations are being recorded, as most relate to paupers who have previously received relief from the parish.

Other documentation relating to those in danger of being removed from Cheltenham has been consulted, and is used in the commentaries that accompany each transcript, to form part of the narrative of each pauper's lot. This documentation includes the Cheltenham Overseers' accounts, ledgers for which are extant from 1835 into 1848, the workhouse registers of admissions and discharges (available from 1835), workhouse births and deaths (both from 1836). Much of this information has also been indexed by Cheltenham Local History

---

[21] "The legal costs involved in fighting settlement cases could be very considerable but the long-term maintenance of a pauper family whose settlement was doubtful or had been gained fraudulently would almost certainly have been far more expensive, so once Overseers are reasonably sure that they could win a case they did not hesitate to bring matters forward" (Powell, p. 176).

[22] The *Cheltenham Chronicle* for 7 March 1839 quoted national figures to the effect that "the total expenditure [on the poor] in 1834 was £7,511,219; in 1837, £4,808,735 showing the saving effected to have been at the rate of 36 per cent". See also comparable figures in Seal, p. 84 and 86.

[23] Powell, p. 151.

Society volunteers for the Gloucestershire Archives. But note that "record keeping by the Cheltenham workhouse master was poor, with few columns in the register completed except for surname and first name and no data provided on age, occupation or religion".[24] A further resource at the County Archives particularly relevant to the non-settled poor in Cheltenham (those resident in Cheltenham but "relieved" by their own parish elsewhere) is styled the "Ledger for keeping the Account of Relief Given to Non-Resident and Non-Settled Poor", though unfortunately the surviving documents date only from 1845 until early 1848.

B. SEASONAL VARIATION IN SETTLEMENT EXAMINATIONS
The distribution of settlement examinations throughout the year indicates a general increase in the colder months, especially from January to March, with less, but by no means negligible, activity in the other seasons. This suggests that although there is a seasonal element to pauper relief, other year-round factors such as sickness, pregnancy, and "want of employment" generally were also significant in Cheltenham.

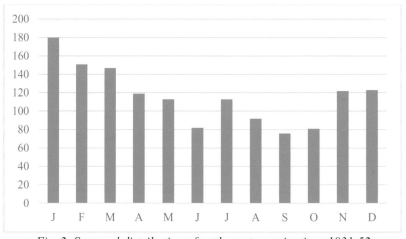

Fig. 2: Seasonal distribution of settlement examinations 1831-52

C. IMMEDIATE FACTORS PROMPTING THE NEED FOR A SETTLEMENT EXAMINATION
Close analysis of the Cheltenham settlement examinations and associated research provide extensive but not exhaustive information about the reasons the paupers documented in this volume required parish relief. Sometimes the reasons are explicitly stated, and at others they can be fairly reliably inferred: this is the case in just over half the examinations (747, or 53.1%).

Surprisingly, only six examinations state unemployment as the motivating cause. It is highly likely that many, though not all, of the 673 examinations where no reason

---

[24] Seal, p. 22.

for the examination is readily apparent were prompted by the head of the family falling out of, or being unable to obtain, employment, but at present this cannot be confirmed. However, most reasons do relate to ability to work.

Leaving this category aside, numerous significant factors are identifiable as the reason for a pauper or a pauper's family having to seek parish relief. Amongst the non-migrant population, the major reason for needing parish relief, on the part of those subjected to settlement examinations, was ill-health, or in a handful of cases, disability. These amount to 26.6% of those cases for which a reason can be determined. Therefore, in over a quarter of these cases, the breadwinner was not well enough to provide for the family, or a dependent family member was ill, which meant that the family dynamics were disrupted to the extent that it was no longer able to function normally. A severer variety of ill-health, generally classified separately in the early to mid-nineteenth century, was "lunacy", either of the pauper or the pauper's spouse (3.5%). The condition in all its forms was overseen in Britain by the Commissioners in Lunacy. In these cases, the examinations show that the afflicted person was likely to be removed to the Gloucester Asylum, where life expectancy once referred seems not to have been high. In some cases, the patient recovered enough to be re-embraced by the family unit, and in others the family took sole responsibility for the care of the "lunatic" without recourse to an asylum.

To some extent related to illness and mental incapacity was the issue of old age and senility (18.6%). The gradual erosion of competence to provide, in a social system which did not offer benefit by right to the elderly, overlaps with ill-health and "lunacy" to constitute cumulatively around 49%, or just under half, of all identifiable reasons for seeking relief. A national system for old-age pensions was not introduced in Britain until the Old Age Pension Act of 1908, when the means-tested benefit was introduced at five shillings per week. Other Liberal measures in the early years of the twentieth century included the National Insurance Act (1911), which introduced sickness benefit for certain paid-up workers (but not for their families). The issue is clearly identified in these examinations from the 1830s onwards, but was not addressed by national government for many years.

Deprivation of the ability to gain an income and provide for oneself and one's family could arrive by a number of other routes. The death of a close relative (particularly that of a husband or wife, but also in the case of unmarried people, that of a father or mother) affected 11.2% of the paupers reviewed in this volume.

Related to this is the absence of a breadwinner. In 49 cases this is known to have been caused by desertion, principally of the husband (6.6% of an examinations), which left the remaining family members unable to provide for themselves. On other occasions (in 4.3% of cases), the breadwinner (usually the husband) was absent because of an army posting, prison, or transportation.

The final major category was pregnancy and childbirth, usually of an illegitimate child (10.8%), predominantly affecting young women. As John Powell observes with reference to Herefordshire, "the most vulnerable people in settlement disputes were young girls who had been abandoned because they were pregnant".[25] In a few cases, the pregnancy of a wife disrupted the family economy enough to require the husband to seek parish relief. There were doubtless further cases of pregnancy which did not result in the birth of a baby, but these are less easy to detect from the records.

The overall picture is one of family suffering, often through no particular reason other than natural causes or misfortune. Even crime and imprisonment might often result for theft from an employer, for example, for money needed to subsist. Without a national system of benefit by right, even if means-tested, the "non-elite" members of society, as they are sometimes called, had no other recourse to fall back upon other than the parish.

D. THE CHELTENHAM WORKHOUSE

Many, but not all, of the poor who awaited their settlement examination in Cheltenham did so in the town's workhouse. The examinations themselves do not normally record place of abode, but from the available information it is clear that some paupers lived outside the workhouse, subsisting on casual "out-relief", whereas many others resided inside the workhouse. References to paupers living inside the workhouse prior to their examination (and indeed afterwards, before they were physically removed) seem to have increased after the Poor Law Amendment Act of 1834. On the other hand, out-relief rose after 1834 "from a low of 365 paupers receiving relief in 1836 to a four-fold increase, to 1,258 in 1840", suggesting a "mild" interpretation of the Act for Cheltenham's own residents (as opposed to those belonging to other parishes).[26] Out-relief always remained a cheaper option than restriction to a workhouse.

Cheltenham had possessed a poor house or workhouse since at least the eighteenth century, but the workhouse known to most of the paupers recorded in this volume was either the "Old" Workhouse situated in what is now Knapp Lane, in a poorer area west of the centre of town, or the "New" Union workhouse built in 1837–41 on the Swindon Road, slightly further from the centre of town to the north-west, to meet the severer requirements of the Poor Law Amendment Act for separating different classes of the poor into different rooms. The "Old" workhouse was not taken out of commission until 1850, and so use of the two workhouses overlapped for a decade. In addition, children were likely to be housed in a workhouse built in 1827 in Charlton Kings.

---

[25] Powell, p. 175.
[26] Seal, p. 88; see also p. 92.

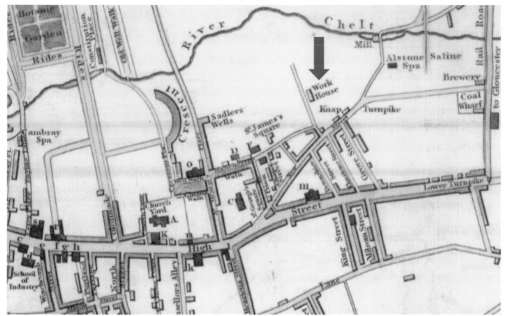

Cheltenham's "Old Workhouse", off New Street to the north-east of town (from Plan of the Town of Cheltenham, Gloucestershire, *published by S. Bettison, c.1820)*

William Sale (**31096SE**: 22 July 1831), removed from Cheltenham to Worcester in 1831, was probably not resident in Cheltenham Workhouse at the time of his examination, as a marginal note reads "No 5 Cross Keys Passage" (a lane off the High Street). Mary Anne Beard (**35006SE**: 19 Mar 1835), on the other hand, stated in her settlement examination of March 1835 that "she is now an inmate of the poor house at Cheltenham where she was admitted with her mother Elizabeth Smith about Six weeks ago or upwards and where her Mother died soon after". References to residence in Cheltenham (or other) workhouses is sometimes included in the settlement examination itself, and at other times is noted in the commentary accompanying each entry.

E. Outcomes of settlement examinations
The Parish Overseers were unlikely to present a pauper for a removal examination unless they felt confident that the pauper and his or her dependants would be removed. The statistics show that the Overseers were overwhelmingly successful, with 80.5% of all settlement examinations in Cheltenham between 1831 and 1852 resulting in removal (1,152 examinants). A further 38 examinants were approved for removal, but died in Cheltenham between the date of the examination and their physical removal, and so were normally buried in paupers' graves in the Old Burial Ground (now the Winston Churchill Memorial Garden). Another pauper (John Partridge **39050SE**: 24 Oct 1839) was set to be removed, but was ordered to be transported two weeks after his settlement examination for larceny by the Gloucestershire County Sessions in Gloucester. Whatever the Poor Law officials' attitude to the poor belonging to Cheltenham, they seem to have

shown a fairly rigorous, uncompromising attitude to paupers who might not rightfully seek relief from the town.

Eighty-two paupers who underwent a settlement examination were adjudged by the magistrates to be residents of Cheltenham, and these were not removed. A disproportionate number of these were examined in the early 1840s, which suggests that the Office of the Magistrates' Clerk, or the Parish Overseers, either suffered from incompetence at the time, or operated an agenda under which they wanted contentious cases settled even if they did not result in removal.

Something over 100 further examination forms were left incomplete or abandoned (typically broken off half-way through, unsigned). These might relate to paupers who had found work and were able to support themselves, or who failed to attend an examination for which the clerks had prepared a partially filled-in form ("Run away": Sarah Hampton **37078RO**: Nov 1837), or to cases which dissolved as evidence was presented, perhaps sometimes in discussion with the receiving parish. A number of these paupers remained in Cheltenham, while others found themselves moving on elsewhere. The stories of some of Cheltenham's paupers, several of which are retold in brief later in this introduction, reveal the significant difficulties encountered by many of the poor at this period around the time they were removed from the town. But despite this, the records make it clear that many returned to Cheltenham after their formal removal.

The chart below plots numbers and percentages of returners, and show that on present evidence 18.5% of removed paupers returned to Cheltenham in the years following their removal. The actual figure is likely to be considerable higher than this, as records are scarce.

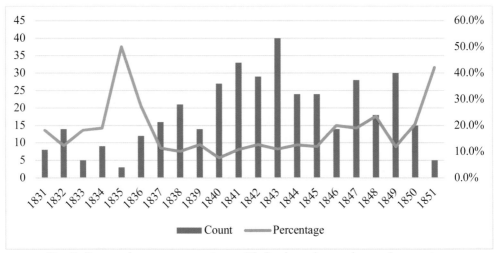

Fig. 3: Removed paupers returning to Cheltenham, by number and percentage

One such returner was blacksmith James Adams, whose story is told in Section 5. But he was just one of many who returned to Cheltenham, either alone or with dependants, to try their luck again in the prosperous Victorian town. Numerically, the highest number of returners occurred in 1843, when the parish was perhaps perceived as becoming more sympathetic towards paupers after the austerity following the initial years of the Poor Law Amendment Act. Sometimes individual paupers or their families returned with the permission of their own parish, as "non-settled" poor. It may have suited their home parish, maybe a small village, to be able to relocate them to Cheltenham, where there was a chance they might benefit from the more active economy. Quarterly Overseers' accounts make regular mention of paupers from elsewhere allowed to reside in Cheltenham, and also of Cheltenham paupers permitted to reside in other places (the "non-resident" poor). It would be a mistake to think that removal was permanent: it often became a legal procedure introduced to satisfy a particular phase in the cycle of poverty.

5. EXAMINATION DAY

This section describes the somewhat forbidding process to which paupers who lived in Cheltenham and had become a "charge" to the parish (by seeking relief) were subject, if the Overseers of the Poor of the parish of Cheltenham determined they might legally "belong" to another parish. This system was tightly controlled by Poor Law legislation and subsequent case law, and the established procedure was theoretically (and usually in practice) followed to the letter, in order to prevent appeals and the quashing of the removal orders which typically marked the end of this stage of the procedure.

A. THE LOCATION OF THE EXAMINATIONS

During the period covered by this volume, the settlement examinations were conducted, for the most part, in the Public Office in Cheltenham High Street, in a room to the rear of the solicitors' offices of Pruen and Griffiths (later Pruen & Co. and then Williams and Griffiths).[27] If a pauper was unable to attend the Public Office, for example because of illness, the law provided that a single magistrate could hold the examination elsewhere (for example, in a gaol, or at a pauper's bedside), though he had to report back to the other magistrate in order to have a removal order drawn up.[28] The magistrates also met regularly in these offices to

---

[27] Rowe, p. 83: "At a large room to the rear of the premises, the meetings of the Magistrates are held. There is also a room at which the Income Tax Commissioners meet." At the end of the nineteenth century the building was used for more Borough business, and it became known as the Municipal Offices. In 1915, these offices moved to new premises in the Promenade, and the original Public Office became a branch of F. W. Woolworth: see *Gloucestershire Echo* (1937), 19 June p. 4, where the writer states that "frequenters to the building in its earlier days would find some difficulty in recognising it now". While the building no longer exists, the house to its left in Rowe's illustration ("The London Warehouse") still stands.

[28] As a result of a dispute with the Guardians of the Poor, newly established in 1835 under a provision of the Poor Law Amendment Act of 1834, meetings were for a short while in the latter part of the 1830s held in the Guardians' office, supervised by their own Clerk, though the meetings soon returned to the Public Office (*Cheltenham Chronicle*: 1840, 25 June). Under the provisions of the Poor (Settlement and Removal) Act of 1809 (49 Geo. 3 c. 124) it was enacted that only one magistrate (rather than the customary two) could

determine minor criminal cases. The Public Office was open for business from 11 a.m. on Tuesdays, Thursdays, and Saturdays, though the magistrates might meet on other days as well.[29]

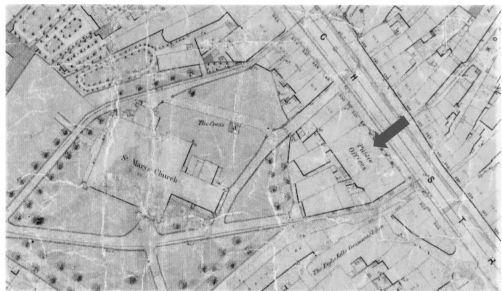

The Public Offices on High Street and backing onto St Mary's churchyard, on the Cheltenham Old Town Survey (1855–7). The Offices included the building at the rear (shown on the Cheltenham Old Town Survey 1855–7, reproduced by kind permission of Cheltenham Borough Council, Gloucestershire Archives, and Cheltenham Local History Society)

B. THE PAROCHIAL ACTORS

The examinations were held in the presence of two Cheltenham magistrates. Magistrates had considerable local powers in relation to parochial matters (sentencing for minor offences, implementing the provision of the Poor Laws, including ruling on settlement and removal, granting ale-house licences, and many other aspects of local life). Their powers, dating from the late Middle Ages, waned during the nineteenth century and many of these powers were gradually assumed by local authorities.

The magistrates were assisted in carrying out their duties by the Clerk to the Magistrates and his staff. The Magistrates' Office would manage the arrangements and paperwork for the magistrates' business, ensuring, for example, that non-settled paupers were removed to their parish of settlement following any removal order.

---

examine an "infirm pauper as to his Settlement", and report back to Petty Sessions: this occurs from time to time in these registers. See, for example, the examination of Thomas Cole (**31076SE**: 21 May 1831 – "confined to bed by sickness, at Alstone"; he died some three months after his settlement examination, and shortly before he could be removed. The officiating magistrate was R. Bransby Cooper.

[29] [Davies] 1840, p. 41.

The Public Office on the High Street in Cheltenham, housed in the same building as the offices of Pruen & Griffiths, solicitor (from Rowe, p. 84)

As well as instituting the central Poor Law Commission, the Poor Law Amendment Act of 1834 introduced aggregated Poor Law Unions managed by local Boards of Guardians for the Poor. Cheltenham's Poor Law Union was established in 1835. The Guardians assumed many of the powers of the old Overseers of the Poor in administrating poor relief. The Clerk to the Guardians of the Poor was responsible for guiding the duties of the Guardians. There was tension between the two Clerks over the distribution of roles immediately after the Poor Law Amendment Act of 1834, and for a short while the Guardians insisted that examinations should be held at their offices, by their Clerk, though this decision was soon reversed by the magistrates. This may help to explain the decline in recorded settlement examinations at this date.

The final principal actors in the following registers, apart from the paupers themselves, were the Parish Overseers. Before the Poor Law Amendment Act their role had been, since medieval times, to manage relief within a parish, to set and collect the poor rate, maintain accounts, compile lists of eligible voters, and other tasks. This was often an unpopular task, for which they were not trained. In

Cheltenham they remained after the Act, but with reduced powers. Their competence was criticised by one of the Cheltenham magistrates, William Gyde, in 1837:[30]

> Mr. Gyde explained that much inconvenience and expense had arisen from the ignorance of the overseers relative to the law of settlement, paupers frequently becoming chargeable for whose [= whom?] removal orders had not been obtained in due time; and others were brought before the Magistrates without a previous examination having taken place before the Overseers, - and the consequence had been, that removals granted under such circumstances, had been appealed against, and the officers of the parish forced to withdraw their orders.

Under the terms of the Poor Relief Act (59 Geo. 3 c.12) of 1819 parochial vestries could appoint a paid Assistant Overseer, to assist or replace unpaid Overseers. By the time of these registers, the Assistant Overseer had the significant role of bringing potentially non-settled paupers to the Magistrates' Office, to established whether there was a case for removal. There were tensions between these various administrative roles, but there was also a large degree of continuity amongst the office-holders over the period covered by these registers. Cheltenham was prone to political in-fighting, and there were repeated accusations against most of the largely Liberal-minded parochial officials of profiteering, political bias, and incompetence. In the light of this, it is remarkable that such an ordered sequence of settlement registers was created and preserved.

William Gyde (c1779–1867), long-standing Cheltenham grocer and magistrate, who officiated at 175 of the settlement examinations transcribed in this volume, between January 1840 and November 1850 (reproduced by kind permission of The Cheltenham Trust and Cheltenham Borough Council)

---

[30] *Cheltenham Chronicle* (1837), 30 November, p. 4.

C. THE EXAMINATION: TRANSCRIPTS

The following transcript records a typical examination, followed by editorial notes on the examinants. Wherever possible, such commentaries throughout this volume show, in the form of a narrative timeline, what happened to the examinants immediately before and after their examination.[31]

43049RO: 6 July 1843 – **James Allen**, blacksmith, and daughter **Mary Ann:** That he has heard and believes he was born in the Parish of Norton in the said County - that when he was fifteen years of age he was apprenticed by Indenture duly stamped to James Caudle of the said parish of Norton Blacksmith for the term of six years – that he served the whole time & slept in his Masters house at Norton aforesaid the whole time – that such Indenture was duly executed – That he has never done any act since to gain a settlement elsewhere – That about 10 years ago he was married in the parish of Addlestrop [= Adlestrop] in the said County to his late Wife Martha now deceased by whom he has one Child Mary Ann aged eight years – That he is now actually chargeable to the said parish of Cheltenham [signed]

James Allen's settlement examination of 6 July 1843 (Gloucestershire Archives)

Each examination has been allocated a unique reference number, consisting of the last two digits of the year of the examination, three digits indicating its number

---

[31] Settlement examinations preferred the term "examinant" (comparable to other legal terms such as "deponent") over "examinee", although "examinee" had existed in English since at least the early sixteenth century. It should be noted that while best efforts have been used to draw up a brief biographical sketch of these paupers, sometimes such information could not be identified safely and unambiguously, and at others incorrect information may have inadvertently been associated with particular people.

in the sequence of examinations for that year, with the final two letters distinguishing the examination as deriving from one of the settlement registers compiled by the magistrates' clerks (SE) or copied into a final removal order (RO). This reference number is also used when cross-referring from other examinations in the series relating to the same pauper.

Examination transcripts are typically presented in the order in which they occur in the settlement examination registers, or (when no settlement register exists for a particular year, from the date of subsequent removal orders). On occasions, this is not a simple chronological order, because the clerks would often enter in advance the introductory matter for a settlement examination record, but the actual examination might be written up slightly later, if delayed, for instance by the non-appearance of a pauper on the date originally determined; on other occasions an expected examination might simply be abandoned for some reason.

The date of the examination or subsequent removal order appears next, followed by a statement of the name of the pauper or paupers under examination, along with any secondary information provided in the formulaic introductory text of the record, the full text of which is omitted here. In the case of James Allen's examination, shown above, the full introductory text, the majority of which derives from the pre-printed removal order pro-forma, reads:

> COUNTY OF GLOUCESTER, TO WIT. THE EXAMINATION of James Allen at present residing in the parish of Cheltenham in the said County, Blacksmith touching the place of his last legal settlement taken before us, two of her Majesty's Justices of the Peace in and for the said County this Sixth day of July One Thousand Eight Hundred and forty three Who upon his oath saith […]

In general, only the texts of the settlement examinations themselves are transcribed in this volume, and any formulaic or pre-printed text, extending for removal orders over four pages, is omitted, with any additional salient aspects summarised in the commentary accompanying each record. The names of the officiating magistrates have also been omitted. In the case of James Allen's examination, these magistrates were D. Latimer St. Clair and William Gyde.

The bulk of the rest of the transcript contains the record of the relevant settlement examination, unabridged and as written out in the original source, to demonstrate as far as possible the tone and content of the magistrates' record.

For each examination, the magistrates appear to have worked initially from a sequence of questions appropriate to the legislation as it existed at the time of the examination, and also perhaps from notes supplied by the Parish Overseers. Although the content purports to reproduce the responses of the examinant (and on occasion is recorded in the first person), the examination record was prepared by the magistrates' clerks to conform to what the magistrates considered appropriate to render the examination least likely to be subject to appeal by the parish to which any removal order would be delivered at the close of the process. It should not be understood to reproduce accurately the pauper's explanations verbatim or in indirect speech. The record was a legal document with a formal agenda, couched in legal phraseology. This is typical of the records of other settlement examinations from this time throughout the country.

The settlement examinations began with questions relating to the name of the pauper and any dependants who might be covered by the removal order, including spouses and dependent children (legitimate or illegitimate) either within "the age of nurture" (seven years of age) or under the age of 16: older children were considered to be independent and so not covered by the relevant Poor Law legislation. At some periods between 1831 and 1852, the examined pauper was required to state his or her age, but sometimes the commentary presents this information from other sources.

The next feature of each examination was central to the outcome: the place of "last legal settlement" of the pauper, and hence in most cases of any dependants, as this was the parish to which they might be removed. This was the aspect most likely to be contested by the receiving parish, and so the details had to be as accurate and comprehensive as possible. Delays in the removal process might occur after the settlement examination if the Magistrates' Office was required to validate paupers' claims, which was often effected by sending clerks or constables (who were at this time under the jurisdiction of the magistrates) to the relevant parish to enquire after birth or employment details, initially at the expense of the Cheltenham rate-payers. Furthermore, the examination might record several potential places of legal settlement, in case the one which was apparently most recent was discovered not to be valid. Towns or villages should be assumed to be in Gloucestershire unless the name of (another) county is given.

The pauper under examination would usually be asked his or her place of birth, since, notably in cases of illegitimacy or paternal settlement, this might become confirmed as the place of settlement. As paupers were under oath, it is normally considered that their responses were likely to be truthful, and this has generally been upheld by modern research into the lives of these Cheltenham paupers.

The place of last legal settlement was determined according to the requirements of existing legislation, and relied upon the concept of "Heads of Settlement", discussed later. In the case of James Allen, he stated that his place of settlement was the parish of Norton, near Gloucester. Apprenticeship, executed according to due legal process, was a valid head of settlement, and so James Allen's statement that he had been legally bound as an apprentice to James Caudle, a blacksmith of Norton, was carefully recorded.

He declared that he was 15 when he started in this apprenticeship (and so his age of apprenticeship was unexceptionable), and that he had continued in his apprenticeship for six years, until the age of 21, which at the time marked a likely term for an apprenticeship. He claimed that he had served the whole of this apprenticeship, which had been properly initiated by a stamped and executed indenture. Crucially, he also stated, doubtless in response to a specific question, that he had "slept in his Masters house at Norton aforesaid the whole time". At times, apprentices might live with their family in a nearby parish, which might invalidate the parish in which the apprenticeship was actually served as the parish of settlement.

The next statement, that "he has never done an act since to gain a settlement", is also important from a legal perspective. If the pauper had subsequently gained a settlement elsewhere, by renting a property for over £10 a year or under any of the other valid heads of settlement, then his parish of settlement would change to the new parish. Most examinations contain a firm statement that a particular claim marked the most recent relevant head of settlement.

Towards the close of the examination, the magistrates moved from settlement claims to dependent relationships. A valid marriage was normally added here, along with the place and approximate date of the marriage, which might be relevant in excluding some heads of settlement. This particularly relates to hiring and service. If the pauper claimed settlement through hiring and service after marriage, then it could not be considered a valid claim. Hiring and service after the Poor Law Amendment Act of 1834 significantly did not confer settlement, but historic service before the act would still be counted. In addition, marriage information might be relevant when the magistrates considered the claims of dependants, especially in the case of female examinants and illegitimate children. Marriage details might be verified by the Magistrates' Office should there be any reason to doubt them.

Marriage information for a male pauper included the forename of his spouse, and whether she was still living (though not her surname, except for a brief passage of time in these records), and also the forenames and age of any dependent children for which the parish of settlement might be responsible. The names of dependants are not included in the introductory text of records from the settlement registers, but they are included in the formal statements of removal in any removal orders.

The examination concludes with a formal statement that the pauper "is now actually chargeable to the said parish of Cheltenham". This was needed as a result of legislation in 1795, which changed the law so that paupers could not, as previously, be removed within 40 days of arriving in a parish just because they were "likely" to become chargeable to the parish, but only after they actually became a charge on the parish by requiring relief from public funds.[32]

The final detail reproduced here is whether the examinant marked or signed the settlement examination record as a true statement, which provides some evidence for levels of literacy over time amongst paupers. Paupers' signatures and marks are found in the original Settlement Registers held in the Magistrates' Office; these were copied onto any subsequent removal order by the magistrates' clerk.

Allen's examination does not involve additional deponents as witnesses, though this would not be uncommon: sometimes a family member (typically a parent), employer, or friend, is required to state birth or other details; at others the Magistrates' Office provides written evidence from an earlier examination and removal, or a medical administrator states details of hospitalisation or institutionalisation.

D. THE EXAMINATION: TIMELINE AND COMMENTARY

Each examination transcript is followed by a short editorial commentary, which gives archive references to the document transcribed and to other related material. It also includes, wherever possible, a short timeline providing additional information about the pauper (and his or her family) in the years immediately before and after the examination, drawn from historical records such as the national censuses, genealogical databases, and contemporary newspapers. These often contain details about the examinant's age, addresses, and family situation around the time of the examination, which have been utilised in the statistical summary above, but which also fill out aspects of the examination, and indicate what happened to the examinant (and his or her family) in the years following the examination.

The commentary is able to reveal, for example, information which might not have been made explicit in the record of the examination, such as whether the examination was needed because of the examinant's old age or infirmity, and whether he or she remained shackled to a life of poverty, or moved on to a more settled existence. Perhaps most significantly, it uncovers whether a pauper who was removed from Cheltenham remained in the parish to which removed, or moved on elsewhere, or even (as is often the case, as it turns out) returned to Cheltenham in the future, either in a more settled condition or to suffer a second or further removal. In such cases (as over), the commentary includes one or more instances of "*(RETURNED)*".[33]

---

[32] The principle of "likely" chargeability was enshrined in Poor Relief Act of 1662 (14 Cha. 2) c.12; the concept of actual chargeability was introduced in 1795 by the Poor Removal Act (35 Geo. 3 c.101). The Settlement of the Poor (England) Act of 1819 extended the 40-day residency requirement to one year.
[33] In the cases of settlement examinations surviving without a parallel removal order, it cannot be assumed that a removal order was in fact drawn up. In these cases, the place of removal is marked as "presumed".

1841: *death of wife Martha in Cheltenham, aged 34 (buried at New Burial Ground on 1 Apr).* **1843: *removed to Norton (Gloucester Union) (apprenticeship).*** **1845–7:** *(RETURNED) from 3Q 1845 until 2Q 1847 daughter Mary (Ann) Allen (10) received parish relief from Gloucester as a non-settled resident of Cheltenham (G/CH/9d/1).* **1851:** *JA (46; blacksmith, born Norton) lived, with housekeeper, in Gas Green, Cheltenham (HO107/1973/550/23).* **1859:** *daughter Mary Ann lived at 22 Henrietta St, Cheltenham when married 26 Sept to Robert Pugh.* [PS/CH/RA/2/6:143 (copy at PS/CH/RA/2/5:517). Removal expenses for "Allen" to Norton 13/- (3Q 1843: D4178).]

In the case of James Allen, the commentary finds that his late wife Martha, mentioned in his examination, had died in Cheltenham at the age of 34, where she was buried in the New Burial Ground, near the workhouse, in early April 1841. Allen must have struggled on with his daughter for a year or so before his difficulties overcame him. The passage in bold notes the outcome of the present settlement examination, which in this case was that the pauper (and his daughter) were removed to Norton, Allen's parish through his apprenticeship, as claimed in the examination. Norton was a constituent parish of the Gloucester Poor Law Union. There is no evidence that the removal was contested, though records do not always survive to demonstrate this. The Overseers' records document expenses of 13 shillings paid to remove James and his daughter to Norton, recoverable by Cheltenham from the Gloucester Union, and this is evidence that the pauper was in all likelihood actually removed.

In this case, the Gloucester Union clearly did accept that the couple were chargeable to them, as Cheltenham records show that the daughter Mary Ann, aged around ten, received parish relief several years later, between 1845 and 1847, from Gloucester, but with the acceptance by both sets of overseers that she could reside in Cheltenham. Her father James also returned to Cheltenham, where he is listed in the 1851 national census living, aged 46 and still a blacksmith, with a housekeeper in Gas Green, Cheltenham, one of the poorer areas of the town. Mary Ann herself remained living in Cheltenham, and was married from Henrietta Street, in the centre of the town, to Robert Pugh in September 1859.

The implications of this additional information are that James Allen was born around 1805, and his daughter about 1835, that their removal to Norton was not opposed, and that both returned to Cheltenham to live after their formal removal, and appeared to maintain a settled existence in the town. In human terms, the outcome of the examination was that Allen was removed to a parish which he may not have known since the termination of his apprenticeship 17 years earlier, and where he perhaps had no current family or friends to support him, or any hope for gainful employment. Similar removals to places where paupers had only worked for a short while in the distant past happened to many examinants, and this was one of the most unsettling features of removal legislation at the time. (Married women taking absent husbands' settlements could even be removed to places they had never been.) It might not be surprising, therefore, that James Allen preferred to try his luck by returning to Cheltenham in search of work. The data feeds into the statistical account of the Cheltenham paupers subject to removal, and extends our appreciation of the day-to-day lives of paupers caught in the network of poverty that enmeshed so many at the time.

6.   THE CRITERIA FOR REMOVAL

The main purpose of a settlement examination was to determine the place of last legal settlement of the examinant, which by the early nineteenth century was established according an increasingly complex set of legislation and case law. Each person was born with a default settlement (though this depended on personal circumstances), or could gain a settlement by any of eight criteria, or "heads of settlement". Once one of these criteria had been fulfilled, the parish or place of residence to which this related became the place of last legal settlement to which a pauper could be removed. If, subsequently, another settlement was gained in the same or another place, then this became the new grounds for the settlement determination.

A. SETTLEMENT BY BIRTH, MARRIAGE, AND PARENTAGE; DERIVATIVE SETTLEMENTS
The default situation for most people was that their place of settlement was their place of birth (this decision was implied by early case law). However, if the place of settlement of the father was known and proved, then this (known as settlement by parentage) took precedence as the place of settlement for a legitimate child. Under the Poor Removal Act of 1795 (but also found earlier) and revised in the Poor Law Amendment Act of 1834, illegitimate children acquired settlement from their birthplace or (until certain ages) that of their mother. Settlements on the basis of parental settlement were known as derivative settlements. In these registers, 6.3% of settlements are adjudged by birth (with a 4.7%-8.2% female/male split), and as many as 38.2% by parental settlement (31.35%–43.68%).[34] These are generally the forms of settlement more frequently claimed by males, and apply to those who have not had the opportunity (or in some cases the inclination) to gain their own independent settlement.

The second staple of settlement law was settlement by marriage (amounting to 19.5% of these records): a wife acquired the settlement of her husband on marriage (including any new settlement subsequently gained by him). She also retained his last legal settlement after his death, unless she remarried or gained another settlement herself. 44.2% of settlement examinations by women relied on settlement by marriage to determine place of settlement.

There were many other possible permutations that exercised the Justices, such as the status of children by a wife's former marriage (who would retain their father's

---

[34] For comparison, between 35% to 55% of males claimed settlement through birth or parental settlement in the south-eastern counties of England between 1831 and 1851: Snell, Fig. 2.5, p. 79.

settlement, but if under seven years of age in our period could not be separated from their mother though relieved by their father's parish). Some of these complexities arise in the settlement examinations in this volume.

The first occurrence of settlement by birth in these registers appears to relate to Edward Summers, who was removed from Cheltenham with his wife Mary Ann to the village of Tuffley in Gloucestershire (**31081SE**: 28 May 1831). His wife accompanied him to Tuffley, as she had acquired her settlement there by marriage. Edward Summers did not remain in Tuffley, but gravitated back to Cheltenham, where he died in 1833.

Charles Mills was the first person in these registers to be removed to the place where his father had gained settlement (**31031SE**: 8 Mar 1831). He was removed with his children Charles, Thomas, and Elizabeth, who were dependent upon him and who had therefore acquired his settlement.

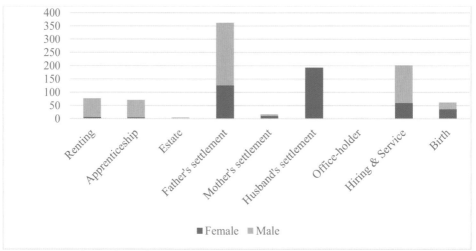

Fig. 4: Numbers of people examined in Cheltenham gaining settlement under the various heads of settlement 1831–52

One of the first women examinants to claim settlement by marriage in these registers was Elizabeth Cummins (**31103SE**: 20 Aug 1831). Her husband John had left her ("absconded"), and this was a situation which the magistrates generally viewed harshly, often making substantial efforts through their clerks or constables to find and punish absent husbands. A deserted wife retained the settlement of her husband by marriage. It appears from the Overseers' accounts that John Cummins was tracked down, and he, his wife Elizabeth, and at least one child were removed to Sudeley, near Winchcombe, where the family had been relieved in the past. Previous relief from a parish was regarded by the magistrates as prima facie evidence that the parish was (at least in the past) the parish of settlement.

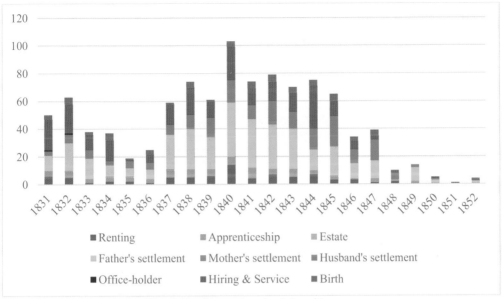

Fig. 5: Settlement heads claimed by year

B. SETTLEMENT BY HIRING AND SERVICE

The commonest way for a person to acquire settlement, other than by birth, parentage, or marriage, was by being hired or engaged for work, and then serving under that hiring for a full and unbroken year (covering 20.4% of these records). In these records, considerably more men (25.6%) claimed settlement through hiring and service than women (13.7%), who were more likely to rely on their husband's settlement. Average length of service under a contract of hiring was around two years: slightly less for men and slightly more for women. The average wage stated was £8 8s 2d per year, though women received on average £6 8s 4d per year, and men slightly more, at £9 8s. It should be remembered that these figures derive from hirings over various periods of the past, though generally in a period of low inflation.[35]

Hiring and service while unmarried was introduced as a criterion for settlement in the Poor Relief Act (3 Will. and Mar. c.11) of 1691. This was a major act for the development of settlement law, which also introduced three other heads of settlement. Any of these settlement heads might have been used previously in determining settlement, but this and other acts *obliged* magistrates to recognise them. There were stringent rules which had to be satisfied in order to acquire settlement by hiring and service, of which the principal ones were that the (former) employee had to be unmarried and childless at the time of service.

---

[35] Thomas Piketty, *Capital in the Twenty-First Century*, transl. Arthur Goldhammer (Belkap Press, Harvard University Press: 2017), p. 137, figure 2.6 ("Inflation since the Industrial Revolution").

The occupation for which the examinant had been hired was not necessarily specified in the examination (66.7% for females and 73.2% for men). Table 1 lists those occupations reported, and their frequency.

Female		Male	
Indoor servant	12	Servant	24
Servant	6	Carter	17
Cook	4	Servant in husbandry	13
Servant-of-all-work	4	Indoor servant	12
Housemaid	2	Cowman/boy	8
Laundry and kitchen maid	2	Groom	7
Maid-of-all-work	2	Footman	5
Nurse maid	2	Coachman	4
Chambermaid	1	Butler	3
Household servant	1	Gardener	3
Lady's maid	1	Postillion	2
Maid & housekeeper	1		
		Butcher	1
Stocking trade	1	Chimney sweep	1
Waiter	1	Milkman	1
		Shepherd	1
		Wagoner	1
	--------		--------
Total	40	Total	103

Table 1: Occupations as stated at time of settlement examination
(household or estate positions shown in buff, other occupations in green)

From this data it is clear that almost all of the women were employed as domestic, "indoor" servants. The men were also mostly employed as servants, some indoor and some as stable hands or farm workers ("servants in husbandry"), with again a small number occupied in trades of some description.

Mary Jones, for example, was "hired as an Indoor servant" in Deerhurst Walton around 1820, when she was still a girl. She later married and had three children, but her husband died. No settlement could be proved for him, so she was removed with her three children to Deerhurst Walton, a village she may not have known well or lived in for many years (**43015RO:** 27 Feb 1843). If the post for which a person was hired is not specified in the settlement examination, it is likely to be for domestic service to the master or mistress of a house.

Hiring contracts might be made informally, or they might be made at the Hiring or "Mop" Fairs that took place regularly about the country, including in Cheltenham. Esther Guest was hired at "Cheltenham first mop" to cabinet-maker Thomas Salmon at four pounds a year, and in fact served him for two years, acquiring settlement in Salmon's place of residence (Cheltenham: **31112SE:** 8 Oct 1831). At this point, the settlement examination was abandoned, as Hester's settlement was presumably adjudged to be Cheltenham, from which she could not be removed. The Overseers perhaps hoped that Esther could be removed to her father's village of Coln Rogers. As a single woman, it is possible that she was pregnant and destitute at the time of her examination. This is not stated in the records; she had an illegitimate child four or five years later, before her marriage to Richard Baylis in 1840.

Hiring agreements had to be for one year, though what "a year" meant might be disputed. William Shinn's examination (**31104SE:** 20 Aug 1831) shows some of the detail to which magistrates might go to elicit the facts: there were rules governing illness during employment, authorised and unauthorised absences, and other irregularities. Employers might move around the country with their servants: in such cases, the general settlement requirement of 40 days' residency would come into play, and usually meant that an employee was settled in the place where his or her contract ended. Edward Morris was employed as a Footman by the Marquess of Salisbury around 1814, and worked for his employer for six years. In his examination, he states that "for the last three months […] I lived in the said service I resided and slept at my said Masters House at Hatfield in the County of Herts" (**48010RO:** 17 Feb 1848). This satisfied the 40-day rule, and so the magistrates had no difficulty in deciding to remove him to Hatfield. Edward Morris returned to Cheltenham, and resided in the workhouse in Cheltenham in 1851, aged 70. Hatfield might relieve him, but it could not provide him with the quality of life to which he was used from his time with the Marquess.

The Poor Law Amendment Act 1834 introduced a major change to the ability of a pauper to acquire a settlement by hiring and service, since it removed hiring and service from the list of criteria by which settlement could be obtained. However, this only related to new contracts, agreed after the Act. Previous hirings would still confer settlement. Keith Snell notes of the 1834 Act, "the abolition of the hiring head of settlement was designed to revive service by removing concern over settlement; but the 1851 census suggests that it had little such effect" for south-east England.[36]

The chart overleaf, showing the percentage of settlement examinations in Cheltenham in which settlement was decided on the basis of hiring, is therefore at first remarkable. Before the 1834 Act, the incidence is high, running at roughly between 30% and 45%; immediately after the Act, and at a period when the Cheltenham authorities were handling a very low incidence rate of settlement examinations, hirings drop to 5% of all settlement examinations in the year.

But after this, the number of settlements claimed by hiring rises, to a ten-year high in 1844. Does this mean that the Cheltenham authorities were flouting the new law? Detailed examination shows that they were not. There were *no*

---

[36] Snell, p. 97.

settlements conferred on the basis of hiring and service after the introduction of the Act in mid-1834; subsequent settlements were adjudicated on the basis of hirings made before (and, in some cases, well before) the Act. Eventually, the incidence of settlement by hiring does drop away, until 1848, when the texts of examinations are no longer available from the registers.

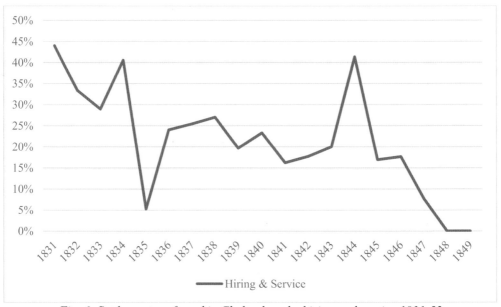

Fig. 6: Settlement conferred in Cheltenham by hiring and service 1831-52

C. SETTLEMENT BY RENTING

Over the period of these registers, 7.8% of examinants claimed settlement by renting a property in a parish, at an average rent of £19 per annum. These examinants were predominantly male (12.8% or 71 people compared with 1.4% female). The various amendments to settlement criteria by renting ensured that, as a settlement head based on the exchange of money, it remained out of reach for many paupers.

The occupancy of property in a town or village might well be considered good grounds for settlement, and the law developed criteria to help magistrates decide. As early as 1662, incomers ("strangers") likely to require parish relief could not be removed if they rented combined property (such as a house and land) worth at least £10 a year (Relief of the Poor (Settlement) Act). Although this marks the origin of settlement by renting, it was reinforced by the Poor Act 1697 (9 & 10 Will. 3 c.11), whereby a person in possession of a certificate from another parish indicating settlement there could gain a settlement in the new parish by taking a lease of at least £10 on a tenement. There were numerous adjustments to the criteria for settlement by renting over time, which tended to make it more difficult for a pauper to achieve, though the basic requirement of a rent of £10 remained throughout: after the Poor Relief Act 1819 (59 Geo. 3 c.12) the tenancy had to be for a separate and distinct dwelling-house for a full year; residency for 40 days became required (though this did not necessarily need to be continuous; the definition of what constituted the rental property changed: two separate pieces of land in a parish, for which a combined rental of £10 was paid, but lacking a dwelling-house, were excluded, for example); in time, it became necessary for the full rent to have been paid in advance, and after the Poor Law Amendment Act of 1834, the lessee had also to have been assessed and to have paid poor rates (s.66). The following chart shows references within the examinations to the payment of poor rates in the context of settlement:

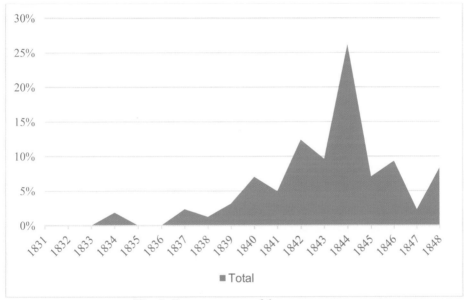

Fig. 7: Paupers assessed for poor rates

Although most paupers who claimed settlement by renting had paid relatively modest rents, several had clearly enjoyed more luxurious lifestyles. One such case is that of John Davis (**44030SE:** 4 May 1844). In 1844, at the time of his settlement examination in Cheltenham, he was an inmate of Cheltenham workhouse, but 25 years earlier he had paid 300 guineas for the five-year rent of a farm in Preston, near Cirencester, as well as £1,800 for the stock living on the farm. That was the last time he had acquired settlement anywhere. By 1841 he had fallen on far harder times, was an inmate of the Cirencester Union workhouse, and is likely to have returned there when the parish of Cheltenham removed him back to the scenes of his earlier, and doubtless long-forgotten success.

D. SETTLEMENT BY APPRENTICESHIP

Apprenticeship became a potential head of settlement under the Poor Relief Act of 1691 (3 Will & Mar. c.11), though apprenticeship itself had existed since at least the Middle Ages in Britain. This was the same act which introduced hiring and service as a head. Apprenticeship might be arranged privately between a family and a master or mistress of a trade, or in the case of pauper families, by Parish Overseers, charities, or (after 1844) by Parish Guardians (7&8 Vict. c.101). In each case, apprentices were bound by an indenture approved by local magistrates (after the Apprentices (Settlement) Act of 1757 (31 Geo. 2 c.11)), and were subject to strict rules enshrined in legislation, relating to residence, the provision of clothing, consent of the apprentice if over 14 years of age, and other regulations.

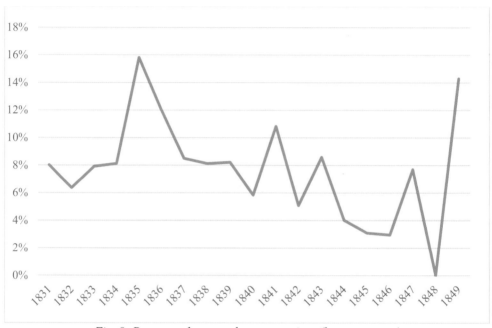

Fig. 8: Paupers who served as apprentices (by percentage)

By the time of these examinations, settlement by apprenticeship was claimed by 7.2% of examinants, though the figure is significantly higher for young men than for young women. Of the 71 instances, 66 relate to males and only 5 to females.[37] The diagram below shows the distribution by year, with an increase in 1835, when the total number of examinations was very low, and a general average of 7.2%. The stories of these apprentices are important, as the evidence shows that having undergone an apprenticeship gave the pauper a trade and therefore (depending on the trade) a better chance of moving away from Cheltenham and recovering from the need to claim relief in future.

Peter Pinching, for example (**40091SE**: 11 Sept 1840), was examined on 11 September 1840 and removed to Great Rissington in eastern Gloucestershire with

---

[37] "Taking all parishes together one should generally expect about an eighth to a tenth of those examined as to settlement to have been apprenticed artisans, claiming settlement on the basis of apprenticeship": Snell, pp. 232-3. Snell was also covering the eighteenth century, before much decline of apprenticeship.

his wife and three children, where he had been bound apprentice to a shoemaker for five years in the 1820s. During the census in the following year he was recorded in Great Rissington as an agricultural labourer. However, in the 1840s the family moved to Stratford-upon-Avon and then, by 1851, to West Bromwich, where Peter had found work as a shoemaker, and his eldest son Walter was a glass-cutter. Similarly, when Miles Arkell (**41032SE**: 29 Apr 1841) was examined, his father informed the magistrates that his son had been apprenticed to a tiler and plasterer in Miserden, in his youth. Miles had lost his wife and was caring for his two daughters at the time of the examination: the family was removed to Miserden. But by 1851 Miles is found lodging in Middlesborough, where he was working as a slater. Those trained as weavers, a declining trade in south Gloucestershire, might be less fortunate, but often the value of an apprenticeship was apparent.

E. REMAINING HEADS OF SETTLEMENT

Settlement could also be claimed by holding an office within a parish, or by the ownership of "estate" (property within the parish). The former head was also introduced by the Poor Relief Act of 1691 (3 Will & Mar. c.11), and the latter by case law in 1712 (though the Poor Relief Act of 1722 (9 Geo. 1 c.7) stipulated that estates had be to worth at least £30 to confer settlement. Recourse to these heads of settlement was necessarily rare, as paupers were unlikely to meet either requirement. In these examinations they occur only twice and five times respectively.

7. PAUPER PROFILES

This section has two parts. The first part documents ten individual stories extracted from the examination transcripts and associated research, to illustrate the variety of issues experienced by examinants. The second part provides general statistics based on the transcribed examinations.

A. PAUPER STORIES

Sometimes, the law produced strange problems for paupers. Eliza Turner (**33057SE**: 10 Aug 1839) was a single woman who was hired in November 1831 by Mrs. Agg of Hewletts, on the boundary of Cheltenham and Prestbury parish, for an annual wage of £5. She served the full year, and so claimed settlement by hiring and service. The magistrates had to consider the nice point whether Eliza's bedroom, on the first floor, was on the Cheltenham or the Prestbury side of the boundary through the house determined by the statutory perambulation.[38] During the annual perambulation of the boundaries, the officials had to walk right through Hewletts house, exiting through the dining-room window. Her bedroom was right

---

[38] "Agg's House [Hewlett's Farm], a conspicuous mansion overlooking the town, was built in two parishes: wherefore a deputation from the crowd [during a perambulation] had to go through one window in the front and out of another at the back": Adams, p. 55.

above the dining room, and Eliza testified that her bed was situated on the Cheltenham side, so that she was at the time technically a resident of Cheltenham. The Poor Law officials seem to have accepted her statement, as the examination form remained incomplete, and it was presumably acknowledged that she should receive relief as a Cheltenham resident at the time of her settlement.

Paupers' horizons were not always limited to the British Isles. When Cyrus Clift (**33074SE**: 10 Dec 1833) was examined in 1833, he and his family were removed to nearby Tewkesbury, where he had once been apprenticed for a short while to a printer. By 1841 Cyrus was a brewer in Tewkesbury, where he and his wife had further children, before returning to Cheltenham. But the family, Nonconformist by religion, did not remain in Cheltenham. In November 1846 they set sail from Liverpool for New York on the SS *Empire* and were listed in the United States census of 1850 as living in Findlay, Hancock, in Ohio, where Cyrus, now aged 48, was a labourer.

Some examinants had little to do with Cheltenham, but arrived in the town in transit. Mary Griffiths (**32015SE**: 8 Mar 1832), recently widowed after the death of her soldier husband at Portsmouth barracks, was travelling to Montgomery in Wales, where she would seek relief from her late husband's place of last legal settlement. She had lost two children since her husband's death. While she was passing through Cheltenham, she was confined and "delivered of a female infant", Mary, baptised in Cheltenham several weeks earlier. She declared that she and her daughter had "no means of Subsistence or of proceeding to her place of Settlement without relief". Cheltenham was legally required to provide relief for "casual" or accidental paupers without means to proceed, and in this case they completed a removal order sending her on to Montgomery. Similar eventualities happened to Brian Kane (**32079SE**: 6 Nov 1832) and to Dan Conigaam (probably Conighan: **32087SE**: 1 Dec 1832).

Sometimes a pauper family managed to escape the poverty trap and establish themselves in successful employment. John Jackson (**38060SE**: 20 Sept 1838) sought relief for himself, his wife and his son from Cheltenham, and they were removed, it seems, to his father's last place of legal settlement in St Clement's, Oxford. By 1841 the family had moved to Welland in Worcestershire, where John was described as "independent" (i.e. not claiming relief). By 1851, they had moved again, to Great Malvern in Worcestershire, where John was a master plasterer employing one man. By 1861, he was living in Colwall, in Herefordshire, employing four men and three boys. For a similar success story, see Charles Tarlton (**36008SE**: 31 Mar 1836).

*The diminutive John Millbank (**33076SE**), Cheltenham's "Muffin Man" and a native of Colchester, selling his wares on the street. As old age crept up on him, he underwent a settlement examination in Cheltenham on Friday 13 December 1833, dying early the following year (reproduced by kind permission of The Cheltenham Trust and Cheltenham Borough Council)*

The ride out of adversity can be bumpy. Edwin Percival (**39029SE**: Mar 1839), a silver-plater, became ill and needed parish relief from Cheltenham, where he had married a year earlier. It seems that he was not removed, as his father (a musician) was Cheltenham-born, despite having left for Ireland 15 years earlier, where he had died. By 1841 Edwin and his wife were still in Cheltenham, but Edwin was by now a coachman. Ten years later, and the family had moved to Ockbrook, Derbyshire, where Edwin, now 35, was a schoolmaster.

Examinations can give us brief glimpses of the hardships of life experienced by children. When Andrew Hall (**39035SE**: 16 May 1839) fell ill, he was brought before the Cheltenham magistrates to explain his settlement. He argued that he should not be removed, as his late father's settlement was in Cheltenham. Indeed, he recalled that his widowed mother had received relief from Cheltenham, and that he himself "remembers going for his said Mother (who then lived in Sherborne Street, Cheltenham) to the Poor House and receiving her allowance which he thinks was a shilling a week".

Marriage legislation could sometimes turn the result of a settlement examination. When Hannah McCarthy (**40100SE**: 3 Nov 1840) fell on the parish, she explained that she had been married about five years earlier in London to John Jones "who since died in Spain". Normally she would have taken her late husband's settlement, but it emerged that "the Marriage Ceremony was not performed in any place belonging to the Church of England" (in this case a Catholic Chapel). At the time, a marriage ceremony between a Catholic and a Protestant was only held valid if consecrated according to the forms of the Established Church in England. As a result, Hannah was removed to Marylebone in London, where her late father had rented a house, and had also received parish relief.

The inhumaneness of the Poor Law legislation did not stop at removing paupers to towns or villages with which they might no longer have any relationship, but separated mothers from illegitimate children who had passed the "age of nurture" (seven years of age). Phoebe Simmonds (**41077RO**, **41078RO**: 18 Dec 1841) was the wife of labourer William Simmonds, and the mother of his daughter Joseph. When the family fell on hard times in December 1841, they were removed from Cheltenham to nearby Badgeworth, where William had been employed ten years earlier, and before his marriage, as a cowman. Immediately after William's settlement examination, Phoebe was examined separately "with regard to her eleven-year-old and illegitimate daughter Ann Lyes, born before Phoebe's marriage to William in Chaceley, Worcestershire. Although Phoebe was removed with her current family to Badgeworth, the law required that Ann be separated from her mother and removed to Chaceley. Happily, by the time of the 1851 census, the family had been reunited in Cheltenham, to which they had returned in the intervening years.

The harsh treatment of Mary Keepax (**45050SE**: 28 Aug 1845) and her sister Elizabeth illustrates the lot of persistent prostitutes in early Victorian England. In August 1845, 29-year-old Mary Keepax was a resident of the Cheltenham Workhouse, awaiting her settlement examination. Her father had died, and her mother had remarried. Seven years earlier, Mary and Elizabeth Keepax had been summoned to appear at the Worcestershire Quarter Sessions on a charge of conspiring with a brothel-owner to steal £90 from an intoxicated client. Mary had been acquitted, but Elizabeth was transported to Van Diemen's Land (Tasmania).

At her later settlement examination, Mary was removed from Cheltenham to the place of her late father's settlement, Claines, in Worcestershire. Her death was registered in Pershore, Worcestershire in the following year. See also the examination for Ann Haskins (**48023RO**), removed to Taynton, and later living as a "Magdalene" (reclaimed prostitute) at the Magdalene Asylum in Gloucester.

The "Lewd Women's Yard" at Cheltenham Union Workhouse, shortly before its demolition (photograph by Steven Blake, 1978; reproduced with permission)

One final experience demonstrates the extremities to which pauper women might be pushed, though in some ways the tale ends on a happy note. In 1851, Susannah Barnett (**51018RO**: 13 Dec 1851) was removed from Cheltenham to Clapton, part of the Stow-on-the-Wold Poor Law Union. Three years later, her five-month-old son Henry, born in the Stow Union Workhouse, was found dead by the side of the Cheltenham road out of Stow. Susannah was charged with manslaughter, and was sentenced to transportation for 20 years. She was sent to London, awaiting transportation, but her sentence was in time commuted and she served it out at the Fulham Refuge, a women's prison then under enlightened management, which prepared women for re-entry into society on release. Susannah was granted a licence to go "at large" in March 1862, and later that year married Joseph Werret, with whom she had several children, living in Cheltenham and then in Staverton.

These are just a handful of the paupers' tales which arise out of research into the Cheltenham settlement examinations between 1831 and 1852. They document the personal tragedies of paupers who suffered the degradations of poverty, sometimes succumbing to their miserable fates, but at others coming through to some form of happier resolution.

B. PAUPER STATISTICS

As well as providing extensive information about individual pauper experiences, these settlement examinations, along with additional research, give considerable detail about the overall situation of people examined for possible removal. This section investigates some of this data from a statistical perspective.

C. WHERE DID THEY COME FROM AND WHERE DID THEY SETTLE?

Birth-place data (not necessarily provided in the examinations, but frequently ascertainable elsewhere) demonstrates that by far the largest number of paupers threatened with removal from Cheltenham had been born in Gloucestershire. Within Gloucestershire, inward migration to Cheltenham was typically from a wide corridor of agricultural areas to the north of Cheltenham down to the south-west, taking in Gloucester and carrying on to the former weaving strongholds in and around Stroud.

As seen in Fig. 9 (opposite), beyond Gloucestershire, most paupers examined came from the adjoining agricultural counties of Somerset and Wiltshire (along with Devon) in the south and west, Herefordshire, Worcestershire, and Warwickshire to the north, and Oxfordshire to the west. However, the traditional picture of west-east migration, ultimately towards London, is counterbalanced by an east-west stream, from Kent, London, Middlesex, Surrey, and Berkshire, a wider and less significant proportion from Wales and East Anglia, and a weaker stream from further north. In the light of the early Irish famine-led migration, the large number of poor labourers embarking from Cobh (Queenstown) in Cork comes through strongly in the early years of the data, along with additional groups from elsewhere in Ireland and from the south of Scotland.

Removal is the other side of the coin. Here, the pattern is similar but not identical (see Fig. 10). Removal was not necessarily to place of birth, but commonly to the place where settlement had been acquired. The data tends to show a preponderance of removals within Gloucestershire, with significant numbers also removed to counties adjoining Gloucestershire. The counties of removal for Irish and Scots paupers were not recorded (their removal being normally to the country), and so do not appear in Fig. 10. Almost 100 Irish and around 30 Scots paupers were removed from Cheltenham to their own countries (all in the 1830s).

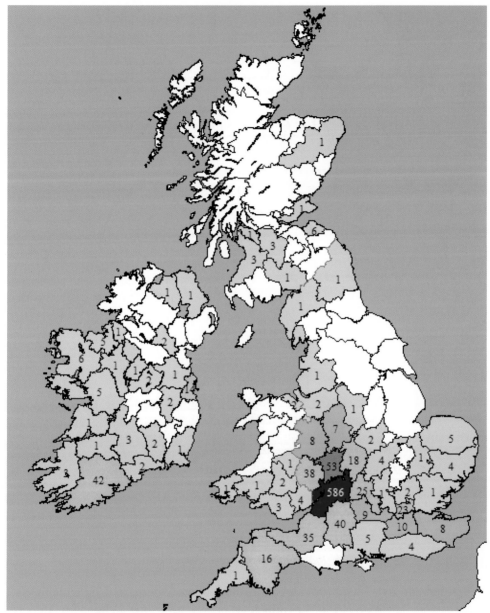

Fig. 9: Pauper birth counties (with numbers of examinants)

Within Gloucestershire, the profile of removal is similar to the profile of birth, with substantial removal back to the agricultural areas north of Cheltenham, continuing again through a wide corridor including Gloucester and down to the former West Country weaving areas.

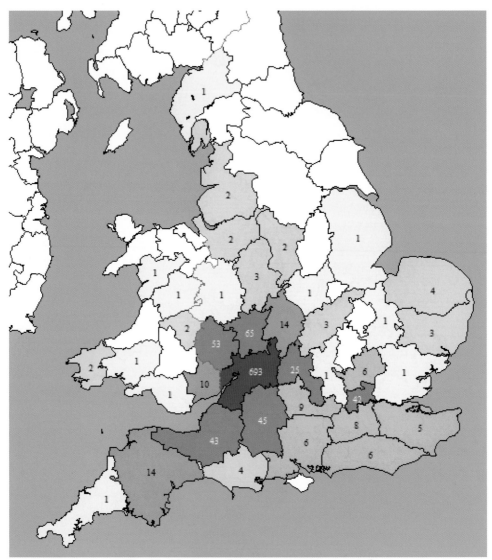

Fig. 10: Places to which paupers were removed

The settlement data also provides information on where in Cheltenham most paupers lived. The map at Fig. 11 (opposite) is derived from Cheltenham addresses in the 1841 census at which examinants lived before, during, or after their settlement examination. The most densely populated (darkest-coloured) areas, in terms of paupers who were subjected to settlement examinations, follow the line of the High Street from the south-east of the town towards the north-west, focusing most significantly around the Lower High Street (close to the old workhouse) and out of the town towards Swindon Village and Tewkesbury. The newer, grander, southern regions of Cheltenham were not areas where paupers resided, unless they had obtained work in domestic service. A final strand, showing the densest area of pauper population, runs south through the area round the Bath Road and on towards Leckhampton.

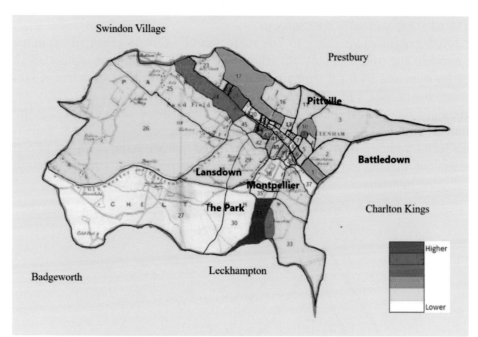

*Fig. 11: Density of population of paupers who were examined as to their place of settlement in Cheltenham Parish, at the time of the 1841 census, by (numbered) enumeration district (*base map from *Parliamentary Papers: Reports from Commissioners on Proposed Division of Counties and Boundaries of Boroughs (1832), Vol. I Part II)*

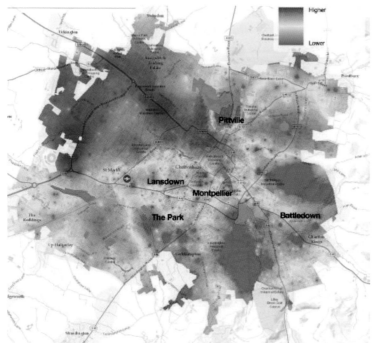

Fig. 12: Cheltenham house prices (2016) for comparison, showing lower prices in the north-west segment of the town, mirroring the poorer areas in 1841; but the dense southern area of poverty in 1841 towards Leckhampton is now shown as relatively prosperous (Knight Frank)

D. THE GENDER AND AGE OF EXAMINANTS

The 1,405 examinations relate to 768 male and 637 female principal examinants. The average age of examinants for whom age is known is approximately 38 years (40.7 for men and 34.6 for women). But these figures mean more when separated into age bands (see Fig. 13). The age distribution here shows that the younger examinants were most likely to be female (and these are often pregnant or unmarried mothers), and that middle-aged men, often widowed and with dependent children, were more likely to need parish relief than middle-aged women, but that in old age both sexes sought parish relief equally, though in diminishing numbers.

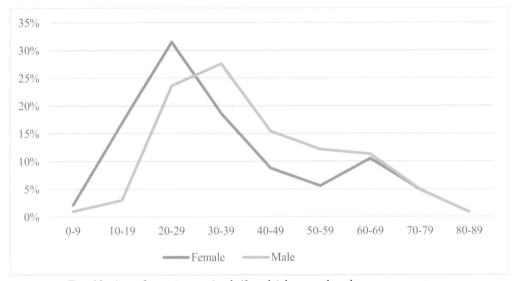

Fig. 13: Age of examinants (male/female) by year bands, as a percentage

These examinations include 123 Irish and Scots migrants (of which 77 were male and 46 female). Their examinations were cursory, and are only recorded between 1831 and 1837 (see section 3.2). Their removals were often noted by the local newspapers, as this was a subject of great popular concern throughout the country.

E. (FORMER) OCCUPATIONS OF PAUPERS

Of those male examinants who stated their occupation, or whose occupation can be determined (to some degree at least) from external evidence, over half were "labourers", though the term can be ambiguous, covering agricultural labourers and general labourers working in manual trades. The other trades noted include those involved in Cheltenham's house-building industry, as much of Cheltenham's Regency-style housing stock dates from this period, and other activities necessary for a thriving resort. But note that some of these trades were practised before their examinations, so do not necessarily document occupations carried on at the time of the examinations.

Male

Labourer	238	Cooper	3	Bracebuckle-maker	1
Shoemaker	30	Miller	3	Carter	1
Stone mason	17	Stableman	2	Chimney-sweep	1
Carpenter	14	Baker	2	Coachman	1
Sawyer	10	Basket-maker	2	Cow-boy	1
Tailor	10	Brewer/Maltster	2	Cutler	1
Gardener	9	Coach-trimmer	2	Drover	1
Servant	8	Currier	2	Fireman & Brazier	1
Painter	7	Flyman	2	Glover	1
Plasterer	7	Footman	2	Groom	1
Blacksmith	5	French polisher	2	Hairdresser	1
Butcher	5	Lathrender	2	Haulier	1
Weaver	5	Paper-maker	2	Ostler	1
Bricklayer	4	Slater	2	Porter	1
Cabinet-maker	4	Tinman	2	Saddletree-maker	1
Clockmaker/Watchmaker	4	Whitesmith	2	Victualler	1
Brickmaker	3	Wood-turner	2	Waiter	1
Chaise-driver	3	Blanket-weaver	1	Woollen clothworker	1
				Total	**439**

Table 2: Occupations stated by male examinants (all examinations)

The occupations listed for female examinants show much less variety, being predominantly related to domestic service, with a small number engaged in shop-work and activities involving needle-work.

Female

Servant	53	Woollen-worker	2
Laundress	13	Clothworker	1
Charwoman	5	Milk woman	1
Dressmaker	3	Milliner	1
Labourer	2	Stocking trade	1
Seamstress	2	Waiter	1
Shopkeeper	2		
		Total	**87**

Table 3: Occupations stated by female examinants (all examinations)

F. LEVELS OF LITERACY

1,113 of the 1,405 examinations are signed with either a mark or a signature. The remaining examinations are either incomplete or fall into the category of orders after 1848 which did not include examinations.

Excluding Irish and Scots migrants, 615 examinations are signed with a mark, and 381 with a signature. Marks are equally spread amongst men and women (309/306), and men were more likely to sign with a signature than women (244/137) (64%).

Amongst the 117 Irish and Scots migrants who provided a mark or signature, the percentage of those who signed with a mark was considerably higher than the other British examinants (72.7% compared with 61.8%). It is noticeable that very few Irish and Scots women signed with a signature (2) (compared with 30 men).

The literacy level amongst the non-migrant group (judged by the ability to write one's signature) was 38.3%, and amongst the smaller migrant group 27.4%. Snell records national male illiteracy levels (between 1754 and 1844) ranging between 59% and 66%, so at the later end of this spectrum, Cheltenham incomers demonstrate a slightly lower level of literacy than the national average.[39]

G. FAMILY STRUCTURES

People attended settlement examinations from a wide variety of family structures. The most extreme case was that of Edward Jones (**50037RO**: 24 Dec 1850), an agricultural labourer who presented himself along with his wife Eliza and their nine dependent children. The family was removed in 1850 to Hanley Castle in Worcestershire.

Of the 1,405 examinants, 112 men with a wife but no children were examined (28.6% of all examinants). The single largest category in terms of percentage was men without a wife or any children (249 in total, or 85.6% of all men); the equivalent figure for spouseless and childless women was numerically higher (392 in total, or 62.1% of all women). The exigencies of pauper life (sickness, lack of work, pregnancy, and old age) meant that survival became extremely difficult if the pauper had no one else to rely upon. A family unit of a man and a woman presenting for examination was likely to have children, making their plight much more pressing. The following chart details various family structures falling into this category.

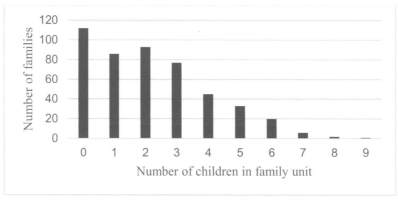

Fig. 14: Dependent children in a family unit with a mother

---

[39] Snell, p. 36, citing data from Roger Schofield.

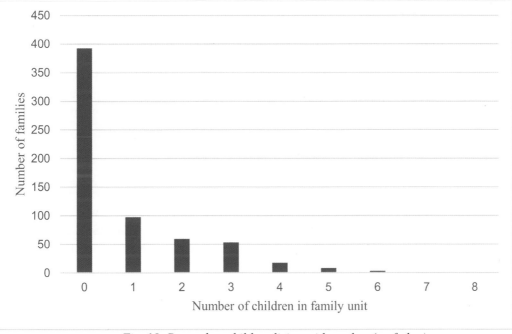

Fig. 15: Dependent children living with mother (no father)

Women with children, who had often lost their husband through death, or who had been abandoned, were statistically more likely to be caring for several children than were men in the same situation. Men left without a wife, typically through death, were often thrown rapidly upon the parish.

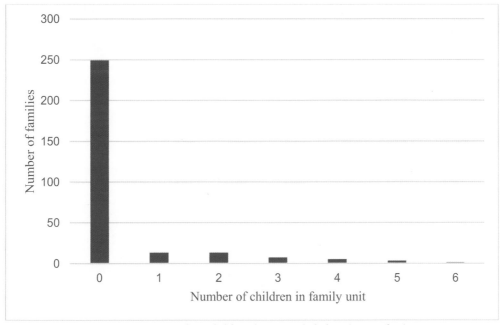

Fig. 16: Dependent children living with father (no mother)

8.   LANGUAGE AND SPELLING IN THE TEXTS

Original spelling is retained throughout these transcriptions. One of the most significant variations from modern practice occurs with the word "expense" and "expenses", which are transcribed in the older variant form "expence" and "expences" when this occurs in the original text. In general texts of the time "expenses" was the dominant form. The use of "aforesaid" or simply "said" is widespread, as are other similar legal expressions.

Examinations are normally presented in the third person, in the style: "That he has a Wife named Margaret and two infant children named Mary Ann and Catherine". However, it is not unusual for speech to be represented as if in the first person. The earliest occurrence of this dates from November 1831: "I was married at Minchinhampton before the child was born" (Mary Davis; **31120SE**: 12 Nov 1831). A graph of the incidence of first-person description in the examinations (by percentage) shows that this became the norm from 1843: see, for example, Solomon Ireland (**43008RO**: 28 Jan 1843).

Whether the examination was reported in the first or the third person, the magistrates' clerks demonstrated some variation in how they presented statements. Information about a pauper's place of birth was not typically supported by paperwork from the relevant parish, but was simply asserted by the pauper. This information might be confirmed later by parish officers. But to indicate that the data was not certain, the clerks would hedge it about with qualification. Sometimes the examinant is reported as saying that he or she had "heard and believes" that they were born in a particular place or that a spouse was employed by a particular person; at others, the formula is simply "understood", or "heard"; other variations might be "as (s)he believes" and "to the best of (his/her) (belief/knowledge/recollection/etc)". The variation is likely to present the office style of the day, or clerical preference, but indicates that in the later years a clear, unambiguous statement was preferred to a qualified one. The chronology of the various styles is shown in the following charts:

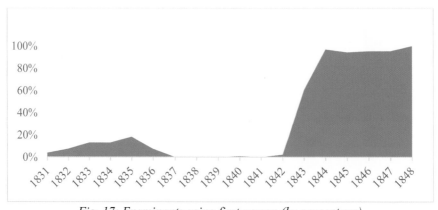

Fig. 17: Examinants using first person (by percentage)

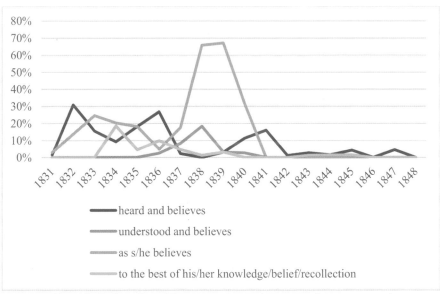

Fig. 18: Styles of qualifying examinants' memory (by percentage)

There are several instances of archaic or dialectal grammar and syntax, some typically characteristic of Gloucestershire and other regional (west-country) forms of English at the time. These have been retained in the transcriptions. The archaic and legalistic "hath" is regularly used, though the modern "has" is also frequent in the texts (see below). The printed pro-formas introduce examinations with "Who saith", though in the examinations third person singulars are (with the exception of "hath") almost universally found in -*s*. Several reports are quoted as if verbatim, in the first person (see below). It is not uncommon for an examination to say, perhaps archaically, that a pauper "is [rather than "hath" or "has"] become chargeable" to the parish of Cheltenham. The third-person singular use of "was", when a plural would be expected, is occasionally found:

> 1842: That we went back to Leonard Stanley and was afterwards relieved by the Parish Officers of King Stanley whilst we were living at Leonard Stanley.

The same text employs a dialectal omission of "has" or "had", which is mirrored in several other examinations, and appears not to be an error:

> That her said husband never done any Act afterwards to gain a settlement and died about 7 months ago.

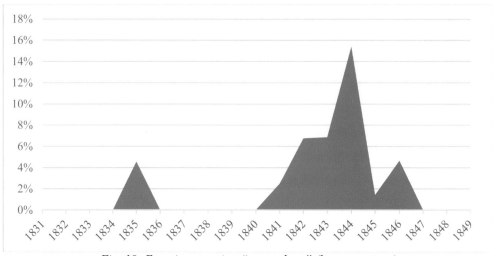

Fig. 19: Examinants using "never done" (by percentage)

The evidence from the settlements associates this idiom principally from the early years of the 1840s, and is likely to relate to a particular clerk.

Usage of "has" in comparison with archaic and legalistic "hath" varies in the examinations recorded, as documented in this chart:

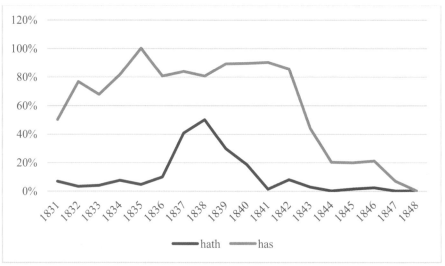

Fig. 20: Usages of "hath" and "has" (by percentage)

It is surprising to find the increase in "hath" consolidated between 1837 and 1841 (probably clerical preference). The tail-off of both forms in the later examinations is explained by the general switch to first-person reporting ("have"), and the occasional occurrence of "never done", as noted above.

A similar archaism occurs when a man refers formally to his wife. In the majority of examinations, the expression "my present wife" is used. However, for a short while, between 1837 and 1842, the idiom "my now wife" is used, peaking at 22.8% of all occurrences in 1840. The use of *now* as an adjective goes back to the Middle Ages, but it is unusual (though not unknown) in this context by the nineteenth century. In both cases, the natural contrast is with "my late wife", though the present idiom is frequently used of a husband's only spouse.

9. DESCRIPTION OF THE REGISTERS

The settlement examinations and removal orders included in this text have been transcribed from six folio manuscript volumes (PS/CH/RA/2/3-8) covering Cheltenham Parish between 1831 and 1852, prepared by the Magistrates' Office in the Public Office, Cheltenham, and preserved in the Gloucestershire Archives. Three volumes contain settlement examinations, and three contain removal orders, which until 7 October 1848 include a copy of the relevant settlement examination.

Each volume includes what appears to be a complete run of documents for a particular chronological range, except for the final volume of removal orders, which may be selective. Overall, there are no chronological gaps between 1831 and 1852, but this continuity masks the fact that there are gaps in the record: settlement examinations are recorded patchily in 1835 (and perhaps at other times), and stop in 1845, and the three volumes of removal orders are not continuous. However, there are many years of overlap, for which both types of record survive. In these cases, the later version (from the removal order) has been selected for transcription, though significant changes from the earlier magistrates' copy are noted.

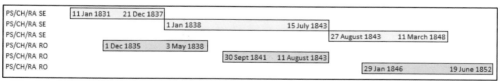

Fig. 21: Overlap of surviving settlement examination (SE) and removal order (RO) registers for Cheltenham

The various volumes, all in stationery binding typical of the period, may be described as follows:

    1) PS/CH/RA/2/3: settlement examinations
Title: CHELTENHAM   PARISH/EXAMINATION   OF   PAUPERS/AS   TO/ SETTLEMENTS/JANUARY 1831
Inside front cover: sticker reading "HARPER/Repository of Arts/Cheltenham"
Dates covered: 31 Jan 1831 to 21 Dec 1837
Contents: A-Z tabbed index (12 leaves); pages numbered 1–507 containing text of settlement examinations; two pages blank and unnumbered at the end.
Page dimensions: 31.9 cm in height by 20.7 cm in width

Description: full parchment binding, title blind-stamped; marbled end-papers and marbled edges on book block.

2) PS/CH/RA/2/4: removal orders
Title: ORDERS/OF/REMOVAL
Removal order pro-formas printed by: Harper, Printer, Free Press Office, Cheltenham
Dates covered: 1 Dec 1835 to 3 May 1838
Contents: 84 pro-formas of printed removal orders (four pages each), completed in script
Page dimensions: 32.5 cm by 20.7 cm
Description: full parchment binding; marbled end-papers

3) PS/CH/RA/2/5: settlement examinations
Title: Examinations/Cheltenham (script)
Dates covered: 1 Jan 1838 to 10 August 1843
Page dimensions: 32.5 cm by 27.7 cm
Contents: A-Z tabbed index (12 leaves, with one unnumbered at front); pages numbered 1–520 containing settlement examinations; 521 numbered but without text; then 57 blank leaves
Description: full parchment binding; marbled end-papers; no spine remaining

4) PS/CH/RA/2/6 removal orders
Title: no writing on cover
Dates covered: 30 Sept 1841 to 10 August 1843
Page dimensions: 32.4 cm by 20 cm
Contents: 147 pro-formas for removal orders (four pages each), completed in script; one blank pro-forma at end
Description: half-leather binding (probably reverse calf) with marbled paper sides; leather very degraded; marbled end-papers; no spine

5) PS/CH/RA/2/7 settlement examinations
Title: no writing on cover
Inside front cover: Made by/L. Dight, Stationery,/170 High Street, Cheltenham
Dates covered: 27 July 1843 to 11 March 1848
Page dimensions: 34 cm by 20.3 cm
Contents: A-Z tabbed index (24 leaves); pages numbered 1–393, with pro-forma headings, containing settlement examinations; 172 leaves blank except for pro-forma headings
Description: full parchment binding, boards; no marbling; broken spine

6) PS/CH/RA/2/8 removal orders
Title: no writing on cover
Dates covered: 29 Jan 1846 to 20 May 1852
Page dimensions: 32.4 cm by 20.3 cm
Contents: 240 pro-formas for removal orders (four pages each) (no settlement examinations included on the 160 completed pro-formas from No 89 (7 Oct 1848) onwards and only single top sheets retained from No 154 to No 167; from No 168 onwards sheets bound in from separate (often light blue) forms; then ten unnumbered pro-formas bound in; finally, 56 blank pro-forma sheets bound in.

10. EDITORIAL METHOD

The body of these settlement examinations have been transcribed verbatim, except for formulaic introductions (which have been briefly summarised) and other matter pre-printed on removal order pro-formas. Additional significant information, such as marginal annotations, has been included in the commentary to each entry.

When the text of a settlement examination is available both in the magistrates' register and a removal order, then the later version, from the removal order, has been selected and any major differences noted in the entry commentary. The originals were written out by any one of a number of clerks, and this edition does not note which clerk was responsible for a particular text.

Formulaic secondary depositions by clerks or medical professionals have normally been summarised within square brackets, to avoid gratuitous repetition, though depositions by relatives or friends of the examinant are normally reproduced in full.

Editorial text within an examination is presented in square brackets. Crossings out by the scribe are usually omitted, unless they contain significant additional information, in which case they are transcribed but struck through.

Initial capitalisation has been retained as in the original, although this does not necessarily correspond to modern style. In particular, the clerks often employed a small initial capital (or a large version of a non-capital letter) for significant nouns, and these have been rendered as regular capitals. In addition, a clerk might not begin a sentence with a capital letter, and this style has also been retained where it occurs. Sometimes, it is not clear whether a particular initial letter was intended to be capitalised, and in these cases a choice has typically been made in favour of capitalisation.

Sentence punctuation is generally quite regular, though on occasions the legal practice of avoiding punctuation is used, and the practice employed in the original text has been retained, though occasional final commas have been converted to full stops. Clerks are generally sparing of apostrophes.

THE SETTLEMENT RECORDS:
1831

31001SE: Tues 11 Jan 1831 – **Henry Spencer**: That he was born in the Parish of Frome in the County of Somerset – that about 6 Years ago he rented a House of Mr Blakeway in the parish of Cheltenham by the Quarter at fifteen pounds a Year – that he occupied the House a whole year and a quarter and paid the whole rent for the time he occupied it [signed]
1785: *an HS baptised at Zion Chapel, Frome, Som 23 Oct.* **1831:** *removal unlikely: settlement probably acknowledged as Cheltenham.* [PS/CH/RA/2/3:1.]

31002SE: [Jan 1831] – **Henry Egerton**: That he has he was born in the parish of Ledbury in the County of Hereford. – That he has heard his Father say that he was settled at Little Hulley [or Hutley; unidentified] and about 8 or 9 Years ago he saw his Father in the Workhouse at Little Hulley. That about three Years ago he was living at Stourbridge and having been taken ill he sent to the overseer of Little Hulley for Relief – That whilst he so resided at Stourbridge the officers of Little Hulley allowed him two Shillings and Six pence for relief – that Mr Hayton who is a Miller at Little Hulley was overseer of the parish and came over [incomplete]
1831: *removal uncertain: examination form incomplete.* **1840:** *perhaps the HE (also Eggerton) buried at New Burial Ground, Cheltenham 30 Sept, aged 30.* [PS/CH/RA//2/3:1.]

31003SE: Tues 25 Jan 1831 – **Thomas Sparkes** (also **Sparks**). *Thomas Harriss of Cheltenham*: That on the 14th. March 1821 he was deputed Bailiff by Richard Snelus to distrain on the Goods and Chattels of his Tenant Thomas Sparkes in a House which Sparkes then rented of Snelus in Cheltenham for the Sum of Five Pounds half a Year but due to Snelus the preceding Christmas. – That he sold the Goods on 2th of March under the distress and that they only produced 3.15.6 out of which the Expences were to be deducted amounting to twelve Shillings, so that the landlord had only three pounds 3/6 towards the Five pounds which was due to him at Christmas 1820. [signed]
Francis Sampson: That he recollects the Sale of Sparkes Effects under the Distress made by Harriss – that the distress was made previously to Ladyday 1821 and only produced 3.15.6 – that he was never present when Sparkes paid Snelus any Sum of money nor does he know of any such payment. [signed] Francis Sampson
Richard Snelus of Cheltenham: That he cannot recollect when it was that Thomas Sparkes took his House but that he took it by the Year at the rent of Ten pounds payable quarterly

That the said Thomas Sparkes entered into possession at the time from whence the rent was payable – that this Examinant is quite sure that the said Thomas Sparkes was not in the House a full Year – that Examinant never received any more than one pound in Cash from the said Thomas Sparkes which was on account of the first half year – That after the first half year was expired he distrained for Four pounds, being the balance of the first half year.

That he is quite positive he never received more than 7.10.0 for Rent from the said Thomas Sparkes – that one pound was received in Money – and the remaining Six pounds ten Shillings was produced by the distresses made by this Examinant [mark]
1829: *TS admitted to Cheltenham Workhouse.* **1831:** *removal unlikely: examination form incomplete.* **1841**: *TS (aged 50; carpenter) lived with wife Ann (50) and daughter Ann (9) in Stanhope St, Cheltenham (HO107/353/9/52/4).* **1851**: *born Cheltenham.* [PS/CH/RA/2/3:2. Removal expenses to Poor House for "Thomas Sparks Carpenter Labour[er]" (5-19 June 1829: P78/1/OV/2/4:15).]

31004SE: Sun 9 Jan 1831 – **John Lloyd** of Cheltenham
1831: *removal uncertain: examination form incomplete.* [PS/CH/RA/2/3:4.]

31005SE: Sat 5 Feb 1831 – **Michael Coleman:** That he is a native of Ireland   That he was born in the town of Tuam in the County of Galway and that he has never done any act to gain a Settlement in England [signed]
1831: *removed to Ireland* (Cheltenham Chron. *10 Feb:* "sent by a pass to Ireland"). [PS/CH/RA/2/3:5.]

31006SE Sat 5 Feb 1831 – **John Martin**, wife **Mary** and two children **Lawrence** and **Thomas:** That he is a native of Ireland and was born in the City of Limerick and has never done any act to gain a Settlement in England That he has a Wife (Mary Martin) and two children Lawrence aged 17 years and Thomas aged 5 years [signed]
1831: *removed to Ireland* (Cheltenham Chron. *10 Feb:* "sent by a pass to Ireland"). [PS/CH/RA/2/3:5.]

31007SE: Sat 5 Feb 1831 – **Thomas Martin:** That he is a native of Ireland and was born in the City of Dublin and that he has never done any act to gain a Settlement in England [signed]
1831: *removed to Ireland* (Cheltenham Chron. *10 Feb:* "sent by a pass to Ireland"). [PS/CH/RA/2/3:6.]

31008SE: Sat 5 Feb 1831 – **Robert Appjohn**: That he is a native of Ireland and was born in the Town of Tuam in the County of Galway. That he has never done any act to gain a Settlement in England [signed]
1831: *removed to Ireland* (Cheltenham Chron. *10 Feb:* "sent by a pass to Ireland"). [PS/CH/RA/2/3:6. Clerk's spelling: "Robert Appi John".]

31009SE: Sat 5 Feb 1831 – **John Butler**, wife **Mary** and son **James**: That he is a Native of Ireland and was born in Smearwick [= Smerwick] in the County of Kerry and that he has [done] no act to gain a Settlement in England. That he, with his wife Mary, and his Son James aged seven years are become chargeable to the parish of Cheltenham [mark]
1831: *removed to Ireland* (Cheltenham Chron. *10 Feb:* "sent by a pass to Ireland"). [PS/CH/RA/2/3:7.]

310010SE: Sat 5 Feb 1831 – **Thomas Dee** of Cheltenham: That he was born in the parish of Cheltenham where he believes his parents were legally settled   That about eleven years ago he rented a House of M^r. Richards in the parish of Saint Luke in the County of Middlesex at Twenty pounds a Year and he paid all Taxes. That he lived in and occupied the said house a whole Year – That he paid three quarter's rent for the said house in money but there was a dispute between him and his landlord about the last quarters rent he having done some work for his said Landlord in the business of a Bricklayer and there was Ten pounds due to him for the said work and for recovery of which he was obliged to bring an action
1831: *removal unlikely: examination form incomplete.* **1833:** *perhaps the TD buried at The Leigh 12 May, aged 45.* [PS/CH/RA/2/3:8.]

31011SE: Tues 8 Feb 1831 – **Ann Holland**, with children **Mary** and **William:** That she is the Wife of James Holland who is a native of Irland [*sic*] as well as herself and that her said husband was born in the parish of Lislee in the County of Cork And that he has never done any act to gain a settlement in England   That she has two children by her said husband Mary aged 3 years and William aged 7 Weeks
1831: *removed to Ireland* (Cheltenham Chron. *10 Feb:* "sent by a pass to Ireland"). [PS/CH/RA/2/3:8. See **31013SE** (James Holland: 10 Feb 1831).]

31012SE: Tues 8 Feb 1831 – **Patrick Bruning**, and wife **Eleanor:** That he is a native of Ireland and was born in the parish of Killabare [perhaps Killaclare] in the County of Mayo   That he is a married man and his wife's name is Eleanor Hayes. That he has never done any act to gain a settlement in England
1831: *removed to Ireland* (Cheltenham Chron. *10 Feb*: "sent by a pass to Ireland"). [PS/CH/RA/2/3:9.]

31013SE: Thurs 10 Feb 1831 – **James Holland:** That he is a native of Ireland and was born in the parish of Lislee in the County of Cork and that he has never done any act to gain a Settlement in England [mark]

1831: *removed to Ireland (*Cheltenham Chron. *17 Feb).* [PS/CH/RA/2/3:9. See **31011SE** (Ann Holland: 8 Feb 1831).]

31014SE: Thurs 10 Feb 1831 – **John Patrick:** That he is a Native of Ireland and was born in Dublin and that he has not done any act to gain a Settlement in England – [signed]
1831: *removed to Ireland (*Cheltenham Chron. *17 Feb).* [PS/CH/RA/2/3:10.]

31015SE: Sat 12 Feb 1831 – **John Sinclair**, wife **Catharine** and son **William:** That he is a native of Ireland and was born in the neighbourhood of Galway in the County of Galway and that he has not done any act to gain a Settlement in England   That he has a Wife named Catharine & one child named William of the age of 12 months [mark]
1831: *removed to Ireland (*Cheltenham Chron. *17 Feb).* [PS/CH/RA/2/3:10.]

31016SE: Tues 15 Feb 1831 – **James Wyeland:** That he was born in the Parish of Muckle Hay [= Mucklelee] in the County of Kilkenny in Ireland
    That he has never done any act to gain a Settlement in England [mark]
1831: *removed to Ireland (*Cheltenham Chron. *17 Feb*: with "wife and two children"). [PS/CH/RA/2/3:11.]

31017SE: [15-22] Feb 1831 – **Elizabeth Foley**, with daughter **Mary:** That she is a native of Ireland and was born near Dublin – That her husband was an Irishman and is now dead   That neither of them ever did any act to gain a Settlement in England
    That she has one Child named Mary aged 14 years – [mark]
1831: *removed to Ireland (*Cheltenham Chron. *17 Feb).* [PS/CH/RA/2/3:11.]

31018SE: [15-22] Feb 1831 – **Margaret Smith**, with son **Edward:** That she is a Native of Ireland and was born at Belfast in the County of Antrim and that she has never done any act to gain a Settlement in England
    That she has a Son named Edward aged Eight Years [mark]
1831: *removed to Ireland (*Cheltenham Chron. *17 Feb).* [PS/CH/RA/2/3:11.]

31019SE: Tues 22 Feb 1831 – **John Woolford**, wife **Elizabeth** and seven children **Mary Ann, Harriet, Frederick, Sarah, Ann, William**, and **John:** That he was born in the parish of Aisey [= Eisey] in the County of Wilts where he believes his parents were legally settled his father having received relief of that Parish –
    That about the 1802 as well as he can remember he was hired at Highworth Mop on Old Michaelmas day by John Hunter of the parish of Staunton [= Stanton] in the said County of Wilts farmer by the year as Cowman at the wages of two pounds –
    That he served the whole year and received all his wages –
    That the year following he was hired by Samuel Pitt of the parish of Aisey aforesaid farmer by the year of the wages or four pounds or Guineas
    That he did not serve his said last Master longer than to the Month of July 1803 in consequence of his having been balloted to serve in the Wiltshire Militia in which he served (in actual Service) till the Month of July 1808
    That in year 1807 he was married to his present wife Elizabeth at the parish of Saint Phillip and Saint Jacob in the City of Bristol and has eight Children now living by her Seven of whom namely Mary Ann aged about fifteen years, Harriett aged about 13 years Frederick aged about twelve years Sarah aged 8 years Ann aged about 6 years William aged about 5 years and John aged about 9 months are now dependant upon him
    That [incomplete]
1817: *JW removed to Stanton, Wilts (presumed) (Gray* **95***: 1 Apr).* **1831:** *removal unlikely: examination form incomplete.* **1840:** *Elizabeth Woolford (aged 54) buried at New Burial Ground, Cheltenham 22 Apr.* **1841:** *Sarah (aged 18; servant) and perhaps Ann (recorded as aged 29; servant) resided at Cheltenham Workhouse (HO107/353/17/16/2 and 3); Harriet was servant in Cheltenham (HO107/353/16/48/12).* **1847:** *Mary Ann Woolford (aged 33) buried at New Burial Ground 22 Oct.* **1851:** *JW (aged 69, widower; pauper, carpenter) apparently resided at Cheltenham Workhouse (HO107/1973/1105/29).* [PS/CH/RA/2/3:12.]

31020SE: Tues 22 Feb 1831 – **Mary Wright:** That she was born in the parish of Baynton [= Bayton] in the County of Worcester where she believes her parents are legally settled

That about six years ago she was hired by D[r]. Rumney of the parish of Saint Nicholas in the City of Worcester by the year at ten pounds wages, that she served the whole year and upwards and received all her wages –

That she has never done any Act to gain a Settlement elsewhere [mark]
1831: *removed to Worcester, Worcs (presumed) (hiring and service).* [PS/CH/RA/2/3:13.]

31021SE: [22-4 Feb 1831] – **Mary Green.**
1831: *removal uncertain: examination form incomplete.* [PS/CH/RA/2/3:13. Removal expenses to Painswick for a "Green" (28 April 1831: P78/1/OV/2/4:32).]

31022SE: Thurs 24 Feb 1831 – **John Cocrane:** That he was born in the Parish of Corfield [unidentified] in the County of Cork and that he has never done any act to gain a Settlement in England [mark]
1831: *removed to Ireland (presumed).* [PS/CH/RA/2/3:14. See **31023SE**: Margaret Cocrane (same date).]

31023SE: Thurs 24 Feb 1831 – **Margaret Cocrane**, widow: That she was born in the parish of Horfield [see previous examination] in the County of Cork and that she has never done any act to gain a settlement in England [mark "of John Cocrane"]
1831: *removed to Ireland (presumed).* [PS/CH/RA/2/3:14. See **31022SE**: John Cocrane (same date).]

31024SE: Thurs 24 Feb 1831 – **John Crofford**, wife and two children **William** and **Margaret:** That he is a native of the Town of Aberdeen in Scotland and has never done any act to gain a settlement in England. That he has a wife and two Children William aged 10 years and Margaret aged two years [mark]
1831: *removed to Scotland (presumed).* [PS/CH/RA/2/3:15.]

31025SE: Sat 26 Feb 1831 – **John Fitzpatrick**, wife and two children **Peter** and **John:** That he was born in the parish of Westport in the County of Mayo   That he has never done any act against a Settlement in England. That he has a Wife and two Children Peter aged 3 years & a half and John aged eleven weeks [signed]
1831: *removed to Ireland (presumed).* [PS/CH/RA/2/3:15.]

31026SE: Sat 26 Feb 1831 – **Richard Cadman:** That he was born in the parish of Westport in the County of Mayo in Ireland – That he has never done any act to gain a Settlement in England [mark]
1831: *removed to Ireland (presumed).* [PS/CH/RA/2/3:16.]

31027SE: Tues 1 Mar 1831 – **Thomas Howell:** That he was born near Castle Bar [= Castlebar] in the Kingdom of Ireland, and that he has done no act to gain a Settlement in England [mark]
1831: *removed to Ireland (presumed).* [PS/CH/RA/2/3:17.]

31028SE: Sat 5 Mar 1831 – **Mary Roke:** That she is a native of Ireland and so is her husband John Roke, who has forsaken her – That she believes her husband was born in Barley Hough [unidentified] in the County of Galway   That her husband has never done any act to gain a settlement in England [mark]
1831: *removed to Ireland (presumed).* [PS/CH/RA/2/3:17.]

31029SE: Sat 5 Mar 1831 – **Ann Boyle**, with son **Michael:** That she is a native of Ireland & was born in Dublin. That she is a Widow and has one Child named Michael Boyle   That neither she or her husband ever did any act to gain a Settlement in England [mark]
1831: *removed to Ireland (presumed).* [PS/CH/RA/2/3:18.]

31030SE: Sat 5 Mar 1831 – **Michael Keys**, wife **Harriet** and daughter **Mary Ann:** That he is a native of Ireland & was born in the parish of Calmoy [= Galmoy] in the County of Kilkenny

That he has a Wife named Harriet and a Daughter aged 2 years & a half old and named Mary Ann Keys   That he has never done any act to gain a Settlement in England [signed]
1831: *removed to Ireland (presumed).* [PS/CH/RA/2/3:18.]

31031SE: Tues 8 Mar 1831 – **Charles Mills**, with children **Charles**, **Thomas**, and **Elizabeth**: That he was born in the parish of Stroud in this County where he believes his parents are legally settled as this Examinant remembers his father receiving relief from the said Parish while living there And this Examinant believes his Grandfather to have been legally settled at Stroud aforesaid That this Examinant has never been hired as a Yearly servant nor rented a tenement at £10 per Annum nor has he done any other Act to gain a Settlement in his own right   That about seven years ago last June he was married to his late wife Maria at the parish of Painswick in this County by whom he has three Children living namely Charles aged seven years Thomas aged near five years and Elizabeth aged near four years – That he is become chargeable to the parish of Cheltenham [mark]
1831: *removed to Stroud (father's settlement).* [PS/CH/RA/2/3:19. Removal expenses to Stroud for "Charles Mills & ch[ildren]" (15 Mar 1831: P78/1/OV/2/4:32).]

31032SE: Tues 8 Mar 1831 – **Ellen Presdee:** That She was born in the parish of Leigh in the County of Worcester where [incomplete and struck out]
1831: *removal uncertain: examination form incomplete.* [PS/CH/RA/2/3:20.]

31033SE: Thurs 10 Mar 1831 – **William Anderson**, wife and three children **Ellen**, **William**, and **Eliza:** That he is a native of Ireland and was born in Shandon Parish in the City of Cork – That he has a Wife and three Children Ellen aged 12 years, William aged 10 years, and Eliza aged 2 years. That he has never done any Act to gain a Settlement in England [mark]
1831: *removed to Ireland* (Cheltenham Chron. *17 Mar*). [PS/CH/RA/2/3:20.]

31034SE: Tues 15 Mar 1831 – **Caroline Cadogan:** That she was born in the parish of Frampton upon Severn [= Frampton on Severn] in this County where she believes her parents were legally settled   That about three years ago she was hired by M^{rs}. Whitmarsh wife of M^r. Whitmarsh of Cheltenham in this County Waiter by the year at the wages of five pounds   That she continued fifteen Months in the said service and received her full wages   That she has done no Act to gain a Settlement since [incomplete]
1831: *removal unlikely: examination form incomplete.* **1832**: a *CC buried 8 June at New Burial Ground, Cheltenham, aged 21.* [PS/CH/RA/2/3:21.]

31035SE: Tues 22 Mar 1831 – **Maria Brain** (also **Breiane**, **Briane**, **Briene**): That she never was informed in what parish she was born – The earliest recollection she has of herself was when she was about 8 or 9 years of age at which time she was living with her mother at Nailsworth in this County   That she lived about twelvemonths with her father and mother at Charlton Kings where her father and mother now reside. That she has never done any Act to gain a Settlement in her [incomplete] [mark]
1828: *MB ("b[ase]-born" at Nailsworth 2 Feb 1813) baptised 1 June in Charlton Kings (parents Thomas and Esther Brain).* **1831**: *removal uncertain: examination form incomplete.* [PS/CH/RA/2/3:22. See **31041SE** (22 Mar 1831); **31044SE** (Mar 1831).]

31036SE: Tues 15 Mar 1831 – **Mary Ann Moore**, single woman: That she was born in S^t. Mary's parish Carlisle in the County of Cumberland where her parents are legally settled   That she has never done any act to gain a Settlement in England [incomplete]
1831: *removal uncertain: examination form incomplete.* [PS/CH/RA/2/3:23.]

31037SE: Thurs 17 Mar 1831 – **James Mayer**, and wife **Sarah:** That he was born in Dublin in Ireland   That he has never gained a Settlement in England   that he has a wife named Sarah and they are become chargeable to the parish of Cheltenham [signed]

1831: *removed to Ireland by pass (*Cheltenham Chron. *24 Mar). Clerk's note: "removed to Gloucester".* [PS/CH/RA/2/3:23.]

31038SE: Sat 19 Mar 1831 – **Dennis Brien:** That he was born as he hath heard & believes in the County of Tipperary in that bit of the United Kingdom called Ireland   That he hath never done any act whereby to gain a Settlement in England And that he hath now actually become chargeable to the Parish of Cheltenham in the said county of Gloucester [signed]
1831: *removed to Ireland (*Cheltenham Chron. *24 Mar).* [PS/CH/RA/2/3:24.]

31039SE: Sat 19 Mar 1831 – **Cornelius Sullivan:** That he was born in the County of Cork in Ireland and has never done any act to gain a Settlement in England And that he is now become actually chargeable to the parish of Cheltenham in the said County of Gloucester [mark]
1831: *removed to Ireland (presumed).* Cheltenham Chron. *24 Mar records a "Patrick Sullivan" "passed to Ireland".* [PS/CH/RA/2/3:25.]

31040SE: Sat 19 Mar 1831 – **Susannah Lane** (also **Susan**), single woman: [That] she was born in the Parish of Longney in the said County where her Parents resided
    That when she was about twelve years old her Mother took her to Eastington in the same County where she resided with a M^{rs}. Jones to nurse her Child for 12 Months but was never hired nor did she receive Wages but her Mistress occasionally gave her Money to buy her Cloathes
    That when she was about fourteen Years of Age she went to Gloucester and was hired by a Mr. Haines of the parish of Saint Nicholas in that City Grocer, at the Wages of Five Pounds per year, with liberty for either Party to dissolve the Contract by giving a Months Notice   That she continued in such service for the whole Year and received the full Wages. That she continued in Mr Haines's Service for Eleven Months longer when she left his Service. That since that time she has never been hired for a Year.
    That she has been residing in Cheltenham for upwards of three Years, occasionally living with her Aunt, and in Lodgings but never rented a Tenement of Ten Pounds per Year nor done any other Act to gain a Settlement [signed Susan Lane]
1831: *removed to Gloucester (presumed) (hiring and service)*; *aged about 20.* [PS/CH/RA/2/3:26-7. Note: "Order of Removal made". Removal expenses for "Susan Lane" (destination not specified) (6 Apr 1831: P78/1/OV/2/4:32).]

31041SE: Tues 22 Mar 1831 – Thomas Brain, labourer, residing in Charlton Kings, relating to settlement of daughter **Maria Brain:** That he was born in the parish of Stone in the County of Stafford – where his Parents were settled – That his father by his Will devised to him a freehold House in the Parish of Stone – which now belongs to him – that she never slept upon the Property so devised by his Father more than about 26 nights.
    That between 5 and 6 Years ago he agreed to rent a House of Mr Clifford on Park Street in the Parish of Charlton King's for a Year at the rent of fifteen pounds, – that the rent was payable quarterly – that he continued in possession under such yearly taking for more than twelve months, – and he paid the Rent for the whole time he occupied. That since that period he has been living at Charlton King's - That Maria Briene – who is present is his legitimate daughter having been born in lawful Wedlock [mark]
[PS/CH/RA/2/3:28. See **31035SE** (22 Mar 1831); **31044SE** (Mar 1831).]

31042SE: Thurs 24 Mar 1831 – **James Scott**, wife and three children **William**, **Michael**, and **Peter**: That he was born as he hath heard and believes in the parish of Lanark in Lanarkshire in that part of the United Kingdom called Scotland
    That he has never done any act to gain a Settlement in England - that he has a wife and three Children namely William aged eight years Michael aged six years and Peter aged sixteen Months that he is become chargeable to the parish of Cheltenham [signed]
1831: *removed to Scotland (presumed).* [PS/CH/RA/2/3:29.]

31043SE: Sat 26 Mar 1831 – **Ann James**: That she was born in the Parish of Hazleton in the County of Gloucester – that on Michaelmas day in the Year 1828 she was hired by Mr Newman of Rose Cottage Cheltenham for a Year at the Wages of Six Guineas – that she was to go into the Service a week after the day on which she was hired – which she accordingly did. – That her hiring was months Wages or Months Warning. – that after she had been with in Mr Newman's Service some time her Mistress said she did not suit her and gave her Warning – That before the month expired being dissatisfied with her place she ran away but on the following day she was induced by her Mother to return back to the service which she accordingly did and her Mistress consented to her going on because she had not got another Servant – that nothing passed further at the end of the month – and she continued on til Michaelmas when her Mistress settled her Wages deducting something but she does not know how much, for the time this Examinant was absent from the Service [mark]
1831: *removal uncertain: settlement probably acknowledged as Cheltenham.* [PS/CH/RA/2/3:30.]

31044SE: [undated] Mar 1831 – Thomas Brain, labourer, residing in Charlton Kings, relating to settlement of daughter **Maria**: That he was born at Darlaston in the Parish of Stone in the County of Stafford where his Parents he believes were settled. – that he lived with his Father until he was about 11 or 12 Years of age. – that he then went to live with his Uncle at Fulford in the Parish of Stone under a yearly hiring at Three Guineas a Year – That he lived with his Uncle as such Servant nearly two Years. – That he then went to a place called the Open Gates [= Oakengates] in Shropshire to work as a Miner – that he never engaged himself as a Yearly Servant after he left his Uncle
That when he was about 21 Years of age he married Ann Clewes in the Parish of Lutterworth in the County of Leicester – that he lived with his said Wife about 21 Years.
That she died and was buried in the Church Yard of Paddington in the County of Middlesex – that he had by her three Children – that between 18 and 19 Years ago he married Esther Smith Widow in the Parish of Darlaston near Bilston in the County of Stafford – that this said Esther Smith had then five Children – that she [*sic*] has only one Child by his said last Wife living whose name is Maria
That she was the eldest Child and was born after their Marriage –
That his said daughter Maria was born in the Parish of Horsley in this County where this Examinant went to work soon after his Marriage
That he never rented a House at the yearly Rent of Ten Pounds [mark]
[PS/CH/RA/2/3:32-3. Note: "Married to Esther Smith his present Wife 2 March 1813". See **31035SE** (22 Mar 1831); **31041SE** (22 Mar 1831).]

31045SE: Tues 29 Mar 1831 – **Mary Hayes**, with granddaughter **Ellen McCarthy**: That She was born as she hath heard and believes in the County of Cork in that part of the United Kingdom called Ireland – That she has never done any act whereby to gain a Settlement in England – And that she hath with her Grand daughter Ellen M^c.Carthy actually become chargeable to the parish of Cheltenham in the said County [mark]
1831: *removed to Ireland (presumed).* [PS/CH/RA/2/3:34.]

31046SE: Tues 29 Mar 1831 – **Thomas Clifford**, labourer, wife **Jane** and son **Charles**: That he was born in the Parish of Swindon in the said County where his Parents resided and which was their legal Place of Settlement
That he never was hired by any Person to serve as a Yearly Servant but that he has served Mr Wiche [reading uncertain] of Cheltenham as a Weekly Servant for several Years, but that he was at Liberty to leave him at any time, upon giving a Weeks Notice   That he has been married to his present Wife Jane upwards of a Year and a half and that he has by his present Wife one Son about three Weeks old who is not yet baptized and they are now chargeable to the parish of Cheltenham [signed]

1831: removed to Swindon (presumed) (his father's settlement): see **37030RO** *(TC: 15 Apr 1837).* [PS/CH/RA/2/3:35.]

31047SE: Thurs 7 Apr 1831 – **James Capper**, wife **Eliza** and children **George** and **Joseph**: That he was born in the Parish of Hartpury in this County but he believes his father was not legally settled there

That when Examinant was about 17 years of age he was hired by John Drinkwater of Sandhurst in this County farmer by the year as a Servant in husbandry at the wages of Three pounds – That he served the full year and received his years wages – That about six years ago being then ill of a fever he applied to the parish Officers of Sandhurst (having been previously become [*sic*] chargeable to the parish of Newent where he then lived and was by them removed by an Order to Sandhurst aforesaid) for relief and was relieved by them – That about seven years ago he married his present wife Eliza at Cheltenham and has two Children namely George aged six years and Joseph aged about three years and a half - That he is now chargeable to the parish of Cheltenham [mark]
1831: removed to Sandhurst (presumed) (hiring and service): see **45010SE** *(JC: 15 Feb 1845) for further information.* [PS/CH/RA/2/3:36.]

31048SE: Sat 9 Apr 1831 – **Maria Larder,** confined to bed by sickness in Cheltenham: That she was born in the parish of Stroud in this County where she believes her parents were legally settled

That when she was about fourteen or fifteen years of age she was hired by M^r. Henry White of Stroud aforesaid Cabinet maker by the week at one Shilling per week   That he gave her some Clothes at times and She continued five years with Mr White and has not gained a Settlement since   That she is become chargeable to the parish of Cheltenham [mark]
*1831: **ML died before removal to Stroud (father's settlement)**; buried at Cheltenham 15 Apr, aged 22.* [PS/CH/RA/2/3:37. Expenses relating to death of Maria Larder (P78/1/OV/2/4:88).]

31049SE: Sat 9 Apr 1831 – **Peter Makin** and four children: I was born in Scotland in the Town of Dumfries & have four Children - I have never done any act to gain a Settlement in England [signed]
1831: removed to Scotland (Cheltenham Chron. 14 Apr: "Peter Makin and family"). [PS/CH/RA/2/3:38.]

31050SE: Sat 9 Apr 1831 – **Timothy Donovan**, wife and three children, **Timothy, Mary**, and **Helen**: That he was born in the Parish of Naas in the County of Kildare in Ireland

That he is married   that his Wife is now living who that she [*sic*] has borne him three Children namely, Timothy aged nine yrs Mary aged 4 and Helen one year and ten months   that he hath never done any act to gain a settlement since he has been in England and that he is now chargeable to the Parish of Cheltenham [signed]
1831: removed to Ireland (presumed). [PS/CH/RA/2/3:38.]

31051SE: Thurs 14 Apr 1831 – **Mary Chambers**, widow, with children **John, Mary**, and **Catherine**: That she was born as she hath heard and believes in that part of the United Kingdom called Ireland   That she hath never done any Act whereby to gain a Settlement in England And that she hath with her Son John and her two Daughters Mary and Catherine actually become chargeable to the Parish of Cheltenham [mark]
1831: removed to Ireland (presumed). [PS/CH/RA/2/3:39.]

31052SE: Thurs 14 Apr 1831 – **John Barrett**, wife **Ellen** and daughter **Betty**: That He Was born as he hath heard and believes in the county of Sligo in that part of the United Kingdom called Ireland   That he had never done any Act whereby to gain a Settlement in England And that he hath with his Wife Ellen and his Daughter Betty actually become chargeable to the Parish of Cheltenham in the said County [mark]
1831: removed to Ireland (presumed). [PS/CH/RA/2/3:39.]

31053SE: Thurs 14 Apr 1831 – **Thomas Mandefield**, wife **Mary** and two sons **James** and **Charles**: That he was born as he hath heard and believes in the City of Edingburgh [= Edinburgh]

in that part of Great Britain called Scotland   That he had never done any Act whereby to gain a Settlement in England And that he hath with his Wife Mary and his two Sons James and Charles actually become chargeable to the Parish of Cheltenham in the said County [mark]
1831: *removed to Scotland (presumed)*. [PS/CH/RA/2/3:40.]

31054SE: Thurs 14 Apr 1831 – **Mary Young**, with daughter **Eliza**: That she was born as she hath heard and believes in the City of Edingburgh [= Edinburgh] in that part of the United Kingdom called Scotland   That she had never done any Act whereby to gain a Settlement in England And that she hath with her Daughter Eliza actually become chargeable to the Parish of Cheltenham in the said County [signed]
1831: *removed to Scotland (presumed)*. [PS/CH/RA/2/3:40.]

0055SE: Thurs 14 Apr 1831 – **Jane Scott**, with children **Nancy** and **John**: That she was born in Scotland and has never done any Act to gain a Settlement in England and that she and her two Children Nancy and John are now chargeable to the parish of Cheltenham [mark]
1831: *removed to Scotland (presumed)*. [PS/CH/RA/2/3:41.]

31056SE: Sat 16 Apr 1831 – **Ann Mustoe**, with son **John**: That she was born at Charlton Kings in this County where she believes her father Thomas Mustoe is legally settled   he had built two Cottages there upon Land leased by him of Miss Bolton
    That this Examinant has never done any Act by Servitude or otherwise to gain a Settlement in her own right
    That she has an illegitimate son named John aged about two years [mark]
1831: *removed to Charlton Kings (father's settlement)*. [PS/CH/RA/2/3:42. Note: "Order made".]

31057SE: Tues 19 Apr 1831 – **John Beard**: That he was born in the parish of Leonard Stanley in the said County [incomplete]
1830: *JB returned from military service in East Indies, where he married wife Mary Ann*. **1831**: *removal uncertain: examination form incomplete*. **1841**: *JB (aged 40, umbrella-maker, previously labourer etc) with family in Westbury on Severn (HO107/369/5/12/18)*. **1851**: *toll collector at Longford, Gloucester, aged 55 (HO107/1961/130/18)*. [PS/CH/RA/2/3:43.]

31058SE: [undated: Apr] 1831 – **William Davis**, wife **Eliza** and daughter **Eliza**: That he was born in the parish of Deptford in the County of Kent where he believes his father is legally settled his said father having formerly rented a house at Deptford aforesaid at £60 a year or upwards
    That on the 29th January 1830 he was married to his wife Eliza of the parish of Hempstead [= Hempsted] in this County by whom he has one Child namely Eliza aged 6 Months
    That this Examinant has never done any Act to gain a Settlement in his own Right by Renting Servitude or otherwise
1831: *removal uncertain: examination form incomplete; perhaps removed to Deptford, Kent (father's settlement)*. [PS/CH/RA/2/3:44.]

31059SE: Sat 23 Apr 1831 – **William Griffin**: That he was born in the parish of Old Swinford [= Oldswinford] in the County of Worcester Where he believes his father was legally settled
    That about fourteen or fifteen years ago he was hired by Edward Pollard Carruthers of Painswick in this County Esquire by the year as Butler at the wages of Fifty Guineas – That he continued nearly two years in the said Service and received all his wages – That he has not done any Act to gain a Settlement since [signed]
1820: *WG removed to Painswick (presumed) (Gray **301**: 6 May) (RETURNED)*. **1831**: *removed to Painswick (presumed) (hiring and service)*. **1841**: *WG (aged 40; labourer) lived in the High, Stourbridge (Oldswinford), Worcs (HO107/1198/10/32/10)*. [PS/CH/RA/2/3:45.]

31060SE: Sat 23 Apr 1831 – **John MacDonald**, wife and five children: That he was born in the City of Glasgow in Scotland. That he has done no act to gain a Settlement in England – That he has a Wife and 5 Children who with him are become chargeable to the parish of Cheltenham [mark]
1831: *removed to Scotland (presumed)*. [PS/CH/RA/2/3:45.]

31061SE: Thurs 28 Apr 1831 – **Ellen Docket**, widow, with daughter **Ellen**: That she was born in the parish of S[t]. Anns in the ~~City of Cork~~ County of Kerry in Ireland – That she hath not gained any Settlement in England

That she and her daughter Ellen are become chargeable to the parish of Cheltenham [mark]
1831: *removed to Ireland (presumed).* [PS/CH/RA/2/3:46.]

31062SE: Thurs 28 Apr 1831 – **Samuel Hyde**: That he was born in the parish of Shurdington in this County where he believes his father was legally settled his said father having informed him that he had gained a Settlement in Shurdington aforesaid by Servitude

That about fifty years ago he was hired by William Rose of Leckhampton in this County farmer as in a yearly Servant in husbandry at about Seven Guineas a year as well as he can remember   That he lived a year in the said Service and he received his full years wages [mark]
1831: *removed to Charlton Kings (presumed) (hiring and service); (RETURNED) died several months after examination (buried 28 Sept at New Burial Ground, Cheltenham, aged 72).* [PS/CH/RA/2/3:46.]

31063SE: Tues 3 May 1831 – Hannah Berry, wife of John Berry, daughter of late Joseph Barnard of Naunton, and sister of **Robert Barnard**: *Hannah Berry:* That she has a brother Robert Barnard who is now confined in the parish Workhouse at Cheltenham being in a deranged state of mind   That her said father Joseph Barnard was the owner of a Cottage and Garden at Naunton aforesaid on which he resided many years till his death in June last

That during the last twelvemonth of his life her said father received weekly pay from the parish officers of Naunton aforesaid

That to the best of her knowledge her said brother never was hired as a yearly Servant in any place whatever nor [has] done any Act to gain a Settlement in his own right except that she has heard that her said brother lived two years with a M[r] Meadows at Frogmill as Ostler – That her said brother would have come into the possession of her said father's Cottage if he could have discharged the claims of the Parish Officers of Naunton aforesaid for having relieved her said father her said brother being her father's legal heir [mark]
Andrew Hathaway, employed by the Guardian of the Poor of Cheltenham: That he made enquiry of M[r]. Meadows respecting the Settlement of the above named Robert Barnard and was informed that he was not an yearly hired Servant – That He filled the situation of Ostler by the week for what he could get [signed]
1831: *probably removed to Naunton (father's settlement).* **1841:** *Hannah Berry (aged 50) lived with husband John (aged 45; agricultural labourer) and two sons at Tally Ho, Guiting Power (near Naunton); brother "Robert Barnet" (48; agricultural labourer) lived in same house (HO107/360/8/7/9).* [PS/CH/RA/2/3:47. Removal expenses (destination unspecified) for "Rob[t]. Barnard" (4 May 1831: P78/1/OV/2/4:32).]

31064SE: Thurs 5 May 1831 – **Mary Eaton**: That she was born in the parish of Wanborough in the County of Wilts where she believes her parents were legally settled –

That her mother after the death of her father being left with a large family received relief from the parish Officers of Wanborough aforesaid

That last Michaelmas two years ago she was hired by Miss Mundy of Wotton Bassett [= Royal Wootton Bassett] in the said County of Wilts by the year at the wages of Eight pounds and she served the whole year and received her full years wages – That she has not done any Act to gain a Settlement since [mark]
1831: *removed to Wootton Bassett, Wilts (hiring and service): see* **38029RO** *(ME: 21 Apr 1838) for further information.* [PS/CH/RA/2/3:48. Note: "Orders [of Removal] made". Removal expenses for ME (destination unspecified) (4 May 1831: P78/1/OV/2/4:32).]

31065SE: Sat 7 May 1831 – **James Maisey**, wife **Mary** and three children **Mary Ann**, **William Henry**, and **George**: That he was born in the parish of Farmington in this County   That about fourteen years ago he was hired by M[r]. Edward Cripps of Cirencester in this County for a Year -

That he was not to receive any wages but lived in M^r. Cripps' house and had his Board Lodging and Clothes in the lieu of wages –

That he lived there the whole year and was again hired in the same Service for another year the whole of which time he served – That he has not since done any other Act by renting Servitude or otherwise to gain a Settlement elsewhere   That about eight years ago he was married to his present wife Mary at Cheltenham by whom he has three children living namely Mary Ann now aged about six years William Henry aged between four and five years and George aged about seven months   That he is become chargeable to the parish of Cheltenham [signed]

1831: *removed to Cirencester (hiring and service).* [PS/CH/RA/2/3:48. Removal expenses for "Maisey & family to Cirencester" (7 July 1831: P78/1/OV/2/4:32).]

31066SE: Tues 17 May 1831 – **Michael Leary**, wife **Julia** and infant child: I was born in Clonikilty [= Clonakilty] in the County of Cork in Ireland – I have a Wife named Julia and an infant child – I have never done any act to gain a Settlement in England [mark]

1831: *removed to Ireland (presumed).* [PS/CH/RA/2/3:50.]

31067SE: Tues 17 May 1831 – **William Lee**, wife **Catherine**, and four children **Thomas**, **Michael**, **William**, and **Richard**: I was born in the County of Cork in Ireland

I have a Wife named Catherine & four children Thomas, Michael, William & Richard – I have never done any act to gain a Settlement in England [mark]

1831: *removed to Ireland (presumed).* [PS/CH/RA/2/3:50.]

31068SE: Tues 17 May 1831 – **Biddy Sullivan**: I am a singlewoman   I was born in the County of Cork – I have never done any act to gain a settlement in England [mark]

1831: *removed to Ireland (presumed).* [PS/CH/RA/2/3:51.]

31069SE: Fri 20 May 1831 – **Thomas Griffin**: That he was born in the County of Cork in Ireland   That he has done no act to gain a Settlement in England [mark]

1831: *removed to Ireland (presumed).* [PS/CH/RA/2/3:51.]

31070SE: Fri 20 May 1831 – **Mary Cochlin**: I am a single woman   I was born in the County of Cork in Ireland   That she has done no act to gain a Settlement in England [mark]

1831: *removed to Ireland (presumed).* [PS/CH/RA/2/3:51.]

31071SE: Fri 20 May 1831 – **Mary Driscole**: I am a singlewoman   I was born in the County of Cork in Ireland   I have never done any act to gain a settlement in England [mark]

1831: *removed to Ireland (presumed).* [PS/CH/RA/2/3:52.]

31072SE: Sat 21 May 1831 – **Elizabeth Lewis**: That she was born in the parish of Bisley in this County where she believes her father is legally settled

That about five or six years ago she was hired by M^{rs}. Turner wife of Evan Turner of Charlton Kings in this County Butcher as a yearly servant at the wages of Four pounds   That she continued in the said Service nearly Three years and received all her wages – That she has not lived a year in any Service since she left M^{rs}. Turners nor done any other Act to gain the Settlement since [mark]

1831: *removed to Charlton Kings (presumed) (hiring and service).* [PS/CH/RA/2/3:53.]

31073SE: Sat 21 May 1831 – **Ann Madden**, with three infant children: I was born in the County of Cork in Ireland   I have 3 infant children

I have a husband who has never gained any Settlement in England [mark]

1831: *removed to Ireland* (Cheltenham Chron. *26 May*). [PS/CH/RA/2/3:53.]

31074SE: Sat 21 May 1831 – **Mary Bruton**, with three children: I was born in the County of Fife in Scotland – I have 3 Children and have never done any act to gain a Settlement in England [mark]

1831: *removed to Scotland* (Cheltenham Chron. *26 May*). [PS/CH/RA/2/3:54.]

31075SE: Sat 21 May 1831 – **Jane Cayle**, with two children: I was born in the City of Dublin   I am a Widow and have 2 Children by my husband who was a native of Scotland and never gained a Settlement in England [mark]
1831: *removed to Scotland (*Cheltenham Chron. *26 May).* [PS/CH/RA/2/3:54.]

31076SE: Sat 21 May 1831 – **Thomas Cole**, confined to bed by sickness, at Alstone: That he was born in the parish of Bishops Cleeve in this County
That he was hired by John Steedman of the parish of Badgworth [= Badgeworth] a great many years ago as a yearly servant from Michaelmas to Michaelmas following.
That he remained in such service the whole year and received the whole year's wages
That he never rented a house at Ten Pounds a year or did any other act to gain a Settlement – That he has frequently relief from the said parish of Badgworth [mark]
1831: *died before removal (presumed) at Cheltenham* shortly after examination (buried at Cheltenham 24 Aug, aged 77). [PS/CH/RA/2/3:55.]

31077SE: Tues 24 May 1831 – **John Dwyer**, wife and three children: That he was born in the County of Kildare in Ireland – That he has never done any Act to gain a Settlement in England That he with his wife and three children are become chargeable to the parish of Cheltenham [signed]
1831: *removed to Ireland (presumed).* [PS/CH/RA/2/3:56.]

31078SE: Tues 24 May 1831 – **Robert Walker**, with three children **Catherine**, **John**, and **Sarah**: That he was born in the County of Ayr in Scotland and That he has never done any Act to gain a Settlement in England – That he has three children namely Catherine aged about 12 years John aged 10 years and Sarah aged 8 years
That he has become chargeable to the parish of Cheltenham [mark]
1831: *removed to Scotland (presumed).* [PS/CH/RA/2/3:57.]

31079SE: 26 May 1831 – **Richard Cavenagh**: That he was born in the County of Meath in that part of the United Kingdom called Ireland – That he has never done any Act to gain a Settlement in England and he is become chargeable to the parish of Cheltenham [mark]
1831: *removed to Ireland (presumed).* [PS/CH/RA/2/3:57.]

31080SE: Thurs 26 May 1831 – **Michael Crawley**, wife **Margaret**, and three children **Michael**, **Catherine**, and **Mary**: That he was born in the County of Cork in Ireland and has never done any Act to gain a Settlement in England – That he has a wife named Margaret and three Children namely Michael aged seven years Catherine aged five years and Mary aged two years –
That he is become chargeable to the parish of Cheltenham [signed Mechal Crawley]
1831: *removed to Ireland (presumed).* [PS/CH/RA/2/3:58. Examination struck out.]

31081SE: Sat 28 May 1831 – **Edward Summers**, and wife **Mary Ann**: That he was born in the parish of Tuffley in this County. That after his parents death when this Examinant was very young he lived as a parish boy with M^r. Parker at one time Overseer of the poor of Tuffley aforesaid – That when he was about nine years old he ran away from the said parish of Tuffley and went to sea on board of a Man of War and remained at Sea about 15 or 16 years – That about six years ago he was married to his present wife Mary Ann at the parish of Hempstead [= Hempsted] in this County – That he has never done any Act to gain a Settlement in his own right That he is become chargeable to the parish of Cheltenham [mark]
1831: *removed to Tuffley (birth).* **1833:** (*RETURNED*) *ES buried at New Burial Ground, Cheltenham 27 Dec, aged 41.* [PS/CH/RA/2/3:59. Removal expenses for "Summers to Tuffley" (26 May 1831: P78/1/OV/2/4:32).]

31082SE: Thurs 2 June 1831 – **Fanny Simpson**, single woman: That she was born in the parish of Cirencester in this County where she believes her father is legally settled, her said father having to this Examinant's knowledge rented a house at Cirencester aforesaid at ten pounds a year for several years - That she is become chargeable to the parish of Parish of Cheltenham [signed Fanney Simpson]

1831: *removed to Cirencester (father's settlement).* [PS/CH/RA/2/3:60. Removal expenses for "F. Simpson to Cirenc^r." (1 June 1831: P78/1/OV/2/4:32).]

31083SE: Sat 4 June 1831 – **Sarah Silman**, single woman: That she was born in the Hamlet of Milton in the Parish of Shipton under Whichwood [= Shipton-under-Wychwood] in the County of Oxford where her Father was legally settled – That about thirteen years ago she left Milton and came to Cheltenham in the County of Gloucester and was hired by Mr. Stokes Haynes for a Year at the Wages of Eight Pounds or Eight Guineas   That she served the whole Year and was again hired for another Year, but quitted the Service before the End of the Year – That she has been in different Services in the Parish of Cheltenham, but never served a Year in any other Place than Mr Haines, nor has she left Cheltenham for any time longer than a Week since she first came into it

That she has done no Act to gain a Settlement in any other Place [mark]

1831: *removal unlikely: settlement probably acknowledged as Cheltenham.* [PS/CH/RA/2/3:61.]

31084SE: Tues 7 June 1831 – **Thomas Martin**.

1831: *removal uncertain: examination form incomplete.* [PS/CH/RA/2/3:62. Expenses for travel "To Gloucester to take examination of Martin" (13 June 1831: P78/1/OV/2/4:59).]

31085SE: Thurs 9 June 1831 – **Daniel Collins**, wife and two children: That he was born in the County of Cork in Ireland and has not done any Act to gain a Settlement in England

That he has a wife and two Children and is become chargeable to the parish of Cheltenham [mark]

1831: *removed to Ireland (presumed).* [PS/CH/RA/2/3:62.]

31086SE: Thurs 16 June 1831 – **James Holder**, wife **Nancy**, and two children **Ann** and **James**: That he was born in the parish of Frampton Cotterell in this County where he believes his parents were legally settled

That when he was about 17 years of age he was apprenticed to Thomas Osborne of Frampton Cotterell aforesaid hatter for seven Years and served the whole time – That about ten years ago he was married to his present wife Nancy at Chertsey in Surry [= Surrey] by whom he has two Children namely Ann aged ten years and James aged eight years

That about six years ago he rented a house of M^r. Gwinnell in Cheltenham at twenty pounds a year that he lived a twelvemonth in the said house and paid the years Rent and taxes for the same

That he afterwards rented a house of William Jordan at Cheltenham at twenty pounds a year and occupied it nearly four years and paid all the rent and taxes [signed]

1831: *removal unlikely: settlement probably acknowledged as Cheltenham.* **1838**: *JH the elder likely to be person of that name (aged 78) buried from the workhouse at Gloucester 18 Oct.* **1841** *Ann Holder (aged 55; greengrocer) lived with son James (15; gardener) at 218 High St, Cheltenham (HO17/353/8/69/21).* **1851**: *JH (28; gardener) was married with young family, and mother (Nancy, 68; domestic duties) and lived with them in Prestbury (HO107/1972/25/5).* [PS/CH/RA/2/3:63.]

31087SE: Sat 18 June 1831 – **Arabella Kellow Herbert**, single woman: That she was born in the Parish of St Mary de Lode in the City of Gloucester – that about 26 Years ago she was hired by Mr Haslem of St Mary de Crypt for a Year and received one Shilling as earnest money –. She was to work twelve Hours a day – she did not work on Sundays – and nothing was said about Sundays – She was not to have any wages her object being to learn the Stocking trade [signed]

1831: *removal uncertain as service was not continuous throughout week.* **1841**: *AKH (aged 50) lived alone in St Mary de Lode, Gloucester.* [PS/CH/RA/2/3:64 (p. 65 blank).]

31088SE: Sat 18 June 1831 – **James Aldridge**, wife **Sarah**, and their six children **Sophia**, **Caroline**, **Sydney**, **Jessie**, **Frederick**, and **Ellen**: That he was born in the Parish of Stroud in the County of Gloucester where his parents were legally settled – that in the year 1826 he served the office of Tythingman of the said Parish and continued in such office three Years.

that in the Year 1819 he was married in the Parish Church of Saint Mary de Lode to Sarah his present wife by whom he has Six Children now living namely Sophia aged 11 Years Caroline 7 Years Sydney Five Years Jessie 4 Years Frederick three Years and Ellen two Years and that he is now chargeable to the Parish of Cheltenham [signed]
1831: *removed to Stroud (office-holding): see* **43076SE** *(JA: 28 Dec 1843) for further information.* [PS/CH/RA/2/3:66. Removal expenses for "Jas. Aldridge & family to Stroud" (30 June 1831: P78/1/OV/2/4:32).]

31089SE: Thurs 30 June 1831 – **Mary Gibson**, with two children **John** and **Thomas**: That she was born in the Town of Ayr in that part of the United Kingdom called Scotland
    that She has never done any Act to gain a Settlement in England
    That she has two children John aged 13 years and Thomas aged 10 years and She is become chargeable to the parish of Cheltenham [mark]
1831: *removed to Scotland (presumed).* [PS/CH/RA/2/3:64.]

31090SE: Thurs 30 June 1831 – **Henry Hooper**, wife **Amelia**, and three children **Mary Ann**, **Caroline**, and **Emma**: That he was born in the Parish of Wottonunderedge [= Wotton-under-Edge] in the said County, the place of Settlement of his Parents as he had heard and believes
    That he has known his father rent a farm at Wottonunderedge aforesaid for several years the rent of which was to the best of this Examinants knowledge and belief upwards of forty pounds a year – That this Examinants Mother occupied the said farm after his father's death for more than a Year
    That he this Examinant has never done any Act by servitude renting or otherwise to gain a Settlement in his own right
    That upwards of five Years ago he was married to his present wife Amelia at Hempstead [= Hempsted] in this County   that he has three Children by her namely Mary Ann aged near six years Caroline aged about three years and an Infant not to get baptized [signed]
1831: *removed to Wotton-under-Edge (father's settlement); unbaptised infant was Emma Hooper, baptised 29 July Cheltenham (buried at Cheltenham 14 Apr 1835).* **1835**: *(RETURNED) HH, widower, married Hannah King 11 May at Cheltenham.* **1841**: *perhaps the HH (aged 35; day labourer) living in Grosvenor St, Cheltenham with daughter Caroline (aged 12) and wife Hannah (HO107/353/4/49/20).* **1851**: *a Caroline Hooper (aged 21; servant, pauper) resided at Cheltenham Workhouse on census night (HO107/1973/1099/19).* [PS/CH/RA/2/3:67: removal suspended as pauper unfit to travel. Removal expenses for "Hooper & family" to "Wotton Underedge" (25 Aug 1831: P78/1/OV/2/4:65).]

31091SE: Thurs 7 July 1831 – **Mary Scott, Mary Mackintosh, Bridget Gordon, Mary Elliot, Ann Manning, Mary McKensie**, with eleven children: [Mary Scott] That she has 3 Children; [Mary Mackintosh] That she has 2 Children; [Bridget Gordon] That she has 2 Children; [Mary Elliot] That she has one child; [Ann Manning] That she has two children; [Mary M^c.Kensie] That she has one child
    And these Deponents farther state their several husbands were natives of Scotland and never did any act to gain a Settlement in England
    And that they and their respective Children and now chargeable to the parish of Cheltenham [marks]
1831: *removed to Scotland (presumed).* [PS/CH/RA/2/3:68.]

31092SE: Thurs 7 July 1831 – **John Drummond**, wife and three children: I am a native of Scotland and have never gained a Settlement in England & with my Wife and 3 Children are become chargeable to the parish of Cheltenham [signed]
1831: *removed to Scotland (presumed).* [PS/CH/RA/2/3:69.]

31093SE: Fri 15 July 1831 – **Amelia Robinson**: That She was born in the parish of S^t. Mary de lode in the City of Gloucester where her parents then resided   that about 15 Years ago she was apprenticed to M^{rs}. Baynham by her aunt Mrs Butters to learn the Millinery business in South

Gate Street in the City of Gloucester aforesaid for the Term of five years at a premium of 50£ to be paid by yearly Installments of 10£   That she served the whole of her time –

[interlinear addition] that the Indenture was on Parchment but whether [end of interlinear addition] [marginal note] there were Seals on or not she cannot tell

I signed the Indenture – it was left with M^r. Sadler Wine Merchant of Gloucester who is dead

I never saw the Indenture afterwards. I did not apply for it after I was out of my time.[end of marginal note]

that she then left and came to reside in Cheltenham, with M^rs. Hinton with whom she entered into an Agreement for twelve months for the purpose of improvement in the Mil[l]inery Business on payment of 10£ for that purpose, during that period she was not employed in any domestic Occupation whatever & that M^rs H[blank] during that period found her in Meat drink and lodgings and that she is now Chargeable to the parish of Cheltenham [signed]

1831: *perhaps removed to Gloucester (apprenticeship).* **1832:** *(RETURNED) death of AR (buried at Cheltenham 5 Mar, aged 27).* [PS/CH/RA/2/3:70; p. 71 contains a list of names of people perhaps associated with the magistrates' work but more generally examinants. "Coach hire to Gloucester to find Settlement of Amelia Robinson" (11 Aug 1831: P78/1/OV/2/4:65).]

31094SE: Thurs 21 July 1831 – **William Sole**, wife **Jane**, and four children, **Mary Ann, Hannah, Caroline**, and **Sarah**: I was born at Winchcomb [= Winchcombe] in this County. – When I was about 16 Years of age I was apprenticed by my Father to Mr Lloyd of Guns Mill [= Gun's Mill] paper Manufacturer until I was 21 Years of age. – I served him under the Indenture until I attained my age and lived and slept the whole time in the parish of Abinghall [= Abenhall] in this County – About three years after I was out of my time I was living at Cheltenham, and applied to the Parish officers of Abinghall for relief · they gave me occasional relief whilst I was living at Cheltenham

I have never done any act to gain a Settlement elsewhere.

I was married 18 Years ago to Jane my present Wife by whom I have four Children living namely Mary Ann aged 14 Years, Hannah aged 11 Years, Caroline aged 9 Years and Sarah aged 5 Years

I am now chargeable to the parish of Cheltenham [signed]

1817: *WS removed to Winchcombe (presumed) (Gray 113: 10 June) (RETURNED).* **1831:** *removed to Abenhall (near Mitcheldean) (presumed) (apprenticeship).* **1841:** *(RETURNED) WS (aged 50; coal merchant) lived with wife Jane and daughter Sarah in Moors Parade, Tewkesbury Rd in Cheltenham (HO107/353/10/4/3).* [PS/CH/RA/2/3:72.]

31095SE: Thurs 21 July 1831 – **William Davis**, wife **Ann** and son **George**: That he was born in the Parish of Sevenhampton in the County of Gloucester – that his Parents were settled there – that he never lived in any Service the whole Year

That he was married about fifteen months ago to Ann Davis his present wife by whom he has an infant Child named George. I am now chargeable to the Parish of Cheltenham [mark]

1831: *removed to Sevenhampton (presumed) (father's settlement).* **1833:** *son Thomas baptised privately at Sevenhampton 18 Apr (died ten weeks later and buried there 23 June).* **1841** *WD (aged 35; agricultural labourer), wife Ann, son George, and two daughters lived in Sevenhampton (HO107/351/13/9/13-10/14).* [PS/CH/RA/2/3:73.]

31096SE: Fri 22 July 1831 – **William Sale**, confined to bed through sickness, wife **Elizabeth** and their son **William**: That he was born in the parish of Bitford [= Bidford] in the County of Warwick where his parents are legally settled – That he is now in his 32nd year   That when he was about 17 years of age he was hired by M^r. James Lee [= Lea] of the Shambles in the parish of St Swithen [= Swithin] in the City of Worcester by the year and remained with him four years and upwards – That his wages for the first year were £4.10 for the second year £5. for the third year Year £8 & for the fourth year 9£

That he received the whole of his wages

That on the 5th. May 1828 he was married to his present Wife Elizabeth at the Parish Church of St Pancras in the County of Middlesex – That he has an infant child by his said [wife] named William aged 1 year & 11 months – That he has never been hired for a Year in any other service or done any act to gain a Settlement except as aforesaid And that he is now chargeable to the parish of Cheltenham [mark]

1831: *removed to Worcester, Worcs (hiring and service).* **1841:** *son perhaps the WS (aged 12) residing at Worcester Union Workhouse (HO107/1209/12/39/7PS/CH/RA/2/3:74. Note: "reported by Mr Cooper to have been taken by him the above being too ill to attend at the office". Margin: "No 5 Cross Keys Passage".* Removal expenses for "Sale Wife & Child to Worcester" (10 Aug 1831: P78/1/OV/2/4:65).]

31097SE: Sat 23 July 1831 – **Thomas Cole**, wife **Sarah** and their son **Daniel**: That he was born in the parish of Welsh Bicknor in the County of Monmouth

That when he was about fourteen or fifteen years of age he was put Apprentice by the parish Officers of the said parish of Welsh Bicknor to Joseph Robins of the same parish Farmer and Maltster and served the whole time for which he was apprenticed but does not recollect the Terms for which he was apprenticed – That about four or five years ago he was hired by Edward Page of Cheltenham Milkman to serve him from Michaelmas to Michaelmas at the wages of [blank] That he served fifteen Months and received all his wages

That last Christmas was twelvemonths he was married to his present wife Sarah at the parish of Prestbury by whom he has one child Daniel aged twelvemonths

1831: *removal uncertain: examination form incomplete.* **1838:** *census evidence from 1851 suggests that family left Cheltenham this year.* **1841:** *TC (aged 35; collier), wife Sarah, Daniel, and four other children lived in Ruardean.* [PS/CH/RA/2/3:75.]

31098SE: Tues 26 July 1831 – **Elizabeth Wilkins**, single woman: That she was born in the parish of Kingstanley [= King's Stanley] in this County where she believes her parents are legally settled – That She has lived in two or three places as a yearly Servant but did not live a whole year in either nor done any other Act to gain a Settlement

That she is become chargeable to the parish of Cheltenham [mark]

1831: *removed to King's Stanley (presumed) (father's settlement).* **1841:** *presumably the EW (aged 56) who lived in King's Stanley as clothworker, in the family of Richard (53) and Hester Wilkins (HO107/370/4/36/14).* **1851:** *EW in King's Stanley, "Pauper formerly worked at cloth Manufacturing" (HO107/1965/331/19).* [PS/CH/RA/2/3:76.]

31099SE: Thurs 28 July 1831 – **Ann Martin**: That She was born in the parish of Stow in the Wold [= Stow-on-the-Wold] in this County   That when she was about twenty years of age she was hired by Mrs Stiles wife to Henry Stiles late of Cheltenham Innkeeper to serve as a yearly servant at the wages of nine pounds   That she lived three years in the said Service and received all her wages – When she left that Service she was hired by Mr. Madegan of Cheltenham as a yearly servant at the wages of Twelve Guineas and continued three years in that Service and received all her wages

That in the year 1821 She was married to her late husband Samuel Martin at the parish of St Pauls in [blank]   That her said husband was an Officer of Excise and she has heard him say that his parents lived at Tewkesbury and that his father who is now dead kept the Star Inn there. That her husband died in August 1824 and was buried at his mothers Expence at Tewkesbury aforesaid – That she believes her said husband never gained a Settlement in his own right

1831: *removal unlikely: examination form incomplete;* *probably the AM buried at Cheltenham 2 Sept, aged 42.* [PS/CH/RA/2/3:77. "Coach hire to Tewkesbury to find Settlement of H. Martin" (11 Aug 1831: P78/1/OV/2/4:65 ("H. Martin" prob. for "Hannah/Anna Martin").]

31100SE: Thurs 18 Aug 1831 – **William Riddell** (also **Riddle**), and wife **Ann**: That he was born at Smedley near Manchester – that he was apprenticed when at the age of 16 or 17 Years by his Father to Mr Roberts of the Parish of Egremont in the County of Cumberland Millwright for 7 Years, that there was a regular Indenture of apprenticeship prepared – that he served the whole of his time at Egremont when the Indenture was delivered up to him and he lately left the same with his Father. That about 14 Years ago he was married to Ann his present wife at Minster in the Isle Shippey [= Isle of Sheppey] in the County of Kent

That he has never done any Act since his apprenticeship to gain a Settlement [signed Wm Riddel]

1831: *removed to Egremont, Cumberland (presumed) (apprenticeship).* [PS/CH/RA/2/3:78.]

31101SE: Thurs 18 Aug 1831 – **William Shinn**, wife **Elizabeth** and two children **Mary Ann** and **Caroline:** That he was born in the parish of Credley [= Cradley] in the County of Hereford where he believes his father is legally settled – That about fourteen years ago he was hired by M^r. Samuel Higgins of the parish of Berrow in the County of Worcester farmer by the year at Six pounds a year   That he lived Three Years at the same place and for the same wages   That he was afterwards hired by M^r. White of the parish of Linton in the County of Hereford by the year at Old Michaelmas for Six Guineas   that he left the said Service at the New Michaelmas following but received his whole year's wages   That about Eight years ago he was married to his present wife Elizabeth at Ellsfield [= Eldersfield] in this County [in fact, Worcs] and has two children by her viz Mary Ann aged near six years and Caroline aged one year   That he is become chargeable to the parish of Cheltenham

[PS/CH/RA/2/3:79. Text struck out and superseded by **31104SE** (20 Aug 1831) (some family details only included here).]

31102SE: Sat 20 Aug 1831 – **George Collingbourne**, wife **Eliza**, and two children **George** and **John:** That he was born in the parish of Badgworth [= Badgeworth] in this County where he believes his parents are legally settled – That about two years ago he rented a house and Shop at N°. 8 Ocean Row Stepney in the parish of Ratcliff in the County of Middlesex of one M^r. Thomas Freelove at twenty pounds a year   That he lived nineteenth [*sic*] Months in the said house and paid all the rent. That in 1825 he was married to his wife Eliza at Poplar in the said County of Middlesex and has two Children by her namely George aged near six years and John aged near two years. That he is become chargeable to the parish of Cheltenham [signed]

1831: *removed to Stepney, Middlesex (presumed) (renting).* **1832:** *son Charles baptised at Limehouse, Middlesex 18 Mar.* **1840:** *GC remarried Sept (St George in the East, Middlesex), to Harriet Jones (née Sharratt).* **1841:** *the family lived in Tower Hamlets, Limehouse with George (15), John (11), and four other children (HO107/701/5/28/7-29/8); GC (aged 38) is described as a milkman.* [PS/CH/RA/2/3:80.]

31103SE: Sat 20 Aug 1831 – **Elizabeth Cummins**, with two children **Mary** and **John:** That her husband John Cummins did about a month ago abscond from and leave her and she does not know where he is

That she believes her said husband to be last legally settled in the parish of Sudeley in this County   That about three years ago her said husband (while living in Cheltenham) received relief from the said parish of Sudeley – She this Examinant having gone to receive the said relief from the parish Officers of Sudeley weekly. That she has two Children by her said husband namely Mary aged 14 years and John aged eleven years [mark]

1831: *removed to Winchcombe (near Sudeley).* [PS/CH/RA/2/3:81 (page 82 blank). Removal expenses for "Cummins Wife & Child to Winchcomb" (25 Aug 1831: P78/1/OV/2/4:65).]

31104SE: Sat 20 Aug 1831 – **William Shinn** (also **Sheen**), wife **Elizabeth** "and family": That he was born in the parish of Credley [= Cradley] in the County of Hereford where he believes his Father was legally settled – That about 14 years ago he was hired by M^r. Samuel Higgins of the parish of Berrow in the County of Worcester Farmer by the year at six pounds a year

That he lived three years at the same place and at the same wages and received the whole of his wages – That he was afterwards hired by M^r. Joseph White of the parish of the Linton in the County of Hereford by the year on Old Michaelmas day for six Guineas   that he left the said last mentioned service on the Tuesday after New Michaelmas day following but received his whole year's wages on that day – On the Monday before that day I went to Gloucester Fair to seek another situation by his Master's permission and returned to his Master's service the same evening and slept in his house that night. – That the next morning his said Master went to Ledbury Fair and asked him before he started if he was going to the fair – That Exam[inan]t answered " Yes Sir if you please"   That his Master then told him to meet him there at "The Oak" public house and said he would pay him his wages – That he did meet him there and received his whole wages – That nothing was said about quitting the service but Examinant considered himself at liberty to find another place immediately which he endeavoured to at the same Fair – That at the New Michaelmas following he went again into the said Joseph White's service and was hired at his house for a year at the wages of Six Guineas – That he was married about six Months after, and from that time received seven shillings a week and left his Master's house where he had lived previous to his Marriage – That he has never done any act to gain a Settlement since his last said service [mark]

1799: *WS baptised at Cradley 7 Apr.* 1831: *removed to Berrow, Worcs (hiring and service).* 1833: *daughter Louisa baptised at Berrow, Worcs 8 Sept.* [PS/CH/RA/2/3:82; replaces 31101SE (18 Aug 1831): William Shinn's service at Linton, Heref not considered to confer settlement. Removal expenses for "Parish Berrow Worcestershire W^m. Shinn Wife & family" (20 Aug 1831: P78/1/OV/2/4:65).]

31105SE: Sat 27 Aug 1831 – **Francis Farmer**, wife **Elizabeth**, and five children **Eliza, Lydia, Charles, Sarah**, and **George**: That he was born in the parish of Whitchurch [probably Shropshire] where he believes his parents were legally settled and where they received relief – That about 14 years ago he was hired by M^r. Thomas Pearce of Langarron [= Llangarron] in the County of Hereford for a year as a servant in husbandry – in the month of May. That he served the whole Year and part of another when he left Mr Pearce's service & received the whole of his wages – That shortly before he so left Mr Pearce's service he married his present Wife Elizabeth by whom he has five children viz Eliza aged 10 years – Lidia aged 8 years Charles aged 6 years, Sarah aged 3½ years and George one year & a half – That he has never done any other act to gain a Settlement [mark]

1818: *the family moved extensively; FF married Elizabeth Griffith at Llangarron, Heref, and their first daughter (Ann) was born there that year.* 1823: *birth of daughter Lydia in Monm.* 1827: *Charles and Sarah both baptised at Smethwick, Staffs.* 1831/2: *removed to Llangarron, Heref (hiring and service).* 1841: *(RETURNED) Lydia lived in Tewkesbury Rd, Cheltenham as servant (HO107/353/9/28/5); her parents were perhaps living in Aston, Birmingham.* 1849: *FF died (buried, aged 56, at Cheltenham 21 Apr).* 1851: *Elizabeth Farmer (aged 59; needlewoman, widow, born Heref) lived at 35 Stanhope St, Cheltenham (HO107/1973/500/20).* [PS/CH/RA/2/3:86; removal perhaps delayed. Removal expenses for "Farmer & family" to "Langarron" (12 Jan 1832: P78/1/OV/2/4:65).]

31106SE: Tues 30 Aug 1831 – **Peter Nugent**, wife **Nancy** and daughter **Ann**: That he was born in the City of Glasgow in that part of the United Kingdom of Great Britain called Scotland   That he has never gained a Settlement in England -

That he has a wife named Nancy and a child named Ann about three years of age   That he is become chargeable to the parish of Cheltenham [mark]

1831: *removed to Scotland (presumed).* [PS/CH/RA/2/3:87.]

31107SE: Thurs 1 Sept 1831 – **James Wanklyn**, and wife **Sarah**: That he was born in the City of Warwick   That in the year 1817 he was hired by Samuel Cave Esquire in the City of Hereford as a Servant at the wages of 10£ for the 1st. year – That he remained in the said service Nine years – the three last years at the wages of £15. That he received the whole of his wages, and married on leaving that service his present Wife Sarah

That he has done no act since to gain a Settlement [signed]

1831: *removed Hereford, Heref (presumed) (hiring and service).* 1851: *JW (aged 45) apparently worked, without wife, as butler in Llandilofawr, Carmarthenshire (HO107/2471/370/5).* [PS/CH/RA/2/3:88.]

31108SE: Tues 6 Sept 1831 – **Joel Tanner**, wife **Charlotte** and daughter **Hannah Maria**: That he was born in the Parish of Chalford in the County of Gloucester – that about Nine Years ago he was hired by Mr Joseph Hawkins of Cheltenham as a Carter by the Year at the Wages of four Guineas – that he served the whole Year and received his full wages.

That the following Year he was hired by Mr Samuel Barber of Tewkesbury for a Year at the Wages of three Guineas – that he lived in Tewkesbury under such hiring a whole Year and received at the end thereof his full Years Wages   that he continued with him about three quarters of a Year afterwards. – That about two Years ago he was married to Charlotte his present Wife by whom he has one Child Hannah Maria aged fourteen Months. – that he has done no Act to gain a settlement since his Service at Tewkesbury [mark]
1831: *removed to Tewkesbury (presumed) (hiring and service): see* **32094SE** *(JT: 26 Dec 1832) for further information.* [PS/CH/RA/2/3:89.]

31109SE: Tues 13 Sept 1831 – **Elizabeth Cooper:** That she was born in the parish of Salperton in this County – which was her mother's place of settlement – That she was not born in wedlock. That when about seven years old she was apprenticed by her reputed Father to Richard Green of Lower Littleworth in the parish of Minchinhampton in this County for the term of seven years to learn the business of Woollen Cloth weaving – That at the time she was so apprenticed she signed a paper or parchment but does not know whether it was an Indenture or not – That she served the whole of the seven years, and half a year afterwards – That she has never since done any act to gain a Settlement by servitude or otherwise [mark]
1831: *removed to Minchinhampton (apprenticeship).* **1841:** *EC (aged 60; pauper) lived in Minchinhampton (HO107/362/7/21/4).* **1851:** *EC at same address, aged 73 (pauper, cloth worker).* [PS/CH/RA/2/3:90. Removal expenses for "Elizabeth Cooper" to Minchinhampton (22 Sept 1831: P78/1/OV/2/4:65).]

31110SE: Sat 17 Sept 1831 – **Amy Cummins:** That she is a single woman
    That she was born at Poulton in Wiltshire as she believes – That she has never done any act to gain a Settlement in any parish in her own right [mark]
Hannah Hughes:
 upon her oath said that she is the Mother of Amy Cummings – That Amy Cummins was not born in Wedlock –
    That She was born in the parish of Poulton in Wiltshire – That She received one Shilling p[er] Week from the parish officers of Poulton for the said Amy Cummings until She was Eight years of age and upwards [mark]
1831: *removed to Poulton, Wilts (birth).* [PS/CH/RA/2/3:91. Removal expenses for "Ann Cummins" to Poulton, Wilts (22 Sept 1831: P78/1/OV/2/4:65).]

31111SE: Thurs 6 Oct 1831 – **Sarah Hobbs:** That She was born in the parish of Hasfield in this County where her parents were legally Settled – That 34 or 35 years ago she was hired by M^{rs}. Loveday wife of M^{r}. William Loveday of Painswick in this County Clothier by the year at about four pounds ten Shillings wages as well as she can remember – That She continued in the same Service two years – When she left that Service She was married to her late husband Robert Hobbs at Painswick aforesaid which was his place of legal Settlement – That she has done no other Act to gain a Settlement – That she is become chargeable to the parish of Cheltenham [mark]
1831: *removed to Painswick (late husband's settlement).* [PS/CH/RA/2/3:92. Removal expenses for "Sarah Hobbs" to Painswick (6 October 1831: P78/1/OV/2/4:65).]

31112SE: Sat 8 Oct 1831 – **Esther** (also **Hester**) **Guest**, single woman: That she was born in the parish of Coln Rogers in this County where she believes her father is legally settled – That three years ago last Michaelmas at Cheltenham first Mop She was hired by M^{r}. Thomas Salmon of Cheltenham Cabinet Maker by the year at four pounds wages and continued there a year and received her wages – and was then hired for another year at the same wages and continued there the whole of the second year and received her whole wages – That she has never done any other Act to gain a Settlement
1831: *removal uncertain: examination form incomplete.* **1837:** *Emily Ellen ("Emma"), illegitimate daughter of EG (single woman, living in St George's Square) baptised at Cheltenham 24 Dec.* **1840:** *(3Q) EG married Richard Baylis(s) in Cheltenham.* **1841:** *the couple lived in Coln Rogers: Richard Bayliss (aged*

60; independent means), Hester Bayliss (30), and Emma Guest (4) (HO107/351/3/3/5). **1845:** *after Richard's death, EG married James Agg in Northleach (2Q).* **1851:** *the family lived in Coln St Dennis: James Agg was master butcher (HO107/1969/222/15).* [PS/CH/RA/2/3:93.]

31113SE: Sat 8 Oct 1831 – **Sarah Ballinger**, single woman: That she was born in the parish of Frampton upon Severn [= Frampton on Severn] in this County where she believes her father is legally settled her said father having carried on business as a Baker there for several years and rented premises there at twenty pounds a year – That she has never gained a Settlement in her own right
1831: *removal uncertain: examination form incomplete.* [PS/CH/RA/2/3:94.]

31114SE: Sat 15 Oct 1831 – **George Crispin**, wife [**Molly**?] and their four children **Charles**, **George**, **Molly**[?], and **Eliza**: [That] he was born at Clonokilty [= Clonakilty] in the County of Cork and that he has never done any act to gain a Settlement in England. That he and [*interlinear*: wife Molly[?]] four Children Charles and George [*interlinear*: Molly[?] and Eliza] are now become chargeable to the Parish of Cheltenham [signed]
1831: *removed to Ireland (presumed).* [PS/CH/RA/2/3:95.]

31115SE: Thurs 20 Oct 1831 – **Miles Sullivan**, wife and three children **Mary**, **Catharine**, and **Brian**: That he was born as he hath heard and believes in the County of Cork in that part of the United Kingdom called Ireland – that he had never done any Act whereby to gain a Settlement in England And that he hath a wife and three children namely Mary aged 7 years Catharine aged three years and Brian an infant about three weeks old and that he is become chargeable to the parish of Cheltenham [mark]
1831: *removed to Ireland (presumed).* [PS/CH/RA/2/3:96.]

31116SE: Fri 28 Oct 1831 – **Joseph Scrivens** (also **Scriven**), confined to bed by sickness, wife **Ann** and unnamed child [**Martha**?]: That he was born at the parish of Horton in the County of Wilts – That about fifteen or sixteen years ago he was hired by M[r]. John Commeline of the parish of Withington in this County farmer at Northleach first Mop by the year as Cowman at the wages of Eight Guineas and when he had served the first year he was hired for another year at nine pounds wages – That he served the whole of the last year and received his whole wages – That a little while after he entered on the third year in the said Service he was married to his first wife Elizabeth by whom he has one child now living namely Susan aged nearly twenty three years who has gained a Settlement in the parish of Cheltenham as he believes   That about four years ago he was married to his present wife Ann at the parish of Cheltenham by whom he has one child not yet babtized [*sic*] about nine months old   That he has done no Act since to gain a Settlement by Servitude renting or otherwise   That at the time of his first wife's death he received relief from the parish officers of Withington aforesaid [mark]
1831: *removed to Withington (presumed) (hiring and service): see* **47007RO** *(JS: 30 Jan 1847) for further information.* [PS/CH/RA/2/3:97.]

31117SE: Sat 29 Oct 1831 – **Philip Evans**, in HM gaol at Gloucester on charge of felony, wife **Mary** and three children **Thomas**, **Marianne**, and **William**: That he was born in the parish of Aston ingham [= Aston Ingham] County of Hereford and that about eight years ago he rented in the parish of Ross County of Hereford a house & shop at the annual rent of Twenty three pounds of M[rs] Powell of Wilton in the same County, that he resided upwards of a year in the said house and paid the whole rent – that he was married in the Church of Abenhale [= Abenhall] County of Gloucester to Mary his present Wife by whom he has three Children viz Thomas nine years old, Marianne eight years old & William seven years old, and that he [has] done no act or deed by which he could gain any subsequent Settlement [signed]
1831: *family removed to (or relieved by) Ross, Heref (presumed) (renting): see* **33023SE** *(wife Mary: 23 Mar 1833) for further information on the family.* [PS/CH/RA/2/3:98.]

31118SE: Tues 8 Nov 1831 – **Thomas Kealley**, wife **Margaret** and two children **Mary Ann** and **Catherine**: That he is a native of the County Monaghan in Ireland

That he has a Wife named Margaret and two infant children named Mary Ann and Catherine – That he has never done any act to gain a Settlement in England and that they are now chargeable to the parish of Cheltenham [signed Thomas Kealey]
1831: *removed to Ireland* (Cheltenham Chron. *10 Nov: "conveyed by passes to Gloucester").* [PS/CH/RA/2/3:99.]

31119SE: Tues 8 Nov 1831 – **Judith Dogan:** That she was born in the County of Cork in Ireland – That she has never done any act to gain a settlement in England and is now chargeable to this parish [mark]
1831: *removed to Ireland* (Cheltenham Chron. *10 Nov: "conveyed by passes to Gloucester").* [PS/CH/RA/2/3:100.]

31120SE: Sat 12 Nov 1831 – **Mary Davis**, with daughter **Maria:** That she is the wife of Thomas Davis by whom she has One Child named Maria aged 4 Years –. I was married at Minchinhampton before the child was born –. I am living at Cheltenham and have been doing so for Five Years last past. – About Six months ago my husband went over to Shurdington for Relief in consequence of a child of ours then lying dead and he brought back from the overseer of Shurdington Ten Shillings to bury our Child [mark]
1831: *removed to Shurdington (husband's settlement):* see **32088SE** *(Thomas Davis: 4 Dec 1832) for further information.* [PS/CH/RA/2/3:100. Removal expenses for "Mary Davis" to Shurdington (10 Nov 1831: P78/1/OV/2/4:65).]

31121SE: Sat 3 Dec 1831 – **Thomas Larkin:** That he has a native of Ireland   That he has never done any act to gain a Settlement in England   That he is now Chargeable to the parish of Cheltenham [mark]
1831: *removed to Ireland* (Cheltenham Chron. *8 Dec).* [PS/CH/RA/2/3:101.]

31122SE: Tues 6 Dec 1831 – **Richard Hillyard** (also **Hilliard**), and wife **Sarah**; also a sworn statement by Peter Butt, Guardian of the Poor: *Richard Hillyard*: That he was born in the parish of S^t. Thomas in the City of Oxford as he believes where he believes his parents were then legally settled. That about twelve years ago he was hired by the Rev^d M^r. Mutlow then residing in the parish of S^t. Mary in the City of Gloucester by the year at the wages of ten Guineas and Clothes months wages or months Warning – This Examinant continued in the said Service One Year and four months and received all his wages – That some months after he left M^r. Mutlows Service he was hired by M^r. John Mills of Miserden in this County by the year at the wages of ten pounds and Clothes – That about eight months after he entered into M^r. Mills' Service he married his present wife Sarah at Miserden aforesaid
   That upon being married his Master said to him "Richard I think now you had better take a pound a Month"   That his said Master afterward paid this Examinant monthly and this Examinant continued in that Service upwards of Seven years [signed]
N.B.
P. Butt: M^r. Mills will prove that Hillyard left his service about the time mentioned by the pauper & that a fresh Hireing took place at £1. p[e]r month & that he let the pauper a small Cottage near his said Dwelling house but had no Communication with his own Residence
   The pauper occupied the said Cottage the whole of his time duering [*sic*] his said Service, under the second hiring. That a short time previous to his leaving his said Master the pauper had misconducted himself & received a Month's Notice to quit, before the expiration of the month, a Servant offered himself, and engaged, when the pauper left & received the whole of the last Months Wages. M^r. Mills stated that if Hilliard had misconducted himself at any time after the Second hireing took place at £1 p[e]r Month he could discharge his said Servant by giving a Months wages or a Months Warning and Vice Versa. [signed]
1831/2: *removed to Gloucester (hiring and service).* **1837:** *the couple had several children, the first born after examination, George, was baptised at Gloucester 21 Feb.* [PS/CH/RA/2/3:102. Expenses for travel to

"Miserdine to investigate settlement of Hilliard" (9 Apr 1832: P78/1/OV/2/4:59)'; removal expenses for "Hillyards family" to Gloucester (5 Jan 1832: P78/1/OV/2/4:65).]

31123SE: Thurs 8 Dec 1831 – **Lucy Crane**, widow: That she was born as she believes in the parish of Saint Michael in the City of Bath – That about nine or ten years ago she was married to her late husband John Crane at the parish of St James in the said City of Bath – that her said husband died about five weeks after they were married And this Examinant does not know and never heard her said husband say where his place of legal Settlement was – That in August 1825 she was hired by Miss Letitia Watts then residing in Cheltenham as a yearly servant as Cook at twelve Guineas wages for a Months warning or a Months wages

That she continued upwards of a Year in that Service until Miss Watts' death and she received all her wages

That about three weeks afterwards she was hired by M^{rs}. Holdship wife of M^{r}. Timothy Holdship of Cheltenham by the year as Cook at twelve Guineas wages a Months warning or a Months wages – That she continued one year and three months in that service and received all her wages

I have never done any other act to gain a settlement [mark]
1819: *Lucy Cryer (bapt. 1797, Bath) married John Crane at Bath, 4 Apr.* **1831:** *removal uncertain: examination form incomplete.* **1840:** *LC married John Palmer, bachelor, at Bath, 21 Jan.* [PS/CH/RA/2/3:103.]

31124SE: Sat 10 Dec 1831 – **Thomas Maquire** (usually **Maguire**): I was born in the County of Waterford in Ireland

I have never done any act to gain a Settlement in England and am now chargeable to the Parish of Cheltenham [mark]
1831: *removed to Ireland (presumed).* [PS/CH/RA/2/3:104.]

31125SE: Sat 10 Dec 1831 – **Edward Bencroft** (also **Bancroft**); also his sister Elizabeth Page: *Edward Bencroft*: That he was born in the parish of S^{t}. George Hanover Square in the County of Middlesex where he believes his father was legally settled   I lived with him in that parish until I was 16 Years of age   That he this Examinant never was in Service nor an Apprentice nor rented a Tenement of Ten pounds yearly nor done any other Act to gain a Settlement in his own right [mark]
Elizabeth Page: That she is about ten years older than her said brother – That she was born in Chandler Street in Grosvenor Square in S^{t}. George's abovementioned where her parents then resided – That some time afterward her parents removed to Queen Street in Grosvenor Square in the same parish – That her said brother was born in Queen Street aforesaid [mark]
1831: *removed to St George, Hanover Square, Middlesex (father's settlement):* see **38011RO** *(EB: 5 Feb 1838) for further information.* Note: "Removed by Saml. Collett Constable". [PS/CH/RA/2/3:105.]

31126SE: Tues 20 Dec 1831 – **Richard Howell**, and wife **Elizabeth**: That he was born in the parish of Bradford in the County of Wilts as he has heard and believes and where he believes his parents were legally Settled His father as this Examinant has heard having carried on business as a Plaisterer [= plasterer] there for several years and rented a house at Fifty pounds a year   That this Examinant has received relief from the parish of Bradford at the time he lived there   That about four years ago he was married to his present wife Elizabeth at the parish of Cheltenham - That this Examinant has not done any Act to gain any Settlement in his own right by renting, Servitude or otherwise [mark]
1831/2: *removed to Bradford, Wilts (father's settlement).* **1832:** *RH buried from Poorhouse, Bradford-on-Avon, Wilts 17 Nov, aged 26.* **1841:** *(RETURNED) widow Elizabeth (aged 50) lived with brother James Shott's family in Stanhope St, Cheltenham (HO107/353/9/41/21).* [PS/CH/RA/2/3:106; removal apparently delayed: expenses for "Howell & Wife" to Bradford (30 May 1832: P78/1/OV/2/4:66).]

31127SE: Tues 20 Dec 1831 – **Augustus Tregarthen Wallis** (also **Wallace**): That he was born in Charlotte Street Black friars Road in [blank]

That in January or February 1819 he took a house of M^r. Mander of Cheltenham Grocer at Thirty Guineas a year – That he occupied the house for six Months –

1831: *removal unlikely: examination form incomplete.* **1833:** *AW buried at New Burial Ground, Cheltenham 22 Nov, aged 39.* [PS/CH/RA/2/3:107.]

31128SE: Thurs 29 Dec 1831 – **Charles Cole**, wife **Hannah**, and son **George**: That about Seven or Eight years ago he was hired by William Cook of the parish of Frocester in this County farmer by the year at the wages of Seven pounds – that he served his full year and received all his wages – That two years ago last Summer he was married to his present wife Hannah at the parish of Stonehouse in this County by whom he has one child – George aged about Eighteen Months – That he has done no other Act to gain a Settlement than as above-stated. That last Spring this Examinant at that time living at Randwick in this County was examined as to his Settlement before the Magistrates at Witminster [= Whitminster] and went to Frocester aforesaid and received parochial Relief from the parish offices there [mark]

1831: *removed to Frocester (hiring and service).* **1832:** *son Samuel baptised 1 July at Frocester (CC described as labourer) but died soon after (buried at Frocester 3 Sept); mother Hannah was buried three days later, aged 33.* [PS/CH/RA/2/3:108. Removal expenses for "Cole Wife & Child" to Frocester (31 Dec 1831: P78/1/OV/2/4:65).]

31129SE: Sat 31 Dec 1831 – **Thomas Aldred**: That he was born in the parish of Cookley in the County of Suffolk where he believes his father was legally settled his father having as this Examinant believes carried on business there as an Innkeeper for several years

That about twenty years ago he rented a Public house at Wimborne in Dorsetshire and a Cottage with it at £12 yearly and occupied it one year and paid the rent – That in the year 1812 he rented an Inn at East Cowes in the Isle of Wight at £50. per Annum and occupied it five years and paid the whole rent – That in 1805 he was married to his late wife Elizabeth at Wimborne aforesaid   That he has a daughter by his said wife about 21 years of Age and is now living with his friends in Bath [signed]

1832: *removed to East Cowes, Isle of Wight, Hants (presumed) (renting).* [PS/CH/RA/2/3:109.]

PUBLIC OFFICE

THURSDAY, FEB. 3. – Before R. Capper and R.B. Cooper, Esqrs – *George Howell*, convicted of keeping a house of ill fame, and in default of finding sureties for his good behaviour, was committed for twelve months, or until bail be found.

SATURDAY. – Before R. Capper, Esq. – *Michael Coleman, John Martin*, his wife and two children, *Thos. Martin, Robt. Appjohn*, and *John Butler*, his wife and child, Irish paupers, having become chargeable to the parish, were sent by a pass to Ireland.

MONDAY. – *Edward Matthews*, committed for trial for having obtained of Mr. Sharland a hat and money, with intent to defraud him thereof, by giving in payment a bank note of a firm which has long been dissolved.

TUESDAY. – Before R. Capper and R. B. Cooper, Esqrs. – *Ann Holland, Patrick*

The Cheltenham Chronicle *(10 February, 1831) reporting on events during the previous week at the Public Office in Cheltenham, where criminal and poor-law cases came before the magistrates. In this case, Irish paupers were returned by passes to Ireland (see **31005SE-310012SE**)*

1832

32001SE: Sat 7 Jan 1832 – **Samuel Barter**, wife **Esther** and two children **George** and **Daniel**: That he was born in the parish of Stroud in this County where he believes his parents were legally settled his father having as this Examinant has heard been apprenticed to a Weaver at Stroud – That he this Examinant has received relief from the parish Officers of Stroud during his illness when he resided there   That he has never done any Act to gain a Settlement in his own right by apprenticeship Servitude renting or otherwise   That about six years ago he was married to his present wife Esther at Stroud aforesaid by whom he has two children living namely George aged three years nearly and Daniel about nine months old – That he is become chargeable to the parish of Cheltenham [signed]
1832: removed to Stroud (father's settlement). 1833: (RETURNED) son Charles Matthew baptised at Cheltenham 3 May; son Daniel buried at Cheltenham 15 June. **1841:** *son George resided temporarily at Bristol Asylum for the Blind; SB (aged 40; labourer) lived in Cheltenham with wife Esther and four children, at Bath Terrace (HO107/353/12/12/18).* [PS/CH/RA/2/3:110. Removal expenses for a pauper to be conveyed to Stroud (5 Jan 1832: P78/1/OV/2/4:65).]

32002SE: Sat 7 Jan 1832 – **William Smith**: That he was born as he has heard and believes in the parish of Chedworth in this County And this Examinant has heard that his mother never was married – That he has lived with M^r. James Mills of Ablington in the parish of Bibury four years and a half – but there was no agreement as to time between them. His Master paid him four pence a day for the Six days in the Week but not for the Sundays – that he gave him five pence for the Working days in the following Year and Six pence a day the third Year and Seven pence a day the last Year. – That he was at liberty to go when he pleased or his Master to discharge him [mark]
1832: removed to Chedworth (birth). **1841:** *probably the WS (aged 35; labourer) living alone in Chedworth (HO107/363/9/7/8).* [PS/CH/RA/2/3:111. Removal expenses for pauper to be conveyed to Chedworth (5 Jan 1832: P78/1/OV/2/4:65).]

32003SE: Sat 7 Jan 1832 – **John Robins**, wife **Ann** and children **Sarah** and **Joseph**: That he was born in the Parish of Quinton in the County of Gloucester where he believes his Parents are settled. – that he was never hired for a Year, or apprenticed, nor did he ever rent a tenement at the yearly Rent of Ten pounds or done any Act to gain a Settlement in his own right

That four Years ago he was married to Ann his present wife by whom he has two Children Sarah aged two Years and Joseph aged 10 months – That he is now become chargeable to the Parish of Cheltenham – [signed]
1832: removed to Quinton (presumed) (father's settlement). 1834: daughter Elizabeth baptised at Quinton 2 Mar. **1841:** *JR (aged 35; agricultural labourer) lived with wife Ann and five children (not including Joseph) at Brickyard House, Quinton (HO107/360/37/12/19).* [PS/CH/RA/2/3:112. Removal expenses for "Robinson [sic] & family" to Quinton (5 Jan 1832: P78/1/OV/2/4:65).]

32004SE: Thurs 12 Jan 1832 – **Jane Clifford**: That she was born in the parish of Leckhampton in this County – This Examinant has heard and believes that her late father William Clifford was last legally settled in the parish of Swindon in this County and her mother now receives relief from the Parish Officers of Swindon aforesaid – That this Examinant has never done any Act to gain a Settlement in her own right [mark]
1832: removed to Swindon (father's settlement); JC pregnant at time of examination; illegitimate daughter Caroline baptised at Leckhampton 22 Apr. 1833: JC married George Jones at Swindon 1 Apr. **1834:** *daughter Eliza baptised at Swindon 8 June.* **1841:** *(RETURNED) the family lived in Naunton Fields, Cheltenham: George (aged 30, labourer); Jane (25), Caroline (9), Eliza (7), Mary (5), and George (1) (HO107/353/12/43/23).* [PS/CH/RA/2/3:113. Removal expenses for pauper to be conveyed to Swindon (5 Jan 1832: P78/1/OV/2/4:65).]

32005SE: Sat 14 Jan 1832 – John Green, relating to sister **Mary Ann Green**, "in a state of insanity": That he is brother to Mary Ann Green a pauper in the Cheltenham Workhouse who now is and has been for some months past in a state of insanity – That the said Mary Ann Green was born at Hyde in the parish of Didbrook in this County where her father and mother were settled – That about five years ago, as he believes, the said Mary Ann Green lived at service at Gotherington in the parish of Bishops Cleeve for 12 months, and has never since lived one year in any service or done any other act to gain a settlement

That within a year from this time his said Sister being pregnant was removed by the parish officers from the hamlet of Maugersbury in the parish of Stow on the Wold to the Hamlet of Gotherington aforesaid from which hamlet she has received relief ever since [signed]
1832: *died before removal; MAG buried at New Burial Ground, Cheltenham 26 Jan, aged 30.* [PS/CH/RA/2/3:114.]

32006SE: Thurs 19 Jan 1832 – **Ann Powell**: That she is the Wife of William Powell to whom she was Married at Ross in Herefordshire about three years ago [insertion] on the 25th of November last

That she knew her Husband when he lived at Kings Capel [= Kings Caple] in Herefordshire as a Servant to Mr Cooke of that parish – that he was in the same Service about two Years – that she was born at Brampton Abbots [= Brampton Abbotts] in Herefordshire where her parents were settled. – [signed]
1832: *removed to Brampton Abbotts, Heref (presumed) (father's settlement, unless husband had acquired settlement at Kings Caple, Heref).* [PS/CH/RA/2/3:115.]

32007SE: Mon 23 Jan 1832 – **Barney Curran**, wife and four children, **Mary Ann**, **Caroline**, **Elizabeth**, and **Michael**: That he was born as he has heard and believes in the county of Westmeath in that part of the united Kingdom called Ireland – That he has never gained a Settlement in England – That he has a wife and four children namely Mary Ann aged fourteen years Caroline aged eight years Elizabeth aged four years And Michael aged about seven years [mark]
1832: *removed to Ireland* (Cheltenham Chron. *2 Feb*). [PS/CH/RA/2/3:116.]

32008SE: Sat 18 [originally apparently 11] Feb 1832 – **Nathaniel Howell**, wife **Hannah** and three children **Henry**, **Thomas**, and **Emily**: That he was born in the parish of Eastington in the said County where he believes his father is legally settled – That he has never gained a Settlement in his own right – That he has at various times received Relief from the parish Officers of Eastington aforesaid and that he now receives three Shillings and six pence per week from the said Parish That about seven years ago he was married to his present wife Hannah at Stroud in the said County by whom he has three children viz Henry aged six years Thomas aged four years and Emella [= Emily] aged six months   That he is become chargeable to the parish of Cheltenham [mark]
1832: *removed to Eastington (father's settlement).* **1834:** *(RETURNED) daughter Louisa Ann baptised at Cheltenham 13 July.* **1841:** *NH (aged 35; labourer) lived off Gt Norwood St in Cheltenham with wife Ann and six children including Henry, Thomas, and Emily (HO107/353/12/26/46-7).* [PS/CH/RA/2/3:117. Removal expenses for "Howell family" to Eastington (13 Apr 1832: P78/1/OV/2/4:66).]

32009SE: Tues 14 Feb 1832 – **Elizabeth Randall**, wife of John Randall, with son **George**: That She was born in the parish of Buckington [presumably = Bulkington] in the County of Wilts – that she has heard and believes that she was born out of Wedlock –

That 14 years ago last December she was married to her husband at Bradford in Wilts aforesaid

That she has heard her said husband say that he belonged to the parish of Avening in the County of Gloucester. That about four years ago she and her husband went to Avening aforesaid (he being then out of employment) and they received relief from the parish Officers there – That this Examinant was present when her said husband applied for relief there and heard him say in answer to questions put to him by the overseer that he had never gained a Settlement in his own right   that his father and grandfather were parishioners there

That she has one Son by her said Husband named George aged about nine years – That her said husband has deserted her and she is now become chargeable to the parish of Cheltenham [mark] **1832:** *removed to Avening (husband's apparent settlement).* **1833:** *EB buried at Avening 25 Dec, aged 35.* [PS/CH/RA/2/3:118. Removal expenses for "E. Randall & Child" to Avening (16 Feb 1832: P78/1/OV/2/4:65).]

32010SE: Sat 18 Feb 1832 – **Thomas Burns**, wife and four children **Ann**, **Mary**, **John**, and **Alice**: That he was born as he has heard and believes in the County of Sligo in Ireland – That he has not gained a Settlement in England – That he has a wife and four Children namely Ann, aged Seventeen Mary aged fourteen John aged Eleven and Alice aged near eight years and he is become chargeable to the parish of Cheltenham [mark]
1832: *removed to Ireland* (Cheltenham Chron. *23 Feb).* [PS/CH/RA/2/3:119.]

32011SE: Sat 18 Feb 1832 – **Michael Cummins**, wife **Ann** and son **William**: That he was born in the County of Wexford in Ireland – that he has a wife named Ann who was also born in Ireland and one Child named William aged two Years. That they are become chargeable to the Parish of Cheltenham [mark]
1832: *removed to Ireland* (Cheltenham Chron. *23 Feb).* [PS/CH/RA/2/3:119.]

32012SE: Tues 21 Feb 1832 – **Jeremiah Manning**, wife and four children: That he was born in the parish of Clonakilty in the county of Cork in Ireland and has not gained a Settlement in England   That he has a wife and four children and is become chargeable to the parish of Cheltenham [mark]
1832: *removed to Ireland* (Cheltenham Chron. *23 Feb).* [PS/CH/RA/2/3:120.]

32013SE: Tues 21 Feb 1832 – **Thomas Horne**: That he was born in Clonakilty in the County of Cork in Ireland and has not gained a Settlement in England and that he is become chargeable to the parish of Cheltenham [mark]
1832: *removed to Ireland* (Cheltenham Chron. *23 Feb).* [PS/CH/RA/2/3:120.]

32014SE: Sat 3 Mar 1832 – **Benjamin Rock**, confined to bed by sickness, wife and their daughter **Sarah Anne**: That he was born in the parish of Saint Mary de Lode or that of St. Nicholas in the City of Gloucester

That about 17 years ago he was apprenticed to M[r]. John Hewlett of the said City Cabinet Maker residing in the parish of St. Michael or of St John – I served the whole of my time – M[r]. Hewlett removed during my apprenticeship and I served the last two years in the parish of St. Michael – I have a wife to whom I was married on the 26th. August 1825 at the parish Church of Cheltenham – I have One child by my said wife named Sarah Anne aged 4 months – I have never done any other act to gain a Settlement and am chargeable to the parish of Cheltenham [mark]
1831: *at daughter Sarah Anne's baptism in Cheltenham 9 Dec, BR described himself as cabinet-maker.*
1832: *died before removal; wife and child apparently removed to Gloucester (apprenticeship); BR buried at New Burial Ground, Cheltenham 14 Apr, aged 29.* [PS/CH/RA/2/3:121. Removal expenses for "Rock & Child" to Gloucester (26 Apr 1832: P78/1/OV/2/4:66).]

32015SE: Thurs 8 Mar 1832 – **Mary Griffiths**, widow of late Thomas Griffiths formerly private in 73rd Regiment of Foot, with daughter **Mary**: That her said late husband died about five Months ago at Portsmouth Barracks. That she was then residing with him. And that two of her Children died there since her said husbands death – She believes her husbands legal Settlement to be in the Town of Montgomery in North Wales

That this Examinant is on her way to the said Town of Montgomery and she has been retarded on her Journey in the parish of Cheltenham through Sickness, having been confined there and delivered of a female infant – That she has no means of Subsistence or of proceeding to her place of Settlement without relief [mark]
1832: *daughter Mary baptised at Cheltenham 26 Feb;* ***removed to Montgomery, Montgomeryshire (presumed) (husband's settlement).*** [PS/CH/RA/2/3:122.]

32016SE: Sat 10 Mar 1832 – **Ellen Bostwick**, wife of John Bostwick, with son **John**: That she was born in the Parish of Walcot in the County of Somerset where her Parents were settled. That on the 10th day of July in the Year 1830 she was married at the Parish Church of Weston Super Mare [in Som] to John Bostwick who at that time was living as a footman with the Misses Vandeleur

– That she lived in the same Service with her Husband at Weston super Mare five months previous to her Marriage and she has heard from her Husband that he had lived with the Ladies Seven Years before her Marriage – and she has also heard that he had 40 Guineas a Year – That her Husband is now abroad in Miss Vandeleur's Service – That on the 13th June last she was delivered of a Male Child in the Parish of Cheltenham

That she has heard her husband say that he was born at Leeds [signed]

1831: at son John's baptism at Cheltenham 26 June, father described as servant. **1832:** *removed to Weston super Mare, Som (presumed) (husband's settlement); EB sentenced for larceny at Lent Assizes in Gloucester; she received two years' imprisonment (HO27/43/248).* **1841:** *EB resided at Bath Union Workhouse (Lyncombe and Widcombe, Som) (aged 40; charwoman) (HO107/931/16/32/12).* **1851:** *probably the "E. B." in Somerset County Lunatic Asylum at Wells (widow, aged 51; "household duties").* **1855:** *probable death of EB 1Q at Bath.* [PS/CH/RA/2/3:123.]

32017SE: Tues 13 Mar 1832 – **Samuel O Brien** (also **Samuel O. Brien**), wife and two children **John** and **Catherine**: That he was born in the County of Dublin in Ireland and has not gained a Settlement in England   that he has a wife and two children namely John aged 17 years and Catherine aged nine months   that he is become chargeable to the parish of Cheltenham [mark]

1832: removed to Ireland (presumed). [PS/CH/RA/2/3:124.]

32018SE: Sat 17 Mar 1832 – **James Hone**, wife **Louisa** and son **William**: That he was born as he has heard and believes in the parish of Maismoor [= Maisemore] in this County out of Wedlock – That his Mother was relieved from the said parish –

About 4 years ago I was hired for my board and lodging by Charles Griffin Bricklayer at Oxenhall in this County for 3 quarters of a year – When that term expired he asked me to remain a year longer with him which I did on the same terms – I have never worked in service or done any act to gain a settlement since – I was married to my present wife Louisa about 13 months ago – I have one child named William aged 4 months – We are now chargeable to the Parish of Cheltenham [mark]

1832: removed to Oxenhall (hiring and service). [PS/CH/RA/2/3:124. *Removal expenses for "Hone Wife & Children" to Oxenhall (15 Mar 1832: P78/1/OV/2/4:65).*]

32019SE: Mon 19 Mar 1832 – **Henry Townsend**, late of Langley Burrell, Wilts: That he was born in the parish of Chippenham in the County of Wilts as he has heard and believes and that his mother Lucy Townsend was not then married – This Examinant has heard his mother say that Joseph Phelps his putative father paid her 10/6 a month towards his maintenance for several years

That when this Examinant was about 12 or 13 years of age he came to Cheltenham with his mother and father in law Edward Stevens (his mother being then married) and was recommended to M[r]. Wildey of Cheltenham Poulterer as a person wanting an Apprentice – That his mother and father in law agreed for Examinant to go upon trial with M[r]. Wildey in order to his being apprenticed – That this Examinant remained from time to time in M[r]. Wildey's employ for upwards of a twelvemont[h], during that period he expected to have been bound to M[r]. Wildey as an apprentice to learn the business of a Poulterer – But no Indenture of Apprenticeship was ever entered into, nor any written Agreement executed – He boarded and lodged at M[r]. Wildey's but received no wages, nor clothes, nor was he at all hired by M[r]. Wildey either by the week month year or otherwise. That a short time previous to his leaving M[r] Wildey a misunderstanding took place between them and Examinant ran away without giving or receiving any kind of Notice – That he did not return nor did he see M[r]. Wildey again until he was brought by Order of removal from the aforesaid parish of Langley Burrow [*sic*]

That he has never done any Act to gain a Settlement in his own right by renting Servitude or otherwise [mark]

1823: *HT married Mary Anne Spier in Chippenham 27 Apr (children baptised at Chippenham).* **1832: removed to Chippenham, Wilts (presumed) (birth).** *1841: HT (aged 40; labourer) lived with wife and four children in The Causeway, Chippenham (HO107/1171/7/7/6).* Note: "Quarter Sessions for the County of Wilts held at Salisbury on Tuesday, 3 April 1832", suggesting appeal. [PS/CH/RA/2/3:125.]

32020SE: Thurs 22 Mar 1832 – Thomas Evans, regarding the settlement of **Thomas Evans**, illegitimate child of daughter Hannah Evans, deceased; also Elizabeth Page, of Cheltenham, midwife: *Thomas Evans, senior*: That his said daughter was about three years ago delivered of her said Child Thomas Evans at her Uncle's house at Charlton Kings and that the said Child is now chargeable to the parish of Cheltenham [signed]

Elizabeth Page: That about three years ago she attended the above named Hannah Evans at Charlton Kings in her capacity of midwife

That the said Hannah Evans was delivered of an illegitimate male infant at Charlton Kings

This Examinant is positive that the infant pauper Thomas Evans now produced is the child of which the said Hannah Evans was so delivered at Charlton Kings aforesaid [mark]

1832: removed to Charlton Kings (presumed) (birth). *1841: (perhaps RETURNED)"pauper" TE is probably the ten-year old Thomas Evans living with grandparents Thomas (aged 65; coal dealer) and Elizabeth Evans in Queen's Place, Tewkesbury Rd, Cheltenham (HO107/353/10/25/16).* [PS/CH/RA/2/3:126. Elizabeth Page, midwife, delivered child of Mary Hopkins: see Gray **421b** (EP: 7 May 1822).]

32021SE: Thurs 22 Mar 1832 – Phebe Archer, regarding the settlement of **Sarah Salmon**, illegitimate child of her late mother Sarah Salmon, deceased; also Elizabeth Page, of Cheltenham, midwife: *Phebe Archer*: That about six years ago her said Mother was delivered of a Male [*sic*] infant in the parish of Prestbury - that the above named Sarah ~~John~~ Salmon is the child of which her said mother was delivered – That her mother never was married – That the said child is now chargeable to the parish of Cheltenham [signed]

Elizabeth Page: That about six years ago she attended the late Sarah Salmon in her said capacity of midwife – That the said Sarah Salmon was delivered of the female illegitimate infant in the parish of Prestbury – That the infant pauper Sarah Salmon now produced is the illegitimate child of which the said Sarah Salmon deceased was so delivered [mark]

1832: removed to Prestbury (presumed) (birth). [PS/CH/RA/2/3:127.]

32022SE: Thurs 5 Apr 1832 – **Thomas Cain**, and wife **Ellen:** That he was born as he has heard and believes in the County of Galway in that part of the United Kingdom called Ireland – That he hath never done any act whereby to gain a Settlement in England – And that he hath together with his Wife Ellen actually become chargeable to the parish of Cheltenham in the said County – [signed]

1832: removed to Ireland (*Cheltenham Chron. 12 Apr*). [PS/CH/RA/2/3:128.]

32023SE: Sat 28 Apr 1832 – **Jane Cougley**, single woman: That he [*sic*] was born at Stroud in the County of Gloucester where his [*sic*] parents were settled – I never was hired for a Year or done any act in my own right to gain a Settlement elsewhere [mark]

1832: removed to Stroud (parents' settlement). [PS/CH/RA/2/3:129. Removal expenses for "Jane Congley [*sic*]" to Stroud 26 Apr 1832 (P78/1/OV/2/4:66); see P320a OV/3/3/3/54 (Stroud parish) Removals to Stroud, 1832.]

32024SE: Tues 1 May 1832 – **Timothy Conolly**, and wife **Ann:** That he was born in the County of Cork in Ireland   that he has not gained a Settlement in England and that he with his wife Ann is become chargeable to the Parish of Cheltenham [mark]

1832: removed to Ireland (presumed). [PS/CH/RA/2/3:130.]

32025SE: Tues 1 May 1832 – **Abraham West:** That he was born in the Parish of Stoke Bruerne in the County of Northampton – that his Parents were settled at Paulerspury in the same county –

that he has never done any Act to gain a Settlement in his own right – that about 10 days ago he was passing through Cheltenham and was there taken very ill and unable to proceed on his Journey [mark]
1832: *removed to Paulerspury, Northants (presumed) (parents' settlement).* [PS/CH/RA/2/3:130.]

32026SE: Thurs 3 May 1832 – **Thomas Trigg**, wife **Mary**, and three children **Elizabeth**, **Mary Ann**, and **Ellen:** That he was born in the Parish of Westbury-upon Severn [= Westbury on Severn] in the County of Gloucester – That about 10 Years ago he was hired by M^r. Thomas Taylor of Awre for a Year at the Wages of Seven Pounds   That he continued in Mr Taylors Service under such yearly hiring a whole Year and for three Quarters of a Year afterwards. – That Seven Years ago he married Mary his present Wife by whom he has three Children namely Elizabeth aged 6 Years, Mary Ann aged 3 Years, and an infant not Christen'd – That he has done no Act to gain a Settlement since his Service at Awre [mark]
1832: *removed to Awre (presumed) (hiring and service); (RETURNED) the "infant not Christen'd" was Ellen, baptised at Cheltenham 1 July (father described as labourer).* **1835:** *daughter Jemima baptised at Cheltenham 17 May.* **1841:** *TT (aged 37; policeman) lived with wife Mary and four children (including Mary Ann, aged 12, and Ellen aged nine) in Sun St, Tewkesbury Rd, Cheltenham (HO107/353/9/38/24).* [PS/CH/RA/2/3:131.]

32027SE: Sat 5 May 1832 – **Richard Herbert;** also brother Thomas: *Thomas Herbert:* That his brother Richard was born in the Parish of Bromsberrow in the county of Gloucester
Richard Herbert: That he was born in the Parish of Bromsberrow in the County of Gloucester.
    That upwards of twenty Years ago he was hired by Mrs Hooper of the Parish of Ledbury [in Heref] for a Year and continued in her Service three Years – that he slept at Mrs Hooper's House at Holles in the said Parish of Ledbury. – That he has never been hired for a Year or rented a House or done any act to gain a Settlement since he left M^{rs}. Hooper's House [mark]
Richard and Thomas Herbert were baptised at Bromsberrow under the surname Harber. **1832:** *removed to Ledbury, Heref (hiring and service).* **1861:** *RH perhaps the Richard Harbor (aged 69; widower) discovered in Greenwich Union Workhouse after career as seaman (RG9/403/77/5).* [PS/CH/RA/2/3:132. Removal expenses for "Richd Herbert" to Ledbury (3 May 1832: P78/1/OV/2/4:66).]

32028SE: Tues 8 May 1832 – **George Davis**, and wife **Mary:** That he was born in the parish of Abbedore [= Abbey Dore] in the County of Hereford where his Parents were legally settled.
    That he was married about thirty Years ago to Mary his present Wife and is now become chargeable to Cheltenham [mark]
1832: *removed to Abbey Dore, Heref (father's settlement); (probably RETURNED) likely to be the George and Mary Davis buried at New Burial Ground, Cheltenham, 10 July 1832 (aged 66) and 10 Aug 1839 (aged 60) respectively.* [PS/CH/RA/2/3:133. Removal expenses for "G Davis & Wife" to Heref (7 June 1832: P78/1/OV/2/4:66).]

32029SE: Tues 15 May 1832 – **Daniel Donovan:** That he was born at Roscarberrey [= Roscarbery] in the County of Cork – and that he has done no Act to gain a Settlement in England [mark]
1832: *removed to Ireland (presumed).* [PS/CH/RA/2/3:134.]

32030SE: Tues 15 May 1832 – Mary Bolton, regarding the settlement of son **Charles Bolton:** That Charles Bolton who is become chargeable to the Parish of Cheltenham is her son – that her said son was born in the Parish of Saint John in the City of Gloucester, where her Husband was legally settled
    That her said son has never done any Act in his own right – That the Parish officers of Saint John aforesaid have relieved her said Son and that he is now of the age of 22 Years [mark]
1832: *removed to Gloucester (father's settlement).* **1837:** *CB (aged 29; inmate of Gloucester Workhouse) buried at St John's, Gloucester 4 Jan.* [PS/CH/RA/2/3:134. Removal expenses to St John's, Gloucester (person unspecified) (10 May 1832: P78/1/OV/2/4:66).]

32031SE: Sat 19 May 1832 – **Matilda Barratt**, inmate of Cheltenham Workhouse: That she was born she has heard and believes in the parish of Widcombe in the City of Bath where she believes her parents were legally settled – That her late father John Barratt carried on business as a Butcher there for several years and rented a large house   that she believes upwards of £10 a year – That she has never done any Act to gain a Settlement in her own right [mark]

1832: *removed to Widcombe, Bath, Som (father's settlement); MB died at the Poor House (buried at St Thomas a Becket's church, Widcombe 12 Sept, aged 19).* [PS/CH/RA/2/3:135. Removal expenses for "Barrett" to Bath (30 May 1832: P78/1/OV/2/4:66).]

32032SE: Tues 22 May 1832 – **Esther Haines**, single woman: That she was born as she has heard and believes in the parish of Painswick in this County where she believes her parents are legally settled, her father William Haines having rented a house there at upwards of Ten pounds a year and carried on business as a Baker –

~~That about Eleven Months ago she was married to her present Husband John Pendry at the parish of [blank] near Ross – That She has never heard her said husband say where his Settlement was – Her said husband is now at work at Upton S^t. Leonards~~ – That she has never done any Act to gain a Settlement in her own right by Servitude or otherwise [mark]

1832: *removed to Painswick (father's settlement).* **1836:** *son John baptised at Painswick 11 Sept (father described as cooper).* **1841:** *EB and husband lived in Butt Green, Painswick (HO107/349/8/13/3): John (aged 30; cooper), Esther (misnamed Elizabeth, 20[= 30?]), and two children. She is correctly named Est(h)er in later censuses.* [PS/CH/RA/2/3:136. Text struck out as EH reverted to single status regarding her claim for relief. Removal expenses for "H. Hunts [*sic*]" to Painswick (30 May 1832: P78/1/OV/2/4:66).]

32033SE: Thurs 26 May 1832 – **Sarah Hampton:** That she was born as she has heard and believes in the parish of Cheltenham – That about two years ago she was hired by M^{rs}. Lawrence of Sandywell Park in the parish of Dowdeswell by the year at the wages of Four pounds – That she continued one year and two months in the said Service and received all her wages – That she has done no other Act to gain a Settlement and she is become chargeable to the parish of Cheltenham [mark]

1832: *removed to Dowdeswell (presumed) (hiring and service):* see **46001SE** *(15 Jan 1846) for further information.* [PS/CH/RA/2/3:137. Removal expenses for "Sick Pauper to Dowdeswell" (7 June 1832: P78/1/OV/2/4:66).]

32034SE: Thurs 7 June 1832 – **Ann Davis:** That she was born in the County of Mayo in that part of the United Kingdom called Ireland and has not gained a Settlement in England
That she is become chargeable to the parish of Cheltenham
1832: *removed to Ireland (presumed).* [PS/CH/RA/2/3:137.]

32035SE: Sat 9 June 1832 – **Sarah Bowley**, widow, and daughter **Ann Burns**, widow: That she was born in the County of Leitrim in Ireland and is become chargeable to the parish of Cheltenham
That she hath not gained a Settlement in England – That she has a daughter named Ann Burns also a widow who is chargeable to Cheltenham parish [mark]
1832: *removed to Ireland (presumed).* [PS/CH/RA/2/3:138.]

32036SE: Sat 9 June 1832 – **Ellen Hughes**, with three children **Daniel**, **Patrick**, and **John:** That She was born in the County of Cork in Ireland and has not gained a Settlement in England. That her husband Jeremiah Hughes is now in London. That she has three Children Daniel, Patrick and John and she is become chargeable to the parish of Cheltenham [mark]
1832: *removed to Ireland (presumed).* [PS/CH/RA/2/3:138.]

32037SE: Tues 12 June 1832 – **Thomas Crook:** That he was born as he has heard and believes in the parish of Steeple Aston [= Steeple Ashton] in the County of Wilts
That upwards of Thirty Years ago he rented a house and land in the parish of Westbury under the Plain [= Westbury] in the said County of Wilts at about fourteen or fifteen pounds a year and paid Taxes and poors [*sic*] Rates and occupied it several years and paid all the rent for the same – That he has done no Act to gain a Settlement since and he is become chargeable to the parish of Cheltenham [mark]

1766: TC *baptised 12 June at Steeple Ashton, Wilts.* **1832:** *removed to Westbury-under-the-Plain, Wilts (renting).* **1837:** *(RETURNED) died at Cheltenham Workhouse 4 Jan (buried at Cheltenham 9 Jan, aged 72).* [PS/CH/RA/2/3:139. Removal expenses for "Thoˢ Crook" to Westbury (21 June 1832: P78/1/OV/2/4:66).]

32038SE: Tues 19 June 1832 – **Hannah Neson** (Mason and Nelson struck out): That her late father John Wood was a travelling Hawker and had not to this Examinants knowledge any fixed place of residence and she has never heard him say where his Settlement was nor where she this Examinant was born   That on the 2ᵈ. day of May 1825 she was married to her late husband Samuel Nelson ~~Mason~~ at Bradley in Staffordshire - that he was a Native of Ireland and had not to this Examinants belief ever gained a Settlement in England
1832: *removal uncertain: examination form incomplete.* [PS/CH/RA/2/3:140.]

32039SE: Thurs 14 June 1832 – Thomas Gibbins (also Gibbens, Gibbons), relating to settlement of daughter **Mary Gibbins**, confined to bed by sickness: That his Settlement is in the parish of Brockworth in this County he having been possessed of a property there and having also received relief from the said parish on account of himself and also on account of his said daughter's illness –
    That his said daughter has never gained a Settlement in her own right and she has lived with this Examinant from her infancy up to the present time [signed]
1832: *removed to Brockworth (father's settlement).* **1834:** *(RETURNED) MG (of Cheltenham) recovered from illness and married Henry Bailey 18 May 1834 at Cheltenham.* **1851:** *MG visitor at brother Thomas Gibbins's house, Brockworth, aged 46 (HO107/1964/509/6).* [PS/CH/RA/2/3:141. Removal expenses for "Mary Gibbins" to Brockworth (22 Aug 1832: P78/1/OV/2/4:66). See **34025SE** (father Thomas Gibbins: 3 Apr 1834).]

32040SE: Tues 19 June 1832 – **Michael Kehoe**, wife and child: That he was born in the County of Dublin in Ireland and has not gained a Settlement in England – That he has a wife and one child and is actually become chargeable to the parish of Cheltenham [signed]
1832: *removed to Ireland (presumed).* [PS/CH/RA/2/3:142.]

32041SE: Tues 26 June 1832 – **Eliza Arkell:** That she was born as she has heard and believes in the parish of Cirencester where she believes her late father John Arkell was legally settled he having received relief from the said parish to this Examinant's knowledge   That a year ago last April She was hired by Mʳˢ. Hughes of the George Hotel in Cheltenham as her indoor servant That Mʳˢ. Hughes asked her what wages she would expect That she told her Seven pounds a year – That she was hired at a month's wages or a month's warning – That she remained there a year and received the whole of her wages at the rate of Seven pounds a year
    That she went for a month on trial
1811: EA born at Cirencester 6 Jan. **1832:** *removal uncertain: examination form incomplete; illegitimate daughter Eliza born soon after examination (baptised at Cheltenham 23 Sept).* **1838:** *EA married James Hunt in Cheltenham 20 Oct, when she (and husband) lived at 261 High St, Cheltenham.* [PS/CH/RA/2/3:142.]

32042SE: Thurs 28 June 1832 – **Thomas Burby**, with son **James:** That he was born in Ireland in the County of Dublin. That he has not done any Act whereby to gain a Settlement in England
    That he and his Son James aged 14 years are chargeable to the parish of Cheltenham [signed]
1832: *removed to Ireland (presumed).* [PS/CH/RA/2/3:143. See Gray **432** (a Thomas Burby from Tallaght, Co Dublin: 8 Oct 1822).]

32043SE: Sat 30 June 1832 – **Sarah Strong**, with children **William** and [unnamed]: That she was born as she has heard and believes in the parish of Kilken [= Cilcain] in the County of Flint - That on the 29ᵗʰ. day of May 1831 she was married to her present husband William Strong at the parish of Cheltenham
    That her said husband has left her and she does not know where he is gone to   That her said husbands place of Settlement is in the parish of Bridgewater [= Bridgwater] in the County of Somerset Her said husband having received relief from the said parish since their Marriage – That she has one Child by her first husband David Miles named William of the age of five years and

one child by her present husband aged 3 Months not yet Baptized – That She has heard her first husband say that he had been apprenticed in the City of Coventry (he was by trade a watchmaker) but She never heard him say in what parish there

That She was married to her said first husband in the parish of Saint Oswald in the City of Chester in the year 1822 [mark]
1832: *removed to Bridgwater, Som (presumed) (husband's settlement): see* **33011SE** *(14 Feb 1833) for further information).* [PS/CH/RA/2/3:144. Removal expenses for "Sarah Strong & Children" (10 Aug 1832: P78/1/OV/2/4:66).]

32044SE: Sat 7 July 1832 – **Ann White:** That she was born as she has heard and believes in the parish of Stroud in this County where she believes her parents were legally settled – her said parents having received relief from the parish officers there   That about two years ago she was hired by M^{rs}. Aspinall wife of Thomas Aspinall of Stroud aforesaid Saddler by the year at five pounds wages – That she remained in the said Service about 13. or 14 months and received all her wages – That she has done no Act to gain a Settlement since [mark]
1832: *removed to Stroud (hiring and service).* **1833:** *an AW married John Pearce at St Lawrence's Church, Stroud 21 July.* **1841:** *the family lived in Whiteshill, Stroud: John (aged 25; cloth worker), Ann (25), and four children (HO107/349/13/24/8).* [PS/CH/RA/2/3:145. Removal expenses for "Ann White" to Stroud (11 July 1832: P78/1/OV/2/4:66).]

32045SE: Thurs 12 July 1832 – **Catherine Collins**, with sons **Michael** and **Timothy:** That she was born in the County of Cork in Ireland and has not gained a Settlement in England – That she and her two Sons Michael and Timothy are become chargeable to the parish of Cheltenham [mark]
1832: *removed to Ireland (presumed).* [PS/CH/RA/2/3:145.]

32046SE: Tues 10 July 1832 – **Sarah Mundy**, with two children **Jane** and **Ann:** That about 9 years ago she was hired by the Revd David Williams of Heytesbury in the County of Wilts by the year as Cook at (as she believes) the wages of 9 guineas   That she continued in that Service until Novr 1825 when she was married to her late husband Thomas Mundy who had entered into the same Service about one year and a quarter before their Marriage – That after their Marriage her said husband continued in M^r. Williams's Service till the first week or somewhat later in the January following, & She is become Chargeable to the parish of Cheltenham and that she had two children by her husband Jane aged five years and Ann aged three years [signed]
1832: *removed to Heytesbury, Wilts (hiring and service).* [PS/CH/RA/2/3:146. Expenses "To Coach hire to Heytisbury [sic] & Steeple Langford" (21 June 1832: P78/1/OV/2/4:59), and removal expenses for "Sarah Mundy & 2 Children" to Heytesbury (11 July 1832: P78/1/OV/2/4:66).]

32047SE: Thurs 19 July 1832 – **Thomas Smith**, wife **Esther**, and five children, **Nathaniel Charles, Emy Maria, Hezekiah Edwins Sands, Athaliah Deborah Hogg**, and **Sarah Hogg:** That he was born as he has heard and believes in the parish of Stroud in the said County where he believes his father Samuel Smith is legally settled his said father having in February 1827 being [= been] removed by an order from the parish of Cheltenham to Stroud aforesaid and resided there ever since and received relief now from the said Parish – That this Examinant has never done any Act to gain a Settlement in his own right by Servitude renting or otherwise   That about 19 years ago he was married to his present wife Esther at the parish of Hasfield and has five children by her namely Nathaniel Charles aged about 18 years Emy Maria aged 16 year[s] Hezekiah Edwin Sands aged 13 years Atheliah [= Athaliah] Deborah Hogg aged about 9 years and Sarah Hogg aged six years – That he is become chargeable to the parish of Cheltenham   That whilst he was Residing with his family at Cheltenham he has received Relief from the Parish Officers of Stroud [signed]
1832: *removed to Stroud (father's settlement).* **1841:** *(RETURNED) the family probably lived in Commercial St, Cheltenham (HO107/353/12/16/26).* **1851:** *TS (aged 63; labourer, born Stroud) and wife Hester lived with daughter Sarah (aged 23; dressmaker, born Stroud) at 2 Victoria St, Cheltenham (HO107/1973/880/18).* [PS/CH/RA/2/3:147. Removal expenses for "Thos Smith & family" to Stroud (22 Aug 1832: P78/1/OV/2/4:66). See **32056SE** (Samuel Smith: 2 Aug 1832).]

32048SE: Thurs 19 July 1832 – **William Strong**, wife **Sarah**, and unnamed child: That he was born in the Parish of Holcomb Regis [= Holcombe Rogus] in the County of Devon – That about 18 or 19 Years ago he was hired to M[r]. James Tottle of the Parish of Bridgwater in the County of Somerset for a Year at the Wages of twelve Guineas. That he lived with him a Year and one day in Bridgwater and received his full Years Wages. – That whilst living at Bridgwater he has received Relief from the officers of the Parish of Bridgwater. – That he has never done any Act since his Service at Bridgwater to gain a Settlement Elsewhere – That in May 1831 he was married to Sarah his present Wife by whom he has one Child aged about three Months not yet Christened [mark]
1832: *removed to Bridgwater, Som (presumed) (hiring and service): see* **33059SE** (7 Sept 1833) *for further information.* [PS/CH/RA/2/3:148. See **32043SE** (wife Sarah Strong: 14 Feb 1833).]

32049SE: Sat 21 July 1832 – **Richard Townsend:** That he was born as he has heard and believes in the parish of Northleach in this County which was his fathers legal place of Settlement his said father having been possessed of property and carried on business as a Hair Dresser there for several years   That his said father's property consisted of a House and Garden wherein he had a life Interest and which his said father (as this Examinant believes) sold for £200

That when he was about fifteen years of Age he was apprenticed by his father to M[r]. Brown of Upton on Severn [Worcs] Plumber and Glazier for seven years and served the whole time, the premium paid with him by his father was £20, That after working at several places, he in April 1794 went to Northleach and carried on his Business as a plumber and Glazier. That this Examinant at that time was the owner of a freehold house at Northleach which was left to him by the will of Mrs Bretherton

That about the year 1800 or 1801 he was appointed at the Court Leet to serve the Office of High Constable for the Hundred of Bradley, in which the parish of Northleach is situate, – That he served the Office Two years,

That he has never done any Act to gain a Settlement elsewhere and he is become chargeable to the parish of Cheltenham [signed]
1832: *removed to Northleach (office-holding).* **1840:** *RT died at Union Workhouse, Northleach (buried there 23 Sept, aged 70).* [PS/CH/RA/2/3:149. Removal expenses for "Rich[d] Townsend" to Northleach (19 July 1832: P78/1/OV/2/4:66).]

32050SE: Sat 21 July 1832 – **John Hitchings** (expanded in examination of 31 July). [PS/CH/RA/2/3:150. See **32054SE** (JH: 31 July).]

32051SE: Tues 24 July 1832 – **Owen McCarthy**, with four children **Alice, Catherine, William,** and **James:** That he was born in the City of Dublin and has not gained a Settlement in England – That he has four Children namely Alice aged ten years Catherine aged eight years William aged four years and James aged about eighteen Months and that he is become chargeable to the parish of Cheltenham [signed]
1832: *removed to Ireland (presumed).* [PS/CH/RA/2/3:151.]

32052SE: [undated: 24-6 July 1832] – **Elizabeth Hale**, single woman; also Charles Shuttleworth, regarding her settlement: *Elizabeth Hale:* That she was born in the Hamlet of Aldbury [perhaps Alberbury] in the County of Salop where she believes her parents are legally settled and now living – That she left home about 4 years ago and went to live as Housekeeper to M[r]. Charles Shuttleworth Butcher in Smallbrook Street Birmingham at the wages of four shillings the week

That she lived in Birmingham about 2 years And received her wages as often as she wanted them but does not know what sum she has received

That she does not recollect that anything was said to her about notice at the time she was hired – That about One year & Eight months ago she left Birmingham with her said Master and went to Gloucester where she lived 6 or 7 months. That she then removed with her Master to Cheltenham and has lived there in his service ever since, That about 3 weeks ago she left his house but has remained in his service

Charles Shuttleworth: [That] about 4 years ago I hired Elizabeth Hale as a serv^t. at 4/- a week – She has generally received her wages by the week – I have paid her nearly all her wages – I always considered that I might discharge her at a week's notice – I do not recollect that any thing was said to her about a month's notice at the time I hired her

But some thing was said about it two years ago
1832: *removal uncertain: examination form incomplete.* [PS/CH/RA/2/3:152-3.]

32053SE: Thurs 26 July 1832 – **Eliza Howse**, single woman**:** That she was born as she has heard and believes in the Town of Woolwich in the County of Kent – I have been informed that I left that town at the age of three months – I recollect myself first in the town of Leicester where my father and mother then lived and have lived nearly ever since – I left it at about the age of Thirteen years – I then went to live at Derby, where I remained some time – About Five years ago I went to reside at Birmingham   After I had been in Birmingham two years I took a house there in Summer Lane (no. 349) at the rent of £16 a year – I occupied it more than 12 months and paid more than Ten pounds rent & the remainder was (I believe) paid for me – I believe I lived in the house 16 months – I took the house by the year to pay the rent monthly. – I have never done any act to gain a settlement since [signed]
1832: *removed to Birmingham, Warks (presumed) (renting).* [PS/CH/RA/2/3:154.]

32054SE: Tues 31 July 1832 - **John Hitchings**, with five children **John**, **Frances**, **George**, **Jane**, and **William:** That he was born in the parish of Kentchurch in the County of Hereford where he believes his parents are legally Settled his said father having been possessed of freehold property there and at present occupying a farm in the parish of Saint Mauns [= St Maughans] Monmouthshire at considerable rent – That in 1809 Examinant was apprenticed to William James of Abergavenny in the County or Monmouth Carpenter and Joiner as an out-door apprentice by Indenture on a Stamp which was duly enrolled & Examinant believes that fourteen pounds was paid with him as an Apprentice fee – That he served three years of the Term of Seven Years and his Master (according to a previous agreement) gave up the Indenture – That about the year 1817 Examinant entered upon and occupied part of a house in the parish of Saint Catherine in the City of Gloucester which had been taken by his brother and Examinant paid Two pounds a year for the same which he duly paid to his said brother and continued in the same for nine years – That Examinant paid all rates and Taxes for the whole of the house to the respective collectors – That from 18th September 1819 to 1824 Examinant rented a Shop in the parish of Saint Nicholas in the said City of Gloucester at Eight pounds a year and that he hath together with his Children actually become Chargeable to the parish of Cheltenham. That in 1817 he was married to his late wife Sarah at S^t. Mary's Gloster [= Gloucester]   that he has five children namely John aged thirteen years Frances aged about Eleven years George aged Seven years Jane age[d] six years and William aged about three years [signed]
1789: *JH baptised at Kentchurch.* **1832:** *removed to Abergavenny (apprenticeship).* **1833:** *death of John (Heath) Hitchings (joiner and cabinet-maker) registered at Holmer, Heref (three sons were given the middle name Heath).* [PS/CH/RA/2/3:155. Removal expenses for "Man & 5 Children" to Abergavenny (16 Aug 1832: P78/1/OV/2/4:66). See **32050SE** (JH: 21 July).]

32055SE: Tues 31 July 1832 - **Sarah Simmonds:** That she was born in the Parish of Cheltenham – that about 17 months ago she was hired by M^{rs}. Smith who lived at No 2 Suffolk Place Cheltenham for a Year at the Wages of ten Guineas – that she served the whole Year in the Parish of Cheltenham – and continued in her Service two Months after her year expired – that she received her full Years Wages of Mrs Smith [mark]
1832: *removal unlikely; presumably settlement adjudged as Cheltenham.* [PS/CH/RA/2/3:156.]

32056SE: Thurs 2 Aug 1832 - Samuel Smith**,** relating to settlement of two sons, **Samuel** and **Joseph,** by first wife**:** That he was born as he has heard and believes in the parish of Stroud in this County where he believes his father Samuel Smith is legally settled his said father having formerly been possessed of real property there and his said father now receives relief there

That he this Examinant has done no Act to gain a Settlement in his own right by apprenticeship servitude renting or otherwise – That in 1807 he was married to his first wife Deborah at Hasfield [*read* Haresfield] in this County by whom he has two Sons namely Samuel aged 20 and Joseph aged 18 who now reside in Cheltenham and are through illness become chargeable to the parish of Cheltenham and that his said Sons were born in the parish of Stroud aforesaid and have not to this Examinants knowledge and belief gained a Settlement in their own right [signed]

1807: *SS married Deborah Hogg (Thomas Smith's sister-in-law) at Haresfield Dec.* **1832: removed to Stroud (presumed) (father's settlement).** *1841: SS's second wife was called Esther; Samuel (aged 50; shoe maker) lived with wife Esther and children Mary and Charles in Lower St, Stroud. Each family was characterised by a preference for unusual Biblical first names (Athaliah, Hephzibur, Hezekiah, Mattaniah).* [PS/CH/RA/2/3:157. Perhaps the removal expenses were included in those for his brother Thomas (22 Aug 1832: P78/1/OV/2/4:66). See **32047SE** (Thomas Smith: 19 July 1832).]

32057SE: [undated - 2-7 Aug 1832] Elizabeth Ceyzer (properly Cayzer**)**, regarding the settlement of daughter **Maria Wilcox:** *Elizabeth Cayzer:* That ~~she was married to her first husband Thomas Wilcox at the parish of Malvern in the~~ her said daughter was born in the parish of Great Malvern in the County of Worcester – That she was not born in Wedlock and that her said daughter has always lived with her and that her said daughter has not to this Examinants knowledge gained a Settlement in her own right [mark]

Maria Wilcox: That She has never lived a year in Service nor been apprenticed nor has she done any other Act to gain a Settlement in her own right [mark]

1810: *MW born at Malvern, Worcs; mother Elizabeth Wilcox later married George Cayzar.* **1832: removed to Gt Malvern, Worcs (birth).** *1837: (RETURNED) Maria married Joseph Powis at Cheltenham.* **1841:** *Elizabeth Cayzar married Thomas Evans at Cheltenham in Mar; Elizabeth (aged 50) and MW (aged 25) and other children lived in Queen's Place, Cheltenham with Thomas Evans (HO107/353/10/25/16).* [PS/CH/RA/2/3:158. Thomas Wilcox was Elizabath Wilcox's father, not her first husband. Removal expenses for "Maria Wilcox" to Malvern (10 Aug 1832: P78/1/OV/2/4:66).]

32058SE: Tues 7 Aug 1832 - **Samuel Jones:** That he was born in the parish of Badgworth [= Badgeworth] in this County where he believes his parents are legally settled – That about the year 1825 he rented a house and Garden of John Finch in the parish of Leckhampton in this County at 23£ per Annum and at the time this Informant began to occupy the said house it was not finished and the agreement between them was that he this Examinant was to pay no rent until it was finished – That he occupied the said house about Nine Months [incomplete]

1832: *removal uncertain: examination form incomplete.* [PS/CH/RA/2/3:159.]

32059SE: Fri 10 Aug 1832 – **Sarah Ridler**, single woman: That she was born at Hardwicke in the County of Gloucester – That about Eleven Years ago she was hired by her Uncle Richard Merrett of the Parish of Haresfield in the said County for a Year at the Wages of five Guineas – That she served the whole of the Year in the Parish of Haresfield and received her full wages – That she continued in the said Service in whole nine Years [*sic*] and since she quitted her Uncle's Service she has done no Act to gain a Settlement. [mark]

1832: *removed to Haresfield (presumed) (hiring and service).* [PS/CH/RA/2/3:160. Removal expenses for "S. Ridler" (destination unspecified) (16 Aug 1832: P78/1/OV/2/4:66).]

32060SE: Thurs 23 Aug 1832 – **James Lippett (**also **Lipet, Lippiatt**), wife **Ann**, and two children **George** and **James:** That he was born in the parish of Cheltenham where he believes his parents were legally settled – That at the age of Fourteen years he was apprenticed to Joseph Jones of the parish of Saint Owens [= St Owen] in the City of Gloucester Cordwainer for seven years by Indenture under the trusts of Townsend's Charity – That he served under the said

Indenture six years and then left his said master's service and has never since done any act to gain a settlement

That on the 23 September 1829 he was married to his present wife Ann at the parish Church of Cheltenham by whom he has two children namely George aged 2 years & a half and an infant aged 5 weeks not yet baptized – That he and his family are now chargeable to the parish of Cheltenham [signed]

1832: *removed to Gloucester (apprenticeship): see* **35007SE** *for further information.* [PS/CH/RA/2/3:161. *Townsend's Charity:* by will of 1682 George Townsend bequeathed £25 to apprentice five poor boys from Cheltenham and other villages, at discretion of trustees. Expenses for "Apprehending Lippett" (6 Sept 1832: P78/1/OV/2/4:59), and removal expenses for "J Lipet" to Gloucester (22 Aug 1832: P78/1/OV/2/4:66).]

32061SE: Thurs 23 Aug 1832 – **John Perkin:** That he was born in the Parish of Chelt [incomplete]
1832: *removal uncertain: examination form incomplete.* [PS/CH/RA/2/3:162.]

32062SE: Thurs 6 Sept 1832 – **Elizabeth Lynall**, single woman: That she was born as she has heard and believes in Woolwich in the County of Kent   That three years ago last May she was hired by M^{rs}. Sturt then of Lake House Cheltenham by the year as Ladys Maid at twelve Guineas a year   That she lived upwards of three years in that Service and received all her wages

That about seven or eight months before she quitted M$^{r[s]}$. Sturts Service The family removed from Lake House Cheltenham and went to reside at Compton Castle in the parish of Compton [= Compton Pauncefoot] in the County of Somerset where the family now reside   That she remained in their family from the time they went to reside at Compton Castle until the twenty ninth of August last and received all her wages up to the time of leaving [signed]
1832: *removed to Compton, Som (presumed) (hiring and service).* [PS/CH/RA/2/3:163.]

32063SE: Thurs 6 Sept 1832 – **John Martin:** [no text].
1832: *removal uncertain: examination form incomplete.* [PS/CH/RA/2/3:164.]

32064SE: [undated: 6-15 Sept 1832] – **Sarah Mason**, widow, with children **William**, **Anne**, and **Caroline:**   That she was born as she has heard and believes in the parish of Stow on the Would [= Stow-on-the-Wold] in this County where she believes her father was then legally settled

That on the twenty first day of May four years ago she was married to her late husband James Mason at the parish Church of Cheltenham and has three Children living by her said husband namely William aged near five years Anne aged near three years and Caroline aged nine weeks – That when she first became acquainted with her late husband She was living as a yearly Servant at Bourton on the Hill [= Bourton-on-the-Hill] with M^r. Hancks who then kept a Public House at that place and she has heard her said husband say that he had lived as a yearly Servant in the said parish of Bourton on the Hill with a Mr Hathaway a farmer – That her said husbands brother now lives at Dunnington [= Donnington] and she believes he can establish the Settlement of her said husband
1832: *examination form incomplete: see* **32083SE** *(SM: 22 Nov 1832) for further information.* [PS/CH/RA/2/3:165.]

32065SE: Sat 15 Sept 1832 – **Jane Tustin**, widow: That she was born in the City of York, that her father was then a Soldier – That she has heard and believes that he was legally settled in the parish of Leckhampton in this County – That on the 4 February 1796 she was married to her late husband George Tustin at Saint Nicholas in Gloucester   that he was then a Soldier – That in 1808 and for two years following her said husband rented a house of a M^r. Sims in the parish of Saint Owen in the said City of Gloucester at ten pounds a year and paid all the rent – That when her said husband died She received relief from the said parish of Saint Owen towards his funeral – This Examinant had several Children by her said husband none of whom are now dependent on her, – When her children were young she had on several occasions received relief from Saint Owens aforesaid   that She is become chargeable to the parish of Cheltenham [signed]

1832: *removed to St Owen's, Gloucester (husband's renting).* **1841:** *JT (aged 70; laundress) lived in Barton St Michael, Gloucester.* **1850:** *JT died at Gloucester, aged 85 (buried 23 June).* [PS/CH/RA/2/3:166. Removal expenses for "Jane Tustin" to Gloucester (20 Sept 1832: P78/1/OV/2/4:66).]

32066SE: Sat 15 Sept 1832 – **Sarah Powell**, single woman**:** That she was born as she believes in the parish of Clomley [= Comley] in the County of Salop where she believes her parents were then legally Settled

That about Seven years ago she was hired by Mrs Crookshank wife of Colonel Crookshank then residing at N°. 6 Oxford Place in the parish of Charlton King's in this County by the year as Cook at twelve pounds a year – and remained there the whole of the year and received all her wages – That She has been in several places of Service since but did not remain a year in any one place   that She is become chargeable to the parish of Cheltenham [mark]
1832: *removed to Charlton Kings (presumed) (hiring and service).* [PS/CH/RA/2/3:167.]

32067SE: Tues 18 Sept 1832 – **Joseph Hooper:** [That] he believes he was born in the parish of Hartpury in this County – That in the year 1787 he was apprenticed to M^r. William Peach of the City of Gloucester Cabinetmaker for Seven years by Indenture at the premium of 42 Guineas which Indenture was duly inrolled – That he served the whole time

That in 1818 he bought a house in the parish of Saint Nicholas in the said City of Gloucester for about Four hundred pounds and paid the purchase money for the same and had it duly conveyed to him – That he also bought other property in the said parish of Saint Nicholas of greater value and paid part of the purchase money thereof

That he resided on each of these said premises

That he has not done any Act to gain a Settlement since by renting or otherwise and he is become chargeable to the parish of Cheltenham [signed]
1832: *apparently removed to Hartpury (birth).* **1836:** *JH lived in Gloucester when he died (buried at Hartpury 30 Aug, aged 63).* [PS/CH/RA/2/3:168. Removal expenses for "Hooper" to Gloucester "&c." and on the same day to Hartpury (20 Sept 1832: P78/1/OV/2/4:66).]

32068SE: Thurs 20 Sept 1832 – **Betty Dobbs**, single woman: That she was born in the parish of Westbury upon Severn where her father & mother resided – I left Westbury ab^t. 30 years ago – I was then at the age of 16 years – Eight years ago I was hired by M^rs. Tippetts at Ledbury Mop and served 2 years with her in the parish of Dimock [= Dymock] and have subsequently served her 5 years in the parish of Donnington in the County of Hereford – I left that service at Old Michaelmas day last and the same day was hired by Timothy Butt and have lived ever since with him in Cheltenham

I received the whole of my wages from M^rs. Tippetts – I am now with child [mark]
1832: *removed to Donnington, Heref (presumed) (hiring and service).* **1835:** *daughter Elizabeth Dobbs baptised 1 Mar at Donnington, Heref.* **1841:** *BD (aged 59; no occupation) lived alone in Gt Heath, Dymock (HO107/350/6/19/10).* [PS/CH/RA/2/3:169.]

32069SE: Sat 22 Sept 1832 – **Elizabeth Nutting** (also **Nutty**), single woman: That she was born at Hardwick [= Bredon's Hardwick] in the parish of Bredon in the County of Worcester where she believes her father was then legally settled – That about two years ago at Old Michaelmas she was hired by M^r. Trinder of Cheltenham as a maid of all work but did not continue a year in that Service nor did receive the whole years wages – That about ten years ago she was hired by M^rs. Holland who kept the Swan Inn in the parish of Tewkesbury by the year at the wages of seven pounds – That she continued for years in that service and had ten pounds wages the last year

That she has not done any act to gain a Settlement since her Service at Tewkesbury and that she is now pregnant [mark]
1832: *removed to Tewkesbury (hiring and service); EN married Thomas Blizard at Tewkesbury 18 Nov, two months after examination; son Charles Blizard Nutting born at this time (he died, aged 16, at Tewkesbury and was buried 25 Aug 1849).* **1841:** *Thomas (aged 40; labourer) and Elizabeth (30) lived in Davis's Alley, off Barton St, Tewkesbury with sons Charles (9) and Thomas (7) and daughter Elizabeth (3)*

(HO107/380/4/30/11). [PS/CH/RA/2/3:170. Removal expenses for "E. Nutting" to Tewkesbury (20 Sept 1832: P78/1/OV/2/4:66).]

32070SE: Sat 22 Sept 1832 – **Joseph Robertson**, and wife **Sarah:** That he was born as he has heard and believes in the out parish of Saint Paul at Bristol where he believes his father was then legally settled – That when Examinant was about fourteen or fifteen years of Age his father removed to the parish of Saint James at Bristol and rented a house there at upwards of ten pounds a year and occupied it several years this Examinant then living with his said father and forming part of his family   That on the 16th. March 1830 he was married to his present wife Sarah at Findon in Sussex – That Examinant has never done any Act to gain a Settlement in his own right by Servitude, renting or otherwise and he is become chargeable to the parish of Cheltenham [signed]
1807: *JR born at Bristol 28 Apr (baptised 21 Mar 1813).* **1832:** *removed to St Paul's, Bristol (presumed) (father's settlement).* [PS/CH/RA/2/3:171.]

32071SE: [undated: 22-9 Sept 1832] – **John Gates:** [no text].
1832: *removal uncertain: examination form incomplete.* [PS/CH/RA/2/3:172.]

32072SE: Sat 29 Sept 1832 – **Isaac Pitt**, wife **Sarah**, and three children **George**, **Edward**, and **Harriet:** That he was born as he has heard and believes at Rushcomb [= Ruscombe] in the parish of Stroud in this County where he believes his parents are legally settled his said father having occasionally received relief at the parish of Stroud aforesaid and Examinant has also received relief from the parish Officers at Stroud. That about 12 years ago he was apprenticed by Indenture for Seven years, to Thomas Barnard of Cainscross in this County Carpenter and served the whole time – That he was an out door apprentice and Slept at his fathers house at Rushcomb going to his Service every morning and returning to his fathers at night – That about six years ago he was married to his present wife Sarah at Stroud aforesaid by whom he has three children living namely George who was born at Rendwick [= Randwick] in this county before this Examinant was married to his said wife and is six years of age Edward aged about four years and Harriet aged about two years – That Examinant has done no Act to gain a Settlement other than as above stated and is become chargeable to the parish of Cheltenham [mark]
1832: *removed to Ruscombe, Stroud (father's settlement).* **1841:** *IP (30; carpenter), wife Sarah (30), George (15) and three other children lived in Birmingham, where Sarah was born (HO107/1144/6/7/6). Isaac spent last years in Stroud Union Workhouse.* [PS/CH/RA/2/3:173. Removal expenses for "Pitt & family" to Stroud (4 Oct 1832: P78/1/OV/2/4:66).]

32073SE: Tues 2 Oct 1832 – **Jane Wilkes**, single woman: That she was born as she believes in the parish of Biddford [= Bidford-on-Avon] in the County of Warwick where she believes her parents are legally Settled – That when she was about thirteen years of age she was hired by M[r]. Osborne of the Hamlet of Broom in the said parish of Biddeford farmer by the year as nurse maid but Examinant does not recollect at what wages – her mother having made the agreement for her – That she remained nearly two years in that Service – That she has not been in Service a year in any place since and is become chargeable to the parish of Cheltenham being pregnant [signed]
1832: *removed to Bidford-on-Avon, Warks (presumed) (hiring and service); JW married George Rice in Bidford- on-Avon 10 Oct, soon after examination.* [PS/CH/RA/2/3:174.]

32074SE: Tues 9 Oct 1832 – **John Lovesy** (also **Lovesey**), and wife **Ellen:** That he was born as he believes in the parish of Eastington in this County his Mother having informed him that he was born there, out of Wedlock and that She had received Relief from the parish Officers there on his Account for his Maintenance

That about six or seven years ago he was hired by M[r]. Gillett of New Barn in the parish of Farmington in this County Inn Keeper and Farmer by the Year and to be paid weekly at four Shillings p[r] week. That he remained one year in the said Service, Sleeping with his Grandmother at Eastington – at the Michaelmas following Examinant was hired by M[r]. Gillett for another year at the same weekly wages and at the following Christmas his Master dying, his Mistress told him he must Sleep in the house for the remainder of the year which he did and received the same weekly wages and Maintenance himself, with the exception of some Meals which his said Mistress occasionally gave him, That on the 15th. August 1831 he was Married to his present wife Ellen at Cheltenham in the said County [mark]

1833: *died before removal; JL died soon after examination (buried at New Burial Ground, Cheltenham 12 Jan, aged 22).* [PS/CH/RA/2/3:175. See **33003SE** (widow Ellen Lovesy: 19 Jan 1833).]

32075SE: Sat 13 Oct 1832 – **Mary (Anne) Preston**, single woman: That She was born as she has heard and believes in the parish of Cheltenham

That about four years ago she was hired at Michaelmas Mop at Gloucester by M^r. James of Ellmore [= Elmore] in this County Farmer by the year at five pounds – That she served a full year and received her years wages – That she has not gained a Settlement since and has become chargeable to the parish of Cheltenham being pregnant [mark]

1832: *removed to Elmore (presumed) (hiring and service).* **1833:** *at examination MP was pregnant with twins, John and Sarah, baptised at Cheltenham 10 Mar; on 22 June she married Charles Daw of Blaisdon at Gloucester (banns previously called twice in Elmore).* **1837:** *son Samuel baptised at Blaisdon 4 June.* **1851:** *the family still lived in Blaisdon: Charles (aged 42; agricultural labourer), Ann (55), John (18; agricultural labourer, now using surname Preston, and Samuel (13).* [PS/CH/RA/2/3:176.]

32076SE: Mon 15 Oct 1832 – **William Clark**, wife **Elizabeth**, and two daughters **Ann Lucretia** and **Elizabeth:** That he was born as he has heard and believes in the parish of Frocester in this County That when he was about fifteen or sixteen years of age he was apprenticed to M^r. John Merret of the parish of Holy Trinity in the City of Gloucester Baker and Confectioner by Indenture for Seven years with the premium of Thirty pounds: that he served about two years and his Master gave him the remainder of his time and returned his friends the sum ~~made his a present~~ of Five pounds

That he slept in his Masters house in the same parish during the said two years – That on the 4th of June 1827 he was married to his present wife Elizabeth at St James Bristol and has two Children Ann Lucretia aged about four years and Elizabeth aged two years and he is become chargeable to the parish of Cheltenham [signed]

1832: *removed to Holy Trinity, Gloucester (presumed) (apprenticeship).* **1841:** *WC (aged 30; baker) lived with second wife Elizabeth and two daughters in Kidderminster (HO107/1208/4/10/12) (equivalent 1851 entry notes born Frocester).* [PS/CH/RA/2/3:177. Removal expenses for "Clarke family" to "parish" (11 Oct 1832: P78/1/OV/2/4:88).]

32077SE: Sat 27 Oct 1832 – **Mary Phillips**, single woman: That She was born as she believes in the parish of Presteigne in the County of Radnor in Wales where she believes her parents were then legally settled - That on the 16th. May 1831 she was hired as a yearly Servant to M^r. Allen then residing in Britannia Square in the parish of Claines in the County of Worcester at Six Guineas wages That she remained in that Service upwards of a year and received all her wages – That in July last year the family came to Cheltenham and she remained as a Servant with them until about a week past [signed]

1832: *removed to Claines, Worcs (hiring and service).* [PS/CH/RA/2/3:178. Removal expenses for "Mary Phillips" to Claines, Worcs (25 Feb 1833: P78/1/OV/2/4 p. 88).]

32078SE: Sat 3 Nov 1832 – **James Whittaker** (also **Whitacre, Whitaker**), wife **Martha**, and four children **Ann, James, Selina,** and **Henry:** That he was born as he has heard and believes in the parish of Stroud in this County where he believes his parents were legally settled his late father John Whittaker having received relief for some years of the parish Officers there when he was incapable of work – That he this Examinant has at several times received Relief from the parish Officers of Stroud aforesaid – And has for about three quarters of a year last past or something more received one Shilling and six pence a week from the said parish to enable him to maintain his family – That he has done no Act to gain a Settlement in his own right by Servitude renting or otherwise

That about 20 years ago he was married to his present wife Martha at Stroud aforesaid and has four Children now dependant [*sic*] upon him namely Ann aged about fifteen years James aged about nine years Selina aged about four years and Henry aged between two and three years, and is now chargeable to the Parish of Cheltenham [mark]

1832: *removed to Stroud (father's settlement).* 1833: *son Christopher baptised at Stroud 18 June, when family lived in Whiteshill district; JW (aged 60; agricultural labourer) lived with wife Martha and two children (including Henry) in Ruscombe, Stroud (HO107/349/13/47/21).* [PS/CH/RA/2/3:179. Removal expenses for "J. Whittaker & family" to Stroud (1 Nov 1832: P78/1/OV/2/4:88).]

32079SE: Tues 6 Nov 1832 – **Brian Kane**, and wife: That he is legally settled in the parish of Saint Mary at Manchester in the County of Lancaster - That on Saturday the third day of November instant he came with his wife and Child to Cheltenham and that in consequence of the illness of his said Child he was retarded on his passage to Manchester and that his said Child has since died [mark]

1832: *temporarily relieved or removed to St Mary, Manchester (place of settlement) (presumed);* *a Margaret Cains was buried at Cheltenham 6 Nov, aged 2 months.* Note: "2/6", expenses incurred by magistrates' office. [PS/CH/RA/2/3:180.]

32080SE: Thurs 8 Nov 1832 – **Elizabeth Townsend**, single woman: I first recollect myself as living at the village of Pilton in Somersetshire with my father & mother – My Father was a farmer and lived on his own estate in Pilton at that time – I left Pilton at about 8 or 9 years of age with my father who then took a farm at West Pennard an adj[oinin]g parish   I lived with him there about 7 years   I remained in that parish until I was of age as I believe, but am not certain – I left West Pennard with my father who then took a farm at Horn bloton [= Hornblotton] in the same County

I lived with him in that parish 2 years – He then left Horn bloton & at the same time I went into service – I was then more than 21 years of age – I was hired for a year but did not live in the service the whole time nor receive a year's wages – I have never since lived a year nor received a year's wages in any service, nor have I ever rented a house at 10£ a year. I am now pregnant [signed]

1832: *removed to Hornblotton, Som (father's settlement).* 1851: *(RETURNED) ET (aged 49; dairy maid) lodged in Henrietta St, Cheltenham (HO107/1973/386/5); father Emanuel (aged 80; farmer) had moved with other family members to Charlton Kings (HO107/353/1/48/22).* **1861:** *ET (aged 65; dressmaker) lodged with friend in Barnes' Yard off Grove St, Cheltenham (RG9/1800/72/42).* [PS/CH/RA/2/3:181. Note: "2/6". Removal expenses for "E. Townsend" to Som (20 Dec 1832: P78/1/OV/2/4:88).]

32081SE: Thurs 8 Nov 1832 – **Robert Davis**, and wife **Ann:** That he was born as he has heard and believes in the parish of Usk in the County of Monmouth –

That about eight or nine years ago he rented a house in Gloucester Place Cheltenham of a M^r. Brown of Pershore in the County of Worcester at twenty four pounds a year and occupied it between three and four years and paid all the Rent and Taxes for the same

That about Eleven or Twelve years ago he was married to his present wife Ann at the parish of Cheltenham and that he has never rented a House or Land at a higher Rent than six pounds a Year nor done any Act since to gain a Settlement elsewhere [signed]

1832: *removal unlikely: settlement probably acknowledged as Cheltenham.* [PS/CH/RA/2/3:182.]

32082SE: Thurs 15 Nov 1832 – **Mary Blackwell:** That she was born as she believes in the parish of Chedworth in this County – That on the 20th. January 1831 she was hired into the service of Lord Segrave in Cheltenham by the year at Ten Guineas wages   That she remained in that service until last April and received her full wages   That she occasionally served at Berkeley and occasionally at Cheltenham – That she left that service at Cheltenham having lived there for three weeks immediately before her discharge [mark]

1832: *removal uncertain: examination form incomplete;* *MB presumably left her employment when she became pregnant.* **1833:** *illegitimate son Obed baptised at Chedworth 19 Mar; presumably the MB of Chedworth who married John Trotman there.* **1834:** *eldest son Robert baptised at Chedworth 31 Aug.* **1841:**

the couple lived in Chedworth (Mary aged 25; John aged 30, agricultural labourer) with three children. [PS/CH/RA/2/3:183.]

32083SE: Thurs 22 Nov 1832 (corrected from 17th Nov) – **Sarah Mason**, widow, with three children **William, Ann**, and **Caroline**: [That] she was born at Stow on the Wold in this County where she believes her father was then legally settled

That on the 21st. day of May four years ago she was married to her late husband James Mason at the parish Church of Cheltenham and has three Children living by her said husband namely William aged about five years Ann aged three years and Caroline aged about three months

That when she first became acquainted with her late husband she was living as a yearly Servant with Mr. Hancks Innkeeper at Bourton on the Hill

That during the period she was such Servant her said late husband was living as a yearly servant with a Mrs. Hancks (a widow as she believes) in the parish of Longborough Gloucestershire – That he remained in such Service as this Examinant believes for upwards of two years – This Examinant further saith that within a week past she has seen the said Mrs. Hancks and she (Mrs. Hancks) admits that this Examinants said late husband was in her Service for two years and upwards as a yearly Servant and she this Examinant is positive that her said husband did not live a year in any Service between that time and the time of their Marriage and that she is now chargeable to the parish of Cheltenham [mark]

1832: *James Mason buried at Cheltenham 8 Sept, aged 29;* **removed to Longborough (late husband's hiring and service).** **1841:** *children apparently being cared for by relatives.* **1845/6:** *(RETURNED) from 2Q 1845 until 4Q 1846 SM and three children received parish relief from Stow-on-the-Wold as non-settled residents in Cheltenham (G/CH/9d/1).* **1851:** *children lived in Corpus St, Cheltenham: Anne (aged 20) and Caroline (18) laundresses at No 5, and William (23; servant) lodged at No 7 with wife Jane and daughter (HO107/1973/817/12 and 818/13).* [PS/CH/RA/2/3:184. Removal expenses for "S. Mason & family" to "Longboro" (6 Dec 1832: P78/1/OV/2/4:88). See **32064SE** (SM: 6-15 Sept 1832) for different information about late husband's employer.]

32084SE: Tues 20 Nov 1832 – **George Peters**, and wife **Margaret**: That he was born in the parish of Brixham near Torbay in the County of Devon where he believes his father & mother were legally settled – That at Xmas 1830 he rented a house of Mr. Hall Painter & Glazier Peters Street Bristol at 14£ a year situated in Newfoundland Lane in the outparish of St. Paul Bristol – That he occupied such house more than a year & a half and paid the whole of the rent – That at the same time he rented a shop at Clifton at £20 a year but never slept on that premises – That he was married to his present wife Margaret at Brixham in the year 1821, but has no child by her [signed]

1832: *removed to St Paul's, Bristol (presumed) (renting).* GP *had numerous business interests in Glos and Oxon, including fishmonger's shops in Nelson Place, Clifton in 1830 and in High St, Cheltenham (see* London Gazette *24 Oct 1834 p. 1908).* **1834:** *his businesses had failed and he was sued for bankruptcy.* **1841:** GP *had died when wife Margaret Peters (aged 45, widow living alone; fish seller) lived in Penn St (near Newfoundland Lane) in St Paul's district of Bristol (HO107/374/5/39/18).* [PS/CH/RA/2/3:185.]

32085SE: Thurs 29 Nov 1832 – **Mary Ann Powell:** That she was born as she believes in the parish of Lidney [= Lydney] in this County – That about 4 Years ago she was hired by Mrs. Falwassar No. 3 Montague Place Cheltenham for a Year at the wages of Ten Guineas Months Warning or Months Wages. That she served the whole Year in the Parish of Cheltenham and received her full years wages – That about three months after she left Mrs. Falwassars Service she was hired by Major Kirwan of Cheltenham for a Year and continued in his service in Cheltenham five weeks when she went with his family to Bath where she remained only about 4 months at the expiration of which time she left this Service [signed] Mary Ann Ball [*sic*]

1832: *removal uncertain: examination form incomplete.* [PS/CH/RA/2/3:186. *Falwassar:* more frequently found in form "Falwasser".]

32086SE: Thurs 29 Nov 1832 – **Hannah Howell:** [no text].

1832: *removal uncertain: examination form incomplete.* [PS/CH/RA/2/3:187.]

32087SE: Sat 1 Dec 1832 – **Dan Conigaam** [prob. = Conigham], wife and three children: That he was born as he believes in the County of Cork in Ireland and has gained no Settlement in England – That he has a wife and three Children and is become chargeable to the parish of Cheltenham that he has been detained on his passage through Cheltenham through the illness of his wife [mark]
1832: *removed to Ireland (presumed).* [PS/CH/RA/2/3:188.]

32088SE: Tues 4 Dec 1832 – **Thomas Davis**, and wife **Mary**: [That] he was born in the parish of Westbury upon Severn in this County – That about ten or eleven years ago last Michaelmas he was hired by M^r. William Cook farmer of the parish of Shurdington in this County by the year at the wages of Four pounds – that he continued in such Service one whole year and received his full years wages

That about three years ago he was married to his present wife Mary at Hampton in this County and he is become chargeable to the parish of Cheltenham That he has done no act since to gain a settlement [mark]
1831: *Mary Davis removed to Shurdington (husband's settlement): see* **31120SE** *(Mary Davis: 12 Nov).*
1832: *removed to Shurdington (presumed) (hiring and service).* [PS/CH/RA/2/3:188.]

32089SE: Tues 4 Dec 1832 – **Daniel Shakespeare** (also **Shakespear**), with two children **Sarah** and **Wanford**: That he was born as he believes in the parish of Newington Bagpath in this County where his parents were legally Settled and This Examinant has at various times and particularly when his late wife was ill received relief from the Parish Officers of the said Parish. That about ten years ago he was married to his late wife Elizabeth at S^t. Pauls Bristol – That his said wife died in last September and he has two Children living by her namely Sarah aged between eight and nine years and Wanford aged about two years That Examinant has never done any Act to gain a Settlement in his own right [signed]
1832: *removed to Newington Bagpath (father's settlement).* **1834:** *DS buried at Newington Bagpath 20 Aug, aged 31.* **1835:** *James Wanford Shakespeare died in London.* [PS/CH/RA/2/3:189. Removal expenses for "Shakespear" to Newington (6 Dec 1832: P78/1/OV/2/4:88).]

32090SE: Sat 8 Dec 1832 – Elizabeth Morgan, widow of James Morgan deceased, relating to settlement of step-children **Charlotte**, **James**, and **George**; also Samuel Huish of Cheltenham, painter: *Elizabeth Morgan*: That on last Whitmonday she was married to her late husband James Morgan at the parish Church of Cheltenham – That there are three Children of her said late husbands by his former wife living with this Examinant who are become chargeable to the parish of Cheltenham namely Charlotte aged about Eleven years James aged about Seven years and George about five years – That her said late husband has not to this Examinants belief rented a Tenement of £10 a year nor (since she knew him) done any other Act to gain a Settlement – That she has heard and believes that her said husband was last legally Settled in Bristol or at Clifton but in which She does not know [signed]
Samuel Huish: That he perfectly well knew the above named James Morgan from his Infancy. that he was born in the parish of Saint Paul in Bristol – Examinant believes that the father of the said James Morgan was legally settled at St Pauls and Examinant recollects the said James Morgan living in a house in Hot Well Road more than two years and that the rent was ten pounds a year or upwards – That Thomas Morgan the brother rented the same house for the said James Morgan and the rent was deducted from the wages which he received from his brother Thomas for whom he then worked as a painter and that James Morgan paid the Taxes for the house himself and Examinant believes that the said James Morgan has not rented a house of £10 a year since [mark]
1832: *James Morgan married Elizabeth Kilby in Cheltenham, 11 June; he was buried at New Burial Ground, Cheltenham on 29 Nov; removed to St Paul's, Bristol (father's settlement) (presumed).* Note: "No 7 Queen St Cheltenham". [PS/CH/RA/2/3:190.]

32091SE: Thurs 6 Dec 1832 – **Mary Ann Dowless** (perhaps for **Douglas** or similar), single woman: That she was born as she believes in the parish of Bisley – and that her Mother was not then married

That when she was about thirteen years of age she was apprenticed by Indenture to M^r. Jacob Lewis of Bisley aforesaid Weaver for five years as In door apprentice – that she served her whole time

That she has not done any Act by Servitude or otherwise to gain Settlement since, That being pregnant she is thereby chargeable to the parish of Cheltenham [mark]
1832: *removed to Bisley (apprenticeship).* [PS/CH/RA/2/3:191. Removal expenses for "Ann Dowdswell [*sic*]" to Bisley (6 Dec 1832: P78/1/OV/2/4:88).]

32092SE: Fri 14 Dec 1832 – Elizabeth Ireland, widow, regarding settlement of daughter **Elizabeth Ireland:** That her said daughter was born in the parish of Miserdine [= Miserden] in this County – this Examinant believes she herself is legally settled at Miserdine aforesaid and has received relief from the parish officers there

That her said daughter is ill and incapable of attending to be examined touching her Settlement

That at Michaelmas day (old Stile) three years ago her said daughter was hired by M^{rs}. Hannah Smith of Brimpsfield in this County to serve as a yearly Servant in husbandry at six pence per week.

That her said daughter lived in the said service two years and received her whole wages [mark]
1832: *removed to Brimpsfield (near Miserden) (hiring and service):* EI buried 30 Dec at Miserden. [PS/CH/RA/2/3:192 (p. 193 blank).]

32093SE: [undated: 14-26 Dec 1832] – **John Harnett**, wife and two children: That he was born in Kingsale [= Kinsale] in the County of Cork in Ireland and has not gained a Settlement in England

That he has a wife and two Children and he is become chargeable to the parish of Cheltenham [signed]
1832/3: *removed to Ireland (presumed).* [PS/CH/RA/2/3:194.]

32094SE: Wed 26 Dec 1832 – **Joel Tanner**, wife **Charlotte**, and two children **Hannah Maria** and **Sarah:** That he was born in the parish of Chalford in this County   That about nine years ago he was hired by M^r. Samuel Barber of Tewkesbury by the year at three Guineas wages – That he lived in such Service a Year and three Quarters and received all his wages – That upwards of three years ago he was married to his present wife Charlotte at Cheltenham and has two Children namely Hannah Maria aged between two and three years and Sarah aged nearly a year – That he has done no Act to gain a Settlement since by renting or otherwise and he is become chargeable to the parish of Cheltenham [mark]
1831: *removed to Tewkesbury (presumed) (hiring and service):* see **31108SE** *(JT: 6 Sept 1831).* **1832:** *(RETURNED) daughter Sarah baptised at Cheltenham 23 Jan.* **1832/3:** *removed to Tewkesbury (presumed) (hiring and service).* **1834:** *(RETURNED) daughter Elizabeth baptised at Cheltenham 19 Oct (JT labourer).* **1841:** *JT (aged 30; fishmonger) lived with wife Charlotte, (Hannah) Maria, and two other daughters at Long's Cottages, off High St, Cheltenham (HO107/353/16/5/5).* **1851:** *the family lived in Barnard's Row, Cheltenham, where JT (aged 42) described himself as costermonger (HO107/1973/653/23).* [PS/CH/RA/2/3:194.]

32095SE: Sat 29 Dec 1832 – **Ellen Maxfield**, widow: That she was born in the City of Edinburgh in Scotland [incomplete]
1832/3: *removed to Scotland (presumed).* [PS/CH/RA/2/3:195.]

1833

33001SE: Mon 7 Jan 1833 – **James Lewis**, labourer, wife **Ann** and children **Mary Ann** and **Charlotte:** That he was born in the parish of Byford in the County of Hereford

That his father died when he was only three Quarters of a Year old – that when he was about 13 Years of age he went to live with his Mother in the parish of Saint Peters in the City of Hereford – that whilst he and his mother were so living at Saint Peters they frequently received relief from the Parish officers of Wellington in the County of Hereford to which parish his Father & his family belonged – that when she died in Saint Peters his said Mother was partly buried at the Expence of the parish of Wellington – that he was once hired in the parish of Withington in the said County but did not serve a full year and having been removed from Saint Peters to Withington the officers of that parish appealed to the Herefordshire Sessions and the order was quashed   that he was subsequently removed to Wellington aforesaid and no appeal was ever made such last-mentioned order [*sic*].

That he has never rented a tenement of the yearly value of ten pounds or done any Act to gain a Settlement   That two Years ago, he was married to Ann his present Wife in the Parish of Cheltenham by whom he has one Child namely Mary Ann aged 16 months and he has also a daughter named Charlotte aged Nine Years or thereabouts by a former wife [mark]
1795: *JL baptised 15 Mar.* **1833:** *removed to Wellington, Heref (father's apparent settlement).* [PS/CH/RA/2/3:196. Removal expenses for "Lewis & family" to Hereford (10 Jan 1833: P78/1/OV/2/4:88).]

33002SE: Tues 15 Jan 1833 – **Patrick O'Brian**, wife and two children: That he was born in the County of Tipperary in Ireland, that he has gained no Settlement in England – That he has a wife and two Children and is become chargeable to the parish of Cheltenham [signed Patrick Brien]
1833: *removed to Ireland* (Cheltenham Chron. *17 Jan*). [PS/CH/RA/2/3:197.]

33003SE: Sat 19 Jan 1833 – **Ellen Lovesy** (also **Lovesey**), widow: That She was born as she believes in the parish of Cheltenham and that her parents were legally Settled there – That Examinant believes that her late husband John Lovesy was last legally settled at the parish of Farmington in this County – That she is chargeable to the parish of Cheltenham – that her husband died last Tuesday [mark]
1833: *burial of husband JL (buried at New Burial Ground, Cheltenham 12 Jan, aged 22).* **1833:** *removed to Farmington (late husband's settlement): see also* **32074SE** *(John Lovesy: 9 Oct).* **1837:** *death of an EL 4Q at Witney, Oxon (near Farmington).* [PS/CH/RA/2/3:198. Removal expenses for "Lovesy's Widow" to Farmington (10 Jan 1833: P78/1/OV/2/4:88).]

33004SE: Sat 19 Jan 1833 – **Ellin Lochlin**, with son **John:** That she was born in the County of Tipperary in Ireland – That Examinants husband Patrick Lochlin has not to this Examinants belief gained a Settlement in England – That she is become chargeable to the parish of Cheltenham   that she has a Son by her said husband named John Lochlin about one year and a half old [mark]
1833: *removed to Ireland* (Cheltenham Chron. *24 Jan*). [PS/CH/RA/2/3:198.]

33005SE: Tues 29 Jan 1833 – **John Burrows:** That he was born in the parish of Whittington in the said County where he believes his parents were legally settled – That Examinant has not gained a Settlement by servitude renting or otherwise and is now chargeable to the parish of Cheltenham

That Examinant received relief about two months ago and several times previously from the said parish of Whittington – That the Overseers of Whittington have acknowledged him as a parishioner [mark]
1833: *removed to Whittington (father's settlement).* [PS/CH/RA/2/3:199. Removal expenses for "Burrows" to "Wittington" (24 Jan 1833: P78/1/OV/2/4:88).]

33006SE: Tues 29 Jan 1833 – **William Hollis** (also **Holliss**), confined to bed by sickness: That he was born as he believes in the parish of Frampton upon Severn in this County – That above a year ago he rented a house in Newmans Row Cheltenham of M^r. John Finch Druggist at £10 [incomplete]
1833: *removal unlikely: examination form incomplete and settlement perhaps likely to be determined as Cheltenham; WH died at Cheltenham soon after examination (buried 16 Feb in Eastington, near Frampton, aged 45).* [PS/CH/RA/2/3:200.]

33007SE: Thurs 31 Jan 1833 – **John Jones:** That he does not know where he was born as his Parents were in the habit of travelling about the Country
   That he has never done any act in his own right to gain a Settlement [signed]
1833: *removal uncertain: evidence inconclusive.* [PS/CH/RA/2/3:201.]

33008SE: Tues 5 Feb 1833 – **Elizabeth Jones:** [incomplete].
[PS/CH/RA/2/3:201. See **33012SE** (EJ: 14 Feb 1833).]

33009SE: Thurs 7 Feb 1833 – **Martha Wood**, single woman: That she was born as she believes in the City of Gloucester where she believes her father Joseph Wood was then legally settled he having for several years carried on the business of a printer there – That her parents left Gloucester about nine years ago and went to Hereford and rented a House in the parish of Saint Peters in Hereford of M^r. Christopher Griffiths at about sixteen pounds a year and occupied the same a whole year and paid the Rent for a Year – That Examinant has not gained a settlement by servitude or otherwise in her own right – that she was part of her father's family at the time he rented the House in Hereford and resided there [signed]
1833: *removed to Hereford (presumed) (father's settlement).* **1839:** *MW lived at 14 Notting Hill when she married musician John Court Wickett 5 Jan.* **1841:** *the couple lived in Tufton St, Westminster: John Wickett (aged 20; Professor of Music) and Martha (aged 20).* [PS/CH/RA/2/3:202.]

33010SE: Tues 12 Feb 1833 – **Martha Dubber**, single woman: That she was born in the County of Oxford but does not know in what parish – That she believes her father Samuel Dubber is [*sic*] last legally settled in the parish of Siddington in this County Examinant having heard him say that he lived in service there And Examinant recollects her said father receiving Relief from the parish Officers there – That about four years ago Examinant was hired by Miss Chapman daughter of the late M^{rs}. Chapman of Nailsworth in the parish of Avening in this County Widow for a year at the wages of four pounds – That she served her full year and received her years wages   That Examinant has not done any act since to gain a Settlement - That She is now chargeable to the Parish of Cheltenham in consequence of her Pregnancy [signed]
1833: *removed to Nailsworth (hiring and service); illegitimate daughter Jane baptised 1 Apr at Avening.* [PS/CH/RA/2/3:203. Removal expenses for "Martha Dubber to Nailsworth" (14 Feb 1833: P78/1/OV/2/4:88).]

33011SE: Thurs 14 Feb 1833 – **Sarah Strong**, with children **John**, **William**, and **Priscilla**: That she has been twice married, her first husband David Miles was a German and never to this Examinants knowledge gained a Settlement in England – That she has two Children now living by him namely John aged nine years and a half and William aged six years – That two years ago come next May she was married to her present husband William Strong at Cheltenham   That he has left her and Examinant does not know where the place of his last legal Settlement is – That she has one Child by her said husband William Strong a female about Eleven Months old not yet baptized – That Examinant was born in the parish of Kilken [= Cilcain] in the County of Flint she believes that her father was legally settled in the said parish of Kilken he having built a house there which was his own property and carried on Business as a Carpenter and Wheelwright for several years   That about fifteen or Sixteen years ago before Examinant was married to her first husband She lived as a Servant with John Myers Esquire of Wavertree [marginal note: 3 Miles from Liverpool] in the parish of Childwall in the County of Lancaster by the year as Cook at twelve Guineas wages and remained in that Service about fourteen Months and received all her wages   Examinant did no other Act to gain a Settlement from the time She left M[r]. Myers' Service till her Marriage with her said first husband [mark]

1832: *removal to Bridgewater, Som (***32043SE:** *30 June) (RETURNED).* **1833:** *place of removal uncertain.* **1849:** *sons John and William Miles and (illegitimate) daughter Priscilla Strong emigrated from Wales (Newport) on SS Medallion, arriving in Boston, Massachusetts 22 Sept.* **1851:** *William Miles may be the William Miles (aged 25) buried at Cheltenham 29 Apr.* [PS/CH/RA/2/3:204. See **33059SE** (husband William Strong: 7 Sept 1833).]

33012SE: Thurs 14 Feb 1833 – **Elizabeth Jones**, wife of John Jones in Gloucester Gaol, with children **James** and **Thomas**: That she never heard her said husband say where his place of legal Settlement is and Examinant believes that her husband does not know the place of his Settlement

That Examinant was born in the parish of Painswick where she believes her father Thomas Birt is legally settled – That Examinant never did any Act previous to her Marriage to gain a Settlement in her own right   That about four years ago she was married to her said husband at Bedwellty in the County of Monmouth and has two Children by him namely James aged near three years and Thomas aged four Months – That she is become chargeable to the parish of Cheltenham [signed]

1833: *removed to Painswick (father's settlement); John Jones was sentenced to three months' imprisonment at Lent Assizes, Gloucester for stealing about five pounds of bacon in Cheltenham.* [PS/CH/RA/2/3:205. Removal expenses for "E. Jones & family" to Painswick (14 Feb 1833: P78/1/OV/2/4:88). See **33008SE** (EJ: 5 Feb 1833).]

33013SE: [between 14 Feb and 2 Mar 1833] – **Thomas Scott**, wife and three children: That he was born as he believes in the City of Edinburgh – That he has never gained a Settlement in England – That he has a wife and three children and is become chargeable to the Parish of Cheltenham [mark]

1833: *removed to Scotland (presumed).* [PS/CH/RA/2/3:206.]

33014SE: [between 14 Feb and 2 Mar 1833] – **Mary Scanlan**, widow, with son **John**: That she was born as she believes in the County of Sligo in Ireland   that She has not gained a Settlement in England

That she has one child namely John Dyer aged a year and a half and she is become chargeable to the Parish of Cheltenham [mark]

1833: *removed to Ireland (presumed).* [PS/CH/RA/2/3:207.]

33015SE: Sat 2 Mar 1833 – **George Orchard**: That he was born at Doddington [= Dodington] in this County

That between six and seven years ago he was hired by Rev[d]. M[r]. Foster of Doddington aforesaid by the year as Groom at the wages of 12 L the first year and continued two years and a half and had 14 £ a year wages afterwards

That Examinant never did any other Act to gain a Settlement since [mark]

1833: *removed to Dodington (presumed) (hiring and service); GO attended the Public Office in Cheltenham charged with stealing a penknife and money from Mr Fisher (*Gloucestershire Chron. *14 Mar); found not guilty of larceny at Gloucester Lent Assizes.* **1851:** *perhaps the GO, formerly private soldier from Glos, who lived (aged 35) in Tower Hamlets with wife Martha (HO107/1546/548/61).* [PS/CH/RA/2/3:207.]

33016SE: Tues 5 Mar 1833 – **Daniel Kelly**: That he was born as he believes in the City of Cork in Ireland – That he has not gained a Settlement in England - and is become chargeable to the parish of Cheltenham

1833: *removed to Ireland (presumed).* [PS/CH/RA/2/3:208.]

33017SE: Tues 5 Mar 1833 – **George King**: That he was born as he believes in the Parish of Saint John's in the City of Coventry – That about 13 Years ago he was hired by Mr Waterfall of Cheltenham Confectioner by the Week at 2/6 a week – that he lived with him about 5 or 6 months

– That about 9 or 10 Years ago he went under a written agreement to serve Messrs King & [blank] as Stone Mason's – There was no regular Indenture
1833: *removal uncertain: examination form incomplete.* [PS/CH/RA/2/3:208.]

33018SE: ?9 Mar 1833 – **Richard Beard**: That he was born in the Parish of Painswick in the said County where his parents were settled – That two Years ago or thereabouts he was hired by M^r. Gregory Druggist of Cheltenham for a Year at the wages of Six pounds to be paid monthly – I continued in the Service 9 months when I left it in consequence of being hurt by a Horse -. As soon as I got well which was about 6 weeks Mr Wm Gregory sent for me and agreed for me to go to him to work again [mark]
1833: *removal uncertain: examination form incomplete.* [PS/CH/RA/2/3:209.]

33019SE: Sat 9 Mar 1833 – **Edward McDonald**: That he was born in the City of Edingburgh [*sic*] and that he has never done any act to gain a settlement in England
1833: *removed to Scotland (presumed).* [PS/CH/RA/2/3:209.]

33020SE: Sat 9 Mar 1833 – **Henry Howard**: I was born in the parish of Saint James in the County of Middlesex   I rented a house in the parish of Prestbury at Ten Guineas a year for four years and paid the whole of the rent   I then came to Cheltenham and took a house at 30£ a year at Michaelmas 1831   I still occupy it & have paid more than a year's rent [signed]
1833: *removal unlikely: settlement probably acknowledged as Cheltenham; HH (shoemaker, late of 15 Henrietta St, Cheltenham) sued for bankruptcy later in year* (London Gazette, 20 Sept, p. 1725). [PS/CH/RA/2/3:210.]

33021SE: Sat 16 Mar 1833 – William Aldridge, in Gloucester Gaol on charge of felony, relating to settlement of wife **Elizabeth** and son **Robert**: That about two years ago he was hired by M^r. John Williams of Dursley, Surgeon, for a Year at the Wages of Eighteen pounds   That he lived with M^r. Williams in Dursley upwards of a Year & received all his wages. That he was married about Six Months ago to his present wife then Elizabeth Webb by whom he has one child an infant. That he hath never done any act except as above to gain any Settlement [mark]
1833: *removed to Dursley (presumed) (husband's hiring and service): see* 38081SE *(EA: 13 Dec 1838) for further information on the family.* [PS/CH/RA/2/3:211.]

33022SE: Sat 23 Mar 1833 – **Mary Jones**, single woman: That she was born as she believes in the parish of Dawson [= Dorstone] in the County of Hereford where she believes her parents were legally settled – That several years ago she was hired by M^r. Thomas Maddox of the parish of Bredwardine in the County of Hereford farmer by the year at about thirty Shillings wages – That she remained in that Service upwards of a year and received all her wages – That She has done no Act to gain a Settlement since and is become chargeable to the parish of Cheltenham [mark]
1807: *an MJ baptised at Dorstone, Heref 1 Feb, daughter of James and Margaret Jones.* **1833:** *removed to Bredwardine, Heref (presumed) (hiring and service).* [PS/CH/RA/2/3:212. Removal expenses for conveying "Paupers to Herefordshire" £2/13/- (28 Mar 1833: P78/1/OV/2/4:88).]

33023SE: Sat 23 Mar 1833 – **Mary Evans**, with children **Thomas**, **Marianne**, and **William**: That her husband Philip Evans has deserted her and she does not know where he is
    Examinant believes that her said husband is [*sic*] last legally settled in the parish of Ross in the County of Hereford he having rented a house there at twenty three pounds a year for two years and paid the rent for the same – That in 1831 her said husband was a prisoner in Gloucester Goal [*sic*] on a charge of felony and while he was there Examinant received relief from the parish Officers of Ross   That she has three children by her said husband Thomas aged twelve Marianne aged ten and William aged eight and she is chargeable to the parish of Cheltenham [mark]
1831: *wife and children removed to (or relieved by) Ross, Heref (presumed) (renting): see* **31117SE** *(husband Philip Evans: 29 Oct); PE sentenced to six months' imprisonment at Michaelmas Gloucester Assizes.* **1833:** *RETURNED) removed to Ross-on-Wye, Heref (husband's renting) (presumed).* [PS/CH/RA/2/3:213. Expenses for conveying "Paupers to Herefordshire" £2/13/- (28 Mar 1833: P78/1/OV/2/4:88).]

33024SE: Sat 23 Mar 1833 – **Daniel Barter**, wife **Ann** and three children **William**, **Esther**, and **Enoch**: That he was born as he believes in the parish of Stroud in this County where he believes his parents are legally settled – they having received relief from the parish officers there for some time and they are now receiving three Shillings per week – And this Examinant received 2/6 per week from that parish for more than a twelvemonth – Examinant having served Apprenticeship at Stroud aforesaid   That about Seven years ago he was married to his present wife Ann at the parish of Stroud aforesaid and has three Children namely William aged 8 years, Esther aged 3 years and Enoch aged one week – That he is become chargeable to the parish of Cheltenham [mark]
1833: *removed to Stroud (father's settlement); baby Enoch died later in year.* **1841:** *DB (aged 35; weaver) and (Hester) Ann lived in Lower St, Ruscombe, Stroud with William (15), Esther (10), and three further children (HO107/349/13/37/1).* [PS/CH/RA/2/3:214. Removal expenses for "conveying Barton [*sic*] & family to Stroud" (28 Mar 1833: P78/1/OV/2/4:88).]

33025SE: Thurs 4 Apr 1833 – **Sarah Lewis;** also John Young Gardner: *Sarah Lewis*: That she was born at Chalford in the parish of Bisley in this County where she believes her parents were legally settled – That she [incomplete]
John Young Gardner: about two Years ago a Man of the Name of Dutton came and looked at a House belonging to this Examinant which he said he wanted for a Young Woman
1833: *removal uncertain: examination form incomplete.* [PS/CH/RA/2/3:215.]

33026SE: ?6 Apr 1833 – **Cornelius Carter**, and wife **Ellen**: That he was born at Glasgow in Scotland and that he has never done any Act to gain a Settlement in England – that in august [*sic*] four years ago he was married to Ellen his present Wife and that they are now chargeable to the Parish of Cheltenham [mark]
1833: *removed to Scotland (presumed).* [PS/CH/RA/2/3:216.]

33027SE: Thurs 2 May 1833 – **Nathaniel** (also **Nathan**) **Sparrow**, wife **Ann**, and children **Amy** and **Charles**: *Nathaniel Sparrow*: That he was born as he believes in the parish of Highworth in the County of Wilts – That his father is now residing in the lodging at M[r]. Coopers in Cheltenham

That he believes his fathers place of last legal Settlement is at Highworth aforesaid – Examinant believes that his said father has occasionally received relief from that parish – That Examinant has also received relief from the said parish of Highworth Towards the support of himself and family whilst he was residing at Cheltenham

That he has done no Act to gain a Settlement in his own right – That about five years ago he was married to his present wife Ann at Bishops Cleeve [= Bishop's Cleeve] in this County and has two Children living namely Amy aged nearly five years and Charles aged four Months – That his wife and child [*sic*] are become chargeable to the parish of Cheltenham [mark]
Ann Sparrow: That She is the Wife of Nathaniel Sparrow and she together with her child now about 4 months old is become chargeable to the parish of Cheltenham [mark]
1833: *removed to Highworth, Wilts (presumed) (father's settlement): see* **38012RO** *(NS: 10 Feb) for further information.* [PS/CH/RA/2/3:217.]

33028SE: Tues 16 Apr 1833 – **George Hill**, and wife **Susan**: That he believes he was born in the parish of Hardwick [= Hardwicke] in this County

That about 25 or 26 years ago he was hired as a yearly Servant by the Rev[d]. M[r]. Rudge of the parish of Saint Catherine at Gloucester by the year as Coachman at about £12 or £13 wages per year – That he lived in the house and was maintained by his Master and found in Livery –

That he lived a whole year in the said Service and received his years wages – That about 21 or 22 years ago he was married to his present wife Susan at Cheltenham – That he is become chargeable to the parish of Cheltenham   That he has never done any other act to gain a Settlement [mark]
1833: *removed to St Catherine's, Gloucester (presumed) (hiring and service).* [PS/CH/RA/2/3:218.]

33029SE: Tues 16 Apr 1833 – **Susan Davis;** also mother Mary Davis: *Susan Davis*: That she believes she was born in the parish of Cherrington [= Cherington] in the County of Gloucester where she believes her parents were legally Settled. that about four years ago she was hired by Mr Edward Smith of Cheltenham by the week at one shilling p[e]r week and received such wages Monthly, and continued in such service two years and a half but lodged during such time with her Mother: there was an understanding between her Master & herself when the agreement took place that a weeks notice should be given or taken on either side on quitting such service, that she has done no other act to gaine [*sic*] a Settlement since [mark]

Mary Davis: That the above named Susan Davis is an illegitimate Child of this Examinant and that She was born in the parish of Cherrington aforesaid   That the Agreement between her said daughter and the said Edward Smith was as above Stated by her said daughter to the best of this Examinant's knowledge and belief [mark]

1833: *removed to Cherington (presumed) (birth).* [PS/CH/RA/2/3:219.]

33030SE: Sat 27 Apr 1833 – **Susannah Cooke** (also **Cook**), with five children **Thomas, Selina, Benjamin, William,** and **Pamela**: That She was born as she believes in the parish of Stroud in this County where she believes her father Thomas Cooke is legally Settled, he at this time receiving pay from the parish Officers there as a pauper   Examinant has never done any Act to gain a Settlement in her own right   Examinant has five Children all born out of lawful Wedlock in the parish of Stroud aforesaid namely Thomas aged 14 years Selina aged 11 years Benjamin aged 8 years William aged 6 years and Pamela aged 2 years and She this Deponent is become chargeable to the parish of Cheltenham [signed Susana Cooke]

1833: *removed to Stroud (presumed) (father's settlement); daughter Pamela Cook buried at Cheltenham 30 May.* **1841:** *Thomas (aged 20; labourer), wife Matilda, and brothers Benjamin (15; labourer) and William (15; labourer), lived in Deacon (also Archdeacon) St, Gloucester (HO107/379/10/12/9).* [PS/CH/RA/2/3:220.]

33031SE: Sat 27 Apr 1833 – **Hannah Evans,** single woman: That she was born as she believes at the parish of Frocester in this County   That her father and mother were legally [settled] in the said parish of Frocester – That she lived one year and received the whole of her wages from M^r. Ford a gentleman farmer at Frocester aforesaid   That she was hired at £5 a year wages a month's notice or a months warning   That she lived at the George Inn Frocester for 3 years after leaving M^r. Ford's

That about five years ago she went to live as waiter at the Bell Inn Cheltenham – That she lived about five years in such service   That when she first went into the situation it was agreed between me and the Mistress that I should have vails [= perquisites; gratuities, tips] instead of wages and I agreed to pay £10 a year for the situation

1833: *removal uncertain: examination form incomplete: see* **44050SE** *(HE: 10 Oct 1844) for further information.* [PS/CH/RA/2/3:221.]

33032SE: Sat 27 Apr 1833 – **Mary Young,** single woman; also mother Mary Young: *Mary Young*: That her Mother Mary Young is a person of Colour and Examinant has heard her Mother say that She (Examinant) was born in Sicily   That She was about six years of Age when first brought into England – They arrived at Bristol – They remained some years in Bristol

Mary Young, mother: [That] her said daughter was born at Palermo in Sicily, her husband belonging at that time to the British Army – That upwards of sixteen years ago – They came to England her husband having previously left the Army on account of the breaking of the regiment   That Examinant never heard her said husband say that he had any Settlement in England

1833: *removal uncertain: examination form incomplete.* **1851:** *MY's mother perhaps the Mary Young (aged 64; charwoman, born India (British subject)) lodging at 6 Townsend Place, Cheltenham (HO107/1973/466/50).* [PS/CH/RA/2/3:222.]

33033SE: Thurs 2 May 1833 – **Ann Swaney** (perhaps **Sweeney**): I was born in the town of Mallow in the County of Cork in Ireland – About 30 years ago I was married to an irishman by a catholic priest in Ireland – I never lived with my said husband in England   I never rented a tenement in England at 10£ a year nor other[wise] gained a settlement

I am now chargeable to the Parish of Cheltenham [mark]

1833: *removed to Ireland (presumed).* [PS/CH/RA/2/3:223. The frequency of related spellings of surname in Mallow according to 1901 census was: Swaney (3 people), Sweeny (6), and Sweeney (36).]

33034SE: Sat 4 May 1833 – **Jeremiah Bryan:** ~~That he was born at Clonakilty in the County of Cork~~
1833: *removal uncertain: examination form incomplete.* [PS/CH/RA/2/3:224.]

33035SE: [undated: 4-7 May 1833] – **Sarah Glyn**, widow, with children **Mary**, **Jane**, and **Martin**: That She was born in the County of Galway in Ireland and has not gained a Settlement in England   That she has three Children namely Mary, Jane and Martin and is now chargeable to the parish of Cheltenham [mark]
1833: *removed to Ireland (presumed).* [PS/CH/RA/2/3:224.]

33036SE: Tues 7 May 1833 – **William Britton** (also **Brittan**): I was born in the Parish of Mar[k]sbury in the County of Somerset – I was apprenticed when I was Eleven years of age by my Father to Thomas Newport of the Parish of Whitechurch [= Whitchurch] in the County of Somerset Taylor until I was 21 Years of age – I served 2 Years under the Indenture of apprenticeship which was prepared by an attorney at Bristol and executed in his presence at my Father's House – I do not know what premium was given – The year I was apprenticed was 1811 or 1812.

after I had served two Years I ran away – Since that time I have never done any act whatever to gain a Settlement [signed]
1833: *removed to Whitchurch, Som (presumed) (apprenticeship).* *Perhaps the WB (also Brittan), born c1800 and imprisoned several times for larceny and assault at Bristol from 1834 onwards (see for example Gloucestershire Chron. 22 Nov, 1834).* [PS/CH/RA/2/3:225.]

33037SE: Sat 25 May 1833 – **Thomas Probert:** That he was born as he has heard and believes at Craysleys [= Crizeley] in the parish of Didley in the County of Hereford   Examinant believes that his late father Thomas Probert was last legally settled in the Extraparochial Hamlet of Treville in the said County of Hereford his said father having received Relief from the Overseers there for some time previous and up to the time of his death and was buried at their expence Examinant being at the time of his father's death about fourteen years of Age and forming part of his family   Examinant lived at Mr Clythe's at Whitfield in the said Hamlet of Treville for 6 or 7 years by the week, but received no Wages – He received relief from the parish Officers there at different times and particularly last Winter being out of Work he was relieved by the parish Officers there – That he has never done any Act to gain a Settlement in his own right and is become chargeable to the parish of Cheltenham – That about a fortnight ago Examinant being on his Journey to the Hamlet of Treville aforesaid was taken ill and rendered unable to proceed on his Journey to his own parish [mark]
1833: *removed to Treville, Hereford (presumed) (father's settlement).* [PS/CH/RA/2/3:226.]

33038SE: Sat 25 May 1833 – **John Miles:** That he was born in the parish of Dymock in this County where he believes his father was legally settled   That in the years 1792 and 1793 he was a yearly Servant to Francis William Thos Bridges of Tibberton Court in the County of Hereford Esquire as a Groom at 16 Guineas a year and Clothes

That he remained 3 years in that Service and received all his wages – That he never did any other Act to gain a Settlement by renting servitude or otherwise   That he is now chargeable to the parish of Cheltenham – That about a month ago he was taken ill on passing through the parish of Cheltenham whilst proceeding on his journey to his own parish [mark]
1833: *removed to Tibberton Court (presumed) (hiring and service).* [PS/CH/RA/2/3:227.]

33039SE: Sat 1 June 1833 – **George Smith**, wife and son **Francis**: That he was born in Dublin That he left Ireland ab^t. 17 or 18 years ago – That about 3½ years ago he quitted a house in Charles

Street Holborn in the parish of Saint Giles ~~which he had rented nearly 4 years at 4£ a year rent~~ – That his father in Law rented the house & that Deponent lived with him – That his father in Law took the house of the Landlord – That he married his wife ab^t. 13 years ago by whom he has one child Francis, aged 10 years [mark]
1833: *removal uncertain: examination form incomplete.* [PS/CH/RA/2/3:228.]

33040SE: Thurs 6 June 1833 – **Ann King** (also **Anne King**), single woman: That She was born as She has heard and believes in the parish of Painswick in this County, where she believes her parents were legally settled her father having carried on business there for several years as a Clothier on an extensive Scale.

That Examinant never did any Act to gain a Settlement in her own right – I am now pregnant – When my father left Painswick my mother was admitted into the Workhouse at Painswick [signed]
1833: *removed to Painswick (presumed) (father's settlement).* [PS/CH/RA/2/3:229.]

33041SE: Thurs 13 June 1833 – **John Conroy**, with children **Luke** and **Biddy**: That he was born in the Kingdom of Ireland in the County of Longford. When I was 15 Years of age – I went into the Army – About 7 or 8 Years ago I lived in a House belonging to Richd Newman in Cheltenham. – I have two Children – Luke aged 10 Biddy aged 13 Years – Luke was born in Cheltenham.

I never rented a House by the Year or done any act to gain a Settlement in England. Biddy was born in Ireland [mark]
1833: *removal uncertain: evidence appears inconclusive.* **1836:** *Luke Conroy, described as a "little urchin", apparently lived in Cheltenham when arrested for stealing two children's bed-gowns from outside house in Prestbury; he was imprisoned for two months in Northleach house of correction and "whipped twice" (*Gloucestershire Chron. *2 July).* [PS/CH/RA/2/3:230.]

33042SE: Sat 29 June 1833 – **Sarah Davis**: I was born in the parish of Mutchdewchurch [= Much Dewchurch] in the County of Hereford – More than 20 Years ago I lived as a Servant with Mr Joseph Wedmore in the Parish of Saint Warnard [= St Weonards] in the County of Hereford for 2 Years nearly

That twenty two Years ago she was married to John Davis at St Nicholas in Hereford – He died about 14 Years ago – he died[?]. That when her Husband was living she applied to him [*sic*] to the Parish officers of Ross for Relief   that he attended a Vestry Meeting and proved that his Settlement was at Ross – that the Parish officers of Ross then allowed them 12^d a Week – that the officers were told by her Husband that he gained a Settlement at Ross by renting a House of Mr Watkins of the Butchers Arms in Ross – that the House was rented about 17 or 18 Years ago at 12£ a Year – that she and her Husband resided in the House so rented of M^r. Watkins more than 40 days

That she is now pregnant with a bastard Child [mark]
1833: *removed to Ross-on-Wye, Heref (late husband's renting) (presumed).* [PS/CH/RA/2/3:231.]

33043SE: Mon 15 July 1833 – **William Calcutt** (also **Calcott**), and wife **Sarah**: That he was born in the parish of Henly [= Henley] in the County of Oxford Where his father was (as deponent believes) legally settled, he having received relief from that parish – That he has never done any act by servitude renting or otherwise to gain a settlement in his own right   That he was married to his present wife Sarah about 17 years ago but has no children [signed]
1833: *WC died before removal; buried at New Burial Ground, Cheltenham 10 Oct, aged 50.* [PS/CH/RA/2/3:232. See another Oxfordshire Calcutt at **33048SE** (Jane Calcutt: 27 July 1833).]

33044SE: Wed 3 July 1833 – James Jones, residing in Lyme Regis, Dorset, regarding son **John Jones**: My Son John Jones was born at Lyme Regis in Dorsetshire. He left home around 11 Years ago when he was of age – I live at Lyme – I Was a Carrier. There was no more than one Parish Church at Lyme Regis

I was an Ostler at the Golden Lion at Lyme for 7 Years

I kept a Public House in 1790 or 1791, at Lyme for 5 Years – I paid 10 Guineas a Year Rent for it – after that I came to Lyme again

I rented a House at Lyme Regis at 12£ a Year for 11 Years – I was living at a House in Lyme when my Son was born – It was in that House that I lived 11 Years – After I quitted that House I took another with Yard and Stables in the same Parish of Lyme Regis for thirteen pounds a Year - I occupied that Eighteen Years – I live in Lyme now and have lived there these last 38 Years [signed]
1833: *removed to Lyme Regis, Dorsetshire (presumed) (father's settlement).* **1851:** *JJ (aged 52; publican, born Lyme Regis) was perhaps the husband of Elizabeth Jones living with two children at 2 George Court, St Martin in the Fields, Middlesex.* [PS/CH/RA/2/3:233.]

33045SE: Sat 27 July 1833 – **Frances Monday** (also **Munday**): That She was born as she has heard and believes in the parish of Saint Peters Mancroft [= St Peter Mancroft] in the City of Norwich, where she believes her late Father James Critchfield was last legally settled he having carried on Business there for several years as a Cutler and Jeweller   That the house her father lived in was his own property – that her father is long since dead and her brother is now living in the same house. That she was married on or about the 25 January in the year 1807 by Banns at St Andrews Church Holborn to Edward Monday who lived with her for sixteen months or thereabouts and then deserted her   That she has not since heard of or seen him. And that she has done no other act to gain a Settlement elsewhere. And this deponent further saith that she has received relief from the Overseers of the Poor of the Parish of Cheltenham, and is now chargeable to the said Parish of Cheltenham [signed]
1790: *FM née Critchfield baptised at Norwich 24 Sept.* **1833:** *removal uncertain: evidence appears inconclusive.* **1841:** *FM (aged 50; waiter) lived in High Street, Cheltenham (HO107/353/14/31/6); she remarried at Cheltenham from 8 St Paul's St North 25 Aug to Jonathan Richards (glover and widower); her father, James Critchfield, was jeweller.* [PS/CH/RA/2/3:234.]

33046SE: Thurs 25 July 1833 – **George Willis**: That he was born in the Parish of Sandhurst in the County of Gloucester where his Parents were legally settled.
    About 11 or 12 Years ago he rented a House in Duke Street Cheltenham of Mr Sawyer at the rent of twenty Guineas a Year payable Quarterly – that he occupied the same two Years and a half and paid the Rent.
    That on the 15 February 1831 he took a House in Saint Clements Danes [= St Clement Danes] Nº 17, in the Parish of Saint Clements Danes, in the County of Middlesex of Mr Brookes by the Year at the rent of fifteen pounds a Year payable Weekly – the rent was to include the Water Rates and Poor rate. The House I rented was behind another. It contained 3 rooms and it was a separate and distinct Tenement – there was no Communication from my Stair Case or House with any other House but the only way in which I had access to it was going through the passage of the front House – When I got through the passage I came into a Court Yard. I then entered one of the Rooms of my House the Communication to which was a door which when locked rendered my House free from access by any other person – There was a Washhouse Common to 4 Servants and two Cocks of Water. I occupied the House a Year and a Quarter and paid Mr Farley the agent of the Land 4/9 a Week as the Landlords proportion of the yearly Rent [mark]
1833: *removed to St Clement Danes, Middlesex (presumed) (renting).* **1841:** *probably the GW (aged 65; occasional waiter) who lived with brother John's family in Sandhurst (HO107/356/12/6/6).*[PS/CH/RA/2/3:235. Compare Gray **30a** (Esther Newman: 4 May 1816) and **30b** (William Allen: 4 May 1816).]

33047SE: Thurs 25 July 1833 – **Staggard** (also **Staggart**) **Cornwall**, and wife **Mary Ann**: That he was born in the parish of Wretham in the County of Norfolk where his father & mother were legally settled – That he has never lived for a year in any service nor rented a tenement at 10£ a year nor been apprenticed – That he married his present Wife Mary Ann at the parish Church in [Prendergast] South Wales – That his said wife was put to bed on Saturday, 20th. July instant as she was passing through the town with him – That he & his said Wife have in consequence become chargeable to the parish of Cheltenham [mark]

1833: *removed to Wretham, Norfolk (presumed) (father's settlement).* SC was a musician who spent much *time travelling around Britain.* **1851:** *SC (aged 45) lived with wife Mary Ann (41), three daughters, and two sons (several of whom were actors or actresses) in St Woollos, Monm. The birthplaces of his children illustrate the family's peripatetic lifestyle: Ellen (20; Taunton), Elizabeth (14; Bedwellty, Monm), John (12; Manchester), Selena (9; Swansea), and George (8; Newport, Monm).* [PS/CH/RA/2/3:236.]

33048SE: Sat 27 July 1833 – **Jane Calcutt** (also **Calcott**), single woman: That she was born as she has heard and believes in the parish of Curbage [= Curbridge] near Witney in the County of Oxford where she believes her late father William Calcott was legally settled – That about three years ago at last Easter she was hired by M[r]. William Boulton of the parish of Saint Giles in the City of Oxford Baker by the year a Months wages or a Months warning at Three pounds twelve Shillings wages – That she continued in the said service in that parish till about the 11th day of December (two years and a half after entering into the same) and then the family removed into the parish of Saint Abbs [= St Ebbe's] in the said City of Oxford and Examinant left on the 20th February following. That she has done no other act to gain a settlement elsewhere and she is now pregnant [signed]
1833: *removed to St Ebbe's, Oxford (presumed) (hiring and service): see* **37076RO** *(9 Nov 1837) for further information.* [PS/CH/RA/2/3:237.]

33049SE: Sat 17 Aug 1833 – **John Metcher**, wife **Sarah**, and three children, **James**, **William**, and **Julia**: That he was born as he has heard and believes in the parish of Southampton – That he believes his father John Metcher is now legally settled in Chipping Norton in Oxfordshire he having a house and Garden there his own property, and carries on the Business of a Plumber on his own Account in the said parish of Chipping Norton   That Examinant never did any Act to gain a Settlement in his own right by Servitude apprenticeship renting or otherwise   That about Seven years ago he was married to his wife Sarah at S[t]. Aldates [= St Aldate's] Gloucester by whom he has three children – James aged about 6 years William aged about 4 years and Julia aged about 18 Months and he is become chargeable to the parish of Cheltenham [signed]
1833: *removed to Chipping Norton, Oxon (presumed) (father's settlement).* **1841:** *(RETURNED) JM (aged 40; plumber), wife Sarah (38), and four children James (14), William (12), John (7), and Emma (1) lived at 28 Park St, Cheltenham (HO107/353/16/49/14).* **1851:** *JM (50; plumber) and Sarah lived with Emma and three younger children in Admiral Buildings, Winchcombe St, Cheltenham.* [PS/CH/RA/2/3:238.]

33050SE: Tues 3 Dec [1 Aug struck out] 1833 – **William Werrett** (also **Wherrett**), wife **Elizabeth**, and daughter **Mary Ann**: That he was born in the parish of Redmarley [= Redmarley D'Abitot] in the County of Worcester   That is Mother was not as he has heard and believes then married   That Examinant has not done any act by Servitude or otherwise to gain a Settlement in his own Right
    A twelvemonth ago last May he was married to his wife Elizabeth at Hempstead [= Hempsted] in this County and has one child Mary Ann aged about ~~Eleven Months~~ one year and he is become chargeable to the parish of Cheltenham [signed]
1833: *removed to Redmarley D'Abitot, Worcs (presumed) (birth).* **1834:** *baptism of son George at wife Elizabeth's home village of Boddington/Staverton (first children Mary Ann and George died early).* **1841:** *WW (aged 25; agricultural labourer) and wife Elizabeth (25) lived in Boddington, with newborn son Joseph (HO107/367/5/4/3). In later censuses the family lived in Staverton.* **1859:** *this examination consulted by magistrates, presumably for another removal from Cheltenham.* **1871:** *death of WW at Cheltenham Union Workhouse.* [PS/CH/RA/2/3:239.]

33051SE: Sat 3 Aug 1833 – **Henry George Williams**: That he was born in the Parish of Kington in the County of Hereford as he [h]as heard and believes, where his father was legally settled his said father having carried on the business of a Cabinet Maker for several years there   That this examinant was apprenticed to his said father by a regular Indenture for seven years when he this examinant was about 14 Years of age - That he served his father as such apprentice for about three years when his father died. That about eighteen months after his father's death he was again apprenticed by regular Indenture to M[r] Henry Brown in the Parish for Old Swinford [=

Oldswinford] – in the County of Worcester for the remainder of the term for which he had previously been bound to serve his said father. That he served the said Henry Brown as such Apprentice for the whole of the term he was bound. That in or about the year 1826 this Examinant's mother took a house for this Examinant at Leominster in the County of Hereford of a Mr Hull at the rent of 25£ a year   That he lived upwards of a twelvemonth in the said House but his mother paid the rent herself and was always rated to the taxes in respect of the said House That he has done no other act to gain a Settlement elsewhere.

That he is become chargeable to the Parish of Cheltenham [signed]

1833: *perhaps removed to Oldswinford, Worcs (apprenticeship):* see **34003SE** *(HGW: 9 Jan 1834) for further information.* [PS/CH/RA/2/3:241; incomplete text of final section struck out on draft at p. 240 of register.]

33052SE: Sat 3 Aug 1833 – **Charlotte Pearce** (also **Pierce**), single woman; also father John Pearce: *Charlotte Pearce*: That she was born at Newnham in this County as she has heard and believes. That her father left the said Parish of Newnham about eleven years ago. That since that time he has rented a house and garden at 17£ a year in the Parish of Leckhampton in this County. That he paid the years rent   that she this Examinant was living as part of her father's family at that time. That she has done no act to gain a settlement in her own right, and that she is become chargeable to the Parish of Cheltenham in consequence of her pregnancy [mark]

John Pearce: That the above statement made by the above named Charlotte Pearce is true and that he has done no other act to gain a settlement elsewhere [signed]

1833: *removed to Leckhampton (presumed) (father's settlement). CP was pregnant with daughter Agnes at time of examination.* **1836:** *(RETURNED) burial of daughter Agnes (aged 2) at Cheltenham Jan.* **1837:** *birth and death of another daughter Agnes at Cheltenham, when CP lived at Field Cottage, Bath Rd.* **1839:** *CP married John Portlock, widower in late thirties: her address then was Manchester Walk, Cheltenham, 25 Mar.* **1841:** *the couple, with the children from John's former marriage, lived in Church St, Charlton Kings (HO107/353/2/19/3).* [PS/CH/RA/2/3:242.]

33053SE: Sat 10 [6 struck out] Aug 1833 – **Ann Edwards**, widow, with son **William**: That she was born as she has heard and believes in the parish of Thatcham in Berkshire – That in the year 1805 her late husband William Edwards rented a house of M^r. John Edwards in upper Ground Street near Black Friars Road in the parish of Christ Church [Southwark] in the County of Surrey by the year at 16£ Rent – That they occupied it half a year and paid half a years rent for the same and also paid land Tax and poors [*sic*] rates for the same house during the time they occupied it – That she has one child by her said husband namely William aged about twelve years

That Examinant believes her late father Thomas Horwood was last legally settled at Hurst in Berkshire he having rented a house at upwards of 10£ a year and carried on business there as a Publican for several years   That her late husband died about 4 months ago [signed]

1833: *removal uncertain: evidence appears inconclusive.* **1841:** *AE (aged 60; charwoman) lived alone in Sidney St, Cheltenham (HO107/353/3/18/31).* **1851** *and* **1861:** *AE lived at 3 York St, Cheltenham, working as needlewoman and sempstress.* [PS/CH/RA/2/3:243.]

33054SE: Tues 6 Aug 1833 – **Elizabeth Hurd** (also **Heard**, **Herd**), single woman: That She was born as She has heard and believes in the parish of Upton Pyne in Devon Shire   That about 5 Years ago She was hired by Mr^s. Sarah Gitchan [prob. Gitshan] wife of M^r. Gitchan of the parish of [St] Mary Steps Church in the City of Exeter at five pounds wages yearly – That She remained nearly two years in the said Service and received all her wages – That Examinant has not done any Act since to gain a Settlement and She is become Chargeable to the Parish of Cheltenham in consequence of her pregnancy. [mark]

1833: *removed to Exeter, Devonshire (presumed) (hiring and service); perhaps returned on appeal:* see **34001SE** *(8 Feb 1834) for further information.* [PS/CH/RA/2/3:244.]

33055SE: Sat 10 Aug [8 struck out] 1833 – **Ann Southam**, single woman: That she was born as She has heard and believes in Ombersley parish in the County of Worcester

That about 9 years ago she was hired by M[rs]. Boulton wife of M[r]. Boulton of the parish of Saint Johns in the County of Worcester Nursery Man by the year at Four pounds wages a months wages or a months warning – That she continued 3 years in that Service and received all her wages – That She has done no Act to gain a Settlement since – That She is become chargeable to the parish of Cheltenham in consequence of pregnancy [mark]
1833: *removed to St John's, Worcester, Worcs (presumed) (hiring and service).* [PS/CH/RA/2/3:245.]

33056SE: [undated: 8-10 Aug] 1833 – **Mary Smith**, widow: That She was born as She has heard and believes in the City of Waterford in Ireland

That she has gained no Settlement in England and is become chargeable to the parish of Cheltenham
1833: *removal uncertain: examination form incomplete.* [PS/CH/RA/2/3:246.]

33057SE: Sat 10 Aug 1833 – **Eliza Turner**, single woman: That She was born as she has heard and believes at Woodchester

That when she was about 3 months old as she has heard She was brought by her parents to Cheltenham where they now reside

That on the 21st. November 1831 She was hired by M[rs]. Agg of Hewletts at five pounds wages a Months wages or a months warning – That she continued in that Service One year and received all her wages. – That Examinant believes that Hewletts house is in the two parishes of Cheltenham and Prestbury – That when the perambulation of Cheltenham parish took place the persons who were then perambulating went through the Dining Room window – That the Bed Room in which Examinant Slept was over the Dining room and as large

That Examinant believes that the part of the Bed room in which she Slept was in the parish of Cheltenham the Bed being always placed on the side next Cheltenham [signed]
1833: *removal unlikely: examination form incomplete; place of settlement probably acknowledged as Cheltenham.* [PS/CH/RA/2/3:247.]

33058SE: Tues 20 Aug 1833 – **Thomas Powell**, wife **Charlotte**, and two children **Mary** and **Harriet**: That he was born as he believes in the parish of Saint Peters [Hereford] in the County of Hereford   That about thirty years ago he was hired by John Bevan of Weston Farm in the parish of Bredwardine in the County of Hereford farmer by the year at Seven Guineas wages and remained a year in that Service and received the whole of his years wages – That about fifteen years ago he married his present wife Charlotte Powell at Cheltenham and has two Children by her namely Mary aged about five years and Harriet aged two years and that he is become chargeable to the parish of Cheltenham [mark]
1833: *removed to Bredwardine, Heref (presumed) (hiring and service).* [PS/CH/RA/2/3:248.]

33059SE: Sat 7 Sept 1833 – **William Strong**: That he was born in the Parish of Holcombe Regis [= Holcombe Rogus] in the County of Devon where his Parents were legally settled – That when he was a young Man he was hired by the Year by M[r] Evans of the parish of Burlescombe in the County of Devon to drive his Team and that he continued in such his service for more than four years – that he was an indoor Servant [mark]
1832: *removed to Bridgewater, Som (see* **32048E**: *19 July 1832) (RETURNED).* **1833:** *removed to Burlescombe, Devon (presumed) (hiring and service).* **1841:** *a WS (or Strang) (aged 65; agricultural labourer) lived with wife Sarah (60) and two daughters, Ann (19) and Jane (8), in Burlescombe, Devon (HO107/202/9/4/2).* [PS/CH/RA/2/3:249. Expenses for "Apprehending W. Strong" (Sept 1833: P78/1/OV/2/4/59). See **33011SE** (wife Sarah Strong: 14 Feb 1833).]

33060SE: Sat 14 Sept 1833 – **Mary Griffiths**: That she was born in the Parish of North Curry in the County of Somerset as she hath heard and believes, where her father was legally settled.

That about the year 1786 she was married to Robert Griffiths at Cliff Church in the Parish of [blank] in the City of Bristol by whom she had three children – That her husband died about the year 1793. That since then two of her children are dead and the third, she believes, is now living but where she cannot say. That she never knew where husband's Parish Settlement was. That about nine or ten years ago she was hired by the Reverend Charles Jervis of Cheltenham for a year at 18 Guineas a year

That she lived upwards of two years in such service and received the whole of her wages. That since that time she has lived in service at different places in Cheltenham for various periods of time and hath not done any other act to gain a Settlement elsewhere   That she is now become chargeable to the Parish of Cheltenham in the County of Gloucester

1833: *removal unlikely: examination form incomplete; place of settlement probably acknowledged as Cheltenham.* [PS/CH/RA/2/3:250.]

33061SE: Tues 17 Sept 1833 – **Sarah Hawker**, single woman: That she was born in the Parish of Longdon in the County of Worcester as she hath heard and believes [incomplete]

1805: *SH baptised at Longdon by Upton, Worcs 24 June.* **1833:** *removal uncertain: examination form incomplete.* [PS/CH/RA/2/3:251.]

33062SE: Sat 12 Oct 1833 – **John Kerney**, with wife **Elizabeth** and six children: I was born as I believe in Ireland. I first left Ireland about 25 years ago – I lived six months in London and afterwards in Bath – I was hired by Mrs Osborne as footman at the wages of 30£ – for a year – She lived in Marlborough Buildings in the parish of Walcot in the County of Somerset – I lived the whole Year and received the whole of my wages   I afterwards returned to Ireland And was married by a Catholic Priest [at St Andrew's Church in Dublin] to Elizabeth Wilkinson about 22 years ago   She has six children living since I married her – About 5 years ago I rented a house in the parish of Walcot (in St James Square) of Mr Howe Woollen draper – at 20£ a year   My family occupied it one year and I paid 10£ in Cash – towards the rent. – I lived all the time in the parish of Walcot 3 or 4 months in the house & used to sleep there occasionally

1833: *removal uncertain: examination form incomplete.* [PS/CH/RA/2/3:252.]

33063SE: Tues 22 Oct 1833 – **Jane Cooper**, with children **John** and **Elizabeth**: That She was born as she believes in the City of Edingburgh [*sic*] in Scotland – That her present husband George Cooper has left her and She does not know where he is

That he is a native of Scotland and has not to this Examinants belief gained a Settlement in England – That She has two children namely John aged Seven years and Elizabeth aged about Seven Months and she is become chargeable to the parish of Cheltenham [mark]

1833: *removed to Scotland (presumed).* [PS/CH/RA/2/3:253. Removal expenses for conveying "Scotch Vagrants to Bristol thence to Scotland" £14/6/2 (27 Mar 1834: P78/1/OV/2/4:88).]

33064SE: Thurs 24 Oct 1833 – **Jane Rose**, widow: That she was born as She believes in the parish of Hatherop in this County –

That her late husband William Rose lived as a yearly Servant with the late M[r]. Durham at Winchcomb Paper Maker for two years at the same time as Examinant lived as a Servant in the same place and that they were married from the same Service – That after their Marriage her said husband served the Office of parish Constable at Winchcomb aforesaid for one whole year – her said husband died about 36 years ago – and Examinant received relief from the parish Officers there since her said husbands death – That Examinant has not gained a Settlement by renting or otherwise in her own right since her said husbands death and that She is become chargeable to the parish of Cheltenham [mark]

1833: *removed to Winchcombe (presumed) (late husband's settlement).* **1841:** *(RETURNED) JR (aged 80; independent; née Hawkins) lived in Sherborne St, Cheltenham with Samuel Hawkins (30) and Ann Waite (45) (HO107/353/5/60/42).* [PS/CH/RA/2/3:254.]

33065SE: Sat 2 Nov 1833 – **Mary Ann Yates**, single woman: That she was born as She believes in the Town of Gibraltar her father being a Soldier in the British army at the time   That Two years and a half ago last July She was hired by M[rs] Bricknell wife of M[r]. Michael Bricknell farmer then living at the Six Chimnies in the Hamlet of Alstone in the parish of Cheltenham

farmer by the year   the first year Examinant received no wages but Clothes and the Second year Examinant was hired by the said M^{rs}. Bricknell at the wages of Two Pounds ten Shillings, that She served a whole year under the last hiring and received her whole years wages and lived half a year more in the same Service [mark]
1833: *removal unlikely: examination form incomplete; place of settlement probably acknowledged as Cheltenham.* [PS/CH/RA/2/3:255.]

33066SE: Tues 5 Nov 1833 – **Bridget Kittrick**: That She is on her journey to the Supposed Settlement of her husband in the parish of Saint Thomas near the City of Exeter but in the County of Devon – That her husband William Kittrick has deserted her and She does not know where he is   That She is unable to proceed on her journey on account of illness and is now chargeable to the parish of Cheltenham [mark]
1833: *removed to St Thomas, Exeter, Devonshire (presumed) (husband's settlement).* [PS/CH/RA/2/3:256.]

33067SE: Tues 12 Nov 1833 – **Michael Marran**, with wife **Eleanor**: That he was born in the County of Sligo in Ireland – That he has never done any Act to gain a Settlement in England – that 14 Years ago he was Married to Eleanor his present Wife in Ireland [mark]
1833: *removed to Ireland after imprisonment (presumed).* **1834:** *MM sentenced to one month's imprisonment at New Year (Epiphany) Assizes at Gloucester, for stealing 50 lbs of lead in Cheltenham (Gloucestershire Chron. 11 Jan).* [PS/CH/RA/2/3:257.]

33068SE: [undated: 16-23 Nov] 1833 – **George Turner**, wife **Ann** and son **William**: That he was born in the Town of Greennock [= Greenock] in the County of Renfrew in that part of the United Kingdom called Scotland and has not gained a Settlement in England
    That he has a wife Ann and one Child named William aged about Seven years and is become chargeable to the parish of Cheltenham [signed]
1833: *pauper and family sent by pass to Tewkesbury: "Scotch paupers" (Gloucestershire Chron. 23 Nov).* [PS/CH/RA/2/3:259.]

33069SE: Sat 23 Nov 1833 – **Thomas Acock** (also **Haycock**), wife **Ann**, and two children **Sarah** and **Joseph**: That he believes he was born in the parish of Northleach where he believes his father Robert Acock was legally Settled his said father having for several years rented a house and land in the said parish of Northleach at upwards of Twenty pounds a year and carried on Business there as a Carpenter
    That Examinant never gained a Settlement in his own right by renting Servitude or otherwise That about eighteen years ago he was married to his present wife Ann at Saint Olds [= St Aldate's] in Oxford and has two children dependent upon him namely Sarah aged near thirteen years and Joseph aged near four years and that he is become chargeable to the parish of Cheltenham [signed]
1833: *removed to Northleach (presumed) (father's settlement).* **1841:** *TA (aged 50; carpenter) lived with wife Ann (50), and children Sarah (15) and Joseph (12) in Northleach (HO107/351/10/9/13).* [PS/CH/RA/2/3:260.]

33070SE: Thurs 28 Nov 1833 – **William Davies**, wife **Eliza**, and two children **Eliza** and **Mary**: That he believes he was born at Deptford in Kent – That his father William Davies is now residing in the parish of Banbury in the County of Oxford and rents a house there at ten pounds yearly – That Examinant has not done any Act to gain a Settlement in his own right by Servitude renting or otherwise – That about four years ago he was married to his present wife Eliza at Hempsted in this County and has two children by her namely Eliza aged about three years and Mary aged one Month and he is become chargeable to the parish of Cheltenham
1833: *removal uncertain: examination form incomplete.* **1836:** *daughter Jane born at Cheltenham late 1836. Soon after this, the family moved to Merthyr Tydfil and then to Abergavenny.* **1851:** *WD (now aged 39) formerly baker and now described as "Clerk and Waggon Officer" (HO107/2446/231/28).* [PS/CH/RA/2/3:261.]

33071SE: Thurs 5 Dec 1833 – **Henry George Williams**: That under the Will of Walter Williams he became entitled to a freehold House in the Parish of Kington in the County of Hereford for his Life – that on his coming of Age he had the Property but did not reside upon it
1833: *removal uncertain: see* **34003SE** *(HGW: 9 Jan 1834) for further information.* [PS/CH/RA/2/3:262.]

33072SE: Sat 14 Dec 1833 – **Michael Leane**, wife and children: That about five weeks ago he his wife and child were passing through Cheltenham on their way for Ireland   That he has been retarded on his Journey by his wife's illness – She being through pregnancy unable to travel And that She has since been delivered of a Child in the parish of Cheltenham [signed]
1833: *removed to Ireland (presumed).* [PS/CH/RA/2/3:263.]

33073SE: [undated: 5-10 Dec 1833] – **Thomas Williams**, and wife **Mary**: That he was born as he believes in the parish of Chidley [prob. Chudleigh] in the County of Devon
    That his father was a Seaman and Examinant knows nothing about his said father's Settlement The [for: That] he never did any Act by renting Servitude apprenticeship or otherwise to gain a Settlement in his own right
    That he married his present wife Mary at Bedminster [then part of Som]
1833: *removal uncertain.* [PS/CH/RA/2/3:264.]

33074SE: Tues 10 Dec 1833 – **Cyrus Clift**, wife **Hannah**, and son **Thomas Augustin**: That he was born as he believes in Marlborough in the County of Wilts   That when Examinant was about 14 years of age he was duly apprenticed by Indenture for the Gloucestershire Society to Thomas Pearce of Tewkesbury in this County Printer Bookseller and Stationer and Bookbinder for Seven years   That he served from the 14th day of March 1823 until some time in October 1824 – That he then ran away and never returned to his said Master and has not done any Act to gain a Settlement Since
    That in July 1830 he was married to his present wife Hannah at S[t]. John's in Margate in Kent and has one child by her namely Thomas Augustin aged about two years and a half and he (Deponent) is become chargeable to the parish of Cheltenham [signed]
1830: *after his marriage CC and family lived in Tewkesbury.* **1833:** *removed to Tewkesbury (presumed) (apprenticeship).* **1834:** *CC described as "of Tewkesbury" when son William baptised at Gloucester in June.* **1841:** *the family lived in Oldbury, Tewkesbury: Cyrus (aged 30; brewer), Hannah (30), Thomas (10), Ann (5), and Mary (3). Further children were born at Tewkesbury and finally (Janette) at Cheltenham (RETURNED).* **1846:** *the Clifts emigrated to New York on "Empire", arriving from Liverpool 30 Nov.* **1850:** *CC (aged 48; labourer), wife, and children lived in Findlay, Hancock, Ohio; CC and wife were Nonconformist, baptising their children in Wesleyan and Bible Christian chapels.* [PS/CH/RA/2/3:265.]

33075SE: Fri 13 Dec 1833 – **Susannah Brown**, single woman: That she was born as She believes at Truro or near Truro in Cornwall
    That She has lived several years in different places as a Servant
    That She lived several years with a Major Tucker as Lady's Maid to M[rs]. Tucker who lived in the Lower College Green Bristol
    That Examinant receives two Shillings weekly from the parish Officers of the Widcomb [= Widcombe] at Bath and has for a considerable time past received such Relief
1833: *removal uncertain.* [PS/CH/RA/2/3:266]

33076SE: Fri 13 Dec 1833 – **John Millbank**: That he was born at Colchester in Essex – That his parents died when he was about 6 or 7 years of age – and he was left chargeable to the parish in consequence [incomplete]
1833: *removal unlikely; examination incomplete.* **1834:** *JM died soon after examination (buried at Cheltenham 17 Mar, aged 84, "after a long and severe illness"); he was "well known in Cheltenham as 'Little John the Muffin-man'"* (Cheltenham Chron. *20 Mar).* [PS/CH/RA/2/3:267. Note: "Miss Hull Bath road". See Illustration.]

33077SE: Tues 24 Dec 1833 – **Sarah Donnell** (also **O'Donnell**): That she was born in Ireland that about thirteen Years ago she went into the Service of M^r. Saml Lesingham at Upton upon Severn [Worcs] as a yearly Servant and continued in his Service nine Years in the said Parish of Upton on Severn – that she has never lived in any place of Service a whole year since or done any act whatever to gain a Settlement and that she is now pregnant [signed]
1833: *removed to Upton-upon-Severn, Worcs (presumed) (hiring and service).* [PS/CH/RA/2/3:268.]

On the 15th inst. in her 79th year, Charlotte Jane Emma, relict of Col. R. Jackson, of the Hon. E. I. Company Service.

On the same day, in Newman's Place, after a long and severe illness, John Milbanke, aged 85, well known in Cheltenham as "Little John the Muffin-man."

---

*The death of John Millbank, Cheltenham's Muffin-man (**33076S**; see illus., p. li), aged 85, recorded in the Cheltenham Chronicle (20 March 1834). Millbank was subjected to a settlement examination in Cheltenham on 13 December 1833, when ill-health meant that he was no longer able to support himself. Newman's Place was a yard off Devonshire Street, running south from the Lower High Street, in one of the poorest areas of the town at the time.*

1834

34001SE: 4 Jan Sat 8 Feb 1833 1834 – **Elizabeth Hurd** (also **Heard, Herd**), single woman: That she was born in the Parish of Upton Pyne in in the County of Devon – that about 9 or 10 Years ago she was hired by Mrs Sarah Gitshan Wife of Mr Samuel Gitshan of the Parish of All Hallows on the Walls in the City of Exeter for a Year at the Wages of five Pounds. That she continued in the Service nearly 2 Years – that she received the whole of her wages for the time she was in that service [and] has never been hired for a Year or lived for a Year, in any Service since – that she is now chargeable to the Parish of Cheltenham [mark]
1833: *removed to Exeter, Devonshire (presumed) (hiring and service): see* **33054SE** *(EH: 6 Aug); EH was mother of Mary (no father noted), baptised 18 Oct at St Sidwell's Church, Exeter; perhaps returned after appeal (RETURNED).* **1834:** *removal uncertain.* **1851:** *both lived at 31 Sherborne St, Cheltenham: EH (aged 61; plain sewer) and Mary (27; laundress) (HO107/1973/149/39).* [PS/CH/RA/2/3:269.]

34002SE: Thurs 9 Jan 1834 – **Eliza White**, single woman: That she was born as she believes at the Parish of Churchdown in this County where She believes her late father Thomas White was last legally settled Examinant having heard her said father say that he had lived as a Servant in the said parish and he having to this Examinants knowledge received relief from the parish Officers of the said parish of Churchdown for many years before his death. – That Examinant never did any Act to gain a Settlement in her own right   That She is become chargeable to the Parish of Cheltenham [mark]
1806: *EW baptised at Churchdown 8 Feb.* **1834:** *removed to Churchdown (presumed) (father's settlement).* **1841:** *EW (aged 35) apparently an inmate of Gloucester Union Workhouse (HO107/379/2/40/3).* [PS/CH/RA/2/3:270.]

34003SE: Thurs 9 Jan 1834 – **Henry George Williams**: That he was born at Kington in the County of Hereford – that when he was about 14 years of age he was apprenticed to Henry Davis his Father who then followed the business of a Cabinet Maker, for 7 Years.
    That he served his Father between 3 and 4 years in Kington when my father died
    I then went to London and staid for a month with my Uncle – that in the Year 1823 or thereabout he was apprenticed to Henry Brown of Old Swinford [= Oldswinford] in the County of Stafford Cabinet Maker for the time of 7 Years. That he served him 18 months or two Years at Old Swinford when they parted – I continued to work there for some time – After I came of age I went to Leominster and lived in a House for 6 months which my mother had taken for me – after that I requested my mother to go and take another House at Leominster at 25 Guineas a Year – it was after the Year 1826 – I did not live in it more than 9 months – I then went to Swansea and took a House at 12 Guineas a Year but I only lived there a quarter of a Year
    I have not taken a House above the rent of nine pounds a Year since I left Swansea [signed]
1833: *HGW perhaps removed to Old Swinford, Heref, with appeal: see* **33051SE** *(HGW: 3 Aug) (RETURNED).* **1834:** *removal uncertain: evidence appears inconclusive.* **1841:** *probably the HW (25; cabinet-maker) living in Market Lane, St Woollos, Newport (HO107/751/17/37/18).* **1843:** *marriage of HW to Sophia Harley in Malpas, Newport, Monm.* **1851:** *HW (45; cabinet-maker) lodged with wife Sophia in Bedwellty, Monm (HO107/2448/537/16).* [PS/CH/RA/2/3:271. See **33071SE** (HGW: 5 Dec 1833).]

34004SE: Sat 11 Jan 1834 – **Ann Wilkins**: I am a single woman – I was born at Defford in the County of Worcester – where my parents were settled – About 2 years & a half ago I came to live in Chelt^m. I was hired by M^r. Wait at the National School for one year at 30/- wages & some clothes – I lived with him a year & a half & received all my wages – On leaving Cheltenham I was hired by M^r. Stevens, Miller, of Overbury at 4 Guineas a year wages, a months wages or a month's warning – After I had been there about 9 months I was taken ill – my brother then came for me & took me away – Before I left I found the situation too hard for me & gave a month's warning – I left at the expiration of the month & received 3£ wages – I was hired at Xmas 1832 by Richard White of Croome [= Croome D'Abitot] Worcestershire until the next Michaelmas at £3 – I was paid the 3£ at Mich[aelm]as – I was then hired again by Richard White for a year at 4£ – A month afterwards I left in consequence of having a sprained ancle – I did not receive any wages for the work – When I left the house my master told me I was to return as soon as I recovered – I lived in lodgings in Croome & my said master used to send me provisions – I am going back to M^r. White's service as soon as I have got some clothes

1812: *baptism of AW's brother Joseph in Defford, Worcs 26 May.* **1834: removal uncertain: examination form incomplete.** *Family tradition (ancestry.com) indicates that AW emigrated to Australia, where she died 11 Jan 1884 at Lyndock Valley, South Australia, fifty years to the day after examination.* [PS/CH/RA/2/3:272-3.]

34005SE: Tues 14 Jan 1834 – **James King**: That about five or six years ago he hired a house of M^r. William Clarke in the parish of Saint Mary De lode in the City of Gloucester at Sixteen pounds a year

That he lived more than a year in the same house and paid all the rent for the same That he has done no Act to gain a Settlement since and is become chargeable to the parish of Cheltenham [signed]

1834: *removed to St Mary de Lode, Gloucester (presumed) (renting).* **1835:** *JK buried at St Mary de Lode, Gloucester, aged 64, 16 Oct, an inmate of Gloucester Workhouse.* [PS/CH/RA/2/3:274.]

34006SE: Thurs 16 Jan 1834 – **Maria Mifflen** (also **Mifflin, Miflin**), otherwise **Maria Bailey** (also **Bayley**), single woman, with daughters **Adelaide** and **Jane**: That She was born she believes in the parish of Maiden Bradley in the County of Wilts   That She has heard and believes that her parents were not married – That when She was about Eleven years of Age She went to live with her Mother and Father in law who then kept a lodging House in Duke Street in the parish of Saint James in the City of Bath – That she continued with them till She was about 15 years old when it was agreed between her father in law and mother that Examinant Should receive yearly wages and she accordingly received five pounds the first year – She being hired in the place of another Servant who left her father in laws Service

That She filled the Situation of Cook and remained as a yearly Servant with them till She was twenty years of Age and received all her wages which was five pounds yearly   But She sometimes had a present given her by her mother to make her wages more   That She is become chargeable to the parish of Cheltenham through pregnancy

Examinant further States that She has two illegitimate Children living namely Adelaide aged about 3 years and Jane aged about 2 years the first was born in Avon Street in Bath and I was then lodging with M^r. Davis – and the youngest was born in Saint James Street near Saint James Church in Bath aforesaid [signed]

1834: *removed to St James, Bath, Som (presumed) (hiring and service).* **1841:** *MM (aged 35; charwoman) lived with daughters Adelaide (10) and Eliza (1) at 9 Galloway Buildings (subsequently North Parade Buildings), Bath.* [PS/CH/RA/2/3:275.]

34007SE: Thurs 23 Jan 1834 – **Ann Simmons** (also **Simmson**), single woman; also mother Mary Simmons: *Ann Simmons:* That she believes she was born in the parish of Upton upon Severn in the County of Worcester where she believes her late father Samuel Simmons was legally settled – That She has never gained a Settlement in her own right   That She is chargeable to the parish of Cheltenham through pregnancy [mark]

Mary Simmons: That the said Ann Simmons was born in the said parish of Upton [upon] Severn [and] that she believes her late husband Samuel Simmons the father of the said Ann Simmons was last legally settled in the parish of Upton upon Severn aforesaid – She having heard her said husband say that he had lived as a yearly servant there and her said husband had relief from the parish Officers there and Examinant also received relief from that parish since her said husband's death on account of her family [mark]

1833: *probably the Ann "Simmson", common-law wife of James Lock.* **1834:** *removed to Upton-upon-Severn, Worcs (presumed) (father's settlement); during examination AS pregnant with son William (HO107/1862/17/26); the children born later in the 1830s were mostly baptised in Dorset.* **1841:** *James Lock (aged 35; agricultural labourer), partner Ann (25), and four sons, lived in Whitchurch Canonicorum, Dorset (HO107/282/10/7/9).* [PS/CH/RA/2/3:276.]

034008SE: Thurs 23 Jan 1834 – **George Chambers**, wife **Martha**, and children **Letitia**, **William**, and **George**: That he believes he was born in the parish of Ledbury in the County of Hereford where he believes his father John Chambers was legally settled

Examinant thinks from what he has heard his Mother say that his father rented a house there at upwards of Ten pounds annually and kept a Shop there And that his said father gained a Settlement in that parish originally by Servitude – Examinant has not gained a Settlement in his own right by servitude renting or otherwise – That about ten years ago he was married to his present wife Martha at Tewkesbury and has 3 Children namely Letitia aged about four years and a half William aged about three years and George aged about Eleven months – That he is chargeable to the parish of Cheltenham [signed]

1834: *removed to Ledbury, Heref (presumed) (father's settlement); death of GC's youngest son George (buried at Ross).* **1839:** *death of GC (registered 2Q at Hereford).* **1841:** *widow Martha Chambers (aged 35; charwoman) lived in Castle St, Hereford with daughter Mary (Letitia) (12) and son William (10) (HO107/433/3/51/4).* **1851:** *the family lived in West St, Hereford, respectively cook/housekeeper, dressmaker, and printer-compositor/reporter.* [PS/CH/RA/2/3:277.]

34009SE: Mon 27 Jan 1834 – **Sarah Wallis**, single woman: That she was born she believes in the parish of Saint Augustine in the City of Bristol

That between two and three years ago She was hired by Miss Stockdale of Westbury upon Trim [= Westbury-on-Trym] near Bristol by the year at five pounds wages – That she lived there the whole year and received all her wages

She was then hired for another year at Six pounds wages and continued about Six months of the second year and then left the Service

That she has done no other Act to gain a Settlement and is become chargeable to the parish of Cheltenham through pregnancy [signed]

1834: *removed to Westbury-on-Trym (presumed) (hiring and service).* [PS/CH/RA/2/3:278.]

34010SE: Sat 25 Jan 1834 – **Archibald Hume**, wife **Jane**, and daughter **Catherine**: That about the 9th. of January Instant he and his wife were passing through Cheltenham on their way to scotland   That he has been retarded on his Journey by his wifes illness, She being through Pregnancy unable to travel & that she has since been delivered of a Child in the Watch house and is become chargeable to the Parish of Cheltenham and has not gained a Settlement in England [signed]

1834: *removed to Scotland (presumed); Catherine Hume, daughter of AH and wife Jane, was baptised at St Mary's, Cheltenham the day after the examination; though both Archibald (weaver) and Jane were born in Scotland, their next children were born in the north of England (Manchester, Leeds, etc).* [PS/CH/RA/2/3:279.]

34011SE: Tues 28 Jan 1834 – **Margaret Lane**, single woman: That She was born as she believes in the parish of Walford in the County of Hereford where she believes her father William Lane is legally Settled

That about 7 or 8 years ago She was hired by Mrs Elizabeth Tipton wife of Thomas Tipton of the Bell Inn in Chepstow in the County on Monmouth by the year at four pounds wages first as nurse Maid and afterwards as house Maid – That she remained in such Service five years and upwards and received all her wages   That when she left that Service She went to the Kings head in Ross kept by Mrs Preston – She was hired by Mrs Preston by the year as house Maid   I was to give her four pounds a year for such Situation and was to receive all the vails [= perquisites;

gratuities, tips] which amounted to 14£ or 15£ a year and upwards   I remained in that Service two years and upwards

This Examinant has not done any other Act to gain a Settlement elsewhere and is become chargeable to the parish of Cheltenham [signed]

1834: *removed to Ross-on-Wye, Heref (presumed) (hiring and service); ML apparently had illegitimate son James, baptised at Cheltenham 20 Jan, a week before examination.* **1837:** *ML married Thomas Brewer in Gloucester 11 June.* **1838:** *baptism of son Thomas at Gloucester 4 Nov.* **1841:** *the family lived in Bell Lane, Gloucester: Thomas (aged 30; servant; Margaret (25), and Thomas (2) (HO107/379/5/6/7).* [PS/CH/RA/2/3:280.]

34012SE: Tues 28 Jan 1834 – **Lucy Dodwell**, single woman: That She was born as she believes in the City of Bristol but in what parish She does not know

That about three years ago She was hired by Mrs Elizabeth Hamlet wife of William Hamlet of Charlton Kings in this County by the year at four pounds wages   That She remained a year and a half and received all her wages – That she has done no Act to gain a Settlement since and is become chargeable to the parish of Cheltenham through pregnancy [mark]

1834: *removed to Charlton Kings (presumed) (hiring and service); baptism of son John (Thomas) Dodwell at Charlton Kings 28 June; LD married Edward Everis, from Cheltenham, at Swindon.* **1839:** *(RETURNED) baptism of daughter Mary Ann at Cheltenham 5 May, when family lived at 55 Stanhope St.* **1841:** *Lucy (aged 25) and Edward (25; labourer) lived with their two children in Stanhope St, Cheltenham (HO107/353/9/51/2).* [PS/CH/RA/2/3:281.]

34013SE: Sun 2 Feb 1834 – **Henry Byne** (incorrectly **Boyne**): [That] he was born in the parish of Penymore [= Pennymoor] in the County of Devon where his Parents were settled. That, when he was Eleven Years of age he was apprenticed by his Mother to M^r. Tibbs of the Parish of Teignmouth in the County of Devon Brazier for Seven Years, that he served the whole time at Teignmouth

That in December 1831 he took a House of M^r. Mustoe in Amb[r]ose Street Cheltenham at the Rent of thirteen pounds – I lived in it a Year and a Quarter – I let out two of the back Rooms and an upper Room to Single Men as Lodgers – at 1/6 a Week each person [signed]

1834: *removal unlikely: examination form incomplete; place of settlement probably acknowledged as Cheltenham.* **1841:** *HB (aged 30; tin-plate worker) and wife Martha lived in Radnor St, Finsbury, Middlesex, with two daughters Hannah (10) and Elizabeth (8) (both girls born Cheltenham, in 1832 and 1834 respectively).* [PS/CH/RA/2/3:272-3.]

34014SE: Tues 4 Feb 1834 – **Sarah Pumfrey** (also **Pomphrey**): That she was born as she believes in the parish of Cold Aston in this County.

That about two years ago she was hired by M^rs. Hancock wife of James Hancock of Charlton Kings in this County Blacksmith by the year at four pounds wages a months warning or a months wages   That she lived in that Service eighteen months and received all her wages –

She has not done any Act to gain a Settlement since and is become chargeable to the parish of Cheltenham through pregnancy [mark]

1834: *removed to Charlton Kings (presumed) (hiring and service); baptism of son George at Charlton Kings 16 July.* **1837:** *SP married Charles Bloxham (also Bloxsom) at Charlton Kings.* **1841:** *the family lived in Charlton Kings: Charles (aged 25; agricultural labourer), Sarah (25), George (7), Charlotte (4), and Eliza (2) (HO107/353/2/8/9).* [PS/CH/RA/2/3:284.]

34015SE: [undated: 4-15 Feb 1834] – John Thomas, relating to the settlement of John Carter (deceased), and hence of surviving **wife**: That he knew and was well acquainted with John Carter in his Life time – 5 Years ago last October I rented two Cottages and Ground in Cheltenham of Mr Squires at twelve pounds a Year – on the 20 October 1828 I let the said Cottages on quitting the same and a portion of the Ground to the said John Carter for a Year at twelve pounds.

Whether Carter lived for the whole Year that he took the Cottages or not I don't know but I received the whole Years [rent] at different times either of the said John Carter or of his Wife after his death

Examination form incomplete. This probably relates to the John Carter whose burial is recorded in Cheltenham, on 26 Nov 1829, aged 29. [PS/CH/RA/2/3:285.]

34016SE: Sat 15 Feb 1834 – **Sarah Hampton**, single woman: That She believes she was born in the parish of Cheltenham

That about five years ago she was hired to go into the Service of W. L. Lawrence Esqre. at Dowdeswell in this County as a yearly Servant - as a Laundry Maid and Kitchen Maid   Captain Stevenson engaged her as a Servant for M^r. Lawrence and She was to have four pounds for the year   She served the year and received her years wages   Examinant has not done any act to gain a Settlement since – that she is become chargeable to the parish of Cheltenham [mark]

1834: *removed to Dowdeswell (presumed) (hiring and service): see* **46001SE** *(15 Jan 1846) for further information.* [PS/CH/RA/2/3:286.]

34017SE: Thurs 20 Feb 1834 – **Sarah Davis** (also **Davies**), single woman: That she was born as she has heard and believes in the parish of Cam in this County where she believes her parents are now legally settled – That at Gloucester first Mop Two years ago last Michaelmas She was hired by M^rs. Williams wife of M^r. Charles Williams of Arlingham in this County farmer for a year at four pounds wages   That She served a twelvemonth under that hiring and received all her wages   That She was then hired for another year at four Guineas but left the Service in about a Month after the last hiring – That she has done no Act to gain a Settlement since   That she is become chargeable to the parish of Cheltenham through pregnancy [mark]

1834: *removed to Arlingham (presumed) (hiring and service); baptism of daughter Elizabeth at Arlingham 22 June.* **1836:** *another illegitimate daughter, Emilla, born at Arlingham (baptised 21 Aug).* [PS/CH/RA/2/3:287.]

34018SE: Sat 22 Feb 1834 – **Hannah Dunkline** (probably **Dunklin** or **Dunkling**), with children: That She was married to her present husband Thomas Dunkline in Birmingham about fifteen years ago   That She does not know nor has ever heard her said husband say where his legal Settlement is – That on the 7th day of February instant she was on her journey with her husband and children to Swansea

That she was retarded in passing thro' Cheltenham through pregnancy and has since been delivered of a male infant And is in consequence chargeable to the said parish of Cheltenham. That her husband has deserted her at Cheltenham [mark]

1834: *removal uncertain: evidence appears inconclusive.* [PS/CH/RA/2/3:288. First draft struck out.]

34019SE: Sat 1 Mar 1834 – Jane Nash, relating to settlement of son **John Nash**: That her ~~illegitimate~~ Son John Nash was born in the Workhouse in the City of Gloucester about 18 months ago – that her Husband was a Sailor and died in the West Indies about 21 months ago   that he left England about 6 Weeks before he died.

And this Examinant saith that about 8 Years ago [s]he was hired by Mr Slade of the Parish of Saint John's in the City of Gloucester for a Year   that she lived with him a full Year and received her whole Years wages – That about Six Years ago she was Married at Bristol in the Parish Church of St Radcliffe [= St Mary Redcliffe] to John Nash her said deceased Husband – but that She knows nothing of his Settlement

That she has received relief for the Child from the Governor of the Workhouse at Gloucester [mark]

1834: *removed to St John's, Gloucester (presumed) (mother's settlement).* [PS/CH/RA/2/3:289.]

34020SE: Sat 1 Mar 1834 – **Ann Lander**, single woman: That she believes she is last legally settled in the parish of Painswick in this County – in which parish She was born   She has heard her mother say that she (Examinant) was born out of lawful wedlock – That Examinant has never

done any Act to gain a Settlement in her own right by Servitude or otherwise   That She was about two years and a ha[l]f ago removed from the parish of Stroud in this County to Painswick aforesaid by an Order of removal and was relieved by the Parish Officer there and she is now become chargeable to the parish of Cheltenham through pregnancy [mark]
1834: *removed to Painswick (birth).* **1835:** *AL (aged 29) buried at Painswick 2 Sept.* [PS/CH/RA/2/3:290 (copy in Painswick overseers' papers: P244 OV/3/3/4/2).]

34021SE: Sat 8 Mar 1834 – **Emma McCann** (also **MacGann**), spinster: That to the best of her knowledge and belief she was born in the Parish of Great Malvern in the County of Worcester where her Parents are legally settled – That about four years ago she was hired by Mrs Card Wife of the Reverend Henry Card Rector of that Parish for a year at 10£ per year – that she lived in that situation upwards of twelve months and received her wages. That about two years ago she was hired to serve as Ladys Maid and Housekeeper in the family of the Archdeacon Carey who then lodged in the Parish of Cheltenham at 12£ per year   That she travelled with this family to Bath & Malvern and afterwards returned to Phœnix Lodge in [Montpellier] Cheltenham with them That she remained in that situation at Phœnix Lodge after her return for upwards of two months. That she left the said service soon after the expiration of nine months from the time of her entering it and has not lived in any other service or done any other act to gain a Settlement elsewhere [signed]
1834: *removed to Gt Malvern, Worcs (presumed) (hiring and service)*; *baptism of son Charles James McCann at Gt Malvern 10 May; he became known as a ventriloquist and mimic, under the name of Charles Du Cann.* **1844:** *EM apparently married to Edward Randle at Ludlow, 4Q.* [PS/CH/RA/2/3:291.]

34022SE: Thurs 13 Mar 1834 – **Thomas Partridge**, wife **Mary**, and children **John** and **Samuel**: That he was born in the parish of Bridgewater [= Bridgwater] in the County of Somerset where he believes his parents are legally settled   That about ten years ago he was apprenticed by the parish Officers of Bridgewater to James Thottle [= Tottle] of Bridgewater aforesaid Inn keeper and farmer for a term of years – That he served about five or Six years and then left
   That about five or six months ago he received One pound five Shillings from M^r. Underdown Assistant Overseer and Governor of the Workhouse at Bridgwater for the purpose of putting him in business as a Hawker of China. About three years ago he was married to his wife Mary at St Mary Redcliff [= Redcliffe] Bristol and has two children by her namely John Harris aged about two years and Samuel Prinn aged thirteen months and is become chargeable to the parish of Cheltenham – That he has done no Act to gain a Settlement otherwise than as above Stated [mark]
1834: *removed to Bridgwater, Som (apprenticeship).* **c1837:** *son Thomas born at Bristol.* **1841:** *TP (aged 35; hawker) lived with wife Mary (30) and three children, John, Samuel, and Thomas in Pile St, Bristol (HO107/373/3/9/13).* [PS/CH/RA/2/3:292. Removal expenses for Bridgwater (17 Apr 1834: P78/1/OV/2/4:128).]

34023SE: Thurs 20 Mar 1834 – **Harriet Jones**, single woman: That She was born as She believes in the parish of Newland in this County   Examinant believes that her father James Jones is last legally settled in the parish of Leckhampton in this County her father having rented a tenement (house and land) in that parish of a M^{rs}. Little at ten pounds a year and paid poors' rates That he occupied the premises about two years and paid the rent for the same – That Examinant has always lived with her parents and has not done any Act to gain a Settlement in her own right and that She is become chargeable to the parish of Cheltenham through pregnancy [mark]
1812: *baptism of HJ at Newland 2 Aug, daughter of James and Jane Jones.* **1834:** *removed to Leckhampton (presumed) (father's settlement)*; *baptism of daughter Harriet 1 May at Cheltenham.* [PS/CH/RA/2/3:293.]

34024SE: Tues 25 Mar 1834 – **Job Twining** (also **Twyning**), of Cheltenham: That he was born in the Parish of Minchinhampton in the County of Gloucester –
[1834: *removed from Leckhampton to Painswick* (P244 OV/3/3/4/3).] [PS/CH/RA/2/3:294. JT's examination was properly registered in PS/CH/RA/2/2:38 (27 Mar 1834). See **37008RO** (JT: 26 Jan 1837).]

34025SE: Thurs 3 Apr 1834 – **Thomas Gibbins**, wife **Mary**, and daughter **Martha**: That he was born as he believes in the parish of Cowley in this County – Examinant believes his place of last legal Settlement to be in the parish of Brockworth in this County he having possessed and lived upon a Cottage and some Land at Brockworth aforesaid in right of his wife which he has Sold – That he has received relief from the parish officers of Brockworth on his own Account when ill and has also received relief from them on Account of his daughter Mary Gibbins at a time when she was ill, And that his said daughter was some time ago sent to the said Parish of Brockworth from Cheltenham by an Order of removal – That about 35 years ago he was married to his present wife Mary at Brockworth aforesaid and has one daughter dependent upon him namely Martha aged about Seventeen years and he is become chargeable to the Parish of Cheltenham [signed]
1834: *removed to Brockworth (estate).* **1841:** *TG (aged 65; agricultural labourer) lived in Bath Rd, Leckhampton (HO107/353/18/50/5).* **1851:** *TG (aged 83; pauper/labourer) lived in Gloucester Union Workhouse (HO107/1961/471/12).* [PS/CH/RA/2/3:295. Removal expenses for "Gibbons & Wife to Brockworth" (17 Apr 1834: P78/1/OV/2/4:128). See **32039SE** (daughter Mary Gibbins: 14 June 1832).]

34026SE: Tues 4 Mar 1834 – **Margaret Wilson**, with children **Margaret**, **William**, **Catherine**, and **Elizabeth**: That on the 24th. day of February last her husband James Wilson deserted her at Newport in this County and She does not know where he where she [*sic*] is –
That to the best of her knowledge and belief her said husband and herself were born in the Town of Lanark in Scotland which they left about four years ago – That her husband hath not to the best of her knowledge done any Act to gain a Settlement in England
That She is become chargeable to the Parish of Cheltenham – That She has four Children neither [*sic*] of whom has gained a Settlement in England [mark] [Listed] Margaret aged 13 years William aged 11 years Catherine aged 7 years Elizabeth aged 3 years
1834: *removed by pass to Bristol for Scotland;* Gloucestershire Chron. *(8 Mar): under provisions of the Poor Removal Act of 1833.* [PS/CH/RA/2/3:296 (marked as a copy). Removal expenses for conveying "Scotch Vagrants to Bristol thence to Scotland" £14/6/2 (27 Mar 1834: P78/1/OV/2/4:88).]

34027SE: Tues 4 Mar 1834 – **Mary Taylor**, widow, with her children **Agnes**, **John**, and **William**: That to the best of her knowledge and belief she was born in the Old Town of Ayr in the County Town of Ayrshire in Scotland which She left about two years and a half ago – That she hath done no Act whereby to gain a Settlement in England and She is become chargeable to the parish of Cheltenham and that She has three Children neither [*sic*] of whom has gained a Settlement in England [signed] [Listing] Agnes aged 14 years John aged 9 years William aged 5 years
1834: *removed by pass to Bristol for Scotland;* Gloucestershire Chron. *(8 Mar): under provisions of the Poor Removal Act of 1833.* [PS/CH/RA/2/3:297 (marked as a copy). Removal expenses for conveying "Scotch Vagrants to Bristol thence to Scotland" £14/6/2 (27 Mar 1834: P78/1/OV/2/4:88).]

34028SE: Tues 15 Apr 1834 – **William Daymond**, and wife **Caroline**: That he was born as he believes in the parish of Saint Pancras in the County of Middlesex where he believes he is last legally settled having served his time to his father Andrew Daymond as a Stone Mason in that parish
That he has on different Occasions received Relief from the parish Officers of Saint Pancras aforesaid
That in February 1833 he was married to his present wife Caroline at Charlton Kings in this County – Examinant further saith that in November last, he, wishing to be admitted into the General Hospital at Bath on account of illness went to London and was examined at Hatton Garden Office as to his Settlement and upon such examination received a Certificate signed by the Minister and parish officers of Saint Pancras aforesaid acknowledging him as having a Settlement there and he received from the said parish officers Three pounds as caution Money upon his being admitted into the said General Hospital at Bath aforesaid   That he remained in the Hospital 13 weeks and was discharged as cured – that he is become chargeable to the parish of Cheltenham [mark]

1834: *removed to St Pancras, Middlesex (presumed) (apprenticeship).* **1835:** *(RETURNED) WD died in June (buried at Cheltenham 29 June, aged 30).* **1838:** *wife Caroline née Williams remarried, to Joseph Compton, in Elmstone Hardwicke mid-year.* [PS/CH/RA/2/3:298.]

34029SE: Thurs 17 Apr 1834 – **Robert Grady**, wife **Julia**, and four children **Edward**, **Robert**, **Mary**, and **Dennis**: That according to the best of his knowledge and belief he was born in the City of Cork in that part of the United Kingdom called Ireland which he left about a twelvemonth ago and hath done no Act thereby to gain a Settlement in England and is become chargeable to the Parish of Cheltenham

That he had a wife named Julia and four Children namely Edward aged about 8 years Robert aged about 6 years Mary aged 3 years and Dennis aged about two years neither [*sic*] of whom has gained a Settlement in England [mark]
1834: *removed to Ireland (presumed).* [PS/CH/RA/2/3:299.]

34030SE: Tues 22 Apr 1834 – **Ann Farebrother**, illegitimate daughter of Richard Judd: *Richard Judd:* That according to the best of his knowledge and belief he was born at Farringdon [= Faringdon] in the County of Berks where he believes his Parents were settled. – that his father possessed Copyhold Property there of the Value of four Hundred Pounds – that he never rented any House of the yearly Value of ten pounds or did any Act to gain a Settlement.

That about 14 Years ago he Cohabited with Hannah Farebrother – that about 9 Years ago she had a Child by this Examinant which was born in the Parish of Shrivenham in the County of Berks – and that the officers of the said parish of Shrivenham have given the said Hannah Farebrother relief for the said Child whilst the Mother and Child were residing here [*sic*] – that the child goes by the Name of Ann Farebrother [signed]
1834: *removed to Shrivenham, Berks (presumed) (birth); death of Richard Judd (aged 40) recorded 6 Aug (National Burial Index: Berks) (in 1833 he had been imprisoned at Gloucester Lent Assizes for one month for stealing two silver spoons from Cheltenham resident:* Cheltenham Chron. *11 Apr).* **1841:** *an Ann Fairbrother (aged 16; servant) lived in Shrivenham, Berks (HO107/27/9/9/12).* [PS/CH/RA/2/3:300. Removal expenses for "Richd. Jad [*sic*] & famy. to Farringdon" (1 May 1834: P78/1/OV/2/4:128).]

34031SE: ~~16 Nov~~ Tues 29 Apr 1834 – **Philip Watkins**, with wife **Ellen**, and three children **Ellen**, **Henry**, and **James**: That he was born as he believes in the parish of Weston [= Weston under Penyard] in the County of Hereford

That about 14 or 15 years ago he was hired as a yearly Servant to M^rs. Westfaling of the Town of Ross in the said County of Hereford

That he lived about four years in the said Service and received all his wages – Examinant believes that the house occupied by the said Lady during his Servitude was situated in four parishes namely Ross, Branton [prob. Brampton (Abbotts)], Upton [Bishop] and Weston aforesaid   That Examinant believes from what he has heard that the Bed Room in which he Slept was situated in the parish of Ross – That he has never done any act since to gain a settlement & has become chargeable to the Parish of Cheltenham

That about six years ago he was married to his present wife Ellen at Cheltenham and has three children namely Ellen aged 5 years Henry aged 3 years and James aged 7 months [mark]
1834: *removed to Ross-on-Wye, Heref (hiring and service); PW (born 1803) was shoemaker.* **1851:** *son James, journeyman shoemaker, lodged at Worcester (HO107/2042/765/47).* [PS/CH/RA/2/3:258; the change of examination date suggests delay such as sickness. Removal expenses for "Philip Watkins & & famy. to Ross" (1 May 1834: P78/1/OV/2/4:128).]

34032SE: Thurs 8 May 1834 – **James Hoare**, wife **Eliza**, and three children **Thomas**, **Mary**, and **Catherine**: That to the best of his knowledge and belief he was born in the County of Mayo in that part of the United Kingdom called Ireland which he left about fourteen years ago, and hath done no Act to gain a Settlement in England and that he hath actually become chargeable to the parish of Cheltenham and that he hath a wife named Eliza and three Children neither of whom

has gained a Settlement in England   [Listing] Thomas aged Seven years Mary aged three years Catherine aged five Months [mark]
1834: *removed to Ireland (presumed).* 1841: *Eliza Hoare (aged 30; charwoman) and daughters Mary (9) and Catherine (8) lived in Kenilworth St, Leamington Priors, Warks (HO107/1135/14/38/29).* [PS/CH/RA/2/3:301.]

34033SE: Thurs 8 May 1834 – **Ann Oakey** (normally **Okey**), single woman: That to the best of her knowledge and belief She was born in the parish of Cirencester in this County where She believes her Father John Oakey is now legally settled

About three years ago her Sister got her a Situation with a M^r. Short of Walcot in the City of Bath Butcher And Examinant was hired by M^{rs}. Short by the year at six pounds wages – That She lived about thirteen Months and received all her wages – in the Parish of Walcot

That Examinant afterwards got a Situation at Cheltenham with M^r. Sims Butcher but remained only between 10 and 11 months in that Service - That She is become chargeable to the parish of Cheltenham through pregnancy [mark]
1834: *removed to Walcot, Bath, Som (hiring and service).* 1841: *an Ann Oakley (aged 25; labourer) lived in Walcot, Bath (HO107/970/8/39/28), though this may not be significant; her parents still lived in Cirencester (HO107/380/54/5).* **1845:** *AO married John Griffin on 19 Oct at Cirencester.* **1851:** *AO (aged 39) lived with husband and four children in Hatherop, near Cirencester (HO107/1968/749/4).* [PS/CH/RA/2/3:302. Removal expenses for "Ann Okey Preg[nan]t to Bath" (5 June 1834: P78/1/OV/2/4:128).]

34034SE: Thurs 15 May 1834 – **Henry Roberts**, and wife **Elizabeth:** That he was born as he believes in the parish of Ashchurch in this County   That several years ago he was hired by M^r. John Moore of Tewkesbury Corn factor and Maltster by the year at 10 Guineas wages and continued two years in that Service and received all his wages – That about 20 years ago he was married to his present wife Elizabeth at Portsmouth and is become chargeable to the parish of Cheltenham

That he has done no other Act to gain a Settlement [signed]
1772: *HR baptised at Ashchurch 28 Jan.* **1834: *removed to Tewkesbury (presumed) (hiring and service).*** **1849:** *an HR (aged 78; of Old Chapel Yard) was buried at Tewkesbury 12 Aug.* [PS/CH/RA/2/3:303.]

34035SE: Thurs 22 May 1834 – **Alexander McGuire**, wife **Susan**, and son **James:** That according to the best of his knowledge and belief he was born in the County of Londonderry in the North of Ireland. About 14 years ago, he was married to Susan his present wife, at Londonderry, by whom he has One child now living, namely, James, aged five months   That he has done no act to gain a Settlement in England [signed]
1834: *removed to Ireland.* [PS/CH/RA/2/3:304. See expenses for "Conveying Irish Vagrants to Bristol from thence to Ireland" £13/4/9 (28 June 1834: P78/1/OV/2/4:128).]

34036SE: Sat 24 May 1834 – **Robert Smith**, and wife **Susan:** I was born in the Parish of Forthampton in this County where my parents were settled – My Father removed to the parish of Purton [= Pirton] in Worcestershire where he rented an estate – I went with him – I remained there with him until I was apprenticed – I was then about 18 years of age – I was apprenticed to Joseph Pardington of Kempsey in Worcestershire Baker – My Father paid a premium of £15 with me – I was present when he paid it – The term was 3 years all of which I served – the Attorney who prepared the indenture or agreement was Mr Staples of Worcester, he also had the care of it – The indenture was not stamped – I lodged in my said Master's house all the time but received no wages – only 1^d. perquisite upon every sack of flour from the Miller – After serving my time I returned to my father's house but remained only 6 or 7 months then 3 months at Fladbury [Worcs] – I then went back to my father's but did not stay half a Year – I lived then 2 years in London as a journeyman baker but was hired by the month – I returned then to Purton but staid only a few months – I never lived one year in one service – in 1798 or 1799 I rented a house in Worcester belonging to M^r. Dillon in the parish of St. Helens in the High St at 27£ a year which I occupied 2 years & paid all the rent   In 1805 I rented a house No 37 Warder [= Wardour] St Soho London at

30l a year & lived there about 2 years & paid one years rent & upwards   The house was at the corner of Ship Yard – I have not rented any house by the year since that time, nor done any other act to gain a settlement   I was married in Marylebone New Church London about 12 or 13 years ago in the name of Robert Smith to my present wife Susan Smith but have no child living by her My wife has had relief from the parish of Cheltenham [signed]
1772: *RS baptised 7 June at Forthampton, son of William and Mary Smith.* **1834: *perhaps removed to Soho, London (renting).*** [PS/CH/RA/2/3:305, 6.]

34037SE: Tues 27 May 1834 – **Mary Cowmeadow**, single woman: That to the best of her knowledge and belief she was born in the parish of Lidbrook [= Lydbrook] in the County of Gloucester   That she believes her parents where [*sic*] legally settled in the parish of Linton in the County of Hereford   that she has been in several services, as a servant, that about 14 Years ago she was hired by M^{rs}. Newcomb the wife of Thomas Newcomb of Bowbridge in the parish of Stroud Clothier for one year, at £8 a year and she remained in the said service upwards of three years and received all her wages   That she has done no other act to gain a Settlement elsewhere [mark]
1834: *removed to Stroud (hiring and service).* **1841:** *(RETURNED) MC (aged 50) lived with younger brother James (40; labourer, born Linton, Heref) and wife Maria (30) in Sidney St, off Hewlett Rd, Cheltenham (HO107/353/3/16/27).* **1851:** *MC at 29 Sidney St, Cheltenham as lodger (aged 66; unmarried, seamstress and pauper) (HO107/1973/26/45).* [PS/CH/RA/2/3:307 (copy at P320a OV/3/3/3/58). See **40053SE** (brother George Cowmeadow: 18 Apr 1840).]

34038SE: Sat 31 May 1834 – **Edward McDermot**, wife and three children, **Mary Ann**, **Ellen**, and unnamed infant: That he was born in the County of Roscommon in Ireland   That he has never done any act to gain a settlement in England
    That he has a wife and three children the eldest Mary Ann aged 5 years Ellen aged 3 years and the other an infant now at the breast [signed]
1834: *removed to Ireland.* [PS/CH/RA/2/3:308. See expenses for "Conveying Irish Vagrants to Bristol from thence to Ireland [...] 13.4.9" (28 June 1834: P78/1/OV/2/4:128).]

34039SE: Tues 10 June 1834 – **James Stevens** (also **Stephens**), and wife **Sarah**: That to the best of his knowledge and belief he was born in the parish of Bisley where his father and mother were legally settled. About six years ago he made application to the parish officers for relief; he had received on several occasions relief from them, that there was no doubt of his being legally settled there –
    That on the 9th. of March in the present year he made a further application and received 10^s/ from the parish – About 3 years ago he was married to his present wife Sarah at S^t. Clemen[t']s Church in the City of Oxford but had no children living   That he is now become chargeable to the parish of Cheltenham [mark]
1834: *removed to Bisley (father's settlement)*: *see* **52001RO** *(Sarah Stevens: 26 Jan 52) for further information on the family.* [PS/CH/RA/2/3:309. Removal expenses for "Stevens & Wife to Bisley" (26 June 1834: P78/1/OV/2/4:128).]

34040SE: Tues 10 June 1834 – **Sophia Munt**, single woman: That to the best of her knowledge and belief she was born in the parish of Wheatley in Oxfordshire where her parents were legally settled. After her fathers death She went to Service and was hired by M^{rs}. Gillett of the Angell Inn at Oxford, where she remained for two years at the wages of £10 a year. That about 2 years ago she was hired by M^r. James Stephens as a yearly servant at £9 a year as chambermaid, where she remained for nearly twelve months and from thence removed with the family to Cirencester and she continued in that service after the expiration of the year for three months   No mention was made of a second hiring – She received all her wages   That she has done no other act to gain a Settlement elsewhere And that she is become chargeable to the parish of Cheltenham through Pregnancy [mark]

1834: *removed to Cirencester (hiring and service); (RETURNED) SM married Robert Smith at St Mary's, Cheltenham 29 Sept.* **1840:** *death of Robert Smith (buried at New Burial Ground, Cheltenham 13 Apr, aged 29).* **1841:** *Sophia Smith (aged 25; charwoman) lived in King St, Cheltenham with sons Frederick (6), with whom she was presumably pregnant at time of examination, and Henry (3; baptised at Cheltenham 29 Oct 1837, when his father was an ostler).* [PS/CH/RA/2/3:310. Removal expenses for "Conveying Sophia Munt preg[nan]t to Cirencester" (28 June 1834: P78/1/OV/2/4:128).]

34041SE: Tues 8 July 1834 – **Henry Heritage**, wife **Elizabeth**, and son **John**: That he was born as he believes in the parish of Saint Mary le Bone in the County of Middlesex – That about 18 years ago as well as he can remember his father who had lived in the parish of S^t. Pancras in Middlesex having left his family and gone to Sea Examinant was relieved by the parish Officers of S^t. Pancras and by them removed by an Order of removal to the said parish of S^t. Mary le Bone against which Order an appeal was made by that parish at the Clerkenwell Sessions and the Order affirmed and that Examinant has at various times both before and since his Marriage received relief from the parish Officers of S^t. Mary le Bone aforesaid – The last time he was relieved by them was about 15 Months ago his wife being ill and he at that time out of work – That he has never done any Act to gain a Settlement in his own right   That in 1826 he was married to his present wife Elizabeth at St Pancras aforesaid and has one child by her namely John aged near 5 years   That he is become chargeable to the parish of Cheltenham [signed]

1834: *removed to Marylebone, Middlesex (presumed) (birth).* **1841:** *HH (aged 40; marble polisher) lived with wife Elizabeth (30; brushdrawer) and son John (12) in Northampton, Northants (HO107/814/5/24/6).* **1851:** *HH (49; stonemason) lived in Islington, Middlesex (HO107/1500/442/24).* **1861:** *HH (57; widower and general labourer) lodged with stonemason in Deptford, Kent; later that year he entered Marylebone Workhouse where, variously "destitute" and sick with rheumatism, he lived from time to time in 1860s until his death, recorded in 3Q 1870 in Pancras.* [PS/CH/RA/2/3:311.]

34042SE: Tues 8 July 1834 – **John Brown**: That to the best of her [*sic*] knowledge and belief he was born in Edinburgh. That he has never done any act to gain a Settlement in England [signed] John Brown

1834: *removed to Scotland (presumed).* [PS/CH/RA/2/3:312.]

34043SE: Tues 8 July 1834 – **Hannah Summers**: That she was born at Twyning in the County of Gloucester where her Parents were settled

1834: *removal uncertain: examination form incomplete.* **1841:** *probably the HS (aged 25) living with young son William (aged 2[?]: obscure) in North Fleet, Twyning (HO107/360/18/14/22).* [PS/CH/RA/2/3:312.]

34044SE: Tues 8 July 1834 – **Mary Harrison**, widow of Joseph Harrison, with son **Thomas**; also Simon Harrison, relating to settlement of daughter-in-law Mary Harrison: *Mary Harrison*: That to the best of her knowledge and belief she was born in Lapworth in Warwickshire where her parents were legally settled   About two years last December she was married to her late husband at Charlton Kings in the said County of Gloucester, by whom she has one child named Thomas aged one year and eight months. She has never heard where her husband was settled. That she is now become chargeable to the parish of Cheltenham [mark]

Simon Harrison: That about nine years ago his son was hired by M^r. Samuel Herbert of Uckington in the said County at Tewk[e]sbury Michaelmas First Mop for a year and received 1^s/ earnest and received twelve Shillings by the week; that he was to sleep in the house and to pay one Shilling weekly for lodging, where he remained one whole year   he again engaged a second year; same wages but lodging free, there he remained as a yearly servant for three years   He then quitted that service and went to M^r. Gardner Brewer Cheltenham in whose service he died. This examinant does not believe he gained any Settlement elsewhere [mark]

1834: *death of MH's husband Joseph;* ***removed to Uckington (late husband's settlement);*** *MH's examination was precipitated by death of husband Joseph (buried 7 May at Elmstone Hardwick, near Uckington, aged 30), though the couple lived in Cheltenham.* **1836:** *MH née Blunt remarried, to widower Robert Goulding, on 19 Oct at Swindon.* **1841:** *(RETURNED) MH (aged 41) and husband Robert (52; brewer) lived in Knapp Place, Cheltenham with son Thomas Harrison (8) (HO107/353/16/57/30).*

[PS/CH/RA/2/3:313-4. Removal expenses for "Mary Harrison to Uckington" (17 July 1834: P78/1/OV/2/4:128).]

34045SE: Thurs 10 July 1834 – **John Wheeler**: That to the best of his knowledge and belief he was born at Barnsley in the said County where his parents were legally settled   About thirteen or fourteen years ago he was hired by M^r. Joseph Cripps of Cirencester as a yearly Servant, in his service he remained a full year at Cirencester and received the whole of his wages [interlinear] that he was also hired by Mr Davis the following Year at Cirencester which he also served – and [illegible] the next year was hired again by Mr Cripps which he also served [end] That he has never done any act to gain a Settlement elsewhere [mark]
1800: *a JW baptised at Barnsley 27 July, son of Joseph and Sarah Wheeler.* **1834: removed to Cirencester (hiring and service).** [PS/CH/RA/2/3:315. See removal expenses to Cirencester (17 July 1834: P78/1/OV/2/4:128).]

34046SE: 31/26 July 1834 – **Louisa James**, single woman; also Elizabeth Sims, relating to settlement of daughter Louisa James: *Louisa James*: That She has heard and believes that She was born in the parish of Saint Nicholas in the City of Gloucester   That her mother had not been nor was at that time married –

And this Examinant has never done any Act to gain a Settlement in her own right

That She is become chargeable to the parish of Cheltenham through pregnancy [signed]
Elizabeth Sims: That she is the mother of Louisa James – that at the time of the birth of the said Louisa James she this deponent was not nor had been married – The said Louisa James was born in the parish of St. Nicholas in the City of Gloucester [signed]
1834: removed to St Nicholas, Gloucester (birth): *see* **40059SE** *(LJ: 20 Apr 1840).* [PS/CH/RA/2/3:316. See removal expenses to Gloucester (31 July 1834: P78/1/OV/2/4:128).]

34047SE: [undated/5] Aug 1834 – Reverend Charles Winstanley of Cheltenham, clerk, and Peter Butt, Guardian of the Poor of the Parish of Cheltenham, regarding the settlement of late Louisa Mills and husband William Mills**,** in respect of children **William**, **James**, and **Thomas Mills**: *Reverend Charles Winstanley*: That about the month of June 1833 he this Examinant applied by letter through the Post Office to the Parish Officers of Lambeth in the County of Surry for relief on behalf of Louisa Mills (the Widow of [blank] Mills who formerly lived at Cheltenham & who died there) and her children   That in the same month of June 1833 he this Examinant received an answer to his said application in which answer he this Examinant was requested as a favor [*sic*] to pay the said Louisa Mills on behalf of the said Parish of Lambeth the sum of four shillings per week & an undertaking that the same should be repaid by the Parish Officers on demand. That this Examinant accordingly paid that sum per week up to the 15 day of May last and has received part of the amount from the Parish Officers of Lambeth. That in the Month of July last the said Louisa Mills died and left 3 Children – That he this Examinant knew the husband of the said Louisa Mills & has heard him say that his Settlement was at Lambeth   That he this Examinant also applied on the husband's behalf for relief to the said Officers in which application (which was by letter thro the post) he this Examinant stated that the said Louisa Mills' husband was a Parishioner of Lambeth Parish [signed]
Peter Butt: That William Mills aged about 11 years James Mills aged about 9 years and Thomas Mills aged about 3 years the three children of [blank] Mills and Louisa Mills mentioned in the Examination of the Rev Charles Winstanley thereunto annexed were brought to the Parish Workhouse of Cheltenham aforesaid on Saturday last and are Actually chargeable thereto [signed]
1833: *death of LM's husband William, chemist (buried at Cheltenham 12 Apr, aged 38).* **1834:** *LM buried at St Mary's, Cheltenham 26 July, by Rev. Charles Winstanley, precipitating examination;* **children removed to Lambeth, Surrey (late father's settlement) (presumed).** **1841:** *Thomas Mills (aged 9; occupation "Hooks & Eyes") resided at Norwood Workhouse (serving Lambeth) (HO107/1059/3/6/8).* [PS/CH/RA/2/3:318-9.]

34048SE: Tues 2 Sept 1834 – **Jane Townsend**, with children **Thomas**, **Jacob**, and **George**: That She is the wife of George Townsend and that her said husband did about a week ago abscond from and leave her – That She does not know where he is

That in June 1830 her said husband was examined at the public Office in Cheltenham as to his Settlement and Examinant believes that from her said husbands Examination as well as what She has heard her said husband and his brother say that he was last legally Settled in the parish of S^t. Mary De lode in the City of Gloucester – but they were not removed upon the said Examination – That She is in consequence of her husband's deserting her become chargeable to the parish of Cheltenham   Examinant has three Children living by her said husband namely Thomas aged about twelve years Jacob aged about Seven years and George aged about five years   That after her Marriage her husband received relief from the parish Officers of Saint Mary De Lode in consequence of his illness [mark]

1834: *removed to St Mary de Lode, Gloucester (husband's settlement): see* **47028RO** *(1 July 1847) for further information.* [PS/CH/RA/2/3:320. Removal expenses for "Jane Townsend to Gloucester" (28 Sept 1834: P78/1/OV/2/4:128). See **41033SE** (husband George Townsend: 3 May 1841).]

34049SE: Tues 16 Sept 1834 – **George Cleveland**, wife **Mary**, and children **George**, **Adelaide**, and **William**: That he was born as he has heard and believes in the parish of Painswick in this County where he believes his father was last legally settled   That about six years ago Examinant received relief from the parish Officers of Painswick and was acknowledged by them as having a Settlement there.

That when Examinant was very young his father Richard Cleveland absconded and left his wife then with four Children   That in consequence of his father's leaving the place his Mother was for several years relieved by the parish Officers of Painswick and always acknowledged as a parishioner there   That Examinant never to his recollection saw his said father nor ever heard how his father gained a Settlement at Painswick – That Examinant was apprenticed to a person of the name of Thomas Glover of Painswick aforesaid hatter and served about three years of the time in Painswick and then left his said Master – That examinant never gained a Settlement elsewhere   That he was married to his present wife [blank] about [blank] in Cheltenham Church and has three Children living by her namely George aged about 6 years Adelaide aged about 3 years and William about two years [mark]

1834: *removed to Painswick (apprenticeship).* **1841:** *(RETURNED) GC (aged 45; labourer) lived with wife Mary (43), George (12), Adelaide (10), and four other children in Devonshire St, Cheltenham (HO107/353/16/28/17).* **1835:** *daughter Rhoda baptised at Cheltenham 16 Aug.* **1851:** *parents and two children lived in New St, Painswick, with George (50) described as "Scavenger Labourer")* *(HO107/1973/626/17).* [PS/CH/RA/2/3:321. Removal expenses for "Cleevland [*sic*] & family to Painswick" (6 Nov 1834: P78/1/OV/2/4:128).]

34050SE: Thurs 18 Sept/2 Oct 1834 – Christian Kear, relating to settlement of daughter **Ann Kear** (also **Care**), single woman: *Christian Kear*: […] That Ann Kear her daughter now receiving relief from the parish of Cheltenham and confined through illness was born in the parish of Leckhampton in this County

That to the best of her knowledge and belief her said Daughter was hired at Evesham first Mop 1832 by M^r. Backford of the parish of Buckland in this County farmer for a year at Six pounds wages and that her said daughter remained the full year in her said Master's Service and received her full years wages

That the said Ann Kear was upon her leaving M^r. Backford's Service hired by M^{rs}. Simmonds wife of Thomas Simmonds of Cheltenham retail Beer Seller for a Month on trial – her daughter remained about Six weeks and was then obliged to leave on account of illness – That she is become chargeable to the parish of Cheltenham having lost the use of her Limbs – That to this Examinants knowledge and belief her said daughter has not done any other Act to gain a Settlement in her own right [signed]

Ann Kear: That at Evesham first Mop in the year 1832 she was hired by M^r. Backford of the parish of Buckland in this County farmer for a year at five pounds fifteen Shillings wages and she served her full year and received her year's wages. That Examinant has done no Act since to gain a Settlement in her own right not having been able to continue in other Services in which She had since engaged through illness   That She has become chargeable to the parish of Cheltenham through illness having lost the use of her legs   That before She lived with M^r. Backford She was hired as a yearly servant by M^r. John Shipway of Gotherington farmer at two pounds for a part of the first year and five pounds the last year   That she served there about a year and a half [mark]
1811: *baptism of AK, after which the family moved to Winchcombe, remaining many years.* **1834: removed to Buckland (northeast Glos) (hiring and service).** **1841:** *CK lived in Gloucester St, Winchcombe, apparently widowed, with seven younger surviving children (HO107/360/20/20/26); husband Thomas and elder daughters Ann and Eliza not at family home.* [PS/CH/RA/2/3:322-3. Removal expenses for "A. Keir p[e]r order" (28 Sept 1834: P78/1/OV/2/4:128).]

34051SE: Thurs 9 Oct 1834 – Sophia Hathaway**,** regarding the settlement of stepson **William Hathaway**: That she believes about 21 years ago her late husband William Hathaway rented a house of M^r. Player[,] Cooper, now deceased, in Barton Street in the parish of Tewkesbury at the yearly rent of £26 or thereabouts, in which house he lived twelve months and upwards and paid the whole rent, and during that period he paid the poor rates and other parochial rates – that his son William resided with them as part of the family, he being then unmarried   Soon after they entered into the said house, she believes that her husband's son William Hathaway was married, and then left Tewkesbury – That she does not know whether the said William Hathaway has gained a Settlement in his own right And this examinant further saith that her husband then went to Worcester where he never rented a house for £10 year. That her husband purchased several houses in the city which are extraparochial but never paid any poor rates for his said property [mark]
1834: *decision at subsequent examination: see* **34052SE** *(13 Oct 1834).* [PS/CH/RA/2/3:324. Expenses "attendant on Mrs. Hathaway from Worcester to give Evidence as to Settlement of Son in law & family" (9 Oct 1834: P78/1/OV/2/4:128).]

34052SE: Mon 13 Oct 1834 – **William Hathaway**, wife **Sarah**, and three children **Emanuel**, **Samuel**, and **William**: That he was born as he has heard and believes in Leech Street in the parish of Saint Michael in the City of Worcester where he believes his father was at that time legally Settled   That his father afterwards purchased several houses in Carden Street which is situate in an extraparochial Place in the said City of Worcester – That at the time of his father's death he lived in one of his own houses in the said Street called Carden Street   Examinant has not done any Act to gain a Settlement in his own right   That about 22 years ago he was married to his late wife Sarah at Wrexham in Denbighshire – That he has 3 Children by his wife now living namely Emanuel aged near 21 years (now living in Tewkesbury) Samuel aged about 10 years and Cecilia aged about four years [signed]
1834: *removed to Tewkesbury (presumably successfully challenged) (father's settlement): see* **35001SE** *(WH: 14 Feb 1835) for further information.* [PS/CH/RA/2/3:317. Note: "Mother in Carden St [Worcester]". See **34051SE** (mother Sophia: 9 Oct 1834).]

34053SE: [undated: between 9 Oct and 6 Dec] 1834 – **Joanna Donn** [perhaps for **Dunne**], widow, with children **John**, **Edward**, and **James**: That she and her two infant Children was upon their journey to Ireland where she is legally settled   That about four weeks ago She was taken ill at Cheltenham being in an advanced State of pregnancy and has been retarded in her journey and delivered of a male infant at Cheltenham aforesaid   That her husband Daniel Donn died about 15 weeks ago   her children are John aged about 6 years and Edward aged two years and 5 months and James the infant newly born [mark]
1834: *removed to Ireland (presumed).* [PS/CH/RA/2/3:325.]

34054SE: Sat 6 Dec 1834 – **Thomas Morgan**, wife **Sarah**, and son **Thomas**: That he believes he was born in the parish of Rendwick [= Randwick] in this County being the illegitimate Child of Emma Morgan – That Examinant never gained a Settlement in his own right by Servitude renting or otherwise howsoever   That in 1829 he was married to his present wife Sarah at Saint James' Church in Bath and has one Child living by his said wife – namely Thomas aged about 4 years – That about two years and a half ago Examinant then living in the parish of Witcombe and Lyncomb [= Widcombe and Lyncombe] near Bath he became chargeable to the said parish in consequence of his said Wife's Insanity and he was examined before the Magistrates at the Guildhall in Bath as to his Settlement and removed by an Order with his wife and children to the said Parish of Rendwick against which order no appeal was made and his wife remained in the poor house there upwards of two years and he is now become chargeable to the parish of Cheltenham in consequence of his wife's insanity [signed]

1809: *baptism of TM at Randwick 25 June, illegitimate son of Amy Morgan.* **1834: *removed to Randwick (presumed) (birth).*** **1841:** *son Thomas (aged 10) lived with family of Emma Furnell, washerwoman, at 4 Ivy Place, Lyncombe and Widcombe, Bath (HO107/931/11/23/38); (also* **1851***) perhaps the TM (42; carpenter) from "Runwick", Glos, living with wife Mary (42; from Swansea) at 7 Crown Terrace, St Pancras, Middlesex (HO107/1498/623/13 and RG9/150/57/26).* [PS/CH/RA/2/3:326.]

> COMMITMENTS TO OUR COUNTY GAOL. - On Saturday, John Martin, charged with stealing at Huntley, a quantity of bread and bacon, the property of J. Lewis. – George Beadle, charged with stealing at Huntley, three fowls, the property of J. Pickering. – Henry Brown, by R. B. Cooper and J. Blagdon, Esqrs., charged with stealing, at Cheltenham, six fowls, the property of Mr. C. Marshall. - John Ashins, by the same Magistrates, charged with stealing, at Cheltenham, two pieces of rosewood, the property of Mr. J. Nicholson. – Monday, William James, charged with assaulting Thomas West, constable of Bisley, and rescuing from his custody J. Matthews, charged with felony. – Tuesday, Richard Judd, by R. B. Cooper, charged with stealing at Cheltenham, two tea-spoons, the property of J. Stroud. – George Smart, charged with stealing, at Avening, about a quarter of a hundred of hay, the property of Mr. S. Holmes. – James and Thomas Berriman, charged with feloniously shooting at H. W. Hancox, at Tunley, on the 2d day of November last, with intent to murder him: also with then and there stealing in the house of the said John Hancox, nine tea-spoons, a punch-ladle, and a pair of silver-mounted spectacles, also his property, and a purse, 6s. in money, pocket-book, a gold ring, a gold brooch, and several pairs of ear-rings, the property of T. Hancox, spinster. – James Matthews, charged with stealing a saddle, the property of W. Skinner, of Bisley.

Destitution can be cumulative. The Cheltenham Journal of 28 January 1833 listed those committed for trial in Gloucester for crimes committed in Cheltenham. Richard Judd, the father of Ann Farebrother (34030SE), was charged with stealing two teaspoons, for which he later received a sentence of three months' imprisonment at the Gloucestershire Lent Assizes. A year or so later Richard Judd attested to his nine-year-old daughter's settlement: as an illegitimate child, it was Shrivenham, Berkshire, the place of her birth. The family were presumably in dire need of money when Richard Judd stole the spoons, his absence caused their family economy to take a further downturn, and eventually they fell upon the parish. The 1841 census seems to show Ann, aged 16, working as a servant in Shrivenham, so she may have begun to rebuild her life.

1835

35001SE: Sat 14 Feb 1835 – **William Hathaway**, with children **Samuel** and **Cecilia**; also Peter Butt, Guardian of the Poor for the Parish of Cheltenham, relating to the settlement of William Hathaway: *William Hathaway*: That he was born as he believes in Leech Street in the parish of Saint Michael Bedwardine in the county of Worcester where he believes his father was at that time legally settled and where he this examinant resided with his mother Mary – That his father afterwards became the proprietor of several houses in Carden Street in the said City of Worcester which Examinant believes is situated in an extraparochial Place   That his father lived in one of his own houses in Carden Street aforesaid of the time of his death

That Examinant has not done any Act to gain a Settlement in his own right by Servitude renting a tenement or otherwise – That upwards of twenty years ago he was married to his late wife Sarah at Wrexham in Denbighshire and has two children namely Samuel aged about Eleven years and Cecilia aged Seven years [signed] William Hathaway

Peter Butt: That the certificate now produced is a true Extract from the Register of Christenings in the said Parish of Saint Michael by which it appears that the said William Hathaway was Christ[d]. in the said Parish of Saint Michael on the Sixth day of September 1784 [signed]

1834: *WH removed to Tewkesbury (successfully challenged) (father's settlement): see* **34051SE** *(9 Oct 1834); wife Sarah buried at Cheltenham 12 July, aged 43.* **1835:** *removed to St Michael Bedwardine, Worcester (father's settlement); burial of WH (aged 50; miniature painter) at Worcester 31 May.* **1851:** *daughter Cecilia (23; gloveress) "Visitor" at Little Fish St, Worcester (HO107/2024/646/31).* [PS/CH/RA/2/3:327. Removal expenses for "Hathay & Child to Tewkesbury" (16 Oct 1834: P78/1/OV/2/4:128); "Law Expences: Appeal Cheltm. v.Tewkesbury Hathaway & Family" (12 Mar 1835: P78/1/OV/2/4:132), and removal expenses for "Conveying W. Hathaway & 2 Children to St. Michael Bedwardine [Worcester]" (12 Mar 1835: P78/1/OV/2/4128). See **34051SE** (mother Sophia: 9 Oct 1834).]

35002SE: Sat 14 Feb 1835 – **Elizabeth Tarling**, with daughter **Charlotte**: That on the twelfth day of August in the Year one thousand Eight hundred and thirty two she was married to Thomas Tarling in the Parish Church of Cirencester in the said County – That she has had one Child by her said Husband named Charlotte now aged a Year and six months – That when she was first Married she and her Husband resided at Cirencester and about twelve months ago they came to reside Cheltenham

that about Sixteen Weeks ago her husband ran away from and left her and her Child chargeable to the Parish of Cheltenham – that she has continued to reside at Cheltenham ever since except for three days when she went to Cirencester – that having been informed and believing that her said Husband was settled in the Parish of Barnsley in this County by hiring and Service with Mr Wilson of Barnesley [*sic*] aforesaid Yeoman she went about three weeks ago to Mr. Townsend who is overseer of Barnsley aforesaid for Relief. that upon that occasion he gave this Examinant for such relief two Shillings and Six pence – that previously thereto Examinant showed him the said Mr Townsend an Examination of her Husband taken before Edward Cripps Esquire on the fourth day of January 1830 in which Examination sworn by the said Thomas Tarling it was stated that about 15 Years ago at Michaelmas he was hired for a Year into the Parish of Barnsley in the said County by [blank] Wilson Yeoman at the Wages of 5£ – that he duly served such year in the said Parish of Barnsley and received the whole of his Wages and that he had done no Act to gain a Settlement elsewhere.

That the said Mr Townsend stated that the said Examination was perfectly satisfactory – and said that he would call at her Mother's House on the following Monday and say what she should have a Week – that on the Monday Examinant saw M[r] Townsend who told him [*sic*] that if she would get an order of removal from Cheltenham they should be obliged to take her but that M[r] Norris wished him not to take her in without an order [mark]

1835: *removed to Barnsley (husband's settlement).* [PS/CH/RA/2/3:328-9. Removal expenses for "conveying E. Tarling & Child to Barnsley p[e]r orders" (12 Mar 1835: P78/1/OV/2/4:128).]

35003SE: Sat 7 Mar 1835 – **Michael Brett**, wife **Margaret**, and daughter **Bridget**: hat he believes he was born in the parish of Tubblecurry [= Tubbercurry] in the County of Sligo in that part of the United Kingdom called Ireland which he left about four years ago and that he hath done no Act whereby to gain a Settlement in England and he is become chargeable to the parish of Cheltenham   That he hath a wife named Margaret and one Child named Bridget aged about four years and which child has not gained a Settlement in England [mark]
1835: *removed to Ireland (presumed).* [PS/CH/RA/2/3:330.]

35004SE: Thurs 19 Mar 1835 – **William Barnes** (properly **Barns**): That he was born in the Hamlet of Woodmancott [= Woodmancote] in the said County where his parents were legally settled as he has been informed and believes   that about a week after Michaelmas in the year 1816 he went to Mr Samuel Merrell of the parish of Twyning Fleet in the County of Gloucester and was by him engaged for a month on trial; my Master then wished to hire me and asked me what he should give me to serve until the Michaelmas, I told him he must give me three pounds; he agreed to give me two pounds and gave me a shilling in earnest. I stopt there until old Michaelmas day and then left and received the whole money and have never lived in any service since for a twelvemonth nor been hired for a year or rented any tenement at ten pounds a year that on the 9 of June 1824 I was married to Ann Edwards in the parish Church of Charlton Kings who soon afterwards deserted me and I have neither seen or heard anything of her since. [mark]
1829: *bigamously married Ann Ivin (see 350055SE: 19 Mar 1835) at Winchcombe 8 Feb; birth of son Joseph (baptised Charlton Kings; WB brickmaker).* **1832:** *birth of son Solomon (baptised Charlton Kings; WB labourer).* **1835:** *removed to Twyning Fleet (presumed) (hiring and service); the couple stayed reunited.* **1839:** *(RETURNED) baptism of daughter Charlotte when family lived at 10 Malvern St, Cheltenham.* **1841:** *the family lived in nearby Elm St, Cheltenham: WB (aged 40; labourer), Ann (25[?]), Solomon (8), Mary Ann (4), and Charlotte (2) (HO107/353/10/3/1).* **1843:** *WB (brickmaker, aged 45) sentenced to six months' hard labour for bigamy at Glos Spring Assizes, 5 Apr (Cheltenham Chron. 13 Apr); Ann Ivin is now described as his "former wife" and was living in "a place near Birmingham" (Gloucestershire Chron. 8 Apr). WB later returned to Woodmancote.* **1881:** *WB "pauper inmate" (widower) of Gloucester St Workhouse, Winchcombe (RG11/2564/129/12).* [PS/CH/RA/2/3:331.]

35005SE: Thurs 19 Mar 1835 – **Ann Ivin**: That she was born in the Parish of Cheltenham in the said County where her parents were legally settled, that she has never been hired for a Year or lived in any service for a Year [incomplete]
1829: *bigamous wife of William Barnes (**35004SE***: 19 Mar 1835).* **1835:** *removal unlikely: settlement form incomplete; settlement probably acknowledged as Cheltenham:* **43032RO** *(15 Apr 1843) for further information.* [PS/CH/RA/2/3:332.]

35006SE: [undated: 19 Mar 1835] – **Mary Ann Beard**; also Jane Tincombe, relating to settlement of niece Mary Ann Beard: *Mary Ann Beard*: That she is now an inmate of the poor house at Cheltenham where she was admitted with her mother Elizabeth Smith about Six weeks ago or upwards and where her Mother died soon after
     That She has often heard her Mother say that she (Examinant) was born in the parish of Holne in the County of Devon – That She believes that her Mother received half a Crown a week from the parish of Holne for her (Examinant) – She has seen her Mother receive the money of a M^r. Hamblin at Holne   That Examinant never knew any thing of her father and never heard her Mother say any thing about her father [mark]
Jane Tincombe (copy of letter addressed from Exeter 19 Mar, 1835): Sir   I feel humbly obliged to you for your information respecting my poor unfortunate Sister – as I could not tell what was become of her – I cannot tell the name of the Overseer of Holne parish and I have not lived there for some years – but I can take an Oath that is her parish as I was with her mother when Mary Ann was born   She was not born under Wedlock and She also received two Shillings and six

pence per week pay for the Child from the parish – he[r] mother was born and always brought up in the same place   I shall be glad for the Child to be sent home as soon as possible And I should also be glad to see the Child as She passes through Exeter - although it is not in my power to do any thing for her – but I will see her taken care of And act a Mother's part by her as far forward as it lays in my power. She dosnt [know] any person herself where her Aunt Beard lives – my name is Jane Tincomb – her mother's own Sister her Aunt Beard is [my] Sister in law – M^r. Hamlyn is a manager of the poor but whether he is an Overseer I do not know

I am Sir Your humble and Oblige[d] Jane Tincombe (Addressed) M^r. Butt Guardian of the poor Cheltenham Gloster

1835: *removed to Holne, Devonshire (birth).* **1841:** *MAB (aged 15) lived at a farm near home village of Holne as one of three young apprentices (HO107/246/11/4/2).* [PS/CH/RA/2/3:332-3. Removal expenses for "Mary Ann Beard to Holne" (14 May 1835: P78/1/OV/2/4:136).]

35007SE: Thurs 23 Apr 1835 – **James Lypiatt** (= **Lippett**), wife **Ann**, and two children **George** and **Elizabeth**: I was born at Cheltenham

I was apprenticed about thirteen years ago with Premium paid out of the Townsends Charity to Joseph Jones of Saint Owens in the City of Gloucester for 7 Years – I served 6 Years with my Master in Saint Owens when I ran away – I never done any act since to gain a Settlement elsewhere – I have been Married 6 Years – I was married to Ann my present wife – and have three Children by her – of which two are living George aged Six Years and Elizabeth aged Nine Months [signed]

1832: *removed to Gloucester (apprenticeship) (32060SE: 23 Aug) (RETURNED).* **1833:** *son James Lippett baptised at Cheltenham 9 July (father was shoemaker).* **1835:** *removed to St Owens, Gloucester (presumed) (apprenticeship); (RETURNED) death of wife Ann died (buried at New Burial Ground, Cheltenham, aged 25, 27 Aug.); JL remarried in Cheltenham 18 Oct, to Eliza Clements.* **1836:** *son Alonza baptised at Cheltenham 18 Sept.* **1841:** *JL (aged 30; shoemaker) moved to St Pancras, Middlesex, with wife Eliza, George (aged 10) and two other children (HO107/685/15/12/18).* **1851:** *JL apparently worked in Liverpool as shoemaker.* **1856:** *JL remarried and started new family in Cheltenham.* **1861:** *JL (aged 52; shoemaker) lived in Cheltenham with wife Johanna (43) and two children (RG9/1801/48/19); son George lived in Evesham with wife and family, and parents probably moved for several years from Cheltenham into Worcs (RG9/2101/29/10).* [PS/CH/RA/2/3:334.]

35008SE: Thurs 30 Apr 1835 – **James Harris**, with children **Ann** and **Mary Ann**: That he was born in the Parish of Saint Mary Magdalen in the City of Oxford. that when he was 4 Years of age he was apprenticed by a Charity called the Grey Coat Charity to Mr. Shackleford of Saint Mary Magdalen in Oxford for 7 Years   that he served his whole time in Saint Mary Magdalen and that since the expiration of his apprenticeship he has never done any act to gain a Settlement elsewhere

That about 9 Years ago he was Married to Sarah Bishop at Saint Mary Magdalen's Church in Oxford – that his Wife is dead but he has two Children living namely Ann aged 14 Years and Mary Ann aged four Years [signed]

1835: *removed after trial to St Mary Magdalen, Oxford, Oxon (presumed) (apprenticeship); on 1 May a JH of Cheltenham was committed for trial at County Sessions on 30 June for larceny (acquitted).* **1841:** *(RETURNED) JH lived at 27 Mount Pleasant, Cheltenham, aged 39, apprentice coachsmith, but without daughters (HO107/353/5/4/3); his former master, William Shackleford, listed as coach maker in Oxford (HO107/891/12/16/24).* [PS/CH/RA/2/3:334.]

35009SE: Sat 2 May 1835 – **Catherine Skey**, with two children **Fanny** and **Lucy**: That She was born as She believes in the parish of West Port in the Town of Malm[e]sbury in the County of Wilts where She believes her father Thomas Bishop is now legally Settled – That about 3 years ago last January she was married to her husband Charles Skey at the parish of West Port aforesaid – That about two years ago in consequence of her husband becoming Chargeable to the said Parish of West port - Her husband and herself and their child were removed by an order from that parish to the parish of Rotherhit[h]e in the County of Surr[e]y   The Order was Suspended during Informant's illness and when She recovered they were Sent to the said parish of West Port and were relieved by the parish Officers there and the person who conveyed them received the

Amount under the Suspension of the said Order - That her husband has not gained any Settlement since their Marriage – That She has two Children by her said husband namely Fanny aged about two years and Lucy aged Seven weeks – That She is become chargeable to the Parish of Cheltenham [mark]

1835: *removed to Rotherhithe, Surrey (apparently husband's settlement); Lucy Skey died two months later in Rotherhithe Workhouse (buried 8 July); Charles Skey had previously been convicted of "sacrilege" (stealing a communion plate from Coberley Church, south of Cheltenham); he was sentenced to death at Gloucester Assizes, commuted to transportation for life to Australia; he left England on the* Aurora *18 June, and arrived in Van Diemen's Land (Tasmania) in Oct.* **1841:** *CS (aged 25; lace maker) and daughter Fanny (6) lived with father, Thomas Bishop, in St Mary Westport, Malmesbury, Wilts (HO107/1181/36/7/6).* **1851:** *Charles Skey drowned while at work as ship's watchman in Hobart Aug, having started new family in Australia.* [PS/CH/RA/2/3:335. Removal expenses for "Conveying Skeys Wife & Child[re]n" to Rotherhithe (4 June 1835: P78/1/OV/2/4:136).]

35010SE: Tues 7 July 1835 – **John Davis**, and wife **Nancy**: That he was born in the parish of Hasfield in the said County.   that when he was about 10 years and a half old he was apprenticed by his father Robert Davis to George Holford then living in the parish of Tirley in the said County Cordwainer   that he served him four years, and was then assigned to John Lloyd then living in the parish of Shurdington in the said County   that after living with him about two years his said last master went to reside in the parish of Hasfield and took this examinant with him where he resided for the last year of his time   that about six years ago he was married in the Parish Church of Hempstead [= Hempsted] to his present wife Nancy   that he became possessed in her right of a house and land in the parish of Ashelworth [= Ashleworth] in the said County which is leasehold for lives of the value one hundred and fifty pounds and has continued in the possession of it ever since and has paid rates for it to the said parish of Ashelworth [signed]

1835: *removed to Ashleworth, near Tewkesbury (estate) (presumed).* **1841:** *probably the JD (40; cordwainer) who lived alone in Woolridge, Hartpury, near Hasfield (HO107/355/2/4/3).* **1844:** *JD (aged 46; living at Gloucester Union Workhouse) buried at Hasfield 25 Aug.* [PS/CH/RA/2/3:336.]

35011SE: Thurs 23 July 1835 – **Elizabeth Cleevely**: That she was borne [*sic*] in the Parish of Painswick in the said County where her parents were legally settled   That she is now about 65 years of Age and a Widow having no Children chargeable to this Parish. – That about 35 yrs ago her husband left her with 4 small Child[n]. and that she was then Compelled to seek relief from the Parish of Painswick aforesaid and received 2/[s]. per Week towards the support of herself and Children for 3 years and that she remained there for a considerable time aftwds the Overseers of the said Parish never having disputed her legal Settlement there – That she has heard and believes that her late husband was Apprenticed to M[r]. Robert Driver of Painswick af[ore]s[ai]d. Cooper but how long he remained as such app[rentic][e]. as aforesaid this Examinant knoweth not – That she has never gained a Settlement in Cheltenham by renting any tenement or otherwise and that she is now Chargeable to the Parish of Cheltenham [mark]

1835: *removed to Painswick (presumed) (father's settlement):* see **36021RO** (EC: 18 June 1836; copy at P244 OV 3/3/4/8). [PS/CH/RA/2/3:337.]

35012SE: Thurs 6 Aug 1835 – **Hannah Yeend**: That she is [the] Wife of Charles Yeend now residing in the Parish of Cheltenham – That she was married to him about 19 years ago – That her said husband rented a house and land in the parish of Staverton in this County at the yearly rent [of] £25 for about 2 years, in the years 1828 & 1829 (as she believes) – That he paid the whole of the rent for two years. That he rented the premises of Tho[s]. Allen, Carpenter – [unsigned]

1835: *removed to Staverton (husband's renting) (presumed).* **1841:** *Charles Yeend apparently committed to Gloucester County Lunatic Asylum (Ancestry: family source); HY (aged approx. 35; servant) lived in High St, Cheltenham (HO107/353/5/25/12).* **1845:** *(RETURNED) HY lived at Waterloo Place, Cheltenham (see* **45015SE:** *James Yeend: 27 Feb).* **1851:** *HY charwoman (50; married but living alone) at 26 Newman's Place, Cheltenham (HO107/1973/638/41).* **1857:** *death of HY at this address (Cheltenham Chron. 15 Sept).* [PS/CH/RA/2/3:338.]

35013SE: Tues 11 Aug 1835 – **Peter Cunningham**: [That] he was a Widower at the time he first came to England – That he has heard and believes that he was born at Kilmore in the County of Mon[a]ghan in Ireland   That he never rented a tenement of any description in England nor has he gained a Settlement there by service or otherwise [mark]
1835: *removed to Ireland (presumed).* [PS/CH/RA/2/3:339.]

35014SE: Tues 11 Aug 1835 – **Samuel Pickering**, and five children: That he was born at Barnsley in the County of York

that his father went afterwards to reside at Marr in the same County where he had property upon which he lived.   that Examinant lived with his father as part of his family at that time. That his father died seized of real property in Marr of which he took a share.

that he was 30 Years of age when his father died

that he has received Relief from the parish officers of Marr – this was about 6 Years ago – He does not know what age he was or when he was married – but he was married to Sarah West his late wife at Silkston[e] in Yorkshire upwards of 20 Years ago – That he had 5 Children by her including the infant now present [mark]
1835: *removed to Marr, Yorkshire (presumed) (father's settlement).* [PS/CH/RA/2/3:339.]

35015SE: Thurs 17 Sept 1835 – **Mary Price**, with three children **Mary Ann**, **Elizabeth**, and **Edward**: That Six years ago last May she was married to James Price her late Husband in the Parish Church of Cheltenham by whom she has three Children now living namely Mary Ann aged 6 Years last June Elizabeth aged 3 Years last October and Edward aged 12 months last December – that her husband died on the fourth of August last – that on the 23 of May 1831 her Husband took a House in Park Street Charlton Kings' of William Clifford at the rent of fourteen pounds a Year   that she and her Husband lived in the said House nearly 3 Years and paid upwards of two Years rent for the same – that on leaving Charlton Kings in February 1834, Her husband took Lodgings by the week and has continued to do so ever since – that the rent paid for such Lodgings was three shillings a week

that her Husband never did any Act to gain a Settlement since she left Charlton Kings [signed]
1835: *removed to Charlton Kings (husband's renting) (presumed)*; *son Edward (James) died soon after examination (buried at Cheltenham 3 Nov).* [PS/CH/RA/2/3:342.]

35016SE: Sat 5 Sept 1835 – **Ellen Williams**, with two children **Ellen** and **Owen**: That she is the Widow of William Williams late of the Parish of Cwmjoy [= Cwmyoy] in the County of Monmouth where his Father was legally settled and that she and her husband lived in the parish about five years. That since her husbands death she has received relief whilst living in the Parish of Cheltenham from the Parish Officers of the said Parish of Cwmjoy (In evidence whereof she now produces the Letter a Copy of which is hereunder written)   That she was married to her said husband at Hempsted in the said County this 20th. day of October 1828   That she had two Children by her said husband Ellen aged about five years and Owen aged about two years and nine months [mark]

> Copy Letter above referred to / Ellen Williams / Enclosed you will receive an Order on the Post Office Cheltenham for £1-19-11   I will send you more soon / Yrs truly / Evan Watkins / Overseer / Cwmyoy / April 4th. 1835. [Addressed to: M^{rs}. Ellen Williams N° 1 Barnards Row New Street Cheltenham]

1835: *removed to Cwmyoy, Monm (presumed) (husband's settlement).* [PS/CH/RA/2/3:344-5 (page 343 blank). Sworn confirmation of marriage by Peter Butt, Guardian of the Poor, omitted; an earlier, similar examination text dated 13 Aug 1835 (p. 340, struck out) states that EW previously married in Co. Cork. Both versions transcribe the relevant section of the Hempsted marriage register, confirming the details given here.]

35017SE: Sat 26 Sept 1835 – **Robert Normanton**, labourer: That he was born in the parish of Farringdon [= Faringdon] in the County of Berks where his parents were settled as he has been informed and believes, that his Mother was frequently relieved by the parish officers of Farringdon aforesaid   that he was never apprenticed or has been hired by the year or rented any house or land of the value of ten pounds a Year nor has served any parish office or done any Act to gain a settlement in his own right and is now chargeable to the parish of Cheltenham [signed] **1832:** *RN (labourer) received six-month prison sentence at Gloucester Michaelmas Assizes for (with others) stealing a pair of trousers in Cheltenham (see* Bristol Mercury *27 Oct).* **1835:** *removed to Faringdon, Berks (presumed) (father's settlement).* **1836:** *death of RN, aged 35 (Berks Burial Index).* [PS/CH/RA/2/3:348.]

35018SE: Thurs 29 Oct 1835 – **Mary MacDonald**, and infant child: That she has heard and believes she was born in the Kingdom of Ireland but in what part she does not know – That about thirty years ago she came to England with her parents, who are both since dead, and continued to reside there up to the present time   That she was married to her husband about two years ago at the Parish Church of Whitechapel in the County of Middlesex and has heard him say that he was born in the City of Cork, That he has since deserted her. That she was passing from Wales through Cheltenham on her way to London whilst in a State of Pregnancy and was retarded on her Journey by being delivered of a Male Child in Cheltenham aforesaid and that she and her said Child have both become Chargeable to the Parish of Cheltenham aforesaid   That to the best of her knowledge and belief her husband has not nor has she ever done any Act whereby to gain a Settlement in England [mark]
1835: *removed to Ireland (presumed).* [PS/CH/RA/2/3:349. Originally inscribed incorrectly in Petty Sessions register (PS/CH/RA/2/2:60) and struck out there.]

35019SE: Sat 7 Nov 1835 – **Benjamin Benfield**: That he was born in the parish of Churchdown in this County – That he was apprenticed to Samuel Cook of Northgate Street in the City of Gloucester (in St John's Parish) Baker & Maltster for 7 years – That he served his whole term – That he has done no other act to gain a Settlement – That he was christened in the parish of Churchdown & is 29 years of age [signed]
1835: *removed to St John's, Gloucester (presumed) (apprenticeship).* **1841:** *BB (aged 30; baker) lived with mother (Hannah; 65) in Pirton Lane, Churchdown (HO107/356/5/3/1).* **1881:** *BB was a pauper inmate of Gloucester Union Workhouse (72; baker) (RG11/2532/105/10).* [PS/CH/RA/2/3:351.]

35020SE: Sat 14 Nov 1835 – **Charles Collier**, stonemason, and wife **Sarah**: That he was born in the Parish of Haresfield in this County where his parents then lived   that in his infancy his parents removed from Haresfield to "Whites Hill" in the Parish of Stroud where his father purchased some Cottages and two Acres of land and is now living   That when he was about fourteen years of Age he entered into an Unstamped Agreement in writing to serve Richard Pew [also Pugh] of Hastings Sussex Stone Mason as an Outdoor servant for three years at 10/ˢ a week – for the first year twelve shillings for the second and fifteen for the third; that he lived with him 15 Months and then left his Service in consequence of the failure in business of his said master. That he has never lived as an hired Servant by the year nor rented any tenement of the value of ten pounds a year or done any Act to gain a Settlement   That on the 15ᵗʰ. June 1834 he married his present Wife Sarah at Cheltenham [signed]
1835: *removed to Stroud (presumed) (father's settlement).* [PS/CH/RA/2/3:353. Expenses for "apprehending Collier deserting his Wife & Child" (18 Nov 1835: P78/1/OV/2/4:136). See **36002RO** (wife Sarah Collier: 26 Jan 1836) and **35023SE** (Richard Pugh: 17 Dec 1835) for further information; also 1836 Stroud overseers' record (P320a OV 3/3/3/60) for Charles (aged 23: address Haresfield) and Sarah Collier (address Cheltenham).]

35021SE: Sat 28 Nov 1835 – John Stevens, of Cheltenham, for sister **Ann Stevens** of Charlton Kings, "lunatic".
1836: *an Ann Stephens (aged 38) was buried at Charlton Kings 13 May.* [PS/CH/RA/2/3:354. Struck out; examination correctly entered in PS/CH/RA/2/2:67. Removal expenses for conveying "Ann Stephens to Asylum" (3 Dec 1835: P78/1/OV/2/4:136).]

35022RO: Tues 1 Dec 1835 – **William Miles**; also Elizabeth Miles, relating to settlement of William Miles: *William Miles:* [Magistrates' register] That he was born at Eastington in the said County which he believes to be his Fathers last legal Place of Settlement, that he recollects his

Father having received Relief from the said Parish of Eastington on several occasions   that he resided with him as part of the family and during the time he received such relief till the age of eighteen and was then hired by M[r]. Darwell of Cheltenham in the said County in whose service he lived about ten months – That he was then hired by Dr Conolly of Cheltenham aforesaid on the third of July 1834 for twelve months and lived with him until the 11th. day of August 1835 and was paid his Wages up to that time. That he has not since lived in any Situation or done any act whereby to gain a settlement elsewhere [signed]

Elizabeth Miles: I am [the] wife of Nathaniel Miles of the parish of Eastington Cloth worker and Mother of William Miles who was born at Eastington aforesaid where I and my said husband were then and still are legally settled [mark]

1814: *WM baptised at Eastington (near Stonehouse) 18 Mar.* **1835: ordered to be removed to Eastington (father's settlement), but perhaps not removed.** **1836:** *a "William Mills" was buried at Cheltenham 14 Mar, aged 22.* [PS/CH/RA/2/4:1: the removal order lacks copy of examination (see PS/CH/RA/2/3:350). Notes: "15 Swindon Place". Removal expenses for "Coach fare to Eastington & back to receive money for Miles expences" (26 May 1836: D4178).]

35023SE: Thurs 17 Dec 1835 – Richard Pugh, relating to the examination of **Charles Collier**: On the 7 July 1828 Charles Collier entered into my employ at Hastings in the County of Sussex under an unstamped agreement in writing which I produced & of which the following is a copy

Memorandum of Agreement made and entered into between Richard Pugh Mason of the one part and Charles Collier of the other part   That the said Charles Collier doth hereby agree and consent for the space of Three years from the date hereof in such le[a]gel [*sic*] terms as an Apprentice to the said Rich[d]. Pugh for to serve him in all respects as he shall appoint or direct as becoming an Apprentice for his instructions   Also the said Charles Collier is to be sober trust[worthy] and honest in all things as may be left to his Charge or Care and that the said Rich[d]. Pugh doth hereby agree to instruct the said Charles Collier agreeable to the branch connected to Mason and Bricklayers Work by the said Rich[d]. Pugh paying to the said Charles Collier at the rate of 10[s]. per week according as the we[a]ther or work may admit during the time of twelve months and the second year the said Rich[d]. Pugh doth agree to pay to the said Charles Collier 12[s]. per week according as before mentioned the first year, and the third year the said Rich[d]. Pugh doth agree to pay to the said Charles Collier at the rate of 15[s]. per week according as before mentioned in the first year   Dated Hastings 7th. July 1828 Richard Pugh / Charles Collier / Witness Thomas Jones

That the said Charles Collier served him (this dep[t].) under the said agreement until the 12th. Sep[r]. 1829 – that there was never any other agreements for service nor any indenture of apprenticeship existing between the said Charles Collier & this deponent [signed]

[PS/CH/RA/2/3:354-6. See **35020SE** (Charles Collier: 14 Nov 1835).]

35024SE: Tues 22 Dec 1835 – **Mary Moor**, single woman: That she was born she has heard and believes in the parish of Birmingham – That she believes her parents were settled in the parish of Great Shelsey [= Gt Shelsley; Shelsley Beauchamp] in the County of Worcester – That between 14 & 15 years ago she was hired by M[rs]. Mountford of Great Shelsey as a servant by the year at 1 Guinea a year wages – That she received the whole of her wages – That she was then hired by Samuel Potter of Upper Sapey in the County of Hereford Farmer by the year at 50[s]/ wages & served him 3 years and received the whole of her wages – That afterwards she was hired by M[r]. William Hunley of the parish of Cotheridge in the County of Worcester Farmer by the year at £6 wages – That she served him 2 years and received the whole of her wages – That she then went into several situations on yearly hirings but did not remain in either of them one year – That in or about the month of September 1832 she was hired by Mrs Gallier in the parish of Clains [= Claines] in the County of Worcester by the year at £6 a year wages, a month's wages or a month's warning – That a week after such last mentioned hiring her said mistress removed to Cheltenham in the County of Gloucester where her husband John Gallier was then living – That she lived with Mr & Mrs Gallier in Jersey Place Cheltenham twelve months all but 3 or 4 days -

That the whole of her 12 months' wages were paid – That before the 12 months expired she hired herself into another situation which she was to enter on the following Monday, but as she was wanted sooner, she entered into the service on the Friday before – That her year with M[r]. Gallier had expired – That she then went into the service of M[rs] Nagle in the Crescent Cheltenham with whom she lived 3 weeks   That about a week or fortnight afterwards she went into Miss Bootham's service in Park Place in Cheltenham [mark]

1835: *removal uncertain: examination form incomplete; perhaps allowed to remain in Cheltenham.* [PS/CH/RA/2/3:358-60.]

Martha Knee was examined by two Cheltenham magistrates, Joseph Overbury and William Pitt, on 25 June 1836 (36023RO). Her removal to Stroud was delayed because of her "sickness, or infirmity": she was probably about 80 years of age, and it was not unusual for the impoverished elderly to seek parish relief in the last years of their life even if they had previously avoided parish charity or the workhouse. The second page of the Removal Order contains notification that her removal was suspended, and then shows that the magistrates were satisfied that she had recovered sufficiently to be sent on to Stroud.

1836

36001SE: Sat 2 Jan 1836 – **Arthur Field**, wife **Bridget**, and four children **Mary, Catherine, Thomas, and Bridget**: That according to the best of his belief he was born at Clonakilty County Cork in Ireland which left about 13 years ago and has never done any Act whereby to gain a Settlement in England – About eight years ago he married his present Wife Bridget in London by whom he has four Children namely Mary aged Seven years Catherine aged 4 years Thomas aged two years and eight months and Bridget aged about fifteen months and that they are now all chargeable to the Parish of Cheltenham & that neither of his said Children have gained a Settlement thereat [signed]
1836: *removed to Ireland (presumed).* **1837:** *(RETURNED) birth of son Jeremiah registered 3Q at Cheltenham.* **1841:** *the family lived in Grove St, Cheltenham, (HO107/353/16/34/29): Arthur (aged 40; labourer), Bridget (31), and six children - Mary (12), Catherine (9), Thomas (8), Bridget (6), Jeremiah (4), and Arthur (1 mo).* [PS/CH/RA/2/3:363; supersedes incomplete text of 22 Dec 1835 (p. 357).]

36002RO: Tues 26 Jan 1836 (examination on 24 Dec 1835/26 Jan) – **Sarah Collier**, wife of Charles Collier; also William Collier of Whites Hill, Stroud, relating to the settlement of daughter-in-law Sarah Collier. *William Collier*: That about 15 years ago he purchased some freehold houses and land in the said Parish of Stroud and which he is still the owner of. That he is the Father of Charles Collier the Pauper who was born in Wedlock   That his Son Charles was born in the Parish of Haresfield in this County

That he (Deponent) had no property at Haresfield

That he purchased some part of the property at Stroud (a house and Garden) before his Son Charles was born

That he has not bought any since his Son was 14 Years of Age   That he has lived at Whites Hill 16 or 17 years. That his said Son Charles is 23 years of age [signed]
Sarah Collier: I was married to my present husband on the 15th. June 1834 at the Parish Church of Cheltenham   I have now chargeable to the Parish of Cheltenham and my husband has deserted me and left me so chargeable to the said Parish [signed]
1836: *removed to Stroud (husband's settlement).* [PS/CH/RA/2/4:2 (copy at P320a OV/3/3/3/60). See **35020SE** (Charles Collier: 14 Nov 1835) and depositions of William Collier (24 Dec 1835) and SC (undated) at PS/CH/RA/2/3:361-2.]

36003RO: Thurs 18 Feb 1836 (examinations on 16 Feb) – **Caroline Mander** (sometimes **Manders**), widow, and daughter **Mary Ann**; also Edward Mander, residing in Stow-on-the-Wold, relating to the settlement of daughter-in-law Caroline Mander. *Caroline Mander*: That on the 27th. day of August 1833 she was married to Thomas Mander now deceased at the Parish Church of Cheltenham by whom she has one Child Mary Ann aged nearly 2 years   That since her Marriage her said husband never did any Act to gain a Settlement in Cheltenham   That she has heard him say the place of his legal settlement was Stow on the Wold

That she and her said Child are now chargeable to the Parish of Cheltenham [signed]
Edward Mander: That he is the Father of Thomas Mander the late husband of Caroline Mander   That about 40 years ago he this Deponent then being a single man was hired by Mr. John Ellis of Stow on the Wold aforesaid by the year at the Wages or £4

That he continued in such service 3 years and received his Wages for that period   That he has never since done any Act whereby to gain a Settlement elsewhere   That the said Thomas Mander was born in Wedlock in the said Parish of Stow on the Wold about 25 years ago and that he this Deponent believes the said Thomas Mander never did any Act to gain a Settlement [mark]
1810: *Caroline Taylor (later Mander) apparently baptised at Chipping Norton 28 June.* **1835:** *burial of Thomas Mander (aged 24) in Cheltenham 21 Sept, precipitating family crisis.* **1836:** *removed to Stow-on-the-Wold (husband's settlement); CM pregnant at time of examination; son Thomas David baptised at*

Cheltenham 22 May. **1841:** *daughter Mary (6) and brother Thomas (5) lived with grandmother Sarah Taylor in Market Place, Chipping Campden (HO107/360/24/9/12); Edward Mander (60; agricultural labourer) continued to live in Stow-on-the-Wold (HO107/366/21/31/17).* **1845:** *CM (widow) apparently married Thomas Sherwood 15 Sept in Chipping Campden.* [PS/CH/RA/2/4:3 (copy at PS/CH/RA/2/3:364).]

36004SE: Sat 20 Feb 1836 – **George Jenkins**, tailor, wife **Mary**, and three children **Eliza**, **Maria**, and **Francis**: That he has heard and believes that he was born in the Parish of Walcot in the County of Somerset and lived with his parents until he was eleven years of age as part of their family   That he was then apprenticed as an Outdoor Apprentice by parchment indentures under seal which are since lost to Charles Shell of Walcot aforesaid Tailor for seven years but after remaining with him as such Apprentice for two years and a half was in consequence of the failure of his said Master in business turned over to William Coxhead of Walcot aforesaid but left such Apprenticeship with him in consequence of his failure in Business   that during his said Apprenticeship he continued to live with his parents as part of their family since which time this Examinant has never Rented a tenement of the value of Ten pounds a year for a period of a year or done any Act whereby to gain a Settlement – That about ten years ago he was married to his present wife Mary at the Church of St Mary Le Port Bristol by whom he has 3 children Eliza aged about 8 years Maria aged about 3½ years and Francis aged about 16 months   That his said wife was a widow when he married her And was living at Bristol with one child by her former husband [signed]
1836: *removed to Walcot, Som (presumed) (apprenticeship).* **1839:** *(RETURNED) son George born at Cheltenham 3Q.* **1841:** *the family, comprising George Jenkins (aged 40; journeyman tailor), Mary (40), Mary (21), Eliza (13), Francis (6), and George (1), lived at 52 Burton St, Cheltenham (HO107/353/16/44/5).* **1851:** *the family lived at Somers Town, St Pancras, Middlesex, with George still journeyman tailor (HO107/1499/8/8).* [PS/CH/RA/2/3:365-6.]

36005RO: Tues 1 Mar 1836 – **Harriett Hulbert**, single woman, residing in Cheltenham Workhouse: That she was born at Birdlip in this said county where her parents resided. That she lived with them as part of their family until about seven years ago when she was hired by M[r]. William Humphris of Didbrook in the said County Farmer (at Cheltenham Mop) for one year and lived in his service for that time and received her whole years Wages. That she has since lived in several situations but never in any one of them for the period of a year. That she has never done any act to gain a Settlement elsewhere and that she is now chargeable to the said parish of Cheltenham [mark]
1813: *HH baptised in Brimpsfield, near Birdlip, 9 May.* **1836:** *removed to Didbrook (hiring and service); HH discharged from Cheltenham (Old) Workhouse 24 Mar for Didbrook (G/CH/60/1) (pregnant when admitted).* **1841:** *perhaps the HH (aged 35; born outside Surrey) recorded as an inmate of Bethlem Hospital in Southwark, Surrey (HO107/1084/10/6/7).* [PS/CH/RA/2/4:4 (copy at PS/CH/RA/2/3:367).]

36006SE: Sat 5 Mar 1836 – **James Craddock**, prisoner in custody on charge of felony, wife **Sarah**, and two children **Martha** and **Lucy**: "I have heard and believe that I was Born at Tewkesbury in the said County – where my Parents reside   I have never been apprenticed, rented a Tenement of the value of Ten pounds a year or done any other Act to gain a Settlement I was married to Sarah my wife at Cheltenham Church about Eight years ago by whom I have two children namely Martha aged five years last August and Lucy aged three years last November["] [mark]
1836: *removed to Tewkesbury (presumed) (birth); JC acquitted at Gloucester Lent Assizes of stealing a quantity of malt and hops for brewing (though he had served six months for larceny in 1830, and had been acquitted of stealing groceries from his master in 1824); (RETURNED) son William born 3 Nov at Cheltenham (10 Bath Terrace).* **1841:** *the family lived at 10 Bath Terrace, Cheltenham: JC (aged 32; greengrocer), Sarah (30), Martha (10), Lucy (8), and William (4).* [PS/CH/RA/2/3:368.]

36007SE: Tues 15 Mar 1836 – **Fanny Connor**: That according to the best of her belief she was born that Youghall [= Youghal] in the County of Cork in Ireland which she left about 6 years ago

and has never done any Act to gain a Settlement in England and that she is now chargeable to the said Parish of Cheltenham [mark]
1836: *removed to Ireland (presumed).* [PS/CH/RA/2/3:369.]

36008SE: Thurs 31 Mar 1836 – **Charles Tarlton**, and wife **Elizabeth**: That to the best of his belief he was Born in the Parish of Dunkerton in the County of Somerset. That about 28 years ago he was bound Apprentice for seven years to Mr Samuel Birt of the Parish of Walcot in the said County of Somerset Boot Closer   That he lived with him as such Apprentice for five years since which time he has never done any Act to gain a Settlement elsewhere. That about nineteen years ago he was married to his present Wife Elizabeth at the Abbey Church in Bath in the said County of Somerset [signed]
1836: *removed to Walcot, Som (presumed) (apprenticeship).* **1841:** *(RETURNED) CT (aged 40; shoemaker) lived with daughter Mary (20) in Sherborne St, Cheltenham (where he had shop) (HO107/353/5/63/48).* **1842:** *after death of wife CT remarried (for the first time).* **1851:** *CT master bootmaker employing two men, living again as widower at 27 Bath St, Cheltenham.* [PS/CH/RA/2/3:370.]

36009SE: Tues 19 Apr 1836 – **James Smith**, wife **Frances Ann**, and two children, **Mary Ann** and **Eliza**: That was born in the Parish of Knapwell in the County of Cambridge – where his parents were settled – That when he was ab^t. 19 years of age he was apprenticed to Joseph Bell of High Street in the parish of St. Peter Cambridge Carpenter by indenture for 2 years – That he served his said master the full term and remained in his service as a Journeyman one year after the expiration of his said Apprenticeship – That he has never done any other act to gain a settlement – That when he was so apprenticed £10 was paid with him as Premium and the indenture was on parchment & stamped and was signed and sealed by Deponent   That he has a wife named Frances Ann to whom he has been married more than 6 years and by whom he has two Children namely Mary Ann aged 5 years and Eliza aged 9 months [signed]
1802: *JS baptised at Knapwell, Cambs on 7 Mar.* **1836:** *removed to St Peter, Cambridge, Cambs (presumed) (apprenticeship); as trained carpenter, this is probably the JS (aged 33) imprisoned at Gloucester Midsummer Assizes for four months (the last month in solitary confinement) for stealing two saws in Cheltenham in Mar (Gloucestershire Chron. 2 July).* [PS/CH/RA/2/3:371.]

36010RO: Tues 26 Apr 1836 (examination 23 Apr) – **Frances Sarah Grimes**, single woman, inmate of Cheltenham Workhouse: That she has heard and believes that she was born in the City of Salisbury (where her parents were legally settled) in the year 1818   That she has lived with her parents [Magistrates' register: as part of their Family] until September last   That about June 1834 her Father removed from Salisbury to the Parish of Burford in Oxfordshire where he purchased a house known by the name of "The Red Lion Inn" in the said Parish and has continued to live there ever since   That she this Examinant has never done any Act whereby to gain a Settlement and that she is now chargeable to the parish of Cheltenham [signed Francis Sarah Grimes]
1836: *FSG admitted to Cheltenham Workhouse 28 Mar, with "bad leg"; discharged for Burford 23 May (G/CH/60/1); removed to Burford (father's settlement).* **1841:** *father John Grimes (aged 48; publican), second wife, and son Thomas lived in High St, Burford, Oxon (HO107/872/17/44/29), but FSG herself was not living with them; she was perhaps the Frances Grimes who lived as servant in Britford, outside Salisbury (HO107/1169/5/8/9).* [PS/CH/RA/2/4:5 (copy at PS/CH/RA/2/3:372). *Removal expenses for conveyance of "Francis Grimes to Burford" (Sept 1836: D4178).*]

36011SE: Sat 23 Apr 1836 – Sarah Jackway, relating to settlement of husband **Charles Jackway:** That she is the wife of Charles Jackway a Lunatic – That her said husband was born as she has heard and believes at the parish of Leonard Stanley in this County – That she has always heard & believed that her said husband's father's place of Settlement was the said Parish of Leonard Stanley   That she was married to her said husband in the said Parish of Leonard Stanley more than 19 years ago – That since that time and about 10 years ago she, her said husband, & their family, received relief from the said Parish of Leonard Stanley several times – That her said husband has never done any act to gain a settlement since his marriage and that She has always heard & believes that his place of Settlement is Leonard Stanley aforesaid [mark]

1836: *removed to* [*Gloucester*] *Asylum, with settlement ascribed to Leonard Stanley (presumed) (father's settlement).* **1841:** *Sarah Jackway (aged 40) apparently lived with daughters Ann (12) and Sarah (7) in Sherborne St, Cheltenham (HO107/353/5/59/41).* **1848:** *CJ's burial probably that recorded in Leonard Stanley on 2 Feb, aged 69.* **1851:** *Sarah Jackway was widow (50) running lodging house in Montpellier Spa Place, with daughter Sarah (now 17) (HO107/1973/1043/22).* [PS/CH/RA/2/3:374. Removal expenses for "Conveyance of Lunatics to Assylum [sic] Charles Jackway" (Sept 1836: D4178).]

36012RO: Tues 26 Apr 1836 (examination 23 Apr) – **Elizabeth Heath Nicholls**, single woman: That she was born as she has heard and believes in the Parish of Buskitt [= Buscot] in the County of Berks[hire] in the year 1814 where her parents were legally settled   That she lived with them as part of their family till she was thirteen years of age when she was hired as a Servant by M^r. Edward Trinder Dyke of the Parish of Highworth in the County of Wilts by the year at the Wages of £2 a year   That she lived in his said service for one whole year and received her full Wages for that time. That she has since been in service with several different persons but never for the period of a year and has never since done any Act whereby to gain a Settlement   That she is now chargeable to the parish [of] Cheltenham [mark]

1836: *"Ann" Nicholls admitted to Cheltenham Workhouse 10 Apr, suffering from "bad leg"; discharged for Highworth 23 May (G/CH/60/1); removed to Highworth, Wilts (hiring and service).* **1841:** *EHN married 4Q in Oxford to Edward Bull.* **1851:** *the couple lived in Abingdon, Oxon, with Edward's niece Ann: Edward (aged 34; groom), Elizabeth (35) (HO107/1688/260/36).* **1854:** *death of EHN in Highworth, Wilts.* [PS/CH/RA/2/4:6 (copy at PS/CH/RA/2/3:373).]

36013SE: Thurs 19 May 1836 – **Mary Rudd:** That in the month of December 1834 she was married to her present husband John Rudd at the parish of Titley in the County of Hereford – That for nearly two years prior to her said marriage her said husband lived in the service of Thomas Monington Esquire of Sansfield [= Sarnesfield] in the said county of Hereford – That she has heard her said husband say that his wages were £52 a year & they were paid quarterly and he had a cottage to live in belonging to his said master in addition to his wages – That she lived in the said service with her said husband 8 months prior to her marriage – That she has heard her said husband say he was born in Yorkshire – That she never heard of his doing any act to gain a settlement in any other place than Sansfield aforesaid – That her said husband left her last Saturday fortnight and has not since returned. That she is in consequence become chargeable to the said Parish of Cheltenham [mark]

1836: *removed to Sarnesfield, Heref (presumed) (husband's settlement).* **1838:** *(RETURNED) son Charles baptised 12 Feb in Cheltenham (where he died after six days).* **1840:** *second son, George Miles, baptised at Cheltenham 4 Oct.* **1841:** *the family lived in Mount Pleasant, Cheltenham: John Rudd (40; servant), Mary (25), and George (9 mo).* [PS/CH/RA/2/3:377.]

36014SE: Sat 21 May 1836 – Ann Wells, wife of William Wells, shoemaker, relating to the settlement of **Eleanor** and **Walter Alfred Murphy**, children of Thomas and wife, Sarah (both deceased): That about Midsummers last Thomas Murphy with his two children Eleanor Murphy aged between 9 & 10 years and Walter Alfred Murphy aged six years came to lodge at this deponent's house   That when they were so lodging there the said Thomas Murphy told her that his own parish and that of his children was Saint George the Martyr in the borough of Southwark   That the said Thomas Murphy died on 28th. Feby last at this deponent's house – That the said Thomas Murphy told her that the said Parish of St George the Martyr was the parish to which himself and his children belonged, during his last illness and about a fortnight before his death – That she had been informed & believes that the said Thomas Murphy's wife died in Cheltenham aforesaid in the month of June last – That the morning after the said Thomas Murphy's death she found two receipts for rent in a box belonging to the said Thomas Murphy of which the following are copies "April 20 1830 Received of Mr Murphy the sum of Two pounds ten shillings for one quarter's rent due Lady day last" (signed) John Prichard

"January 18 1831 Received of M^r. Murphy the sum of two pounds for one quarters rent due Christmas last past £-10=0=0 (signed) John Prichard"
1836: *removed to St George's, Southwark, Surrey (presumed) (father's settlement).* **1841:** *(RETURNED) Walter Alfred Murphy (aged 10; baptised Southwark 1830 as Albion Walter Murphy) was an inmate of Charlton Kings Workhouse (HO107/353/2/53/1), "deserted" (G/CH/60/2: recorded at workhouse from at least 1837); Eleanor Murphy (14; servant) resided at Cheltenham Union Workhouse (HO107/353/17/16/3).* [PS/CH/RA/2/3:378-9.]

36015RO: Thurs 26 May 1836 (examination 21 May) – **James Yeend**, and wife **Elizabeth:** [Magistrates' register] That he was born as he believes in the parish of Elmstone Hardwicke in the said County, where his parents were legally settled – That he rented a house & some land at Boddington in the said County for about sixteen years, at the rent of Eight Guineas for the first three years, Ten Guineas for the three next & Ten pounds for the remaining time that he occupied that he occupied the said premises – That he paid the whole of the rent and all taxes – That he has not done any act since that time whereby to gain a Settlement elsewhere. That he has a wife named Elizabeth. That they are now chargeable to the parish of Cheltenham [mark]
1836: *removed to Boddington (near Elmstone Hardwicke) (renting).* **1838:** *(perhaps RETURNED) an Elizabeth Yeend (aged 65) buried at Cheltenham 10 Feb.* **1839:** *a James Yeend of Woodmancote buried at Bishop's Cleeve, aged 61, 4 Jan.* [PS/CH/RA/2/4:7; the removal order lacks copy of examination (PS/CH/RA/2/3:380).]

36016RO: Sat 28 May 1836 (examination 24 May) – **Ann Willicombe**, wife of Aaron Willicombe, and daughter **Hannah:** [Magistrates' register] That she joined her husband Aaron Willicombe in Cheltenham aforesaid about seven months ago – That her said husband has told her that he gained a settlement in the Parish of Dunster in the county of Somerset by hiring and service before his marriage – That she has never heard her said husband mention the name of his master or mistress at Dunster – That she married her said husband at Bath about a year and a half ago – That she has one child by her said husband named Hannah aged 7 months. That she this deponent lived in the service of M^r. Samuel Tucker of the parish of Westbury Leigh in the County of Wilts as a yearly servant at the wages of 8£ a year, 15 years, and received the whole of her wages – That she was married in less than 12 Months after quitting such service   That she did no act to gain a settlement after quitting such service – nor has her s^d. husband ever done any such act to her knowledge – That her said husband has left her & she is now chargeable to the Parish of Cheltenham [mark]
1834: *an Aaron Willicombe complained formally to Cheltenham magistrates against Charles Wiles, "for wages for labour as a carpenter", 1 May.* **1835:** *infant daughter of Aaron (carpenter) and AW was christened Hannah 13 Dec in Cheltenham.* **1836:** *removed to Westbury Leigh, Wilts (hiring and service).* **1851:** *AW (aged 50; widow, grocer, born West Knoyle, Wilts) lived with daughter Hannah in The Street, Batheaston, Som (HO107/1943/509/13).* **1871:** *AW probably the Hannah Willicombe (aged 35; nurse, from Glos) who emigrated to New Zealand on Charlotte Gladstone.* [PS/CH/RA/2/4:8. The removal order lacks copy of examination (PS/CH/RA/2/3:381-2); earlier unsigned examination on 5 May (p. 375) includes her birthplace as West Knoyle, Wilts.]

36017RO: Thurs 9 June 1836 (examination 31 May) – **Hannah Mitchell**, single woman: That she was born as she has heard and believes in the parish of Tetbury in the said County of Gloucester   That as she was informed and believes she was not born in Wedlock
    That about three years ago she was hired by Mr Laker of Moreton [= Morton] near Thornbury in this County as a yearly servant at the wages of £5 a year - That she lived in such service one year and a quarter and received the whole of her wages – That she has never lived 12 months in any service since that time nor has done any other act to gain a settlement   That she is now chargeable to the parish of Cheltenham [mark]
1815: *HM, "base child" of Mary Mitchell, baptised at Tetbury 8 Oct.* **1836:** *HM unable to look after herself: when admitted to Cheltenham Workhouse 25 Mar she was classified "Insane", with infant son George (who died at workhouse 29 Apr at 5 weeks); discharged for Thornbury 6 July (G/CH/60/1); removed to*

Thornbury (hiring and service). **1841:** *(RETURNED) HM married widower Richard Cooke of Sherborne St at Cheltenham 8 Mar, when living at 2 Sussex Place; (census); HM lived at 10 Russell Place, Cheltenham, with husband and young (step?)son: Richard G. Cooke (aged 44; auctioner's porter, born Maugersbury), Hannah (38; born Tetbury, and Richard (3; born Cheltenham) (HO107/1973/475/11).* [PS/CH/RA/2/4:9 (copy at PS/CH/RA/2/3:383).]

36018SE: Thurs 16 June 1836 – **Martha Stewart**, wife of Charles Stewart, and four children, **Charles**, **James**, **Mary**, and **Harriet**: That her husband has deserted her – That 13 years ago last March her husband rented a house in Mount Pleasant Cheltenham by the year at the Yearly rent of 12 Guineas and lived in such house at the said rent for two years and paid the whole of the rent that he continued in such house for three Years and upwards afterwards at ten Guineas a Year and her husband has [*sic*] not left Cheltenham until last September when he deserted her   that she has four children who with herself are chargeable to the parish of Cheltenham – That her said husband has done no act to gain a settlement since renting the said house in Mount Pleasant Place as aforesaid [mark]
1835: *when MS's daughter Harriet was baptised at Cheltenham 14 Jan, husband Charles was described as "labourer".* **1836:** *removal unlikely: place of settlement probably acknowledged as Cheltenham.* **1841:** *MS (aged 40; charwoman) lived with four children Charles (20), James (13; both servants), Mary (10), and Harriet (5) in Barnard's Row, south of Lower High St, Cheltenham.* [PS/CH/RA/2/3:388.]

36019SE: Thurs 16 June 1836 – **Maria Phelps**, single woman, inmate of Cheltenham Workhouse: That she was born in the parish of Awre in the said County as she has been informed and believes where her parents were settled   that the first service she was ever in was with the Misses Coppin at Belle Vue Hotel Cheltenham where she has been for the last three years and has received six pounds a year wages but the agreement was made by her Aunt Mrs Olive with the Misses Coppin and she was not present – that she is now in the Workhouse at Cheltenham [mark]
1819: *MP baptised (father unnamed) in Awre 18 July.* **1836:** *removal uncertain: place of settlement perhaps acknowledged as Cheltenham; "Pregnant & Ill" when admitted to Cheltenham Workhouse 10 June; illegitimate daughter Maria born 10 Aug at workhouse (baptised 28 Aug 1838) (G/CH/67/1), from which MP was discharged after three months (G/CH/60/1).* **1841:** *likely to be the MP (aged 20) working as servant, living in High St, Cheltenham (HO107/353/7/25/6); daughter Maria probably lived with family of Caleb Hulin (aged 20; blacksmith) in Awre.* **1842:** *infant MP readmitted to workhouse 6 Oct (aged 7; "clean") (again in 1845, aged 9) (G/CH/60/2&3).* **1845:** *MP re-admitted to Cheltenham Workhouse 1Q and remained there for much of year (G/CH/60/4).* [PS/CH/RA/2/3:389.]

36020RO: Sat 18 June 1836 (examination 16 June) – **Benjamin Toleman**: That he has been informed and believes that he was born in the parish of Mangotsfield in the said County where his parents were settled – That about 17 or 18 years ago he was hired by Sir William Call of the parish of Saint George Hanover Square London for a year at the yearly wages of twenty five guineas   that he served the whole year and received his years wages and continued in such service a year and a half longer – That he has never been in any service by the year since nor rented any house or land of the annual value of ten pounds nor served any parish office or done any act to gain a settlement elsewhere   that he is now chargeable to the parish of Cheltenham [signed]
1836: *removed to St George, Hanover Square, Middlesex (hiring and service).* **1841:** *BT (aged 60; no occupation given) lived in St George Hanover Square Workhouse (HO107/734/10/35/5).* [PS/CH/RA/2/4:10 (copy at PS/CH/RA/2/3:387).]

36021RO: Sat 18 June 1836 (examination 16 June) – **Elizabeth Cleevely**, widow.
1835: *removed to Painswick (presumed) (father's settlement)* **(35011SE:** *EC 23 July 1835).* **1836:** *removed to Painswick.* **1841:** *EC (aged 70) lived alone in Painswick (HO107/349/8/52/20).* [PS/CH/RA/2/4:11; removal order lacks copy of examination (PS/CH/RA/2/3:390).]

36022RO: Sat 18 June 1836 (examination 16 June) – **John Wood,** wife **Maria**, and five children: That he was born in the parish of Cheltenham in the said County as he has been informed and believes -

That he has heard that his father left his Wife this Examinants mother when Examinant was about two years and a half old – That he lived with his Mother in Cheltenham until he was about twenty years of age – That during that time his Mother frequently received relief from the Overseers of Cheltenham   That in the spring of last year his Mother died in the Cheltenham Workhouse and was buried at the expence of the parish of Cheltenham – That he has never been at service or apprenticed or done any act to gain a settlement in his own right but has always worked at the brickmaking business That he is now chargeable to the Hamlet of Uckington [mark]

1836: *removed from Uckington to Cheltenham (mother's settlement).* [PS/CH/RA/2/4:1 (comparable examination at Cheltenham Petty Sessions 7 June). PS/CH/RA/2/4:14 instructs John Wood, wife Maria, and five children to be removed to Cheltenham (July 1836; examination dated 7 July). These Orders should properly have been entered in Cheltenham Petty Sessions register.]

36023RO: Mon 27 June 1836 (examination 25 June) – **Martha Knee**, single woman: That she was born she has heard and believes in the parish of Kingstanley [= King's Stanley] in the said County. That she lived eleven years at the parish of Stroud in the said County as a hired Servant to M^r. Freebury, Baker. She also lived with D^r. Darke in the said Parish of Stroud as a yearly servant to him the said D^r. Darke – That she received the wages of eight pounds a year from the said D^r. Darke and that she lived with him and received her wages for ten years – That she has not done any act by service or otherwise to gain Settlement elsewhere   And that the Officers of the said parish of Stroud have given her the relief of 1^s/6^d a week until one month last past And that the said parish of Stroud has never disputed her Settlement but for the last month past she has been refused relief from that parish and has now become chargeable to the parish of Cheltenham [mark]

1836: *removed to Stroud (hiring and service).* **1837:** *probably the MK (aged 81; single, and an inmate of Minchinhampton Workhouse) buried at Minchinhampton near Stroud 7 July.* [PS/CH/RA/2/4:13 (copy at PS/CH/RA/2/3:391); removal postponed as pauper unfit to travel. Removal expenses for "M. Knee" to Stroud (30 Mar 1837: D4178).]

36024RO: Fri 22 July 1836 – **John Stratford**, wife **Ann**, and five children **Thomas** (8), **John** (6), **Hannah** (4), **Emma** (2), and unnamed infant of five months (**William**).

1836: *removed from Leckhampton to Miserden.* [PS/CH/RA/2/4:15 (Cheltenham parish); pauper said to be unfit to travel. Properly in Cheltenham Petty Sessions register, 2 July. See P198a OV/3/2/19 (Leckhampton records) for further details.]

36025RO: Mon 8 Aug 1836 (examination 5 Aug) – **Mary Hill**, single woman: That she was born as she has heard and believes in the parish of Bisley in the said County – That she never saw her father but that her mother died about thirteen years at ago and that she had heard her mother say that her father was never lawfully married to her – That she this Examinant has never rented a house or any other tenement of the value of ten pounds per year – That she has never been out to service for the space of a year at one service and that she has never gained a settlement in any parish by her own act And that she is now chargeable to the parish of Cheltenham aforesaid [mark]

1836: *removed to Bisley (birth): perhaps see* **47011RO** *(MH: 15 Feb 1847).* [PS/CH/RA/2/4:16 (copy at PS/CH/RA/2/3:392). Removal expenses for "Hill Johnson & Jordan" £1/11/-. (30 Mar 18374178).]

36026SE: [undated: 8 – 24 Aug 1836] – [blank] Postlethwaite, of Prestbury, regarding the settlement of **William Henry Goone**: That the said William Henry Goone rented a house in the parish of Broadway in the County of Worcester of M^r. Thomas Smith in the year 1830 and 1831 at as She believes the yearly rent of at least twenty pounds   that she is quite positive he lived in such house upwards of a year [incomplete]

1836: *removal uncertain: examination form incomplete.* [PS/CH/RA/2/3:393; text struck out as examination does not relate to Cheltenham parish.]

36027RO: Fri 12 Aug 1836 – **Sarah Herbert**, and three children, **Edward, Mary,** and **Charles**.

1836: *removed from Leckhampton to Bisley.* [PS/CH/RA/2/4:17; entered incorrectly in register; see PS/CH/RA/2/2:78).]

36028RO: Wed 24 Aug 1836 (third examination 6 June 1836) – **Ann Clarke** (also **Clark**), wife of Richard Clarke, and daughter, **Caroline**, inmates of Cheltenham Workhouse; also Mary Ann Clarke, and Richard Clarke relating to the settlement of daughter-in-law and wife Ann Clarke. *Mary Ann Clarke*: That she is the mother of Richard Clarke the Husband of Ann Clarke – that the said Richard Clarke was born in the Outparish of Saint Philip and Jacob [Bristol] in the County of Gloucester – that she believes the said Richard Clarke has never himself gained a settlement.

That her Husband James Clarke was Apprenticed to one [blank] Wilcox Shoemaker and that he has been living in the City of Hereford for the space of eight years last past and to the best of her belief the said James Clarke has done nothing since his apprenticeship to gain a settlement elsewhere than in the Parish of Saint Peter in Hereford [mark] [From earlier unsigned examination of 2 June 1836] That her husband James Clarke rented a house in Cheltenham for seven [? obscure] years and a half at ten pounds for the last four years and the husband of the said Ann Clarke lived with them during the whole time

Ann Clarke: That she was married to Richard Clarke in the Parish Church of Cheltenham on the 16th day of March 1835 – that her said husband as she believes has lived in Cheltenham for the last seventeen years – that she has heard her Husband say he was born in Bristol – that she has one child by the said Richard Clarke which was born in Cheltenham about seven months since named Caroline   that her said Husband left her about seventeen weeks ago and that she hath become chargeable to the Parish of Cheltenham aforesaid [mark] [From earlier unsigned examination of 2 June 1836] she this Deponent hath not heard and does not know where her said husband was born

Richard Clarke: [Magistrates' register] That he was born as he has heard & believes in the City of Bristol – That when he was about 2 years of age his father James Clarke left Bristol and went to Hereford to live, where he had been apprenticed – That this deponent has not lived with his said father since he was 2 years of age – That his father now lives at Hereford – That about 12 or 14 years ago his said father was removed by the Parish of Cheltenham where he then lived and where this deponent's mother had become chargeable, to the Parish of Saint Peter Hereford – That his said father has resided in the said Parish of S^t. Peter ever since – That this deponent does not believe his said father has done any act to gain a Settlement since his apprenticeship – That this deponent was born as he believes in wedlock – That he has a Wife named Ann and an infant Child named Caroline aged 4 months   That his said wife and child are become chargeable to the said Parish of Cheltenham [mark]

1836: *removed to St Peter, City of Hereford, Heref (husband's settlement); AC and daughter Caroline admitted to Cheltenham Workhouse 4 Aug, after desertion of husband Richard; discharged after 7 weeks and 2 days, and readmitted on 24 Sept, when AC again "Pregnant", with son Richard (after three days they were removed to Hereford (G/CH/60/1)).* **1841:** *(RETURNED) AC (aged 25; shoe binder) and children Caroline (5), and Richard (4) lived in Newman's Place, Cheltenham (HO107/353/16/8/11) (1851 census shows AC born at Brockhampton). [PS/CH/RA/2/4:19 (copies at PS/CH/RA/2/3:384-6, 394-5). Removal expenses for "Ann Clarke" to Hereford Union (D4178).]*

36029RO: Wed Aug 31 Aug 1836 – **Elizabeth Jones**, widow of George Jones, and four children, **Mary, Caroline, William, Sarah Ann**: That in the year one thousand eight hundred and twelve she was married to the said George Jones at Newland in the Forest of Dean in the said County by whom she has four Children now living namely, Mary Aged twenty two years who is now in a very sickly state of health   Caroline aged eleven years – William aged five years and Sarah Ann aged two years – that her and her late Husband lived in a House which her Husband rented of Mr William Verrinder situate in the Hamlet of Barton Saint Mary in the said County in the year one thousand eight hundred and eighteen for the space of two years – that the rent was Twenty eight Pounds and her Husband paid a years rent and upwards – that in the year one thousand eight hundred and twenty one she was removed with her family (her Husband then being confined in Gloucester Prison for Debt) by an order of removal from this Parish to the said Hamlet of Barton Saint Mary and there received weekly relief from the Overseers for a considerable time and was acknowledged to be a Parishioner there – that her said late Husband has done no other Act to gain a

settlement elsewhere than in the aforesaid Hamlet of Barton Saint Mary and that she and her said four Children are now chargeable to the said Parish of Cheltenham 31st day of August 1836
1836: *removed to Barton St Mary in Gloucester (husband's settlement).* **1841:** *EJ (aged 45; laundress) lived with three younger children, Caroline, William, and Sarah Ann in Moorend Rd, Leckhampton (HO107/353/18/24/17).* [PS/CH/RA/2/4:18 (earlier copy at PS/CH/RA/2/3:396).]

36030SE: Fri 16 Sept 1836 – **Esther** (also **Hester) Harvey**, single woman, inmate of Cheltenham Workhouse: That she was born in the Parish of Cam in the said County of Gloucester in or about the Year one thousand Eight hundred and sixteen. – When She was about Eleven Years of Age She was hired as a Servant by Thomas Arnold of the Parish of Cheltenham aforesaid Fruiterer for a Year at the Wages of six pence a Week. – That she duly served the said Thomas Arnold the whole of such Year and continued in his service nearly another Year. – That she hath not done any Act to gain a Settlement since the said hiring and service and that she had lately become and now is chargeable to the said Parish of Cheltenham [signed]
1836: *removal unlikely: place of settlement probably acknowledged as Cheltenham; EH (aged 20; "Pregnant") admitted to Cheltenham Workhouse 10 Sept; discharged after two weeks (G/CH/60/1); illegitimate male child William born 3 Oct at workhouse (G/CH/67/1).* **1837:** *William buried at New Burial Ground, Cheltenham, 16 May.* **1840:** *EH, servant living in Cheltenham, married Matthew Mann (painter and glazier) 31 May at St John's Church, Gloucester.* **1841:** *the couple (both aged 30) lived in Sherborne St, Gloucester.* [PS/CH/RA/2/3:397.]

36031SE: [undated: 16 – 21 Sept 1836] – **James Johnson**: That he is about thirty six Years of Age but that he cannot tell where he was born. – That about [incomplete]
1836: *removal uncertain: examination form incomplete.* [PS/CH/RA/2/3:398; text struck out.]

36032RO: Wed 21 Sept 1836 – **Hannah Tombs**, spinster: That she is about 64 Years of Age That She is the Daughter of John Tombs formerly of Northleach in the same County Glazier That She was born and Christened at Northleach aforesaid where are Father was then living and settled   That She lived there until She was about ten or eleven Years old   That She then went to live with her Uncle John Butler who resided at N°s 40 and 42 Wells Close [= Wellclose] Square in London Haberdasher, with whom she lived many Years and until he died   That she afterwards continued to live with his Son who succeeded him in business on the same premises   That she lived with her said Uncle and Cousin altogether 40 Years and upwards and during the whole of such time she was never hired nor received any Wages but She worked as a Domestic and had a Little Money occasionally given to her by them – That they purchased all the Clothes she had during the whole of the time and not having been hired She always felt herself quite at liberty to leave them whenever she pleased without being liable to be called to any account for so doing – About 12 Years ago She left London and came to live in Cheltenham with her brother Roberts Tombs Haymaker at his request with whom she lived about six Years when he died   She has ever since lived with his Widow but never was hired by nor received any Wages from either of them but they found her Clothes and other necessaries   That she has always considered Northleach (the place of her birth) to be her to only legal place of settlement and that she is now chargeable to the said Parish of Cheltenham [mark]
1836: *to be removed to Northleach (father's settlement), but died before removal; buried at New Burial Ground, Cheltenham 7 Oct, aged 64.* [PS/CH/RA/2/4:19 (copy PS/CH/RA/2/3:399-400); order suspended as pauper unfit to travel. Removal expenses for "Tombs" to Northleach (D4178); expenses for "funeral H Tombs" (D4178).]

36033SE: Wed 5 Oct 1836 – **Mary Haddington**, with four children **Owen, Ellen, James**, and **Mary Ann**: That she is the Wife of Owen Haddington – that the said Owen Haddington was as she has heard and believes born at Cork in the Kingdom of Ireland and that she has never done any thing to gain a Settlement at any place in England – that she the said Mary Haddington was born in or about the year one thousand seven hundred and ninety three at Dublin in the Kingdom of Ireland and that she was married to the said Owen Haddington at Dublin about 25 years ago

and that she has never done any Act to gain a Settlement in any Parish in England – that she has four Children by her said Husband Owen Haddington aged 9 years Ellen Haddington aged six years – James Haddington aged four years – and Mary Ann Haddington aged fourteen months that her said Husband has deserted her and she is now become chargeable to the Parish of Cheltenham [mark]
1836: *removed to Ireland (presumed).* [PS/CH/RA/2/3:401.]

36034RO: Thurs 24 Nov 1836 – **Daniel Fluck**.
[PS/CH/RA/2/4:20; see **36036RO**.]

36035RO: Thurs 24 Oct [probably Nov] 1836 – **Elizabeth Granger**, single woman, inmate of Cheltenham Workhouse: That she is about forty eight years of age and was born in the Parish of Grittleton in the County of Wilts where her father who was a labourer named John Granger was legally settled as she hath always understood and believes

That she this Examinant never was a hired Servant nor ever did any Act whatever to gain a legal Settlement and that she is now chargeable to the said Parish of Cheltenham. [mark]
1836: *EG admitted to Cheltenham Workhouse 22 Oct, aged 48, "Pregnant","Ill & Destitute" (G/CH/60/1); removed to Grittleton, Wilts (father's settlement).* [PS/CH/RA/2/4:21 (copy at PS/CH/RA/2/3:402); order suspended as pauper unfit to travel. Removal expenses for "E Granger" to Grittleton, Wilts (D4178).]

36036RO: Thurs 24 Nov 1836 – **Daniel Fluck**: [That] he was born in the parish of Stroud in this County where his Parents were legally settled – I am now about forty five years of age – about thirty two years ago I was Apprenticed to Sampson Peyton of Stroud aforesaid Cordwainer for 7 years as indoor apprentice - I served about 3 years of the time and then went to Sea

I was apprenticed by the Mercers Company in London and a Premium of £10 was paid with me.

I remained at Sea until the 11th September 1815 and then returned to Stroud and followed my business of Shoemaker - I have never rented a Tenement of 10^l a year or upwards or done any other Act to gain a Settlement – I am now chargeable to the Parish of Cheltenham – [mark]
1836: *to be removed to Stroud (apprenticeship), but died before removal; DF died 30 Dec at Cheltenham Workhouse.* **1837:** *buried (aged 45) at New Burial Ground, Cheltenham 2 Jan.* [PS/CH/RA/2/4:22 (copy at PS/CH/RA/2/3:405); order suspended as pauper unfit to travel.]

36037RO: Thurs 24 Nov 1836 – **Thomas Adams,** inmate of Cheltenham Workhouse: That he was born in the Parish of Ellingham in the County of Norfolk where his Parents were legally settled – that his Father worked for Mr John Magett who was a Master Miller at Ellingham as his Foreman for many years and kept Cows of his own – that his Father rented a small Meadow and an Orchard as well as a House and had a right of Common for Pasturage of Cattle in Ellingham – that when he was a young man he was hired to a Mr Baker of Ditchingham in Norfolk for a year but did not remain with him longer than eleven months when he left on account of illness – that he did not return to his said Service – that he has never done any Act to gain a settlement in his own right and is now become chargeable to the Parish of Cheltenham – that he is about sixty four years of age [mark]
1836: *TA (aged 64; miller, very "ill & Destitute") admitted to Cheltenham Workhouse 25 Oct (G/CH/60/1); removed to Ellingham, Norfolk (father's settlement).* [PS/CH/RA/2/4:23 (copy at PS/CH/RA/2/3:406); order suspended as pauper unfit to travel. Removal expenses for "T. Adams" to Ellingham, Norfolk £9/17/2 30 (Mar 1837: D4178).]

36038RO: Sat 26 Nov 1836 – the three infant children, **Sarah Ann**, **John**, and **Harriet Farley** of Jane Jordan of Cheltenham, wife of Michael Jordan, 28 Malvern Place, by former husband Samuel Farley: That she is about 32 years of age – That she was born in the Parish of Halling [= Hawling] in this County where her Father was legally settled – That about sixteen years ago she was married to Samuel Farley of Halling aforesaid Labourer and resided in that Parish with her Husband about two years – That about fourteen years ago she this Examinant and her said Husband left the said parish of Halling and went to live in the Parish of Swindon in the said County where her said

Husband was lastly legally settled he having acquired such Settlement by Servitude with Mr Thomas Newman ffarmer of that place - That they continued to reside in the said Parish of Swindon until the death of her said Husband which happened about eleven years ago – that during their residence at Swindon aforesaid they were relieved at various times by the Parish Officers there and she this Examinant continue to receive such relief for and on account of her said Children until within about nine months ago – that she this Examinant has three Children by her said deceased Husband (namely, Sarah Aged about 14 years – John Aged about 12 years – and Harriet aged about 11 years) all of whom are now chargeable to the said Parish of Cheltenham [mark]

1836: *removed to Swindon (mother's settlement).* **1841:** *(RETURNED) Michael Jordan (aged 45; labourer) and Jane Jordan (35) lived with four children and Harriet (16) from Jane's previous marriage, in Elm St, Cheltenham; Sarah Farley (18) was servant living in Stanhope St.* [PS/CH/RA/2/4:24 (copy at PS/CH/RA/2/3:403. Removal expenses for "Hill Johnson & Jordan" 1/11 (30 Mar 1837: D4178). See Gray **446** (Samuel Farley: 4 Feb 1823).]

36039RO: Sat 26 Nov 1836 – Mary Page, wife of William Page of Cheltenham, marble mason and mother of **James Whiting**: That she was born at Bisley in the County of Gloucester and that her maiden name was Whiting - that she was the Daughter of Robert Whiting of Bisley aforesaid and that he was legally settled at Bisley – that on the sixteenth day of September 1828 she was put to Bed of the said James Whiting who is illegitimate and was born in the Parish of Bisley – that in the month of October 1828 Examinant attended before the Magistrates sitting at Stroud for the purpose of deposing to the Father of such Child which she accordingly did and an order of affiliation was duly made on such party – that James Moore of Cheltenham Dancing Master was the Father of such Child – that Examinant has since been married to William Page of Cheltenham marble mason and has several children by him all whom are chargeable to the Parish of Cheltenham. That she has regularly received pay from the Parish of Bisley on account of the said James Whiting up to the month of April last past and that the said James Whiting is now chargeable to the Parish of Cheltenham [mark]

1836: *removed to Bisley (father's settlement): see* **42012RO** *(Mary Page: 7 Feb 1842) for further information.* [PS/CH/RA/2/4:25 (copy at PS/CH/RA/2/3:407-8).]

36040RO: Thurs 1 Dec 1836 – **John Northam**: That about sixteen years ago he was hired by the Reverend Joseph Cheston of the College Green in the Parish of Saint Mary de Lode in the City of Gloucester as Footman at the wages of Thirty Pounds a year and that he served the whole of such year – that he has since attended before the late James Wood Esquire when Mayor of Gloucester for the purpose of being examined as to his Settlement and that an order was thereupon made on the said Parish of Saint Mary de Lode to make him a weekly payment which was done for a considerable time and that since he has occasionally been relieved by the Parish Officers of the said Parish and that he has also been received in the Workhouse and supplied with medical attendance when ill – that he has done no Act to gain a Settlement in any other Parish and that he is not chargeable to the Parish of Cheltenham [mark]

1836: *JN (aged 61) admitted to Cheltenham Workhouse 1 Dec, "Out of Work" and "Destitute" (G/CH/60/1); removed to St Mary de Lode, City of Gloucester (hiring and service).* [PS/CH/RA/2/4:26 (copy at PS/CH/RA/2/3:409-10). Removal expenses for "Northam" to Gloucester (30 Mar 1837: D4178).]

36041SE: [undated: 1-8 Dec 1836] – **Ellen Driscol**, widow, regarding the settlement of daughters **Mary** (aged about 13) and **Catharine** (aged about 9): That she was born at Clanakilkie [= Clonakilty] in the County of Cork Ireland   that about fifteen years since She was married to John Driscol of Clanakilkie at Clanakilkie in the County of Cork, that she has two Children by the said John Driscol namely the said Mary Driscol and Catharine Driscol   that the said John Driscol has never done any thing to gain a Settlement in England   that the said John Driscol died at Cheltenham on the 19th day of November last past and that she this Examinant and her said two Children are become chargeable to the Parish of Cheltenham   That this Examinant has never done any Act to gain a settlement in England [mark]

1836: *removed to Bristol for Ireland.* [PS/CH/RA/2/3:411. Removal expenses for "Driscol Pauper to Bristol" (D4178).]

36042SE: [undated: 1-8 Dec 1836] – **Charlotte Barnes**, wife of Richard Barnes: [no text].
1836: *removal uncertain: examination form incomplete.* [PS/CH/RA/2/3:421; introduction struck out.]

36043RO: Thurs 8 Dec 1836 – **John Bastin**: That he is now aged about 62 years – that he was born in the Parish of Charlton Kings – that about thirty five years since he was hired by Mr Baylis of Highleadon near Gloucester as his Carter at the wages of Ten Pounds by the year and that he remained in his service for the period of five years – that about thirty three years ago he was married to Mary Holder of Highleadon aforesaid at the Parish Church of Rudford of which Parish Highleadon is a Hamlet – that he had one Child by his said wife named Eliza now aged about thirty two years who is now married and settled in the Parish of Cheltenham   that he and his Wife lived with Mr Baylis for about three years after they were married and that his wife has been dead about thirty years – that he maintained and supported his said Daughter till she was of the age of 9 years when she went to live with his Brother Richard Bastin at the Parish of Charlton Kings and that when she was about twelve years old she was hired by Mr John Greening of Charlton Kings for a twelvemonth to take care of his Children – that since his Daughter was so hired he has never contributed to her support in any way whatever – that about nineteen years ago he was hired by Mr John Proctor of Pirton in the County of Worcester as his Carter for one year at the wages of Ten Pounds and that he lived in such Service the entire twelvemonth and received his wages – that since such Period he has done no Act to gain a settlement in any other Parish and that he is now chargeable to the Parish of Cheltenham [mark]
1836: *removed to Pirton, Worcs (hiring and service).* **1841:** *JB (aged 65; agricultural labourer) lived alone in Pirton (HO107/1206/19/5/17).* [PS/CH/RA/2/4:27 (copy at PS/CH/RA/2/3:413-14). Removal expenses for "Bastin" to Pirton, Worcs (30 Mar 1837: D4178).]

36044RO: Sat 31 Dec 1836 – **William Bousher** (also **Bowsher**): That he is now aged thirty seven years or thereabouts – that he was born in the Parish of Walcot in the City of Bath and that he is the son of John Bowsher formerly of Saint Ann's Court in Walcot aforesaid Coachman and who was legally settled in such Parish – that when he was about eleven years old he was admitted into the Blue Coat School at Bath and was apprenticed by the said School when he was about fourteen years old to one William Brown of the Parish of Walcot aforesaid Cabinet Maker with whom he remained six months when the said William Brown absconded from Bath – that he this Examinant hath never since done any Act to gain a settlement in any other Parish or Place and that he is now chargeable to the Parish of Cheltenham [signed] W^m. Bousher
1836: *to be removed to Walcot, Bath, Som (father's settlement), but died before removal.* **1837:** *(RETURNED) WB died at Cheltenham Workhouse 5 Feb (buried New Burial Ground, Cheltenham, 8 Feb).* [PS/CH/RA/2/4:28 (copy at PS/CH/RA/2/3:415); order suspended as pauper unfit to travel.]

The official crest used on Cheltenham Removal Orders from 1841. The modern typeface and artistic design replace the earlier more stolid and formulaic design

1837

37001SE: Sat 7 Jan 1837 – **John Neale**: That he was born in the Parish of Athlone in the County of Westmeath in the Kingdom of Ireland and that he has never done any thing to gain a Settlement in England and that he is now chargeable to the Parish of Cheltenham [unsigned]
1837: *removed to Ireland.* [PS/CH/RA/2/3:416. Expenses: "Relief in kind" for "Neale" 2/6 (7 Mar 1837: D4178), and removal expenses for "Neale – Irish Pauper" 3/4 (30 Mar 1837: D4178).]

37002RO: Mon 9 Jan 1837 – Charlotte Belgrove, regarding the settlement of three nieces **Mary Ann** (10 years old), **Charlotte** (7), and **Emily Cruze** (4), children of John Cruze: That the Father John Cruze left and deserted the said three Children in the month of February one thousand eight hundred and thirty five, that the said John Cruze was legally settled in the Parish of Great Shurdington in the County of Gloucester by being the Owner of a certain Freehold Messuage and Lands situate in the Parish of Great Shurdington and that the said Mary Ann Cruze Charlotte Cruze and Emely Cruze are now chargeable to the Parish of Cheltenham [mark]
1837: *removed to Gt Shurdington (father's settlement).* **1841:** *(RETURNED) CB lived with husband and five children in Naunton Fields, Cheltenham (HO107/353/12/43/22); John Cruze worked as brickmaker and lived with four daughters (including the three listed) in the Heath, Willenhall, Wolverhampton, Staffs (HO107/985/3/13/17).* **1842:** *Emma (10) and Charlotte Cruz (9) were inmates of Charlton Kings Workhouse for children (Cheltenham Union), while father John Cruze was "in the Hospital".* **1843:** *Emma and Charlotte lived in workhouse (discharged Sept) (G/CH/60/2).* **1851:** *John Cruze, widower, worked as drain-pipe maker and lived with three daughters in back West Lane, Wick and Abson (HO107/1956/233/22).* [PS/CH/RA/2/4:29 (copy at PS/CH/RA/2/3:417).]

37003RO: 9 Jan 1837 – **Elizabeth Hancock,** single woman: That in the month of April one thousand eight hundred and thirty two she was hired by Thomas Edwards of the Parish of Prestbury Esquire as an indoor Servant at the wages of Ten Pounds a year – that she remained in his Service till he removed to Cheltenham in the month of December one thousand eight hundred and thirty five or January one thousand eight hundred and thirty six and that she continued in his Service till the month of June last past – that she is now chargeable to Parish of Cheltenham [mark]
1837: *removed to Prestbury (hiring and service);* on 8 Feb EH gave birth to illegitimate son, John, at Cheltenham Workhouse (G/CH/67/1); he died after 4 days. [PS/CH/RA/2/4:30 (copy at PS/CH/RA/2/3:418). Removal expenses for "Hancock &c" (D4178).]

37004RO: 9 Jan 1837 – **James Boustead** (also **Bowstead**), wife **Elizabeth** (also **Betsy, Eliza**), and three children **Elizabeth** (aged 6), **Joseph** (4), and **Mar**y (ten weeks), residing in Waterloo Place, Cheltenham: That in the month of December one thousand eight hundred and twenty five he took of William Moore of the Parish of Upton upon Severn in the County of Worcester a Messuage and Garden situate near the Pig market in the Parish of Upton upon Severn at the rent of Eleven Guineas Per annum and occupied the same for the space of one year and a half during which he was duly rated to the relief of the Poor and paid the rent and rates ["taxes" added] – that he has not since done any thing to gain a legal Settlement – that he was married to his said wife at Worcester in the year one thousand eight hundred and twenty eight and that he has by her three Children namely, the above mentioned Elizabeth Joseph and Mary and that they are now all become chargeable to the Parish of Cheltenham [signed]
1836: *daughter Mary baptised at Upton upon Severn, Worcs 25 Dec (though 1851 census states birthplace as Cheltenham).* **1837:** *removed to Upton upon Severn (renting).* **1838:** *(RETURNED) son Robert born at Cheltenham.* **1841:** *JB (aged 35; independent means) lived with wife Eliza (30), and children Joseph (10), Elizabeth (8), Mary (4), and two younger sons in Pilley Field, Leckhampton (HO107/353/18/53/11).* **1851:** *the family lived in Stanhope St, Cheltenham, where James (aged 43) and eldest son Joseph (19) were journeyman carpenters (HO107/1973/502/23).* [PS/CH/RA/2/4:31 (copy at PS/CH/RA/2/3:419). Removal expenses for "Boustead & family" (D4178).]

37005RO: Thurs 12 Jan 1837 – Martha Johnson, residing in parish of Saint Philip and Jacob, Bristol, relating to the settlement of son **James Johnson**, wife **Elizabeth** (also **Eliza**), and three children **Martha**, **William**, and **Mary**: That she is the Widow of Robert Johnson of the Parish of Saint Philip and Jacob in the County of Gloucester Labourer – that she was married to the said Robert Johnson at the Parish of Stapleton in the County of Gloucester and that the said Robert Johnson was legally settled in the said Parish of Saint Philip and Jacob – that from the Period of her Marriage with the said Robert Johnson till his death which happened about thirteen years ago they resided in the Parish of Saint Philip and Jacob and that her Husband received relief from the said Parish for some time previous to his decease and that she this Examinant is now living in Lamb Street in the same Parish and received relief from the Parish – that she is the Mother of James Johnson by her said Husband Robert Johnson and that she was born in Lamb Street in the said Parish of Saint Philip and Jacob about thirty four years since – that her said Son was never apprenticed nor has he done any Act which she is aware of to obtain a settlement himself – that her said son was married to his present Wife Elizabeth about ten years since, and that by her he has three Children Martha aged about eight years, William aged about four years, and Mary aged about one year all of whom are now chargeable to the Parish of Cheltenham [mark]
1837: *removed to St Philip and Jacob, Bristol (father's settlement).* **1841:** *(RETURNED) JJ (aged 38; painter), wife Elizabeth (39), Martha, William, and Mary, plus two further children, lived in Sidney St, Cheltenham (HO107/353/3/18/30); all children born at Cheltenham.* [PS/CH/RA/2/4:32 (copy at PS/CH/RA/2/3:420-1). Removal expenses for "Hill Johnson & Jordan" 1/11 (30 Mar 1837 (D4178).]

37006SE: Thurs 19 Jan 1837 – **Daniel Murphy**, wife **Mary**, and two children, **Denney** and **Michael**: That he was born in the City of Cork in the Kingdom of Ireland about thirty two years ago; and that about ten months since he came over to England and that he has never done any act to gain a Settlement in England, that he has a Wife Mary Murphy and two Children Denney Aged about two years and Michael aged about five weeks, and that they are now chargeable to the Parish of Cheltenham [mark]
1837: *perhaps removed to Ireland; perhaps the DM fined by Cheltenham magistrates later in year for being drunk and disorderly in the High St, and assaulting police (*Cheltenham Chron. *13 July).* [PS/CH/RA/2/3:422.]

37007RO: Thurs 26 Jan 1837 – **Christian Smith**, wife of William Smith, labourer: That she was born in the Parish of Bradfield in the County of Suffolk in the year 1800 where her Father John Vickers who was a Shoemaker lived – that she was married to her present Husband the said William Smith at Saint Mary Abbots Church in the Parish of Kensington on the fourteenth of February last, and this Examinant has been told by her said Husband and verily believes that he was born at Fornham Saint Genevieve in the County of Suffolk where his Father was legally settled and that he hath never done any act to gain a settlement himself – that in the month of December last her said Husband deserted her and she is now chargeable to the Parish of Cheltenham [signed]
1837: *removed to Fornham St Genevieve, Suffolk (husband's settlement).* **1841:** *CS probably reverted to her maiden name and lived (aged 40) as servant at Rainsford Lodge, Chelmsford (HO107/325/9/3/1).* [PS/CH/RA/2/4:33 (copy at PS/CH/RA/2/3:423).]

37008RO: Thurs 26 Jan 1837 – **Job Twining** (also **Twyning**), shoemaker: That he is the Son of Samuel Twining and Esther his wife formerly of Minchinhampton in this County – that he was born at a place called Blackditch [= Black Ditch] in the said Parish of Minchinhampton and is now about 56 years of age – that when he this Examinant was about seven years old his Father was drowned in the Stroud Canal and this Examinant's Mother was left with five children – that she went before the Magistrates at Painswick for the purpose of proving her Parish when an order was made for her and her children to be removed to the Parish of Painswick in this County (to which Parish this Examinant's Father belonged he having been apprenticed and served his time to a Weaver there) from which Parish they received relief for a length of time – that about three years ago this Examinant was living in Charles Street in the Parish of Leckhampton in this

County from whence he was removed by an Order of the Magistrates of Cheltenham to the said Parish of Painswick and was placed in the Workhouse there where he remained a considerable time – that he has not since done any Act to gain a Settlement elsewhere – and that he is now chargeable to the Parish of Cheltenham [signed]

1805: *JT married Leah Phillips in Woodchester, near Stroud.* **1834:** *JT removed from Leckhampton to Painswick: see* **34024SE** *(JT: 25 Mar).* **1837:** *(RETURNED)* ***removed to Painswick (father's settlement).*** **1838:** *JT buried at Minchinhampton 23 Jan, aged 57, from Minchinhampton Workhouse.* **1841:** *Leah (aged 60; cloth-worker) lived with son Samuel (30; also cloth-worker; by 1861 shoemaker) in Rodborough, near Stroud (HO107/362/8/19/5).* **1851:** *Leah lived in Painswick.* [PS/CH/RA/2/4:34 (copies at PS/CH/RA/2/3:424 and P244 OV 3/3/4/9). Removal expenses for "J. Twining" to Stroud (D4178). See **34024SE** (JT: 25 Mar 1834).]

37009RO: Thurs 26 Jan 1837 – **William Collings** (also **Collins**), stonemason, wife **Mary**, and six children **William**, **Frederick**, **Mary Ann**, **Eliza**, **Catharine**, and **Henry**: That he was born in the Parish of Martin Hussington [properly Martin Hussingtree] in the County of Worcester where his Father Edward Collings who is a Labourer now resides and is legally settled – that about thirteen years ago he was married to his present Wife Mary at Liverpool in the County of Lancaster by whom he has six Children (namely, William now aged about twelve years – Frederick aged about ten years – Mary Ann aged about six years – Eliza aged about four years, Catharine aged about one year and nine months and Henry aged about three months all of whom are now chargeable to the Parish of Cheltenham – that he never was apprenticed, nor has he ever done any act to gain a settlement in his own right [signed]

1837: ***removed to Martin Hussingtree, Worcs (father's settlement).*** [PS/CH/RA/2/4:35 (copy at PS/CH/RA/2/3:425). Removal expenses for "Collins" to "Martin Essington" £2/18/4 (30 Mar 1837: D4178).]

37010RO: Thurs 26 Jan 1837 – **Susan Lippiatt** (also **Lyppiatt**), single woman: That she is the Daughter of Peter Lippiatt Labourer and that she was born at Almondsbury in the County of Gloucester about 17 years ago who was legally settled at Almondsbury – that from her earliest recollection she was living in the Workhouse at Almondsbury – that when she was about ten years old she was hired by the Parish Officers to one Jacob Thomas of Almondsbury as his Servant and she lived with him three years – that when she left his Service she returned to the Poor house and that she has never done anything to gain a Settlement in her own right and that she is now chargeable to the Parish of Cheltenham [mark]

1836: *perhaps the SL imprisoned for two days 6-7 Dec at Glos Epiphany Sessions for stealing five pounds and a half sovereign.* **1837:** ***removed to Almondsbury (near Bristol) (father's settlement).*** [PS/CH/RA/2/4:3 (copy at PS/CH/RA/2/3:426); order suspended 23 Feb – 1 Apr as pauper unfit to travel. Removal expenses for "S. Lyppiatt" to Almonsbury (30 Mar 1837: D4178).]

37011RO: Thurs 26 Jan 1837 – **Sarah Pearce** (also **Pearse**), widow, inmate of Cheltenham Workhouse: That she was born in the parish of Shiffnell [= Shifnal] in the County of Salop – that about 26 years since she was married to Henry Pearce at Old Bathwick Church in the City of Bath – that about 9 years since her Husband died – that she does not know and never heard to what Parish her Husband belonged – that about thirty years since she was hired by [blank] Sapt at the wages of 10^l. a year and she lived with him at N° 9 Old Crescent in the Parish of Walcot in the City of Bath for two years, and received her wages – that since that period she has done no act to gain a settlement in her own right – [mark]

1836: *SP admitted to Cheltenham Workhouse 10 Sept (aged 69; widow, of Wesleyan Methodist religion, "not Able"); discharged after two weeks and immediately readmitted ("Idiot"), discharged, and readmitted 1 Dec (G/CH/60/1).* **1837:** ***removed to Walcot, City of Bath, Som (hiring and service).*** **1839:** *SP died at workhouse (buried at Walcot, Bath 5 July, aged 71).* [PS/CH/RA/2/4:37 (copy at PS/CH/RA/2/3:427). Removal expenses for "S. Pearce" to Bath (30 Mar 1837: D4178).]

37012RO: Thurs 16 Feb 1837 – **Ann Probyn** (also **Probben, Probin***)*, single woman, and infant daughter: That she was born in the Parish of Upton-Bishop in the County of Hereford where her Father William Probyn Labourer resided for many years and was legally settled – that in the month of December 1833 she was hired as an indoor Servant to a M^r. Wilson of Montpellier Villas in Cheltenham aforesaid at the wages of Six Pounds – that she remained in such Service for thirteen months and received her wages – that she has never done any other Act to gain a Settlement in her own right – that on the 21st January last she this Examinant was delivered of a Female Bastard Child and is now chargeable to the Parish of Cheltenham [mark]

1837: *to be removed to Upton Bishop, Heref (father's settlement), but transferred to Gloucester Asylum.*
1841: *AP not living with parents William and Ann Probyn in Upton Bishop (HO107/421/21/23/3).* [PS/CH/RA/2/4:38 (copy at PS/CH/RA/2/3:428). Removal expenses for "A Probin" to Gloucester Asylum 1/1 (30 Mar 1837: D4178).]

37013RO: Thurs 16 Feb 1837 – **James Smith**, labourer, wife **Ann**, and four children **John**, **James**, **Henry**, and **William**: That he is 29 years of age – that he was born in the Parish of Catherston Lew[e]ston in the County of Dorset to which Parish his Father belonged – that his Father died when he was very young, and he was then taken into the Poor house of such last named Parish and maintained there – that he has never done any act to acquire a settlement in his own right – that about ten years ago he was married to Ann Mustoe in the Parish Church of Cheltenham by whom he has three Children, namely, John, aged about nine years – James aged about six years and Henry aged about three years – that his wife died about nine months since – that about six months since he was married to his present Wife Ann (Summers) in Cheltenham, and that she has an illegitimate male Child William, aged about two years, and that he and his said three Children and his said Wife and her illegitimate Child are now chargeable to the Parish of Cheltenham [mark]

1837: *removed to Catherston Leweston, Dorset (father's settlement).* [PS/CH/RA/2/4:39 (copy at PS/CH/RA/2/3:429). Removal expenses for "J Smith &c" to Catherston Leweston £9/17/- (June 1837: D4178).]

37014RO: Thurs 2 Mar 1837 – **John Tate Harrison**, labourer: That he is the Son of Thomas Harrison who kept the Bengal Wharf Limehouse Hole in the Parish of Bermondsey in the County of Surrey and was legally settled in that Parish   that his Father died when he was very young when he was taken by an Uncle with whom he remained till he was about 14 years old when he went to Sea   that he has never done any act to gain a Settlement in his own right and that he is now chargeable to the Parish of Cheltenham [signed]

1837: *removed to Bermondsey, Surrey (father's settlement).* [PS/CH/RA/2/4:40 (copy at PS/CH/RA/2/3:432); pauper deemed unfit to travel until 1 Apr 1837. Removal expenses for "J. T. Harrison" to Bermondsy 2/- (30 Mar 1837: D4178).]

37015RO: Thurs 2 Mar 1837 – **Sarah Stevens**, widow: That she is the Widow of James Stevens who as this Examinant believes was born in the Parish of Bisley in the said County of Gloucester where her [*sic*] Father was legally settled

that to the best of this Examinant's belief her said Husband never did any Act to gain a Settlement

that in the year 1834 her said Husband was examined before the Magistrates at Cheltenham as to the place of his Settlement and was thereupon removed with this Examinant to the said Parish of Bisley from which they received parochial relief for some time   that shortly afterwards this Examinant and her Husband Came to Cheltenham where her said Husband died on the eighth day of February instant – that this Examinant believes her place of Settlement is at Bisley aforesaid and that she is now chargeable to the said Parish of Cheltenham [mark]

1837: *removed to Bisley (husband's settlement):* see **52001RO** (26 Jan 52) *for further information.* [PS/CH/RA/2/4:4 (copy at PS/CH/RA/2/3:430). Removal expenses for "S Stevens" to Bisley 16/6 (June 1837: D4178).]

37016SE: Thurs 2 Mar 1837 – **Mary Murphy**, with daughter **Mary**: That she was born in the County of Cork in that part of the United Kingdom called Ireland, where her Husband was also born – that about twenty two years ago this Examinant was married to the said Timothy Murphy in Ireland by whom she hath four Children now living, namely Michael aged twenty years or thereabouts – Mary aged sixteen years or thereabouts Hannah aged twelve years or thereabouts and John aged ten years or thereabouts – that all her said Children reside in Ireland, except the said Mary who is now living in Cheltenham – that her said Husband hath done no Act whereby to gain a Settlement in that part of the United Kingdom called England and that she this Examinant hath actually become and is now chargeable to the Parish of Cheltenham in the County of Gloucester aforesaid [mark]

1837: *removed to Ireland.* [PS/CH/RA/2/3:431. Removal expenses for "Murphy. Irish Pauper" £2/18/4 (30 Mar 1837: D4178). See **37051SE** (daughter MM[?]: 5 Aug 1837).]

37017RO: Thurs 2 Mar 1837 – **Elizabeth Coles**, single woman: That she is the Daughter of Joseph Coles of Standish in the County of Gloucester Labourer, and was born there about twenty years since   that in the year 1830 she was hired by M^{rs}. Agg of the Golden Heart Inn in the Parish of Painswick as an indoor Servant at the Wages of four pounds a year and that she lived with her nearly four years and received her Wages   that since that period she has done no Act to gain a Settlement and that she is now chargeable to the Parish of Cheltenham [mark]

1837: *removed to Painswick (hiring and service).* [PS/CH/RA/2/4:42 (copies at PS/CH/RA/2/3:433 and P244 OV/3/3/4/10). Removal expenses for "E Coles" to Painswick 16/6 (June 1837: D4178).]

37018RO: Sat 4 Mar 1837 – **James Saunders**: That about 26 years since He was hired by Colonel Thornton of Spye Park in the Parish of Bromham in the County of Wilts as groom at the Wages of twenty Six pounds a year and that he lived in the House, that he remained in Colonel Thorntons Service two years and a half and received his Wages   that since that period He has done no Act to gain a Settlement in his own right and that he is now chargeable to the Parish of Cheltenham [signed]

1837: *removed to Bromham, Wilts (hiring and service).* [PS/CH/RA/2/4:43 (copy at PS/CH/RA/2/3:434), stating that JS resided at 26 Rutland St, (St Paul's), Cheltenham. Removal expenses for "J Saunders to Bromham" £3/15/- (June 1837: D4178).]

37019RO: Thurs 9 Mar 1837 – **John Alsop**, labourer: That he was born at Stoke Orchard in the County of Gloucester about sixty five years ago   that he is the Son of Samuel Alsop who was legally settled in the Parish of Twining   [= Twyning] having there rented and occupied a farm that he was apprenticed to one Charles Roberts in the Parish of Ripple [Worcs] Shoemaker but did not remain with him about [for "above"] Eighteen Months – that he has never done any act to gain a Settlement in his own right and that he is now Chargeable to the Parish of Cheltenham [mark]

1837: *ordered to be removed to Twyning (father's settlement):* *but JA and wife Mary are removed to Ripple, Worcs (see* **37025:** *1 Apr 1837).* [PS/CH/RA/2/4:44 (copy at PS/CH/RA/2/3:435), stating that JA resided at 67 Stanhope St, Cheltenham. Expenses for "Removing J. Allsop [*sic*] Staverton [confused with next: Ripple] 1 [-/-]" (June 1837: D4178).]

37020SE: Thurs 9 Mar 1837 – **Charles Povey**, wife **Sarah**, and two children **Caroline** and **Helena**: That he was born in the Parish of Wootton under Edge [= Wotton-under-Edge] where his Father Charles Povey was legally settled – that he is now 23 years old – that he has a Wife named Sarah, & two Children one named Caroline about twelvemonth [*sic*] old and a Female Child born the 23^d November last, that he has done no Act to gain a Settlement in his own right [mark]

1837: *removed to Wotton-under-Edge (father's settlement):* *see* **43020RO** *(CP: 4 Mar 1843) for further information.* [PS/CH/RA/2/3:436.]

37021SE: [undated: 9-18 Mar 1837] – **Charlotte Weare**, single woman: That she is the Daughter of Robert Weare of Chalford Woolscourer who is legally settled in the Parish of Bisley in the County of Gloucester   that she was born at Chalford on the Sixth day of October 1813 – that she has never done any Act to gain a Settlement in her own right & that she is now chargeable to the Parish of Cheltenham

1837: *removal uncertain: examination form incomplete.* [PS/CH/RA/2/3:437.]

37022RO: Sat 18 Mar 1837 – **Elizabeth Hale**, single woman: That she is the Daughter of Thomas Hale of Ruardean Woodside who was legally settled in the Parish of Blakeney in the

County of Gloucester – that she was born about seventeen years ago – that about three years since her father died leaving her Mother with herself and three other Children – that shortly after her Father died her Mother took two of her Sisters to Blakeney and applied to the Parish Officers there for assistance to Clothe two of her Sisters who were going into Service, and that the Parish Officers did Clothe them – that her Mother died about eighteen Months' since – that Examinant has never done any Act to gain a Settlement in her own right and that she is now chargeable to the Parish of Cheltenham [mark]

1837: *removed to Blakeney (father's settlement).* [PS/CH/RA/2/4:45 (copy at PS/CH/RA/2/3:438). Removal expenses for "E Hale" to Blakeney £1/5/- (June 1837: D4178).]

37023RO: Sat 1 Apr 1837 – **Daniel Davis**, wife **Elizabeth**, and son **Alfred**: That he is the Son of Daniel Davis Labourer who lived at and was settled in the Parish of Kings Stanley in the County of Gloucester and that he was born at Kings Stanley aforesaid on the 7th May 1779   that he was married to his present Wife Elizabeth at Stroud about 18 years since and that by her he has one Son Alfred aged about 7 Years   that he has never done any thing to gain a Settlement in his own right and that he and his said Wife and Son are now Chargeable to the Parish of Cheltenham [mark]

1837: *removed to King's Stanley (father's settlement):* see **47010RO** *(Elizabeth Davis: 6 Mar 1847) for further information on family.* [PS/CH/RA/2/4:46 (copy of examination at PS/CH/RA/2/3:439); order suspended until 29 Apr as pauper unfit to travel.]

37024RO: Sat 1 Apr 1837 – **Thomas Paginton**, wife **Elizabeth**, and daughter **Elizabeth**: That he is the Son of Thomas Paginton Labourer who lived at and was settled in the Parish of Malmesbury in the County of Wilts   that he was born at Malmesbury on the 7th April 1793 and that he has never done any thing to gain a Settlement in his own right

That he was married to his present Wife Elizabeth at Charlton Kings about 5 years since and that he has one Child Elizabeth by a former Wife aged about 13 years   that he his said Wife and Child are Chargeable to the Parish of Cheltenham [mark]

1837: *not removed to Malmesbury, Wilts (father's settlement), as TP died before removal; buried at New Burial Ground, Cheltenham, aged 44, on 1 Aug.* [PS/CH/RA/2/4:4 (copy at PS/CH/RA/2/3:367, where address given as Newman's Place, Cheltenham); order suspended as pauper unfit to travel, but reimposed on wife and daughter 31 July. Removal expenses for "Paynter [*sic*] & daugh[ter]" to Malmesbury £2/4/- (30 Sept 1837: D4178); also "E. Pagington [*sic*]" to Asylum £1/1/- (15 Oct 1838: D4178).]

37025RO: Sat 1 Apr 1837 – **John Alsop** and wife **Mary**: That he is legally settled in the Parish of Ripple in the County of Worcester by having been apprenticed to one Charles Roberts of Ripple Shoe Maker and Served him under the Apprenticeship Indentures upwards of a twelvemonth   that he was Married to his present Wife Mary formerly Mary Cole about 40 years ago at Twyning [= Twining] in the County of Gloucester And that some years since he attended the Magistrates at Upton for the Purpose of deposing to his Place of Settlement when an Order was made on the said Parish of Ripple and that he was taken into the Poor House there and has since received Relief from the said Parish of Ripple   That he has since done no act to gain a Settlement elsewhere and that he and his said Wife are now Chargeable to the Parish of Cheltenham [signed]

1837: *removed to Ripple (apprenticeship) (see* **37019RO***).* [PS/CH/RA/2/4:48 (copy at PS/CH/RA/2/3:441); order suspended until 29 July as pauper unfit to travel.]

37026SE: Sat 1 Apr 1837 – **Mary Blake**, widow: That She is about 63 Years Old and was born at ~~Liverpool~~ Corophin [= Corofin] in the County of ~~Lancaster~~ Clare ~~and that She is the Daughter of John Baker of the same Parish Labourer who as She believes was legally settled there.~~ That about 40 years ago she was married at ~~Liverpool~~ Corophin in the County of Clare to One Thomas Blake who was a Soldier in the 89 Regiment and who was a native of Corophin aforesaid and who died at S[t] Domingo   ~~That she cannot tell to what Parish the said Thomas Blake belonged~~ That for the last 35 Years she has been living with one ~~John~~ Lewis Donelly but that she was never Married to him   That she has never done any thing to gain a Settlement in her own Right in England and that she is now chargeable to the Parish of Cheltenham [mark]

1837: *removed to Ireland (presumed).* [PS/CH/RA/2/3:442.]

37027SE: Sat 1 Apr 1837 – **Mary Ann Roche**, with unnamed child: That She is the Daughter of Miles Roche a Native of Dublin in the Kingdom of Ireland and that She was born at Dublin in the Month of May 1819   that She has never done any thing to gain a Settlement in England and that She is now chargeable to the Parish of Cheltenham – and that she has [an] infant illegitimate Child born one Month since [mark]
1837: *removed to Ireland.* [PS/CH/RA/2/3:443. Removal expenses for "M A Roche" to Cork £2/18/8 (18 Dec 1837: D4178).]

37028RO: Sat 1 Apr 1837: [form blank.] [PS/CH/RA/2/4:49.]

37029RO: Thurs 6 Apr 1837 – **John Lane**, wife **Sarah**, and three children **Mary**, **Hannah**, and **John**: That he is the Son of Edward Lane Butcher who lived at and was legally Settled in the Parish of Staverton in the County of Gloucester and that he was born at Staverton in the year 1794. That he has never done any Act to gain a Settlement in his own right   that he was married at Hampstead [= Hempsted] about 14 years since to his present Wife Sarah and that by her he has 3 Children Mary aged about 11 years Hannah aged about 9 years and John aged about 6 years and that he and his said Wife and Children are now Chargeable to the Parish of Cheltenham [signed]
1837: *removed to Staverton (father's settlement).* **1838:** *birth of an Amelia Lane registered at Staverton 2Q.* **1841:** *(RETURNED) SL (aged 44), Hannah, John, and Amelia (aged 3) lived in Stanhope St, Cheltenham (JL absent).* **1851:** *the family lived at 41 Queen St, Cheltenham. JL (aged 57), like son John, was labourer on railway; wife Sarah said to be aged 49.* [PS/CH/RA/2/4:50 (copy PS/CH/RA/2/3:444). Removal expenses for "J. Lane" to Ripple [confused with preceding: Staverton] 9/6 (June 1837: D4178).]

37030RO: Sat 15 Apr 1837 – **Thomas Clifford**, labourer, wife **Jane**, and four children **Charles**, **Thomas**, **William**, and **John**: That he was born in the Parish of Swindon in the said County where his Father John Clifford Labourer resided for many years and was legally Settled – That he this Examinant about seven years ago was married to his present Wife Jane in the Parish Church of Bredon in the County of Worcester by whom he has four Children now living (namely) Charles aged about six years Thomas aged about four years William aged about two years and John aged about one year – That he this Examinant hath never done any act to gain a Settlement in his own right and that he is now chargeable to the Parish of Cheltenham [signed]
1831: *probably removed to Swindon (father's settlement): see* **31046SE** *(TC: 29 Mar); son Charles baptised at Cheltenham 19 Oct (where father described as labourer).* **1833:** *next son Thomas baptised at Cheltenham 30 Jan.* **1837:** *removed to Swindon (father's settlement).* **1841:** *(RETURNED) TC (aged 35; groom, but carpenter in 1851), wife Jane and six children (as above with younger Jane and James, both born Cheltenham) lived in Worcester St, Cheltenham (HO107/353/9/60/20-1).* [PS/CH/RA/2/4:5 (copy at PS/CH/RA/2/3:445). Removal expenses for "Clifford" to Swindon 5/- (June 1837: D4178).]

37031RO: Sat 22 Apr 1837 – **Guy Robert**, otherwise **Robert Guy**: That he is the Natural Son of Elizabeth Guy the Daughter of George Guy formerly of Claydon Farm in the Parish of Aschurch [= Ashchurch] in the County of Gloucester where he this Examinant was born about 56 years ago – And this Examinant further Saith that he hath never done any Act to gain a Settlement, And that he hath become And is now Chargeable to the said Parish of Cheltenham [signed]
1837: *removed to Ashchurch (birth).* **1849:** *(RETURNED) GR ("houseless & destitute") admitted to Cheltenham Workhouse 16 Mar (discharged later that year) (G/CH/60/6).* **1851:** *Robert Guy (age unclear; unmarried, porter) visited 37 Rose and Crown Passage, off High St, Cheltenham.* **1852:** *buried at New Burial Ground, Cheltenham 20 Dec, aged 70.* [PS/CH/RA/2/4:52 (copy at PS/CH/RA/2/3:446). Removal expenses for "Guy" to Ashchurch 17/6 (June 1837: D4178).]

37032RO: Sat 22 Apr 1837 – **Joseph Coleman**, labourer: That he is about 45 years of age and was born in the Parish of Vernham Dean [= Vernhams Dean] in Hampshire, where his Father Richard Coleman, who was a Labourer resided for many years and was legally settled – that about 15 or 16 years ago he this Examinant was hired to one Thomas Webb of the Parish of

Vernham Dean aforesaid Farmer in the capacity of Shepherd for a year – that he this Examinant duly served the said Thomas Webb for the said term of a year and during the whole of that time resided and slept in his said Master's House in the Parish of Vernham Dean aforesaid and that since such servitude he has not done any act to gain a settlement – that he hath become and is now chargeable to the Parish of Cheltenham [mark]

1837: *to be removed to Vernhams Dean, Hants (hiring and service), but died before removal*; *JC buried at New Burial Ground, Cheltenham 21 Sept.* [PS/CH/RA/2/4:53 (copy at PS/CH/RA/2/3:447); order suspended as pauper unfit to travel.]

37033RO: Mon 24 Apr 1837 – **William Bullock**, shoemaker, wife **Susan**, and five children **Charles**, **Isabella**, **William**, **John**, and **Thomas**: That he is the Son of William Bullock formerly of the Parish of Leckhampton in the said County Shoemaker who was legally settled in such Parish – that Examinant was born at Leckhampton aforesaid about thirty one years since – that he was examined at the Public Office Cheltenham on the 18th. day of October 1826 as to the place of his then last legal settlement, and an order was made for the removal of himself and his Wife Susan to the said Parish of Leckhampton from whence they received relief accordingly – that he has done no act since to gain a Settlement elsewhere – and that he his said Wife and their five Children (namely) Charles aged about 10 years – Isabella aged about 6 years - William aged about 5 years – John aged about 4 years and Thomas aged about 12 months are chargeable to the Parish of Cheltenham [signed]

1837: *removed to Leckhampton (father's settlement)*. 1839: *(RETURNED) wife Susanna Bullock died at Cheltenham (buried at New Burial Ground 3 June).* **1840:** *WB (shoemaker, living at 26 Charles St, Cheltenham) remarried, to Sophia Powis, widow with several children, 19 Jan in Cheltenham.* **1841:** *the combined family lived at Temperance Cottage, Naunton Crescent, Cheltenham, with WB aged 35; shoemaker, wife and four children from her previous marriage, plus Isabella Bullock (aged 11), William (9), John (8), and Thomas (5) (HO107/353/12/59/17); Charles Bullock (aged 15) apparently lived with grandmother Isabella and uncle in Leckhampton (HO107/353/18/54/13).* [PS/CH/RA/2/4:54 (copy at PS/CH/RA/2/3:449). Removal expenses for "Bullock" to Leckhampton 5/- (June 1837: D4178).]

37034SE: Sat 29 Apr 1837 – **Ann Downing**, single woman: That she is now in the 20th year of her age – That she is the Daughter of Robert Downing now residing at Westmancote in the Parish of Bredon in the County of Worcester Carpenter but who at the time of this Examinants birth resided at Upton upon Severn in the said County of Worcester.

That about six Years ago she this Examinant was hired as an in-door Servant by John Fletcher of the Parish of Cheltenham in the said County for the Year: – that she served the said John Fletcher the whole of that term in the said Parish of Cheltenham and received her Wages since which period she has not done any Act whatever to gain a legal Settlement: – that she hath become and is now chargeable to the said Parish of Cheltenham [mark]

1837: *removal unlikely: place of settlement probably acknowledged as Cheltenham*; *birth of illegitimate son 9 June at Cheltenham Workhouse (G/CH/67/1); the child died next day (buried at New Burial Ground, Cheltenham, 12 June).* **1851:** *AD had married Philip James (aged 68; cabinet-maker) and the couple lived with daughter Ann (3) in Montpelllier Retreat, Cheltenham (HO107/360/18/23/5).* [PS/CH/RA/2/3:448.]

37035RO: Thurs 4 May 1837 – **James Williams**, labourer, wife **Mary Ann**, and six children **William, Frederick, Mary Ann, Eliza, Catherine**, and **Henry**. *James Williams*: That he is legally settled in the Parish of Upton Bishop in the County of Hereford by having been apprenticed to one John Smallman a Shoemaker of Upton Bishop aforesaid for seven years and duly served his time since which he has done no Act to gain a Settlement – that about 22 years ago he this Examinant was married at Saint Swithin's Church in the City of Worcester to Mary Ann Crump and by her he has a Son named Joseph – that about 14 years ago he left his Wife and that she has now as he believes six other Children [mark]

Mary Ann Williams: That she is the Wife of James Williams above named – that she has seven Children (namely) Joseph aged about 21 years who is now maintaining himself – and that she has also 6 other Children (namely) William aged about 12 years – Frederick aged about 10 years – Mary Ann

aged about 6 years – Eliza aged about 4 years – Catherine aged about 2 years and Henry aged about six months all of whom are now chargeable to the Parish of Cheltenham [signed]
1837: *removed to Upton Bishop, Heref (apprenticeship).* [PS/CH/RA/2/4:55 (copy at PS/CH/RA/2/3:451); p. 450 contains incomplete copy of Mary Ann Williams's deposition. Removal expenses for "Williams" to Upton Bishop, Heref £3/5/- (June 1837: D4178).]

37036RO: Thurs 18 May 1837 – **Samuel Hart**, watchmaker: That he is thirty-six years of age – that about 17 years ago he rented a House of a Mr Davies (who was a Builder) situate in Cleeveland Street [= Cleveland St] Fitzroy Square in the Parish of Saint Pancras in the County of Middlesex at 45^l a year which he occupied for about 12 years and paid the rent and taxes – that soon after this Examinant entered upon such House he was married (according to the rules and ceremonies of the Jews) to his present Wife Louisa by whom he has four Children now living (namely) Simeon aged about 13 - Charlotte aged about 12 – Adelaide aged about 5 and a half and Rebecca aged about 3 and a half years – that since such renting and occupation as aforesaid he this Examinant has never done any Act whereby to gain a Settlement and that he is now chargeable to the Parish of Cheltenham aforesaid [signed]
1837: *removed to St Pancras, Middlesex (renting).* [PS/CH/RA/2/4:56 (copy at PS/CH/RA/2/3:452).]

37037RO: Thurs 18 May 1837 – **Betty** (also **Elizabeth***)* **Butt**, wife of James Butt: That she is about 75 years of age – that about sixty years ago she was married to her present Husband James Butt in the Parish Church of Bisley in the said County of Gloucester in which Parish her said Husband who is a Shoemaker was as she verily believes born and legally settled – that she hath had issue by her said Husband eight Children three of whom are now living namely, Isaac Jacob and Susan – that the said Jacob and Susan are both married and settled, but that the said Isaac who became blind soon after his birth and has ever since continued so, is now living in the said Parish of Bisley from which he has occasionally received relief and this Examinant further saith that her said Husband hath never as she believes done any act to gain a settlement since his birth – that he some time since deserted her and that she hath since become and is now chargeable to the Parish of Cheltenham [mark]
1837: *removed to Bisley (husband's settlement).* **1841:** *EB died at Stroud Union Workhouse (buried at Bisley 22 Feb, aged 81); Isaac Butt lived in Stroud Union Workhouse (Bisley hundred) (aged 50; agricultural labourer).* **1846:** *death of James Butt in Stroud Union Workhouse (buried at Bisley 29 Jan, aged 78).* **1848:** *Isaac's workhouse death was followed by burial at Bisley 2 May, aged 61.* [PS/CH/RA/2/4:57 (copy at PS/CH/RA/2/3:453); order suspended as pauper unfit to travel until 17 June. Removal expenses for "Butts" to Bisley 18/- (June 1837: D4178).]

37038RO: Thurs 25 May 1837 – **George Fouch**: That he was born at Bromsgrove in the County of Worcester in or about the year 1761 – that when he was about 14 years old he was apprenticed to John Frost of the Parish of Tewkesbury in the said County of Gloucester Patten maker for seven years which he duly served – that soon after such apprenticeship he entered into Business on his own account in the said Parish of Tewkesbury where he rented a House of his Uncle Samuel Wilkins for which he paid 10^l a year and all rates and taxes – that he continued in the occupation of the said House as tenant to the said Samuel Wilkins for about 10 years when the said Samuel Wilkins died – that the said Samuel Wilkins devised the said House to this Examinant's Mother for her life and afterwards to this Examinant absolutely – that this Examinant's Mother lived with this Examinant in the said House until her death which took place in about 16 months afterwards – that this Examinant took down and rebuilt the said House and continued to reside and carry on his business therein until the year 1814 when he sold the said House and went to reside in London – that since he so left the said Parish of Tewkesbury he has not done any Act to gain a settlement in any other Parish and that he hath now become chargeable to the said Parish of Cheltenham [signed]
1837: *removed to Tewkesbury (renting).* **1841:** *GF (aged 80; clog-cutter) lived in Oldbury, Tewkesbury (HO107/380/7/15/25); son George (aged 30) lived as innkeeper with his family in High St, Tewkesbury (HO107/380/5/7/9).* **1845:** *death of GF in Tewkesbury Workhouse (buried 26 Feb, aged 81).*

[PS/CH/RA/2/4:58; copy of examination in PS/CH/RA/2/3:454-5. Removal expenses for "G. Fouch" to Tewkesbury 17/- (June 1837: D4178).]

37039SE: Mon 5 June 1837 – **Richard Allman** (also **Almond**, **Adams**), with wife **Charlotte**, and son **William**: That he was born in or about the year 1803 in the Parish of Chetwynd in the County of Salop where his Father John Allman who was a Labourer then resided – that this Examinant hath heard and believes that his said Father was legally settled in the Parish of Stoke upon Teme in the said County of Salop by hiring and service – that when this Examinant was about 16 or 17 years of age he enlisted as a Soldier in the 24th Regiment of foot, in which regiment he continued about two years when he left it – that he hath since been working, as a Journeyman Painter, at various places but that he hath never been apprenticed or hired for a year, or otherwise done any act to gain a legal Settlement – That about two or three years ago he was married in the name of John Adams in the Parish Church of Saint Mary De Cript [= St Mary de Crypt] in the City of Gloucester, to Charlotte his now Wife, then Charlotte Barnard, Singlewoman, by whom he has one Child living named William aged about two years, and that his said Wife is now pregnant of another Child – that he this Examinant is now chargeable to the Parish of Cheltenham aforesaid
1837: *removal uncertain: examination form incomplete.* [PS/CH/RA/2/3:456. Note: "this Pauper, who was in custody, made an arrangement with Mr Fagg (one of the Overseers) and left the Office without completing his examin"". RA married in 1835 under name "Richard Adams" (not "John Adams").]

37040RO: Sat 8 July 1837 – Robert Moss, stonemason, relating to settlement of grandchildren by son William Moss, **Esther**, **William**, **Elizabeth**, and **James Moss**, children of William Moss, stonemason: That he was born in the Parish of Stow on the Wold in the said County of Gloucester where his Father was, as he hath heard and believes legally settled – that his said Father died in one of the Alms Houses there about 7 or 8 years ago – and this Examinant further saith that about 48 years ago he was lawfully married in the Parish Church of Stow on the Wold aforesaid to Ann his now wife by whom (amongst other Children) he has a son named William now aged about 43 years who was also born in the said Parish of Stow on the Wold, and who about 23 years ago was married in the Parish Church there to one Mary Hookham (who died about 18 years ago) by whom he had three Children one of whom is married and settled, another of whom is dead and a third named Sarah now aged about 17 is living with this Examinant – That about 15 or 16 years ago this Examinant's said Son William was married at Birmingham (as this Examinant has heard and believes) to a second wife formerly Ann Mills Singlewoman (since also deceased) by whom he has 5 Children now living (namely) George aged about 14 years – Esther aged about 12 years – William aged about 10 years - Elizabeth aged about 8 years & James aged about 5 years – That this Examinant never did any Act to gain a Settlement between the birth of his said Son William & the time of his attaining his age of 21 years and that his said Son William (as he this Examinant believes) has never done any Act to gain a Settlement in his own right – that this Examinant's said Son William has lately deserted his four last named Children who have become and are now chargeable to the said Parish of Cheltenham [signed]
1837: *removed to Stow-on-the-Wold (father's settlement):* *see* **39054SE** *(William Moss: 11 Nov 1839) for further information.* [PS/CH/RA/2/4:59 (copy at PS/CH/RA/2/3:459-60); see also *G/CH/60/2* 1836 27 June, etc).]

37041SE: [undated: 8 July 1837] – **William Freeman**: [incomplete]
[PS/CH/RA/2/3:458.]

37042SE: Mon 10 July 1837 – **Michael Crawley**, with wife **Catherine**, and two children **Mary** and **Ann**: That he is a Native of Ireland   that he was born at Tom my leage [= Timoleague] in the County of Cork, that he has never done any Act to gain a Settlement in England ~~and that he is now chargeable to the Parish of Cheltenham~~. He further saith that about 6 years ago He was married to his present Wife Catherine (Nield) in the City of London, that his Wife was a Native of Sheebeen [perh. Skibbereen] in the County of Cork & that he has by her two Children, Mary

aged about 3 years and Ann aged about 2 years   that he his said Wife & Children are now chargeable to the Parish of Cheltenham [mark]
1837: *apparently removed to Ireland.* **1841:** *(RETURNED) MC (aged 35; labourer, born in Ireland) lived in Devonshire St, Cheltenham with wife Catherine (30; born in Ireland) and two daughters Mary (8) and Ann (5) (HO107/353/16/28/17).* [PS/CH/RA/2/3:457. Note: "Order made".]

37043RO: Mon 17 July 1837 – **Grace Thomas** and daughter **Isabella**: That she is about 44 years of age and was born in the City of Bath in the County of Somerset – That about 14 years ago she was lawfully married in the Parish Church of Walcot in the said City of Bath to James Thomas of the Parish of Saint George in the City of Bristol Steam Engineer by whom she has a Child named Isabella now living and aged about 14 years – That about 10 years ago her said Husband left her and although she has not heard from him ever since she about three years ago received information that he was in Flanders. That she always understood from her said Husband that he was legally settled in the said Parish of Saint George in the said City of Bristol – That soon after her said Husband left her she applied for relief to the Parish of Lawford's Gate (outside the Gate) and was passed to the said Parish of Saint George and received 1/0 from the Overseer there for the purpose of bringing her Husband to Justice –but that he immediately left the Country and avoided apprehension – That about 5 years ago this Examinant received relief from the Parish officers of Tewkesbury in the said County of Gloucester in consequence of being ill there and that soon afterwards she was taken from thence by an order of removal to the said Parish of Saint George and received 2/6 Per week for several weeks from the Parish officers there until she became better and that she hath since received occasional relief from that Parish – That she and her said daughter have become and are now chargeable to the said Parish of Cheltenham [mark]
1837: *not removed to St George, Bristol (husband's settlement), as pauper died before removal;* GT *buried at Cheltenham 22 Nov.* [PS/CH/RA/2/4:60 (copy at PS/CH/RA/2/3:461); order suspended as pauper unfit to travel. See **37084RO** (daughter Isabella Thomas: 9 Dec 1837).]

37044RO: Thurs 13 July 1837 – **John Greening**, labourer, and children **Ann** and **Thomas**: That he is about fifty nine years of age and was born in the Parish of Boddington in the County of Gloucester where his Parents at that time resided – That about thirty four years ago he this Examinant was hired for a year as a Servant in Husbandry by Henry Buckle of Heydon [= Haydon] Farm in the said Parish of Boddington Farmer at the wages of Ten Pounds – that he duly served the said year during the whole of which he resided in his said Master's House and received his wages and that since that time he has not done any Act whatever to gain a legal settlement – That about 32 or 33 years ago he this Examinant was married in the Parish Church of Cheltenham in the said County of Gloucester to Elizabeth his late wife deceased then Elizabeth Scrivens Singlewoman and has the following issue now living by her namely John aged 23 years Charles aged 21 years (both of whom are settled) and Ann aged 19 years and Thomas aged 9 years both now living with this Examinant – That he this Examinant hath become and is now chargeable to the said Parish of Cheltenham [mark]
1822: *removed to Boddington (Gray 412: 6 Feb).* **1837:** *(RETURNED)* **removed to Boddington (hiring and service).** **1839:** *(RETURNED) JG (aged 59) buried at Cheltenham 4 Dec.* **1841:** *JG's youngest son probably the Thomas Greening (aged 13) at Charlton Kings Workhouse (HO107/353/2/54/2), alongside several young Scrivenses: see* **41053SE** *(Thomas Greening: 18 Sept 1841).* [PS/CH/RA/2/4:61 (copy at PS/CH/RA/2/3:462). Removal expenses for "Greening & fam[ily]" to Boddington   5/- (13 Feb 1838: D4178). See **51014RO** (daughter-in-law Honora Greening: 5 Aug 1851).]

37045SE: Sat 15 July 1837 – William Murrell, relating to the settlement of sister **Mary Murrell**, single woman: That he is the Brother of the said Mary Murrell – that in the year 1776 his said Sister as he hath heard and believes was born in the Parish of Cheltenham where their Father Thomas Murrell resided for many years, and in which Parish (as he this Examinant has always understood and believes) he was legally settled – That about thirty years ago this Examinant's said Father rented a House in Worcester Street Cheltenham of one Thomas Haywood at 10[l]. a year – that he occupied the said House for 12 months and as this Examinant believes paid rates and taxes for the same – That he this Examinant believes his said Father never did any subsequent Act to gain a Settlement, and that to the best of this informant's belief his said Sister never did any act whereby she gained a Settlement in her own right, and that she is now chargeable to the said Parish of Cheltenham [mark]

1837: *died before removal or permission to remain; MM buried 24 July at New Burial Ground, Cheltenham.* [PS/CH/RA/2/3:463.]

37046SE: Sat 22 July 1837 – **John Fox**, labourer, residing at Cheltenham Workhouse: That he was born in the Parish of Broadway in the County of Worcester where his Father John Fox (now of Cheltenham Baker) lived for many years and as this Examinant has always understood and believes was legally settled – That about 25 years ago this Examinant was hired for the year by [blank] Hawkins then of Cheltenham aforesaid Brickmaker and Limeburner at the wages of 18^s Per week – that he accordingly entered upon and continued in such service for the space of 12 months during the whole of which he resided in his said Master's House and regularly received his wages – That about 15 years ago he this Examinant was lawfully married in the Parish Church of Cheltenham to his present wife Mary (then Mary Thomas Widow) – That about 7 years ago he left his said wife and has not lived with her since, that he is now chargeable to the Parish of Cheltenham [mark]

1837: *removal unlikely: place of settlement probably acknowledged as Cheltenham.* [PS/CH/RA/2/3:464.]

37047RO: Sat 22 July 1837 – **John Price**, blacksmith, wife **Catherine,** and children **Mary, John** and **Thomas**, the last four residing in Cheltenham: [Examination of Catherine Price] That 6 years ago last May she was lawfully married to her said Husband in the Parish Church of Saint Michael in the City of Gloucester by whom she has had three Children all of whom are now living – namely Mary aged about 5 years, John aged about 3 years and Thomas aged about 7 months – That in the Month of April 1821 her said Husband was by Indenture regularly bounden as an indoor apprentice to Charles Townsend then of the Parish of Ross in the County of Hereford Blacksmith but since deceased for the term of 5 years and this Examinant has repeatedly heard her Husband say and she verily believes that he left his said apprenticeship during the third year thereof up to which time he duly served his said Master – That last March twelve Months this Examinants said Husband took and entered upon a House N°. 6 Witcomb [= Witcombe] Place Cheltenham of William Henry Collins at the rent of 12$^£$ a year and is still occupying such House but has never paid More than 8..2..6 on account of such rent the last 2$^£$ of such sum having been levied by Distress in the Month of May last – that previous to such rental her said Husband never rented a House at 10$^£$ a year nor as she this Examinant believes has he ever done any act since his said apprenticeship to gain a legal Settlement – That about a fortnight ago her said Husband left her and her Children and she has not heard of him since and they are become Chargeable to the Said Parish of Cheltenham [signed]

1837: *removed to Ross, Heref (apprenticeship).* **1841:** *the couple were reconciled, and JP (aged 35; blacksmith) lived with wife Catherine (35), Mary (9), and John (7), with new sister Catherine (3; apparently born Ross), in Westbury-on-Severn (HO107/369/5/28/19).* **1851:** *(RETURNED) the family lodged at 10 Grove St, Cheltenham (HO107/1973/590/6), with two more small children; son John worked as blacksmith, and Catherine as dressmaker.* **1871:** *JP and Catherine lived in Little Witcombe, Badgeworth (RG10/2662/15/6).* [PS/CH/RA/2/4:62. Removal expenses for "C. Price & 3 Child[re]n" to Ross £1/16/- (30 Sept 1837: D4178).]

37048RO: Sat 29 July 1837 – **Elizabeth Chapman**, widow: That she is about 49 years of age - that about 22 years ago she was lawfully married in the Parish Church of Bright Elmstone [= Brighthelmstone = Brighton] in the County of Sussex to her late Husband Edward Chapman who was then a Sergeant in the 3rd Regiment of the line called the Old Buffs which Regiment about 6 years afterwards was broken up when her said Husband was allowed a pension and became a Watchman in the Parish of Saint Mary Le Bone [= Marylebone] in the County of Middlesex – That about 15 years since her said Husband rented a House N° 9 Turks row opposite the Royal Military assylum [*sic*] at Chelsea in the County of Middlesex of a Mr Anderson who was then a

Baker and Brewer of Chelsea College by the year but what the rent was she this Examinant does not now recollect, but she has heard her Husband say and she verily believes that it was upwards of 10$^£$ a year   that her said Husband and herself occupied the said house for about 6 years when her Husband died suddenly   that she this Examinant has done no Act whatever in her own right to gain a Settlement and that she is now Chargeable in the Parish of Cheltenham [mark]

1837: *removed to Chelsea, Middlesex (renting); EC died (aged 49) at Cheltenham Workhouse (buried at New Burial Ground, Cheltenham 27 Oct).* [PS/CH/RA/2/4:63 (copy at PS/CH/RA/2/3:466); order suspended as pauper unfit to travel.]

37049RO: Sat 5 Aug 1837 – **John Whitehead**, wife **Ann**, and three sons **Edward**, **William,** and **Henry**: That he is the Son of William Whitehead of Tewkesbury Toll Gate Keeper

That he was born at Tewkesbury about 32 years since where his Father who was then a Stocking Weaver Resided and was legally settled   that about 20 years since He was apprenticed to Mr Charles Malvern of Tewkesbury Brush Maker by Indenture for 7 years as an Out Door Apprentice and regularly served his Apprenticeship and that during such Apprenticeship He lived and Slept at his Father's House in Tewkesbury   that about 12 years since he was married at the Parish Church of St Nicholas in the City of Gloucester to his present Wife Ann and by her has three Children Edward aged about 7 years, William aged about 3 years and Henry aged about 18 Months   that in the latter end of the year 1834 He took & rented of Mr Hatch of Stoke Orchard in the County of Gloucester a Cottage Tenement at the rent of £10 per annum and lived there and paid his rent for More than 12 Months but he was never rated to the Relief of the Poor, for the same or paid any rates: – that he has never done any other Act to gain a Settlement and that he his said Wife and Children are now Chargeable to the Parish of Cheltenham [signed]

1837: *removed to Tewkesbury (apprenticeship).* **1841:** *(RETURNED) Ann Whitehead (aged 33; laundress) lived with two sons Edward (10) and William (5) (husband absent) in Whitehart Row, Cheltenham (HO107/353/9/13/20). As late as 1895 William Whitehead (aged 58; height 5' 6", dark-brown hair) was imprisoned at HMP Wakefield for a fortnight as a "casual pauper" refusing work.* [PS/CH/RA/2/4:64 (copy at PS/CH/RA/2/3:467-8). Removal expenses for "Whitehead" to Tewkesbury 18/- (30 Sept 1837: D4178).]

37050SE: Sat 5 Aug 1837 – **Michael Mahoney**, residing in Milsom St, Cheltenham: That he was born at Fermoy [County Cork] in the Kingdom of Ireland and that he has never done any Act to gain a settlement in England & he is now chargeable to Chelt^m Parish [mark]

1837: *removed to Ireland.* [PS/CH/RA/2/3:469. Removal expenses for "Mahoney Irish Pauper" £1/5/8 (30 Sept 1837: D4178).]

37051SE: Sat 5 Aug 1837 – **Mary Murphy**: [That] She is the Daughter of Timothy Murphy and Mary his Wife and was born in the County of Cork in the Kingdom of Ireland, that she has never done any act to gain a Settlement in her own right & She is now chargeable to the Parish of Cheltenham [mark]

1837: *removed to Ireland.* [PS/CH/RA/2/3:469. Removal expenses for "Murphy Irish Pauper" £2/13/10 (30 Sept 1837: D4178). See **37016SE:** probably mother MM: 2 Mar 1837.]

37052RO: Sat [5] Aug 1837 – **James Snook**: That he is the Son of Esau Snook formerly of Stalbridge in the County of Dorset Baker who was legally settled there   that his Father died when he was An Infant and that he was then residing at Milbourne Port [= Milborne Port]   that he was removed by An Order of the Magistrates from that place to Stalbridge where he was maintained and kept by the Parish Officers of Stalbridge, till he was grown up   that he has never done any Act to gain a Settlement in his own right and is Chargeable to the Parish of Cheltenham [signed]

1826: *JS married Jemima Hamblen at Purse Caundle, Dorset, in July; later in year he (aged 21; labourer) served several months in Dorchester gaol for smuggling (prison record shows him blind in one eye, with cut over right eyebrow, and marked by smallpox).* **1833:** *despite having legitimate children, Jemima had an illegitimate son; the Purse Caundle register notes "her Husband having run away".* **1837:** ***ordered to be removed to Stalbridge, Dorset (father's settlement); probably death of "James Snooks" recorded in Cheltenham Workhouse 3 Sept and burial on 5 Sept in New Burial Ground.* **1838:** *Jemima remarried.* **1841:**

Jemima listed in Purse Caundle with daughter Selina Snook and son George by second husband George Young (HO107/291/6/4/2); she was soon widowed again. [PS/CH/RA/2/4:65 (copy at PS/CH/RA/2/3:470).]

37053RO: Mon 14 Aug 1837 – **Richard Goff** (also **Gough**), labourer: That about 39 years ago he was born as he believes at Cundover [= Condover] in the County of Salop where his Father who was a Farmer and Maltster resided for many years - That at Michaelmas in or about the year 1811 he this Examinant was hired at Tewkesbury Mop by one Mrs Lode of the Parish of Hanley Castle in the County of Worcester Widow and Baker to be her Servant for the term of a year at the wages as this Examinant believes of 5^l   that he lived and slept in the house and duly served such year and received his wages, since which time he has never done any act whereby to gain a settlement and that he has become and is now chargeable to the Parish of Cheltenham [mark]
1837: *removed to Hanley Castle, Worcs (hiring and service): see* **44051** *(RG: 10 Oct 1844) for further information.* [PS/CH/RA/2/4:66 (copy at PS/CH/RA/2/3:471); order suspended as pauper unfit to travel. Removal expenses for "R Gough" to Hanley Castle, Worcs 18/- (30 Sept 1837: D4178).]

37054RO: Mon 28 Aug 1837 – **Sarah Ward**, widow, with three children **Henry**, **John**, and **Ellen**: That she was born at Hignham [= Highnam] in the County of Gloucester about 31 years ago where her Father William Pimble who was a Labourer resided for many Years – That in the summer of the year 1823 she this Examinant was hired to Jeremiah Hopkins of Tirley in the said County of Gloucester as an indoor Servant at the wages of eight Guineas   That she lived in such service about a year and three quarters and received her Wages – That her late Husband John Ward was also a hired Servant of the said Jeremiah Hopkins and lived with him at the same time as she this Examinant did   That he lived there for two Years and that they both left such Service at Michaelmas in the year 1824   That at the following Christmas she this Examinant was lawfully married to the said John Ward in the Parish Church of Tirley aforesaid by which Marriage She has two Children now living namely Henry aged about seven Years and John aged about five years That her said Husband died about two Years and three quarters ago and that about 6 or 7 Months Previous to his death he received relief from the Parish Officers of Tirley aforesaid who also paid his Funeral Expenses – That She this Examinant continued to receive relief therefrom for some time after his death when it was discontinued because she refused to go into the Poor House   That since the death of her said Husband She this Examinant hath not done any Act whereby to gain a Settlement – That about a Month ago She this Examinant was delivered of a female Bastard Child and that this Examinant is now chargeable to the parish of Cheltenham [mark]
1837: *removed to Tirley (husband's settlement).* **1839:** *(RETURNED) SW (née Pimble) remarried, to Enoch Dyer, in Cheltenham 4Q.* **1841:** *SW (aged 40) lived with husband (53; labourer), his daughter Eliza, her children Henry (10), John (8), and Ellen (3; the unnamed child in examination), and their joint child James (6 weeks) in Queen St, Cheltenham (HO107/353/9/34/17).* **1851:** *with SW widowed again, children by first marriage reverted to maiden name (HO107/1973/360/29).* [PS/CH/RA/2/4:67 (copy at PS/CH/RA/2/3:472). Removal expenses for "Ward & 3 Child[re]n" to Tirley 18/6 (30 Sept 1837: D4178).]

37055RO: Thurs 7 Sept 1837 – **Mary Lansdown**, widow: That she is a Widow; that her Husband has been dead upwards of twelve years, that she is legally settled in the Parish of Walcot in the County of Somerset having rented of M^r. Edward Grimter [prob. = Grinter] a House in Richmond Place at the rent of twelve pounds a year and occupied it for the space of three years and paid all rent and rates – The Tenancy commenced at Michaelmas 1826 – She has done no act since to gain a Settlement and is now become chargeable to the Parish of Cheltenham [signed]
1837: *removed to Walcot, Bath, Som (renting).* **1840:** *probably the ML, servant, who died of "Decay of Nature" on 7 Nov at 5 Upper Dover St, Walcot, Bath.* [PS/CH/RA/2/4:68 (copy at PS/CH/RA/2/3:473). Removal expenses for "M. Lansdown" to Bath £1/19/- (9 Oct 1837: D4178).]

37056SE: Thurs 7 Sept 1837 – Elizabeth Welch, wife of John Welch, relating to the settlement of (step)mother **Sophia Stubbs**, widow: That she is the Daughter of William Stubbs formerly of Cheltenham Carpenter, the Husband of the said Sophia Stubbs, that her said Father was born and bred at Staverton in this County and was the Son of [blank] Stubbs who lived there   that her

Father rented several Houses in Cheltenham but none of them to the amount of Ten pounds a Year   that her Father was never apprenticed but learnt his trade from his Father at Staverton that her father died last Friday Week [mark]

1837: *removal uncertain: evidence appears inconclusive; William Stubbs buried at St Mary's, Cheltenham 25 Aug, aged 58; he had married Sophia Poulson (both previously widowed) at Cheltenham 13 Sept 1831.*
1841: *SS probably the housekeeper (age recorded as 45) living at 4 Fountain Passage, High St, Cheltenham.*
1843: *SS buried (aged 55) at Cheltenham 13 Nov.* [PS/CH/RA/2/3:474. Note: "11th Sept   The above named Sophia Stubbs came to be exam^d in support of the above, when Mr Cooper & the 2 Magistrates then present understanding the relief afforded by this Parish was only a Coffin for her late Husband's burial they declined taking her exam^n."]

37057SE: Thurs 21 Sept 1837 – **Ann Rice**: That in the year 1814 she was lawfully married at Saint Ann's [= St Anne's] Church in the Parish of Saint Ann Soho in the City of Westminster to John Rice – That about 12 or 13 years ago her said Husband rented two Houses situate in Mount Pleasant Place Cheltenham of one Thomas Gunnell then and now of Cheltenham Carpenter at the rent of 40$^£$ or Gu[ine]as Per Annum – that her said Husband occupied such Houses and carried on his business of a Baker for about 2 years and a half and duly paid the rent and taxes – That about 10 years ago, and during such occupation as aforesaid her said Husband left her and went away with another Woman – That about 4 or 5 years ago she this Examinant was on a visit to her Husband's Father (who then lived and as she believes now lives at Irthling Borough [= Irthlingborough] in the County of Northampton) her Husband came there to see his Father but immediately afterwards went away and she has not heard of him since – That she is not aware that her said Husband since he left Cheltenham has done any act to gain a Settlement elsewhere, and that she is now chargeable to the said Parish of Cheltenham [signed]

1837: *removal unlikely: place of settlement probably acknowledged as Cheltenham; AR died soon after examination (buried at New Burial Ground, Cheltenham, 4 Nov, aged 49).* [PS/CH/RA/2/3:475.]

37058SE: Sat 23 Sept 1837 – **Richard Jones**, wife **Mary**, and two children **Eliza** and **Charlotte**; also James Jones, lime-burner, relating to settlement of son Richard Jones. *James Jones:* That his said Son Richard Jones is about 26 years of age and was born in the Parish of Newland in the County of Gloucester where he this Examinant then resided, That in or about the year 1813 he left Newland aforesaid and went to live at Gloucester – That he remained in Gloucester for 7 or 8 years when he left and went to reside in the Parish of Leckhampton – That about 2 or 3 years afterwards he left Leckhampton and came to reside in Exmouth Street [off Bath Rd] in the Parish of Cheltenham at a House he took of a Mr Earle (who then kept the Duke of Wellington Inn in Cheltenham) at 10^l a year – That he lived in such House for about two years during which time he paid the rent but whether he paid any Taxes he does not now recollect – That he this Examinant has since rented several Houses in this Parish under 10^l a year – That at Midsummer 1836 he this Examinant took and entered upon and is now in the occupation of a House belonging to Mr Price of Saint Georges Place [= St George's Place, running south from the Lower High St] Attorney at Law, situate in Baker Street [off Swindon Rd] in the Parish of Cheltenham at the rent of 12^l. a year – That he has paid all rent up to Midsummer last and all Taxes which have been demanded of him [mark]

Richard Jones: That three years ago last april he was lawfully married at the Parish Church of Avenhall [= Abenhall] in this County to Mary his Present Wife then Mary Meredith Singlewoman by whom he has two Children now living (namely, Eliza aged about 3 years and Charlotte aged about 2 years – That he this Examinant was never apprenticed nor has he ever done any Act in his own right whereby to gain a Settlement – That his said Wife and Children have lately become chargeable to this Parish.

1837: *removal unlikely: place of settlement probably acknowledged as Cheltenham.* **1838:** *Eliza apparently buried 24 Nov (aged 4) at New Burial Ground, Cheltenham.* **1841:** *RJ (aged 30; lime-burner) lived in Alstone Place, Cheltenham, with father James (60; lime-burner), wife Mary (25), daughter Charlotte (5) and other family members (HO107/353/10/23/13).* [PS/CH/RA/2/3:476-7.]

37059RO: Sat 7 Oct 1837 – **James Davison**, wife **Sarah**, and four children **Sarah**, **Charlotte**, **Thomas**, and **William**: That he is about 48 years of age and that he was born at a place called Hobnails in the Parish of Alderton in this County where his Father and Mother lived for many years – That when he was about ten or eleven years of age he went out as a Farmer's Servant and lived in various situations until Michaelmas in or about the year 1808 when he was hired at Cheltenham Mop to John Oakey then of Heyden [also Haydon] in the Parish of Boddington Baker as his Servant for a year at the wages of 9^l – That he lived there for 2 years during the whole of which time he eat [= ate] drank and slept at his Master's House and received his wages – That soon after he this Examinant left Mr Oakey's Service he was married at the Parish Church of Hempstead [= Hempsted] near Gloucester in this County to his present Wife Sarah formerly Sarah the Daughter of Mrs Lane of the Golden Valley Singlewoman by whom he has four Infant Children unable to support themselves (namely) Sarah aged about 11 years - Charlotte aged about 9 years – Thomas aged about 5½ years and William aged about 3½ years – That since he left Mr Oakey's Service he has done no Act whereby to gain a settlement and has become chargeable to the Parish of Cheltenham [mark]
1837: removed to Boddington (hiring and service); JD died soon after examination (buried at Cheltenham 1 Nov, aged 48). **1841:** *wife Sarah (aged 50; agricultural labourer), daughter Sarah (16), and William (7) lived in Haydon Green, Staverton (HO107/354/27/8/12); daughter Charlotte (14) was servant living in Gloucester Rd, Cheltenham (HO107/353/10/52/10). [PS/CH/RA/2/4:69 (copy at PS/CH/RA/2/3:478); order suspended as pauper unfit to travel. Removal expenses for "Davidson [sic] & fam[il]y" to Boddington 6/- (7 Oct 1837: D4178).]*

37060SE: Sat 7 Oct 1837 – **Thomas Warren**, wife **Elizabeth**, and two children **Thomas** and **Elizabeth**: That he was born in or about the year 1811 in the Parish of Upton upon Severn in the County of Worcester where his Father John Warren who was a Gardener then resided – That shortly after this Examinant's birth his said Father came to reside at Cheltenham and about 14 years ago took a House there called Bank Cottage situate on Keynsham Bank [London Rd] with about two Acres of land adjoining it from a Miss Addis of Cainscross near Stroud at 24^l Per Annum and that he continued to rent and occupy the same until within about two years since, when he left it and took a House and land in the same Parish belonging to Mr Hurlstone which he now occupies at the rent of 18^l. a year – That about 5 years ago he this Examinant was married at the Parish Church of Cheltenham aforesaid to Elizabeth his now Wife (formerly Elizabeth Stubbs Singlewoman) by whom he has two Children namely Thomas aged about 2 years and Elizabeth aged about 1¾ year - That he this Examinant hath never done any act to gain a settlement in his own right, and that he and his said Wife and Children have become and are now chargeable to the said Parish of Chelt^m [signed]
1837: removal unlikely: place of settlement probably acknowledged as Cheltenham; an Elizabeth Warren was buried at Cheltenham 25 Aug 1837, aged 23, but this predates examination. **1838:** *TW remarried, to Sarah Shute, at Charlton Kings 15 Oct.* **1841:** *the family lived in Mill Lane, Prestbury: TW (aged 30; gardener), Sarah (42), Thomas (7), and Elizabeth (5). [PS/CH/RA/2/3:479.]*

37061SE: Sat 7 Oct 1837 – **Ann Richardson**, wife of Henry Richardson, blacksmith, with two children **William** and **Henry**: That she was born in the Parish of Saint George in the East in the Borough of Southwark where her Father who was an Irishman and a Bricklayer or Bricklayer's Labourer lived as she has heard and believes for many years – That about 4 years ago she was lawfully married in the Catholic Chapel in the City of Bristol to the said Henry Richardson who as she has heard and believes was born in the City of Cork in Ireland – That at the time of the said Marriage and for some time afterwards, her said Husband worked as a Journeyman Blacksmith in Bristol and that they have since been travelling about the Country having no fixed residence – That she has two Children by her said husband (namely) William aged 2½ years and Henry aged about 3 months – That about 2 months ago her said Husband left her in Bristol and she has not heard of him since. That she verily believes her said Husband has never done any Act whereby to

gain a Settlement in England and that she and her said two Children are become chargeable to this parish. [mark]
1837: *removed to Ireland (presumed).* [PS/CH/RA/2/3:480.]

37062RO [form crossed out and word "Irish" written, presumably relating to **37061SE**.]

37063RO: Mon 9 Oct 1837 – **John Warden** and wife **Martha**: That he was born in or about the year 1817 in the Parish of Cheltenham where his Father Francis Warden Shoemaker then lived – That when he this Examinant was about 10 years old he was apprenticed by the Parish Officers of Cheltenham aforesaid to William Harding of that place Chimney Sweeper for seven years – That he served six years and three quarters of that term with the said William Harding when he died and that he served the remaining three months with his Widow Mary Harding – That at the expiration of the said seven years he this Examinant went to London and was hired for a year as a Journeyman Sweep to one [blank] Bennett of Welbeck Street in the Parish of Saint Mary le Bone at the wages of 5^l. – That he served about 11 months, and three weeks of this term when in consequence of some disagreement between them he left the said [blank] Bennett and went to Oxford where he was hired for a year by Mary Buckland of the Parish of Saint Peter le Bailey Chimney Sweeper at the wages of 4^l. – That he served her the said year living and sleeping on her Premises and at the expiration thereof received his wages after which he served her the two following years at the wages of 5^l a year – That on leaving her Service he was hired for a year to Luke Stephens of the said Parish of Saint Peter le Bailey Chimney Sweeper at the wages of 5^l – That he entered upon such last mentioned Service and lived with the said Luke Stephens about 3 months when in consequence of a quarrel between them he left him and came to Cheltenham where he hath ever since remained – That since his said servitude in the said Parish of Saint Peter le Bailey Oxford he has done no act to gain a settlement elsewhere – That about 18 months ago he this Examinant was lawfully married at the Parish Church of Cheltenham to Martha his now Wife (then Martha Bowen) by whom he has had one Child which is since dead – That he hath become and is now chargeable to the said Parish of Cheltenham [mark]
1837: *removed to St Peter le Bailey, Oxford, Oxon (hiring and service).* **1841:** *(RETURNED) JW (aged 24; sweep) and wife Martha lived in Swindon Parade, Elm St, Cheltenham (HO107/353/9/63/27). They remained in Cheltenham over subsequent censuses, with a gradually increasing family (in 1851 young son Henry (9) described as a "Sweep" (HO107/1973/625/14)).* [PS/CH/RA/2/4:70 (copy at PS/CH/RA/2/3:481-2). See expenses for "endeav[ourin]g to apprehend Warden" 13/- (31 Mar 1838: D4178).]

37064RO: Thurs 26 Oct 1837 – **William Greenaway**, shoemaker, and wife **Sarah**: That he was born as he believes in or about the year 1782 in the Parish of Purton in the County of Wilts where his Father Joseph Greenaway as he believes was also born and settled – That when this Examinant was about 14 years old he was apprenticed by Indenture to William Coward of the said Parish of Purton shoemaker for 7 years on which occasion his Father paid a Premium of 12 Guineas with him – that he duly served the whole of his time during which he lived and slept in his said master's House – That when he this Examinant was about 24 or 25 years old he was lawfully married at the Parish Church of Purton aforesaid to one Esther Bridgeman who about 5 years afterwards left him and he has not heard of her for the last 18 years – that he had 3 Children by such marriage all of whom are settled and this Examinant further saith that fully believing his said Wife to be dead he on the 10th day of August 1835 was married at Ratcliffe Church [= St Mary Redcliffe] Bristol to Sarah his present Wife then Sarah Wakeman [also Wakeham] Widow by whom he has no Child And this Examinant lastly saith that since his said apprenticeship in the said Parish of Purton he has not done any Act whatever to gain a Settlement elsewhere and that in consequence of illness he and his said Wife have become and are now chargeable to the Parish of Cheltenham [signed]
1837: *removed to Purton, Wilts (apprenticeship); WG died at Cheltenham Workhouse 21 Nov (burial in New Burial Ground, Cheltenham 24 Nov).* **1841:** *some of WG's children by first marriage to Esther Bridgeman (John, Mary Jane, and Alfred) had settled back in Purton. Esther (also Hester) Greenaway may*

well have been alive at time of his second marriage (a Hester Greenaway died at nearby Cricklade 1Q 1850). [PS/CH/RA/2/4:71 (copy at PS/CH/RA/2/3:483); order suspended as pauper unfit to travel.]

37065RO: Thurs 26 Oct 1837 – **Ann White** (no examination text with removal order): That she is about Sixteen Years of Age and was born in the Parish of Alverstoke in the County of Hants: – That she has always understood and believes that the place of Settlement of her Father who was a Soldier and named George White was at Dunsbourn Rous [= Duntisbourne Rouse] in the County of Gloucester but how such Settlement was acquired she this Examinant does not know: that her Father and Mother died when she this Examinant was quite Young, and that after their decease she this Examinant was taken into the Work house at Alverstoke aforesaid where she remained until about 6 Years ago when she was removed or taken to a place called Sapperton in the said County of Gloucester and placed in the House of a Woman named Esther Birtles [perh. Bittles] where she was maintained and kept as she believes by the Parish Officers of Dunsbourn Rous aforesaid: – that she remained there about 12 Months when she went to the House of M^r. Richardson who kept a public House at Daglingworth where she remained a Year and a half doing the work of the House [*i.e.* housework] for which she was fed, the Parish of Dunsbourn Rous finding her Cloathes: that she afterwards went to M^r. Boulton a Farmer at Dunsborne Rous and lived in his House, doing the Work of the House for which he found her Victuals and Cloathes: that she lived there about 2 Years: that she came to Cheltenham about 3 Months ago, and hath become chargeable to the Parish: [mark]
1837: *removed to Duntisbourne Rouse (father's settlement).* **1842:** *this is perhaps the AW (daughter of George White) married to Joseph Pates at Alverstoke 5 May (died Mar 1850 at Chelsea).* [PS/CH/RA/2/4:72 (text reproduced from PS/CH/RA/2/3:485).]

37066RO: Thurs 26 Oct 1837 – **John Guest** (also **Gist**), wife **Maria**, and two children **William** and **Ann**: That he is about 27 years old and was born at Dix[t]on in the Parish of Alderton in the County of Gloucester where his Father then lived – That about fourteen years ago he this Examinant was hired as a Cow-boy to Lydia Young of the Parish of Eldersfield Widow for the term of a year at the wages of 30 shillings – that he duly served the said year during the whole of which he lived and slept at his Mistresses House – that since that time he has never done any Act to gain a legal settlement in any other Parish either by servitude or otherwise – That about six years ago he was lawfully married at Bishop's Cleeve in the said County of Gloucester to Maria his now Wife then Maria Kear [also Carr] by whom he has 2 Children now living namely William aged about 5 years and Ann aged about 3 years – And this Examinant lastly saith that by reason of severe illness he has become and his [*sic*] now chargeable to the Parish of Cheltenham [mark]
1837: *removed to Eldersfield, Worcs (hiring and service); JG died soon after examination.* **1841:** *wife Maria (aged 32) lived with Joseph Hooper (28; waterman) and two children, William (9) and Ann (7), in Upton-upon-Severn (HO107/1206/6/7/7).* [PS/CH/RA/2/4:7) (copy at PS/CH/RA/2/3:486); order suspended until 18 Nov as pauper unfit to travel. Removal expenses for "Guest" to Eldersfield £1/-/- (18 Nov 1837: D4178).]

37067RO: Thurs 26 Oct 1837 – **Jane Kerby**, single woman: That she is about seventeen years of age and was born as she hath heard and believes in the Parish of Minchinhampton in the said County where her Father Britton Kerby who was a stonemason was lawfully settled – That she this Examinant has never done any Act in her own right to gain a Settlement since her birth and that in consequence of severe illness she hath lately become and is now chargeable to the Parish of Cheltenham [mark]
1837: *removed to Minchinhampton (father's settlement).* [PS/CH/RA/2/4:74 (copy at PS/CH/RA/2/3:487); order suspended until 11 Dec as pauper unfit to travel. Removal expenses for "Jane Kerby" to Horsley (12 Dec 1837: D4178).]

37068SE: Sat 28 Oct 1837 – **Esther Bullock**, widow, with six children **Noah, Eliza, John, Priscilla, Charles,** and **Alfred**: That about 19 years ago she was lawfully married to her late Husband John Bullock of Cheltenham aforesaid Labourer at the Parish of Arlingham in this County by whom she has six Children now living (namely) Noah aged about 16 – Eliza aged

about 14 John aged about 12 – Priscilla aged about 10 – Charles aged about 8 and Alfred aged about 5 Years – That in the month of August last her said Husband met with an accident and was taken to the Infirmary at Gloucester where he died – That whilst he was there her said Husband told her and she believes it to be true that about 23 years ago he was hired for a year at the wages of £7 by a Mr Hale of Cheltenham as a Carter and that he lived in Mr Hale's Service two successive years during the whole of which he was lodged and boarded in his Master's House in consequence of which he considered Cheltenham to be his Parish as he never afterwards did any act to gain a settlement elsewhere – That about twelve months ago this Examinant had a Child buried at the expense of the Parish of Cheltenham and that shortly before the death of her said Husband he became chargeable to the Parish of Cheltenham and she and her said Children are now likewise chargeable thereto [mark]
1837: *removal unlikely: place of settlement probably acknowledged as Cheltenham.* **1841:** *EB (aged 40; independent, widow) lived in Exmouth St, Cheltenham with family: Eliza (15), John (15; labourer), Priscilla (10), and Alfred (8) (HO107/353/12/37/11).* [PS/CH/RA/2/3:488.]

37069RO: Thurs 2 Nov 1837 – **Samuel Edwards**, labourer, wife **Joanna**, and four children, **Caroline, James, Elizabeth**, and **Mary Ann**: That he is about 26 years of Age and was born in the Parish of Twining [= Twyning] in the County of Gloucester where his parents then resided: that about 8 years ago he this Examinant was hired for a year by Alexander Page of the Parish of Leckhampton in the said County Gardener at the wages of six pounds: that he duly served the said year and at the expiration thereof received his wages and afterwards lived with the said Alexander Page a second year and that during the whole of his said Servitude he was boarded and lodged in his master's house at Leckhampton aforesaid, since which time he has not done any act to gain a settlement elsewhere: that about seven years ago he was lawfully married in the Parish Church of Tewkesbury in the said County of Gloucester to Joanna his now Wife (then Joanna Hourgin [= Hogan]) by whom he has 4 Children now living – namely Caroline aged about 6 years, James aged about 5 years, Elizabeth aged about 2½ years and Mary Ann aged about eleven months: and this deponent lastly saith that he, his Wife and Children aforesaid are become chargeable to the Parish of Cheltenham [mark]
1837: *removed to Leckhampton (hiring and service).* **1841:** *(RETURNED) SE (aged 30; labourer) lived with Julia [= Joanna?] (30; from Ireland) and three children James (8), Elizabeth (6), and Mary (4) in Stanhope St, Cheltenham (HO107/353/9/53/5).* [PS/CH/RA/2/4:75 (copy at PS/CH/RA/2/3:492 - note at wife's name: "was born at Chacely a Bastard").]

37070RO: Thurs 2 Nov 1837 – **John Cox**, labourer: That he hath heard and believes that he was born in the Parish of Bishops Cleeve in this County in or about the year one thousand seven hundred and seventy nine: that he hath also heard and believes his Father John Cox was then living as a Shepherd to M^r. Arkell of Whittington Court in this County where he lived for upwards of 30 years and was legally settled – that in or about the year 1798 this examinant went as a hired servant to Mrs Hill of the Parish of Leigh in this County Farmer at the wages of four Guineas a year and continued in her service for three years during which time he lived and slept in her house and received his Wages: that on leaving Mrs Hills service he enlisted as a Soldier in the South Gloucester Militia in which Regiment he served upwards of eleven years: that when he had served about five years of that time he was lawfully married to his late Wife Sarah (then Sarah Hawkins Widow) at the Parish Church of Brighton (where his Regiment was then stationed) by whom he has one Daughter named Sarah now living and who has been married about five years: that since he left the service of Mrs Hill he has done no act whereby to gain a settlement – that his late Wife is now lying dead in the Parish of Cheltenham to which Parish he hath become chargeable [signed]
1837: *Sarah Cox, whom JC married in Brighton 1808, died occurred shortly before examination (buried at New Burial Ground, Cheltenham 2 Nov); removed to The Leigh (hiring and service);* **1841:** *JC lived in The Leigh (aged 60; widower and agricultural labourer) (HO107/354/25/7/10).* **1851:** *JC listed in The Leigh as pauper (agricultural labourer) (HO107/1974/42/26* [PS/CH/RA/2/4:76 (copy at PS/CH/RA/2/3:490-1). See Gray **91** (father John Cox: 11 March 1817).]

37071SE: Sat 4 Nov 1837 – **Ann Whittle**: That she is about 21 years of age and that she hath heard and believes that she was born a Bastard in the Parish of Redmarley D'Abitot in the County of Worcester – That she never knew her Father or Mother the latter of whom as she hath understood and believes left her when she was about five or six years old – That she this Examinant was brought up as she understood with her Grandmother who received a weekly allowance from Redmarley Parish by way of assisting her so to do. – That when she this Examinant was about 15 years old she was hired for a year as an indoor Servant to M^r McMichael then of Cheltenham Tea dealer at the wages of 30^s/. – that she duly served the said year and continued in his Service nearly another year   And this Examinant lastly saith that since such hiring and service with the said M^r McMichael she has done no Act whereby to gain a Settlement and that she has lately become and is now chargeable to the Parish of Cheltenham [mark]
1837: *removal unlikely: place of settlement probably acknowledged as Cheltenham.* [PS/CH/RA/2/3:484.]

37072RO: Mon 6 Nov 1837 – Ann Mucklewean, widow, relating to settlement of grandchildren **John Ingram** and **Sarah Ingram**, the children of James and Sarah Ingram, inmates of Charlton Kings Workhouse for children (Cheltenham Union): That she has always understood and believes that she was born in the Parish of Newent in the said County of Gloucester where her father Andrew Webley who was a Tailor was legally settled and in which Parish he died. That she this Examinant never did any Act in her own right to gain a legal Settlement. That when she was about 18 years of age she was lawfully married in one of the Churches at Worcester to her late Husband James Mucklewean deceased who at that time and for many years afterwards was a Sergeant in the 4th Regiment of foot – commonly Called the King's Own – That her said Husband was a Native of Ireland and never to the best of her belief gained a Settlement in England. That she this Examinant had several Children by her said Husband and amongst them a Daughter named Sarah who was born in or about the year 1809 at Horsham in Surrey where this Examinant was then Staying with her Husband whose Regiment was Stationed at the Barracks there – That about 10 years ago this Examinant's said daughter (who as this Examinant believes never did any Act in her own right whereby to gain a Settlement) was lawfully married at Newtown Hamilton [= Newtownhamilton] in the County of Armagh in Ireland to James Ingram a Native of that Country and who likewise as this Examinant believes never gained a Settlement in England That her said Daughter has 3 Children now living by her said Husband (namely) John aged about 8 years Sarah aged about 6 years and Elizabeth aged about 5 years. That about 12 Months ago her said Daughter Sarah Ingram and her said 3 Children were received into the Poor house of Newent aforesaid where they remained about 9 Months after which they came to this Examinant's Lodgings in Cheltenham and remained with her until about a Fortnight since when the said Sarah Ingram went away and took her younger Child with her leaving the two others with this Examinant, who by reason of this Examinant's inability to maintain and provide for them have become Chargeable to the said Parish of Cheltenham [mark]
1837: *removed to Newent (father's settlement): see* **42027RO** (Ann McKlwain: 21 Mar 1842) for further information on the family. [PS/CH/RA/2/4:77 (copy at PS/CH/RA/2/3:489-90). Removal expenses for "Ingram" to Newent &c £1/12/9 (14 Nov 1837: D4178). See also *G/CH/60/2* 1837 19 Oct, p. 18).]

37073SE: Thurs 9 Nov 1837 – **Ann Carey** (otherwise **Hawker**), single woman: That about 19 years ago as she hath been informed and believes she was born a Bastard of the body of Elizabeth Hawker then of the Parish of <u>Cheltenham</u> Singlewoman by one John Carey who was a Chaisedriver there and who soon after this Examinant's birth was lawfully married to her said Mother at Cheltenham – That she hath also been informed and believes that the said John Carey died when she was an infant and that her said Mother also died shortly afterwards – That about 4 or 5 years ago she this Examinant was hired as [a] Servant to one M^r. Margarett of the said Parish of Cheltenham Baker for a year at the wages of one shilling Per week   That she duly served the whole of the said year during which she was boarded and lodged in her said Master's House and received her wages And this Examinant further saith that since hiring and service in the said

Parish of Cheltenham she hath not done any Act to gain a Settlement elsewhere and that in consequence of severe illness she hath lately become and is now chargeable to that Parish [mark] **1837: *removed unlikely: place of settlement probably acknowledged as Cheltenham.*** **1840:** *an AC buried at New Burial Ground, Cheltenham 1 Aug, aged 22.* [PS/CH/RA/2/3:493.]

37074RO: Thurs 9 Nov 1837– **Sarah Neale**, single woman: That she is about 22 years of age and that she was born as she hath been informed and verily believes in the Parish of Frampton Upon Severn [= Frampton-on-Severn] in the said County of Gloucester where her Father George Neale who was by Trade a Carpenter was legally settled and resided till the time of his death which happened about four years ago, and that her Mother still resides in that Parish – That she this Examinant hath never done any Act in her own right whereby to gain a Settlement and that she hath lately become and is now Chargeable to the Parish of Cheltenham [mark]
1837: *removed to Frampton-on-Severn (father's settlement).* **1841:** *SN's mother Hester (aged 60; schoolmistress) still lived in Frampton-on-Severn, with Sarah's siblings William (20; labourer) and Eliza (15) (HO107/370/2/15/5); SN was probably in service elsewhere (perhaps at Frenchay, near Winterbourne).* **1847:** *(RETURNED) SN married Thomas Sadler in Cheltenham Aug.* **1851:** *SN (34) and Thomas (37; agricultural labourer) lived at 58 Stanhope St, Cheltenham (HO107/1973/502/25).* [PS/CH/RA/2/4:78 (copy at PS/CH/RA/2/3:494); order suspended as pauper considered unfit to travel until 11 Dec. Removal expenses for "S. Neale" to Frampton-on-Severn (12 Dec 1837: D4178).]

37075SE: Thurs 9 Nov 1837 – **Ann Collier**: That upwards of 40 years ago she was lawfully married in the Parish Church of Staverton in this County to her late Husband who was then a Post Boy at the George Hotel Cheltenham   That on being married they went to live in a House in Admiral Buildings in <u>Cheltenham</u> which her Husband rented of a Mr Timbrell of Cheltenham Sawyer at the rent of 12^l a year – That they occupied the said House a great number of years during a portion of which the rent was reduced to 10^l a year but never below that sum – That during the whole of his tenancy her said Husband paid all rates and taxes for the said House – That after such occupation as aforesaid her said Husband never did any Act whatever whereby to gain a settlement – That her said Husband about 3 Weeks ago met with a severe accident which she verily believes caused his death in consequence of which she hath become chargeable to the said Parish of Cheltenham [mark]
1837: *removal unlikely: place of settlement apparently acknowledged as Cheltenham (husband's settlement)*; *husband Robert buried at New Burial Ground, Cheltenham 4 Nov, aged 63.* **1841:** *presumably the AC (aged 70; independent) living in Tewkesbury Rd, Cheltenham (HO107/353/9/36/21) (buried aged 73 at New Burial Ground, Cheltenham 24 Apr 1845).* [PS/CH/RA/2/3:495.]

37076RO: Thurs 9 Nov 1837 – **Jane Calcutt** (also **Calcott**), single woman, and two illegitimate children **Alfred** and **John**: That she is about 23 years of age and was born she believes in the Parish of Kerbridge [= Curbridge] in the County of Oxford where her Father William Calcutt who was a Labourer was legally settled – That when she this Examinant was about fifteen years old she was hired for a year by William Bolton of the Parish of Saint Ebbe's in the City of Oxford Baker at the wages of seven pounds   That she duly served the said year and continued in the service of the said William Bolton the two following years living and sleeping in his House the whole of the time – that since such hiring and service in the Parish of Saint Ebbe's she hath never done any act to gain a settlement elsewhere – That she hath two illegitimate Children (to wit) Alfred born in the said Parish of Saint Ebbe's and now aged about 4 years and John born in the Parish of Cheltenham aforesaid about eight months ago and that she this Examinant and her said Children are now chargeable to the said Parish of Cheltenham [signed]
1833: *removed to St Ebbe's, Oxford* (**33048SE:** *JC: 27 July*) *(RETURNED).* **1837: *removed to St Ebbe's, Oxford (hiring and service)*;** *on 6 Nov 1837 Alfred Calcut admitted to Charlton Kings Workhouse for Children (Cheltenham Union) (discharged to mother's care 6 Dec (behaviour "Good")) (G/CH/60/2 p. 19).* **1840** *JC married William Ewins in Oxon 4Q.* **1841:** *JC (aged 25) and husband William (40; labourer) lived with two children Alfred (8) and John (3) in Broadwater Court, Queen St, Oxford (HO107/891/15/9/9).* **1851:** *the family lived off Queen St, Oxford in Arnold's Yard, with Jane's two older children (both errand*

boys) and five children by marriage (HO107/1728/480/10). [PS/CH/RA/2/4:79 (copy at PS/CH/RA/2/3:496). Removal expenses for "Calcutt" to Oxford, Oxon £2/19/6 (9 Dec 1837: D4178). See Gray **482** (father William Calcott: 16 August 1823) and another Oxfordshire Calcutt at **33043SE** (William Calcutt: 15 July 1833).]

37077SE: Sat 11 Nov 1837 – Nathaniel Wiles, regarding settlement of son **Benjamin Wiles**, lunatic: That he is upwards of 66 Years old and was born as he believes in the Parish of Frampton upon Severn [= Frampton-on-Severn] in the said County of Gloucester where his Father was legally settled: That upwards of forty Years ago he this Examinant was lawfully married in the Parish Church of Painswick in this County to Mary his now Wife by whom he has now living among other Children the said Benjamin his Son now aged about thirty eight Years who was born in the said Parish of Painswick: That in the Year 1820 he this Examinant took a Public House called the Crown Inn in the Parish of Wotton under Edge [= Wotton-under-Edge] at the Yearly Rent of forty Pounds which he continued to rent for the space of 3 successive Years during which he paid all rates and taxes for the same: that since that period he this Examinant hath never done any Act to gain a Settlement in any other Parish: that this Examinant's said Son Benjamin never was emancipated from him and never did any Act in his own right whereby to gain a Settlement and that he is now of unsound mind. – [signed]
1837: *place of settlement determined as Wotton-under-Edge (presumed) (father's settlement). BW's admission to the Gloucester Lunatic Asylum in 1828 is described in Leonard Smith's* Cure, Comfort and Safe Custody *(1999: p. 102): "The conversation of Benjamin Wiles (29), a 'steady and industrious' Cheltenham carpenter, became incoherent and religiose, with 'most ridiculous Ideas' regarding the Devil" (see also HO22/70/2 no. 248); "Preaches continually if any one will listen to him".* **1849:** *death of Nathaniel Wiles, carpenter, registered at Cheltenham 4Q.* [PS/CH/RA/2/3:497. Removal expenses to Gloster Asylum £4/-/- (14 Nov 1837: D4178).]

37078RO: [blank] Nov 1837 – **Sarah Hampton**: [no examination filed with removal order; text from magistrates' register]. That she was born as she hath heard and verily believes in the Parish of Cheltenham aforesaid – That about eight years ago she this Examinant was engaged by Captain Stevenson to go as a hired Servant to live with Walter Lawrence Lawrence [*sic*] Esquire of the Parish of Dowdeswell in this County as a Laundry and kitchen Maid at the wages of four Pounds for a year   That she duly served such year, lived and slept in her said Masters House, and received her Wages – That since such hiring and service as aforesaid she this Examinant has never done any Act whereby to gain a settlement – That she is now in a state of Pregnancy and is chargeable to the said Parish of Cheltenham.
1837: *removed to Dowdeswell (presumed) (hiring and service): see* **46001SE** *(SH: 15 Jan 1846) for further information.* [PS/CH/RA/2/4:[unnumbered]. Pencilled note: "Run away". Perhaps see removal expenses for "Sweeney" to Northleach 11/- (29 Nov 1837: D4178).]

37079SE: Thurs 16 Nov 1837 – **Elizabeth Kellow**, widow of William Kellow, late of Cheltenham, with two children **Amelia** and **William Peter**; also Elizabeth Green, widow of Peter Kellow and wife of John Green, regarding the settlement of daughter-in-law Elizabeth Kellow. *Elizabeth Green*: That she is about 42 years of age and that she was as she has always understood and believes [born] in the Parish of Bengeworth in the County of Worcester where her Parents then resided – That in or about the year 1812 she was lawfully married in the Parish Church of Saint James in the City of Bristol to her former Husband Peter Kellow deceased who died at Cheltenham in the year 1817 without ever having as this Examinant believes acquired a Settlement in his own right – That by her said Marriage with the said Peter Kellow she this Examinant had a Son named William Kellow born in or about the year 1813 at Evesham in the s^d County of Worcester – That in the year 1819 (about two years after her said Husband's decease) she this Examinant was hired to Elizabeth Burt Widow who then kept the Shakespear Inn in the Parish of Cheltenham aforesaid for the term of a year at the wages of Five Pounds – That she duly served the said year and received her wages, since which she this Examinant hath never done any Act in her own right whereby to gain a Settlement   That her said Son William Kellow, who never did any Act in his own right whereby to gain a Settlement, died on or about the 12th. day of September last in the Parish of Cheltenham aforesaid leaving a Widow named Elizabeth Kellow and two Infant Children namely Amelia aged about six years and William Peter aged about sixteen months – [signed]

Elizabeth Kellow: That she is the Daughter of Thomas Archer formerly of Cheltenham aforesaid Plasterer who was legally settled in that Parish where she this Examinant was born about 28 Years ago: That she this Examinant never did any act in her own right whereby to gain a Settlement: That about Seven Years ago she was lawfully married in the Parish Church of Cheltenham aforesaid to the said William Kellow by whom she has two Children now living namely Amelia aged about 6 Years and William Peter aged about 16 months and that she this Examinant is now pregnant: – That she hath always understood and believes that her said Husband never did any Act to gain a Settlement, and that he died at Cheltenham aforesaid on the 12th day of September last: – that she this Examinant and her said Children have become and are now chargeable to the said Parish of Cheltenham [signed]

1837: *removal unlikely: place of settlement probably acknowledged as Cheltenham; daughter Elizabeth born at Cheltenham (or early 1838).* **1841:** *the family lived in Burton St, Cheltenham: EK (aged 30; charwoman), Amelia (9), Peter (5), and Elizabeth (3).* [PS/CH/RA/2/3:499-500. See Gray **138** (mother EK: 16 Sept 1817) (mother born Sollass, formerly living as vagrant).]

37080RO: Sat 18 Nov 1837 – **Edward Bencroft** (also **Bancroft**): That he is about fifty four years of age and that he was born in the Parish of Saint George Hanover Square in the County of Middlesex where his Father John Bencroft who was by Trade a Painter lived and as he this Examinant hath always understood and believed was legally settled – And this Examinant further saith that he hath never done any Act whereby to gain a Settlement in his own right and that he hath become and is now chargeable to the said Parish of Cheltenham [mark]

1837: *removed to St George Hanover Square, Middlesex (father's settlement): see* **38011RO** *(EB: 5 Feb) for further information.* [PS/CH/RA/2/4:80 (copy at PS/CH/RA/2/3:501).]

37081SE: Mon 20 Nov 1837 – **Sarah Main**, widow, with son **Jesse**: That she is about fifty Years of Age and was born as she believes in the Parish of Dymock in the County of Gloucester where her Father John Finch then resided: That when she was about sixteen Years of Age she was hired for a Year as an indoor servant to M^r. Fream [also Freame] of the Parish of All Saints, Worcester at the Wages of 7[£] or 8[£] and that she duly served the said Year in that Parish: that she was then hired for a Year to Major Atkinson of Sion House Bedminster in the County of Somerset at the Wages of 14[£] and lived in his service 3 successive Years in that Parish: that from the time of such last mentioned hiring and Service up to the time of her Marriage she did not do any Act whereby to gain a settlement: That about 16 Years ago this Examinant was lawfully married in the Parish Church of Saint Paul Bristol to her late Husband William Main by whom she has one Child now living with her named Jesse Main aged about 14 Years ~~That about 2 Years~~ after this Examinant's Marriage her husband was hired for a Year to Robert Morris then of the Parish of Cheltenham Banker and that he lived in his service for a Year accordingly during the whole of which he was lodged and boarded in his Master's House: that since such last mentioned service she this Examinant is not aware that her said Husband ever did any act to gain a Settlement: – that about 8 Years ago her said Husband left her and as she believes went to Guildford in the County of Surry [= Surrey] where he was employed as a Waiter at an Inn but whether he was hired as a servant she does not know: that ~~she hath understood~~ he afterwards went to Chichester and was employed as a Waiter at the Dolphin Inn there but whether he was a hired servant or how long he lived there she this Examinant does not know: that he afterwards went as Waiter to the Swan Inn at Chichester where as she this Examinant understood and believes he died about 3 Years ago: And this Examinant saith that she hath become and is now chargeable to the said Parish of Cheltenham: ~~That about 2 years ago she was hired by M^{rs}. Alexander the Wife of Captⁿ. Alexander of Cheltenham as a Servant at the Wages of 16 Guineas and lived in such service~~ [signed Sarah Man]

1837: *removal unlikely: place of settlement probably acknowledged as Cheltenham: abbreviated version in magistrates' register at* **38079SE** *(SM: 8 Dec 1838).* [PS/CH/RA/2/3:503.]

37082SE: Thurs 30 Nov 1837 – **Eliza Hill**, single woman, with son **William**: That she is about Eighteen Years of Age: that she does not know where she was born but recollects being at Lechlade in the County of Gloucester went about six Years old in which Parish her Father and Mother were then living: that her Father was a Soldier and died about 8 Years ago in Chelsea Hospital and that her Mother died some time before him: that she this Examinant never heard her Father or Mother say where their Settlement was or where she this Examinant was born: that she this Examinant was delivered of a male illegitimate Child in the Parish of Cheltenham about 3 weeks ago and that she and her said Child are now chargeable to that Parish. – [mark]
1818: *EH baptised 16 Aug at Lechlade, daughter of William (then blacksmith) and Ann Hill.* **1837**: *removal uncertain; no removal order found in register; illegitimate son William baptised 1 Dec, while mother was resident at Poor House in Cheltenham.* **1838**: *William buried 27 Jan, aged two months, at New Burial Ground, Cheltenham.* [PS/CH/RA/2/3:504.]

37083RO: Fri 8 Dec 1837 – **Elizabeth Walter**, widow: That she is about 38 years of age and was born as she believes in the Parish of Clerkenwell in the County of Middlesex where her Father and Mother then resided – That about 8 years ago she was lawfully married in the Parish Church of Saint Helier in the Island of Jersey to her late Husband Samuel Walter who was a Ship Carpenter there – That during the life time of her said Husband she frequently heard him say and she verily believes that he was born in the Parish of East Loo[e] in the County of Cornwall where his Father who was a Fisherman resided for many years and was legally settled and that he (her said late Husband) was bounden as an indoor apprentice to a Mr Minet then of the Parish of East Loo aforesaid Ship Carpenter (since deceased) for seven years with whom he served the whole of his time. That by her said marriage she this Examinant has a Son named Samuel who is now about seven years Old – That about two years ago she applied to the Parish Officers of East Loo aforesaid for money to enable her to take her said Son to London for the purpose of placing him in the Mariners School there (through the Medium of the Mariners Orphan Society) – That she received from the said Parish Officers the sum of 25^s/ to enable her to take and place her said son in such School where he now is – That her said Husband died about 5½ years since and she verily believes he never did any act after his said apprenticeship, nor has she this Examinant since his death done any Act whereby to gain a settlement and that she is now chargeable to the said Parish of Cheltenham [mark]
1837: *removed to East Looe, Cornwall (husband's settlement).* [PS/CH/RA/2/4:81 (copy at PS/CH/RA/2/3:505); *order suspended until 6 Jan 1838 as pauper unfit to travel. Removal expenses for "E. Walters" to East Looe, Cornwall £12/11/11 (Jan 1838: D4178). The Merchant Seamen's Orphan Asylum, founded 1827 to care for children whose fathers had been lost at sea, was originally located at 4 Clark's Terrace, London, and in 1834 moved to New Grove, Bow Rd, London.*]

37084RO: Sat 9 Dec 1837 – **Isabella Thomas**, single woman: That she is in the 15th year of her age and is as she believes the Daughter of Grace Thomas (who died at Cheltenham about a fortnight ago) by her Husband James Thomas formerly at the Parish of St George near Bristol in the County of Gloucester Steam Engineer – That she this Examinant has no recollection whatever of her Father, who as she has always understood from her Mother left her when she this Examinant was about 4 years of age – That she this Examinant frequently heard her said Mother say that her Father's legal settlement was in the said Parish of Saint George from which she had on many occasions received Parochial relief – And this Examinant saith that she hath never done any Act in her own right whereby to gain a Settlement – That for some time before her said Mother's death she became chargeable to the Parish of Cheltenham and died in the Poor house there and that this Examinant is now chargeable to the said Parish [mark]
1837: *removed to Saint George, Bristol (father's settlement).* **1841**: *perhaps the IT (aged 20) who lived in family of John Thomas in Bristol (60; cooper) (HO107/375/1/9/13).* [PS/CH/RA/2/4:82 (copy at

PS/CH/RA/2/3:506). Removal expenses for "Isabella Thomas" to Bristol £2/4/- (29 Nov 1837: D4178). See **37043RO** (mother Grace Thomas: 17 July 1837).]

37085SE: Sat 16 Dec 1837 – **David Vizard** (also **Vizzard**), labourer, wife **Mary**, and children **William**, **Fanny**, **Jane**, and **Handy**: That he is about 31 Years of Age and was born as he believes in the Parish of Broadway in the County of Worcester where his Father John Vizard who was a Carpenter was settled: That about 13 or 14 Years ago he this Examinant was hired for a Year as an indoor Servant to Edward Fricker of Cheltenham Surgeon at the Wages of four Guineas (in addition to Cloathes) and that he duly served the said Year accordingly and continued in M^r. Fricker's service some time afterwards: That since such service he this Examinant hath never done any Act whatever whereby to gain a Settlement: – That about 8 Years ago he was lawfully married in the Parish Church of Broadway aforesaid to Mary his now Wife (then Mary Mealing Singlewoman) by whom he has four Children living namely William aged about Six Years, Fanny aged about 4 Years, Jane aged about 3 Years and Handy aged about 1 Year: - [signed]

1837: *children Fanny (aged 5) and Jane Vizard (7) admitted to Charlton Kings Workhouse for children (Cheltenham Union) on 7 Dec; **removal unlikely: place of settlement probably acknowledged as Cheltenham**. **1838:** Fanny and Jane discharged to father's care 27 Jan (behaviour "Good") (G/CH/60/2/3 pp. 20, 23, etc). **1839:** son Charles born at Broadway, Worcs 3Q. **1841:** the family lived in Church St, Broadway: David (aged 30; agricultural labourer), Mary (30), Fanny (8), Jane (5), Handy (3), and Charles (1) (HO107/1204/10/9/10). **1842:** Fanny, Jane, and Handy received (condition "Clean") into Charlton Kings Workhouse, when parents were admitted inmates of Cheltenham Workhouse. **1851:** the family lived in Gas Green, Cheltenham: David (40) on parish relief, "dung gatherer"; Handy (12) and Charles (10) also dung-gatherers, and Fanny (18) charwoman (HO107/1973/549/20). [PS/CH/RA/2/3:507. Expenses for "Apprehending Watts/at Vizard [braced together]" £2/11/- (15 Dec 1837: D4178). See G/CH/60/2 1837 Dec, etc).]*

37086SE: Thurs 21 Dec 1837 – **William Watts**, wife **Mary Ann**, and two children **William** and **Mary Ann**: That he is about forty six Years of Age and was born as he believes in the Parish of Minchinhampton in the County of Gloucester where his Father Samuel Watts who was likewise a Stonemason was settled: That when this Examinant was about 14 Years old he was apprenticed for 7 Years to George Evans of Minchinhampton Stonemason: that he served him about 5½ Years when he died: That when he was about 25 Years old he came to Cheltenham and having established himself in business there Rented a House of George Snelus in that Parish at 12 Pounds a Year for 2 successive Years and that he afterwards rented a House in the same Parish from John Snelus at 10 Guineas a Year, since which he hath not done any act whereby to gain a Settlement: That about 23 Years ago he this Examinant was lawfully married in the Parish Church of Minchinhampton aforesaid to Mary Ann his present Wife then Mary Ann Tilley Singlewoman by whom he has 2 Children now living (namely) William aged 22 Years and Mary Ann aged about 20 years: – [signed]

1837: *removal unlikely: place of settlement probably acknowledged as Cheltenham. **1838:** Mary Ann Watts left husband WW, citing "ill-usage", around this time. **1851:** she is perhaps the Mary Ann Watts (aged 60; cook, born Worcester) who resided at Cheltenham Workhouse; WW (aged 51; stonemason) lived with Eliza Fudger (46; huxter's shopkeeper), her daughter Louisa (9; school) and illegitimate sons with WW: Charles (3) and George Fudger (1; both born Worcester) in Upper Quay, Worcester (HO107/2042/196/27). **1861:** WW (67; stonemason) lived with the Fudgers, now as head of household (RG9/2090/24/41). **1857:** wife Eliza became chargeable to Cheltenham and WW was arrested for desertion (see Worcestershire Chron. 18 Feb); WW committed to serve one month in gaol in default of fine. [PS/CH/RA/2/3:[508]. Expenses for "Apprehending Watts/at Vizard [braced together]" £2/11/- (15 Dec 1837: D4178).]*

37087RO: Thurs 21 Dec 1837 – **William Wicksey**, labourer, wife **Elizabeth**, and three children **Phoebe**, **Jane**, and **William**, residing in Lower Alstone, Cheltenham: That he is about twenty nine years of age and that he was born as he believes in the Parish of Upper Guiting in the said County of Gloucester where he hath understood his Father was Settled: – That about fourteen years ago he this Examinant was hired as a Servant in Husbandry by William Lane of the Parish of Charlton

Abbotts in the said County of Gloucester Farmer for the year: That he duly served the said Year and Continued in the Service of the said William Lane a year afterwards   that since such hiring and Service he this Examinant hath not done any Act whereby to gain a Settlement   that about eight years ago he was lawfully married in the Parish Church of Temple Guiting in this County to Elizabeth his now Wife by whom he hath 3 Children now living namely Phœbe aged about 7 years Jane aged about 4 years and William aged about 2 years   That he this Examinant hath received occasional relief from the said Parish of Charlton Abbotts and that he his said Wife and Children are now Chargeable to the Parish of Cheltenham [mark]

1837: *removed to Charlton Abbots (near Winchcombe) (hiring and service).* **1841:** *WW (aged 35; agricultural labourer) lived with wife Elizabeth (25), and children Jane (8), William (5), and Mary (1), and also father Thomas and younger brother Joseph, in Kineton, Temple Guiting (HO107/360/9/5/4).* **1851:** *WW (aged 44; widower, agricultural labourer) lodged with children William (14; agricultural labourer), Mary (11), and Fanny (9) in Gloucester St, Winchcombe (HO107/1971/105/45). PS/CH/RA/2/4:83 (copy at PS/CH/RA/2/3:[509]).]*

37088SE: Thurs 21 Dec 1837 – **Mary Budd**: That she is about to 18 Years of Age and that she was born as she believes in London but in what Street or Parish she does not know: That her Father died when she was quite an infant and her Mother died when this Examinant was about 9 Years old: that she never heard her Mother say any thing about her own or her Father's Settlements: That she this Examinant hath never done any Act in her own right whereby to gain a Settlement: That she is now pregnant and hath become chargeable to the Parish of Cheltenham [mark]

1837: *removal uncertain: evidence appears inconclusive.* **1838:** *illegitimate male child stillborn at Cheltenham Workhouse 20 Jan. [PS/CH/RA/2/3:[510].]*

*Joseph Brown (**38019RO**), tailor, sent back to Middlesex, where he had been apprenticed*

*Charles Fluck (**38021RO**), a 19-year-old labourer, removed to Hawling, Glos, his father's place of settlement*

*Eliza Sole or Soul (**38045SE**), single woman, from Painswick. Probably allowed to remain in Cheltenham. Clerk notes in pencil that she is in the Workhouse about to give birth*

Pauper signatures: 37% of paupers signed their settlement examination; the majority placed a cross as their mark

1838

38001RO: Mon 1 Jan 1838 – **James Prosser**, labourer, wife **Mary**, and four children **Sarah**, **Caroline**, **Edith**, and **Elizabeth**: That he is about 45 years old and that he was born as he believes at Martley in the County of Worcester where his Father William Prosser who was also a Labourer as he this Examinant always understood was settled – That when he this Examinant was about 10 years old he went out as a servant in Husbandry and lived in various situations until he was about 20 years of age when he was hired to M^r. William Lamb of the Pigeon house Farm in the Parish of Eldersfield in the said County of Worcester for a year at the wages as he this Examinant believes of £8　　That he duly served such year during the whole of which he slept in his Master's House – That he afterwards continued to work on the said Farm at various times for several years – That about 20 years ago he was lawfully married at the Parish Church of Eldersfield aforesaid to Mary his now Wife by whom he had 10 Children 7 of whom are now living – That four of such Children (namely) Sarah aged about 14 years Caroline aged about 7 years – Edith aged about 4 years and Elizabeth aged about 4 months are now dependant [*sic*] upon this Examinant for support　　That on many occasions when he this Examinant lived at Eldersfield he was relieved by the Parish Officers there and that about 10 weeks before last Michaelmas he received the sum of 15^s/- from that Parish for the purpose of enabling him to bury one of his Infant Children And this Examinant saith That since such hiring and service at Eldersfield aforesaid he has not done any Act whereby to gain a Settlement elsewhere and in consequence of severe illness he has become and is now chargeable to this Parish [mark]
1838: *birth of daughter Elizabeth in Cheltenham just before examination;* **removed to Eldersfield, Worcs (hiring and service).** **1841:** *JP (aged 45; agricultural labourer) lived with wife Mary (45), and four children Mary (20; servant), William (15; agricultural labourer), Caroline (12), and Elizabeth (7) in Lime St, Eldersfield, Worcs (HO107/1204/5/20/9).* **1843:** *birth of next child in Eldersfield.* [PS/CH/RA/2/484; order lacks examination text (taken from PS/CH/RA/2/5:1). Removal expenses for "Paupers Prosser & fam[il]y" to Eldersfield £1/3/- (Jan 1838: D4178).]

38002RO: Thurs 4 Jan 1838 – **Francis Cox**, labourer: That he is about 46 years of age and that he was born as he hath always understood and believes in the Parish of Burford in the County of Oxford where his Father and Mother resided: – that about 9 years ago he this Examinant was hired for a year by [blank] Joy Esqre. then of <u>Draycot</u> Near Reading in the County of Berks as his Coachman: – That this Examinant accordingly entered upon such service and when he had lived with the same [blank] Joy about a fortnight his said Master removed from Draycot to Hartham Park in the Parish of Corsham in the County of Wilts where this Examinant duly served the remainder of his year: – that since this service he hath done no act whereby to gain a settlement and that he hath become and is now chargeable to the said Parish of Cheltenham [mark]
1838: *removed to Corsham, Wilts (hiring and service).* **1851:** *an FC (aged 59; porter) was a pauper inmate of Cheltenham Workhouse (HO107/1973/1093/7), though listed as born in Glos.* [PS/CH/RA/2/4:85 (copy at PS/CH/RA/2/5:2). Removal expenses for "Francis Cox" to Corsham, Wilts £2/16/6 (Febuary 1838: D4178).]

38003RO: Sat 13 Jan 1838 – **Elizabeth Clarke** (also **Clark**), widow: That she is about 58 years old – That about 20 years ago she was lawfully married in the Parish Church of Tetbury in the said County of Gloucester to her late Husband Jonathan [Watson] Clarke who died about 13 years ago　　That she frequently heard her said Husband say and she verily believes that he was apprenticed to a Tinman and Brazier (whose name she does not now recollect) of the Parish of Saint Peter and Saint Paul in the City on Bath and that he duly served his apprenticeship accordingly in such Parish after which he never did any act whereby to gain a settlement – That upon the death of her said Husband the Parish officers of Saint Peter and Saint Paul aforesaid promised to allow this Examinant a Weekly Payment towards her support but being able to do without it she never received it. That in or about the year 1821 this Examinant came to reside in

the Parish of Cheltenham and that a few weeks before Christmas 1832 being unable by reason of infirmity to do any work she applied to the Parish officers of Saint Peter and Saint Paul aforesaid for relief which they refused to grant unless she would go into the Poor house there   That this Examinant declined doing so whereupon the Parish officers gave her a few shillings to enable her to return to Cheltenham again where she has been living ever since – That she has never done any Act in her own right whereby to gain a legal Settlement and in consequence of severe illness she has now become chargeable to the said Parish of Cheltenham [mark]
1825: *EC removed to St Peter and St Paul, Bath (see Gray* **558, 583** *(EC: 5 July, 28 Oct), where birthplace given as Tetbury) (RETURNED).* **1838:** *removed to St Peter and St Paul, Bath (husband's settlement).* [PS/CH/RA/2/4:86 (copy at PS/CH/RA/2/5:4; incomplete copy p. 3); order suspended until 5 July as considered to be pauper unfit to travel. Removal expenses for "E. Clarke" to Bath £3/6/- (17 July 1838: D4178).]

38004RO: Sat 13 Jan 1838 – **Elizabeth Parke**, widow, with two children **George** and **Elizabeth**: That she is the Widow of George Parke to whom she was lawfully married in the Parish Church of Saint Mary Le Bone in the County of Middlesex about 17 years ago – That about 3 years after this marriage [magistrates' register note: before her marriage] her said Husband was hired for a year as Groom to Sir Thomas Wilson of Charlton in the County of Kent Baronet – That he duly served the said year and continued in the service of the said Sir Thomas Wilson until the time of his death which happened about 3 years ago – That by her marriage as aforesaid she has 2 Children now living (namely) George aged about 11 years and Elizabeth aged about 7 years who together with this Examinant have become and are now chargeable to the Parish of Cheltenham [mark]
1838: *removed to Charlton, Kent (husband's settlement).* [PS/CH/RA/2/4:87 (copy at PS/CH/RA/2/5:5: note: "the s^d. George Parke; he was hired for a Year as Groom to [struck out] Sanctuary Esqr of the P[ari]sh Wasenham [= Weasenham] in the Co: of Norfolk in whose service he lived for 2 successive Years after which he never did any act whereby to gain a Settlement: That since her s^d. husband died she has rece[ive]d relief from the s^d P[ari]sh of Wasenham"; order suspended as pauper unfit to travel. See **38015RO** (EP: 17 Feb 1838).]

38005RO: Sat 13 Jan 1838 – **William Saunders**, labourer, with wife **Ann**: That he is about 28 years old and that he was born as he believes in the Parish of Prestbury in this County where his Father Edward Saunders as he has been informed and believes lived for 30 years or more and was legally settled – That his said Father has oftentimes told him and he verily believes that he acquired a settlement in the said Parish of Prestbury by having been hired as a Servant in Husbandry for a year at the Hyde Farm in that Parish where he lived for two successive years after which he never did any Act to gain a Settlement elsewhere   That he this Examinant has been living in the said Parish of Prestbury all his life time but has never done any act whereby to gain a Settlement in his own right – That about 4½ years ago he this Examinant was lawfully married at the Parish Church of Prestbury aforesaid to Ann his present Wife formerly Ann Morgan Singlewoman – That he is now in consequence of illness chargeable to the Parish of Cheltenham [mark]
1838: *removed to Prestbury (father's settlement).* **1841:** *(RETURNED) WS (aged 30; labourer) and wife Ann (35) lived in Mount Pleasant, Cheltenham (HO107/353/6/16/26).* [PS/CH/RA/2/4:88 (copy at PS/CH/RA/2/5:8); order suspended as pauper unfit to travel.]

38006RO: Sat 13 Jan 1838 – **Charles Linham**, servant: That he was born as he believes in the Parish of Purton [also Puxton; probably Puriton] near Bridgwater in the County of Somerset where his ffather James Linham who was a Mason was as he this Examinant believes legally settled – That he this Examinant went out to Service when he was about 14 years of age and lived in several places until the year 1833 or 1834 when he was hired for a year as under Butler to Sir William Welby of Denton Hall in the Parish of Denton in the County of Lincoln in whose Service he duly lived the said year after which he never did any Act whereby to gain a legal Settlement And this Examinant saith that he hath lately become and is now chargeable to the Parish of Cheltenham [signed]

1838: *removed to Denton, Lincs (hiring and service) (quashed on appeal): see* **38032RO** *(CL: 23 Apr 1838) for further information.* [PS/CH/RA/2/4:89 (copy at PS/CH/RA/2/5:9); order suspended as pauper unfit to travel. Note: "this order was appealed against at Easter sessions 1838 and quashed on the ground that Linham did not live 12 months with Sir William Welby". Pencilled notes in text replacing details of three years' service as footman to Sir William Welby with service to William Blane Esq. of Winkfield, Berks.]

38007SE: Sat 13 Jan 1838 – **Mary Ann George**: That she is between 17 and 18 Years of Age and that she was born as she believes in the <u>City of Worcester</u>: That at Michaelmas 1832 she this Examinant was hired for a Year as a Household Servant to Thomas Davis of the <u>Parish of Cheltenham</u> aforesaid Painter at the Wages of five Pounds which Year she duly served accordingly since which time she has not done any act whereby to gain a Settlement: And this Examinant lastly saith that she hath lately become and is now chargeable to the said Parish of Cheltenham [mark]
1838: *removal unlikely: place of settlement probably acknowledged as Cheltenham.* [PS/CH/RA/2/5:10.]

38008RO: Mon 15 Jan 1838 – **James Smith**, and children **James** and **Emma**: That he is about 36 years of Age and that he was born as he believes in the Parish of Repton in the County of Derby where his Father William Smith a Labourer was as he this examinant has always understood and believes legally settled: – That when he this examinant was about 12 years old he went as an indoor Servant to Mr Gregory a Schoolmaster of Repton aforesaid with whom he lived two successive years - That he then went as an indoor Servant to a Doctor Tabberer of that Parish with whom he lived 12 Months and upwards when he was afterwards hired for a year by a M^r. Walton of the same Parish in whose service he continued three successive years during the whole of which time he lived and slept in his Master's House – That on leaving Mr Walton's service he went to live with a Mr Boultby of Newton Cerney [= Newton Solney] in the County of Derby with whom he lived 12 months when he returned to Repton and was again hired by his former Master Mr Walton in whose service he lived two years during which he was boarded and lodged in his Master's House – That since such last named servitude he has done no act whereby to gain a settlement – That about six years ago he was examined before the Magistrates of Repton aforesaid as to his Settlement when he was relieved by the Parish Officers there and has on other occasions since that period been relieved by them – That in the year 1820 this examinant was lawfully married at the Parish Church of Saint Philip and Saint Jacob at Bristol to Mary his late Wife (who died about seven years ago) by whom he has three Children now living (namely) James aged about 15 years, William (now living with his Uncle at Bristol aforesaid) aged about 14 years, and Emma aged nearly 10 years – That in consequence of severe illness he this examinant and the said James and Emma his Children have become and are now chargeable to the Parish of Cheltenham [mark]
1838: *removed to Repton, Derbys (hiring and service).* [PS/CH/RA/2/4:90 (copy at PS/CH/RA/2/5:6); order suspended as pauper unfit to travel.]

38009SE: Mon 15 Jan 1838 – **Charles Povey**, labourer, wife **Sarah**, and two children **Caroline** and **Ellen**: That he is 24 Years of Age and that he was born as he hath always understood and believes in the Parish of <u>Wotton under Edge</u> [= Wotton-under-Edge] in the said <u>County of Gloucester</u>: That his Father died when he this Examinant was very Young but that his Mother is now living at Wotton under Edge aforesaid: That he hath frequently heard her say and he verily believes that his Father was legally settled in that Parish: That he this Examinant hath never done any Act in his own right whereby to gain a Settlement: That about three Years and 3 Months ago he was lawfully married in the Parish Church of Cheltenham to Sarah his now Wife by whom he has 2 Children namely Caroline aged about 2 Years and a half and Ellen aged about 14 Months: – [mark]
1838: *removed to Wotton-under-Edge (presumed) (father's settlement): see* **43020RO** *(CP: 4 Mar 1843) for further information.* [PS/CH/RA/2/5:11.]

38010SE: Sat 27 Jan 1838 – **Benjamin Simmonds** (also **Simmons**), labourer, and wife **Susan**: That he is about 42 years of age and that he was born as he believes at Stoke Orchard in the

Parish of Bishop's Cleeve in the said County – That when he this Examinant was about 14 or 15 years Old he was hired as under Carter to Mr John Healing of Walton Hill in the Parish of Deerhurst Farmer for a year at the wages of £5 which year he duly served – That he was next hired to Mr Charles Yeend of Elmstone Hardwick [= Elmstone Hardwicke] in the said County Farmer as a Servant in Husbandry for a year at the wages of 13^l. which year he likewise duly served – That after such last mentioned Servitude this Examinant came to Cheltenham and worked about at different places for some time when he was hired by Mr Richard Dawes of Cheltenham aforesaid Common Carrier for a year at the wages of 7^s/ Per week and his board and lodgings – That he used to go about the Country with his Masters Waggon and Horses and on some occasions remained out on his Master's business for a night or two together during such year – That he afterwards continued in Mr Dawes's Service on the same terms for two years during which time he used to go out frequently to Beaconsfield and other places with his Master's Waggon and Horses and was occasionally about for a week at a time but he always considered his home to be at M^r. Dawes's – That about 3 years ago he was lawfully married at the Parish Church of Cheltenham to Susan his now Wife (formerly Susan West Singlewoman)   That since his Servitude as aforesaid with Mr Dawes, he has done no Act whereby to gain a Settlement and that he [is] now chargeable to this Parish [mark of Benjamin Joseph Simmons]
1838: removal unlikely: place of settlement probably acknowledged as Cheltenham. 1851: *probably the Benjamin Simonds (aged 60; labourer, born Bishop's Cleeve) lodged at 5 King St, Cheltenham (HO107/1973/409/51) (married, but not living with wife at time of census).* [PS/CH/RA/2/5:12.]

38011RO: Mon 5 Feb 1838 – **Edward Bencroft**, labourer: That he is about fifty four years of age and that he was born as he hath always understood and believes in the Parish of Saint George Hanover Square in the County of Middlesex where his Father John Bencroft who was by trade a Painter lived and as he this Examinant likewise understood and verily believes was legally settled – And this Examinant further saith that on or about the year 1831 he became chargeable to the Parish of Cheltenham by having received Parochial relief there in consequence of which he was examined as to the place of his Settlement and removed by an Order of 2 Justices to the said Parish of Saint George Hanover Square from which he subsequently received relief – That about 14 months since this Examinant again came to Cheltenham in search of employment where he hath remained ever since – That from the time of his birth he hath never done any Act in his own right whereby to gain a Settlement and that he hath lately become a second time chargeable to the said Parish of Cheltenham [mark]
1831/7: *previous removals to St George, Hanover Square, Middlesex: see* **31125SE** *(EB: 10 Dec 1831) and* **37080RO** *(18 Nov 1837) (RETURNED).* **1838: removed to St George, Hanover Square (father's settlement). 1841:** *EB (pauper aged approx. 50, born Middlesex) lived as an inmate of St George Hanover Square Workhouse (HO107/688/16/70/1); EB, pauper, died of "Apoplexy" on 22 Dec at St George's Workhouse, Chelsea, aged 51.* [PS/CH/RA/2/4:91 (copy at PS/CH/RA/2/5:13). Removal expenses for "Bencroft" to St George, Hanover Square £2/5/9 (27 Feb 1838: D4178).]

38012RO: Sat 10 Feb 1838 – **Nathan** (also **Nathaniel**) **Sparrow**, labourer, wife **Ann**, and children **Charles** and **Charlotte**: That he is about 33 years of age and that he was born as he hath always understood and believes in the Parish of Highworth in the County of Wilts where his Father Nathan Sparrow then resided and where he believes he is legally settled – And this Examinant saith that he hath never in his own right done any Act whereby to gain a settlement – That about ten years ago he this Examinant was lawfully married in the Parish Church of Bishop's Cleeve in the said County of Gloucester to Ann his now Wife then Ann Page Widow by whom he has 2 Children now living born in Wedlock (namely) Charles aged about 5 years and Charlotte aged about 4 years – That about 2 months before his Marriage his said Wife had an illegitimate Child which is now living and which was born in the said Parish of Bishop's Cleeve And this Examinant lastly saith That he his said Wife and Children have become and are now chargeable to the Parish of Cheltenham [mark]

1833: *removed to Highworth, Wilts (father's settlement): see* **33027SE** *(NS: 2 May) (RETURNED).* **1834:** *birth of daughter Charlotte registered at Cheltenham though apparently born at Highworth (census: HO107/1833/271/4).* **1835:** *son John born at Cheltenham.* **1838:** ***removed to Highworth, Wilts (father's settlement)****; Ann Sparrow buried 30 Mar at St Mary's, Cheltenham.* **1841:** *children Charles (aged 8) and Charlotte (aged 8; both "pauper in the house") were resident at Highworth Union Workhouse, Wilts (HO107/1178/15/31/3).* **1851:** *daughter Charlotte was an inmate of Highworth and Swindon Union Workhouse, aged 16.* **1857:** *marriage of Charles (under spelling "Sparrough").* [PS/CH/RA/2/4:92 (copy at PS/CH/RA/2/5:14); note: "Sum[mon]s issued to bring this man up to have the above taken"; order suspended until 7 Apr as pauper unfit to travel. Removal expenses for Cole to accompany "N Sparrow & family" to Highworth £2/7/6" (9 Apr 1838: D4178). See **38066SE** (Jane Sparrow: 3 Nov 1838) (illegitimate daughter Amy buried at Bishops Cleeve 25 Feb 1840, aged 14.]

38013SE: Thurs 8 Feb 1838 – Thomas Priestley, labourer, regarding the settlement of **Frances Rodway**, illegitimate daughter of Rose Rodway, deceased, formerly of Cheltenham and late of Kensington, Middlesex: That the said Rose Rodway died on the Seventeenth day of January last at Kensington aforesaid   That the said Frances Rodway is her Child and is now in the fourth Year of her Age: That for the space of 17 Months or thereabouts prior to the death of the said Rose Rodway he this Examinant cohabited with her during which time he frequently heard her say that she gained a Settlement at Cheltenham about the Year 1830 by having been hired and served a Year to Dr Allardyce there: That this Examinant believes that the said Rose Rodway was never married: that the said Frances Rodway hath become and is now chargeable to the said Parish of Cheltenham [signed]
1838: *removal unlikely: place of settlement probably acknowledged as Cheltenham.* **1839:** *FR died of "Scrofula" on 1 Jan at Purton, Cricklade, Wilts, aged 4 (buried 3 Jan).* [PS/CH/RA/2/5:15.]

38014RO: Sat 17 Feb 1838 – **Sarah Matthews**, single woman: That she is about 32 years of age and that she was born as she believes in the Parish of Frome Silwood [= Frome Selwood] in the County of Somerset where her Father John Matthews at that time resided – That she hath frequently heard her said Father say and she verily believes that his Parish is at Sutton Veney [= Sutton Veny] in the County of Wilts – That about 9 years ago when this Examinant was ill at Frome Silwood aforesaid her Examination was taken there as to her Settlement upon which occasion it was ascertained that Sutton Veney was her Parish – And this Examinant further saith that she hath never done any Act in her own right whereby to gain a settlement – That about three months ago she came to Cheltenham in search of employment but not having been able to procure any she hath been driven to the necessity of applying for and obtaining relief from that Parish to which she is now chargeable [mark]
1838: *removed to Sutton Veny, Wilts (father's settlement).* [PS/CH/RA/2/4:93 (copy at PS/CH/RA/2/5:7: a sentence in magistrates' register (struck out) notes that SM's father was a weaver. Removal expenses to Sutton Veny Wilts for "S. Matthews" (16 Mar 1838: D4178).]

38015RO: Sat 17 Feb 1838 – **Elizabeth Parke**, widow, with two children **George** and **Elizabeth**: That she is the Widow of George Parke to whom she was lawfully married in the Parish Church of Saint Mary Le Bone in the County of Middlesex about 17 years ago – That about three years previously to such marriage her said Husband was hired for a year as Groom to [blank] Sanctuary Esquire of the Parish of Weasenham Saint Peters or North in the County of Norfolk in whose Service he lived two Successive years after which he never did any Act whereby to gain a Settlement. That since her said Husband's decease she has received relief from the said Parish of Weasenham – That by her marriage with the said George Parke as aforesaid She has two Children now living (namely) George aged about 11 years and Elizabeth aged about 7 years who together with this Examinant has [sic] become and are now Chargeable to the said Parish of Cheltenham [mark]
1838: *removed to Charlton, Kent (presumably appealed): see* **38004** *(EP: 13 Jan); removed to Weasenham St Peter's or Weasenham North, Norfolk (husband's settlement).* [PS/CH/RA/2/4:9) (copy at

PS/CH/RA/2/5:17). Removal expenses to Weasenham, Norfolk for "Parks & family" £13/3/3 (8 May 1838: D4178).]

38016RO: Sat 17 Feb 1838 – **Henry Whitall**, glover, with wife **Catherine**: That he is about forty one years of age and that he was born as he believes in the Parish of Saint Helens in the City of Worcester where his Father William Whitall who was a Glover at that time resided and was as he this Examinant also believes legally settled – That when he this Examinant was about 11 or 12 years old he was bounden apprentice by Indenture to his said Father for 7 years – That he served about 3 years of such term in the said Parish of Saint Helens when his father went to reside in the Parish of <u>All Saints</u> at Worcester aforesaid in which this Examinant served 2 years more of his said apprenticeship – that he then quarrelled with and left his Father and was assigned for the remainder of his term to one Thomas Digger of the Parish of Saint Martin in the said City of Worcester Glover but that he did not serve the said Thomas Digger any portion of such term the assignment being made for the purpose of enabling this Examinant to obtain his freedom – That since his Servitude with his Father he hath not done any Act whereby to gain a settlement – That about 5 years ago he this Examinant was legally married to Catherine his present Wife (then Catherine Salmon Widow) in consequence of whose severe illness he has become and is now chargeable to the said Parish of Cheltenham [signed]
1838: *removed to All Saints, Worcester (apprenticeship).* **1851:** *HW (aged 54; glover) lived with new wife Ann (50; born Worcester) in Bromley, Kent* [PS/CH/RA/2/4:9 (copy at PS/CH/RA/2/5:17, with extensive editing: Catherine Whitall had two children, now provided for, from previous marriage, and none as result of marriage to HW.); order was suspended because of Catherine Whitall's sickness; Pencilled notes "20 Newman's Place. Wife very ill" and "Suspension as to wife".]

38017RO: Sat 17 Feb 1838 – **Eliza Powell**, single woman: That she is about 24 years of age and that she was born as she believes in the Parish of Beckington in the County of Somerset where her Father Samuel Powell who was a Stage Coachman resided – That her Mother as she had been informed and believes died in Beckington aforesaid about 12 months after this Examinants birth and that her Father died at Bath about 6 years since – That about 2 years ago last May she this Examinant in consequence of illness went in the Poor house of Cheltenham aforesaid where she remained about 11 weeks – That she went from Cheltenham to Bath and lived in various places as a Servant but was never hired for a year – That about eighteen months since she returned to Cheltenham and in consequence of illness hath become and is now chargeable to that Parish – That she has never done any Act in her own right whereby to gain a Settlement – [mark]
1802: *an EP baptised at Beckington, Som 3 Mar, to Samuel and Maria Powell; early burial for this child has not been found; if this is examinant, then she was about ten years older than examination records indicate.* **1838:** *removed to Beckington, Som (birth).* **1841:** *perhaps the EP (aged 35; born Som) living at 4 Church St, Bath and employed as nurse (HO107/969/2/29/54).* [PS/CH/RA/2/49 (copy at PS/CH/RA/2/5:21); order suspended until 12 Mar because of sickness or infirmity). Removal expenses for "Powell" to Beckington, Som (16 Mar 1838: D4178).]

38018SE: Sat 17 Feb 1838 – **Sarah Holdey**: That she is about 37 years old and that she was born as she believes in the Parish of Cowley in the said County where her Father James Mitchell now resides and where as she believes he is legally settled – That when she this Examinant was about 20 years old she was hired for a year to Absolem [= Absolom] Holland of Cheltenham aforesaid Eating house Keeper at the wages of 4^l. – That she served the whole of such year (during which she slept and boarded in her Master's House) and received her wages – That for 3 or 4 years afterwards she was out of a situation after which she was hired by Miss Thornton of Cheltenham aforesaid Milliner as an indoor Servant for a year at the wages of 8^l. which year she duly served and received her wages   That in or about the year 1829 she was lawfully married at the Parish Church of Cheltenham aforesaid to Charles Holdey Labourer to whom she had a short time before sworn a Child with which she was then pregnant which Child was born in about 2 months after her marriage and died when about a year and a half old – That on her delivery of such Child

her said Husband deserted her and she has never seen him since – That she never heard him say any thing whatever as to his place of Settlement nor has she any knowledge whatever respecting it, and that she is now chargeable to the Parish of Cheltenham aforesaid. [mark]
1838: *not removed, as place of settlement adjudged to be Cheltenham.* [PS/CH/RA/2/5:20. Pencilled note: "Chelt^m Parish".]

38019RO: Mon 5 Mar 1838 – **Joseph Brown**, tailor: That he is 24 years old and that he was born as he hath heard and believes in the Parish of Bloomsbury in the County of Middlesex where his Father Francis Brown (who was a Tailor) was as he this examinant verily believes legally settled – That in or about the year 1829 he this Examinant was bounden by Indenture as an indoor Apprentice to Messieurs Cooke and Son of N°. 54 Great Queen Street in the Parish of Saint Giles in the Fields in the said County of Middlesex Tailors for the term of 6 years – That he served about 2 years of such Apprenticeship when he left his said Masters and did not afterwards returned to them – That a short time after this he took lodgings in the Great Wild Street in the said Parish of Saint Giles in the Fields in which he followed the Business of a Tailor and Dealer in second hand Clothes – That he paid 2 shillings a week for such Lodgings which he occupied about a year and a half – That he then quitted them and has ever since travelled about the Country as a Dealer in Old Clothes having no fixed place of residence – That since his Apprenticeship he has never done any act whereby to gain a settlement – That in consequence of severe illness he hath become and is now chargeable to the Parish of Cheltenham [signed]
1838: *to be removed to Saint Giles in the Fields, Middlesex (apprenticeship), but apparently died before removal;* presumably the JB buried at New Burial Ground, Cheltenham, aged 25, 10 Aug. [PS/CH/RA/2/4:97 (copy at PS/CH/RA/2/5:19, containing pencilled note: "46 Stanhope S^t; very ill").]

38020SE: Mon 12 Mar 1838 – **John Davis**, labourer, and children **John** and **William** (and stepdaughter **Mary Ann Parls**): That he is about 26 years of age and that he was born as he believes in the Parish of Ledbury in the County of Hereford where as he hath understood and believes his Father John Davis was also born and in which he now resides and is legally settled: That he this Examinant hath never done any act in his own right whereby to gain a Settlement: That about 5 Years ago he was lawfully married in the Parish Church of Cheltenham aforesaid to his late Wife then Susan Parls [= Pearls] by whom he hath 2 Children now living namely John aged about 4 Years and William aged about 8 Months: That before her Marriage with this Examinant his said late Wife had an illegitimate Daughter named Mary Ann Parls born in the Parish of Cheltenham: That by reason of the illness and subsequent death of his said Wife he this Examinant has become chargeable to the said Parish of Cheltenham [signed] John Davies
1832: *Susan Davis's illegitimate daughter Mary Ann(e) baptised at Cheltenham 25 May.* **1838:** *removal uncertain: order apparently not issued;* Susan Davis buried at New Burial Ground, Cheltenham 8 Mar, aged 26, and son William buried there (aged eleven months) on 16 June. **1841:** John Davis (aged 25; labourer) remarried and lived with new family (Cecilia, 25; John, 7; Mary, 5, Elizabeth 5 mo) in Ballinger's Passage, off High St, Cheltenham (HO107/353/16/27/15). [PS/CH/RA/2/5:22. Note: "No Orders[?]".]

38021RO: Thurs 15 Mar 1838 – **Charles Fluck**, labourer: That he is about 19 years of age and that he was born as he believes in the Parish of Halling [= Hawling] in the said County of Gloucester where his Father William Fluck who was a labourer as he hath always understood was settled   That he believes the Parish Officers of Halling on many occasions afforded his said Father relief and assisted him in Paying the rent of the Cottage there in which he resided – That prior to Michaelmas 1834 he this Examinant was never hired to any person for a year and that he has never in his own right done any Act whereby to gain a Settlement – That in consequence of illness he this Examinant hath lately become chargeable to the Parish of Cheltenham [signed]
1838: *removed to Hawling (father's settlement).* **1841:** *CF (aged 25; agricultural labourer) lived in Hawling (HO107/360/11/4/3).* [PS/CH/RA/2/4:98 (copy at PS/CH/RA/2/5:24). Removal expenses to Hawling for "Chas Fluck" accompanired by Jesse Castle 8/- (5 Apr 1838: D4178).]

38022SE: Thurs 15 Mar 1838 – **James Glanville**, labourer, and wife **Elizabeth**: That he is about 61 Years of Age and that he was born as he believes in the Parish of Cheltenham where his Father who was a Soldier was at that time quartered: That when he this Examinant was about 14 Years old he was apprenticed by Indenture for 7 Years to John Murrell a Stonemason of Woolwich in the County of Kent which he duly served: That soon after the expiration of his term he enlisted as a Soldier and continued in His Majesty's service about 22 Years when he received his discharge: that he then came to Cheltenham and worked at his business, living in Lodgings: that with the exception of about 2 Years during which he was absent in London working as a Journeyman Stonemason and occupying Lodgings he has lived in Cheltenham up to the present time: that upwards of 2 Years ago he took a House (N°. 25 King Street Cheltenham) of Mr William Haines at 12$^£$ a Year which he has occupied ever since but has not paid any Rates for Taxes for it:

That about 30 Years ago he was lawfully married to his present Wife Elizabeth Glanville by whom he has 4 Children none of whom are now living with him: That he hath lately become chargeable to the Parish of Cheltenham.

1838: *removal unlikely: place of settlement probably acknowledged as Cheltenham; JR's wife Elizabeth died soon after examination (buried at New Burial Ground, Cheltenham 4 Apr); JR (mason) quickly remarried, to Mary Ann Gammon, spinster, at Cheltenham 24 July: address 2 Rutland St, St Paul's, Cheltenham; JR's father James apparently Sergeant in Royal Artillery.* **1839:** *son Alexander baptised at Cheltenham 7 Feb.* **1841:** *James and Alexander lived in Rutland St (HO107/353/7/59/22).* [PS/CH/RA/2/5:25.]

38023RO: Fri 16 Mar 1838 – **Elizabeth Ireland**, single woman: That she is about 26 years of age and that she was born as she has always understood and believes in the Parish of Whitchurch in the County of Hereford where her Father Thomas Ireland who was a Miller occupied considerable Property and was legally settled – That when she this Examinant was about 14 years old she was hired for a year to John Watkins a Confectioner of Abergavenny in the County of Monmouth at the wages of 4^l. and that she continued in his service upwards of 2 years – That she was then hired for a year to William Bowen a Confectioner of Newport in the said County of Monmouth at the wages of Five Pounds – That she duly served the said year during which she lived in her Masters House and was afterwards hired by him again and remained in his Service 3 successive years – That since such Service with the said William Bowen at Newport aforesaid she has not done [any] act whereby to gain a Settlement and that she had she hath lately become and is now chargeable to the parish of Cheltenham [mark]

1838: *removed to Newport, Monm (hiring and service).* [PS/CH/RA/2/49) (copy at PS/CH/RA/2/26).]

38024RO: Sat 17 Mar 1838 – **Eli Daniels** the younger, labourer, wife **Esther** (also **Hester**), and two infant children, **Charlotte** and **Louisa**: That he is about 32 years of age and that he was born as he hath always understood and believes at Stroud in the County of Gloucester where his Father Eli Daniels the Elder then resided – That he hath heard his Father say that his Parish was at Stroud and that he obtained relief from it – That he this Examinant hath never done any Act in his own right whereby to gain a Settlement – That about six weeks before Christmas last in consequence of severe illness he applied for and obtain relief from the Parish Officers of Stroud aforesaid And this Examinant states that about four years and a half ago he was lawfully married at Cheltenham to Esther his now Wife (then Esther White) by whom he has one Female Child born in Wedlock about a fortnight ago – That a short time before his marriage with his said Wife she had an illegitimate Child named Louisa born in the said Parish of Stroud – That he this Examinant hath lately become chargeable to the Parish of Cheltenham. [signed]

1838: *removed to Stroud (father's settlement); daughter Charlotte baptised at Cheltenham 29 Apr.* **1840:** *(RETURNED) daughter Charlotte buried at Cheltenham 18 July.* **1841:** *Hester Daniels (aged 25, charwoman) and daughter Louisa (7) lived in Exmouth Court, Cheltenham at her mother's house (HO107/353/12/37/10); perhaps ED (aged 40; weaver) lived alone in Stroud at this time (HO107/349/13/37/1).* **1843:** *birth of son Joseph Thomas, while both lived in Exmouth Court with Hester's mother.* [PS/CH/RA/2/4:100 (copy at PS/CH/RA/2/5:27); order suspended as Esther Daniel unfit to travel; "Constables Expenses" for apprehending "E

Daniels" 13/- (late[?] Mar 1838: D4178), and removal expenses to Stroud for "E. Daniels & fam[i]ly" £1/6/- (10 Apr 1838: D4178).]

38025RO: Mon 26 Mar 1838 – **Thomas Tyler**, labourer, and wife **Sophia**: That he is about twenty two years of Age and that he was born as he believes in the Parish of Lugwardine in the County of Hereford where his Father John Tyler lived and in which Parish he obtained a Settlement by having rented a Tenem^t. and other Property there of the value of seventeen pounds a Year: That he this Examinant hath never done any act in his own right whereby to gain a Settlement: That about two years ago he was lawfully married in the Parish Church of Newent in the County of Gloucester to Sophia his now Wife then Sophia Smith Singlewoman.

That in consequence of the illness of his said Wife and the want of employment he this examinant hath become chargeable to the Parish of Cheltenham [signed]

1838: *removed to Lugwardine, Heref (father's settlement).* **1841:** *TT (aged 25; labourer) lived in West Bromwich, Staffs, with wife Sophia (25; born Swansea) and daughter Caroline, born at West Bromwich the previous year.* [PS/CH/RA/2/4:101 (copy at PS/CH/RA/2/5:28).]

38026RO: Thurs 5 Apr 1838 – **Thomas Sparks**, wife **Jane Caroline**, and children **Frederick**, **Caroline**, and **Thomas**: That he is about 34 years of age and that he was born as he hath heard and believes at Silverhill in the County of Kent   That when he this Examinant was about 19 years of age he was apprenticed by Indenture to Charles Frost of the Parish of Saint Peter in the City of Bristol Printer for 5 years – That he served about two years of that term when the said Thomas [*sic*: "Charles" in magistrates' register] Frost died – That about 2 years after his death this Examinant bound himself Apprentice by Indenture for the term of 5 years to Joseph Matthews of the Parish of Saint John the Baptist in the said City of Bristol Printer – That he served about 4 years and 3 quarters of such last mentioned term to the said Joseph Matthews who then relinquished business in favor [*sic*] of his Brother Matthew Matthews to whom he this Examinant was assigned for the remainder of his time which he duly served – That he this Examinant was an outdoor Apprentice and that during the last forty days and upwards of his time he boarded in King Street in the Parish of Saint Nicholas in the said City of Bristol – That since the completion of his said last mentioned Apprenticeship he hath never done any Act whereby to gain a settlement – That between 2 and 3 years ago he applied for and obtained relief from the Parish Officers of Saint Nicholas aforesaid – that about 6 years ago he was lawfully married in the Parish Church of Saint Philip at Bristol to Jane Caroline his present Wife by whom he has 3 Children now living (namely) Frederick aged about 5 years – Caroline aged upwards of 3 years and Thomas aged about 2 years and that his said Wife is again Pregnant and near her confinement That he hath become chargeable to the Parish of Cheltenham [signed]

1838: *ordered to be removed to St Nicholas, Bristol (apprenticeship); (11 April) birth of Jane Sparks's daughter Mary at Regent Place, Cheltenham.* **1839:** *mother Jane (née Griffiths) and then Mary died (Apr and July respectively) at Bristol.* **1841:** *the family (Thomas: 35), Frederick (9), Caroline (6), and Thomas (5) entered Stapleton (Bristol) Poor Asylum (HO107/378/15 passim).* [PS/CH/RA/2/4:102 (incomplete copy at PS/CH/RA/2/5:29; full copy at page 31); order suspended as Jane Caroline Sparks was unfit to travel (pregnancy). Removal expenses to Bristol for "Sparks & family" £2/13/- (2 May 1838: D4178).]

38027RO: Thurs 5 Apr 1838 – **David Evans**: That he is about 25 years Old And that he was born as he hath always understood and believes in Machynlleth in the County of Montgomery where his Parents resided: – That his Father's name was David and that he died about 18 years ago: – That during his lifetime this Examinant frequently heard him say and this Examinant verily believes that his said Father was lawfully Settled in the Parish of Towyn [= Tywyn] in the County of Merioneth: – That this Examinant's Mother received Relief from the Parish Officers of Towyn aforesaid And this Examinant Saith that he hath never done any Act in his Own Right whereby to gain a Settlement and that he hath lately become and is now Chargeable to the Parish of Cheltenham [mark]

1838: *removed to Tywyn, Merionethshire (father's settlement).* [PS/CH/RA/2/4:103 (copy at PS/CH/RA/2/5:32); order suspended as pauper unfit to travel. Removal expenses to Tywyn, Merionethshire for "D Evans" £8/3/8 (18 June 1838: D4178).]

38028RO: Mon 16 Apr 1838 – **Hela Hillman**, single woman: That she is about 21 years of age and that she was born as she believes at Catswood in the Parish of Bisley in the said County where her Father Nathaniel Hillman who was a Stonemason at that time resided – That she has heard her said Father say and she verily believes that he belonged to the Parish of Miserdine [= Miserden] in the said County and she well remembers that he received Parochial relief from that Parish during his residence at Catswood aforesaid – That she this Examinant was employed by Nathaniel Marling of the Parish of Stroud in this County Clothier to work at his Factory as a weekly Servant at the wages of 4ˢ/– Per week in whose employ she remained about 2 years leaving it in the month of March 1834 having resided during such time in the House of her Father – That she has never done any act whereby to gain a settlement in her own right and has become and is now chargeable to the Parish of Cheltenham [mark]
1838: *HH gave birth to stillborn male child at Cheltenham Workhouse 28 Feb (G/CH/67/1); removed to Miserden (father's settlement).* Her parents Nathaniel and Sarah Hillman resided in Miserden at time of 1841 and 1851 censuses. [PS/CH/RA/2/4:104 (copy at PS/CH/RA/2/5:33). Removal expenses to Miserden for "Hillman" £1/6/- (8 May 1838: D4178).]

38029RO: Sat 21 Apr 1838 – **Mary Eaton**, single woman: That she was born as she believes in Wanborough in the County of Wilts and that she is about 28 years old – That when she was about 9 years of age she went out as a weekly Servant and lived as a Servant in various situations until about 9 or 10 years ago when she was hired by the Misses Munday of Harrisgrate Farm in the Parish of Wotton Basset [= Wootton Bassett] in the said County of Wilts as an indoor Servant but at what wages she this Examinant does not now recollect – That she duly served the whole of such year and received her wages since which she has continued to reside and work for various Farmers in Wotton Basset aforesaid where she has been acknowledged and at various times occasionally relieved by the Parish Officers there – That since serving the Misses Munday as aforesaid she has never been hired for a year nor has she done any Act whereby to gain a settlement and in consequence of severe illness she has become and is now chargeable to the Parish of Cheltenham aforesaid [mark]
1831: *removed to Wootton Bassett, Wilts (hiring and service): see* **31064SE** *(ME: 5 May). ME pregnant at time of examination and removal, and daughter Ann baptised 28 Aug, at Wootton Bassett (RETURNED).*
1838: *to be removed to Wootton Bassett, Wilts (hiring and service), but died before removal; ME (aged 28; living in Rutland St, Cheltenham) buried at New Burial Ground, Cheltenham 21 May, aged 28.* [PS/CH/RA/2/4:105 (copy at PS/CH/RA/2/5:35); order suspended as pauper unfit to travel.]

38030RO: Tues 24 Apr 1838 – **Emma Hopson**, single woman: That she was born as she believes at Speenham Land near Newbury in Berkshire – That about 11 or 12 years ago she was hired as Ladies Maid for a year by Mʳˢ. Walker then residing at Nᵒ 5 Princes Buildings Clifton at the wages of Ten Pounds a year, that she duly served such year –That her said Mistress was in the habit of visiting various places and she this Examinant accompanied her said Mistress – That she remained in Mʳˢ. Walkers service about four years – That at the time Examinant left Mʳˢ Walker's Service she was lodging at Mʳˢ Bary's at the Vineyards in the Parish of Walcot Bath – that her said Mistress had been lodging at the said Mʳˢ Barys upwards of three months and that she this Examinant left Mʳˢ Walker's Service while she was lodging at the Vineyards in the Parish of Walcot Bath – That since Examinant left Mʳˢ· Walker's Service she has done no Act to gain a settlement in any other place [signed]
1838: *to be removed to Walcot, Bath (hiring and service), but died before removal; EH died at Cheltenham Workhouse 21 May (buried at New Burial Ground, Cheltenham 26 May, aged 28).* [PS/CH/RA/2/4:106 (copy at PS/CH/RA/2/5:38); order suspended as Emma Hopson unfit to travel (see also D4178, 13 June 1838).]

38031RO: Mon 23 Apr 1838 – **John Marshall**, labourer, and son **William Marshall**: That he was born as he believes in the Parish of Didbrook in the said County and that he is now about 45 years old – That in the early part of his life he went out as a servant in Husbandry and lived in various situations until about 25 years ago when he was hired to one William Wood of Barton Farm in the Parish of Temple Guiting in this County Farmer for the term of a year at the wages of 14¹ – That he lived in such Service the whole of such year during which he slept in his Masters House – That about 5 weeks after the completion of such service he this Examinant was lawfully married to one Elizabeth Newman of Lower Guiting in this County where he took a House at the rent of 4¹ a year and continued to work as a day Labourer for the said William Wood for several years – That by such marriage he has four Children now living all of whom are out in the world except his eldest son named William aged about 22 years who is living with this Examinant and has never done any act in his own right whereby to gain a settlement nor has he this Examinant since his servitude with Mʳ Wood done any Act whereby to gain a settlement   That in consequence of the severe illness of himself and his said son they are become chargeable to the Parish of Cheltenham [mark]
1832: *Elizabeth Marshall of Lower Guiting buried 24 June, aged 39.* **1838:** *removed to Temple Guiting (hiring and service).* **1841:** *(RETURNED) JM (59; agricultural labourer) and son William (20; agricultural labourer) lived in Alstone, Cheltenham (HO107/353/10/35/5).* [PS/CH/RA/2/4:107 (copy at PS/CH/RA/2/5:34); order suspended as both men unfit to travel until 18 June. Removal expenses to Temple Guiting for "J. Marshall" £1/2/- (19 June 1838: D4178). See **50017RO** (JM: 27 May 1850).]

38032RO: Mon 23 Apr 1838 – **Charles Linham**, labourer: That he was born as he believes in the Parish of Purton [probably Puriton] near Bridgewater [= Bridgwater] in the County of Somerset where his Father James Linham who was a Mason was as he believes legally settled – That he this Examinant went out to service when he was about 14 years of age and lived in several places 'till about the year 1828 – That about the year 1828 he was hired for a year as Footman by Wᵐ Blane Esqʳᵉ. of the Parish of Winkfield in the County of Berks in whose Service he lived residing in the House for three years – That since such service he has done no act to gain a legal settlement and he is now chargeable to the Parish of Cheltenham [signed]
1838: *removed to Denton, Lincs (quashed on appeal): see* **38006RO** *(CL: 13 Jan 1838); removed to Winkfield, Berks (hiring and service).* [PS/CH/RA/2/4:108, superseding that of 13 Jan 1838 (copy PS/CH/RA/2/5:37).]

38033RO: Thurs 26 Apr 1838 – **Hannah Weger** (more commonly **Wager**): That she is about 55 years of Age and that she was born as she believes in the parish of Painswick in the said County That about 24 years ago she this examinant was hired for a year by Mʳˢ. Loveday of Painswick aforesaid as an indoor Servant of all work at the Wages of £5 – That she lived in Mrs Loveday's Service 15 Months, That since that period she this examinant has been employed by various persons in Painswick aforesaid by the week until about three years ago when she came to reside at Cheltenham. That She has done no Act since she left Painswick whereby to gain a legal Settlement and is now chargeable to the parish of Cheltenham, That about [blank: "five" added in magistrates' register] years ago she received relief from the said Parish of Cheltenham [mark]
1838: *removed to Painswick (hiring and service): see* **46031RO** *(HW: 13 June 1846).* [PS/CH/RA/2/4:109 (copy at PS/CH/RA/2/5:39). Removal expenses to Painswick for "H. Weger" 15/4 (24 May 1838: D4178).]

38034RO: Thurs 26 Apr 1838 – **William Bristol**, and three children, **Matilda**, **William**, and **George**: That he is about 28 years of Age and that he was born as he believes in some part of Somersetshire but in what parish he cannot tell, that this examinants Father is now living at Fisherton Anger near to Salisbury in the County of Wilts where he went to reside when this examinant was about 2 years of Age and in which parish he for many years rented property exceeding in value One Hundred pounds a year and consequently acquired a Settlement there, that he this examinant has never done any Act in his own right whereby to gain a Settlement. That about ten years ago he was lawfully married at Brightelmstone in the County of Sussex to Mary his late Wife (then Mary Campbell) by whom he has three Children now living namely Matilda Aged about 7 years William Aged about 2 years and a half and George Aged about eighteen months: That in consequence of the illness and recent death of his said Wife he has become chargeable to the Parish of Cheltenham [signed]

1809: *WB baptised at Kingstone, near Ilminster, Som 25 June, son of George and Mary Bristol.* **1838:** *wife Mary buried at New Burial Ground, Cheltenham 9 Mar;* **removed to Fisherton Anger, Wilts (father's settlement).** **1839:** *(RETURNED) sons William and George died at Charlton Kings (presumably at the workhouse): William (4) was buried at Charlton Kings 15 Apr and George (aged 4) 13 May.* **1841:** *daughter Matilda (aged 9) was an inmate of Charlton Kings Workhouse for pauper children (HO107/353/2/54/2)* **1851:** *(after period in service) Matilda was an inmate of the Female Refuge in Winchcombe St, Cheltenham (HO107/1973/179/43).* **1871:** *WB (aged 60; umbrella-maker) lived in Swansea, married to Ann (50; born Cork) (RG10/5452/46/35).* [PS/CH/RA/2/4:110 (copy at PS/CH/RA/2/5:23).]

38035RO: Tues 24 Apr 1838 – James Andrews, in Gloucester gaol, with reference to wife **Elizabeth**, and three children **Elizabeth**, **James**, and **Caroline**: That about 2 years Ago he Rented a House in Cheltenham at £12 per annum but was distrained on for the Rent and never paid any Rates That he is the legitimate Son of Thomas Andrews who is Settled and now living in Trowbridge in the County of Wilts, That he this examinant was apprenticed by Indentures duly stamped and executed to John Haines of Trowbridge Cordwainer for Seven years   That he served the said John Haines in his house in Trowbridge for three years and a half under such Indentures which were then given up, That about seven Seven years Ago he was married to his present Wife then Elizabeth Brown by whom he has three Children namely Elizabeth aged 6 years, James aged three years and Caroline aged one year and his Wife and Children and now chargeable to Cheltenham [mark]

1838: *James Andrews was convicted of two counts of larceny and sentenced to a year in Gloucester Gaol 7 Mar (he had already served three months there in 1835 for receiving stolen goods); on 19 Apr Elizabeth and James Andrews were admitted to Charlton Kings Workhouse for children (Cheltenham Union) (discharged to mother's care 20 May: behaviour "Good");* **removed to Trowbridge, Wilts (husband's apprenticeship);** *mother Elizabeth (29) received into Charlton Kings Workhouse from Cheltenham Workhouse with 15-month-old daughter Caroline (G/CH/60/2 pp. 33, 35).* **1841:** *(RETURNED) the family lived in Union St, Fairview, Cheltenham: James (aged 29; shoemaker), Elizabeth (30), Elizabeth (10; born Stroud), James (6), Caroline (4), and Ruth (1: last three born Cheltenham) (HO107/353/12/14/23); a persistent offender, James was almost immediately convicted again, with associates, of robbery at new Queen's Hotel in Cheltenham; he was sentenced to transportation for ten years; wife and children removed to Trowbridge, Wilts (husband's settlement): see* **41056RO** *(EA: 30 Sept 1841).* **1845/6:** *from 2Q 1845 until 3Q 1846 Elizabeth and four children received parish relief from Melksham, Wilts as non-settled residents in Cheltenham (G/CH/9d/1).* **1851:** *the family lived at 2 Butt's Passage, Sherborne St, Cheltenham (HO107/1973/154/48): Elizabeth (42; widow, shoebinder, born Horsley), Elizabeth (22; nursemaid), James (15; labourer), Caroline (14; servant), Ruth (11; scholar).* [PS/CH/RA/2/4: (no copy). Removal expenses to Trowbridge, Wilts for "Andrews & family" £8/14/- (15 Nov 1838: D4178), and £3/4/10 (19 Nov 1838: D4178).]

38036RO: Thurs 3 May 1838 – **Henry New**: That he was born as he believes in the Parish of Stanton in the County of Worcester and that he is about 67 years of Age, That about 8 years since he rented a House [magistrates' register: at £20 per annum] in the Parish of Charlton Kings of Mr Warder – That he occupied such House as a beer House for three or four years and that he duly paid the Poors Rates during such period, that he has not since done any Act to gain a Settlement elsewhere and he is now chargeable to the Parish of Cheltenham

1838: *removed to Charlton Kings (renting).* **1841:** *(RETURNED) burial of HN (aged 71) at New Burial Ground, Cheltenham 3 Feb.* [PS/CH/RA/2/4 (copy at PS/CH/RA/2/5:40).]

38037SE: Sat 12 May 1838 – **Richard Barnfield**, stonemason, with wife **Susannah**, and daughter **Grace**: That he is about 65 years old and that he was born as he believes in the Parish of Stroud in the said County where his Father Richard Barnfield who was also a Stonemason resided but who belonged (as he this Examinant has heard him say and as he verily believes) to the Parish of Painswick in the same County in consequence of his having been apprenticed there – That about 41 years ago he this Examinant was lawfully married at the Parish Church of Stroud aforesaid to Susannah his present Wife by whom he has had 4 Children all of whom (except the youngest named Grace aged about 20 and who is living with this Examinant) are married and settled – That he this Examinant has always been acknowledged by the Parish Officers of Painswick aforesaid as belonging to that Parish and on many occasions has received Parochial Relief therefrom (he never having done any Act to gain a Settlement in his own right) nor has his said Daughter Grace ever done any Act to gain a settlement in her own right – That he has become and is now chargeable to the said Parish of Cheltenham. – [mark]

1838: *removed to Painswick (father's settlement).* **1841:** *(RETURNED) eldest daughter Elizabeth (then Elizabeth Davis) lived in Bath Terrace, Cheltenham with her family (near Exmouth St, where her daughter was born in 1837) (HO107/353/12/13/21).* **1844:** *RB ran stonemason's business from 4 Exmouth Court, Exmouth St, Cheltenham (*Harper's Directory). **1851:** *RB (aged 75; mason) and wife Susan (75; cloth worker) lived at Union Cottage, Union St, Cheltenham (HO107/1973/896/50).* **1853:** *death of RB, aged 81, at Cheltenham Union Workhouse, his wife predeceasing him by almost a year.* [PS/CH/RA/2/5:41. Removal expenses to Painswick for "Barnfield & Wife" £1/-/6 (31 May 1838: D4178).]

38038SE: Sat 9 June 1838 – **Hannah Price**, single woman: That she is about 24 years of age and that she was born as she believes at Ham near Berkeley in this County in which Parish she has been informed and believes her Father William Price who was a Labourer lived and died – That her mother is still living there. That about 7 years ago she this Examinant was hired as Maid of all work to Mr Laite who then Kept the White Hart Inn in Berkeley aforesaid for the term of a year at the wages to the best of [her] recollection of 3^l. That she continued in Mr Laites' Service nearly three successive years with an advance of wages each year – That during the whole of such time she slept in her masters house and received her Wages – That soon after she left the White Hart Inn aforesaid she was hired as Cook to M^{rs}. Michael of the Berkeley Arms Inn at Berkeley aforesaid for a year at the wages of 7^l That she remained in such last service about a month after the completion of the year when she left having received her wages   That during the whole of such time she slept in the House of her Mistress – Since which she has done no act to gain a settlement and in consequence of illness she has become chargeable to the Parish of Cheltenham. [mark]

1838: *removed to Berkeley (presumed) (hiring and service).* [PS/CH/RA/2/5:42. Pencilled note: "(Order)".]

38039SE: Mon 11 June 1838 – **Margaret Hayward** (also **Haywood**), wife of John Hayward, with children **George** and **Mary Ann**: That she is about 33 years of age and that she is the Daughter of George Davis of Devonport in the County of Devon at which place she believes she was born. That about 14 years ago she was lawfully married at Stonehouse East, near Devonport aforesaid to her present Husband by whom she has two Children (namely) George aged about 8 years and Mary Ann aged about 12 days – That she hath always understood and believes that her said Husband obtained a Settlement by having been apprenticed and served his time to one Mr Sibley a Bricklayer of the Parish of Aston in the County of Warwick – That about 5 years ago (when her Husband deserted her in Birmingham) she underwent an Examination at the Public Office there and was afterwards together with her said Son George removed to the said Parish of Aston and remained in Erdington Workhouse there about 13 weeks – That her said Husband left her in Wolverhampton a Fortnight before last Christmas and she has not heard of him since nor has she any Idea where he now is – That ~~having been believed to be brought to Bed in the Workhouse of Cheltenham she became~~ she hath lately become and is now chargeable to the Parish of Cheltenham [mark]

1838: *Mary Ann Haywood, daughter of John Haywood (bricklayer) and Margaret, born at Poor House, Cheltenham, (baptised at St Mary's, Cheltenham the day before the examination);* **removed to Aston, Birmingham, Warks (husband's settlement).** [PS/CH/RA/2/5:43. Pencilled note: "(Orders)". Removal expenses to Aston, Birmingham, Warks for "M Hayward & family" £3/3/- (14 July 1838: D4178).]

38040SE: Sat 16 June 1838 – **Thomas Michell** (also **Mitchell**), tailor, with wife **Margaret**: That he is about 30 years of age and that he was born as he believes in the Parish of Coln Saint Rogers [= Coln Rogers] in this County where his Father who was a Labourer formerly resided but who belonged to the Parish of Bibury in the said County to which Parish this examinant well remembers his said Father being removed. That he never did any Act to gain a settlement

elsewhere – That he this Examinant when about 17 years old was hired as indoor Servant to Mr Lemmon of <u>Chipping Sodbury</u> in this County Surgeon for the term of a year at the wages of 5^l that he continued to live in such service for three successive years and received his wages – That soon afterwards this Examinant was hired as indoor Servant to Miss Rooke of the <u>Parish of Prestbury in this County</u> for the term of a year at the wages of 12^l that he duly served such year and remained in her Service for 6 months afterwards during the whole of such time he slept in his Mistress's House and received his wages. That about 5 years ago in consequence of severe illness he this Examinant applied to the Parish Officers of Prestbury aforesaid from which Parish he received relief   That in the month of October last he was lawfully married in the Parish of Cheltenham aforesaid to Margaret his present Wife (formerly Margaret McGowen Singlewoman) who is now in a state of Pregnancy in the Workhouse of Cheltenham – That since his service with Miss Rooke in Prestbury aforesaid he has never done any Act whereby to gain a settlement [signed]
1838: *removed to Prestbury (presumed) (hiring and service); Elisha [later Elijah], son of Thomas (tailor) and [Martha] Mitchell, born at Poor House, Cheltenham (baptised 21 Aug).* **1851:** *(RETURNED) TM (aged 40; tailor) lodged with three children at home of wife's sister, 4 Burton St, Cheltenham (HO107/1973/600/26). He had several more children in the 1850s.* **1861:** *TM lived at 8 Park St, Cheltenham (RG9/1800/59/16), still practising as tailor.* [PS/CH/RA/2/5:44. "T" in surname struck out at first occurrence. Expenses for "Apprehending Mitchell desert[in]g Wife 1.5.0" (June 1838: D4178).]

38041SE: Sat 16 June 1838 – **Edward Loose**, with wife **Sarah**, and five children **Leonard, Richard, Joseph, Ellen**, and **John**: That he is about 31 Years old and that he was born as he believes in the Parish of Holkham in the County of Norfolk where his Father William Loose who was at that time & for many Years afterwards Gamekeeper to the present Earl of Leicester then resided: That about 15 Years ago his said Father was hired for a Year as Gamekeeper to George Graham Blackwell of Ampney Park in the Parish of Ampney Crucis in the County of Gloucester Esqre. which Year he duly served and that he continued in M^r. Blackwell's service until the time of his death which happened about 12 Months ago [marginal insertion] That his said Father rented about 5 or 6 Acres of Land in the said Parish of Ampney Crucis for 2 or 3 Years & paid Rates & taxes for the same [end of insertion]: that this Examinant lived with his said Father and assisted him in his employment during the time he so lived with M^r. Blackwell but he this Examinant never did any Act in his own right whereby to gain a Settlement: that his Mother is now living and since his Father's death has obtained relief from the said Parish of Ampney Crucis: That about 12 Years ago he this Examinant was lawfully married at Ampney Crucis aforesaid to Sarah his now Wife (then Sarah Phipps) by whom he has 5 Children namely Leonard aged 11 Years, Richard aged 10 Years, Joseph aged 9 Years, Ellen aged 7 Years & John aged 14 Months: that he this Examinant hath lately become chargeable (by reason of the illness of his family) to the Parish of Cheltenham [signed]
1838: *removed to Ampney Crucis (father's settlement).* **1839:** *death of son John soon after examination (registered in Cheltenham 2Q); birth of Elizabeth registered at Cheltenham 3Q.* **1841:** *(RETURNED) EL (aged 32; labourer) lived with family Sarah (32), Leonard (13), Richard (12), Joseph (11), Ellen (9), and Elizabeth (1), in Bath Terrace, Cheltenham (HO107/353/12/13/21).* [PS/CH/RA/2/5:45. Expenses for "Apprehending Loose desert[in]g Wife" (June 1838: D4178), and removal expenses for "E Loose & family" to Ampney Crucis £1/12/- (14 July 1838: D4178).]

38042SE: Sat 16 June 1838 – **Mary Ann Hodgkins**, widow, with children **Joseph, John**, and **George**: That she is about 26 Years of Age and that she is the Widow of Joseph Hodgkins who died in the Month of March 1834: That about 9 Years ago she was lawfully married at Shipton under Wichwood [= Shipton-under-Wychwood] in the County of Oxford to the said Joseph Hodgkins who after 5 or 6 Years before such Marriage was hired for the Year to a M^r. Slater who kept the Plume of Feathers Inn at Postcombe in the Parish of Lewknor in the said County of Oxford: that he duly served such Year during which time he was lodged and boarded in his Master's House and at the expiration of it received his Wages: that he continued in M^r. Slater's service some time after this and never afterwards did any Act whereby to gain a Settlement: that

by her said Marriage she this Examinant hath 3 Children namely Joseph aged 8 Years, John aged 6 Years & George aged 4 Years: that this Examinant hath frequently received Relief since her Husband's death from the said Parish of Lewknor, and that in consequence of the illness of her family she hath lately become chargeable to the Parish of Cheltenham. [signed]
1838: *removal uncertain; perhaps not removed to Lewknor (husband's settlement); see* **42033RO** *(MAH: 7 Apr 1842) for further information.* [PS/CH/RA/2/5:46.]

38043SE: Wed 20 June 1838 – **Mary [Ann] Cooper**, single woman, with daughter **Mary Ann**: That she is about 23 Years of Age and that she was born as she believes at a place called [inserted: near the Town of] Swansea in the County of Glamorgan where her Parents then resided: That about 8 Years ago she this Examinant was hired for a Year as a Servant of all work to a M[r]. Thomas Steel of the Parish of Coleford in the said County of Gloucester Blacksmith at the Wages of 4 Pounds: that she duly served such Year during which she lived in her said Master's House and at the expiration thereof received her Wages, and that she continued to live in M[r]. Steel's service the four following Years: that since that period she has not done any Act whereby to gain a Settlement: That on the [blank] instant she this Examinant was delivered in the Poor house of Cheltenham of a female illegitimate Child and that she is now chargeable to that Parish.
1838: *removed to Coleford (presumed) (hiring and service); MAC's illegitimate daughter Mary Ann born at Poor House, Cheltenham (baptised 3 July), but died there aged two weeks (buried at New Burial Ground, Cheltenham 7 July).* [PS/CH/RA/2/5:47.]

38044SE: Mon 2 July 1838 – **James Stone**, whitesmith, with wife **Louisa**, and four children **William, Louisa**, and two further unnamed children: That he is about 27 Years of Age and that he was born as he believes in the Parish of Maisemore in the County of Gloucester: That about 12 Years ago he this Examinant was hired for a Year as an indoor Servant to Charles Griffin of the Parish of Oxenhall in the said County of Gloucester Stonemason which Year he duly served in that Parish since which he has not done any act to gain a Settlement elsewhere: that when he this Examinant was ill about 7 Years ago he applied for and obtained relief from the said Parish of Oxenhall: – That about 8 Years ago he was lawfully married in the Parish Church of Prestbury to Louisa his now Wife (then Louisa Townsend) by whom he has four Children, namely William aged about 7 Years, Louisa aged about 6 Years and two others one aged about 4 Years and the other aged about 12 months not yet baptized: – That this Examinant hath become chargeable to the Parish of Cheltenham [mark]
c1834: *two unnamed children born to James and Louisa Stone: Eliza(beth) and Charlotte.* **1837:** *unnamed child aged about 4 was Alfred Stone (baptised 23 Aug at Cheltenham); JS described as "Smith", living at 35 Townsend St, Cheltenham.* **1838:** *removed to Oxenhall (presumed) (hiring and service).* **1841:** *William Stone (aged 12), Elizabeth (9), Charlotte (8), Alfred (4), and later daughter Julia (6 months; born when family lived in Duke St, Cheltenham)) lived as paupers at Newent Workhouse (near Oxenhall) (HO107/350/10/64/1); (RETURNED) JS (aged 40) apparently commercial traveller living in St James's Terrace, Suffolk Parade, Cheltenham with daughter Louisa (9) and an Emma Stone (25) (HO107/353/13/28/12).* **1851:** *Louisa Stone (38; laundress, widow) lived at 5 Cakebridge Row, Prestbury Rd, Cheltenham, with Eliza (17; dressmaker), Charlotte (15; servant), Alfred (12; scholar), and Julia (9; scholar) (HO107/1973/60/44).* [PS/CH/RA/2/5:48. See "Louisa Stone Relief in kind 1[.0]" (31 Mar 1838: D4178).]

38045SE: Sat 7 July 1838 – **Eliza Sole** (also **Chew**), single woman; also Robert Sole of Painswick, weaver. *Eliza Sole:* That she is about 25 years of age and that she was born as she believes in the Parish of Painswick. that she is the Daughter of Esther the Wife of Thomas Chew formerly of the Parish of Painswick Weaver, who was as this Deponent has been informed and believes legally settled in the Parish of Standish in the said County that about 8 years since this Dependent went to Service in the Parish of Cheltenham and she then applied to the Parish of Standish for assistance that the Parish Officers thereupon gave her the Sum of One Pound to Enable Her to purchase Clothes. that about 8 Years since She was hired by Mary Harding of the Parish of

Cheltenham for one twelvemonth at the Wages /6 [= 6d.] a Week & lived with her for the space of 18 Months – that since that period She has done no Act to gain a Settlement [signed Eliza Sawl]

Robert Sole: That the said Eliza Chew otherwise Sole is the Daughter of Esther the wife of Thomas Chew formerly of the Parish of Painswick aforesaid Weaver both of whom are dead but that the said Thomas Chew as this Examinant has been informed and believes was legally settled in the Parish of Standish in the said County – that the said Esther Chew died about 21 years since at Painswick aforesaid and the Parish officers of Standish aforesaid paid the expenses of her Funeral - that the said Eliza Chew otherwise Sole came to live with this Examinant and thereupon the Parish allowed to this Examinant towards her maintenance the sum of 2^s/a week – that such payment was made for the space of two years – that at the expiration of that period the Parish reduced the pay to 1^s/– a week and continued to pay it for about two years longer   that about 8 years since when the Pauper was going to service she applied to the Parish officers of Standish aforesaid to supply her with Clothes and they gave her a Pound to purchase the same. [signed]

Although her parents were married, Eliza Chew was the "baseborn" daughter of her mother and an unnamed father (Stroud register). **1838: removal unlikely: place of settlement acknowledged as Cheltenham**; *Eliza Chew's illegitimate son, William Sole (also Soule) baptised 6 Dec at Cheltenham. On Eliza Chew's mother's death, she was taken in by the Sole family.* **1841**: *Robert Sole of Painswick (aged 40; labourer) and wife Sarah lived with two children in Union St, Cheltenham (HO107/353/12/15/24).* [PS/CH/RA/2/5:49. Later interlinear pencilled notes: "Standish Parish never p^d her any wages; gave her 6^d now & then; no 2nd hiring & left with[ou]t notice & was in a sit[uatio]n to do so; in Ho[use] ab^t to be confined". PS/CH/RA/2/5:51; note: "belongs to Cheltenham Parish".]

38046SE: Sat 21 July 1838 – Mary Bayliss, laundress, wife of Thomas Bayliss, regarding the settlement of **Dinah Holliday**: That the said Dinah Holliday was hired by her as Servant of all work, at Cheltenham Michaelmas Mop 1832, by the week, that she remained in her said service for about 18 months and was regularly paid her Wages by the Week, that she this examinant gave the said Dinah Holliday a weeks Notice to leave her employ in the month of March or April 1834 and that at the expiration of such week the said Dinah Holliday quitted her service [signed]
[PS/CH/RA/2/5:50. Expenses for maintaining pauper under order of removal (to Withington) for Dinah Holliday 10/6 (1 May 1838: D4178). See **38051SE** (DH: 26 July 1838).]

38047SE: Thurs 19 July 1838 – **Margaret Mitton** (also **Mytton**), widow: That she is about 70 Years of Age and that she was born as she believes in the Parish of Tewkesbury in the said County of Gloucester where her Father Francis Mann was settled: That about 50 Years ago she this Examinant was lawfully married in the Parish Church of Tewkesbury aforesaid to her late Husband William Mitton who was a stockingmaker then residing at Cheltenham but who as this Examinant frequently heard him say and as she verily believes gained a Settlement by Apprenticeship in the said Parish of Tewkesbury: That in about 3 or 4 Years after her Marriage her said Husband went into the Army and continued in it several Years: – That her said Husband died about 25 Years ago and that she hath become and is now chargeable to the Parish of Cheltenham. – That she, this Examinant recollects her said husband Renting a House near the Mythy [= Mythe] at Tewkesbury at £10 pounds a year but that he never Rented a House at £10 p^r. annum in the Parish of Cheltenham and that her said husband never Rented any House except at Cheltenham and Tewkesbury and that she believes he never did any Act except as above mentioned whereby to gain a settlement [mark]
1824: *removed to Tewkesbury: see Gray* **512** *(MM: 17 Apr) (RETURNED).* **1838: died before removal to Tewkesbury (husband's settlement)**; *MM buried at New Burial Ground, Cheltenham 28 July.* [PS/CH/RA/2/5:52.]

38048SE: Thurs 19 July 1838 – Francis Caffell, plasterer, regarding the settlement of daughter **Eliza Caffell**, single woman, "of unsound mind": That his said daughter is about 24 Years of Age and that she was born at Shepton Mallet in the County of Somerset: and that to the best of this Examinant's belief she has never done any act in her own right whereby to gain a Settlement: That when he this Examinant was about 12 Years old he was bounden Apprentice by Indenture to

Charles Palmer of the Parish of Frome in the said County of Somerset Plasterer and Tiler for 7 Years which term he duly served in the said Parish of Frome: That about 15 Years ago this Examinant rented about Seven Acres of Land in the Parish of <u>Hartpury</u> in the said County of Gloucester of one James Bradstock at 14$^£$. Per Annum and that he continued to rent and cultivate such land for the space of 3 Years or thereabouts and duly paid the Rent for the same since which he has not done any act whereby to gain a Settlement: And this Examinant lastly saith that his said Daughter who is of unsound Mind hath become and is now chargeable to the said Parish of Cheltenham [signed]

1838: *removed to or regarded to be the responsibility of Hartpury (presumed) (father's settlement).* **1841:** *(16 March) death of EC (formerly servant) registered at the County Lunatic Asylum, Wotton, near Gloucester, aged 25, of a "decline"; parents Francis (aged 51; plasterer) and Ann (50) then lived in Cleeveland St, Cheltenham (HO107/353/9/31/).* [PS/CH/RA/2/5:53.]

38049SE: Mon 23 July 1838 – **Joseph Williams**, labourer, with wife **Elizabeth**, and three children **Louisa**, **William**, and **John**: That he is about 30 Years of Age and that he was born as he believes in the Parish of Rendcomb in the County of Gloucester where his Father Joseph Williams now lives and in which Parish he this Examinant hath always understood and believes legally settled: that his said Father now holds and has for many Years held the situation of Parish Clerk there: that he this Examinant hath never done any Act in his own Right whereby to gain a Settlement: That about five Years and a half ago he was lawfully married in the Parish Church of Rendcomb aforesaid to Elizabeth his now Wife (then Elizabeth Shill) by whom he has 3 Children now living namely Louisa aged about 4 Years, William aged about 2 Years and a half and John aged about 12 Months: And this Examinant lastly saith that in consequence of the illness of his said Children he hath become chargeable to the Parish of Cheltenham [mark]

1838: *removed to Rendcomb (presumed) (father's settlement); son John (born 1837) buried at New Burial Ground, Cheltenham 1 Dec.* **1841:** *(RETURNED) JW (aged 30; labourer), wife Elizabeth (27), Louisa (8) and William (6) lived in Lower Gas Green, Cheltenham (HO107/353/10/20/6).* [PS/CH/RA/2/5:54.]

38050SE: Thurs 19 July 1838 – **John Barrett** (also **Barratt**), shoemaker, with wife **Mary**, and four children **William**, **Eliza**, **Richard**, and **Alfred**: That he is about 36 years old and that he is the Son of Richard Barrett formerly of the Parish of Temple Guiting in this County Shoemaker deceased, in which Parish he this Examinant was born and is legally settled. That about 9 years ago he this Examinant was lawfully married to his present Wife Mary (formerly Mary Ornsby [= Hornsby] Singlewoman) at the Parish Church of Bourton on the Water in this County by whom he has 4 Children all of whom are now living (ie) William aged about 8 years – Eliza aged about 4 years – Richard aged about 3½ years and Alfred aged about 1 year – That about 4 years ago he this Examinant in consequence of a swelling in his neck which rendered him unable to work, applied to the Parish Officers of Temple Guiting aforesaid (in which Parish he then resided) for Parochial relief, who accordingly allowed him the sum of 5^s/– a week for six Weeks when his ailment becoming worse he was afterwards allowed 7^s/– a week for several weeks and until his recovery – That he this Examinant hath never done any Act whereby to gain a Settlement in his own right and has lately become chargeable to the said Parish of Cheltenham. [mark]

1838: *removed to Temple Guiting (presumed) (birth).* **1841:** *JB (aged 35; agricultural labourer) lived in Temple Guiting with wife Mary (27), and four children William (11), Eliza (8), Richard (6; born Temple Guiting), and Alfred (3; born Cheltenham) (HO107/360/9/16/6).* [PS/CH/RA/2/5:55.]

38051SE: Thurs 26 July 1838 – **Dinah Holliday**, single woman: That she is about 22 years of Age   that she was born as she believes in the Parish of Withington in the said County of Gloucester where her Father Edward Holliday was a Stonemason then and from that time up to the period of his death which happened about 9 years ago resided and in which as she this Examinant has always understood and believes he was legally settled   that her mother is still living there, that about six months ago she this examinant in consequence of illness applied to the parish Officers there for relief who allowed her two Shillings a week for the space of 5 months or thereabouts, that soon after obtaining such Relief she underwent an examination as to the place of her Settlement and having on that occasion stated that she gained a Settlement by having been hired for a year by a Mrs Baylis [= Bayliss] of the parish of Cheltenham and duly serving such year, she this Examinant was shortly afterwards removed by the parish Officers of Whittington to the said parish of Cheltenham but this examinant has since discovered that she made a mistake in stating that she was hired to the said M^{rs}. Baylis for a year and is now convinced that she was only hired to her by the week and consequently that she did not gain a Settlement by such hiring and service in Cheltenham, This examinant further saith that she [has] never done any Act in her own right whereby to gain a Settlement and that she hath lately become chargeable to the said parish of Cheltenham [mark]

1838: *removed to Withington (presumed) (father's settlement).* [PS/CH/RA/2/5:56. See **38046SE:** Mary Bayliss: 21 July 1838).]

38052SE: [undated: between 26 July and 11 Aug 1838] – **William Sheward**, with wife **Jane**, and six children, **Jane**, **Betsy**, **Etty**, **William**, **Thomas**, and **Mary Ann**: That he is about 48 years old   that about 14 years since He rented a House of Mr Henry Haines situate in Lower Park Street Cheltenham at the Rent of Eleven pounds a year and occupied it for 14 or 15 months. – that about 7 years since He rented of Mr Thomas Bowle a House situate in Sherborne Street Cheltenham at the Rent of Ten pounds a year and occupied it till within the last Seven Months – and paid the Rent for it. He has one Son Theophilus by a former Wife aged about 22 years who is now living in Coventry. About 20 years since He was married to his present Wife Jane and by her has Six Children Jane aged about 12 years, Betsy aged about 10 years, Etty aged about 8 years – William aged about 6 years Thomas aged about 4 years and Mary Ann aged about 2 years all of whom are now chargeable to the Parish of Cheltenham [signed]

1838: *children Esther (Etty), Thomas, and (Mary) Ann Sheward admitted to Charlton Kings Workhouse 11 Apr;* **removal unlikely: place of settlement probably acknowledged as Cheltenham.** **1839:** *children readmitted to workhouse when "deserted by [their] Father" (G/CH/60/2); death of wife Jane in Cheltenham (buried at New Burial Ground, 5 Feb).* **1840:** *WS (born Kidderminster, tin-plate worker) remarried in Stafford 2Q to Mary Hodson.* **1841:** *four of children by WS's former marriage resided at Charlton Kings' Workhouse (Esther/Etty, aged 11; William, 8; Thomas, 7, and Mary Ann, 5) (HO107/353/2/54/2); WS's elder son Theophilus (aged 25; watch gilder) lived with his family in Spon St, Coventry (HO107/1152/12/45/12); WS (declared aged 40; journeyman brazier) lived with new wife Mary (3), and daughter Mary (3 mo), in St Chad St, Stafford.* **1844:** *daughter Jane (17) admitted to Cheltenham Workhouse at various times (G/CH/60/4).* [PS/CH/RA/2/5:57.]

38053SE: Sat 11 Aug 1838 – **Benjamin White**, shoemaker, with wife **Beata**, and four children **Henry**, **William**, **George**, and **Harriet**: That he is about 32 years of age and that he was born as he believes in the Parish of Stroud in the said County of Gloucester where his Father Joseph White who was also a Shoemaker was settled and from which Parish he received Parochial relief for many years previously to his death – That his Mother now receives relief therefrom, and that he this Examinant has also been relieved by the said Parish – That about 12 years ago he was lawfully married at Stroud aforesaid to Beata his now Wife (formerly Beata Cratchley Singlewoman) by whom he has four Children (ie) Henry aged about 10 years – William aged about 8 years – George aged about 4 years & Harriet aged about 4 months – That he this Examinant has never done any Act whatever whereby to gain a Settlement in his own right and that in consequence of the severe illness of himself and Family he has become chargeable to the said Parish of Cheltenham [signed]

1838: *removed to Stroud (father's settlement); son William buried at New Burial Ground, Cheltenham 16 Aug, aged 8 years 6 mo.* **1840:** *(RETURNED) son Samuel (the couple's third son Samuel over sixteen years) baptised 20 Dec at St Mary's, Cheltenham, when family lived in Upper Bath St.* **1841:** *the family lived off Gt Norwood St, Cheltenham: BW (aged 35; labourer), Beata (35), Henry (13), George (5), Harriet (3), and Samuel (1) (HO107/353/12/7/10). Later the family moved to 6 Francis St (by 1843) and then Exmouth Court (by 1848) in Cheltenham. Although Benjamin described himself as a shoemaker, he was weaver when he lived in Stroud and labourer in Cheltenham.* [PS/CH/RA/2/5:58. Removal expenses for "White & family" to Stroud £1/5/- (1 Sept 1838: D4178). See **38071SE** (John Cratchley: 8 Nov 1838).]

38054SE: Mon 3 Sept 1838 – **Ann Bowkett**, single woman, with son **Joseph**: That she is it is about 30 Years of Age and that she was born as she believes in the Parish of Ledbury in the County of Hereford where her Father Joseph Bowkett who is a Shoemaker now resides and in which she hath been informed he is legally settled: – That about Seven Years ago she this Examinant was hired for a Year as Cook to a M^r. Hart then of the Parish of Charlton King's in the County of Gloucester at the Wages of 10 Guineas: that she duly served the said Year during the whole of which she lived in her Master's House and that she remained in his service about 2 Months afterwards: that since such hiring and Service she hath not done any act whereby to gain a Settlement: That about 6 weeks since she was delivered of an illegitimate Male Child in the Poor House of Cheltenham to which Parish she is now chargeable. – [signed]
1838: *illegitimate son Joseph Read Bowkett baptised at Cheltenham 21 Aug; **removed to Charlton Kings** (presumed) (hiring and service).* **1841:** *(RETURNED) AB (aged 36; servant) resided at Cheltenham Workhouse with Joseph (3).* **1842:** *birth of illegitimate daughter, Sarah Mary, in workhouse (baptised 24 Oct).* [PS/CH/RA/2/5:59. Expenses for maintaining pauper under order of removal (to Charlton Kings" for "Bowkett & Child" £1/1/- (6 Dec 1838: D4178).]

38055SE: Mon 20 Aug 1838 – Sarah Stevens, widow, regarding the settlement of **Caroline Davis**, single woman, daughter by first husband, Robert Davis: That her said Daughter is the Daughter of Robert Davis formerly of Saint Clements in the City of Oxford Shoemaker who a short time previous to the birth of her said Daughter deserted this Examinant and eight Children then living in consequence of which desertion this Examinant was obliged to go to into the Workhouse there in which House her said Daughter was born – That her Father (Examinant's said Husband) died in the Parish of Saint Clements aforesaid about 9 years ago soon after which her said Daughter was received into the Workhouse at Oxford where she remained about 4 years when she was placed out by the Officers of the Parish of Saint Clements aforesaid as a Servant with a Mrs Weaving in Walton Place where she remained for about a week and on leaving, she was again placed out by them with a Mr Mitchell a Compositor there, with whom she remained about 4 months when she again went into the Poor House and remained there until about 12 months ago – That her said Daughter is about 15 years of age and has never done any Act whereby to gain a Settlement in her own right nor did she this Examinant during her widowhood do any Act whereby to gain a Settlement in her own right – That her said Daughter is now in the Workhouse of Cheltenham aforesaid. [mark]
1838: *removed to St Clement's, Oxford, Oxon (presumed) (father's settlement).* **1841:** *CD (aged 15) lived with Martha Faulkner (20) and Martha Frankum (15) in St Thomas St, Oxford (HO107/891/17/13/18); the* Oxford Journal *(18 Dec) reported that CD and Martha Frankum were convicted of disorderly conduct in Oxford Workhouse, and were imprisoned for 14 days; Faulkner and Davis are described in newspapers as "common prostitutes", and Davis appears to have had numerous encounters with the law in the 1840s.* [PS/CH/RA/2/5:60. See **38067SE** (Sarah Stevens: 1 Nov 1838).]

38056SE: Mon 3 Sept 1838 – **Henry Blanchard**, drover: That he is about 24 years of Age and that he was born as he believes in the Poor house of the Parish of Wimbourne Minster [= Wimborne Minster] in the County of Dorset of the body of Isabella Blanchard Singlewoman who as he hath always understood and believes was legally settled in that Parish – That he remained in the Poor house of Wimbourne Minster for several months – That about three years ago the Parish Officers of Wimbourne Minster aforesaid allowed this Examinant 1^s/6^d Per week as Out Relief of that Parish – That since that period this Examinant has been travelling about the Country as a Drover having no fixed residence and never having done any Act whereby to gain a settlement – That he hath lately become and is now chargeable to the Parish of Cheltenham aforesaid. [mark]
1838: *removed to Wimborne Minster, Dorset (birth).* [PS/CH/RA/2/5:61. Removal expenses for "H. Blanchard" to Wimbourne Minster, Dorset £4/16/- (5 Oct 1838: D4178).]

38057SE: Mon 3 Sept 1838 – **Charles Hiscocks** (also **Hiscox**), gardener, with wife **Ann**, and four children **Harriet**, **Hiram**, **Ann**, and **Ellen**: That he is about 45 years Old and that he was born as he believes in the Parish of Almondsbury in the County of Gloucester where his Father James Hiscocks a Farmer resided – That about 25 years ago he was hired for a year as Cowman by Mr Richard Williams of the Marsh in the Parish of Almondsbury aforesaid at the wages of £3 including board and lodging – That he duly served the whole of such year and entered upon a like service for a second year but after remaining about 3 months he left such Service on Account of illness. That about 24 years ago he this Examinant was lawfully married to Ann his present Wife (then Ann Bailey) at the Parish Church of Minchinhampton in this County by whom he has 8 Children four of whom (that is to say it) Harriet aged about 15 years Hiram aged about 9 years Ann aged about 7 years and Ellen aged about a year and a half are now chargeable to the Parish of Cheltenham aforesaid – That about 4 years ago in consequence of illness Examinant applied to the Parish Officers of Almondsbury aforesaid for relief and upon that occasion he received from them a Sovereign – That since the hiring and service above mentioned he has not done any Act whereby to gain a settlement and in consequence of illness he has become and is now chargeable to the said Parish of Cheltenham. [mark]

1838: *removed to Olveston (hiring and service).* **1841:** *(RETURNED) CH (aged 45; gardener) lived with wife Ann (40; laundress) and five children Thomas (15; porter), Charles (14; porter), Hiram (12; porter), Ann (10), and Ellen (5) in Lime Kiln Row, St Paul's, Cheltenham.* [PS/CH/RA/2/5:62; in later copy (**38065SE:** 18 Oct 1838) Richard Williams's address given as the Marsh, Olveston. Removal expenses for "Hiscocks" to Olveston £1/19/11 (9 Nov 1838: D4178). See **42043SE** (CH: 9 May 1842).]

38058SE: Thurs 20 Sept 1838 – **William Thornton**, cooper: That he is about 43 years of age and that he was born as he believes in the Parish of Towcester in the County of Northampton where he hath always understood and as he verily believes his Father was legally settled – That when he this Examinant was about 14 years old he was bounden Apprentice by Indenture to a Mr William Sheppard of Towcester aforesaid Cooper for the term of seven years   That he duly served the whole of his time during which he boarded and lodged in his Masters House, since which he has not done any Act whereby to gain a settlement elsewhere   That in consequence of illness he has become chargeable to the Parish of Cheltenham aforesaid. [signed]

1838: *removed to Towcester, Northants (apprenticeship).* [PS/CH/RA/2/5:63. Removal expenses to Towcester for "W. Thornton" 10/6 (19 Nov 1838: D4178).]

38059SE: Thurs 20 Sept 1838 – **Susan Smith**, single woman: That she is about 23 years of age and that she was born as she believes in the Parish of Eastnor in the County of Hereford where her Father Charles Smith who was a Lath Render [= a person who splits wood to form laths for building] lived for many years, but who as she hath frequently heard him say and as she verily believes was born in the Parish of Ledbury in the said County of Hereford in which Parish she hath frequently heard him say and as she likewise verily believes he was settled – And this Examinant further said that she had never done any Act whereby to gain a Settlement in her own right and that in consequence of illness she has become and is now chargeable to the said Parish of Cheltenham. [mark]

1838: *removed to Ledbury (presumed) (father's settlement).* [PS/CH/RA/2/5:64.]

38060SE: Thurs 20 Sept 1838 – **John Jackson**, with wife **Mary**, and son **John**: That he was born as he believes in the Parish of Henley upon Thames in the County of Oxford where his Father Elias Jackson a Carpenter then resided – That about 8 or 9 years ago his said Father rented a House of a Mr Jackson in the Parish of Saint Clements Oxford at the rent of £10 a year and upwards and duly paid the Poor rates – That he occupied such House about two years and paid the Rent – That during such period his Father received Relief from the said Parish of Saint Clements – That he this Examinant never did any Act whereby to gain a Settlement in his own right   That about 2 years ago he was lawfully married at the Parish Church of Welland in the County of Worcester to Mary his present Wife (then Mary Eaton Singlewoman) by whom he has one Child named John Eaton about 11 weeks old who together with this Examinant and his said Wife are become chargeable to the Parish of Cheltenham aforesaid. [signed]

1838: *John Eaton Jackson baptised at Cheltenham 5 Aug, when family lived at 13 Witcomb Place, Cheltenham; JJ was plasterer;* **removed to St Clement's, Oxford, Oxon (presumed) (father's settlement).** **1841:** *lived in Welland, Worcs, where John and Mary had married: John (aged 20; independent), Mary (28), John (3), and new baby William (5 mo; born Welland) (HO107/1203/4/8/10).* **1851:** *JJ employed one man (in Gt Malvern, Worcs).* **1861:** *JJ employed 4 men and three boys (in Colwall, Heref).* [PS/CH/RA/2/5:65.]

38061SE: Mon 1 Oct 1838 – **William Simmonds** (also **Simmons**), labourer, with wife **Phoebe**, and two children **Ann** and **Joseph**: That he is about 40 years old and that he was born as he believes in the Parish of Pitchcomb [= Pitchcombe] in the said County of Gloucester where his Father was settled. That about 11 or 12 years ago he was hired for a year by Daniel Theyer of Little Shurdington in the Parish of Badgeworth in the said County Farmer, as Cowman at the wages of 6^l. which year he duly served and was again hired by him for another year at the wages of 7^l but in consequence of an accident he left in about 6 months – That within 12 months afterwards he was again hired as Cowman to M[r] William Bubb of Little Shurdington aforesaid Tanner for a year at the wages of 5^l. which year he duly served – That on leaving Mr Bubb's Service he was again hired by the aforesaid Daniel Theyer as Cowman for a year at the wages of 5^l. which he also duly served and slept in his Master's House   That about 7 years ago he was lawfully married at the Parish Church of Bishop's Cleeve in this County to Phœbe his now Wife (then Phœbe Lyes Singlewoman) by whom he has 2 Children now living (ie) Ann aged about 8 years an illegitimate Child and Joseph aged about a year and a half   That since such last hiring and Service he has not done any Act whereby to gain a settlement and in consequence of sickness he has become and is now chargeable to the Parish of Cheltenham aforesaid [mark]
1838: *removed to Badgeworth (presumed) (hiring and service): see* **41077RO** *(WS: 18 Dec 1841) for further information.* [PS/CH/RA/2/5:66.]

38062SE: Sat 6 Oct 1838 – Ruth Harding, wife of John Harding, labourer, regarding the settlement of brother **William Elliot** (also **Elliotts**), late of Cheltenham, haulier (lunatic): That she is the Daughter of William Elliot formerly of the Parish of Wotton under edge [= Wotton-under-Edge] in the said County of Gloucester Haullier deceased who was the lawful Father of the above named William Elliott – That she hath frequently heard her said Father say and she verily believes that he acquired a Settlement by hiring and service in the said Parish of Wotten under edge – That about 24 years ago her said Father applied to the said Parish for relief and went into the Poor house there where he remained for some years until he was enabled to provide for himself and Family when he left – That about 19 years ago he died in the said Parish and was as she hath understood and believes buried at the expence of such Parish – That her Mother afterwards received relief therefrom and was also buried at the expence thereof – That this Examinant's said Brother William Elliot has never done any Act whereby to gain a settlement in his own right, and in consequence of Lunacy he has lately become chargeable to the Parish of Cheltenham aforesaid from when he has been removed to the Assylum [*sic*] of this County at Gloucester. [mark]
1838: *removed to Gloucester Asylum.* **1841:** *Ruth Harding (aged 35; baptised Ruth Elliotts)) and husband John (40; labourer) lived in Naunton Crescent, Cheltenham (HO107/353/12/59/17); William Elliott(s) is not recorded in Gloucester Asylum on census night.* [PS/CH/RA/2/5:67. Removal expenses for "Elliott" to Asylum £1/1/- (1 Oct 1838: D4178).]

38063SE: Sat 6 Oct 1838 – **Charles Cooper**, labourer, with wife **Ann**, and daughter **Elizabeth**: That he is about 26 years of age and was born as he believes in the Parish of Fulham in the County of Middlesex where his Father John Cooper who was a chaisedriver then resided   That about 8 years ago he this Examinant was hired as Groom for a year by Mr Richard McAdams of Northend in the Parish of Fulham aforesaid at the wages of 6^l that he duly served such year and remained in his Service a second year at the wages of the 7^l. – That about 6 years ago examinant was hired for a year by M^r. Aldridge of Claremont Cottage in the Parish of Fulham aforesaid as Groom and Gardener at the wages of 12^l. – That he duly served such year and received his wages   That about 3½ years ago this Examinant was lawfully married at the Parish Church of Isleworth in the said County of Middlesex to his present Wife Ann (formerly Ann Stevens Singlewoman) by whom he has one Child named Elizabeth about 17 months old – That about 9 months ago he this Examinant applied to the Parish Officers of Fulham aforesaid and received out door relief for several weeks therefrom. That since such Hiring & service as aforesaid he this Examinant hath done no Act whereby to gain a Settlement and is now chargeable to the Parish of Cheltenham aforesaid. [signed]

1838: *removed to Fulham, Middlesex (hiring and service); Ann Cooper must have been heavily pregnant during the examination, as birth of son Charles was registered 4Q (baptised at Cheltenham 14 Jan 1839); CC (gardener) resided at Cheltenham Poor House with his family.* **1841:** *the family lived at one of Taylor's Bone Houses, Fulham Fields, Middlesex: CC (aged 25; labourer), Ann (25), Elizabeth (4), and Charles (2) (HO107/689/13/8/9).* [PS/CH/RA/2/5:68. Pencilled note: "orders to be suspended" (presumably because of wife's pregnancy). Removal expenses to Fulham for "Cooper" £4/9/- (24 Jan 1839: D4178).]

38064SE: [undated: between 6-18 Oct 1838] – **James Blackmore**, bricklayer, with wife **Ann**: That he is about 56 Years of Age and that he was born as he believes in the Parish of Oakham [perhaps Holcombe or Okehampton] in the County of Devon: That about 13 Years ago he this Examinant took a House situate in the Bath Road in the Parish of Cheltenham at 12$^£$. a Year which he continued to rent and occupy for several Years during which he paid Rates and taxes for such House: That since such renting he has not done any Act whereby to gain a Settlement: That about 29 - Years ago he was lawfully married in the Parish Church of S^t. Augustine Bristol to Ann his now Wife then Ann Lovett [also: Lovatt]: That in consequence of illness he is unable to support himself or his Wife: that his Wife hath lately received relief from the Parish of Cheltenham. – [mark]

1838: *removal unlikely: place of settlement probably acknowledged as Cheltenham.* **1839:** *JB died of "asthma" at 12 Clare Parade (now Kew Place), Cheltenham, aged 56, on 2 Sept; AB died of "apoplexy" at Cheltenham Workhouse, aged 56, on 11 Sept; they were buried respectively on 7 and 14 Sept at New Burial Ground, Cheltenham.* [PS/CH/RA/2/5:69.]

38065SE: Thurs 18 Oct 1838 – **Charles Hiscocks**.
[PS/CH/RA/2/5:70; **38057SE** (CH: 3 Sept 1838) gives Richard Williams's address at the Marsh as Olveston, not Almondsbury.]

38066SE: Sat 3 Nov 1838 – Jane Sparrow, regarding the settlement of granddaughter **Amy** (also **Amey**) **Page**, infant: That the said Amy Page is between 11 and 12 years Old and that she was born in the Parish of Bishop's Cleeve in the said County of the body of Ann Page formerly of that Parish Singlewoman who about four months after the birth of the said Child was married at Bishop's Cleeve aforesaid to this Examinant's son <u>Nathan Sparrow</u> whom she hath lately left a Widower – That such Child was affiliated upon this Examinant's said Son Nathan and an Order made upon him for the payment to that Parish of 1/6 weekly towards her support – That she is now in the workhouse of Cheltenham aforesaid [mark]

1838: *removed to Bishop's Cleeve (father's settlement).* **1840:** *burial of AP (consistently "Amey" in baptismal and burial records) at Bishop's Cleeve 20 Apr aged 14 (address Winchcombe).* [PS/CH/RA/2/5:71; examination supplementary to **38012RO** (Nathan Sparrow: 10 Feb 1838). Removal expenses to Bishop's Cleeve for "A. Page" 7/6 (30 Nov 1838: D4178), and 5/- (30 Nov 1838: D4178).]

38067SE: Thurs 1 Nov 1838 – Sarah Stevens, widow, regarding the settlement of daughter **Caroline Davis**, single woman, by first husband Robert Davis: That the said Caroline Davis is the Daughter of this Examinant by her first Husband Robert Davis late of Saint Clements near the City of Oxford Shoemaker who died there about 9 years ago – That she this Examinant hath frequently heard the said Robert Davis say and she verily believes that he gained a settlement some years before his marriage with this Examinant in the Parish of All Saints in the City of Oxford by having lived as a hired Servant for a year with one Mr Ricketts an Attorney at that Parish – That the said Robert Davis on several occasions to the knowledge of this Examinant received relief from the said Parish of All Saints some time before his death and that after his decease this Examinant continued to receive relief therefrom for some time – That about 18 years ago this Examinant's said late Husband having become chargeable to the Parish of Kensington Gravel Pitts in the County of Middlesex he (together with this Examinant and their Family) were removed therefrom by an Order of two magistrates to the said Parish of All Saints the Parish Officers of which received them and gave them relief - That the said Caroline Davis hath never in her own right done any act whereby to gain a settlement and that she hath become and is now chargeable to the Parish of Cheltenham. [mark]

1838: *removed to All Saints', Oxford, Oxon (father's settlement).* [PS/CH/RA/2/5:72. Removal expenses to All Saints', Oxford for "C. Davis" 7/6 and £2/5/9 (27 Nov 1838: D4178). See **38055SE** (Sarah Stevens: 20 Aug 1838).]

38068SE: Thurs 1 Nov 1838 – **Elizabeth Stonham** (also **Stoneham**), single woman; also Hannah Stonham, single woman, relating to the settlement of sister Elizabeth Stonham. *Elizabeth Stonham*: That she is about 17 years of age and that she was born as she believes in the Parish of Calne in the County of Wilts where her Father John Stonham who is a Shoemaker then resided but who is now living at Old Sodbury in the said County of Gloucester in which last mentioned Parish she has frequently heard him say he was settled by having served his Apprenticeship there – That she this Examinant hath never done any Act whereby to gain a Settlement in her own right and that she hath lately become chargeable to the Parish of Cheltenham. [mark]

Hannah Stonham: That she is about 25 years of age and that she is the Sister of the said Elizabeth Stonham who is about 17 years old and who was born in the Parish of Calne in the County of Wilts where her Father John Stonham Shoemaker at that time lived but who now resides at Old Sodbury in the said County of Gloucester. That she this Examinant hath frequently heard her said Father say and she verily believes that he gained a Settlement in the said last named Parish by having been apprenticed and served his time to one M[r]. Isaacs a Shoemaker of that place and that after such an apprenticeship he never gained a settlement elsewhere – That this Examinant recollects her said Father having received relief from the said Parish of Old Sodbury about 6 or 7 years ago – That her said Sister Elizabeth Stonham hath never done any Act in her own right whereby to gain a settlement [mark]

1838: *removed to Old Sodbury (father's settlement).* **1841** *(RETURNED) ES (aged 20; servant) resided at Cheltenham Union Workhouse (HO107/353/17/16/3).* [PS/CH/RA/2/5:73. Removal expenses to Old Sodbury for "E Stoneham" 10/6 (15 Nov 1838: D4178) and £2/13/5 (23 Nov 1838: D4178).]

38069SE: Thurs 1 Nov 1838 – **Lot Organ**, labourer, with wife **Sarah**, and three children **Merryman**, **Lot**, and **John**: That he is about 31 years of Age, and that he was born as he believes in the parish of Badgeworth in this County where his Father Merryman Organ then resided and was legally Settled, that he has he[a]rd his said father say and he verily believes that he gained such Settlement by hiring and Service with M[r]. Oakey of that place, and has actually been releieved [*sic*] by the parish of Badgeworth aforesaid – examinant further saith that he has never done any Act in his own right whereby to gain a Settlement.

That about 7 or 8 years Ago examinant was lawfully married at the parish Church of S[t] Mary's Gloucester, to his present Wife Sarah (then Sarah Bryan) by whom her [*sic*] has three Children viz – Merryman Aged about 6 years, – Lot Aged about four Years and John Aged about 1/4 years, who together with examinant has in consequence of his said Wifes illness become chargeable to the parish of Cheltenham [signed]

1838: *removed to Badgeworth (presumed) (father's settlement).* **1840:** *(RETURNED) at Walter's baptism 7 June address given as Gloucester Rd, Cheltenham.* **1841:** *LO (aged 35; labourer) lived with his family (Sarah, 25; Merryman, 7; Lot, 5; John, 4; and Walter, 12 mo) in Lower Gas Green, Cheltenham (HO107/353/10/20/6); LO appears to have had several brushes with the law, including ten months' imprisonment imposed at County Sessions at Gloucester 19 Oct (for stealing five bushels of wheat).* **1843:** *Merryman, Lot, and Walter Lot admitted to Charlton Kings Workhouse for children (Cheltenham Union) from 12–14 Dec (G/CH/60/2), while Lot, Sarah, and other members of the family were admitted as inmates of Cheltenham Workhouse 8 Dec (G/CH/60/4).* [PS/CH/RA/2/5:74.]

38070SE: Mon 5 Nov 1838 – **George Hewlings**: That he is about 64 years of age, and that he was born as he believes at Stonehouse in this County to which Parish his Father belonged – That when he this Examinant was about 20 years old he rented and occupied a House in the Parish of Stroud in this County of a Mr Drew at 16 Guineas Per annum for several years, since which he hath rented and occupied other Houses there at above 10^l Per Annum each, the last of which (situate in Bowbridge Lane there) he about 12 years ago rented of one Mr Chalmers at 14^l. a year – That he occupied such House for nearly two years and paid the rent – since which he hath done no Act whatever whereby to gain a Settlement – That about 10 years since he was lawfully married to Hester his present Wife at Pitchcomb [= Pitchcombe] aforesaid who about 6 months afterwards deserted him and has not lived with him ever since – That about 12 months ago his said Wife who then lived at Pitchcomb aforesaid applied to the Parish Officers there for relief and therefrom received relief from that Parish upon which this Examinant was examined before two Magistrates at Stroud aforesaid as to his Settlement from which time this Examinant's said Wife (who is older than this Examinant) has been in receipt and still continues to receive a weekly allowance from that Parish to which he belongs – That in consequence of severe illness he has become and is now chargeable to the Parish of Cheltenham aforesaid [mark]
1838: *died before removal to Stroud (renting); death registered at Cheltenham 4Q (buried at New Burial Ground, aged 65) on 26 Nov.* [PS/CH/RA/2/5:75. Expenses received from Stroud for relief and burial of "Geo: Hewlings" £1/7/- (1 Dec 1838: D4178).]

38071SE: Thurs 8 Nov 1838 – **John Cratchley**, labourer: That he is about 80 years of Age and was born as he believes in the parish of Randwick in this County where his Father Daniel Cratchley then resided, that he has he[a]rd his said father say and he verily believes that he (examinants father) gained his Settlement in the parish of Stroud by Apprenticeship with a M^r. Moss of that place.
    That he (this examinant) has upon several occasions received relief from the parish of Stroud, and that upon one occasion about 20 years ago he was received as an inmate of the Stroud Workhouse where he remained about three months, that about nine months ago he (this Examinant) applied to the parish officers of Stroud for Relief and was allowed a Shilling a week for about six months   that he has never (in his own right) done any Act whereby to gain a legal Settlement elsewhere, and is now chargeable to the parish of Cheltenham [mark]
1838: *removed to Stroud (father's settlement); JC died at Stroud Workhouse soon after examination (buried 23 Dec, aged 80).* [PS/CH/RA/2/5:76. Expenses received from Stroud for maintenance of "Jno. Cratchley" 10/6 (1 Dec 1838: D4178), and removal expenses to Stroud 17/6 (30 Nov 1838: D4178). Beata Cratchley (see **38053SE** Benjamin White: 11 Aug 1838) was also born at Randwick, Stroud.]

38072SE: Thurs 15 Nov 1838 – **Mary Hunt**, widow: That she is about 65 years old and that she is the Widow of William Hunt late of Greet in the Parish of Winchcomb [= Winchcombe] in the said County Labourer deceased who previous to his marriage gained a Settlement in the Parish of Prestbury in the same County by having been hired and lived as a Servant to Mr Wells of the Hyde Farm in that Parish Tanner for the term of a year   That about 10 years ago this Examinant, her said Husband and their two Children, were removed by the Order of two Justices from the Parish of Dumbleton in this County to which Parish they had become chargeable to the said Parish of Prestbury and by such Parish acknowledged as belonging thereto   That about 5 years ago her said Husband applied to the same Parish of Prestbury for relief and were [*sic*] relieved by the Officers thereof accordingly since which she has done no Act to gain a settlement and that she is now ~~in the Poor house~~ chargeable to the Parish of Cheltenham aforesaid [mark]
1838: *removed to Prestbury (presumed) (late husband's settlement): see* **40044SE** *(MH: 12 Mar 1840) for further information.* [PS/CH/RA/2/5:77.]

38073SE: Thurs 15 Nov 1838/undated – **Priscilla Turner**, single woman, residing at Cheltenham Workhouse; also Charlotte Turner, relating to the settlement of mother Priscilla Turner. *Priscilla Turner*: That she is about 39 years old and that she was born as she believes in the Parish of Stroud where her Father Samuel Turner (who was a Weaver) then resided – That she hath frequently heard her Mother Mary Turner say and she verily believes that she was legally settled in the Parish of Minchinhampton in this County and That her Father was examined before the Justices at Rodborough and proved his Parish to be at Minchinhampton when he enlisted and went for a Soldier – And this Examinant further saith That she has never been married nor has she ever done any Act in her own right whereby to gain a Settlement and that she is now chargeable to the Parish of Leckhampton within the Union of Cheltenham aforesaid [mark]

Charlotte Turner: That she is about 23 years of age   That she is the Daughter of the said Priscilla Turner and that she was born as she believes in the Parish of Minchinhampton in the said County where she has always understood and believes her Mother was legally settled – That this Examinant has frequently heard her said Mother say and she verily believes that she gained her Settlement in right of her (this Examinant's) Grandmother Mary Turner who for many years received relief from the said Parish of Minchinhampton which was frequently paid to this Examinant by the Officers of that Parish for and on account of her said Grandmother – That about 6 months ago this Examinant's said Grandmother died at the Parish of Stroud but was buried at the expense of the said Parish of Minchinhampton [signed]

1838: *Mary Turner (aged 73) was buried at Stroud 1 Apr;* **removed to Minchinhampton (presumed) (father's settlement). 1841:** *PT (42; no occupation) lived with daughter Charlotte Smith (née Turner) (25; dressmaker) and grandson Walter Henry Smith (4 mo) in Charles St, Leckhampton (HO107/353/18/6/7).* [PS/CH/RA/2/5:78-9. Note: "(Leckhampton Pauper)".]

38074SE: Mon 26 Nov 1838 – **Hannah Edwards**, widow: That she is about 63 years Old and that she is the Widow of Joshua Edwards formerly of the Parish of Cheltenham aforesaid Bricklayer deceased to whom she was lawfully married in the Parish Church of Charlton Kings in the said County about 30 years ago – That she was frequently told by her said Husband and she verily believes that he was born in Magpie Lane in the Town and Parish of Cheltenham aforesaid – That some years after their Marriage her said Husband took a House No 11 in Ambrose Street Cheltenham of one Mr Mustoe a Carpenter at the rent of 11^l. – That he occupied such House a whole year and paid the rent and taxes for the same after which he never did, neither [h]as she this Examinant since his decease ever done any Act whereby to gain a Settlement And that she is now in the Workhouse of Cheltenham aforesaid – And this Examinant lastly saith that on the occasion of her Husband's death a Coffin was provided for him at the expence of the said Parish of Cheltenham. [mark]

1838: *removal unlikely: place of settlement probably acknowledged as Cheltenham.* **1839:** *an HE (aged 67) buried at New Burial Ground, Cheltenham 8 Feb.* [PS/CH/RA/2/5:80.]

38075SE: [undated: 26 Nov 1838] – **George Slide**, chaise-driver: That he is about 42 years of age and that he was born as he believes in the Parish of Aston Cantlow in the County of Warwick to which Parish his Father belonged

That when he this Examinant was about 14 years of Age he went soon after Michaelmas to live as a Servant with Mr Thomas Evans of Aston Cantlow aforesaid Farmer with whom he remained 'till the following Michaelmas when he was hired by him for a year but at what wages he does not recollect – That he duly served the said year and slept in his Master's House during the whole of such servitude. That on leaving this situation he went to Studley Mop where he was hired as a Servant to one Mr Green of Oldborough otherwise Oldberrow in the County of Worcester Farmer for the term of a year to look after his Horses – That he duly served such year during which he boarded and slept in his Master's House and at the expiration thereof received his wages but what they were he this Examinant does not now recollect – That he hath since lived in various situations as Post Boy but has not been hired for a year neither has he ever since done any Act whereby to gain a settlement and that in consequence of illness he has become chargeable to the Parish of Cheltenham.

1838: *removal uncertain: examination form incomplete.* **1843:** *GS (aged 46) put on trial at Warks County Sessions 26 June for larceny; found "Not Guilty" (despite previous conviction).* **1855:** *GS buried 12 Mar (aged 70) at Aston Cantlow (residing at Alcester Union Workhouse).* [PS/CH/RA/2/5:81. Pencilled note: "This man promised to attend the Office on Monday last; he can't be found to day Thursday [29 Nov 1838]".]

38076SE: Thurs 29 Nov 1838 – **Thomas Colstone** (also **Coulstone**), labourer: That he is about 68 years of Age and was born as he believes in the Parish of Kemerton in this County where his father John Coulstone who was a Carpenter then resided, that he has herd [*sic*] his said father say and he verily believes that he was legally Settled in the parish of Ashchurch in this County and that he gained his Settlement there by Hiring & Service, That about 2 years Ago in consequence of an Accident, examinant was relieved by the Parish of Ashchurch and sent to the Union Workhouse at Tewkesbury where he remained about a Month at the expense of the said Parish of Ashchurch, Examinant further saith that he has never done any Act in his own right whereby to gain a Settlement elsewhere and is now chargeable to the parish of Cheltenham [mark]
1838: *removed to Painswick (father's settlement).* **1841:** *no Colstones in Tewkesbury Workhouse on census night, though a TC (aged 6) resident there was buried at Ashchurch 18 Feb.* [PS/CH/RA/2/5:82. Removal expenses for "Colstone" to Painswick[?] 13/- (27 Dec 1838: D4178).]

38077SE: Sat 1 Dec 1838 – **Mary Haines**: That she is about 80 years of age and that she was born as she believes in the Parish of Saint John in the County of Worcester where her father Edward Fowlkes who was a Farmer then resided – ~~That she hath always understood and verily believes that her said Father was the Owner of considerable Property in the Parish of Saint John aforesaid~~ That about 50 years ago she this Examinant was lawfully married at the Parish Church of Saint Augustines at the back [= St Augustine the Less] Bristol to Edward Haines a Hair Dresser who left her about 40 years ago since which she has not heard of him ~~nor does she this Examinant know to what Parish he belonged. That she is now an inmate in the Cheltenham Poor house~~ [signed]
1838: *removed to St John's, Worcester, Worcs (birth): see* **39032SE** *for further information.* [PS/CH/RA/2/5:83. Expenses received from Worcester for "M Haines" 10/6 (24 Dec 1838: D4178), and removal expenses to Worcester £1/12/- (27 Dec 1838: D4178).]

38078SE: Mon 3 Dec 1838 – **John Soper**, plasterer.
[PS/CH/RA/2/5:84; corrected version of examination transcript at **38080SE** (13 Dec 1838).]

38079SE: Sat 8 Dec 1838 – **Sarah Main**, widow, with son **Jesse**: That she is about 50 years of age and that she was born as she believes in the Parish of Dymock in the County of Gloucester where her Father John Finch then resided – That when she was about 16 years old she was hired for a year as an indoor servant to M^r. Fream of the Parish of All Saints, Worcester at the wages of £7 or 8^l. a year and that she duly served the said year in that Parish – That she was then hired for a year to Major Atkinson of Sion House, Bedminster in the County of Somerset at the wages of 14^l. and lived in his Service three successive years in that Parish – That from the time of such last mentioned hiring and service up to the time of her marriage she did not do any Act whereby to gain a Settlement – That about 17 years ago she this Examinant was lawfully married in the Parish Church of Saint Paul Bristol to her late Husband William Main by whom she has a Son named Jesse Main aged about 15 years now living – That she this Examinant never heard her said Husband say where he was born nor any thing whatever with reference to his Parish nor is she aware that he ever did any Act whereby to gain a Settlement in his own right. That she this Examinant has become and is now chargeable to the Parish of Cheltenham aforesaid. [illegible signature; mark]
1837: *removal unlikely: place of settlement probably acknowledged as Cheltenham: see* **37081SE** *(SM: 20 Nov).* **1838:** *removed to Bedminster, Som (hiring and service); son Jesse (aged 15) imprisoned for four months with hard labour at Gloucester County Sessions 3 July for embezzlement; his "bad behaviour" in prison was noted (Prison Hulk Register: ancestry).* **1839:** *Jesse Main sentenced to transportation for seven years for stealing seven gold rings from master in Stroud at County Sessions 31 Dec; sent to Warrior hulk at Woolwich Dockyard.* **1842:** *Jesse Main transported to Van Diemen's Land (Tasmania) 9 Apr.* **1841:** *(probably RETURNED) SM is perhaps the Sarah Maine (aged 55; but listed as independent, born outside*

the county) who lived in Grove St, Cheltenham. **1842:** *SM probably the Sarah Maine buried 7 Apr at New Burial Ground, Cheltenham.* [PS/CH/RA/2/5:85; this is an abbreviated version of examination of 20 Nov 1837, omitting second section detailing husband's career. Removal expenses to Bedminster, Som for "S. Main" 2/- (3 Jan 1839: D4178).]

38080SE: Thurs 13 Dec 1838 – **John Soper**, plasterer, with wife **Charlotte**, and two sons **John** and **Arthur**: That he is about 38 years of age and that he was born as he believes in the Parish of Saint David in the City of Exeter where his Father Arthur Soper then resided – That when he this Examinant was about 16 years of Age his said Father placed him as an ~~indoor~~ Apprentice by Indenture to Joseph Brindley of the Parish of Saint George in the said City of Exeter for the term of 7 years – That he duly served about 4 years of such term, the two last of which he boarded and lodged in the House of his Father situate in the said Parish of ~~Holy Trinity~~ Saint David in the said City of Exeter and received 7^s/– a week from his Master to enable him to pay his said Father for such Board and Lodging, - That about 7 years ago he this Examinant received relief from the united Parishes of Exeter and remained in the Union Workhouse there about 3 months. – That about 6 years ago he was lawfully married at the Parish Church of Saint Mary Major in Exeter aforesaid to Charlotte his present Wife (then Charlotte Sugg) by whom he has two Children (namely) John aged about 5 years and Arthur aged about 4 months – That he this Examinant has become and now is chargeable to the said Parish of Cheltenham. [signed]
1838: *when Arthur Soper was baptised 5 Oct the family lived at 3 Portland Square, Cheltenham;* **removed to St David's, Exeter, Devon (apprenticeship).** **1841:** *the family lived in Exeter (St Mary Steps, "Under the Town Walls": John (aged 40; plasterer), Charlotte (25), John (7), and Arthur (2) (HO107/267/11/19).* [PS/CH/RA/2/586; a slightly corrected later version of examination transcript of 3 Dec 1838. Removal expenses to Exeter, Devon for "J. Soper & fam[ily]" £7/12/6 (7 Jan 1839: D4178).]

38081SE: Thurs 13 Dec 1838 – **Elizabeth Aldridge**, widow, with son **John**: That her maiden name was Elizabeth Webb and that she was born as she believes about 27 Years ago in the Parish of Wenhaston in the County of Suffolk where her Father Robert Webb who was a Farmer was legally settled and in which Parish he died when this Examinant was about 14 Years old: that soon after her Father's death she went out to service & lived in various situations until her Marriage: That about 7 Years ago she was lawfully married in the Parish Church of Dursley in the said County of Gloucester to William Aldridge who died abroad about 6 Years ago: That she hath frequently heard her said Husband say and she believes that a few Years before his Marriage with this Examinant he was hired for a Year by the present Lord Moreton with whom he lived as Groom for about 3 Years in the Parish of Woodchester and that he was afterwards hired for a Year by M^r. John Williams a Surgeon of Dursley whom he served for such Year in that Parish and that after such last mentioned hiring and Service he did not do any Act Whereby to gain a Settlement: That she has no Child by her said Husband but that she has an illegitimate Child named John born in the Parish of Cheltenham about 18 Months ago which has become chargeable to that Parish: That since her Husband's death she hath not done any Act whereby to gain a Settlement [signed]
1833: *removed to Dursley (presumed): see 33021SE (William Aldridge: 16 Mar); William Aldridge of Dursley sentenced to fourteen years' transportation at Gloucester Lent Assizes for stealing two pigs (Cheltenham Chron. 7 Mar reports his committal to Assizes; see also BGAS Record Series vol. 1, p. 2); Robert William Aldridge baptised 9 May at Cheltenham; WA sailed on Lloyds 19 Aug, arriving New South Wales 18 Dec.* **1838:** *RETURNED; John Wilks Aldridge was baptised at Cheltenham 9 July;* **removed to Dursley (late husband's settlement) (presumed).** [PS/CH/RA/2/5:87.]

38082SE: Sat 29 Dec 1838 – **Thomas Underwood**, servant, with wife **Mary Ann**, and son **William**: That he is about 28 years of age and that he was born as he believes in the Parish of Twyning in this County to which Parish his father Thomas Underwood Labourer belongs. That when he this Examinant was about 16 years old he went out to Service and lived in various situations until he was about 21 years old   That in the year 1831 he was hired for a year to Mr John Boodle of the Parish of Saint George Hanover Square in the County of Middlesex as Footman at the wages of 20 Guineas   that he duly served such year and continued to remain in the same situation and upon the same terms for nearly the 3 following years during the whole of which time he slept and boarded in his said Master's House and received the whole of his Wages, since which he has not done any Act whereby to gain a Settlement   That in the year 1833 or 1834 he this Examinant was married at All Souls Church in the said Parish of Mary Le Bone to his present Wife Mary Ann (formerly Mary Ann Price) by whom he has one Child named William Joseph Pittman [= Pitman] Underwood nearly 4 years old and that his said Wife now residing in this Parish is in a state of pregnancy [signed]

1838: *not removed to St George, Hanover Square, Middlesex: see* **44009SE** *(18 Jan 1844) for further information on the family).* [PS/CH/RA/2/5:88. Pencilled note: "No orders".]

CITY COURT. – Friday, Dec. the 10th, Caroline Davis and Martha Frankum, for disorderly conduct in the workhouse, were committed for 14 days, last 7 days solitary confinement. – Tuesday, Dec. 14, John Hyatt, for indecent language in the Parks, fined 5s. and costs.

Caroline Davis, a common prostitute, and companion of the prisoner, was charged as a vagrant.

Thomas Curtain stated that on Saturday night last he proceeded to a house in St. Thomas's to apprehend Scotty, (the prisoner in the above case,) whom he was about handcuffing, when Davis siezed [*sic*] him by the hair, and pulled him backwards with great violence, being at the same time very riotous, and making use of the most disgusting language. Committed to the House of Correction for fourteen days.

Caroline Davis was the subject of a settlement examination in Cheltenham in 1838 (38055SE and 38067SE), but she was well-known in the late 1830s and 1840s to the Oxford newspapers. Here, she is charged with disorderly conduct in the Oxford workhouse in 1841 (Oxford Chronicle 18 December) and with swearing and riotous behaviour in the St Thomas's area of Oxford four years later (Oxford Chronicle 17 May 1845)

1839

39001SE: Sat 5 Jan 1839 – **Harriet Pearce**, single woman, with daughter **Mary Anne**: That She is about twenty two years of Age and was born as she believes in the Parish of Rodborough where her Father John Pearce Labourer then resided – That she has frequently heard her said Father say and she verily believes that he was legally settled in the Parish of Randwick in the County of Gloucester – That Examinant recollects that when her Father died her Mother applied to the Parish Officers of Randwick for relief and received therefrom the sum of two shillings a week – That her said Mother has continued to receive relief from the said Parish person[al]ly ever since – That She (examinant) has never done anything in her own right whereby to gain a settlement – That she has an infant Female illegitimate Child And that she and her said Child are now chargeable to the Parish of Cheltenham [mark]
1839: *removed to Randwick (father's settlement); daughter Mary Anne baptised at Randwick 14 July.* **1840:** *Mary Anne buried at Randwick, aged sixteen months, 18 Apr; HP then an inmate of Stroud Union Workhouse.* [PS/CH/RA/2/5:89. Pencilled note: "Order incomplete". Removal expenses to Randwick for "H. Pearce" £1/3/6 (31 Jan 1839: D4178).]

39002SE: Thurs 10 Jan 1839 – **Hannah Workman**, single woman: That she is about 32 years of age and was born as she believes in the Parish of Cam in this County where her Parents then resided: – That about seven years ago She was hired for a Year to M^r. Wheeler Nurseryman of the Parish of S^t. John in the City of Gloucester at the wages of five pounds a year: – That she duly served that year and received her full Wages: – That about two years and a half ago She applied in consequence of her pregnancy to the Parish Officers of Cam for relief and was removed by orders of removal to the said Parish of Saint John Gloucester and remained in the Union Workhouse there for about seven weeks until the death of her Child since which time she has not done any act whereby to gain a Settlement and in consequence of Pregnancy is now chargeable to the Parish of Cheltenham. [signed]
1839: *removed to Gloucester (hiring and service); daughter Louisa baptised 1 Mar at St Catherine's, Gloucester.* **1840:** *death of HB's mother (buried 18 Apr, aged 31, at St John the Baptist, Gloucester).* **1840:** *Louisa (aged 2½) was an inmate of Gloucester Union Workhouse, St Catherine's, Gloucester (HO107/379/2/41/19).* [PS/CH/RA/2/5:90. Pencilled note: "Order". Removal expenses to Gloucester for "H. Workman" 14/- (1 Feb 1839: D4178).]

39003SE: Thurs 17 Jan 1839 – **Israel Winstone** (also **Whinstone**, **Winston**), shoemaker, with wife **Harriet**, and daughter **Martha**: That he is about 26 years of age and that he was born as he believes in the Parish of Bisley in the said County in which Parish his Father William Winstone has lived for many years and Paid Parochial rates for property there (which he still occupies) where he is legally settled – That he this Examinant when about 15 years old was placed with George Parker of Bisley aforesaid as an Outdoor apprentice but for what term he this Examinant does not now recollect. that no Indenture was ever made – but that he faithfully served his said Master for 4 years and for the last three years thereof was paid weekly wages towards his support – That during the whole of the time he boarded and lodged in his said Father's House in the said Parish of Bisley – That about 2 and a half years ago he was lawfully married in the Parish Church of Cheltenham aforesaid to Harriet his present Wife (formerly Harriet Antill Singlewoman) by whom he has one Child named Martha aged about one year & 10 months and that his said Wife is now far advanced in Pregnancy – That he this Examinant has never done any Act save his said apprenticeship whereby to gain a settlement in his own right and in consequence of illness he has become chargeable to the said Parish of Cheltenham. [signed Isreal Winston]
1839: *at examination Harriet pregnant with Samuel Winstone (born 16 St George's St, 12 February), who seems not to have survived into 1841 census; **removed to Bisley (presumed) (apprenticeship).** **1841:***

daughter Martha died 2 Jan of a "decline"; IW (aged 25; cordwainer) and wife Harriet (25) lived in Eastgate St, Gloucester (HO107/379/8/8/11). [PS/CH/RA/2/5:91.]

39004SE: Thurs 10 Jan 1839 – **Elizabeth Arnold**, single woman: That she is about 23 Years of Age and was born as she believes in the Parish of Cam in the County of Gloucester where her Parents then resided both of whom died when she this Examinant was quite Young: that she hath never done any act in her own right whereby to gain a Settlement and that in consequence of illness she hath become and is now chargeable to the Parish of Cheltenham. [mark]
1839: *removed to Cam (father's settlement).* **1841:** *(perhaps RETURNED) perhaps the EA (aged 25) who lived as servant in Lawrence's Passage, Bath Road, Cheltenham (HO107/353/12/39/14).* [PS/CH/RA/2/5:92. Note: "Order".]

39005SE: Sat 12 Jan 1839 – **Richard Merrett**, labourer: That he is about 61 Years of Age and was born as he believes in the Parish of Miserdine [= Miserden] in the County of Gloucester where his Father John Merrett resided and was as this Examinant has frequently heard him say and as he verily believes legally settled: That he this Examinant hath never in his own right done any act to gain a Settlement: That about six Years ago he became chargeable to the Parish of Painswick from which he was removed by an order of 2 Magistrates to the said Parish of Miserdine, where he received relief in consequence of the illness of his then Wife who is since dead: And this Examinant lastly Saith that he is now chargeable to the Parish of Cheltenham. [mark]
1839: *removed to Miserden (father's settlement).* **1841:** *RM (age given as 70; agricultural labourer) was an inmate of Stroud Union Workhouse, of which Miserden was constituent parish (HO107/349/13/67/7).* **1851:** *RM (aged 70, widower; labourer) lived in Miserden (HO107/1964/317/26).* [PS/CH/RA/2/5:93. Note: "Order". Removal expenses to Miserden for "R Merrett" (and E Gill to Horsley) £1/1/6 (4 Feb 1839: D4178).]

39006SE: Sat 19 Jan 1839 – **Sarah Faulkes**, widow, with two daughters **Elizabeth** and **Rose**: That she is 34 years of age and that she was born as she believes in the Parish of Stroud in this County. That on the 5th. of november 1830 she was lawfully married at the Parish Church of Rodborough in this County to William Faulkes Labourer by whom she has two Children namely Elizabeth aged about 7 years and Rose aged about 5 years who together with herself are now chargeable to the said Parish of Cheltenham. That she has frequently heard her said Husband say and she verily believes he was legally settled in the Parish of Bisley in this County – That on the 30th of april last her said Husband died at Westbromwich in consequence of which she became chargeable to that Parish and was removed therefrom by orders of Removal to the Parish of Stroud which Orders she believes was [*sic*] appealed against and the adjoining Parish of Bisley aforesaid ultimately agreed to receive this Examinant and Family till the question was legally settled between Stroud & Westbromwich and that Mr Shill the Guardian of Bisley told Examinant that she belonged to that Parish – That she was allowed for 4⁰/– a week by the said Parish of Bisley until August last [signed Sarah Faulks]
1839: *removed to Bisley (husband's settlement).* [PS/CH/RA/2/5:94. Removal expenses to Bisley for "Faulks & fam[ily]" £1/13/6 (11 Feb 1839: D4178).]

39007SE: Sat 19 Jan 1839 – **Thomas Farmer**, gardener, wife **Jane**, and four children **Albert**, **John**, **Mary**, and **Jane**: That he is about 43 years of age and that he was born as he believes in the Parish of Twyning in this County where his Father John Farmer then resided in a House of his Own worth about 300^l and that he also rented Land in the same Parish at 15^l Per Annum and paid taxes for the same   That he this Examinant has never done any Act in his own right whereby to gain a legal Settlement   That about the year 1822 he this Examinant was lawfully married at the Parish Church of Cheltenham to his present Wife Jane (whose maiden name was Mason) by whom he has four Children now living (namely) Albert aged about 14 years, John Aged about 10 years, Mary aged about 6 years & Jane aged about 3 years – That he this Examinant has become chargeable to the Parish of Cheltenham aforesaid [signed]
1839: *removed to Twyning (father's settlement).* **1841:** *TF (aged 40; labourer) lived with his family (Jane, 40; Albert, 14; John, 11; Mary, 10, and Jane, 5) in Crooked Alley, Tewkesbury (HO107/380/5/13/21).* **1851:**

(RETURNED) the family lived at 19 Grove St, Cheltenham (HO107/1973/591/9). [PS/CH/RA/2/5:95. Removal expenses to Twyning for "Farmer" 19/6 (9 Feb 1839: D4178).]

39008SE: Mon 14 Jan 1839 – **Elizabeth Gill**, single woman: That she is about 29 Years of Age and was born in the Parish of Horsley in the County of Gloucester where her Father then resided and still lives: That she hath frequently heard her said Father say and she verily believes that he is settled in that Parish from which he now receives relief: And this Examinant further saith that she hath never in her own right gained a Settlement by hiring and Service or otherwise and that in Consequence of pregnancy she hath become chargeable to the Parish of Cheltenham. [mark]
1839: *removed to Horsley (father's settlement).* 1841: *presumably the EG (aged 28) who lived alone as a servant in High St, Stroud (HO107/349/14/18/30).* **1848:** *EG buried at Horsley 4 June, aged 37.* [PS/CH/RA/2/5:96. Removal expenses to Miserden for "R Merrett & Horsley E Gill" £1/1/6 (4 Feb 1839: D4178).]

39009SE: Sat 19 Jan 1839 – **William Cossens**, blanket-weaver: That he is about 63 years of age and that he is the Son of Thomas Cossens formerly of Whitney [= Witney] in the County of Oxford Labourer to which Parish he belonged and received relief therefrom for very many years previous to his death. That he this Examinant has also occasionally received relief therefrom and has been in the Workhouse there in consequence of illness for 3 or 4 weeks together – That he has never done any Act whereby to gain a Settlement in his Own right and that in consequence of sickness he has become chargeable to the Parish of Cheltenham. [mark]
1839: *removed to Witney (father's settlement).* 1841: *probably the "William Collems" (aged 67; weaver) who lived alone at Bridge St, Witney (HO107/872/31/19/5).* **1842:** *WC, pauper, died of "Debility" on 2 Oct at the Union Workhouse, Witney, age registered as 56.* [PS/CH/RA/2/5:97. Removal expenses to Witney, Oxon for "W. Cossens" £1/16/- (28 Feb 1839: D4178).]

39010SE: Tues 22 Jan 1839 – **Samuel Baughan**, with wife **Ann**: That in or about the Month of May 1830 he was Removed from the parish of Cheltenham by orders of Removal to the parish of Bisley in this County together with his present Wife Ann Baughan   that such order[s] of Removal were not appealed against – that he has not done any Act since that period to gain a legal Settlement elsewhere and in consequence of illness he is now chargeable to the parish of Cheltenham [mark]
1839: *removed to Bisley (previously determined as his settlement)*; *wife Ann buried at New Burial Ground, Cheltenham 15 Feb, three weeks after husband's examination.* **1841:** *(RETURNED) SB (aged 81) buried at Cheltenham on 11 Feb.* [PS/CH/RA/2/5:98. Note: "Orders made". Removal expenses to Bisley for "Baughan & Wife" £1/14/8 and 19/6 (22 Nov 1839: D4178).]

39011SE: Fri 1 Feb 1839 – **William Millard**, tailor, wife **Mary**, and two children **James** and **Margaret**: That he is about 44 Years old and that he was born as he believes in the Parish of Tetbury in the County of Gloucester: That when he this Examinant was about 14 Years of Age he was bounden Apprentice by Indenture to George Lamb of the said Parish of Tetbury Tailor for 7 Years which Apprenticeship he duly served since which he has not done any act whereby to gain a Settlement: That about 14 years Years ago he was lawfully married in the Parish Church of Cheltenham to Mary his present Wife (then Mary Humphris) by whom he has 2 Children now living, namely James aged about 6 Years and Margaret aged about 3 Years: That about 6 Years ago he this Examinant applied for and obtained relief from the said Parish of Tetbury and that he, his Wife and Children are now chargeable to the said Parish of Cheltenham. [mark]
1839: *removed to Tetbury (apprenticeship).* 1841: *WM (45; journeyman tailor) lived in Cirencester with wife Mary (40), son James (7) and daughter Margaret (5).* [PS/CH/RA/2/5:99. Removal expenses to Tetbury for "Millard" £2/4/- (23 Feb 1839: D4178).]

39012SE: Fri 1 Feb 1839 – **Thomas Belcher**, labourer, and wife **Ann**: That he is 37 Years old and was born as he believes in the Parish of Shipton Oliffe in the County of Gloucester: That at Michaelmas 1822 he was hired for a Year as Milkman to Thomas Ballinger of the Parish of Charlton Kings in the said County of Gloucester Farmer at the Wages of £9: 10: 0: that he duly served such Year and received his Wages; immediately after which he was hired for a Year by

Samuel Burroughs of the Same Parish Farmer which Year he likewise duly served: That he afterwards rented a Farm in this Said Parish of Charlton Kings of one William Flatcher at the rent of 100[l]: Per Annum which he occupied upwards of 2 Years & duly paid the Rent & all Rates and taxes for this Same: that he has not since done any act whereby to gain a Settlement: That about 14 Years ago he was lawfully married at Charlton Kings to his first Wife Lucy Smith (who died in 1827) by whom he has a Daughter now living named Lucy aged about 13 Years: That about 2 Years ago he was lawfully married to his present Wife then Ann Sisom at the Parish Church of Sevenhampton but has no Child living by her: That in Consequence of illness this Examinant & his Wife have become chargeable to the Parish of Cheltenham [signed]

1839: *removed to Charlton Kings (presumed) (renting).* **1840:** *daughter Caroline baptised at Charlton Kings 30 Aug.* **1841:** *TB (aged 35; agricultural labourer), wife Ann (25), and daughter Caroline (2; incorrectly listed as "Ann") lived at Vineyards Farm Cottage, Charlton Kings (HO107/353/2/31/2), where they remained in 1851 census.* [PS/CH/RA/2/5:100.]

39013SE: Sat 2 Feb 1839 – **William Brunsdon**, cordwainer: That he is about 77 years of Age and was born as he believes in the parish of Winstone in this County. That when he was about 16 years of Age his father bound him Apprentice by Indenture for 7 years to Thomas Broadsmith of North Cerney in this County Shoemaker and paid a premium of Eight Guineas with him. That he duly served his said Master till he was 21 years of Age during the whole of which time he boarded and lodged in his said Master's House   that since such Apprenti[ce]ship he has not done any Act whereby to gain a legal Settlement and is now chargeable to the parish of Cheltenham [mark]

1839: *removed to North Cerney (apprenticeship); WB died soon after examination (buried at Cirencester 14 Mar, aged 77); the burial register gives his last address as Cirencester Union Workhouse, North Cerney.* [PS/CH/RA/2/5:101. Removal expenses to Cerney for "Brunsden" 17/6 (23 Feb 1839: D4178).]

39014SE: Wed 6 Feb 1839 – **John Davis**, labourer, wife **Ann**, and daughter **Elizabeth**: That he is about 34 years of age and that he was born as he believes in the Parish of Hawkesbury in the said County where his Father Richard Davis then lived, But who afterwards went to live in the Parish of Boxwell in the said County in which Parish as this Examinant hath always understood and verily believes he was legally settled and upon his death (which happened about 9 years ago) this Examinant's mother was allowed a weekly payment of 1[s]/– from that Parish up till the time of her death now upwards of 12 months since   That about 6 years ago he this Examinant was lawfully married at Tetbury in the said County to Ann his now Wife formerly Ann Clymer Singlewoman by whom he has one Child now living named Elizabeth about 3 years old. That about 12 months ago this Examinant's said Wife applied to the Officers of Tetbury Union (of which Union the Parish of Boxwell aforesaid forms a part) and received relief therefrom for several weeks together – That he this Examinant has never done any Act in his own right whereby to gain a settlement and in consequence of very severe illness has become and now is chargeable to the said Parish of Cheltenham. [signed]

1839: *removed to Boxwell (father's settlement).* [PS/CH/RA/2/5:102. Removal expenses to Boxwell for "J. Davis" and another to Marston Maisey £2/4/- (4 Mar 1839: D4178).]

39015SE: Mon 11 Feb 1839 – **John Gale**, labourer: That he was born as he believes in the Parish of Norton & Lynchwick [= Norton and Lenchwick] in the County of Worcester where his Father lived   that he is 34 years of age & that when he was about fourteen years of age He was hired for one year to Mr Peyton of the Parish of Dumbleton in the County of Worcester [bordering Glos] at the Wages of Three pounds – that he duly served such year, boarding and lodging in the House and received the whole of his Wages since which hiring and service He has not done any Act to gain a Settlement and he is now chargeable to the Parish of Cheltenham [mark]

1839: *removed to Dumbleton (hiring and service).* **1841:** *JG (aged 35; agricultural labourer) lived in Lenchwick with mother and brothers (HO107/119/4/5/3).* [PS/CH/RA/2/5:103. Removal expenses to Dumbleton for "J. Gale" £1/11/- (6 Mar 1839: D4178).]

39016SE: Tues 12 Feb 1839 – **Martha Hayward**, widow: That she is about 63 years of age and that she was born as she believes at Abbey Dore in the County of Hereford – That when she was about 14 years of age she was hired for the term of a year as Servant to a Mr Davis of the Parish of Nantmel in the County of Radnor and duly served such year, during which she boarded and lodged in her Master's House and received her wages – That she entered upon a second year's service with her said Master and continued therein as such servant from year to year for six successive years during the whole of such time having boarded and slept in her said Master's House in the Parish of Nantmel aforesaid and received her Wages – That when she this Examinant was about 21 years of age she was lawfully married at the Parish Church of Disserth in Radnorshire to John Wilcox Butcher who has since died but that she does not nor never did know to what Parish he belonged That she has since been married at the City of Hereford to one Charles Hayward who was a Navigator [= "navvy", construction worker] & who about 15 years ago died at Monmouth That soon after their Marriage her said Husband left her and she Never knew to what Parish he belonged. That she has become chargeable to this Parish [mark]
1839: *removed to Nantmel, Radnorshire (hiring and service):* see **49019RO** *(MH: 12 Mar 1849) for further information.* [PS/CH/RA/2/5:104. Removal expenses for "Hayward" £5/-/- (1Q 1840: D4178) and to Nantmel, Radnorshire £22/4/8 (2Q 1840: D4178).]

39017SE: Tues 12 Feb 1839 – **Mary Price**, widow: That she is about fifty four years of age, - and that she was married in the year 1812 at the Parish of Hempstead [= Hempsted] near Gloucester in the County of Gloucester to James Price who was as this Deponent hath heard and believes legally settled in the Parish of Abergavenny in the County of Monmouth and who died and was buried at that Parish. That she hath lately become chargeable to the Parish of Cheltenham [mark]
1839: *removed to Abergavenny (husband's settlement).* **1841:** *probably the MP (aged 68; labourer's widow, blind, born Clifford, Heref) who lived in Abergavenny (HO107/2446/229/25).* [PS/CH/RA/2/5:105. Removal expenses to Abergaveny £2/11/- (21 Feb 1839: D4178).]

39018SE: Fri 22 Feb 1839 – **George Allen**, labourer, wife **Elizabeth**, and son **George**: That he is about 35 Years of Age and was born as he believes in the Parish of Saint James in the City of Bath in which Parish his Father John Allen ~~who was a Labourer~~ now resides and is legally settled: that his said Father occasionally receives relief from that Parish and that he this Examinant about 4 Years ago being unwell applied to Mr. Douglas the Relieving Officer there and also obtained Relief therefrom: that he hath never in his own right done any act whereby to gain a Settlement: That about 15 Years ago he was lawfully married to his wife then Elizabeth Pitman by whom he has a Son named George aged about 14 Years: That in Consequence of severe illness he is now chargeable to the Parish of Cheltenham [mark]
1839: *died before removal to St James's, Bath (father's settlement); the burial of a GA (aged 39) recorded at New Burial Ground, Cheltenham 15 Mar.* [PS/CH/RA/2/5:106. Note: "orders under suspension to be made". Removal expenses to St James Bath 2/4 (25 Mar 1839: D4178).]

39019SE: Tues 26 Feb 1839 – **William Edwards**, labourer: That he is about 30 years of age and that he was born as he believes at the Parish of Marston-Maisey [= Marston Meysey] in the County of Wilts where [h]is parents have ever since resided and are legally settled – That about 4 years ago he this Examinant was lawfully married at the Parish Church of Castle Eaton in the said County of Wilts to Mary Ann his Present Wife (then Mary Ann Febery [also Freebury/Freebery]) who died about 12 months ago leaving a Child named Mary Ann now about 3 years old who is living with this Examinant's Father – That about 3 years ago his said Father who was ill for about 6 or 7 weeks and unable to work, received relief during that period from the said Parish of Marston-Maisey – That he this Examinant has never done any act whereby to gain a settlement in his own right and severe illness has caused him to become chargeable to the Parish of Cheltenham aforesaid. [mark]
1839: *removed to Marston Meysey (father's settlement).* **1841:** *WE (aged 30) lived with his parents and daughter (Mary) Ann (6), in Marston Meysey (HO107/1178/19/6/6).* [PS/CH/RA/2/5:107. Removal expenses to Boxwell for "J. Davis" and another to Marston Maisey £2/4/- (4 Mar 1839: D4178).]

39020SE: Thurs 28 Feb 1839 – **Julia Smith**, single woman, with daughter **Mary Ann**: That she is about Eighteen Years of Age and was born in the Hamlet of Westmancote in the Parish of Bredon in the County of Worcester where her Parents then resided: That about 10 Years ago her Father Thomas Smith who is a Butcher went to reside at Overbury in the said County of Worcester where he rented and still continues to rent a House and Land for which he has paid together about Twenty six Pounds a Year and all Rates and taxes: That this Examinant hath never done any act in her own right whereby to gain a Settlement: That she hath lately been confined in the Parish of Cheltenham with a female illegitimate Child and is now chargeable to that Parish. [signed]
1839: *illegitimate daughter Mary Ann baptised at Cheltenham just before examination, 24 Feb; **removed to Overbury, Worcs (father's settlement) (uncertain).** **1840:** death of JS (she lived in Leckhampton and was buried at Cheltenham 11 Dec); daughter (aged 2) became a pauper inmate of Charlton Kings Workhouse (HO107/353/2/55/3).* [PS/CH/RA/2/5:108.]

39021SE: Sat 2 Mar 1839 – **Charlotte Ewer**, widow: That she is about 64 Years of Age and that she is the Widow of Thomas Ewer late of the Parish of Bushey in the County of Hertford Gardener to whom she was lawfully married in the Parish Church of Saint Mary Lambeth in the County of Surrey in the Month of October 1817: That her said Husband was settled in the said Parish of Bushey from which he received Parochial relief for some time previous to his death and that he was buried at the expense of that Parish: That she this Examinant hath obtained relief from the said Parish of Bushey on many occasions since her Husband's death: That she hath never done any Act since she became a Widow whereby to gain a Settlement in her own right and that she is now chargeable to the Parish of Cheltenham in the County of Gloucester. – [mark]
1839: *removed to Bushey (presumed) (husband's settlement).* [PS/CH/RA/2/5:109.]

39022SE: Mon 4 Mar 1839 – **Betsey** (also **Elizabeth**) **Ingram**, widow, with children **Thomas**, **George**, and **John**: That she is about 49 years of age and that she was born as she believes in the Parish of Cheltenham aforesaid where her Husband Thomas Ingram, who was a Plasterer, lately died – That about 23 years ago she was lawfully married at the Parish Church of Cheltenham aforesaid to her said late Husband, who, as she has frequently heard him say and she verily believes was legally settled in the Parish of Boddington in this County – That her said late Husband's father received relief from that Parish and that her said Husband never did any Act whereby to gain a settlement in his own right and that he also received relief therefrom upon several occasions – That by her said late Husband she has 3 Children (namely) Thomas aged about 18 years – George aged about 9 years and John aged about 7 years and that she hath become chargeable to the Parish of Cheltenham aforesaid [mark]
1839: *BI's husband Thomas buried at New Burial Ground, Cheltenham on 20 Feb; **removed to Boddington (husband's settlement).** **1841:** (RETURNED) "Elizabeth Ingram" (aged 45; washerwoman) lived with two sons George (11) and John (9) in Elmstone Road, Cheltenham (HO107/353/16/30/21).* [PS/CH/RA/2/5:110. Removal expenses to Boddington for "Ingram" 7/- (15 Aug 1839: D4178). Perhaps compare Gray **539** (Thomas Ingram: 24 Feb 1825).]

39023SE: Mon 4 Mar 1839 – **John Juggins**: That he is about 49 Years of Age and was born as he believes in the Parish of Withington in the County of Gloucester where his Father William Juggins was settled: That about 22 Years ago he was hired as a Yearly Servant by George Long of Arle in the Parish of Cheltenham Farmer at the Wages of Six Pounds: that he duly served the said Year during which he lived in his Master's House: That he afterwards rented and occupied for a Year a House in Cheltenham of one M^r. Spencer of the Knapp and paid a Rental of ten Pounds a Year & likewise paid Taxes: that he this Examinant except by the means aforesaid hath never done any act whereby to gain a Settlement and that he is now chargeable to the Parish of Cheltenham. – [mark]
1839: *not removed: settlement probably acknowledged as Cheltenham (renting).* **1842:** *a JJ (aged 45; labourer, widower), whose father was William Juggins (labourer), married Hannah Niblett (38; spinster) at Down Hatherley 28 Mar.* **1841:** *this JJ lived (45; agricultural labourer) lived in the next village, Norton (HO107/356/11/14/5).* **1844/5:** *JJ (55) and Ann (40; for Hannah) were inmates of Cheltenham Workhouse from 17 Oct 1844 until 6 Mar 1845.* **1847:** *death of Hannah Juggins, aged 44 (buried 25 June at New Burial*

Ground, Cheltenham). **1848:** *at various times JJ ("houseless & destitute") was admitted to Cheltenham Workhouse, on account of old age (G/CH/60/5/6).* **1861:** *JJ (63; dairyman) lodged in Worcester St, Cheltenham (RG9/1800/17/28).* [PS/CH/RA/2/5:111: Note: "No order." See **41081RO** (nephew John Juggins: 18 Dec 1841).]

39024SE: Tues 12 Mar 1839 – **Abraham Hawes**, labourer, wife **Eliza**, and three children **Thomas**, **William**, and **Mary**: That he is about 48 years of age: – That he was born in the Parish of Drayton in the County of Norfolk where his Father Mark Hawes who was a Labourer resided and was legally settled: – That he this Examinant has never done anything in his own right whereby to gain a settlement: – That about nine years since he was lawfully married to his present Wife (then Eliza Singer) at Newbury in the County of Berks and by her has three Children namely Thomas aged about 5 years, William aged 2 years and 10 months, and Mary aged about 14 Months: – That about 4 years ago he was at Drayton aforesaid and from an accident to his hand was obliged to apply to the Parish Officers of the said Parish of Drayton for relief and that he received 4^s/6^d a week for four Months from the said Parish: – That in consequence of illness He this Examinant & his said Wife and three Children have become and are now chargeable to the Parish of Cheltenham aforesaid [mark]
1839: *removed to Drayton, Norf (father's settlement); deaths of children Mary and William registered in Bath 4Q.* **1841:** *AH (aged 50; shoemaker) lived with wife Eliza (30) and son Thomas (7) in Wellington Place, Walcot, Bath, Som (HO107/970/1/14/20).* **1849:** *death of AH in Bath (registered 4Q).* [PS/CH/RA/2/5:112. Removal expenses for "A Hawes & others" to London and Drayton, Norfolk £4/11/1 (15 May 1839: D4178) and to Norwich for "Hawes & family" £1/4/8 (13 June 1839: D4178).]

39025SE: Sat 9 Mar 1839 – **Richard Woolley**, carpenter, wife **Sarah** ("in a state of derangement"), and daughter **Mary Ann**: That he is about twenty seven years of age and that he was born as he believes at the Parish of Wellington in the County of Hereford where his Father Samuel Woolley who was a Weaver lived and as he believes was legally settled. that he has never been apprenticed or done any thing to gain a Settlement in his own right – That He was legally married in the Parish Church of Cheltenham to his present Wife Sarah formerly Sarah Hawkes and by her has One Daughter named Mary Ann aged about three years and a half that in Consequence of his said Wife being in a state of derangement She is become chargeable to the Parish of Cheltenham [signed]
1839: *removed to Wellington, Heref (father's settlement); wife Sarah removed to Gloucester Asylum.* **1841:** *(RETURNED) the family lived in Gt Norwood St, Cheltenham: RW (aged 30; mason); Sarah (35), and Mary Ann (5) (HO107/353/12/21/37).* [PS/CH/RA/2/5:113. Removal expenses to Wellington, Heref £1 10/- and 5[/- (25 Mar 1839: D4178); also removal expenses to Gloucester Asylum for "Sarah Wooley" £1/1/- (13 June 1839: D4178).]

39026SE: Sat 9 Mar 1839 – **Richard Alder**, labourer, wife **Charlotte,** and daughter **Sarah (Anne)**: That he is about 36 Years old and that he was born at King['s] Stanley in the County of Gloucester where his Father Nathanial Alder, as he believes, was born and legally settled: that he died there about 2 Years ago: – That he this Examinant was never apprenticed neither was he ever hired to any person for a Year and that he never rented any Property of the Value of Ten Pounds a Year; or did any Act in his own right whereby to gain a Settlement: That about 8 or 9 Years ago he was lawfully married in the Parish Church of Minchinhampton to Charlotte his now Wife (then Charlotte Dangerfield) by whom he has one Child named Sarah aged about 2 years. – [signed]
1839: *removed to King's Stanley (father's settlement) (uncertain); the Alders were living in Leckhampton before and after the examination.* **1840:** *son Charles baptised at Leckhampton 19 Oct (buried there 2 Jan 1841).* **1867:** *daughter Sarah (Anne) married in Leckhampton.* [PS/CH/RA/2/5:114.]

39027SE: Tues 12 Mar 1839 – **George Bristol**, labourer: That he is about 60 years old   That upwards of 20 years ago he took and rented three several Houses and premises adjoining each other situate in the Parish of Fisherton-Anger [= Fisherton Anger] in the County of Wilts, of a Gentleman whose name he does not now remember but who was an Attorney residing at Salisbury - That the largest and best of such Houses adjoined a Public House called the Coach and Horses   That the rent of such several Houses was 22^l. a year besides Taxes which he duly paid – That he underlet one of such Houses at 5^l. and another at 6^l. a year and held them for upwards of two years during which time he occupied the largest. That about 7 years ago in consequence of the illness of his then Wife he applied to the Parish Officers of Fisherton-Anger aforesaid for relief and received an allowance of Half a Crown a Week therefrom for a period of 14 or 15 weeks – That since such rental as aforesaid he this Examinant has done no act whatever to gain a settlement and is now chargeable to the Parish of Cheltenham [signed]

1839: *died before removal to Fisherton Anger, Wilts (apparent place of settlement)*; *died at Cheltenham 2Q (buried at St Mary de Lode, Gloucester 27 May from the workhouse, aged 60).* [PS/CH/RA/2/5:115. Note: "Orders susp^{bm}".]

39028SE: [undated: 12-23 Mar 1839] – **William Marshall**, labourer: That he is about 77 years of Age and that he was born in the Parish of Nonbeauchamp [= Naunton Beauchamp] in the County of Worcester – That nearly 20 years ago he took and rented of a Mr Bartleet then of Redditch in the County of Worcester a Messuage and large Garden situate near Maul's Elm [later Maud's Elm] in the Parish of Cheltenham aforesaid at the Rent of 18 or 19^l a year   That he held and occupied such Premises for three successive years and duly paid the Rent and Taxes – That on quitting such Premises he took and rented a House situate in Grove Street in the Parish of Cheltenham aforesaid of one John Humphris at the rent of 12^l. a year, in which he lived for 5 or 6 successive years and paid the rent and Taxes since which he has done no Act to gain a settlement That in consequence of illness he has become and is now chargeable to the Parish of Cheltenham aforesaid.

1839: *removal unlikely: settlement probably acknowledged as Cheltenham.* **1841:** *WM buried at New Burial Ground, Cheltenham 4 Jan, aged 77.* [PS/CH/RA/2/5:116.]

39029SE: [undated: 12-23 Mar 1839] – **Edwin Percival** (also **Percivall**), labourer, with wife **Sarah**: That he is about 23 Years of age and that he was born as he believes in the said Parish of Cheltenham where his Father George Percival who was a Musician was also born, then resided, and was as this Examinant believes legally settled: – That soon after this Examinant's birth his said Father went to Ireland where he died about 15 years ago – That he this Examinant in the month of April last was lawfully married in the Parish Church of Cheltenham aforesaid to Sarah his now Wife (then Sarah Thayer Singlewoman)   That he has never done any Act in his own right whereby to gain a settlement and that in consequence of illness he has become and is now chargeable to the Parish of Cheltenham aforesaid.

1838: *when EP (of Park St, Cheltenham) married, his occupation was "Silver Plater".* **1839:** *removal unlikely: settlement probably acknowledged as Cheltenham (father's settlement).* **1841:** *EP (aged 25; coachman) lived with wife Sarah (29) and son Charles (2 mo; born Cheltenham) in Montague Place, London Road, Cheltenham (HO107/353/14/18/30).* **1851:** *the family lived in Ockbrooks, Derbys, where Edwin (35) was schoolmaster (HO107/2141/397/12).* [PS/CH/RA/2/5:117.]

39030SE: [undated: 12-23 Mar 1839] – **Thomas Hobbs**, stonemason, with wife **Barbara**: That he is about 63 years of age and that he was born as he believes in the Parish of Painswick in this County – That when he was about 12 or 14 years Old he was hired at Cheltenham Mop for the term of a year to a Mr Corbett then a Grocer of that place, as an indoor Servant at the wages of 2^l. That he continued in such service for that and the following year and received his wages having an advance of 10^s/– the last year – That about 40 years ago he was lawfully married at the Parish Church of Painswick aforesaid to Barbara his now Wife (then Barbara Atkins Singlewoman) That about 9 years ago he took and rented a House in which he has ever since resided, situate and being N° 25 Queen Street in Cheltenham aforesaid of Mr Robert Williams at 10^l. a year which rent he paid for two years and upwards when it was increased to 10 Guineas but has lately been reduced to 9^l.– That his said Landlord paid the Taxes, and in consequence of severe illness he this Examinant has become and is now chargeable to the Parish of Cheltenham aforesaid.

1839: *removal unlikely: settlement probably acknowledged as Cheltenham (renting)*; *TH died soon after examination (buried at New Burial Ground, Cheltenham 6 Apr, aged 63).* **1841:** *wife probably the Barbara Hobbs (aged 60; independent – i.e. not a pauper) living in Shipton Oliffe (HO107/351/14/8/9).* **1844:** *wife buried 3 May, aged 66.* [PS/CH/RA/2/5:118. Perhaps compare Gray **34** (Thomas Hobbs: 11 June 1816).]

39031SE: Sat 23 Mar 1838 [i.e. 1839] – **Sarah Sollis**, widow: That she is about 78 years old and is the Widow of Samuel Sollis who died at Evesham in the County of Worcester about 29 years ago – That about 25 years ago she went to live with a Mrs Birt (who at that time kept the Shakespeare Inn in Cheltenham aforesaid), as a hired Servant at the wages of 10^l a year – That she continued in such Service for three successive years and upwards during such time sleeping and boarding in her said Mistresses House from whom she received her wages – That on leaving such service she this Examinant went to live with her Daughter who occupied a House in the High Street of Cheltenham (nearly opposite the Shakespeare) That about 18 months afterwards her said Daughter gave up the Possession of such House to this Examinant who held it as she believes as tenant to Mr John Lea for 12 months and upwards at the rent of £ 25 which she paid – That she this Examinant then took and rented a House in Park Street Cheltenham of a Mr Allen a Shoemaker at 13^l. a year which House she occupied for three successive years and paid the rent and Taxes – That she then went as a hired Servant to M^r. Goode (who kept the Royal Oak Inn) at the wages of 10^l. a year in whose service she continued for 12 years and upwards and boarded and lodged in the House during that period – That about 5 years ago she took and rented a House situate in Knapp-Place Cheltenham of Mr Vines, Stonemason, at the rent of 11^l – which she occupied for 3 successive years paying for the 2^d year an additional rent of 1^l. and for the 3^d year a further additional rent of 2^l. together with all Rates and Taxes since which she has done no Act to gain a settlement and is now chargeable to the Parish of Cheltenham aforesaid. [mark]
1839: *removal unlikely: settlement probably acknowledged as Cheltenham (renting).* **1851:** *probably the SS who lived with daughter in King St, Cheltenham (aged 88; formerly "nurse") (HO107/1973/407/46).* **1855:** *this SS buried at Cheltenham 10 Jan, aged 97.* [PS/CH/RA/2/5:119.]

39032SE: Thurs 25 Apr 1839 – **Mary Haines**: That she is about 80 years Old and that she was born as she believes in the Parish of Saint John in the County of Worcester where her Father Edward Fowlkes who was a Farmer then resided – That about 50 years ago she this Examinant was lawfully married at the Parish Church of Saint Augustines at the back [= St Augustine the Less] in Bristol to Edward Haines who was a Hairdresser and who about 40 years ago deserted her, since which she has not heard of him   That the said Edward Haines in or about the year 1793 and since his marriage as aforesaid obtained a legal settlement in the Parish of Richmond in the County of Surrey by renting a House and Garden situate in Norman Row there by the year at 16^l. that he took such House by the year and occupied it for a year and upwards under such renting and paid a year's rent for the same   That she this Examinant has since her said marriage actually received Parochial Relief from the said Parish of Richmond to which Parish she now belongs not having gained a settlement elsewhere: That she is now chargeable to the Parish of Cheltenham aforesaid [signed]
1838: *removed to St John's, Worcester, Worcs (birth): see **38077SE** (MH: 1 Dec 1838) (RETURNED).* **1839:** *removed to Richmond (husband's settlement).* **1841:** *MH (aged 80; pauper, staymaker) in Richmond Union Workhouse, Surrey (HO107/1075/13/16/1); died at Richmond 1Q 1843.* [PS/CH/RA/2/5:120. Removal expenses to St John Bedwardine, Worcester, Worcs for "M Haines" £3/3/- (10 Apr 1839: D4178) and to Richmond £4/19/3 (13 June 1839: D4178).]

39033SE: Sat 4 May 1839 – **John Randall** (also **Randel**), labourer: That he is about 56 Years of Age and that he was born as he believes in the Parish of Prestbury in the County of Gloucester: That when he this Examinant was old enough to work he went out as a Servant in husbandry and lived in various situations the last of which was at Rudford in the County of Gloucester on which occasion he was hired for a Year by Thomas Phelps of that place Farmer at the Wages of 12$^£$.: That he duly served such Year during the whole of which he lived in his Master's House: that such

hiring and service took place about 30 Years ago, since which he has never done any act whereby to gain a Settlement: That he has lately become chargeable to the Parish of Cheltenham. [mark]
1839: *removed to Rudford (hiring and service).* [PS/CH/RA/2/5:121. Removal expenses to Rudford for "John Randall" 19/- (28 May 1839: D4178).]

39034SE: Mon 13 May 1839 – **Maria Wright**, single woman: That she was born as she believes in the Parish of <u>Bromyard</u> in the County of Hereford and is about 22 years old – That she is the Daughter of William Wright some time since of that Parish Hatter – That she has often heard her said Father say and she verily believes that he was apprenticed and served his time in the same Parish and that it was his place of legal Settlement – That about 5 or 6 years ago she this Examinant went to live as a hired Servant for a year at the White Hart Gloucester but did not serve 12 months – That she has never done any act in her own right whereby to gain a settlement and that severe illness has caused her to become chargeable to the Parish of Cheltenham aforesaid. [signed]
1839: *removed to Bromyard, Heref (father's settlement);* death registered at Bromyard, Heref soon after removal 3Q. [PS/CH/RA/2/5:122. Removal expenses to Bromyard £1/19/- (17 May 1839: D4178), to Bromyard for "Maria Wright" 15/11 (13 June 1839: D4178) and £1/10/- (14 Sept 1839: D4178).]

39035SE: Thurs 16 May 1839 – **Andrew Hall**, plasterer: That he was born as he believes in the Parish of Cheltenham aforesaid about 25 years ago – That he is the Son of Thomas Hall then of that Parish Carpenter who as this Examinant has heard and believes died there soon after this Examinant's birth leaving this Examinant and an elder Brother - upon which as this Examinant has often heard his mother say and he verily believes that she was driven to this Parish for relief and continued to receive relief therefrom for 7 or 8 years – That when he this Examinant was considered old enough to go, and during the latter part of that period he well remembers going for his said Mother (who then lived in Sherborne Street Cheltenham) to the Poor House and receiving her allowance which he thinks was a shilling a week – That he has never been apprenticed nor has he ever done any Act whereby to gain a settlement in his own right and that illness has caused him to become an inmate of the said workhouse of Cheltenham [signed]
1839: *removal uncertain: settlement probably acknowledged as Cheltenham (father's settlement).* **c1848:** *son Cornelius born in Ireland; AH's wife was Irish.* **1851:** *AH (aged 34; plasterer) lodged without his family in Risca, Monm (HO107/2453/144/14).* **c1858:** *daughter Mary born at Pontypool, Monm.* **1861:** *(RETURNED) the family lived in Stanhope St, Cheltenham: Andrew (46; plasterer); Mary (40); Cornelius (13; scholar); Mary (3; born Cheltenham), Elizabeth (1; also born Cheltenham).* [PS/CH/RA/2/5:123.]

39036SE: Tues 21 May 1839 – **William Waite** (also **Wait**), labourer: That he is about 42 years of age and that he was born as he believes in the Parish of Lawfords Gate Bristol. That when he this Examinant was about 12 or 13 years old he was bounden by Indenture as an Outdoor Apprentice to one Thomas Vaughan of Merchant Street in the Parish of Saint James in the City of Bristol Fancy Chairmaker for 7 years but that his Father resided in Wade Street in the Parish of <u>Saint Phillips</u> and Jacob in the same City – That his s^d. Master having become Bankrupt he this Examinant served only three years or thereabouts of his term during the whole of which he boarded and slept in his said Father's House in Saint Phillips and Jacob aforesaid – Since which he has not done any act to gain a settlement, and in consequence of indisposition he is now in the Cheltenham Workhouse [signed]
1839: *removed to St Philip and St Jacob, Bristol (presumed) (apprenticeship).* **1841:** *(RETURNED) WW (aged 45; gardener) lived in Mount Pleasant, Cheltenham with niece Eliza (15), daughter of brother Emmanuel, who lived in St Philip and St Jacob, Bristol (HO107/353/6/16/26).* **1849:** *WW died at Cheltenham 4Q.* [PS/CH/RA/2/5:124.]

39037SE: Sat 15 June 1839 – **Ann Bridges**, widow, with two children **Charles** and **Richard**: That she is about 32 years of age   That about 13 years ago she was lawfully married at the Parish Church of Hope Mansell in the County of Hereford to William Bridges Veterinary Surgeon – That he has often told her and she verily believes that he never did any act to gain a settlement in his own right but that he belonged to the Parish of his Father Richard Bridges formerly of the Parish of Colne-engain [= Colne Engaine] in the County of Essex where he was born. That about five years ago she this Examinant was residing with her said Husband in Saint John's Gloucester from whence he ran away and left her for which offence he was apprehended and brought back when his Examination was taken as to his place of settlement upon which himself and Family were removed by Orders of removal to the said Parish of Colne-engain where they remained chargeable for some months when her Husband again deserted her and she has never lived with him since. That by her said marriage she has two Children now living (namely) Charles aged about 12 years and Richard aged about 7 years - That her said Husband as she has heard and believes, died suddenly in the month of July 1838 near Berkeley in this County – That in consequence of illness she has become chargeable to the Parish of Cheltenham aforesaid. [signed]

1839: *removed to Colne Engaine, Essex (presumed) (husband's settlement).* [PS/CH/RA/2/5:125.]

39038SE: Thurs 11 July 1839 – **Edward Stiles** (also **Styles**), gardener, wife **Sarah**, and three children **Charles**, **Elizabeth**, and **Harriet**: That he is about 34 years old and that he was born as he believes at Kempsey in the County of Worcester where his Father William Stiles who was a Labourer was legally settled – That in or about the month of August 1823 he this Examinant was hired as a Servant for a year to William Wall Esquire then a Banker of the Parish of Saint Nicholas in the City of Worcester at the wages of 10^l with board and lodging – That he remained in such Service upwards of 12 months and received his full wages during which his said Master resided in the Winter Season in the Parish of Saint Nicholas aforesaid, and in the Summer Season at the Parish of Great Malvern in the said County of Worcester in which last named Parish he lived with and served his said Master for the last 6 months during which time he slept in his House there – That since such Service he this Examinant has never done any act whereby to gain a settlement – That about 9 years ago he was lawfully married at Saint Peter's Church Worcester to his present wife then Sarah Ballinger, by whom he has 3 Children (namely) Charles aged about 8 years Elizabeth aged about 6 years and Harriet aged about 4 years and that he hath become chargeable to the Parish of Cheltenham. [signed]

1839: *removed to Malvern, Worcs (hiring and service).* **1840:** *ES convicted of felonies on several occasions in Glos and Worcs, and received one month's imprisonment, for example, at Worcs County Sessions 29 June (for stealing coal).* **1841:** *Edward (Henry) Stiles (aged 38; agricultural labourer) lived with wife Sarah (37) and children Charles (11), Elizabeth (8) and Harriet (6) in Gt Malvern, Worcs (HO107/1205/6/34/12).* **1845:** *at Worcs County Sessions 30 June ES convicted of stealing a kettle in Kempsey, Worcs, and transported to Tasmania.* **1845/6:** *(RETURNED) from 4Q 1845 until 4Q 1846 Sarah and four children received parish relief from Upton-upon-Severn, Worcs as non-settled residents in Cheltenham (G/CH/9d/1).* [PS/CH/RA/2/5:127. *Removal expenses for "Styles" to Malvern, Worcs 15/- (12 July 1839: D4178).*]

39039SE: Thurs 20 June 1839 – **Edward Jay**, painter: That he is about 73 years of age and was born as he believes in the Parish of Saint James Clerkenwell in the County of Middlesex where his Father William Jay who was a Collector of Taxes was settled   That when he this Examinant was about 15 years old he was bounden Apprentice by Indenture to Thomas Stowers of King Street Snowhill in the Parish of Saint Sepulchres in the City of London Coach Painter for the term of seven years   That he served about 3½ years of such Apprenticeship with the said Thomas Stowers when he was assigned to one Henry Blanchard of Great Queen Street in the Parish of Saint Giles in the Fields in the said County of Middlesex Coach Painter with whom he lived about a year and a half when he was assigned for the remainder of his term to one Mr Marshall also a Coach Painter residing in King Street Holborn in the said County of Middlesex but who carried on his business in Great Queen Street aforesaid and with whom this Examinant completed his said Apprenticeship – That during the whole of the period last aforesaid he this Examinant boarded with his said Master in King Street aforesaid but slept at the House of Mrs Henley situate in Queens Court Great Queen Street aforesaid – That since his said Apprenticeship he has never done any Act whereby to gain a Settlement and that he hath become chargeable to the Parish of Cheltenham aforesaid. [signed]

1840: *died before removal to St Giles-in-the-Fields, Middlesex; buried at New Burial Ground, Cheltenham 25 Mar, aged 73.* Examination struck out, despite considerable editing. [PS/CH/RA/2/5:128; earlier version strucked out on p. 126 of magistrates' register.]

39040SE: Sat 13 July 1839 – **Susannah Fisher**, with children **John**, **William**, **Emily**, and **Ambrose**: That she is the lawful Wife of Ambrose Fisher who has deserted her and left her and her four Children chargeable to the parish of Cheltenham. That upwards of twelve months Ago she became chargeable to the parish of Charlton Kings in consequence of the desertion of her said Husband who was apprehended by the parish Officers of Charlton Kings aforesaid and examined touching the place of his last legal Settlement, That she has heard her said husband say and she verily believes that he is legally Settled in the parish of Tetbury in this County and that he gained such Settlement through his father who was the owner of Property in Tetbury aforesaid – That the Mother of the said Ambrose Fisher is now living at Tetbury and possessed of some property there that she does not believe her said husband ever did any Act to gain a Settlement elsewhere [signed Susanna Fisher]
1839: *removed to Tetbury (husband's settlement); orders appealed Oct 1839 (Gloucestershire Chron. 19 Oct) (order provisionally confirmed).* **1841:** *the couple lived in Tetbury: Ambrose Fisher (aged 40; stonemason); Susanna (34), and children John (12), William (8), Emily (6), and Ambrose (4) (HO107/362/12/7/10).* **1881:** *Ambrose (76; unemployed stonemason) and Susanna (77) had been living in Minchinhampton for many years (RG11/2549/17/29).* [PS/CH/RA/2/5:129. Note: "This and the Exam[inatio]n of Ambrose Fisher (see Out Parish Book fo 123) sent with orders made this day" to the appeal. Removal expenses to Tetbury £1/19/- (13 July 1839: D4178), and for "Mrs. Fisher & family" 6/10 (early 1840: D4178).]

39041SE: Mon 15 July 1839 – **Mary Severn**, with three children **Martha**, **Elizabeth**, and **William**: That she is about 25 years of Age and was married to Samuel Severn a Wheelwright at the parish Church of Berrow in the County of Worcester in the month of September 1833. That she has three Children by such Marriage (namely) Martha Aged about 6 years, Elizabeth Aged about 3 years, and William Aged about 12 months who together with herself have in consequence of the desertion of her said husband become chargeable to the parish of Cheltenham   That her said husband is the Son of John Severn of the parish of Berrow aforesaid And that she has understood and believes that her said Husband was bounden Apprentice by Indebenture [for "Indenture"] for 7 years to Thomas Gillham of the parish of Upton on Severn [= Upton-upon-Severn] in the said County of Worcester Wheelwright – That he duly served such Apprenticeship, and boarded & lodged in his said Masters House in the parish of Upton on Severn aforesaid and received his Indebentures at the termination of the said term since which time he has done No Act whereby to gain a legal Settlement elsewhere [mark]
1839: *removed to Upton-upon-Severn (late husband's settlement).* **1840:** *son William buried, aged 2 years and 6 mo 20 Sept at St Martin's Church, Birmingham.* **1841:** *Samuel Severn (aged 30; wheelwright) apparently reconciled with wife Mary (25); they lived with daughter Elizabeth (4) in Aston, Birmingham (HO107/1149/8/24/1).* [PS/CH/RA/2/5:130. Removal expenses to Upton-upon-Severn for "Severn & 2 Ch[ildren]" 19/6 (6 Aug 1839: D4178) and £1/4/- (7 Aug 1839: D4178).]

39042SE: Mon 22 July 1839 – **Sarah Williams**, single woman: That she is about 76 years old & that she was born as she believes in the Parish of Hay in the County of Brecon of the body of Martha Williams then of that place Widow – That she this Examinant has often been informed by her said Mother and she verily believes that she (her said mother) was legally settled in that Parish by having married her first Husband who was a Tailor residing there and belonging thereto and not having gained a settlement in her own right. That upwards of 30 years ago she this Examinant received, and until about 2 years ago continued to receive relief more or less from the said Parish of Hay when it was discontinued – That she has not done any Act whatever whereby to gain a settlement in her own right and that she has become chargeable to the Parish of Cheltenham aforesaid. [mark]

1839: *died before removal to Hay, Breconshire.* **1840:** *buried at New Burial Ground, Cheltenham 7 Jan, aged 77.* [PS/CH/RA/2/5:131.]

39043SE: Thurs 1 Aug 1839 – Hannah Ivin, regarding the settlement of granddaughter **Jane Ivin**: That her Son William Ivin (the Father of the said Jane Ivin) was many years ago bounden Apprentice by Indenture for 7 years to Mr Checkett[s] of the Hamlet of Norton by Kempsey [= Norton Juxta Kempsey] in the Parish of Kempsey in the County of Worcester Carpenter and Wheelwright – That he served about 5 years of such term and then left his said Master's Service That during the time of such his servitude he boarded and lodged in the said Hamlet of Norton in the Parish of Kempsey aforesaid – That her said Son was lawfully married at the Parish Church of Cheltenham aforesaid about six years since and that Jane Ivin the Pauper was born in Wedlock – That her said Son and his Wife are both dead and have left their said Daughter wholly unprovided for and that She has become chargeable to the said Parish of Cheltenham – That her said Son never did any act to gain a Settlement after his said Apprenticeship. [mark]
1839: *removed to Norton Juxta Kempsey (father's settlement).* **1841:** *(RETURNED) JI (aged 6; servant) lived with grandparents, William (55; carpenter) and Hannah (55) Ivin in (St) James St, Cheltenham (HO107/353/4/41/4).* **1843:** *Hannah Ivin buried at New Burial Ground, Cheltenham 21 Jan.* **1851:** *William (aged 67; carpenter) inmate of Cheltenham Workhouse (HO107/1973/1093/7).* **1891:** *JI had presumably been taken in by the church, as she (56) was a Sister of Mercy living in Dover (RG12/741/28/50).* [PS/CH/RA/2/5:132. Removal expenses to Norton Juxta Kempsey for "Jane Iving" 7/6 (24 Aug 1839) and 15/6 (28 Sept 1839: D4178).]

39044SE: Thurs 1 Aug 1839 – **John Wells**, carpenter, with wife **Hannah**: That he is about 52 years of Age, and that he was born as he believes in the parish of Stow on the Wold in this County That about 33 years ago he was lawfully married at the parish Church of Oddington in this County to his present wife then Hannah Williams

That about 14 years Ago he purchased three Old Houses in Chapel Street and Little George Street Horseferry Road opposite Lady Dakers [= Dacre's] Alms Houses in the parish of Saint Margretts [= St Margaret's] in the City of Westminster, That he pulled down the said Old Houses and built Nine Small Houses upon the same ground. That he received the Rents of the said Houses for about 10 years and resided for some years in one of the said Houses himself, that he paid Rates and Taxes for the said property during the said period, That the said Houses were Sold about three years Ago by order of the Mortgagee and that since that period he has not done any Act to gain a Settlement elsewhere and in consequence of illness is now chargeable to the Parish of Cheltenham [signed]
1839: *died before removal to St Margaret's, Westminster; JW buried at New Burial Ground, Cheltenham 14 Sept, aged 52; widow removed to his place of settlement (renting) in St Margaret's, Westminster.* [PS/CH/RA/2/5:133. Removal expenses to London for "Mrs. Wells" £4/3/- (28 Sept 1839: D4178) and to St Margarets, London for "Maintenance of Wells & Wife under order" £5/6/3 (12 Oct 1839: D4178).]

39045SE: Mon 19 Aug 1839 – **Martha Stephens**, single woman, and unnamed daughter: That she is about 20 years of age and that she was born as she believes in the Parish of Wotten under Edge [= Wotton-under-Edge] in the said County of Gloucester That she is the legitimate Daughter of Samuel Stephens a Labourer who is legally settled in the Parish of Dursley in the same County – That she has heard her Parents say and she verily believes that her said Father gained such settlement by living as a yearly Servant for upwards of twelve months with a M^r. Harris of Dursley aforesaid Farmer, – That many years ago her said Father was removed by an order of removal from the said Parish of Wotten under Edge to the said Parish of Dursley from which Parish he has several times received Relief That her said Father has not done any Act since the above hiring and service whereby to gain a legal Settlement That about seven months ago she this Examinant was delivered of a Female Bastard Child which together with herself is now chargeable to the Parish of Cheltenham aforesaid and that she has never done any Act in her own right whereby to gain a legal Settlement. [mark]

1839: *removed to Dursley (father's settlement).* [PS/CH/RA/2/5:134. Removal expenses to Dursley for "M Stephens & child" £1/1/- (13 Sept 1839) and 15/6 (14 Sept 1839: D4178). See **45019SE** (father Samuel Stephens: 27 Mar 1845).]

39046SE: Mon 14 Oct 1839 – **Isaac Carter**, labourer: That he is about 67 years of age and that about 16 years ago he was hired as an indoor Servant for the term of a year by M^rs. Judith Thompson of Cheltenham aforesaid (the Widow of Henry Thompson formerly of the same Place Esquire deceased) at the wages of 20 Guineas and his Livery   That he served the said year under such hiring and continued in such service for nine months afterwards since which he has not done any Act whereby to gain a settlement   That he is now chargeable to the said Parish of Cheltenham [signed]
1839: *removal unlikely: settlement probably acknowledged as Cheltenham (hiring and service).* **1841:** *IC (aged 65; labourer) lived in Sherborne St, Cheltenham (HO107/353/6/8/11).* **1848:** *death of IC (buried at New Burial Ground, Cheltenham on 13 Apr, aged 77).* [PS/CH/RA/2/5:135.]

39047SE: Wed 16 Oct 1839 – **James Paish** (also **Pash**), labourer, with wife **Elizabeth**: Who upon his Oath saith that he is about 32 years old and that he was born as he believes in the Parish of Fairford in this County in which Parish his Father John Paish who was a Labourer resided and was legally settled and where he this Examinant likewise resided until he was about 15 years old when he went out to Service but hath never been hired for a year nor has he ever done any Act whereby to gain a Settlement in his own right – That he is now chargeable to the said Parish of Cheltenham   That about 14 years ago he was lawfully married at the Parish Church of Cirencester to Elizabeth his present Wife (formerly Simpson) by whom he has had three Children ~~which are now living~~ all of whom are dead. [mark]
1839: *removed to Fairford (father's settlement).* [PS/CH/RA/2/5:136. Constable's expenses for "Apprehending Jas Paish" 2/6 (2 Nov 1839: D4178); similarly 22 Nov for Mr Russell to Fairford to serve suspended removal order £1/10/-.]

39048SE: Mon 21 Oct 1839 – **John Dugan** (also **Doogan**), labourer, wife **Mary**, and two daughters **Julia** and **Louisa**: That he is about 29 years of age – That about 12 years ago he was hired as an indoor Servant to Mr Healy of Cheltenham aforesaid Winemerchant for the term of a year at the wages of Seven Pounds   That he served under such hiring the whole of the year and continued to live in the same Service for two years afterwards at advanced wages – That about seven years ago he was lawfully married at the Parish Church of Charlton Kings in this County to Mary his present Wife then Mary Tocknell Singlewoman by whom he has two Children now living vizt. Julia aged about three years and Louisa aged about four months   That about three years after such marriage he took and rented a House of Mr Thomas Haines of Cheltenham aforesaid Builder, situate in Windsor Terrace there and N° 6 at 18^l. a year   That he held such House under such taking the whole year and Paid the rent and Rates but did not during such time actually occupy such House inasmuch as he let two Rooms therein to undertenants   That since such hiring and service with Mr Healy as aforesaid he this Examinant has done no Act whereby to gain a Settlement and in consequence of illness he has become chargeable to the Parish of Cheltenham aforesaid. [signed]
1839: *removal unlikely: settlement probably acknowledged as Cheltenham.* **1841:** *JD (aged 25; "gas man", born Ireland) lived in High St, Cheltenham with wife Mary (30), and two daughters Julia (4) and Louisa (2) (HO107/353/8/39/10). A gas man was either a worker for a gas company, or someone who lit (and extinguished) gas-powered street lamps.* [PS/CH/RA/2/5:137.]

39049SE: Mon 11 Nov 1839 – **John Knight**, labourer, with wife **Charlotte**: That he is about 70 years of age and that he was born as he believes in the Parish of Fretherne in this County where his Father Robert Knight was legally settled by Estate being the Owner of a Freehold Cottage and Land there: – That about 34 years ago he this Examinant was lawfully married at the Parish Church of Stroud in this County to Charlotte his present Wife (formerly Charlotte Cooke Singlewoman) by whom he has had six Children two of whom are now living and placed out in the world – That about 20 years ago he this Examinant became chargeable to and received relief from the said Parish of Fretherne   That in the Spring of the year 1835 he this Examinant took or hired a House and Premises of M[r] Bidmead of Cheltenham aforesaid Plumber situate in the Old Well Lane there for the term of a year at the rent of £23..8..0   That he occupied such Premises under the said taking the whole of the year, during which he carried on the trade or business of a Retailer of Beer to be drunk on the Premises and Paid the Rent and also the Poor rates to which he was assessed in respect thereof when in consequence of being unable through illness to apply for a renewal of his licence it was arranged that his Son Henry Knight should be assessed to the Poor rates for the said Premises and take out a Licence in his own name which was accordingly done and he soon afterwards left the Premises   That he this Examinant continued to occupy such Premises until about Michaelmas 1837 (when the House was taken down), immediately upon which he took and rented another House in Cheltenham aforesaid, at the corner of Union Street [&] Bath Road there, of M[r] Matthew Lane, Bricklayer, for the term of a year at the Rent of £12 – That he occupied such House under the said taking until Midsummer last and during the whole of such occupation he paid the rent and also the Poor rates to which he was assessed in respect thereof   That he also during the whole of such occupation carried on the business of a Retailer of Beer, to be consumed on the Premises since which he has not done any Act whereby to gain a Settlement and in consequence of severe illness has become and now is chargeable to the Parish of Cheltenham aforesaid. [mark]

1839: *removal unlikely: settlement probably acknowledged as Cheltenham (renting).* 1841: *JK (aged 70; labourer) and his Charlotte (60; weaver) lived in Upper Bath St, Cheltenham (HO107/353/12/10/15).* **1850:** *death of JK (buried at New Burial Ground, Cheltenham 22 Nov, aged 79).* **1851:** *Charlotte Knight (68; widower, born Stroud) lived with grand-daughter Ann (16; born Stroud) in Gt Norwood St, Cheltenham (HO107/1973/910/8). [PS/CH/RA/2/5: pages 145-6 (fair copy of (undated) edited draft in magistrates' register p. 138.]*

39050SE: Thurs 24 Oct 1839 – **John Partridge**, labourer, prisoner in custody, wife **Mary Ann**, and three children **Elizabeth, Ellen**, and **Frederick**: That he is about twenty five years of age – that about twelve years ago he was hired by M[rs] [blank] Arkell of Boddington in the said County as an indoor Servant for a twelvemonth   that he remained in her Service there three years and received his Wages since which time he has never done any Act to gain a Settlement elsewhere. His Wages at M[rs] Arkells were £2-15-0 the first year, three pounds the Second and four pounds the third and last year   About Seven years ago He was married to his present Wife Mary Ann Harris at S[t] Marys Gloucester and by her has three Children viz[t]. Elizabeth aged 4 years Ellen aged about three years and Frederick aged about two years: Last Summer Examinant was ill and applied to the Parish Officers of Boddington for Relief and was relieved by them for the space of the Five Weeks [mark]

1839: *JP transported for larceny and no orders of removal drawn up;* *JP (aged 25) was convicted at Glos County Sessions 31 Dec of stealing a sheep at Uckington, Elmstone Hardwicke, and sentenced to transportation to Australia for ten years.* **1841:** *daughter Ellen (Elenor; 5) lived with maternal grandparents John (70) and Sarah Harris (65) and uncle Henry (39) in Uckington, while Elizabeth (8) lived with JP's parents in Staverton (HO107/354/27/4/7) (as also in 1851 (HO107/1972/331/4)).* **1842:** *wife is perhaps the Mary Ann Harris buried at Cheltenham 9 June, aged 31. [PS/CH/RA/2/5:139. Note: "No Orders". See* **39063SE** *(Mary Ann Harris: 30 Nov 1839).]*

39051SE: Sat 2 Nov 1839 – Henry Green Trinder, yeoman and Overseer of the Poor, regarding the place of settlement of the infants **Elizabeth Duck** and **Louisa Duck**, inmates of Charlton Kings Workhouse for children (Cheltenham Union): That in consequence of having been engaged in making various enquiries relative to the Settlement of the above name[d] Elizabeth Duck and Louisa Duck he has understood and verily believes That John Duck formerly of Lacock in the County of Wilts Labourer as appears by the register of marriages of that Parish, was lawfully married there and that the two Children above named were born in Wedlock – That the said John Duck was killed about two years ago, leaving a Widow (the mother of the said Children) him surviving – That the last legal Settlement of the said John Duck was in the Parish of Chippenham in the said County of Wilts – That during his life time he frequently received relief from that Parish and after his death his Widow and the Children above named became chargeable to the same Parish for several months as Paupers legally settled there. That the said Children are now become chargeable to the Parish of Cheltenham aforesaid. That the said Widow Duck was lawfully married a second time, at Lacock aforesaid on the 27th of August 1838 to one William Rogers a Labourer, and that on or about the 26th day of September last she died in the Parish of Cheltenham aforesaid leaving the said two Children and that the said William Rogers has deserted the said Children. [signed]

1839: *removed to Chippenham, Wilts (father's settlement)*; *Sarah and Eliza Duck admitted to Charlton Kings Workhouse as orphans (condition: "Itch") from 2 Nov until 29 Nov 1839, when they were removed to Chippenham under this order.* **1841** *ED (aged 11) was an inmate of Lacock Workhouse, Wilts; although there is no mention of an LD, Elizabeth is accompanied in the workhouse by John Duck (9) and Sarah Duck (9; perhaps Sarah Louisa) (HO107/1172/6/1).* [PS/CH/RA/2/5:140. Removal expenses to Chippenham, Wilts for "Maintenance of Ducks Children" 15/- and £2/17/- (29 Nov 1839: D4178).]

39052SE: Mon 4 Nov 1839 – **Richard Morris**, gardener, wife **Maria**, and five children **Jesse**, **Emily**, **George**, **Thomas**, and **James**: That he is about 45 years of age and that he was born as he believes in the Parish of Saint Mary's Longford in this County where his Father William Morris who was a Gardener was legally settled   That he gained such Settlement there by the Purchase of four Acres of Land in the said Parish for which he paid 800[l]. That he this Examinant has never done any Act in his own right whereby to gain a Settlement   That in the year 1817 he was lawfully married at the Parish Church of Saint Mary's Longford aforesaid to his present Wife Maria (formerly Maria Alford Singlewoman) by whom he has five Children (namely) Jesse aged about 20 years – Emily aged about 15 years George aged about 7 years Thomas aged about 5 years and James aged about 2 years and 9 months – That about 6 or 7 years ago he this Examinant became chargeable to the said Parish of Saint Mary's Longford – That neither of the Children above named ever did any Act whereby to gain a Settlement and that he this Examinant together with them and his said Wife are now chargeable to the Parish of Cheltenham aforesaid. [mark]

1839: *removed to St Mary's, Longford (presumed) (father's settlement).* **1841:** *(RETURNED) Richard Morris (aged 40; labourer) lived with wife Maria (30), and children Emma (20), George (12), Jesse [= James] (6), in Upper Gas Green, Cheltenham (HO107/353/10/19/3-4).* [PS/CH/RA/2/5:141.]

39053SE: Thurs 7 Nov 1839 – **Ann Douglas**, widow: That She is about 71 years of age: that in the year 1808 She was lawfully married at the Parish Church of Hempstead [= Hempsted] near Gloucester to Alexander Douglas a Gardener by whom She has one Son aged about thirty years. That she has been informed by her said Husband that he was legally settled in the Parish of Donnington in the County of Hereford by having lived for three years as an indoor yearly Servant with [blank] Freeman of that Place during which time he lived in the said Parish and received his Wages – That her Husband died about two years after her Marriage. That soon after her Husband's death Examinant was obliged to apply to the Hamlet of Wotton near Gloucester where She was then living for relief for her infant Son. The Parish Officer of Wotton went with the Examinant to Donnington when the Parish Officers of that Parish allowed the Examinant to the best of her recollection three shillings a Week for the Maintenance of the Child which allowance they paid till the Child was seven years old. Examinant is now chargeable to the Parish of Cheltenham [signed Ann Douglass]

1839: *removed to Donnington (late husband's settlement).* **1841:** *(perhaps RETURNED) perhaps the AD (aged 70) who lived in Rosehill St, Charlton Kings (HO107/353/1/6/6).* **1851:** *an AD (70; widow, born Birkenhead) was a pauper inmate of Cheltenham Workhouse (HO107/1973/1091/3).* [PS/CH/RA/2/5:144. Removal expenses for "Douglas" to Donnington £1/3/6 (3 Dec 1839: D4178).]

39054SE: Mon 11 Nov 1839 – **William Moss**, stonemason, residing in Rugeley, Staffs, with four children **Hester**, **William**, **Elizabeth**, and **James**: That he is about 45 years of age   that he was born at Stow on the Wold in the County of Gloucester where his Father Robert Moss who was a Stone Mason lived and was settled. Examinant never did any thing to gain a Settlement in his own right. About twenty five years since he was married to Mary Hookham since deceased and by her had two Children who are both emancipated. About Eighteen years since he was again married to his late Wife Ann Mills at Birmingham Old Church since deceased and by her he has five Children George aged about Sixteen years. Hester aged about fourteen years William aged about twelve years Elizabeth aged about Seven years and James aged about Six years. the four latter of whom are now chargeable to the Parish of Cheltenham neither of whom have done any thing to gain a Settlement in their own right [signed]

All five of Robert Moss's children by Ann Mills (who died before July 1837) were born at Rugeley, near Lichfield, between 1823 and 1834. **1837:** *Esther, William, Elizabeth, and James Moss admitted as inmates of Charlton Kings Workhouse 27 June, after desertion by father; removed to Stow-on-the-Wold (father's settlement): see* **37040SE** *(grandfather Robert Moss: 11 Nov 1839); on 11 July father reclaimed them (behaviour in workhouse was recorded as "Good"), and they were all removed.* **1838:** *(RETURNED) children were again deserted and admitted to Charlton Kings Workhouse 4 Oct, again removed to Stow-on-the-Wold 2 Dec (G/CH/60/2 p. 16, etc).* **1839:** *(RETURNED)* **removed to Stow-on-the-Wold (father's settlement).** **1841:** *WM (aged 49; stonemason) lived with sons George (18; stonemason) and William (12) in Tamworth St, Lichfield, Staffs (HO107/1008/2/16/24); youngest son James (5; pauper) was an inmate of Stow-on-the-Wold Workhouse (HO107/366/21/43/1); daughter Hester (16) is perhaps a pauper inmate of Leek Union Workhouse, Staffs (HO107/1005/8/52/1); William's father Robert (70; stonemason) lived in Francis St, Cheltenham, with granddaughters Sarah (20) and Ann (15) (HO107/353/12/41/19) (Sarah may be William's oldest surviving daughter, mentioned in examination).* **1851:** *William and son George lived in Walsall, Staffs, as stonemasons (HO107/2023/562/13).* [PS/CH/RA/2/5:147. Removal expenses to Stow-on-the-Wold for "Maintenance of Moss's Children" £1/16/- and for "Removal" of "Moss Children" to Stow-on-the-Wold £1/3/- (2 Dec 1839: D4178).]

39055SE: Mon 11 Nov 1839 – **Charlotte Dyer**, single woman, and son **Daniel**: That she is about 30 years of Age and was born as she believes in the parish of Nailsworth in this County   that she is the daughter of Susannah Dyer who was legally Settled in the Parish of Nailsworth aforesaid – That about 6 years ago she was delivered of a Male Bastard Child in the said Parish of Nailsworth and received One Shilling and Six pence a week for several months for the Maintenance of her said Child from the parish Officers there   That about 4 or 5 years ago in consequence of the illness of her Mother she applied to the parish Meeting at Nailsworth for an allowance for the Maintenance of her Mother and was allowed One Shilling a week for several months which examinant received from Mr Simpkins the Relieving Officer of Nailsworth. That her said Mother died about 12 months ago not having done any Act to gain a subsequent Settlement nor has Examinant ever done any Act in her own right to gain a Settlement elsewhere & that she and her said Son are now chargeable to the said parish of Cheltenham [mark]

1833: *illegitimate son Daniel baptised at Horsley near Nailsworth 26 May.* **1839:** *from 26 Nov until 9 Dec Daniel Dyer (condition: "Scald head") was an inmate of Charlton Kings Workhouse for children (Cheltenham Union) (G/CH/60/2);* **removed to Nailsworth (mother's settlement).** **1841:** *(RETURNED) CD (aged 25; charwoman) lived with son Daniel (8) in Sherborne St, Cheltenham.* [PS/CH/RA/2/5:149 (no examination on p. 148). Removal expenses for "Dyer" to Nailsworth £1/-/6 (9 Dec 1839: D4178).]

39056SE: Thurs 14 Nov 1839 – **Harriet Risbey** (also **Risby**), single woman, residing at Cheltenham Union Workhouse, and son **Samuel**: That she is about 22 Years of Age and that she is the Daughter of Samuel Risbey late of the Parish of Minchinhampton in the said County of Gloucester Stonemason who hath lately gone to and is now as she believes residing in the City of London: That at the time of this Examinant's birth her said Father resided at Avening in the said County and continued there until this Examinant was about 12 Years old when he went to live at a place called the Box in the said Parish of Minchinhampton where he rented a House of one M^r. Walkley at Five Pounds a Year and a Stone quarry of one M^r. Playne at Ten Pounds a Year, and that he continued to rent and hold such respective Properties together for some Years, and she believes that since such rentings her Said Father hath not done any Act whereby to gain a Settlement: And this Examinant further saith that she hath never done any act in her own right whereby to gain a Settlement: That on or about the 17th. September last she was delivered in the

Parish of Leckhampton in this County of a Male bastard Child of which John Jervis [also Jarvis] of the Parish of Cheltenham Brewer is the Father, and that she and her said Child are now chargeable to the Said Parish of Leckhampton. – [signed Harriot Risbey]

1839: *removed to Minchinhampton (presumed) (father's settlement).* **1841:** *HR (aged 25) and son Samuel (2) lived in Stroud (HO107/349/12/4/2)*; *John Jarvis (45; brewer) lived in Francis St, Cheltenham, with son John (10) and daughter Fanny (5) (HO107/353/12/42/20).* [PS/CH/RA/2/5:150; the examination probably belongs in Petty Sessions register, as examinant was chargeable to Leckhampton, not Cheltenham.]

39057SE: Sat 16 Nov 1839 – **John Robins**, servant, wife **Lydia**, and son **Richard**: That he is about 46 years old and that he was born as he believes at the Parish of Newton St Loe in the County of Somerset – That his Father John Robins who was a Gardener was as he this Examinant hath always understood and believes legally settled in the Parish of Walcot in the City of Bath where he was the Owner of a House and other Property and where he died about 20 years ago – That he this Examinant went out to Service when about 13 years old, and lived in various situations until his first Marriage: That the last situation in which he so lived was with Captain Wilson of N° 6 Old Sydney Place in the Parish of Bathwick in the said Co[unt]y of Somerset by whom he was hired for a Year at the wages of 12^l. That he served the whole of such year under such hiring in the said Parish of Bathwick and received his wages – That shortly afterwards he was married at the Parish Church of Chelsea in the County of Middlesex to one Mary Sunderland (since deceased) by whom he has two Children both now out at Service but who have until recently been supported by him – That since such hiring and service as last aforesaid he has not done any Act whereby to gain a settlement – That about 15 months ago he was married within about a mile of Swansea to Lydia his present Wife (then Prideaux) by whom he has a Child named Richard aged about 11 weeks and that he this Examinant hath lately become and is now chargeable to the Parish of Cheltenham. [signed]

1839: *settlement was probably Bathwick (hiring and service), but orders drawn up were not executed.* **1841:** *JR (aged 45; servant) lived with wife Lydia (35) and son Richard (1) in Clarence St, Cheltenham (HO107/353/15/7/9).* **1851:** *Lydia (35; married, dressmaker) lived with son Richard (11) in Bath (HO107/1941/200/45).* [PS/CH/RA/2/5:151. Note: "Order not executed".]

39058SE: Thurs 21 Nov 1839 – **Elizabeth Checketts**, single woman: That she is about 38 years old and that she was born as she believes at Whittington near Worcester in the County of Worcester where her Father Thomas Checketts, who was a Carpenter and Joiner was born, lived for many years, and was legally settled – That when she this Examinant was about 13 years old she went out to service and lived in various situations until about 17 years ago when she was hired as Maid and Housekeeper to M^{rs}. Sheldon of N° 5. in the Crescent of Cheltenham in the Parish of Cheltenham aforesaid for the term of a year at the wages of £12   That she continued in such Service nearly five years at the same wages the whole of which she received. That during the former part of her said servitude she occasionally travelled with her said Mistress but during the latter part thereof namely, two years and upwards, she duly served her said Mistress in the said Parish of Cheltenham to which she this Examinant is now chargeable. That since such hiring and service with Mrs Sheldon, she this Examinant hath not done any Act whereby to gain a Settlement. [signed]

1839: *settlement in Cheltenham is implied by following examination: see* **39059SE** *(Elizabeth Checketts: 21 Nov 1839).* [PS/CH/RA/2/5:152. Note: "The last 40 Days & upwards in Bath".]

39059SE: Thurs 21 Nov 1839 – Elizabeth Checketts, single woman, regarding the settlement of illegitimate son **John Checketts**: That she is about 38 years of Age and that she was born she believes at Whittington near Worcester in the County of Worcester where her Father Thomas Checketts who was a Carpenter and Joiner was legally settled   That she has acquired a Settlement in the Parish of Cheltenham aforesaid by hiring and Service – That about 18 years ago she was delivered of a Male Bastard Child named John, at the Parish of Saint Peter in the City of Worcester where he was shortly afterwards christened   That such Child has ever since been under this Examinant's Care and that he together with this Examinant are now chargeable to the Parish of Cheltenham aforesaid [signed]

1839: *removal unlikely: settlement probably acknowledged as Cheltenham (mother's settlement).* [PS/CH/RA/2/5:153. Note: "With whom was she hired and how long in the S^d. Service; the o[the]r Exam^n. opposite tells". See **39058SE** (Elizabeth Checketts: 21 Nov 1839).]

39060SE: Thurs 21 Nov 1839 – **Thomas Marchant**, servant: That he is about 37 years of age and that he was born as he believes at Petworth in the County of Sussex   That in the month of April 1818 he was hired for the term of a year as Servant to Lord Charles Henry Somerset of the Parish of Aldsworth in this County at the wages of Sixteen Guineas   That he remained in his said Master's Service as such Yearly Servant about seven years during which he travelled about to various places until the year 1826 or 1827, when his said Master died at Brighton – That shortly afterwards he this Examinant went from thence with Lady Somerset and the Family to London and resided in the Parish of Saint Mary Le Bone in the County of Middlesex with his said Mistress about two months when he received a months Notice to leave the said Service at the expiration of which time he received his full wages and left the said Service Since which he has not done any Act whereby to gain a Settlement and that he is now chargeable to the Parish of Cheltenham aforesaid. [signed]

1839: *apparently removed to Marylebone (hiring and service).* [PS/CH/RA/2/5:154. Removal expenses for "Marchant" to London £4/16/- (1Q 1840: D4178).]

39061SE: Sat 23 Nov 1839 – **Charlotte Barnett** (formerly Charlotte Phelps), single woman, with two sons, **William** and **Joseph**; also Joseph Barnett, labourer, relating to the settlement of son Samuel Barnett. *Joseph Barnett*: That he is about 44 years of Age and that he was born as he believes in the Parish of Brimpsfield in the said County – That upwards of 20 years ago he this Examinant was lawfully married at the Parish Church of Charlton Kings in this County to Mary his present Wife and that the above named Samuel Barnett is one of the Children of such marriage born in Wedlock – That about three or four years previous to his said marriage he this Examinant was hired by one John Richardson of the Parish of Stanton in the said County Farmer to be his Carter for the term of year – That after he had served about six months of such last mentioned hiring in that Parish his said Master took a Farm in the Parish of Coberley in the same County and sent this Examinant to work there – That he went there accordingly and staid about two months after which he returned to the Parish of Stanton and served the remainder of his year being about three months – That since such hiring and service he this Examinant has never done any Act whereby to gain a Settlement and that his said Son Samuel Barnett hath never to the best of this Examinant's belief done any Act in his own right whereby to gain a Settlement [mark]

Charlotte Barnett: That she is about 27 years old – That about 18 months ago she was lawfully married to the said Samuel Barnett at the Register office in Cheltenham aforesaid by which marriage she has one Child named Joseph aged about seven months   That previously to such marriage she had a Bastard Child called or named William Phelps now aged about six years and nine months who was born in the said Parish of Cheltenham   That both such Children are now living – That about 12 months ago her said Husband was transported for several years for stealing Coals   That to the best of this Examinant's belief her said Husband never did any Act whereby to gain a Settlement in his own right – That she and her said two Children are now chargeable to the said Parish of Cheltenham [signed]

1839: *SB (aged 19) had been sentenced to transportation for seven years at Glos County Sessions 1 Jan, for larceny (stealing coal), following previous conviction of nine months' imprisonment in 1837; **SB's place of settlement was apparently determined to be Stanton (father's settlement), where wife and children were removed.** **1841:** (RETURNED) wife Charlotte (28; a charwoman) lived with sons William (8) and Joseph (2) in Fairview St, Cheltenham (HO107/353/5/40/3). **1845:** Charlotte and one child received parish relief from Winchcomb as non-settled residents in Cheltenham 4Q (G/CH/9d/1). **1851:** Charlotte (37; labourer's wife, born Ramsgate, Kent) lived without husband but with son Joseph (12) in Sherborne St, Cheltenham.* [PS/CH/RA/2/5: pages 155-6; amended fair copy report on pp. 142-3, which includes a significant passage struck out: "that about 3 or four years previous to his said Marriage he this Examinant was hired by ~~and did~~

contract and engage to serve one M[r]. Hughes of Noverton Mill in the Parish of Prestbury in this county Miller for one year at the wages of £8: That he served his said master under that hiring one whole year in the said Parish of Prestbury and received a full years wages since which he this Examinant has never done any Act […]". Removal expenses for "Barnett" to Stanton £1/3/- (1Q 1840: D4178).]

39062SE: Sat 30 Nov 1839 – **Lucy Shaw**, with two children **Henry** and **Maria**: That she is about 25 Years of Age and that she is the lawful Wife of Samuel Shaw formerly of Gloucester Hair Dresser, to whom she was married about 8 or 9 years ago at the parish Church of Saint Aldgate [= Aldate] there and by whom she has two Children namely Henry Aged about 7 years and Maria Aged about 6 years who together with this Examinant are now chargeable to the parish of Cheltenham

That she hath understood and verily believes that her said husband is legally Settled in the Parish of Saint Aldgate aforesaid and that he gained such Settlement there by Apprenticeship with M[r]. Wilkins Hair Dresser to whom he was bound by Indenture for 7 years and that during the continuance of such Apprenticeship he slept at the House of M[r] Bullock Auctioneer & appraiser of Northgate Street in the parish of Saint Aldgate aforesaid and that since such Apprenticeship her said husband has not done any Act to gain a Settlement elsewhere [mark]
1839: *place of settlement was presumably determined to be St Aldate, Gloucester (husband's settlement):* see **40051SE** *(LS: 23 Mar) for further information.* [PS/CH/RA/2/5:157. Note: "Saint Mary de Crypt in Glo[uceste]r ap[d]."]

39063SE: Sat 30 Nov 1839 – **Mary Ann Harris**, single woman, with children **Elizabeth**, **Eleanor**, and **Frederick**: That she is about 28 years of Age and that she was born as she believes at Uckington in this County

That about 8 or 9 years ago she was hired for a year by M[rs]. Holland the Wife of M[r]. John Holland of Tewkesbury Park in the parish of Tewkesbury as Nurse Maid at the Wages of Seven Pounds, that she duly served the entire year and received her full wages since which time she has not done any Act to gain a settlement.

That she has three illegitimate Children viz Elizabeth who was born in the month of February 1834 at a House in the parish of Staverton in this County belonging to James Cavell, Elenor Aged about 4 years and Frederick Aged about 2 years, all of whom together with this Examinant are now chargeable to the Parish of Cheltenham [signed Mary ann Harriss]
1839: *removed to Tewkesbury (presumed) (hiring and service).* [PS/CH/RA/2/5:158. Removal expenses for "Harris" to Tewkesbury 11/- (1Q 1840: D4178). See **39050SE** (John Partridge: 24 Oct 1839).]

39064SE: Sat 30 Nov 1839 – **John Jeremiah Roney**[?]: That he is about 25 years of Age and that he was born as he believes in the parish of Cheltenham   That in or about the year 1830 he was hired for a year as Under Butler to the Dowager Marchioness of Salisbury at No. 20 Arlington Street Picadilly [= Piccadilly] in the parish of Saint James's Westminster at the Wages of £15 a year   that he duly served the said year & received his full Wages & resided in the said Parish the whole period, that he continued in the same service about another year when he left and has not done any Act since whereby to gain a Settlement and that through illness he is now chargeable to the Parish of Cheltenham [signed]
1839: *removed to St James's, Westminster (presumed) (hiring and service).* [PS/CH/RA/2/5:159.]

1840

40001SE: Thurs 9 Jan 1840 – **Mary Hardyman**, widow, with daughter **Hannah**: That she is the Widow of Joseph Hardyman late of Cheltenham aforesaid Waggoner deceased to whom she was lawfully married at the Parish Church of Didbrook in this County about five years ago – That by such marriage she has one Child named Hannah aged about 12 months now living – That she this Examinant has often heard her said late Husband say and she verily believes that he was the son of John Hardyman formerly of the Parish of Temple Guiting in this County Labourer deceased; that his said Father was legally settled in that Parish and that he himself was born and also legally settled there never having done any Act whereby to gain a Settlement in his own right – That she this Examinant is now chargeable to the said Parish of Cheltenham. – [mark]
1839: *Joseph Hardemann of Cheltenham buried at Elmstone Hardwicke 2 Oct, aged 27.* **1840:** *removed to Temple Guiting (husband's settlement).* **1841:** *(RETURNED) MH (aged 26; sempstress) lived with daughter Hannah (2) in Queen's Place, Cheltenham (HO107/353/10/26/19).* [PS/CH/RA/2/5:160. Pencilled note: "Temple Guyting". Removal expenses to Bredon [error for Guiting] for "Hardyman" 14/- (2Q 1840: D4178).]

40002SE: Thurs 9 Jan 1840 – **Richard Cheney**, basket-maker, wife **Sarah**, and children **Naomi**, **Sarah**, **Richard**, and **Jonathan**: That he is about 42 years of age – That about 13 years ago he took and hired a House Stable and Coal Yard situate in the White Hart row in the Parish of Cheltenham aforesaid of a M^r. Thomas Evans, then a Coachman, for the term of a year at the Rent of 20^l; That he occupied such Premises under the said taking a year and quarter during which time he paid the rent and Taxes for the same – That on leaving these Premises he went to reside in a House situate in Burton Street in the same Parish of Cheltenham which he rented or hired of William Young then and now a Broker of Cheltenham at the rent of 11^l. a year That he occupied such last named Premises about three successive years during the whole of which time he also paid the Rent and Taxes in respect thereof. That about 16 years ago he was lawfully married at the Parish Church of North-Killworth [= North Kilworth] in the County of Leicester to Sarah his present Wife (then Sarah Vickers Singlewoman) by whom he has five Children now living (namely) Ann aged about 12 years - Naomi about 10 - Sarah about 8 - Richard about 6 and Jonathan about 4 years and that his Wife is now pregnant. That since such last named renting and occupation he this Examinant has not done any Act whereby to gain a Settlement and that in consequence of an accident which bafel [= befell] him about 3 years ago and which still disables him he together with his said Wife and the 4 youngest Children have become and are now chargeable to the Parish of Cheltenham aforesaid. [mark]
1840: *removal unlikely: settlement probably acknowledged as Cheltenham (renting).* **1841:** *RC (aged 40; labourer) lived with wife Sarah (35), and children Naomi (12), Sarah (10), Richard (8), and Jonathan (6) in Cleveland Passage, Tewkesbury Road, Cheltenham (HO107/353/9/28/4).* **1851:** *the family lived in Norwood Terrace, Cheltenham (HO107/1972/183/2): RC born at Swinford, Leics, and wife at Spalding, Lincs.* [PS/CH/RA/2/5:161. Pencilled note: "Chelt^m."]

40003SE: Thurs 9 Jan 1840 – **Richard Lowe**, French polisher: That he is about 67 years of age and that he was born as he believes in the Hamlet of Little Shurdington in the Parish of Badgeworth in the said County where his Father Thomas Lowe who was a Labourer was legally settled by having rented and occupied a House there upwards of 50 years – That in or about the year 1817 he this Examinant was lawfully married in the Parish Church of Cambridge to Elizabeth his present Wife (then Elizabeth Ferrance Singlewoman) That his said Wife is now an inmate of the Lunatic Assylum [*sic*] at Gloucester That in or about the year 1820 he rented or hired a House and Shop situate in Clarendon Place Somers Town in the Parish of Saint Pancras in the County of Middlesex of a Mr June then of Bishop's-Gate Street within Shoemaker for the term of a year at the rent of 32^l. That he occupied such premises for three successive years or thereabouts and carried on the Grocery business therein – That during the whole of such rental

and occupation he Paid the rent and all Parish taxes since which he has not done any Act whereby to gain a legal settlement – That he has become and now is chargeable to the Parish of Cheltenham aforesaid. [signed]
1840: *RL's settlement determined to be St Pancras (renting), but he apparently died before removal.* **1840:** *an RL (aged 68) was buried at New Burial Ground, Cheltenham on 11 Jan.* [PS/CH/RA/2/5:163. Pencilled note: "St Pancras London". The document was struck out, suggesting that Richard Lowe died before he could be removed. Removal expenses (destination omitted) for "Lowe" £1/-/- (1Q 1840: D4178), and to St Pancras (perhaps towards burial) for "Lowe" 7/6 (2Q 1840: D4178).]

40004SE: Sat 11 Jan 1840 – **Joseph Wollen**, sawyer, wife **Elizabeth**, and five children **Samuel, William, Joseph, Eliza**, and **Mary**: That he is about 40 years old   That in or about the year 1831 he took and rented a House N° 1. in Moore's Parade [= Moor's Parade] in the Parish of Cheltenham aforesaid of a Mr Rene for the term of a year at the rent of 10 Guineas   That he occupied such house the whole of the year and paid the rent and one rate for the same   That in or about the year 1833 he took and rented another House situate in the same Parish (at Westall) of Mr Brazenhall Bricklayer for the term of a year at the rent of £13   That he occupied such House the whole of the year during which time he carried on the business of a Retailer of Beer therein – that he paid the full year's rent and Parish taxes   That about 15 or 16 years ago he this Examinant was lawfully married at the Parish Church of Cheltenham to Elizabeth his present Wife (formerly Maisey) by whom he has 5 Children now living (namely) Samuel aged about 11 years - William aged about 9 – Joseph aged about 5 - Eliza about 3 and Mary aged about 8 weeks   That he has become chargeable to the Parish of Cheltenham aforesaid and has never done any Act since such last named rental and occupation whereby to gain a Settlement. [signed]
1840: *removal unlikely: settlement probably acknowledged as Cheltenham.* **1841:** *"Eliza" Wollen (aged 34; charwoman) lived with children Samuel (11), William (8), Joseph (6), Eliza (4), and Mary (1) in Waterloo Place, Wellington St, Cheltenham; JW (41) is perhaps in St Lawrence's Workhouse, Reading* (HO107/35/9/4/4). **1843:** *birth of daughter, Hannah, in Cheltenham.* **1851:** *JW present, when family lived at 7 Soho Place, Cheltenham* (HO107/1973/545/12-13). [PS/CH/RA/2/5:164. Pencilled note: "Chelt^m query: The whole of the Rent was not paid at Moors place or Westall".]

40005SE: Mon 13 Jan 1840 – **Maria Page**, single woman: That she is about 63 Years of Age and that she was born at Painswick in this County where her father Robert Page who was a Carpenter was settled: That when she was about 24 Years of Age she went out to service and lived in various situations in and about the Neighbourhood of London: That about 17 Years ago she was hired by the Year as a Servant of all work to a M^r. Rock of Kingsland Road in the Parish of Hackney in the County of Middlesex at the Wages of 10 Pounds: that she duly served the said Year and continued in the same service the 9 following Years: that on leaving this situation she came to Cheltenham and remained out of place 2 or 3 Years when she was hired to Miss Freeman of the Baths there but that since such hiring and service in the said Parish of Hackney she hath not done any act whereby to gain a Settlement: That she hath lately become chargeable to the Said Parish of Cheltenham. – [mark]
1840: *removed to Hackney (hiring and service).* **1841:** *MP (aged 60) was a pauper inmate of Hackney Workhouse* (HO107/698/13/25/11). **1842:** *MP, pauper, died of "Bronchitis" on 8 Oct at the Workhouse, Hackney, Middlesex, aged 71. Freeman's "warm and tepid" Baths were opened on Cheltenham High St in 1787.* [PS/CH/RA/2/5:165. Pencilled note: "Hackney London".]

40006SE: Mon 13 Jan 1840 – **William Walker**, labourer, wife **Mary**, and daughter **Mary**: That he is about 23 Years of Age and that he was born at Oxford but in what Parish that he does not recollect knowing - That about 9 Years ago he was hired as a Servant in Husbandry for the term of a Year (namely from Michaelmas to Michaelmas) to Richard Purnell of Holwell Downs in the Parish of Westwell in the County of Oxford Farmer: That he duly served the said Year and continued in Mr Purnell's service for about 5 following Years, since which he has not done any act whereby to gain a Settlement: That about 12 Months ago he was lawfully married in the Catholic Chapel in Cheltenham to Mary his now Wife (then Mary Donovan) by whom he has one

Child named Mary aged about 13 Weeks: That he has lately become chargeable to the Parish of Cheltenham. [mark]
1840: *removed to Westwell, Oxon (hiring and service).* **1841:** *(RETURNED) Mary Walker (aged 23; charwoman, born Ireland) lived with daughter Mary (18 mo) in Newman's Place, Cheltenham.* [PS/CH/RA/2/5:166. Pencilled note: "Westwell Oxon".]

40007SE: Fri 17 Jan 1840 – **Ellen Yates**: That about six years ago she was lawfully married at the Parish Church of Eastington in this County to Henry Yates of that Parish Labourer but who had previously enlisted for a Soldier and in consequence of this Examinant being far advanced in pregnancy he was fetched from Woolwich, where the Regiment was stationed, by the Parish authorities of Eastington aforesaid for the purpose of so marrying her – That in a few days after such marriage her said Husband left her and went back to his Regiment and she has only seen him once since which was about five years ago – that the Child with which she was pregnant as aforesaid was still born – That she has frequently heard her said Husband say and she verily believes that he belonged to, was born and legally settled in the said Parish of Eastington to which Parish his Father William Yates who was a Labourer also belonged and in which he was legally settled and that her said Husband never did any Act whereby to gain a settlement in his own right. That at the time of her delivery as aforesaid (about 15 weeks after her marriage) having occasion for assistance she applied to the Officers of the said Parish of Eastington for relief and received from them 1/6^d a week for about 8 weeks. That she is now in the Workhouse of Cheltenham in a very advanced state of Pregnancy. [mark]
1840: *removed to Eastington (husband's settlement); birth of son Edwin.* **1841:** *EY (aged 25) lived with Edwin (2) in Eastington (near Stonehouse) (HO107/370/1/23/6).* [PS/CH/RA/2/5:167. Removal expenses for "Yates" [destination omitted] 18/6 and for "Yates" to Eastington £1/8/- (1Q 1840: D4178).]

40008SE: Sat 18 Jan 1840 – **James Ingram**, labourer, and wife **Margaret**: That he is about fifty Years of Age and that he was born in the Parish of Cheltenham where his Father James Ingram who was for many Years a Labourer in the employ of M^r. Ballinger of the Old Farm there was as he this Deponent hath always understood and believes legally settled: That in the Year 1812 he this Examinant was hired as Groom for a Year by M^r. John Ferryman then of Cheltenham aforesaid: that he entered that service but after having been in it about 4 Months he enlisted for a Soldier in the North Gloucester Militia after which he volunteered into the 56th. Regiment of Foot in which he continued until he received his discharge in the Year 1831: That about 10 Years ago this Examinant was lawfully married to Margaret his now Wife by whom he has never had any Issue: That he hath lately become chargeable to the said Parish of Cheltenham and hath never done any Act in his own right whereby to gain a Settlement. [mark]
1840: *removal uncertain: his settlement was perhaps acknowledged as Cheltenham (perhaps father's settlement).* **1841:** *JI (aged 50, labourer) lived with wife Margaret (40; born Ireland) in Grove St, Cheltenham (HO107/353/16/35/30).* [PS/CH/RA/2/5:168. Note: "Chelt^m. How does this E[xaminan]t gain a Settl[e]m[ent] in Chelt[enha]m". Removal expanses to (destination omitted) for "Ingram" 10/- (1Q 1840: D4178).]

40009SE: Sat 18 Jan 1840 – **James Ponsford**, sawyer: That he is about 32 Years of Age and that he was born as he believes at Long Ashton in the County of Somerset where his Father was as he believes settled: That in the Year 1819 he was hired for a Year by William Allen of Cheltenham aforesaid Victualler at the Wages of Five Pounds: that he duly served such Year and was again hired by M^r. Allen for a second Year at the increased Wages of Six Pounds which second Year he likewise duly served: that he had not since done any act whereby to gain a Settlement, and that he has lately become chargeable to the Said Parish of Cheltenham. [signed]
1840: *removal unlikely: his settlement was apparently acknowledged as Cheltenham (hiring and service).* **1841:** *JP (aged 33; sawyer) boarded in Cliffe Pypard, Wilts (HO107/1179/4/25/16).* [PS/CH/RA/2/5:169. Pencilled note: "Chelt$^{m.}$".]

40010SE: Thurs 23 Jan 1840 – **William Wells** (also **Wills**), labourer, and wife **Hannah**: That he is about 52 years old – That he is the Son of Thomas Wells formerly of Cheltenham aforesaid

Labourer and who when he this Examinant was about 7 or 8 years of age enlisted for a Soldier and has since died in the Army   That his said Father was as he this Examinant has heard and believes born and legally settled in this Parish where he this Examinant was also born – That soon after his said Father went for a Soldier as aforesaid his Mother went after him leaving this Examinant and three other Children unprovided for in consequence of which he this Examinant went into the Workhouse of Cheltenham aforesaid where he remained for about two years when he left and provided for himself – That about 27 years ago he was lawfully married at the Parish Church of Cheltenham aforesaid to Hannah his now Wife (formerly Cutriss [= Gutridge]) who never had issue – That he has never done any Act whereby to gain a Settlement in his own right and for want of employment has become chargeable to the Parish of Cheltenham aforesaid. [mark]
1840: *removal unlikely: settlement probably acknowledged as Cheltenham (father's settlement).* 1850: *a Hannah Wills was buried at Cheltenham 6 Nov, aged 64.* [PS/CH/RA/2/5:170. Pencilled note: "Chelt^m".]

40011SE: Sat 25 Jan 1840 – **Thomas Dixon**, labourer, wife **Mary**, and two sons **George** and **Thomas**: That he is about 34 years old and that he was born as he believes in the Parish of Cheltenham aforesaid   That he is the Son of Joshua Dixon some time since of that Parish Coach-body Maker but who died in London about 18 months ago – That he was told by his said Father when on his death Bed and he verily believes that he was legally settled in this Parish and that he gained such Settlement by having rented and occupied a House in the same Parish for 5 or 6 years at the rent of 25^l a year – That about 4 years ago he this Examinant was lawfully married at the Parish Church of Saint Mary Le Bone in the County of Middlesex to Mary his wife (then Mary Mellady Widow) who had four Children by her previous marriage (namely) Anthony Mellady aged about 10 years Mary Ann about 8 Jane about 5 and Joseph aged about 3½ years   That such Children are at present living with this Examinant's Sister in Law in Herefordshire – That by his present Wife he has two Children vizt, George aged about 2 years and Thomas aged about 4 months – That he this Examinant has never done any Act whereby to gain a settlement in his own right and that in consequence of illness he has become chargeable to the Parish of Cheltenham aforesaid. [signed]
1840: *removal unlikely: his settlement was apparently acknowledged as Cheltenham (father's settlement).* [PS/CH/RA/2/5:171. Pencilled note: "Chelt^m".]

40012SE: [undated – about 25 Jan 1840] – **William Grinnell** (also **Gwinnell**), sawyer, wife **Elizabeth**, and four daughters **Caroline**, **Matilda**, **Elizabeth**, and **Sarah Ann**: That he is about 36 years old and that he was born as he believes in this Parish where his Father John Grinnell (who was also a Sawyer) was As he this Examinant also believes likewise born and legally settled, having lived here all his life time   That about 14 years ago he this Examinant was lawfully married at Hempsted in this County to Elizabeth his now Wife (then Price) by whom he has four Children now living (namely) Caroline aged about 13 years Matilda about 7 – Elizabeth about 6 and Sarah Ann about 4 years – That he has never done any Act whereby to gain a Settlement in his own right and for want of employment has become chargeable to the said Parish of Cheltenham
1840: *removal unlikely: his settlement was apparently acknowledged as Cheltenham (father's settlement).* 1841: *WG (35; sawyer) lived with wife Elizabeth (35), and children Matilda (10), Elizabeth (7), and Sarah (5) in Grove St, Cheltenham. (HO107/353/16/32/24).* [PS/CH/RA/2/5:172. Pencilled notes: "Not taken", and "Chelt^m".]

40013SE: Thurs 23 Jan 1840 – **Walter Boket** (also **Bowkett**), painter and glazier, wife **Ann**, and children **Betsy**, **William**, and **Henry**: That he is about 44 years of age – That when he was about 11 or 12 years old he was apprenticed (but not by Indenture) to Francis Carruthers then of Cheltenham Painter and Glazier for seven years which he duly served – That in about a month after the expiration of his said apprenticeship he went to live as a hired Servant (a Footman) to Colonel Lennon then of N° 4 Bath Villas in the Parish of Cheltenham aforesaid at the wages of Eleven Guineas – and his Livery – That he continued in the Colonel's Service at the same place two years and upwards and received his wages. That on leaving such Service he was lawfully married at the Parish Church of Cheltenham to Ann his now Wife (then Ann Stephens

Singlewoman) by whom he has three Children (namely) Betsy aged about 15 - William about 11 and Henry about 9 years. That some 16 or 17 years ago being out of employment he received outdoor relief on one or two Occasions from the Officers of this Parish – That about 4 years since (his shoulder being put out which rendered him unable to work) he received relief from this Parish for about a fortnight. That ever since his hiring and Service with Colonel Lennon as aforesaid he has followed his Trade but has not done any Act whereby to gain a settlement, and for want of employment he has become chargeable to the Parish of Cheltenham aforesaid. [mark] **1840: *removal unlikely: settlement was apparently acknowledged as Cheltenham (hiring and service).*** **1841:** *WB (aged 45; painter) lived with wife Ann (50), and children Elizabeth (15), William (12), and Henry (10) in Hereford Passage, Cheltenham (HO107/353/8/63/10).* **1851:** *WB, wife Ann, and youngest son Henry were inmates of Cheltenham Workhouse (HO107/1973/1100/20 and 1101/23).* [PS/CH/RA/2/5:173. Pencilled note: "Chelt^{m}".]

40014SE: [undated – about 25 Jan 1840] – **Thomas Davis**, labourer: That he is about 35 years old and that he was born as he believes at Chalford in this County where his Father Aaron Davis then resided. That when he this Examinant was about 3 years old his said Father, as he has been informed and believes came to reside at Cheltenham where he lived until the time of his death which happened about 7 months ago, and worked as a Pumper to the late and present Mr Thompson – That about 22 years ago his said Father took and rented a House situate at Alstone in this Parish of Mr Henry Ward Fishmonger at 10^l a year – That he occupied such House for two or three years during which time he also rented and occupied some Land at Bays Hill there – that he actually paid the rent. That his Sister Sophia about 12 years ago received relief from this Parish (to wit) 1^s/6^d a week for some years. That his Father has frequently told him that this was his Parish. That he has never done any Act whereby to gain a settlement in his own right and has become chargeable to the said Parish of Cheltenham aforesaid. **1840: *removal unlikely: settlement probably acknowledged as Cheltenham, where his father was settled.*** *Pumper: a person who pumps water at a spa: Henry and then Pearson Thompson, large Cheltenham property developers, owned the Montpellier Spa in the town.* [PS/CH/RA/2/5:174.]

40015SE: Thurs 23 Jan 1840 – **Charles Emms**, basket-maker, wife **Edith**, and children **Charles** and **Mary Ann**: That he is about 31 years of age and that he was born as he believes at Chipping Campden in this County where his Father Richard Emms who was a Butcher was legally settled That about 9 years ago he this Examinant took and hired a House and Shop N° 11 in Winchcomb Street in the Town and Parish of Cheltenham aforesaid of M^rs. Newbury at the rent of 28^l a year. That he actually occupied such House under such yearly hiring for three successive years and upwards and paid the rent for the same during that period – since which he has not done any Act to gain a settlement   That about 8 years ago he was legally married at the Parish Church of Cheltenham to Edith his now Wife (then Edith Ayers Singlewoman) by whom he has two Children namely Charles Richard aged about 6 years and Mary Ann aged about 5 years – That in consequence of illness he has become and now is chargeable to the said Parish of Cheltenham. [signed] **1840: *removal unlikely: settlement probable acknowledged at Cheltenham.*** **1841** *CE (aged 30; basket-maker) lived with wife Edith (40), and children Charles (7) and Maryann (6) in Milsom St, Cheltenham (HO107/353/8/60/1).* [PS/CH/RA/2/5:175. Pencilled note: "query as to paym^t of one years Rent".]

40016SE: Thurs 23 Jan 1840 – **James Johnson** (also **Johnston**), cooper, wife **Maria**, and son **Benjamin**: That he is about 25 years of age and that he was born in the Parish of Cheltenham aforesaid as he verily believes. That he is the Son of Benjamin Johnson who is a Cooper and an old resident here – That his said Father has been the Owner of several Cottages and Land situate at a place called the Cold Baths in Cheltenham aforesaid. That Examinant believes he is still interested in Property there and that he belongs to and is legally settled in this Parish – That he this Examinant has never gained a settlement in his own right – That about 7 Years ago he was lawfully married at the Old Church of Cheltenham to Maria his Wife (then Maria Bailey

Singlewoman) by whom he has one Child named Benjamin about 4 years old – That his said Wife is near her Confinement with a second Child and that he has become chargeable to the Parish of Cheltenham [signed]

1840: *removal unlikely: settlement probably acknowledged as Cheltenham (father's settlement); Maria Johnson was pregnant at time of examination with son James, baptised at Cheltenham 4 Mar, when family lived in Cold Bath (near the Old Spa), in central Cheltenham; James Johnson was committed to Quarter Sessions for larceny (later acquitted) (Cheltenham Chron. 27 Feb); he is probably the JJ committed and acquitted of larceny on at least two other occasions.* **1841:** *JJ (25; cooper), wife Maria (30), and children Benjamin (6) and James (1) lived in Cold Bath Cottages, next-door to Benjamin Johnson (90; cooper) (HO107/353/15/46/1).* [PS/CH/RA/2/5:176. Pencilled note: "Chelt^{m}".]

40017SE: Thurs 23 Jan 1840 – **Joseph Palmer**, carpenter and joiner, wife **Sarah**, and children (**John**), **Sophia**, and **Esther**: That he was born as he hath understood and believes in Burford Oxfordshire about 30 years ago to which Parish his Father at that time belonged – That about 18 years ago his said Father left Burford and came to reside in Cheltenham where he took and rented a House in Saint James's Street but of whom Examinant does not know at 28^l a year   That he occupied such House only about 6 months when he went to reside in Rutland Street (where he lived upwards of 12 months) and Examinant has no doubt that he paid upwards of 10^l a year rent – That from thence he went into Newman's Row or Place where he held and occupied a House of Mr Newman upwards of 2 years but Examinant believes as a weekly tenant – That his said Father ultimately took and rented a House in Ambrose Street in Cheltenham aforesaid by the year at the rent of 14^l. of Old Mr Mustoe. That he occupied such House as a yearly tenant 5 or 6 years successively and actually paid the rent during the whole time since which he has not done any Act whereby to gain a legal Settlement nor has he this Examinant ever done a like Act and that he now [is] chargeable to the Parish of Cheltenham aforesaid   That about 5 years ago he was lawfully married in Cheltenham Parish Church to Sarah his now Wife (then Barnard) by whom he has 3 Children (namely) ~~John aged about 7 years~~ Sophia aged about 3 and Esther about 2 years and that his said wife ~~is very far advanced in pregnancy~~ was this morning delivered of a daughter. [signed]

1840: *JP committed to appear with James Johnson* (**40016SE**) *at County Sessions in Gloucester Jan. for stealing a plane and saw (both acquitted); like Johnson, Palmer was also apparently involved in other petty crime in Cheltenham;* **removal unlikely: settlement probably acknowledged as Cheltenham (father's settlement)**; *daughter Ann baptised at Cheltenham 4 Mar, when family lived in Cold Bath, Cheltenham.* **1841:** *daughters Sophia (aged 5) and Esther (3) lived in Grove St, Cheltenham, apparently in same house as William Grinnell (see* **40012SE**) *(HO107/353/16/32/24); JP (35; carpenter) lived with wife Sarah (30), and daughter Ann (1) in the Common, Minety, Wilts (until 1844 in Glos) (HO107/354/20/27/12).* [PS/CH/RA/2/5:177. Pencilled notes: "X Q[uer]y is John who is a Bastard full 7 if he be the mo[the]r sho[ul]d be exam[ine]d as to his birth place & he may be removed there"; "Chelt^m except John".]

40018SE: Sat 15 Feb 1840 – **William Pinchin**, labourer, wife **Hannah**, and children **Sarah** and **George**: That he is about 28 years of age and that he was born as he hath been informed and believes in the Parish of Shipton-Solars [= Shipton Sollars] in this County where his Father Daniel Pinchin Labourer, is now living and where as he this Examinant hath also been informed and believes he hath resided all his life time and is legally settled. That about 4 years ago he this Examinant was married at the Parish Church of Cheltenham aforesaid to Hannah his now Wife (then Mills) by whom he has two Children (namely) Sarah aged about 4 years and George aged about 2 years – That his said Wife is very far advanced in Pregnancy – That 2 years ago this winter he this Examinant being out of employ applied to the then Overseer of the said Parish of Shipton Solars for relief from whom he received 1/- by way of loan – That he has never done any Act where by to gain a settlement in his own right and that he has become chargeable to the Parish of Cheltenham aforesaid. [signed]

1840: *removed to Shipton Sollars (father's settlement); death of son George (buried at Shipton Oliffe and Shipton Sollars 14 June).* **1841:** *WP (aged 25; agricultural labourer) lived with wife Hannah (25) and children Sarah (5) and Daniel (1) in Shipton Sollars (HO107/351/15/2/12).* [PS/CH/RA/2/5:178. Pencilled note: "22 Feby. The Order herein was suspended & a Copy of Order suspended & also the Exam[inatio]n made to be sent off". Further note: "Shipton Solars". For an earlier, undated draft of examination see p. 162 of Cheltenham magistrates' register. Removal expenses to Shipton for "Pinchin" 11/- and 12/- (1Q 1840: D417).]

40019SE: Sat 25 Jan 1840 – **Henry Clifford**, labourer, wife **Ellen**, and children **Frederick** and **Charlotte**: That he is about 24 years Old and that he was born as he believes at Leckhampton in this County – That he is the Son of William Clifford some time since of the Parish of Swindon in the same County Milkman who as this Examinant hath always understood and believes was born and legally settled in that Parish. That he died in Cheltenham about 14 years ago – That he this Examinant remembers that soon after the death of his said Father a question arose as to his last legal place of Settlement and this Examinant his mother and two Brothers were removed to Upton Saint-Leonard in this County the legallity [*sic*] of which removal was afterwards questioned and as this Examinant hath understood and believes tried and that they ultimately returned to the said Parish of Swindon as their proper place of Settlement. That Examinant's mother hath ever since received occasional relief and is now as he believes receiving a weekly allowance from that Parish – That last Summer he was legally married to his now Wife (then Ellen Chesterman Singlewoman) who previous to such marriage had two illegitimate Children one named Frederick aged about 4 years and the other named Charlotte aged about 3 years both of whom are now living with this Examinant. That he has never done any Act whereby to gain a settlement in his own right and for want of employment he has become chargeable to the said Parish of Cheltenham. [mark]
1834: *HC is perhaps the Henry Clifford (18) involved in petty crime and indicted for theft in Cheltenham and sentenced to six months' imprisonment* (Cheltenham Chron. *9 Jan*). **1840: removed to Swindon (father's settlement). 1841:** *(RETURNED) HC (aged 25; labourer) and wife Ellen (25) lived in Francis St, Cheltenham with Ellen's illegitimate children Frederick (7) and Charlotte (5), and with their daughter Elizabeth (3 mo), baptised at Cheltenham 14 Apr, when HC is described as a brickmaker (HO107/353/12/41/19); Ellen moved to Horsefair St, Charlton Kings with her children, including two further illegitimate children (John) Edwin (4; a scholar) and Emma (1), both born at Charlton Kings (HO107/1972/164/24).* **1843:** *death of HC at Cheltenham Hospital 9 June of heart disease (buried 14 June, aged 26).* [PS/CH/RA/2/5:179. Pencilled note: "Swindon". See Gray **586** (mother Mary Clifford: 8 Nov 1825), referred to here, and **43070SE** (brother James Clifford: 4 Dec 1843).]

40020SE: Sat 25 Jan 1840 – **Susan Shurmer** (also **Shermer**; formerly Wood), and son **Thomas**: That she was born as she believes in Tewkesbury in this County and that she is about 54 years old. That her Father as she hath been informed and believes deserted his Family when this Examinant was quite young and when she was about 8 or 9 years old her Mother having departed this life she went to live with her Aunt at Shurdington who brought her up until she became about 15 or 16 years old when she this Examinant went out to Service and was hired for the term of a year to a Mr Smith who then kept the 8. Bells Inn in Cheltenham aforesaid   That she served the whole of such year under such hiring as an indoor Servant – That some months afterwards she was again hired for a year to the Misses Surman who then lived at (now) N° 94 High Street in Cheltenham aforesaid as an indoor Servant at the wages of 5^l. that in consequence of the death of her said Mistresses (who were both buried on the same day) about 3 months previous to the expiration of her term she continued her service with their nephew Mr Surman then and now a Straw bonnet manufacturer residing in Cheltenham with whom she completed her full year under the same hiring and from whom she received her full years wages at the expiration thereof – since which she has not done any Act to her knowledge or belief whereby to gain a Settlement except having ab[out] 20 years ago last October lawfully married one Samuel Shurmer at Cheltenham Parish Church with whom she lived in Cheltenham aforesaid about 8 years and who during that time did not to her knowledge gain a settlement nor is she aware to what Parish he belonged   That he was then transported for life and went out of the Country and she has never since heard of him   That by such Marriage she has a son named Thomas who was born in this Parish and is now about 15 years old and under her Care   That she has become chargeable to the Parish of Cheltenham. [mark]
1840: removal unlikely: settlement probably acknowledged as Cheltenham (hiring and service). 1841: *SS (aged 50; laundress) lived alone in Cleveland Passage, Tewkesbury Road, Cheltenham (HO107/353/9/27/3).*

1851: *SS (65; charwoman and widow) lived with son Thomas (26; labourer) in King Street, Cheltenham (HO107/1973/410/52).* [PS/CH/RA/2/5:180. Pencilled note: "Chelt^(m)".]

40021SE: Sat 25 Jan 1840 – **John Smith**, labourer, wife **Priscilla**, and eight children **Mary, Thomas, Eliza, Henry, Sarah, Martha, John**, and **Rosetta**: That he is about 35 years of age and that he was born as he believes in the Parish of Great Hampton [= Hampton] in the County of Worcester where his Father Henry Smith who was a Labourer lived and died when he this Examinant was quite an Infant and where as he hath been informed and believes his said Father resided for many years and was legally settled – That his Mother also died at Great Hampton aforesaid when he was about 6 years old upon whose death he was bred up with an Uncle at Rodborough in this County   That about 6 years ago he this Examinant took and hired a House N°. 11 in Sidney St in Cheltenham aforesaid of Mr Jeanes Plumber and Glazier at the Rent of 12^l a year which he still holds and although it has been assessed to the Poor Rates he has never paid any having been excused therefrom on Account of Poverty – That with the exception of the first year of such tenancy he has never actually occupied the said House having occasionally let a portion thereof to Undertenants - That about 14 years ago he was lawfully married at Rodborough aforesaid to his now Wife Priscilla (then Smith) by whom he has 8 Children now living (namely) Mary Aged about 13 Thomas about 11, Eliza about 10 – Henry about 9 – Sarah about 8 – Martha about 5 John about 2 years and Rosetta about 13 months   That he has never done any Act whereby to gain a Settlement in his own right and that he has become chargeable to the Parish of Cheltenham aforesaid. [mark]

1840: *removed to Gt Hampton, Worcs (father's settlement).* **1841:** *(RETURNED) JS (aged 45; labourer) lived with his family in Sidney St, Cheltenham: Priscilla (37), Mary (15), Thomas (13), Eliza (12), Henry (10), Sarah (8), Martha (5), John (4), Rosina (2), and George (5 mo); George Smith baptised at Cheltenham 12 Sept, when family lived at 11 Sidney St.* [PS/CH/RA/2/5:181. Pencilled note: "Great Hampton".]

40022SE: [undated] 1840 – **James Stevens**, sawyer, wife **Elizabeth**, and three children **William, Mary Ann**, and **Sarah**: That he is about 44 years of Age and that he is the Son of James Stevens late of Cheltenham aforesaid Sawyer deceased and was born as he believes in the City of Cork in Ireland where his Father then resided   that he came over to England with his said Father when about 16 years old but his Father has never gained a Settlement in England – That when Examinant was about 19 years old he was hired as Servant for the term of a year by a Miss Tucker at that time a Boardinghouse Keeper residing at N° 4 Portland Street in the Town and Parish of Cheltenham aforesaid at the wages of 4^l. – That he served the whole of the year as an under Servant under such hiring and received his full years wages since which he has not done any Act to gain a Settlement – That about 9 years ago he was lawfully married at Saint Clements Church Oxford to Elizabeth his now Wife then Stiles by whom he has 3 Children now living vizt. William aged about 7 Mary Ann about 5 and Sarah aged about 4 years   That for want of employment he has become and now is chargeable to the Parish of Cheltenham.

1840: *removal unlikely: settlement probably acknowledged as Cheltenham (hiring and service).* [PS/CH/RA/2/5:182. Pencilled note: "Chelt^(m)".]

40023SE: Mon 27 Jan 1840 – **George Cornwall**, labourer, wife **Elizabeth**, and five children **Zachariah, George, Eliza, James**, and **Edwin**: That he was born as he believes in the Parish of Dymock in the said County of Gloucester where his Father George Cornwall lived, that when he was about fifteen years of age he was hired by William Hill of Lilly hawes [= Old Lilly Hall] in the Parish of Ledbury in the County of Hereford Farmer as an in Door Servant at the Wages he believes of Four Pounds a year for a year & served his time under such hiring in that Parish and received his Wages. that about Eleven years ago he was married at Dymock aforesaid to his present Wife Elizabeth (then Elizabeth Smith Spinster) and by her has five Children now living namely Zachariah aged about ten years George aged about 9 years, Eliza aged about seven years James aged about five years and Edwin aged about three years, that since his said Service with Mr Hill He has never done any Act in his own right to gain another Settlement – that about three years since when he was living at Newent, He from illness was obliged to apply to his Parish for Relief – & that he accordingly applied to the Parish Officers of Ledbury and was by them together with his Family taken into the Poor House there & relieved, that from illness He his Wife and Children are now become chargeable to the Parish of Cheltenham [mark]

1840: *removed to Ledbury (hiring and service).* **1841:** *(RETURNED) baptism of (John) Charles 6 June, when the family lived at 7 Charles St, Cheltenham.* **1851:** *the family lived at 12 Bath Terrace, Cheltenham (HO107/1973/877/12): George Cornwall (aged 45; labourer), Elizabeth (42), Zachariah (21; labourer), James (16; labourer), Edwin (14) and three younger children.* [PS/CH/RA/2/5:183. Removal expenses for "Cornwell" to Ledbury £2/8/9 (1Q 1840: D4178).]

40024SE: Sat 1 Feb 1840 – **John Gardner** (also **Gardiner**), labourer, and children **Joseph, Rhoda**, and **Ralph**: That he is about 47 years old and that he was born as he believes in the Parish of Bisley in this County   That his Father James Gardner (who was a Weaver) was legally settled there and always resided in that Parish and from which he occasionally received relief – That he this Examinant has never done any Act whereby to gain a Settlement in his own right – That about 20 years ago he was lawfully married in the Parish Church of Bisley aforesaid to Fanny Rowles who is dead by which marriage there are three Children now living (namely) Joseph aged about 17 years Rhoda aged about 13 years and Ralph aged about 8 or 9 years – That Examinant hath become chargeable to the Parish of Cheltenham aforesaid. [mark]

1840: *removed to Bisley (father's settlement).* **1841:** *JG remarried at Bisley 14 Feb, to Phoebe Pegler (both give their address as Chalford; John was clothworker); JG (aged 48; cloth worker) lived in Bisley with Phoebe (48) and son Ralph (10).* [PS/CH/RA/2/5:184. Pencilled note: "Bisley". Removal expenses to Bisley for "Gardner" £1/8/6 (1Q 1840: D4178).]

40025SE: Sat 1 Feb 1840 – **Maria Warton**, wife of Peter Warton, and children **William** and **Sarah**: That about 10 years ago she was lawfully married in the Parish Church of Saint Thomas in the City of Oxford to her said Husband   That her Husband's Father is dead. That she believes he was legally settled in the Parish of Saint Clements in the County of Oxford where her said Husband was as she has heard and believes born. That her said Husbands Mother was an acknowledged Parishioner there and that about 12 months ago she received outdoor relief from that Parish weekly – That about 12 months ago being deserted by her Husband she applied to the Parish Officers of Saint Clements aforesaid for relief and was with her Son William received into the workhouse there – That her said Husband has done no act Act to gain a Settlement as she verily believes. That by her said Marriage she has two Children now living viz[t]. William aged about 7 years and Sarah aged about 9 months – That in consequence of her Husband having deserted her she has become chargeable to the Parish of Cheltenham aforesaid [signed]

1840: *removed to St Clement's, Oxford, Oxon (husband's settlement).* **1841:** *the couple, apparently reconciled, lived in Gloucester, perhaps with Maria's parents: Peter Warton (aged 30; engineer), Maria (30), William (9), Sarah (3), and new baby Ann (6 weeks) (HO107/379/9/41/31/).* **1851:** *Peter Warton (30; engineer, born Oxford) lived alone as lodger in Northampton (HO107/1740/136/26).* [PS/CH/RA/2/5:185. Pencilled note: "S[t] Clements Oxon". Removal expenses to Oxford for "Wharton" £3/18/- (1Q 1840: D4178).]

40026SE: Tues 4 Feb 1840 – **Ann Elliot**, single woman: That she is the Daughter of William Elliot some time since of the Parish of Wootten Underedge [= Wotton-under-Edge] in this County Labourer deceased to which Parish he belonged and in which he was legally settled and that she was born as she believes in the Parish of Westley [= Westerleigh] in the same County about 30 years ago – That her said Father soon after her birth was residing in the said Parish of Westley when he removed from that place to the said Parish of Wootten Underedge to which Parish he applied for relief in consequence of which he and his Family were received into the Workhouse there and her Father and Mother remained there until their respective deaths – That her said Father died in Wootten Underedge aforesaid about 19 years ago and was buried at the expence of that Parish – That she has never done any Act whereby to gain a settlement in her own right and is now chargeable to the Parish of Cheltenham aforesaid [mark]

1840: *removed to Wotton-under-Edge (father's settlement).* **1841:** *(perhaps RETURNED) perhaps the AE (aged 35; plain sewer) who lived alone in Hanover St, St Paul's, Cheltenham (HO107/358/8/9/13).* **1842:** *perhaps the AE buried at New Burial Ground, Cheltenham on 22 Aug, aged 32.* [PS/CH/RA/2/5:186. Pencilled note: "To Wootten under Edge". Removal expenses to Wotton-under-Edge for "Elliott" £1/2/- (1Q 1840) and £2/-/6 (3Q 1841: D4178).]

40027SE: Sat 8 Feb 1840 – **John Mullens** (also **Mullings**), tailor, wife **Mary Ann**, and children **John**, **Sarah**, and **Mary Ann**: That he is about 31 years of age and that he was born as he believes in the Parish of Saint Thomas in the City of Bristol – That when he was about between 10 and 11 years old he was bounden by Indenture as an indoor Apprentice to one William Cowd a Tailor of the Parish of Lympston [= Lympstone] in the County of Devon until he arrived at the Age of 21 years – That he served seven years of his said apprenticeship in the said Parish of Lympston during which time he boarded and lodged in his said Master's House – That his Father John Mullens was also settled in that Parish by having been apprenticed there – That since this Examinant's said apprenticeship he has [not] done any Act whereby to gain a Settlement and that he has become chargeable to the Parish of Cheltenham That about 9 years ago he was married at Cheltenham Parish Church to Mary Ann his now Wife by which Marriage he has three Children now living (viz) John about 8 years Sarah about 4 years and Mary Ann about 11 months old – [signed]
1840: *removed to Lympstone, Devon (apprenticeship);* *"John Mullings", tailor, died of "Decline" on 13 June at Topsham, Devon.* **1841:** *(RETURNED) Ann "Mullings" (aged 29; charwoman) lived with three children John (10), Sarah (6), and Mary (2) at 3 Roper's Walk, Cheltenham.* **1851:** *Ann "Mullens" was laundress (36; widow) with her children John (19; labourer) and Mary Ann (12; scholar) living with her mother at 8 Roper's Row [= Roper's Walk], Cheltenham.* [PS/CH/RA/2/5:187. Pencilled note: "To Lympston Devon". Removal expenses to Lympstone for "Mullent [sic]" £8/7/6 (1Q 1840: D4178).]

40028SE: Fri 14 Feb 1840 – **George Wintle**, labourer, and wife **Elizabeth**: That he is about 32 years old and that he was born as he believes in the Parish of Tirley in this County where as he verily believes his Father John Wintle who was also a Labourer was legally Settled and where he died about 14 months ago That about 18 years ago he this Examinant was hired as Servant for the term of a year to Mr John Staite [also Staight, etc] of Tirley aforesaid Farmer at the wages of 5^d. [an hour] or thereabouts That he duly served his said Master under such hiring the whole of the year and received his full wages during which time he boarded and lodged in his said Master's House and since which he has never done any Act to gain a Settlement – That about 16 years ago he was lawfully married at the Parish Church of Cheltenham aforesaid to Elizabeth his now Wife (then Slocombe) but has no child living by such Marriage. That about 6 years ago he was examined at Beckford (in this County) as to his Settlement, having had relief from Tirley aforesaid, when he was acknowledged to belong thereto – That he is now chargeable to the Parish of Cheltenham aforesaid. [mark]
1840: *removed to Tirley (hiring and service).* [PS/CH/RA/2/5:188. Removal expenses for Wintle to Tirley 10/- and 14/- (1Q 1840: D4178).]

40029SE: Sat 8 Feb 1840 – **Sophia James**, single woman, and brothers **William** and **Benjamin**: That she is about 18 years old – That she is the Daughter of Thomas James late of Cheltenham aforesaid Razor-Grinder, who hath lately been sentenced at Gloucester to 7 years transportation – That her Mother is dead, and she is not aware where her Father is settled – That she had been informed and believes that she was born in this Parish [and] that her said two Brothers (namely) William aged about 8 years, and Benjamin aged about 6 years were also born in this Parish – That she hath never done any Act to gain a settlement and she and her Brothers are become chargeable to the same Parish. [mark]
1840: *removal unlikely: her settlement was probably accepted as Cheltenham.* [PS/CH/RA/2/5:189.]

40030SE: [undated] – **Isaac Hancock**, chaise-driver, wife **Martha**, and two children **Sarah Ann** and **Elizabeth**: That he is about 51 years old – That in or about the year 1826 he took and rented a

House N° 6 Admiral Buildings in the Parish of Cheltenham aforesaid of a Mr Timbrell (who then lived near) for the term of a year at the rent of 16¹. That he occupied such House under such hiring the whole of that and the following year at the same rent, when it became reduced to 14¹. a year – That he has ever since occupied the same House as a yearly tenant at the last named rental which rent he has duly paid – That about [blank] years ago he was lawfully married at Hawkesbury in this County to his present Wife Martha (then Crew) by whom he has two Children now living (namely) Sarah Ann aged about 16 years and Elizabeth aged about 14 years – That in consequence of sickness he has become chargeable to the Parish of Cheltenham aforesaid.

1840: *removal unlikely: settlement probably acknowledged as Cheltenham (renting).* **1841:** *Martha Hancock (aged 50; laundress) lived in Admiral's Buildings, Winchcombe St, Cheltenham; husband Isaac (50; post-boy) was patient at Bath General Hospital, Upper Borough Walls, Bath, which specialised in mineral-water cures for the poor.* **1848:** *Martha Hancock died at 4 Admiral's Building, Cheltenham 15 Jan, aged 55; IH died at Cheltenham General Hospital 2Q.* [PS/CH/RA/2/5:190.]

40031SE: Fri 14 Feb 1840 – **James Booy**, plasterer, and wife **Mary Ann**: That he is about 23 years of age and that he was born as he hath been informed and believes in the Parish of Castle Combe in the County of Wilts where his Father John Booy who was also a Plasterer was legally settled – That his said Father about 8 years since being ill and unable to work applied to the said Parish of Castle Combe for relief and received relief therefrom up to the time of his death which happened about 5 years since. That about 2 years ago he was lawfully married at the Parish Church of Cheltenham aforesaid to Mary Ann his now Wife (formerly Barrett) but has no Child living – That he has never done any Act whereby to gain a settlement in his own right and that he has become chargeable to the said Parish of Cheltenham. [mark]

1840: *probably ordered to be removed to Castle Combe, Wilts (father's settlement), but died before removal; death of JB in Cheltenham Aug, aged 23.* [PS/CH/RA/2/5:191. Removal expenses for "Booy" to Castle Combe, Wilts £2/1/6 and £4/8/- (1Q 1840: D4178).]

40032SE: Mon 17 Feb 1840 – **Jane Maycock**, widow, and four children **Charlotte**, **Thomas**, **Elizabeth**, and **Sarah**: That she is about 33 years of age and that she is the Widow of Joseph Maycock late of this Parish Servant deceased – That she has heard him say and she verily believes that he was born in the Parish of Aldsworth in this County, that when a Boy he lived with a Mʳ Sadler of that Parish Livery Stable Keeper but whether as a hired Servant he did not state, and that his Father was settled in and received relief from that Parish. That about eleven years ago she was lawfully married to her said Husband at Saint Martin's Church Worcester by whom she has four Children now living (namely) Charlotte aged about 9 years Thomas aged about 4 years Elizabeth aged about 2 years and Sarah aged about 4 months – That to her knowledge or belief her said Husband never did any Act whereby to gain a settlement in his own right except That at or about Midsummer 1836 he took or hired a House N° 21 in Mount Pleasant in Cheltenham aforesaid by the year at the rent of 14¹. of Mr Holford of that Place Builder which House he held and occupied under such hiring up to the time of his death (in January last) and paid the rent (except the last 6 months) and also the Poor rates in respect thereof That during the whole of such occupation as aforesaid her said Husband at various times let or hired out one Room in the said House to Lodgers ready furnished and sometimes Lodgings to Single Persons by the week. [signed]

1840: *burial of Joseph Maycock in Cheltenham 31 Jan; removed to Aldsworth (husband's settlement).* **1841:** *(RETURNED) JM (aged 30; upholsteress) lived with children Charlotte (10), Thomas (5), and Sarah (1) in Fairview St, Cheltenham (HO107/353/4/3/1).* [PS/CH/RA/2/5:192. Removal expenses for "Maycock" to Aldsworth 15/- (2Q 1840: D4178).]

40033SE: Thurs 20 Feb 1840 – **John Dyer**, sawyer, wife **Ann**, and children **George** and **Charlotte**: That he is about 40 years of age – That when he was about 18 years old he was hired at Winchcomb Mop as a Servant in Husbandry for the term of a year to Mʳ Richard Fisher then of the Parish of Prestbury in this County Farmer at the wages of 9¹. – That he duly served his said Master under such hiring the whole of such year in the said Parish of Prestbury during which he boarded and slept in his said Master's House and received his full years wages – That about 17 years ago he was lawfully married at the Parish Church of Cheltenham aforesaid to Ann his now Wife (then Freeman) by whom he has had several Children two of whom are now living (namely) George aged about 10 years and Charlotte aged about 8 years and that his said Wife is now near her confinement – That about 11 years ago for want of employment, he became chargeable to this Parish when he was examined as to his place of Settlement and himself and Family were taken to and received and acknowledged by the Parish officers of Prestbury aforesaid as belonging to that Parish and received the sum of 20^0/– by way of relief from the Overseer there – That some time since (on the death of a Son) he applied to the Parish officers of Prestbury aforesaid to enable him to bury him and was accordingly relieved – That since such hiring and service as aforesaid he has not done any Act whereby to gain a Settlement and that he has now become chargeable to the Parish of Cheltenham aforesaid – [signed]

1840: *removed to Prestbury (presumed) (hiring and service)*; *son Thomas born at Cheltenham.* **1841:** *(RETURNED) the family lived in Duke St, Cheltenham: John (aged 40; sawyer), Ann (35), George (13), Charlotte (10), and Thomas (1) (HO107/353/3/29/10).* **1851:** *the family lived at 2 Back Mount Pleasant in Cheltenham (HO107/1973/202/38): John born at Didbrook, and the family consisted of himself (50; sawyer), Ann (46; laundress), and four sons Thomas (10), John (8), David (6), and William (4; all born Cheltenham).* [PS/CH/RA/2/5:193. See Gray **611** (JD: 21 Feb 1826) (daughter Caroline aged 16 mo).]

40034SE: Sat 22 Feb 1840 – **James Evans**, cabinet-maker, wife **Mary**, and four children **Elizabeth**, **Georgiana**, **Mary**, and **James**: That he is about 34 years of age and that he was born as he believes at Wootten-under-Edge [= Wotton-under-Edge] in this County where his Father James Evans who is a Surveyor of Roads has lived for very many years and where he now lives. That in the year 1826 he was lawfully married at the Parish Church of Saint James Bristol to Mary his now Wife (then Mary Ferris Singlewoman) by whom he has four Children now living (namely) Elizabeth aged about 10 years – Georgiana aged about 7 years – Mary aged about 4 years and James aged about 2 years   That two years ago last August he took or hired a Cottage and Garden in Sandford Field Cheltenham of Mr William Gwinnell Plasterer, by the year at the rent of 12^l. which was afterwards reduced to 11^l. at which it now stands. That he has occupied such house as a yearly tenant under such hiring until the present time and has paid upwards of two years rent and also the Poor rates in respect thereof for a little period. That in consequence of severe illness he has become chargeable to the Parish of Cheltenham aforesaid. [signed]

1840: *removal unlikely: settlement probably acknowledged as Cheltenham (renting)*; *JE died 24 Mar, soon after examination, at Field Cottage, Sandford, Cheltenham, aged 34; on 18 Apr three children (James, Mary, and new daughter Ann: all born Cheltenham) baptised at Cheltenham, when family lived at Field Cottage.* **1841:** *(RETURNED) Mary Evans (aged 30; charwoman) lived with five children in Union St, Cheltenham (HO107/353/5/44/11).* **1844:** *Mary Evans re-married, to James Lloyd, widowed cabinet-maker, 23 Dec.* **1851:** *Mary (46), new husband, Georgiana (18; dressmaker), James (13; errand boy), and Ann (11; scholar) lived at 37 Union St, Cheltenham (HO107/1973/137/15).* [PS/CH/RA/2/5:194.]

40035SE: Sat 22 Feb 1840 – **George Liddington** (also **Leddington**), labourer, wife **Elizabeth**, and son **George**: That he is about 30 years old and that he is the Son of Edward Liddington of the Parish of Down [= Downe] in the County of Kent Labourer where this Examinant was born as he believes and where his said Father is legally settled – That his said Father has occasionally received relief therefrom. That about 4 years ago he this Examinant was lawfully married at the Parish Church of Bromley in the said County of Kent to one Sarah Baker who is since dead – That by such marriage he has a Son named George about 3 years old – That about 18 months ago he was lawfully married to a second Wife at the Parish Church of Orpington in the said County of Kent, named Elizabeth (then Elizabeth Woole Singlewoman) who together with his said Son are now in the Workhouse of Cheltenham aforesaid to which Parish he has become chargeable in consequence of a scaleded [*sic*] foot   That he has never done any Act whereby to gain a settlement in his own right. [mark]

1840: *removed to Downe, Kent (father's settlement).* [PS/CH/RA/2/5:195. Removal expenses for "Liddington" to Downe, Kent £8/10/5 (2Q 1840: D4178).]

40036SE: Mon 24 Feb 1840 – **William Hill**, stone-sawyer, wife **Ann**, and three children **Charles**, **Alfred**, and **William**: That he is about 25 years old and that he was born as he believes at the Parish of Minchinhampton in this County where his Father George Hill who is a Labourer has lived for nearly 20 years last past, and where he now lives and is legally settled. That about 6 years ago he this Examinant was lawfully married at the Parish Church of Woodchester in this County to his now Wife Ann (then Ann Lane [= Lynn], Singlewoman) by whom he has 3 Children now living (namely) Charles aged about 10 years Alfred aged about 6 years and a newly born male Infant not yet christened – That he this Examinant hath on various occasions received relief from the Said Parish of Minchinhampton and has ever been acknowledged by that Parish as belonging thereto, never having done any Act whereby to gain a settlement elsewhere – That he is now chargeable to the Parish of Cheltenham aforesaid [mark]
1840: *removed to Minchinhampton (father's settlement);* (RETURNED) *son William baptised at Cheltenham 27 Aug, when the family lived at 15 Chapel St, Cheltenham.* **1841:** *the family lived in Woodchester, though William was away on census night: Ann (25), Alfred (7), William (1) (HO107/362/14/24/12). Their new children over next decade were born at Stroud.* **1851:** *the family lived in Stroud (HO107/1965/214/5).* [PS/CH/RA/2/5:196. Removal expenses for "Hill" to Minchinhampton 18/- and £1/12/- (1Q 1840: D4178).]

40037SE: Thurs 27 Feb 1840 – **Elizabeth Richards**, and daughters **Elizabeth** and **Mary**: That she is about 35 years of age and that she was born as she believes at Ledbury in the County of Hereford where are Father Richard Yarnall [= Yarnold] who was a Brewer always resided and was legally settled   That about seven years ago she was lawfully married at the Parish Church of Cheltenham aforesaid to James Richards a Carpenter by whom she has two Children now living (namely) Elizabeth aged about 6 years and Mary aged about 4 months – That she has heard her said Husband say, and she verily believes, that he was born at Monmouth in the County of Monmouth to which place his Family belonged – That about 3 years ago her said Husband – having deserted her and left her destitute she went to Monmouth and saw his Father. that she remained with him a short time there when she applied for relief and went into the Workhouse of Monmouth where she remained about two years – That during that time a Child of hers by her said Husband died and was buried at the expence of that Parish – That her said Husband to her knowledge never gained a Settlement in his own right. That he has lately deserted her and her said two Children whereby she has actually become chargeable to the Parish of Cheltenham aforesaid. [signed]
1840: *removed to Monmouth, Monm (husband's settlement):* see **42051RO** *for further information.* [PS/CH/RA/2/5:197. Removal expenses for "Richards" to Monmouth, Monm £2/3/4 (1Q 1840: D4178).]

40038SE: 27 Feb 1840 – **Darius Sims**, stone-sawyer, wife **Eliza**, and son **Henry**: That he is about 23 years of age and that he was born as he hath been informed and believes in the Parish of Minch[inh]ampton in this County where his Father – Richard Sims who is a Labourer is now living – That he hath resided there for very many years and as Examinant hath been informed and verily believes is legally settled there having gained such Settlement by hiring and Service with a Mr Bartleet of that place Baker – That about 4 years ago he this Examinant was lawfully married at Minchinhampton aforesaid to Eliza his now wife (then Blackwell) by whom he has a Child named Henry about 3½ years old – That about 2 years ago being unable to work he applied to the Parish officers of Minchinhampton aforesaid for relief and obtained relief therefrom for a short time when he worked at Stone breaking for such Parish and was paid 10^d Per day by the said Officers for about a fortnight. That he has never done any Act whereby to gain a settlement in his own right and that he is now chargeable to the said Parish of Cheltenham [signed]
1840: *removed to Minchinhampton (father's settlement); Eliza Sims was pregnant with son Hephzibah at time of husband's examination; (RETURNED) Hephzibah's birth registered at Cheltenham 3Q (baptised 20*

Sept), when family lived in Burton St. **1841:** *the family lived in Minchinhampton: Darius Sims (aged 22); Eliza (24), Henry (4), Hephzibah (1) (HO107/362/7/25/13).* [PS/CH/RA/2/5:198. Removal expenses for "Sims" to Minchinhampton £1/1/- (2Q 1840: D4178).]

40039SE: Sat 29 Feb 1840 – **Isaac Williams**, labourer, and sons **Francis** and **William**: That he is about 29 years old and that he was born as he believes in the Parish of Minchinhampton in this County – That his Father is legally settled in the Parish of Brimpsfield in the same County from whence he has received Parochial relief and now works for the Parish Officers there – That about 13 years ago he this Examinant was hired as an indoor Servant to M^r. Walter Watkins of Stroud in this County Farmer for the term of a year at the wages of one shilling a week – That he duly served the said Walter Watkins under such hiring in the said Parish of Stroud and received his full years wages namely 52^s/– in addition to which he had his maintenance and Lodgings in his said Masters House since which he has done no act whereby to gain a settlement   That at Christmas 1838 in consequence of sickness he applied to the Parish Officers of Stroud aforesaid for relief and was relieved by them for about a month   That about 8 years ago he was married to his late Wife Elizabeth at Stroud aforesaid by whom he has two Children now living (vizt) Francis aged about 4 years and William aged about 2 years and that he has become chargeable to the said Parish of Cheltenham. [mark]
1840: *removed to Stroud (presumed) (hiring and service).* **1841:** *IW (aged 30; labourer) lived with sons Francis (6) and William (3) in Stroud (HO107/349/12/7/8).* [PS/CH/RA/2/5:199.]

40040SE: 29 Feb 1840 – **Samuel Johnson**, brickmaker, wife **Eliza**, and son **George**: That he is about 24 years of age and that he was born as he believes in the Parish of Kings-Thorpe [= Kingsthorpe] in the County of Northampton where his Father Samuel Johnson as he has heard and verily believes was also born and where he has lived all his life time and is legally settled – That about four years ago last Christmas he this Examinant was lawfully married at the Parish Church of Coventry in the County of Warwick to Eliza his now Wife (then Eliza Russell Singlewoman) by whom he has a Child named George about two years old – That he has never done any Act whereby to gain a Settlement in his own right and that in consequence of severe illness he has become chargeable to the Parish of Cheltenham aforesaid. [mark]
1840: *removed to Kingsthorpe, Northants (presumed) (father's settlement).* **1851:** *SJ (aged 40; brickmaker) lived with wife Eliza (36) in Kingsthorpe, Northants (HO107/1740/358/6).* [PS/CH/RA/2/5:200.]

40041SE: Mon 9 Mar 1840 – Mary Clifford, relating to the settlement of son **Edward Clifford**: That she is about 56 years old and is the wife of James Clifford formerly a Labourer of Calne in the County of Wilts to whom about 22 years ago she was lawfully married in the Church of that Parish – That she hath frequently heard her said Husband say and she therefore verily believes that he was legally settled in the said Parish of Calne – That by such marriage they have amongst other Children the said Edward Clifford their son who will be 21 years of age some time in May next – That when she had been married about 4 years and was living with her said Husband and two Children at the Parish of North Liddiard [= Lydiard Millicent] in the said County of Wilts her said Husband applied to the Overseer of that Parish for relief and having obtained relief therefrom he together with this Examinant and their said two Children were removed therefrom to the said Parish of Calne and were received into the Workhouse there – That about six months afterwards her said Husband Deserted her, in consequence of which she this Examinant and her said two Children went to her Friends at North Liddiard aforesaid since which as she hath been informed and believes her said Husband has been an inmate of Calne Workhouse – That she is not aware that he ever gained a settlement in his own right, nor has her said Son ever done any Act whereby to gain a settlement in his own right and that in consequence of infirmity her said Son has become chargeable to the said Parish of Cheltenham aforesaid. [mark]
1840: *removed to Calne, Wilts (father's settlement).* [PS/CH/RA/2/5:201. Removal expenses for "Clifford" to Calne, Wilts £3/9/6 (2Q 1840: D4178).]

40042SE: Thurs 12 Mar 1840 – **Sarah Humphris**, widow, and son **Job**: That she is the Widow of Job Humphris late of the Parish of Cheltenham Labourer (in which Parish he died about seven months ago) to whom she was lawfully married at the Parish Church of Cheltenham aforesaid on or about the 23^d of August 1837. That he was legally settled at the Parish of Upper Slaughter in this County that being as she believes the place of his birth and he never having done any Act whereby to gain a settlement in his own right – That her said late Husband's Father who now resides at Upper-Slaughter aforesaid is also settled in that Parish and is receiving relief therefrom. That by Examinant's said Marriage she has one Child named Job aged about 6 months, and that she has become chargeable to the Parish of Cheltenham aforesaid. [signed]

1839: *Job Humphris (aged 25; railway labourer) died during railway excavation work, after a tram wheel crushed his leg (Gloucester Journal 24 Aug).* **1840: *removed to Upper Slaughter (husband's settlement).*** **1841:** *son Job (aged 1) lived with maternal grandfather John Pain (also Payne) in Bishop's Cleeve (HO107/354/1/9/12); mother Sarah Humphris died 12 Nov of "apoplexy" at Guiting Power, aged 65.* [PS/CH/RA/2/5:202. Removal expenses to Upper Slaughter 5/4 (1Q 1840: D4178), "Humphris 17/- (1Q 1840: D4178); and for "Humphris" to Guiting 17/- (2Q 1840: D4178).]

40043SE: Sat 14 Mar 1840 – **George Long**, painter, and wife **Elizabeth**: That he is nearly 32 years of age and that he was born as he has been informed and believes at the Parish of Abergavenny in the County of Monmouth where his Father Henry Long who is a Glazier and Painter has resided for the last 40 years and where he still resides and is legally settled   That about 8 years ago he this Examinant was lawfully married at the Parish Church of Llandogo in Monmouthshire aforesaid to Elizabeth his now Wife (then Elizabeth Mumford Singlewoman) but has no Child now living by such Marriage – That he has never done any Act whereby to gain a settlement in his own right and that in consequence of illness he has become and now is chargeable to the Parish of Cheltenham aforesaid [signed]

1840: *removed to Abergavenny, Monm (father's settlement).* **1841:** *GL (aged 30; painter) lived with wife Elizabeth (30; laundress) in Abergavenny, Monm (HO107/742/10/16/24).* [PS/CH/RA/2/5:204. Removal expenses "Long" to Abergavenny £3/14/6 (2Q 1840: D4178).]

40044SE: Thurs 12 Mar 1840 – **Mary Hunt**, widow: That she is about 66 years of age and that she is the Widow of one William Hunt to whom she was married at Winchcomb [= Winchcombe] about 40 years ago and who as she hath understood and verily believes was legally settled in the Parish of Prestbury in the said County he having gained such settlement by hiring and service with a M^r. Welles about 33 years ago who at that time lived at the Hyde Farm in that Parish – That about 30 years ago her said Husband having become chargeable to the Parish of Dumbleton in this County he was examined as to his then place of settlement and removed by Orders of Removal to his said Parish of Prestbury from which Parish he received relief for about twelve months, since which he has never done any Act whereby to gain a settlement, nor has she this Examinant since his decease (which happened at Greet about 2 years ago last Christmas) done any Act by which she has gained a Settlement and that she is now chargeable to the Parish of Cheltenham aforesaid [mark]

1837: *death of William Hunt at Greet, Winchcombe Dec, aged 61.* **1838:** *removed to Prestbury (presumed) (late husband's settlement): see* **38072SE** *(MH: 15 Nov) for further information.* **1840: *removed to Prestbury (husband's settlement).*** **1841:** *(RETURNED) MH (aged 55; "On Poor Book") lived in Cheltenham with son Benjamin (30; labourer),his wife Elizabeth (24) and daughter Sarah A (1) in Grove St (HO107/353/16/35/31).* **1851:** *MH (75; agricultural labourer) was an inmate of Winchcombe Union Workhouse (HO107/1971/111/56).* [PS/CH/RA/2/5:205. Removal expenses for "Hunt" to Prestbury 2/6 (2Q 1840: D4178).]

40045SE: 12 Mar 1840 – **William Midgley**, stableman: That he is about 30 years old and that he was born as he believes in the Parish of Saint Mary in the Borough of Pembroke [= Pembroke St Mary, Pemb] – That about 11 or 12 years ago he was hired as Coachman and Groom to one Charles Callan an Attorney who resided in the said Parish of Saint Mary aforesaid for the term of a year at the wages of 20 Guineas and his Livery   That he duly served his said Master as an indoor servant in the said Parish of Saint Mary aforesaid under such hiring the whole of the year and continued in the same Service under a like hiring the following year at the like wages in the same Parish. That he received his full two years wages. ~~That he is now in the Workhouse of Cheltenham aforesaid to which Parish he is chargeable.~~ That in or about the month of the following April he went as a Weekly Servant in the House, to Mr Stokes in the Parish of Roche [= Roch] in the said County of Pembroke who was a Coroner at the wages of 20^l and after remaining there until the following Michaelmas he was hired as an indoor Servant to that Gentleman for the term of a year at the wages of 20^l. and a suit of Clothes   That he duly served the whole of the year under such hiring in the said Parish of Roche and received his full years wages since which he has done no Act whereby to gain a Settlement and has become chargeable to the Parish of Cheltenham aforesaid. [signed]

1840: *apparently died before removal to Roch, Pemb (hiring and service); (31 May) death of WM, servant, of "consumption" at Cheltenham Workhouse, aged 30.* [PS/CH/RA/2/5:206. Removal expenses for "Midgley" to Roche, Pemb £1/12/- (2Q 1840: D4178).]

40046SE: 12 Mar 1840 – **Henry Barber**, labourer: That he is about 22 years of Age and was born as he believes at Reading in the County of Berks where his Father William Barber who was a Victualler at that time resided – That about 8 years ago he this Examinant was hired as Postillion in the Service of The Right Honourable Lord Hill of Cockrane House in the Parish of Paddington in the County of Middlesex at the wages of 16^l. That he duly served the whole year under such hiring as an indoor servant in the said Parish of Paddington and also the following year therein under a like hiring and received his full two years wages Since which he has not done any Act whereby to gain a settlement and that in consequence of infirmity he has become an inmate in the Parish Workhouse of Cheltenham aforesaid [mark]

1840: *removed to Paddington, Middlesex (hiring and service).* [PS/CH/RA/2/5:207. The London residence of General Rowland Hill, 1st Viscount Hill, was Westbourne House, Paddington. Removal expenses for "Barber" to Paddington, Middlesex £4/7/- (2Q 1840: D4178).]

40047SE: Mon 16 Mar 1840 – **Ann Harrod**, single woman: That she is about 50 years of Age and that she was born as she believes at Hooknorton [= Hook Norton] in the County of Oxford. That about 10 or 11 years ago she was hired for a year as Servant to a Mrs Arnott (who at that time resided at Earlscroome [= Earls Croome] in the County of Worcester) at the wages of 8^l. That she lived in her Service about 5 years when she died in the Parish of Prestbury in this County about Christmas in the year 1834 – in which Parish she served her said Mistress as an indoor Servant the last half year – That she received her full wages, since which she has not done any Act whereby to gain a settlement and that she is now chargeable to the said Parish of Cheltenham. [mark]

1840: *removed to Earls Croome, Worcs (or Prestbury) (presumed) (hiring and service).* [PS/CH/RA/2/5:208; fair copy of struck-out version on p. 203.]

40048SE: Sat 21 Mar 1840 – **William Holder**, labourer, and wife **Charlotte**: That he is about 40 years of age and that he was born as he believes at Aston-upon-Carron [= Aston on Carrant] in the Parish of Ashchurch in this County where his Father Thomas Holder who is a Labourer was as he hath been informed and believes also born and where he is now living and legally settled having gained such settlement by hiring and service there – That when he this Examinant was about 17 years old he was hired as Carter to one William Nind of Aston upon Carron aforesaid Tanner for the term of a year at the wages of 4^l 10^s 0^d or 5^l. – That he duly served his said Master under such hiring the whole of the year in the said Hamlet of Aston-upon-Carron during which he boarded and slept in his said Master's house and received his full year's wages Since which he has not done any Act whereby to gain a settlement – That about 14 years ago he was lawfully married at the Parish Church of Winchcomb [= Winchcombe] in this County to his now Wife (then Charlotte Craddock Singlewoman) but has no Child by such Marriage And that he has become and now is chargeable to the Parish of Cheltenham aforesaid. [mark]

1840: *settlement probably determined to be Ashchurch (presumed) (hiring and service); however, WH seems to have been removed to Gloucester Asylum.* 1841: *Charlotte Holder (aged 40) apparently in Tewkesbury Union Workhouse, without husband (HO107/380/7/38/3).* [PS/CH/RA/2/5:209. See Removal expenses for "Holder" to Gloucester Asylum £1/1/- (2Q 1840: D4178).]

40049SE: Tues 24 Mar 1840 – **John Tanner**, labourer, and wife **Mary**: That he is about 34 years old and that he was born as he believes in the Parish of Randwick in this County – That his Father John Tanner belongs to and is legally settled in that Parish where he resides and from whence he is receiving a weekly allowance as an acknowledged Parishioner – That he this Examinant about 3 years ago last Christmas was lawfully married at the Parish Church of Leonard Stanley to his now Wife (then Mary Lustre [= Lusty] Singlewoman) but has no Child thereby   That he has never done any Act whereby to gain a settlement in his own right and that in consequence of severe illness he has become chargeable to the Parish of Cheltenham aforesaid. [signed]

1840: *removed to Stroud (father's settlement); from 1834 Randwick (father's settlement) was part of Stroud Poor Law Union.* **1841:** *(RETURNED) JT (aged 30; labourer) and wife Mary (30) apparently lived in Victoria St, Fairview, Cheltenham (HO107/353/8/4/3).* **1851:** *the couple lived as gardener (aged 44) and housekeeper (36) at house of John Ovey, Clerk to Poor Law Inspector, 29 Grosvenor Place, Cheltenham (HO107/1973/251/31).* [PS/CH/RA/2/5:210. Pencilled note: "Very ill at N°. 10 King Sᵗ". Removal expenses to Stroud for "Tanner" 17/- (2Q 1840: D4178).]

40050SE: 24 Mar 1840 – **Samuel Cornbill**, porter, wife **Ann**, and three children **Mary Ann**, **John**, and **Lucy**: That he is about 29 years old and that he was born as he believes at Stow on the Wold in the said County and is the Son of Charles Cornbill some time since of that Parish Baker where he was also born and bred and is legally settled – That about 6 years ago he this Examinant was lawfully married at the Parish Church of Cheltenham to Ann his now Wife (then Ann Pike Singlewoman) by whom he has three Children (namely) Mary Ann aged about five years John Robert Rufus about two years and a Female Infant about a fortnight old not yet christened – That he has never done any Act whereby to gain a settlement in his Own right and severe illness has caused him to become chargeable to the said Parish of Cheltenham. [signed]

1840: *removed to Stow-on-the-Wold (father's settlement); Lucy Elizabeth Cornbill baptised at Cheltenham 29 Mar; SC died soon after examination (buried at New Burial Ground, Cheltenham 16 Apr, aged 29).* **1841:** *(RETURNED) death of Lucy (buried 30 Mar at Cheltenham); the family lived in Columbia St, Fairview, Cheltenham: Mary Cornwell [sic] (aged 40; dressmaker), Elizabeth Cornwell (30), Mary Cornwell (5), and (John) Robert (3) (HO107/353/5/56/34).* **1851:** *the family lived in the same street: Ann Cornbill (46; widow, sempstress), Mary A. (16), and Robert (13; scholar) (HO107/1973/143/26).* [PS/CH/RA/2/5:211. Pencilled note: "Very ill in Clarence Sᵗ". Removal expenses to Stow for "Cornbill" 19/6 (2Q 1840: D4178). See **40066SE** (brother Thomas Cornbill: 16 May 1840), **40070SE** (Ann Cornbill: 7 July 1840), **40071SE** (Charles Cornbill: 7 July 1840).]

40051SE: Mon 23 Mar 1840 – **Lucy Shaw**, and two children **Henry** and **Maria**: That she is about 25 years of age and that she is the lawful Wife of the said Samuel Shaw some time since of Gloucester Hairdresser to whom she was married about 8 or 9 years ago at the Parish Church of Saint Aldate there, and by whom she has two Children (namely) Henry aged about 7 years and Maria aged about 6 years. That she hath understood and verily believes that her said Husband is legally settled in the Parish of Saint Mary de Cript [= Crypt] in the City of Gloucester having gained such Settlement there by Apprenticeship with Mʳ Wilkins Hairdresser of that Parish to whom he was bounden by Indenture for seven years   That he duly served four years of such term with his said Master in the said Parish of Saint Mary de Cript aforesaid during which he boarded and slept in his said Master's House when they agreed to part and since which he has never to the knowledge or belief of this Examinant done any Act whereby to gain a settlement – and that she and her said two Children have become chargeable to the Parish of Cheltenham aforesaid [mark]

1839: *son Henry Shaw (aged 7) and daughter Maria (5) admitted to Charlton Kings Workhouse for children (Cheltenham Union) on 2 Nov, "deserted" (G/CH/60/2); place of settlement was presumably determined to be St Aldate, Gloucester (husband's settlement): see* **39062SE** *(LS: 30 Nov) for further information (RETURNED).* **1840:** *removed to St Mary de Crypt, Gloucester (presumed) (husband's settlement).* **1841:** *LS (aged 26) lived with two children Henry (9) and Maria (7) at parents' house in Haresfield, near Stroud (HO107/370/10/8/9); she had perhaps separated from husband:* Gloucestershire Chron. *12 Nov 1836 related that "Samuel Shaw, a hair-dresser" was committed to the Quarter Sessions for larceny (he was acquitted); the same paper reported on 7 July 1838 "Samuel Shaw, 21" was imprisoned by the Gloucester City Sessions for a week for assaulting* *his wife.* [PS/CH/RA/2/5:212. Text struck out indicates that LS's husband left about four years earlier. Removal expenses for "Shaw" to [destination unspecified] 6/- (1Q 1840: D4178).]

40052SE: Sat 28 Mar 1840 – **Mark Lee**: That he is about 60 years of age   That he was born in the parish of Northwick in this County as he hath been informed and believes   That about 30 years ago and before he was married he was hired by Mr Thomas Hewitt a farmer residing at Alveston in this County as a servant in husbandry for a year at the wages of Three pounds ten shillings per year. That he lived with his said master under such hiring for a whole year and received all his wages   That he continued in such service for the further space of two years. That he has never done any other act to gain a settlement and he is become chargeable to the Parish of Cheltenham aforesaid [signed]
1840: *removed to Alveston (hiring and service);* *ML died soon after removal (buried at Olveston, near Alveston 12 July).* [PS/CH/RA/2/5:213. Removal expenses for "Lee" to Olveston £1/9/- (2Q 1840: D4178).]

40053SE: Sat 18 Apr 1840 – **George Cowmeadow**, waiter, wife **Jane**, and four children **Fanny**, **Henry**, **Charles**, and **George**: That he is about 45 Years of Age and that he was born as he believes in the Parish of Linton in the County of Hereford where his Father Thomas Cowmeadow possessed a small Estate which he occupied and farmed and where he was legally settled: That when he this Examinant was about ten or Eleven Years old he went out to Service and lived in various situations as a hired Servant by the Year the last of which was with Miss Wordie of Cambray Street Cheltenham to whom he was hired as an indoor Servant about 18 Years ago and with whom he lived nearly 2 Years: – that since such last mentioned hiring and Service he has been employed in different situations as a Waiter but has not done any act whereby to gain a Settlement: That about 10 Years ago he was lawfully married at the Spa Church Gloucester to Jane his now Wife by whom he has 4 Children namely Fanny aged 9 Years, Henry aged 5 Years, Charles aged 4 Years and an infant not yet baptized aged about a fortnight: That in consequence of illness and want of Employment he this Examinant hath lately become chargeable to the Parish of Cheltenham. – [mark]
1840: *removal unlikely: settlement acknowledged as Cheltenham (hiring and service).* **1841:** *GC (aged 46; servant) lived with wife Jane (33), and children Fanny (110, Henry (8), Charles (6), and new "infant" George (12 mo) in Union St, Cheltenham (HO107/353/5/49/20-1).* **1841:** *death of GC (buried at New Burial Ground, Cheltenham 20 Dec), aged 45.* **1843:** *Jane Cowmeadow (laundress) remarried, to Thomas Lawrence (gardener), in Churchdown 30 May* [PS/CH/RA/2/5:215. Pencilled note: "Chelt^{m}". See **34037SE** (sister Mary Cowmeadow: 27 May 1834).]

40054SE: 18 Apr 1840 – **William Andrews**, fireman and brazier: That he is about 77 years old and that he was born as he believes in the Parish of Boulton [perhaps Bolstone] in the County of Hereford – That he belongs to and is legally settled in the Parish of All Saints in the City of Hereford having gained such Settlement by Apprenticeship with a Mr Callow formerly of that Parish Fireman and Brazier   That about 2 years ago when he this Examinant and his late Wife were residing at Ross he, in consequence of his said Wife's illness applied to the Parish Officers of All Saints aforesaid for relief upon which he was examined as to his place of Settlement at Hereford aforesaid and acknowledged as belonging to the said Parish of All Saints from which Parish he has ever since received and is now receiving relief – That since living with M^r. Callow he has never done any Act whereby to gain a settlement and that he is now chargeable to the Parish of Cheltenham aforesaid. [mark]
1840: *removed to All Saints, Hereford, Heref (apprenticeship).* **1841:** *(RETURNED) WA (aged 75; brazier) lived with daughter Maria (35) and her husband Thomas Jones (50; labourer) in Barnard's Row, Cheltenham (HO107/353/15/56/20).* [PS/CH/RA/2/5:216. Pencilled cross at foot of page perhaps indicates that removal order was not drawn up, but see removal expenses for "Andrews" to Hereford, Heref £2/7/6 (2Q 1840: D4178).]

40055SE: 18 Apr 1840 – **James Morgan**, painter, and wife **Catharine**: That he is about 61 years of age. That about 14 years ago he took and rented a House situate in lower Park Street in the

Town and Parish of Cheltenham of M[r] Merryman then of that place Butcher at the Rent of 12[l] or Gu[ine]as Per Ann[um] – That he occupied such House upwards of twelve months and paid more than 12 months rent for the same, since which he has done no Act whereby to gain a settlement That in or about the year 1815 he was lawfully married at Wotten under Edge [= Wotton-under-Edge] in this County to his now Wife (then Catharine Denham Widow) and that he has become and is now chargeable to the Parish of Cheltenham aforesaid. [signed] James Morgan

1840: *removal unlikely: settlement acknowledged as Cheltenham (renting).* **1841:** *JM (aged 60; painter) lived with wife Catherine (60) in Fairview St, Cheltenham.* [PS/CH/RA/2/5:217. Pencilled note: "Chelt[m]".]

40056SE: 18 Apr 1840 – **Samuel White**, saddle-tree maker: That he is about 61 years old. That when about 16 years old he was apprenticed by Indenture by the then Parish authorities of Stonehouse in this County to one John Harries then of the Parish of <u>Horseley</u> [= Horsley] in the same County Saddle tree Maker for the term of 7 years   That he duly served his said Master as such Apprentice for six years of the said term in the last named Parish during which he boarded and slept in his said Master's House in the same Parish since which he has not done any Act whereby to gain a settlement – That he has a Wife named Elizabeth (formerly Poulson [also Polson]) to whom he was married at Rodboro' in this County about 18 years ago but has not lived with her for some 7 or 8 years last past. – That she has had four Children by him, the youngest of whom is about 11 years old and neither of them are living with this Examinant, who has become chargeable to the Parish of Cheltenham aforesaid. [mark]

1840: *removed to Horsley (perhaps subsequently to Stroud) (apprenticeship).* **1845:** *perhaps the SW who died at Stroud (buried at Horsley 11 July, aged 66).* [PS/CH/RA/2/5:218. Pencilled cross at foot of page perhaps indicates that removal order was not drawn up, but see removal expenses for "White" to Horsley £1/1/6 (2Q 1840: D4178), and subsequently to Stroud 19/- (3Q 1840.]

40057SE: Mon 20 Apr 1840 – **Thomas Matthews**, chaise-driver, wife **Maria**, and two children **William** and **Alfred**: That he is about 70 years of age – That about 20 years ago he took and lived in a House situate in a place in Cheltenham aforesaid called Thornton's Passage by the year of M[r] Thomas Sheldon then of the York Hotel Boarding house at the rent of 24[l]. – That he held and occupied such House as a yearly tenant for about four years during the whole of which period he paid all rent in respect thereof since which he has done no Act whereby to gain a Settlement   that about 13 years ago he was lawfully married at Cheltenham Old Church to Maria his second Wife (then Maria Thomas Singlewoman) by whom he has two Children now living (namely) William aged about five years and Alfred aged about 13 months – That he has become chargeable to the Parish of Cheltenham aforesaid. [mark]

1840: *removal unlikely: settlement probably acknowledged as Cheltenham (renting).* **1841:** *TM (aged 60; servant) lived with wife Maria (39), and children William (6), Alfred (2), and Ann (five mo) in Newman's Place, Cheltenham, (HO107/353/16/10/15).* **1847:** *death of TM (buried at Cheltenham 1 May, aged 76).* [PS/CH/RA/2/5:219. Pencilled note: "Chelt[m]". Removal expenses to (destination omitted) for "Matthews" 3/- (1Q 1840: D4178) (perhaps not TM).]

40058SE: 20 Apr 1840 – **Eliza Williams**, single woman: That she is in the 19th. year of her age and that she was born as she believes in the Parish of Monington-on-Wye [= Monnington-on-Wye] in the County of Hereford and is the illegitimate Daughter of Lucy Williams some time since of that place Singlewoman who hath since married one James Hooper of Minsterworth in this County Labourer – ~~and verily believes that her said Father gained a settlement in the said Parish of Minsterworth by hiring and service previous to such marriage with a Gentleman named Ellis of that Parish~~ – That she this Examinant hath never done any Act whereby to gain a settlement in her own right and that she has become chargeable to the Parish of Cheltenham aforesaid. ~~That she has always been an acknowledged Parishioner of Minsterworth aforesaid   having been taken into the Overseers House (named John Stephens) where she remained about a month when she was placed out by him with one William Sims a Farmer of that Parish with who she lived from Lady day till Michaelmas when she left and hired herself for a year to one M[r] Robinson of Hasfield in this County on which occasion the~~

~~Parish Officers of Minsterworth aforesaid provided her with necessary Clothing to enable her to enter~~
~~such service where she remained about 4 months only~~ [mark]
1840: *removed to Monnington-on-Wye (presumed) (birth).* [PS/CH/RA/2/5:220; a longer, undated version
appeared (struck out) earlier in the magistrates' register, p. 214, apparently in the belief that JH's settlement
was relevant to that of Eliza Williams (significant text added above from earlier version, and then struck
out).]

40059SE: 20 Apr 1840 – **Louisa James**, single woman, regarding her settlement and that of
daughters **Elizabeth** and **Charlotte**: That she is about 34 years of age – That she is the
illegitimate Daughter of Elizabeth James (afterwards Syms [also Sims]) who formerly resided at
the Parish of Saint Nicholas in the City of Gloucester in which Parish this Examinant (as she has
been informed and verily believes) was born – That she has had two illegitimate Children
(namely) Elizabeth aged about 9 years who was born in the Parish of Leckhampton in this
County, and Charlotte aged about 5 years and a half (the said Charlotte having been born in the
month of September 1834) That she has never done any Act whereby to gain a settlement in her
own right and that she and her said Children are now chargeable to the Parish of Cheltenham
aforesaid. [signed]
1834: *removed to St Nicholas, Gloucester (birth): see* **34046SE** *(LJ: 31 July).* **1840:** *(RETURNED) removed
to St Nicholas, Gloucester (presumed) (birth); daughter Elizabeth was apparently removed to
Leckhampton:* Cheltenham Chron. *23 Apr 1840 - Public Office* [...] *A little child was brought into the office,
which had been found upon the step by a door. Its mother, Louisa James, who is deranged, had come from
Gloucester on Thursday, and had left the child, and gone no one knew whither. Orders were given that the
mother should be sought for and the child restored to her.* **1841:** *LJ probably died at St Nicholas, Gloucester
(buried at Gloucester 13 Jan, when age recorded as 26); daughter Charlotte (aged 7) was an inmate of
Gloucester Union Workhouse (HO107/378/2/41/5).* **1842:** *Elizabeth James is probably the person of that
name buried (aged 11) at New Burial Ground, Cheltenham, on 14 Mar.* [PS/CH/RA/2/5:221. Notes: "2
Orders" and "the words written with red Ink in the Exam[inatio]n annexed to ~~Elizabeth's~~ Orders of removal
of Elizabeth, to Leckhampton". Removal expenses to Leckhampton for "James" 2/6 (2Q 1840: D4178).]

40060SE: 20 Apr 1840 – **Samuel Wise**, tailor, and wife **Margaret**: That he is about 62 years old
– That at or about Christmas 1831 he took and hired a House situate in the Parish of Hanwell in
the County of Middlesex of a Mr John Rotton at the rent of £12 year – That he held and occupied
such House for two successive years and upwards at that rent which together with Parochial taxes
he duly paid since which he has not done any Act whereby to gain a settlement – That he and his
Wife Margaret (formerly Margaret Troughton [also Troutton]) to whom he was married at
Stepney about 35 years ago, are now chargeable to the Parish of Cheltenham aforesaid. [mark]
1840: *removed to Hanwell, Middlesex (renting).* **1841:** *(RETURNED) SW (aged 60; tailor) lived with wife
Margaret (60) in Sherborne St, Cheltenham (HO107/353/6/9/12).* **1847:** *death of SW (buried 9 Apr at New
Burial Ground, Cheltenham, aged 69).* **1851:** *widow Margaret (73; pauper, formerly servant, born
Winchcombe) lodged in Sherborne St, Cheltenham (HO107/1973/151/41).* [PS/CH/RA/2/5:222. Removal
expenses for "Wise" to Hanwell, Middlesex £3/3/- (2Q 1840: D4178).]

40061SE: 20 Apr 1840 – **John Clarke**, flyman: That he is about 22 years of age, and that he was
born as he believes in the Parish of Saint Philip and Jacob [Bristol] in this County and that he is
the Son of James Clarke of the Parish of Saint Peter's in the City of Hereford Shoemaker who has
resided there for many years last past and in which he is legally settled – having as he this
Examinant hath been informed and verily believes gained such settlement by Apprenticeship with
one Zacharia Wilcox of that place Shoemaker – That for several years he has (as this Examinant
has been informed and verily believes) been an acknowledged Parishioner of Saint Peter's
aforesaid from whence he has occasionally received relief – That he this Examinant has never
done any Act whereby to gain a settlement in his own right and that he is now chargeable to the
Parish of Cheltenham aforesaid – [mark]
1840: *removed to St Peter's, Hereford, Heref (father's settlement).* [PS/CH/RA/2/5:223. Pencilled cross at
foot of page perhaps indicates that removal order was not immediately drawn up. Removal expenses for

"Clarke" to Hereford, Heref £1/16/6 (2Q 1840: D4178); see also "Clarke" to "Church Agburn" £2/17/- (2Q 1840) and "Clark" to Hereford £2/16/- (4Q 1840: D4178).]

40062SE: [undated – Apr 1840] – **Thomas Brown**, cabinet-maker, wife **Ann**, and four children **William**, **Henry**, **James**, and **Eliza**: That he is about 40 years of age, and that he was born as he believes in the Parish of Newcastle upon Tyne in Northumberland – That when he was about 13 years old he was bounden as an indoor apprentice by Indenture to one Benjamin Harmer then of Cleeveland Street in the Parish of Mary Le Bone in the County of Middlesex for the term of seven years – That after serving about four years of such term with his said Master he was assigned by him to one John Wellsman of Warder Street [= Wardour St] Soho in the Parish of Saint Anne's in the said County of Middlesex with whom he served the remainder of his time as an <u>outdoor</u> apprentice – That after such Assignment as aforesaid he lodged in the House of Mr Lovegrove in Wells Street in the said Parish of Mary Le Bone for about twelve months when he went to lodge in Saint Anne's Court in the Parish of Saint Anne's aforesaid and lodged there for some six or seven months when he went to lodge a[n]d sleep in Edmund Street Battle Bridge in the Parish of <u>Saint Pancras in the Fields</u> where he continued to lodge for the remainder of the term of his Apprenticeship of seven years as aforesaid when his Master delivered to him his said Indentures since which he has not done any Act whereby to gain a legal settlement – That about five years ago he was lawfully married at Aston Church Birmingham to Ann his now Wife (then Ann Young Singlewoman) by whom he has four Children (namely) William aged about 7 Years Henry about 5; James about 2½ and Eliza aged about 4 months – That he has become chargeable to the Parish of Cheltenham aforesaid.
*1840: **removal uncertain: examination form incomplete.** 1841: TB (aged 41; cabinet-maker) lived with wife Ann (30), and children William (8), Henry (6), James (3), and Eliza (1) in Sidney St, Cheltenham (HO107/353/3/17/28).* [PS/CH/RA/2/5:224.]

40063SE: Fri 24 Apr 1840 – **Stephen Arundell**, labourer, wife **Elizabeth**, and son **Daniel**: That he is about 73 years old and that he was born as he believes in the Parish of Bisley in this County to which Parish his Father Daniel Arundell belonged. That when he this Examinant was about 21 years old he went out as a Servant in Husbandry and lived in various situations. That about 50 years ago (and previous to his first marriage) he was hired by Mr John Jones then of Brockworth in this County Farmer for the term of a year as Cowman, at the wages of 4^l. That he duly served the whole of such year under the said hiring in the said Parish of Brockworth during which he boarded and slept in his said Master's house and received his full years wages – That about 25 years ago he was lawfully married at Painswick in this County to Elizabeth his present Wife (then Elizabeth Browning Widow) by whom he has had three Children two of whom are now living, one married and settled, and the other named Daniel, who is between 12 and 13 years of age, is living with this Examinant   That on many occasions previous to the year 1830 he this Examinant received outdoor relief from the said Parish of Brockworth. That since such hiring and service as aforesaid he has not done any Act whereby to gain a settlement and that he is now chargeable to the Parish of Cheltenham aforesaid. [signed]
*1840: **settlement determined as Brockworth (hiring and service); husband and wife died before removal, dependent children were presumably removed**; SA died soon after examination (buried at New Burial Ground, Cheltenham on 14 May, aged 73); wife Elizabeth died within a month (buried at Cheltenham on 13 June, aged 63).* [PS/CH/RA/2/5:225. Removal expenses for "Arundel" to Brockworth 12/- (2Q 1840: D4178).]

40064SE: [undated – Apr 1840] – **Elizabeth Hooper**, widow, and children **Henry** and **William**: That she is the Widow of Richard Hooper some time since of Cheltenham aforesaid Labourer where as she hath been informed and verily believes he was born and bred and where he died seven years ago last month never having done any Act whereby to gain a Settlement   That a short time previous to his death he received outdoor relief from this Parish – That about 19 years ago they were married at Hempsted near Gloucester – That about 8 months after his death as aforesaid she had a Child since named Henry, and about 3 years afterwards she had another Child named William both of which Children were born in this Parish and are now living – That in consequence of severe illness she has become chargeable to the Parish of Cheltenham aforesaid.

1840: *examination form incomplete and removal unlikely: settlement probably acknowledged as Cheltenham.* [PS/CH/RA/2/5:226.]

40065SE: Thurs 30 Apr 1840 – **Jane Ellis** (also **Stephens**), single woman: That she is upwards of 18 years of Age and that she was born as she believes in the Parish of Chertsey in the County of Surr[e]y and is the illegitimate Daughter of Harriet Ellis by one Williams Stephens whom she (the said Harriet Ellis) has since married – That in or about the month of May last she left the Workhouse at Newtown which forms part of the Union wherein Chertsey is situate, after having been an inmate there for about ten months – That she has never done any Act whereby to gain a settlement in her own right, and that she has become and is now an inmate of the Workhouse of Cheltenham aforesaid. [mark]

1840: *removed to Chertsey (birth).* [PS/CH/RA/2/5:227. Removal expenses for "Ellis" to Chertsey £5/15/6 (2Q 1840: D4178).]

40066SE: Sat 16 May 1840 – **Thomas Cornbill**, baker, wife **Sarah**, and two children **William** and **Charles**: That he is the Son of Charles Cornbill some time since of the Parish of Stow-on-the-Wold in the said County Baker, where he this Examinant was born as he believes about 36 years ago and with whom he was brought up to his Trade – That when he was about 17 years old he was hired as an indoor Servant for the term of year to Mr Rouse then a Baker of the Parish of Chipping-Norton in the County of Oxford at the wages of 6^l – That he served his said Master under such hiring the whole of the year in the said Parish of Chipping-Norton and received his full year's wages – That on or about 13th March 1827 he was lawfully married at Saint Luke's Church, Chelsea, to Sarah his now Wife (then Sarah Atkins Singlewoman) by whom he has had four Children two of whom are now living (namely) William aged about 9, and Charles aged about 6 years – That since such hiring and Service as aforesaid he has not done any Act whereby to gain a settlement and that in consequence of severe illness he has become chargeable to the Parish of Cheltenham aforesaid. [signed W [*sic*] Cornbill]

1840: *settlement determined as Chipping Norton (hiring and service); TC's dependent family removed there; TC died shortly after examination (buried at Cheltenham 2 July, aged 36).* **1848:** *wife Sarah remarried, in Lambeth, to James Partington (soldier) 28 May (son Charles went to sea).* **1854:** *William Cornbill married Louisa Baker in 3Q at St George Hanover Square.* **1857:** *Charles married Sarah Jane King at St Luke's Church Chelsea 13 Sept (he entered Fulham Road Workhouse in 1880s).* [PS/CH/RA/2/5:228. Pencilled note: "[illegible] G. E. Williams 1st case" (George Edmunds Williams was Clerk to the Cheltenham Magistrates). Removal expenses to Chipping Norton for "Cornbill" £1/11/6 (2Q 1840: D4178). See **40050SE** (Samuel Cornbill: 24 Mar 1840).]

40067SE: Tues 19 May 1840 – **Ann Baylis**, widow: I was born as I have heard and believe at the Parish of Bishop's Cleeve in this County - about 30 years ago I was married to my late Husband John Baylis at the Parish Church of Bishop's Cleeve – I continued with my Husband to live at Cleeve for about nine or 10 years after we were married – We then came to Cheltenham, where we lived until the death of my Husband which happened between three and four years' [*sic*] ago – We never rented a House of the annual value of Ten Pounds in Cheltenham – I have lived in Cheltenham since the death of my Husband but have done no Act to gain a settlement there – During the time my Husband was alive, I was relieved by the Parish Officers of Bishop's Cleeve whilst we were living in Cheltenham – My Husband's Settlement was in that Parish as I have heard and believe – I am now chargeable to the Parish of Cheltenham. [mark]

1840: *removed to Bishop's Cleeve (husband's settlement).* [PS/CH/RA/2/5:229. Removal expenses for "Baylis" to Bishop's Cleeve 7/3 (2Q 1840: D4178).]

40068SE: Mon 29 June 1840 – **Charlotte Dunn**, single woman: That she is about 23 years of age – That about eight or nine years ago she gained a Settlement in the Hamlet of Baulking in the Parish of Uffington in the County of Berks by hiring and service with a Mr George of that place Farmer –

soon after which she was examined at Farringdon [= Faringdon] in the said County of Berks as to her Settlement and an Order was thereupon made for her removal to the Parish of Baulking aforesaid which Order was appealed against at Abbingdon [= Abingdon] in the same County and fully confirmed Since which she has done no Act whereby to gain a Settlement and that she is now chargeable to the Parish of Cheltenham aforesaid [mark]
1840: *removed to Baulking, Berks (hiring and service).* [PS/CH/RA/2/5:230. Removal expenses for "Dunn" to Baulking, Berks £2/9/- (3Q 1840: D4178).]

40069SE: [undated] – **Sarah Coleman**, widow: That she is about 65 years of age, and […]
1840: *removal uncertain: examination form incomplete.* **1841:** *probably the SC (aged 70) who lived in Sherborne Place, Cheltenham (HO107/353/5/9/12).* [PS/CH/RA/2/5:231.]

40070SE: Tues 7 July 1840 – **Ann Cornbill**, widow, and three children **Mary Ann, Robert**, and **Lucy**: That six year's [*sic*] ago the third of March last she was married to her late husband Samuel Cornbill in Cheltenham Old Church. that she has had by him three Children who are now living Viz^t. Mary Ann aged five years Robert aged two years and Lucy aged four months, that her said husband has not since her said Marriage rented a Tenement of the annual value of Ten pounds nor ever done any act to her knowledge to gain a settlement in his own right. That she is now chargeable to the Parish of Cheltenham [signed]
1840: *removed to Painswick (presumed) (husband's settlement):* *see* **40071SE** *for further information on the family.* [PS/CH/RA/2/5:232.]

40071SE: 7 July 1840 – Charles Cornbill, regarding the settlement of late son, **Samuel Cornbill**: That he was born in the parish of Stow on the Wold in the said County where his parents were legally settled as he has been informed and believes. That about sixteen years ago he went with his family including his said Son (who was then about thirteen years of age) to the Parish of Painswick in the said County and there rented a house of William Welch at £15 year   that he lived with his family in such house four years and paid three years rent or more. that he afterwards rented a house in the same Parish of Painswick of Miss Knight at £16 a year exclusive of the Taxes, that he paid her a years rent or more   That his said Son remained with him until he was married - that his said Son never lived in any service for a year or [has] done any Act to gain a settlement in his own right to this Examinants knowledge and belief [signed]
1840: *removed to Painswick (father's settlement).* [PS/CH/RA/2/5:232. Removal expenses for "Cornbill" to Painswick 15/- (3Q 1840: D4178). See **40050SE** (Samuel Cornbill: 24 Mar 1840).]

40072SE: Thurs 9 July 1840 – **Elizabeth Jelf** (also **Jelfs**), widow, and three children **John, Elizabeth**, and **Mary Ann**: That she was born as she has heard and believes at the Parish of Rodley in this County where her Parents were legally settled – That she lived with her parents until the age of Seventeen – That she then went to Service to Mr Henry Butt of the Hamlet of Hucclecote in the parish of Churchdown in this County – That she was hired to serve him for a twelvemonth at the wages of 50^s/– That she lived in such service the twelvemonth and received the whole of her wages – That she was married about ten years ago at the Parish Church of St John in the City of Gloucester to her late husband Joseph Jelf – that he died on the third of last May – That she has three children by her said husband namely John aged 10 years Elizabeth aged seven years and Mary Ann aged three years   That during the time of her living with him he never Rented a Tenement of the yearly value of Ten Pounds or did any act to her knowledge to gain a Settlement – that she is now chargeable to the Parish of Cheltenham. [mark]
1840: *removed to Hucclecote (hiring and service).* **1841:** *(RETURNED) EJ (aged 30; charwoman) lived with children John (14; errand boy), Elizabeth (8), Mary (4), and new baby Joseph (8 mo) in Burton St, Cheltenham (HO107/353/16/23/7).* [PS/CH/RA/2/5:233. Removal expenses for "Jelf" to Hucclecote 14/- (4Q 1840: D4178).]

40073SE: Fri 10 July 1840 – **John Knight**: That he was born in the parish of Saul in the said County as he has been informed and believes. That about three years ago he took a house of

Matthew Lane at the corner of Commercial Street in Cheltenham for a year at the yearly rent of twelve pounds and to pay the Taxes   that he lived in such house one year and three quarters and paid all the rent. that he was assessed to the Poor Rates and duly paid the same and all other rates which were demanded of him.. that he has been in Lodgings ever since.. that he has been chargeable to the Parish of Cheltenham the three last quarters of a year [mark]

1840: *removal unlikely: settlement probably acknowledged as Cheltenham (renting); perhaps the JK (aged 61) who was, according to the following day's* Gloucester Journal, *sentenced at Gloucester Sessions to six months' imprisonment with hard labour for stealing a wheelbarrow in Cheltenham; he had previously been in trouble with the authorities on several occasions, and in Jan 1841 was convicted again, and sentenced to seven years' imprisonment.* [PS/CH/RA/2/5:234.]

40074SE: Sat 11 July 1840 – Henry Bailey, bricklayer, of Cheltenham, relating to wife **Mary Bailey** (also **Bayly**), "lunatic": That at Christmas in the year 1837 he rented a Tenement in Little Norwood Street in the Parish of Leckhampton in the said County for one year at the rent of Ten Pounds – That he continued to live in that Tenement until the month of July 1839 – That he paid the whole of the rent for that period – That he was assessed to the Poor Rates for the Parish of Leckhampton in respect of the same Tenement for the time he lived there and paid all the rates that were demanded of him – That after he left Leckhampton Parish he took Lodgings at Cheltenham and has not since done any Act whereby to gain a Settlement – That in the year 1834 he was married to his present wife Mary at the Old Church Cheltenham – That his said wife is a Lunatic and he is unable to maintain her – [mark]

1834: *Henry Bailey married Mary Gibbens 18 May: see* **32039SE** *(her father Thomas Gibbins: 14 June 1832), where her father states that she is ill, and* **34025SE**). **1840:** *removed to Lunatic Asylum in Gloucester (husband's settlement); Leckhampton was probably deemed her parish.* **1841:** *Henry Bailey (aged 25; bricklayer) lived in Little Norwood St, Leckhampton (HO107/353/18/33/3); wife Mary (32; formerly servant) was an inmate of Glos Lunatic Asylum in Kingsholme, Gloucester (HO107/356/9/49/2).* [PS/CH/RA/2/5:235. Removal expenses for "Bailey" to Gloucester £1/1/- (1Q 1841: D4178).]

40075SE: 11 July 1840 – **Henry Moss**, and children **Mary Ann**, **Caroline**, and **Elizabeth**: That he was born at Painswick in the said County as he has heard and believes – that he is now About forty years of age – That about twenty five years ago he was bound apprentice by Indenture to Mr George Ireland of Painswick aforesaid Weaver – That he served such Apprenticeship for three years and one month in the said Parish of Painswick – That he was then assigned by Deed to M^r. Thomas Cook of Painswick aforesaid Weaver for the remainder of the said term of Seven Years – That he served the Remainder of the full term as such apprentice with the said Thomas Cook in the said Parish – that he slept at the house of the said Thomas Cook in Painswick during his service with him – That about sixteen years ago he was married to his late wife Sarah at the parish Church of Minchinhampton in this County by whom he has three children namely Mary Ann aged 14 years Caroline aged 8 years and Elizabeth aged 5 years –

That he has never done any other act to gain a Settlement and That he is now chargeable and his Children to the Parish of Cheltenham [mark]

1840: *death of wife Sarah Moss in childbirth (buried 18 Apr 1840 at Cheltenham, aged 40); daughter Sarah survived only one week (the family then lived at 13 Commercial St, Cheltenham, having lived in 1837 in Norwood Terrace); removed to Painswick (apprenticeship); daughter Elizabeth died at time of father's examination (buried at Cheltenham 17 July, aged 5).* **1841:** *daughter Mary Ann Moss (aged 15) probably lived in Sun St, Cheltenham and worked as servant (HO107/353/9/39/26).* **1849:** *HM made deposition at daughter Caroline's settlement examination at Cheltenham:* **49051RO** *(HM: 10 Oct).* **1851:** *HM (48; agricultural labourer, born Painswick) lived with Elizabeth (48; agricultural labourer, also born Painswick) at Painswick (HO107/1964/216/14).* [PS/CH/RA/2/5:236. Removal expenses for "Moss" to Painswick 15/6 (3Q 1840: D4178).]

40076SE: Mon 13 July 1840 – **Elizabeth Lewis**, single woman: That she was born in the parish of Highworth in the County of Wilts as she has been informed and believes. that her mother Sarah Ann Sparrow late Lewis belonged to Highworth aforesaid as she has heard and believes.

that she has also heard that she is an illegitimate Child of her said Mother – that about Six years ago she was in the Workhouse at Highworth for nine days from whence her Mother fetched her that she has done no Act to gain a settlement in her own right. that she is now chargeable to the Parish of Cheltenham [mark]
1840: *removed to Highworth, Wilts (mother's settlement).* [PS/CH/RA/2/5:237. Removal expenses for "Lewis" to Highworth £2/18/6 (3Q 1840: D4178).]

40077SE: [undated] Aug 1840 – **Timothy Riorden**, blacksmith: That he was born in the City of Cork in the Kingdom of Ireland and served his apprenticeship in the said City   that about Eleven years ago he rented a house situate and being Nº 10 Cornwall buildings in the Parish of Walcot in the City of Bath at twenty six pounds a year including Taxes. that he continued in such house about three years and paid the whole of the rent – That five years ago he rented a house [incomplete]
1840: *removal uncertain: examination form incomplete.* [PS/CH/RA/2/5:238.]

40078SE: [undated] Aug 1840 – **John Smith Amplett** (also **Amphlet, Hamplet, Hamplett**): That he was born in the Parish of Twy[n]ing in the said County where his parents were legally settled as he has been informed and believes   that about seventeen years ago he rented a house in the parish of Cheltenham and five acres of Ground at thirteen pounds a year - that he continued in such house about thirteen years and paid his rent   that he paid his poor rates to the said Parish of Cheltenham   that he then went into Lodgings at Staverton at one shilling and six pence a week and continued there until he came to Cheltenham Workhouse [mark]
1840: *not removed: settlement acknowledged as Cheltenham (renting).* **1841:** *JSA (aged 74) was an inmate of Cheltenham Workhouse (HO107/353/17/1).* **1844:** *death of JSA in Cheltenham 1Q.* [PS/CH/RA/2/5:239. Pencilled note: "Cheltm".]

40079SE: Mon 3 Aug 1840 – **Sarah Hawkins**, single woman, and son **William**: That she was born as she has heard and believes At the Parish of Pilton near Shepton Mallett [= Shepton Mallet] in Somersetshire Where her parents were legally settled – That with the exception of being out at service for six months she continued to live with her parents until Christmas 1834 – That since That time she has been living at different places but never did any act whereby to gain a Settlement – That on Friday the 24ᵗʰ. July last she was delivered ~~at the workhouse~~ of a male child – That herself and child are now chargeable to the parish of Cheltenham – [signed]
1840: *removed to Pilton, Som (father's settlement).* **1841:** *SH (aged 21) lived with newborn baby (name "n[ot] k[nown]; 10 mo) with her father James Hawkins, in Pilton, Som (HO107/963/9/15/2); baptism of baby William Hawkins at Pilton 20 June.* [PS/CH/RA/2/5:241 (previous page blank). Removal expenses for "Hawkins" to Pilton, Som £2/14/- (3Q 1840: D4178).]

40080SE: Thurs 13 Aug 1840 – **Rachael** (also **Rachel**) **Collet** (also **Collett**), single woman: That she was born in the Parish of Burwascot [= Buscot] in the County of Berks where her father and Mother were settled as She has heard and believes, that She has done no Act to gain a settlement in her own right. That she is now chargeable to the Parish of Cheltenham [signed]
1840: *removed to Buscot, Berks (father's settlement).* **1841:** *RC (aged 20) lived with parents in Buscot, Berks (HO107/27/5/4/2).* [PS/CH/RA/2/5:242. Removal expenses for "Collett" to Buscott, Berks £1/9/- (3Q 1840: D4178).]

40081SE: Fri 14 Aug 1840 – **David Thomas**, wife **Sarah**, and two children **Henry** and **Mary**: That on the 22ᵈ. day of March 1839 he rented a house 21 Tewkesbury Road in the Parish of Cheltenham at the rent of Eleven pounds fourteen shillings a year – that he lived in that house the year and four months – That he paid ten months rent and left goods in his Landlord's hands for more than the amount due to him for rent – That he was rated in respect of this house and paid all the rates – That he has a wife named Sarah Thomas and two Children named Henry Thomas aged 6 years and Mary Thomas aged 15 months – That he his wife and family are now chargeable to the Parish of Cheltenham. [signed]
1840: *see following examination:* **40082SE** *(DT: 18 Aug 1840).* [PS/CH/RA/2/5:243.]

40082SE: Tues 18 Aug 1840 – **David Thomas**, wife **Sarah**, and two children **Henry** and **Mary**: That he was born in the Town of Carmarthen as he has heard and believes   That when he was about Eighteen or Nineteen years of age he was hired by David Tennant Esquire of Pantyquad [= Pant-y-gwydir] in the parish of Swansea in the County of Glamorgan for a year at the yearly wages of Twenty Guineas   that he served the whole year and nearly another year and received the whole of his wages   That he has done no act since either by servitude or otherwise to gain a settlement elsewhere –

That he was married to his present Wife Sarah about Seven Years ago at the Parish of St Mary's Tenby in the County of Pembroke and by whom he has two Children namely Henry of the age of six years and Mary of the age of fifteen months [signed]

1840: *(3 Oct) DT died at 29 St Paul's St North, aged 32 of a "decline", before removal; family removed to Swansea, Glam (hiring and service).* **1841** *(RETURNED) widow Sarah Thomas née Birt (aged 25; dressmaker) lived with daughter Mary (2) in Sun St, Cheltenham.* **1851:** *Sarah (37; widow, dressmaker) lived with mother Sarah Birt (81; annuitant) at 17 Queen's Retreat, Cheltenham (HO107/1973/967/14).* [PS/CH/RA/2/5:244. Removal expenses for "Thomas" to Swansea, Glam £5/16/- (3Q 1840, and £8/14/- (4Q 1840: D4178). See **40081SE** (DT: 14 Aug 1840), written out in a different hand.]

40083SE: [undated] Aug 1840 – **Mary [Ann] Miller**, widow: [no text].
1840: *removal unlikely: examination form incomplete: see* **43016RO** *(MAM: 4 Mar 1843).* [PS/CH/RA/2/5:245.]

40084SE: Thurs 20 Aug 1840 – **Joseph Sadler**, baker, wife **Hannah**, and two children **Esther** and **Joseph**: That he was born at Pagan Hill [= Paganhill] in the Parish of Stroud in the said County where his parents were legally settled as he has heard and believes. ~~That he has heard that his father gained a Settlement there by renting a house at more than £10 a year~~ – that his father still lives at Pagan Hill aforesaid – That about six years ago he was married to his present Wife Hannah (then Roberts) at the Parish of Kingstanley [= King's Stanley] by whom he has two Children namely Esther of the age of Three Years and Joseph of the age of Eighteen Months

That he has never done any act to gain a settlement in his own right. That he is now chargeable to the Parish of Cheltenham [signed]

1840: *removed to Stroud (father's settlement).* **1841:** *(RETURNED) death of JS (buried at New Burial Ground, Cheltenham 25 Jan, aged 28); his family lived in Cheltenham in Beaufort Buildings: Susannah (for "Hannah"[?], aged 30; laundress), Esther (3), and Joseph (2).* [PS/CH/RA/2/5:246. Removal expenses for "Sadler" to Stroud 13/- (3Q 1840) and £1/3/- (4Q 1840: D4178).]

40085SE: Sat 29 Aug 1840 – **Sarah Hurfurt**, wife of George Hurfurt, and four children **Elizabeth**, **William**, **James**, and **Emily**: That about Eight years ago she was married to her present husband at Cheltenham aforesaid. that she knew the Father and Mother of her said husband who resided at Weston [in Bath] in the County of Somerset. that she has heard and believes that the Father of her said husband gained a Settlement in the said Parish of Weston by rent of a House there of the annual value of thirteen Guineas for two or three years. that last Winter twelvemonth she and her said husband and three of their Children were living at Weston aforesaid and were relieved by the Parish officers there for three weeks. that her said husband deserted her about seventeen weeks ago, that she has had by her said husband four Children, to wit, Elizabeth of the age of seven years William of the age of five years James of the age of three years and Emily of the age of four months – that she and her said Children are now chargeable to the Parish of Cheltenham

That since her said Marriage her said husband has not rented a Tenement of the annual [value] of Ten pounds or done any act to gain a settlement in his own right. that she has heard her said husband say he never lived in any service by the year or done any act to gain a settlement in his own right previous to their Marriage [mark]

1840: *removed to Weston, Som (husband's settlement).* **1841:** *the couple, reunited, lived in Weston, Som: George (aged 30; gardener; Sarah (25), Elizabeth (8), William (6), James (4), Emily (1)*

(HO107/931/23/31/13), where they continued to live and have further children. [PS/CH/RA/2/5:247. Removal expenses for "Harfurt" [*sic*] to Weston, Som £3/13/- (4Q 1840: D4178).]

40086SE: Fri 18 Sept 1840 – **Mary Ann Wadley**, single woman, and children **Henry** and **John**: That she was born at the Parish of Kemmerton [= Kemerton] in the said County where her parents were legally settled as she has been informed and believes. That in the year 1830 she was hired by Mrs Gist of the Parish of Dixon [= Dixton; until 1831 Alderton with Dixton] by the year a months wages or a months warning that she lived at Dixon aforesaid for A little more than a Year And then went with the family to the Grange in the Parish of Didbrook in the said County where she continued until and after the year 1834 under the same hiring and left there in the Year 1836 –

That she has done no Act since to gain a Settlement elsewhere – That she has been lately delivered of a male bastard Child and she is with such Child and another of the name of Henry aged Six years chargeable to the Parish of Cheltenham [signed]
1840: *MAW apparently remained in Cheltenham until her subsequent examination: see* **40109SE** *(MAW: 12 Dec) for further information.* [PS/CH/RA/2/5:248.]

40087SE: Sat 12 Sept 1840 – **Eliza Hooper**, single woman: That she was born in the Parish of Tibberton in the said County as she has heard and believes. that she has heard and believes [that] her Parents were legally settled in the Parish of Minsterworth in the said County – That her Mother died about Eight years ago in the said Parish of Tibberton and was buried at the Expence of the Parish officers of Minsterworth. that her Father was very ill about four years ago and was relieved by the Parish officers of Minsterworth aforesaid whilst he was living in the said Parish of Tibberton That about four years ago she was relieved by the Parish officers of Minsterworth for about six months That she has never done any Act to gain a Settlement in her own right – That she is now chargeable to the Parish of Cheltenham [mark]
1840: *removed to Minsterworth (father's settlement).* [PS/CH/RA/2/5:249. Removal expenses for "Hooper" to Minsterworth 13/6 (4Q 1840: D4178).]

40088SE: [undated] Sept 1840 – **James Pearce**: That he was born in the Parish of Stroud in the said County but his parents were legally settled in the Parish of Randwick in the said County as he has been informed and believes That about twenty seven years ago he was hired by Mr Cooke of N° 1 Portland Place Cheltenham for a Year. That he served the whole year and received his years wages

That he has never done any act to gain a settlement elsewhere [incomplete]
1840: *examination incomplete and removal unlikely: settlement probably acknowledged as Cheltenham.* [PS/CH/RA/2/5:250.]

40089SE: [undated] 1840 – **John Parrott**: That he was born in the Parish of Cheltenham in the said County where his parents were legally settled as he has been informed and believes – that he has never been hired by the year or rented a Tenement of the annual value of ten pounds not done any act to gain a settlement in his own right. That he is now chargeable to the said Parish of Cheltenham
1840: *examination incomplete and removal unlikely: settlement probably acknowledged as Cheltenham.* [PS/CH/RA/2/5:251.]

40090SE: Thurs 10 Sept 1840 – **Sarah Dutton**, widow, with two children **Joseph** and **Mary**: That about twenty two Years ago she was married to her late husband John Dutton in the parish Church of Bisley in the said County, that her said husband was born in the said Parish of Bisley where his parents were legally settled as she has been informed and believes

That her said husband lived in his own house in the said Parish of Bisley for about twenty years and sold the said house for seventy pounds – that her said husband nor has she since his death done any act to gain a settlement in any other Parish than Bisley – that about a Year and a half ago she received relief from the Parish officers of Bisley whilst living in Cheltenham – That

she has two Children by her said husband namely Joseph of the age of nine years and Mary aged about seven years who with herself are now chargeable to the Parish of Cheltenham [mark]
1836: *death of husband John, butcher (buried at Bisley 24 Nov, aged 48).* **1840:** *removed to Bisley (husband's settlement).* **1841:** *(RETURNED) SD (aged 50) lived in Sandford St, Cheltenham, with two independent children Henry (25; butcher) and Ann (20; servant), and with Joseph (10) and Mary (10) (HO107/353/13/13/19).* [PS/CH/RA/2/5:251. Removal expenses for "Dutton" to Bisley 18/- (4Q 1840: D4178).]

40091SE: Fri 11 Sept 1840 – **Peter Pinching**, wife **Sarah**, and three children **Emma**, **Walter**, and **Eliza**: That he was born at Eyford in the County of Gloucester where his parents were legally settled as he has been informed and believes   That when he was about Eighteen years of age he was apprenticed by Indenture to William Newman of Great Rissington in the said County Cordwainer for five years. that he served the whole of his time at Great Rissington aforesaid. That he has done no Act since to gain a settlement elsewhere

That he was married to his present Wife Sarah at St Marys Church Cheltenham by whom he has three Children to wit Emma aged nine Years Walter aged Seven Years and a half and Eliza of the Age of three months. That he is now Chargeable to the Parish of Cheltenham [mark]
1840: *removed to Gt Rissington (apprenticeship).* **1841:** *PP (aged 30; agricultural labourer) lived in Gt Rissington with wife Sarah (35) and children Emma (9), Walter (8), Eliza (11 mo) (HO107/366/6/4/7). The family later moved to Stratford upon Avon, Warks where their next three children were born in mid 1840s.* **1851:** *the family lived in West Bromwich, Staffs: PP (44; shoemaker), Sarah (46), Walter (18; glass-cutter), Eliza (10; scholar), Thomas (8; scholar), Joseph (5; scholar), and John (3) (HO107/2025/108/11).* [PS/CH/RA/2/5:252. Removal expenses for "Pinchin" to Gt Rissington £1/-/6 (3Q 1840, and £1/4/- (4Q 1840: D4178).]

40092SE: [undated] Sept 1840 – **Stephen Keeler**, with (or relating to the settlement of) wife **Matilda**: That he was born in the Parish of North Tudenham [= North Tuddenham] in the County of Norfolk where his parents were legally settled as he has been informed and believes   that when he was Eleven years of age he was hired to Richard Paul of North Tudenham aforesaid for a year that he served the whole year and received his years wages. That he has done no Act to gain a settlement elsewhere   that about seven years ago he was relieved by the Parish officers of North Tudenham aforesaid. That about four Years ago he was married to his Wife Matilda at Hastings in the County of Sussex. That his Wife is now chargeable to the Parish of Cheltenham [signed]
1840: *settlement likely to have been determined as Gt Tuddenham (hiring and service); wife Matilda died at Cheltenham (buried at New Burial Ground 11 Nov, aged 25).* **1841:** *SK (aged 30; hatter) lived in room at Cross Keys, Cross Keys Yard, Oxford, Oxon (HO107/891/15/7/6).* **1847:** *SK remarried in Oxford, to Alice Browning, and started new family.* [PS/CH/RA/2/5:253.]

40093SE: Sat 3 Oct 1840 – **Frances Thurston**, single woman: That she was born in the Parish of Dursley in the said County where her parents were legally settled as she has been informed and believes. That she has never been hired by the year nor done any act to gain a settlement elsewhere [incomplete]
1840: *removal uncertain: examination form incomplete.* See **40094SE** (brother Thomas Thurston: [undated] 1840).

40094SE: [undated] 1840 – **Thomas Thurston**: That he was born at Dursley in the said County where his parents were legally settled as he has been informed and believes. that is Father was Parish Clerk of Dursley for several years

That in September 1834 he rented N°. 6 Burton Street Cheltenham at 16£ a year   that he lived in it five years and paid the rent to Mrs Townsend the Landlady

That he has rented N°. 8 in the same Street for near 2 years at 14£ a year. That he has paid a year and a half rent to Mr Pensom - that he has paid two or three poor rates. [signed]
1840: *settlement perhaps determined as Cheltenham (renting).* **1841:** *TT (20) in service in Lansdown Terrace, Cheltenham (HO107/353/11/27/13); sister Frances (aged 30) lived with parents Thomas (50; cordwainer) and Frances (50) Thurston at 209 High St, Cheltenham (HO107/353/8/71/24).*

[PS/CH/RA/2/5:254. The surname is spelled "Thurstone" by the magistrates' clerk. See **40093SE** (sister Frances Thurston: 3 Oct 1840).]

40095SE: 3 Oct 1840 – **William Holder**, stonemason, wife **Esther**, and three children **George**, **Charles**, and **Eliza**: That he was born in the Parish of Randwick in the said County where his parents were legally settled as he has heard and believes – that about fourteen years ago his Mother was relieved by the Parish officers of Randwick aforesaid. that about the same time he was also relieved by the Parish officers of Randwick. that he has never done any act to gain a settlement in his own right   That Eight years ago last Whitsuntide he was married to his present Wife Esther at Randwick aforesaid by whom he has three Children George aged seven years Charles aged six years & Eliza aged four years   That he is now chargeable to the said Parish of Cheltenham [mark] *1840: removed to Randwick (father's settlement). 1841: (RETURNED) WH (aged 36; mason) lived with wife Esther (35) and children George (8), Charles (7), Eliza (5), and William (6 mo) in Whaddon Lane, Cheltenham (HO107/353/3/44/4). 1843: the family lived at 17 Exmouth Court, Cheltenham when William and Esther's son Samuel was baptised 16 Apr.* [PS/CH/RA/2/5:255. Removal expenses for "Holder" to Randwick 3/- and £1/1/- (4Q 1840: D4178).]

40096SE: Tues 20 Oct 1840 – Thomas Phillips, tailor, relating to settlement of son **John Phillips** and wife **Elizabeth**, and two children **Louisa** and **Harriet**:
That about fourteen years ago he rented a house in Sherborne Street Cheltenham of Mr John Shott at twelve pounds a year   that he lived there a whole year and paid a years rent, that he then went to York Street Cheltenham and rented a house at Fourteen pounds a year of Mr Moreland – and stopt there three years and paid all the rent, but he has never paid any poor rates   that he has rented no house out of Cheltenham Since he left York Street   that about four and thirty years ago he was married to his present Wife Mary at the Cathedral Church Hereford. [mark]
[Additionally] That his Son John by his said Wife is now aged about thirty four years and was married about Eleven Years ago to his present Wife Elizabeth at the Parish Church of Cheltenham – That his said Son came with him to Cheltenham from Ross about twenty five years ago and lived with him as part of his family during the whole time he lived in Sherborne Street, and left him whilst he was in York Street – that his said Son never rented a house of the annual value of Ten pounds nor went into any service nor done any act to gain a settlement in his own right [mark]
1840: removal unlikely: father's settlement probably acknowledged as Cheltenham. 1841: wife Elizabeth (20; ironer) lived in Sherborne St with two daughters Louisa (7) and Harriet (5) (HO107/353/6/9/12); father Thomas Phillips (aged 65; tailor) lived with wife Mary (50), also in Sherborne St (HO107/353/6/9/12). [PS/CH/RA/2/5:256.]

40097SE: Thurs 29 Oct 1840 – **John Grant**, labourer, wife **Mary**, and five children **Job**, **Patience**, **Esther**, **Susan**, and **Robert**: That he was born in the Parish of Saintbury in the said County ~~where his parents were legally settled~~ as he has been informed and believes – that about Sixteen years ago he was hired by Mr Thomas Wadham of the parish of Exhall in the County of Warwick Farmer for a year. that he served the whole year and received his whole years wages. that he has never been hired by the year since nor lived in any Service for a year or rented a Tenement of the annual value of ten pounds or done any act to gain a settlement elsewhere   that Eight years ago last April he was married to his present Wife Mary at Church Honeybourne by whom he has five Children Job aged near Eight years Patience aged six years Esther aged four years Susan aged three years and Robert aged one year   that he is now chargeable to the Parish of Cheltenham aforesaid. [mark]
1840: removed to Exhall, Warks (father's settlement). 1841: Mary Grant (aged 35; charwoman) lived with children Job (9), Patience (7), Esther (6), Susan (5), Robert (2), and John (3 mo) in Alcester, Warks (HO107/124/1/6/4). 1842: death of Patience Grant (buried at Alcester 31 Aug, aged 7). The family (including John) appear to have emigrated to the United States by late 1840s. 1860: the family was recorded in U.S. Federal Census of 1860 in Wonewoc, Juneau, Wisconsin: John Grant (47; farmer), Mary (51), Robert (21), Charles; 12, born New York), and Esther (8; born Wisconsin) (Federal Census p. 1017). [PS/CH/RA/2/5:257. Removal expenses for "Grant" to Exhall, Warks £2/7/- (4Q 1840: D4178).]

40098SE: Mon 2 Nov 1840 – **George Goodman**, plasterer: That he was born in the Parish of Burford in the County of Oxford where his parents were legally settled as he has been informed and believes

That in the year 1825 he rented a house in Bath Terrace Cheltenham of Mr Smith Butcher at Eighteen pounds a year. that he lived in such house about a Year and a half and paid the year and half rent. that he has never rented a house at ten pounds a Year since nor done any act to gain a settlement elsewhere [signed]

1840: *removal unlikely: settlement probably acknowledged as Cheltenham (renting); GG (labourer) arrested for deserting wife and children, leaving them chargeable to Cheltenham, and committed for three months to Northleach prison* (Cheltenham Chron. *5 Nov*). [PS/CH/RA/2/5:258. "Constables expenses" "apprehending Goodman" £4/9/- (4Q 1840: D4178).]

40099SE: 2 Nov 1840 – **Ann Cox**, wife of George Cox, and three children **William, Sarah**, and **Thomas**: That on the 25 day of December 1832 she was married to her said husband at the Parish Church of Charlton Kings in the said County. that she has frequently heard and believes that her said husband was born at Charlton Kings aforesaid and that his parents were legally settled at Charlton Kings. that she has heard her husband say he never gained a settlement in his own right. that since their said Marriage her said husband has never rented a house of the annual value of ten pounds nor done any other act to gain a settlement

that She has by her said husband three Children to wit William aged five years Sarah aged three Years and Thomas aged one year and nine Months

That her said husband has deserted her and she is now chargeable to the Parish of Cheltenham [signed]

1840: *removed to Charlton Kings (husband's settlement); AC heavily pregnant at time of examination.* **1841:** *AC was an inmate of Cheltenham Workhouse and William (6) and Sarah (3) were inmates of Charlton Kings Workhouse for children (Cheltenham Union) (discharged 14 May) (G/CH/60/2); (RETURNED) AC (aged 31; charwoman) lived with children (William (5), Sarah (3), Thomas (1), and George (4 mo) in Major's Row, Cheltenham (HO107/353/11/4/3).* [PS/CH/RA/2/5:259. Removal expenses for "Cox" to Charlton Kings 2/6 (4Q 1840: D4178).]

40100SE: Tues 3 Nov 1840 – **Hannah McCarthy** (~~alias Jones~~): That she was born in the Parish of Mary le bone in the County of Middlesex   that her Father rented a house for Nine or ten years in Gees Court in the said Parish of Mary le bone at more than twenty pounds a year during which time she lived with her said Father, that he left such house about Nine or 10 years ago and went into Lodgings and did not afterwards rent a house of the annual value of ten pounds

That her said Father died about seven years ago in the Workhouse belonging to the said Parish of Mary le bone and was buried at the Expence of that Parish. That she never lived in any service by the year or rented a Tenement of the annual value of ten pounds

That about five years ago she was married at the Catholic Chapel in Spanish place London to John Jones who since died in Spain as She has been informed and believes, but the Marriage Ceremony was not performed in any place belonging to the Church of England

That she is now chargeable to the Parish of Cheltenham [mark]

1840: *removed to Marylebone (father's settlement).* [PS/CH/RA/2/5:260. Legally, the Magistrates were correct to investigate the curcumstances of the marriage: see W. G. Lumley's *Popular Treatise of the Law of Settlement and Removals* (1842, ed. 2), p. 40: "Catholics may now be married by a Catholic Priest, according to the form of the Roman ritual, in any chapel or other place. But a marriage between a Catholic and a Protestant according to that ritual is not valid. On the other hand, a marriage between a Protestant and a Catholic, according to the forms of the established church is valid." As the marriage was not considered valid under English law, the magistrates did not enquire into husband's settlement. Removal expenses for "McCart[h]y"to Marylebone £3/9/- and £5/3/- (4Q 1840: D4178).]

40101SE: 3 Nov 1840 – **Elizabeth Tinkler**, single woman: That she was born in Bristol as she has been informed and believes

That about twelve years ago she was hired by Mr Fisher of Fulham Park house in the Parish of Fulham in the County of Middlesex for a Year at the wages of Ten Guineas

That she served the whole year and received her whole years wages – That she has done no act to gain a settlement since   That she is now chargeable to the Parish of Cheltenham

1840: *removal uncertain: examination form incomplete.* **1850:** *an ET buried at New Burial Ground, Cheltenham 4 May, aged 55.* [PS/CH/RA/2/5:261.]

40102SE: 3 Nov 1840 – **Hannah Barnard**, single woman: That she was born at Bagpath in the parish of Minchinhampton in the said County where her parents were legally settled as she has been informed by her Father and believes – That her Father died about four or five years ago and was buried at the Expence of the Parish officers of Minchinhampton aforesaid – That she has never been hired by the Year nor done any Act to gain a settlement in her own right

That she is now chargeable to the Parish of Cheltenham [mark]

1808: *baptism of HB in Minchinhampton.* **1840:** *removed to Minchinhampton (father's settlement).* **1842:** *probably the HB who complained officially about her treatment at Horsley prison near Minchinhampton, where she suffered from consumption* (Gloucester Journal *19 Nov); the complainant was named as "Jane Barnard", but it was stated "at Cheltenham, that the name was that of Hannah, not Jane Barnard".* [PS/CH/RA/2/5:262. Removal expenses for "Barnard" to Minchinhampton 16/- (4Q 1840: D4178).]

40103SE: Sat 21 Nov 1840 – **Henry Richards**, labourer, wife **Elizabeth**, and three children **Susan, John**, and **Thomas**: That he was born in the Parish of Buckland in the County of Berks where his parents were legally settled as he has been informed and believes – That about seven or eight years ago orders were made by magistrates at Farringdon [= Faringdon] for his removal from the Parish of Langford together with his Wife Elizabeth and One Child named Susan (now aged nine Years) to the said Parish of Buckland, that he was then relieved by the Overseer of Buckland

That he has not rented a house at 10£ a year or done any act to gain a settlement in his own right. That he has now three Children namely Susan aged nine Years John aged Six Years and Thomas aged four years – That he is now Chargeable to the Parish of Cheltenham [signed]

1840: *removed to Buckland (father's settlement).* [PS/CH/RA/2/5:263. Removal expenses for "Richards" to Buckland £1/15/- (4Q 1840) and £3/8/- for 1Q 1841: D4178).]

40104SE: 21 Nov 1840 – **William Bowden**, and wife **Elizabeth**: That he was born in the Parish of Holy Trinity in the City of Chester where his parents were legally settled as he has been informed and believes   that he was apprenticed by Indenture to John Mellor of the said Parish of Holy Trinity Plumber for seven Years   that he served five years of the said term in the said Parish of Holy Trinity when his Master died

That he has done no Act since to gain a Settlement elsewhere

That about thirty years ago he was married to his present Wife Elizabeth

That he is now chargeable to the Parish of Cheltenham [mark]

1840: *removed to Chester, Ches (apprenticeship).* **1841:** *WB buried at Holy Trinity, Chester 15 Feb, aged 64.* [PS/CH/RA/2/5:264. Removal expenses for "Bowder" to Chester, Ches £7/6/- (1Q 1841: D4178).]

40105SE: Sat 28 Nov 1840 – **Eliza Apperley**, single woman: That she was born in the Parish of Eastington in the County of Gloucester where her parents were legally settled as she has been informed and believes. that about Nine years ago she was in the Workhouse at Eastington aforesaid and from thence she lived with Mr Smith at Eastington aforesaid as a Servant for three years and a half – that she has not rented a tenement at ten pounds a year

That she is now chargeable to the Parish of Cheltenham [mark]

1840: *removed to Eastington (near Stroud) (father's settlement); EA presumably pregnant at time of examination (daughter Elizabeth baptised 27 June 1841, at Eastington).* **1841:** *EA (aged 21; servant) was an inmate of Wheatenhurst Union Workhouse at Eastington (near Stroud) (HO107/370/62/1).* [PS/CH/RA/2/5:265. Removal expenses for "Apperley" to Eastington 18/- (4Q 1840: D4178).]

40106SE: 28 Nov 1840 – **James West**, labourer: That he was born in the Parish of Dunster in the County of Somerset where his parents were legally settled as he has been informed and believes.

That he has never done any act to gain a settlement in his own right. that some years ago he was relieved by the Parish Officers of Dunster

That he is now chargeable to the Parish of Cheltenham [mark]

1840: *removed to Dunster, Som (father's settlement).* [PS/CH/RA/2/5:266. Removal expenses for "West" to Dunster, Som £3/13/- (4Q 1840: D4178).]

40107SE: Tues 1 Dec 1840 – William Ellery, regarding the settlement of son **James Ellery**, labourer: That he was born in the Parish of Wootton Underedge [= Wotton-under-Edge] in the said County where his parents were legally settled as he has been informed and believes – that he has never done any Act to gain a settlement in his own right – That his said Son James was born at Wooton under edge aforesaid And has never done any Act to gain a settlement in his own right and is now chargeable to the Parish of Cheltenham [signed]

1840: *removed to Wotton-under-Edge (father's settlement).* **1841:** *(13 Jan) death of JE at Wortley, Wotton-under-Edge, aged 29 (cause not given), father William present at death.* [PS/CH/RA/2/5:267. Removal expenses for "Ellary" to Wotton-under-Edge £1/4/- (4Q 1840) and £1/16/6 (1Q 1841: D4178).]

40108SE: Thurs 3 Dec 1840 – **Edwin Belcher**, wife **Ann**, and four children **Mary Ann**, **Agnes**, **Adelaide**, and **Jesse**: That he was born in the Parish of Painswick in the said County where his parents were legally settled as he has been informed and believes. That about thirteen Years ago he was hired at the first Mop at Gloucester to Mr Beckett of the Parish of Churchdown in the said County for a Year at the wages of Three pounds fifteen shillings   that he served the whole year and received his years wages. that he was then hired again by Mr Beckett for another year at the wages of Five pounds and served that whole year and received his Wages

That he has never lived in any service for a Year Since nor rented a Tenement of the annual value of Ten pounds or done any Act to gain a Settlement elsewhere. That he is now Chargeable to the Parish of Cheltenham – That about Eight years ago he was married to his present Wife Ann at the Parish of St Mary de lode in the City of Gloucester by whom he has four Children to wit Mary Ann aged seven years Agnes aged six years Adelaide aged four years and Jesse nine weeks [mark]

1840: *removed to Churchdown (hiring and service):* see **47025RO** *(EB: 12 June 1847).* [PS/CH/RA/2/5:268; pencilled cross at foot of page perhaps indicates that removal order was not immediately drawn up. Removal expenses for "Belcher" to Churchdown 14/6 (1Q 1841: D4178).]

40109SE: Sat 12 Dec 1840 – **Mary Ann Wadley**, single woman, formerly servant, and son **John**: That she was born in the Parish of Kemmerton [= Kemerton] in the County of Gloucester where her parents were legally settled as she has been informed and believes. That in the year 1830 she was hired by Mr Gist who was then living in Cheltenham for a Year   that she remained in Cheltenham about twelve months and then went to Shurdington and lived there about twelve months under the same hiring. that she then went to Dixon [= Dixton] in Alderton to reside and she continued with the family there under a hiring by the year for about two years and in the year 1834 she went with the family to Wormington Grange and continued there for about a Year

That she has done no Act since to gain a Settlement since, That about four months ago she was delivered of a Male bastard Child named John in the Parish of Cheltenham   That she is now chargeable to Cheltenham [signed Mary Anne Wadley]

1840: *removed to Alderton (hiring and service):* see also **40086SE** *(MAW: 18 Sept 1840); illegitimate son John baptised at Cheltenham 23 Oct, while Mary Ann remained in Cheltenham Workhouse.* **1841:** *John died 2 Feb at Winchcombe Workhouse of "Cold", aged 4 mo; buried at Alderton; AW (aged 22) is the Maria Wadley living with mother Maria in Kemerton (HO107/367/7/5/4).* [PS/CH/RA/2/5:269. Removal expenses for "Wadley" Alderton 16/- (1Q 1841: D4178).]

40109SE: Sat 12 Dec 1840 - **William Buckle**, stonemason, and wife **Sarah**: That he was born in the Parish of Prestbury in the said County where his parents were legally settled as he has been informed and believes – that his father died about 24 years ago and afterwards his Mother and himself and the rest of the family were relieved by the Overseer of Prestbury. that he has never done any Act to gain a settlement in his own right – that about six years ago he was married to his present Wife Sarah at St Swithin's Church in the City of Worcester   that he is now chargeable to the parish of Cheltenham [mark]

1840: *removed to Prestbury (presumed) (father's settlement).* **1841:** *(RETURNED) WB (aged 25; stonemason) lived with wife Sarah (25; glover) in Townsend St, Cheltenham (HO107/353/9/8/11).* **1851:** *WB (37; stonemason) and Sarah (38; glover) lived with their niece Emma Long (8; scholar) at 6 Carlton Place West, St Paul's, Cheltenham (HO107/1973/445/8).* [PS/CH/RA/2/5:270.]

40111SE: Fri 18 Dec 1840 – Ann Townsend, of Bath, regarding the settlement of brother **Charles Townsend**, in the Lunatic Asylum, Gloucester: That about twenty years ago her Father Robert Townsend rented a house in the parish of Walcot near Bath in the County of Somerset by the year at ten pounds a Year where he resided until about seven years ago when he died. That her Brother the said Charles Townsend who is now about twenty three years of age resided with her said Father in the Said house from the time he went there until his said death –. That her said Brother has never been an apprentice or hired Servant or rented a Tenement of the annual value of ten pounds or done any act to gain a settlement in his own right [signed]

1840: *ordered to be removed to Bath (presumed) (father's settlement);* *(26 Dec) death of CT at Gloucester Lunatic Asylum, of "Appoplexy", aged 30.* [PS/CH/RA/2/5:271. Removal expenses for "Townsend" to Bath £1/15/- (1Q 1841: D4178).]

40112SE: Tues 22 Dec 1840 – **Mary Sadler**, single woman: That she was born in the Parish of Blakeney in the said County where her parents were legally settled

1840: *removal unlikely as result of death: examination form incomplete; MS buried at New Burial Ground, Cheltenham 28 Dec, aged 54.* [PS/CH/RA/2/5:272.]

40113SE: 22 Dec 1840 – **Richard Corah**, labourer: That he was born in the Parish of Kegworth in the County of Leicester

That he has heard his Father say he belonged to Breason [= Breaston] near Sawley in the County of Derby

That he remembers his Father being relieved by the Parish officers of Breason aforesaid

That he has done no act to gain a settlement in his own right

That he is now chargeable to the Parish of Cheltenham

1840: *removed to Breaston, Derbys (father's settlement).* **1841:** *RC (aged 20; agricultural labourer) lived with father in Kegworth, Leics (HO107/594/28/8/8), and subsequently became an innkeeper and brewer in Kegworth.* [PS/CH/RA/2/5:273. Removal expenses for "Corah" to Breason, Derbys £2/17/6 and £4/6/- (1Q 1841: D4178).]

40114SE: Thurs 24 Dec 1840 – **Hannah Williams**, single woman, and daughter **Lucy**: That She was born in the Parish of Llangarron in the County of Hereford where her parents were legally settled as she has heard and believes

That she has never done any Act to gain a Settlement in her own right

That about six weeks ago she was delivered of a female bastard Child named Lucy in the Parish of Cheltenham and she is now chargeable to the said Parish of Cheltenham [mark]

1840: *removed to Llangarron, Heref (father's settlement).* [PS/CH/RA/2/5:274. Removal expenses for "Williams" to Langarran £2/11/8 (1Q 1841: D4178).]

1841

41001SE: Sat 2 Jan 1841 – **Harriet Bayly**, single woman: That She was born in the Parish of Eastington in the said County where her parents were legally settled as She has been informed and believes – that she has done no act to gain a settlement in her own right   That She is now chargeable to the Parish of Cheltenham [mark]
1841: *removed to Eastington (father's settlement)*; *presumably the Harriet Baily (aged 25) who lived as servant in Eastington (near Northleach) (HO107/370/14/23)*. [PS/CH/RA/2/5:275. Removal expenses for "Bailey" to Eastington £1/17/- (1Q 1841: D4178).]

41002SE: 2 Jan 1841 – **Joseph Hinton**, cooper, wife **Hannah**, and two children **George** and **Ann**: That he was born in the Parish of St Marys Cricklade in the County of Wilts as he has heard and believes – That about seven Years ago he rented a house in the parish of Cirencester in the County of Gloucester for a Year at the rent of Fourteen pounds a year   that he continued in such house a Year and A half and paid all the rent and was duly rated to and paid all the poor rates in respect of such house for such time – That he has done no act since to gain a settlement elsewhere. that he is now Chargeable to the parish of Cheltenham   that about 24 years ago he was married to his present wife Hannah at Ashton Keynes Wilts by whom he has two Children George aged 15 Years and Ann aged Eleven years [signed]
1841: *removed to Cirencester (renting)*; *(RETURNED)* (6 June) *JH (aged 40; cooper) lived with wife Hannah (45; laundress) and children Joseph (22; shoemaker), George (15; shoemaker), Sarah (15; shoebinder), and Ann (10) in Milsom St, Cheltenham (HO107/358/8/50/33-51/34)*. **1851:** *JH and wife lived at 54 Sherborne St, Cheltenham (HO107/1973/152/44)*. [PS/CH/RA/2/5:276. Removal expenses for "Hinton" to Cirencester 17/6 (1Q 1841: D4178). See **41006SE** (son Joseph Hinton: 16 Jan 1841), **41016SE** (daughter Sarah Hinton: 28 Jan 1841).]

41003SE: Mon 4 Jan 1841 – **James Worth**, labourer: That he was born in the Parish of Dunster in the County of Somerset where his parents were legally settled as he has been informed and believes – That he has never done any act to gain a settlement in his own right
    That some years ago he and his family were relieved by the Parish officers of Dunster
    That he is now chargeable to the Parish of Cheltenham [mark]
1841: *removed to Dunster, Som (father's settlement)*. [PS/CH/RA/2/5:277. Removal expenses for "Worth" to Dunster, Som £5/5/6 (1Q 1841: D4178).]

41004SE: Sat 9 Jan 1841 – **Elizabeth Aldridge**, single woman: That she was born in the Parish of Bisley in the said County where her parents were legally settled as she has heard and believes. That she has done no act to gain a settlement in her own right. That she is now chargeable to the Parish of Cheltenham [mark]
1841: *removed to Bisley (father's settlement)*. [PS/CH/RA/2/5:278. Removal expenses for "Aldridge" to Bisley £1/5/- (1Q 1841: D4178).]

41005SE: Tues 12 Jan 1841 – **Joseph Scrivens**, labourer, and children **Martha**, **Caroline**, and **Henry**: That near 20 years ago he was hired by Mr Commeline of the Parish of Withington in the said County for a year at the wages of Nine Guineas   that he served the whole year and received his years wages - That he was then hired again by the said Mr Commeline for another year and served that year   that he has done no act since to gain a settlement elsewhere – ~~That about seven years ago he was married to his late [wife] Ann who is now dead at Cheltenham by whom~~ he has three Children vizt Martha aged ten years Caroline aged five years and Henry aged four years all born in lawful wedlock
    That he is now chargeable to the Parish of Cheltenham [mark]
1841: *removed to Withington (hiring and service)*: see **47007RO** *(JS: 30 Jan 1847) for further information*. [PS/CH/RA/2/5:279. Removal expenses for "Scrivens" to Withington 14/6 (1Q 1841: D4178).]

41006SE: Sat 16 Jan 1841 – **Joseph Hinton**, cordwainer: That when he was about 12 Years old he was apprenticed by Indenture to Joseph Perrin of the parish of Cirencester in the said County Cordwainer for seven Years   that he served three years of the said term with his said Master and lived in his Masters house at Cirencester

That the Indenture was then cancelled by the Magistrates at Cirencester in consequence of the ill treatment of his Master

That he has done no Act since to gain a settlement elsewhere –. That he is now chargeable to the Parish of Cheltenham [mark]

1841: *removed to Cirencester (apprenticeship); (RETURNED) (6 June) JH (aged 22; shoemaker) lived with family in Milsom St, Cheltenham (HO107/358/8/50/33-51/34).* **1851:** *wife Elizabeth lived with parents-in-law at 54 Sherborne St, Cheltenham (HO107/1973/152/44), while JH (38; shoemaker, born Ashton Keynes, Wilts) was imprisoned in Northleach Gaol (HO107/1969/383/25).* **1861:** *JH (40; general labourer) lived with wife Elizabeth (38) at the Old Toll Gate, Cricklade Road, Swindon (RG9/1272/20/34).* [PS/CH/RA/2/5:280. Removal expenses for "Hinton" to Cirencester 17/6 (1Q 1841: D4178). See **41002SE** (father Joseph Hinton: 2 Jan 1841).]

41007SE: Thurs 14 Jan 1841 – **William Cox**, labourer, and son **Isaac**: That about 19 years ago he was hired by Farmer Greenwood of the Parish of Charlton Kings in the said County for a Year at the wages of Four pounds ten shillings   that he served the whole year and received his years wages

that in a Year afterwards he was again hired by the said Farmer Greenwood for another year which he also served and received his years wages down – That he has done no act since to gain a settlement elsewhere   That about the 16 years ago he was married to his late Wife Ann now dead at Hatherley [properly Hatherop] by whom he has one child named Isaac aged 15 Years – That he is now Chargeable to the Parish of Cheltenham [mark]

1840: *wife probably the Ann Cox buried at New Burial Ground, Cheltenham 22 Apr, aged 37.* **1841:** *removed to Charlton Kings (hiring and service); (RETURNED) (6 June) Isaac Cox (15; labourer) lived in Exmouth Court, Cheltenham; father perhaps the William Cox (60; agricultural labourer) living alone in Southrop (HO107/352/12/5/4).* **1851:** *WC at same address (aged 75; widower and agricultural labourer) (HO107/1969/11/15).* [PS/CH/RA/2/5:282. Removal expenses for "Cox" to Charlton 2/6 (1Q 1841: D4178).]

41008SE: Sat 20 Feb 1841 – **John Smith**, sawyer, and wife **Elizabeth**: That in the year 1818 he was hired by Colonel Newport of the Hamlet of Hanley William in the County of Worcester for a year at the yearly wages of £20   that he continued in such service a whole year and received his years wages. That he has done no act since to gain a settlement elsewhere   That 9 years ago last November he was married to his present wife Elizabeth at Evesham. That he is now chargeable to the Parish of Cheltenham [signed]

1841: *removed to Hanley William, Worcs (hiring and service); (RETURNED) (6 June) JS (aged 45; sawyer) and wife Elizabeth (30) lived in Bath Terrace, Cheltenham (HO107/353/12/13/21).* [PS/CH/RA/2/5:283. Removal expenses for "Smith" to Hanley William, Worcs £2/6/- (1Q 1841: D4178).]

41009SE: Mon 18 Jan 1841 – **Benjamin Briggs**, bricklayer: That he was born in the Parish of Billingshurst in the County of Sussex where his parents were legally settled as he has been informed and believes. That his Father died about six Years ago and was relieved by the Parish officers of Billingshurst up to his death and was buried at their Expence. That he has done no Act to gain a Settlement in his own right – That he is now chargeable to the Parish of Cheltenham [mark]

1841: *removed to Billingshurst, Sussex (father's settlement).* [PS/CH/RA/2/5:284. Removal expenses for "Briggs" to London £4/1/- (1Q 1841: D4178).]

41010SE: Tues 19 Jan 1841 – **James Sparks** (also **Sparkes**), clock-maker, wife **Ann**, and two children **Edward** and **Ann**: That he was born in the City of Coventry where his parents were legally settled as he has been informed and believes   that when he was about 14 Years of Age he was apprenticed by Indenture to Mr Caldicot of Coventry aforesaid Silk Dyer for seven years - that he served two Years of the said term with his said Master and slept in Coventry when his Master failed – that he has never done any act to gain a settlement since – That about 7 or 8 years ago he was married to his present wife Ann at Llangolan [= Llangollen] in Denbighshire by whom he has two Children viz Edward aged 8 Years and Ann aged a fortnight   That he is now chargeable to the Parish of Cheltenham [mark]

1841: *daughter Anne baptised at Cheltenham the day before examination, when family lived at 5 Worcester St, Cheltenham (JS described as "clock-fitter");* ***removed to Coventry, Warks (presumed) (apprenticeship).*** **1851:** *the family lived in Wolverhampton: JS (36; clock-maker), Amelia (36; sempstress: the name is perhaps in error), and Edward (17; puddler, heating and stirring iron in furnace) (HO107/2018/570/16).* **1881:** *JS (64; silk dyer) was an inmate of Coventry Poor Law Union Workhouse (RG11/3070/117/4).* [PS/CH/RA/2/5:285.]

41011SE: Wed 20 Jan 1841 – Jane Birt, widow, with reference to the settlement of son **George Birt**, with his wife **Hannah Maria**, and daughter **Amelia**: That her late husband William Birt was born in the Parish of Boddington in the said County and was legally settled there as she has heard and believes – That her husband was frequently relieved by the Parish officers of Boddington up to his death which happened about Eight years ago. That her said Son George was born in the said Parish of Boddington and has never done any act to gain a settlement in his own right. That about four Years ago her said Son was married at Cheltenham to his present Wife Hannah Maria by whom he has one Child named Amelia aged 4 Years. That his said Wife and Child are chargeable to the Parish of Cheltenham and her said Son is now a Prisoner for felony confined to the County Goal [= Gaol] at Gloucester [mark]

1841: ***removed to Boddington (presumed) (father's settlement);*** *GB acquitted of "larceny" at Gloucester County Adjourned Sessions 3 Mar, but not at home on census night (6 June); (RETURNED) wife Hannah (aged 31) lived with daughters Amelia (4) and Eliza (6 weeks) in Malvern St, Cheltenham (HO107/353/10/5/4).* **1851:** *the couple lived at 1 Waterloo Place, Cheltenham: GB (41; sawyer), Hannah M. (44; charwoman), Emelia (14), Ellen (7), Emma (4; all three at home), and James (1) (all children born Cheltenham) (HO107/1973/492/5).* [PS/CH/RA/2/5:285 [i.e. 286]. Removal expenses for "Birt" to Boddington 8/- (1Q 1841: D4178).]

41012SE: Sat 23 Jan 1841 – **Thomas Dodwell**, labourer, and children **Mary Ann, Samuel, Charles**, and **Josiah**: That he has heard his Father say and he believes it to be true that his said Father gained his settlement in the Hamlet of Southam and Brockhampton in the said County by hiring and service there. That about 14 or 15 Years ago he was relieved by the Overseers of the said Hamlet of Southam and Brockhampton whilst he was residing in Cheltenham. That he has never done any act to gain a settlement in his own right. That about 30 years Ago he was married to his late Wife Charlotte now deceased at Cheltenham by whom he has four Children. Viz^t Mary Ann aged 14 years Samuel aged 12 Years Charles aged 10 years and Josiah aged 7 years   That he is now Chargeable to the Parish of Cheltenham [mark]

1841: *removed to Southam and Brockhampton (presumed) (father's settlement); (RETURNED) (6 June) TD (aged 50; labourer) and his children Charlotte (20), Elizabeth (19), Mary (17), Samuel (15), Charles (13), and Josiah (6) lived in Stanhope St, Cheltenham (HO107/353/9/51/3).* **1851:** *TD (63; widower and pauper, born Cheltenham) lived in Cheltenham, lodging at the house of Thomas Compton (with whom he had shared his house in 1841) at 10 Bloomsbury Place (HO107/1973/611/49).* [PS/CH/RA/2/5:286, replacing examination (p. 281) of 14 Jan, in which TD stated that his father's settlement was Winchcombe. Removal expenses for "Dodwell" to Winchcombe 7/6 (1Q 1841: D4178). See **41012SE** (brother David Dodwell: [23?] Jan 1841) and Gray **277** (a TD, born in Cheltenham: 4 January 1820).]

41013SE: [23?] Jan 1841 – **David Dodwell**, labourer, wife **Hannah**, and three children **Baylis, Hannah**, and **Sarah**: That he has heard and believes it to be true that his Father gained his Settlement in the Hamlet of Southam and Brockhampton in the said County by hiring and service there   That he has never done any act to gain a settlement in his own right   That about Six years ago he was married to his present Wife Hannah by whom he has three Children Baylis aged five Years Hannah aged four Years and Sarah aged two Years – That he is now chargeable to the Parish of Cheltenham [mark]

1841: *removed to Southam and Brockhampton (father's settlement); (RETURNED) (6 June) DD (aged 25; labourer) lived with wife Hannah (25) and children Baily (6), Hannah (5), and Sarah (2) in Elm St, Cheltenham (HO107/353/9/62/25).* **1851:** *the family lived at 10 Elm St, Cheltenham: DD (32; labourer, born Tewkesbury), Hannah (31), and seven children, all born Cheltenham (HO107/1973/517/13).* [PS/CH/RA/2/5:287. Removal expenses for "Dodwell" to Southam 11/6 (1Q 1841: D4178). See **41012SE** (brother Thomas Dodwell: 23 Jan 1841).]

41014SE: 23 Jan 1841 – **George Deacon** (also **Dakon**), labourer, wife **Elizabeth**, and five children **George**, **Martha**, **Helen**, **Absalom**, and **Eli**: That he was born in the Parish of Avening in the said County where his parents were legally settled as he has been informed and believes. That about 8 or 9 Years ago he was relieved by the Parish officers of Avening   That he has never done any act to gain a settlement in his own right   That about 15 Years ago he was married to his present Wife Elizabeth at the Parish of Charrington [= Cherington] by whom he has five Children George aged ten years Martha aged Eight years Helen aged five Years Absalom aged three years and Eli aged 1 Year & 9 months. That he is now chargeable to the Parish of Cheltenham [mark]
1841: *removed to Avening (father's settlement); (RETURNED) (6 June) GD (aged 35; labourer) lived with wife Elizabeth (35) and six children George (10), Martha (8), Ellen (6), Absalom (4), Eli (2), and Joseph (three mo), in Naunton Fields, Cheltenham (HO107/353/12/43/22).* **1851:** *the family lived in Upper Bath St, Cheltenham: GD (aged 47; labourer, born Stroud), Elizabeth (47; born Rodborough), and seven children (all born Cheltenham) (HO107/1973/874/7).* [PS/CH/RA/2/5:288. Removal expenses for "Deacon" to Avening £1/-/- and £1/17/6 (1Q 1841: D4178).]

41015SE: Mon 25 Jan 1841 – **Richard Crowder** (also **Crowther**, **Crouder**), labourer, wife **Hannah**, and four children **Henry**, **Charlotte**, **Rachael**, and **Emanuel**: That about fourteen years ago he was hired by Solomon Sellman of the parish of Ashleworth in the said County Labourer for a Year   that he served the whole Year and received his Years wages   That he has done no act since to gain a settlement elsewhere – That about ten Years ago he was married to his present Wife Hannah at Frampton upon Severn by whom he has four children Henry aged 9 Years Charlotte aged 7 Years Rachael aged 5 Years and Emanuel aged 3 Years. That he is now chargeable to the Parish of Cheltenham [mark]
1841: *removed to Ashleworth (hiring and service); (RETURNED) (6 June) RC (aged 30; labourer) lived with wife Hannah (30) and children Henry (9), Charlotte (7), Rachael (5), and Emanuel (2) in Waterloo Place, Cheltenham (HO107/353/9/55/11).* **1846:** *perhaps the RC (35) imprisoned for ten weeks for larceny at Gloucester County Sessions of 30 June.* **1851:** *RC (40; ostler) and Hannah (36) lived in Pigott St, Lee Bank, Birmingham (but without children); Charlotte Crowder (16; pauper) was an inmate of Gloucester Union Workhouse (HO107/1961/471/11), and Henry Crowder (20; house keeper, described as an inmate) lived with a family near Tram Road, Gloucester (HO107/1962/452/29).* [PS/CH/RA/2/5:289. Removal expenses for "Crowther" to Ashleworth 18/6 (1Q 1841: D4178).]

41016SE: Thurs 28 Jan 1841 – **Sarah Hinton**, single woman: That she was born in the Parish of St Marys Cricklade in the County of Wilts as she has heard and believes – That about 7 Years ago her father rented a house in Cirencester at Fourteen pounds a year. that he resided in such house a Year and a half and paid all the rent and was duly rated to and paid all the poor rates in respect of such house for such time. that She lived with her Father the whole of that time. That she has never done any Act to gain a settlement in her own right – That She is now chargeable to the Parish of Cheltenham [signed]
1822: *SH baptised at St Mary's, Cricklade 24 Feb, daughter of Joseph and Hannah Hinton.* **1841:** *removed to Cirencester (father's settlement); (RETURNED) (6 June) the family lived in Milsom St, Cheltenham: Joseph Hinton (aged 40; cooper), Hannah (45; laundress), Joseph (22; shoemaker), George (15; shoemaker), Sarah (15; shoe-binder), and Ann (10) (HO107/353/8/50/33).* **1846:** *SH married Charles Dodson in 2Q at Winchcombe.* **1846:** *the couple lived in Sherborne St, Cheltenham: Charles Dodson (32; shoemaker); Sarah Hinton (29; shoe-binder); her parents lived at 54 Sherborne St (HO107/1973/153/46).* [PS/CH/RA/2/5:290. Removal expenses for "Hinton" to Cirencester 15/6 (1Q 1841: D4178) and £1/-/- (3Q 1841: D4178). See **41002SE** (father Joseph Hinton: 2 Jan 1841).]

41017SE: Mon 25 Jan 1841 – **Jacob Barnes**, plasterer, wife **Charlotte**, and daughter **Ann**: That he was born in the Parish of Broad Somerford [= Gt Somerford] in the County on Wilts where his parents were legally settled – that his father died about 20 years ago and was relieved by the Parish officer of Broad Somerford up to his death and was buried at their Expence   That he has done no Act to gain a settlement in his own right

That about 7 years ago he was married to his present Wife Charlotte at Cheltenham by whom he has ~~two Children~~ one Child Ann aged 5 Years

That he is now chargeable to the Parish of Cheltenham [signed]

1841: *removed to Gt Somerford, Wilts (father's settlement); (RETURNED) JB buried at Cheltenham 7 June, aged 30; he was absent from home in Jersey St the previous evening when the census was taken: Charlotte Barnes (aged 25; charwoman), Alfred (10), Ann (6). Alfred not noted in father's examination as he was born out of wedlock and so was not regarded by parish as dependant.* [PS/CH/RA/2/5:291. Removal expenses for "Barnes" to Gt Somerford, Wilts £1/9/- and "Barnes" to Gt Somerford £2/15/6 (1Q 1841: D4178).]

41018SE: Sat 6 Feb 1841 – **Martha Alexander**, widow, and son **John**: That about fifteen years ago she was married to her late husband William Alexander at the Parish of Hempstead [= Hempsted] in the said County – That her husband died about Eight years ago. That she has heard her said husband say and she believes it to be true that he was born in the Hamlet of Chaceley in the County of Worcester [now in Glos] and that her said husband never did any act to gain a settlement in his own right. That she has one Child by her said husband named John now aged about 14 Years. That since her said husbands death she has been relieved by the Parish officers of Chaceley aforesaid whilst she was residing in the Parish of Cheltenham

That she and her said Son are now chargeable to the said Parish of Cheltenham [mark]

1841: *removed to Chaceley, Worcs (husband's settlement); (RETURNED) (6 June) MA (aged 50; washerwoman) lived in Elm St, Cheltenham with Matilda (16), John (12), and Henry (10) (HO107/353/10/4/2); the presence of Matilda and Henry is unexplained.* [PS/CH/RA/2/5:293. Removal expenses for "Alexander" to Chaceley, Worcs 16/6 (1Q 1841: D4178).]

41019SE: [blank] Feb 1841 – **Richard Smith**, labourer: That he [incomplete].

1841: *removal uncertain: examination form incomplete.* [PS/CH/RA/2/5:294.]

41020SE: Mon 15 Feb 1841 – **John Powers**, labourer, wife **Sarah**, and four children **Mary, George, Thomas**, and **James**: That about 18 Years ago he was hired by Mr Moss of the Parish of Brockworth in the said County Farmer for a year at the yearly wages of seven pounds   that he served the whole Year and received his Years wages and continued in such service Six Years afterwards. That he has done no act since to gain a settlement elsewhere – That about fifteen years ago he was married to his present Wife Sarah at Brockworth aforesaid by whom he has four Children Viz^t. Mary aged 11 years George aged 7 years Thomas aged 4 years and James aged 4 months

That he is now chargeable to the Parish of Cheltenham [mark]

1841: *removed to Brockworth (hiring and service): see* **49031RO** *(JP: 8 June) for further information.* [PS/CH/RA/2/5:295. Removal expenses for "Powers" to Brockworth 13/6 (1Q 1841: D4178).]

41021SE: Thurs 18 Feb 1841 – **Thomas Bishop**, labourer: That about fifty years ago he was hired by Mr Thomas Arkell of the Parish of Boddington in the said County Farmer for a Year at the wages of Seven Guineas   that he served the whole year and received his years wages. That he has done no act since to gain a Settlement elsewhere – That about ten Years ago he was relieved by the Parish officers of Boddington whilst he was residing in the Parish of Staverton

That he is now chargeable to the Parish of Cheltenham [mark]

1841: *removed to Boddington (hiring and service); (RETURNED) probably the TB (aged 60; agricultural labourer) who lived with the family of son John Bishop (25; agricultural labourer) in Gloucester Road, Cheltenham (HO107/353/10/53/12). A John Bishop, son of Thomas and Sarah Bishop (married at Boddington on 28 June 1796), was baptised at Staverton 3 July 1807.* [PS/CH/RA/2/5:296. Removal expenses for "Bishop" to Boddington 6/- (1Q 1841: D4178).]

41022SE: Mon 8 Mar 1841 – **Mary Sabin**, single woman: That she was born in the Parish of Saint Marys in the Borough of Warwick where her parents were legally settled as she has heard and believes. That her Father died about three years ago and was buried at the Expence of the Parish officers of Saint Mary's aforesaid   that she was afterwards relieved by the Parish officers of Saint Marys

That she has done no act to gain a settlement in her own right And is now actually chargeable to the said Parish of Cheltenham [mark]

1812: *MS baptised at St Mary's, Warwick, Warks 19 May.* **1839:** *father John buried at Barford, Warks 6 Jan.* **1841:** *removed to St Mary's, Warwick, Warks (father's settlement).* [PS/CH/RA/2/5:297, replacing examination of [blank] Feb 1841where MS says she was born in the parish of St Nicholas, Warwick (PS/CH/RA/2/5:292. Removal expenses for "Sabin" to Warwick, Warks £2/2/6 (2Q 1841: D4178).]

41023SE: Thurs 11 Mar 1841 – **Hannah Taylor**, single woman: That in the Year 1832 She was hired by Mr John Dudfield of the Parish of Charlton Kings in the said County Innkeeper for a Year at the yearly wages of Five pounds   that she served the whole Year and received her years wages. That she has done no act to gain a settlement since – That She is now actually chargeable to the said Parish of Cheltenham [mark]

1841: *removed to Charlton Kings (hiring and service).* [PS/CH/RA/2/5:298. Removal expenses for "Taylor" to Charlton Kings 2/6 (2Q 1841: D4178).]

41024SE: Sat 27 Mar 1841 – **Esther Lait** (written **Lake** in error; also **Laite, Laight**), widow, and five children **Ann, Mary, Ellen, Amelia,** and **Sarah Ann**: That about 15 Years ago She was Married to her late husband Joseph Lake at Cubberley [= Coberley] in the said County by whom she has five Children Viz^t Ann aged 14 years Mary aged 11 years Ellen aged 9 years Amelia aged Six years and Sarah Ann aged 3 Years. that her said husband died about 5 weeks ago. That She has heard her husband say that about 16 years and half ago he was hired by Mr Guy of Cubberley aforesaid Farmer for a year, that She knows that her said husband served the whole year – And that he never done [*sic*] any act afterwards to gain a settlement – That She and her said Children are now chargeable to the said Parish of Cheltenham [mark]

1841: *husband Joseph Lait buried at Cheltenham 22 Feb;* **removed to Coberley (husband's settlement);** *(RETURNED) son Joseph baptised 25 July at Cheltenham; Esther Lait (aged 36; independent) lived in Bath Road, Cheltenham with daughters Mary (11), Ellen (9), Amelia (6), and Sarah (3) HO107/353/13/9/12).* **1851:** *EL (47; charwoman, born Eyford) lived in Eaton Place, Cheltenham with daughters Mary (22; lace-maker) and Sarah Ann (13; scholar) (HO107/1973/797/30); Ellen Lait (19) lived with maternal grandparents in Cubberley (HO107/1972/257/2).* [PS/CH/RA/2/5:299. See removal expenses to Coberley £1/2/6 (2Q 1841: D4178).]

41025SE: Sat 3 Apr 1841 – **Daniel Davis**, labourer, wife **Elizabeth**, and two children **Alfred** and **Susannah**: That he was born in the Parish of King's Stanley in the said County where his parents were legally settled as he has been informed – That he has never done any act to gain a settlement in his own right – that he remembers his Father was relieved by the Parish officers of King[s] Stanley aforesaid about Eight Years ago. That about twenty two Years ago he was married to his present Wife Elizabeth at Stroud by whom he has two Children Alfred aged ten years and Susannah aged near four Years – That he is now chargeable to the said Parish of Cheltenham [mark]

1841: *removed to King's Stanley (father's settlement):* see **47010RO** *(Elizabeth Davis: 6 Mar 1847) for further information on family.* [PS/CH/RA/2/5:300. Removal expenses for "Davis" to King's Stanley £1/10/- (2Q 1841: D4178).]

41026SE: Fri 23 Apr 1841 – **Hannah Smith**, single woman: That she was born in the Parish of Badgworth [= Badgeworth] in the said County where her parents were legally settled as she has heard and believes

That about Six years ago her Father received relief of the Parish officers of Badgworth

That she has done no act to gain a settlement in her own right   That she is now chargeable to the Parish of Cheltenham [signed]

1841: *removed to Badgeworth (father's settlement).* [PS/CH/RA/2/5:301. Removal expenses for "Smith" to Badgeworth 7/- (2Q 1841: D4178).]

41027SE: Sat 24 Apr 1841 – **Elizabeth Horlick**, single woman: That she was born in the Parish of Painswick in the said County where her parents were legally settled as she has heard and believes

That she has done no act to gain a settlement in her own right And is now chargeable to the Parish of Cheltenham aforesaid [signed]

1841: *removed to Painswick (father's settlement);* (6 June) EH (aged 20; servant) lived with mother Mary (55; independent) in Painswick (HO107/349/8/47/10). **1844:** marriage of EH to William Leech (also Leach), local clothworker, in Painswick 27 Feb. **1851:** Elizabeth (34; clothworker) lived with husband William (33; clothworker) and three children John (4), Elizabeth (2), and Catharine (6 mo) at Vatch Mill, Stroud (HO107/1965/221/19). [PS/CH/RA/2/5:302. Removal expenses for "Horlick & Cook" to Painswick £1/-/- (2Q 1841: D4178).]

41028SE: 24 Apr 1841 – **John Lovadon Verrier**, cordwainer, wife **Charlotte**, and five children **Joseph**, **Rachael**, **Livinia**, **George**, and **Elizabeth**: That he was born in the Parish of Curry Mallett [= Curry Mallet] in the County of Somerset as he has heard and believes that about thirty two years ago he was apprenticed by Indenture to William Vicary of Ashbrittle in the County of Somerset for Four years that he served the said term and slept at his Masters house at Ashbrittle the whole of that time. That he has done no act since to gain a settlement elsewhere. that about Seventeen Years ago he was married to his present Wife Charlotte at Radcliffe Church Bristol [= St Mary Redcliffe, Bristol] by whom he has five Children namely Joseph aged 15 Years Rachael aged 13 years Lavina aged 11 years George aged 9 years and Elizabeth aged 7 Years. That he is now chargeable to the Parish of Cheltenham [signed]

1841: *removed to Ashbrittle, Som (presumed) (apprenticeship).* **1851:** (RETURNED) JLV (aged 54; cordwainer) lived with wife Charlotte (62) and children Rachael (23; shoebinder), Livinia (22); shoebinder), George (20; cordwainer), and Elizabeth (19; shoebinder) at 6 Devonshire St, Cheltenham (HO107/1973/631/26). Son Joseph (also shoemaker) was imprisoned for stealing on at least two occasions in 1840s. **1861:** death of wife Charlotte (buried at New Burial Ground 29 Jan, aged 74). **1868:** death of JLV, aged 75, at Cheltenham Workhouse (buried at New Burial Ground 4 Aug 1868). JLV's middle name also transcribed Loveoben and Loveband. [PS/CH/RA/2/5:303.]

41029SE: Tues 27 Apr 1841 – **William Cooke** (also **Cook**), labourer, wife **Sarah**, and four children **Eliza**, **Henry**, **Cornelius**, and **Thomas**: That he was born in the Parish of Randwick in the said County, where his parents were legally settled as he has been informed and believes That he has never done any act to gain a settlement in his own right. That about Sixteen Years ago he was married to his present Wife Sarah at Stroud by whom he has had since his said Marriage four Children to wit Eliza aged 12 years Henry aged 6 years Cornelius aged three years and Thomas aged four months That he is now chargeable to the Parish of Cheltenham [mark]

1841: *removed to Randwick (presumed) (father's settlement);* WC was not at home on census night (6 June); (RETURNED) wife Sarah (aged 35) lived with four children Eliza (14), Henry (6), Cornelius (3) and Thomas (1) in Commercial St, Cheltenham (HO107/353/12/18/30). **1851:** WC (50; labourer) lived with Sarah (49), Henry (16; errand boy), Cornelius (12; scholar), (Thomas) Felton (10; scholar), Alfred (6; scholar, born Cheltenham), and John (4), at 3 Back of Railway Inn, near Providence Terrace, Gt Norwood St, Cheltenham (HO107/1973/900/58). [PS/CH/RA/2/5:304. Removal expenses for "Horlick & Cook" to Painswick £1/-/- (2Q 1841: D4178).]

41030SE: 27 Apr 1841 – William Cooke, labourer, relating to the settlement of **James Cooke** (also **Cook**), otherwise **Smith**: That between sixteen and seventeen Years ago the said James Cook [sic] otherwise Smith was born in the Parish of Randwick in the said County and is the natural Child of this deponents now wife then Sarah Smith and was christened by the name of James Cook and has ever since lived with this deponent as one of his family being reputed to be his Son That the said James Cooke otherwise Smith has never done any act to gain a settlement in his own right and is now residing in and chargeable to the Parish of Cheltenham [mark]

1841: *removed to Randwick (father's settlement)*; *probably the JC (aged 15; butcher) who lived in High St, Cheltenham (6 June) (HO107/353/16/27/14).* [PS/CH/RA/2/5:305. Removal expenses for "Smith" to Randwick 15/- (2Q 1841: D4178).]

41031SE: Thurs 29 Apr 1841 – Mary Constable, relating to the settlement of daughter **Eliza Ann Sainsbury**: That the said Eliza Ann Sainsbury is an illegitimate Child of this Examinant and was born between 18 and 19 years ago in the Parish of Burghclere in the County of Hants and was relieved by the Parish officers there until she was about Eight years of age. That her said Daughter has never done any act to gain a settlement in her own right   And is now chargeable to the Parish of Cheltenham [signed]

1841: *removed to Burghclere, Hants (birth)*; *(6 June) EAS's mother, then Mary Constable (aged 35), lived with husband William Constable (35; shoemaker) and their five children in Grosvenor Cottages, off Albion St, Cheltenham (HO107/353/4/30/25).* **1843:** *death of EAS registered 4Q at Kingsclere, Hampshire.* **1845/6:** *Mary Constable and husband William died at Cheltenham in 1845 and 1846 respectively.* [PS/CH/RA/2/5:306. Removal expenses for "Sainsbury" to Burghclere, Hants £3/9/- and £4/14/6 (2Q 1841: D4178).]

41032SE: 29 Apr 1841 – John Arkell, stonemason, residing in Miserden, relating to the settlement of son **Miles Arkell** (also **Arkwell**, **Harkwell**) and two daughters **Mary Ann** and **Martha**: That his said Son was born in the Parish of Miserdine [= Miserden] in the said County That when his said Son was about 15 years of age he was apprenticed by Indenture to Thomas Lediard of the parish of Stroud in the said County Tiler and Plasterer for seven years   That he served until he was 21 years of age under such Indenture and slept in the parish of Stroud during the whole time. That his said Son has done no act since to gain a settlement elsewhere   That about 20 years ago his said Son Married his late Wife at Oxford by whom he has two Children Mary Ann aged about fourteen Years and Martha aged about twelve Years who are both chargeable to the Parish of Cheltenham. [mark]

1841: *son Miles Arkell and daughters under care of Overseers of Miserden;* ***removed to Stroud (apprenticeship)***; *Martha Arkell (aged 10, "deserted by Father", behaviour "Very Good") was admitted as an inmate of Charlton Kings Workhouse for children (Cheltenham Union) 26 May until removal to Stroud (G/CH/60/2); John Arkell (aged 75; mason) lived in Miserden (6 June) (HO107/349/6/1/1); daughters Mary Ann (11) and Martha Miles (10) were then inmates of Stroud Union Workhouse HO107/349/13/65/3); Miles's son Miles lived in St Ebbe's, Oxford (also in 1851).* **1851:** *Miles Arkell (52; slater and widower) lodged in Middlesborough (HO107/2383/296/25).* **1854:** *probably death of Miles Arkell (buried at St Olave, Southwark 1 Aug, aged 56).* [PS/CH/RA/2/5:307. Removal expenses for "Arkell" to Stroud 16/- (2Q 1841: D4178).]

41033SE: Mon 3 May 1841 – **George Townsend**, carpenter, wife **Jane**, and two children **Jacob** and **Sarah**: That upwards of thirty years ago he was hired by M[rs] Hunt of the Parish of Saint Mary de lode in the City of Gloucester for a year   that he served the whole year and received his years wages   that he continued in such service for years afterwards   That he has done no act since to gain a settlement elsewhere

That about six years ago he was relieved by the Parish officers of Saint Mary de lode while he was residing in Cheltenham

That about twenty years ago he was married at the said Parish of Saint Mary de lode to his present wife Jane by whom he has two Children namely Jacob aged fourteen years and Sarah aged seven years. That he is now chargeable to the Parish of Cheltenham [mark]

1841: *removed to St Mary de Lode, Gloucester (hiring and service).* [PS/CH/RA/2/5:308. Removal expenses for "Townsend" to Gloucester 9/6 (2Q 1841: D4178). See **34048SE** (wife Jane: 2 Sept 1834) and **47028RO** (1 July 1847).]

41034SE: Mon 10 May 1841 – **Joshua Birt** (also **Bert**, **Burt**), labourer, wife **Rachael**, and four children **Mary**, **Jeremiah**, **Job**, and **Amelia**: That he was born in the Parish of Painswick in the said County where his parents were legally settled as he has heard and believes. That his father is now and has been for some time receiving relief from the Parish officers of Painswick, that he has done no act to gain a settlement in his own right

That about Eight years ago he was married to his present Wife Rachael at Stroud by whom he has four Children to wit Mary aged seven years Jeremiah aged five years Job aged three years and Amelia aged Three months. That he is now Chargeable to the Parish of Cheltenham [mark]

1841: *removed to Painswick (presumed) (father's settlement); (6 June) JB (aged 30; labourer) lived with wife Rachael (25) and children Eliza (9), Mary (7), Jeremiah (5), Job (3), and Amelia (3 mo), in Exmouth St, Cheltenham (HO107/353/12/40/17). When Joshua lived in the Stroud area, he had been a weaver; after moving to Cheltenham he was consistently described as a labourer.* **1843:** *(RETURNED) daughter Harriet baptised in Cheltenham 25 June.* **1847:** *death of wife Rachael (aged 34) at Cheltenham (buried at New Burial Ground 9 Nov).* **1851:** *JB (44; labourer) lived with children Eliza (19; at home), Mary (17; at home), Job (12; scholar), Amelia (9; scholar), and Harriet (7) in Exmouth Court, Cheltenham (HO107/1973/854/12).* [PS/CH/RA/2/5:310; see **41035SE** (wife Rachael Birt about illegitimate daughter Eliza: 15 May 1841).]

41035SE: Sat 15 May 1841 – Rachael Birt (also Bert, Burt), relating to the settlement of **Eliza Smith**: That in the month of October 1831 she was delivered of a female illegitimate Child the said Eliza Smith in the Parish of Stroud in the said County who is now chargeable to the Parish of Cheltenham [mark]

1832: *baptism of (Frances) Eliza Jane, illegitimate daughter of RB (née Smith) 20 May, at Stroud.* **1833:** *Rachael Smith married Joshua Birt in Stroud 25 Apr.* **1841:** *removed to Stroud (birth).* [PS/CH/RA/2/5:311. *Removal expenses for "Birt" to Stroud £1/4/6 (2Q 1841: D4178). See* **41034SE** *(husband Joshua Birt: 10 May 1841); examination necessary because of illegitimacy of wife's (and probably his) daughter Eliza.*]

41036SE: Thurs 13 May 1841 – Ann Loveday, widow, residing in Staverton, relating to the settlement of daughter-in-law **Rhoda Loveday**, wife of late John Loveday, and her son **Thomas**: That the said John Loveday was her Son and that Eleven years ago last Michaelmas She was present with him at Tewkesbury when he was hired by Mr Isaac Yeend of the Parish of Elmstone Hardwicke in the said County Farmer for a year at the yearly wages of Six pounds

that her said Son served the whole year and received his years wages. That her said Son has done no act since to gain a settlement

That about nine years ago her said Son was relieved by the Parish Officers of Elmstone Hardwick aforesaid whilst he was residing in the Parish of Boddington

That about Six years ago her said Son was married to Rhoda Kear [also Care] at St. Marys Church Gloucester by whom he had one Child named Thomas now aged five years. That her said Son is now dead and his said Wife and Child are now chargeable to the said Parish of Cheltenham [mark]

1841: *John Loveday buried 10 May, from County Gaol in Gloucester; he had been sentenced to two months' imprisonment at County Adjourned Sessions 3 Mar for (with two others) stealing a quantity of iron plates belonging to the Cheltenham Tram Railway Company (see Cheltenham Chron. 18 Feb); dependent family was removed to Elmstone Hardwicke (hiring and service); (6 June) widow Rhoda Loveday (aged 30; charwoman) lived with son Thomas (5) in Elm St, Cheltenham (HO107/353/10/4/2).* **1851:** *(RETURNED) Rhoda (52; labourer and pauper, born Longdon, Worcs) lived with Thomas (14; labourer, born Boddington) at 9 Swindon Parade, Cheltenham (HO107/1973/518/14).* [PS/CH/RA/2/5:312. *Removal expenses for "Loveday" to Elmstone Hardwick 6/6 (2Q 1841: D4178). See* **48001RO** *(AL: 3 Jan 1848),* **50009RO** *(AL: 16 Mar 1850).*]

41037SE: Tues 18 May 1841 – **Mary Ann Adams**, widow, with three children **Frederick, Jane,** and **Walter;** also William Adams, residing in Poulton, Wilts, relating to the settlement of her husband, his late son James Adams. *William Adams:* That his said Son James was born at Fairford in the County of Gloucester

That in the year 1827 his said Son was hired by John Caswell of the said Parish of Fairford Baker for a Year   that he served the whole Year.

That his said Son has never done any act since to this Examinants knowledge and belief to gain a settlement elsewhere [signed]

Mary Ann Adams: Who upon her Oath saith that about Eight years ago she was married to her late husband James Adams in the Parish Church of Cheltenham by whom she has two Children Frederick aged seven Years and Jane aged four Years. That her said husband has been dead about three Years   that he never done [*sic*] any act to gain a settlement during their Marriage. that she has done no act to gain a settlement since her husbands death. that seven weeks ago she was delivered of a Male bastard Child named Walter in the said Parish of Cheltenham

That she and her said three Children are now actually chargeable to the said parish of Cheltenham [signed] **1838:** *death of husband James Adams (buried at Fairford 27 Oct, aged 28).* **1841: removed to Fairford (Cirencester Poor Law Union) (late husband's settlement);** *death of illegitimate son Walter aged two mo (buried at Cheltenham 28 May; (6 June) MAA (aged 28; servant) inmate of Cheltenham Union Workhouse; son Frederick (aged 6) lived in Fairford with family of Henry and Elizabeth Greening (HO107/352/7/39/3).* [PS/CH/RA/2/5:313a/b; page 309 of the register contains undated and unsigned sheet for MAA, with only introductory information completed. Removal expenses for "Adams" to Cirencester £1/1/- (2Q 1841: D4178).]

41038SE: Thurs 20 May 1841 – **William Barnes**, stonemason: That he was born in the Parish of Churchdown in the said County   that when he was about thirteen years and a half old he was Apprenticed by Indenture to William Gardner of the Parish of Tewkesbury in the said County Stonemason for seven years. That he Served the whole time and slept in his Masters house until the expiration of the term. that he has done no Act since to gain a settlement elsewhere   That about twenty years ago he was relieved by the Parish officers of Tewkesbury whilst he was residing at Gloucester

That he is now chargeable to the Parish of Cheltenham [signed]

1841: *removed to Tewkesbury (apprenticeship); (6 June) WB (aged 66; carpenter [error?]) was an inmate of Cheltenham Union Workhouse (HO107/353/17/16/2).* **1847:** *(RETURNED) death of WB at 1 Chapel St, Cheltenham (aged 72; stonemason) (buried 12 Feb).* [PS/CH/RA/2/5:314. Removal expenses for "Barnes" to Tewkesbury 12/- (2Q 1841: D4178).]

41039SE: [blank] May 1841 – **John Ursell**, stonemason, and wife **Charlotte**: That he was born in the Parish of Cirencester in the said County where his parents were legally settled as he has been informed and believes

That about twenty years ago he rented a house in the said Parish of Cirencester at upwards of twenty pounds a Year of Lord Bathurst. that he lived in such house about two years. that he has done no act since to gain a settlement elsewhere. That about ten Years ago he was married to his present Wife Charlotte at the Parish Church of Leckhampton. That he is now chargeable to the said Parish of Cheltenham [signed]

1841: *removed to Cirencester (presumed) (renting); (6 June) JU (aged 75; mason) and wife Charlotte (50) lived at 8 Commercial St, Cheltenham (HO107/353/12/20/35).* **1842:** *(RETURNED) death of JU (buried at New Burial Ground, Cheltenham 8 June, aged 80); wife Charlotte sent to Cirencester Union Workhouse.* **1845:** *death of wife Charlotte, aged 57 (buried at Cirencester 16 Jan).* [PS/CH/RA/2/5:315.]

41040SE: [blank] June 1841 – **Solomon Vines**, labourer, and son **Alfred**: That he was born in the Parish of Randwick in the said County where his parents were legally settled as he has been informed and believes. that both himself and his Father have been relieved by the Parish officers of Randwick aforesaid: that he has never done any act to gain a settlement in his own right.

That he has one Child named Alfred aged nine Years by his late wife Ann. That he is now chargeable to the said Parish of Cheltenham

1841: *removal uncertain: examination form incomplete: see* **41069RO** *(SV: 18 Nov 1841) for further information.* [PS/CH/RA/2/5:316.]

41041SE: Thurs 3 June 1841 – **Thomas Barnett**, labourer: That he was born in the Parish of Dowdeswell in the said County where his parents were legally settled as he has been informed and believes – That he has done no act to gain a settlement in his own right. That about a twelvemonth ago he was relieved by the Parish Officers of Dowdeswell whilst he was living at Charlton Kings – That he is now chargeable to the Parish of Cheltenham aforesaid [mark]

1841: *removed to Dowdeswell (father's settlement).* **1843:** *death of TB in Northleach Workhouse (Dowdeswell was part of Northleach Poor Law Union) (buried 24 Nov, aged 86).* [PS/CH/RA/2/5:317.

Removal expenses for "Barnett" to Dowdeswell 5/- (2Q 1841), 10/- (3Q 1841: D4178), and 12/6 (3Q 1843: D4178).]

41042SE: Tues 15 June 1841 – **Charlotte Smith**, single woman, and daughter **Amelia**: That she was born at Cirencester in this County where her parents lived – That she lived with her Father until she was fourteen years of age. That then she continued to live at the same house with her sisters – That she lived there until within the last two years – That she never rented a house at all. That she has heard her father and mother were settled at Cirencester – that they were both born there – that she has heard her father say so – That when she was about twelve years of age She and her three sisters and her brother were inmates of the Cirencester Workhouse and were relieved by the Parish – That one of her sisters named Harriet is in that Workhouse now – That she has never done any act to gain a settlement in her own right – That she is now chargeable to the Parish of Cheltenham – That she has one child named Amelia Smith of the age of four months [mark]
1841: removed to Cirencester (presumed) (father's settlement). 1843: death of CS (buried at Cirencester, aged 23). 1851: daughter Amelia (10) was an inmate of Cheltenham Workhouse (HO107/1973/1097/14)); Amelia's sister Harriet (aged 15) listed as an inmate of Cirencester Union Workhouse on census night (6 June). [PS/CH/RA/2/5:318.]

41043SE: Thurs 1 July 1841 – **George Hale**, labourer: That he was born in the Parish of Minchinhampton in the said County where his parents were legally settled as he has been informed and believes   That he has never done any act to gain a settlement in his own right
    That he is now chargeable to the said Parish of Cheltenham [signed]
*1841: ordered to be removed to Minchinhampton (father's alleged settlement) (appealed and quashed): see **41064SE** (GH: 23 Oct 1841), where he is described as "weaver".* [PS/CH/RA/2/5:319.]

41044SE: 1 July 1841 – **Mary Kings**, single woman: That She was born in the Parish of Saint Mary's Bury Saint Edmunds in the County of Suffolk where her parents were legally settled as she has been informed and believes   That she has done no act to gain a settlement in her own right. That she is now chargeable to the said Parish of Cheltenham [mark]
1841: removed to Bury St Edmunds, Suffolk (father's settlement). [PS/CH/RA/2/5:320. Removal expenses for "King" to Suffolk £8/10/- (3Q 1841: D4178).]

41045SE: Mon 2 Aug 1841 – **Moses Mundy** (also **Monday**, **Munday**), labourer, and wife **Sarah**: ~~That about 30 Years ago he was hired by Mr Hooper of the Parish of North Nibley in the said County Farmer for a year at the wages of Five pounds   that he served the whole year and received his years wages~~ he has heard and believes that his parents were legally settled in the Parish of North Nibley in the said County – that he has never done any act to gain a settlement in his own right   That his Father is dead and his Mother is now receiving relief from the Parish officers of North Nibley aforesaid. that about ~~twenty five~~ fifteen years ago he was married at Uley to his present wife Sarah – That about seven years ago he was relieved by the Parish officers of North Nibley aforesaid whilst he was residing in the Parish of Uley. That he is now chargeable to the Parish of Cheltenham [mark]
1841: (6 June) MM (aged 45) lived in Bath Terrace, Cheltenham with David (15; labourer), son by first marriage (HO107/353/12/12/20); removed to North Nibley (father's settlement). 1842: probable death of wife Sarah in Dursley Union Workhouse 6 Jan, aged 64; remarriage of MM, to Sarah Smith, at Leckhampton 24 July. 1851: (RETURNED) the couple lived at 8 Bath Terrace, Cheltenham: Moses (58; labourer, born Swanley) and Sarah (56; laundress) (HO107/1973/878/14). [PS/CH/RA/2/5:321. Removal expenses for "Munday" to North Nibley £2/1/6 (3Q 1841: D4178).]

41046SE: 2 Aug 1841 – **Mary Parkinson**, widow: That about Fifty years ago she was married to her late husband William at Bolton le Moor [= Bolton le Moors] in the County of Lancaster - that She has heard her said husband say and she believes it to be true that he was apprenticed by Indenture to Mʳ Williams of the parish of Liverpool in the said County of Lancaster Slater and Plasterer for seven years and that he served the whole time, – That her said husband never rented a Tenement of the annual value of ten pounds nor did any act to gain a settlement elsewhere

That her said husband died about twenty four Years ago at Liverpool aforesaid and was buried at the Expence of the Parish officers there – That She has done no act to gain a settlement in her own right since her husbands death. That She has herself been relieved by the Parish officers of Liverpool and been in the Workhouse there – That she is now chargeable to the Parish of Cheltenham [mark]

1841: *removed to Liverpool, Lancashire (husband's settlement).* [PS/CH/RA/2/5:322. Perhaps see removal expenses for "Patterson" to Liverpool £5/5/9 (3Q 1841: D4178).]

41047SE: 2 Aug 1841 – **Reuben Yates** (also **Yeates**), cordwainer, and wife **Margaret**: That when he was about seventeen years of age he was apprenticed by Indenture to Joseph Copner then of Barton Saint Mary in the County of Gloucester for four years   that he served about the first two years of the term with his Master at Barton Saint Mary aforesaid and then removed with his Master to the Parish of Upton Saint Leonards in the said County where he served the remainder of his term. That he has never done any act to gain a settlement elsewhere

That about nine months ago he was married to his present wife Margaret at the Parish of Cheltenham aforesaid   That he is now chargeable to the said parish of Cheltenham [mark]

1841: *removed to Upton St Leonards (apprenticeship):* see **49011RO** *(RY: 30 Jan 1849) for further information on family.* [PS/CH/RA/2/5:323. Removal expenses for "Yates" to Upton St Leonards 2/- (3Q 1841: D4178).]

41048SE: Mon 9 Aug 1841 – **John Ivin** (also **Iuens, Iving, Ivins, Ivein, Ivens**), wife **Ann**, and two children **Piety** and **Charles**; also Solomon Ivin, regarding the settlement of son John Ivin.

Solomon Ivin: That thirty three years ago he was hired by M'r Cambridge of the Township of Acton Turville in the said County Farmer for a year   that he served the whole year and received his years wages – That he has never done any act since to gain a settlement elsewhere

John Ivin: That he had never done any act to gain a settlement in his own right   That about three years ago he was married to his present Wife Ann at Cheltenham by whom he has two Children viz Piety aged two years and Charles aged five months

That he is now chargeable to the Parish of Cheltenham

1841: *removed to Acton Turville (father's settlement):* see **48028** *(JI: 29 Nov 1848) for further information.* [PS/CH/RA/2/5:324. Removal expenses for "Ivens" to Acton Turville £3/6/6 (3Q 1841: D4178).]

41049SE: Thurs 19 Aug 1841 – **Mary Stevens** (also **Stephens**), widow: That her husband Henry has been dead about thirty one years. That about fourteen years ago she was hired by M'r Garner of the Parish of Elmstone Hardwicke in the said County for a year at the wages of Eight pounds that she served the whole year and received her years wages and continued in such service three years afterwards at the same wages

That she has done no act since to gain a settlement elsewhere – That she is now chargeable to the Parish of Cheltenham [mark]

1841: *(6 June) MS (aged 75; independent) lived alone in Naunton Fields, Cheltenham (HO107/353/12/43/23); removed to Elmstone Hardwicke (hiring and service).* **1847:** *(RETURNED) death of MS in Cheltenham (buried 10 Sept at New Burial Ground, aged 86); at time of death MS lived at 11 Bath Terrace, Cheltenham.* [PS/CH/RA/2/5:325. Removal expenses for "Stevens" Elmstone Hardwicke 7/6 (3Q 1841: D4178).]

41050SE: Wed 25 Aug 1841 – **John Nicholls** (also **Nichols**), labourer: That in the year 1800 he was hired by M'r Harrison of the Parish of Collard [perhaps for Callow]   in the County of Hereford for a Year at the wages of twenty pounds   that he served the whole year and received his years wages and continued in the same service another year   That in the year 1803 he rented a Cottage and Stable of M'r Taylor in the Parish of Saint Andrew in the City of Worcester by the Year at a little above Eleven pounds a Year and continued in the occupation of it for about nine Years and paid the rent for the same   That he has never done any act since to gain a settlement elsewhere   That he is now chargeable to the said Parish of Cheltenham [signed John Nichols]

1841: *removed to St Andrew, Worcester, Worcs (renting).* [PS/CH/RA/2/5:326. Removal expenses for "Nicholls" to Worcester, Worcs £1/-/6 (3Q 1841: D4178).]

41051SE: 25 Aug 1841 – **James Tomlin**: That about fifteen years ago he rented a house in the parish of Tottenham in the County of Middlesex for a Year at the rent of fifteen pounds – that he continued in such house three Years and paid all the rent and was duly rated and paid all poor rates in respect of the same. That he has done no act since to gain a settlement elsewhere. that about four years ago he was relieved by the parish officers of Tottenham aforesaid whilst he was residing in the parish of Saint Martin in the fields – That he is now chargeable to the Parish of Cheltenham aforesaid [signed]

1837: *JT was removed to Tottenham from Castle St Workhouse, Westminster, aged 64.* **1841:** *(6 June) JT (aged 70; labourer) lived in Gratton Terrace, Cheltenham (HO107/353/12/20/35);* **removed to Tottenham, Middlesex (renting).** **1846:** *death of JT, aged 73 (buried at All Hallows, Tottenham). [PS/CH/RA/2/5:327. Removal expenses for "Tomkins" [sic] to Tottenham £5/2/6 (3Q 1841: D4178).]*

41052SE: Tues 31 Aug 1841 – **Elisha Smith**, wife **Ann**, and three children **Jane, Elisha**, and **Hannah**: That his parents are legally settled in Ampney Crucis in the said County as he has heard and believes & where they are now living

That he has done no act to gain a settlement in his own right – That about Seven Years ago he was Married to his present Wife Ann at the parish Church of Cheltenham by whom he has three Children vizt Jane aged six years Elisha aged four years and Hannah one Year and a half

That he is now chargeable to the said Parish of Cheltenham [signed]

1841: *ES was absent from home on census night (6 June): wife Ann (aged 30; charwoman) and children Jane (6), Elisha (4), and Hannah (1) lived in Newman's Place, Cheltenham (HO107/353/16/8/11);* **removed to Ampney Crucis (father's settlement).** **1842:** *(RETURNED) daughter Anna (probably Hannah) baptised at Cheltenham 1 Feb, when ES (formerly labourer) gave his occupation as "Policeman"; the family lived at 22 Newman's Place.* **1843:** *death of ES (buried at Ampney Crucis 11 July, aged 28). [PS/CH/RA/2/5:328. Removal expenses for "Smith" to Ampney Crucis £1/9/- (3Q 1841: D4178).]*

41053SE: Sat 18 Sept 1841 – Mary Artus, regarding the settlement of nephew **Thomas Greening**: That the said Thomas Greening is now about 13 years of age and is the Son of her Sister Elizabeth Greening and John Greening. that the said John Greening and his Wife were about 15 years ago removed by the Parish officers of Cheltenham to the Parish of Boddington in the said County the Parish officers of which latter Parish relieved them several times afterwards

That the said John Greening and his Wife are now dead and [had] never to her knowledge done any Act to gain a settlement after their Removal to Boddington aforesaid – That the said Thomas Greening has never done any act to gain a settlement in his own right and is now chargeable to the said Parish of Cheltenham [mark]

1837: *removed with family to Boddington: see* **37044RO** *(father John Greening: 13 July 1837) (RETURNED).* **1841:** *TG (aged 13) was an inmate of Charlton Kings Workhouse for children (Cheltenham Union) (HO107/353/2/54/2), where he had lived occasionally since at least 25 Jan 1840 when admitted, aged 11, as orphan (G/CH/60/2);* **removed to Boddington (father's settlement).** **1851:** *not found on census (probably at sea).* **1856:** *TG, stoker, married Ellen Grayson on 1 Dec in Sheffield, Yorks.* **1861:** *the couple lived in Rotherham: TG (32; labourer, born Cheltenham), Ellen (32), and son Thomas (7 mo) (RG9/3504/70/7).* [PS/CH/RA/2/5:329. Removal expenses for "Greening" to Boddington 2/6 (4Q 1841: D4178).]

41054SE: 18 Sept 1841 – **Ann Cook** (also **Cooke**), and son **Richard**; also Esther Holder, regarding the settlement of brother Samuel Cook, husband of Ann Cook.

Esther Cook: That her parents are legally settled in the Parish of Randwick in the said County as she has heard and believes   that her father has been several times relieved by the Parish Officers of Randwick aforesaid   that her said Brother has never to her knowledge and belief done any Act to gain a settlement in his own right [signed Esther Houlder]

Ann Cook: That about three Years ago she was married to her present husband Samuel Cook in the Tower of London by whom she had one Child named Richard aged one year

That her husband belongs to the Rifle Brigade and is now at Malta. That she is now chargeable to the Parish of Cheltenham [signed] Ann Cooke

1841: *removed to Randwick (husband's settlement).* **1861:** *Richard Cook was Corporal in Royal Horse Artillery, stationed at Woolwich (RG9/405/148/26).* [PS/CH/RA/2/5:330. Removal expenses for "Cooke" to Randwick 17/6 (4Q 1841: D4178).]

41055SE: Thurs 30 Sept 1841 – **Thomas Holland**, labourer, wife **Esther**, and three children **Ann**, **Henry**, and **Charles**: That he was born in the Parish of Lechlade in the said County where his parents were legally settled as he has been informed and believes – that about ten years ago he was relieved by the Parish Officers of Lechlade aforesaid while he was residing at Cirencester

That he has never done any act to gain a Settlement in his own right. That about twenty nine years ago he was married to his present Wife Esther at Lechlade aforesaid by whom he has three Children Ann aged about ten Years Henry aged Eight years and Charles aged five years

That he is now chargeable to the said Parish of Cheltenham [mark]

1841: *(6 June) TH (aged 45; ostler) lived with wife Catharine (née Hester; 45; washerwoman) with children Ann (13), Henry (10), and Charley (4) in Burton St, Cheltenham (HO107/353/16/26/12);* ***removed to Lechlade (father's settlement).*** **1844:** *(RETURNED) death of Catharine Holland (buried 12 Mar at New Burial Ground, Cheltenham).* **1845:** *daughter Ann died (buried at New Burial Ground, Cheltenham 8 Dec, aged 17).* **1846:** *arrest of TH for stealing pair of boots in Cheltenham, and sentenced to three months' imprisonment.* **1847:** *Charles Holland apparently accused of stealing lead (with two others) in Cheltenham in Mar (Cheltenham Chron. 1 Apr) (not guilty).* **1849:** *death of TH in Faringdon Workhouse, aged 58 (burial in Cirencester 6 Oct).* [PS/CH/RA/2/5:331. Removal expenses for "Holland" to Lechlade £2/1/- (4Q 1841: D4178).]

41056RO: 30 Sept 1841 – **Elizabeth Andrews** and four children, **Elizabeth**, **James**, **Caroline**, and **Ruth**: That she is the Wife of James Andrews who was transported at the last Assizes holden for the said County And that she and her said husband and their three children was [*sic*] about four years ago removed by the Parish Officers of Cheltenham to the Parish of Trowbridge in the County of Wilts which order was not appealed against – That her said husband has done no act since to gain a settlement – That she has now four children by her said husband Viz^t. Elizabeth aged ten years James aged seven years Caroline aged five years and Ruth aged one year – That she is now chargeable to the said Parish of Cheltenham [mark]

1841: *removed to Trowbridge, Wilts (husband's settlement):* see **38035RO** *(EA: 24 Apr) for further information on the family.* [PS/CH/RA/2/6:1 (copy at PS/CH/RA/2/5:332). Removal expenses for "Andrews" to Trowbridge, Wilts £3/11/6 (4Q 1841: D4178).]

41057RO: Sat 2 Oct 1841 – Leah Thomas Lea, widow, regarding the settlement of son **John Lea**: That she is the Widow of Richard Lea who was a Miller and Baker at Malm[e]sbury in the County of Wilts who gained a settlement there by renting a Tenement about 30 Years ago at twenty pounds a Year and had a considerable copyhold property of his own at Malmsbury and sold it for Six hundred pounds a few months before his death which happened about 15 Years ago

That he nor has this Examinant done any Act to gain a settlement since – That her said Son was born at Malmsbury and has never done any act to gain a settlement in his own right. That he is now chargeable to the said Parish of Cheltenham [signed]

1841: *removed to Malmesbury, Wilts (father's settlement), but pauper apparently died before removal took place;* JL *buried at New Burial Ground, Cheltenham 16 Oct, aged 21.* [PS/CH/RA/2/6:2 (copy at PS/CH/RA/2/5:333); suspended as pauper unfit to travel. Note: "Order should have been to the Parish of Westropp [= Westrop] Malmsbury – Abandoned - The Pauper Since Dead.] Removal expenses to Malmesbury for "Lea" £1/10/6 (4Q 1841: D4178).]

41058RO: 2 Oct 1841 – **David Patten** (also **Paten**, **Pattern**): That he was born in the Parish of Stonehouse in the said County where his parents were legally Settled as he has been informed and believes

That his parents have been several times Relieved by the Parish Officers of Stonehouse and are now receiving two shillings a week from them   that he has done no act to gain a settlement in his own right and is now chargeable to the said Parish of Cheltenham [signed]

1799: *DP born 18 Feb (baptised at Randwick, Countess of Huntingdon's Connexion), to William and Elizabeth Patten.* **1841:** *(6 June) William and Elizabeth Patten both lived in Randwick: William Patten (aged 70; woollen spinner), Elizabeth Patten (65) (HO107/370/14/35/5);* **removed to Stonehouse (father's settlement).** **1861:** *DP perhaps the David Patton (62; plasterer, born Stroud) recorded as patient at Queen's Hospital, Birmingham, Warks (RG9/2137/64/4).* [PS/CH/RA/2/6:3 (copy at PS/CH/RA/2/5:334).]

41059RO: Tues 5 Oct 1841 – **Thirza Wilkins**, single woman, and daughter **Elizabeth Wilkins**: That she was born in the Parish of Arlingham in the said County. that about ten years ago she was hired by Mr Hollester [also Hollister] of the Parish of Painswick in the said County as a servant of all work by the Year at Four pounds a Year – that she served the whole year and received her years wages – That She has done no act since to gain a settlement elsewhere. That about 13 weeks ago she was delivered of a female Bastard Child named Elizabeth in the Parish of Cheltenham And she is now actually chargeable to the said Parish of Cheltenham [mark]
1841: *TW (aged 20; servant) lived in Winchcombe St (6 June) (HO107/353/6/48/8);* **removed to Painswick (hiring and service);** *daughter Elizabeth died aged six months (buried at Painswick 10 Dec 1841).* **1849:** *death of TW 3Q in Bridgwater, Som, where brother Nathaniel trained for Master Mariner's licence (awarded 1851).* [PS/CH/RA/2/6:4 (copy at PS/CH/RA/2/5:335). Removal expenses for "Wilkins" to Painswick 15/- (4Q 1841: D4178).]

41060RO: Thurs 7 Oct 1841 – **Emanuel** (also Immanuel) **Bridges**, stonemason, wife **Rose**, and six children **Ann**, **William**, **Rosanna**, **Mary**, **Prudence**, **Eliza**: That he was born in the Parish of Chedworth in the said County where his parents were legally settled as he has been informed and believes. But he has never done any act to gain a settlement in his own right. That two years ago he was relieved by the parish Officers of Chedworth aforesaid
    That about 13 years ago he was married to his present Wife Rose at the said Parish of Chedworth by whom he has six children to wit Ann aged ten years William aged 8 years Rosanna aged 6 years Mary aged three years Prudence aged 2 years & Eliza aged 6 weeks. That he is now actually chargeable to the said Parish of Cheltenham [signed]
1841: *removed to Chedworth (father's settlement):* see **47001RO** *(EB: 9 Jan 1847).* [PS/CH/RA/2/6:5 (copy at PS/CH/RA/2/5:336. Removal expenses for "Bridges" to Chedworth 18/6 (4Q 1841: D4178).]

41061SE: Tues 12 Oct 1841 – **Susan Blenman** (also **Blinman**), single woman: [no text].
1841: *removal uncertain: examination form incomplete:* see **46004SE** *(future husband John Walton: 23 Jan 1846) for further information on family.* [PS/CH/RA/2/5:337. Removal expenses for "Blenman" to Cirencester 13/- (4Q 1841: D4178). See **41065SE** (father Henry Blenman: 25 Oct 1841).]

41062RO: Sat 23 Oct 1841 – **John Alsop** (also **Allsop**), cordwainer, and two children **John** and **Joseph**: That the first place he remembers himself was residing with his Father in the Parish of Saint James' in the City of Bristol and continued to live with him until this Examinant was about 14 Years of age   That during the time he so lived with his Father his said Father rented a house in the said Parish of Saint James' at more than twenty pounds a Year for as long as he can remember
    That he was Apprenticed by Indenture to Thomas Garland of the said Parish of Saint James's Cordwainer for five years and served four Years and three quarters of the said term during the whole of which time and for a considerable time afterwards he lodged in the Parish of Saint Pauls in the said City of Bristol – That he has never done any act since to gain a settlement elsewhere
    That about seven Years ago he was married to his late Wife Sarah (lately deceased) in the Parish Church of Cheltenham by whom he has two Children to wit John aged six years and a half and Joseph aged three years and a half.
    That he is now chargeable to the Parish of Cheltenham aforesaid [mark]
1841: *(6 June) the family lived at 37 Rutland St, Cheltenham: JA (aged 27; shoemaker), Sarah (20), and children John (6) and Joseph (3) (HO107/353/7/65/34); Sarah Alsop died shortly before examination (buried at New Burial Ground, Cheltenham on 8 Oct, aged 32;* **removed to St Paul's, Bristol (apprenticeship).** **1844:** *(RETURNED) birth of son, Henry, to JA and Elizabeth Griffin (baptised at Cheltenham 15 Sept 1844), under name of Griffin.* **1845:** *JA remarried, to Elizabeth Griffin, in Cheltenham on 15 Feb.* **1846:** *second son, Charles, baptised at Cheltenham 31 May, when parents lived at 36 Rutland St.*

1851: *the family lodged at 37 Rutland St (next-door to Elizabeth Griffin's parents at 36): JA (37; shoemaker, born Bristol), Elizabeth (26; washerwoman), and children John (17; labourer), Joseph (18; shoemaker), Henry (7; scholar), and Charles (5; scholar) (HO107/1973/358/25). [PS/CH/RA/2/6:6 (copy at PS/CH/RA/2/5:340). Removal expenses for "Alsop" to Bristol £2/6/- (4Q 1841: D4178).]*

41063RO: 23 Oct 1841 – **William Dix** (also **Dicks**), labourer, wife **Louisa**, and two children **John** and **Ellen**: That the first place he remembers himself was living with his Father in the Parish of Charlton Kings in the said County with whom he resided in that Parish until he was about twenty Years of age   That during that time his father lived in his own house for about 16 years which House he sold for about thirty five pounds to Mr Gael – That he has done no act to gain a settlement in his own right   That near three Years ago he was married to his present Wife Louisa in the Parish Church of Cheltenham by whom he has two Children to wit John aged one Year and nine months and Ellen aged three Months   That he is now actually chargeable to the said Parish of Cheltenham [mark]
1841: *WD absent from home on census night (6 June): wife Louisa (aged 20) lived in Worcester St, Cheltenham with son John (2) (HO107/353/9/61/22); removed to Charlton Kings (father's settlement); (RETURNED) children John and Ellen Dix baptised 16 Dec at Cheltenham, when family were inmates of workhouse. **1844:** family again inmates of workhouse late Feb (G/CH/60/4). **1846:** death of son John Dix (buried at New Burial Ground, Cheltenham, aged 6). **1851:** WD (34; labourer) lived with wife Louisa (30) and five children in Leckhampton (HO107/1972/211/25). [PS/CH/RA/2/6:7 (copy at PS/CH/RA/2/5:338). Removal expenses for "Dix" to Charlton Kings 2/6 (4Q 1841: D4178). See **41066SE** (mother Jane Dix, confirmed husband's and hence William's settlement was Charlton Kings: 1 Nov 1841), **42002RO** (brother Robert Dix, removed from Cheltenham to Charlton Kings: 6 Jan 1842).]*

41064SE: 23 Oct 1841 – **George Hale**, weaver: That the first place he remembers himself was living with his Father at a place called Bewley [= Burleigh] in the parish of Minchinhampton in this county [incomplete]
1841: *GH (aged 70; cloth-worker) lived (6 June) in Sherborne St, Cheltenham, with Hannah Hale; ordered to be removed to Minchinhampton (father's alleged settlement) (appealed and quashed): see **41043SE** (GH: 1 July 1841); removal uncertain: examination form incomplete; (RETURNED) GH married Hannah 15 Nov in Cheltenham. **1843:** deaths of GH and Hannah in Cheltenham, aged 80 and 79 respectively. [PS/CH/RA/2/5:339. Removal expenses for "Hall" [sic] to Minchinhampton £1/14/- (4Q 1841: D4178).]*

41065SE: Mon 25 Oct 1841 – Henry Blenman, cordwainer, residing in Cirencester, regarding the settlement of daughter **Susan Blenman**: That [t]he said Susan Blenman is an illegitimate Child and was born in the parish of Cheltenham in the said County about 25 years ago and has done no act to gain a settlement in her own right [incomplete]
[PS/CH/RA/2/5:341. See **46004SE** (future son-in-law John Walton: 23 Jan 1846).]

41066SE: Mon 1 Nov 1841 – Jane Dix, residing in Cirencester, regarding the settlement of son **William Dix**: That she was married to her husband Robert Dix about twenty six years ago in the parish Church of Charlton Kings in the said County   that she well knew her husband for about four years previously   that about two years before her said marriage her said husband was hired by Mr Faulkner of Eastend farm in the said Parish of Charlton Kings from Christmas until the Michaelmas following when he was again hired by the same person for a Year   that her said husband served the whole year and we [sic] were married in about two or three days afterwards

That she and her said husband never rented a tenement of the annual value of ten pounds nor done [sic] any act to gain a settlement elsewhere   that the said William Dix is her Son by her said husband [mark]
[PS/CH/RA/2/5:342. See **41064RO** (son William Dix: 23 Oct 1841), **42002RO** (son Robert Dix: 6 Jan 1842).]

41067SE: [blank] Nov 1841 – **Margaret Murphy** (perhaps **Marphy**), widow: That she is near 70 Years of age   That about 32 years ago she was married to her late husband Philip who died about four years ago at the Cove [= Cobh] of Cork in Ireland by a Catholic Priest – [incomplete]

[PS/CH/RA/2/5:343. Examination struck out.]

41068RO: Thurs 18 Nov 1841 – **Thomas Andrews**, labourer: That the first place he remembers himself was in the Parish of Northleach in the said County that he has never been hired for a Year or rented a tenement of the annual value of ten pounds or done any act to gain a Settlement in his own right That near 12 months ago he was admitted into the Workhouse at Northleach where he continued for about 11 months and was chargeable to that Parish That he is now actually Chargeable to the Parish of Cheltenham aforesaid [signed]

1841: *(6 June) TA (aged 30) was an inmate of Northleach Workhouse at Eastington (HO107/351/10/38/1); removed to Northleach (father's presumed settlement).* **1851:** *TA again an inmate of Northleach Workhouse (37; unmarried, born Northleach) (HO107/1969/132/16).* **1871:** *death of TA (buried at Northleach 31 Jan, aged 57).* [PS/CH/RA/2/6:8 (copy at PS/CH/RA/2/5:344). Removal expenses for "Andrews" to Northleach £1/1/- (4Q 1841: D4178).]

41069RO: 18 Nov 1841 – **Solomon Vines**, labourer, and son **Alfred**: That the first place he remembers himself was at Randwick in the said County which place he left about 6 or 7 Years ago. that his Father belonged to that Parish and received relief from the Parish Officers of that Parish for about twenty two Years until his death which happened about two Years ago That he this Examinant hath done no act to gain a settlement in his own right. That about twenty years ago he was married to his late Wife Ann at Randwick aforesaid who is now dead and by whom he has one Child named Alfred aged ten Years

That he and his said Child are now chargeable to the said Parish of Cheltenham [signed]

1834: *death of Ann Vines in Randwick, aged 38 (buried 5 Mar).* **1840:** *a SV fined for drunkenness (Cheltenham Chron. 5 Nov).* **1841:** *(6 June) SV (aged 38; labourer; at Randwick formerly (billy-)spinner) lived with youngest son Alfred (8) at 2 Park Place, Cheltenham (HO107/353/16/46/9); removal uncertain: examination form incomplete: see* **41041SE** *(SV: June 1841); removed to Randwick (father's settlement).* **1851:** *SV (43; agricultural labourer and widower) lodged with Collier family in Tuffley (HO107/1962/462/12).* [PS/CH/RA/2/6:8 (copy at PS/CH/RA/2/5:345). Removal expenses for "Vines" to Randwick £1/6/6 (4Q 1841: D4178).]

41070SE: [undated: Nov 1841] – **Mary Reeves**: [no text].

1841: *(6 June) an MR (aged 23; servant born outside Glos) worked in Pittville Terrace, Cheltenham; removal uncertain: examination form incomplete.* [PS/CH/RA/2/5:346. Removal expenses for "Reeves" to Lechlade £2/1/- (4Q 1841: D4178).]

41071RO: Sat 11 Dec 1841 (examinations on 9 Dec and 27 Nov respectively) – Samuel Coombes, joiner, regarding the settlement of son George West Coombes and consequently of his wife **Mary Coombes** and their infant son, **Josiah**:

Samuel Coombes: That about ten years ago he rented a house by the year in the Parish of Leckhampton in the said County at £18.18.0. a Year and continued in such house about five years and a half and is now chargeable to the said Parish of Leckhampton. That the said George Coombes is his Son by his late Wife Fanny. That his said Son has never done any act to gain a settlement in his own right [signed]

Mary Coombes: That in the Month of December last year she was married to her husband George Coombes at Cheltenham by whom she has an Infant Boy now unchristened. that her said husband has deserted her and she is become chargeable to the said Parish of Cheltenham [signed]

1840: *marriage of Mary Ann Thackwell, daughter of Josiah Thackwell of Marsh Lane, Cheltenham and George Coombes at Cheltenham 27 Dec.* **1841:** *(6 June) Mary Coombes (aged 18; laundress, known as "Thackwell", born outside Glos) lived without George with mother and younger sister in Marsh Lane, Cheltenham (HO107/353/8/26/8); (31 Oct) birth of son Josiah at The Marsh, Cheltenham; removed to Leckhampton (George Coombes's settlement).* **1842:** *death of son Josiah in Cheltenham 1Q.* [PS/CH/RA/2/6:12 (copy at PS/CH/RA/2/5:347). Removal expenses for "Coombes" to Leckhampton 2/6 (1Q 1842: D4178).]

41072SE: Sat 20 Nov 1841 – Robert Godfrey, labourer, relating to the settlement of wife **Elizabeth** and daughter **Louisa**: That the first place he remembers himself was in the Parish of Cheltenham

that about 18 months ago he rented a house in Albert Street Cheltenham of Mr Jones at five shillings a week   that he continued in such house a full year and paid all rent due in respect thereof   that he was duly rated and paid the Poor Rates in respect of such house – That his Wife and Child are now chargeable to the said Parish [signed]

1839: *Robert Godfrey (porter working at Royal Hotel, Cheltenham) married Elizabeth Pitt in Cheltenham 17 June.* **1840:** *daughter Louisa Harriet Godfrey baptised at Cheltenham 1 Nov, when Robert Godfrey was porter living in Albert St.* **1841:** *the couple apparently separated, and on census night (6 June) Robert (age given as 15; porter) lived at home with parents in Albert St, Cheltenham (HO107/353/9/4/3), while Elizabeth (25) and Louisa (1) lodged with Charles and Harriet Godfrey at 38 Ann St, Birmingham (HO107/1144/3/14/21);* **removal unlikely: settlement probably acknowledged as Cheltenham.** **1851:** *Elizabeth (35; widowed, born Cheltenham) worked as housekeeper and cook at 13 Devonshire Place, Marylebone, London (HO107/1487/216/6), while daughter Louisa (10; scholar) lived with maternal grandparents Joseph and Louisa Pitt at 54 Stanhope St, Cheltenham (HO107/1973/502/24).* [PS/CH/RA/2/5:348.]

41073RO: Fri 3 Dec 1841 – **George Corbett** (also **Corbet**), labourer, wife **Hannah**, and two children **Caroline** and **William**: That last Michaelmas ten years he was hired by Richard Organ of Little Witcomb [= Little Witcombe] in the Parish of Badgworth [= Badgeworth] in the said County as a Carter for a Year at £4. or £5 a year   that he served the whole year and received his year's wages   That he was then hired by Charles Brunsdon of Uphatherly [= Up Hatherley] in the said County for a Year at the wages of five pounds. That he continued in such service until three weeks before the end of the Year when the contract was dissolved by mutual Consent and he was paid wages for only the time he served   That he has never done any act since to gain a settlement. that about Eight years ago he was married to his present Wife Hannah at Saint Mary de lode Church Gloucester by whom he has two Children to wit, Caroline aged near Eight years and William aged six years – That he is now actually chargeable to the said Parish of Cheltenham [mark]

1841: *GC died of consumption on 4 December at Tivoli Place, Cheltenham, aged 25, before his removal; family removed to Badgeworth (hiring and service).* **1845:** *remarriage of widow Hannah, to Richard Newman (both of Hatherley Cottage, Cheltenham) 25 Dec.* **1851:** *the family lived in Badgeworth: Richard Newman (42; agricultural labourer), Hannah (38), Caroline (17), and William (15) (children all born Badgeworth) (HO107/1972/305/1).* [PS/CH/RA/2/6:10 (copy at PS/CH/RA/2/5:349). Removal expenses for "Corbett" to Badgworth 11/- (4Q 1841: D4178).]

41074RO: Thurs 9 Dec 1841 – **Thomas Mott**, labourer, wife **Hannah**, and six children **Mary Ann**, **Thomas**, **Eleanor**, **Edwin**, **Henry**, and **George**: That about thirty years ago he was apprenticed by Indenture to Messrs Lloyd of Winchcomb [= Winchcombe] in the said County Paper Makers for seven years – That he served the whole time and slept in Winchcomb the whole of the time

That he has done no act since to gain a Settlement. That about 23 Years ago he was married to his present Wife Hannah at the Parish Church of Badgworth [= Badgeworth] by whom he has six children now forming part of his family neither of whom has gained a settlement in their own right Viz^t Mary Ann aged 18 Years Thomas aged 13 Years Eleanor aged 10 years Edwin aged four years Henry aged 2 years and George aged 7 months   That he is now chargeable to the Parish of Cheltenham aforesaid [signed]

1841: *(6 June) TM (aged 40; agricultural labourer, born Cheltenham) lived with wife Hannah (40) and six children in Major's Row, Cheltenham (HO107/353/11/4/3-5/4);* **removed to Winchcombe (apprenticeship).** **1851:** *(RETURNED) the family lived at 3 Park St, Cheltenham: TM (53; labourer), Hannah (62), five children, and Ann Mott (80) (HO107/1973/603/32-33).* [PS/CH/RA/2/6:11 (copy at PS/CH/RA/2/5:350). Removal expenses for "Mott" to Winchcombe 18/- (1Q 1842: D4178).]

41075RO: Sat 11 Dec 1841 – **Ann Coates**, single woman: That the first place she remembers herself was in the Parish of Chedworth in the said County   That about 12 Years ago her Father was relieved by the Parish Officers of Yanworth in the said County whilst he was residing at Chedworth. That she accompanied her Father and Mother about that time from Chedworth to Yanworth in which latter place they resided in a Cottage belonging to the Parish of Yanworth – That she has done no act to gain a settlement in her own right And is now chargeable to the said Parish of Cheltenham [mark]

1841: *perhaps the AC (aged 50; dressmaker) who lived in Chedworth (6 June) (HO107/363/9/13/21);* **removed to Yanworth (father's settlement).** **1861:** *AC perhaps visitor (aged 74; unmarried, and dressmaker, born Chedworth) at house of Thomas Walker (farmer) at Compton Abdale (RG9/1788/68/24).* [PS/CH/RA/2/6:13 (suspended as pauper unfit to travel (suspension not lifted) (copy at PS/CH/RA/2/5:351). Removal expenses for "Coates" to Yanworth 13/- (4Q 1841) and £1/13/6 (1Q 1842: D4178).]

41076RO: Thurs 16 Dec 1841 – **Elizabeth Jones**, wife of William Jones, and five children **Richard**, **Eliza**, **Henry**, **Amos**, and **Matilda**: That about nineteen years ago she was married to her said husband in the Parish Church of Rodborough in the said County   that at the time of her Marriage her said husband was about Eighteen years of age and had up to that time always lived with his Father as part of his family in the Parish of Stroud in the said County where he was born. that her said husband's Father had for several years before she was married rented a House at Stroud aforesaid of the annual value of at least thirty pounds and where he has lived ever since – That her said husband has never done any act to gain a settlement in his own right. That she has five Children by her said husband now living with her neither of whom has been emancipated to wit, Richard aged 17 years Eliza aged 14 years Henry aged 11 years Amos aged 8 years and Matilda aged 4 years. That her said husband is now confined in Gloucester Gaol for felony and She and her Children are now actually chargeable to the said Parish of Cheltenham – That about 11 years ago she was relieved by the Parish officers of Stroud aforesaid [mark]

1841: *(6 June) EJ (aged 30; charwoman, born Stroud) lived with children Richard (15; labourer), Henry (12), Amos (8), and Matilda (4) in Sherborne St, Cheltenham (HO107/353/5/59/41);* **removed to Stroud (husband's settlement).** **1842:** *William Jones (39) convicted at County Sessions on 4 Jan of stealing wheelbarrow and pickaxe from his employer, Carter & Bailey, Road Contractors, of Bishop's Cleeve; son Richard accused of involvement (not guilty) (Cheltenham Chron. 25 Nov 1841); Richard Jones sentenced to twelve months' imprisonment with hard labour and severe whipping at Northleach Gaol for involvement in stealing twenty-six rabbit and hare skins (Gloucestershire Chron. 5 Mar 1842).* **1849:** *EJ (widow) married John Nichols at St Peter's, Leckhampton 19 Nov.* **1851:** *(RETURNED) the family lived at 15 Tivoli St, Cheltenham: John Nichols (41; day labourer), Elizabeth (46; laundress, born Stroud), Henry (21; plasterer, born Stroud), and Matilda (14; laundress, born Cheltenham) (HO107/1973/926/41-927/42).* [PS/CH/RA/2/6:13 (copy at PS/CH/RA/2/5:352). Removal expenses for "Jones" to Stroud £1/2/6 (1Q 1842: D4178).]

41077RO: Sat 18 Dec 1841 – **William Simmonds** (also **Simmons**), labourer, wife **Phoebe**, and child **Joseph**: That about ten years ago he was hired by Mr Daniel Theyer of Little Shurdington in the Parish of Badgworth [= Badgeworth] in the said County as Cowman at £5 a Year   that he served the whole year and received his Years wages   That he has done no act since to gain a settlement elsewhere   That soon after he left Mr Theyers he was married to his present Wife Phoebe in the Parish Church of Bishops Cleeve by whom he has one Child named Joseph aged 4 Years   That he is now actually chargeable to the said Parish of Cheltenham [mark]

c1795: *WS born at Pitchcombe.* **1838:** *removed to Badgeworth (presumed) (hiring and service): see* **38061SE** *(WS: 1 Oct) (RETURNED).* **1841:** *WS (aged 40; agricultural labourer), wife Phoebe (30; charwoman), Ann ([1]2), and Joseph (4) lived in Major's Row, Cheltenham (HO107/353/11/4/2).* **1841:** **removed to Badgeworth (hiring and service).** **1851:** *(RETURNED) the family lived at same address: WS (56; agricultural labourer), Phoebe (47), and Ann Lyes (21) (HO107/1973/962/4).* [PS/CH/RA/2/6:17 (copy at PS/CH/RA/2/5:353). Removal expenses for "Simmond" to Badgeworth 10/- (1Q 1842: D4178). See **41078RO** (Phoebe Simmonds: 18 Dec 1841).]

41078RO: 18 Dec 1841 – Phoebe Simmonds, with regard to illegitimate daughter **Ann Lyes**: That the said Ann ~~Simmonds~~ Lyes is an Illegitimate Child of hers now aged 11 Years and was

born in the parish of Chaceley in the County of Worcester and has done no act to gain a settlement in her own right and is now Chargeable to the said Parish of Cheltenham [mark]
1831: *baptism of AL in Bishop's Cleve on 6 Nov.* **1841:** *removed to Chaceley, Worcs (birth).* **1851:** *(RETURNED) AL lived with mother Phoebe Simmonds and stepfather William in Major's Row, Cheltenham (see notes to* **38061SE** *William Simmonds 1 Oct 1838).* [PS/CH/RA/2/6:18 (copy at PS/CH/RA/2/5:356). Removal expenses for "Lyes" to Chaceley, Worcs 19/- (1Q 1842: D4178). See **41077RO** (William Simmonds: 18 Dec 1841).]

41079RO: 18 Dec 1841 – **Richard Hemming** (also **Hemmings, Emmins**), labourer, wife **Jane**, and child **Thomas Lucas**: That the first place he remembers himself was in the Parish of Prestbury in the said County where he lived with his parents until he was about twenty Years of Age   That he has never been hired by the Year or done any act to gain a settlement in his own right   That about Eleven years ago he was relieved by the Parish officers of Prestbury

That about four months ago he was married to his present Wife Jane at Pontypool who has a Child named Thomas Lucas (by her first husband Thomas Lucas) who is now only six Years old That he is now chargeable to the said Parish of Cheltenham [mark]
1841: *removed to Prestbury (father's settlement).* **1851:** *RH (aged 52; labourer, born Prestbury) lived in Aberystruth, Monm, with wife Jane (55), and stepson Thomas Lucas (16; labourer) (HO107/2447/250/11).* [PS/CH/RA/2/6:15 (copy at PS/CH/RA/2/5:354).]

41080RO: 18 Dec 1841 – **John Juggins**, labourer, wife **Mary**, and son **William**: That the first place he remembers himself was in the Parish of Withington in the said County and [he] was an illegitimate Child of Mary Juggins   That about Eight years ago he was removed by orders from the Parish of Prestbury to the said Parish of Withington which orders were not appealed against and he received relief from the Parish Officers of Withington and has done no act to gain a settlement since – That about ten years ago he was married at Salperton to his present Wife Mary by whom he has one Child named William aged seven years – That he is now chargeable to the said Parish of Cheltenham [mark]
1841: *(6 June) JJ (aged 30; labourer) lived with wife Mary (40) and son William (7) in Commercial St, Cheltenham (HO107/353/12/17/28); removed to Withington (birth).* **1851:** *JJ lived in Withington: JJ (42; pauper, agricultural labourer, born Withington), Mary (56), William (17; agricultural labourer) (HO107/1969/275/1).* [PS/CH/RA/2/6:16 (copy at PS/CH/RA/2/5:355). Removal expenses for "Juggins" to Withington 17/6 (1Q 1842: D4178). See **39023SE** (uncle John Juggins: 4 Mar 1839).]

41081RO: Mon 20 Dec 1841 (examination 18 Dec) – **William Ringwood**, tailor, wife **Esther**, and five children **James, Esther, Emma, Harriet**, and **Henry**: That the first place he remembers himself was in the Parish of Saint Mary Magdalen Bridgenorth [= Bridgenorth] in the County of Salop where his parents resided and where they are legally settled That he has never done any act to gain a settlement in his own right   that about twenty six years ago he was married to his present wife Esther at Saint Michaels Church Worcester by whom he has five Children now living with him Viz^t. James aged 13 Years Esther aged 11 Years Emma aged 8 Years Harriet aged 5 Years and Henry aged 8 Months

That he is now actually chargeable to the said Parish of Cheltenham [mark]
1841: *(6 June) WR (aged 45; journeyman tailor) lived with wife Hester (41) and family in Prospect Terrace, Fairview, Cheltenham (HO107/353/4/6/6); ordered to be removed to St Mary Magdalen, Bridgnorth, Shropshire (father's apparent settlement) (abandoned).* **1842:** *death of WR (buried at New Burial Ground, Cheltenham, aged 46, 27 Sept.* **1843:** *death of wife Esther (buried at Cheltenham 9 Feb, aged 43).* **1848:** *daughter Hester Ringwood married Joseph Steventon in Sedgley, Staffs 20 Mar, and subsequently emigrated to America, before returning to live eventually back in Cheltenham; son James Ringwood also married in Staffs in this year, to Caroline Pulley. The children were presumably cared for by relatives in Shropshire.* **1850:** *death of son (William) Henry Ringwood in Bridgnorth 1Q.* **1851:** *daughter Emma Ringwood (17) worked as servant in Bridgnorth (HO107/1986/272/6); daughter Harriet Ringwood (15; shoebinder) lived with uncle and aunt in Poplar, Middlesex (HO107/1556/673/25).* [PS/CH/RA/2/6:19 (WR considered unfit to travel and order suspended on 20 Dec) (copy at PS/CH/RA/2/5:357). Note: "Order abandoned Pauper

belongs to Chelt- by rent[in]g in Queen Street". Removal expenses to Bridgenorth for "Ringwood" £2/2/- (4Q 1841: D4178).]

41082RO: Tues 21 Dec 1841 – **Joseph Casey** (also **Ceasey**), labourer and wife **Elizabeth**: That the first place he remembers himself was in the Parish of Minchinhampton in the said County where he resided with his parents until he was upwards of twenty Years of age – That he has never been hired by the year or rented a tenement of the annual value of ten pounds or done any act to gain a Settlement in his own right   That about fifteen Years ago he was relieved by the Parish officers of Minchinhampton aforesaid for five or six weeks

That about 37 years ago he was married to his present Wife Elizabeth in the Parish Church of Horsley. That he is now actually chargeable to the said Parish of Cheltenham [mark]

1841: *removed to Minchinhampton (father's apparent settlement): see* **47002RO** *(JC: 9 Jan 1847) for further information on family.* [PS/CH/RA/2/6:22 (Elizabeth Casey considered unfit to travel and order was suspended 21 Dec (suspension not lifted)) (copy at PS/CH/RA/2/5:358). Removal expenses for "Casey" to Minchinhampton £1/7/6 (1Q 1842: D4178).]

41083RO: Thurs 23 Dec 1841 – **Elizabeth Sprouse** (more often **Spruce**, **Spruse**), widow: That she was married to her late husband Joseph Sprouse at Swansea in the County of Glamorgan

That about twenty five years ago she was sent by orders of removal from the Parish of Newport in the County of Gloucester to the Parish of Brockworth in the same County which orders were not appealed against – that she continued at Brockworth for many years and was relieved by the Parish officers there for many Years   that she was relieved by the Parish officers of Brockworth about two Years ago And have [*sic*] done no act to gain a settlement elsewhere   That she is now chargeable to the said Parish of Cheltenham [mark]

1841: *(6 June) ES (aged 60; plain sewer, born Swansea) lived in Queen St, Cheltenham (HO107/353/9/32/10); removed to Brockworth (husband's presumed settlement).* **1845-7:** *(RETURNED) from 2Q 1845 until 2Q 1847 she received parish relief from Gloucester as a non-settled resident of Cheltenham (G/CH/9d/1).* **1851:** *ES (70; widow, born Swansea) lodged at 9 Corpus St.* **1853:** *death of ES (buried at Cheltenham, aged 73, on 16 Aug).* [PS/CH/RA/2/6:21 (copy at PS/CH/RA/2/5:359). Removal expenses for "Sprouse" to Brockworth 11/- (1Q 1842: D4178).]

Inquests. – The following inquests have recently been taken by J. Cooke, Esq.: - In the Forest of Dean, on James Batt, aged 55, who was at work in a coal-pit, when the roof fell upon him and killed him on the spot. Verdict – *Accidental Death.* – At Sudeley, Forest of Dean, on Thomas Sterry, aged 70, who retired to rest in good health, but was found dead in his bed the next morning. – Verdict – *Died by the visitation of God.* – At Cheltenham, on Job Humphries, aged 29, a railway labourer, who was employed to cart away the earth from the excavations. In doing this, a tram is drawn to the edge of what is called "the tip", and being emptied of its contents, it propels itself back again for some distance. The deceased, in endeavouring to get out of the way, fell down, and the tram wheel passing over him, inflicted a shocking compound fracture of the thigh. Amputation was performed at the Cheltenham Hospital, but the deceased died soon after undergoing the operation. Verdict – *Accidental Death.*   (*Gloucestershire Chronicle*, 31 Aug. 1839)

---

*Poverty was often precipitated by misfortune. In this case, John Humphris (also Humphries), husband of Sarah, was killed in a tragic railway accident in Autumn 1839. Seven months later Sarah and her little son Job, destitute, were examined by the Cheltenham magistrates as to their settlement (**40042SE**) and removed to Upper Slaughter, the late John Humphris's home village.*

1842

42001RO: Sat 1 Jan 1842 – **James Pryor**, labourer: That about twenty years ago he was hired by M^r. Thomas Lewis of the Parish of Malmesbury in the County of Wilts by the year at Twelve guineas a year – that he served the whole Year and received his years wages – that he continued in the same service three years afterwards

That he has done no act to gain a settlement since – ~~That about four Years ago he was married to his present Wife Eliza.~~ That he is now chargeable to the said Parish of Cheltenham [mark]
1842: *removed to Malmesbury, Wilts (hiring and service).* [PS/CH/RA/2/6:22 (copy at PS/CH/RA/2/5:360, from which the passage struck out derives). Removal expenses for "Pryer" to Malmesbury £2/-/6 (1Q 1842: D4178).]

42002RO: Thurs 6 Jan 1842 – **Robert Dix** (also **Dicks**), labourer, wife **Sarah**, and sons **Charles** and **Isaac**: That the first place he remembers himself was in the Parish of Charlton Kings in the said County where he resided with his parents until he was about fifteen years of Age. That he has never done any act to gain a settlement in his own right

That about four years ago he was married to his present Wife Sarah by whom he has two Children Viz^t. Charles aged two Years and Isaac aged four months   That he is now Chargeable to the said Parish of Cheltenham [mark]
1841: *RD (aged 20; agricultural labourer) lived with wife Sarah (20) and son Charles (1) in Swindon Road, Cheltenham (HO107/353/9/17/29); birth of son Isaac registered at Cheltenham 4Q (baptised 6 Oct 1841, when his father Robert was a brickmaker, living at 233 High St, Cheltenham.* **1842:** *removed to Charlton Kings (father's settlement). Subsequent children were born at Cheltenham (RETURNED).* **1847:** *RD (27) imprisoned at Northleach for two months for stealing 2,500 bricks in Cheltenham (Gloucester County Sessions, 23 Mar).* **1851:** *the family lived in Barton St Michael, Gloucester: Robert (29; brickmaker, born Cheltenham), Sarah (29; washerwoman), Charles (11), Isaac (9), Sarah Ann (7), and Robert (5; all children "scholars") (HO107/1962/277/41).* **1861:** *the family, with further six children, lived in Gloucester Road, Cheltenham (RG9/1800/40/9).* [PS/CH/RA/2/6:23 (copy at PS/CH/RA/2/5:360, from which the passage struck out derives). Removal expenses for "Dix" to Charlton Kings 2/6 (1Q 1842: D4178). See **41063RO** (brother William Dix, removed to Charlton Kings: 23 Oct 1841.]

42003RO: Wed 12 Jan 1842 (examination on 11 Jan) – **Jonathan Payne**, prisoner in Gloucester Gaol, wife **Ann**, and five children **William**, **James**, **George**, **Frederick**, and **Elizabeth Jane**: That 11 Years ago last Michaelmas he was hired for a year by Mr Biddle of the Parish of Stroud in the County of Gloucester at the wages of nine shillings per week   that he resided with Mr Biddle in Stroud within three days of the following Michaelmas, when his last week having ended three days before Michaelmas day Mr Biddle paid him his wages and discharged him.

That at Michaelmas 1822 he was hired for a Year (being then a single man) by Mr John Bryant then living at Lower Slaughter in the County of Gloucester at the wages of one guinea. That he lived with Mr Bryant in Lower Slaughter the whole Year and received all his wages, since which he has done no act whereby to gain a settlement. That ten Years ago he was Married at Barnsley to his present wife Ann by whom he has five Children namely, William aged 9 years James aged 7 years, George aged five 5 Years Frederick aged 2 Years and Elizabeth Jane aged seven months and that his said family are now Chargeable to the Parish of Cheltenham in the County of Gloucester not having gained any settlement there [signed]
1842: *removal to Lower Slaughter (hiring and service) (abandoned):* see **42034RO** *(JP: 7 Apr) for further information.* [PS/CH/RA/2/6:24 (no copy in magistrates' register). Notes: "This Order was abandoned; the pauper after removed to Painswick". Removal expenses to Lower Slaughter for "Payne" £1/3/6 (1Q 1842: D4178).]

42004RO: Sat 15 Jan 1842 – **Sarah Trew** (also **Treu**, **True**), widow, children **Harriet** and **Elizabeth**, and stepson **William**: That about ten Years ago she was married to her late husband

William Trew in the Parish of Leckhampton in the said County   that her said husband died in September last

That three Years ago last Michaelmas her said husband took a House and Garden in the said Parish of Leckhampton at £36 a year and continued to occupy the same until near, and paid the rent for the same, to Michaelmas last, and was duly rated to and paid all parochial rates in respect of the Same   That she has done no act to gain a Settlement elsewhere – That she has two Children by her said husband Viz^t Harriet aged Eight Years and Elizabeth aged five years. That her said husband had a Child named William now aged twelve years, by a former Wife who is now living with this Examinant and said Child and herself and her two Children are now chargeable to the said Parish of Cheltenham [signed]

1841: *ST (aged 35, born Heref) lived with husband William (35; gardener) and children Charles (14; servant), William (12; gardener), and Elizabeth (5) in Painswick Road, Leckhampton (HO107/353/18/23/15); Charles Trew was another child of William and first wife Mary Ann (died 1831); burial of husband William Trew at Cheltenham 29 Sept, aged 39.* **1842: removed to Leckhampton (husband's settlement). 1851:** *(RETURNED) the family ran a lodging-house at 11 Lansdown Parade, Cheltenham: ST (48; lodging-house keeper, widow), Harriet (17; dressmaker), Elizabeth (14), and niece Ann Jones (16; servant) (HO107/1973/1007/24).* [PS/CH/RA/2/6:25 (copy at PS/CH/RA/2/5:362). Removal expenses for "Trew" to Leckhampton 2/6 (1Q 1842: D4178).]

42005RO: Mon 17 Jan 1842 – **William Forty**, stonemason, wife **Elizabeth**, and six children **Josiah**, **James**, **William**, **Ann**, **Frank**, and **Fred**: That in the Year 1834 he rented a House Garden and Orchard in the Parish of Buckland in the said County at Sixteen pounds. that he continued in the occupation of it for upwards of three years and paid upwards of three Years rent – That he was duly rated to and paid all parochial rates in respect of the same for that time   That he has done no act since to gain a settlement elsewhere   That near twenty two Years ago he was married to his present Wife Elizabeth at Buckland aforesaid by whom he has six Children Josiah aged 13 Years James aged 11 Years William aged 9 Years Ann aged 7 Years Frank aged 5 Years and Fred aged 2 years   That he is now chargeable to the said Parish of Cheltenham [signed]

1841: *WF (aged 45; stonemason, born Stow-on-the-Wold) lived with wife Elizabeth (30; laundress) and children Josiah (13; porter), James (10), William (8), Sarah A (6), Frank (4), and John Frederick (1) in Lime Kiln Row, St Paul's, Cheltenham (HO107/358/8/53/38).* **1842: ordered to be removed to Buckland (renting) (abandoned). 1851:** *the family lived at 11 Hamilton Place, St Paul's, Cheltenham: William (55; stonemason), Elizabeth (51), Josiah (22; boot-closer), James (20; mechanical dentist), Ann (16; milliner), Frank (13; errand boy), and Frederick (11; scholar) (HO107/1973/337/44); although William Buckland was born at Stow, wife and first child were born at Laverton, the next three children at Buckland, and Frederick at Cheltenham.* [PS/CH/RA/2/6:26 (copy at PS/CH/RA/2/5:363). Note: "This Order was abandoned; the man not removed".]

42006RO: 17 Jan 1842 – **Hannah Garner**, single woman: That the first place she remembers herself was in the Parish of Bisley in the said County where her parents were legally settled   That her Father has been dead about twelve Years and she has frequently seen him relieved by the Parish officers of Bisley aforesaid previous to his death and was buried partly at the Expence of the Parish officers there – that She has never done any act to gain a settlement in her own right and is now chargeable to the said Parish of Cheltenham [mark]

1841: *perhaps Hannah Gard(i)ner; a Hannah Gardiner (aged 66; pauper) lived in Bisley (HO107/349/3/34/13).* **1842: removed to Bisley (father's settlement);** *(17 July) death of Hannah Gardiner, "warper", of "Mortification in the lower extremities", at Chalford, Bisley, aged 69.* [PS/CH/RA/2/6:27 (copy at PS/CH/RA/2/5:364). Removal expenses for "Garner" to Bisley £1/2/- (1Q 1842: D4178).]

42007SE: [blank] Jan 1842 – **William Goode**, stonemason, wife **Ann**, and two children **John** and **James**: That the first place he remembers himself was in the Parish of Berkeley in the County of Somerset where he resided with his parents until he was about seventeen years of Age that he then went into the Army and Served therein until about five Years ago when he was discharged   That he has done no act to gain a settlement in his own right   That about five Years

ago he was married to his present Wife Ann at St Pauls Church Bath that he has one Child by a former Wife named John aged seven Years and he has one Child by his present Wife named James aged four Years. That he is now Chargeable to the said Parish of Cheltenham
1842: *removal uncertain: examination form incomplete.* [PS/CH/RA/2/5:365.]

42008RO: Thurs 20 Jan 1842 – **William Cook**, wife **Mary**, and two children **Susan** and **John**: That when he was about ten years of Age he was apprenticed by Indenture to Nathaniel King of the Parish of Painswick in the said County Woollen Cloth Weaver for seven Years that he served the whole term and slept the whole time in his Masters house at Painswick

That he has never been hired by the Year or rented a tenement of the annual value of ten pounds or done any act to gain a settlement elsewhere That he has several times been relieved by the Parish Officers of Painswick. That about 28 Years ago he was married to his present Wife Mary at Painswick aforesaid by whom he has two Children now living with him, Viz Susan aged 12 Years and John aged 10 Years That he is now Chargeable to the said Parish of Cheltenham [mark]
1842: *removed to Painswick (apprenticeship):* see **48031RO** *for further information on WC and family.* [PS/CH/RA/2/6:28 (copy at PS/CH/RA/2/5:364). Removal expenses for "Cooke" to Painswick 17/9 (1Q 1842: D4178).]

42009RO: 20 Jan 1842 – **Samuel Meddings**, bricklayer, and wife **Sarah**: That about Forty years ago he was hired by Mr Turnberrow of the Parish of Welland in the County of Worcester for a Year that he served the whole Year and received his Years wages. that in about three Years afterwards he was sent by orders of removal from the Parish of Castle Morton [= Castlemorton, Worcs] to the said Parish of Welland which orders were not appealed against and he has since been relieved by the Parish officers of Welland. That he has done no act to gain a settlement elsewhere. That about three Years ago he was married to his present Wife Sarah at Cheltenham That he is now chargeable to the Parish of Cheltenham [mark]
1841: *SM (aged 55; bricklayer) lived with wife Sarah (35) in Sherborne St, Cheltenham (HO107/353/5/62/46).*
1842: *removed to Welland, Worcs (hiring and service).* **1851:** *SM (64; bricklayer, born Worcester) lived with wife Sarah (42; gloveress) in Upper Quay, Worcester (HO107/2042/167/60).* [PS/CH/RA/2/6:29 (copy at PS/CH/RA/2/5:367). Removal expenses for "Meddings" to Welland, Worcs £1/11/- (1Q 1842: D4178).]

42010RO: 20 Jan 1842 – **William Prosser**, labourer, and wife **Ann**: That the first place he remembers himself was in the Parish of Earls Croome [= Earls Croome] in the County of Worcester where he resided until the last five years That he has been relieved by the Parish officers of Earls Croome aforesaid – That his parents have been several times relieved by the Parish officers of Earls Croome That he has never done any act to gain a settlement in his own right. that about two years ago he was married to his present Wife Ann at Cheltenham – That he is now chargeable to the said Parish of Cheltenham [mark]
1842: *removed to Earls Croome, Worcs (father's settlement).* **1851:** *WP (aged 41; agricultural labourer, born Earls Croome, Worcs), wife Ann (30), and daughters Mary (3) and Elenor (1) lived in Ombersley, Worcs (HO107/2046/264/45).* [PS/CH/RA/2/6:30 (copy at PS/CH/RA/2/5:368).]

42011RO: Sat 29 Jan 1842 – Thomas Webb, labourer, regarding the settlement of son **Thomas Webb**, in Gloucester Gaol, and **Sarah Webb**, wife of Thomas Webb the Younger, and her two children **Sarah Jane** and **John**. *Thomas Webb:* That when he was about thirteen Years of Age he was Apprenticed by Indenture to John Scott of the Parish of Nayland in the County of Suffolk Blacksmith for seven years that he served the whole time and slept in his Masters house the whole term. that he has never been hired by the Year or rented a Tenement of the annual value of ten pounds or done any Act to gain a settlement elsewhere. That he was lawfully married to his present Wife Margaret about twenty seven years ago And the said Thomas Webb is his Son by his said Wife and is now aged about twenty five years. That his said Son has never done any act to gain a settlement in his own right [mark]
Sarah Webb: That about four years ago she was Married to her said husband at Plymouth Old Church by whom she has two Children to wit Sarah Jane aged two years and a half and John aged

five months – That since her Marriage her said husband has not rented a Tenement of the annual value of ten pounds or done any Act to gain a Settlement in his own right. That her said husband is now confined in Gloucester County Gaol for felony and She and her two Children are chargeable to the Parish of Cheltenham [mark]

1841: *TW (aged 20; labourer) lived with wife Sarah (20) and daughter (Sarah) Jane (2) at 4 Hereford Passage, Hereford Place, Cheltenham (HO107/353/8/64/10).* **1842: order to be removed to Nayland, Suffolk (father's settlement)) (abandoned);** *on 1 Mar TW was found not guilty of stealing (with others) two legs of mutton at Cheltenham, at County Adjourned Sessions (Gloucestershire Journal 5 Mar).* [PS/CH/RA/2/6:31 (copies at PS/CH/RA/2/5:369-70). Note: "This Order was abandoned Thomas Webb the Elders Wife was living and receiving relief in Nayland he Married a Second Wife and this Pauper was a Son belonging to her and born in Cheltenham".]

42012RO: Mon 7 Feb 1842 – Mary Page, regarding the settlement of illegitimate son, **James Whiting**: That the said James Whiting is an illegitimate Child of hers now of the age of thirteen Years and was born in the Parish of Bisley in the said County and has done no act to gain a settlement in his own right and is now chargeable to the said Parish of Cheltenham [signed]

1836: *removed to Bisley (father's settlement): see* **36039RO** *(Mary Page: 26 Nov).* **1840:** *(RETURNED) JW admitted to Charlton Kings Workhouse for children (Cheltenham Union) from 9–11 Dec, when mother was an inmate of Cheltenham Workhouse (G/CH/60/2).* **1842: removed to Bisley (birth).** [PS/CH/RA/2/6:32 (copy at PS/CH/RA/2/5:371). Removal expenses for "Whiting" to Bisley £1/2/6 (1Q 1842: D4178).]

42013RO: 7 Feb 1842 – William Smith, relating to the settlement of his brother James Smith, and **Martha Smith**, wife of James Smith, and her son, **Alfred**:

William Smith: That he remembers his said Brother being born in the Parish of Chippenham in the County of Wilts where his parents were legally settled   That his said Brother has never been hired by the Year or rented a Tenement of the annual value of ten pounds or done any act to gain a settlement in his own right [mark]

Martha Smith: That about two years ago she was married in Cheltenham to her said husband James Smith by whom she has one Child named Alfred now aged three months – That her said husband deserted her about Eight months ago and she has not heard of him since and she and her Child are become chargeable to the Parish of Cheltenham [mark]

1842: removed to Chippenham, Wilts (husband's settlement). 1844: *(RETURNED) son George baptised at Cheltenham 6 Oct; father apparently James Smith's brother William.* **1851:** *MS (aged 45; charwoman and widow, born Stroud) lived with two children, Ann (15; scholar) and Richard Rodway (11; scholar), by former husband, groom William Rodway (died 1839, aged 27), Alfred Smith (10; scholar), son of James Smith, and two subsequent children, apparently with William Smith, in Albion St, Cheltenham (HO107/1973/211/2).* [PS/CH/RA/2/6:33 (copies at PS/CH/RA/2/5:372). Removal expenses for "Smith" to Chippenham £3/8/- (1Q 1842: D4178).]

42014RO: Sat 19 Feb 1842 – **Richard Tipper**, bricklayer, and son, **Thomas**: That when he was about fifteen years of age he was apprenticed by Indenture to Thomas Jones of the Parish of Bewdley in the County of Worcester Bricklayer for seven years: that he served six years and nine months of the time and slept in his Masters house at Bewdley the whole of that time

That he was never hired by the Year or rented a tenement of the annual value of ten pounds or done any act to gain a settlement elsewhere

That about fifteen years ago he was removed by orders of removal from the said Parish of Cheltenham unto the said Parish of Bewdley and which orders were not appealed against and he was in the Workhouse at Bewdley for about seven Weeks   That about 33 years ago he was married to his late Wife Elizabeth at Cheltenham aforesaid who is now dead by whom he has one Child now living with him named Thomas aged 15 Years   That he is now chargeable to the said Parish of Cheltenham [mark]

1841: *RT (aged 65; bricklayer) lived with son Thomas (12) in Stanhope St, Cheltenham (HO107/353/9/52/4).* **1842: removed to Bewdley, Worcs (apprenticeship). 1851:** *(RETURNED) RT (72; bricklayer, pauper, born*

Worcester) was an inmate of St Paul's Workhouse, Cheltenham (HO107/1973/1092/5). [PS/CH/RA/2/6:38 (copy at PS/CH/RA/2/5:373). Removal expenses for "Tipper" to Bewdley, Worcs £2/5/- (1Q 1842: D4178).]

42015RO: Wed 16 Feb 1842 (examination on 14 Feb) – **John Lloyd**, cordwainer: That when he was about ten years of Age he was apprenticed by Indenture to Richard Wood of the Parish of Shurdington in the said County Cordwainer for seven Years that he served the whole of the term and slept in his Masters house the whole time that about twenty five years ago he rented a Cottage and Washhouse and a piece of Land at Chargrove in the Parish of Shurdington aforesaid at ten pounds one shilling per Year and continued in the occupation of it for upwards of Eight years

That he has done no act since to gain a settlement elsewhere. That he is now chargeable to the said Parish of Cheltenham [mark]

1841: *JL (aged 50; cordwainer, born outside Glos) lived in Stanhope St, Cheltenham (HO107/353/9/51/2).* **1842:** ***died before removal to Shurdington (renting) (abandoned on death of pauper).*** [PS/CH/RA/2/6:35 (copy at PS/CH/RA/2/5:374). Note: "This Order was abandoned; the Pauper is Supposed to belong to Ledbury from apprenticeship – since dead".]

42016SE: [blank] [blank] 1842 – **Jehu Minott**, blacksmith, wife **Mary**, and daughter **Helen**: That about 12 months ago he was married to his present Wife Mary in the Parish Church of Prestbury in the said County by whom he has one Child named Helen aged 6 weeks. That he has never done any act to gain a settlement in his own right and is now chargeable to the said Parish of Cheltenham [incomplete]

1841: *marriage of JM (aged 23; smith) to Mary Giles (23; servant) 5 July in Prestbury.* **1842:** *daughter Ellen (also Helen) baptised 30 Jan, when family lived at 22 Sherborne St, Cheltenham;* ***removal uncertain: examination form incomplete.*** **1845:** *death of JM (buried at New Burial Ground, Cheltenham 22 Jan, aged 25).* [PS/CH/RA/2/5:375.]

42017RO: Mon 14 Feb 1842 – **George Clutterbuck**, labourer, wife **Jane**, and four children **William**, **Elizabeth**, **Selina**, and **Frederick**: That the first place he remembers himself was in the Parish of Norton in the said County. that about 15 or 16 Years ago he was hired by M^rs. Cook of the said Parish of Norton for a Year at the wages of fifty shillings and served the whole Year and received his Years wages That he has done no act to gain a settlement elsewhere. that near nine Years ago he was married to his present Wife Jane at the said Parish of Norton by whom he has four Children William aged 7 Years Elizabeth aged 5 Years Selena aged 3 Years and Frederick aged 8 months. That he is now chargeable to the said Parish of Cheltenham [mark]

1841: *GC (aged 25; labourer) lived with wife Jane (20) (daughter of Solomon and Charlotte Ivin:* **42019RO**)*, and children William (7), Elizabeth (5), Selina (2), and Frederick (five mo) in Elm St, Cheltenham (HO107/353/10/4/2).* **1842:** ***removed to Norton (hiring and service). (RETURNED)*** *Their subsequent children were born at Cheltenham.* **1851:** *the family lived "near Gloucester Road", Cheltenham: GC (39; labourer, born Cheltenham), Jane (39), William (16), Elizabeth (14), and five other children (HO107/1973/1002/15-1003/16).* [PS/CH/RA/2/6:34 (copy at PS/CH/RA/2/5:376). Note: "I hereby acknowledge that George Clutterbuck is a Parishioner belonging to the Parish of Norton; Thomas Long Overseers".]

42018RO: 16/18 Feb 1842 (examination on 14 Feb) – **Patrick Pitman** (also **Pittman**), French polisher, wife **Ann**, and children **Ann** and **Elizabeth**: That the first place he remembers himself was in the Parish of Didbrook in the said County that about twenty five Years ago he was relieved by the Parish Officers of Didbrook aforesaid for about six months. That he has never been apprenticed or hired by the Year or rented a Tenement for a Year at the annual value of ten pounds or done any act to gain a settlement elsewhere

That about Eight Years ago he was married to his present Wife Ann in the Parish Church of Cheltenham by whom he has two Children Viz Ann aged four Years and a half and Elizabeth aged two Years and a half

That he is now chargeable to the said Parish of Cheltenham [signed]

1833: *John (Patrick?) Pitman, baptised at Didbrook in 1817, married Ann Robins on 12 Nov in Cheltenham.* **1841:** *the couple lived with their family at 209 High St, Cheltenham with John Robins (30; shoemaker, born*

Ireland), presumably Ann's brother: John (30; chiropodist), Ann (25, born Ireland), Ann (4), Elizabeth (2), and Mary (seven mo) (HO107/353/8/71/24). **1842: removed to Didbrook (Winchcombe Union) (birth). 1843:** *(RETURNED) death of John Pitman (buried at New Burial Ground, Cheltenham on 22 Nov, aged 37: described by* Cheltenham Chron. *23 Nov as "carver and polisher").* **1845-6:** *from 1Q 1845 until 2Q 1846 Ann and two children received parish relief from Winchcombe as non-settled residents of Cheltenham (G/CH/9d/1).* **1851:** *daughters Ann (14; apprentice to Straw Bonnet Mak[er]") and Elizabeth (11; scholar) lived at 16 Hanover St, St Paul's, Cheltenham (mother was absent from home on census night) (HO107/1973/325/21). A Patrick Boyne Pitman was baptised at Didbrook 2 Mar 1806, illegitimate son of Margaret Pitman.* [PS/CH/RA/2/6:36 (copy at PS/CH/RA/2/5:377). Removal expenses for "Pittman" to Didbrook 19/6 (1Q 1842: D4178).]

42019RO: Thurs 17 Feb 1842 – **Solomon Ivin** (also **Iven**, **Ivens**), labourer, wife **Charlotte**, and children **Mary**, **James,** and **Hannah**: That About thirty three Years ago he was hired by Mr Cambridge of the Parish of Acton Turville in the said County for a Year at the wages of Eight pounds   that he served the whole Year – and received his Years wages. That he has not been hired for a Year since or done any act to gain a settlement elsewhere   That about thirty Years ago he was married to his present Wife Charlotte at the Parish of Winchcomb [= Winchcombe] in the said County by whom he has three Children now living with him Viz^t Mary aged 16 Years James aged 14 Years and Hannah aged nine Years

   That he is now chargeable to the said Parish of Cheltenham [mark]

1842: removed to Acton Turville (hiring and service): *see* **48018RO** *(SI: 18 Nov 1848).* [PS/CH/RA/2/6:37 (copy at PS/CH/RA/2/5:378). Removal expenses for "Ivens" to Acton Turville £2/18/- (1Q 1842: D4178). See **42017RO** (daughter Jane Clutterbuck: 14 Feb), **48021RO** (James Ivin: 18 Nov 1848), **48022RO** (Hannah Ivin: 18 Nov 1848).]

42020RO: 26/28 Feb 1842 (examination on 26 Feb) – **Ann Ellah** (also **Ella**, **Ellard**, **Eloe**), single woman: That the first place she remembers herself was in the Parish of Tewkesbury in the said County where she resided until within the last twelve months. That her Father died in the Workhouse at Tewkesbury aforesaid about three years ago and she remained in the Workhouse there about three months after the death of her Father – That she has done no act to gain a settlement in her own right and is now chargeable to the said Parish of Cheltenham [mark] [examination struck out]

1839: *death of father Edward in Tewkesbury Workhouse (buried at Boddington on 18 Mar, aged 70); AE charged with "maliciously and wilfully attempting to set fire to the Workhouse", and committed to Tewkesbury Borough Gaol for one year; discharged on 28 June 1840, her character described as "very bad" (prison register).* **1841:** *mother Sarah remarried, to Charles Cresswell, both of Boddington, on 22 Mar; the family lived in Boddington: Charles Cresswell (aged 29; agricultural labourer), Sarah (40; agricultural labourer), Ann (15; agricultural labourer), and her two sisters Mary (6) and Charles (10; servant).* **1842: ordered to be removed to Tewkesbury (father's settlement) (abandoned). 1849:** *death of mother, Sarah, registered at Tewkesbury 2Q.* [PS/CH/RA/2/6:39 (copy at PS/CH/RA/2/5:379). Note "This Girl belongs to Boddington and was accepted without Orders". Removal expenses to Tewkesbury for "Ellah" 13/- (1Q 1842: D4178).]

42021RO: 26 (corrected to Thurs 24) Mar 1842 – **Henry Foley**, labourer: That the first place he remembers himself was the Parish of Codford Saint Peters [= Codford St Peter] in the County of Wilts which place he left about 23 Years ago and where his parents resided until about 30 Years ago   that his Father rented a Farm there at about £50 or £60 a Year for several Years

   That he has never been hired for a Year or rented a Tenement of the annual value of ten pounds or done any act to gain a Settlement in his own right – That he is now chargeable to the said Parish of Cheltenham [mark]

1793: *baptism of HF in Codford St Peter, Wilts.* **1842: removed to Codford St Peter, Wilts (father's settlement).** **1843:** *perhaps the HF (bachelor; carpenter) who died of "Paralysis" at the Union Workhouse, Warminster (Codford's poor-law district) on 21 May, aged 61.* [PS/CH/RA/2/6:42 (copy at PS/CH/RA/2/5:380).]

42022RO: Sat 5 Mar 1842 – **Thomas Bosley**, labourer: That 17 Years ago last Michaelmas he was hired by Mr Powell of the Parish of Fownhope in the County of Hereford Farmer at three shillings a week and continued in such service and slept in his Masters house four Years under the same hiring and received all his wages. That he has not been hired by the year since or done any act to gain a settlement elsewhere   That he is now Chargeable to the said Parish of Cheltenham [mark]
1842: *removed to Fownhope, Heref (hiring and service).* [PS/CH/RA/2/6:41 (copy at PS/CH/RA/2/5:381).]

42023RO: 5 Mar 1842 – **Mary (Ann) Miller**, widow, and three children **Mary Ann**, **Frederick**, and **Louisa**: That about 19 Years ago She was married to her late husband Charles Miller at the Parish of Saint Georges Hanover Square London – That about five years ago her said husband rented a house of Mr Sadler in the Parish of Charlton Kings by the Year at £12 a Year
   That he continued in such house about 15 Months and paid all the rent   That he was duly rated to and paid all poor rates in respect of the same   That her said husband [has] done no act afterwards to gain a settlement [and] died two years ago last January. That she has three Children by her said husband now living with her Viz^t Mary Ann aged 11 Years Frederick aged 9 Years and Louisa aged 3 Years. She is now chargeable to the said Parish of Cheltenham [signed]
1842: *removed to Charlton Kings (husband's settlement) (abandoned): see* **43016RO** *(MAM: 4 Mar 1843).* [PS/CH/RA/2/6:42 (copy at PS/CH/RA/2/5:382). Note: "This Order was abandoned.]

42024RO: 5 Mar 1842 – **William Newman**, butcher, wife **Sarah**, and three children **Joseph**, **John**, and **George**: That the first place he remembers himself was in the parish of Oddington in the said County where his Father resided on property of his own until his death
   That he has never done any act to gain a Settlement in his own right
   That about five years ago he was married to his present Wife Sarah at the parish of Cheltenham by whom he has three Children to wit Joseph aged three years and a half John aged two years and George aged five months
   That he is now chargeable to the said Parish of Cheltenham [signed]
1841: *WN (aged 30; journeyman butcher) lived with mother, Elizabeth Newman (70), wife Sarah (25), and two sons Joseph (2) and John (1) in Townsend St, Cheltenham (HO107/353/9/10/14).* **1842:** *death of WN's mother Elizabeth (buried at Oddington 25 Feb, aged 70);* **ordered to be removed to Oddington (father's settlement) (abandoned).** **1851:** *(RETURNED) the family lived in Stanhope St, Cheltenham: William (43; agricultural labourer, born Oddington), Sarah (44), Joseph (12; agricultural labourer), scholars John (10), George (9), Henry (7), and Elizabeth (6), as well as William (3; all children born Cheltenham) (HO107/1973/501/22).* [PS/CH/RA/2/6:43 (copy at PS/CH/RA/2/5:383). Note: "This order was abandoned".]

42025SE: [blank] Mar 1842 – William Hyett (also Hyatt), residing in Sudeley, regarding the settlement of **Robert Andrews**: That about Michaelmas in the Year 1823 but he believes it was after Michaelmas he hired the said Robert Andrews to serve him until the Michaelmas following at the sum of Eight pounds in the parish of ~~Sudeley~~ Snowshill in the said County   that he served him in that Parish until the third of May following when Examinant and the said Robert Andrews went to Winchcomb [= Winchcombe] Parish in the said County where the said Robert Andrew served him until Michaelmas and then left his service [signed]
1842: *removal uncertain: examination form incomplete.* [PS/CH/RA/2/5:384.]

42026RO: Fri 11 Mar 1842 – **John Weston** (also or incorrectly **Wesson**), cutler, and wife **Ann**: That in the month of December 1833 he rented a house in Suffolk Street in the parish of Leckhampton in the said County by the Year at twenty four pounds a year   That he continued in such house two Years and paid the whole rent for the same   That he was duly rated to the poor rates in the said Parish for that time and he paid all such rates – That he has never rented a Tenement of the annual value of ten pounds since nor done any Act to gain a Settlement elsewhere. That about 35 Years ago he was married to his present wife Ann at Banbury in Oxfordshire – That he is now chargeable to the said Parish of Cheltenham [mark]

1841: *JW (aged 50; cutler) lived with wife Ann (53) and son Robert (24; hawker) in Fairview St, Cheltenham (HO107/353/4/3/1).* **1842:** *removed to Leckhampton (renting).* **1847:** *(RETURNED) probable death of wife Ann (buried 27 May aged 58 at New Burial Ground, Cheltenham).* **1857:** *remarriage of JW (73; razor-setter, and widower), to Mary Sparrow (61; widow), in Cheltenham 14 Nov.* **1861:** *JW (75; razor-grinder, born Warks) lived in Gas Green, Cheltenham, with wife Mary (63) (RG9/1800/39/8).* **1867:** *death of JW, aged 75, in Cheltenham (buried at the cemetery on 25 Jan).* [PS/CH/RA/2/6:44 (copy at PS/CH/RA/2/5:385).]

42027RO: Mon 21 Mar 1842 – Ann McKlwain (also McIlwain, Mucklewean), relating to the settlement of daughter **Sarah Ingram**, widow, and her children **Sarah** and **Elizabeth**: That about 43 Years ago she was married to her late husband James McKlwain at Saint Andrews' in the City of Worcester that her said husband was born in Ireland and [had] never done any act to gain a settlement in England and died about 14 Years ago. That the first place she remembers herself was in the Parish of Newent in the said County of Gloucester where her Father and Mother were legally settled and where her Father died about six years ago and was previously relieved by the Parish Officers of Newent aforesaid – That the said Sarah Ingram is her Daughter by her said husband and she was never hired as a Servant by the year and was married to her late husband James Ingram at Newtown Hamilton in the County of Armagh Ireland about 16 years ago – That her said Daughters husband died about nine year Years ago at Newton Hamilton aforesaid never having done any act to gain a settlement in England. That her said Daughter had three Children by her said husband two of whom are now living with her Viz^t Sarah aged 11 Years and Elizabeth aged 9 years – that her said Daughter and her three Children went to Newent aforesaid about six years ago and were inmates of the Workhouse there for about 12 months – That her said Daughter and two Children are now chargeable to the said Parish of Cheltenham [mark]
1837: *removed to Newent (father's settlement): see* **37072RO** *(Ann Mucklewean: 6 Nov) (RETURNED).* **1841:** *Sarah (aged 34) lived with children John (14) and Elizabeth (8; both born Ireland), at mother's house in Bath Terrace, Cheltenham (HO107/353/12/13/20); mother (respelt "Ann McLowen", later also McIlwain; aged 60) also shared house with two of Sarah's brothers (both tailors).* **1845-8:** *from 2Q 1845 until 1Q 1848 Sarah and two children received parish relief from Newent as non-settled residents of Cheltenham (G/CH/9d/1).* **1851:** *Sarah Ingram (48; pauper, needlewoman, and widow, born Horsham, Surrey) was an inmate of Newent Union Workhouse (HO107/1960/171/5); daughter Sarah probably the Sarah J. Ingram (unmarried; 19, born Ireland) who worked as a servant at Grovefield House, Cheltenham (HO107/1973/952/31).* **1861:** *death of Ann McIlwain died (buried at Leckhampton 6 May, aged 81).* **1842:** *removed to Newent (mother's settlement).* [PS/CH/RA/2/6:45 (order suspended as SA unfit to travel; lifted 19 Apr) (copy at PS/CH/RA/2/5:386). Removal expenses for "Ingram" to Newent 12/- (1Q 1842: D4178).]

42028RO: Sat 26 Mar 1842 – **Mary Gardner**, single woman: That about Eleven years ago she was hired by Mrs Beard of the Parish of Saint Nicholas in the City of Gloucester for a Year at the wages of Four pounds that she served the whole year and received her years wages. That about Eighteen months ago she was removed by orders from the Parish of Stroud in the said County to the said Parish of Saint Nicholas which orders were not appealed against That she has done no act since to gain a settlement And is now chargeable to the said Parish of Cheltenham [mark]
1842: *removed to St Nicholas, Gloucester (hiring and service).* **1846:** *death of a Mary Gardiner (35) recorded at workhouse in Gloucester (buried at St Nicholas, Gloucester on 16 June).* [PS/CH/RA/2/6:46 (copy at PS/CH/RA/2/5:387.]

42029SE: [blank] [blank] 1842 – **Sarah Evans**, single woman: [no text].
1842: *removal unlikely: examination form incomplete.* [PS/CH/RA/2/5:388.]

42030RO: Mon 4 Apr 1842 – Mary Smith, widow, relating to the settlement of daughter **Margaret Smith**: That about 19 years ago she was married to her late husband William Smith at the Parish of Leonard Stanley in the said County by whom she had the said Margaret Smith now aged 15 Years
That about six years ago she and her said husband and Children were residing at Leonard Stanley aforesaid and being out of work her Husband applied to Mr Fowler Overseer of Leonard Stanley for relief and was by him taken before the Magistrates at Stroud to be examined as to his

Parish and in two or three days afterwards we were taken by Mr Fowler to Mr Hobbs the Overseer of King['s] Stanley in the said County by whom we were relieved

That we Went back again to Leonard Stanley and were afterwards relieved by the Parish Officers of Kings Stanley whilst we were living at Leonard Stanley [insertion] That her said husband done no act no act [*sic*] afterwards to gain a settlement and died about four months ago [end of insertion]

That my said Daughter has done no act afterwards to gain a settlement in her own right and is now Chargeable to the said Parish of Cheltenham [mark]

1842: *removed to King's Stanley (father's settlement): see* **47036RO** *(MS: 11 Sept 1847)*. [PS/CH/RA/2/6:47 (copy at PS/CH/RA/2/5:389).]

42031RO: 4 Apr 1842 – **John Burrows** (also **Burroughs**), stonemason, wife **Maria**, and seven children **Elizabeth**, **Maria**, **John**, **William**, **Eliza**, **James**, and **Charles**: That the first place he remembers himself was in the Parish of Minchinhampton in the said County where his Father has been living ever since. That he has never done any act to gain a settlement in his own right   That about 15 Years ago he was married to his present Wife Maria at the Parish of Minchinhampton aforesaid by whom he has Seven Children Viz. Elizabeth aged 14 Years Maria aged 12 Years John aged 10 Years William aged 8 Years Eliza aged 6 Years James aged 4 Years and Charles aged two Years   That he is now Chargeable to the said Parish of Cheltenham [mark]

1841: *the family lived in Stanhope St, Cheltenham: Maria Burrows (aged 30) (husband John absent on census night), John (11), William (10), Eliza (7), James (5), and Charles (3) (HO107/353/9/44/36) (for several years before this they had lived in Little Dean).* **1842:** *removed to Minchinhampton (father's presumed settlement).* **1843:** *(RETURNED) son Joseph baptised 31 Dec at Cheltenham, when family lived in Stanhope St.* **1851:** *the family lived at 16 Phillip St, Leckhampton: John (45; stonemason, born Minchinhampton); Maria (42), and six children (HO107/1972/187/11).* [PS/CH/RA/2/6:48 (order suspended as Maria Burrows unfit to travel; suspension not lifted) (copy at PS/CH/RA/2/5:390).]

42032RO: 4 Apr 1842 –**Matilda Dowell** (also **Dowle**), single woman; also Mary Dowell, widow, relating to the settlement of daughter, Matilda Dowell.

Mary Dowell: That about 44 Years ago she was married to her late husband Thomas Dowell on in the parish of Pendock in the County of Worcester

that She had been acquainted sometime previously with her husband whilst he was a Servant in the Parish of Eldersfield in the County of Worcester. That she and her said husband were several times relieved Afterwards by the Parish Officers of Eldersfield whilst we were residing in the Parish of Painswick – That my husband who is now dead never rented a Tenement of the annual value of ten pounds or done any Act to gain a Settlement after our Marriage   That the said Matilda Dowell is my Daughter by my said husband [mark]

Matilda Dowell: That she has never done any act to gain a settlement in her own right and is now chargeable to the said Parish of Cheltenham [mark]

1841: *MD (aged 25) lived in Regent St, Cheltenham (HO107/353/14/47/2).* **1842:** *removed to Eldersfield, Worcs (father's settlement).* **1851:** *MD apparently worked (aged 30) as house servant at 33 Montpelier Road, Brighton, Sussex (HO107/1646/347/38).* **1861:** *MD (aged 40) lived as cook in Painswick, where baptised in 1815 (RG9/450/141/25).* [PS/CH/RA/2/6:49 (copies PS/CH/RA/2/5:391-2).]

42033RO: Thurs 7 Apr 1842 (examination on 4 Apr) – **Mary Ann Hodgkins**, widow, and three children **John**, **George**, and **William**: That she is about thirty years of age and that she is the Widow of Joseph Hodgkins who died in the month of March 1834

That about 13 Years Ago she was lawfully married at Shipton under whichwood [= Shipton-under-Wychwood] in the County of Oxford to the said Joseph Hodgkins who about 5 or 6 years before her Marriage was hired for a Year to Mr Slater who kept the Plume of Feathers Inn at Postcombe in the parish of Lewknor in the said County of Oxford   that he duly served such Year during which time he was lodged and boarded in his Masters house and at the expiration of it received his wages. That he continued in the same service Sometime after and never afterwards did any act whereby to gain a settlement. that she has by her said husband two Children now living with her John aged 10 Years and George aged 9 Years

That she hath an illegitimate Child now aged One Year and a half named William That this Examinant has frequently received relief since her husbands death from the said Parish of Lewknor

That she is now become chargeable to the said Parish of Cheltenham [mark]

1838: *removal uncertain; perhaps not removed to Lewknor (husband's settlement): see* **38042** *(MAH: 16 June).* **1840:** *son William born at Cheltenham 2Q (baptised 20 June, when MAH lived at 4 Page's Row, York St).* **1841:** *MAH (aged 25; governess) lived with three sons John (10), George (8), and William (illegitimate: 12 mo) in York St, Fairview, Cheltenham (HO107/353/5/47/17).* **1842:** *removed to Lewknor, Oxfordshire (husband's settlement).* **1843:** *(RETURNED) death of MAH in Cheltenham in 3Q.* **1851:** *son George resident at Thame Union Workhouse, Oxon, while John earned living as bootmaker in London.* [PS/CH/RA/2/6:50 (order suspended as MAH was unfit to travel; lifted 23 June) (copy at PS/CH/RA/2/5:393). Removal expenses for "Hodgkins" to Lewknor £4/1/- (3Q 1842: D4178).]

42034RO: 7 Apr 1842 – **Jonathan Payne**, miller, wife **Ann**, and five children **William**, **James**, **George**, **Frederick**, and **Elizabeth (Jane)**: That at Michaelmas day 1828 he then being unmarried was hired by Robert Gibbs of the Parish of Moreton in the Marsh in the said County for a Year that he served the whole year and received his years wages That at Cirencester first Mop in the Year 1830 he was hired by M[r] John Biddle of the parish of Stroud in the said County Mealman from the Michaelmas following for a Year at the wages of nine Shillings a week that he entered into such service the day before Michaelmas and continued in such service a whole year and received his years wages and slept the three last months of the term at his Masters house in the parish of Painswick in the said County That he has done no act since to gain a settlement elsewhere. That about 10 Years ago he was married to his present wife Ann at the Parish Church of Barnsley by whom he has five Children namely William aged 9 Year James aged 7 Years George aged 5 Years Frederick aged 2 Years and Elizabeth Jane aged 10 Months That he is now chargeable to the Parish of Cheltenham aforesaid [signed]

1841: *JP (aged 30; miller) lived with wife Ann (30) and five children in Prospect Place, Bristol (HO107/377/14/58/9); on 2 Nov JP (miller living in Bristol) was committed for trial at County Sessions on 4 Jan 1842 where he (35) was sentenced to six weeks' imprisonment with hard labour at Lawford's Gate, Bristol for "larceny by servant", i.e. embezzling money from his master in Cheltenham (see* Cheltenham Chron. *13 Jan 1842).* **1842:** *removal to Lower Slaughter (hiring and service) (abandoned): see* **42003RO** *(JP: 12 Jan);* **removed to Painswick (hiring and service).** **1851:** *the family lived at 6 Upper Cheese Lane, Bristol: JP (44; miller's journeyman, born Bristol), Ann (42), William (18; porter), James (16; porter), George (14; "works at Cotton Factory"), Frederick (12; scholar), Mary Ann (7; scholar), Harriett (5; scholar), and Henry (nine mo) (HO107/1954/731/53-54).* [PS/CH/RA/2/6:51 (copy at PS/CH/RA/2/5:394).]

42035SE: [blank] [blank] 1842 – Jane Green, widow, regarding the settlement of niece **Jane Wakefield**: That the said Jane Wakefield is the Daughter of this Examinants Brother Thomas Wakefield by Mary his Wife and is now of the age of Eighteen Years [incomplete]
[PS/CH/RA/2/5:395. See **42053RO** (JW: 2 July 1842).]

42036RO: Wed 13 Apr 1842 – **Elizabeth Luker**, single woman: That the first place she remembers herself was in the Parish of Charlton Kings in the said County where she has resided all her life time until within the last two Months – That her Father Charles Luker died about Four years ago in the said Parish of Charlton Kings having previous to his death been relieved by the Parish Officer there several times and which Parish Officer provided a Coffin for his Funeral – That she has never been hired for a year or done any Act to gain a settlement in her own right, and is now Chargeable to the said Parish of Cheltenham – [mark]

1838: *death of EL's father Charles (buried at Charlton Kings on 17 Jan, aged 50).* **1839:** *death of mother Ann on 12 Jan, aged 53.* **1841:** *EL (15; servant) lived in Ryeworth, Charlton Kings.* **1842:** *ordered to be removed to Charlton Kings (father's apparent settlement) (abandoned).* **1847:** *marriage to John Ingles, gardener 23 Aug: both lived in Bath Road, Cheltenham.* **1850:** *birth of first child, James (baptised 5 May), when family lived in Leckhampton.* **1851:** *the family lived at 12 Croft St, Charlton Kings: Joseph (24; agricultural labourer), Elizabeth (28, born Charlton Kings), and James (11 mo) (HO107/1972/225/17).*

[PS/CH/RA/2/6:52 (order suspended as EL unfit to travel; suspension was not lifted) (copy at PS/CH/RA/2/5:396).]

42037RO: 13 Apr 1842 – **John Stallard**, coach-trimmer, and four children **Sarah, James, Henry**, and **George**: That the first place he remembers himself was in the Parish of Clifton in the said County where his Parents resided and lived in a House at the Rent of One Hundred pounds a year for several years – That about 30 Years ago he was apprenticed by Indenture to John Clark of Milk Street Saint Pauls in the City of Bristol Coach Maker for Seven Years – That he served the whole time and slept in the Parish of Clifton the whole of the term – That he has never rented a Tenement of the annual value of Ten pounds or done any Act to gain a Settlement elsewhere – That about Six Years ago he was relieved by the parish Officers of Clifton aforesaid – That he has Four Children by his late Wife Mary Ann now deceased (Viz^t.) Sarah aged 12. Years, James aged 10 Years, Henry aged 8. Years, and George aged Six years – That he and [his] said Children are now Chargeable to the said Parish of Cheltenham – [signed]
1838: *sons Henry John, James, and George baptised at Cheltenham 29 Apr, when the family lived at 29 Ambrose St, Cheltenham.* **1841:** *the family lived in Kingsholm, Gloucester: John (55; coach-maker), Mary Ann (stated as 20), William (20; coach-maker), Sarah (11), James (9), Henry (7), and George (4) (HO107/379/7/37/15); wife (Mary) Ann Stallard died (aged 38) at Cheltenham, soon after giving birth to son, John (both buried 21 June).* **1842:** *removed to Clifton (apprenticeship).* **1843:** *death of JS (buried 18 Aug at Clifton).* **1851:** *sons Henry (16) and George (14) pauper inmates of Clifton Union Workhouse at Stapleton (HO107/1955/427/3), and their elder brother James (19; coach-trimmer) was visitor at house of William Stallard and family, 31 Sherborne St, Cheltenham (HO107/1973/149/39).* [PS/CH/RA/2/6:53 (copy at PS/CH/RA/2/5:397).]

42038RO: Thurs 14 Apr 1842 – **Thomas Daniels**, weaver: That the first place he remembers himself was in the Parish of Minchinhampton in the said County   that when he was about twelve years of age he was apprenticed by Indenture to John Harris of the said Parish of Minchinhampton Weaver for seven years   that he served the whole term and slept in his Masters house the whole time. that he has never rented a tenement of the annual value of ten pounds or done any act to gain a settlement elsewhere
   That he is now chargeable to the said Parish of Cheltenham [mark]
1842: *removed to Minchinhampton (apprenticeship): see* **43075SE** *(TD: 28 Dec 1843) for further information.* [PS/CH/RA/2/6:54 (copy at PS/CH/RA/2/5:398).]

42039RO: Thurs 28 Apr 1842 – **Anne Hulbert**, widow: That about thirty one years ago she was married to her late husband William Olive Hulbert at the parish Church of Wootton under edge [= Wotton-under-Edge] in the said County. That her said husband then rented a House Garden and Orchard of a Mr Tombs in the Parish of Upton Saint Leonards in the said County at about £12 a Year. That we continued in the occupation of such premises for about three Years after our Marriage And paid All the rent. That my said husband during that time rented several acres of Land in the same Parish of Mr Howell of about the annual value of twenty pounds   That her said husband then left her to endeavour to get the situation as Bailiff and She has not seen him since   that she has heard he died about four years after he left her. That about 11 Years ago she was relieved by the Parish officers of Upton Saint Leonards. That she has done no act since to gain a settlement in her own right and is now actually Chargeable to the said Parish of Cheltenham [signed]
1841: *AH (née Hooper) (aged 65) lived in Grosvenor St, Cheltenham with relations Henry Hooper (35; labourer), Hannah (40; independent), and Caroline Hooper (12) (HO107/353/4/49/20).* **1842:** *removed to Upton St Leonards (husband's settlement).* [PS/CH/RA/2/6:55 (copy at PS/CH/RA/2/5:399).]

42040SE: [blank] [blank] 1842 – **Edward Hiscocks**, stonemason: That he has never done any act to gain a settlement in his own right and is now Chargeable to the said Parish of Cheltenham
1842: *removal uncertain: examination form incomplete.* [PS/CH/RA/2/5:400. See **42043SE** (father Charles Hiscocks: 9 May 1842).]

42041SE: [blank] [blank] 1842 – **Richard Webb**, labourer: [no text].

1842: *removal uncertain: examination form incomplete.* [PS/CH/RA/2/5:401. See perhaps removal expenses for "Webb" to North Cerney 18/- and 15/- (4Q 1842: D4178).]

42042SE: Mon 9 May 1842 – **Thomas Parker**, labourer, wife **Mary Ann**, and two children **Frederick (James)** and **Vashti**: That he is 24 Years of age   that the first place he remembers himself was in the Parish of Sapperton in the said County where his Father and Mother resided and where they have resided all his lifetime and are now living there – That his Fathers name is William and his Mothers name is Catharine Parker. that he left his parents when he was about 16 or 17 Years of age and went to work by the week in various parishes

That he has never lived in any service for a Year or rented a Tenement of the annual value of ten pounds or done any act to gain a settlement in his own right   That three years ago last October he was married at Sapperton aforesaid to his present Wife Mary Ann by whom he has two Children Frederick James aged 3 Years and Vashti aged 2 Years. That he is now actually chargeable to the said Parish of Cheltenham [mark]

1841: *Mary Parker (aged 20; dressmaker) lived in Swindon Place, Cheltenham with son Frederick (2) and daughter Vashti (1); (TP not at home on census night) (HO107/353/9/17/28).* **1842:** *removed to Sapperton (presumed) (father's settlement); TP was at the same time examined at the Public Office in Cheltenham for leaving his wife chargeable to parish; he was ordered to defray parish's expenses, but wife was "rather loath to return home with him" (Cheltenham Chron. 12 May); (RETURNED) son William baptised at Cheltenham 12 June, when family lived at 20 Swindon Place.* **1851:** *the family lived at 36 Park St, Cheltenham: TP (33; labourer, born Sapperton), Mary Ann (34), and three children (HO107/1973/607/40).* [PS/CH/RA/2/5:402.]

42043SE: 9 May 1842 – Charles Hiscocks, gardener, relating to the settlement of son **Edward Hiscocks** (also **Hiscox**): That he is about 49 Years of age. That the first place he remembers himself was in the Parish of Almondsbury in the said County where his father resided and rented a Farm of about 100 acres of Land there. that about 29 Years ago he was hired by Mr Richard Williams of the Marsh in the Parish of Olveston in the said County for a Year at the wages of Three pounds including board and lodging   that he duly served such Year and slept in his Masters house at Olveston aforesaid the whole of the time   that he continued in such three months longer but then left it on account of illness. That he has done no act since to gain a Settlement elsewhere

That three years ago last October he was removed with his Wife and family from Cheltenham aforesaid to Olveston aforesaid by orders of removal which Orders were not appealed against. That about 26 or 27 Years ago he was married to his present Wife Ann at the parish Church of Minchinhampton by whom he has his said Son Edward [mark]

1841: *EH (aged 20; apprentice) lived in Tivoli Place, Cheltenham (HO107/353/11/58/25).* **1842:** *removed to Olveston (presumed) (father's settlement).* **1843:** *(RETURNED) EH married Elizabeth Parry in Cheltenham on 18 June, when he lived at 3 Suffolk Road, as gardener.* **1844:** *birth of son William Edwin (baptised 24 Mar, when family lived at 4 Albert St, Cheltenham.* **1845:** *birth of daughter Elizabeth Jemima registered 1Q at Cheltenham (baptised 1 Feb 1846) (address: 6 Marsh Cottages, Cheltenham); death of EH (buried 15 Nov at Cheltenham, aged 29).* [PS/CH/RA/2/5:403. See **42040SE** (son Edward Hiscocks: [undated] 1842), where Edward is said to be a stonemason, and **38057SE** (Charles Hiscocks: 3 Sept 1838), resulting in his removal with wife Ann and four younger children to Olveston. [PS/CH/RA/2/5:403.]

42044SE: Tues 10 May 1842 – **Sarah Brown**: That she is now in the 72nd Year of her age. That about 40 Years ago she was married to her first husband John Hawes at the Parish of Stow on the Wold [= Stow-on-the-Wold] in the County of Gloucester   that in about three weeks after we were married we came to Cheltenham and rented a house in the High Street there at thirty pounds a Year   that we lived in that house one Year and then bought it at £900 and paid 50£ in part of the purchase money – that we then lived in that house for about 9 Years and sold it to Mr Mackay for £1200. We then took 415 in the High Street of Mr Newbury at £80 a Year and continued in the occupation of it for about twenty Years at that rent. My husband died in 1816 leaving one child by me who died in 1818   That since her husbands death she has rented the said house N° 415 in the High Street up to within the last three weeks at £47 a Year and paid several Years rent and taxes for the same. That about twenty Years ago she was married to John Brown in the parish

Church of Cheltenham who left me the same day and I have never seen or heard of him since. that the said John Brown was a Frenchman and never to her knowledge and belief done any act to gain a settlement in England

That she is now actually chargeable to the said Parish of Cheltenham [mark of Sarah Hawes]
1841: *Sarah Hawes (aged given as 60; lodging house-keeper) lived alone in High St, Cheltenham (HO107/353/14/9/13).* **1842:** *removal unlikely: settlement probably acknowledged as Cheltenham.* **1847:** *death of SB (buried 27 Feb at Cheltenham, aged 78). Her second husband was called William (not John) Brown, according to Cheltenham marriage register of 1822 (14 Dec).* [PS/CH/RA/2/5:404.]

42045RO: Sat 14 May 1842 – **Betty Cooke** (also **Cook**), single woman; also Michael Cooke, labourer, residing in Brockhampton (Sevenhampton parish), regarding the settlement of daughter Betty Cooke:
Betty Cooke: That she is in the 21 Year of her age. That she has never done any act to gain a settlement in her own right and is now chargeable to the Parish of Cheltenham [mark]
Michael Cooke: That at Cheltenham first mop about thirty one years ago he was hired by James Barnes of the parish of Tirley in the said County Farmer as a Carter for a year at the wages of Seven pounds that he served the whole year and received his wages That the year following he was hired by M[r]. Reeves of the parish of Badgworth in the said County Farmer for a year at the wages of nine guineas that he continued in such service until about a fortnight before the end of the year when he and his Master quarrelled and the Contract was dissolved by mutual consent and he was paid his wages only up to that time That he has never been hired for a year since or rented a tenement of the annual value of ten pounds nor done any act to gain a settlement. that about 15 or 16 years ago he was relieved by the parish officers of Tirley aforesaid whilst he was residing in the Parish of Whittington. that about 23 years ago he was married to his first wife Maria at the parish of Cam in this County by whom he had his said Daughter Betty now aged 21 years [mark]
1842: *removed to Tirley (father's settlement); BC married John Pocket(t) on 7 Nov at Northleach.* **1849:** *son Thomas baptised at Blakeney, East Dean 14 June (John Pockett was by then collier).* **1851:** *Betty (aged 29, born Whittington), husband John (44; agricultural labourer), and Thomas (2) lived in East Dean (HO107/1959/326/32). Note: "Not entered on list".* [PS/CH/RA/2/6:56 (copy at PS/CH/RA/2/5:405-6).]

42046RO: Sat 21 May 1842 – **Mary Ann Miller**, widow, and three children **Mary (Ann)**, **Frederick**, and **Louisa**: That she is About 36 years of age and was born in the parish of Saint George Hanover Square in the County of Middlesex where she resided with her parents until she was 17 Years of age when she was married to her late husband Charles Miller in the parish Church of Saint George Hanover Square aforesaid who died two years ago last January and was buried at Cheltenham aforesaid

That she has no knowledge whatever of the settlement of her said husband he never having done any act since their Marriage to gain a settlement. That during the whole of the time she lived with her said parents her Father John Breese rented a house N[o] 10 Poland Street in the said Parish of Saint George Hanover Square at about twenty pounds a year of M[r] Howard and paid the rent to him and in which House her Father resided for two Years and a half after she left him and died in such house and was buried in the burial Ground belonging to the said Parish of St George That since her husbands death she has done no act to gain a settlement in her own right That she has now living with her three Children by her said husband Mary Ann aged 11 Years Frederick aged 9 Years and Louisa aged 3 years

That she and her said Children are now actually Chargeable to the said Parish of Cheltenham [signed]
1831: *an MAM was committed for one month by the Cheltenham magistrates for being idle and disorderly (Chelt. Chron. 20 Jan; see also 24 Feb, 14 Apr, 26 May).* **1842:** *ordered to be removed to St George's Hanover Square, Middlesex (father's settlement) (abandoned): see* **43016RO** *(MAM: 4 Mar 1843) and Justice of the Peace 10 December, p. 765.* [PS/CH/RA/2/6:57: copy at PS/CH/RA/2/5:407). Note: "Abandoned; removed to St James' Westminster".]

42047RO: 21 May 1842 – **Elizabeth Liddiard** (also **Lydiatt**): That about twenty four years ago she was married to John Liddiard at the Parish Church of Saint Clement in the City of Worcester – that her said husband deserted her about 15 Years ago   That her said husband has done no act to gain a settlement since her said Marriage.

That about 15 Years ago she was removed by the Parish Officers of Cheltenham aforesaid to the Parish of Upton upon Severn in the County of Worcester by orders, that such orders were not appealed against

That about five Years ago she was relieved by the Parish officers of Upton upon Severn aforesaid whilst she was residing in the Parish of Cheltenham and had half a crown a week. That she is now actually chargeable to the said Parish of Cheltenham [mark]

1842: *died before removal to Upton-upon-Severn, Worcs (husband's presumed settlement); death of EL in Cheltenham (buried 10 Oct at Upton-upon-Severn, aged 44).* [PS/CH/RA/2/6:58 (copy at PS/CH/RA/2/5:408).]

42048RO: Mon 30 May 1842 – **John Witts**, labourer: That he was born in the parish of Bisley in the said County where he resided with his parents until he was about twenty Years of age when he went into the Marines and continued in that service Eleven years and a half when he was discharged and then went back to Bisley and continued there about ten years   That he has never been hired by the year or rented a tenement of the annual value of ten pounds or done any act to gain a settlement in his own right   That he has been several times relieved by the parish officers of Bisley aforesaid and his Wife and Child were buried at their Expence – That he is now chargeable to the said Parish of Cheltenham [mark]

1841: *probably the JW (aged 50; labourer) who lived alone in Stanhope St, Cheltenham (HO107/353/9/50/1).* **1842:** *removed to Bisley (father's presumed settlement).* **1861:** *JW probably a pauper inmate of Stroud Union Workhouse, aged 76 (RG9/1775/102/2).* **1867:** *probable death of JW, aged 82 at Stroud.* [PS/CH/RA/2/6:59 (copy at PS/CH/RA/2/5:409).]

42049RO: Fri 3 June 1842 – **John Hopkins**, labourer, wife **Sarah**, and son **James**: That at Tewkesbury fair held on the 10 of October 1827 he was hired by James Chadd of the parish of Elmstone Hardwick[e] in the said County Farmer for a Year as Carter at the wages of nine pounds   that he served the whole year and slept in his Masters house at Elmstone Hardwick aforesaid the whole time and received his whole Years wages – That he has never been hired for a Year since or rented a tenement of the annual value of ten pounds or done any act to gain a settlement elsewhere. that ten Years ago last May he was married in the parish Church of Cheltenham to his present Wife Sarah by whom he has one Child named James aged six years That he is now actually chargeable to the said Parish of Cheltenham. [mark]

1842: *removed to Elmstone Hardwicke (hiring and service).* [PS/CH/RA/2/6:60 (copy at PS/CH/RA/2/5:410).]

42050SE: Thurs 2 June 1842 – **Samuel Bloom,** tailor, and wife **Hannah**: That he is in the fiftieth Year of his age. That about 27 Years ago he was married at the parish Church of Hempstead [= Hempsted] to his present Wife Hannah. that his said Son William would be about 24 Years of age now if he was living. That about 20 Years ago he rented a house of Charles Williams situate in Clare Street Bath road in the said parish of Cheltenham by the quarter at the rate of £12 a Year that he [incomplete]

1841: *SB (aged 45; journeyman tailor born outside Glos) lived with wife Hannah (45) and children Susan (20), George (15), Josiah (10), and Mary (8) in Cleveland Passage, Tewkesbury Road, Cheltenham (HO107/353/9/28/4).* **1842:** *removal unlikely: settlement probably acknowledged as Cheltenham.* **1846:** *death of SB (buried at New Burial Ground, Cheltenham on 3 Dec, aged 54).* **1851:** *Hannah Bloom (62; widow) lived with four children (one on leave from Marines) in Aston, Birmingham (HO107/2060/42/13-43/14).* [PS/CH/RA/2/5:411. Text struck out.]

42051RO: Sat 25 June 1842 – **Elizabeth Richards**, widow, and daughter **Elizabeth**: That about nine years ago She was married to her late husband James Richards now deceased at the parish

Church of Cheltenham aforesaid by whom she has one Child named Elizabeth aged eight years. that her said husband was born at Monmouth as she has heard and believes and never done any act to gain a settlement in his own right   That two years ago last March she and her said Child and another Child named Mary then aged four months and since dead were removed by orders of removal from the Parish of Cheltenham aforesaid to the said Parish of Monmouth which orders were not appealed against and she remained in the Workhouse there for a year until April 1841 when she again came to Cheltenham and has been living there ever since in Lodgings at half a Crown a week and has done no act to gain a settlement – That she and her said Child are now actually chargeable to the said Parish of Cheltenham [signed]

1840: *ER removed to Monmouth (husband's settlement): see* **40037SE** *(ER: 27 Feb).* **1841:** *daughter Mary died 21 Mar at Monmouth Workhouse; (RETURNED) ER (aged 35; charwoman) lived with daughter Elizabeth (5) in Sherborne St, Cheltenham (HO107/353/5/62/46).* **1842:** *removed to Monmouth, Monm* ***(husband's presumed settlement)**; earlier in June she adjusted her statement to say she returned to Cheltenham in Apr 1841 (before census of 6 June); death of ER registered 4Q at Monmouth.* **1861:** *daughter Elizabeth (26) lived with uncle's family in Monmouth (RG9/3987/85/9).* [PS/CH/RA/2/6:61 (copy at PS/CH/RA/2/5:412). Removal expenses for "Richards" to Monmouth, Monm £2//11/6 (3Q 1842: D4178).]

42052RO: 25 June 1842 – **Sarah Yem** (also **Yemm**), single woman, and daughter **Maria**: That about twelve Years ago She was hired by the Rev^d. Edward Prowse Jones in the Parish of Edgeworth in this County for a Year at the wages of three pounds ten shillings   that she served the whole year and received her years wages   that she was then hired again by Mr Jones for another Year at the wages of five pounds and served the whole year and received her Years wages. That she was again hired by Mr Jones for another Year but served only about nine months. That she has done no act since to gain a settlement elsewhere   That she has an Infant Child named Maria with which she was delivered a fortnight ago   That she is now actually chargeable to the said Parish of Cheltenham [mark]

1842: *removed to Edgeworth (hiring and service).* **1851:** *on census night Maria Yem (aged 8; scholar) was visiting aunt Elizabeth Savory and uncle Thomas at 45 Duke St, Cheltenham (HO107/1973/39/3).* [PS/CH/RA/2/6:62 (copy at PS/CH/RA/2/5:412). Removal expenses for "Yem" to Edgeworth 18/- (3Q 1842: D4178).]

42052SE: Sat 2 July 1842 – **Richard Oakey,** carpenter: That he was born in the parish of Leigh in the said County where he resided until he was about twenty two Years of age. That his Father rented a Farm in the said Parish of Leigh for several Years at above twenty pounds a Year [incomplete]

1842: *removal uncertain: examination form incomplete.* [PS/CH/RA/2/5:412: text struck out. See **42055RO** (RO: 4 July 1842).]

42053RO: 2 July 1842 – **Jane Wakefield,** single woman; also Charlotte Brown, wife of James Brown, residing in Cirencester, relating to the settlement of sister Jane Wakefield:

Jane Wakefield: That she has never been hired as a Servant for a year or done any act to gain a settlement in her own right – That she is now chargeable to the said Parish of Cheltenham.

Charlotte Brown: That she is in the 30th year of her age – That her Father Thomas Wakefield died in the year 1830 in a Public House called the three tons [= Three Tuns] in the parish of Cirencester in the County of Gloucester which house he had rented for upwards of three years next preceding that time at £20 a year. that he paid all the rent for the same to M^r. Smith the Landlord who is now dead   that she and her Sister lived with her said Father in the said house the whole time – That she was married soon after the death of her Father and her said Sister Jane came to Cheltenham and lived with her Grandmother until about a twelve month ago – [signed]

1824: *baptism of JW at Fairford 21 Mar; father was shoemaker.* **1842:** *removed to Cirencester (father's* ***settlement).** 1851: *perhaps the JW (aged 26; unmarried) in service at Siddington (HO107/1968/289/5).* [PS/CH/RA/2/6:63 (copy at PS/CH/RA/2/5:415). Removal expenses for "Wakefield" to Cirencester 15/6 (3Q 1842: D4178), and perhaps see removal expenses for "Wakefield" to Bristol £4/2/- (2Q 1843: D4178). See **42035SE** (Jane Green: [undated] 1842).]

42054SE: [blank] July 1842 – Mary Oakey, widow, residing in The Leigh, relating to the settlement of son **Richard Oakey**: That about forty two Years ago she was married to her late husband William Oakey in the parish Church of Leigh aforesaid by whom she had her said Son Richard now aged about 31 years. that after she and her husband was [*sic*] married her said husband rented a small farm of Mr Beckett in the said Parish of Leigh at twenty two pounds a Year and continued in the occupation of it about Eleven years and paid all the rent. that he rented a small farm of Mrs Hill in the said Parish of Leigh at twenty pounds a Year for five years and paid all the rent – that her said husband never done any act afterwards to gain a settlement and died about twenty Years ago in the said Parish of Leigh and was buried there. That her said Son was born in the said Parish of Leigh in the first mentioned Farm and lived with her and his Father until he was about fifteen years of age [incomplete]
[PS/CH/RA/2/5:416 (copy at PS/CH/RA/2/5:416). See **42055RO** (RO: 4 July 1842), for which this was not needed, as settlement was judged based on his hiring and service, not father's settlement.]

42055RO: Mon 4 July 1842 – **Richard Oakey**, carpenter, wife **Hannah**, and three children **George**, **Mary**, and **Martha**: That he is now about 31 Years of age – That when he was about Fifteen years of age and unmarried he was hired by M^r. James Lee of the Parish of Leigh in the said County, Farmer, for a year at the Wages of Three pounds – That he served the whole Year and slept the whole time at his Master's House in Leigh aforesaid and at the end of the term he received his whole Years wages   That he has done no Act since to gain a settlement elsewhere and is now Chargeable to the Parish of Cheltenham – That about Eleven years ago, he was married to his present Wife Hannah in the Parish Church of Cheltenham by whom he has three Children (Viz^t.) George aged ten years, Mary aged Eight years, and Martha aged eight Months – [signed]
1842: *removed to The Leigh (hiring and service); (RETURNED) daughter Martha baptised at Cheltenham 25 Dec, when family lived at 9 Worcester St.* **1848:** *birth of daughter Sarah Coates Oakey registered at Cheltenham 4Q.* **1851:** *wife Hannah Oakey (aged 40; no occupation) lived with Martha (9), William (7), and Sarah (2) at 8 Worcester St, Cheltenham (HO107/1973/514/6), while husband RO (40; carpenter) and son George (18; carpenter) lodged in The Leigh (HO107/2043/67/23).* **1861:** *the family lived at 6 Tewkesbury Road, Cheltenham: Richard (52; carpenter), Hannah (51), George (29; carpenter), and William (16; blacksmith) (RG9/1800/26/9).* [PS/CH/RA/2/6:64 (copy at PS/CH/RA/2/5:417). Removal expenses for "Oakey" to The Leigh 10/- (3Q 1842: D4178). See **42052SE** (RO: 2 July 1842), **42054SE** (mother Mary Oakey: 4 July 1842).]

42056RO: Sat 9 July 1842 – **Mary Turner**, widow: That she is the Widow of David Turner who died on the 15th day of June last. That in the month of October 1816 she and her said husband and four of their Children were removed by orders of removal from the said Parish of Cheltenham to the Parish of Dowdeswell in the said County which orders were not appealed against – That she and her said family returned to Cheltenham and were relieved by the Parish officers of Dowdeswell for two or three months whilst they residing in Cheltenham – That her said husband never rented a Tenement of the annual value of ten pounds or done any act to gain a settlement since he was removed to Dowdeswell as aforesaid
     That she is now actually chargeable to the parish of Cheltenham aforesaid [mark on magistrates' original]
1841: *David Turner (aged 65; labourer) lived with wife Mary (50) in Tewkesbury Road, Cheltenham (HO107/353/9/30/9).* **1842:** *David Turner died at Cheltenham (buried 18 June, aged 66);* **removed to Dowdeswell (husband's presumed settlement)**; *(perhaps RETURNED) MT buried at Cheltenham 17 Nov (aged 64).* [PS/CH/RA/2/6:65 (copy at PS/CH/RA/2/5:418). Removal expenses for "Turner" to Dowdeswell 10/6 (3Q 1842: D4178).]

42057RO: Sat 27 Aug 1842 – Mary Ann Moreton, relating to the settlement of son, **George Page**, his wife **Mary Ann**, and two children **George** and **Mary**: That the said George Page is an illegitimate Child of hers with which she was delivered about 32 Years ago in the Queens lying in Hospital Bayswater London (which Hospital was duly licensed)   That she had previously done no act to gain a settlement in her own right

That her Father belonged to the Parish of Hackney in the County of Middlesex having been born in that Parish and never rented a Tenement of the annual value of ten pounds or done any act to gain a settlement elsewhere   That her Fathers Father was an Inmate of the Workhouse in Hackney aforesaid for two Years and upwards previous to his death and died in that Workhouse about 35 Years ago

That said Son has never done any act to gain a settlement in his own right and is now actually chargeable to the said Parish of Cheltenham

That Eight Years ago her said Son was married in the Parish Church of Cheltenham to his present Wife Mary Ann by whom he has two Children namely George aged seven years and Mary aged sixteen months [signed]

1841: *GP (aged 30; shoemaker), wife Mary Ann (25), and children George (7), Benjamin (3), and Mary Ann lived at 4½ Milsom St, Cheltenham (HO107/353/8/59/1).* **1842: *ordered to be removed to Hackney, Middlesex (mother's settlement) (abandoned);*** *see* Justice of the Peace *10 Dec p. 765.* **1845:** *the family lived in Cheltenham 3Q, when son William's birth was registered.* **1851:** *the family lived at 5 Bloomsbury Place, Cheltenham: GP (38; pauper shoemaker), Mary Ann (33; pauper), George (15; errand boy), Mary Ann (10; scholar), William (6; scholar), and Benjamin (4) (HO107/1973/611/48).* [PS/CH/RA/2/6:66 (order suspended as GP was unfit to travel; lifted 26 Sept) (copy at PS/CH/RA/2/5:419). Note: "Abandoned". Removal expenses to Hackney for "Page" £3/3/-" (3Q 1842), and £6/11/6 (4Q 1842: D4178).]

42058RO: Thurs 14 July 1842 – **Joel Poulston**, labourer, wife **Mary Ann**, and three children **Samuel George, Frederick**, and **Jane**: [That] his Father is legally settled in the parish of Stroud in the said County where he is now receiving relief of the Overseers of the Poor of the said parish of Stroud and has for some years past and in which parish his Father has been settled all his lifetime – that he this examinant has never done any act to gain a settlement in his own right – that about seven or eight years ago he was releived [*sic*] by the Overseer (M[r]. Shell) of the said Parish of Stroud for two or three months whilst he was residing at Ebley in the parish of Stonehouse. That about thirteen years ago he was married to his present Wife Ann at the parish of Stonehouse by whom he had three children Viz[t]. Samuel George aged 12 years Frederick aged 5 years and Jane aged 16 months – that he is now actually chargeable to the said Parish of Cheltenham [signed]

1841: *JP (aged 35; labourer, born Ebley, Stonehouse) lived with wife Ann (30), and children Samuel (10), Frederick (4), and Jane (two mo) in Suffolk St, Cheltenham (HO107/353/18/9/13).* **1842: *removed to Stroud (father's settlement);*** *(RETURNED) death of Jane Poulston in Cheltenham (buried at New Burial Ground 18 Nov, aged 21 mo).* **1845:** *birth of son Edwin at Cheltenham 2Q.* **1851:** *the family lived in Berkeley Avenue, Winchcombe St, Cheltenham (HO107/1973/174/32).* [PS/CH/RA/2/6:67 (copy at PS/CH/RA/2/5:420).]

42059RO: Fri 15 July 1842 – **William Prust**, labourer, wife **Grace**, and two children **Mary Ann** and **Joseph**: That about 31 years ago, being then unmarried, he was hired by M[r]. John Howe of the Parish of West Leigh [= Westleigh] in the County of Devon Farmer for a Year at the Wages of Seven pounds, that he served the whole year and received his years wages and slept in his Master's house at West Leigh aforesaid the whole time – That he was again hired for another year and served the whole time with M[r]. Howe in the same parish – That he was again hired for another Year to the same person and served the whole time at West Leigh aforesaid   That he has done no Act since to gain a settlement elsewhere – That about 28 Years ago he was married at the Parish Church of West Leigh aforesaid to his present Wife Grace, by whom he has two Children now living with him Viz[t]. – Mary Ann aged 11 Years, and Joseph aged 5½. Years – That he is now chargeable to the Parish of Cheltenham aforesaid – [signed]

1841: *WP (aged 55; no occupation given) lived with wife Grace (50) and children Mary (11), Thomas (7), and Joseph (5) in Westleigh, Devon (HO107/221/13/10/24-5).* **1842:** *death of son Thomas Prust (buried at New Burial Ground, Cheltenham 15 Apr);* ***removed to Westleigh, Devon (hiring and service).*** **1851:** *the family lived in Westleigh, Devon: WP (70; agricultural labourer, born Bideford, Devon), Grace (64; born Westleigh), and son Joseph (16; groom, born Westleigh) (HO107/1893/552/9).* [PS/CH/RA/2/6:68 (copy at PS/CH/RA/2/5:421). Removal expenses for "Prust" to West Leigh £10/7/6 (3Q 1842: D4178).]

42060RO: 15 July 1842 – **Mary Smith**, widow: That about 19 Years ago, she was married to her late Husband William Smith at the Parish of Leonard Stanley in the said County. That about Six Years ago her husband being out of work and residing at Leonard Stanley aforesaid applied to M^r. Fowler Overseer of Leonard Stanley for relief and was by him taken before the Magistrates at Stroud to be examined as to his parish, and in two or three days afterwards she and her said Husband and Children were taken by M^r. Fowler to M^r. Hobbs the Overseer of King Stanley [= King's Stanley] in the said County by whom we were relieved

That we went back to Leonard Stanley and was [*sic*] afterwards relieved by the Parish Officers of King Stanley whilst we were living at Leonard Stanley – That her said husband [has] never done any Act afterwards to gain a settlement and died about Seven months ago – That She has done no Act since her Husbands death to gain a settlement, and is now chargeable to the said Parish of Cheltenham. – [mark]

1842: *removed to King's Stanley (husband's settlement).* [PS/CH/RA/2/6:69 (copy at PS/CH/RA/2/5:422). Removal expenses for "Polson" to Stroud and to King's Stanley £1/2 (3Q 1842: D4178). See **47036RO** (MS: 11 Sept 1847).]

42061RO: Mon 25 July 1842 – **James Strain** (also **Strayn**, **Streign**; incorrectly **Strange**), labourer, wife **Susannah**, and three children **Frederick**, **James**, and **Mary Ann**: That his Father William Strange belonged to the parish of Bisley in the said County and was relieved by the Officer of that parish for many Years and died in the Workhouse there about Eleven Years ago where he had been an Inmate for Two or three years before. That he this Examinant hath done no act to gain a settlement in his own right – That about Fifteen years ago being ill he became chargeable to the Parish of Saint Michael in the City of Gloucester, and was taken by M^r. James Bullock the Overseer of that parish before the Magistrates at Gloucester and was by them removed from the said Parish of Saint Michael to the said Parish of Bisley by Order to which latter place he was taken and was relieved by the Overseer there – That such Orders were not appealed against –

That Eight Years last November he was married in the Parish Church of Stroud to his present Wife Susannah by whom he has Three Children. Viz^t. – Frederick aged Six years, James aged two years and a half, and Mary Ann aged three months

That he is now chargeable to the Parish of Cheltenham Aforesaid [mark]

1804: *baptism of JS in Bisley 10 Apr.* **1841:** *JS (aged 30; labourer) lived with wife Susan(nah) (30), and sons Frederick (11) and James (1) in Exmouth St, Cheltenham (HO107/353/12/40/17-41/18).* **1842:** *removed to Bisley (father's settlement).* **1851:** *(RETURNED) the family lived in Exmouth Court, Cheltenham: JS (52; labourer), Susan (50), Frederick (14), James (11), and Mary Ann (9; all scholars) (HO107/1973/853/10).* [PS/CH/RA/2/6:70 (copy at PS/CH/RA/2/5:423). Removal expenses for "Strain" to Bisley 19/- (3Q 1842: D4178).]

42062RO: Thurs 4 Aug 1842 – **Elizabeth Tucker**, single woman: That she was born in the Parish of Sturry in the County of Kent, That her Mother Sarah Tucker died in the said Parish of Sturry about 17 Years ago and her Father Charles Tucker died in the same Parish in the Year 1839 having for sometime previously to his death been relieved by the Parish Officers of Sturry aforesaid. That about ten Years ago she being ill was relieved by Mr Rammell the Overseer of the said Parish of Sturry for two or three months

That she has done no act to gain a settlement in her own right and is now chargeable to the said Parish of Cheltenham [mark]

1841: *ET presumably the servant (aged 25) living and working at Cambrian Villa, Charlton Kings (HO107/353/2/18/1).* **1842:** *removed to Sturry, Kent (father's presumed settlement).* **1844:** *(RETURNED) ET married widower William Bond (labourer) at Cheltenham 7 June; both lived in Rutland St, St Paul's, Cheltenham; Sarah baptised at Charlton Kings 27 Oct.* **1851:** *the family lived at 7 Church St, Charlton Kings: William Bond (40; labourer), Elizabeth (35, born Sturry, Kent), Mathew (17; bootmaker), William (12), Sarah (6), and Jane (1; all children born Charlton Kings) (HO107/1972/136/3); Mathew and William were children of William Bond's first wife Rebecca (buried at Charlton Kings 11 Oct 1841).*

[PS/CH/RA/2/6:71 (order suspended as ET unfit to travel; lifted 18 Nov.) (copy at PS/CH/RA/2/5:424). Removal expenses for "Tucker" to Sturry, Kent £4/16/6 (3Q 1842) £6/4/9 (4Q 1842: D4178).]

42063RO: Mon 8 Aug 1842 – **Margaret Rich**, single woman: That she is about Eighteen Years of age, and is the Daughter of Benjamin and Mary Rich – That she believes her said Father gained his Settlement in the Parish of Bedminster in the County of Somerset by Apprenticeship – That her said Father died when she was about two years old – That as long as she can remember her Mother resided in the Parish of Saint James in the City of Bristol with her Children including this Examinant until October 1839 when her said Mother died – That during the whole of that time her Mother received relief from the Parish Officers of Bedminster aforesaid – whilst she resided in the Parish of Saint James' – That She this Examinant hath done no act to gain a Settlement in her own right And is now Chargeable to the said Parish of Cheltenham [mark]
1839: death of MR's mother Mary in Bristol 4Q. **1841:** *Margaret and siblings remained in Bristol: William Rich (20; journeyman tailor, Susan (15), Catherine (15), Margaret (14), Thomas (13; apprentice tailor), and Eliza (8; all children born Ireland) (HO107/372/8/16/26).* **1842: removed to Bedminster, Som (father's settlement). 1851:** *MR (24; servant) was visitor at house of John Healey, tailor in St George Hanover Square, Westminster (HO107/1475/17/26); MR married Charles Taylor in Westminster 15 Dec.* [PS/CH/RA/2/6:72 (copy at PS/CH/RA/2/5:425). Removal expenses for "Rich" to Bedminster £1/13/6 (3Q 1842: D4178).]

42064RO: Tues 9 Aug 1842 – **John Lusty**, weaver, and wife **Mary**: That he is about 70 Years of age and as long as he can remember his Father rented a House and Land in the Parish of King Stanley [= King's Stanley] in the said County at twelve pounds a Year and continued in the Occupation of it until his death which happened About 30 Years ago. that he this Examinant hath done no act to gain a settlement in his own right. That about 37 Years ago he was married to his present Wife Mary at the Parish Church of Woodchester. That he is now Chargeable to the Parish of Cheltenham aforesaid [signed]
1841: JL (aged 65; weaver) lived with wife Mary (60) in Fairview St, Cheltenham. **1842: removed to King's Stanley (father's settlement). 1843:** *(RETURNED) death of JL at Cheltenham (buried at King's Stanley 9 Apr, aged 70).* **1844:** *death of Mary Lusty (buried 22 Jan at New Burial Ground, Cheltenham, aged 70).* [PS/CH/RA/2/6:73 (order suspended as JL unfit to travel; order discharged with respect to wife) *(copy at* PS/CH/RA/2/5:426). Removal expenses for "Lusty" to King's Stanley 18/- (2Q 1843: D4178).]

42065RO: Thurs 11 Aug 1842 – **Robert Young**, carpenter, and wife **Sarah**: That in the Year 1835 he rented a house of Edward Borton in the Parish of Leckhampton in the said County at ten pounds ten shillings a year and continued in the occupation of such house for one Year and a half and paid all the rent for the same   That he was duly rated to all Poor rates made for the said Parish during that time and paid each of such rates
   That he has done no act since to gain a Settlement elsewhere – That near two years ago he was married to his present Wife Sarah in the Parish Church of Cheltenham And he is now chargeable to the said Parish of Cheltenham [signed]
1841: RY (carpenter) married Sarah Carter at Cheltenham 18 Jan; both had been married before, and lived at 1 The Knapp; (6 June) the couple lived in Cirencester: RY (aged 60; journeyman carpenter) and Sarah (60). **1842: removed to Leckhampton (renting). 1846:** *(probably RETURNED) probably the RY buried at Cheltenham 4 Dec, aged 79.* **1847/9:** *wife Sarah Young probably buried at Cheltenham either on 28 Oct 1847 (aged 77) or 22 Nov 1849 (aged 74).* [PS/CH/RA/2/6:74 (copy at PS/CH/RA/2/5:427). Removal expenses for "Young" to Leckhampton 2/6 (3Q 1842: D4178).]

42066RO: Wed 24 Aug 1842 – Sarah Packer, residing in Burford, relating to the settlement of daughter, **Sarah Taylor**, single woman: That about thirty Years ago she was married to her late husband William Taylor in the Parish Church of Burford in the County of Oxford where her said husband lived all his lifetime and died 19 Years ago last July – That her said husband belonged to the said Parish of Burford and was frequently relieved by the Parish Officers there   That after the death of her said husband she and her four Children were relieved by the Parish Officers of Burford for three or four Years. that her said Daughter Sarah is now aged about 21 Years and was born in and lived with this Examinant at Burford aforesaid until about five Years ago and never done any Act to gain a settlement in her own right   That her said Daughter is now Chargeable to the Parish of Cheltenham [mark]

1842: *ST in final stages of pregnancy; **removed to Burford, Oxfordshire (father's settlement);** daughter Sarah Ann born 4Q (baptised at Cheltenham 24 Oct, when ST was single woman living at Cheltenham Union Workhouse).* **1845:** *(RETURNED) ST married Daniel Mustoe in Cheltenham 12 Oct (address 44 Sherborne St).* **1851:** *the family lived at 12 King St, Cheltenham: Daniel Mustoe (aged 30; porter), Sarah (30), and Sarah Ann (8; scholar) (HO107/1973/408/48).* [PS/CH/RA/2/6:75 (order was suspended as ST unfit to travel, presumably through pregnancy; lifted 18 Nov) (copy at PS/CH/RA/2/5:428). Removal expenses for "Taylor" to Burford 17/- (3Q 1842) £1/2/- (4Q 1842: D4178).]

42067RO: 24 Aug 1842 – Henry Wheeler, cordwainer, relating to the settlement of illegitimate son of his late wife Hannah, **Henry Jones**: That the said Henry Jones is an illegitimate Child of his late Wife Hannah who died about three weeks ago. That the said Henry Jones was born in the Parish of Bisley in the said County near ten years ago and has done no act to gain a settlement elsewhere and is now chargeable to the said Parish of Cheltenham [mark]

1841: *HJ (aged 10) lived with mother Hannah (30) and stepfather Henry Wheeler (25; shoemaker) in Bisley (HO107/349/5/5).* **1842:** *mother Hannah Wheeler buried at New Burial Ground, Cheltenham 10 Aug; **removed to Bisley (birth).*** [PS/CH/RA/2/6:76 (copy at PS/CH/RA/2/5:429). Removal expenses for "Wheeler" to Bisley £1/-/- (3Q 1842: D4178). See **42068RO** (HW: 3 Sept 1842).]

42068RO: Sat 3 Sept 1842 – **Henry Wheeler**, cordwainer: That he was born in the Parish of Bisley in the said County where his Father has resided as long as this Examinant can remember and lived in his own property and is still residing there on his own property   That this Examinant hath never done any act to gain a settlement in his own right. And is now actually chargeable to the Parish of Cheltenham aforesaid [mark]

1842: *removed to Bisley (father's presumed settlement).* **1848:** *(RETURNED) HW married Maria Matthews in Cheltenham 4Q.* **1851:** *HW (36; shoemaker) lodged in Birmingham (HO107/2053/240/16); wife Maria (46; charwoman) lived with daughter Sophia (2) and five children from former marriage at 25 Newman's Place, Cheltenham (HO107/1973/638/40).* [PS/CH/RA/2/6:78 (copy at PS/CH/RA/2/5:430). See **42067RO** (HW: 24 Aug 1842).]

42069RO: 3 Sept 1842 – **Robert Robbins** (also **Robins**), labourer, and wife **Mary**: That he was born in the parish of Chedworth in the said County where his parents were legally settled

That about thirteen Years ago whilst he was residing in the said Parish of Cheltenham he received relief from the Overseers of Chedworth aforesaid for more than twelve months at five shillings a week

That he has done no act to gain a settlement in his own right   That about forty Years ago he was married to his present Wife Mary. That he is now actually chargeable to the said Parish of Cheltenham [signed]

1841: *RR (aged 60; shoemaker) lived at 9 Milsom St, Cheltenham with wife Mary (50; born Ireland), and non-dependent son Robert (20; also born Ireland) (HO107/353/8/61/5).* **1842: *removed to Chedworth (Northleach Union) (father's settlement).*** **1844:** *(RETURNED) probably the Robert Robins who died at Cheltenham, aged 65 (buried at New Burial Ground 18 Mar).* **1845:** *wife Mary probably the Mary Robins buried at Cheltenham 29 May, aged 61; in 2Q 1845 Mary received parish relief from Northleach as a non-settled resident of Cheltenham (G/CH/9d/1).* **1848:** *son Robert Robins (shoemaker, of 1 New St, Cheltenham) married widow Mary Anne Smith 3 Sept at St Paul's Church, Cheltenham.* [PS/CH/RA/2/6:77 (copy at PS/CH/RA/2/5:430). Removal expenses for "Robins" to Chedworth 14/- (3Q 1842: D4178). See **49029RO** (son Robert Robbins: 17 May 1849).]

42070RO: Wed 14 Sept 1842 – **John Dee** (also **Pressdee**), labourer, wife **Maria**, and six children, **Ann**, **Mary**, **Eliza**, **Sarah**, **John**, and **Emma**: That as long as he can remember his Grandfather Joseph Dee lived upon an Estate of his own situate in the parish of Ledbury in a County of Hereford and died there about 17 Years ago. That upon his said Grandfathers death the said Estate descended to his Father Edward Dee who has resided there ever Since and is now living upon such Estate

That this Examinant hath done no act to gain a Settlement in his own right. That Sixteen Years ago he was married to his present Wife Maria in the Parish Church of Ledbury aforesaid by whom he has six Children to wit Ann aged 15 Years Mary aged 12 Years Eliza aged 9 Years Sarah aged 7 Years John aged 5 Years and Emma aged 2 Years   That about Eight Years ago part of his family being then ill he was relieved by the Parish Officers of Ledbury Aforesaid

That he is now actually chargeable to the said Parish of Cheltenham [mark]

1842: *ordered to be removed to Ledbury, Heref (father's settlement) (abandoned): see* **42090RO** *(JD: 29 Dec 1842) for further information.* [PS/CH/RA/2/6:81 (copy at PS/CH/RA/2/5:432 (Maria Dee unfit to travel: order abandoned on death of Maria Dee). Removal expenses for "Dee" to Ledbury £1/-/- (3Q 1842: D4178).]

42071RO: Mon 12 Sept 1842 – **Esther** (also **Hester**) **Ward**, wife of Joseph Ward, and three children, **Mary Ann**, **Joseph**, and **Esther**: That about Seven Years ago She was married to her said husband in the Parish Church of Leckhampton in the said County – that her said husband deserted her about Seven weeks ago and she does not know where he is – That she was born in the Parish of Saint Philip and Jacob in the City of Bristol   That her said Husband was born in the said Parish of Philip and Jacob in which Parish his parents rented a house at twelve pounds a Year as long as she can remember until the last six years when the last of his parents (his mother) died in that parish – That two years and a half ago she was relieved by the parish Officers of Saint Philip and Jacob aforesaid for several weeks, and that her said husband has never rented a tenement of the annual value of Ten pounds or done any Act to gain a settlement elsewhere – That she has three Children by her said husband, namely Mary Ann aged 5 Years, Joseph aged three Years and Esther aged 8 weeks – That she and her said Children are now actually chargeable to the said parish of Cheltenham [mark]

1842: *ordered to be removed to St Philip and St Jacob, Bristol (husband's settlement) (abandoned).* **1845:** *despite separation, birth of next child Elizabeth registered at Shrewsbury, Shropshire 2Q.* **1846:** *tragic death of daughter Esther* (Eddowes's Journal, *25 Nov).* **1851:** *EW (aged 30; dyer's widow) lived in Shrewsbury with children Mary Ann (13) Joseph (11), and Elizabeth (6).* [PS/CH/RA/2/6:79 (copy at PS/CH/RA/2/5:433). Notes: "Order Abandoned"; "Mary Ward Widow of Joseph Ward Carpenter rented a house No. 1 Church Alley; she then lived in the last house in the court and died there 8 Years ago; City of Bristol".]

42072RO: 14 Sept 1842 – **Samuel Boddington**, labourer, and wife **Maria**: That about Seven Years ago he rented a house of the Revd Henry Cooper in the parish of Leckhampton in the said County at twenty five pounds a Year and continued in the same house a whole Year and paid the whole years rent   that he then rented the same house at twenty pounds a Year for another Year and occupied it for that Year and paid the whole rent   That he then rented the same House for three successive years at Eighteen pounds a year and occupied it the three Years and paid all the rent That he was duly rated to all Poor rates made in the said Parish of Leckhampton for the Said five years and paid the whole of them – that he has done no Act since to gain a settlement elsewhere. That about nine years ago he was married to his present Wife Maria in the Parish Church of Horsley in the said County   That he is now actually Chargeable to the said Parish of Cheltenham [signed]

1841: *SB (aged 65; gardener, called in "error" John) lived with wife Maria (50) in Brunswick St, Cheltenham (HO107/353/8/13/20).* **1842:** *removed to Leckhampton (renting).* **1851:** *the couple were visitors at 14 Commercial St, Cheltenham: SB (78; farm servant, born Hellidon, Northants) and wife Maria (66; cloth worker, born Horsley) (HO107/1973/891/41).* [PS/CH/RA/2/6:82 (copy at PS/CH/RA/2/5:433). Note: "31 Brunswick St[ree]t". Removal expenses to Leckhampton for "Bod[d]ington" 2/6 (4Q 1842: D4178).]

42073SE: [blank] Sept 1842 – **John Moss**, with wife **Hannah**: That about twenty three years ago he then being single and never having been married he was hired by Major Brookes of Westal house in the parish of Cheltenham in the said County for a Year at twenty five Guineas a Year and Clothes that he continued in such service under that hiring two years and received the whole of his wages

That about fifteen Years ago he rented a house in Duke Street Cheltenham of a Mr Morris at Fourteen pounds a Year and lived in such house the whole year and paid the whole rent. that he has been living in Cheltenham ever since as a Lodger and [has] done no Act to gain a settlement elsewhere – that about twenty one Years ago he was married to his Wife Hannah in the parish Church of Swindon in the County of Wilts

That he is now chargeable to the said Parish of Cheltenham [signed]

1841: *JM (aged 60; independent) apparently lodged with wife Hannah (55) at house of clerk William Burgiss in Corpus St, Cheltenham (HO107/353/14/20/35).* **1842: *removal unlikely: settlement probably acknowledged as Cheltenham.*** **1851:** *JM (65; pauper and widower, formerly wheelchairman, born Cheltenham) was an inmate of Cheltenham Workhouse in St Paul's (HO107/1973/1091/3).* [PS/CH/RA/2/5:435.]

42074RO: Thurs 22 Sept 1842 (examinations on 17 and 22 Sept respectively) – Pethahiel Purnell, carpenter, residing in King's Stanley, relating to the settlement of daughter, **Mary Purnell**, single woman:

Pethahiel Purnell: That when he was about 13 Years of age he was apprenticed by Indenture to John Harding of Wootton under edge [= Wotton-under-Edge] in the said County for seven Years – that he served three years of the said term and slept the whole of that three Years in the said Parish of Wootton under edge when his Master failed and he was discharged   that in the Year 1823 he this Examinant purchased a piece of Land in the Parish of Leonard Stanley in the said County at the sum of thirty pounds of a Captain Holbrow which purchase money he duly paid and erected a House upon part of the Land – that he lived in such house from the time he erected it which was in the year 1824 until February last when he went to reside in Kings Stanley – That he has done no Act since to gain a settlement – That his said Daughter was born in Leonard Stanley aforesaid and has done no act to gain a settlement in her own right and left me long before February last [signed] Pethahiel Purnell

Mary Purnell: That she was born in the parish of Leonard Stanley in the said County – that she has never been hired for a Year or done any Act to gain a settlement in her own right, and is now actually Chargeable to the said Parish of Cheltenham [mark]

1841: *death of mother Ann (buried at Leonard Stanley 18 Mar); MP (aged 15; servant) lived in service in Portland Square, Cheltenham (HO107/353/6/20/34); father Pethahial Purnell (45; carpenter, born Hereford) lived in Leonard Stanley with his other children (HO107/370/5/2).* **1842: *removed to Leonard Stanley (father's settlement).*** [PS/CH/RA/2/6:82 (order suspended as MP unfit to travel; lifted 9 Dec) (copy at PS/CH/RA/2/5:436-7). Removal expenses for "Purnell" to Leonard Stanley 14/- (3Q 1842) and 2/6 (4Q 1842: D4178).]

42075SE: [blank] Oct 1842 – Edward Press Dee, labourer, residing in Ledbury, Heref, relating to the settlement of son **John Dee**: That he is in the seventy eighth year of his Age   that when he was about nine years old and unmarried he was hired by Mr Bennett of the Parish of Ledbury aforesaid for a Year at the wages of twenty six shillings that he served the whole Year and slept in his Masters house at Ledbury the whole time & received his years wages –

That being unmarried he was afterwards hired by Mr Partridge a Carrier in the Parish of Colwall in the said County of Hereford for a Year at 26 shillings a Year and served the whole year and slept in his Masters house at Colwall the whole time & received his years wages – that he was then hired by Mr Bossard of Briers Court in Ledbury aforesaid for a year in which service he lived four successive Years his wages increasing every year   the last year he had three pounds ten shillings   that he slept in his Masters house at Briers Court aforesaid the whole time and received All his wages   that he then went to work for several persons at weekly Wages but was never hired for a Year afterwards. That about 43 Years ago he was Married to his first Wife Susanna in the parish Church of Eastham in the County of Worcester by whom he had his said Son John now aged 38 Years who was born in Hanley Child in the said County of Worcester That about twenty three years ago and before his said Son was emancipated he this Examinant rented a House and Garden of Mr John Hulland [app. = Holland] in the Parish of Stoke Bliss in the said County of Hereford Miller for a Year at the rent of ten pounds six shillings a Year which house he occupied for two Years and paid the rent   That he has not rented a tenement of the annual value of ten pounds since [incomplete]

[PS/CH/RA/2/5:438 (text struck out). See **42076RO** (JD: 14 Oct 1842).]

42076RO: Fri 14 Oct 1842 – **John Dee**, labourer, and six children, **Ann**, **Mary**, **Eliza**, **Sarah**, **John**, and **Emma;** also father Edward Press Dee (also Pressdee), residing in Ledbury, Heref:

John Dee: That he is now in the thirty eighth year of his age – that he is the Son of Edward Press Dee who lives at Wellington Heath in the Parish of Ledbury in the County of Hereford

That this Examinant never did any act to gain Settlement in his own right – That about Sixteen Years ago he was married to his late Wife Maria now deceased in the Parish Church of Ledbury Aforesaid by whom he has six Children namely Ann aged 15 Years Mary aged 12 Years Eliza aged 9 Years Sarah aged 7 Years John aged 5 Years and Emma aged two Years. That he remembers his Father renting a House and Garden at Stoke Bliss [Heref]   That he this Examinant lived with his Father there

That he is now actually chargeable to the said Parish of Cheltenham [mark]

Edward Press Dee: That he is now in the seventy eighth Year of his Age   That when he was about Eleven years of age he being then unmarried and having no Child or Children he was hired by Mr Bossard of Briers Court in the parish of Ledbury Aforesaid to serve him for a Year   That he lived in M^r. Bossards service four successive years and recieved [*sic*] for the last year Three pounds wages. That he slept in his Masters house at Ledbury aforesaid the whole four Years and received All his wages   That after he left Mr Bossards service he never was hired by any person for a Year nor served at any place under a Yearly hiring. That about forty three Years ago he was married to his first Wife Susannah at the Parish Church of Eastham in the County of Worcester by whom he had his said Son John now aged 38 Years

That his said Son was born at Hanley Child in the said County of Worcester. That about 23 Years ago and before his said Son was emancipated he this Examinant rented a house and Garden of Mr John Hulland [app. = Holland] Miller in the Parish of Stoke Bliss in the said County of Hereford for a Year at the rent of ten pounds six shillings a Year   that he occupied the said House and Garden for two Years and paid the rent for the same. That he has not since rented a tenement of the annual value of ten pounds nor done any Act to gain a settlement in his own right other than as next is mentioned. That about twelve months after the death of this Examinants Father which happened 17 Years ago last August he went to reside upon some Cottages and Gardens which belonged to his Father and which descended to this Examinant as his Eldest Son and heir at Law situate in Wellington Heath in the said parish of Ledbury. That he has lived there ever since   That about three months before he went to live there after his said Fathers Death this Examinants said Son John was married to his Wife Maria   that when he came to live there his said Son John was living at the Cottages with his Wife. That this Examinant was at work at Ludlow from the time of his Fathers death until three or four months after the Marriage of his said Son John [mark]

1842: *ordered to be removed to Stoke Bliss, Heref (father's settlement) (abandoned):* see 42090RO *(JD: 29 Dec 1842) for further information.* [PS/CH/RA/2/6:83 (copy at PS/CH/RA/2/5:439-40. See **42075SE** (Edward Press Dee: [undated] Oct 1842).]

42077RO: Sat 15 Oct 1842 – Henry Whittick, painter, grandfather of **Harriet Whittick** (also **Wittick**): That he is in the 56th year of his age – That about Twenty nine years ago he rented a House of M^r. Dodd situate in the Parish of Saint Nicholas in the City of Gloucester at Twenty pounds a year – that he continued in the occupation of such House for about Twelve years and paid all his Rent – That he has not rented a Tenement of the annual value of Ten pounds or done any act since to gain a settlement elsewhere – That in the year 1817 he was married to his present Wife Mary in the Parish Church of Saint Nicholas Aforesaid by whom he had a Daughter named Mary who was born about twelve months before he was married and was an illegitimate Child of his said Wife –

That such Child Mary was born in the said Parish of Saint Nicholas Gloucester in the House he so rented of M^r. Dodd – That his said Daughter lived with him as one of his Family until within the last three years and never did any act to gain a Settlement in her own right – That his said

Daughter never was married, and about Five years ago was delivered of the said Harriet Whitwick in the parish of Cheltenham in a house occupied by this Examinant at Half a Crown a week – That the said Harriet Whittick has done no act to gain a Settlement And is now Chargeable to the said Parish of Cheltenham [signed]
1838: *HW baptised 2 Feb from 28 Grove St, Cheltenham.* **1841:** *HW lived with grandparents Henry (55; painter) and Mary (Ann) (45) and uncle James (10) in Grove St, Cheltenham (HO107/353/16/34/28-9); death of grandmother Mary Ann (buried at Cheltenham 20 July, aged 57).* **1842:** **removed to St Nicholas, Gloucester (mother's settlement).** **1846:** *uncle James (14) in receipt of poor relief in Cheltenham.* **1849:** *death of grandfather Henry Whittick, aged 63 (buried at Cheltenham 11 Sept).* **1851:** *HW (14; pauper, scholar) was an inmate of Gloucester Union Workhouse, St Catherine's, Gloucester (HO107/1961/468/6).* [PS/CH/RA/2/6:84 (copy at PS/CH/RA/2/5:441). Removal expenses for "Whittick" to Gloucester 8/- (4Q 1842: D4178). See **46015RO** (HW: 5 Mar 1846).]

42078RO: Thurs 3 Nov 1842 – **Ann Agate**, and son **James:** That on the twenty second day of January 1825 she was married to her present husband James Agate in the parish Church of S^t. Marylebone in the County of Middlesex by whom she has one Child now living with her named James aged twelve Years. that at Michaelmas 1829 her said husband rented a house situate and being N° 8 Praed Street in the Parish of Paddington in the County of Middlesex at the Yearly rent of thirty four pounds. that her said husband and herself actually resided in such house for two Years and a half at that rent and paid the whole of such rent that the Landlords name was Marmaduke Matthews That she and her said husband occupied the same house for another following year at the reduced rent of thirty pounds and resided in it the whole time and paid the whole rent that the Number of such house was the last year altered to Number 12 That her said husband was duly rated to and paid all such Poor rates and other Rates and taxes during the whole of the time he occupied such house That she and her said husband soon afterwards went into service and her said husband hath not rented any house or tenement of the annual value of ten pounds or done any act to gain a settlement since. That her said husband is now in France and she is unable to support herself and Child and she and her said Child are actually become chargeable to the said Parish of Cheltenham [signed]
1842: **removed to Paddington, Middlesex (husband's settlement).** **1851:** *AA (aged 50, born Marylebone, Middlesex) lived with son James (21; blind) in Paddington, Middlesex (HO107/1467/63/13).* **1861:** *AA (59; needlewoman, widow) and James (31; blind) lived in Paddington (RG9/9/117/1).* [PS/CH/RA/2/6:85 (copy at PS/CH/RA/2/5:442). Removal expenses for "Agate" to Paddington £4/14/6 (4Q 1842: D4178).]

42079RO: Sat 5 Nov 1842 – **Elizabeth Poulson** (also **Polson**, **Powlson**), widow, and daughter **Emma**; also Sarah Poulson, residing in Bisley, wife of the late John Poulson, relating to the settlement of her son James Poulson.
Elizabeth Poulson: That about twenty six years ago she was married to her late husband James Poulson in the Parish Church of Bisley in the said County by whom she has one Child now living with her named Emma aged nine years who was born in the said Parish of Bisley. that her said husband died on the 14th of August last at Cheltenham Aforesaid never having rented a tenement of the annual value of ten pounds or done any act to gain a settlement in his own right since his Marriage to her
  That she and her said Child are now actually chargeable to the said Parish of Cheltenham [mark]
Sarah Poulson: That about fifty eight Years ago she was married to her said late husband John Poulson in the Parish Church of Bisley in the said County who was born in the said Parish of Bisley and where he resided all his lifetime she having known him from his early Childhood. that her said husband died about twelve Years ago in the said Parish of Bisley. that she had by her said husband her said late Son James who was born in the said Parish of Bisley about fifty years years ago and who continued to live with his said Father and this Examinant until he was married to his first Wife which was when he was about twenty one Years of Age that her said Son continued to live in the said Parish of Bisley until about five Years ago when he came to Cheltenham to work and [has] never done any act to gain a settlement in his own right [mark]

1841: *James Poulson (aged 50; labourer, though previously weaver) lived with wife Elizabeth (45) and four children Eliza (20), Jesse (10), Emma (8), and James (2) in Worcester St, Cheltenham (HO107/353/9/61/22).* **1842:** *death of sons Jesse Poulson (buried at New Burial Ground, Cheltenham on 11 May, aged 12) and James Poulson (registered at Cheltenham 3Q 1842); death of husband James Poulson (buried at Cheltenham 17 Aug);* **removed to Bisley (husband's presumed settlement).** **1843:** *daughter Eliza married.* **1847:** *death of EP in Stroud Workhouse (buried 21 Apr, aged 52).* **1851:** *daughter Emma (18) in service at 3 Bedford Buildings, Clarence St, Cheltenham (HO107/1973/701/17).* [PS/CH/RA/2/6:86 (copy at PS/CH/RA/2/5:443-4. Removal expenses for "Polson" to Stroud and "Smith" to King's Stanley £1/2/- (3Q 1842) to Bisley £1/3/6 (twice) and to Bisley 19/- (4Q 1842: D4178).]

42080RO: Thurs 24 Nov 1842 – **Mary Ann Miller**, widow, and three children **Mary Ann**, **Frederick**, and **Louisa**: That She is about thirty six years of age – that about nineteen years ago she was lawfully married to her late husband Charles Miller in the parish Church of Saint George Hanover Square London – that her said Husband died two years ago last January in the said Parish of Cheltenham – That about Five or six years ago her said Husband rented a house and Garden of M^r. Sadler in the parish of Charlton Kings in the said County at the Yearly Rent of Twelve pounds   That her said Husband and herself resided in such house for more than a year and paid the whole years rent – that her said husband was duly rated to the poor rate for the said parish of Charlton Kings in respect of such house and paid the same – That her said husband never afterwards done any act to gain a settlement elsewhere – That she has done no act since her Husbands death to gain a settlement in her own right – That she has three Children by her said Husband now living with her – namely Mary Ann aged Eleven years – Frederick aged nine years and Louisa aged three years – That she and her said Children are now actually chargeable to the said Parish of Cheltenham – [signed]
1842: **ordered to be removed to Charlton Kings (husband's presumed settlement) (order abandoned):** *see* **43016RO** *(MAM: 4 Mar 1843).* [PS/CH/RA/2/6:87 (copy at PS/CH/RA/2/5:445).]

42081RO: Mon 28 Nov 1842 – **Jane Adams**, single woman: That the first place she remembers herself was in the Parish of Horsley in the said County where her parents were settled – That she is the daughter of Samuel and Hannah Adams – That she has been relieved by the Parish Officers of Horsley aforesaid for near Eighteen Years last past during which time she has been living in Cheltenham   That she has done no act to gain a settlement in her own right and is now actually chargeable to the Parish of Cheltenham aforesaid – [mark]
1841: *(Clara) Jane Adams (aged 33) lived with family of George Blackwell (labourer) in Shackle's Pike, Hewlett Rd, Cheltenham (HO107/353/3/42/1).* **1842:** **died before removal to Horsley (father's settlement);** *death of JA (buried at New Burial Ground, Cheltenham 6 Dec).* [PS/CH/RA/2/6:88 (order suspended as JA unfit to travel; suspension not lifted) (copy at PS/CH/RA/2/5:446). Note: "This Girl died before the Notice could be served".]

42082RO: Thurs 1 Dec 1842 – **Richard Freeman**, labourer: That about thirty three years of ago he then being unmarried and having no Child or Children he was hired by Captain Charles Boultbee of the Parish of Horsley in the said County as Groom for a Year at the Wages of Fifteen pounds – That he continued in such service the whole Year and received his Years Wages and slept in his Master's house at Horseley [= Horsley] aforesaid the whole time – That he continued in such service for six or seven years afterwards and was married after he had been in such service two years but his Wife is now dead – That he has done no act since to gain a settlement elsewhere and is now actually Chargeable to the said parish of Cheltenham – [signed]
1835: *presumably the RF, Cheltenham coachman and sometime lodging-house keeper, whose bankruptcy hearing is listed in* London Gazette *26 June, p. 1242.* **1841:** *wife Elizabeth (aged 50; spinner) apparently an inmate of Stroud Union Workhouse (HO107/349/13/69/10); death of wife Elizabeth at Stroud 25 Oct, aged 51 (buried at Horsley).* **1842:** **removed to Horsley (hiring and service).** [PS/CH/RA/2/6:89 (copy at PS/CH/RA/2/5:447). Removal expenses for "Freeman" to Horsley £1/2/6 (1Q 1843: D4178).]

42083RO: Mon 5 Dec 1842 (examination on 3 Dec) – **John Harris**, cordwainer, and wife **Elizabeth**: That he is about 62 Years of age, and the first place he remembers himself was in the

Parish of Haresfield in the said County where his Father and Mother resided and his said Father gained a Settlement in that parish, by renting a Farm there for several Years at more than 10£. a year and resided there up to his death which happened about 58 Years ago That his Mother died about 13 years ago in the said Parish of Haresfield – That he has never done any Act to gain a settlement in his own right; That about twenty years ago he was relieved several times by the Parish officers of Haresfield aforesaid whilst he was residing in the City of Gloucester – That about twelve years ago he was relieved by the Overseer Mr Grizzell of the said Parish of Haresfield with a sum of Two pounds ten shillings   that he was then living in the Parish of Cheltenham – That about 40 Years ago he was married to his present Wife Elizabeth in the parish of Saint Michael in the City of Gloucester That he is now actually Chargeable to the said parish of Cheltenham [mark]

1842: *removed to Haresfield (father's settlement).* **1843:** *(RETURNED) JH stated that he lived in Cheltenham: see* **43058SE** *(JH for son William Harris: 31 Aug).* **1851:** *JH (aged 69; cordwainer, born Haresfield) lived with wife Elizabeth (69) in Westgate St, Gloucester (HO107/1961/257/16).* [PS/CH/RA/2/6:90 (copy at PS/CH/RA/2/5:448). Removal expenses for "Harris" to Haresfield £1/4/- (1Q 1843: D4178).]

42084RO: 5 Dec 1842 (examination on 3 Dec) – **Henry Holman**, labourer: That he is about 37. Years of age – That the first place he remembers himself was in the parish of Saint Andrew Plymouth in the County of Devon in which parish his Father rented a house of a M^r. Wills Druggist situate in Broad Street at Forty pounds where his Father resided until this Examinant was about Sixteen Years of age – That his Father then rented a House in Thick's Lane Saint Andrew aforesaid of a M^r. Mumford at ten pounds a Year and resided there until his death which happened about Six years ago – That this Examinants Mother is now Chargeable to the said Parish of Saint Andrew – That he has never done any act to gain a settlement in his own right and is now actually Chargeable to the said Parish of Cheltenham [signed]

1831: *HH (22nd Regiment, discharged) imprisoned in Bodmin Gaol.* **1841:** *apparently the HH (aged 35; labourer) held in Exeter City Prison, St David's, Exeter, on census night (HO107/266/11/2/2); on 19 Oct he was sentenced to one day's imprisonment at Devon County Sessions, for larceny.* **1842: removed to St Andrew, Plymouth, Devon (father's settlement).** **1843:** *HH committed for larceny and vagrancy 7 Mar at Dorchester Prison (hard labour; 21 days).* **1851:** *HH (age given as 38; born Exeter) had probably re-enlisted, and was stationed as private in 28th Regiment at barracks in Salford, Manchester (HO107/2224/27).* [PS/CH/RA/2/6:91 (copy at PS/CH/RA/2/5:449). Note: "This Pauper was received in the Workhouse at Plymouth – but did not belong to the Parish of Saint Andrew". Removal expenses to Plymouth for "Holman" £7/10/6 (4Q 1842: D4178).]

42085RO: Wed 7 Dec 1842 – **John Silvester**, miller: That about Eight years ago he rented a House and Mill situate in the parish of Edgbaston in the County of Warwick the property of Lord Calthorpe at one hundred and thirty pounds a year and continued to reside in the same for six years at that rent and paid the whole of the rent, that he was duly rated to all Poor and other Parochial rates in respect of such Property during that time and paid the whole of such Rates: That he has done no act to gain a settlement since and is now actually chargeable to the said Parish of Cheltenham – [signed]

1841: *JS (aged 70; millwright) lived with wife Elizabeth (70) in King Edward's Place, Ladywood, Birmingham (HO107/1140/1/35/22).* **1842: ordered to be removed to Edgbaston, Warks (renting) (order abandoned).** **1846:** *death of JS (buried at King's Norton, Birmingham 12 Sept, aged 76).* **1847:** *wife Elizabeth buried at King's Norton, Birmingham 24 May, aged 77.* [PS/CH/RA/2/6:93 (copy at PS/CH/RA/2/5:450). Note: "Pauper left the Town". Removal expenses to Edgbaston for "Silvester" £2/4/- (2Q 1843: D4178).]

42086RO: 7 Dec 1842 – **Mary Ann Carless**, widow: That she is in the fifty seventh year of her Age – That about Thirty three years ago she was married to her late husband Thomas Carless in the parish of Saint George Hanover Square London   That her said husband who was a Joiner and builder there rented a house Shop and premises in Saint Owens Street without in the parish of Saint Owen in the City of Hereford at twenty pounds a Year of his Father Joseph Carless where he resided with this Examinant until his death which happened about twenty four years ago. that her said husband paid the whole of his rent   that her said husband about four years after her said Marriage served the Office of Overseer for the said Parish of Saint Owen   That her said husband was duly rated to the Poor rates of the said Parish of Saint Owen for the time he so lived there and paid such rates   That she has done no act to gain a settlement since her said husbands death – That she is now actually chargeable to the said Parish of Cheltenham. [signed]

1842: *removed to St Owen, Hereford, Heref (husband's settlement).* **1845:** *MAC remarried, to Charles Wainscott, in Hereford 11 Dec.* **1849:** *MAC (Turnpike Gate Keeper) died 14 Sept at Clehonger, Heref, aged 64.* [PS/CH/RA/2/6:92 (copy at PS/CH/RA/2/5:451). Removal expenses for "Carless" to Hereford, Heref £2/6/6 (1Q 1843: D4178).]

42087RO: Tues 13 Dec 1842 – **John Goodall** (also **Goodhall, Goodwill**), labourer, wife **Rebecca**, and three children **Charles, William,** and **Amelia**: That he was born in the Parish of Quinnington [= Quenington] in the said County where his Parents were legally settled – That he has never done any Act to gain a settlement in his own right – That about Six years ago, he was married to his present Wife in the Parish Church of Charlton Kings in the said County by whom he has three Children, namely, Charles aged five years William aged two years, and Amelia aged nine months   That he is now actually chargeable to the said Parish of Cheltenham [mark]

1841: *JG (aged 27; labourer, subsequently also gardener) was prisoner at Gloucester County Gaol (HO107/356/10/10/3); wife Rebecca (25; agricultural labourer) lived with two sons Charles (4) and William (1) at Prescott (HO107/367/15/2/13).* **1842:** *removed to Quenington (father's settlement).* **1844:** *son Edwin Timothy baptised 16 June at Leckhampton; (RETURNED) two further children were born at Cheltenham.* **1848:** *on 8 Sept the family sailed as steerage passengers on the "Ajax" for New Zealand, arriving at Port Chalmers, Dunedin, Otago 8 Jan 1849.* **1851:** *JG (labourer) listed as eligible for jury service in Otago (Otago Witness, 8 Mar p. 1) and subsequent children born at Otago.* [PS/CH/RA/2/6:94 (copy at PS/CH/RA/2/5:452). Removal expenses for "Goodall" to Quenington £1/18/- (1Q 1843: D4178).]

42088SE: [blank] Dec 1842 – **Esther Price**, single woman, and daughter **Sarah**: That she is the Daughter of Thomas Price and Esther his Wife and is now in the twenty second Year of her Age. that she has never been hired for a Year or done any act to gain a settlement in her own right That about five weeks ago she was delivered of a female bastard Child in the said parish of Cheltenham and is now Actually chargeable to that Parish

1841: *EP (aged 20) lived with mother Esther (50; independent) and brother James (25; porter) in Swindon Place, Cheltenham (HO107/353/9/15/24).* **1842:** *removal uncertain: examination form incomplete; "female bastard child" baptised Sarah 29 Dec, while EP was an inmate of Cheltenham Workhouse.* **1843:** *death of Sarah at seven weeks (buried at Cheltenham 9 Jan).* [PS/CH/RA/2/5:453.]

42089RO: Sat 24 Dec 1842 – **John Dobbins**, labourer, wife **Maria**, and four children **Thomas, William, John,** and an infant male [**George**]: That about Twenty seven years ago he being then unmarried and having no Child or Children he was hired by M^r. Jones of the Parish of Mitchel Dean [= Mitcheldean] in the said County Farmer and Currier for a Year at the Wages of Eight pounds. That he served his said Master under such hiring for three years and received the whole of his Wages and slept in his Masters house at Mitchel Dean aforesaid the whole time – That he has never done any act since to gain a settlement elsewhere – That about Ten years ago he was married to his present Wife Maria in the Parish Church of Cheltenham aforesaid by whom he has four Children, namely Thomas aged nine years, William aged Seven years, John aged two years and an Infant Male Child aged three Months. That he is now actually become chargeable to the said Parish of Cheltenham in consequence of being out of Employ and his Wife being very ill [signed]

1841: *JD (aged 35; labourer) lived with wife Maria (30), and sons Thomas (8), William (6), Charles (4; died later that year), and John (8 mo) at 2 Park Place, Lower High St, Cheltenham (HO107/353/16/46/9).* **1842:** *"infant male child" was George Dobbins, born 4Q; removed to Mitcheldean (hiring and service).* **1843:** *(RETURNED) death of George (buried 14 Dec), when family lived in Brunswick Terrace, Cheltenham; subsequent children all born at Cheltenham.* **1851:** *the family lived at 1 Cullen Place, Swindon Road, Cheltenham: JD (45; general labourer, born Leigh, Worcs), Maria (38), Thomas (18; errand boy), William (16; errand boy), John (10; scholar), Edwin (7; scholar), James (3), Mary Ann (5), Maria (1)*

(HO107/1973/484/29). [PS/CH/RA/2/6:95 (copy at PS/CH/RA/2/5:455). Removal expenses for "Dobbins" to Mitcheldean £1/17/- (1Q 1843: D4178).]

42090RO: Thurs 29 Dec 1842 – **John Pressdee** (also **Dee**), labourer, and five children **Maria**, **Eliza**, **Sarah**, **John**, and **Emma**; also Thomas Price, yeoman and Overseer of the Poor, and Thomas Weaver, shopkeeper, both of Eastham, Worcestershire. *John Pressdee*: That about Eight years ago he was residing in the Parish of Eastham in the County of Worcester and with Maria his Wife and three Children, namely Ann then aged about Seven years – Mary then aged about three Years, and Eliza then aged about Eight Months – we were removed from that parish to the parish of Ledbury in the County of Hereford by an Order of two Magistrates acting in and for the County of Worcester, we were all taken by Thomas Weaver (who was employed by Thomas Price the then Overseer of Eastham aforesaid) to Ledbury aforesaid and delivered over to M^r. Dukes the then Overseer of the said parish of Ledbury by whom we were relieved for about a fortnight, and M^r. Dukes then gave me two pounds to get my Furniture from Eastham – I then took a House at Ledbury at Two pounds a year and resided in it Five years, and then came to Cheltenham and took a House at Half a Crown a week and lived in it about 15. Months I then went to the Parish of Leckhampton in the County of Gloucester and rented a House in Charles Street in that parish at thirteen pounds a Year and resided there about 14 Months and paid 11. pounds towards my Rent, but was not rated to the Poor Rate, and paid no Poor Rate – I then came into Cheltenham and rented a House at Half a Crown a week and continued there up to the present time – I have done no act to gain a settlement since I was removed to Ledbury – I was married about 16 Years ago to my late Wife Maria now deceased in the Parish Church of Ledbury aforesaid, by whom I have now five Children living with me namely Mary aged 12 Years, Eliza aged 9. Years, Sarah aged 7. Years John aged 5. Years, and Emma aged two Years – That I am now actually Chargeable to the said Parish of Cheltenham [mark]

Thomas Price: [produces removal order for family from Eastham to Ledbury and confirms that Thomas Weaver was charged with delivering them to Ledbury, and that the removal was not appealed against]

Thomas Weaver: [confirms that he delivered the family to the Overseers at Ledbury in March 1834].

1841: *Maria Dee (aged 38; laundress) lived with children Ann (14), Mary (10), Eliza (8), Sarah (5), John (3), and Emma (4 mo) in Charles St, Cheltenham (JD absent from home on census night) (HO107/353/18/5/5).* **1842:** *ordered to be removed to Ledbury, Heref (father's settlement) (abandoned): see* **42070RO** *(JD: 14 Sept); death of Maria Dee mid Sept 1842 (buried at New Burial Ground, Cheltenham 24 Sept, aged 37); ordered to be removed to Stoke Bliss, Heref (father's settlement) (abandoned): see* **42076RO** *(JD: 14 Oct);* **removed to Ledbury, Heref (father's settlement).** **1846:** *(probably RETURNED) probable death of JD in General Hospital at Cheltenham on 24 Dec (buried five days later, aged 42) (his father had declared that he was 38 in 1842).* [PS/CH/RA/2/6:96 (papers for order include first page of removal order from Eastham, Worcs to Ledbury, Heref, signed on 28 Feb 1834) (copy at PS/CH/RA/2/5:457-9). Removal expenses for "Pressdee" to Ledbury, Heref £1/10/- (twice) (4Q 1842), to Eastham, Worcs £3/6/- and £2/11/-, and Ledbury, Heref £1/14/- (1Q 1843: D4178).]

1843

43001RO: Thurs 5 Jan 1843 – **John Barton**, labourer, wife **Ann**, and six children **Henry**, **Albina**, **Jane**, **Matilda**, **Robert**, and **Charles**: That about Seventeen or Eighteen Years ago he (then being unmarried and having no Child or Children) was hired by Mr Benjamin Bisco of the Parish of Norton in the County of Gloucester Farmer for a Year as Carter at the wages of Six pounds   that he served the whole year and received his years wages and slept in his Masters House at Norton aforesaid the whole time – That he has never been hired for a Year since or rented a Tenement of the annual value of Ten pounds or done any act to gain a Settlement elsewhere – That about thirteen Years ago he was married to his present Wife Ann at the Parish Church of Saint Mary de lode in the City of Gloucester, by whom he has Six Children, namely, Henry aged Twelve Years, Albina aged ten years, Jane aged Eight Years – Matilda aged Six years, Robert aged Four Years, and Charles aged eighteen months. That he is now actually chargeable to the said Parish of Cheltenham – [mark]
1841: *JB (aged 40; agricultural labourer) lived with wife Ann (30) and six children in Arle, Cheltenham (HO107/353/10/52/11).* **1843:** *removed to Norton (hiring and service).* **1844:** *(RETURNED) daughter Emma baptised at Cheltenham 7 Jan, when family lived in Golden Valley.* **1845:** *JB, wife Ann, and six children received parish relief from Gloucester as non-settled residents of Cheltenham 3Q (G/CH/9d/1).* **1846:** *son William baptised at Gloucester 17 June.* **1851:** *the family lived in Kingsholm, Gloucester: JB (51; labourer, born Staverton), Ann (46; tailoress, born North Nibley), and children Henry A. (20; labourer), Albina (19; laundress), Jane (17; laundress), Matilda (16), Robert (12), Charles (10), Emma (8), and George (3) (HO107/1961/377/26).* [PS/CH/RA/2/6:97 (copy at PS/CH/RA/2/5:460). Removal expenses for "Barton" to Norton 15/- (1Q 1843: D4178).]

43002RO: 5 Jan 1843 – **William Siniger** (also **Sinigar**, **Sinnigar**), plasterer, wife **Ann**, and five children **James**, **Elizabeth**, **Priscilla**, **Charles**, and **Henry**; also father Daniel Siniger, weaver, currently living in Coaley. *Daniel Siniger:* That the first place he remembers himself was in the Parish of Cam in the said County – That about Twenty Years ago he rented a house in the said Parish of Cam of Thomas Hadley at Ten pounds a Year, and resided in such house for one Year – and paid the whole Rent for the same – That he then rented a House in the said Parish of Cam of Mr Reuben Hill at Ten pounds a year, and resided in such House Two years and paid the whole Rent – That he has never Rented a house of the annual value of Ten pounds since or done Any Act to gain a settlement elsewhere – That about Forty three years ago he was married to his present Wife Elizabeth in the Parish Church of Saint Mary de Lode in the City of Gloucester by whom he had his said Son William who continued to reside with him in the said Parish of Cam as part of his family until about Fourteen years ago when his said Son was married – That he has been several times relieved by the Parish Officers of Cam aforesaid – [signed Daniel Sineger]
William Siniger: That he has never done any Act to gain a settlement in his own right. – That he resided with his Father and Mother Daniel Siniger and Elizabeth his Wife in the Parish of Cam in the said County until his Marriage which took place about Fourteen years ago in the parish Church of Dursley in the said County, That his Wife's name is Ann by whom he has Five Children – namely James aged Six Years, Elizabeth aged Four Years, Priscilla aged three Years, Charles aged Two years, and Henry aged three weeks – That he is now actually chargeable to the said Parish of Cheltenham [signed Wm. Sineger]
1841: *WS (aged 35; plasterer), wife Ann (30), and four children James (4), Elizabeth (2), Priscilla (18 mo), and Charles (4 mo) lived with Daniel Siniger (55; agricultural labourer and pensioner) and wife Elizabeth (50) in Waterloo Place, Cheltenham (HO107/353/9/54/9-55/10).* **1842:** *birth of son Henry registered at Cheltenham 4Q.* **1843:** *removed to Cam (renting).* **1844:** *birth of son (Albert) George registered at Dursley (born Cam) 2Q.* **1851:** *the family lived in Woodmancote, Dursley: WS (46; plasterer, born London, Middlesex), Ann (42; born Dursley), and eight children, the first five born at Cheltenham, and the remainder at Cam and then Dursley (HO107/1958/383/15).* [PS/CH/RA/2/6:98 (copy at

PS/CH/RA/2/5:461). Removal expenses for "Sinigar" to Coaley 12/- and to Cam £1/17/6 (1Q 1843: D4178).]

43003RO: Wed 11 Jan 1843 – **Sarah Jefferies**, single woman; also father John Jefferies, basketmaker, currently residing in Cirencester. *John Jefferies*: That he is in the 54th. year of his age. That when he was about Fifteen years old, being then unmarried and having no Child or Children, he was hired by M[r]. Thomas Colan [also Colen] of Cricklade Street Cirencester in the said County for a year at the wages of Thirty shillings, that he served under such hiring Four Years at increased wages of One Guinea a Year, and slept in his Master's house at Cirencester aforesaid the whole time and received all his wages – That when he left his said Masters service he apprenticed himself by Indenture duly Stamped to Thomas Skinner of Dyer Street Cirencester Aforesaid Basket maker for Three years - that he served the whole years and slept in his Master's house at Cirencester aforesaid the whole time   That he has never done any act since to gain a settlement elsewhere – That about Thirty two Years ago he was married to his late Wife Mary in the parish Church of Cirencester aforesaid by whom he had his said daughter Sarah who continue[d] to live with him as part of his Family at Cirencester Aforesaid until about two or three years ago – That his said daughter is now about Twenty two Years of Age and unmarried [mark] *Sarah Jefferies*: That she is about Twenty two years of age, that she has never done any act to gain a settlement in her own right and is now actually chargeable to the said parish of Cheltenham [mark]
1843: *removed to Cirencester (father's settlement).* [PS/CH/RA/2/6:99 (copy at PS/CH/RA/2/5:463-4). Removal expenses for "Jefferies" to Cirencester 9/9 and 18/- (1Q 1843: D4178).]

43004RO: Thurs 12 Jan 1843 – **Charles Stephens**, painter, wife **Ann**, and seven children **William**, **Charlotte**, **Charles**, **Julia**, **Mary Ann**, **John**, and **Frederick**: That he is in the Fifty second year of his age – That the first place he remembers himself was in the Parish of Redmarley D'Abitot the County of Worcester where he resided with his Father Joseph Stephens, and his Mother Mary Stephens until he was about Sixteen years of age, that during the whole of that time his said Father resided in a house of his own with a Garden and two Orchards of the annual value of Twenty pounds at Redmarley D'Abitot aforesaid and his said Father continued to reside in such House and premises until his death which happened about Nine Years ago when the said House Gardens and Orchards descended to this Examinants Brother Richard as his fathers eldest Son and Heir at Law – That he has never done any act to gain a settlement in his own right   That Ten or eleven Years ago he became Chargeable to the said Parish of Redmarley D'Abitot and [and] was relieved by The Parish Officers there for nearly two years. That about twenty five years ago he was married to his present Wife Ann in the Parish Church of Redmarley D'Abitot aforesaid by whom he has seven Children now living with him as part of his Family – namely William aged 21 Years, Charlotte aged 18 Years, Charles aged 16 Years Julia aged 13 Years, Mary Ann aged 10 Years, John aged 7 Years and Frederick aged One Year, neither of which Children have done any act To gain a settlement in their own right. That he is now actually chargeable to the said Parish of Cheltenham [signed]
1841: *the family lived in York Buildings, St Paul, Bristol: CS (aged 45; painter), Ann (40), and children Charlotte (15), Julia (10), Mary Ann (7), and John (5) (HO107/374/5/23/4).* **1843:** *removed to Redmarley D'Abitot, Worcs (father's settlement).* **1851:** *CS (59; painter and glazier, born Redmarley D'Abitot, Worcs) lived with wife Ann (51; milliner and dressmaker, born Dymock) and children Charlotte (26, born Redmarley) and Mary Ann (18; born Pendock, Worcs; both milliners and dressmakers), and Frederick (9; scholar, born Bristol) (HO107/2043/117/59).* [PS/CH/RA/2/6:100 (copy at PS/CH/RA/2/5:465). Removal expenses for "Stephens" to Redmarley D'Abitot, Worcs £1/12/- (1Q 1843: D4178).]

43005RO: Thurs 19 Jan 1843 – **William Hemming** (also **Hemmings**), labourer, wife **Sarah**, and two children **Elisha** and **Ann;** also Richard Hemming, labourer, relating to the settlement of his son William. *Richard Hemming*: That about Thirty one years ago being then unmarried and having no Child or Children he was hired by Thomas Smith of the Parish of Beckford aforesaid Horse Doctor for a Year at the yearly wages of Nine pounds – That he continued in such service for three Years under such hiring and received all his Wages and slept in his said Masters house at Beckford aforesaid the whole time – That he has never done any act to gain a Settlement since – That about Twenty eight years ago, he was married to his present Wife Eve in the parish Church of Beckford aforesaid by whom he had his said Son William, now aged about Twenty seven Years who lived with this Examinant at Beckford aforesaid until he was about twenty Years of Age, and never during that time done any act to gain a settlement in his own right. – [mark]

William Hemming: That he has never done any act to gain a Settlement in his own right – That three Years last Michaelmas he was married to his present Wife Sarah in the Parish of Cheltenham aforesaid, by whom he has two Children, namely Elisha aged three Years, and [Sarah] Ann aged nine Months – That he is now actually Chargeable to the said parish of Cheltenham – [signed]

1841: *WH (25; porter, born Beckford) lived with wife Sarah (21) and son Elisha (1) in Mount Pleasant, Cheltenham (HO107/353/6/14/22).* **1843:** *removed to Beckford (now in Worcs) (father's settlement).* **1845:** *(RETURNED) birth of son Richard registered at Cheltenham 3Q.* **1851:** *the family lived in Boodles Passage, Rutland St, St Paul's, Cheltenham (HO107/1973/365/39).* [PS/CH/RA/2/6:101 (copy at PS/CH/RA/2/5:466-7). Removal expenses for "Hemming" to Beckford 6/- and 14/6 (1Q 1843: D4178).]

43006RO: Sat 21 Jan 1843 – **Edward Faulkner**, labourer: That about Fifteen Years ago being then unmarried and having no Child or Children he was hired by M^r. Richard Owen of Knighton Farm in the Parish of Inkberrow in the County of Worcester at about a Month after Michaelmas to serve until the Michaelmas following at One shilling and nine pence per week which time he served And was then hired for a Year by the said Richard Owen at Inkberrow Aforesaid At One shilling and nine pence per week until Lady day, and two shillings a week from Lady day to Michaelmas and continued in such service after the being so hired for a Year, Five years at the same wages and resided in his said Master's House at Inkberrow aforesaid the whole Five years and received all his Wages – That he has never been hired for a Year since or done any act to gain a settlement elsewhere – That he was never married and is now actually chargeable to the said Parish of Cheltenham [mark]

1841: *EF (aged 60; agricultural labourer) lived alone in King St, Cheltenham (HO107/353/8/47/27).* **1843:** *removed to Inkberrow, Worcs (hiring and service).* **1851:** *as he was never married, he is perhaps not the EF (70; nurseryman's labourer, and widower) who was an inmate of Oversley Union Workhouse, Warks (HO107/2075/248/15).* [PS/CH/RA/2/6:102 (copy at PS/CH/RA/2/5:468). Removal expenses for "Faulkner" to Inkberrow, Worcs £1/11/6 (1Q 1843: D4178).]

43007RO: Thurs 26 Jan 1843 – **Henry Lewis**, cordwainer, wife **Sarah**, and six children, **Henry**, **George**, **William**, **Emma**, **Elizabeth**, and **Thomas**: That about Four years ago he rented a House of M^r. William Togwell on the London road in the parish of Charlton Kings in the said County at the Yearly Rent of Sixteen pounds and paid the whole Rent and resided in said house the whole time – and for a year afterwards – That he was duly rated to the Poor rates in respect of such house in the said Parish of Charlton Kings during the whole time he resided there as aforesaid and paid such rates – That he has done no act to gain a Settlement since – That about Eighteen Years ago he was married to his present Wife Sarah in Saint Paul's Church Bristol, by whom he has Six Children, namely Henry aged 14 years – George aged 11 Years, William aged 9. Years – Emma aged 5. Years, Elizabeth aged 4 years, and Thomas aged 18. Months. – That he is now actually chargeable to the said Parish of Cheltenham [signed]

1841: *HL (aged 30; shoemaker) lived with wife Sarah (30), and children Henry (13), George (11), William (7), Emma (4), Elizabeth (2), and Thomas (1 week) in Park St, Cheltenham (HO107/353/16/46/10).* **1843:** *removed to Charlton Kings (renting).* **1844:** *(RETURNED) birth of son James registered at Cheltenham 1Q.* **1851:** *the family lived at 4 Knapp Place, Cheltenham: HL (44; shoemaker, born Bristol), Sarah (44; born America), Emma (14), Elizabeth (12), Thomas (9; scholar), James (7; scholar), Charles (3), and Frederick (2 mo; all children born Cheltenham) (HO107/1973/601/29).* [PS/CH/RA/2/6:103 (copy at PS/CH/RA/2/5:469). Removal expenses for "Lewis" to Charlton Kings 2/6 (1Q 1843: D4178).]

43008RO: Sat 28 Jan 1843 – **Abiah** (also **Abia**) **Ireland**, single woman; also father Solomon Ireland, labourer, residing in Painswick, relating to the settlement of daughter. *Solomon Ireland*: I was married to my late Wife Sarah at the Parish Church in Painswick about twenty two Years ago next Whitsuntide – The said Abiah Ireland is one of the children of that Marriage – She has never to my knowledge done an Act to gain a Settlement in her own Right – About 31 Years ago I was hired at Gloucester Mop by William Cowley of Slimbridge in this County to serve for a Year at the Wages of £3..10..0.. I went into his service and served the Whole Year and received all my Wages – I slept at my said Master's house at Slimbridge aforesaid during the whole time – I never did an Act to gain a Settlement since that time, – About twelve Years ago I was chargeable to the Parish of Painswick where I was then living   The said Abiah Ireland was living with Me – I was removed with her by Order of Removal from Painswick to Slimbridge aforesaid. We were taken to Slimbridge by M^r. Baylis the Overseer of Painswick   He took us to the Workhouse at Slimbridge and we received were there [mark]
Abiah Ireland: That She is in the Nineteenth year of her age and has never done any Act to gain a Settlement in her own right and is now actually chargeable to the said Parish of Cheltenham [mark]
AI was, apparently, known by the more common name Eliza. **1841:** *AI (aged 15; servant) lived alone in Fairview St, Cheltenham (HO107/353/5/41/5).* **1843:** *removed to Slimbridge (father's settlement); AI was pregnant at time of examination; son William baptised at Cheltenham 17 Mar, when both mother and child were inmates of Cheltenham Workhouse.* **1851:** *AI lived with future husband Robert Bucknell in Coberley: Robert Buckell (26; agricultural labourer, born Coberley), Eliza (28, born Painswick), William (9; born Cheltenham) (HO107/1972/261/10).* **1856:** *(RETURNED) AI married Robert Buckell (under her real name of Abia Ireland) in Cheltenham 9 Oct, while she resided at 3 Hamilton Place, St Paul's, Cheltenham.* [PS/CH/RA/2/6:104 (order suspended as AI unfit to travel; lifted 28 May) (copy at PS/CH/RA/2/5:470-1). Removal expenses for "Ireland" to Painswick 6/-, to Slimbridge 17/- (1Q 1843), and to Slimbridge £1/2/6 (2Q 1843: D4178).]

43009RO: Mon 30 Jan 1843 – **Henry Millard,** labourer; also father John Millard, whitesmith, relating to the settlement of son. *John Millard*: That the first place he remembers himself was in the parish of South Cerney in the said County where he resided with his Father Edmund Millard. That his said Father at the time he so lived with him resided upon an Estate of his own consisting of a House Stables, Shops Garden and premises called by the Sign of the Plough Inn situate in the said Parish of South Cerney of the annual value of Seven or Eight pounds and his said Father resided in the same premises until he sold the same about forty years ago to M^r. Edmund Miles – That he continued to live with his father until the Premises were sold – The Estate was worth considerable [*sic*] more than forty pounds – That his said Father never done any act afterwards to gain a settlement – That this Examinant never done any act to gain a settlement in his own right – That about 26. Years ago he was married to his present Wife Mary at the parish Church of Bisley in the said County by whom he had his said Son Henry now aged near 18. years [signed]
Henry Millard: That he has never done any act to gain a Settlement in his own right, and is now actually chargeable to the said parish of Cheltenham [mark]
1841: *HM (aged 15) lived with family in Duke St, Cheltenham: John Millard (40; whitesmith), Mary (40), Ellen (6), and Elizabeth (4) (HO107/353/3/29/9).* **1843:** *removed to South Cerney (father's settlement).* **1846:** *HM married Ann Roberts on Christmas Day, when he lived at 6 New St, Cheltenham, as labourer.* **1847:** *birth of daughter Elizabeth Jane registered at Birmingham 4Q.* **1848:** *at baptism of Elizabeth Jane 5 July at St Martin's, Birmingham HM described as "coach-body painter".* **1850:** *(RETURNED) birth of daughter Susannah registered at Cheltenham 4Q; at baptism, the family lived in Duke St, Cheltenham.* **1861:** *on census night HM absent from home (he is listed with the family in Birmingham in later censuses), and Ann (39; boot binder, born Cheltenham) is recorded with children Elizabeth (13), Susannah (11; servant), George (7; scholar), and Frank (11 mo, born Birmingham) (RG9/2140/92/41).* [PS/CH/RA/2/6:105 (copy at PS/CH/RA/2/5:472-3). Removal expenses for "Millard" to South Cerney £1/3/- (1Q 1843: D4178).]

43010RO: Mon 6 Feb 1843 (examination on 2 Feb) – **Martha Webber,** widow, and infant son **William**: That about twenty three years ago I was bound apprentice by Indenture, stamped with a One pound stamp to serve Mary Wilcox of the Parish of Saint James in the City of Bath Dressmaker to learn Dressmaking and Millinery for the term of three years as an indoor apprentice - My Father was dead at the time – My Mother signed the Indenture myself and Miss Wilcox – M^r. Clarke of Queen Square was the Attorney who prepared the Indenture – he read it to me and was witness to the Indenture – I served the whole of my apprenticeship with Miss Wilcox for the three years and worked for her three months afterwards – the premium was Forty Guineas and was paid by my Mother – Mary Wilcox lived at N°. 3 Saint James Parade in Saint James' Parish Bath. I lived with her at that house and slept there during the three years and three months – As much as eight or nine years ago I burned the Indenture thinking it was of no use to me to keep – I have done no act since to gain a settlement – I was married 10 years ago last June to my late Husband William Webber at Chippenham near Bath – he died about six Years ago – I know nothing of his Settlement – Three weeks ago last Sunday I was delivered of a male bastard child at Cheltenham – I and my child are now actually chargeable to the Parish of Cheltenham – [signed]

1843: *removed to St James, Bath (apprenticeship):* see **49047RO** *(MD: 22 Sept 1849) for further information on MD.* [PS/CH/RA/2/6:106 (copy at PS/CH/RA/2/5:474).]

43011RO: Sat 11 Feb 1843 – Jane Williams, wife of John Williams, labourer, relating to the settlement of illegitimate daughter **Elizabeth Turk**: On the fourteenth of November one thousand eight hundred and thirty I was delivered of a female Bastard child in the Parish of Long Newton in the County of Wilts – The said Elizabeth Turk is such Bastard Child   I was at service at Long Newton aforesaid at the time I was so delivered and had been in that service about three months previously – I was a singlewoman at the time   My Maiden name is Jane Turk   I was married to my present husband John Williams at Tetbury in this County in 1834   the Child is now living with me   I am unable to support her – She is now actually chargeable to the said Parish of Cheltenham [mark]

1841: *ET (aged 15; baptised at Tetbury 22 May 1831) lived with maternal grandparents Thomas and Susannah Turk (both aged 75) in Tetbury (HO107/362/11/45/24).* **1842:** *death of Susannah Turk in Tetbury.* **1843:** *death of Thomas Turk in Minchinhampton;* ***removed to Long Newton, Wilts (now in Glos) (birth).*** **1851:** *Elizabeth Williams may be the EW (20; general servant, born Tetbury) who lived at 3 Dodd's Cottages, North Place, Cheltenham (HO107/1973/283/36).* [PS/CH/RA/2/6:107 (copy at PS/CH/RA/2/5:477). Removal expenses for "Turk" to Long Newton £1/12/6 (1Q 1843: D4178). See **43012RO** (John Williams: 15 Feb 1843) for further information about ET's mother and stepfather.]

43012RO: Wed 15 Feb 1843 (examination on 10 Feb) – **John Williams**, labourer, wife **Jane**, and three children **Edwin**, **Mary Ann**, and **Eliza**: I am in the Thirty fourth Year of my age – About three years and a half ago I took a House of M^r. Saddler N°. 2. Charlton Place in the Parish of Charlton Kings in the said County at the Rent of Eleven pounds a year – I went into the house the same day that I took it and continued to occupy it for a year and a half – I paid all the Rent commencing from the day I took it up to the time I left   I was assessed to the Poors rate for the Parish of Charlton Kings in respect of such house during the time I so lived there and paid all the rates during that time – I have done no act since to gain a settlement elsewhere – I was married to my present Wife Jane at Tetbury in this County in the year 1834 by whom I have three Children now living namely, Edwin aged Seven Years, Mary Ann aged Four Years, and Eliza aged Two Years and a half – I and my said Wife and my said Children are now actually chargeable to the said Parish of Cheltenham [mark]

1841: *JW (30; labourer) lived with wife Jane (30; in fact baptised at Tetbury in early 1807) and children Edwin (7), Mary (Ann) (3), Eliza (10 mo; both born Charlton Kings), and wife's niece Matilda Turk (15; servant – cousin of Elizabeth Turk in the removal order* **43011RO** *Elizabeth Turk: 11 Feb 1843) in Corpus St, Cheltenham (HO107/353/14/20/34).* **1843:** ***died before removal to Charlton Kings (renting); family removed****; JW died at 17 Corpus St of "Dropsy", aged 34; buried at Cheltenham 14 Mar.* **1844:** *(RETURNED) Elizabeth (aged 13), Edwin (8), Mary (6), and Eliza (4) were all inmates of Charlton Kings Workhouse for children (their condition was recorded as "Filthy" and Mary also had a "Sore Head" on admission (Cheltenham Union); their mother was then an inmate of Cheltenham Workhouse (G/CH/60/3); the family entered Cheltenham Workhouse for a week 17 Apr (G/CH/60/4).* **1847:** *Jane Williams had been imprisoned for two weeks for stealing two silver teaspoons and other articles from lodging-house at Albert Place, Cheltenham (Cheltenham Chron. 12 Aug).* **1851:** *Edwin Williams (15) lived* *with cousin Matilda Turk (24; dressmaker) and her son George (9 mo) in Swindon Place, Cheltenham (HO107/1973/423/12); Jane Williams is likely to be the Jane Williams (44; laundress and widow) imprisoned at Gloucester County Jail (HO107/1961/245/14).* [PS/CH/RA/2/6:108 (copy at PS/CH/RA/2/5:475 (struck out) and 476). Removal expenses for "Williams" to Charlton Kings 2/6 (1Q 1843: D4178).]

43013RO: Tues 21 Feb 1843 (examination on 20 Feb) – **James Niblett**, labourer, wife **Ann**, and four children **Elizabeth**, **James**, **Eliza**, and **Samuel**: I am about Fifty years of Age – I was born in the Parish of Painswick in this County as I have always heard and believed – My Father's name was Thomas Niblett   he received relief from the said parish of Painswick for some Months and died in the Workhouse of Painswick about Forty one years Ago. I was in the Painswick Workhouse at the time of his death and remained there and was relieved there for Nine Years after his death   I was again relieved by the said parish of Painswick about the year One thousand eight hundred and twenty nine – I was relieved backwards and forwards for about Four Years – I have never done any Act whereby to gain a settlement in my own right – About Twenty two years ago, I was married to my present Wife Ann at the Parish Church of Horsley in this County and have by her Four Children: namely, Elizabeth aged Fourteen years – James aged Twelve Years – Eliza aged Nine Years and Samuel Aged Seven Years, all born in lawful wedlock – I and my said Wife and Four Children are now actually chargeable to the said Parish of Cheltenham [signed]
1841: *JN (aged 45; agricultural labourer) lived with wife Ann (45) and six children, Harriet (21), William (15), Elizabeth (10), James (10), Eliza (9), Samuel (6), in Painswick (HO107/349/8/51/19).* **1843: *removed to Painswick (father's settlement).* 1845:** *(RETURNED) death of JN in Cheltenham (buried 4 Mar at New Burial Ground, aged 52).* **1846:** *son James Niblett probably sentenced to transportation to Australia in (aged 15) for stealing a copper furnace in Prestbury, following a previous conviction; he committed suicide, a victim of the "Silent System", in Millbank Prison, Pimlico, London, the following year (Colonial Times 6 Apr, 1847): the prison held convicts awaiting transportation.* **1851:** *Ann Niblett (56; hawker, and widow) lived with youngest son, Samuel (16; porter) at 4 Rutland St, Cheltenham (HO107/1973/365/38).* [PS/CH/RA/2/6:109 (copy at PS/CH/RA/2/5:478). Removal expenses for "Niblett" to Painswick 19/6 (1Q 1843: D4178).]

43014RO: Mon 20 Feb 1843 – Harriet Roff, wife of Robert Roff, labourer, regarding the settlement of illegitimate daughter **Harriet Jones**: On the thirteenth of April one thousand eight hundred and thirty four I was delivered of a female Bastard Child in the parish of Leckhampton in the said County – The said Harriet Jones is such Bastard Child   I was a singlewoman at the time   My Maiden name is Harriet Jones – I was married to my present husband Robert Roff in the month of June one thousand eight hundred and thirty four – The Child is now living with me. I am unable to support her – she is now actually chargeable to the said Parish of Cheltenham [mark]
1841: *HJ was not living with mother Harriet Roff (aged 25) and her other three sisters at 2 Hereford Passage, Cheltenham on census night (HO107/353/8/64/9): brickmaker Robert Roff was also absent from home then.* **1843: *removed to Leckhampton (birth).* 1850:** *death of HJ's mother (buried, aged 37, at Cheltenham 24 Oct).* [PS/CH/RA/2/6:110 (copy at PS/CH/RA/2/5:479). Removal expenses for "Jones" to Leckhampton 2/6 (1Q 1843: D4178).]

43015RO: Mon 27 Feb 1843 – **Mary Jones**, widow, and three children **Keziah**, **Edwin**, and **George**: I was born in the County of Worcester   About nineteen years ago being then unmarried and having no child or children I was hired at Tewkesbury Mop Fair to serve M^r. Phillips of Deerhurst Walton in the said County of Gloucester   I was hired to serve him from Michaelmas to Michaelmas as an Indoor servant at the wages of Six pounds   The Mop was held before Michaelmas day   I went into the service the same Michaelmas I was hired and continued there the whole year and received all my wages   I resided and slept the whole time in M^r. Phillips' house which is situate in Deerhurst Walton aforesaid   I have never done any act to gain a Settlement in my own right since that time   I was married about seventeen years ago to my late Husband William Jones of St Mary de lodes Church in the City of Gloucester. My husband died at Cheltenham about thirteen months ago. I have three Children by my said Husband namely Keziah aged fifteen years Edwin aged thirteen years and George aged five years   My said husband never did any act to my knowledge to gain a Settlement – his father and mother and all his relatives are to the best of my belief dead. I and my said three children are now actually chargeable to the said Parish of Cheltenham – [mark]

1841: *MJ (aged 30) lived with husband William Jones (40; labourer) and four children Keziah (13), Edwin (11), George (4), and Charles (4 mo) in Stanhope St, Cheltenham (HO107/353/9/54/8); son Charles buried at Cheltenham 3 July, aged 6 months.* **1842:** *death of husband William (buried at Cheltenham, aged 45, 31 Jan).* **1843:** **removed to Deerhurst Walton (hiring and service).** **1851:** *George Jones (15; pauper, born Cheltenham) is perhaps the boy of that name listed as an inmate of Tewkesbury Workhouse (the registration district for Deerhurst Walton) (HO107/1974/497/12).* [PS/CH/RA/2/6:111 (copy at PS/CH/RA/2/5:480). See **45008SE** (daughter Keziah Jones: 8 Feb 1845).]

43016RO: Sat 4 Mar 1843 (examinations on 27 Feb and 4 Mar) – **Mary Ann Miller**, widow, and three children **Mary Ann**, **Frederick**, and **Louisa**; also Edmund Ward, of 28 Granby St, Hampstead Rd, Middlesex, landlord's agent, and James Saddler, landlord, of Charlton Kings, relating to the settlement of Mary Ann Miller. *Edmund Ward*: On the Ninth of February 1831, as Agent for my Sister Frances Spackman I let a House and premises situate and being No. 6. Upper James Street Golden Square in the Parish of Saint James Westminster to Charles Miller at the Rent of Fifty two pounds ten shillings a year payable quarterly – One half quarters rent to become due on the 25th. of March then next – the said Charles Miller to pay all taxes and Rates – the said Charles Miller took immediate possession of the Premises and he and his Family occupied them to Lady day 1835. – I received the whole of the Rent from the said Charles Miller for the time he so occupied the said Premises, except the Rent for the last three quarters he lived there – I am certain he paid me the first three years Rent – About a year after I let the House my said Sister died and the property became mine – I continued Charles Millers tenancy at the same Rent and upon the same terms as before – the said Mary Ann Miller is the Widow of the said Charles Miller – [signed]

Mary Ann Miller: I was married to my late Husband Charles Miller at the Parish of Saint George Hanover Square in London about twenty one years ago – About nine or ten years ago my Husband rented a House in the Parish of St. James' Westminster in the County of Middlesex – Mr. Ward was the landlords Agent – The house my husband rented was No. 6. Upper Saint James Street Golden Square, in the said Parish of Saint James. We lived in the house for more than a year. I think a year and a half but I cannot tell exactly how long. I don't know how much the rent was but I am certain it was more than twelve pounds a year – I saw some of it paid. We came direct from St. James Westminster to Cheltenham where I have been about seven or eight years. When we came to Cheltenham we took a house in High Street and lived in it five or six months. We then went into lodgings and continued there about the same time. We then went into the Parish of Charlton Kings in the said County of Gloucester – I think this was in 1835. I was informed by my husband that he took a house of Mr. Saddler at twelve pounds a year – he said there were no taxes. We lived there about fifteen months. I saw three pounds rent paid to Mr. Saddler while we lived there – I think this was the first quarter's rent - the only other rent I recollect having seen paid was some silver under a pound – This was for arrears for the last quarter. I have no receipt for the rent. I paid one shilling for the poor rate. My husband never did any other act to gain a settlement in the said Parishes of Cheltenham and Charlton Kings or either of them and did no act to gain a settlement after he left Mr. Saddler's house. About three years ago last January my husband died. I have never since his death done any act to gain a settlement in the said Parishes of Cheltenham and Charlton Kings or either of them elsewhere. I have three children by my said husband now living with me namely Mary Anne aged eleven Years Frederick aged nine years and Louisa aged between three and four years   I and my said children are now actually chargeable to the said Parish of Cheltenham [signed]

James Saddler: I live at the Back of Charlton Place in Charlton Kings Parish. I recollect letting a house and garden in Charlton Place to the late Charles Miller the husband of Mary Ann Miller about six years ago last Michaelmas. I let it for a year at twelve pounds a year – He came with his wife and family – he paid me the first quarter's rent. I let him go on to the two next quarters as he was very ill. When that half year became due I distressed him. The things were valued – M^r. Cossens was the Bailiff. Two pounds nineteen shillings and sixpence was paid me leaving three pounds and sixpence due – Charles Miller signed a paper to move in a week afterwards – Charles Miller went out at Christmas – he had been in nearly fifteen months. I was paid altogether One sixpence short of twelve pounds leaving the said sum of three pounds and sixpence in arrear for the half year I have mentioned. There was not ten pounds paid on account of the first years rent – [mark]

1840: *husband Charles (hatter) buried at New Burial Ground, Cheltenham 4 Feb, aged 40; inconclusive settlement examination at Cheltenham: see* **40083SE** *(MAM: Aug).* **1841:** *MAM (30; milliner) lived with children Mary (11), Frederick (9), and Louisa (2) in Hewlett St, Cheltenham (HO107/353/4/20/4).* **1842:** *removed to St George's, Hanover Square, Middlesex: see* **42023RO** *(MAM: 5 Mar),* **42046RO** *(21 May) (RETURNED),* **42080RO** *(24 Nov) (RETURNED).* **1843:** *removed to St James, Westminster, Middlesex (husband's settlement).* **1851:** *(RETURNED) MAM (42; dressmaker, born London, Middlesex) lived with daughter Louisa (11; scholar) at 4 Queen's Buildings, Cheltenham (HO107/1973/252/33); daughter Mary Ann (20) was then servant in Walcot, Bath (HO107/1943/421/43).* [PS/CH/RA/2/6:116 (copies at PS/CH/RA/2/5:481-2 and 485). Removal expenses for "Miller" to Westminster, Middlesex £1/17/- (2Q 1843: D4178).]

43017RO: Thurs 2 Mar 1843 – **William Barton**, labourer, wife **Ann**, and child **Priscilla**: About sixteen Years ago being unmarried and not having any child or children I was hired at Gloucester Michaelmas Mop by M^r. Henry Bubb of the Parish of Frampton upon Severn in this County to serve him for a twelve month as a Cowman at the wages of Three pounds. I served the whole year and slept in my said Master's House at Frampton upon Severn aforesaid and received all my wages   I then was hired by Mr Thomas Evans of the same place to serve him for a twelvemonth at the wages of Five pounds – I lived in his service the twelvemonth – and slept in his house at Frampton upon Severn aforesaid and received all my wages   The same Michaelmas I left M^r. Evans I was hired again by the said Henry Bubb at Gloucester Mop to serve him for another twelvemonth – as Cowman at the wages of Five pounds   I served him the whole year and never slept out of his house at Frampton upon Severn aforesaid during the time I received all my wages – I have not since done any act whereby to gain a settlement – I was never married and had no child or children until I was married to my present Wife Ann at Boddington in this County about ten years ago by whom I have one child namely Priscilla aged seven years – I and my said Wife and child are now actually chargeable to the said Parish of Cheltenham – [mark]

1841: *WB (aged 34; labourer) of Frampton-upon-Severn committed to prison on 16 Feb for two months for larceny (stealing old iron plates); by census night (6 June) he (age given as 30; labourer) lived with mother Jane (70) and daughter Priscilla (5) in Waterloo Place, Cheltenham (wife Ann was absent on census night) (HO107/353/9/55/11).* **1843:** *removed to Frampton-upon-Severn (hiring and service).* **1846/9:** *(RETURNED) WB tried for larceny (acquitted) and again in 1849 while living in Cheltenham.* **1849:** *death of WB 7 Oct, aged 49, while living in Stanhope St, Cheltenham.* **1851:** *wife Ann (49; charwoman and widow) lived with daughter Priscilla (16; charwoman) at 36 Stanhope St (HO107/1973/500/20).* [PS/CH/RA/2/6:113 (copy at PS/CH/RA/2/5:483). Removal expenses for "Barton" to Frampton-upon-Severn £1/8/- (1Q 1843: D4178).]

43018RO: 2 Mar 1843 – **William White**, shoemaker, wife **Emma**, and four children **George, Rosina, Elizabeth,** and **Henry**: About the year 1836. I rented a House and yard situate in Little Norwood Street in the parish of Leckhampton in this County belonging to M^r. King at the rent of Ten pounds a year – I lived in the house about Fifteen Months and paid the whole of the Rent for that time – I was duly Assessed to the Poor Rates for Leckhampton Parish in respect of such house for the time I so lived there and paid all the same – I have done no act since to gain a settlement – I was married to my present Wife Emma about Fifteen years ago at the parish Church of Pitchcomb [= Pitchcombe] in this County by whom I have Four Children, now living with me, namely George aged fourteen years – Rosina aged nine years, Elizabeth aged Seven years, and Henry aged a year and nine months – I and my Wife and my said Four Children are now actually chargeable to the said parish of Cheltenham – [signed]

1841: *WW (aged 30; shoemaker) lived with wife Emma (35) and five children George (12), Rosanna (8), Harriet (6), Elizabeth (5), and Henry (1) in Upper Bath Rd, Cheltenham.* **1843: removed to Leckhampton (renting).** **1851:** *(RETURNED) WW (42; shoemaker, born Stroud) lived with wife Emma, and five children, Roseanna (18; shoebinder), Henry (10; scholar), Albert (4), Mary Ann (2), and James (1: all children born Cheltenham) at 1 James' Cottages, Tivoli St, Cheltenham.* [PS/CH/RA/2/6:112 (copy at PS/CH/RA/2/5:483).]

43019RO: 4 Mar 1843 – **John Newman**, labourer, wife **Eliza**, and five children **John, Elizabeth, Sarah, Eliza,** and **Maria**: About Fourteen Years ago being unmarried and having no Child or Children I was hired by M^r. Shill of the parish of Charlton Kings in the said County to serve him as a Carter for a Year, namely from Michaelmas to Michaelmas at the Wages of Six shillings a week – I served my said Master at Charlton Kings aforesaid under that hiring for more than a twelve month and received all my Wages – I slept at Charlton Kings aforesaid during the time – I have done no act since to gain a Settlement – About ten years ago I was married to my present Wife Eliza at the Parish Church of Charlton Kings aforesaid by whom I have Five Children now living with me namely John aged nine years, Elizabeth aged seven years – Sarah aged Five years – Eliza aged three years and Maria aged One year – I and my said Wife and Children are now actually chargeable to the said parish of Cheltenham [mark]

1843: removed to Charlton Kings (hiring and service); *(RETURNED) daughter Maria Newman was baptised at Cheltenham 26 Mar, when family lived in Upper Alstone, Cheltenham; they still lived in Alstone when daughters Susannah and Caroline were baptised, in 1845 and 1847 respectively.* **1848:** *JN killed in tragic railway accident Sept leaving "a wife and six children, the eldest 14 and the youngest 10 months (Cheltenham Chron. 21 Sept) (buried at Cheltenham 18 Sept, aged 36).* **1850:** *widow Eliza remarried 7 Apr in Churchdown to Caleb Butt, bricklayer, and they soon emigrated to Canada.* **1851:** *not all of the children emigrated, and Eliza Newman (12) was apparently a pupil of the "Upper Class" at the Orphan Asylum in Cheltenham (HO107/1973/169/23), whilst Sarah Newman (13; scholar) lived with grandparents William and Elizabeth Smith in Charlton Kings (HO107/1972/139/8).* **1861:** *the Census of Canada shows that the family lived in Agnes St, York, Ontario: Caleb Butt (aged 41; bricklayer and Wesleyan Methodist), Eliza (42), Maria (17), Caroline (12), and four other children born in Canada.* [PS/CH/RA/2/6:115 (copy at PS/CH/RA/2/5:486). Removal expenses for "Newman" to Charlton Kings 2/6 (2Q 1843: D4178). Note: "This Order was appealed against and confirmed 19th. April 1843".]

43020RO: 4 Mar 1843 – **Charles Povey**, wife **Sarah**, and four children **Caroline, Charles, Eli,** and **Rhoda**; also father Charles Povey the Elder, weaver, of North Nibley, relating to the settlement of son Charles. *Charles Povey the Elder*: About Twenty Six years ago I rented a tenement and Workshop situate in the Parish of Wotton under Edge in the said County – I rented it of a M^r. Hambling of Wootton [*sic*] under Edge aforesaid at the yearly rent of Twelve Guineas I lived in the said House for three years and paid all the rent for the time I so occupied it I have done no act since to gain a settlement since that time – About thirty four years ago I was married to my present Wife Sarah Povey at the Parish Church of North Nibley aforesaid by whom I had the said Charles Povey the Younger born in lawful wedlock. – [signed]

Charles Povey the Younger: "I am about Thirty Years of age – I have never done any Act whereby to gain a settlement in my own right – About Eight years ago I was married to my present Wife Sarah at the Parish Church of Cheltenham aforesaid. –

I have four Children by my said Wife now living, namely Caroline aged seven years, Charles aged five years – Eli aged three years, and Rhoda aged One year – I and my said Wife and said Four Children are now actually chargeable to the said parish of Cheltenham – [signed]

1834: *CP imprisoned for three months (Gloucester Epiphany Assizes) for stealing three geese.* **1837: removed to Wotton-under-Edge (father's settlement):** *see* **37020SE** *(CP: 9 Mar); unnamed child called Helena (RETURNED).* **1838:** *before examination CP awaiting trial at County Adjoined Sessions 7 Mar; removed to Wotton-under-Edge (presumed) (father's settlement): see* **38009SE** *(CP: 15 Jan 1838). CP imprisoned for one month for larceny; son Charles baptised at Cheltenham.* **1841:** *CP (aged 30; plasterer) lived with wife Sarah (24) and four children Caroline (5), Helena (4), Charles (3), and Eli (1; incorrectly "Elizabeth") in Stanhope St, Cheltenham (HO107/353/9/53/7-54/8).* **1843: removed to Wotton-under-Edge (father's settlement);** *Eli and Rhoda died later in 1843, with the family still in Cheltenham: Eli was buried 13 Nov, aged 4, and*

Rhoda 13 Dec. CP had been involved in petty crime since at least 1833 at the age of 20; he was regularly imprisoned for short periods in Gloucester Gaol into the 1880s, for drunkenness, being a "rogue and vagabond", assault on his (second) wife, etc, often while an inmate of Wotton Workhouse. **1851:** *CP not at home on census night in Wotton-under-Edge: Sarah Povey (35; charwoman), Caroline (16; "works at Woollen Cloth Factory"; born Cheltenham) (HO107/1958/105/32).* **1870:** *Gloucester prison records describe CP's dark hair, large oval face, fresh complexion, and tattoos, aged 57: Adam, Eve, Serpent & Tree, with also female figure on left arm and Mermaid on right.* **1891:** *CP (aged 79; plasterer, widower) was a pauper inmate of Wotton-under-Edge District Union Workhouse.* **1899:** *CP died at Gloucester Workhouse.* [PS/CH/RA/2/6:114 (copy at PS/CH/RA/2/5:487). Removal expenses for "Povey" to North Nibley £2/3/- (1Q 1843) and to Wotton-under-Edge £1/16/- (2Q 1843: D4178).]

43021RO: Sat 11 Mar 1843 – **Jeremiah Sutton**, labourer, wife **Ann**, and six children **Mary Ann, Robert, James, George, Thomas,** and **Esther**: That about twenty six years [ago] being then unmarried and having no Child or Children he was hired by James Cartwright of Dripsill Farm in the Parish of Great Malvern in the County of Worcester Farmer for a year as Carter at the wages of Five pounds   that he served the whole Year and received the whole of his wages and slept in his Masters house at Dripsill aforesaid the whole time

   That he has never done any act since to gain a settlement elsewhere – that about seventeen years ago, he was married to his present wife Ann at the parish Church of Charlton Kings in the County of Gloucester by whom he has six Children namely Mary Ann aged 15 years Robert aged 13 years James aged 11 years George aged 8 years Thomas aged 3 years and Esther aged 6 months – that he is now actually chargeable to the said Parish of Cheltenham – [signed]

1841: *JS (aged 40; labourer) lived with wife Ann (35) and sons Robert (12), James (10), George (8), and Thomas (1) in Kingsholm, Gloucester (HO107/379/7/43/27).* **1843:** *removed to Gt Malvern, Worcs (hiring and service).* **c1844:** *daughter born at Cheltenham.* **1851:** *the family lived in Gt Malvern, Worcs: JS (51; labourer, born Oxenton), Ann (52, born Worcester), James (21; labourer, born Cheltenham), George (19; labourer, born Cheltenham), Elizabeth (7), and William (5; born Gt Malvern, Worcs) (HO107/2043/156/60).* [PS/CH/RA/2/6:117 (copy at PS/CH/RA/2/5:488). Removal expenses for "Sutton" to Gt Malvern, Worcs £1/16/- (2Q 1843: D4178).]

43022RO: 11 Mar 1843 – **Ann Haskings**, wife of John Haskings, in Gloucester Infirmary: That twenty five years ago the 22^d. of September last she was married to her present husband John Haskings in S^t. Michael's Church in Bath – That her said husband is now very ill and confined in the Infirmary at Gloucester – that about 22 years ago she and her said husband became chargeable to the said Parish of Saint Michaels Bath and her said husband was examined as to his settlement before two Magistrates at Bath and was by them removed to the parish of Bradford in the County of Wilts by the Overseers of S^t. Michael Bath – that she and her said husband were received by the Parish Officers of Bradford aforesaid and relieved by them   that she and her said husband soon afterwards returned to S^t. Michaels Bath and were relieved by the Parish Offices of Bradford for several weeks at two shillings a week whilst she and her said husband were residing at S^t. Michaels Bath aforesaid. That the said orders of removal from S^t. Michaels Bath to Bradford were not appealed against – That her said husband has never done any act to gain a settlement since – That she is now chargeable to the said Parish of Cheltenham [mark]

1843: *removed to Bradford, Wilts (husband's settlement).* **1848:** *(RETURNED) deaths of both Ann and John Haskings, buried at Cheltenham: Ann (aged 57) 21 Jan and John (aged 55) 8 Apr).* [PS/CH/RA/2/6:118 (copy at PS/CH/RA/2/5:489). Removal expenses for "Haskins" to Bradford, Wilts £2/13/- (2Q 1843: D4178).]

43023RO: 11 Mar 1843 – **William Hawkes**, labourer, and wife **Mary**: That he was born in the parish of Fawler in the County of Oxford   that about 13 years ago he became chargeable to the Parish of Claines in the County of Worcester and was taken by the Overseers of that parish before two Magistrates and examined as to his parish and he and his Wife were removed by such Magistrates from Claines aforesaid to Fawler aforesaid by order of removal   that he and his Wife were taken by the Overseers of Claines and delivered to the Overseers of Fawler aforesaid and were received by them   that the orders of removal were not appealed against – That he has done no act since to gain a settlement – That about 26 years ago he was married in Paddington Church London to his present wife Mary – That he is now actually chargeable to the said Parish of Cheltenham [mark]

1843: *removed to Fawler, Oxon (father's presumed settlement).* [PS/CH/RA/2/6:119 (copy at PS/CH/RA/2/5:492). Removal expenses for "Hawkes" to Fawler, Oxon £2/19/- (2Q 1843: D4178).]

43024RO: Thurs 16 Mar 1843 – **John Matthews** (also **Mathews**), cordwainer, wife **Susannah,** and three children **John, Sarah**, and **Susannah**: That when I was about Fourteen Years of age I was apprenticed by Indentures from the Blue School Charity in Cirencester to George Catterell [also Catterill; perhaps for Cockerell] of the parish of Cirencester in the said County Cordwainer for the term of Seven Years to learn the business of a Cordwainer. The Indenture was duly executed by my said Master and by myself in the presence of a Witness and duly attested by such Witness

I was an out door apprentice but served my said Master in Cirencester aforesaid the whole time and slept in that parish the whole time – The Indenture was given up to me at the end of my Apprenticeship, but I have either lost or mislaid it about two Years ago – There was no Counterpart of such Indenture I have never done any act to gain a settlement since – That Seven years ago last October I was married in the parish Church of Cheltenham to my Wife Susannah by whom I have three Children, namely, John aged Six years Sarah aged Four years and Susannah aged twenty months – I am now actually chargeable to the said Parish of Cheltenham [signed]

1841: *JM (aged 30; cordwainer) lived with wife Susan(nah) (30), and two children John (5) and Sarah (2) in Vine's Cottages, St Paul's, Cheltenham (HO107/353/8/15/25-16/26).* **1843:** *removed to Cirencester (apprenticeship); (RETURNED) daughter Eliza baptised at Cheltenham 29 Oct, when family lived in King St.* **1845:** *son Joseph baptised at Cheltenham 19 Oct (Victoria Place, prob. Fairview).* **1847:** *daughter Mary baptised at Cheltenham 31 Oct (Corpus St).* **1851:** *the family lived in Montpellier Retreat, Cheltenham: JM (47; shoemaker, born Cirencester), Susannah (40; born Abergavenny, Monm), John (14, born Cirencester), Janet (12), Susannah (9), Eliza (7), Joseph (5), Mary (3), and Charlotte (1) (HO107/1973/1063/2).* [PS/CH/RA/2/6:120 (copy at PS/CH/RA/2/5:491). Removal expenses for "Matthews" to Cirencester 19/- (2Q 1843: D4178).]

43025SE: Sat 18 Mar 1843 – **Ann Jeynes**, and three children **Job, William**, and **Betsy**, relating to the settlement of husband **Charles Jeynes** (also **Janes, Jeans**), "lunatic": That about twenty three years ago she was married to her present husband Charles Jeynes who is now a Lunatic in the parish Church of Cheltenham aforesaid by whom she has three Children now living with her namely John [for Job] aged 17 years William aged 14 years and Betsy aged 8 years   that she and her said husband has [*sic*] lived in Cheltenham aforesaid ever since their Marriage and her said husband has never during that time rented a Tenement of the annual value of ten pounds or done any act to gain a settlement

That during the time she and her said husband were so residing in Cheltenham they have three or four times been relieved by the Overseer of the parish of Newent in the said County; that she has herself made personal application to the parish officers of Newent aforesaid for relief and was by them acknowledged to belong to that parish in consequence of her said husband having been apprenticed at Newent aforesaid [mark]

1841: *CJ (50; labourer) lived with wife Ann (40) and children Job (15; labourer), William (9), and Betsy (6) in New St, Cheltenham (HO107/353/16/20-21/2).* **1843:** *family removed to Newent (husband's settlement).* **1845-6:** *(RETURNED) from 4Q 1845 until 4Q 1846 CJ, wife Ann, and two children received parish relief from Newent as non-settled residents of Cheltenham (G/CH/9d/1).* **1851:** *CJ (61; building labourer, born Newent) recovered and lived with wife Ann (54; born Cirencester) and son William (19; building labourer) at 30 New St, Cheltenham (HO107/1973/627/19); daughter Elizabeth (17) was house servant at 3 Montague Place, Cheltenham (HO107/1973/823/22).* [PS/CH/RA/2/5:492. Removal expenses for "Jeynes" to Newent 14/- (1Q 1843: D4178). See also **45003SE**: Jeans.]

43026RO: Mon 20 Mar 1843 – **James Spencer**, labourer; also father John Spencer, relating to son's settlement. *John Spencer*: That the first place he remembers himself was in the parish of

Horsley in the said County where he has resided all his life time until within the last seven years and has several times been relieved by the Overseers of that parish.

That he has never done any act to gain a Settlement either by service renting a Tenement or otherwise – That about thirty five years ago he was married to his present Wife Elizabeth in the Parish Church of Horsley aforesaid by whom he had his said Son James, now aged about twenty eight years who was born in the said parish of Horsley [mark]

James Spencer: That he was never hired for a year or rented a Tenement of the annual value of Ten pounds, or done any act to gain a settlement in his own right And he is now actually chargeable to the said parish of Cheltenham

I came from Horsley to Cheltenham [signed]

1843: *removed to Horsley (presumed) (father's settlement)*: *see* **45036SE** *(Charles Maisey: 23 June 1845) for further information.* [PS/CH/RA/2/6:121 (copy at PS/CH/RA/2/5:493). Removal expenses for "Spencer" to Horsley £1/1/- (2Q 1843: D4178). See **43047RO** (father John Spencer: 26 June 1843).

43027RO: Sat 25 Mar 1843 – **Thomas Cornock** (also **Cornick**), labourer, and wife **Elizabeth**: That about Ten years ago I was living in the parish of Frocester in the said County and being out of employ became chargeable to that parish – I was taken by the Overseer of that parish before the Magistrate at Whitminster Inn and examined as to my parish – I was then removed by Orders of Removal from the Parish of Frocester aforesaid to the Parish of Uley in the said County and together with my Wife and four Children was delivered to the Overseer of the said parish of Uley and together my said Wife and Children were placed in the Workhouse at Uley aforesaid where we remained Five Months – That the said Order of removal was not appealed against – I have done no act since to gain a Settlement

I was married to my Wife Elizabeth in the year 1816 in the parish Church of Frocester aforesaid – My Children have all left me   I am now actually chargeable to the said Parish of Cheltenham [signed]

1841: *TC (aged 55; woollen cloth-worker) lived with wife Elizabeth (50) and with Oliver Cornock (3) in Eastington, near Stroud (HO107/370/1/40/9).* **1843: *removed to Uley*. 1848:** *at son Caleb's wedding in Gloucester 12 June TC described as "traveller" (at own wedding in 1816, he was a "shearman").* **1851:** *TC (61; born Stonehouse) lived with wife Elizabeth (60; born Frocester) in Charlton Kings (HO107/1972/75/9); (RETURNED) Elizabeth died later in the year (buried at Cheltenham 2 July, aged 60.* [PS/CH/RA/2/6:122 (copy at PS/CH/RA/2/5:494). Removal expenses for "Cornock" to Uley £1/6/- (2Q 1843: D4178).]

43028RO: Thurs 30 Mar 1843 – **George Denning**, lathrender, wife **Eliza**, and five children **Martha, Joseph, Thomas, Ann**, and **Elizabeth**: I am 47. Years of age – my Father and Mother are both dead, I have heard my Father George Jennings [= Dennings] gained his settlement in the parish of Dursley in the said County by hiring and service to Capt[n]. Moss of that parish – I remember when I was about Six years of age living in the parish of Cam in this County – and was relieved by the Overseer of Dursley aforesaid for upwards of a year whilst I was living in the parish of Cam – When I was about 7 years of age the Overseer of Dursley wished me to go into the Workhouse at Dursley aforesaid and refused to relieve me any further – I did so – I was then taken to by my Grandfather at Wickwar because I should not go into the Workhouse who kept me till I was about 11 years of age – I have never been hired for a year or done any act to gain a settlement in my own right. – About 19. years ago I was married in the parish Church of Minchinhampton to my present Wife Eliza by whom I have five Children, namely, Martha aged 11. Years, Joseph aged 9. years – Thomas aged 5. years, Ann aged 4 years and Elizabeth aged 18. Months – I am now actually chargeable to the said parish of Cheltenham [mark]

1841: *the family lived in Townsend St, Cheltenham: GD (aged 40; lath-render), Elizabeth (30), and four children Martha (10), Joseph (8), Thomas (5), and Ann (3) (HO107/353/9/10/14).* **1843: *removed to Dursley (father's settlement)*. 1849:** *death of wife Elizabeth Denning (née Phillpott) (buried at Gloucester, aged 45).* **1851:** *GD (52; lath-cleaver and widower, born Dursley) lived in Warwick with son Joseph (19; lath-cleaver) (HO107/2073/521/42); daughter Ann (12; woolcarder, born Cheltenham) lived with uncle Daniel Phillpott and his family in Minchinhampton (HO107/1966/157/19).* [PS/CH/RA/2/6:123 (copy at PS/CH/RA/2/5:495).]

43029RO: Tues 4 Apr 1843 – **Jane Bell**, widow: That about twenty six years ago she was married to her late husband Anthony Bell in the parish of Saint Michaels Coventry – That her husband was then a soldier in the 73rd Regiment of Foot and about twenty years ago was sent to the East Indies. That she has understood from the War Office that her said husband died about thirteen or fourteen years ago in the East Indies – That at the time her said husband went to the East Indies she went to the Parish of Luckington in the County of Wilts to reside where she has heard her said husband was born and legally settled – That soon after she went to Luckington to reside she received relief from the Overseers of that parish and continued to receive such relief for about four years – That she then went to reside in the City of Bath and remained there for about three or four Years during the whole of which time she received relief from the Overseer of Luckington aforesaid – That she then went to reside in the City of Bristol and remained there two or three years and during the whole of that time she received relief from the Overseer of Luckington aforesaid   That she has never done any act to gain a settlement in her own right since her said husbands death and is now actually chargeable to the said Parish of Cheltenham [mark]
1843: *removed to Luckington, Wilts (husband's settlement): see* **45029SE** (JB: 23 May 1845). [PS/CH/RA/2/6:124 (copy at PS/CH/RA/2/5:496). Removal expenses for "Bell" to Luckington, Wilts £2/-/- (2Q 1843: D4178).]

43030RO: Thurs 6 Apr 1843 – **Elizabeth Hignell**, widow, and three children **Elizabeth**, **Harriet**, and **Mary**; also mother-in-law Mary Hignell, single woman, relating to the settlement of late son Thomas Hignell.
Mary Hignell: That her said Son Thomas Hignell was born in the parish of Saint Mary Magdalen in the City of Oxford near 39 years ago and was an illegitimate Child of this Examinant   that her said Son never done any act to gain a settlement in his own right – [mark]
Elizabeth Hignell: That about ten years ago she was married to her late husband Thomas Hignell in the parish Church of Cheltenham aforesaid by whom she has three children namely Elizabeth aged four years Harriet aged three years and Mary aged fourteen months. That her said husband died about a month ago. That he never done any act to gain a settlement in his own right since her Marriage – that she is now actually chargeable to the said Parish of Cheltenham [mark]
1843: *Thomas Hignell buried at New Burial Ground, Cheltenham 10 Mar, aged 40;* ***removed to St Mary Magdalen, Oxford (husband's settlement).*** **1845:** *EH (widow) married Robert Sampson 15 Sept at St Nicholas Church, Gloucester.* **1845-6:** *from 3Q 1845 and 4Q 1846 EH and three children received relief from City of Oxford as non-settled residents of Cheltenham (G/CH/9d/1).* **1851:** *(RETURNED) the family lived at 25 Hermitage Place, Cheltenham: Robert Sampson (50; servant), Elizabeth (40; born Northleach), Harriet (11; scholar), Mary (10; scholar), Hannah (5; scholar), and Charles (3: all children born Cheltenham) (HO107/1973/861/26).* [PS/CH/RA/2/6:125 (copy at PS/CH/RA/2/5:497). Notes on unnumbered page at end of Removals register: Mrs Hignell St Helens Court Oxford near Broad St; Son Thomas; Removal expenses to Oxford for "Hignell" £2/2/6 (2Q 1843: D4178).]

43031RO: Thurs 13 Apr 1843 – **William Spencer**, shoemaker: That when he was about 21. years of age he was hired by M^r. Addersall of the George Inn London Coney [= London Colney] in the parish of Shenley in the County of Herts as Ostler for a year at the Wages of Six Guineas – that he served the whole year and received his years wages and slept in his Master's house at Shenley aforesaid the whole time   That he was then unmarried and had no Child or Children – That about Fifteen Years and a half ago, he was removed from the parish of Welling in the County of Herts to the said Parish of Shenley by Orders of removal and delivered by M^r. Freeman the Overseer there – That such Orders were not appealed against – That he has been several times relieved by the parish Officers of Shenley aforesaid –
That he has never done any act to gain a settlement since he lived with M^r. Addersall at Shenley aforesaid
That he is now actually chargeable to the said parish of Cheltenham – [mark]
1843: *removed to Shenley, Herts (hiring and service).* [PS/CH/RA/2/6:126 (copy at PS/CH/RA/2/5:498). Removal expenses for "Spencer" to Shenley, Herts £4/14/6 (2Q 1843: D4178).]

43032RO: Sat 15 Apr 1843 – **Ann Ivens** (also **Ivin**), single woman, and two illegitimate children **Mary Ann** and **Charlotte**; also Thomas Boodle, Assistant Overseer, relating to the settlement of Ann Ivens. *Ann Ivens*: That she is the daughter of Solomon Ivens and Charlotte his Wife, who were removed by orders of Removal from the said Parish of Cheltenham to the parish of Acton Turville in the said County, about thirteen months ago – That she has never done any act to gain a settlement in her own right and is now actually chargeable to the said parish of Cheltenham – That she has two illegitimate Children, namely, Mary Ann aged Seven years and Charlotte aged four years – neither of whom have done any act to gain a settlement – [mark]

Thomas Boodle: [confirms removal of 17 Feb 1842 and states that it was not appealed against] **1829**: *bigamous wife of William Barnes (***35004SE***: 19 Mar 1835).* **1835**: *removal examination:* **35005SE** *(AI: 19 Mar 1835) (RETURNED).* **1841**: *AI (aged 25) lived with the father of (at least some of) her children, William Barnes (40; labourer), Solomon (8), Mary Ann (4), and Charlotte (2) in Elm St, Cheltenham (HO107/353/10/3/1-4/2).* **1843**: *William Barnes sentenced to six months' hard labour for bigamy (***35004SE***: 19 Mar); **removed to Acton Turville (father's settlement)**.* **1844**: *(RETURNED) Mary Ann Ivens (aged 7) inmate of Charlton Kings Workhouse for children (Cheltenham Union) in July (G/CH/60/3).* **1845**: *living in* "*a place near Birmingham*" *(Gloucestershire Chron. 8 Apr).* **1849**: *mother Ann married John Coombs at Cheltenham.* **1851**: *AI (34) lived with John Coombs (27; labourer), and three children at 7 Swindon Parade, Cheltenham: all of the family born at Cheltenham (HO107/1973/518/14).* [PS/CH/RA/2/6:127 (copies at PS/CH/RA/2/5:499). See **42019RO** (Solomon Ivin: 17 Feb 1842), **48028RO** (John Ivin: 29 Nov 1848).]

43033RO: 15 Apr 1843 – Ann Ivens, single woman, relating to the settlement of illegitimate son **Solomon Ivens**: That the said Solomon Ivens is an illegitimate Child of hers with which she was delivered in the parish of Charlton Kings in the said County on the 26th day of March, 1832. That said Son has never done any act to gain a settlement in his own right, and is now actually chargeable to the said parish of Cheltenham [mark]

1841: *Solomon Barnes (illegitimate son of Ann Ivin and William Barnes) lived with family in Elm St, Cheltenham: William Barnes (40; labourer), Solomon (8), Mary Ann (4), and Charlotte (2) (HO107/353/10/3/1-4/2); SI (aged 10) admitted to Charlton Kings Workhouse for children (Cheltenham Union) from 24 Sept until 14 Dec (G/CH/60/2), and Cheltenham Workhouse in Oct.* **1843**: ***removed to Charlton Kings (birth)**; SI admitted to Cheltenham Workhouse Dec (G/CH/60/4).* **1855**: *while living in Woodmancote, SI discharged of stealing coat of John Coombs, private in North Gloucester Militia, and presumably new stepfather (Cheltenham Chron. 27 Nov).* **1861**: *SI (30; agricultural labourer) lodged in Charlton Kings, at North St (RG9/1793/35/4).* [PS/CH/RA/2/6:128 (copy at PS/CH/RA/2/5:500). Notes on unnumbered page at end of Removals register: "Ann Ivens Daughter of Solomon Ivens married 13 years ago the 7 of February to W[m] Barnes at Winchcomb; To Prove the s[d] Marriage, by Ann Ivens W[m] Barnes was married about 19 years ago at Charlton Kings to Ann Edwards Daughter of George Edwards - Prove this Marriage To Prove Ann Edwards (alias Barnes) was alive since the 2[d] Marriage [to] George Edwards W[m] Barnes has a Sister of the name of Woodward at Ham". Removal expenses to Charlton for "Ivens" 2/6 (2Q 1843: D4178). For family references see **43032RO** (Ann Ivin: 15 Apr 1843).]

43034SE: Mon 24 Apr 1843 – Richard Cook (also Cooke), labourer, relating to the settlement of wife **Hannah Cook**, "lunatic": That about fifteen or sixteen years ago being then unmarried and having no Child or Children he was hired by M[r] John Wood of the parish of Notgrove in the said County Farmer for a Year as general servant at the wages of Four pounds that he served the whole year and received his years wages and slept in his Masters house at Notgrove aforesaid the whole time. that he has never done any act to gain a settlement since. That on the Eighth day of March 1841 he was married to his present Wife Hannah in the parish Church of Cheltenham aforesaid

That his said wife is now a Lunatic and become chargeable to the parish of Cheltenham aforesaid

1841: *Richard Cooke (porter and widower, living in Sherborne St, Cheltenham) married Hannah Mitchell (spinster, of 2 Sussex Place, Cheltenham) at Cheltenham 8 Mar; perhaps lived in Oriel Place, Bath Rd, Cheltenham: RC (30, servant), Anna (25, servant) (HO107/353/13/64/41).* **1843**: ***removal unlikely; examination form incomplete.*** **1847**: *son Richard Thomas born 2Q (baptised at Cheltenham 18 July, when family lived in North St, Cheltenham, and Richard was porter).* **1851**: *RC (44; auctioneer's porter, born*

Maugersbury), Hannah (38), and Richard Thomas (3) lived at 10 Russell Place, Cheltenham (HO107/1973/475/11). [PS/CH/RA/2/5:501 (text struck through).]

43035RO: Mon 8 May 1843 – **Susannah Tagg**, widow: I am Seventy eight years of age – I was married to my late Husband John Tagg in the parish Church of Saint George Hanover Square London about the month of August 1791. – My said Husband died about twenty years ago – About Forty eight years ago my said husband rented the old Queen's Head Public House Lower Green in the parish of Saint Nicholas Deptford in the County of Kent at a great deal more than Ten pounds a year – I and my said Husband lived in such House about Eight years at that Rent –

My said Husband never did any act afterwards to gain a Settlement – I have never done any act to gain a Settlement since my Husband's death. – I am now actually chargeable to the said parish of Cheltenham [mark]

1843: *removed to St Nicholas, Deptford, Kent (husband's settlement).* [PS/CH/RA/2/6:129 (order suspended as ST unfit to travel; lifted 10 Aug) (copy at PS/CH/RA/2/5:502). Removal expenses for "Tagg" to Deptford, Kent £4/3/- (2Q 1843) and £6/11/6 (3Q 1843: D4178).]

43036RO: Mon 24 Apr 1843 – **John Blackmore** (also **Blackmoor**), carpenter, wife **Mary**, and three children **Mary Ann**, **James**, and **Sarah**: I am about Sixty years of age – When I was about Seventeen Years of age I was hired by M^r. Hart of Sinkley [*i.e.* St Loe's] School in the parish of Minchinhampton in the said County as general servant at three pounds a year for a Year – I was then unmarried and had no Child or Children – I served the whole Year and received my years wages and slept in my Master's house in the said Parish of Minchinhampton the whole time – I have done no act since to gain a settlement – About twelve Years ago I was living in the parish of Stroud and was relieved by the parish Officers of Minchinhampton aforesaid for about three or four Years whilst I was so living at Stroud

I was married to my Wife Mary about thirty seven Years ago in the parish Church of Hasfield in the said County by whom I have three Children now living with me namely Mary Ann aged near sixteen years – James aged fourteen years and Sarah aged twelve years neither of which Children have gained a settlement. – I am now actually chargeable to the said parish of Cheltenham [mark]

1843: *removed to Minchinhampton (hiring and service): see* **47012RO** *(JB: 20 Feb 1847) for further information on JB and family.* [PS/CH/RA/2/6:130 (copy at PS/CH/RA/2/5:503). Removal expenses for "Blackmore" to Minchinhampton £1/11/- (2Q 1843: D4178).]

43037RO: Thurs 27 Apr 1843 – Elizabeth Manning, widow, residing in Bromsgrove, Warks, relating to the settlement of son **George Manning**, brace-bucklemaker, in Gloucester Asylum: I was married to my late husband Thomas Manning Brace Buckle maker at the parish Church of Wolverhampton on the 9th day of March 1802

My said Son George was born in the parish of Birmingham in the County of Warwick on the 15 day of November 1807

About 35 Years ago, my said husband rented a house in Henrietta Street Birmingham aforesaid belonging to Mr Wasdale at £30 a Year and we lived in such house five years. My said husband then rented a house in Tanter Street Birmingham aforesaid of Mr Archer at twenty Guineas a Year and we lived in such house five years. My said husband then rented a house in Navigation Street Birmingham aforesaid of Mr Gough at twenty three pounds a year. We lived there Eight years. My husband was rated to the poor rates for Birmingham aforesaid for each such house and paid them

My husband never afterwards rented a house of the annual value of ten pounds or done any act to gain a settlement and died about nine years [ago] at Birmingham aforesaid

My said Son was never apprenticed nor hired as a Yearly servant or done any act to gain a settlement in his own right   my said Son worked with his Father in his trade of a brace buckle maker aforesaid until he was Eighteen Years of age when he inlisted into the Army in the 4th Regiment of Dragoon Guards and served therein for about fourteen years [mark]

1843: *removed to Gloucester Asylum, whence to Birmingham, Warks (father's settlement); GM (labourer) died of "Fever" on 13 June at Bromsgrove, Warks (since 1844, Worcs), where he was buried 19 June.* [PS/CH/RA/2/6:131 (examination copied from PS/CH/RA/2/5:504). Note: "Removed to the Lunatic

Asylum". Removal expenses to Bromsgrove for "Manning" 10/- and to Birmingham £1/4/- (2Q 1843: D4178).]

43038RO: Mon 1 May 1843 – **Thomas Pickering,** butcher, and wife **Hannah**: The first place I remember myself was in High Street in the Parish of Saint Thomas in the City of Winchester where I resided with my Father and Mother, until I was about thirty five years of age

My said Father resided in his own house in High Street Saint Thomas' aforesaid until his death which happened about Eighteen years ago – I have never done any Act to gain a Settlement in my own right – About Fourteen Years ago I was married to my present Wife Hannah in Saint Sepulchre's Church London – About Twelve months ago I was chargeable to the Parish of Clerkenwell in the County of Middlesex, and was with my Wife by Orders of Removal taken to the said Parish of Saint Thomas Winchester and there left – And such Orders were not appealed against – I am now Chargeable to the said Parish of Cheltenham. [signed]
1841: TP (aged 40; journeyman butcher) lived with wife Hannah (35) at 11 Hosier Lane, St Sepulchre, London (HO107/728/4/11/16). **1843: removed to St Thomas, Winchester, Hants (father's settlement).** [PS/CH/RA/2/6:132 (copy at PS/CH/RA/2/5:505). Removal expenses for "Pickering" to Winchester, Hants £4/14/- (2Q 1843: D4178).]

43039RO: Sat 6 May 1843 – **John Bown** (also **Bawn**), labourer, wife **Sophia**, and son **John**; also Joseph Bown, gardener, of Kemerton, relating to the place settlement of brother John Bown. *Joseph Bown*: I am upwards of Fifty years of age – My Father and Mother lived at Kemerton aforesaid from when I can first recollect up to the time of their death – My Mother died about thirty years ago and my Father about twenty years ago – both of them died at Kemerton aforesaid – and were buried there – My Father owned a Freehold Cottage House and two Orchards in Kemerton aforesaid worth more than a hundred pounds – My Father and Mother occupied that property to the time of their death – I recollect when my said Brother John was born – I am some years older than him   I was at home at the time when my Mother was confined at his birth   He was born in the Cottage House of which I have spoken – My Father then owned the Cottage and I lived there with him –
John Bown: The first place I recollect myself in was at my Father's Cottage at Kemerton in this County – I continued to live with my Father at Kemerton aforesaid until he died – I was then about nine Years of age – I have never done any act to gain a Settlement in my own right – I am now actually chargeable to the said parish of Cheltenham – That about 7 Years ago I was married to my wife Wife Sophia at Cheltenham by whom I have one Child named John aged Five years – [mark]
1841: JB (aged 40; porter) lived with wife Sophia (25) and two children John (3) and Henry (9 mo) in Sherborne St, Cheltenham (HO107/353/5/62/46). **1842:** *death of Henry (buried at New Burial Ground, Cheltenham 22 Aug, aged 1 year and 11 months).* **1843: died before removal; son John removed to Kemerton (father's settlement)**; *JB was buried at New Burial Ground, Cheltenham 12 Sept, aged 42; wife Sophia buried 9 Oct, aged 32.* **1847:** *son John buried at Kemerton 1 Apr, aged 8.* [PS/CH/RA/2/6:134 (order suspended as JB was unfit to travel; lifted with regard to surviving son John Bown 7 Nov 1843) (copy at PS/CH/RA/2/5:506-7). Removal expenses for "Bown" to Kemmerton 10/- (2Q 1843) and 12/6 (4Q 1843: D4178).]

43040RO: Mon 8 May 1843 – **Judith Shelton,** widow: About Forty seven years ago I was married to my late husband George Shelton at the parish Church of Rodborough in this County – he died at Cheltenham aforesaid twelve years ago last December – During my husband's life time he left me with five small Children – I was living at the time in the parish of Avening in this County – I applied to my husbands parish at Coaley in this County for relief   I went myself to the parish Officers there and asked for relief for myself and Children – they relieved me and paid me Five shillings a week for the support of my said Children for four or five years afterwards During some part of the time that I received this relief I was living at Avening aforesaid and during the remainder of the time at Minchinhampton in the said County   I never lived at Coaley – My husband's settlement was at Coaley   I have heard him frequently say Coaley was his parish – I know that some of his family lived there – I recollect during his life time when he was very ill and living at Cheltenham aforesaid he received relief from the parish officers of Coaley aforesaid – After his death I applied to them for relief and they paid me sixpence a week for about six months and during the whole of that time I was living at Cheltenham aforesaid – they then refused to give me further relief unless I came home to Coaley aforesaid   I have done no act to gain a settlement since my said Husband's death – I am now actually chargeable to the said parish of Cheltenham [mark]

1843: *removed to Coaley (husband's settlement).* **1851:** *(RETURNED) JS (aged 74; widow, born Rodborough) lived with daughter and son-in-law Sarah and William Sparrow at 5 Lawrence Court, Cheltenham (HO107/1973/854/13.* **1853:** *death of JS in Cheltenham Union Workhouse 3 Jan (buried two days later).* [PS/CH/RA/2/6:133 (copy at PS/CH/RA/2/5:508). Removal expenses for "Shelton" to Coaley £1/-/- (2Q 1843: D4178). See **49015RO** (son-in-law William Sparrow: 10 Feb 1849).]

43041RO: Thurs 11 May 1843 – **Mary Pincott,** single woman, inmate of Cheltenham Workhouse; also mother Mary Pincott, relating to daughter Mary's settlement. *Mary Pincott the elder*: That in the year 1807. she was married to her late Husband Thomas Pincott in the Parish Church of Stroud in the said County – That her said Husband has been dead about six years – that her said Daughter is aged about twenty years – and was born in the parish of Bisley in the said County – that her said husband belonged to the said Parish of Bisley as she has heard - and she remembers his being relieved by the Overseer of that parish – That she has been acknowledged by the parish Officers of Bisley to belong to that parish since her husband's death – and for the last six Months she has received a shilling a week from the parish Officers of Bisley aforesaid during which time she has been residing in Cheltenham. [mark]

Mary Pincott the younger: That she has never done any act to gain a settlement in her own right, and is now actually chargeable to the said parish of Cheltenham – [mark]

1843: *removed to Bisley (father's settlement):* see **45021SE** *(MP: 5/7 Apr 1845).* [PS/CH/RA/2/6:135 (order suspended as Mary Pincott unfit to travel; lifted 29 June) (copy at PS/CH/RA/2/5:509). Removal expenses for "Pincott" to Bisley 15/- (2Q 1843) and 19/- (3Q 184: D4178).]

43042RO: Thurs 18 May 1843 – **Henry Vincent,** labourer, and wife **Ann:** About Forty years ago I was hired by Henry Spacier [also Spacer; apparently Spicer] Esquire of the parish of Topsham in the County of Devon for a Year as Coachman at the wages of Twenty five Guineas – I served the whole year and received my years wages, and slept in my Master's house at Topsham aforesaid the whole time – I had then never been married and had no Child or Children, I was married soon afterwards to my present Wife Ann in the parish Church of Ashpreithton [prob. Ashprington] in the said County of Devon – I have never rented a tenement of the annual value of Ten pounds or done any act to gain a settlement since my service at Topsham aforesaid – I am now actually chargeable to the said parish of Cheltenham [signed]

1821: *removed to Topsham, Devon (hiring and service): see Gray 353 (HV: 16 Jan 1821).* **1843:** *removed to Topsham, Devon (hiring and service).* **1851:** *HV (aged 84; pauper, born Selworthy, Som) lived with wife Ann (77; from Milford Haven, Pemb) in High St, Topsham, Devon (HO107/1866/259/19).* [PS/CH/RA/2/6:136 (copy at PS/CH/RA/2/5:510).]

43043RO: 18 May 1843 – **Thomas Fisher,** wife **Ann,** and two children **Edwin** and **Mary Ann**; also mother, Mary Fisher, relating to the settlement of Thomas Fisher. *Mary Fisher*:That about 42 Years ago She was married to her late Husband Nathaniel Fisher in the parish Church of Kings Stanley [= King's Stanley] in the said County by whom she had her said Son Thomas now aged about twenty five years who was born in the Parish of Kings Stanley aforesaid – That her said Husband has been dead about Twenty years – That since her husband's death, she has been several times relieved by the Parish Officers of Kings Stanley aforesaid – That she has been living in Cheltenham the last Five years and about three weeks ago she received relief from the parish Officers of Kings Stanley aforesaid on account of one of her Children who is afflicted and living with her [mark]

Thomas Fisher: That he has never done any act to gain a settlement in his own right –

That Two years ago last September he was married in Cheltenham to his present Wife Mary by whom he has two Children – Edwin aged two years, and a Female Infant Child now aged 5. days – That he is actually chargeable to the said parish of Cheltenham – [mark]

1841: *TF (aged 30; labourer) lived in Rutland St, Cheltenham with wife Mary (20; independent) and son Edwin (6 mo) (HO107/353/7/62/28).* **1843:** *removed to King's Stanley (father's settlement); birth of daughter Mary Ann registered at Cheltenham 2Q (baptised 19 May at Cheltenham).* **1844:** *(RETURNED) death of son Edwin in Cheltenham 4Q.* **1847:** *baptism of William Henry in Cheltenham 26 Dec, when family lived in Sherborne St, Cheltenham.* **1850:** *daughter Lucy Ann baptised 16 June, from their home in Duke St, Cheltenham.* **1851:** *the family lived at 13½ Fairview St, Cheltenham: TF (33; labourer), Mary (31), William Henry (4), and Lucy Ann (10 mo) (HO107/1973/110/45).* [PS/CH/RA/2/6:137 (copy at PS/CH/RA/2/5:511). Removal expenses for "Fisher" to King's Stanley £1/4/6 (2Q 1843: D4178).]

43044RO: Sat 10 June 1843 – **Richard Sisom** (also **Sisam, Sissum, Sisum**), labourer, wife **Mary Ann**, and child **Alfred:** I am 32 Years of age, the first place I remember myself was living with my Father and Mother at Brockhampton in the parish of Sevenhampton in the said County – When I was about five years old my Father died, and my Mother myself and my Sister were placed in a Cottage house belonging to John Lovering at Brockhampton aforesaid and for which the Overseer of Sevenhampton aforesaid paid the rent until the death of my Mother which happened about 15. or 16 Years ago – My Mother was buried at the expence of the parish of Sevenhampton aforesaid I have never done any Act to gain a Settlement in my own right – About Four years ago I was married to my present Wife Mary Ann in the parish Church of Sevenhampton aforesaid by whom I have one Child named Alfred aged three years –

I am now actually Chargeable to the said parish of Cheltenham [mark]

1843: *removed to Sevenhampton (father's settlement): see* **47018RO** *(RS: 15 May 1847) for further information on RS and family.* [PS/CH/RA/2/6:138 (copy at PS/CH/RA/2/5:512). Note: "21st October committed to Northleach for 14 days for becoming chargeable a Second time". Removal expenses to Sevenhampton for "Sisom" 15/- (3Q 1843: D4178).]

43045RO: 10 June 1843 – **Frances Johnson**, wife of William Johnson, convicted felon in Horsley Gaol, and three children **James, Sabina** (= **Albina**; also **Vina**), and **Susan:** That about 21 Years ago she was married to her present husband William Johnson in the parish of Bisley in the said County by whom She has three Children namely James aged Seven Years – Sabina aged Five Years and Susan aged Two Years – That she has heard and believes that her husband gained his settlement in the parish of Brimpsfield in the said County by hiring and service with Mr. John Winning of that Parish – That about Five Years ago she and her husband and Family were living in the parish of Leckhampton in the said County and became chargeable to that parish – That herself and her husband and her two first named Children with another Child were removed by Orders of Removal from the said Parish of Leckhampton to the said Parish of Brimpsfield and delivered to the Overseer there who received them – That such Order of removal was not appealed against – That her said Husband has never done any Act to gain a settlement since and is now confined in the Prison of Horsley as a convicted Felon – That she and her said Children are now actually chargeable to the said Parish of Cheltenham [mark]

1843: *FJ (aged 30) lived with husband William (45; labourer) and children James (6), Albina (5), and Virginia (4 mo) in Sherborne St, Cheltenham (HO107/353/5/62/47).* **1843:** *William Johnson convicted of stealing four silk handerkerchiefs and other articles and imprisoned in Horsley Gaol for twelve months with hard labour (Gloucestershire Chron. 7 Jan 1843); removed to Brimpsfield (husband's settlement).* **1851:** *(RETURNED) the family lived at 1 Exmouth Court, Exmouth St, Cheltenham: William Johnson (66; shepherd, born Chedworth), Frances (50; charwoman), Albina (18; servant, born Brimpsfield), and Susan (10; scholar, born Cheltenham) (HO107/1973/853/10).* [PS/CH/RA/2/6:139 (copy at PS/CH/RA/2/5:513). Removal expenses for "Johnson" to Brimpsfield 15/- (3Q 1843: D4178).]

43046RO: Thurs 22 June 1843 – **Thomas Goode** (also **Good**), cordwainer, inmate of Cheltenham Workhouse, wife **Ann**, and seven children **Hannah, John, Edward, Thomas, Mary Ann, Susannah**, and **Caroline:** That he is the Son of John and Martha Goode and now aged about 37 years. that his said Father as he has heard and believes gained a settlement in the parish of Taynton in the County of Gloucester by hiring and service. that he remembers his said Father was several times relieved by the Overseers of Taynton aforesaid – That this Examinant has never done any act to gain a settlement in his own right – that about 14 years ago this Examinant was living in the parish of Staunton in the County of Worcester and applied to M^r. Fishpool the then Overseer of Taynton for Relief and was by him relieved and the sum of ten shillings was given him – that about eleven or twelve years ago he was still living in the parish of Staunton aforesaid and again applied to M^r. Fishpool who was then Overseer of Tainton aforesaid for relief – that he went with M^r. Fishpool before the Bench of Magistrates at Newent and was examined as to his parish who informed M^r. Fishpool that this Examinant belonged to Taynton and M^r. Fishpool then gave the Examinant a Sovereign. That about 18 years ago he was married to his present Wife Ann in the parish Church of Pendock by whom he has seven children namely Hannah aged 14 years John aged 12 years Edward aged 7 years Thomas aged 5 years Mary Ann aged 3 years Susanna aged 2 years and Caroline aged 4 months – That he is now actually chargeable to the said Parish of Cheltenham [signed]

1841: *the family lived in Stanhope St, Cheltenham: Ann Goode (35), Hannah (13), John (9), Edwin [= Edward] (5), Thomas (3), Mary (2), Susan (3 mo) (HO107/353/9/52/5) (TG was absent on census night).* **1843: *removed to Taynton (Newent Union) (father's settlement)***; *the family were inmates of Cheltenham Union Workhouse mid-year (discharged June 28/16 July) (G/CH/60/4).* **1844:** *the family entered Newent Workhouse, where son Thomas died (buried at Taynton 30 Apr, aged 6).* **1851:** *TG (45; cordwainer, born Gloucester City) lived with wife Ann (45; shoebinder, born Hereford) and three children Mary Ann (12; scholar, born Evesham, Worcs), Susannah (11; scholar, born Cheltenham), and Caroline (8; scholar; born Malmesbury, Wilts) in Culvert St, Newent (HO107/1960/184/31).* [PS/CH/RA/2/6:140 (copy at PS/CH/RA/2/5:514). Removal expenses for "Goode" to Taynton £1/6/6 (3Q 1843: D4178).]

43047RO: Mon 26 June 1843 – **John Spencer**, labourer, wife **Elizabeth**, and two children **Jane** and **Hannah:** That the first place he remembers himself was in the parish of Horsley in the said County where he has resided all his life time until within the last Seven Years and has several times been relieved by the Overseers of that parish – That he has never done any Act to gain a Settlement by service, renting a Tenement or otherwise

That about thirty five years ago he was married to his present Wife Elizabeth in the parish Church of Horsley aforesaid by whom he has two Children, living with him, namely Jane aged Eighteen years, and Hannah aged Fourteen years neither of whom hath done any act to gain a settlement – That he is now actually Chargeable to the said parish of Cheltenham [mark]

1841: *JS (aged 50; labourer) lived with wife Elizabeth (50) and daughter Amelia (23; laundress) in Victoria Place, Cheltenham (HO107/353/12/26/46).* **1843: *removed to Horsley (father's presumed settlement).*** **1851:** *(RETURNED) JS (64; labourer, born Horsley) lived at Vine Cottage, near Victoria Place, Cheltenham with wife Elizabeth (63) and children Hannah (22; boarder, born Horsley), William (31, labourer, born Horsley), and Mary Ann (26; washerwoman, born Cheltenham) (HO107/1973/882/23).* [PS/CH/RA/2/6:141 (order suspended as Elizabeth Spencer unfit to travel (suspension not lifted) (copy at PS/CH/RA/2/5:515). Removal expenses for "Spencer" to Horsley 15/- (3Q 1843: D4178). See **43026RO** (JS for son James: 20 Mar 1843).]

43048RO: Thurs 6 July 1843 – **William Bufton**, labourer, wife **Jemima**, and two children **William** and **Mary:** That about 14 or 15 years ago being then unmarried and having no child or Children he was hired by M^{rs}. Daniel Capel then residing at Gloucester for a year at the wages of thirty pounds   that he served her near two years at Gloucester and then came with her to Prestbury in the said County   that he lived with his said Mistress two years at N°. 2 Tatchley Villa in Prestbury aforesaid   That he was hired each year – That he left M^{rs}. Capel's service at Prestbury aforesaid and was immediately afterwards married to his present Wife Jemima at Cheltenham – That about Six Years ago he rented a House at Prestbury aforesaid of M^r. Richard Seabright called Field Cottage at Twelve pounds a year, that he continued in such house three years, and paid all the Rent – That he was duly rated to and paid all the Poor rates in respect of such house and has done no act since to gain a settlement elsewhere – That he has by his said Wife two Children namely William aged Eight years and Mary aged Five years – That he is now actually Chargeable to the said parish of Cheltenham – [mark]

1841: *WB (aged 45) was in service to Mrs. Susan Capel at Prestbury House, Burgage St, Prestbury (HO107/354/26/18/7); his wife Jemima (35) lived elsewhere in Burgage St with children William (8) and Mary (3) (HO107/354/26/19/9).* **1843: removed to Prestbury (renting).** **1850:** *(RETURNED) death of WB (buried, aged 60, at Cheltenham 8 June).* **1851:** *Jemima (erroneously "Jane") Bufton (48; born Redmarley, Worcs) was domestic servant working for Mrs Capel at Prestbury House (HO107/1972/29/12); son William Bufton (16) was apparently servant living at 15 Brunswick St, Cheltenham (HO107/1973/318/6).* [PS/CH/RA/2/6:142 (copy at PS/CH/RA/2/5:516). Removal expenses for "Bufton" to Prestbury 2/6 (3Q 1843: D4178).]

43049RO: 6 July 1843 – **James Allen**, blacksmith, and daughter **Mary Ann:** That he has heard and believes he was born in the Parish of Norton in the said County - that when he was fifteen years of age he was apprenticed by Indenture duly stamped to James Caudle of the said parish of Norton Blacksmith for the term of six years – that he served the whole time & slept in his Masters house at Norton aforesaid the whole time – that such Indenture was duly executed – That he has never done any act since to gain a settlement elsewhere – That about 10 years ago he was married in the parish of Addlestrop [= Adlestrop] in the said County to his late Wife Martha now deceased by whom he has one Child Mary Ann aged eight years – That he is now actually chargeable to the said parish of Cheltenham [signed]

1841: *death of wife Martha in Cheltenham, aged 34 (buried at New Burial Ground on 1 Apr).* **1843: removed to Norton (Gloucester Union) (apprenticeship).** **1845-7:** *(RETURNED) from 3Q 1845 until 2Q 1847 daughter Mary (Ann) Allen (10) received parish relief from Gloucester as a non-settled resident of Cheltenham (G/CH/9d/1).* **1851:** *JA (46; blacksmith, born Norton) lived, with housekeeper, in Gas Green, Cheltenham (HO107/1973/550/23).* **1859:** *daughter Mary Ann lived at 22 Henrietta St, Cheltenham when married 26 Sept to Robert Pugh.* [PS/CH/RA/2/6:143 (copy at PS/CH/RA/2/5:517). Removal expenses for "Allen" to Norton 13/- (3Q 1843: D4178).]

43050RO: Sat 15 July 1843 – **Mary Smith**, widow of Daniel Smith, and son **Daniel**; also Elizabeth Smith, mother of Daniel Smith the elder, relating to his settlement. *Elizabeth Smith*: That about forty three years ago she was married to her late husband Daniel Smith at the parish of Boddington in the said County   that her said husband died about six weeks ago in Cheltenham

That she was delivered of her said Son Daniel at Longford in the said County about twenty three Years ago who died three months ago in Cheltenham

That about eighteen years ago her said husband rented a House in Sweet Briar Street in the parish of Saint Mary de lode in the City of Gloucester of Mr Morgan at nine pounds a year   that her said husband resided in that house upwards of Eight years and paid the first five years rent – that Mr Counsel of Gloucester was landlord of the house part of that time   That in about two years after her said husband began to rent said house he rented a piece of land adjoining the said house in the said parish of Saint Mary de lode at one pound a Year – that he continued to occupy such Land jointly with the said house for two Years and paid the rent for the same – that her said husband never afterwards done any act to gain a settlement – that her said son never done any act to gain a settlement in his own right and was about two years ago married to his present wife Mary in the parish of Cheltenham [signed]

Mary Smith: That about two years ago she was married to her late husband Daniel Smith at the parish of Cheltenham aforesaid by whom she has one Child named Daniel aged nine months – that her said husband has done no act to gain a settlement since their Marriage – that her said husband died three months ago at Cheltenham aforesaid – That she is now actually chargeable to the said parish of Cheltenham – [signed]

1843: *father-in-law Daniel Smith (aged 57; labourer) lived in Queen St, Cheltenham, with wife Elizabeth (56) (HO107/353/9/35/18).* **1843:** *husband Daniel buried 13 May at New Burial Ground, Cheltenham, aged 23; his father Daniel (gardener) buried there three weeks later, 1 June, aged 66;* **removed to St Mary de Lode, Gloucester (husband's settlement).** **1845-6:** *(RETURNED) from 3Q 1845 until 2Q 1846 MS and two children received parish relief from Gloucester as non-settled residents of Cheltenham (G/CH/9d/1).* **1851:** *son Daniel is probably the Daniel Smith (9; scholar) who was an inmate of Gloucester Union Workhouse in*

St Catherine's, Gloucester (HO107/1961/467/4); his grandmother probably the Elizabeth Smith buried 7 Apr at Cheltenham, aged 66. [PS/CH/RA/2/6:144 (copy at PS/CH/RA/2/5:519-20). Removal expenses for "Smith" to Gloucester 2/- (3Q 1843: D4178).]

43051SE: Thurs 13 July 1843 – **Charles Nicholls**, with wife **Deborah**: I am about twenty nine years of age. The first place I remember myself was living in the Parish of Horsley in the said County with my Father George Nicholls and my Mother Hannah his wife with whom I lived in the said parish of Horsley as part of their Family until I was about twenty four years of age   that my said Father and Mother rented a house as long as I can remember of Mr Cornelius Farmlowe [= Farmilo(e)] in the said Parish of Horsley at Four Pounds a Year until about 6 years ago   that for several Years during that time my Father rented Land in the Said parish of Horsley at Eight pounds a Year. That my Father left Horsley aforesaid about four years ago for Australia and has not returned since

    That I have done no Act to gain a settlement in my own right   that about four Years ago I was married to my present Wife Deborah in the said parish of Horsley [mark]
1839: *apparent emigration of CN's parents and other siblings as free settlers to Sydney, New South Wales.* **1841:** *CN (aged 25) worked as footman in Avening Court, Avening (HO107/362/1/3/1); wife Deborah (20) lived with father Samuel Alder and family four miles away, in Horsley (HO107/362/4/45/6); the couple had a daughter, Martha, soon after examination, baptised at Avening, where Charles remained a servant.* **1843:** *removal to Horsley (father's settlement) uncertain without further documentation: see* **49071RO** *(Deborah Nicholls: 22 Dec) for further information.* **1847:** *(RETURNED) son (Samuel) Charles Nicholls baptised at Cheltenham 8 Aug 1847, when family lived in Bath Rd.* **1849:** *son George Thomas born at Cheltenham.* **1851:** *wife Deborah (30; monthly nurse, born Horsley) lived at "back of Mount Pleasant", Cheltenham, with son George (1) (HO107/1973/168/21); Charles (36) was then working as servant to stockbroker in West Ham, Essex (HO107/1768/478/9).* [PS/CH/RA/2/5:[521].]

43052RO: Thurs 27 July 1843 – **Edith Gardner** (also **Gardener**, **Gardiner**; living as **Bundy**, also **Bunday**, **Bundey**), single woman; also Martha Bunday, wife of George Bunday, mason, and mother of Edith Gardner, relating to her settlement. *Edith Gardner*: I am a Singlewoman and have never been married – I have never done any act whereby to gain a Settlement in my own right – I am now actually Chargeable to the said parish of Cheltenham [mark]
Martha Bunday: About twenty four years ago I was delivered of an illegitimate daughter named Edith Gardner – I was then unmarried and had never been married – I was confined with the said Edith Gardner in the parish of Saint Nicholas in the City of Gloucester and the said Edith Gardner was born in the said parish of Saint Nicholas – I was in lodgings in that parish at the time – I was married to my present husband in the said parish of Corse about twenty two years ago [mark]
1841: *EG (Edith Bundy; aged 20) lived as servant in Pittville Terrace (south side of Clarence Rd), Cheltenham (HO107/353/6/49/11).* **1843:** *EG admitted as an inmate of Cheltenham Workhouse 13 July; illegitimate daughter Harriet born at workhouse 1 Aug (baptised at Cheltenham 11 Aug); both discharged from workhouse 27 Sept 1843 (G/CH/60/4); removed to St Nicholas, Gloucester (birth).* **1844:** *daughter Harriet died at Gloucester aged 11 mo (buried at St Nicholas, Gloucester, 5 July).* **1851:** *Edith Bundy (32) was dairymaid living in service in Upton Bishop, Heref (HO107/1976/85/14).* **1861:** *EG in service at Friern Barnet, Middlesex, aged 42 (RG9/790/27/11).* **1871:** *EG lived in Corse (51; dressmaker), caring for half-brother Samuel's daughter Edith Ellen (5) (RG10/2609/42/1).* **1880:** *death of EG at Corse (buried 18 Nov, aged 62).* [PS/CH/RA/2/6:145 (order suspended as EG was unfit to travel; not noted as lifted) (copy at PS/CH/RA/2/7:1). Removal expenses for "Gardner" to Gloucester 7/3 (3Q 1843: D4178).]

43053RO: 27 July 1843 – **John James**, labourer, and wife **Sarah**: About Forty years ago being then unmarried and having no Child or Children I was hired by M^r. Richard Minching of the parish of Haselton [= Hazleton] in the said County Farmer to serve him as his Servant for a year at the wages of four pounds a Year – The hiring was to serve him from Michaelmas to Michaelmas   I served him the whole year and received all my wages and slept and resided in my Masters house at Haselton aforesaid the whole time   At the end of my first years service I was hired again by the said Richard Minching to serve him as his servant for another year at the wages of five pounds a year   I served him the whole year and received all my wages and slept and resided in my said Masters house in the said Parish of Haselton the whole year   I have never done any act since whereby to gain a settlement

About four years ago I was married to my present Wife Sarah at the Parish Church of Cheltenham in the County of Gloucester – I and my said Wife are now actually chargeable to the said parish of Cheltenham [mark]

1839: *marriage of JJ and Sarah Mitchell 11 Aug at Cheltenham: they lived respectively in York St, and in Chapel St, Cheltenham.* **1843:** *removed to Hazleton (hiring and service).* **1851:** *(RETURNED) the couple apparently lived in Hall's Court, Cheltenham: JJ (aged 76; labourer, born Naunton) and Sarah (50; born Cowley) (HO107/1973/164/12).* [PS/CH/RA/2/6:146 (copy at PS/CH/RA/2/7:2). Removal expenses for "James" to Haselton 16/- (3Q 1843: D4178).]

43054RO: Thurs 10 Aug 1843 – **Edward Caudle** (also **Caudel**), labourer, wife **Mary Ann** and two children **Jane** and **Susannah:** That about Sixteen years ago being then unmarried and having no Child or Children he was hired by the late M[r]. Henry Rooke the parish of Prestbury in the said County as Gardener at the wages of Ten pounds for a Year – That he served the whole Year and received his Years wages and slept in his Master's house at Prestbury aforesaid the whole time –

That he has done no act since to gain a Settlement – That about Eleven Years ago he was married to his late Wife Jane in the parish of Cheltenham, who died about Four Years ago, by whom he has two Children, namely Jane aged Ten Years, and Susannah aged Seven Years –

That about Three years ago he was married to his present Wife Mary Ann at Birmingham – That he is now actually Chargeable to the said parish of Cheltenham [mark]

1841: *EC (aged 32; labourer) lived with wife Mary (Ann) (25) and daughter Jane (7) in Worcester St, Cheltenham (HO107/353/9/59/18); younger daughter Susan (4) apparently lived with her uncle's family in Hailes (HO107/360/10/5/4).* **1843:** *removed to Prestbury (hiring and service); the family were admitted to Cheltenham Workhouse from 31 Aug until 7 Sept (G/CH/60/4).* **1845:** *(RETURNED) death of EC at Worcester St, Cheltenham (Cheltenham Chron. 18 Dec) (buried at Cheltenham 12 Dec, aged 37).* **1848:** *wife Mary Ann died of "Scrophula" 19 July at Deacon St, Gloucester, aged 46; buried at St Nicholas, Gloucester 24 July.* **1851:** *Jane Caudle (17) worked as live-in servant for William Turk, maltster, at Hamilton Cottage, Charlton Kings (HO107/1972/107/31).* [PS/CH/RA/2/6:147 (copy at PS/CH/RA/2/7:3); see page 518 of the previous register PS/CH/RA/2/5 for incomplete draft of examination (dated [blank] July 1843, and struck through). Removal expenses for "Caudle" to Prestbury 7/- (3Q 1843: D4178).]

43055SE: Fri 11 Aug 1843 – **George Walkley** (also **Wakeley**), labourer, wife **Susan**, and five children, **Thomas**, **Pamela**, **Emma**, **Louisa**, and **Dan**; also mother, Mary Walkley, single woman, residing in King's Stanley, regarding the place of his settlement. *George Walkley*: I am a Labourer at present residing at Cheltenham in the said County. I have never done any act whereby to gain a settlement in my own right – About twenty years ago I was married to my present wife Susan in the Parish Church of Rodborough in the said County of Gloucester and have by her eight Children now living and all born in lawful wedlock – they are Hannah aged nineteen Years – Ann aged eighteen years – Maria aged sixteen years – Thomas aged fifteen years – Pamela aged twelve years – Emma aged nine Years – Louisa aged eight years and Dan aged four years – I and my said wife and five of my said children namely Thomas aged fifteen years – Pamela aged twelve years – Emma aged nine years – Louisa aged eight years – and Dan aged four years – are all now actually chargeable to the said Parish of Cheltenham [mark]

Mary Walkley: I am a Singlewoman living at Kingstanley in this County   About thirty eight years ago I was delivered of an illegitimate son the above named George Walkley. I was then unmarried and have never been married – I was confined with the said George Walkley in the said Parish of Kingstanley and the said George Walkley was born in that parish   I was living at a house called the Sandpitts in the said Parish of Kingstanley at the time I was delivered

1841: *GW (aged 30; clothworker) lived in King's Stanley with wife Susan (35) and seven children, Maria (15), Thomas (14; agricultural labourer), Pamela (13; servant), Emma (7), Louisa (6), Charlotte (4), and Dan (2) (HO107/370/4/36/14-15); on 29 June GW (36) probably sentenced to two years' imprisonment with hard labour for stealing a ewe at Woodchester, near King's Stanley (Cheltenham Chron. 8 July).* **1842:**

daughter Charlotte died at Cheltenham (buried at New Burial Ground 5 May, aged 5). **1843: *removed to King's Stanley (Stroud Union) (birth).*** **1844:** *(RETURNED) birth of daughter Charlotte registered to GW and Susan 3Q at Cheltenham.* **1845-6:** *from 1Q 1845 until 4Q 1846 GW, wife Susan, and four children received parish relief from Stroud as non-settled residents of Cheltenham (G/CH/9d/1).* **1851:** *the family lived at 6 Worcester Place, Cheltenham: GW (45; hawker), Susan (50; fruiterer), Emma (16; hawker), Louisa (15; hawker), Daniel (11; hawker); Charlotte (6; servant girl), along with Susan's mother Ann Dangerfield (72; weaver and pauper; born Leonard Stanley); all of George's family here were born at King's Stanley except Charlotte, born at Cheltenham (HO107/1973/515/8).* [PS/CH/RA/2/7:4. Removal expenses for "Walkley" to King's Stanley £1/13/6 (3Q 1843: D4178).]

43056SE: 14/17 Aug 1843 – **Esther** (also **Hester**) **Hope**, widow, and three children **Henry**, **Thomas**, and **George**; also mother-in-law, Maria Hope, widow, residing in Newent, regarding the place of settlement of daughter-in-law Esther Hope. *Maria Hope:* I am the widow of John Hope who died at Newent aforesaid about thirteen or fourteen years ago – I was married to him in Newent about thirty years ago – I had four children by him born in lawful wedlock at Newent - Thomas Hope was the eldest of such children – he married the above named Esther Hope at Cheltenham aforesaid and died there about four or five weeks since – I have lived in Newent aforesaid ever since I was about twelve years of age – it is my Parish – My husband lived there all the time from my Marriage until he died – and was buried at Newent – it was his Parish. he was born there – he was a Gardener and worked with his Father at Newent when I married him – Since my husband's death I have been in the Workhouse at Newent for nearly a month and supported by the Parish. When I came out of the Workhouse the Parish officers paid me two shillings a week for relief – I now receive that sum from them – My said Son Thomas continued to live with me until he was fourteen years of age – when he was put apprentice to Samuel Lewis of Newent aforesaid Plumber Glazier & Painter. After my son had been apprenticed to him about two years the said Samuel Lewis left Newent – and he is now gone to America. My said Son told me he had not served his term with the said Samuel Lewis, and that he must learn his trade to finish it by journey work. My said Son Thomas did not serve the five years with the said Samuel Lewis – Before his time was out he came as a Journey man to work for Charles Harbell [uncertain] of Newent aforesaid Plumber & Glazier. My said Son Thomas never did to my knowledge any act to gain a Settlement in his own right. – My said Son Thomas Hope worked for the said Charles Harbell as a journeyman and on his own account in the beginning of June 1828 at Newent aforesaid and continued to work with him until 1830 – [mark]
Esther Hope: I was married to my late husband at the Old Church in Cheltenham about nine years ago. he died at Cheltenham the ninth of last July. I have three children by him now living with me namely Henry aged seven years   Thomas aged five years and George aged three years   I and my said three children are now actually Chargeable to the Parish of Cheltenham – I knew my late husband about a twelvemonth before I married him. He never did any act to gain a Settlement after my marriage – during the time I knew him before the marriage he was working by the week as a Journeyman – [signed]
1841: *Thomas Hope (aged 30; plumber) lived with wife Esther (25) and three children John (Henry) (5), Thomas (3), and George (2) in York St, Cheltenham (HO107/353/5/47/16).* **1843:** *death of Thomas Hope (buried at New Burial Ground, Cheltenham 13 July, aged 32);* ***removed to Newent (husband's settlement).*** **1846:** *(RETURNED) the family rented house in Sun St, Cheltenham, when Esther Hope was complainant in assault case in Cheltenham (Cheltenham Chron. 30 Apr).* **1851:** *EH (38; widow, born London) was employed as nurse in house in Paddington, where eldest son John (Henry) (14; born Cheltenham) also worked as page (HO107/1467/818/8); EH's other two children lodged in Poplar Cottage, Elmstone St, Cheltenham: Thomas (14) and George Hope (12), both "scholars" born Cheltenham (HO107/1973/630/24).* [PS/CH/RA/2/7:5-6. Removal expenses for "Hope" to Newent £1/5/6 (3Q 1843: D4178).]

43057SE: Thurs 24 Aug 1843 – **Mary Ann Hardwidge**, inmate in Cheltenham Workhouse, and two children **Henry** and **Charles:** I am a native of the parish of Axbridge in the County of Somerset and am 23 years of age. I was married Seven Years ago last Christmas in the parish

Church of Axbridge aforesaid to my husband Richard Hardwidge by whom I have two Children namely Henry aged seven Years and Charles aged four Years   I always lived in Axbridge aforesaid until my said Marriage – I lived with my said husband in Axbridge aforesaid for three Years after our Marriage and rented a house there for that time at five pounds a Year. I and my husband then went to Bristol where we remained about three months in Lodgings. We then came to Cheltenham – where We have been residing ever since in Lodgings at one Shillings and nine pence a week until March last when my said husband deserted me and I do not know where he now is   I and my said Children are now chargeable to the parish of Cheltenham [signed]

1841: *MAH's sons Henry (aged 4) and Charles (2) were inmates of Axbridge Union Workhouse, Som (HO107/967/11/28/8); father Richard (24) lived in Cheltenham, as Constable at the Rural Constabulary Barracks (HO107/353/17/3/2).* **1843:** *husband Richard imprisoned at Northleach House of Correction, aged 25, for being "idle and disorderly", receiving a sentence of one calendar month with hard labour; MAH and children admitted into Cheltenham Workhouse on 20 July;* **removed to Axbridge (husband's settlement).** **1848:** *MAH is perhaps the person of that name who emigrated without family to America (New York) July, aged 30, aboard the* Liberty. **1851:** *Henry Hardwidge (14; born Axbridge) lived as house servant at home of George Brice, innkeeper, in Compton Bishop, Som (HO107/1937/32/9).* [PS/CH/RA/2/7:7. Removal expenses for "Hardwidge" to Axbridge £2/9/- and £4/10/6 (3Q 1843: D4178).]

43058SE: Thurs 31 Aug 1843 – John Harris, relating to the place of settlement of son **William Harris**, "lunatic": That he is about Sixty three years of age and the first place he remembers himself was in the parish of Haresfield in the said County where his parents resided as long as he can remember and his Father gained a settlement in that parish by renting a Farm there and residing upon it for several years at more than ten pounds a Year and resided there up to his death what [*sic*] happened about 58 Years ago   That his Mother died about thirteen Years ago in the said parish of Haresfield That he has never done any act to gain a settlement in his own right

   That about twenty Years ago he was several times Relieved by the Overseers of Haresfield aforesaid whilst he was residing in the City of Gloucester

   That about twelve Years ago he was relieved by Mr Grizzell the then Overseer of Haresfield aforesaid with a sum of two pounds ten shillings and was then residing in the said parish of Cheltenham

   That in the month of December last he was with his Wife removed by orders of removal from the said parish of Cheltenham to the said Parish of Haresfield by whom he was received and relieved. That such orders of removal were not appealed against. That about forty Years ago he was married to his wife Elizabeth in the parish of Saint Michael in the City of Gloucester by whom he had his said Son William now aged twenty nine years   that his said Son has never done any act to gain a settlement in his own right. That his said Son is now actually Chargeable to the said parish of Cheltenham – That his said Son is a Lunatic and cannot give evidence about his Settlement [mark]

1843: *removed to Haresfield (father's settlement).* [PS/CH/RA/2/7:8. Removal expenses for "Harris" to Haresfield £1/15/- (3Q 1843: D4178). See **42083RO** (John Harris: 5 Dec 1842).]

43059SE: Fri 1 Sept 1843 – **Elizabeth Beale**, inmate of Cheltenham Workhouse; also father John Beale, cordwainer, currently residing in Tirley, relating to the settlement of daughter.

John Beale: That about twenty seven years ago I was married to my late Wife Mary in the parish of Saint Mary de lode in the City of Gloucester by whom I had my said Daughter Elizabeth who was born in the said parish of Tirley about Eighteen years ago. About 16 or 17 Years ago I was appointed Constable for the said parish of Tirley at a Court Leet and Court Baron of the Right Honourable Earl Coventry and served such office for the space of two successive Years and resided in the said parish during the whole of that time with my said Wife and Daughter in a house which I rented there. I have done no act since to gain a settlement [signed]

Elizabeth Beale: I have never done any act to gain a settlement in my own right   I am now actually chargeable to the parish of Cheltenham aforesaid [mark]

1841: *EB (aged 15) lived as servant at house of Sarah Merrick, High St, Tewkesbury (HO107/380/4/5/4).* **1843:** *EB an inmate of Cheltenham Workhouse variously between 31 Aug 1843 and 27 Mar 1844*

(G/CH/60/4); removed to Tirley (father's settlement); birth of daughter Maria registered 4Q at Tewkesbury (baptised at Tewkesbury 21 Jan 1844, when Elizabeth lived in High St, Tewkesbury). **1844:** *(RETURNED) Maria apparently died aged 2 (buried 22 Aug at Cheltenham).* **1851:** *EB (aged 25, born Tirley) lived as servant in Tirley, in house of John Hayward, butcher (HO107/1973/699/13).* [PS/CH/RA/2/7:9. Removal expenses for "Beale" to Tirley 16/- (3Q 1843: D4178).]

43060SE: Wed 6 Sept 1843 – **William Hooper**, butcher, wife **Esther**, and five children **Jane**, **William**, **Richard**, **George**, and **Samuel**: I am about thirty two years of age   About twenty one Years ago I was apprenticed by Indenture duly executed by Solomon Hopson of Pagan Hill in the parish of Stroud in the said County Butcher for the term of Seven Years. I duly served the whole term and slept in my Masters house at Pagan Hill aforesaid the whole time

I have never done any act to gain a settlement elsewhere. About fourteen years ago I was married to my present Wife Esther in the parish Church of Stroud aforesaid by whom I have five Children namely Jane aged twelve Years William aged Eleven Years Richard aged nine Years George aged six Years and Samuel aged three Years. I and my said Wife and Children are now actually chargeable to the said parish of Cheltenham [signed]

1841: *WH (aged 30; labourer) lived with wife Esther (30), and children Jane (12), William (9), Richard (6), George (4), and Samuel (1) in Upper Bath Rd, Cheltenham (HO107/353/12/9/13).* **1843:** *removed to Stroud (apprenticeship).* **1844:** *(RETURNED) birth of son Charles registered at Cheltenham 2Q; both Charles and Samuel baptised at Cheltenham 17 Nov.* **1846:** *birth of daughter Rhoda registered 4Q 1846 at Cheltenham.* [PS/CH/RA/2/7:10. Removal expenses for "Hooper" to Stroud £1/2/- (4Q 1843: D4178).]

43061SE: Sat 23 Sept 1843 – **Elizabeth Perrott** (also **Perrot**), widow: I am about seventy six years of age   In the year 1792 I was married to my late husband Richard Perrott in the parish of Painswick in the said County. In the year 1805 my said husband purchased a house at the top of Vicarage Lane in the said parish of Painswick of M[r]. Edward Gardner for Three hundred pounds and paid the purchase money for it   My said husband resided in such house with myself for about four Years after he purchased it and died there about thirty four years ago. I resided in such house for about two years after my husbands death. I have never done any act to gain a settlement since – I have been constantly relieved by the parish officers of Painswick aforesaid for about Sixteen or Seventeen Years last past during the whole of which time I have been residing in the said parish of Cheltenham   The Parish officers of Painswick aforesaid only at present allowing me Eighteen pence a week it is insufficient for my support and I have applied to the parish officers of Cheltenham for relief and am now actually chargeable to the said Parish of Cheltenham [signed Elizebeh Perrtt]

1843: *removed to Painswick (her or husband's settlement by estate).* **1844:** *(RETURNED) EP died at Cheltenham (buried 10 May at New Burial Ground).* [PS/CH/RA/2/7:11. Removal expenses for "Perrott" to Painswick 10/- (3Q 1843: D4178). See Gray **530** (EP: 9 Oct 1824) (born Miserden, son Edwin), **44053SE** (daughter Elizabeth Perrott: 26 Oct 1844).]

43062SE: Sat 30 Sept 1843 – Thomas Gale, servant, relating to the place of settlement of son **Thomas Gale:** That in the Year 1813 being then unmarried and having no Child or Children he was hired by Samuel Stephens Esquire of the parish of Awliscombe in the County of Devon as Groom for a Year at the Yearly wages of Fifteen Guineas   that he served his said Master two years under such hiring and received all his wages: that he travelled about with his said Master to several places during his service but he is quite positive he slept in his Masters house in the said parish of Awliscombe for more than the last forty days of such service   that he has never done any act to gain a settlement since. that soon after he left his said Masters service he was married to his present Wife Elizabeth in the parish of The Holy Trinity in the City of Exeter by whom he had his said son Thomas now aged near twenty eight years   that his said Son has never been hired for a Year or done any act to gain a settlement in his own right. That his said Son is now Insance [for "Insane"] and actually chargeable to the said parish of Cheltenham [signed]

1843: *removed to Awliscombe, Devon (father's settlement).* [PS/CH/RA/2/7:12. Removal expenses for "Gale" for Awliscombe, Honiton, Devon £3/6/- (4Q 1843: D4178).]

43063SE: Sat 7 Oct 1843 – Mary Barrett, wife of John Barrett, relating to the settlement of son **John Lamb:** About 29 Years ago I was married to my first husband William Lamb in the parish Church of Shipton Moyne in the said County Tailor. That I was delivered of my said [son] John about 28 years ago in the said Parish of Shipton Moyne. I have heard that my said husband William Lamb gained a settlement in the Parish of Tetbury in the said County by apprenticeship to his Father David Lamb of the said Parish of Tetbury Tailor

That soon after the birth of my said Son John my said husband William Lamb deserted me and my two Children and I have not seen him since

Upon such desertion I became chargeable to the Parish of Minchinhampton in the said County and was with my two Children of whom my said [son] John was one removed by orders from the said Parish of Minchinhampton to the said Parish of Tetbury and delivered to the Overseer there. I then went to live with my Father in the parish of Shipton Moyne aforesaid and was relieved for about Eight Years by the parish officers of Tetbury aforesaid whilst I was so residing in the Parish of Shipton Moyne. My said husband [William] Lamb has been dead some years   The orders of removal were not appealed against [signed]
[PS/CH/RA/2/7:13. See **43065SE** (JL: 17 Oct 1843).]

43064SE: Thurs 12 Oct 1843 – **Sarah Wager**, widow, with children **Thomas**, **Rosina** (also **Rosa**), and **Samuel**; also John Cugley, tailor, residing in Stroud, relating to the settlement of daughter Sarah Wager. *John Cugley*: I am about 61 years of age and have lived in the said parish of Stroud all my lifetime, in the year 1805 I was married to my wife Martha in the parish of Bisley in the said County by whom I had my said Daughter Sarah Wager now aged twenty eight years who was born in the said parish of Stroud [signed]
Sarah Wager: I am about twenty eight years of age. I lived in the parish of Stroud in the said County with my Father John Cugley and his Wife Martha until I was married which was in the parish Church of Stroud on the 26 of August 1837 to my late husband Thomas Wager who died a week ago in Cheltenham. In a few weeks after my Marriage I and my husband came to Cheltenham to reside and lived in a house there at Six pounds a Year ever since   my husband never done any act to gain a Settlement since my said Marriage – I have never heard where my said husband was settled

His Father and Mother are both dead and I do not know where any of his family are living

I have three Children now living with me which I had by my said husband namely Thomas aged five years Rosina aged three years and Samuel aged fifteen months   I am now actually chargeable to the said parish of Cheltenham [mark]
1841: *SW (aged 20) lived with husband Thomas (20; labourer) in Soho Place, Coach Rd, Cheltenham, with children Thomas (2) and Rosaline (1) (HO107/353/10/22/11).* **1843:** *death of husband Thomas Wager (buried at Cheltenham 7 Oct, aged 30);* **removed to Stroud (father's presumed settlement).** **1845-6:** *(RETURNED) from 1Q 1845 until 4Q 1846 SW and three children received parish relief from Stroud as non-settled residents of Cheltenham (G/CH/9d/1).* **1851:** *mother Martha Cugley (76; housekeeper, born Bisley) looked after SW's children as guardian, in Coach Rd, Cheltenham: Thomas (12; scholar), Rosaline (11; scholar), and Samuel (8) (HO107/1973/546/14).* **1854:** *SW remarried 20 June 1854, to car proprietor Richard Green, at Whitnash (near Leamington), Warks.* **1861:** *the couple lived with two of Richard Green's children and Rosaline Wager in Leamington (RG9/222/61/32).* [PS/CH/RA/2/7:14, 15. Removal expenses for "Wager" to Stroud £1/-/- (4Q 1843: D4178).]

43065SE: Tues 17 Oct 1843 – **John Lamb**, wife **Harriet**, and daughter **Harriet:** I have never done any act to gain a settlement in my own right   About seven years ago I was married to my present Wife Harriet in the parish Church of Cheltenham by whom I have one Child named Harriet aged three Years

I am now actually chargeable to the said Parish of Cheltenham [signed]
1841: *JL (aged 25; labourer) lived with wife Harriet (20) and two children Mary (6) and Harriet (7 mo) in Victoria St, Fairview, Cheltenham (HO107/353/4/10/13).* **1843: removed to Tetbury (father's settlement).** **1844:** *(RETURNED) JL buried at New Burial Ground, Cheltenham 12 Jan.* **1849:** *widow Harriet remarried 1*

Apr at Cheltenham, to William Hill, labourer. [PS/CH/RA/2/7:16. Removal expenses for "Lamb" to Tetbury 19/- (4Q 1843) and £1/6/- (1Q 1844: D4178). See **43063SE** (mother Mary Barrett for JL: 7 Oct 1843).]

43066SE: Tues 31 Oct 1843 – **James Hiscocks** (also **Hiscox**), inmate of Cheltenham Workhouse: That about Six Years ago he rented a house in Cricklade Street in the parish of Cirencester in the said County of M^r. Smith at thirty pounds a Year   that he resided in such house from that time until about four months ago – that he paid the first five years rent. that he was duly rated to all poor rates made for the said parish of Cirencester for the said time and paid all such rates for the first five Years he resided in such house. that he has done no act to gain a settlement since and is now actually chargeable to the said parish of Cheltenham [signed]
1841: *JH (aged 71; publican) lived with Samuel Hiscock (26; baker) in Cricklade St, Cirencester (HO107/380/1/28/3).* **1843:** *removed to Cirencester (renting).* **1853:** *death of JH at Cirencester Union Workhouse (buried 28 Dec, aged 85).* [PS/CH/RA/2/7:17. Removal expenses for "Hiscox" to Cirencester 13/6 (4Q 1843: D4178).]

43067SE: Sat 18 Nov 1843 – **Charles Steer**, labourer and inmate of Cheltenham Workhouse: That in the Year 1834 being actually charg[e]able to the parish of Walcot near Bath he was duly removed by orders of removal from the said Parish of Walcot to the parish of St Michael in the City of Bath   that he was received by virtue of such orders into the Workhouse of the said Parish of St Michael and supported there for about three Months. That such orders of Removal were not appeal against or in any way abandoned   that the said orders of Removal are now in the custody or possession of the Overseers of the said Parish of Saint Michael. that since the time of the said Removal into the said Workhouse this Examinant hath done no act whereby to gain a settlement. that he is now actually chargeable to the said parish of Cheltenham [signed]
1843: *perhaps removed to St Michael's, Bath, where accepted previously, though supporting documentation is absent.* **1844:** *CS discharged from Cheltenham Workhouse 28 Feb (G/CH/60/4).* [PS/CH/RA/2/7:18.]

43068SE: 18 Nov 1843 – **Samuel Stone**, labourer, with wife **Eliza**: I am about 39 Years of age. About 28 Years ago being then unmarried and having no Child or Children I was hired by Mr Barry then residing in the Crescent Minories in the parish of St Botolph Aldgate in the City of London as Postillion [*sic*] for a Year at the wages of Fifteen pounds. That he [*sic*] served five Years under such hiring and slept in his [*adjusted to* my] Masters house at the Crescent aforesaid the greater part of the time and certainly for the last three or four Months before I was discharged. I have done no Act since to gain a settlement. About nine years ago I was married to my present Wife Eliza in the parish Church of Cheltenham
   I am now actually chargeable to the said Parish of Cheltenham [signed]
1843: *SS charged Nov at Public Office in Cheltenham with ill-treating and deserting wife Eliza, countering that she had sold his goods and absconded with another man; SS ordered to pay 3s. per week to support his wife and to be examined as to settlement* (Cheltenham Chron. *23 Nov*); ***removed to St Botolph Aldgate, London (hiring and service).*** [PS/CH/RA/2/7:19. Removal expenses for "Stone" to London £4/1/6 (1Q 1844: D4178).]

43069SE: Sat 2 Dec 1843 – **Mary Barnes**, widow: I am about 66 years of age. I was born in the parish of Sedgeley [= Sedgley] in the County of Stafford and where I resided until I was about 25 years of age when I was married to my late husband William Barnes in the parish Church of Sedgeley aforesaid   after I was married I continued to live with my said husband in Sedgeley aforesaid until his death which happened about 25 Years ago   I continued to live in Sedgeley aforesaid for about five years after my husbands death when I came to Cheltenham and have resided in a house in Elm Street there ever since at a rent of two shillings a week and have rented no other property
   I am now actually chargeable to the said parish of Cheltenham [mark]
1843: *removal uncertain: evidence appears inconclusive.* **1847:** *probably the MB who died 11 Jan at 3 Worcester St, Cheltenham, aged 66 (Cheltenham Chron. 21 Jan).* [PS/CH/RA/2/7:20.]

43070SE: Mon 4 Dec 1843 – **James Clifford**, labourer, wife **Elizabeth**, and child **Sarah Ann**; also Mary Clifford, widow, relating to the settlement of son James Clifford. *Mary Clifford*: I am 68 Years of age. About 42 Years ago I was married to my late husband William Clifford in the parish of Swindon in the said County who died about 18 Years ago in Cheltenham   soon after my husbands death I with my Children became Chargeable to the said parish of Cheltenham and were removed from thence by orders of removal to the Parish of Upton St Leonards in the said County which orders were appealed against and quashed my said husbands settlement being upon the trial of such appeal at Gloucester Sessions proved to have been in the parish of Swindon in the said County by Birth. That I have ever since been relieved by the Overseers of Swindon whilst I have during that time resided in the parish of Cheltenham   About twenty six Years ago I was delivered of my said Son James in the parish of Cheltenham [mark]

James Clifford: I have never been hired for a Year or rented a tenement of the annual value of ten pounds or done any act to gain a settlement in my own right

About Eight weeks ago I was married to my present Wife Elizabeth at Cheltenham by whom I have one Child name is Sarah Ann aged Six weeks   I am now actually chargeable to the said Parish of Cheltenham [mark]

1843: *birth of daughter Sarah Ann (baptised 30 Nov), when family lived in Naunton Fields in Cheltenham;* ***removed to Swindon (father's settlement)****; death of Sarah Ann at nine weeks and also of her mother (aged 23) (both buried at New Burial Ground, Cheltenham 28 Dec).* [PS/CH/RA/2/7:21, 22. Removal expenses for "Clifford" to Swindon 2/6 (1Q 1844: D4178). See Gray **586** (mother Mary Clifford: 8 Nov 1825), referred to here, and **40019SE** (brother Henry Clifford: 25 Jan 1840).]

43071SE: Sat 9 Dec 1843 – **George Price**, labourer, wife **Eliza**, and three children **Caroline**, **George**, and **Sarah Ann**: I am about thirty two Years of age   about Sixteen Years ago being then unmarried and having no Child or Children I was hired by Mr Symonds of Hailesmore in the parish of Pauntley in the said County Farmer for a Year to drive the Oxen at the wages of two pounds ten shillings. I served the whole Year and received my Years wages and Slept in my Masters house at Pauntley aforesaid the whole time. I was then again hired by the said Mr Symonds for another Year at the wages of two pounds fifteen shillings which year I also served and received my wages and slept in my Masters house at Pauntley aforesaid the whole of that Year. I have done no act since to gain a settlement   Five Years ago last July I was married to my present Wife Eliza in the parish Church of Cheltenham by whom I have three Children namely Caroline aged four Years George aged two Years and a half and Sarah Ann aged seven months

I am now actually chargeable to the said Parish of Cheltenham [mark]

1839: *daughter Caroline baptised 20 Oct, when family lived in Malvern Place, Cheltenham.* **1841:** *GP (aged 30; agricultural labourer) lived with wife Eliza (25) in Alstone, Cheltenham (HO107/353/11/5/4-5).* **1843:** ***removed to Pauntley (hiring and service).*** **1846:** *(RETURNED) birth of daughter Eliza at Alstone (baptised 31 May).* **1849:** *baptism of son Joseph at Alstone (25 Feb).* **1850:** *baptism of daughter Jane at Alstone (22 Sept).* **1851:** *the family lived at Higgs Cottage, Alstone Rd, Alstone, Cheltenham: GP (40; labourer, born Ross-on-Wye, Heref), Eliza (37), Caroline (11; scholar), Sarah Ann (7; scholar), Joseph (3; scholar), and infant Jane (HO107/1973/571/3).* [PS/CH/RA/2/7:23. Removal expenses for "Price" to Pauntley £1/7/- (1Q 1844: D4178).]

43072SE: Thurs 14 Dec 1843 – **Thomas Sturmey** (also **Sturmy**), cordwainer, wife **Elizabeth**, and five children **Edward**, **William**, **Esther**, **Henry**, and **Mary**: When I was about fourteen Years old I was apprenticed by Indenture duly stamped executed and attested to Job Adkins of Dumbleton in the said County of Gloucester Cordwainer for the term of seven Years   I served the whole term and slept in my Masters house at Dumbleton aforesaid the whole time   I produce such Indenture the subscribing Witness to which is now dead. the name "Thomas Sturmey" thereto subscribed is my hand writing – the Mark thereto subscribed is the mark of the said Job Adkins who is now dead. I have done no act since to gain a settlement   About thirteen year Years ago I was married to my present Wife Elizabeth in the parish Church of Didbrook in the said County by whom I have five Children namely Edward aged Eleven Years William aged nine Years Esther aged seven Years

Henry aged four Years and Mary aged nine months. I am now actually chargeable to the said parish of Cheltenham [signed]

1841: *TS (aged 30) lived with wife Elizabeth (30) and children Edward (9), William (7), Esther (5), and Henry (2) in Barnet's (Barnard's) Row, Cheltenham (HO107/353/15/55/19).* **1843: removed to Dumbleton (apprenticeship). 1849:** *(RETURNED) birth of son (John) George registered at Cheltenham 3Q.* **1851:** *the family lived at 5 Hall's Court, Fairview, Cheltenham: TS (44; shoemaker and letter-carrier, born Winchcombe), Elizabeth (38; dressmaker, born Didbrook), and children Edward (19; porter, born Winchcombe), William (17; butcher, born Winchcombe), Henry (12; scholar, born Cheltenham), Mary (8; born Cheltenham), and George (1; "at home", born Cheltenham) (HO107/1973/164/13).* [PS/CH/RA/2/7:24. Removal expenses for "Sturmey" to Dumbleton 17/9 (1Q 1844: D4178).]

43073SE: Thurs 21 Dec 1843 – **Sarah Hurn** (also **Hurne**), single woman, inmate of Cheltenham Workhouse: That about thirteen Years ago being then unmarried and having no Child or Children I was hired by Mr William[s] Foreman of the Plough Inn in the parish of Old Sodbury in the Said County for a Year at the Wages of Five Pounds   I continued in such service five Years under such hiring and received all my wages and Slept in my said Masters house at Old Sodbury aforesaid the whole time   I have done no act since to gain a settlement. I am now actually chargeable to the said parish of Cheltenham [mark]

1843: removed to Old Sodbury (hiring and service). 1844: *presumably the SH buried at Yate, near Chipping Sodbury 2 Mar, aged 57.* [PS/CH/RA/2/7:25; G/CH/60/4. Removal expenses for "Hurn" to Sodbury £1/7/- and £1/14/- (1Q 1844: D4178).]

43074SE: Sat 23 Dec 1843 – **Peter Whithorn** (also **Whitton, Witham, Whiton, Witten, Wittern**), labourer, wife **Sarah**, and three children, **Ann**, **Edward**, and **Henry:** The first place I remember myself was in the parish of Bredon in the County of Worcester   As long as I can remember my Father John Whithorn was the Owner of a House and an Acre of Land in the said Parish of Bredon and in which house my said Father and my Mother Ann Whithorn with myself resided for several Years up to the death of my said Father which happened about 16 Years ago – My Mother and myself resided in such house for about two years after my Fathers death when I left my said Mother. I have never been hired for a Year or rented a tenement of the annual value of ten pounds or done any act to gain a settlement in my own right   About Nine years ago I was married to my present Wife Sarah in the parish Church of Cheltenham by whom I have three Children namely Ann aged seven Years Edward aged three Years and Henry aged fourteen months. I am now actually Chargeable to the said parish of Cheltenham [signed]

1841: *PW (aged 25; railway labourer) lived with wife Sarah (25) and children Ann (5) and Edward (1) in Kingswood, Chippenham, Wilts (HO107/1172/5/13/18-19).* **1842:** *son Henry baptised at Ledbury, Heref 28 July.* **1843: removed to Bredon (father's settlement). 1847:** *(RETURNED) birth of son John registered at Cheltenham 4Q.* **1848:** *John baptised 23 Jan at Tewkesbury; death registered 3Q at Cheltenham.* **1851:** *the family had moved to Vale St, Birmingham: PW (34; labourer, born Bredon, Worcs), Sarah (38; born Wootton Bassett, Wilts), Edward (11; born Wootton Bassett, Wilts), and Henry (6; born Ledbury, Heref) (HO107/2055/302/45).* [PS/CH/RA/2/7:26. Removal expenses for "Whithorn" to Bredon 18/3 (1Q 1844: D4178).]

43075SE: Thurs 28 Dec 1843 – **Thomas Daniels**, weaver: The first place I remember myself was in the parish of Minchinhampton in the said County where my parents resided. When I was about twelve Years of age I was apprenticed by Indenture by the Parish Officers of Minchinhampton aforesaid to John Harris of the same Parish Weaver for the term of Seven Years. I served the whole term and slept in my Masters house at Minchinhampton aforesaid the whole time   at the end of the term my said Master delivered to me the Indenture but I have since lost it   I have done no act since to gain a settlement. I am now actually chargeable to the said Parish of Cheltenham – There was only one Indenture [mark]

1842: *removed to Minchinhampton (apprenticeship): see* **42038RO** *(TD: 14 Apr 1842).* **1843: removed to Minchinhampton (presumed) (apprenticeship).** [PS/CH/RA/2/7:27.]

43076SE: 28 Dec 1843 – **James Aldridge**, labourer, wife **Esther**, and children **Ellen**, **William Henry**, and **Thomas:** The first place I remember myself was in the parish of Stroud in the said

County where my parents have resided ever since   My Father James Aldridge resided there in a house of his own for many years which he Mortgaged about twelve Years ago for forty pounds. I have never done any act to gain a settlement in my own right. About twelve Years ago I was removed by orders from the said Parish of Cheltenham to the said Parish of Stroud and delivered to the Overseer there who put me and my family into the Workhouse there. the orders of removal were not appealed against   About twenty four Years ago I was married to my first Wife Sarah in the parish Church of Saint Mary de lode in the City of Gloucester who died about Eleven Years ago by whom I have one Child named Ellen aged thirteen years, About three Years ago I was married to my present Wife Esther in the said parish Church of Saint Mary de lode by whom I have two Children namely William Henry aged two years and a half and Thomas aged one Year I am now actually chargeable to the said Parish of Cheltenham [signed]

1831: *JA removed to Stroud (office-holding): see* **31088SE** *(JA: 18 June).* **1832:** *death of first wife Sarah in Ruscombe, Stroud (buried at Randwick 18 Oct).* **1841:** *(RETURNED) JA (aged 40; labourer) lived with children Sophia (20), Jessie (13), Frederick (11) and Ellen (10) in Stanhope St, Cheltenham (HO107/353/9/53/7).* **1843: *removed to Stroud (presumed) (father's settlement).*** **1845:** *(RETURNED) death of son Thomas (buried at New Burial Ground, Cheltenham 5 Aug, aged 2).* **1848:** *death of son William (buried at New Burial Ground, Cheltenham 17 Jan, aged 7).* **1851:** *JA (57; labourer, born Stroud) lived at 23 Cleeveland St, Cheltenham, with second wife Esther (43; charwoman, born Uley), daughter Eliza (2; born Cheltenham), and Esther's son George Glanville (15; dustman, born Cheltenham) from previous marriage (HO107/1973/446/11).* [PS/CH/RA/2/7:28. See Removal expenses for "Aldridge" to Bisley £1/12/6 and £1/10/- (4Q 1843) and to Minchinhampton £1/9/6 (1Q 1844: D4178).]

43077SE: Thurs 4 Jan 1844 – **Hannah Welch**, widow: About forty Years ago I was married to my late husband John Welch in the parish Church of Swindon in the said County who died about twelve months ago   I have heard and believes [*sic*] that my husband gained a settlement in the Parish of Tibberton in the said County by hiring and service there before he was married

About Eighteen Years ago we were relieved by the parish Officers of Tibberton whilst we were residing in the parish of Cheltenham and were continued [*sic*] to be relieved for about ten years successively by the Parish Officer of Tibberton aforesaid during the whole of which time we were living in the said Parish of Cheltenham. My said husband never done any act to gain a settlement since our Marriage and I have done no act to gain a settlement since his death   I am now actually chargeable to the said Parish of Cheltenham [mark]

1844: *removed to Tibberton (Newent Poor Law Union) (husband's settlement)*; *John Welch buried at New Burial Ground, Cheltenham 4 Feb, aged 70.* **1845-8:** *(RETURNED) from 3Q 1845 until 1Q 1848 widow Hannah (67) received parish relief from Newent as a non-settled resident of Cheltenham (G/CH/9d/1).* **1851:** *HW (72; formerly labourer's wife, born Swindon) lived in Kingsditch Lane, Cheltenham (HO107/1973/529/36).* [PS/CH/RA/2/7:29. Removal exprenses for "Welch" to Tibberton 17/6 (1Q 1844: D4178).]

1844

44001SE: 4 Jan 1844 – **William Bacon**, carpenter, inmate of Cheltenham Workhouse, wife **Diana** (also **Dianna**, **Dinah**), and three children **Charles**, **Matilda**, and **Robert:** I am about thirty Years of age   when I was 15 Years of age I was apprentice [*sic*] by Indentures by the Parish officers of Kirkby Mallory in the County of Leicester to James Spiers of the parish of Earls Shilton [= Earl Shilton] in the said County of Leicester Carpenter and Joiner to serve from that time until I was twenty one Years of age

A Premium of Fifteen pounds was paid with me and the Indentures were properly executed. I served under such Indentures about three years and a half when my Master failed   I slept in my said Masters house at Earls Shilton aforesaid the whole three years and a half   My said Master then gave me up the Indenture and the same was burnt

I have done no act since to gain a settlement

I was married in the year 1835 to my Wife Diana in the parish Church of Lyminster in the County of Sussex by whom I have three Children namely Charles aged seven years Matilda aged four years and Robert aged four months. I am now actually chargeable to the said parish of Cheltenham [signed]

1844: *Charles (aged 7) and Matilda Bacon (7) were inmates of Charlton Kings Workhouse for children from 13 Jan until 7 Feb (G/CH/60/3); they and the rest of the extended Bacon family had been admitted into Cheltenham Workhouse on 4 Jan (G/CH/60/4);* **removed to Earl Shilton, Leics (apprenticeship).** **1845:** *birth of daughter Caroline registered at Chichester, Sussex 2Q.* **1851:** *Diana Bacon (aged 50; tramp and vagrant) states that she is a widow (Newick, Sussex: HO107/1643/167/1).* **1871:** *Robert (aged 26; labourer) and Charles Bacon (40; labourer) lived with mother Diana (aged 72; place of birth unknown) in Ore, Sussex (RG10/1027/102/72).* [PS/CH/RA/2/7:30. Removal expenses for "Bacon" to Earl Shilton, Leics £4/14/- (1Q 1844: D4178). See **44002SE** (Diana Bacon for Mary Ann Smedley: 6 Jan), **44003SE** (Diana Bacon for Caroline Shepherd: 6 Jan), **44018SE** (Diana Bacon for Sarah Shepherd: 5 Feb 1844).]

44002SE: Sat 6 Jan 1844 – Diana Bacon, wife of William Bacon, relating to the settlement of daughter **Mary Ann Smedley**, inmate of Cheltenham Workhouse: My Maiden name was Smedley   About Sixteen years ago (never having been then married) I was delivered of my said Daughter Mary Ann who is an illegitimate Child in the parish of Limpsfield in the County of Surrey the Parish officers of which Parish allowed half a crown a week for about five Years for her support – my said Daughter has never done any act to gain a settlement in her own right having lived with me to the present time   My said daughter is now actually chargeable to the said Parish of Cheltenham [mark]

1844: *removed to Limpsfield, Surrey (birth).* [PS/CH/RA/2/7:31. Removal expenses for "Smedley" to Limpsfield, Surrey £5/6/6 (1Q 1844: D4178). See **44001SE** (William Bacon: 4 Jan 1843).]

44003SE: 6 Jan 1844 – Diana Bacon, wife of William Bacon, relating to the settlement of daughter **Caroline Shepherd** (also **Shephard**, **Sheppard**, **Shepperd**), inmate of Cheltenham Workhouse: My Maiden name was Smedley   about 14 Years ago I was married to my late husband James Shepherd who died in the Month of August 1832 and was buried at Cuckfield in the County of Sussex. On the 18th of March 1834 I was delivered of my said Daughter Caroline in the parish of Lindfield in the County of Sussex who is an illegitimate Child. I was married to my present husband William Bacon in the year 1835 at Lyminster in the County of Sussex

My said Daughter has never done any act to gain a settlement and is now actually chargeable to the Parish of Cheltenham [mark]

1844: *removed (at least initially) to Lindfield, Sussex (birth); Caroline Shepherd (as Caroline Bacon) was an inmate of Charlton Kings Workhouse for children from 13 Jan until 5 Feb (G/CH/60/3).* **1851:** *CS perhaps the Caroline Sheppard (aged 17; barmaid) who lived and worked at the White Hart, Henfield, Sussex (HO107/1647/505/22).* [PS/CH/RA/2/7:32. Removal expenses for "Shepperd" to Lindfield, Sussex £4/16/- (1Q 1844: D4178). See **44001SE** (William Bacon: 4 Jan 1843).]

44004SE: Thurs 11 Jan 1844 – **John Bennett**, gardener, wife **Mary**, and three children **Charles**, **Elizabeth**, and **James:** I am about 53 years of Age. About 31 years ago being then unmarried and having no Child or Children I was hired by Mr Brookes of Sheep Street in the parish of Stow on the Wold in the said County Solicitor for a Year as Gardener at Four pounds a year. I served the whole year [and] received my years wages and slept in my said Masters house at Stow on the Wold aforesaid the whole Year

I have never since done any act to gain a settlement. I was married to my present Wife Mary about twenty nine years ago in the parish Church of Stow on the Wold aforesaid. I resided at Stow on the Wold aforesaid after my said Marriage until about Eight years ago when I came to Cheltenham aforesaid. I have resided in Bloomsbury place Cheltenham for the last seven Years and rented a house there for the first two years of which I paid twelve pounds a Year and for the next five years ten pounds a Year   I have never paid any poor rates or any other Rates or taxes since I have been in Cheltenham. I have by my said Wife three Children now living with me namely Charles aged 15 Years Elizabeth aged 11 Years and James aged 5. Years. I am now actually Chargeable to the said Parish of Cheltenham [mark]

1841: *JB (aged 45; gardener) lived with wife Mary (40) and children Mary (20), George (18), Henry (16), Charles (14; journeyman baker), Thomas (12), Elizabeth (9), and James (2) in Bloomsbury Place, Cheltenham (HO107/353/16/54/24).* **1844:** *removed to Stow-on-the-Wold (hiring and service).* **1851:** *(RETURNED) the family lived in Lower Swell, near Stow-on-the-Wold, with Mary Bennett's father: Robert Bettridge (83; carpenter and widower), JB (58; gardener, born Longborough), Mary (54; born Stow), Thomas (21; labourer), Elizabeth (19), and James (11; children all apparently born Stow), (HO107/1970/326/19).* [PS/CH/RA/2/7:33. Removal expenses for "Bennett" to Stow-on-the-Wold £1/6/6 (2Q 1844: D4178). See **51019RO** (Henry Bennett: 6 Dec 1851).]

44005SE: 11 Jan 1844 – **Thomas Simmonds** (also **Simmons**), labourer, wife **Lucy**, and daughter **Ann:** About Eighteen years ago being then unmarried and having no Child or Children I was hired by Mr John Warder of the Parish of Swindon in the said County Farmer for a Year as Carter at the wages of twelve pounds   I served three Years under such hiring and received all my wages and slept in my said Masters house at Swindon aforesaid the whole time   I have done no act since to gain a settlement. About 14 or 15 Years ago I was married to my Wife Lucy in the parish Church of Cheltenham by whom I have one Child named Ann aged three Years. I am now actually chargeable to the said parish of Cheltenham [mark]

1841: *TS (aged 40; agricultural labourer) lived with wife Lucy (30) and daughter Ann (6 mo) in Ryeworth, Charlton Kings (HO107/353/1/27/16).* **1844:** *removed to Swindon (hiring and service).* **1846:** *(RETURNED) daughters Mary and Sarah baptised 1 Feb at St Peter's Church in Cheltenham, when family lived at 4 Swindon Parade, Swindon Rd.* **1847:** *death of Mary Simmonds at 12 months (buried at Sevenhampton 18 Feb), though she lived in Swindon.* **1848:** *death of wife Lucy (buried at Swindon 10 June, aged 40).* **1850:** *death of TS (buried at Swindon 4 July, aged 48).* **1851:** *daughter Sarah (aged 5; scholar, born Cheltenham) lived with Lucy's sister Ann Collett and husband John in Stanway (HO107/1971/179/8).* [PS/CH/RA/2/7:34. Removal expenses for "Simmons" to Swindon 2/6 (1Q 1844: D4178).]

44006SE: 11 Jan 1844 – **Rachael Sparrow**, wife of Thomas Sparrow, labourer, relating to the settlement of son **George Wilkins:** My maiden name was Wilkins. About fifteen years ago being then unmarried and having no Child or Children I was hired by Mr John Ferrabee of the Thrupp in the Parish of Stroud in the said County Engineer for a Year at the wages of Six pounds. I served the whole year [and] received my wages and slept in my said Masters house at Thrupp in the parish of Stroud aforesaid the whole time. I continued in Such service for near two Years afterwards   I was not in any service afterwards for a Year or done any act to gain a settlement in my own right

About Eight Years ago I was delivered of my said Son George in the parish of Minchinhampton in the said County who is an illegitimate Child

Two years last August I was married to my said husband Thomas Sparrow in Cheltenham aforesaid

My said Son George is now actually Chargeable to the said Parish of Cheltenham

About ten years ago I became chargeable to the parish of Saint Mary le bone in the County of Middlesex and was taken by the Overseer of that Parish before two Magistrates and examined as to my Parish who thereupon made orders for my removal to the said Parish of Stroud. I was taken to Stroud with such orders and received by the Overseers of the said Parish of Stroud who relieved me for some time

Such orders of removal were not appealed against [mark]

1841: *GW (aged 5) lived with mother Rachael Wilkins (30) in Bisley (HO107/349/3/19/5).* **1844: *removed to Stroud (mother's settlement)****; GW admitted to Cheltenham Workhouse 24 Apr for a week (G/CH/60/4). One or more George Wilkinses became involved in petty crime in Cheltenham and elsewhere in Glos in the 1840s and it is probable that he served at least one prison sentence for larceny.* **1847:** *a GW (11) was imprisoned for two months for larceny at Glos County Sessions on 5 Feb 1847.* **1851:** *a GW (15; errand boy, born Stroudwater) was a prisoner at the Northleach House of Correction at Hampnett (HO107/1969/382/25); mother Rachael Sparrow (39; laundress, born Minchinhampton) lived in Elm Place, Elm St, Cheltenham with husband Thomas Sparrow (56; labourer, born Bisley), and children Thomas (6; scholar, born Cheltenham) and Lucy Ann (3; born Cheltenham) (HO107/1973/430/27).* [PS/CH/RA/2/7:35. Removal expenses for "Wilkins" to Stroud 12/6 (1Q 1844: D4178).]

44007SE: Sat 13 Jan 1844 – **William Pitman** (also **Pittman**), labourer, wife **Hannah**, and four children **Thomas**, **James**, **Charles**, and **Jesse**: About fifteen years ago being then unmarried and having no Child or Children I was hired by Mr Joseph Yeend of the Parish of Elmstone Hardwicke in the said County Farmer for a Year as Carter at the wages of Seven pounds

I served the whole year and received my Years wages and slept in my Masters house at Elmstone Hardwicke aforesaid the whole time. I have done no Act since to gain a settlement   I was married to my present Wife Hannah in the parish Church of Bishops Cleeve about thirteen years ago by whom I have four Children namely Thomas aged 11 Years James aged six Years Charles aged four Years and Jesse aged one Year and a half   About Eleven Years ago I was removed by orders of removal from the Hamlet of Southam and Brockhampton to the said Parish of Elmstone Hardwicke and delivered to the Overseer there who have [*sic*] relieved me several times since and where I have resided until Michaelmas last. Such orders were not appealed against. I am now actually chargeable to the said parish of Cheltenham [mark]

1833: *baptism of son Thomas at Bishop's Cleeve, 7 July.* **1835:** *baptism of son George at Elmstone Hardwicke, 14 June.* **1841:** *WP (aged 30; agricultural labourer) lived with wife Hannah and three boys in Elmstone Hardwicke (HO107/369/9/3/2).* **1844: *removed to Elmstone Hardwicke (hiring and service).*** **1846:** *sons George and William baptised at Elmstone Hardwicke 18 May.* **1851:** *WP (41; born Eldersfield, Worcs) lived with wife Hannah (41; born Prestbury) and three sons Charles (10), Jesse (8), and George (4; all born Elmstone Hardwicke) in the Green, Elmstone Hardwicke.* [PS/CH/RA/2/7:36. Removal expenses for "Pittman" to Elmstone Hardwicke 9/6 (1Q 1844: D4178). See WP's earlier examination (PS/CH/RA/2/2, p. 10: Southam to Elmstone Hardwicke) on 12 Jan 1833.]

44008SE: 13 Jan 1844 – **John Lewis**, butcher, wife **Ann**, and son **Thomas**: About twelve Years ago being then unmarried and having no Child or Children I was hired by Edward [presumably for: Edwin] Danter of the Colonnade Cheltenham Butcher at the wages of Eight pounds. I served the whole Year and slept in my Masters premises in Cheltenham aforesaid the whole time – I cannot swear I received the twelve months wages. – I could have left the said Edward Danter at any time during the year. I received my wages now and then – sometimes he gave me a few shillings. It was sometime in the summer I went into his service and I think I lived with him a year and a quarter altogether. When I was going on the same Road I sometimes did errands for other people and they paid me for it. I only recollect receiving two pounds from him   I do not remember what else he paid me – he was in my debt when he went away. he did not pay me a year's wages. it was towards the spring of the Year when I left. I was not hired a second time by him but continued my Service as before. I lived with Mr Slack the butcher before I went to M^r. Danter – I went straight from Mr Slack's service into Mr Danter – he persuaded me to leave Mr Slack. – I went direct from M^r. Danter's services to Mr Ryan's – I was out of place more than a day. Mr Field was Foreman to M^r

Ryan. I was hired by Mr Ryan at Ten pounds a year to serve him for a twelvemonth in his business as a Butcher in Cheltenham – I served him the whole twelvemonth and received my years wages and slept in his house at Cheltenham aforesaid – At the time I was hired to Mr Ryan I was not married nor had I any child or Children – I have continued ever since in Cheltenham – Seven years ago I was married at the Parish Church in Cheltenham to my present wife Ann by whom I have one child named Thomas aged six years – I and my said wife and child are now actually chargeable to Cheltenham aforesaid

1841: *JL (aged 25; labourer) lived with wife Ann (20) and son Thomas (5) at Back of 213 High St, Cheltenham (HO107/353/8/70/23).* **1844: removal unlikely: settlement was probably acknowledged as Cheltenham. 1851:** *the family lived in Hereford Place, Cheltenham: JL (37; butcher), Ann (38; née Cox), and Thomas Cox (14; scholar, all three born Cheltenham); Thomas is apparently Ann's child (HO107/1973/427/21).* [PS/CH/RA/2/7:37.]

44009SE: Thurs 18 Jan/[blank] Jan 1844 – **Mary Ann Underwood**, widow, and children **William**, **James**, and **Louisa**; also John Boodle, gentleman, 42 Connaught Square, Paddington, Middlesex, relating to the settlement of the late Thomas Underwood, servant, lately residing in Cheltenham and husband of Mary Ann Underwood. *John Boodle*: In the Month of February 1831 I hired the said Thomas Underwood he then being to the best of this Examinants knowledge and belief unmarried and having no Child or Children for a Year as Footman at the wages of Twenty Guineas. I was then residing at N° 42 Lower Brook Street in the parish of Saint George Hanover Square in the County of Middlesex   the said Thomas Underwood served me the whole Year and Slept in my house in Lower Brook Street in the Parish of Saint George aforesaid the whole Year with the exception of about two months in the Autumn of that Year when I resided at Southend but he returned with me to my said residence in Brook Street aforesaid certainly before the month of December in that Year and resided with me there until the end of the Year for which I so hired him And received his Years wages. the said Thomas Underwood continued in my Service as a Yearly Servant at the wages aforesaid from that time until the Month of December 1834 during the whole of which time he resided in my house in Brook Street in the parish of Saint George aforesaid with the exception of about two months in the Autumns of each of the Years 1832 and 1833 – [signed]

Mary Ann Underwood: In the Month of May 1833 I was married to my late husband Thomas Underwood in the parish Church of All Souls S^t. Mary le bone London. My said husband was then living as Footman to M^r. John Boodle of 42 Lower Brook Street in the parish of Saint George Hanover Square in the County of the Middlesex – My said husband never did any act to gain a settlement after he left Mr Boodles service and died about four Years ago in Cheltenham aforesaid. I have done no act since my husbands death to gain a settlement

I have by my said husband two Children namely William aged Eight Years and James aged five Years – I have one Child aged about sixteen months who is illegitimate   I and my said Children are now actually chargeable to the said Parish of Cheltenham [mark]

1835: *baptism of son William in Tewkesbury 14 June.* **1837:** *at Tewkesbury Borough Sessions 29 July a Thomas Underwood (28) was sentenced to six months' imprisonment for larceny.* **1838:** *family not removed to St George, Hanover Square, Middlesex: see* **44009SE** *(18 Jan 1844) for further information on the family.* **1839:** *son James Joseph baptised at Cheltenham 10 Mar, when Thomas (labourer) and family lived in Queen St, Cheltenham; (9 Dec) Thomas Underwood died of "Paralysis" at Milsom Street, Cheltenham (buried at Cheltenham 12 Dec, aged 30).* **1841:** *widow MAU (25; independent) lived with children William (6) and James (1) in household of John Butt, tailor, in Rutland St, Cheltenham (HO107/353/7/60/24); unnamed illegitimate child mentioned in examination was Louisa, born at Cheltenham c1842.* **1844: removed to St George Hanover Square, Middlesex (husband's settlement). 1845:** *(RETURNED) birth of son Charles in Cheltenham.* **1851:** *MAU (32; widow, born Kemerton) lived with four children William (13, born Tewkesbury), James (11, born Cheltenham), Louisa (8), and Charles (6) at 70 New St, Cheltenham (HO107/1973/651/19).* [PS/CH/RA/2/7:38, 39. Removal expenses for "Underwood" to Middlesex £5/10/6 (1Q 1844: D4178).]

44010SE: Sat 20 Jan 1844 – **Thomas Teakle** (also **Takel**, **Teacle**, **Teakkel**), hairdresser, wife **Ann**, and five children **Sophia**, **Elizabeth**, **James**, **Charles**, and **Edward**: About Eleven years ago I rented a house of the Reverend M[r]. Lloyd in the parish of Newnham in the said County at ten pounds a Year   I resided in such house about Eighteen months and paid all my rent   I was duly rated to the Poor Rate for such house for upwards of a Year and paid such rates   I immediately afterward rented a house of M[r] John Plasted in the said Parish of Newnham at ten pounds ten shillings a Year and continued as tenant to him for about 15 months. In the Year 1838 I rented a house of William Roberts in the said Parish of Newnham at twenty pounds a Year   I resided in such last mentioned house about three years and paid all my rent. I was duly assessed to the Poor rates of the said Parish of Newnham in respect of such last mentioned house for the three Years I so resided in it and paid all such rates

I have done no act since to gain a settlement

About Eleven Years ago I was married to my present Wife Ann in the parish Church of Newnham aforesaid by whom I have five Children namely Sophia aged 9 Years Elizabeth aged 7 Years James aged 4 Years Charles aged 2 Years and Edward aged 10 months – I am now actually Chargeable to the said Parish of Cheltenham [signed]

1841: *TT (aged 30; hairdresser) lived with wife Ann (30) and children Sophia (7), Elizabeth (5), James (3), Charles (1) and Ann (1 month) in Townsend St, Cheltenham (HO107/353/9/8/10).* **1843:** *birth of son Edward registered at Cheltenham 1Q.* **1844:** *removed to Newnham (renting); (RETURNED) birth of son Thomas registered at Cheltenham 3Q; later children also born at Cheltenham.* **1851:** *the family lived in Grafton Passage, Lower High St, Cheltenham: TT (40; wire-worker, born Stroud), Ann (38; born Newnham), Sophia (14), Elizabeth (13), James (11), Charles (9; all born Newnham), Edward (7), Thomas (6), Ann (3), and Ellen (1) (HO107/1973/271/12).* [PS/CH/RA/2/7:40. Removal expenses for "Teakle" to Newnham £1/12/6 (1Q 1844: D4178).]

44011SE: 20 Jan 1844 – **Martha Leonard** (also **Lenard**), widow: About 16 or 17 Years ago my husband Andrew Leonard rented a house in Grove Street Cheltenham aforesaid of M[rs]. Willis at ten pounds a Year   I am quite sure I and my said husband resided in such house for upwards of a Year and paid a full Years rent. I have never lived out of Cheltenham since. My husband has been dead About 12 or 13 years [mark]

1830: *husband Andrew Leonard buried at Cheltenham 28 Jan, aged 43. In the 1830s widow ML was taken before Cheltenham magistrates on several occasions for disorderly conduct (Cheltenham Chron. 19 Jan 1832, 22 Mar 1838).* **1841:** *ML (aged 63) lived alone in Little's Row, New St, Cheltenham (HO107/353/15/56/20).* **1844:** *removal unlikely: late husband's settlement was probably acknowledged as Cheltenham.* **1851:** *ML (74; pauper, charwoman, and widow, born Stroud) lodged with the Eaves family at 4 Roper's Row, Cheltenham (HO107/1973/672/6).* **1852:** *death of ML in Cheltenham 9 Sept (buried four days later, aged 76).* [PS/CH/RA/2/7:41.]

44012SE: Thurs 25 Jan 1844 – **Mary Ann Murphy**, widow: On the twenty second day of September 1825 I was married to my late husband John Murphy in the parish Church of Stepney in the County of Middlesex. About three weeks or a month previous to my said Marriage my said husband rented a house N[o]. 87 Luke [= New?] Crane in the parish of S[t]. Paul Shadwell in the County of Middlesex of M[r] Patterson at twenty four pounds a Year   I and my said husband resided in such house four Years and a half and paid all the rent. I paid the rent Quarterly several times myself – my said husband done no act to gain a settlement afterwards and died about thirteen Years ago in the said Parish of S[t]. Paul Shadwell. I have several times been relieved by the Parish officers of Saint Paul Shadwell since my husbands death. I have done no act to gain a settlement since my husbands death. I am now actually chargeable to the said Parish of Cheltenham [mark]

1844: *probably removed to St Paul, Shadwell, Middlesex (husband's presumed settlement).* [PS/CH/RA/2/7:42.]

44013SE: Sat 27 Jan 1844 – **Stephen Mullett**, tailor, wife **Eliza**, and three children **Joseph**, **Mary**, and **Betsy**: I am about forty six years of age and am the Son of Steven Mullett and Elizabeth his Wife   A little more than forty Years ago my said Father rented a house in Tottenham Court road in the parish of St Pancras in the County of Middlesex at the rent of about fifty Guineas a Year and resided in such house for about ten years. My said father then took a house of Mr Rutland in Brill Terrace Somers Town in the said parish of S^t. Pancras at about thirty pounds a Year and resided in such last mentioned house about Six Years   he immediately afterwards rented a house of Mr Hopeman in Providence Place Kentish Town in the said parish of S^t. Pancras at about thirty pounds a Year and resided in such last mentioned house about three or four years in which said last house my said Father died. I resided with my said Father until the time of his death. I have never done any act to gain a settlement in my own right. My said Mother died about Three Years ago. About six years and a half ago my said mother was admitted an Inmate in the Workhouse belonging to the said Parish of St Pancras and continued therein for about Eighteen Months when I took her out of such Workhouse and supported her until her death. About Nineteen Years ago I was married to my present Wife Eliza in the parish Church of Saint Martin's Birmingham by whom I have three Children namely Joseph aged seventeen Years who has never been away from me Mary aged three Years – and Betsy aged one Year and a half – I am now actually chargeable to the said Parish of Cheltenham [signed Steven Mullett]

1841: *SM (aged 40; journeyman tailor) lived with wife Eliza (35) and children Joseph (15) and Mary (1) in Milk St, Birmingham (HO107/1142/2/46/12).* **1844: removed to St Pancras, Middlesex (father's settlement). 1851:** *the family lived in Aston, Birmingham: SM (52; tailor, born St Pancras), Eliza (45, born Coventry, Warks), and Mary (10, born Birmingham) (HO107/2060/354/10). [PS/CH/RA/2/7:43. Removal expenses for "Mullett" to St Pancras, Middlesex £7/1/6 (1Q 1844: D4178).]*

44014SE: Thurs 1 Feb 1844 – **Samuel Tarling** junior, carpenter, wife **Sarah** and three children **Charles**, **Emma**, and **Hannah**; also Samuel Tarling senior, carpenter, residing in Prestbury, relating to the settlement of son Samuel Tarling. *Samuel Tarling, senior:* About Twenty five years ago I purchased a piece of Land in the parish of Prestbury in the said County of Mr Wheeler for Seventy pounds and paid the purchase money to him for it   I immediately afterwards erected a house upon such Land and have resided in it ever since   About thirty four years ago I was married to my present Wife Hannah in the parish Church of Prestbury aforesaid by whom I had my Said Son Samuel Tarling now aged about thirty three years. My said Son was born in the said Parish of Prestbury and resided with me there until he was about twenty one Years of Age when he left me [signed]

Samuel Tarling, junior: I have never done any act to gain a settlement in my own right   About nine Years ago I was married to my Wife Sarah at the parish Church of Cheltenham by whom I have three Children namely Charles aged Eight Years Emma aged five Years and Hannah aged two Years and a half   I am now actually chargeable to the said Parish of Cheltenham [signed]

1841: *ST junior lived at Field View Cottage, Whaddon Lane, Cheltenham, with wife Sarah (35), and children Charles (5) and Emma (3) (HO107/353/3/50/16).* **1844: removed to Prestbury (father's settlement). 1851:** *(RETURNED) the family lived at 10 Whaddon Lane, Cheltenham: ST (40; carpenter, born Denby, Worcs), Sarah (46, born Hardwicke), and children Emma (13; scholar) and Anna/Hannah (9; both born Cheltenham) (HO107/1973/61/47-62/48). [PS/CH/RA/2/7:44, 45. Removal expenses for "Tarling" to Prestbury 2/6 (1Q 1844: D4178).]*

44015SE: Sat 3 Feb 1844 – **Robert Dix**, labourer, wife **Jane** and daughter **Elizabeth:** I am about fifty years of age. About thirty one years ago being then unmarried and having no Child or Children I was hired by Thomas Faulkner of Eastend farm in the parish of Charlton Kings in the said County Farmer for a Year at the wages of Eleven Guineas   I served the whole year and received my Years wages and slept in my said Masters house at Charlton Kings aforesaid the whole time

In three or four days after I left my said service I was married to my present Wife Jane in the parish Church of Charlton Kings aforesaid by whom I have one Child named Elizabeth aged fifteen Years. I have never rented a Tenement of the annual value of ten pounds or done any act to gain a settlement elsewhere

About twenty six Years ago I took possession of a piece of Land in the said Parish of Charlton Kings which had been inclosed many years previously and erected a Cottage upon it and resided in such Cottage about Sixteen Years and sold the same about nine Years ago to Mr Gael who purchased the same of me for the said Parish of Charlton Kings for thirty pounds which I received I am now actually chargeable to the said Parish of Cheltenham [mark]

1841: *wife Jane Dix (aged 45) and daughter Elizabeth (10) lived in Sun St, Cheltenham (HO107/353/9/37/23); RD absent on census night.* **1842:** *at Gloucester County Sessions 4 Jan JD (45) found not guilty of larceny.* **1844:** ***removed to Charlton Kings (hiring and service).*** **1851:** *a Jane Dix (64; widow, born Chedworth) lived with sister Mary Hall in London Rd, Charlton Kings (HO107/1972/129/32).* [PS/CH/RA/2/7:46. Removal expenses for "Dix" to Charlton Kings 2/6 (1Q 1844: D4178).]

44016SE: 3 Feb 1844 – **John Hall**, wife **Eliza**, and four children **George**, **Mary Ann**, **Frederick**, and **Caroline**: About five Years ago I rented a house of Philip Lane situate in Victoria Street in the Hamlet of Barton St Michael in the County of Gloucester for a Year at the rent of twelve pounds. I resided in such house for a whole Year and paid the first half Years rent after the said rate of twelve pounds. at the end of the first half year my said Landlord Philip Lane agreed to take five pounds for the second half year which I also paid

I was duly assessed to all poor rates made for the said Hamlet during the Year and paid the whole of such rates in respect of such House. I have done no act to gain a settlement since. About fourteen Years ago I was married to my present Wife Eliza in the parish Church of Saint Mary de lode Gloucester by whom I have four Children namely George aged ten Years Mary Ann aged Eight years Frederick aged two Years and a half and Caroline aged Eight months

I am now actually chargeable to the said Parish of Cheltenham [mark]

1841: *JH (aged 30; agricultural labourer) lived in Alstone, Cheltenham with wife Eliza (31) and children George (8), Mary Ann (5) and Frederick (Thomas) (3 mo; baptised 2 Apr, when family lived in Coach Rd, Cheltenham) (HO107/353/10/38/9).* **1844:** ***removed to Gloucester (renting).*** **1847:** *(RETURNED) baptism of daughter Eliza in Cheltenham 25 July, when family lived in Golden Valley, Cheltenham.* **1851:** *JH (30; agricultural labourer, born Ashleworth) lived in Gloucester Rd, Cheltenham with wife Eliza (41, born Gloucester) children George (15), Mary Ann (13) and Frederick (10) (all born Gloucester), and Caroline Amelia (8) and Eliza (3) (both born Cheltenham) (HO107/1973/953/33).* [PS/CH/RA/2/7:47. Removal expenses for "Hall" to Gloucester 9/9 (1Q 1844: D4178).]

44017SE: Mon 5 Feb 1844 – **Thomas Gage** junior, labourer, inmate of Cheltenham Workhouse, wife **Charlotte**, and children **Mary** and **Ellen**; also Thomas Gage senior, labourer, residing in Minchinhampton, relating to the settlement of son Thomas Gage junior. *Thomas Gage, senior*: The first place I remember myself was in the parish of Minchinhampton in the said County where my parents resided and where I have resided all my life time   I was married to my present Wife Sarah about twenty seven Years ago in the parish Church of Minchinhampton aforesaid by whom I had my said Son Thomas aged twenty six years who was born at Walls Quarr[y] in the said Parish of Minchinhampton and resided with me until he was about twenty years of age in the said Parish of Minchinhampton. I have never done any act to gain a settlement in my own right [mark]

Thomas Gage, junior: The first place I remember myself was in the parish of Minchinhampton in the said County where I resided with my Father Thomas Gage and my Mother Sarah Gage until I was about twenty Years of age. I have never done any act to gain a settlement in my own right. I was married to my present Wife Charlotte in the Parish Church of Charlton Kings in the said County about two Years and a half ago by whom I have two Children namely Mary aged 15 Months and Ellen aged six weeks   I am now actually Chargeable to the said Parish of Cheltenham [mark]

1844: ***removed to Minchinhampton (birth or father's settlement).*** **1846-:** *(RETURNED) births of other children registered at Cheltenham from 2Q onwards.* **1851:** *TG (aged 36; agricultural labourer, born Minchinhampton) lived in Cleeveland St, Cheltenham, with wife Charlotte (32; ironer, born Cheltenham), and children Mary Ann (9), Ellen (8), Emma (5), and Thomas (3) (all scholars, born Cheltenham), and also Charlotte (7 mo; born Cheltenham) (HO107/1973/446/11).* [PS/CH/RA/2/7:48, 49; G/CH/60/4). Removal expenses for "Gage" to Minchinhampton £1/5/9 (1Q 1844: D4178).]

44018SE: 5 Feb 1844 – Diana Bacon, wife of William Bacon, relating to the place of settlement of daughter **Sarah Shepherd**: I am the Wife of William Bacon. About 14 Years ago I was lawfully married to my first husband James Shepherd by whom I had my said Daughter Sarah Shepherd now aged 13 Years who was born in the parish of Lyminster in the County of Sussex

My said husband died about six months after the birth of my said Daughter   Immediately after the death of my said husband James Shepherd I applied to the Overseers of Lyminster for relief who relieved me for about two or three years whilst I resided in that Parish. I then went to reside at Croydon in Surrey and took my said Daughter with me And the Parish officers of Lyminster aforesaid continued to relieve me for about two years whilst I so resided in the parish of Croydon. My said Daughter has done no act to gain a settlement and is now actually chargeable to the said Parish of Cheltenham – my said daughter has lived with me all her life time. [mark]

1844: *SS (as Sarah Bacon) was an inmate of Charlton Kings Workhouse for children from 13 Jan until 27 Feb (G/CH/60/3);* **removed to Lyminster, Sussex (presumed) (birth).** **1861:** *apparently the Sarah (Ann) Porter (aged 28; beggar) living with John Bacon (18; beggar) and other relations in Newick, Sussex (RG9/585/144/22).* [PS/CH/RA/2/7:50. Removal expenses for "Shepperd" to Lyminster, Sussex £7/2/6 (1Q 1844: D4178). See **44001SE** (William Bacon: 4 Jan 1843).]

44019SE: Thurs 8 Feb 1844 – Ann Herbert, widow, relating to the settlement of daughter **Ellen** (also **Helen**) **Herbert**, an inmate of Cheltenham Workhouse: About thirty Years ago I was married to my late husband William Herbert in the parish Church of Stroud in the said County by whom I had my said Daughter Ellen now aged about twenty three years who was born in the said Parish of Stroud. My said husband died about fifteen years ago in the said Parish of Stroud   I was relieved by the Overseers of the said Parish of Stroud for about seven or eight years after my said husbands death. My said Daughter continued to live with me at Stroud aforesaid as part of my family until about seven years ago and never done any act to gain a settlement in her own right. My said Daughter is now in the Cheltenham Workhouse and chargeable to the said Parish of Cheltenham [mark]

1844: *removed to Stroud (father's presumed settlement).* **1851:** *(RETURNED) EH (aged 30; dressmaker, born Stroud) lodged at 38 New St, Cheltenham (HO107/1973/628/20).* [PS/CH/RA/2/7:51; G/CH/60/4]. Removal expenses for "Herbert" to Stroud £1/6/- (1Q 1844: D4178).]

44020SE: [blank] Feb 1844 – **James Betteridge** (also **Bettridge**), wood-turner, wife **Jane**, and five children **Caroline**, **Sarah**, **James**, **John**, and **Mary**: I am about thirty seven years of age when I was Eighteen Years of age I articled and hired myself to Charles Shettleworth of Smallbrook Street in the parish of Birmingham in the County of Warwick Woodturner for the term of three Years   I served two years of the said term and slept in Birmingham aforesaid the whole time when my Master failed and the agreement was delivered up and destroyed

I was then unmarried and had no Child or Children – I have done no Act since to gain a settlement. I was married about Eleven Years ago at Saint Philips Church Birmingham to my present Wife Jane by whom I have five Children namely Caroline aged ten Years Sarah aged six years James aged four Years John aged two Years and Mary aged three Months. – I am now actually chargeable to the said Parish of Cheltenham [signed]

1844: *removed to Birmingham, Warks (apprenticeship): see* **45001SE** *(JB: 9 Jan 1845) for further information.* [PS/CH/RA/2/7:52. Removal expenses for "Bettridge" to Birmingham, Warks £1/4/- (1Q 1844: D4178).]

44021SE: Sat 10 Feb 1844 – **Harriet Beesley** (also **Beasley**, **Besley**), widow, and three children **Emma**, **Edward**, and **Henry**: In the Year 1832 I was married to my late husband Henry Beesley in Saint Martins Church Birmingham by whom I have three Children Emma aged nine Years Edward aged Eight Years and Henry aged three Years

My said husband died three years ago last September at Cheltenham   About Eight years ago my said husband rented a house of Mr Jukes in Bond Street Dudley in the County of Worcester at ten pounds a Year. I and my said husband resided in such house at the said rent of ten pounds [for] fifteen Months and my said husband paid all the rent for the same. My said husband was duly rated to and paid all the poor rates made in the said Parish in respect of such house for the said fifteen months

My said husband never afterwards done any act to gain a settlement. I have done no act to gain a settlement since my said husbands death.

I and my said Children are now actually chargeable to the said Parish of Cheltenham [signed]
1844: *removed to Dudley, Worcs (husband's settlement); see* **45033SE** *(HB: 14 June 1845) for further information.* [PS/CH/RA/2/7:53. Removal expenses for "Beesley" to Dudley, Worcs £3/-/6 (3Q 1843: D4178). Note: "13 St Anne's Terrace [Cheltenham]".]

44022SE: Sat 17 Feb 1844 – **Sarah Ann Boxer**, and son **Henry:** I am about twenty five years of age   three years ago last December I was married to my present husband John Boxer in the parish Church of Saint Martins in the fields London

My said husband was a native of Calcutta in the East Indies and came to England about six Months before we were married   my husband has never done any act to gain a settlement in England. He left me a week ago last Monday and I do not know where he now is   I have not heard of him since – I am the Daughter of William Riley and Elizabeth his Wife and lived with my parents until I was about Nineteen years of age   I lived with them about seven years in the parish of Burslem in the County of Stafford in a small Cottage

About thirteen or fourteen Years ago whilst we were so residing in the said Parish of Burslem I went with my Father to the Overseer of the Township of Endon in the said County of Stafford and my said Father was relieved by such Overseer. I have never done any act to gain a settlement. I have one Child by my said husband named Henry aged 18 months. I am now actually chargeable to the said Parish of Cheltenham [mark]
1844: *removed to Endon, Staffs (father's presumed settlement).* [PS/CH/RA/2/7:54. Removal expenses for "Boxer" to Endon, Staffs £4/18/- (1Q 1844: D4178).]

44023SE: 17 Feb 1844 – **Ann Lane**, widow: About thirty Years ago I was married to my late husband Charles Lane in the parish Church of Colesbourne in the said County who died about three years ago. I have heard that my said husband was apprenticed to the late Mr Court of the Parish of Chedworth in the said County Blacksmith, who has been dead many years. Soon after my said Marriage I and my said husband went to reside in a Cottage belonging to my said husband in the said Parish of Chedworth and resided in such Cottage for about 14 Years. My said husband was possessed of such Cottage and the one adjoining which he let for three pounds a Years before I married him. About Sixteen Years ago my said husband sold the said two Cottages to M^r. Bridges of Chedworth aforesaid for about Sixty or Seventy pounds and received the purchase money

My Husband then went into Lodgings and done no act afterwards to gain a settlement. I have done no act since my said husbands death to gain a settlement

I am now actually chargeable to the said parish of Cheltenham [mark]
1844: *removed to Chedworth (husband's settlement).* [PS/CH/RA/2/7:55. Removal expenses for "Lane" to Chedworth 18/6 (1Q 1844: D4178).]

44024SE: Thurs 7 Mar 1844 – **Caroline Stanley**, single woman, inmate of Cheltenham Workhouse: I am about 46 years of age   In the Month of January 1832 being then unmarried and having no Child or Children I was hired by Richard Godson Esquire of N° 22 Woburn place in the parish of Saint George Bloomsbury in the County of Middlesex Barrister at Law for a Year at the wages of twelve Guineas a Months wages or a months warning. I served two Years under such hiring received my wages and slept in my said Masters house at Woburn Place aforesaid the whole time. I have done no act since to gain a settlement – I am now actually Chargeable to the said Parish of Cheltenham [signed]
1841: *perhaps the CS (aged 40; servant) residing in Berkeley Place, Cheltenham, and born outside Glos (HO107/353/4/21/6).* **1844:** *perhaps removed to St George Bloomsbury, Middlesex (hiring and service).* [PS/CH/RA/2/7:56; G/CH/60/4).]

44025SE: [blank] Mar 1844 – **William Haynes** (also **Haines**): About Thirty Years ago I rented a House Corn Mill and Land situate at Aston upon Carrant [= Aston on Carrant] in the parish of Ashchurch in the said County of Mrs Parsons at twenty six pounds a Year. I resided in such house and occupied the same and the said Mill and Land for Six Years and paid the rent for the same – I was duly assessed to and paid all Poor Rates in respect of the said house Mill and Land in the said Parish of Ashchurch   I have done no act since to gain a settlement. I am now actually chargeable to the said Parish of Cheltenham [signed]
1844: *removed to Ashchurch (renting).* **1845:** *death of WH, aged 54 (buried at Ashchurch 20 Feb).* [PS/CH/RA/2/7:57. Removal expenses for "Haynes" to Ashchurch 9/6 (2Q 1844: D4178).]

44026SE: Tues 12 Mar 1844 – **Mary Ball**, single woman; also Ann Paysh, residing in Bisley, relating to the settlement of daughter Mary Ball. *Ann Paysh*: I am the wife of William Paysh and was married to him about ten Years ago at Bisley aforesaid. I was delivered of my said Daughter Mary Ball about thirty one Years ago in the said Parish of Bisley who is an illegitimate Child of mine   My Maiden name was Ball. I was delivered of such Child in the Workhouse at Bisley aforesaid   my said Daughter was in the Workhouse at Bisley many Years [mark]
Mary Ball: I am the Daughter of Ann Paysh and now aged about thirty one Years of age   I remember being in the Workhouse at Bisley several Years. I have never done any act to gain a settlement in my own right   I am now actually Chargeable to the said Parish of Cheltenham and an Inmate of the Workhouse there [mark]
1844: *removed to Bisley (Stroud Union) (presumably birth)*; *MB died at Stroud Workhouse, aged 31 (buried at Bisley 12 Aug).* [PS/CH/RA/2/7:58, 59. Removal expenses for "Ball" to Bisley 18/6 (2Q 1844: D4178).]

44027SE: Fri 29 Mar 1844 – **Hannah Cardwell** (properly **Cordwell**), widow: I am about Seventy Years of Age. About forty eight years ago I was married to my late husband Thomas Cardwell at Alston [= Alstone] in the County of Worcester where we resided for about two years after our Marriage. My husband was Settled in the Hamlet of Alston aforesaid by Apprenticeship to his Uncle Isaac Peart of that Hamlet Carpenter and Wheel[w]right who is dead. About thirty Years ago I and my said husband were residing in the Parish of Tredington in the County of Gloucester and my husband being then ill applied to the Overseers of Tredington for relief and was taken by the Overseers to the Magistrates at Tewkesbury and sworn to his Parish
My said husband myself and three Children were thereupon taken by orders of removal from the said Parish of Tredington to the said Hamlet of Alston and delivered to the Overseer there who received us and relieved us. Such orders were not appealed against. My said husband never afterwards done any act to gain a settlement. I have never done any act since his death to gain a settlement
About three years ago I was residing in the parish of Sedgebrook in the County of Worcester and applied to Mr New the then Overseer of Alston aforesaid for relief. He relieved to me with the sum of One Sovereign whilst I was so residing in Sedgeberrow
I am now actually chargeable to the said parish of Cheltenham [mark]
1844: *removed to Alstone, Worcs (husband's settlement).* **1845-6:** *(RETURNED) from 4Q 1845 until 4Q 1846 HC (aged 72) received parish relief from Winchcombe as a non-settled resident of Cheltenham (G/CH/9d/1).* **1848:** *death of HC (buried at New Burial Ground, Cheltenham on 18 Feb, aged 74).* [PS/CH/RA/2/7:60. Removal expenses for "Cardwell" to Alstone 17/3 (2Q 1844: D4178).]

44028SE: Tues 9 Apr 1844 – **Matilda Stephens**, wife of Edwin Stephens, and two children **Ellen** and **Sarah**; also Samuel Stephens, relating to the settlement of son Edwin Stephens, husband of Matilda Stephens. *Samuel Stephens*: About forty four Years ago being then unmarried and having no Child or Children I was hired by Mr John Harris of Castle Farm in the parish of Dursley in the said County Farmer for a Year at the wages of either Five or Six pounds   I served the whole Year and received my years wages and slept in my said Masters house at Castle Farm in Dursley aforesaid the whole time. I was married to my present wife Mary at Wootton under edge [= Wotton-under-Edge] in the year Year 1804 by whom I had my said Son Edwin who was born in the year

1816 in the said Parish of Dursley   my said Son continued to reside with me at Dursley until he was about 17 years of age when he left me and was married about five years ago last October

I never done any act to gain a settlement after my said hiring and Service at Dursley until after my said Son left me and was married – My said Son never was apprenticed or hired for a Year or done any act to gain a settlement in his own right [mark]

Matilda Stephens: Five Years ago last October I was married to my present husband Edwin Stephens in the parish Church of Cheltenham aforesaid – I have had two Children since my said Marriage namely Ellen aged three years and Sarah aged seven weeks. My said husband has never done any act to gain a settlement since my said Marriage. My said husband deserted me two Years ago and I have not seen him since nor do I know where he is. I and my said two Children are now actually Chargeable to the said Parish of Cheltenham [mark]

1841: *MS (aged 20) lived with husband Edwin (25; bricklayer) and daughter Ellen (7 mo) in Naunton Crescent, Cheltenham (HO107/353/12/59/16).* **1844:** *daughter Sarah (apparently illegitimate) born at Cheltenham Workhouse (baptised Cheltenham 29 Mar);* ***removed to Dursley (husband's settlement).*** **1853:** *when Matilda Green had married Edwin Stephens in 1837, his name was given as "Edward": Edward Stephens (36; bricklayer, from London) sailed for Tasmania on the "Panama", with daughter Ellen (9), and Elizabeth Stephens (36; needlewoman and laundress).* [PS/CH/RA/2/7:61, 62. Removal expenses for "Stephens" to Dursley 19/- (2Q 1844: D4178). See **45019SE** (father-in-law Samuel Stephens: 27 Mar 1845).]

44029SE: Sat 4 May 1844 – **Thomas Welch**, labourer, inmate of Cheltenham Workhouse: About fifty years ago when I was unmarried and without child or children I was hired by William Johnson of the Parish of Hanley Castle near Upton upon Severn in the County of Worcester to serve him in that Parish for one year as a Carter at the wages of Seven Pounds ten shillings – I went immediately into the service of the said William Johnson and continued in the same service for the space of one whole year thence ensuing. I resided and slept at my Master's in Hanley Castle aforesaid during the whole of the time I was in his said Service – I continued in the same service for the space of four years afterwards and resided and slept at Hanley Castle aforesaid during the whole of the time – I have done no act to gain a Settlement elsewhere. I am now an Inmate of the Workhouse at Cheltenham aforesaid and actually chargeable to that Parish [mark]

1841: *TW (aged 70; labourer, born Glos) lived alone in Sherborne St, Cheltenham (HO107/353/5/63/48).* **1844:** ***removed to Hanley Castle, Worcs (hiring and service).*** [PS/CH/RA/2/7:63 (G/CH/60/4). Removal expenses for "Welch" to Hanley Castle, Worcs 12/- and 18/6 (2Q 1844: D4178).]

44030SE: 4 May 1844 – **James Davis**, inmate of Cheltenham Workhouse: About twenty five years ago I rented of Thomas Master of Cirencester Esquire a tenement consisting of a separate and distinct dwelling house and buildings and about two hundred and twenty acres of Land situate in the Parish of Preston in this County for the term of five Years at the rent or sum of Three hundred Guineas a Year   There was no Lease or Agreement in Writing with me   I bought the stock upon the Farm and paid One thousand Eight hundred pounds for it to Messrs Wood and Lane the assignees of Edward Sutton the previous tenant   both Mr Wood and Mr Lane are dead. I held the said dwelling house and buildings and occupied the said Land for the said term of five years the time of my so renting it as aforesaid   I paid the full rent of Three hundred Guineas a Year during the whole term for the same to John Kan the Steward of the said Thomas Master

During the whole of the said five years I resided constantly in the said Parish of Preston at the said Dwelling House. I have done no Act to gain a Settlement elsewhere. I am now an Inmate of the Cheltenham Workhouse [signed]

1841: *JD (aged 66) was an inmate of Cirencester Union Workhouse (Preston was part of Cirencester Poor Law Union) (HO107/380/3/64/6).* **1844:** ***removed to Preston (renting).*** [PS/CH/RA/2/7:64 (G/CH/60/4). Removal expenses for "Davis" to Preston 18/- (2Q 1844: D4178).]

44031SE: 4 May 1844 – **Thomas Vaisey**, weaver: I am above Eighty Years of age. When I was about twelve years of age unmarried and without child or children I was hired into the parish of Cam in this County by Joseph Millard of that Parish Dairyman to serve him for one year – at the wages of three guineas – I went immediately after into the service of the said Joseph Millard and continued in the Same Service for the space of one whole year thence ensuing. I resided and slept during the whole of the time at my Master's house at Cam aforesaid. I received my Years wages. I was hired a second year to serve the said Joseph Millard for a twelvemonth at the wages of four guineas – I was unmarried and without child or children. I served my said Master at Cam aforesaid and resided and slept there for the last mentioned twelvemonth and received my wages. I continued to live with my said Master at Cam aforesaid for as much as ten years. I have never done any act to gain a Settlement elsewhere. I am now actually chargeable to the said Parish of Cheltenham [mark]

1844: *ordered to be removed to Cam (presumably quashed) (hiring and service)*: *see* **44042SE** *(TV: 18 July)*. [PS/CH/RA/2/7:65.]

44032SE: 4 May 1844 – **Sarah Sears**, widow, and six children **Elizabeth, Charlotte, Thomas, William, Sarah**, and **John:** I am the Widow of John Sears who died at Cheltenham aforesaid in November 1842 – I was married to the said John Sears at the Parish Church of Cheltenham aforesaid about eleven years ago. About six years ago my said husband hired from Mr Hall of Evesham in the County of Worcester Draper the Agent of Mr Dixon of Worcester for the term of one year thence next ensuing at the rent of Thirty Two pounds a tenement consisting of a separate and distinct dwelling house and out offices called The Rose and Crown Inn situate in the parish of Saint Laurence [= Lawrence] in Evesham aforesaid. I was present when my said husband hired the same – My said husband actually occupied all the said premises under the said hiring, in the said Parish of Saint Laurence from the said commencement of his said tenancy for three years thence next ensuing. I lived with him at the said Rose and Crown Inn during the whole time and to my knowledge he resided there in the same parish of Saint Laurence during his said Tenancy. The whole of the rent was paid for the three Years at thirty two pounds a year. I made the payments myself of two half years rent of Sixteen pounds each to the said Mr Hall for part of the time my said husband so rented of him as aforesaid – My said husband was assessed to the Poor Rates made for the relief of the Poor of the said Parish of Saint Laurence during the same three Years of his living in that Parish in respect of all the said premises called the Rose and Crown Inn and the same rates were duly paid – I paid most of them myself – My said husband never did any act to gain a settlement elsewhere. I have never done any act to gain a settlement since my said husbands death. I am now actually chargeable to the said Parish of Cheltenham – I have six children living with me and actually chargeable to the said Parish namely Elizabeth aged ten years Charlotte aged eight years Thomas aged six years William aged five years Sarah aged four years and John aged one year and seven months – the children of my marriage with John Sears [signed]

1844: *removed to St Lawrence, Evesham, Worcs (husband's settlement)*: *see* **47017RO** *(SS: 12 Mar 1847) for further information on SS and family*. [PS/CH/RA/2/7:66-7. Removal expenses for "Sears" to Evesham, Worcs £1/3/3 (2Q 1844: D4178).]

44033SE: Sat 11 May 1844 – **Elizabeth Hossington**, single woman, inmate of Cheltenham Workhouse; also Cornelius Hossington, pilot, residing in Newton, Glam, relating to the settlement of daughter Elizabeth Hossington. *Cornelius Hossington*: About twenty four years ago I rented a Tenement consisting of a separate and distinct dwelling house situate and being N°. 2 Coronation Place Back Street in the Parish of Saint Nicholas in the City of Bristol of M^r. Atwood for a year at the rent of Fourteen pounds a year. I resided in the said dwelling house from the time of my so taking it for two years next ensuing and paid the full two years rent for the same – I then rented a tenement consisting of a separate and distinct dwelling house situate and being N°. 5 Coronation Place aforesaid in the said Parish of Saint Nicholas of the same Landlord for a year at the rent of Sixteen Pounds a year – I resided in such last mentioned dwelling house for two years from the time of my so taking it and paid the full two years rent for the same – I was duly assessed to all the Poor rates made for the relief of the Poor in the said Parish of Saint Nicholas in respect of the said Houses during the respective times I resided in them as aforesaid and paid all such rates. I have never done any act to gain a settlement elsewhere. I was married to my late Wife Wenny [= Gwen] at the Parish Church of Saint Mary Swansea about thirty two years ago by whom I had my said daughter Elizabeth born in lawful wedlock and now aged about thirty one years – she resided with me during the whole time I lived at N°. 2 and N°. 5 Coronation Place aforesaid – she left when she was about sixteen years of age – she has never done any act to gain a Settlement to my Knowledge – [mark]

Elizabeth Hossington: I am about thirty one years of age. I recollect residing with my Father and Mother at N°. 2 and N°. 5 Coronation Place in the Parish of Saint Nicholas in the City of Bristol. I left my Parents when I was about Sixteen years Old. I have never done an Act to gain a Settlement in my own right. I am now an Inmate of the Cheltenham Workhouse. I am now actually chargeable to the said Parish of Cheltenham – [mark]

1844: *removed to St Nicholas, Bristol (father's settlement).* 1851: *EH (aged 37; general servant, born Swansea) lived at 78 Coleshill St, Hanover Square, London (HO107/1477/209/27).* **1854:** *EH married mariner Robert Clarke Huntley 9 Jan at St Luke's Church, Finsbury, London.* [PS/CH/RA/2/7:67, 68; G/CH/60/4). Removal expenses for "Hossington" to Bristol £1/3/6 (2Q 1844: D4178).]

44034SE: Thurs 16 May 1844 – **Eliza James**, single woman, inmate of Cheltenham Workhouse, with daughter **Mary Ann**; also Margaret Robins, residing in King's Stanley, relating to the settlement of niece Eliza James: *Margaret Robins*: I am the Wife of Abraham Robbins of Kings Stanley aforesaid Carrier and am the Sister of the late Thomas James of Kings Stanley aforesaid Cloth worker who died there at the latter end of the Year 1834. I was present at my Brothers Marriage with Ann Harris at the Parish Church of Kings Stanley aforesaid about twenty five Years ago. She died at Kings Stanley aforesaid about twelve years ago   Eliza James is his Daughter by that Marriage. My said Brothers last place of legal settlement is at Wootton under edge [= Wotton-under-Edge] in this County. he gained his Parish by taking his Fathers William James's settlement

My said Brother never done any act to gain a settlement in his own right. He always lived close by where I lived. I produce an order under the hand and seals of H C Clifford T J L Baker and H J Clifford three of Her Majestys Justices of the peace of and for the said County of Gloucester and dated the Eleventh day of February 1841 for the removal of the said William James from the said Parish of Kings Stanley to the said Parish of Wootton under edge. I recollect William James being removed with such orders to Wootton under edge

He was received as a Parishioner there, but returned to Kings Stanley aforesaid in about a week after he was so removed And has ever since been relieved by the Parish officers of Wootton under edge aforesaid during the whole of which time he has been living at Kings Stanley aforesaid. I recollect orders of removal were made for the removal of my said Brother from Kings Stanley to Wootton under edge aforesaid just before the time of his death. The Orders were suspended and my Brother died. After his death his Widow and six Children were duly removed to Wootton under edge aforesaid and received there has Parishioners [mark]

Eliza James: I am the Daughter of Thomas James and Ann his Wife who resided at Kings Stanley [= King's Stanley] in this County – They are both dead –

I have never done any act to gain a settlement in my own right   I am an inmate of the Cheltenham Workhouse and actually chargeable to the said Parish of Cheltenham. I was delivered of a female bastard child named Mary Ann aged eight months in the parish of Cheltenham. [signed]

1844: *removed to Wotton-under-Edge (father's settlement).* [PS/CH/RA/2/7:69, 70 (G/CH/60/4). Removal expenses for "James" to Wotton-under-Edge £1/8/0 (2Q 1844: D4178).]

44035SE: Thurs 23 May 1844 – **John Simmons** (also **Simons**), wife **Maria**, and two sons **Samuel** and **John**: About sixteen Years ago when I was unmarried and without child or children I was hired into the Parish of Prestbury in this County by Thomas Atkins of that Parish Farmer to serve him for one year at the wages of Five pounds.

I went into the service of the said Thomas Atkins and continued in the same service for the space of one whole year thence ensuing and received my years wages. I resided and slept during the whole of the time at my Master's house at Prestbury aforesaid – I have done no act to gain a settlement elsewhere. About ten years ago I was married to my present wife Maria in the parish Church of Charlton Kings by whom I have two children namely Samuel aged four years and John aged six months. I and my said wife and my said two children are now actually chargeable to the said Parish of Cheltenham – [mark]

1841: *JS was absent on census night; wife Maria (aged 35) lived with son Samuel in Exmouth St, Cheltenham (HO107/353/12/40/16).* **1844: *removed to Prestbury (hiring and service).*** **1847:** *(RETURNED) death of JS at Cheltenham (buried at New Burial Ground 7 June):* Cheltenham Chron. *17 June describes him as gardener, aged 38, of Hatherley Lane, Cheltenham.* **1851:** *Maria Simmons (44; widow, born Ruscombe, near Stroud) lived in Hatherley Court, Cheltenham with two sons Samuel (8) and John (6), both born Cheltenham (HO107/1973/949/25).* [PS/CH/RA/2/7:71. Removal expenses for "Simmons" to Prestbury 2/6 (2Q 1844: D4178).]

44036SE: Tuesday 21 May 1844 – **Mary Walker**, single woman, inmate of Cheltenham Workhouse, with son **Alfred**; also William Walker, joiner, residing in Wybunbury, Ches, relating to the settlement of daughter Mary Walker. *William Walker*: About twelve or thirteen years ago I rented a Tenement consisting of a separate and distinct Dwelling House and about five Acres of Land situate in the parish of Wybunbury aforesaid at Wybunbury Moss for the term of one whole year at the rent of Fourteen pounds twelve shillings. I occupied the said premises under the said taking from the commencement of my tenancy up to the present time I have the same house and Land in my holding now I paid the said Yearly rent of Fourteen pounds twelve shillings for the said term of one Year and have continued to pay the same Yearly ever since About three or four Years since my rent was reduced to Thirteen pounds twelve shillings. I have resided in the said Dwelling House at Wyburybury aforesaid during the whole of my said tenancy During the whole of the fifteen years I have occupied the said premises I have been duly assessed to all the Poor Rates made for the relief of the Poor of the said Parish of Wyburybury in respect of the said dwelling house and Land and had duly paid the same

I have never done an act to gain a settlement elsewhere I was married to my Wife Margaret about twenty nine years ago at the Parish Church of Wyburybury aforesaid by whom I had my said Daughter Mary Walker who was born in lawful wedlock

My said Daughter resided with me at Wybunbury aforesaid until she was about Eighteen years of age [signed]

Mary Walker: I am the Daughter of William Walker and Margaret his Wife and am now aged About twenty seven Years I lived with my said Father and Mother in the parish of Wybunbury in the County of Chester until I was about Eighteen years of age. I have done no act to gain a settlement in my own right. I was delivered of a Male bastard Child named Alfred about nine weeks ago in the Parish of Cheltenham – I and my child are now Inmates of the Union Workhouse at Cheltenham and actually chargeable to that Parish [signed]

1844: *removed to Wybunbury, Ches (father's settlement)*; *MW (resident in Wybunbury, Ches) married John Statham (labourer, widower) at Wybunbury 7 Oct.* **1851:** *the couple lived in Bignall End, Staffs: John Statham (aged 42; iron miner, born Audley, Staffs), Mary (32; born Basford, Ches), Elizabeth (18; dressmaker, born Audley, Staffs), John (11; iron miner, born Audley, Staffs), Alfred Walker (7; "at home", born Cheltenham), Mary Statham (5); "at home", born Audley, Staffs), Henry (3; born Audley, Staffs), and John Walker (19; lodger and iron miner, born Wybunbury, Ches) (HO107/2001/663/29).* [PS/CH/RA/2/7:72, 73 (G/CH/60/4). Removal expenses for "Walker" to Wybunbury, Ches £6/2/- (2Q 1844: D4178).]

44037SE: Sat 8 June 1844 – **Priscilla Trinder**, widow, inmate of Cheltenham Workhouse: About twenty two Years ago I was married to my late husband John Trinder in the Parish Church of Tewkesbury in the said County

About two years after I was married I and my said Husband were removed by orders of removal from the Parish of Tewkesbury to the Parish of Shipton Sollars in the said County and delivered with a copy of such order to the Overseer there who received us and relieved us. The said order of removal was not appealed against. About fourteen or fifteen Years ago I and my said husband were residing in the parish of Sevenhampton in the said County and my husband being ill I applied to M[r] John Bee the then Overseer of the said Parish of Shipton Sollars for relief who relieved to me and continued to do so for four or five weeks at two shillings and sixpence a week during the whole of which time I and my said husband continued to reside in the said Parish of Sevenhampton. My said husband has never done any act to gain a settlement since and died at Manchester about two Years ago I have done no act since his death to gain a settlement

I am now actually chargeable to the said Parish of Cheltenham [mark]

1844: *removed initially to Shipton Sollers (husband's presumed settlement): see* **45026SE** *(PT: 2 May 1845).* [PS/CH/RA/2/7:74. Note: "This order was erroneous in removing to Shipton Sollers instead of to Shipton Oliffe – and new orders made see page 155". Removal expenses to Shipton Oliffe for "Trinder" 12/6 and to Severnhampton 15/3 (3Q 1844: D4178).]

44038SE: Sat 15 June 1844 – **Elizabeth Barnes**, widow: I am about Seventy three years of age – About fifty years ago I was married to my late husband William Barnes in the Parish Church of Stanton in the County of Worcester – About Thirty six years ago my said husband rented a separate and distinct tenement consisting of a House and five Acres of Land of M[r]. Whittle in the parish of Stanton aforesaid by the year at the yearly rent of Eighteen pounds and resided in such house and occupied the Land for the space of nine years under such hiring at the said rent and paid the same – My said husband never afterwards done any act to gain a Settlement and died about three years ago at Stanton aforesaid – My said husband was constantly relieved by the Parish Officers of Stanton aforesaid for about Seven years previous to his death – I have done no act to gain a settlement since my said husbands death and have been constantly relieved by the Parish Officers of Stanton aforesaid from my husbands death until about 8 Weeks ago when I came to Cheltenham

I am now actually chargeable to the said Parish of Cheltenham – [mark]

1844: *removed to Stanton, Worcs (husband's settlement).* [PS/CH/RA/2/7:76. Removal expenses for "Barnes" to Stanton, Worcs £1/-/6 (3Q 1844: D4178).]

44039SE: Thurs 13 June 1844 – **Richard Hill**, servant, wife **Maria**, and two children **William** and **Mary**: I am about sixty seven years of age. About fifty six years ago when I was unmarried and without child or children I was hired into the Parish of Yazor in the County of Hereford by M[r]. Robert Price of Foxley in the said Parish of Yazor to serve him for one year at the wages of twelve pounds I went immediately on the hiring into the service of the said Robert Price and continued in the same service for one whole year thence ensuing and received my years wages I resided and slept during the whole of the year at my Master's house at Foxley in the parish of Yazor aforesaid – I was hired again a second year and served my said Master at Foxley aforesaid for nine years and resided and slept during the time at Foxley – I have done no act since to gain a settlement elsewhere – About eighteen years ago I was married to my present Wife Maria at the Parish Church of Maynooth in the County of Kildare in Ireland by whom I have two Children now living with me namely William aged seventeen years and Mary aged thirteen years – My said Child William has never been out to service or done any act to gain a settlement in his own right – he has always lived with me I and my said Wife and children are now actually chargeable to the said Parish of Cheltenham – We have been relieved by the relieving officer Peter Butt – [signed]

1841: *RH (60; footman) lived with wife Maria (40; stay-maker) and children Richard (14; shop boy), William (12), and Mary (10) in Sidney St, Cheltenham (HO107/353/3/17/29).* **1842:** *Richard Hill the younger convicted 12 Apr of house-breaking at County Assizes at Gloucester (punishment: three strokes and whipped); father RH senior (66) also sentenced to three months' imprisonment, for receiving stolen goods.* **1843:** *Richard Hill junior convicted of larceny ("cutting a bag from the arm of Mary Ann Price": Cheltenham Chron. 9 Feb), for which – as second conviction – he was transported to Tasmania for seven years.* **1844:** *removed to Yazor, Heref (hiring and service).* **1851:** *(RETURNED) Maria Hill (45; pauper, born King's Stanley) lived as lodger with Mary Johnson (perhaps relation) at 57 Burton St, Cheltenham (HO107/1973/597/21); children William (22; journeyman poulterer) and Maryann (20; general servant) (both born Cheltenham) lived in house of relations Robert and Maria Jackson at 16 Sun St, Cheltenham*

(HO107/1973/506/32). [PS/CH/RA/2/7:77 (earlier, signed version of this text struck out on p. 74). Removal expenses for "Hill" to Yazor, Heref £3/4/- (3Q 1844: D4178).]

44040SE: 15 June 1844 – **James Sweet**, cabinet-maker, inmate of Cheltenham Workhouse: I am about seventy four Years of age   About twenty nine Years ago I rented a Tenement consisting of a separate and distinct dwelling House situate and being N° 4 Kings Mead in the Parish of Walcot in the County of Somerset of Mr Peacock for a Year at the rent of fifty Guineas a Year.. I resided in such house from the time of my so taking it for about Seven Years and paid upwards of the first six years rent

I have done no act since to gain a settlement elsewhere

I am now an Inmate of the Cheltenham Workhouse and actually chargeable to the Parish of Cheltenham aforesaid [signed]

1841: *JS (aged 70; cabinet-maker) lived in Bell St, Shaftesbury, Dorset (HO107/295/4/4/2).* **1844:** *removed to Walcot, Bath, Som (renting).* **1846:** *JS died at Walcot (buried from workhouse, aged 77, 3 Nov).* [PS/CH/RA/2/7:78; G/CH/60/4. Removal expenses for "Sweet" to Bath, Som £1/8/9 (3Q 1844: D4178).]

44041SE: 15 June 1844 – **George Stone**, labourer; also Thomas Stone, labourer, relating to the settlement of his son George Stone. *Thomas Stone*: About twenty five Years ago being then unmarried and having no Child or Children I was hired by George Yeates of the Star Public House on the Quay in the parish of St Nicholas in the City of Gloucester for a Year at the Yearly wages of Six pounds I served the whole Year and slept in my Masters house in the said Parish of St Nicholas the whole time   I was again hired to him for another Year and served that and the following Year with the said George Yeates and slept in his house in the said Parish of St Nicholas the whole time. I have done no Act since to gain a settlement. About twenty two years ago I was married to my present Wife Jane in the parish Church of Hempstead [= Hempsted] in the said County by whom I had my said Son George now aged about twenty Years. My said Son George has always lived with me and never done any act to gain a settlement in his own right My said Son is now actually Chargeable to the said Parish of Cheltenham

About Eighteen Years ago I was chargeable to the said Parish of Cheltenham and together with my said Wife and Son George were removed by orders of removal from the said Parish of Cheltenham to the said Parish of Saint Nicholas and delivered to the Overseers there who received us and relieved us. such orders of removal were not appealed against [mark]

George Stone: I have never done any act to gain a settlement in my own right. I am now actually chargeable to the said Parish of Cheltenham having received relief from the Relieving officer [mark]

1841: *GS (aged 15) lived in Albert St, Cheltenham with parents Thomas Stone (35; dealer in rags) and Jane (35), and siblings Emma (15), Mary (13), Edward (11), Thomas (5), Jane (3), and Samuel (1) (all except Jane born Cheltenham) (HO107/353/9/7/9).* **1844:** *removed to St Nicholas, Gloucester (father's settlement).* **1845-7:** *(RETURNED) from 3Q 1845 until 2Q 1847 GS received parish relief from Gloucester as a non-settled resident of Cheltenham (G/CH/9d/1).* **1851:** *his family lived at 34 Albert St, Cheltenham: Thomas Stone (57; a labourer), Jane (47; a charwoman), George (21; labourer, born Cheltenham, "blind"), Edwin (14; labourer), Jane (9; scholar) (HO107/1973/454/26).* [PS/CH/RA/2/7:79, 80. Removal expenses for "Stone" to Gloucester 7/6 (3Q 1844: D4178). See Gray **615** (father Thomas Stone: 3 Mar 1826).]

44042SE: Thurs 18 July 1844 – **Thomas Vaisey** (also **Vasey, Veisy, Vesey**), weaver: I am above 80 Years of Age. Between forty and fifty years ago I bought of Thomas Maser of the parish of Kingswood in the County of Wilts [= Glos] Clothier an Estate in possession in Freehold Land situate in the said Parish of Kingswood consisting of a Dwelling House and Garden close by the Turnpike road near to the said Thomas Masers Clothing Mill for the sum of Three hundred and fifty pounds The said Land was conveyed to me in fee and I had the Deed of Conveyance and paid the purchase money. I took possession of the said Estate immediately on my acquisition thereof and continued in the possession thereof and resided upon the same from that time until Seven Years ago. I built Several houses upon the said Land and sold the Land and houses to William Long of the said Parish of Kingswood about Seven Years ago. About thirty Years ago I served the office of Parish Constable for the said Parish of Kingswood for one entire year and resided in such Parish the whole year. I have lived with my Daughter Mary Ann Vizard at Cheltenham since I left Kingswood and have done no Act since I left Kingswood to gain a settlement elsewhere

I am now actually chargeable to the said Parish of Cheltenham [mark]

1841: *TV (aged 78; labourer) lived in Suffolk St, Leckhampton (HO107/353/18/9/12) with daughter Mary (Ann) Vizard (39; shoe-binder) and sons William (12) and Rufus (8).* **1844:** *ordered to be removed to Cam (presumably quashed) (hiring and service): see* **44031SE** *(TV: 4 May 1844);* ***removed to Kingswood, Wilts (estate).*** **1849:** *death of TV at Leckhampton (buried 26 June, aged 86).* [PS/CH/RA/2/7:81. Removal expenses for "Vaisey" to Kingswood, Wilts 19/6 (3Q 1844: D4178).]

44043SE: Fri 26 July/1 Aug 1844 – **Martha Tale** (also **Teale**), widow, inmate of Cheltenham Workhouse; also Joseph Crump, farmer, residing in Dumbleton, relating to the settlement of Martha Tale, widow of William Tale, deceased. *Joseph Crump*: About thirty three Years ago I occupied a Farm called the Layfield farm in the said Parish of Dumbleton. I Knew the said William Tale   About that year at Michaelmas I hired the said William Tale who was then unmarried and had no Child or Children to serve me for one Year from that time at the Parish of Dumbleton aforesaid. he came into my service immediately and remained with me the whole Year and resided and slept at my house in Dumbleton aforesaid the whole time   he continued a long time afterwards in my Service. I knew the said Martha Tale and She worked for me for sometime   The said William Tale lived with me up to the time of his marriage with the said Martha Tale   they were fellow Servants [signed]

Martha Tale: About twenty nine years ago I was married to my late husband William Tale in the parish Church of Dumbleton in the said County who was then living in service with Mʳ. Joseph Crump of the said Parish of Dumbleton and in which service we continued for about two Years after our Marriage. My said husband never done any act afterwards to gain a settlement and died about twenty six Years ago at Dumbleton aforesaid. I have done no act since my said husbands death to gain a settlement in my own right. I am now an Inmate at the Workhouse at Cheltenham and actually Chargeable to the said Parish Of Cheltenham [mark]

1844: ***removed to Dumbleton (Winchcombe Union) (husband's settlement).*** **1847:** *death of MT in Winchcombe Workhouse, aged 73 (buried at Dumbleton 22 Jan).* [PS/CH/RA/2/7:82, 84. Removal expenses for "Tale" to Dumbleton 18/3 (3Q 1844: D4178).]

44044SE: Thurs 1 Aug 1844 – **Thomas Lewis**, labourer, wife **Susannah**, and four children **Thomas**, **James**, **Philip**, and **Mary:** I am about 43 years of Age   In the Month of August 1825 being then unmarried and having no Child or Children I was hired by John Lloyd Esquire of the Bullwalk [now Bulwalk] in the parish of Saint Mary in the Town of Brecknock [also Brecon] for a Year as Groom at the wages of Eighteen pounds and my Clothes   I served the whole year and slept in my Masters house at the Bullwalk in the parish of Saint Marys aforesaid the whole Year and received all my wages. I was again hired to my said Master Mʳ Lloyd for another Year who continued to reside at the Bullwalk Sᵗ Mary's aforesaid until he removed from thence to a Mansion house belonging to the said John Lloyd called Dennis which is situate in the parish of Sᵗ. Davids Brecknock aforesaid in which last place I continued with my said Master and slept in his house at Dennis parish of Sᵗ Davids aforesaid for upwards of two months when I left my said Masters Service in the Month of April 1827. I have done no act since to gain a settlement elsewhere. About Eleven Years ago I was married to my present Wife Susannah at the parish Church of Merthyr Tidvil [= Tydfil] by whom I have four Children namely Thomas aged nine years James aged six years Philip aged 4 Years and Mary aged two Years   I and my said Wife and Children are now actually chargeable to the said Parish of Cheltenham [mark]

1841: *TL (aged 30; groom) lived with wife Susan (30), and sons Thomas (7), James (4), and Philip (2) in Sherborne St, Cheltenham (HO107/353/6/11/16).* **1842:** *the family lived at 17 Columbia St, Cheltenham when daughter Mary Ann was baptised at Cheltenham 11 Sept.* **1844:** ***removed to Brecknock, Brecknockshire (Breconshire) (hiring and service).*** **1845:** *birth of daughter Margaret registered at Cheltenham 3Q.* **1851:** *(RETURNED) TL (48; groom, born Brecon), wife Susannah (45; born Cockyard,*

Heref), and children Thomas (15; scholar, born Carmarthenshire), James (13), Philip (10), Mary Ann (7), Margaret (5), and William (2), all born Cheltenham and all "scholars" except William, lived at 69 Duke St, Cheltenham (HO107/1973/43/11). [PS/CH/RA/2/7:83. Note: "I found my own clothes the first year; I had a fresh agreement the second year & went with him before sent Home." Removal expenses to Brecknock for "Lewis" £2/12/6 (3Q 1844) and £5/17/6 (4Q 1844: D4178).]

44045SE: Mon 12 Aug 1844 – **Phoebe Gee**, single woman: I am now aged about twenty one years. I was born at the Parish of Lower Heyford in the County of Oxford where my Parents lived and were settled. I lived with my Mother at Lower Heyford aforesaid from my birth until I was eighteen years of age when for the first time I went out to service. I do not know where my Father is. I have not known any thing of him for many years. My Mother Sarah Gee died at Lower Heyford aforesaid near three years ago. She received relief from Lower Hayford [*sic*] for many years before she died. I have frequently seen M[r]. Hoare the Relieving Officer of the Bicester Union in which the parish of Lower Heyford is situate relieve her. he paid her two shillings a week. While I lived with my Mother the year that she died I was relieved by M[r] Hoare and received regularly eighteen pence a week from him for several weeks – When the payment was stopped I was taken into the Union Workhouse at Bicester aforesaid and was maintained there for some time – this was about two years ago. – I have done no act to gain a Settlement in my own right. I am now actually chargeable to the Parish of Cheltenham, and am an Inmate of the Union Workhouse there. [mark]
1844: *removed to Lower Heyford, Oxon (father's settlement); PG's son William Gee, born 15 August at Union Workhouse, Cheltenham, (and died 3Q at Cheltenham); PG (aged 21) was admitted into Cheltenham Workhouse 4Q (G/CH/60/4).* [PS/CH/RA/2/7:85. Removal expenses for "Gee" to Lower Heyford, Oxon £2/4/6 (4Q 1844: D4178).]

44046SE: 12 Aug 1844 – **Mary Ann Hemming**, single woman, inmate of Cheltenham Workhouse, with daughter **Emma:** About twelve years ago when I was unmarried and without child or children I was hired into the Parish of Severnstoke [= Severn Stoke] in the County of Worcester by M[r] Horniblow of the Park Farm in that Parish Farmer to serve him for one year from Michaelmas to Michaelmas – I was hired at the Upton Mop and went direct from there into M[r]. Horniblow's service and continued in his Service the whole year and received my full years wages. During the year I resided and slept at my Master's house in Seven stoke aforesaid. I was the Housemaid there. I have done no act since to gain a Settlement. I am now actually chargeable to the Parish of Cheltenham and an inmate of the Union Workhouse there. I was delivered of a female bastard child named Emma two months ago at the Cheltenham Workhouse. [mark]
1844: *MAH admitted to Cheltenham Workhouse 18 Apr (discharged with daughter 2 Oct (G/CH/60/4); removed to Severn Stoke, Worcs (hiring and service).* **1851:** *(RETURNED) MAH (aged 30; charwoman, born Castlemorton, Worcs) lodged, with daughter Emma (6; scholar) and also with older daughter Sarah, at house of Robert Jackson and family at Newman's Place, Cheltenham (HO107/1973/637/39).* [PS/CH/RA/2/7:86. Removal expenses for "Hemming" to Severn Stoke, Worcs 19/6 (3Q 1844: D4178).]

44047SE: [blank] Aug 1844 – Thomas Lock, labourer, residing in Stanway, relating to the settlement of brother, **John Lock** (also **Locke**), inmate of Cheltenham Workhouse: I am about Forty Years of Age and the Son of Robert Lock and Ann his Wife
   I remember about thirty years ago being removed with my Father and Mother from Peglesworth [= Pegglesworth] in the said County to the Parish of Winchcomb [= Winchcombe] in the said County where my Father continued to reside from that time until his death which happened about Seventeen Years ago. My said Father received relief from the Overseers of Winchcomb aforesaid for nearly the whole time he so lived there and was buried at the Expence of the said Parish of Winchcomb. My Mother continued to reside in the said Parish of Winchcomb from the death of my said Father until her death which happened about three Years after the death of my said Father and she was relieved con[s]tantly by the Overseers of Winchcomb at so much per week until her death and was buried at the Expence of the said Parish of Winchcomb. My said Brother John was born in the said Parish Winchcomb [mark]

1844: *removal to Winchcombe (father's settlement) uncertain: examination form not signed by* **magistrates. 1851:** *JL (aged 33; agricultural labourer, born Winchcombe) was a visitor 25 Ivy St, Portsea, Hampshire (HO107/1659/279/6).* [PS/CH/RA/2/7:87; G/CH/60/4.]

44048SE: [blank] [blank] 1844 – **Ann Harpin**, widow, and two children **Ann** and **Thomas:** About Nine years ago I was married to my late husband Charles Harpin in the Parish Church of Cheltenham aforesaid by whom I had two Children now living namely Ann aged five years and and [*sic*] Thomas aged one Year and ten Months. My said husband died in Cheltenham aforesaid the 10th day of September 1843. My said husband never done any act to gain a settlement since our said Marriage.

I have done no act to gain a settlement since my said husband's death. I and my said Children are now actually chargeable to the said Parish of Cheltenham

1841: *AH (aged 23; shoe-binder) lived with daughter Ann (2) and son Thomas (1 month) in Rutland St, Cheltenham (HO107/353/7/59/23); Charles Harpin absent on census night.* **1842:** *death of Thomas (buried at Cheltenham 29 Jan).* **1843:** *husband Charles Harpin buried at Cheltenham 16 Oct.* **1844:** *removal unlikely: examination form incomplete; probably adjudged to be settled in Cheltenham.* **1845:** *AH remarried in Cheltenham to Francis Kingett: both lived at 62 Rutland St at marriage.* **1846:** *birth of son Thomas registered at Cheltenham 2Q.* **1851:** *Ann Kingett (née Harpin; 33, born Winchcombe) lodged with husband Francis (25; labourer, born Cheltenham) with children Thomas (4), William (2), and Ann (11; from Ann's first marriage) at Regent Place, Cheltenham (HO107/1973/353/14).* [PS/CH/RA/2/7:88.]

44049SE: Thurs 10 Oct 1844 – **William Roberts**, labourer, residing at 2 Upper Bath St, Cheltenham, **Hannah**, and six children **Emma**, **Hannah**, **Ellen**, **Elizabeth**, **Martha**, and **Ann**; also wife Hannah Roberts, inmate of Cheltenham Hospital and Dispensary, Edward John Young, house agent, the Promenade, Cheltenham, and James Vobes, builder, residing in Leckhampton, relating to the settlement of William Roberts. *Hannah Roberts*: About the latter end of the year 1836 I rented for and on account of my said husband of William Baldwin of Charles Street in the Parish of Leckhampton in the said County Stone Mason for the term of one year at the rent or sum of sixteen pounds a year a tenement consisting of a separate and distinct dwelling house situate and being N°. 17 in Charles Street aforesaid in the parish of Leckhampton aforesaid – My said husband entered into possession of the said premises immediately after they were so rented which was upon Mr Baldwin the Landlord leaving them and actually occupied all the said premises under the said renting in the said Parish from the said commencement of his tenancy until about the Spring of the year 1838. I am certain he resided there for more than a year and a half – I paid the said yearly rent for the time my husband occupied the said premises – During his said tenancy he resided constantly in the said Parish of Leckhampton. My said husband was duly assessed to the Poor Rate of the said Parish of Leckhampton in respect of the said premises for one year during the time he so occupied them and I paid the same – [mark]

William Roberts: I recollect living at Number 17 Charles Street in the Parish of Leckhampton in the said County. I recollect going there in the year 1836 and I know I was there more than a twelvemonth but I cannot say exactly how long. I know that my child Ellen was born there on the twenty ninth of May 1837 and that I occupied the said premises and resided there for some months afterwards. I did not rent the said premises myself. My wife rented them for me – she always paid the rent and poor Rates for me. I have never done any act to gain a Settlement since I left 17 Charles Street aforesaid. I was married to my wife Hannah about the year 1827 in the Parish Church of Hempstead [= Hempsted] near to the City of Gloucester by whom I have six children now living with me namely Emma aged 14 years Hannah aged 11 years Ellen aged 7 years Elizabeth aged 5 years Martha aged 3 years and Ann aged 14 months. I and my said wife and said children are now actually chargeable to the said Parish of Cheltenham. On last Friday I was relieved by Peter Butt the Relieving officer of the said Parish of Cheltenham with six quartern loaves and two shillings in money. [mark]

Edward John Young: [confirms that William Roberts was the tenant of Isaac New's property, 17 Charles Street, and paid rent of £16 from Lady Day 1837 until Lady Day 1838 and perhaps longer]

James Vobes: [confirms that William Roberts was assessed to the poor rate (7s 6d) for his house on Charles St on 16 October 1837]
1841: *Hannah Roberts (aged 40; charwoman) lived with seven children in Exmouth St, Cheltenham (husband William absent on census night) (HO107/353/12/39/15).* **1844: *removed to Leckhampton (renting).*** **1845:** *(RETURNED) Hannah died, aged 45 (buried at Cheltenham 22 Aug).* **1848:** *WR (of Bath Terrace, Cheltenham) remarried, to widow Elizabeth Dyke, 1 Oct.* **1851:** *the family lived at 19 Commercial St, Cheltenham: WR (43; labourer, born Frampton-on-Severn), Elizabeth (44; servant, born Yarpole, Heref), Emma (14; scholar), Ellen (13; dressmaker), Martha (10; scholar), and Ann (1) (all children born Cheltenham) (HO107/1973/892/42).* [PS/CH/RA/2/7:92, 93, 97, 98. Removal expenses for "Roberts" to Leckhampton 8/6 (4Q 1844: D4178).]

44050SE: 10 Oct 1844 – **Hannah Evans**, single woman, inmate of Union Workhouse, Cheltenham, and daughter **Sarah:** I am now about forty four years of age. When I was about nineteen years of age and unmarried and without child or children I was hired into the Parish of Froucester [= Frocester] in the said County by Messrs William and Nicholas Ford of that Parish Gentlemen to serve them for one year in that Parish. I was hired in the Summer time and immediately after the hiring went into the Service of my said Masters and continued in their Service the whole year and received my wages in full. I resided and slept in my said Masters House in Froucester aforesaid during the whole of that year – I have never done any act to gain a Settlement elsewhere. About eight years ago last January I was delivered of my illegitimate child Sarah who is now with me in the said Workhouse. We have been inmates of the said Workhouse about three months – we are now actually chargeable to the said Parish of Cheltenham – [signed]
1833: *inconclusive examination in Cheltenham:* **33031SE** *(HE: 27 Apr).* **1844: *removed to Frocester (hiring and service);*** *HE admitted to and discharged from Cheltenham Workhouse at various times in 1844 and 1845 (G/CH/60/4).* **1851:** *(RETURNED) HE (aged 50; born Frocester and living as widow) and daughter Sarah (16; born Cheltenham) worked as servants at 2 The Promenade (lodging-house) in Cheltenham (HO107/1973/739/52).* [PS/CH/RA/2/7:94 (similar text at 30 Sept 1844, page 89, struck out as examining magistrate died before removal order could be prepared). Removal expenses for "Evans" to Frocester 15/9 (4Q 1844: D4178).]

44051SE: 10 Oct 1844 – **Richard Goff** (also **Gough**), labourer, inmate of Union Workhouse, Cheltenham; also William Cole, greengrocer, of 288 High St, Cheltenham, relating to the settlement of Richard Goff. *Richard Goff*: I am about forty five years of age. About thirty one years ago being then unmarried and without child or children I was hired into the parish of Hanley Castle in the County of Worcester by M^rs. Lode of that Parish Widow and Baker for a year at the wages I believe of five pounds. I was hired at old Michaelmas and served to the next old Michaelmas when I left her said Service. I served the whole year and resided and slept during the year in my said Mistress' house at Hanley Castle aforesaid. I have never done an act to gain a Settlement elsewhere. About seven Years ago I was chargeable to the said Parish of Cheltenham and removed from thence by orders of Removal to the said Parish of Hanley Castle and was received there as a Parishioner. I was maintained at the Workhouse there for some weeks. I am now actually chargeable to the said Parish of Cheltenham [mark]
William Cole: [produces removal order of 14 Aug 1837 and confirms he conveyed Richard Goff to Hanley Castle]
1837: *removed to Hanley Castle, Worcs: see* **37053RO** *(RG: 14 Aug) (RETURNED).* **1844: *removed to Hanley Castle (hiring and service).*** **1845:** *(RETURNED) RG recorded as inmate of Cheltenham Workhouse mid-year.* **1848:** *RG admitted to Cheltenham Workhouse 25 June (G/CH/60/4/6); perhaps the Richard Gough (aged 49) buried at Cheltenham 7 Oct.* [PS/CH/RA/2/7:94, 96 (similar text of 30 Sept 1844, page 90, struck out as examining magistrate died before removal order could be prepared). Removal expenses for "Gough" to Hanley Castle, Worcs 14/6 (4Q 1844: D4178).]

44052SE: Sat 26 Oct 1844 – **John Troughton**, butcher, residing at 42 Stanhope St, Cheltenham, wife **Sarah**, and daughter **Mary:** Three years ago last Michaelmas I rented a separate and distinct Tenement consisting of a dwelling house and orchard and about one acre and a quarter of Land situate in the hamlet of Uckington in the Parish of Elmstone Hardwick [= Elmstone Hardwicke] in the said County from Sir Anthony Lechmere Baronet for the term of one whole year commencing on the twenty ninth day of September One thousand eight hundred and forty one at or for the sum of twelve pounds a year   I resided in and actually occupied all the said premises under the said yearly hiring in the said hamlet from the said commencement of my tenancy for the term of one whole year   I paid the said yearly rent of twelve pounds for the said term of one year – I was assessed to the Poor rates of the said Hamlet of Uckington in respect of the said tenement for the said one year during the time I so occupied it and paid the same. I have done no act to gain a settlement since. About thirty years ago I was married to my present wife Sarah at the Parish Church of Elmstone Hardwick aforesaid by whom I have two children now living with me namely Mary aged twenty five years and Sarah aged twenty four years – My said two children have always resided with me as part of my family and have never done an act to gain a Settlement in their own right. – they are both unmarried – I and my said wife and my said child Mary are now actually Chargeable to the said Parish of Cheltenham – and have received from Peter Butt the Relieving officer of the said Parish of Cheltenham on account of that Parish relief in bread and money. I received from him one shilling [signed]

1819/22: *at baptism of Mary and Sarah Troughton at Elmstone Hardwicke (1819 and 1822) their parents' "abode" was stated as "Bedlam".* **1841:** *the family lived in Uckington, Elmstone Hardwicke: JT (aged 50; butcher), Sarah (50), Mary (22), and Sarah (19) (HO107/354/24/5/4).* **1844: *removed to Elmstone Hardwicke (Cheltenham and Tewkesbury Unions) (renting).*** **1845:** *(RETURNED) John and Sarah Troughton (64 and 60 respectively) admitted to Cheltenham Workhouse in 2Q (discharged 23 Apr); Mary buried at Elmstone Hardwicke, aged 25 ("abode" given as Cheltenham) 6 Jan; Sarah buried at Elmstone Hardwicke, aged 23 ("abode" Cheltenham) 11 June.* **1851:** *JT (71; butcher, born Winchcombe) and Sarah (66; born Uckington) lived in Uckington (HO107/1972/6/4).* [PS/CH/RA/2/7:99. Removal exprenses for "Troughton" to Uckington 7/- (4Q 1844: D4178).]

44053SE: 26 Oct 1844 – **Elizabeth Perrott**, single woman, residing at 24 Lower Park St, Cheltenham, and daughters **Julia** and **Mary Ann:** I am now about fifty one years of age – About the years 1815 or 1816 being unmarried and without child or children I was hired into the Parish of Charlton Kings in the said County by Miss Paine of that Parish who then kept a Boarding School to serve her for one year at her Establishment at Charlton Kings aforesaid – The School was conducted by Miss Paine and Miss Watts   I went immediately into Miss Paine's Service and continued in the service under the same hiring for the space of one whole year thence Ensuing – I resided and slept at the House of my said Mistress at Charlton Kings aforesaid during the said year – I received my full years wages of Miss Paine. She was the manager of the School and Miss Watts was an assistant – I have never done an act to gain a Settlement since   Several years ago I think about twenty four years I was taken ill with a fever at Bath and applied to Mr Finch the then overseer of Charlton Kings aforesaid for relief. The Parish officers of Charlton Kings allowed me five shillings a week for six or seven weeks – I was then living with my Mother in Grove Street Cheltenham. My mother's name is Elizabeth Perrott. She died in last May. Fourteen years ago last Christmas I was delivered of an illegitimate child named Julia in Cheltenham. Nine years ago last Michaelmas I was delivered of an illegitimate child named Mary Ann in Cheltenham   I and my said two children are now actually Chargeable to Cheltenham. We have lately been relieved by Peter Butt the Relieving officer of Cheltenham with loaves of bread and four shillings in money at the charge of the said Parish of Cheltenham [signed]

1843: *EP's mother, Elizabeth Perrott, examined by Cheltenham magistrates: see* **43061SE** *(Elizabeth Perrott: 23 Sept).* **1844: *removed to Charlton Kings (hiring and service).*** **1851:** *(RETURNED) EP (aged 58; widow and dressmaker, born Painswick) lived at 7 Chapel St, Cheltenham, with daughters Julia (20) and Mary Ann (15; both boot-binders born Cheltenham) (HO107/1973/656/29); the family lived under the name of "Pitt".* **1861:** *Elizabeth Perrott Pitt died at Cheltenham, aged 68 (buried at New Burial Ground 5 Mar).* [PS/CH/RA/2/7:100. Removal expenses for "Perrott" to Charlton Kings 2/6 (4Q 1844: D4178).]

44054SE: Sat 2 Nov 1844 – **Benjamin Tustin**, labourer, residing at 11 Lower Park St, Cheltenham, with wife **Elizabeth:** I am sixty five years of age. I am the Son of Jonathan and Grace Tustin Parishioners of Painswick in the said County. they are both dead. I was at home with my Parents until I was between fifteen or sixteen years of age. When I was about sixteen years of age unmarried and without child or children I was hired into the Parish of Painswick in the said County by M^{rs}. Knight of that Parish Widow and Clothier to serve her for three years from the time of hiring. I went immediately into the service of Mrs Knight and continued in the same for the space of three years thence next ensuing. I slept at Painswick aforesaid during my said Service and I completed the whole three years of my said service in the said Parish of Painswick while I resided and slept there – I never went to service to be hired for a year before or after that time – I was in the Army about twenty one years – and then left the Army and returned to the said Parish of Painswick. About a year and a half after this I was married to my wife Elizabeth at the Parish Church of Painswick aforesaid – I continued to live at Painswick for two or three years and then we came to Cheltenham – after we had been at Cheltenham a little time I and my wife were taken ill. While we were so living at Cheltenham I received relief from the Parish officers of Painswick to the amount of twenty shillings. Within a twelvemonth after this I was removed by orders of removal by the Parish officers of Cheltenham to the Parish of Painswick aforesaid and taken to the Workhouse there with my said wife and my two children named Elizabeth and William. I was received with my said wife and children into the said Workhouse and maintained there. The Parish officers of Painswick aforesaid then provided us a house to live in at the charge of the said Parish of Painswick and situate in the George Court in Painswick aforesaid. We lived there about six months when I rented a House myself at Painswick aforesaid. I have never done any act to gain a Settlement elsewhere than at Painswick aforesaid. I and my said wife are now actually chargeable to the said Parish of Cheltenham. I have received relief from Peter Butt the Relieving officer of Cheltenham namely two loaves of bread and two shillings in money. [mark]
1844: *removed to Painswick (renting):* see **49062RO** *for further information.* [PS/CH/RA/2/7:101. Removal expenses for "Tustin" to Painswick 17/9 (4Q 1844: D4178).]

44055SE: 2 Nov 1844 – **John Stone,** clockmaker, residing at 22 Swindon Place, Cheltenham, wife **Eleanor**, and six children **William, Henry, Edward, John, Jane,** and **Elizabeth;** also Joseph Lane, shoemaker, residing in Barnwood, relating to the settlement of John Stone.
John Stone: I am thirty one years of age   When I was about fourteen years old I was bound apprentice to Joseph Lane of the Parish of Barnwood in the said County Shoemaker for a premium and consideration of twelve pounds for the term of seven years by the Indenture of Apprenticeship which Joseph Lane this day produces. The signature John Stone is mine and I saw Joseph Lane make his mark on it. – I served and lived with my said Master in the Parish of Barnwood aforesaid for five years when we separated by mutual Consent and I became free and went away from him. I completed the last forty days of my said service under the said Indenture in the said Parish of Barnwood while I there resided and slept. I have never done an act to gain a settlement elsewhere than at Barnwood. I was married to my wife Eleanor about eleven years ago at the Parish of Churchdown in the said County by whom I have Six children now living with me namely William aged ten years Henry aged eight years Edward aged six years John aged four years Jane aged two years and Elizabeth aged nine months. I and my said wife and my said Six Children are now actually chargeable to the said Parish of Cheltenham. I have received from Peter Butt the Relieving officer of Cheltenham relief in bread and five shillings a week in money [signed]
Joseph Lane: I produce an Indenture of Apprenticeship bearing date the fifth day of September 1826 by which the said John Stone was bound to serve me from the day of its date as an apprentice for the term of seven years thence next ensuing. The Indenture was duly executed by me and the said John Stone. He served me under the said Indenture for between four and five years residing all the time in my House in the Parish of Barnwood aforesaid – we had a little dispute and mutually agreed to separate – I have held the Indenture in my possession Since – he

became free with my consent and took his Clothes and things from my house and never returned to serve or live with me [mark]
1844: *removed to Barnwood (apprenticeship):* see **47023RO** *(JS: 12 June 1847) for further information.* [PS/CH/RA/2/7:101, 105. Notes: "At House". Removal expenses to Barnwood for "Stone" 17/6 (4Q 1844: D4178).]

44056SE: 2 Nov 1844 – **William Baylis**, labourer, with wife **Elizabeth**; also Ann Liddington, wife of John Liddington, labourer, residing in Chosen [= Churchdown], relating to the settlement of brother William Baylis.
Ann Liddington: I know the said William Baylis. He is my brother. – I am some years older than my said brother – Our parents Isaac Baylis and Elizabeth Baylis lived at the Parish of Winchcomb [= Winchcombe] in the said County as long as I can remember. They are both dead. I lived at home with my said Parents at Winchcomb aforesaid until I was as much as twenty years of age – I recollect my said brother William being born – he was born at my Said Parents house at Winchcomb aforesaid and lived at home with them until he was about fourteen years of age. He never did an Act to my knowledge to gain a Settlement in his own right. – [signed]
William Baylis: I am about fifty years of age   I never did an act whereby to gain a Settlement in my own right   My Father and Mother lived at Winchcomb [= Winchcombe] as long back as I can remember and continued to live there until their deaths. They are both dead – I always understood their Parish was Winchcomb. I do not know of my own knowledge where their Parish was. I do not know any one to whom to refer. I recollect that I lived at Winchcomb until I was fourteen or fifteen years of age. – My Sister Ann is older than me and lived at home at Winchcomb at my Fathers house for many years after my birth. I was married to my wife Elizabeth at Penryn in Cornwall thirteen years ago last May. I and my said wife are now actually chargeable to the said Parish of Cheltenham [signed]
1809: *WB, son of Isaac and Elizabeth Baylis, baptised at Winchcombe 14 May, four years after sister Ann.*
1844: *removed to Winchcombe (father's presumed settlement or WB's settlement through birth).* [PS/CH/RA/2/7:102, 104. Notes: [Ann Liddington] "At House". Removal expenses to Winchcombe for "Baylis" 8/- (4Q 1844: D4178).]

44057SE: Thurs 21 Nov 1844 – **James Barnett**, labourer, residing in Grove St, Cheltenham, with wife **Eliza:** I am now about thirty six years of age. When I was about nineteen years of age and unmarried and without child or children I was hired into the Parish of Chestlet [= Chislet] in the County of Kent by M'' Nean of that Parish Farmer to serve him for one whole year in that Parish – Immediately after the hiring I went into the service of my said Master and continued in his said service under the said yearly hiring for the said term of one year – and received my wages in full. I resided and slept in my said Master's house at Chestlet aforesaid during the whole of that year – I have never done an Act to gain a Settlement elsewhere. Near two years ago I was married to my present Wife Eliza at the Parish Church of Saint Mary de Lode in Gloucester. I and my said Wife are now actually chargeable to the said Parish of Cheltenham – We have received relief from Peter Butt the Relieving Officer relief [*sic*] in bread – Chestlet was my Father's Parish and he lives there now, and I was born there as I have heard and believe [mark]
1844: *removal unlikely as pauper died before removal; JB died "at his residence", 14 Grove St, Cheltenham 12 Dec (buried, aged 36, at New Burial Ground, Cheltenham 18 Dec (Cheltenham Chron. 26 Dec).* [PS/CH/RA/2/7:107 (see also shorter but similar struck-out draft on p. 106). Removal expenses for "Barnett" to Chislet, Kent £4/17/6 (4Q 1844) and £6/15/6 (1Q 1845: D4178).]

44058SE: Mon 2 Dec 1844/30 Nov – **Ann Dix**, single woman, residing at Union Workhouse, Cheltenham; also Joseph Dix, labourer, residing in Badgeworth, relating to the settlement of daughter Ann Dix.
Joseph Dix: I am about forty years of age   when I was about nineteen Years of Age and then unmarried and having no Child or Children I was hired by M'' William Smith of Highnam in the Parish of Churcham in the said County Farmer for a Year as Cowman from Michaelmas to

Michaelmas at the wages of six pounds   I continued in such Service the whole of the Year and resided and slept in my said Masters house at Highnam aforesaid the whole Year and received my year's wages. About twelve or thirteen years ago my Wife was ill and I was then residing in the Parish of Badgworth aforesaid and applied for Relief to the then Overseer of Highnam who continued to relieve me for five or six months during the whole of which time I was living in Badgworth aforesaid   My Wife then died and the Overseer of Highnam gave me a Sovereign towards the Expence of her funeral   I have done no act to gain a settlement since my said hiring and service as aforesaid

About Twenty Years ago I was married to my first wife Elizabeth at Hempstead [= Hempsted] Church by whom I had my said Daughter Ann born in lawful wedlock now of the age of 19 Years who continued to live with us as part of my family until about four Years ago [mark]

Ann Dix: I am about nineteen years of age. I am the daughter of Joseph and Elizabeth Dix. I always lived at home until about four years ago. I have never done an act to gain a Settlement in my own right. I am now actually chargeable to the said Parish of Cheltenham – [mark]

1844: *removed to Highnam, Churcham (father's settlement): see* **47004RO** *(AD: 30 Jan 1847) for further information.* [PS/CH/RA/2/7:108, 112. Note: [AD] "at Workhouse". Removal expenses to Highnam for "Dix" 15/- (1Q 1845: D4178).]

44059SE: 2 Dec 1844 – **Mary Ann Lockett**, single woman, inmate of Union Workhouse, Cheltenham; also Sarah Ruck, wife of Anthony Ruck, labourer, residing at Hunting Butts Cottage, Prestbury, relating to the settlement of niece Mary Ann Lockett.

Sarah Ruck: I know the said Mary Ann Lockett - she is now an Inmate of the Cheltenham Union Workhouse – she is about nineteen years of age. I recollect her birth at the house of my Father Peter Lockett Labourer in the Parish of Broadway in the County of Worcester   she is the daughter of my Sister Lydia Lockett who was confined of the said child at the House of my said Father in Broadway aforesaid – she is a bastard child – my said Sister was never married. My Father and her are both dead. When the said Mary Ann Lockett was about five years of age she came to live with me at Woodmancote in the Parish of Bishops Cleeve in this County. – While she was so living with me at Woodmancote aforesaid I applied to the Relieving officer of Broadway aforesaid for relief for her. He gave her relief weekly for several years while she resided with me at Woodmancote aforesaid – I recollect three times being present myself when he gave relief for her while she was so living with me at Woodmancote aforesaid – I recollect about five years ago receiving a month's relief from him for the said child – The said Mary Ann Lockett continued to live with me up to last Michaelmas   She never to my knowledge did an act to gain a Settlement [mark]

Mary Ann Lockett: I am nineteen Years of age the twelfth of next January. The first place I recollect myself in is the Parish of Broadway in the County of Worcester where I was born as I have heard and believe. I was taken from Broadway and lived several years with Sarah Ruck my Mother's Sister at Woodmancote in the Parish of Bishops Cleeve in this County and afterwards at Prestbury in this County. The overseer of Broadway paid two shillings a week for my relief while I lived at Woodmancote   When I was a little girl he gave me a pair of shoes and some other little things. I lived with my Aunt up to last Michaelmas. I never did an act to gain a Settlement in my own right. I am now actually chargeable to the said Parish of Cheltenham – [mark]

1841: *MAL (aged 10; baptised "Mary Lockett") lived with aunt Sarah Ruck (40; servant) and uncle Anthony Ruck (35; agricultural labourer) at Hunting Butts Farm Cottage, Prestbury (HO107/354/26/8/10-11).* **1844:** *removed to Broadway, Worcs (mother's settlement or MAL's settlement by birth).* **1845:** *MAL discharged from Cheltenham Workhouse 8 Jan 1845.* [PS/CH/RA/2/7:109, 110; G/CH/60/4). Removal expenses for "Lockett" to Broadway, Worcs 16/- (1Q 1845: D4178).]

44060SE: 2 Dec 1844 – **Thomas Cleevely** (also **Cleveley, Clevely**), labourer, inmate of Union Workhouse, Cheltenham, wife **Anne**, and four children, **Jane**, **George**, **Esther**, and **John:** I am now about thirty six years of age. About fourteen years ago being unmarried and without child or children I was hired into the hamlet of Southam in the Parish of Bishops Cleeve in this County by M[r] George Hone of Cockbury Farmer to serve him for a year from Michaelmas to Michaelmas as a Carter at the wages of Seven Pounds a Year. I entered immediately after the said hiring into his said Service and continued to work for him the whole year at Southam aforesaid and received my wages in full. I resided and slept during the whole of the twelvemonth at Mr Hone's house in Southam aforesaid. – I have never done an Act to gain a settlement since. – In the August after I left Mr Hone's said Service I was married to my present Wife Anne at the Parish Church of Winchcomb [= Winchcombe] in this County by whom I have four children namely Jane aged eleven years George aged ten years Esther aged five years and John aged two years. I and my said wife and my said four children are now actually chargeable to the said Parish of Cheltenham. [mark]

1841: *TC (aged 30; labourer) lived with wife Anne (30) and four children in London Rd, Charlton Kings (HO107/353/1/23/10).* **1844:** *removed to Southam (hiring and service).* **1843-5:** *(RETURNED) at various times the family were inmates of Cheltenham Workhouse (G/CH/60/4).* **1845:** *daughter Emma baptised 25 Jan 1845 at Cheltenham, when parents still inmates of Cheltenham Workhouse, and Jane, George, and Esther were inmates of Charlton Kings Workhouse for children (Cheltenham Union) (G/CH/60/3).* **1847:** *birth of Ann Elizabeth registered at Cheltenham 2Q.* **1851:** *TC (43; labourer, born Hatherley) lived with wife Anne (41; born Gretton), and children Jane (18), Hester (10), John (9), Emma (6), Ann Elizabeth (3; last three "scholars"), and Thomas William (1) at 2 Little's Row, New St, Cheltenham (HO107/1973/652/20).* [PS/CH/RA/2/7:111. Note: "at Workhouse". Removal expenses to Southam for "Cleevely" 5/- (4Q 1844) and 9/- (1Q 1845: D4178).]

44061SE: Sat 21 Dec 1844 – **Ambrose Dance**, labourer, residing in Fiddler's Green, near Gloucester Rd, Cheltenham, wife **Hannah**, and three children **Dinah, James**, and **Daniel:** About twenty six or twenty seven years ago when I was unmarried and without child or children I was hired into the Parish of Beckford in the said County [now Worcs] by M[r]. Richard Smith of Didcote in the said Parish Farmer to serve him at the said Parish of Beckford for one year from Michaelmas to Michaelmas as Carter. Accordingly upon the hiring I went into the service of the said Richard Smith and continued in the same service at the said Parish of Beckford for the space of one whole year thence ensuing – I resided and slept at my said Master's house in the said Parish of Beckford during the whole of my said year's service with him under the said yearly hiring. I received my years wages in full. After the said one year was expired being still unmarried and without child or children I was again hired by my said Master to serve him for one whole year at the said Parish of Beckford. I continued thenceforth in his said Service at the said Parish of Beckford for the said last mentioned one year and received my wages for the same service. I completed the last forty days of my said service in the said Parish of Beckford while I there resided and slept. I have done no act since to gain a Settlement. About six years ago I was working at the Hamlet of Uckington in the Parish of Elmstone Hardwick [= Elmstone Hardwicke] in the said County when I applied to the Parish officers of the said Parish of Beckford for relief. The Officers of the said Parish allowed me seven shillings and sixpence a week for eleven or twelve weeks while I resided in the Parish of Staverton in the said County. I have applied myself several times to Benjamin Slack the Relieving officer of the said Parish of Beckford for the said weekly relief and have from time to time received the same from him while I still resided in the said Parish of Staverton. About twenty two years ago last Michaelmas I was married to my present wife Hannah at the Parish of Boddington in the said County by whom I have three children now living with me namely Dinah aged nineteen years James aged twelve years and Daniel aged nine years. They have always lived at home with me and neither of these have done an act to gain a Settlement. I and my said wife and my said three children are now actually chargeable to the said Parish of Cheltenham and have received relief from Peter Butt the Relieving officer in bread. [mark]

1844: *removed to Beckford (hiring and service):* see **50038RO** *(AD: 24 Dec 1850) for further information on AD and family.* [PS/CH/RA/2/7:113. Removal expenses for "Dance" to Beckford 16/9 (1Q 1845: D4178).]

44062SE: 21 Dec 1844 – **William Tale** (also **Teal, Teale, Teil**), labourer, residing at 7 Elm St, Cheltenham, wife **Sarah**, and son **George**; also George Tale, labourer, residing in Elmstone Hardwicke, relating to the settlement of son William Tale.

William Tale: I am now about thirty years of age – I lived with my Father George Tale until within a twelvemonth of my being married. I was married to my present wife Sarah at the Parish Church of Elmstone Hardwick [= Elmstone Hardwicke] in the said County six Years ago last Michaelmas. I have never done an act to gain a Settlement in my own right. My said Father is legally settled at the Hamlet of Uckington in the said Parish of Elmstone Hardwick – I recollect about twenty five years ago my said Father's being removed with me as part of his Family by orders of removal from the hamlet of Bangrove [= Bengrove] in the said County to the said Hamlet of Uckington – We were received as Parishioners of the said Hamlet of Uckington and maintained at the expence of the said Hamlet and the said orders were not appealed against. I recollect at the time of my Mother's death twelve or thirteen years ago my said Father was chargeable to the said hamlet of Uckington while he resided in the said Parish of Elmstone Hardwick – The overseer of the said Hamlet allowed my said Father at that time half a Crown a week for several weeks while he is so resided in the said Parish of Elmstone Hardwick and out of the said hamlet of Uckington. I have applied to the said Overseer for the money myself on behalf of my said Father and received it for him. I have one child by my said Wife named George aged five years. I and my said wife and my said child are now actually chargeable to the said Parish of Cheltenham. We have received relief in bread from Peter Butt the Relieving officer. [mark]

George Tale: My Parish is Uckington in the said Parish of Elmstone Hardwick in the said County. I am near sixty years of age. When I was about twenty years of age I was hired by Mr John Roberts of Uckington aforesaid Farmer to serve him for a Year at Uckington aforesaid as Under Carter. I was unmarried and without child or children at the time of the said hiring. I served the whole Year at Uckington aforesaid and received my years wages – I resided and slept at my said Master's house at Uckington aforesaid during the said year under the said hiring. I have done no act to gain a Settlement elsewhere. I was removed by orders from Bengrove in the said County to the hamlet of Uckington aforesaid about twenty five Years ago. The Parish officers of Uckington aforesaid then put me into a Parish house and relieved me every week regularly for several weeks. I had relief from them weekly while I lived at Elmstone Hardwick aforesaid and not in the Hamlet of Uckington aforesaid – This was just before my wife died about twelve years ago. The Parish officers gave me twenty shillings to bury her. I was married to my wife Sarah at Winchcomb [= Winchcombe] in the said County about thirty five years ago by whom I had my said Son William [mark]

1841: *WT (aged 25; labourer) lived with wife Sarah (20) and son George in St Paul's St North, Cheltenham (HO107/353/8/25/7).* **1844:** *removed to Uckington (father's settlement).* **1845:** *(RETURNED) George Teal (5) admitted as an inmate of Charlton Kings Workhouse for children (Cheltenham Union) 17 Jan (G/CH/60/3), when parents admitted to Cheltenham Workhouse (G/CH/60/4).* **1848:** *daughter Mary Ann baptised at Elmstone Hardwicke 26 Apr.* **1851:** *the family lived in Elmstone Hardwicke: WT (36; railway labourer, born Bengrove), Sarah (28; born Cawston, Norfolk), George (11; scholar, born Alstone, Cheltenham), Mary Ann (3) and Alfred (4 mo: both born Elmstone Hardwicke) (HO107/1974/4/1).* [PS/CH/RA/2/7:114, 115. Removal expenses for "Tale" to Uckington 7/- (1Q 1845: D4178).]

44063SE: 21 Dec 1844 – **Elizabeth Dickason** (more often **Dickenson**), widow residing in Coach Rd, Cheltenham: About thirty two Years Ago I was married to my late husband John Dickason in the Parish Church of Walsall in the County of Stafford   About Eleven or twelve [years] ago my said husband rented a separate and distinct tenement consisting of a Dwelling house and about two acres and a half of pasture Land of Miss Harvey situate in the parish of Swindon in the said County for a Year at the Yearly rent of Thirty pounds. I and my said husband continued to reside in such house and occupied the said Land at such Yearly rent for the space of about Eight or nine Years and paid the whole of the rent for the same

My said husband was duly rated to all the Poor Rates made for the said Parish of Swindon during the whole of the time we so resided there and paid all such Rates. My said husband never done any act to gain a settlement afterwards and died about three Months ago in Cheltenham aforesaid. I have done no Act since his death to gain a settlement. I am now actually chargeable to the said Parish of Cheltenham having been relieved by the Relieving officer for that Parish with a loaf of Bread [mark]

1844: *John Dickenson buried 30 Sept at New Burial Ground, Cheltenham, aged 68;* **removed to Swindon (husband's settlement).** **1847:** *(RETURNED) death of ED (buried at New Burial Ground, Cheltenham 17 July, aged 65).* [PS/CH/RA/2/7:118. Removal expenses for "Dickason" to Swindon 2/- (1Q 1845: D4178).]

44064SE: Sat 28 Dec 1844 – **Samuel Cook** (also **Cooke**), labourer, wife **Sarah**, and six children **Harriet**, **Eliza**, **John**, **Jane**, **Samuel**, and **Sarah**; also Nathaniel Cook, labourer, residing in Randwick, relating to the settlement of son Samuel Cook**.**

Nathaniel Cook: I am about Seventy nine Years of Age and have resided in the said Parish of Randwick all my lifetime and where I was born   I have never been hired for a Year or rented a tenement of the annual value of ten pounds or done any other Act to gain a settlement in my own right. About forty nine Years ago I was married to my late Wife Elizabeth in the parish Church of Randwick aforesaid by whom I had my said Son Samuel now aged about thirty six years. My said Son Samuel was born in the said Parish of Randwick and lived with me there as part of my family until he was about fifteen years of age

I have been receiving relief from the Parish officers of Randwick aforesaid for nearly two Years last past. I have always heard and believe that my Fathers Parish was Randwick aforesaid   He has been dead for some years and I cannot tell any body living who can give evidence about his settlement [mark]

Samuel Cook: I am about thirty Six Years of age. the first place I remember myself was living with my Father Nathaniel Cook and my Mother Elizabeth Cook in the parish of Randwick in the said County and with whom I resided in that Parish until I was about fifteen Years of age   I have never been hired for a Year or rented a tenement of the annual value of ten pounds or done any other Act to gain a Settlement in my own right   About fifteen Years ago I was married to my present Wife Sarah in the Parish Church of Randwick aforesaid by whom I have six Children namely Harriet aged fourteen Years Eliza aged Eleven years John aged nine years Jane aged seven years Samuel aged four [years] and Sarah aged two years   I am now actually chargeable to the said Parish of Cheltenham [mark]

1841: *SC (aged 30; agricultural labourer) lived near the Lansdown turnpike, Cheltenham, with wife Sarah (35), and children William (13), Harriet (11), Eliza (7), John (4), and Jane (3) (HO107/353/11/9/13).* **1844: removed to Randwick (father's presumed settlement).** **1845:** *(RETURNED) birth of daughter Elizabeth registered 3Q at Cheltenham.* **1847:** *death of SC's wife Sarah in Cheltenham (buried at New Burial Ground 23 Jan); SC (coal dealer and widower, son of Nathaniel Cook) remarried 23 Feb to Eliza Walkley (servant) in Rodborough.* **1851:** *the family lived in Birmingham, Warks: SC (40; agricultural labourer, born Randwick), Eliza (36), and children Jane (11; born Randwick), Samuel (8; rope-spinner), and Elizabeth (6; scholar at home; last two born Cheltenham) (HO107/2051/313/12).* [PS/CH/RA/2/7:119, 120. Removal expenses for "Cooke" to Randwick £1/-/9 (1Q 1845: D4178).]

1845

45001SE: Thurs 9 Jan 1845 – **James Betteridge**, wood-turner, residing at 5 Hungerford Rd, Cheltenham, wife **Jane**, and five children **Caroline**, **Sarah**, **James**, **John**, and **Mary;** also Mary Betteridge, single woman, residing in Camden Terrace, Cheltenham, relating to the settlement of brother James Betteridge.

James Betteridge: I am about thirty seven years of age. I have never done an act to gain a Settlement in my own right – My Grandfather and my Father's Parish is Drayton in the County of Oxford – I was born at Drayton as I have heard and believe. I have a Sister named Mary living at Cheltenham who is older than me and knows that I was born at Drayton – My Father was acknowledged a Parishioner at Drayton and I recollect his receiving relief from the Parish Officers of Drayton for his eldest Son. – I was married to my present wife Jane about eleven Years ago at Saint Phillips [*sic*] Church Birmingham by whom I have five children namely Caroline aged eleven years Sarah aged seven years James aged five years John aged three years and Mary aged ten months. I and my said wife and my said five children are now actually Chargeable to the said Parish of Cheltenham. We have received relief in bread and other things from Peter Butt the Relieving officer for several weeks past. My Father received the said relief for his said Eldest Son John for several years namely for about twenty six twenty seven and twenty eight years ago up to my said brother John's death about twenty Six years ago. All my Brothers and Sisters but Mary Betteridge and my Father and Mother are dead. My Father died about fifteen years ago and my Mother died about two years after him. I lived at home at my Father's house at Drayton aforesaid from my birth until I was about sixteen years of age. I recollect my said Father's residing at the Parsonage House at Drayton aforesaid for several years I resided there with him as part of his family [signed]

Mary Betteridge: I lived at home with my Father and Mother at Drayton in the County of Oxford from my birth until I was near eighteen years of age. I recollect my said brother James Betteridge when he was about eighteen months old living at my said Father's house at Drayton aforesaid. I am older than he is. I was at home at the time of his birth. My Father and Mother are both dead. I am the eldest Member of the Family now living. I have no doubt my said brother was born at Drayton aforesaid. I am about six years older than my said brother – The first time I left my home at Drayton aforesaid was about the time of the birth of my Sister Caroline who was born the Christmas twelvemonth after my said brother James. I dont know that I had ever slept from home before this time - My Father Thomas was a Farmer living at Drayton aforesaid. I recollect his residing at the Parsonage house at Drayton aforesaid as much as eight or ten years. I know that he resided there the year of 1814 and had resided there some years before as well as some years after that year – I resided there with him the whole time as part of his Family and so did my said brother James   he was the tenant of Mr John Richmond Senior who then lived at Drayton aforesaid. The Parsonage was a large house with a garden in front and behind – My Father was then in respectable circumstances and carried on the baking business for a few years. There was a large oven and bakehouse on the Premises – [signed]

1841: *JB (aged 30; wood-turner) lived in Holloway Head, Birmingham with wife Jane (30), and children Caroline (8), Sarah (4), James (2), and Jonathan (10 mo) (HO107/1147/6/32/7).* **1844:** *removed to Birmingham, Warks (apprenticeship): see* **44020SE** *(JB: Feb 1844) (RETURNED).* **1845:** *removed to Drayton, Oxon (father's settlement); (RETURNED) death of JB in Cheltenham (buried 25 Apr, aged 38).* **1851:** *surviving family lived at 4 Queen's Retreat, Cheltenham: Jane Betteridge (42; sempstress and widow, born Fillongley, Warks), Sarah (14; servant, born Birmingham, Warks), James (12; labourer in Rope Walk, born Birmingham), John (10; scholar) and Mary (7; both born Cheltenham).* [PS/CH/RA/2/7:116, 117. Removal expenses for "Betteridge" to Drayton, Oxon £2/-/6 (1Q 1845) and £4/3/- (2/3Q 1845: D4178).]

45002SE: Mon 13 Jan 1845 – **Jane Tipper**, single woman, residing at Union Workhouse, Cheltenham: I am about twenty one years of age. I was born at the Parish of Stroud in the said

County as I have heard and believe. I have never done an act to gain a Settlement in my own right. I lived at home with my Father Abraham Tipper until I was about thirteen years of age, up to the time of his death which happened about eight years ago. My said Father died at Gloucester – Immediately after my said Father's death I was actually chargeable with my youngest brother James, between four or five years of age to the Parish of Saint Mary de Crypt in the City of Gloucester and we were both taken into the Gloucester Union Workhouse. We remained in the said Workhouse about two months and were then removed by orders of removal to the said Parish of Stroud. Mr Estcourt the Mayor's officer of Gloucester took us from Gloucester and left us at the House of the overseer of Stroud The overseer took us to the Stroud Union Workhouse. I remained in the said Workhouse for some weeks. When I went out to service, the said orders of removal were not appealed against. My said Father's Parish was Stroud. I left my said brother in the said Stroud Workhouse. I am actually chargeable to the said Parish of Cheltenham and am maintained in the said Workhouse of Cheltenham – [signed]
1845: *removed to Stroud (father's presumed settlement); JT was an inmate of Cheltenham Workhouse from 12 Dec 1844 until 28 May 1845 (G/CH/60/4).* [PS/CH/RA/2/7:121. Removal expenses for "Tipper" to Stroud 17/6 (1Q 1845: D4178).]

45003SE: Mon 20 (twice)/25 Jan 1845 – Elizabeth Jeans, widow, residing in Newent, relating to the settlement of son **Charles Jeans** (also **Janes, Jeanes, Jeynes**), inmate of Gloucester County Lunatic Asylum; also Frederick Thomas Griffiths, solicitor, and Mr Charles Edward Prior, surgeon, currently residing in Gloucester, relating to the settlement of Charles Jeans. *Frederick Thomas Griffiths*: [confirms baptism of Charles, son of Richard and Elizabeth Jeans, on 31 July 1790, at Newent]
Elizabeth Jeans: I have read the extract produced by Frederick Thomas Griffiths touching the place of the last legal settlement of my said Son. The Charles Jeans there mentioned is my said Son by Richard Jeans my late husband – he was born in the Parish of Newent in the said County in the year 1790. I was married to my said husband Richard Jeans at the said Parish of Newent about sixty years ago and have always lived in the said Parish of Newent since my said marriage – All my children were born in the said Parish of Newent – my said Son Charles lived at the said Parish of Newent until he was grown up and went for a Soldier. he never did an act to my knowledge to gain a Settlement out of the said Parish of Newent – My late husband Richard Jean's [*sic*] Parish is Newent and I am an acknowledged Parishioner of the said Parish of Newent and have been for many years last past and [am] in receipt of a weekly allowance from the Parish officers for my support. [mark]
Charles Edward Prior: [confirms that Charles Jeans has been an inmate of Gloucester County Lunatic Asylum since 18 Mar 1843, and that he has incurred costs of £22 over past calendar year for maintenance, medicine, clothing, and care]
1841: *CJ (aged 50; labourer) lived with wife Ann (40), and children Job (15; labourer), William (9), and Betsy (6) in New St, Cheltenham (HO107/353/16/20/1-21/2).* **1845:** *removed to Newent (father's settlement). (RETURNED) CJ must have recovered from the mental problems which arose in 1843 as in 1851 he is still living in New St, Cheltenham (30): CJ (61; building labourer, born Newent), Ann (54; born Cirencester), and William (19; building labourer, born Cheltenham) (HO107/1973/627/19).* [PS/CH/RA/2/7:122, 123, 126. Removal expenses for "Janes" to Newent 14/- (1Q 1845: D4178). See also **43025SE**: Jeynes.]

45004SE: Sat 25 Jan 1845 – **Ann Paul**, widow, residing in Streathers Passage, Mount Pleasant, Cheltenham, and three children **James**, **Elizabeth**, and **Esther:** I am the Widow of James Paul late of the Parish of Stroud in the said County Dyer who died seven years ago. I was married to my said husband at Hawkesbury Church in the said County about the year 1831. About three years before my said husband's death that is to say about the year 1835 my said husband purchased of Mr William Hopson of Stroud aforesaid Gentleman for the sum of Sixty Four pounds a cottage buildings and garden situate at the Upper part of the Town of Stroud in the said Parish of Stroud – My said husband rebuilt the said premises and lived therein with me until his death in 1838. My said husband resided in the said Parish of Stroud from the time I married him until his death. I continued to reside in the said house for some months after my said husband's death and have been in receipt of the rents and profits thereof since I left it. I have done no act to gain a Settlement elsewhere than in the said Parish of Stroud. I have three children by my said husband now living with me as part of my family namely James aged thirteen years – Elizabeth aged twelve years and Esther aged nine years. I and my said children are now actually chargeable to the said Parish of Cheltenham   I have received one loaf of bread from Peter Butt the Relieving officer of Cheltenham [signed]

1841: *AP (aged 25; servant) lived at 4 Briggs's Court, New St, Cheltenham, with children James (9), Elizabeth (8), and Hester (5) (HO107/353/15/57/22-23).* **1845: removed to Stroud (husband's settlement).** **1846:** *(RETURNED) from 3Q until 4Q AP and three children received parish relief from Stroud as non-settled residents of Cheltenham (G/CH/9d/1).* **1850:** *death of AP 1 Sept, pauper lunatic at Gloucester Asylum, the day after she was certified insane and sent to the asylum* (Cheltenham Chron. *5 Sept).* **1851:** *children Elizabeth (17) and Hester (14; both bonnet-makers, born Stroud) lived in lodging house in Grove St, Cheltenham (HO107/1973/633/31); son James (19; general porter; born Cheltenham) lodged at 275 High St, Cheltenham, with beer-house keeper (HO107/1973/615/1).* [PS/CH/RA/2/7:124. Removal expenses for "Paul" to Stroud £1/1/- (1Q 1845: D4178).]

45005SE: 25 Jan 1845 – **Jane Sollis** (also **Sallis**, **Sollice**), widow, residing at 8 Queen's Place, Tewkesbury Rd, Cheltenham, and daughter **Priscilla:** I am the widow of John Sollis who died at the Parish of Hawling in this County about eleven years ago. I was married to him twenty eight years ago at the Parish Church of Hemstead [= Hempsted] in the said County. I have one child by my said husband named Priscilla aged seventeen years now living with me who has been always ill from her birth and has never done an act to gain a Settlement in her own right. My said husband's Parish was Hawling aforesaid. he gained his Parish there by hiring and service there while he was single and unmarried with Mr Ruck of that Parish Farmer. he lived with Mr Ruck two years – my said husband was chargeable to the said Parish of Hawling for as much as eight or nine Years before he died. He lost his sight and was incapable of labour. he was buried at the expence of the said Parish of Hawling. About five years ago I and my said daughter Priscilla were chargeable to the said Parish of Hawling and received relief from the overseer for five or six weeks in money and bread. I have never done an act to gain a Settlement since my said husband's death. I and my said daughter Priscilla are now actually chargeable to the said Parish of Cheltenham. [mark]

1845: removed to Hawling (husband's settlement): *see* **47019RO** *(Priscilla Sollis: 15 May 1847) for further information on JS and family.* [PS/CH/RA/2/7:125. Removal expenses for "Sollis" to Hawling 18/9 (1Q 1845: D4178) and 7/3 (2Q 1846: D4178).]

45006SE: Thurs 30 Jan 1845 – **Harriet Beesley** (also **Beasley, Besley**), widow, and three children **Emma, Edward,** and **Henry:** I am the Widow of Henry Beasley late of the parish of Dudley in the County of Worcester who died at Cheltenham aforesaid in December 1840 – I was married to my said Husband in the year 1832 – at Saint Martin's Church in Birmingham by whom I have three Children now living with me, namely Emma aged ten years – Edward aged nine years and Henry aged four years – After my said Marriage (that is to say) in the year 1835 – my said late Husband Henry Beesley in my presence took and rented of Luke Jukes of Dudley aforesaid Maltster for the term of one whole year commencing on the Twenty fifth day of December 1835 – at the Rent of Ten pounds a year – a Tenement consisting of a separate and distinct dwelling house situate in Bond Street in the parish of Dudley aforesaid – My said Husband actually occupied all the said premises under the said yearly renting in the said Parish of Dudley from the said commencement of his said tenancy until June 1837 – being One Year and six months – I lived there during that time – The said yearly Rent of Ten pounds was paid to the said Luke Jukes for the said term of One year – I had the Receipts for the said Rent signed by the said Luke Jukes, but which Receipts I have lost – During the whole of my said husband's said tenancy he resided and slept upon the said premises in the said Parish of Dudley – My said husband was assessed to the poor rate for the said Parish of Dudley in respect of the said Tenement so rented by him of the said Luke Jukes as aforesaid for the said One year and six months he so occupied the same as aforesaid – and I saw that the same rates were duly paid – I

had the Receipts for the said rates and they are now lost – My said Husband did no act afterwards to gain a Settlement – I have done no act since my said Husband's death to gain a Settlement - I and my said three children are now actually chargeable to the said parish of Cheltenham [signed]
1845: *apparently removed to Dudley, Worcs (husband's settlement): see* **45033SE** *(HB: 14 June 1845) for further information.* [PS/CH/RA/2/7:127.]

45007SE: Sat 8 Feb 1845 – **James Brown**, labourer: About Eighteen Years ago being then unmarried and having no Child or Children I was hired into the Parish of Wormington in the said County by the late Josiah Guest [= Gist] Esquire of the Grange in that Parish to serve him for a Year as Coachman at the wages of Twenty Eight Guineas. I served the whole year under such hiring and resided and slept in my said Masters house at the Grange in the said Parish of Wormington the whole year and received my Years wages   I have done no act since to gain a settlement   I am now actually chargeable to the said Parish of Cheltenham having been relieved by the relieving officer of that Parish with Bread and lodging [signed]
1845: *removed to Wormington (presumed) (hiring and service).* [PS/CH/RA/2/7:128.]

45008SE: 8 Feb 1845 – **Keziah** (also **Kesiah**) **Jones**, single woman; also Charles Maisey, magistrates' office, relating to the settlement of Keziah Jones.
Keziah Jones: About two Years ago I and my Mother Mary Jones Widow and my two Brothers Edwin then aged 13 Years and George then aged five Years became chargeable to the said Parish of Cheltenham and were by the Parish officers of that Parish sent by Orders of removal from thence to the Parish of Deerhurst Walton in the said County and delivered to the Overseers of that Parish who received us   Such Orders of removal were not Appealed against   I have done no Act to gain a settlement – I am now actually Chargeable to the said Parish of Cheltenham having been relieved by the relieving officers of that Parish with two loaves of Bread [mark]
Charles Maisey: [confirms removal of Mary Jones and family to Deerhurst Walton by order of 7 Feb 1843 and that there was no appeal]
1843: *removed to Deerhurst Walton (mother's settlement): see* **43015RO** *(mother Mary Jones: 27 Feb) for further information.* **1845:** *(RETURNED) removed to Deerhurst Walton (mother's settlement).* [PS/CH/RA/2/7:129, 131. Removal expenses for "Jones" to Deerhurst 12/-" and 14/6 (1Q 1845: D4178).]

45009SE: 8 Feb 1845 – **Mary Hunt**, single woman: About fifteen years ago being then unmarried and having no Child or Children I was hired into the Parish of Walcot Bath in the County of Somerset by Mrs Haviland of Brock Street in the parish of Walcot aforesaid to serve her in that Parish for a Year at the wages of ten Guineas a Year a months wages or a months warning   I served two years and nine months under such hiring and resided and slept in my said Mistresses house in Brock Street Walcot aforesaid the whole time   I left her service on account of ill health and remained out of place for about four or five months when being still unmarried and having no child or children   I was hired by Mrs Wall of Cavendish place in the said Parish of Walcot for a Year at the wages of Nine Guineas a months wages or a months warning   I served two years and about six Months under such last mentioned hiring and resided and slept the whole time in my said Mistress Mrs Walls house in Cavendish place Walcot aforesaid   I have done no act to gain a settlement since I am now actually chargeable to the said Parish of Cheltenham having been relieved by the relieving officer of that Parish with two shillings and a loaf of Bread [mark]
1845: *removed to Walcot, Bath, Som (hiring and service).* [PS/CH/RA/2/7:130. Note: Removal expenses to Walcot for "Hunt" £1/13/- (1Q 1845: D4178).]

45010SE: Sat 15 Feb 1845 – **James Capper**, labourer, residing at 11 Malvern Place, Cheltenham, wife **Eliza**, and seven children **George, James, William, Charles, Henry, John, Edwin**: About thirty one Years ago being then unmarried and having no Child or Children I was hired into the Parish of Sandhurst in the said County by Mr John Drinkwater of that parish Farmer for a Year at the wages of three pounds ten Shillings   I served the whole year in that Parish under such hiring and resided and slept in my said Masters house at Sandhurst aforesaid the whole year and received my years wages. I have done no act since to gain a Settlement   Twenty years ago last Christmas I was married to my present Wife Eliza at Cheltenham Church by whom I have Eight Children seven of whom are now living with me namely George aged Nineteen Years James aged twelve Years William aged ten Years Charles aged Eight Years Henry aged six years John aged three years and Edwin aged Eleven months. Neither of my said Children have done any act to gain a settlement in their own right. I am now actually chargeable to the said Parish of Cheltenham having received relief from the receiving office of that Parish in Bread [mark]

1831: *removed to Sandhurst (presumed) (hiring and service): see* **31047SE** *(JC: 7 Apr); one or more JC of Cheltenham was imprisoned for short periods in 1830s and 1840s for larceny.* **1841:** *JC (aged 40; labourer) lived in Little Norwood St, Leckhampton with wife Eliza (30) and children James (10) and Charles (5) (HO107/353/18/34/4); other children lived with grandparents William (aged 72; agricultural labourer) and Hannah Capper in Rudford near Hartpury (HO107/355/6/5/5).* **1843:** *probably the JC (44) found not guilty of larceny at Gloucester County Assizes 5 Apr (RETURNED).* **1845:** ***removed to Sandhurst (hiring and service).*** **1847:** *(RETURNED) son David baptised at Cheltenham 14 Nov.* **1850:** *daughter Eliza baptised at Cheltenham 27 Oct, when family lived in Elm St, Cheltenham; son David buried at Cheltenham 21 Nov.* **1851:** *wife Eliza buried, aged 47, at New Burial Ground, Cheltenham 13 Mar; on census night JC (57; labourer, born Newent) lived at 16 Elm St, Cheltenham with children Henry (13; labourer), Edwin (5; scholar) and Eliza (6 mo) (HO107/1973/516/10).* [PS/CH/RA/2/7:132. Removal expenses for "Capper" to Sandhurst 19/6 (1Q 1845: D4178).]

45011SE: Thurs 20 Feb 1845 – Sarah Phillips, widow, residing at 2 Cornwall Row, St Michael's, Bath, and Charles Edward Prior, surgeon, residing in Gloucester, relating to the settlement of **Mary Ann Phillips**, inmate of Gloucester Lunatic Asylum.

Sarah Phillips: I am upwards of Sixty Years of age – I am the Aunt of Mary Ann Phillips at present a patient in the Gloucester Lunatic Assylum – she is the daughter of Charles and Susanna Phillips who lived in the Parish of Walcot in the said County of Somerset several years before and after the birth of the said Mary Ann Phillips there – The said Charles Phillips died in the said Parish of Walcot about ten years ago and was buried at the expence of the said Parish of Walcot – His wife was relieved by the Parish officers of Walcot weekly with money from the time of her husband's death up to the time of her own death about eight or nine years ago and the said Mary Ann Phillips was then living with her in the said Parish of Walcot as part of her Family. When she died she was buried at the expence of the said Parish of Walcot – One of her children named James with Eliza [*sic*] were taken into the Parish of Walcot's Workhouse by me immediately after the death of their said Mother and they were received there as Parishioners of Walcot – James has continued in the Workhouse ever since up to the present time chargeable to the said Parish of Walcot – I recollect the said Mary Ann Phillips being born in the said Parish of Walcot in the year 1822. Her said Parents then lived at N° 21 Milk Street in the said Parish of Walcot – I lived then within two or three doors of them in the same Street and attended upon the Mother at the confinement – The said Mary Ann Phillips has never done an Act to gain a Settlement in her own right   I produce a copy from the register of baptisms in the said Parish of Walcot made the seventeenth day of this month by which the said Mary Ann Phillips appears to have been born 1ᵈ May 1822 - [mark]

Charles Edward Prior: [confirms that Mary Ann Phillips was an inmate of Gloucester County Lunatic Asylum from 1 Oct 1844, and has incurred charges of £9 for maintenance, medicine, clothing, and care]

1845: ***died before removal to Walcot, Som (father's presumed settlement)***; *MAP died on 14 Mar of "Epilepsy" at the Gloucester Asylum, aged 22.* [PS/CH/RA/2/7:133, 136.]

45012SE: 20 Feb 1845 – **James Strange**, labourer, wife **Elizabeth**, and daughter **Rhoda Ann**; also Daniel Strange, labourer, residing in Poole Keynes, Wilts, relating to the settlement of son James Strange.

Daniel Strange: About thirty one years ago being then unmarried and having no Child or Children I was hired into the said parish of Poole by Mʳ Stephens of that Parish Farmer for a Year at the wages of twelve shillings a week for the Winter and fifteen shillings a week for the summer. I served the said Mr Stephens the whole Year under that hiring and resided and slept in his house at Poole aforesaid the whole time   I have done no act since to gain a settlement

About thirty Years ago I was married to my late Wife Maria in the parish Church of Poole aforesaid by whom I had my said Son James who was born in the said Parish of Poole about twenty eight years ago

I have been receiving relief from the said Parish of Poole for several Years last past. [mark]

James Strange: I am about twenty eight Years of age   the first place I remember myself was in the parish of Poole in the County of Wilts where I resided with my parents Daniel Strange and Maria his Wife until I was about twenty years of age

I have never done any act to gain a settlement in my own right   Four years ago last Michaelmas I was married to my present Wife Elizabeth in the parish Church of Poole aforesaid by whom I have one Child named Rhoda Ann aged three Years   I am now actually Chargeable to the said Parish of Cheltenham having been relieved by the relieving officer of that Parish with four, one shilling loaves of Bread [signed]

1845: *removed to Poole Keynes, Wilts (father's settlement): see* **52002RO** *(JS: 26 Jan 1852) for further information.* [PS/CH/RA/2/7:134. Removal expenses for "Strange" to Poole Keynes, Wilts £1/9/- (3Q 1845: D4178).]

45013SE: Wed 26 Feb 1845 – **Lucy Sheargold** (also **Shergold**), single woman, residing at 5 Fairview St, Cheltenham, and daughter **Alice:** In the Year One thousand Eight hundred and thirty two being then unmarried and having no Child or Children I was hired by Mr William Lingham of Broad Street in the parish of All Saints in the City of Worcester Baker to serve him in the said Parish of All Saints for a Year at the wages of ten pounds a Year, a months wages or a months warning

I served the whole Year under such hiring and received my years wages and resided and slept in my said Masters house in Broad Street in the parish of All Saints aforesaid the whole Year. I have done no act since to gain a settlement. I was delivered of a female bastard Child on the twenty second day of January last.

I am now actually chargeable to the said Parish of Cheltenham having been relieved by the relieving Officer of that Parish with Bread Meat tea sugar & other Articles [signed]

1841: *LS (aged 25; servant) lived in household of Charles Hale, music-seller in Crescent Terrace, Cheltenham (HO107/353/15/12/18-19).* **1845:** *illegitimate daughter Alice born at 5 Fairview St, Cheltenham, 22 Jan; removed to All Saints, Worcester (hiring and service) (appealed against).* **1851:** *LS (38; cook, born Shelsley Beauchamp, Worcs) lived in Claines, Worcs (HO107/2042/302/62); daughter Alice remained in Cheltenham as "nurse-child" in family of Mary Cox (50; ironer) at Hill Field, Gloucester Rd.* [PS/CH/RA/2/7:137. The Churchwardens and Overseers of All Saints, Worcester appealed against the decision to remove LS to their parish 22 Mar 1845: P78/1/OV/3/5.]

45014SE: Thurs 27/24 Feb 1845 – **Elizabeth Britton** (also **Brittain**), wife of Joseph Britton (transported); also Mary Britton, widow, residing in Sedgeberrow, near Evesham, Worcs, relating to the settlement of daughter-in-law, Elizabeth Britton.

Mary Briitton: I am the widow of Edward Brittain Labourer. I was married to him about thirty years ago at the Parish of Ripple in the said County of Worcester by whom I had my Son Joseph born in lawful wedlock – His parish was Upton upon Severn [= Upton-upon-Severn] in the said County of Worcester – he gained his Parish there by being hired when he was unmarried and without child or children about four years before our said Marriage by Mr Ricketts of that Parish Farmer for a year and serving in that Parish under that hiring for the said year and residing at Mr Rickett's house in that Parish during the said year to the best of my knowledge   I lived with my said husband at Upton upon Severn aforesaid for five years after our said Marriage when my said Son Joseph was born there – about four months after our marriage – Mr Ricketts is dead - [mark]

Elizabeth Britton: About thirteen Years ago I was married to my husband Joseph Brittain in the Parish Church of Charlton Kings in the said County   My said Husband was transported about two Years and a half ago   He never done any act to my knowledge to gain a settlement either by renting a tenement of the annual value of ten pounds or otherwise   I am now actually chargeable to the said Parish of Cheltenham having been relieved by the relieving officer of that Parish with sum of Four shillings [mark]

1841: *EB (aged 30; servant) lived alone in Sun St, Cheltenham (HO107/353/9/38/25), while husband Joseph Britton (28; alias Joseph Williams, "tramper") served an eighteen-month sentence for stealing a copper furnace; Joseph had been in constant trouble with the law for theft since his teens.* **1843:** *at Epiphany Sessions at Gloucester 3 June Joseph sentenced to one day in Penitentiary followed by transportation for ten years, for stealing another copper furnace and an iron bar; he was transferred from local gaol to hulk* Justitia *at Woolwich.* **1845:** *removed to Upton-upon-Severn, Worcs (husband's settlement).* **1845-6:** *(RETURNED) from 2Q 1845 until 4Q 1846 EB (35) received parish relief from Upton-upon-Severn as a non-settled resident of Cheltenham (G/CH/9d/1).* **1851:** *Joseph (40; labourer, born Upton-upon-Severn, Worcs, perhaps not transported) lodged with wife EB (39, born Charlton Kings) in Wednesbury, Staffs (HO107/2027/206/18).* **1881:** *the couple moved to Hargate Lane, West Bromwich: Joseph Britton (72; labourer, born Worcs) and EB (69; born Charlton Kings) (RG11/2850/57/9).* [PS/CH/RA/2/7:138, 139. Removal expenses for "Britton" to Upton-upon-Severn 19/6 (2-3Q 1845: D4178). See also removal expenses for "Britton" to Upton-upon-Severn 12/- (2Q 1848: D4178).]

45015SE: 27 Feb 1845 – **James Yeend**, labourer, wife **Amelia**, and son **James**; also Hannah Yeend, residing in Waterloo Place, Cheltenham, relating to the settlement of son James Yeend.

Hannah Yeend: About twenty seven Years ago I was married to my Husband Charles Yeend in the parish Church of Elmstone Hardwicke in the said County by whom I had my said Son James now aged about twenty three Years. My said Husband is insane and has been confined in the Lunatic Assylum for more than Eight years last past

About fourteen years ago My said husband rented a separate and distinct tenement consisting of a House Garden Orchard and about six Acres of Land situate in the parish of Staverton in the said County of Mr Thomas Allen for a Year at the rent of twenty five pounds a Year   I and my said Husband resided in such house and occupied the said Land under such renting for near two years My said husband paid the whole of the first years rent

He never afterwards did any act to gain a settlement [signed]

James Yeend: I have never done any act to gain a settlement in my own right. About two years ago I was married to my present Wife Amelia at Cheltenham aforesaid by whom I have one Child named James aged twelve months

I am now actually chargeable to the said Parish of Cheltenham having been relieved by the relieving officer of that Parish with several loaves of Bread [mark]

1845: *perhaps removed to Staverton (father's presumed settlement).* **1849:** *birth of daughter Mary registered at West Bromwich, Staffs; (RETURNED) Thomas baptised at Cheltenham 2Q.* **1851:** *JY (aged 28; gas works labourer, born Elmstone Hardwicke) lived with wife Amelia (28; born Cheltenham) and children James (7), Mary (4), and Thomas (1) at 2 Newman's Place, Cheltenham (HO107/1973/635/34).* [PS/CH/RA/2/7:140, 141. See **35012SE:** (Hannah Yeend: 6 Aug 1835).]

45016SE: Sat 1 Mar 1845 – **John Golsby** (also **Goldsby, Goldsbey, Gouldsby**), currier [probably for "carver"], residing at Union Workhouse, Cheltenham, wife **Mary** and children **Joseph** and **Edwin:** I have always considered that I belonged to the Parish of Sandridge in the County of Hertford, and that Parish has frequently acknowledged me as a Parishioner – About fifteen or sixteen years ago I was living in the Parish of Saint Peters in the Town of S^t. Albans in the said County of Hertford and in consequence of my being out of employment I applied to Jonathan Parsons the then Overseer of Sandridge aforesaid for some support - he relieved me with bread whilst I was so living in the said Parish of S^t. Peters and provided me with a ticket to obtain work in my said Parish of Sandridge. I was set to work on the Roads and was paid on account of the said Parish of Sandridge for some weeks afterwards   About five years ago I was living in the Parish of Abbey in the said Town of Saint Albans and was again in distress and applied to Mr Greenwood the then relieving officer of S^t. Alban's Union and he relieved me with bread and meat for about a week and then removed me with my wife and two children into the Union

Workhouse in S^t. Albans aforesaid and the said relief was given me and I was maintained in the said Workhouse for several weeks at the charge of the said Parish of Sandridge. I and my wife and family have been received five times into the said Union Workhouse and maintained there at the charge of the said Parish of Sandridge. I know that my name is entered in the books of the said Union to the account of the said Parish of Sandridge. I never did an act to gain a Settlement in my own right. Sandridge was my Father Thomas Golsby's Parish – he gained his Parish there by hiring and service for a year with Mr Bowger of Sandridge Lodge as Gardener near forty years ago and has been to my knowledge acknowledged as belonging to that Parish I recollect his wife being insane about seventeen years when she lived with my Father in Saint Peter's Parish in the said Town of Saint Albans and went afterwards to live at the Three horse Shoes public house in Harpenden Parish in the said County of Hertford – she was removed from that Parish to the Workhouse of Sandridge aforesaid and received there as a Parishioner where she remained several weeks. I was married to my present wife Mary about twelve years ago at the said Parish of Saint Peters in St Albans by whom I have my said two children named Joseph aged eleven years and Edwin aged eleven months. My wife and said last named children are now with me in the Cheltenham workhouse actually chargeable to that Parish [signed]

1841: *JG (aged 30; agricultural labourer) lived with wife Mary (Ann) (30; weaver and pauper) and children Joseph (7) and Sarah (1) at St Albans Workhouse, Herts (HO107/447/7/31/8).* **1845: removed to Sandridge, Herts (father's settlement). 1848:** *death of Mary Golsby at Union Workhouse, St Albans (buried 2 Jan).* **1850:** *JG (wood-turner and widower, living in Star St, Paddington) remarried Ann Levitt 1 May at St James, Paddington, Middlesex.* **1851:** *the couple lived in Paddington, Middlesex: JG (45; turner, born St Albans) and Ann (40; charwoman) (HO107/1467/718/45); Edwin Golsby (7; scholar and pauper) was an inmate of St Albans Union Workhouse (HO107/1713/531/8).* [PS/CH/RA/2/7:142-3; G/CH/60/4. Removal expenses for "Golsby" to Sandridge, Herts £8/-/- (2-3Q 1845: D4178).]

45017SE: Sat 8 Mar 1845 – **James Benson**, labourer: In the Month of January in the year One thousand Eight hundred and thirty three being then unmarried and having no Child or Children I was hired by Mrs Milford of the Parish of Prestbury in the said County for a Year to serve her in the said Parish of Prestbury at the wages of twenty six pounds I served my said Mistress under the said hiring the whole year and resided and slept in my said Mistresses house at Prestbury aforesaid the whole time   I received my said years wages. I have done no act since to gain a settlement   About Six years ago I was married to my present wife Elizabeth in the parish Church of Leckhampton in the said County by whom I had one Child named William now aged five years. My Wife has been living apart from me the last four years and upwards

I am now actually chargeable to the said Parish of Cheltenham having been relieved by the relieving Officer of that Parish with Bread [mark]

1841: *JB (aged 35; born Ireland), already separated from wife and child, lived as servant at Marle Hill, Prestbury (HO107/354/26/7/8).* **1845: removed to Prestbury (hiring and service). 1851:** *son William (10; scholar) lived as "nurse-child" at 42 Norwood St, Cheltenham, home of Elizabeth Studd (HO107/1972/10/11).* **1861:** *EB (45; cook, born Cam, Dursley) lived under maiden name of Shelton as servant at Carshalton House, Carshalton, Surrey (RG9/418/39/7).* **1866:** *marriage of son William to Ann Stone at Lambeth 1 Jan, giving father's name as "unknown".* [PS/CH/RA/2/7:144. Removal exprenses for "Benson" to Prestbury 2/6 (2-3Q 1845: D4178).]

45018SE: Thurs 13 Mar 1845 – **Elizabeth Cowley** (also **Coley**), single woman, residing at 10 Bath Terrace, Cheltenham; also Martha Cowley, widow, residing at same address. *Martha Cowley*: About twenty Seven Years ago I was married to my late husband Stephen Cowley in the Parish Church of Stroud in the said County My said husband was a native of Stroud aforesaid. My said husband died about Eighteen Years ago in Stroud aforesaid. About five years before my husbands death his Father Stephen Cowley died and thereupon a Freehold House and Garden situate at Ruscomb [= Ruscombe] in the said Parish of Stroud descended to my said husband as his said Fathers only Son and Heir at law   My said Husband entered into the possession of the said House and Garden and resided upon it for about five years before and up to his death I continued to reside in the same House and Garden for about two years after my said husband's death   I received relief from the Parish officers of Stroud for about three years after my said husbands death. I had by my said husband my said Daughter Elizabeth now aged about twenty one years

My said Daughter was born in the said Parish of Stroud [mark]

Elizabeth Cowley: I have never done any act to gain a settlement in my own right   The first place I remember myself was living with my Mother Martha Cowley in the Parish of Stroud in the said County

I am now actually chargeable to the said Parish of Cheltenham having been relieved by the relieving officer of that Parish with Bread [mark]

1841: *EC (aged 15) lived with sister Sarah (26; laundress) off Providence Terrace, Gt Norwood St, Cheltenham (HO107/353/12/8/10); mother Martha (50; laundress) lived in Stroud (HO107/349/13/25/11).* **1845:** *removed to Stroud (father's settlement);* *EC entered Cheltenham Workhouse soon after examination, and remained there till 16 Apr (G/CH/60/4).* **1851:** *(RETURNED) EC ("Betsey, 23; washerwoman, born Ruscombe, Stroud) lodged with mother Martha (65; on parish relief, born Tetbury) at 5 Bath Terrace, Cheltenham (HO107/1973/876/10).* [PS/CH/RA/2/7:145, 146. Removal expenses for "Cowley" to Stroud 15/- (2-3Q 1845: D4178).]

45019SE: Thurs 27 Mar 1845 – **Samuel Stephens**, residing in St George's Square, Cheltenham, with wife **Mary:** In the Year One thousand Eight hundred and forty one I rented a house Situate and being Nº 15 Norwood Terrace in the Parish of Leckhampton in the said County of Mʳ Ball Agent for Mʳ Cooper for a Year at the yearly rent of Eleven pounds   I continued to reside in such House which was a separate and distinct tenement for two years and a half at that rent and paid the whole rent for that period

I was duly rated to all Poor Rates made for the said Parish of Leckhampton in respect of such House for the whole of the time I so resided in it and paid the whole of such rates   I have done no act since to gain a settlement. About forty two Years ago I was married to my present Wife Mary in the parish Church of Wootton under edge [= Wotton-under-Edge] in the said County. I and my said Wife are now actually chargeable to the said Parish of Cheltenham having been relieved by the relieving officer of that Parish [mark]

1845: *probably died before removal to Leckhampton (renting); SS (aged 62; gardener, living at 14 St George's Square) buried at New Burial Ground, Cheltenham 2 June* (Cheltenham *Chron.* 5 June). [PS/CH/RA/2/7:147. Removal expenses for "Stephens" to Leckhampton 2/6 and 2.6 (2-3Q 1845: D4178). See **39045SE** (daughter Martha Stephens 19 Aug 1839), **44028SE** (son Edwin Stephens: 9 Apr 1844).]

45020SE: Sat 5 Apr 1845 – **Elizabeth Barrett**, single woman, residing at 29 Gratton Terrace, Gt Norwood St, Cheltenham: I am About Sixty Seven Years of age. About forty three Years ago being then unmarried and having no Child or Children I was hired by Mr Thomas Pye of the Parish of Chepstow in the County of Monmouth Victualler for a year at the wages of Three pounds   I served him in the said Parish of Chepstow under such hiring for three Years and resided and slept in my said Masters house at Chepstow aforesaid the whole time and received the whole of my wages

I have done no act to gain a settlement since

I am now actually chargeable to the said Parish of Cheltenham having been relieved by the relieving officer of that Parish [mark]

1845: *removed to Chepstow, Monm (hiring and service).* [PS/CH/RA/2/7:148. Removal expenses for "Barrett" to Chepstow, Monm £1/19/6 (2-3Q 1845: D4178).]

45021SE: Sat 5/7 Apr 1845 – **Mary Pincott**, single woman, and two children **Ann** and **Isaac;** also Charles Maisey, magistrates' office, relating to the settlement of Mary Pincott.

Mary Pincott: I am the Daughter of Thomas Pincott and Mary his Wife who belonged to the Parish of Bisley in the said County   I have never done any act to gain a settlement in my own right – In the month of June one thousand Eight hundred and forty three I was sent by Orders of Removal from the said Parish of Cheltenham to the said Parish of Bisley and delivered to the Overseers there who received me and relieved me   Such orders of removal were not appealed

against. I have two illegitimate Children namely Ann aged two Years and a Male Child named Isaac aged three Months   I and my said two Children are now actually chargeable to the said Parish of Cheltenham having been relieved by the relieving officers of that Parish [mark]
Charles Maisey: [confirms that Mary Pincott was removed to Bisley under order of 11 May 1843]
1841: *MP (aged 19) lived as servant in Priory Terrace, Cheltenham (HO107/353/3/14/23).* **1843:** *birth of illegitimate daughter (Mary) Ann at Cheltenham Workhouse 28 May (G/CH/60/4); removed to Bisley (father's settlement): see* **43041RO** *(MP: 11 May); (Mary) Ann baptised at Bisley 15 July, while both lived in Bisley Workhouse; (RETURNED) they resided at Cheltenham Workhouse at various times in 1843 and 1844 (discharged 5 June 1844).* **1845:** *removed to Bisley (husband's settlement); birth of illegitimate son Isaac (baptised at Cheltenham 1 June), from 26 Park St, Cheltenham.* **1846:** *death of Isaac (buried 12 Jan, when he and mother resided at Stroud Workhouse).* **1849:** *death of MP at Stroud Workhouse, aged 26 (buried at Bisley 15 Aug).* **1851:** *daughter Ann (7; at school) was a pauper inmate of Stroud Union Workhouse, as was grandmother Mary Pincott (71; weaver and widow, born Overton, Flintshire) (HO107/1965/297/7). [PS/CH/RA/2/7:149, 150. Removal expenses for "Pincott" to Bisley 17/- and £1/9/- (2-3Q 1845: D4178).]*

45022SE: Sat 12 Apr 1845 – **Edmund Jones**, currier, residing at 9 Columbia St, Cheltenham: On or about the twenty fourth day of October 1822 I was bound apprentice by Indenture to Richard Pountney of Birmingham in the County of Warwick Currier to learn his art and serve him after the manner of an apprentice from the said 24th. day of October 1822 for the term of Seven years thence next following. I produce the said Indenture which bears date the day I have named and was duly executed by myself and by my Father John Jones and my Master Richard Pountney in my presence. – I served my said Master as such apprentice for the whole of the said term and worked during the time at his Establishment at the corner of Colmore Street in [*sic*] Worcester Street in Birmingham aforesaid – I was an outdoor apprentice and resided and slept during the said term and of my said service with the said Master at the house of my Sister Frances Oseland Widow in Vauxhall Lane nearly opposite to the Vauxhall Tavern in the Parish of Aston nigh Birmingham aforesaid – When I had fulfilled my time my said Master gave up to me the said Indenture. I have never done an Act to gain a Settlement since. I am now actually chargeable to the said Parish of Cheltenham and am in receipt of bread and other food from Peter Butt the relieving officer of Cheltenham. [signed]
1841: *EJ (aged 36; currier) lived with Elizabeth Caldwell (38) and children Thomas (10), John (8), Anne (6), Mary (4), and William (6 mo) in Winchcombe St, Cheltenham (HO107/353/6/17/26).* **1845:** *death of Elizabeth Caldwell 22 Feb at 9 Columbia St, Cheltenham, aged 39 (Cheltenham Chron. 6 Mar) (buried at New Burial Ground on 28 Feb); removed to Aston, Warks (apprenticeship).* **1846:** *(RETURNED) William Jones (4) buried at New Burial Ground, Cheltenham Jan.* **1851:** *burial of Frederick Jones (5) at New Burial Ground, Cheltenham. [PS/CH/RA/2/7:151. See removal expenses for "Jones" for Aston, Warks £1/14/- (2-3Q 1845: D4178). See* **45023SE** *(EJ for Thomas Jones: 12 Apr 1845),* **45030SE** *(EJ for Ann, Mary, and William Jones: 29 May 1845).]*

45023SE: 12 Apr 1845 – Edmund Jones, currier, residing at 9 Columbia St, Cheltenham, relating to the settlement of illegitimate child **Thomas Jones**: I have never been married – the said Thomas Jones is my child – he was fourteen years of age on the seventh of November last – I was in the house at the time of his birth. Elizabeth Caldwell was the mother of the child – she was never married. She died at Cheltenham on the twenty second of last February. I had lived with her eighteen months before the birth of the said child and continued to live with her up to the time of her death – the said Thomas Jones was born at the house of Mr. Curtis the [furniture] broker situate at the corner of the new burial ground in Walcot Street in the parish of Walcot adjoining Bath in the County of Somerset. – The said Thomas Jones has never been away from me – and has done no act to gain a Settlement in his own right. he is now actually chargeable to the said Parish of Cheltenham and is in receipt of bread from Peter Butt the relieving officer of Cheltenham – [signed]
1841: *TJ (aged 10) lived with parents in Winchcombe St, Cheltenham (HO107/353/6/17/26).* **1845:** *removed to Aston, Warks (father's settlement). [PS/CH/RA/2/7:152. See removal expenses for "Jones" to Aston £1/14/- (2-3Q 1845: D4178). See* **45022SE** *(EJ: 12 Apr 1845).]*

45024SE: Sat 19 Apr 1845 – **Elizabeth Fletcher**, widow, residing at 48 Burton St, Cheltenham: About forty two Years Ago I was married to my late husband Richard Fletcher in the Parish Church of Kings Stanley [= King's Stanley] in the said County. About thirty three years ago my said husband rented a separate and distinct tenement consisting of a House and Garden of Mr John Webster situate in the said Parish of Kings Stanley for a Year at the annual rent of ten Guineas   I and my said husband resided in such house for thirteen Years at the rent and paid the whole thirteen years rent   My said husband done no act to gain a settlement elsewhere and died about twenty years ago in the said Parish of Kings Stanley   After my husbands death I resided in a house of my own in the said Parish of King's Stanley for about two or three Years and have done no act to gain a settlement elsewhere   I am now actually Chargeable to the said Parish of Cheltenham having been relieved by the relieving officer of that Parish with Bread [mark]
1845: *removed to King's Stanley (husband's settlement).* [PS/CH/RA/2/7:153. Removal expenses for "Fletcher" to King's Stanley 15/0 (2-3Q 1845: D4178)]

45025SE: Thurs 8 May 1845 – **Solomon Chapman**, labourer, residing at 3 Melbourne Cottages, Fairview, Cheltenham, wife **Elizabeth**, and five children **John**, **William**, **Elizabeth**, **Charles**, and **Edwin**; also Sarah Chapman, widow, residing at the Rooks Grove, Rodborough, relating to the settlement of her Solomon Chapman. *Sarah Chapman*: I am the widow of William Chapman late of the said Parish of Rodborough Labourer deceased. I was married to him at the Parish Church of Stroud in the said County about Sixty Years ago by whom I had my said Son Solomon born in lawful wedlock – my said husband died at the said Parish of Rodborough about eleven years ago – My said Son Solomon is now about forty five years of age and was born in King's Court in the said Parish of Rodborough at the house there in which I and my said husband William Chapman then resided – he lived at home with us at the said Parish of Rodborough as part of our family until he was married when he was between twenty and thirty years of age – about The same year that my said Son Solomon was born at the said Parish of Rodborough as aforesaid my said husband William Chapman rented a tenement consisting of a Cottage and garden ground attached thereto situate in King's Court in the said Parish of Rodborough of M^r. Ellams [also Hellams] of that Parish Shoemaker being of the value of Ten Pounds a year at the rent of Ten Pounds a year. we resided in the said Cottage and occupied the said garden from the time of our so renting it as aforesaid for several years thence next following and duly paid the said rent for the Same. About forty years ago while my said Son Solomon lived at home with us at the said Parish of Rodborough as part of our family as aforesaid my said husband William Chapman purchased by public Auction a freehold Cottage and about three acres of land situate in King's Court in the same said Parish of Rodborough for two hundred pounds and the said Estate was duly conveyed to him. – he took possession of the said Estate immediately on the acquisition thereof and continued in such position from thence until his death which happened about eleven years ago as aforesaid and always resided in the said Parish of Rodborough during the time of such possession – Upon his death the property was divided between me and my children according to the Will of my said husband. I have continued to reside in the said Parish of Rodborough since my said husband's death – and shall be eighty one years of age in next June – [mark]
Solomon Chapman: I am now about forty five years of age – I am the Son of William and Sarah Chapman – My Parents always resided in the Parish of Rodborough in the said County from the time I can first recollect until I left to be married when I was about twenty eight Years of age. I lived at home with them at the said Parish of Rodborough until I left them to be married as aforesaid. My Father William Chapman died at the said Parish of Rodborough about eleven years ago and left me by Will four freehold Cottages situate at King's Court in the said Parish of Rodborough for my life. I resided in one of such Cottages for four years and received the rent of the others until they were all sold about seven years ago. I have done no act to gain a settlement elsewhere than in the said Parish of Rodborough – I was married to my present wife Elizabeth at the Parish Church of Salperton [error for: Sapperton] about seventeen years ago by whom I have

five children now living with me namely John aged thirteen years William aged ten years Elizabeth aged six years Charles aged four Years and Edwin aged two years. I and my said wife and said children are now actually chargeable to the said Parish of Cheltenham and are in receipt of bread and money from Peter Butt the relieving officer of Cheltenham [signed]

1841: *SC (aged 40; labourer) lived with wife Elizabeth (30) and five children Sarah (11), John (8), William (5), Elizabeth (2) and Charles (1) in Bath Terrace, Cheltenham (HO107/353/12/12/18).* **1845:** *removed to Rodborough (estate).* **1851:** *the family lived in Oxygen St, Aston, Warks: SC (50; labourer, born Rodborough), Elizabeth (39; dressmaker, born Bredon, Worcs), and three children (HO107/2061/110/28).* [PS/CH/RA/2/7:154, 156. Removal expenses for "Chapman" to Rodborough £1/4/3 (2-3Q 1845: D4178)]

45026SE: Fri 2 May 1845 – **Priscilla Trinder**, widow, residing at Union Workhouse, Cheltenham: About twenty two Years ago I was married to my late husband John Trinder in the Parish Church of Tewksbury [= Tewkesbury] in the said County – About two years after we were married I and my said husband became chargeable to the said Parish of Tewksbury and were relieved by the Parish officers of Tewksbury and then removed by orders of removal from thence to the Parish of Shipton oliffe in the said County as the place of my husband's legal Settlement. We were received as Parishioners at Shipton oliffe aforesaid and maintained at the expence of that Parish and the orders of removal were not appealed against – About fourteen or fifteen Years ago I and my said husband were living in the Parish of Sevenhampton in the said County and my husband being ill there I applied to M[r] John Bee the then overseer of the said Parish of Shipton oliffe who relieved us with two shillings and sixpence a week for the then next four or five weeks and during the whole of those four or five weeks I and my said husband were living in the said Parish of Sevenhampton – I fetched the money from M[r] Bee every week – My said husband did no act to gain a Settlement since his said removal to the said Parish of Shipton oliffe. he died at Manchester in the County of Lancaster about two years ago. – In last January I was received into the Northleach Union Workhouse and remained in there more than a month at the charge of the said Parish of Shipton Oliffe. I am now actually chargeable to the said Parish of Cheltenham. [mark]

1844: *PT inmate of Cheltenham Workhouse variously from 17 Apr 1844 (G/CH/60/4); removed initially to Shipton Sollers (husband's presumed settlement): see* **44037SE** *(PT: 8 June).* **1845:** *PT finally discharged from Cheltenham Workhouse 4 June; removed to Shipton Oliffe (husband's presumed settlement).* **1850:** *PT (née Good) married Thomas Nicholls, labourer, at Kidderminster, Worcs, 2 Dec.* **1851:** *the couple lived in Ashchurch: Thomas Nicholls (aged 62; agricultural labourer, born Ashchurch) and Priscilla (61; born Tewkesbury).* [PS/CH/RA/2/7:155. Removal expenses for "Trinder" to Shipton Olliff 9/6 (2-3Q 1845: D4178).]

45027SE: 8 May 1845 – William Wilmore, labourer, residing in Ripple, Worcs, relating to the settlement of brother **Arthur Wilmore.**

1845: *replaced by subsequent examination: see* **45051SE** *(WW for sister-in-law Ann Wilmore: 13 Sept 1845); AW buried 4 June 1845 at New Burial Ground, Cheltenham, aged 45.* [PS/CH/RA/2/7:157.]

45028SE: [blank] July 1845 – Ann Wilmore, widow, relating to the settlement of late husband **Arthur Wilmore** (also **Willmor**, **Willmore**).

1845: *examination form incomplete, and replaced by subsequent examination: see* **45051SE** *(WW for sister-in-law Ann Wilmore: 13 Sept 1845).* [PS/CH/RA/2/7:157.]

45029SE: Fri 23 May 1845 – **Jane Bell**; also Charles Maisey, magistrates' office, relating to the place of last legal settlement of Jane Bell. *Charles Maisey*: [confirms the removal of Jane Bell to Luckington, Wilts under order dated 4 Apr 1843]

Jane Bell: About twenty eight Years ago I was married to my late husband Anthony Bell in the parish of S[t]. Michaels Coventry – he was then a Soldier in the 73[d] Regiment of Foot   About twenty two Years ago he was sent to the East Indies   I have understood from the War office that he died about fifteen Years ago in the East Indies   At the time my said husband went to the East Indies I went to the Parish of Luckington in the County of Wilts to reside there   I have heard that my said husband was born and legally settled there   Soon after I went to Luckington to reside I received relief from the Overseers of that Parish and continued to receive relief for about four years. I then went to reside in the City of Bath and remained there about three or four Years during the whole of which time I received relief from the Overseers of Luckington aforesaid. I then went to reside in the City of Bristol and remained there two or three Years and during the whole of that time I received relief from the Overseers of Luckington aforesaid   About two years ago I was removed from the said Parish of Cheltenham to the said Parish of Luckington, which orders were not appealed against   I have done no act to gain a Settlement Since my husbands death   I am now actually chargeable to the said Parish of Cheltenham having been relieved with food and Lodging [mark]

1843: *removed to Luckington, Wilts (husband's settlement): see* **43029RO** *(JB: 4 Apr).* **1845: *perhaps died before removal to Luckington, Wilts (husband's settlement)**; presumably the JB buried at New Burial Ground, Cheltenham 17 June, aged 64.* [PS/CH/RA/2/7:158, 159. Removal expenses for "Bell" to Luckington £1/11/6 and £1/5/- (2-3Q 1845: D4178).]

45030SE: Thurs 29 May 1845 – Edmund Jones, currier, residing at 4 Grove St, Cheltenham, relating to the settlement of illegitimate children **Anne, Mary,** and **William Jones:** Elizabeth Caldwell was the mother of the said Children – they were born namely the said Anne Jones about ten years ago last April the said Mary Jones about eight years ago last November and the said William Jones about four years ago last October – they were all born in the Parish of Cheltenham in the house where I lived with the said Elizabeth Caldwell   I was in the house at the time of their several births. they are all illegitimate. the said Elizabeth Caldwell died at Cheltenham in last February. her name was Elizabeth Caldwell – she was a native of Hopton near Mortimer Cleobury in Shropshire where her Father John Caldwell who is a Tailor now lives. The said Anne Jones Mary Jones and William Jones are now actually chargeable to the said Parish and are maintained with bread and lodging at the expence of this Said Parish. [signed]

1841: *Anne (aged 6), Mary (4), and William Jones (6 mo) lived with parents in Winchcombe St, Cheltenham (HO107/353/6/17/26).* **1844:** *baptism of son Frederick 10 Apr, when family lived in Mount Pleasant, Cheltenham.* **1845: *removal uncertain: evidence appears inconclusive.*** **1846:** *death of William (buried at New Burial Ground, Cheltenham 20 Jan, aged 4).* **1851:** *death of Frederick, aged five (buried at Cheltenham 4 Feb); Anne is perhaps the Ann Jones (17; house servant) working at Beaufort Buildings, Cheltenham (HO107/1973/93/9).* [PS/CH/RA/2/7:160. See **45022SE** (Edmund Jones: 12 Apr 1845).]

45031SE: 29 May 1845 – **Hannah** (also **Hanna**) **Driver**, single woman: The first place I remember myself was in the parish of Painswick in the said County where I resided with my Father and Mother Nathan Driver and Hannah his Wife until I was about twenty six Years of age. I have never done any act to gain a settlement in my own right either by servitude, renting or otherwise. About seven Years ago being then chargeable to the Parish of Walcot in the City of Bath I was removed by orders of removal from the said Parish of Walcot to the said Parish of Painswick and delivered to Mr Constable the then Overseer of that Parish by whom I was received and relieved That such orders of removal were not appealed against. I returned back to Walcot Parish in about a week after having been so removed and was relieved by the Parish officers of Painswick aforesaid for about twelve months with a shilling a week during the whole of which time I continued to reside in the said Parish of Walcot. I am now actually chargeable to the said Parish of Cheltenham having been relieved by the relieving officer of that Parish with Bread. [signed]

1845: *removed to Painswick (father's presumed settlement): see* 47038RO *(HD: 16 Sept 1847) for further information.* [PS/CH/RA/2/7:161. Removal expenses for "Driver" to Painswick 11/- (2-3Q 1845: D4178).]

45032SE: Sat 31 May/6 June 1845 – **Elizabeth Davis**, widow, and children **Alfred** and **Susannah;** also Charles Maisey, magistrates' office.

Elizabeth Davis: About twenty nine Years ago I was married to my late husband Daniel Davis in the Parish Church of Stroud in the said County by whom I have two Children namely Alfred aged fourteen Years and Susannah aged about Eight years. My said husband died the Eighth day of May instant. My said husband never rented a tenement of the annual value of ten pounds or did any act to gain a settlement since my Marriage to him. I have heard and believe that my said husband was born in the Parish of Kings Stanley [= King's Stanley] in the said County. About four Years ago I and my said husband and two Children were removed by orders of removal from the Parish of Cheltenham to the said Parish of Kings Stanley and delivered to Mr Pinnegar the then Overseer of that Parish by whom we were relieved. that such orders of removal were not appealed against. I am now actually chargeable to the said Parish of Cheltenham having been relieved with food and money by the relieving officer of that Parish [mark]

Charles Maisey: [confirms removal of Daniel Davies, wife Elizabeth, and two children to King's Stanley under order dated 5 Apr 1841]

1845: *removed to King's Stanley (husband's presumed settlement)*: see **47010RO** *(6 Mar 1847) for further information.* [PS/CH/RA/2/7:162, 163. Removal expenses for "Davis" to King's Stanley 16/- (2-3Q 1845: D4178).]

45033SE: Sat 14 June 1845 – **Harriet Beesley**, widow, residing at 56 Burton St, Cheltenham, with three children **Emma**, **Edward**, and **Henry**; also Dr Thomas Beale Cooper, residing at the Mansion House, Bengeworth, near Evesham, Worcs, and Joseph Beesley, tailor, residing at No 12 Gt Pulteney St, St James, Middlesex, relating to the settlement of Harriet Beesley.

Joseph Beesley: The said Harriet Beesley is the Widow of my late brother Henry Beesley who died at Cheltenham in 1840. I remember my said brother Henry being apprenticed to John Nock of Wolverhampton Street Dudley in the County of Worcester Tailor in the year 1820. I was then living near Dudley – My said Brother Henry was apprenticed by the [Blue Coat] Charity School at Evesham – for the term of seven years – My said brother Henry served with his said Master John Nock under the said apprenticeship at the house of the said John Nock in Dudley aforesaid from the time of his said apprenticeship until some time in the year 1826 when he went away for some little time without his said Master's consent and afterwards at my request returned to Dudley – During the whole of the said six years namely from the year 1820 until my said brother Henry went away from his said Master in the year 1826 my said brother Henry boarded and lodged and resided in his said Master John Nock's house in Dudley aforesaid. I was living at Dudley the greater part of the time. While my said brother Henry was away from Dudley as I have mentioned I went to his said Master John Nock at the request of my said brother and enquired how much he would take to cancel the Indenture. The said John Nock said he would take Ten Pounds to cancel them and I paid him the Ten Pounds. The Indenture of apprenticeship was given up to me and I gave it to my said brother Henry. I believe my said brother destroyed the Indenture as soon as I gave it him I think he threw it on the fire I believe the signature to the Indenture now produced is his handwriting [signed]

Dr Thomas Beale Cooper: [confirms that he is acting as a trustee for the Blue Coat Charity School, Bengeworth, one object of which is to apprentice boys; he produces the duplicate indenture of 24 Apr 1820 apprenticing Henry Beesley, with father William Beesley's consent, to John Nock, tailor, of Dudley, Worcs, with a receipt for £5 indicating that the first year of the apprenticeship had been served]

Harriet Beesley: I am the Widow of Henry Beesley late of the Parish of Dudley in the County of Worcester who died at Cheltenham aforesaid in December 1840. My said husband was the brother of Joseph Beesley now present. I was married to my said husband about the year 1832 at S^t. Martin's Church in Birmingham in the County of Warwick by whom I have three children living with me namely Emma aged eleven years Edward aged ten years and Henry aged four years – I have heard from my said husband that about the year 1820 he was apprenticed by the Blue Coat School near Evesham to John Nock of Dudley aforesaid Tailor for the term of seven years. After his death I had all his papers. I have used every endeavour to find the Indenture but cannot – it must have been mislaid or destroyed by my said husband. – In the year 1835 my said husband took and rented of Luke Jukes of Dudley aforesaid Mal[t]ster for the term of one whole year Commencing on the 25th. day of December 1835 at the rent of Ten Pounds a tenement consisting of a separate and distinct dwelling house situate in Bond Street in the Parish of Dudley aforesaid – My said husband actually occupied the said tenement under the said yearly renting and resided upon it in the Said Parish of Dudley from the said commencement of his tenancy until June 1837 being one year and six months – I lived there with him during the whole time – The said yearly rent of Ten Pounds was paid to the said Luke Jukes for the said term of one year for which the said tenement was rented as aforesaid – I had the receipts for the said rent signed by the said Luke Jukes but which receipts I lost after my said husband's death – My said husband was assessed at the Poor Rates of the Said Parish of Dudley in respect of the said Tenement so rented by him of the said Luke Jukes as aforesaid for the said one Year and six months he so occupied and resided upon the same as aforesaid and I saw that the same rates were paid. I had the receipts for the said rates but they are now lost with the other papers – My said husband did no act afterwards to gain a Settlement elsewhere than in Dudley aforesaid. I have done no act since his death to gain a Settlement. I and my said children are now chargeable to and actually receiving relief in bread and money from the said Parish of Cheltenham. [signed]

1841: *husband Henry buried at New Burial Ground, Cheltenham 26 Dec, aged 33.* **1841:** *HB (30; tailoress) lived in Winchcombe Place, Winchcombe St, Cheltenham with children Emma (7), Edward (6), and Henry (2 mo) (HO107/353/6/6/6).* **1844:** *removed to Dudley, Worcs (husband's settlement): see* **44021SE** *(HB: 10 Feb) (RETURNED).* **1845:** *apparently removed to Dudley, Worcs (husband's settlement): see* **45006SE** *(HB: 30 Jan) (RETURNED);* ***removed to Dudley, Worcs (presumed) (husband's settlement).*** **1851:** *HB (40; tailoress and widow, born (S)eckington, Warks) lived in Bradford St, Aston, Birmingham, Warks with two daughters Emma (17; born Dudley) and Elizabeth (2; born Birmingham, and registered as if daughter of Henry (tailor, deceased) and Harriet Beesley (HO107/2060/171/8); both sons were "visitors" in Birmingham: Edward (15; baker) at house of Thomas Lamsbury, bedstead-maker (HO107/2052/636/38) and Henry (10) at home of Robert Durden (56; baker) in Inge St, Birmingham (HO07/2052/788/15). [PS/CH/RA/2/7:164-7.]*

45034SE: Thurs 19 June 1845 – **Elizabeth Holland**, widow: About thirty seven Years ago I was married in the parish Church of Staplehurst in the County of Kent to my late husband William Holland who died about thirty five Years ago –

I have heard and believes [*sic*] that my said husband was born in the Parish of Bodiham [= Bodiam] in the County of Sussex and was legally settled there at the time of his death. Upon the death of my said husband I went to the Overseer of the said Parish of Bodiham with my only Child which I had by my said husband who acknowledged us as belonging to the said Parish and the said Overseer agreed to allow me two shillings and six pence per week for the support of my said Child which allowances of two shillings and six pence a week the Parish officers of Bodiham aforesaid paid for about ten Years during the whole of which ten Years my said Child was residing in the Parish of Mardan [= Marden] in the County of Kent and I was residing at various places of service during such time at Maidstone in Kent in the Borough of Southwark and at Islington and Hornsey

I have done no act since my husbands death to gain a settlement in my own right. I am now actually chargeable to the said Parish of Cheltenham having been relieved by the relieving officer of that Parish with Bread and Money [mark]

1845: *removed to Bodiam, Sussex (husband's settlement).* [PS/CH/RA/2/7:168. Removal expenses for "Holland" to Bodiham, Sussex £5/7/6 (2-3Q 1845: D4178).]

45035SE: Wed 25 June/8 July 1845 – **Sarah Stevens** (also **Stephens**), widow; also William Cole, relating to the place of settlement of Sarah Stevens. *Sarah Stevens*: I am the Widow of James Stevens who was legally settled in the parish of Bisley in the said County by birth as I have heard and believes [*sic*]   In the Year 1834 I and my said husband were removed by orders of removal from the said Parish of Cheltenham to the said Parish of Bisley and delivered to the Overseer there who received us and relieved us   I and my said husband soon afterwards came to Cheltenham and my said husband died there on the Eighth day of February 1837. In a few weeks afterwards I was removed by orders of removal from the said Parish of Cheltenham to the said Parish of Bisley and delivered to the Overseer there who received me and relieved me   Neither of such orders of removal were appealed against. I have done no act since my husbands death to gain a settlement

I am now actually chargeable to the said Parish of Cheltenham having been relieved by the relieving officer of that Parish with Bread and Money [mark]
William Cole: [produces order of removal of 2 Mar 1837, confirms that he delivered Sarah Stevens to Bisley, and that the removal was not appealed against]
1845: *removed to Bisley (husband's settlement): see* **52001RO** *(26 Jan 52) for further information.* [PS/CH/RA/2/7:169, 171. Removal expenses for "Stevens" to Bisley 12/3 (2-3Q 1845: D4178).]

45036SE: Mon 23 June 1845 – Charles Maisey, magistrates' office and cabinet-maker, of Rutland St, Cheltenham, relating to settlement of **James Spencer**, "lunatic": [produces a removal order of 20 Mar 1843 and confirms that he delivered James Spencer to Horsley]
1843: *removed to Horsley (presumed) (father's settlement): see* **43026RO** *(JS: 20 Mar 1843) (RETURNED).* **1845:** *removed to Horsley (father's settlement).* [PS/CH/RA/2/7:170. Removal expenses for "Spencer" to Horsley 13/- (2-3Q 1845: D4178).]

45037SE: Thurs 26 June 1845 – **Maria Hill**, single woman; also Mary Hill, residing in Bisley, relating to the settlement of daughter Maria Hill.
Mary Hill: The Said Maria Hill is an illegitimate Child of mine and was born in the Parish of Bisley in the said County about twenty three years ago [mark]
Maria Hill: I have never done any act to gain a settlement in my own right   I am now actually chargeable to the said Parish of Cheltenham having been relieved by the relieving officer of that Parish with Bread. [signed]
1845: *removed to Bisley (birth): see* **47005RO** *(MH: 30 Jan 1847) for further information.* [PS/CH/RA/2/7:172, 173. Removal expenses for "Hill" to Bisley 12/6 (2-3Q 1845: D4178). See **47011RO** (Mary Hill: 15 Feb 1847).]

45038SE: Sat 28 June/5 June [probably for July] 1845 – **Richard Hill**, labourer, residing at 3 Rutland St, Cheltenham; also George Hill, innkeeper, residing in Stroud, relating to the settlement of brother Richard Hill: *George Hill*: I am about forty four Years of Age and am the Son of Richard Hill and Priscilla his wife who have long since been dead
I remember my Brother the said Richard Hill being born in his and my parents house in a place then called Lamb Lane but now called Church Street in the said Parish of Stroud about the year one thousand Eight hundred and twelve
At the time of my said Brothers birth my Father rented a house in the said Lamb Lane at about ten pounds a Year and resided in such house several Years. When my said Brother was about thirteen Years of age my said Father rented a public house called the Greyhound on Badbrooke [= Badbrook] Lane then called but now Gloucester Street at the rent of Thirty five pounds a Year and resided in such house about Five years during the whole of which time my said Brother resided with my said Father as part of his family. My Father died at the said public house called the Greyhound and I took to the house afterwards [signed]
Richard Hill: The first place I remember myself was residing with my Father and Mother Richard Hill and Priscilla his Wife in the Parish of Stroud in the said County with whom I continued to reside in the said Parish of Stroud until the death of my Father
I have done no act to gain a settlement in my own right – I am now actually chargeable to the said Parish of Cheltenham having been relieved by the Relieving Officer of that Parish with Money and Bread [signed]
1845: *removed to Stroud (father's settlement).* **1846-7:** *(RETURNED) from 1Q 1846 until 1Q 1847 RH (aged 33) received parish relief from Stroud as a non-settled resident of Cheltenham (G/CH/9d/1).* **1848:** *death of RH at 3 Rutland St, Cheltenham (buried 20 Nov, aged 37) (Cheltenham Chron. 9 Nov).* [PS/CH/RA/2/7:174, 175. Removal expenses for "Hill" to Stroud £1/4/6 (2-3Q 1845: D4178).]

45039SE: Thurs 3 July 1845 – **Maria Coates**, widow and inmate of Cheltenham Workhouse: About thirty Years ago I was married to my late husband Thomas Coates in the Parish Church of Saint Johns in the City of Gloucester   I have heard and believes [*sic*] that my said husband was born in the parish of Saint Mary de lode in the said City of Gloucester and never done any act to gain a Settlement in his own right. He died six years ago last December, between four and five Years ago I was Several times relieved by the Overseer of the said Parish of Saint Mary de lode in the said City whilst I was residing in the Parish of Saint Nicholas in the said City

I have done no act since my husbands death to gain a settlement. I am now actually chargeable to the said Parish of Cheltenham being an inmate of the Union Workhouse there [mark]
1841: *MC (aged 55) lived in Rutland St, Cheltenham (HO107/353/7/62/26).* **1845: *removed to St Mary de Lode, Gloucester (husband's settlement).*** **1851:** *MC (68; servant, widow, and pauper, born Gloucester) was an inmate of Gloucester Union Workhouse (HO107/1961/467/4).* [PS/CH/RA/2/7:176 (G/CH/60/4). Removal expenses for "Coates" to Gloucester 7/6 (2-3Q 1845: D4178).]

45040SE: [blank] July 1845 – **Elizabeth Anderson**, and four children **John**, **Robert**, **George**, and **Elizabeth:** I was married to my husband Moses Anderson about thirteen years ago last October in the parish Church of Shipley [= Shiplake] in the County of Oxford by whom I have four Children John aged Eight years Robert aged seven years George aged four years and Elizabeth aged three months [incomplete]
1845: *examination form incomplete;* *see* **45052SE** *(EA: 25 Sept 1845).* [PS/CH/RA/2/7:177.]

45041SE: Thurs 10 July 1845 – **William Pimble** (also **Pymble**), labourer, wife **Ann**, and son **Robert:** In the Year 1813 I with my wife and three Children were removed by an order of removal by the Overseer of the Hamlet of Littleworth in the said County to the Parish of Dymock in the said County and delivered to the Overseer there who received us and relieved us. Such order of removal was not appealed against. In the year one thousand Eight hundred and twenty seven I and my wife and three Children were removed by orders of removal from the said Parish of Cheltenham to the said Parish of Dymock and delivered to the Overseer there who received us and relieved us   Such last Order of removal was not appealed against. I have done no act since to gain a settlement   About twenty five years ago I was married to my present Wife Ann in the Parish Church of Cheltenham by whom I have one Child named Robert aged thirteen years

I am now actually chargeable to the said Parish of Cheltenham being now in the receipt of two shillings a week from the relieving officer of that Parish [mark]
1845: *removed to Dymock (his settlement as indicated by earlier removals)*: *see* **47015RO** *(WP: 20 Mar 1847) for further information.* [PS/CH/RA/2/7:178. Removal expenses for "Pimble" to Dymock £1/6/6 (2-3Q 1845: D4178). See also removal order of 1827 held in Dymock Parish records (P125 OV 3/3/6).]

45042SE: Mon 14 July 1845 – **Sarah Browning**, single woman, residing at 4 York St, Cheltenham; also Moses Browning, labourer, residing at 4 York St, Cheltenham, and Frederick Thomas Griffiths, solicitor, relating to the settlement of Sarah Browning**.**
Moses Browning: I am upwards of Seventy Years of age – the said Sarah Browning is my lawful Sister – we are the children of John and Mary Browning both of whom have been dead several years. my said Sister is Younger than me – I continued at home with my said Parents at the Parish of Woodchester in the said County from the time of my birth there until I was able to maintain myself by my work and then I left home – My said Sister was born before I left home – she was born at the house where my said Parents lived in the said Parish of Woodchester when I was about five years of age. I can recollect her when she was very young. My Said Mother never lived in any other Parish than Woodchester aforesaid from the time I can first recollect until the time of her death which happened about twenty two years since. I can recollect living with my Mother at Woodchester before my said Sister was born and I am sure she continued to live at the same house until the time of her death. [mark]
Sarah Browning: I am the daughter of John and Mary Browning late of the Parish of Woodchester in the said County deceased. I am the Sister of Moses Browning who lodges at the same house with me. I am about sixty six years of age. The first place I remember myself living in is at my Parents House in the Said Parish of Woodchester – I lived with them there until my Father died about forty years ago – I lived with my Mother at the same house after his death until her death about twenty two years ago. For about six or Seven years before my said Mother's

death she was regularly relieved with eighteen pence a week up to the time of her death by the then overseer of the said Parish of Woodchester – I have frequently applied to him for the weekly money for her and received it during the seven years I have mentioned – When she died I applied to the overseer for the funeral and she was buried at the expence of the said Parish of Woodchester. – I have never done an Act to gain a Settlement in my own right. I always worked in the factories at Woodchester aforesaid for more than twenty years – [mark]

Frederick Thomas Griffiths: [confirms register entry for birth in Woodchester of Sarah, daughter of John Browning 23 Aug 1779]

1845: *removed to Woodchester (father's presumed settlement)*: see **49027RO** *(SB: 12 May 1849) for further information*. [PS/CH/RA/2/7:179-81. Removal expenses for "Rone" to Painswick and "Browning" to Woodchester £1/6/6 (2-3Q 1845: D4178).]

45043SE: Thurs 17 July 1845 – **Thomas Nicholls** (also **Nichols**), residing at the Coach Road Cheltenham, wife **Hannah**, and children **Sophia**, **Elizabeth**, and **Thomas:** In the Year one thousand Eight hundred and forty two I rented a separate and distinct tenement consisting of a Dwelling House of John Curtis situate and being in Park Street in the parish of Charlton Kings in the said County for a Year at the rent of Ten pounds a Year   I resided in such house for one Year and a half under such renting and paid the whole rent for the same. I was duly rated to Poor Rates made for the said Parish of Charlton Kings in respect of such Dwelling House during my said tenancy and paid the same and for which I received the receipts of the assistant Overseer of that Parish and they are now in my possession   I have done no act since to gain a settlement   I was married to my present Wife Hannah in the parish Church of Painswick about six Years ago by whom I have three Children Sophia aged four years and a half Elizabeth aged three years and Thomas aged fifteen months

   I am now actually chargeable to the said Parish of Cheltenham being now receiving relief [of] three shillings a week and Bread from the relieving officer of that Parish [signed]

1841: *TN (aged 30; tailor) lived in Slad, near Stroud, with wife Hannah (30; dressmaker) and daughter Sophie (7 mo) (HO107/349/8/5/5).* **1845:** *removed to Charlton Kings (presumed) (renting); death of TN, aged 35 (buried 10 Oct at New Burial Ground, Cheltenham).* **1851:** *(RETURNED) the family lived in Alstone, Cheltenham: Hannah Nicholls (39; needlewoman and widow), Sophia (10), Elizabeth (8; both scholars, born Painswick), and Thomas (7; scholar, born Charlton Kings) (HO107/1973/963/7).* [PS/CH/RA/2/7:182. Note: "At home".]

45044SE: 17 July 1845 – **Mary Ann Rone** (also **Roan**), single woman, residing at 4 Grove St, Cheltenham; also Martha Rone, single woman, residing near Gloucester Turnpike Gate, Painswick, relating to the settlement of illegitimate daughter Mary Ann Rone**.**

Martha Rone: The said Mary Ann Rone is my daughter. She was born in or about the year 1823 in the said Parish of Painswick in the said County. I had not then ever been married. I have lived in the said Parish all my life time and am living there now. I am in the forty sixth year of my age. – My said daughter Mary Ann Rone lived with me at the said Parish of Painswick until she was about seventeen years of age. [mark]

Mary Ann Rone: I am about twenty two years of age. I am the illegitimate daughter of Martha Rone who now lives at Painswick. The first place I remember myself in is in the said Parish of Painswick in the said County where I lived until I was about seventeen years of age. I have never done any act to gain a Settlement in my own right. I am now actually chargeable to the said Parish of Cheltenham and am maintained in the Poor House there at the expense of that Parish. [mark]

1841: *MAR (aged 15) lived with mother Martha and family in Vicarage Lane, Painswick (HO107/749/8/36/14).* **1845:** *removed to Painswick (presumed) (birth).* **1849:** *MAR married Robert William Halliday at St George, Bloomsbury 19 Aug.* **1851:** *the couple lived with son in St Giles-in-the-Fields, Finsbury: Robert Halliday (29; engraver, born London), Mary Ann (27; born Painswick), and George (1 mo; born London) (HO107/1509/231/5).* [PS/CH/RA/2/7:183, 184. Note: "At home". Removal expenses to Painswick for "Rone" and to Woodchester for "Browning" £1/6/6 (2-3Q 1845: D4178).]

45045SE: Mon 21 July 1845 – **Joseph Maiden** (also **Maidon**), labourer, wife **Frances**, and son **John**; also William Tovey, schoolmaster, currently residing in Gloucester St, Winchcombe, relating to the settlement of Joseph Maiden, son of Sarah Maiden. *William Tovey:* I know the said Joseph Maiden now present. I am eighty seven years of age and have lived in the said Parish of Winchcomb [= Winchcombe] all my life time – I recollect the said Joseph Maiden being born. I knew his Mother Sarah Maiden very well – she went by the name of Sarah Oxford – the said Joseph Maiden was an illegitimate child. I recollect the said Sarah Maiden being confined with him – he was born in the said Parish of Winchcomb about sixty four or sixty five Years ago. I knew the House in which his said Mother lived at the time of her confinement in the said Parish of Winchcomb – I knew the said Sarah Maiden from when she was about ten years of age until she left Winchcomb when she was about forty years of age and during the whole of that time she regularly lived at Winchcomb aforesaid. I recollect the said Joseph Maiden living at Winchcomb with her when he was very Young. [signed]

Joseph Maiden: I am the illegitimate child of Sarah Maiden otherwise Sarah Oxford. My said Mother is dead. I believe I was born at the Parish of Winchcomb [= Winchcombe] in the said County on the twenty first day of December 1781 – The first place I remember myself living in is the said Parish of Winchcomb. I have never done an act to gain a Settlement. I was married to my wife Frances at the Parish Church of Cheltenham in the year 1818 by whom have one Son now living with me namely John aged nineteen years. My said Son has never been from home or done an act to gain a Settlement in his own right. I and my Said wife and said Son are now actually chargeable to the said Parish of Cheltenham and are receiving relief in bread and money from Peter Butt the relieving officer of the said Parish of Cheltenham – I produce an Extract from the Register of Births of the said Parish of Winchcomb which I saw written by Mr Harvey the Vicar – and taken from the Parish Register - I am the person referred to in the said Extract. [mark]

1841: *JM (aged 55; chairman) lived with wife Frances (62; seamstress) and son John (12) in Rutland St, Cheltenham (HO107/353/7/63/30-1) (Joseph had previously enlisted in 35th Foot Soldiers in 1811, aged 27).* **1845: removed to Winchcombe (presumed) (birth). 1850:** *Frances Maiden died at Winchcombe (buried there, aged 70, 7 June).* **1851:** *JM (69; agricultural labourer) was an inmate of Winchcombe Union Workhouse (HO107/1971/110/54), whilst son John (28; labourer) lodged at 7 York St, Cheltenham (HO107/1973/146/32).* **1853:** *John Maiden married Pamela Heaven at Cheltenham 3 July, when both lived at 7 Burton St, Cheltenham.* [PS/CH/RA/2/7:185, 186, and inset. See also inset copy of entry of 30 Dec 1781 from Winchcombe Baptismal Register attested by John R. Harvey, vicar (p. 94). Removal expenses for "Maiden" to Winchcombe 13/- (2-3Q 1845: D4178).]

45046SE: Mon 28 July 1845 – **Hannah Payne** (also **Paine**), widow, residing in Exmouth Court, Cheltenham: I am the Widow of Thomas Payne deceased. I was married to my said Husband at the Parish of Berkeley in this County about thirty years ago. My said Husband died in Cheltenham aforesaid about thirteen years ago. My said Husband's Parish is Frocester near Dursley in the said County. About twelve months after my said husband's death I was living in Bath Street in the said Parish of Cheltenham and in consequence of ill health I applied to the Parish officers of Frocester aforesaid for relief. The overseer of the said Parish of Frocester came to me at Cheltenham to see me. he gave me a few shillings – and told me if I wanted any more relief I was to come to Frocester. About seven years ago my Mother in Law Sarah Payne died where I lived in Cheltenham aforesaid and in consequence of her death I went to the said Parish officers of Frocester and applied for relief at the Board Room at Eastington in which Union Frocester is. – They relieved me with a few shillings. I lived in Bath Street in Cheltenham aforesaid as much as thirteen years and left Bath Street about five years ago. My said Mother in Law Sarah Payne lived with me in Bath Street aforesaid during the whole time I lived there. She was acknowledged by the Officers of Frocester aforesaid to belong to that Parish. She regularly received half a Crown a week from the Parish Officers of Frocester aforesaid for relief while she was so living with me in Bath Street aforesaid for twelve months before she died – I have often fetched the money for her myself –. ~~I have two children by my said late husband now living with me named William aged~~ I am now actually

Chargeable to the said Parish of Cheltenham – and have received Eighteen pence and a loaf of bread from Peter Butt the relieving officer of the said Parish of Cheltenham – [mark]
1845: *removed to Frocester (husband's settlement).* **1847:** *(RETURNED) HP died at Exmouth Court in Cheltenham 18 June* (Cheltenham Chron. *1 July) (buried at New Burial Ground, aged 66).* [PS/CH/RA/2/7:187. Removal expenses for "Payne" to Frocester 12/- (2-3Q 1845: D4178).]

45047SE: 28/31 (twice) July 1845 – **Mary Ann Capener** (also **Capenor**, **Cipener**), residing at 13 Bloomsbury Place, Cheltenham, with five children **Elizabeth**, **Maria**, **George**, **Thomas**, and **Mary**; also James Capener, carpenter, residing at 5 Columbia St, Gloucester, and James Capener, wheelwright, residing in Brockworth, relating to the settlement of sister- and daughter-in-law (respectively) Mary Ann Capener, widow of Daniel Capener, deceased. *James Capener, brother-in-law*: The late Daniel Capenor was my brother. He died last January. About fifteen years ago I and my said brother purchased a piece of freehold land for building situate in Columbia Street in the said Parish of Saint John the Baptist in the said City of Gloucester for upwards of Thirty Pounds of Mr Counsel Attorney of Gloucester – We built a Cottage and Workshop upon the Land within a twelvemonth after we had purchased it as aforesaid and then both of us took possession of the same and continued in such possession from thence until it was sold about Seven years ago – During the time we so possessed the said Estate my said Brother resided in the said Parish of Saint John the Baptist. Between thirteen and fourteen Years ago I and my said brother purchased another piece of freehold land for building situate in Columbia Street aforesaid in the said Parish of Saint John the Baptist for about thirty five pounds of the said M^r. Counsel. We built a cottage upon this land – I took to the first mentioned Cottage workshop and land and my said brother took to the last mentioned cottage and land – We took possession of the same and continued in such possession from thence until both were sold about Seven years ago. During the time my said brother so possessed the said last mentioned Cottage and land he resided in the said Parish of Saint John the Baptist. –
James Capener, father-in-law: The said Mary Ann Capener is my daughter in law. She married my late Son Daniel Capener at the Parish Church of Painswick about twelve years ago. My said Son Daniel died last February   My settlement is in the Parish of Brockworth aforesaid   My Grand Father was a Wheel[w]right there and died at about sixty five years ago seized of an Estate in the Parish of Brockworth aforesaid consisting of a Cottage workshop and building and garden situate near to the Horseferry Turnpike Gate on the road from Cirencester to Gloucester – Upon my said Grandfather's death my late Father William Capener Carpenter and Wheelwright took possession of the said Estate and continued in such possession from thence until his death which happened about sixteen Years ago. he resided upon the said Estate in the said Parish of Brockworth for more than fifty years up to the time of his death. I was born there as I have heard and believe. I lived with my Father there until I was twenty four years of age. I was then married and left him for about five years then came back to live with him in the said Cottage and premises with my family and continued to reside there with him until his death which happened about sixteen years ago. My said Son Daniel Capener was then living with me in the said Cottage as part of my Family and had never been away from home to stay – he continued to live with me as part of my Family in the said Parish of Brockworth until he was married at Painswick as aforesaid. After my said Father's death I took possession of the Said Estate and have continued to reside upon it ever since as my own property. I have no brother living but Daniel who is younger than Me. My said Son Daniel lived with me at the Parish of Brockworth aforesaid for three or four years after I came into possession of the said Estate and while I resided upon it as aforesaid [signed] James Capener
Mary Ann Capener: I am the Widow of the late Daniel Capener the Son of James Capener now present. I was married to my said husband at the Parish Church of Painswick in this County about twelve years ago last June. I have five children by my said husband and now living with me namely Elizabeth aged ten years Maria aged eight years George aged five years Thomas aged two years and Mary aged one year. My said husband died in London on the tenth of February last and

had lived there for five Years before and up to his death   he did no act there to gain a Settlement. I and my said five children are now actually chargeable to the said Parish of Cheltenham and are now in receipt of money and bread from Peter Butt the relieving officer of the said Parish of Cheltenham – [signed] Mary Ann Capener

1841: *MAC (aged 30) lived with husband Daniel Capener (35; journeyman carpenter) and children Elizabeth (6), Maria (4), and George (1) at 1 Exeter Place, Chelsea, London (HO107/687/5/27/48).* **1845:** *Daniel Capener buried, aged 39, at St Luke, Chelsea, London;* **removed to Brockworth (Gloucester Union) (husband's settlement).** **1845-6:** *(RETURNED) from 4Q 1845 until 4Q 1846 MAC and five children received parish relief from Gloucester as non-settled residents of Cheltenham (G/CH/9d/1).* **1851:** *MAC (36; laundress, born Miserden, lived with children Elizabeth (16), Maria (14; both born Gloucester), George (11; born Painswick), Thomas (7), and Mary (5; both born London) in Alstone Rd, Cheltenham (HO107/1973/557/5).* [PS/CH/RA/2/7:188-90. Removal expenses for "Capenor" to Brockworth 8/- (2-3Q 1845: D4178). Evidence of James Capenor, carpenter, struck out; note: "Settlement lost by residence in London after it was acquired 4 & 5 W^m. 4 C 76 Sec. 68" (= Poor Law Amendment Act (1834): residence lost by virtue of living more than ten miles away from established settlement).]

45048SE: Sat 2/7 Aug 1845 – **Thomas Caudle** (also **Cawdel**), labourer, wife **Elizabeth**, and daughter **Phoebe**; also Joel Caudle, labourer, residing in Charlton Kings, relating to the settlement of son Thomas Caudle. *Joel Caudle*: I am Sixty two Years of age. In the year One thousand Eight hundred and three I was living with Mary Jones Singlewoman at the Parish of Totness [= Totnes] in the County of Devon by whom I had my said Son Thomas who was born in the said Parish of Totness   I was married to the said Sarah Jones about four years after the birth of my said Son Thomas at the parish Church of Salehurst in Sussex. The said Thomas Caudle continued to live with me as part of my family until his Marriage [signed]

Thomas Caudle: I have never done any act to gain a settlement in my own right

On the twelfth of August 1827 I was married to my present Wife Elizabeth in the parish Church of Hempstead [= Hempsted] in the said County by whom I have one Child living with me named Phoebe aged about ten years

I am now in the receipt of Seven shillings a week from the relieving officer of Cheltenham and have been chargeable to that Parish for some time past [mark]

1841: *TC (aged 35; navigator: "navvy" or construction worker) lived in High St, Brentford, Essex with wife Elizabeth (40), and daughter Phoebe (5); none born Essex (HO107/324/8/48/5).* **1845:** *removal uncertain: evidence appears inconclusive.* **1846:** *Elizabeth Caudle died of "Debility" on 7 Mar at The Vineyards, Alstone, Cheltenham, aged 49 (buried at New Burial Ground 13 Mar).* [PS/CH/RA/2/7:191, 192. Note to deposition of Joel Caudle: "the Mother was married at the time Thomas Caudle was born to a Man named Clements".]

45049SE: Mon 11 Aug 1845 – **William Collins**, residing in Fairview St, Cheltenham, with wife **Hannah:** My Father William Collins was a native of the Parish of Linton in the County of Hereford in which place he died last November. My said Father received relief regularly for Eight or Nine years previous to his death from the Overseers of the said Parish of Linton   My Mother Susan Collins has been dead about thirty years. About twenty five years ago I was relieved by the Overseers of the Parish of Linton aforesaid with a Sovereign whilst I was residing in the City of Hereford. I have never done any act to gain a settlement in my own right. About thirty years ago I was married to my wife Hannah at the Parish Church of All Saints in the City of Hereford. I am now receiving relief from the relieving officer of the said Parish of Cheltenham [mark]

1845: ***WC died before removal to Linton, Heref (father's settlement); widow Hannah removed to Linton:*** *see* **47024RO** *for further information on family.* [PS/CH/RA/2/7:193. Removal expenses for "Collins" to Linton, Heref 17/6 (2-3Q 1845: D4178).]

450495SE: 11 Aug 1845 – **Catharine Jones**, widow, and two children **Edward** and **Rosina,** residing in Rutland St, Cheltenham: I was Married to my late husband Benjamin Jones in Monmouth Church about twelve years ago. he has been dead about five Years. About ten years Years ago I and my said husband were removed by orders of removal from the Parish of Newland in the said County to the Parish of Dinastow [= Dingestow] in the County of Monmouth and delivered to the Overseer there who received us and relieved us. Such orders of removal were not appealed against   We soon afterwards returned to Newland and were relieved by the Parish Offices of Dinastow aforesaid for four or five months at four shillings a week during the whole of which time We resided in Newland aforesaid   I was relieved by the Parish officers of Dinastow aforesaid last January twelve months whilst I was residing in the Parish of Cheltenham aforesaid

My said husband never done any act to gain a settlement since his removal to Dinastow and I have done no act to gain a settlement since his death. I am now in the actual receipt of relief from the relieving officer of Cheltenham aforesaid   I have two Children by my said husband now living with me namely Edward aged ten Years and Rosina aged five years [mark]

1845: *removed to Dinastow, Monm (husband's presumed settlement). For further information see* **47031RO.** [PS/CH/RA/2/7:194. Removal expenses for "Jones" to Dinastow, Mon 3/16/6 (2-3Q 1845: D4178).]

450498SE: 11 Aug 1845 - The examination of **Sarah Gigg**, widow, residing at 35 Sherborne Street, Cheltenham: About fifty years ago I was married to my late husband Thomas Gigg in the parish Church of Saint Mary de Crypt in the City of Gloucester. My husband died about ten years ago in the parish of Chippenham in the County of Wilts

About twenty seven years ago my said husband rented the Cock Public house situate in the High Street in the parish of Chippenham aforesaid of Sir Samuel Fludgyer [= Fludyer] at the yearly rent of twenty five pounds. I and my said husband resided and slept in the said Cock public House Chippenham aforesaid the whole year and paid the whole years rent. I and my said husband continued to reside and sleep in the said Cock public house for the next six years at the reduced rent of Sixteen pounds as a yearly tenant to the said Sir Samuel Fludgyer and his son afterwards

We paid all the rent for the same. We then rented a house in the Shambles in Chippenham aforesaid of M^r. [uncertain] by the year at the yearly rent of ten pounds and resided and slept in that house until the death of my said husband and paid all the rent for the same

I continued to reside in the said last mentioned house for two years after the death of my said husband as a yearly tenant at the rent of ten pounds a year   I paid all the rent for the same. I and my said husband were rated to and paid all the Poor and other rates in respect of both the Said houses during the whole time we occupied them. I have done no act, since to gain a settlement elsewhere. I am now actually chargeable to the said Parish of Cheltenham having been relieved by the relieving officer of that Parish with half a Crown [mark]

1841: *SG (aged 66; independent) lived with her sister in Sherborne St, Cheltenham (HO107/353/5/63/48).* **1845:** *perhaps removed to Chippenham (husband's presumed settlement); RETURNED.* **1851:** *SG (85; former laundress) lived with her sister at 35 Sherborne St, Cheltenham (HO107/1973/150/40).* [PS/CH/RA/2/7:195.]

45050SE: Thurs 28 Aug 1845 – **Mary Keepax** (also **Kepax**, **Keppax**), single woman, inmate of Union Workhouse, Cheltenham; also Mary Pate, twine-spinner, wife of William Pate, residing in Pershore, Worcs, relating to the settlement of daughter Mary Keepax, single woman. *Mary Pate*: About thirty Years ago I was married to my late husband Samuel Keepax at the Parish Church of Claines in the County of Worcester   the said Mary Keepax is my daughter by my said husband and is now about twenty nine years of age. She was born at the said Parish of Claines where I and my said husband were then living. My said husband died at the said Parish of Claines about ten Years after our said Marriage. From the time of our said Marriage until his death we resided upon the same premises in the said Parish of Claines. We occupied a tenement consisting of a Cottage garden and ground situate near the River Severn at a place Called Fosters Bank situate in the Parish of Claines belonging to one Mr Lavender being of the value of Sixteen Guineas a Year and where my said daughter was born – We resided for the said ten years after our said marriage on the said tenement – Immediately after my said husband's death I rented the said tenement in the said Parish of Claines from year to year at the said rent of Sixteen Guineas a year – I occupied the said premises under the said taking from the time of my said husband's death for two years and One quarter of a year thence next ensuing – And the said yearly rent of Sixteen Guineas was actually paid by me for the first year and three quarters of a Year of the said term of two years and one quarter of the year and Mr Lavender distrained my goods for the remainder of the rent due to him – During my said tenancy I resided constantly in the said Parish of Claines and the said Mary Keepax resided with me there the whole two years and one quarter of the year as part of my Family. [mark]

Mary Keepax: I am now an Inmate in the Cheltenham Union Workhouse and actually chargeable to the Parish of Cheltenham in the said County. I was born at the Parish of Claines in the County of Worcester as I have heard and believe - and I am now about twenty nine years of age. I am the daughter of Samuel and Mary Keepax now Mary Pate – I have done no act to gain a Settlement in my own right. [mark]

1838: *sister Elizabeth sentenced to be transported to Van Diemen's Land at Worcs Epiphany Sessions; sister Mary acquitted; it was alleged that the two sisters and brothel-owner, Jane Glover, had stolen £90 in notes from an intoxicated client (*Berrow's Worcester Journal *9 Nov 1837, etc).* **1845: *removed to Claines, Worcs (father's settlement).* 1846:** *death of MK registered at Pershore 1Q.* [PS/CH/RA/2/7:196, 197. Removal expenses for "Keepax" to Claines, Worcs £1/10/- (2-3Q 1845: D4178).]

45051SE: Sat 13 Sept 1845 – **Ann Wilmore** (also **Willmor**, **Willmore**), widow, and four children **Jane**, **Job**, **William**, and **Charles;** also William Wilmore, residing in Ripple, Worcs, relating to the settlement of sister-in-law Ann Wilmore. *Ann Wilmore:* About twenty one years ago I was married to my late husband Arthur Wilmore in the Parish Church of Cheltenham in the County of Gloucester by whom I have four children Jane aged sixteen years Job aged twelve years William aged six years and Charles aged three years. My said husband never did any act to gain a settlement since our marriage nor since he left the Parish of Ripple in the County of Worcester - My said husband has been dead about four months. I and my said children are now actually chargeable to the said Parish of Cheltenham having been relieved by the releiving [*sic*] officer of that parish with bread and money – [mark]

William Wilmore: I am in the fifty second year of my age and am the son of Thomas Wilmore and Hannah his Wife. I remember my Grandfathers dying between forty and fifty years ago and thereupon a copy hold tenement consisting of a house garden and about eight acres of land situate in the parish of Ripple in the county of Worcester and which had been for many years previously and up to his death was [*sic*] my said Grandfathers property came to my said Father who was the only son and heir at law of my said Grandfather – My said Grandfathers name was Thomas Wilmore – My said Father resided upon such tenement for nearly thirty years and up to his death which happened about twenty one years ago - I remember my Brother the said Arthur Wilmore being born in my said fathers said house at Ripple aforesaid about forty years ago – I was living in the said house at the time – My Mother has been dead about sixteen years – My said Brother resided with my said father in the said house from the time of his birth until his said fathers death as part of my said fathers family – After my said fathers death my said Brother continued to reside in the said house with his mother the said Hannah Wilmore until the time of his marriage with Ann Farley now Ann Willmore – he lived with his said Brother as part of her family until his said marriage. And never did any act to gain a settlement in his own right – to my knowledge. [mark]

1845: *Arthur Wilmore buried at New Burial Ground, Cheltenham 4 June, aged 45; examination form incomplete, and replaced by subsequent examination: see* **45028SE** *(Ann Wilmore for brother Arthur Wilmore: July 1845);* ***removed to Ripple, Worcs (husband's settlement).*** **1845-6:** *(RETURNED) from 4Q 1845 until 2Q 1846 AW and four children received parish relief from Upton-upon-Severn, Worcs as non-settled residents of Cheltenham (G/CH/9d/1).* **1851:** *AW (aged 49; washerwoman, born The Leigh) lodged with two sons William (11) and Charles (8) at 17 Cleeveland St, Cheltenham (HO107/1973/447/12).* [PS/CH/RA/2/7:198, 199. Removal expenses for "Wilmore" to Ripple, Worcs 11/6 (2-3Q 1845: D4178) and 14/- (3Q 1846: D4178). See **45027SE** (William Wilmore for brother Arthur Wilmore: 8 May 1845).]

45052SE: Thurs 25 Sept 1845 – **Elizabeth Anderson**, inmate of Union Workhouse, Cheltenham, and four children **John William**, **Robert**, **George**, and **Elizabeth**; also Thomas Millard, of the liberty of Eye and Dunsden, Sonning, Oxon, relating to the settlement of Elizabeth Anderson. *Thomas Millard*: [confirms that he delivered Moses Anderson and wife Elizabeth from Sonning to Taplow, Bucks under order of 1 Dec 1831 (produced)]

Elizabeth Anderson: About fourteen years ago I was married to Moses Anderson at the Parish of Shiplake in Oxfordshire – by whom I have four children namely John William aged eight years Robert aged seven years George aged five years and Elizabeth aged six months. My said husband has deserted me and my children and we are now actually chargeable to the said Parish of Cheltenham and Inmates of the Union Workhouse – I have not heard of my husband for the last six months and I do not know where he now is or whether he is now living. – About seven or eight months after our said marriage I and my said husband became chargeable to the Parish of Sonning in the County of Oxford and were removed by the order of removal which Thomas Millard now produces to Taplow in the County of Buckingham the place of my said husband's Settlement – we were received at the said Parish of Taplow as Parishioners and the said order was not appealed against. When my first child named William – died about thirteen years ago I and my said husband were living in the Parish of Maidenhead in Berkshire and my said child was then buried at the expence of the said Parish of Taplow [mark]

1841: *EA (aged 29) lived with children John (4), Robert (3), and George (1) in Oaksey, Wilts; husband absent on census night (HO107/1181/29/16/24).* **1845: removed to Taplow, Bucks (husband's settlement).** **1850:** *husband probably the Moses Anderson whose death was registered at Bishop's Stortford, Herts 2Q; EA remarried, to George Field, 3Q at Eton, Bucks.* **1851:** *the family lived with George Field's mother in Taplow, Bucks: Mary Howard (72; pauper, widow of labourer), George Field (42; labourer, both born Elverton [= Elvetham?], Hants), Elizabeth Field (39; charwoman, born Nuffield, Oxon), John William Anderson (19; carter's boy, born Maidenhead, Berks), Robert Anderson (12; baker's boy), George Anderson (10; scholar, both born Oaksey, Wilts), and Elizabeth Ann Anderson (6; scholar, born Cheltenham) (H)107/1718/734/14).* [PS/CH/RA/2/7:200, 201]. Removal expenses for "Anderson" to Taplow, Bucks £3/9/3 (2-3Q 1845: D4178). See **45040SE** (EA: July 1845).]

45053SE: 25 Sept 1845 – **James Dominey** (also **Domeny, Domnay, Domney**), labourer, residing at 60 Duke St, Cheltenham, wife **Jane**, and four children **Emma**, **William**, **Ellen**, and **Josiah**; also Samuel Domney, haulier, residing in Uley, relating to the settlement of brother James Domney. *James Domney*: I am the Son of John Domnay formerly of the Parish of Uley in the County of Gloucester Milkman deceased and was born at the said Parish of Uley as I have heard and believe. My said Father died when I was about fourteen years of age seized of a freehold Estate situate at Windsor in the said Parish of Uley and consisting of a Cottage or Tenement and garden there in which he lived from the time I can first recollect until his death. I lived with him there as part of his Family. Upon his death the said Tenement descended to my Eldest brother Samuel Domnay of the said Parish of Uley Haulier as my Father's Eldest Son and heir at Law. My said brother took possession of the said Estate and continued to live there with my Mother until her death which happened about the year 1809 and I lived with them there as part of the Family. My mother was ill for several years before her death and was relieved with relief weekly from the said Parish of Uley. After her death my brother continued in the occupation of the said Tenement I lived with him there as much as a twelvemonth – About thirty five years ago I was out of work and applied to the Overseers of the said Parish of Uley for relief the Overseers of the said Parish of Uley allowed two or three shillings a week I forget which for as much as five months afterwards and during the whole of that time I was living in the said Parish of Cheltenham and my wife and family were living in the Parish of Kings Stanley [= King's Stanley] in the said County. I left Kings Stanley to get work in Cheltenham. I have never done an Act to gain a Settlement in my own right – I was married to my present wife Jane at the Parish Church of Cheltenham in the said County about thirteen years ago next March by whom I have four children now living with me namely Emma aged seven years William aged four years Ellen aged two years and Josiah aged five months. I and my said wife and said children are now actually chargeable to the said Parish of Cheltenham. [mark]

Samuel Domney: The said James Domnay now present is my Brother and about five years and a half younger than me. I was at home when he was born. I recollect his being born in my Father John Domnay's house at the said Parish of Uley about sixty two years ago – My said Father was seized of a Tenement and Garden situate in the said Parish of Uley at a place called Windsor there which belonged to my Grandfather Christopher Domnay and descended by heirship to my said Father and descended from my said Father to me – The first time I can recollect my said Father was living there and he bred up his Family there and died there – [signed Sam¹ Domnay]

1845: *birth of Joseph (not Josiah) Domney registered at Cheltenham 2Q 1845;* **removed to Uley (father's settlement):** *see* **48025RO** *(JD: 25 Nov 1848) for further information.* [PS/CH/RA/2/7:202, 203. Removal expenses for "Dominey" to Uley 16/6 (2-3Q 1845: D4178).]

45054SE: 25 Sept 1845 – **Harriet Saunders** (also **Sanders**), single woman; also Henry Saunders, labourer, relating to the settlement of daughter Harriet Saunders. *Henry Saunders*: About twenty years ago next Christmas I was married to my present wife Harriet at the Parish of Bisley in this County by whom I had my said daughter Harriet Saunders – About thirty four years ago when I was about twelve years of age unmarried and without child or children I was hired into the Parish of Randwick in the County of Gloucester by Samuel Laurence of that Parish Farmer to serve him for one Year in the said Parish from the time of my said hiring at the wages of fifty two shillings the year. Accordingly I entered immediately into the service of the said Samuel Laurence and Continued in the same service under the said yearly hiring for the space of one whole Year thence ensuing. I resided and slept during the whole of my said year's service at the House of my said Master situate in the said Parish of Randwick. I have done no act to gain a Settlement since. – About sixteen years ago I and my said wife and family were living in the Parish of Stroud in the said County and were taken ill – and I applied for relief to the overseers of the said Parish of Randwick. they relieved me with bread and money for about five weeks and during the whole of this time I and my family were residing in the said Parish of Stroud. [mark] *Harriet Saunders*: I am about eighteen years of age. I am the daughter of Henry Saunders and Harriet his wife. I never left home until I was about twelve years of age. I have never done an Act to gain a Settlement in my own right. I am now actually chargeable to the said Parish of Cheltenham. On Friday last I received a loaf of bread from the Relieving officer of Cheltenham. [mark]

1845: *removed to Randwick (father's settlement): see* **48032RO** *(HS: 21 Dec 1848) for further information.* [PS/CH/RA/2/7:204, 205. Removal expenses for "Saunders" to Randwick 5/9 (2-3Q 1845: D4178).]

45055SE: Thurs 16 Oct 1845 – **Joseph Collins**, labourer, residing at 3 Providence Terrace, Gt Norwood St, Cheltenham, with wife **Mary:** I am in the seventy eighth year of my age – About fifty years ago next May I was married to my wife Mary at the Parish Church of Fladbury in the County of Worcester. When I was about twenty three years of age unmarried and without child or children I was hired into the Parish of Holy Cross near Pershore in the County of Worcester by James Evans of that Parish Farmer to serve him as Under carter for one year from the time of my said hiring. Accordingly on that day I went into the service of the said James Evans and continued in the same service under the said Yearly hiring for the space of one whole year thence ensuing and received my years wages. I resided and slept during the whole of my said years service with the said James Evans in the said Parish of Holy Cross under the said Yearly hiring at the Farm house of my said Master situate in the said Parish of Holy Cross. I have never done an act to gain a Settlement elsewhere. About forty five years ago I was living in the Parish of Fladbury in the said County of Worcester and applied to the Parish officers of Holy Cross aforesaid for relief. they allowed me five shillings a week for the first month after my said application and afterwards four shillings a week for the next Eight or nine months and during the whole of this time I was living in the said Parish of Fladbury. I and my said wife are now actually chargeable to the said Parish of Cheltenham – and have received a loaf of bread from Peter Butt the Relieving officer of Cheltenham [mark]

1841: *JC (aged 70; independent) lived with wife Mary (70) and daughter Susannah (35; servant) in Hartley Cottages, Bath Rd, Cheltenham (HO107/353/12/32/1).* **1845:** *removed to Holy Cross, near Pershore, Worcs* *(presumed) (hiring and service).* **1848:** *(RETURNED) JC died at 3 Providence Terrace, Cheltenham 28 Mar (buried, aged 79, at New Burial Ground).* **1849:** *death of wife Mary (buried at New Burial Ground, Cheltenham, aged 79, 28 May).* [PS/CH/RA/2/7:206.]

45056SE: 16 Oct 1845 – **Agnes Owen**, widow, residing at 23 Burton St, Cheltenham, with eight children **Teresa**, **Mary**, **Agnes**, **Clara**, **Cecilia**, **Catherine**, **Joseph**, and **Lucy:** I am the widow of Joseph Owen who died at Cheltenham about two months since. I do not know where my late husband was born nor do I know where his place of settlement was. His Father and Mother are both dead – he has no brother or Sister or any relation that I know of – I never heard him say where his Parish was. I was married to him in the year 1828 at Kingston Church near Portsmouth. I have eight children by my said husband now living with me namely Tereza aged 14 years Mary aged 12 years Agnes aged 10 years Clara aged 8 years Cecilia aged six years Catherine aged 4 years Joseph aged 2 and a half years and Lucy aged seven or eight months. My Parish is the Parish of Portsea in the Borough of Portsmouth in the county of Hants. About twenty one years ago when I was unmarried and without child or children I was hired into the said Parish of Portsea by Captain Finlayson to serve him as Maid of all work for one year from the time of my said hiring – Accordingly on that day I went into the service of the said Captain Finlayson in the said Parish of Portsea and continued in the same service under the same Yearly hiring for the space of one whole Year thence ensuing and received my years wages. I lived with him there for three years and four months – I resided and slept during the whole of my said Service with the said Capt[ai]n Finlayson at his House situate in the said Parish of Portsea. I and my said children are now actually chargeable to the said Parish of Cheltenham and are in receipt of relief in bread and money from Peter Butt the relieving officer of Cheltenham – [signed]
1841: *AO (aged 35) lived with husband ("Dennis" perhaps in error, 40; greengrocer, both born Ireland) and children Teresa (10), Mary (8), Agnes (5), Cecily (3), Clara (1), and Catherine (3 mo) in East St, Southampton, Hants (HO107/416/3/28/2).* **1845:** *death of husband Joseph Owen in Cheltenham, aged 46 (buried at New Burial Ground 12 Aug); removed to Portsea, Hants (hiring and service).* **1851:** *daughters Cecily (12) and Catherine (8; both scholars in workhouse, born Southampton, Hants) were inmates of Portsea Island Union Workhouse, Hants (HO107/1657/562/18).* **1861:** *mother Agnes (56; clear starcher and widow, born Barry (for "Kerry"), Ireland lived with daughter Theresa (24; needleworker, born Cheltenham) at 35 Cumberland St, Chelsea, Middlesex (RG9/37/11/18).* [PS/CH/RA/2/7:207. Removal expenses for "Owen" to Portsea £6/19/9 (2-3Q 1845: D4178).]

45057SE: Thurs 30 Oct 1845 – **John Winter**, carpenter, residing at 20 Rutland St, Cheltenham: I am about sixty six years of age. – My Grand father William Winter was a Weaver at the Parish of Wincanton in the County of Somerset. He lived on an Estate of his own in the said Parish of Wincanton consisting of four acres of land called "Long Close" – He died at Wincanton aforesaid about fifty six years ago possessed of the said Estate. – He resided in the said Parish of Wincanton from the time I can first recollect until his death and occupied the said Estate being a period of five or six years. My Father William Winter was his eldest Son and heir at Law and as such took possession of the said Estate upon my Grandfather's death and occupied the same from thence until his death about thirty years ago and during the whole time resided in the said Parish of Wincanton and carried on the business of a Weaver there. – My said Father was the owner of two freehold cottages situate near the Dolphin Inn in the High Street of Wincanton aforesaid – My said Father lived at one of such Cottages from the time I can first recollect him until his death and I lived with him there as part of his family for as much as twenty years. About twenty six years ago I rented from M[r] Lindsey of Wincanton Currier for the term of one year at the rent of Twenty Four pounds a year a tenement consisting of a separate and distinct dwellinghouse situate in Mill Street in the said Parish of Wincanton. I held and occupied the said tenement under the said Yearly renting from thence for three years next ensuing and paid the full rent of Twenty Four pounds a year for the same for the said three years. During such my three years tenancy I resided constantly in the said Parish of Wincanton. I have done no act to gain a Settlement since. I am

now actually chargeable to the said Parish of Cheltenham and have received relief in bread and Money from the Relieving officer Peter Butt of the said Parish [signed]
1841: *JW (aged 60; carpenter) lived at house of James Brimson (54; plasterer) in Rutland St, Cheltenham (HO107/353/7/57/18).* **1845: removed to Wincanton, Som (renting).** *[PS/CH/RA/2/7:208. Removal expenses for "Winter" to Wincanton, Som £2/11/- (2-3Q 1845: D4178).]*

45058SE: Thurs 13 Nov 1845 – **Sarah Ford**, widow: I am now about sixty five years of age. When I was about twenty three years of age unmarried and without child or children namely about the year 1803 I was hired into the Parish of Dursley in the said County of Gloucester by The Reverend Mr Williams of that Parish to serve him as Servant of all work for a twelvemonth at the wages of Eight Guineas a Year. Accordingly I went into the service of the said Mr Williams and continued in the same service under the said yearly hiring for the space of one whole year thence ensuing and received my years wages. I resided and slept at the house of the said Mr Williams situate in the said Parish of Dursley during the whole of my said Years service with him in the said Parish of Dursley. I remained in the service of the said M^r. Williams for the next eight years as a yearly Servant to him and received my wages yearly and constantly resided and slept at his house in the said Parish of Dursley during the whole of the time – and when I left his service in the year 1812 I had not been married – nor had had a child – About the month of April in the year 1812 I was married to my late husband Joseph Ford at the Parish Church of Temple in the City of Bristol. My said husband died about the year 1822 – His Settlement was in the said Parish of Dursley and the Parish officers of the said Parish of Dursley acknowledged me as a Parishioner after his death and regularly relieved me with four shillings a week for more than a twelvemonth thence ensuing. About four years before my said husband's death namely about the year 1818 My said husband rented a house at Woodmancote in the said Parish of Dursley of Mr Robert Smith of the said Parish of Dursley Gardener being of the yearly value of ten pounds. I recollect the time of the renting from my Son Henry having been born at that house. My said husband occupied the said house for more than forty days from the time of his said renting and resided in the said Parish of Dursley during his said tenancy and occupation for upwards of five months. – All this was before the year 1819. – I am now actually chargeable to the said Parish of Cheltenham and am receiving two shillings and sixpence a week from Peter Butt the relieving officer of Cheltenham [mark]
1841: *SF (aged 70; charwoman) lived with son Joseph (20) at 5 Hereford Place, Cheltenham (HO107/358/8/63/9).* **1845: removed to Dursley (husband's settlement). 1850:** *probably the SF buried at Dursley, aged 75, 23 Oct. [PS/CH/RA/2/7:209. Removal expenses for "Ford" to Dursley 13/- (2-3Q 1845: D4178).]*

45059SE: Sat 15 Nov 1845 – **Edmund Edward Carter**, coachman, wife **Sarah**, and children **George Edward** and **Ellen Mary**; also Mary Carter, wife of Edmund Edward Carter, residing at 2 Limekiln Rd, Cheltenham, relating to the settlement of illegitimate son Edmund Edward Carter.
Mary Carter: The said Edmund Edward Carter is my Son – he was born on the eighth day of June in the year 1817 or 1818 I am not certain which in the Parish of Dymock in the County of Gloucester. I had not then ever been married. I was confined at the house of my Father John Price situate at More oak in the said Parish of Dymock – [signed]
Edmund Edward Carter: I am the illegitimate Son of Mary Carter – and am now about twenty eight years of age. I have never done an Act to gain a Settlement in my own right. I and my wife and children are now actually chargeable to the said Parish of Cheltenham and in consequence of illness I am attended by Mr Hyatt the Medical officer of the said Parish – and am in receipt of two shillings and three loaves of bread weekly from Peter Butt the relieving officer of the said Parish. I was married to my Present wife Sarah at the Parish Church of Cheltenham aforesaid about five Years ago by whom I have two children living with me – namely George Edward aged three years and Ellen Mary aged nine months. [signed]
1817: *EEC baptised (as Edmund Edward Price) at Dymock 9 June, son of Mary Price, servant.* **1841:** *EEC (aged 24; coachman) lived with wife Sarah (20) at back of 12 Commercial St, Cheltenham (HO107/353/12/26/47).* **1845:** *children Mary Ellen and George Edward both baptised (under surname Price)*

at Cheltenham 2 Feb, when family lived at 2 Limekiln Place; **EEP died before removal to Dymock**; *buried at Cheltenham 11 Dec, aged 27.* **1847**: *(RETURNED) widow remarried, 28 June, to widower and shoemaker, Francis Taylor; Sarah Carter lived in St Paul's St, Cheltenham.* **1851**: *the family lived at Court 21, House 9, in Moor St, Birmingham, Warks: Francis Taylor (38; a shoemaker, born Bath, Somerseet), Sarah (29; a dressmaker, born Coleford), William Taylor (14; wire-worker, born Bath, Som), and Sarah's son George Carter (8; scholar; apparently born London (HO107/2054/58/14).* [PS/CH/RA/2/7:210, 211.]

45060SE: Sat 22 Nov 1845 – **Lucy Alder**, widow, residing at 23 Exmouth St, Cheltenham, and children **Alfred**, **Edwin**, **Jane**, and **Thomas:** I am the Widow of Thomas Alder who died fifteen years ago last February at the Parish of Kings Stanley [= King's Stanley] in this County. About twenty four years ago I was married to my said husband at the Parish Church of Kings Stanley aforesaid by whom I have four children now living with me namely Alfred aged twenty years Edwin aged seventeen years Jane aged fifteen Years and Thomas aged nine years. – My said husband was settled in the said Parish of Kings Stanley and was buried partly at the expence of that Parish and had About half a crown a week from that Parish for a month previous to his death. About eighteen years ago my said husband rented of his Father Nathanial Alder for the term of one year at the rent of Ten pounds a year a tenement consisting of a separate and distinct dwelling house situate in the said Parish of Kings Stanley. he occupied the said premises under the said yearly renting from the said day of commencing tenancy for the term of three years thence next ensuing and actually paid the yearly rent of Ten pounds a year for the said three years – During his said tenancy my said husband resided constantly in the said Parish of Kings Stanley and I lived with him all the time there. Immediately after my husband's death I received relief at six shillings a week from the said Parish of Kings Stanley for four years thence ensuing. About ten years ago I was residing in the said Parish of Cheltenham and applied to the overseers of the said Parish of Kings Stanley to give me relief for myself and children. The overseers of Kings Stanley aforesaid allowed me four shillings a week relief for about nine Months thence following and during the whole of the time I resided in the said Parish of Cheltenham. I have done no act to gain a settlement since. My said four children have not nor hath either of them done an act to gain a settlement – they have lived at home with me all their life time and are too ill to attend to be examined. I am now actually chargeable to the said Parish of Cheltenham and am in receipt of seven shillings a week from Peter Butt the Relieving officer [mark]
1845: *removed to King's Stanley (husband's settlement).* **1851**: *(RETURNED) LA (aged 58; widow, "at home", born Cam) lived with children Edwin (22; gardener), Jane (19; plain-sewer), and Thomas (15; gardener; all three born King's Stanley) at 2 Hermitage Place, Bath Rd, Cheltenham (HO107/1973/858/21).* **1859**: *LA died 5 Jan at 7 Commercial St, Cheltenham (buried at New Burial Ground 10 Jan, aged 67) (Cheltenham Chron. 11 Jan).* [PS/CH/RA/2/7:212.]

45061SE: Wed 26 Nov/undated 1845 – **Esther Paget (also Patchet)**, single woman; also Esther Lambert, residing near the Baptist Chapel, Sheepscombe, relating to the settlement of granddaughter Esther Paget.
Esther Lambert: The said Esther Paget is my Granddaughter   She was born at Painswick in the said County about twenty one years ago. Her Father Richard Paget lived in Painswick aforesaid from the time of her birth until his death about nine years ago. His Settlement was in Painswick aforesaid. When he died he was buried at the expence of the said Parish of Painswick – The said Richard Paget had another daughter named Jane Paget. She is now living in Bristol. The Parish officers of Painswick have acknowledged her as a Parishioner and allow her eighteen pence as a week relief though she is living in Bristol aforesaid. She has had this relief about two years. I receive the money for her from Mr Constable the relieving officer of the Stroud Union and send it to her at Bristol. The said Esther Paget is the Sister of the said Jane Paget – [mark]
Esther Paget: [incomplete].
1845: *removal uncertain: examination form incomplete.* **1847**: *EP, of 4 New St, Cheltenham (father: Richard Paget, shepherd) married Joseph Seward, of 5 Elm St, Cheltenham.* **1851**: *the couple lived at 5 Elm St, with Joseph's sister: Joseph Seward (25; painter, born Cheltenham), Esther Seward (26; boot-binder,*

born Painswick), and Eliza Seward (17; occasional servant, born Cheltenham) (HO107/1973/517/13).
[PS/CH/RA/2/7:213, 214.]

45062SE: Thurs 27 Nov 1845 – **William Hatton**, inmate of Cheltenham Workhouse: About the year 1821 when I was unmarried and without child or children I was hired into the Parish of Saint James in the County of Middlesex by John Higford Esquire of Albany House in that Parish to serve him as Butler for one Year from the time of such hiring – Accordingly I went Into the service of the said John Higford and continued in the same service under the said Yearly hiring for the space of twelve whole years thence ensuing. I completed the last forty days of my said service with the said John Higford at his residence Newark House in the Parish of Hempstead [= Hempsted] in the County of Gloucester while I there resided and slept. I have never been married. ~~and have never had a child~~. – I lived as much as eight months with the said John Higford at Newark House aforesaid and then left his service and have not since done an act to gain a settlement. – I am now actually chargeable to the said Parish of Cheltenham and am an Inmate of the Cheltenham Workhouse chargeable to that Parish. [signed]
1845: removed to Hempsted (Gloucester Union) (hiring and service). 1847: WH died at Gloucester Union Workhouse (buried at Gloucester, aged 46, 28 May). [PS/CH/RA/2/7:215. Removal expenses for "Hatton" to Hempsted 3/- (2-3Q 1845: D4178).]

45063SE: 27 Nov 1845 – **Celia Organ**, widow: I am the Widow of Charles Organ who died about eight years ago. I was married to him about forty years ago at the Parish Church of Berkeley in this County. I am in the seventy fourth year of my age and actually chargeable to the said Parish of Cheltenham and am in receipt of half a crown a week from Peter Butt the relieving officer of Cheltenham. About the year 1828 just before Christmas my said husband rented from John Gardner of Cheltenham aforesaid Brewer from year to year commencing from Christmas at the rent of Ten pounds a year a tenement consisting of a separate and distinct dwellinghouse with garden attached situate in the Parish of Staverton in the said County near to the Pheasant Public House in that Parish My said husband occupied the said premises under the said yearly renting from the said day of commencing tenancy for four years thence next ensuing and the said yearly rent of Ten pounds was actually paid by my said husband for the said term of four years   During his said tenancy my said husband resided constantly in the said Parish of Staverton – My said husband never did an Act afterwards to gain a Settlement. I have done no act to gain a Settlement since his death. I produce nine receipts for rent paid during the said four years. I have lost the other receipts [mark]
1845: removed to Staverton (husband's settlement). 1847: CO died at Kingsholme, Gloucester (buried at St Mary de Lode, Gloucester 2 Oct, aged 77). [PS/CH/RA/2/7:216. Removal expenses for "Organ" to Staverton 4/6 (2-3Q 1845: D4178).]

45064SE: Thurs 4 Dec 1845 – **Joshua Stevens**, labourer, wife **Jane**, and three children **Sarah**, **Joshua**, and **Ellen**; also Mary Stevens, widow, residing in Chedworth, relating to the settlement of son Joshua Stevens.
Mary Stevens: The said Joshua Stevens is my Son. He was born on the sixteenth day of August about the year 1817 in the said Parish of Chedworth – I was born there as I have heard and believe and have lived there all my lifetime. I was married to my late husband Joshua Stevens at the said Parish of Chedworth about thirty or forty years ago. My said husband was transported about fifteen years ago and I have not heard of him Since – His Parish was Chedworth – His Father's Parish was there. he is dead. About fifteen years ago I was relieved by the overseers of the said Parish of Chedworth with money. My said Son Joshua lived mostly at home until he was married about nine Years ago. [mark]
Joshua Stevens: I am the Son of Joshua and Mary Stevens and aged about twenty eight years – I have never done an Act to gain a Settlement in my own right. I was married at the Parish of Chedworth in this County about nine years ago to my present Wife Jane by whom I have three children now living with me namely Sarah aged nine years Joshua aged six years and Ellen aged three years. I and my said wife and my said three children are now actually chargeable to the said

Parish of Cheltenham and am in receipt of two shillings and sixpence and five loaves weekly from Peter Butt the Relieving officer of the said Parish of Cheltenham. About seven years ago I was relieved by the Parish officers of the said Parish of Chedworth with seven shillings a week for two Weeks [signed]

1841: *JS (aged 20; agricultural labourer) lived with wife Jane (20), and children Sarah (5) and Joshua (2) in Chedworth (HO107/363/9/10/15).* **1845:** *removed to Chedworth (father's settlement).* **1851:** *(RETURNED) the family lived at 36 Queen St, Cheltenham: Joshua Stevens (35; general labourer), Jane (33; washerwoman), Joshua (12; all three born Chedworth), and Ellen (9; scholar, born Cheltenham (HO107/1973/479/19).* [PS/CH/RA/2/7:217, 218. Removal expenses for "Stevens" to Chedworth 12/6 (2-3Q 1845: D4178).]

45065SE: Sat 6 Dec 1845 – **James Hole**, tinman, with wife **Elizabeth:** I am now about fifty two years of age – When I was about twenty three years of age unmarried and without child or children I was hired into the Parish of Old Cleeve in the County of Somerset by Mr Coles of that Parish Farmer to serve him as Wagonner for one year from the time of my said hiring – Accordingly I went into the service of the said Mr Coles and continued in the same service under the said yearly hiring for the space of one whole year thence ensuing and received my years wages – I resided and slept during the whole of my said year's Service at the house of my said Master situate in the said Parish of Old Cleeve. I have never done an Act to gain a Settlement elsewhere. I was married to my wife Elizabeth at the Parish of Thornbury in the County of Gloucester about two years ago – I and my said wife are now actually chargeable to the said Parish of Cheltenham and have been relieved with bread and meat by Peter Butt the Relieving officer of the said Parish of Cheltenham. [mark]

1845: *removed to Old Cleeve, Som (hiring and service).* [PS/CH/RA/2/7:219. Removal expenses for "Holes" to Old Cleeve, Som £3/6/- (2-3Q 1845: D4178).]

45066SE: Thurs 18 Dec 1845 – **Ann Bubb**, widow: I am the Widow of Joseph Bubb deceased – and am upwards of Seventy years of age. I was married to my late husband at the Parish of Avening in this County about fifty Years ago. My said husband never did an act to my knowledge to gain a Settlement in his own right. – He died at Avening aforesaid about sixteen years ago. His Father Henry Bubb was settled in the Parish of Elkstone in this County as I have heard and owned a freehold Estate there. About eight or ten years before my said husband's death my said husband made application to the overseers of the said Parish of Elkstone to give him relief – Accordingly the said overseers of the said Parish of Elkstone allowed my said husband about twenty shillings a year and some times more from that time up to his death towards payment of his rent and during the whole of the time my husband was receiving such relief he was residing in the said Parish of Avening. Immediately after my said husband's death while I was residing in the said Parish of Avening I made application to the overseers of the said Parish of Elkstone for relief – Accordingly soon after that the Overseers of that Parish allowed me four shillings a week which I received for about twelve weeks while I still resided in the said Parish of Avening – They continued to allow me two shillings a week for about half a Year and which relief I received while I still resided in the said Parish of Avening. I have never done an act to gain a Settlement since my said husband's death and am now actually chargeable to the said Parish of Cheltenham and am receiving relief in bread and money from Peter Butt the Relieving Officer of Cheltenham – [signed]

1845: *removed to Elkstone (husband's settlement).* [PS/CH/RA/2/7:220. Removal expenses for "Bubb" to Elkstone 8/- (2-3Q 1845: D4178).]

45067SE: 18 Dec 1845 – **John Jordan**, labourer, wife **Eliza**, and five children **Henry**, **Joseph**, **Edwin**, **Jane**, and **John:** I am now about forty two years of age. About Lady Day seventeen years ago when I was unmarried and without child or children I was hired into the Parish of Churchdown in the said County by Mr Lawrence of that Parish Farmer to serve him as Carter from the time of my hiring namely Lady Day to the following Michaelmas   Accordingly on that day I went into the service of the said Mr Lawrence and Continued in the same service for the space of one year and six months thence next ensuing – I resided and slept during the whole of my said service in the said Parish of Churchdown at the Farm House of my Master there situate. At the Michaelmas aforesaid while I was still unmarried and without child or children my said Master hired me to serve him as Carter for one year at the wages of Seven pounds I think – Accordingly I continued in the same service for the space of the said one year under the said yearly hiring and received my years wages. I completed the last forty days of my said service in the said Parish of Churchdown while I there resided and slept. About sixteen years ago after I left Mʳ Lawrence's Service I was married to my Wife Eliza at the said Parish of Churchdown by whom I have five children namely Henry aged fifteen years Joseph aged eleven years Edwin aged nine years Jane aged seven years and John aged four years. About a twelvemonth after I was married I was relieved by the Parish officers of Churchdown with three shillings a week for fourteen weeks. I and my said wife and children are now actually chargeable to the Said Parish of Cheltenham and have received four loaves of bread from Peter Butt the Relieving officer of Cheltenham aforesaid [mark]

1845: *removed to Churchdown (presumed) (hiring and service).* **1847:** *(RETURNED) baptism of Eliza Sophia in Cheltenham 23 May.* **1851:** *the family lived at 21 Tivoli St, Cheltenham: John Jordan (46; day labourer, born Coberley), Eliza (42; born Longney), Henry (20; born Churchdown), William (18; born Badgeworth, both day labourers), Joseph (16), Edwin (14), Jane (12), John (9), Eliza (4), Walter (1 mo; all six born Cheltenham) (HO107/1973/925/38-9).* [PS/CH/RA/2/7:221.]

45068SE: 18/25 Dec 1845 – **Elizabeth Staite** (also **Stait**, **State**), widow, and three children **John**, **Patience**, and **Mary Ann**; also George Staite, residing in Gretton, relating to the settlement of late brother Richard, husband of Elizabeth Staite. *George Staite*: I am About forty seven Years of Age. I perfectly well remember my Brother the said Richard Staite being born about thirty eight years ago in the said Hamlet of Gretton in a house belonging to my Father John Staite in which he resided in the said Hamlet about thirty Eight Years ago which house was given to my said Father by his Father Richard Staite   My Father and Mother resided in the said House until my said Fathers death.

   About twenty one years ago I rented a Farm in the said Hamlet of Gretton and resided there and hired my said Brother Richard as Carter for a Year at the wages of six pounds   My said Brother continued in my service for a whole year under such hiring and received his years wages and resided and slept in my House at Gretton aforesaid the whole year

   My said Brother had not at the time of the said hiring been married and had no Child or Children – [signed]

Elizabeth Staite: I am the Widow of the late Richard Staite who was the brother of George Staite of Gretton. I was married to my said late husband about fifteen years ago at the said Parish of Cheltenham by whom I have three children namely John aged about eleven years Patience aged about seven years and Mary Ann aged about four years – My said husband died at Cheltenham about six weeks ago. My said husband never did an act to gain a settlement to my knowledge. I am now actually chargeable to the said Parish of Cheltenham and am in receipt of three loaves of bread and one shilling and sixpence from Peter Butt the Relieving officer of that Parish. [signed]

1845: *removed to Gretton (husband's settlement): see* **47016RO** *(ES: 12 Mar 1848) for further information.* [PS/CH/RA/2/7:222, 224. Removal expenses for "Staite" to Gretton 8/3 (2-3Q 1845: D4178).]

45069SE: Sat 20 Dec 1845 – **James Heaven**, shoemaker: I am about seventy six years of age. I have never done an Act to gain a Settlement in my own right. My Parish is Frocester in the said County where my late Father Jacob Heaven and my Grandfather were Settled. About twenty years ago while I was residing in the Parish of King's Stanley in the said County I applied to the Overseers of the said Parish of Frocester for relief – They gave me on that occasion an allowance of sometimes two shillings a week and sometimes two shillings and sixpence a week for several weeks while I still resided in the said Parish of King's Stanley. – About a twelvemonth afterwards I was removed by order of removal from the said Parish of King's Stanley to the said Parish of Frocester and there was no appeal against the Same – The Parish officers of Frocester aforesaid allowed me to live rent free in a Parish House there for some years. I returned to King's Stanley about seven years

ago and being ill and unable to work again applied to the overseers of the said Parish of Frocester for relief – They allowed me on that occasion one shilling and sixpence a week from that time while I still resided in the said Parish of King's Stanley until I came to Cheltenham aforesaid about two years ago – Since I have been in Cheltenham the said overseers have continued to allow me the said one shilling and sixpence a week up to within the last eight weeks when the payment was discontinued – I am now actually chargeable to the said Parish of Cheltenham and am in receipt of bread and four shillings in money from Peter Butt the Relieving officer of that Parish [signed]
1845: *removed to Frocester (father's settlement).* **1851:** *(RETURNED) JH (aged 81; shoemaker, widower, deaf, born Leonard Stanley) lived at 5 Union St, Cheltenham (HO107/1973/895/49).* **1861:** *death of JH whilst an inmate of Eastington (Stroud) Union Workhouse, aged 91 (buried 2 Apr at Frocester).* [PS/CH/RA/2/7:223. Removal expenses for "Heaven" to Frocester 7/6 (2-3Q 1845: D4178).]

45070SE: Sat 27 Dec 1845 – **William Cook** (also **Cooke**), **Mary**, and children **Susan** and **John**; also Thomas Boodle, Assistant Overseer of the Poor of Cheltenham, relating to the settlement of William Cook: *Thomas Boodle:* [confirms that William Cook, wife and children were removed to Painswick under order of 20 Jan 1842, and that there was no appeal]
William Cook: I am the person who with my wife and two children are named in the order of removal now produced by Thomas Boodle. I and my said wife and two children were duly removed to the Parish of Painswick in the said County by virtue of the order within a short time after it bears date. I have done no act to gain a Settlement since. My wife Mary in the said Order named is still living and also my two children therein also named that is to say Susan aged fifteen years and John aged thirteen years. I and my said wife and said two children are now actually chargeable to the said Parish of Cheltenham [mark]
1845: *removed to Painswick (apprenticeship):* see **48031RO** *for further information on family.* [PS/CH/RA/2/7:225, 226. Removal expenses for "Cooke" to Painswick 10/6 (2-3Q 1845: D4178).]

*Cheltenham Overseers' Accounts (D4178), showing expenses for the removal of nine paupers to various parish within and outside Gloucestershire on 4 August 1846, as a result of their settlement examinations. The first column shows the Magistrates' officer responsible for transporting the pauper to the relevant parish, followed by the surname of the pauper, the destination parish, and the cost of the removal. Hannah Weger (**46031RO**) tells how she was originally hired as a servant in Painswick around 1814: because she had not acquired any later settlement, she was returned to Tewkesbury in 1846, as she had been earlier in 1838.*

1846

46001SE: Thurs 15 Jan 1846 – **Sarah Hampton**, single woman, inmate of Cheltenham Union Workhouse; also Charles Griffiths, in relation to the settlement of Sarah Hampton. *Charles Griffiths*: [produces removal order of 15 Feb 1834, confirming that Sarah Hampton was ordered to be removed to Dowdeswell]
Sarah Hampton: I am the person named in the Order of removal this day produced by Charles Griffiths – and dated the 15th day of February 1834. Within a short time after the date of the said Order I was removed by virtue of the same from the said Parish of Cheltenham unto the Parish of Dowdeswell in the said County and was received into the Dowdeswell workhouse where I remained for about five months. There was no appeal against the said Order. I have done no act since to gain a Settlement. I am now actually chargeable to the said Parish of Cheltenham and maintained in the public Workhouse there. [signed]
1832: *removed to Dowdeswell (presumed) (hiring and service): see* **32033SE** *(SH: 26 May 1832) (RETURNED).* **1834:** *removed to Dowdeswell (presumed) (hiring and service): see* **34016SE** *(15 Feb 1834) (RETURNED).* **1837:** *removed to Dowdeswell (presumed) (hiring and service): see* **37078RO** *(Nov 1837).* **1838:** *birth of daughter Rebecca at Union Workhouse, Northleach (baptised 13 Mar); child's death registered almost immediately.* **1841:** *(RETURNED) SH (aged 28; servant) worked at 8 (now 49) Pittville Lawn, Cheltenham (HO107/353/6/35/14).* **1846:** *removed to Dowdeswell (presumed) (hiring and service).* **1847:** *an SH (23) admitted to Cheltenham Workhouse with "Dropsy" 4Q (G/CH/60/5).* **1851:** *(RETURNED) SH (aged 37; unmarried, born Cheltenham) lived at Wellington House, Wellington St, Cheltenham (HO107/1973/760/20).* [PS/CH/RA/2/7:227-8. Removal expenses for "Hampton" to Dowdeswell 6/- (4Q 1845/1Q 1846: D4178).]

46002SE: 15 Jan 1846 – **Charles Underwood**, blacksmith, wife **Maria** and two children **George** and **Rosina**: About twenty one years ago I took and rented of one Mr Long from year to year at the rent of Ten Pounds a year a tenement consisting of a separate and distinct dwellinghouse and premises Situate in the Hamlet of Hucclecote in the County of Gloucester. I occupied the said premises under the said yearly tenancy from the time of my so taking it for the term of ten years thence next ensuing and the said yearly rent of ten pounds was actually paid by me for the said term of ten years. During my said tenancy I resided constantly in the said hamlet of Hucclecote. I have done no act to gain a settlement since   I am now actually chargeable to the said Parish of Cheltenham. I was married to my Wife Maria at the church of Saint Mary de Lode in the City of Gloucester about the year 1822 by whom I have two children namely George aged twenty years and Rosina aged ten years – my said children have always lived with me and have never done an act to gain a settlement in their own right [signed]
1846: *removed to Hucclecote (renting): see* **47041RO** *(wife Maria Underwood: 22 Nov 1847) for further information on the family.* [PS/CH/RA/2/7:229. Removal expenses for "Underwood" to Hucclecote 9/- (4Q 1845/1Q 1846: D4178).]

46003SE: Sat 17 Jan 1846 – **Isaac Vines**, carpenter, wife **Elizabeth**, and children **Jacob** and **Lucy**: About nine years ago I purchased a piece of freehold land situate in the Parish of Littleton Drew in the County of Wilts adjoining to the Turnpike Road leading from Chippenham to Sodbury and near to the Gib Public House of Edward Thompson of Littleton Drew aforesaid Beerhouse keeper for the sum of Forty Pounds. About the time I have mentioned it was Conveyed to me and I paid the purchase money for it. Directly after I had so purchased the land I commenced building a house upon it which I completed in about twelve months. Immediately after its completion I took possession of the said house and land and continued in such possession from thence for three years next ensuing and resided uninterruptedly during that time in the said Parish of Littleton Drew. After I had built the house I mortgaged it and the land and the mortgagee sold it about six years ago. After it was so sold – namely about five years ago I rented of Mr Bezer [= Beazer] of Castle Coomb [= Castle Combe] Gentleman from year to year

commencing from Lady Day at the rent of Twelve pounds a year a tenement consisting of a separate and distinct dwellinghouse and garden Situate in the said Parish of Littleton Drew – I occupied the said premises under the said yearly hiring in the said Parish from the Commencement of my said tenancy for twelve months and resided in the said Parish of Littleton Drew during the time – I paid the said yearly rent of Twelve pounds for the said term of one Year. I was rated to the poor rate of the said Parish of Littleton Drew in respect of the said tenement for the said one Year and paid the same – About eight years ago I was appointed Constable for the said Parish of Littleton Drew for one year thence ensuing at a Court of the Lord of the Manor of Badminton – I executed the said office in the said Parish during one whole year from such appointment accordingly and during the whole of that period I resided and slept in the said Parish of Littleton Drew. I was married to my Wife Elizabeth about thirty years ago at the said Parish of Littleton Drew by whom I have two children now living with me – namely Jacob aged twelve years and Lucy aged nine years. I and my said wife and children are now actually chargeable to the said Parish of Cheltenham [signed]

1846: *presumably the IV charged at the Public Office in Cheltenham with being drunk and disorderly (Cheltenham Chron. 8 Jan);* **removed to Littleton Drew, Wilts (renting). 1851:** *IV (aged 60; journeyman carpenter, born Holt, Wilts) lodged in Nettleton, Wilts (HO107/1836/73/8); wife Elizabeth (59; born West Kington, Wilts) worked as house servant in Langley Burrell, Chippenham, Wilts) (HO107/1836/614/15); Jacob Vines (18; agricultural labourer, born Littleton Drew) lodged with Edward Thompson in Littleton Drew (HO107/1836/5/3); Lucy Vines (15) worked as "nurse girl" in Swindon, Wilts (HO107/1833/629/16 [PS/CH/RA/2/7:230. Removal expenses for "Vines" to Littleton Drew, Wilts £2/7/6 (4Q 1845/1Q 1846: D4178).]*

46004SE: Fri 23 Jan 1846 – **John Walton**, wife **Susannah**, and children **Charles**, **Alice**, and **Louisa:** About twenty seven years ago when I was unmarried and without child or children I was hired into the Parish of Pebworth in the said County by Charles Tysay [= Tysoe] of that Parish to serve him for one year from the time of my said hiring – at the wages of Eight Guineas a year. Accordingly I went into the service of the said Charles Tysay and continued in the same service under the said yearly hiring for the space of one whole year thence ensuing and received my whole year's wages. I completed the whole of my said years service in the said Parish of Pebworth and resided and slept there uninterruptedly during the time.

After I had completed my said years service and being still unmarried and without child or children I was hired again by the said Charles Tysay to serve him for another year. I continued in this service the whole of the second year – I completed the last forty days of my said service with the said Charles Tysay in the said Parish of Pebworth while I there resided and slept. I have done no act to gain a settlement since. About eighteen years ago I was married to my deceased wife Mary at the Parish of Charlton Kings in the said County by whom I have two children now living with me namely Charles aged fifteen years and Alice aged eleven years. After my said wife's death and about three years ago I was married to my present wife Susannah at the Parish of Cheltenham aforesaid by whom I have one child namely Louisa aged eight months. My said children have always lived with me and have never done an act to gain a Settlement in their own right. I and my said wife and said three children are now actually chargeable to the said Parish of Cheltenham – [mark]

1841: *(6 June) future wife Susan Blenman (aged 24) lived with her family in Cricklade St, Cirencester (HO107/380/1/34/15); Susan's removal uncertain: examination form incomplete: see **41061SE** (Susan Blenman: 12 Oct 1841).* **1842:** *Susan Blenman married John Walton (labourer, living in Sherborne St, Cheltenham) 3 Nov (address given as Union St, Cheltenham).* **1844:** *her sister Sophia married in Gloucester.* **1846: removed to Pebworth (hiring and service). 1849:** *her mother Elizabeth died at Cirencester (buried 23 May, aged 55). After this, Susan's father Henry (shoemaker) emigrated with daughter Harriet to United States, and they were subsequently joined by shoemaker son Henry and his family, living in Detroit, Michigan.* **1851:** *(RETURNED) JW (aged 54; gardener, probably in Blockley, Worcs) and wife Susan (34; born Cheltenham) lived with two daughters Emily Louisa (6; scholar at home) and Harriet (1; both born Cheltenham) in Birdlip Cottages, Cheltenham (HO107/1973/888/34); Charles (20; farm labourer) and Alice (16; servant), JW's children by first wife, lived respectively in Bretforton,*

Worcs   (HO107/2044/363/27)   and   at   3   Suffolk   Parade,   Cheltenham   (HO107/1973/1067/10).
[PS/CH/RA/2/7:231. Removal expenses to "Walton" to Pebworth £1/3/- (4Q 1845/1Q 1846: D4178).]

46005RO: Thurs 29/31 Jan 1846 (examination on 29 Jan) – **James Colville** (also **Colwell**); also John Curtis, carpenter, residing in Charlton Kings. *John Curtis:* I know the said James Coalville who is now living at M^r. Phipps house on the Bath Road in Cheltenham. I knew his Father James Colville who left England about three years ago and has not since returned - About the year 1832 the said James Colville the Elder took and rented of me from year to year commencing in the Spring at the Rent of Eleven pounds a year or twelve pounds a year I am not certain which a tenement consisting of a separate and distinct dwelling house and Garden situate in Park Street in the said parish of Charlton Kings - He actually occupied all the said premises under the said yearly Tenancy in the said parish from the said commencement of his tenancy until about four years and a half ago, being a period of upwards of eight years – he paid the said yearly rent above mentioned for the said term of Eight years - During his said tenancy he resided constantly in the said parish of Charlton Kings – [signed]
James Colville: I am the son of James Colville – My Father went to America about three years ago - and has not since returned to England   I remember my said Father renting of M^r. John Curtis of Charlton Kings in the said County Carpenter at Twelve pounds a year a House situate and being in Park Street in the said Parish of Charlton Kings - until about Four years and a half ago - He occupied the said House for about Nine years, and during the last Forty days of his said tenancy resided in the said parish of Charlton Kings – He resided constantly in the said House during the whole of the time he so occupied it as aforesaid – and I lived with him as part of his Family – I am now actually chargeable to the said parish of Cheltenham – I have done no act to gain a Settlement in my own right – [mark]
1841: *JC (aged 15, born Glos) lived with family in Park St, Charlton Kings (HO107/353/1/8/10).* **1846: died before removal to Charlton King (father's settlement)**; *death of JC at Victoria Place, Cheltenham (Cheltenham Chron. 19 Feb) (buried 11 Feb at New Burial Ground, aged 22; like father, lathrender.* **1861:** *parents recorded in Toronto, Canada in Canadian census: James Colwell (66; Wesleyan Minister) and wife Jessie (65).* [PS/CH/RA/2/8:1 (copy at PS/CH/RA/2/7:232-3). Note: "Dead".]

46006RO: Thurs 12/13 Feb 1846 (examination on 5 Feb) – **Ann Saunders**, and three children **Frederick**, **John**, and **Ann Elizabeth**; also brother-in-law, James Saunders, writer and accountant, of 5 Thomas St, Walcot, Bath, Somerset. *Ann Saunders:* I am the Widow of the late John Saunders deceased who was the brother of James Saunders now present. I was married to my said husband in Walcot Church Bath about twenty one years ago. – He died about twelve months ago – I have three Children by my said husband now living with me – namely Frederick aged twelve years – John aged Six years, and Ann Elizabeth aged Fourteen months – I and my said Children are now actually chargeable to the said Parish of Cheltenham – My said husband never did an act to my knowledge to gain a Settlement – I always understood from him that his Parish was Beckington in the County of Somerset – that he was born there and lived there until he was nearly thirty years of age – that his father Father kept a School there and had acted as Churchwarden of the Parish [signed]
James Saunders: The said Ann Saunders now present is the Widow of my deceased brother John Saunders – I am some years older than my said Brother – I recollect his being born at Beckington in the County of Somerset at the house of our Father William Saunders who kept a School there – My Father and Mother have been dead several years – My said Father lived in Beckington aforesaid for about thirty eight years until the year 1825, when he came to live at Bath. I lived with him the whole of the thirty eight years at Beckington – Within a year or two after my said brother's birth, namely in the year 1796 or 1797 my said Father purchased a Freehold Estate consisting of about half an Acre of Land situate in the said Parish of Beckington for about Seventy Guineas upon which to build a House and called the Premises Mountpleasant   he took possession of the said Estate immediately on his acquisition thereof and continued in such

possession from thence until the year 1822 - being a period of Twenty five years, and during the time he so possessed the said Estate he resided in the said parish of Beckington

In the year 1822, my said Father rented the said House and Premises of M[r]. Benjamin Newth of Bebington [perhaps Babington] in the County of Somerset (who became the purchaser thereof) from year to year at the Rent or Sum of Forty Pounds a year – My said Father occupied the said house and Land from the time of his said renting to 1825, being upwards of two years and paid the full two years Rent of Forty Pounds for the same – During such his tenancy he resided constantly in the said Parish of Beckington – About the year 1807 my said Father was appointed at Beckington aforesaid Churchwarden of the said Parish of Beckington – He executed the same Office in the said Parish of Beckington during the whole of Seventeen years from such appointment accordingly and during the whole of that period resided and slept constantly in the said Parish of Beckington – My said brother lived at home with my Father at Beckington aforesaid until he was about Twenty nine years of age – [signed]

1846: *removed to Beckington, Som (father's settlement).* **1851:** *(RETURNED) AS (aged 48; shopkeeper, born Frome, Som) lived at 21 Sandford St, Cheltenham with children Frederick J. (17; porter, born Bath, Som), John (11; scholar, born Dursley), and Ann Elizabeth (6; scholar, born Cheltenham) (HO107/1973/801/39-802-40).* [PS/CH/RA/2/8:2 (copy at PS/CH/RA/2/7:234-5). Note: "Ann Saunders & 3 Children" delivered to Beckington 16 Mar 1846 by Charles Maisey.]

46007RO: Sat 14/19 Feb 1846 (examination on 12 Feb) – **Elizabeth Bullock**, single woman: I am now upwards of sixty five years of age, I was born in the Parish of S[t]. Catharine's in the City of Gloucester as I have heard and believe where my Parents were legally settled – My Father and Mother have been dead some Years – and I am the eldest of their Children now living – From the time of my birth, namely about the year 1780 until about the year 1815, my said Father Thomas Bullock who was a Gardener rented a tenement consisting of a house and Garden situate where Wellington Parade is now built in the said Parish of S[t]. Catharine being of the value of Twenty pounds a year of M[r]. Saddler of Gloucester – During the whole of this time, namely for thirty five years my said Father resided in the said Parish of S[t]. Catharine and occupied the said tenement and I resided with him there as part of his Family. About the year 1815, my said Father and Mother removed to the house of my brother John Bullock situate in the Parish of Saint John the Baptist in the said City of Gloucester and called the Plough Public House – While my Mother Mary Bullock was living at my said Brother John's house, situate in the said Parish of Saint John the Baptist and about a Year after we went there as aforesaid she applied to the Parish Officers of Saint Catharine aforesaid for relief, and they relieved her with Two shillings a week for several weeks afterwards while she resided in the said Parish of St John the Baptist – While I was residing in the said Parish of Cheltenham about Five years ago I went over to Gloucester and applied to the Overseers of the said Parish of Saint Catharine for relief accordingly immediately afterwards the Overseers of that Parish allowed me a Shilling a week which I received for Four Weeks while I still resided in the said Parish of Cheltenham – I am now actually chargeable to the said Parish of Cheltenham. [mark]

1846: *removed to St Catharine's, Gloucester (father's settlement):* **47026RO** *(EB: 12 June 1847) for further information.* [PS/CH/RA/2/8:3 (copy at PS/CH/RA/2/7:236). Note: "Elizabeth Bullock" delivered to St Catharine, Gloucester 12 Mar 1846 by Charles Maisey.]

46008RO: Thurs 19/21 Feb 1846 (examination on 19 Feb) – **Jane Payton**, widow: I am now sixty nine Years of age – I am the widow of the late Edward Payton who died at Upton on Severn [= Upton-upon-Severn] in the County of Worcester about eighteen years ago – I was married to my said husband at Totness [= Totnes] in the County of Devon about the year 1794, where we lived until about the year 1810, and thence came to Upton on Severn aforesaid – where we resided uninterruptedly from the year last mentioned until my said husband's death – My husbands settlement was in the parish of Bosbury in the County of Hereford – his Father Samuel Payton was settled there – About nine or ten years before my said husband died namely about the years 1817, and 1818, and 1819, I applied to the Overseers of the said Parish of Bosbury for some support – For several times during these years they relieved to me with Money sometimes two shillings and sometimes three shillings at a time whilst I and my said husband resided in the said Parish of Upton on Severn

About six years before my said husband died namely about the years 1822, and 1823, I applied again to the Overseers of the said Parish of Bosbury for some support – They relieved me with One shilling A week for more than a twelvemonth afterwards – and during the whole of that time I and my said husband resided in the said parish of Upton on Severn - During my said husband's last illness and while he still resided in the said parish of Upton on Severn he was relieved for almost two years by the Overseers of the said Parish of Bosbury with Two shillings a week. When my said husband died, I received from the said Overseers two Sovereigns to pay the expences of his Funeral – My said husband never did an act to my knowledge to gain a Settlement. I have never done an act to gain a Settlement since his death. I am now actually chargeable to the said Parish of Cheltenham, and have been relieved by the Relieving Officer of that Parish with Bread – [signed]

1846: *removed to Bosbury, Heref (husband's settlement).* 1851: *(RETURNED) JP (aged 73; nurse, born Totnes, Devon) lodged at 16 Hereford Place, Cheltenham (HO107/1973/429/25).* [PS/CH/RA/2/8:4 (copy at PS/CH/RA/2/7:237). Notes: "Jane Payton" delivered 16 Mar 1846 to Bosbury by Charles Maisey.]

46009RO: Thurs 26/28 Feb 1846 (examination on 21 Feb) – **Caroline Eyles** (also **Iles**, **Isles**) and **Mary**, illegitimate children of Martha Eyles, deceased; also Richard Turner, Assistant Overseer, North Cerney. *Richard Turner*: [confirmed that Martha Eyles and two children were removed from North Cerney to Painswick under order of 20 March 1843, and that the order was not appealed against]

The said Martha Eyles was about the age of Thirty one years when I so removed her and had two Children one named Caroline who at that time was living with her Grandmother Hannah Eyles at the said parish of North Cerney and the other named Mary who was an Infant in arms and was removed by me with the said Martha Eyles – The said Martha Eyles hath since died

Caroline Eyles: I and my said Sister Mary are now actually Chargeable to the said parish of Cheltenham – I am about ten years of age   my sister Mary is near three years of age – Our Mother Martha Eyles died about three weeks ago – I lived with my Grandmother Hannah Eyles at North Cerney in the said County until I came to my Mother at Cheltenham about a year and a half ago – I lived with my Grandmother some years before this   I do not know how long [mark]

1846: *mother Martha Iles buried at New Burial Ground, Cheltenham 2 Feb, aged 42 (daughters Caroline and Mary had been born at Cowley and Stroud Workhouse respectively); **removed to Painswick (mother's settlement), until aged 16.** 1851:** *ME (aged 8; pauper, at school) was an inmate of Stroud Workhouse (HO107/1965/298/8).* **1861:** *Caroline (baptised 1836) may be the CE (22; born Cirencester) who worked as General Servant to accountant in Kensington, Middlesex (RG9/22/18/28).* [PS/CH/RA/2/8:5 (copies at PS/CH/RA/2/7:238-9). Note: "Catherine & Mary Eyles" delivered to Painswick 24 Mar 1846 by Charles Maisey.]

46010RO: 26/28 Feb 1846 (examination on 26 Feb) – **Henry Hawkes**, labourer, **Mary**, and four children **Harriet**, **John**, **Henry**, and **Thomas**; also father William Hawkes, labourer, residing in Shackles Pike, Hewlett Rd, Cheltenham. *William Hawkes*: The said Henry Hawkes is my Son. He was born at the Parish of Sevenhampton in this County about Thirty two years ago – I recollect his being removed from the Parish of Leckhampton to the said Parish of Sevenhampton about five years ago – I was then living in Sevenhampton

About Forty three years ago when I was unmarried and without Child or Children I was hired into the said Parish of Sevenhampton by Edward Kearsey of that parish Farmer to serve him for one year from the time of my said hiring – Accordingly on that day I went into the service of the said Edward Kearsey and continued in the same for the space of one whole year thence ensuing – I completed the last forty days of my said service under the said yearly hiring in the said Parish of Sevenhampton and slept and resided at the House of my Master there called Puckham Farm during the whole time – I have done no act to gain a Settlement since

About thirty six years ago I was married to my Wife Ann at the said Parish of Sevenhampton by whom I had my said Son Henry. – [mark]

Henry Hawkes: About the Month of April 1841, I was removed by Orders of Removal from the Parish of Leckhampton in the said County to the Parish of Sevenhampton in the said County as the place of my Settlement – I was born there as I have heard and believe – and my Parents were legally settled there – I have never done an act to gain a Settlement in my own right – There was no Appeal against the said Order – I was married to my said Wife Mary Ann at the said parish of Cheltenham about ten years ago by whom I have Four Children, namely Harriet aged nine Years – John aged Six Years – Henry aged Four Years and Thomas aged Six Months – I and my said Wife and said four Children are now actually chargeable to the said Parish of Cheltenham – [mark]

1841: *HH (aged 27; labourer) lived with wife Mary (25) and son John (2) in Charles St, Leckhampton (HO107/353/18/1); daughter Harriet (4) lived with grandparents William and Ann Hawkes in Sevenhampton (HO107/351/13/9/12).* **1846: removed to Sevenhampton (father's settlement). 1848:** *(RETURNED) birth of son Job 3Q at Cheltenham.* **1851:** *the family lived at 15 Albert St, Cheltenham: HH (37; labourer, born Sevenhampton), Mary Ann (31; laundress, born London), John (12; driver of a coal cart, born Sevenhampton), Job (3), and William (7 mo; both born Cheltenham) (HO107/1973/451/21); Harriet Hawkes (14; born Brockhampton) worked as servant for John Pleydell, butcher, at 251 High St, Cheltenham (HO107/1973/610/46).* [PS/CH/RA/2/8:6 (copies at PS/CH/RA/2/7:240-2, where HH's first examination of 26 Feb struck out with note "Retaken at page 242 in consequence of the order of removal not being found"). Note: "Henry Hawkes Wife & four Children" delivered by Charles Maisey; removal expenses to Sevenhampton for "Hawkes" 7/3 (2Q 1846: D4178).]

46011RO: 26/28 Feb 1846 (examination on 26 Feb) – **George Sterry**: When I was about sixteen Years of age unmarried and without Child or Children namely about the year 1801, I was hired into the Parish of Barnwood in the said County by M^r. William Holtham of that parish to serve him as Carter's boy for one year from the time of my said hiring. Accordingly at that time I went into the service of the said William Holtham and continued in the same under the same yearly hiring for the space of one whole year thence ensuing – I resided and slept at the House of my said Master situate at Barnwood aforesaid, and completed the whole of my said service in the said parish of Barnwood while I there resided and slept – I have done no act to gain a Settlement since.

I am now an Inmate of the Cheltenham Workhouse actually Chargeable to the Parish. [mark]

1846: *removed to Barnwood (hiring and service): see* **47032RO** *(GS: 5 July 1847) for further information.* [PS/CH/RA/2/8:7 (copy at PS/CH/RA/2/7:243). Note: "George Sterry" delivered to Barnwood 24 March 1846.]

46012RO: Sat 28/30 Feb 1846 (examination on 26 Feb) – **Reuben Yates** (also **Yeates**), wife **Margaret**, and two children **Solomon** and **Mary**; also George Wilson, relating to the settlement of Reuben Yates.

George Wilson: [confirms removal of Reuben Yates and wife to Upton St Leonard's under order of 2 Aug 1841, and that the removal was not appealed against]

Reuben Yates: I am the person who with my wife Margaret am named in the order of removal now produced by George Wilson and dated the second of August 1841. We were duly removed from the said parish of Cheltenham unto the Parish of Upton Saint Leonards in the said County within a short time after the said Order bears date. – I have done no act to gain a Settlement since – I was married to my said Wife Margaret between six and eight years ago at the said parish of Cheltenham by whom I have two Children namely Solomon aged five Years and Mary Aged three Years – I and my said Wife and Children are now actually chargeable to the said parish of Cheltenham – [mark]

1846: *removed to Upton St Leonard's (apprenticeship): see* **49011RO** *(RY: 30 Jan 1849) for further information on family.* [PS/CH/RA/2/8:8 (copies at PS/CH/RA/2/7:244-5). Removal expenses for "Yates" to Upton St Leonards 8/6 (2Q 1846: D4178). See **46016RO** (wife Margaret Yates: 5/7 Mar 1846).]

46013RO: Thurs 5/7 Mar 1846 (examination on 5 Mar) – **John Slade**, son of John and Hannah Slade (also **Sly**); also mother, Hannah Slade, in-patient at Gloucester Infirmary, and Frederick

Thomas Griffiths, solicitor, relating to the settlement of John Slade. *Hannah Slade*: I am the Widow of the late John Slade otherwise Sly who died at the parish of Great Barrington in this County about six Months ago – I believe my husband was married to me in the name of Sly. We were generally called "Sly" but sometimes "Slade". Previous to my Marriage with the said "John Slade" otherwise "Sly" my place of Settlement was in the parish of Little Barrington in the said County by right of my first husband named William Alborough who died at the parish of Bisley about thirty eight years ago. Soon after his death I was removed to the said parish of Little Barrington with my two Children and we were then received there as Parishioners. From the time of my Marriage with the said John Slade otherwise Sly namely about thirty years ago up to his death as aforesaid he resided constantly in the said parish of Great Barrington with his family – when I married him he had four Children by his former wife Elizabeth – namely his Son John then aged about twelve years – Thomas – and two daughters. He lived in the said parish of Great Barrington several years before I married him – and I understood from him that his settlement was in the said parish of Great Barrington and that he gained his settlement there by hiring and service – His said Son John was born in the said parish of Great Barrington about forty three years ago and lived at home with his Father in that parish until he was about twenty years of age as part of his family – During the last illness of the said John Slade otherwise Sly and about six weeks before he died he received from the Officers of the said parish of Great Barrington two loaves of bread and eighteen pence a week up to his death, and during the whole of this time he resided in a house at Little Barrington in the said parish of Great Barrington – From the time of his death I was relieved by the Officers of the said Parish of Great Barrington with two loaves of bread and One shilling a week for about four months thence ensuing and then the said parish Officers gave me a ticket of admission into the Gloucester Infirmary. I received from them five shillings to bring me down to the Infirmary – and they promised to bring me back to the said Parish of great Barrington as soon as I got better at their expence [mark]

John Slade: I am the Son of John and Elizabeth Slade otherwise Sly and was born in the parish of Great Barrington in the said County as I have heard and believe about the tenth day of October 1802. The first place I remember myself in was in the said parish of Great Barrington, and I lived at home with my Father in that parish until I was about twenty years of age – My Father and Mother are both dead, and I have no elder brother or sister living – I have never done an act to gain a settlement in my own right. I am now an Inmate of the Cheltenham Union Workhouse – I am the person named in the Extract this day produced – [mark]

Frederick Thomas Griffiths: [confirms baptism record for John, son of John and Elizabeth Sly, on 10 Oct 1802 at Gt Barrington]

1845: *JS admitted to Cheltenham Workhouse 23 Apr.* **1846: removed to Gt Barrington (father's settlement).** **1848:** *stepmother Hannah buried at Gt Barrington 1 May, aged 64; JS died at Stow-on-the-Wold Workhouse, aged 46 (buried at Gt Barrington 19 May).* [PS/CH/RA/2/8:9 (order suspended as JS unfit to travel) (copies at PS/CH/RA/2/7:246-8). Note: "John Slade" delivered to Gt Barrington 31 March 1846 by Charles Maisey.]

46014RO: 5/7 Mar 1846 (examination on 5 Mar) – **Thomas Chew**, inmate of Cheltenham Union Workhouse: About seven or eight years ago I was removed by Orders of Removal from the Parish of Rodborough in the said County to the parish of Standish in the said County as the place of my Settlement – My Wife Elizabeth and my Children were removed with me and we were received at the said parish of Standish as parishioners, and there was no appeal against the said Order –

We were in the Workhouse and maintained at the charge of the said parish of Standish for several months afterwards – About six years ago, while I was residing in the parish of Stroud in the said County I applied to the Overseers of the said parish of Standish for relief – accordingly the Overseers of that parish allowed me four shillings a week which I received for several weeks afterwards while I still resided in the said parish of Stroud – My Grandfather Thomas Chew's Settlement was in the said Parish of Standish which he gained by hiring and service there – My Father Thomas Chew was settled in that parish – he died in Gloucester Infirmary about sixteen or eighteen years ago – For more than a twelvemonth before his death, and while he was living in the said parish of Rodborough the Overseers of the said Parish of Standish allowed him a Sum of Money weekly – I think Two shillings a week up to the time of his being taken to Gloucester Infirmary which was a fortnight before his death and during the whole time that he received such relief he was residing in the said parish of Roborough –

I have never done an act to gain a Settlement in my own right – I am now actually chargeable to the said parish of Cheltenham and am an Inmate of the Union Workhouse there. – [mark]
1842: *death of wife Elizabeth in Cheltenham (buried at New Burial Ground 29 Sept, aged 73).* **1846:** *removed to Standish (father's settlement).* [PS/CH/RA/2/8:10 (copy at PS/CH/RA/2/7:249). Note: "Thos. Chew" delivered to Standish 30 March 1846 by Charles Maisey.]

46015RO: 5 Mar 1846 – **Henry Whittick**, wife **Mary Ann**, and son **James**: About the year 1816, I rented from Robert Dodd of the City of Gloucester Mal[t]ster from year to year at the rent of Ten Guineas a year a Tenement consisting of a separate and distinct Dwelling-house Situate in Westgate Street in the Parish of Saint Nicholas in the City of Gloucester near to the Lower George Inn - I held the said dwelling house from the time of my so renting it for upwards of eight years thence next ensuing and I paid the whole rent of Ten Guineas a year for the same - During such my tenancy I resided in the said parish of Saint Nicholas constantly and was charged to the public Rates and taxes of the said Parish of Saint Nicholas in respect of the said tenement during the said eight Years and paid the same - While I was residing in the said parish of Cheltenham about eight or ten years ago I applied to the Overseers of the said Parish of Saint Nicholas for relief – they gave me on that occasion an allowance of four shillings a week for seven or eight months thence ensuing and while I was still residing in the said parish of Cheltenham – I am now actually chargeable to the said Parish of Cheltenham – I was married to my Wife Mary Ann about sixteen years ago at the said parish of Saint Nicholas by whom I have one Child named James aged fourteen years. My said Child has never done an act to gain a Settlement in his own right. [signed]
1846: *removed to St Nicholas, Gloucester (renting).* [PS/CH/RA/2/8:11. Note: "Henry Whittick & Son" delivered to St Nicholas, Gloucester 6 Apr 1846 by Charles Maisey. See **42077RO** (HW for granddaughter Harriet Whittick: 15 Oct 1842) for further information on HW and family.]

46016RO: 5/7 Mar 1846 (examination on 5 Mar) – Margaret Yates, wife of Reuben Yates, relating to the settlement of children **Ann**, **Caroline**, and **Martha Gaze**: About eighteen years ago I was married to my late Husband William Gaze at Bully [= Bulley] in the Parish of Churcham in this County by whom I had my said three Children namely Ann aged fourteen years - Caroline aged twelve years, and Martha aged ten years – They were all born in the Parish of Churchdown in the said County where I resided with my said Husband interruptedly from the time of our marriage until his death there about Seven years ago – My said husband was a Parishioner there and his Parents were settled there as I have heard and believe – About six months before my said Husband's death he was allowed by the Overseers of the said Parish of Churchdown Eight or Nine shillings a week regularly. After my said husband's death I applied to the said Overseers for relief, they allowed me Five shillings a week from the time of his death, until my Marriage with my present husband Reuben Yates about Six years ago, being for upwards of twelve months – During eight months of this time and when I received such relief I was residing with my Family in the said Parish of Cheltenham – The money was sometimes sent to me at Cheltenham, at other times I have fetched it myself, my said three Children are now actually Chargeable to the said Parish of Cheltenham – [mark]
1846: *removed to Churchdown (mother's settlement).* [PS/CH/RA/2/8:12 (copy at PS/CH/RA/2/7:251). Removal expenses for "Gaze" to Churchdown 7/3 (2Q 1846: D4178). See **46012RO** (Reuben Yates: 28/30 Feb 1846).]

46017RO: Wed 11/12 Mar 1846 (examination on 11 Mar) – **John Barton**, wife **Priscilla,** and five children **John**, **Hannah**, **Ann**, **William**, and **Fanny**; also Ruth Tiley, widow, residing in Corsham, Wilts, and Frederick Thomas Griffiths, solicitor.
John Barton: I am an Inmate of the Cheltenham Union Workhouse

I was born at Corsham in the County of Wilts about forty two years ago – My Parents John and Mary Barton were settled there – they are both dead – About thirty three years ago my said Father John Barton took and rented a tenement consisting of a Cottage and about two Acres and a half of Land situate by the Cross Keys in the said parish of Corsham, the Cottage belonging to John Manby of Corsham Farmer being of the value of Five pounds a Year – and the Land belonging to William Hulbert of Corsham Brewer and being of the value of Six pounds a year – I lived with my said Father at the said Cottage during his said tenancy – He resided for forty days and upwards in the said parish of Corsham in the said tenement under the said tenancy – About seventeen years ago my said Father rented the Roebuck Inn in the said parish of Corsham at the Rent of Sixteen pounds a year – and occupied the said premises under the said taking for upwards of a year –

About the years 1813, 1814, and 1815 the Overseers of the said parish of Corsham allowed my said Father twenty shillings a month, and afterwards sixteen shillings a month for two or three years – I have been several times with my Father when he received such relief. – About twelve Years ago last Christmas I was married to my Wife Priscilla in Saint John's Church in the City of Gloucester by whom I have five Children namely John aged Eleven years – Hannah aged Nine years, Ann aged Seven years, William aged Five years – and Fanny aged two years – I and my said Wife and Children are now actually chargeable to the said parish of Cheltenham – I have never done an act to gain a settlement [mark]

Ruth Tiley: I know John Barton now present   He is the Son of John and Mary Barton late of the said parish of Corsham. I knew his parents very well   I remember his father renting the two acres and a half of land situate by the Cross Keys in the said parish of Corsham. – I recollect the said John Barton being born at the said parish of Corsham about forty two years ago – His parents at that time lived in the said Parish of Corsham in the house just the opposite to where I lived – I attended upon his Mother in her confinement and nursed the Child, and took him to Church to be baptized about two years afterwards – I am sure he was born in the said parish of Corsham – [mark]

Frederick Thomas Griffiths: [confirms from Corsham register birth and baptism of John, son of John and Mary Barton on 14 Feb and 7 Sept 1804 respectively]

1846: *removed to Corsham, Wilts (father's settlement).* 1847: *death of Priscilla Barton at Corsham, Wilts (buried 8 June).* **1851:** *the family lived in Priory Lane, Corsham: JB (aged 46; agricultural labourer: previously also horse-keeper, born Corsham), John (16; agricultural labourer), Hannah (14; both born Gloucester), Ann (13), and William (9; both born Northleach); Fanny Barton (7) was "visitor" at 29 Grosvenor Place, Cheltenham (HO107/1973/251/31).* **1870:** *Fanny Barton married to Edward Jackway 7 Mar, from 29 Grosvenor Place, Cheltenham.* [PS/CH/RA/2/8:13 (copies at PS/CH/RA/2/7:252-4). Note: "John Barton Wife & 5 Children" delivered to Corsham 4 Apr 1846.]

46018RO: Thurs 19 Mar 1846 – **John Pillinger**, labourer; also sister Maria Lampett. *John Pillinger*: I am about fifty years of age. I was born in the Parish of Ledbury in the County of Hereford as I have heard and believe where my Parents Edward and Hannah Pillinger were legally settled – they are both dead. I was maintained in the Workhouse at Ledbury aforesaid from the first time I can recollect until I was about fifteen years of age. About the year 1810 when I was unmarried and without child or children I was hired to serve Capt[ai]n Jones of the said Parish of Ledbury in husbandry – I served him in the said Parish of Ledbury from the time of, and under the said hiring for two years and resided and slept during the whole of my said service in his House at Ledbury aforesaid – My Master found me in meat drink lodging and clothes but I received no wages. – and no time was mentioned – I was to be his servant and I went there and lived in his service for two years without interruption – About twenty seven years ago I and my wife Mary were chargeable to the Parish of Tewksbury [= Tewkesbury] in the County of Gloucester and were then removed by order of removal from the said Parish of Tewksbury to the said Parish of Ledbury and received in that Parish as Parishioners – there was no appeal against the said order – I am now actually chargeable to the said Parish of Cheltenham, and an Inmate of the Union Workhouse there. [mark]

Maria Lampett: I am the daughter of Hannah Pillinger deceased the Mother of John Pillinger now present – The said Hannah Pillinger lived with me at the Parish of Tewksbury in the said County for several years before she died – she died there about ten years ago – While she was residing in the said Parish of Tewksbury and about five years before her death – being helpless and unable to work [removal order text follows] I went by her direction to the Overseers of the said parish of Ledbury and applied to them for relief for her   accordingly they gave me some shillings for her and from that time allowed her three shillings a week I believe, which she received monthly up to the time of her death while she still resided in the said parish of Tewkesbury – I have often received the relief for her. I know that she had it monthly because she lived with me in Tewkesbury and had no other means of support. – [mark]

1846: *removed to Ledbury, Heref (hiring and service, or father's settlement).* [PS/CH/RA/2/8:14 (copies at PS/CH/RA/2/7:255-6). Note: "John Pillinger" delivered to Ledbury, Heref 20 Apr 1846 by Charles Maisey.]

46019RO: 19 Mar 1846 – **Mary Hill**, singlewoman: I am about Sixty four years of age –. I am the illegitimate daughter of Mary Hill – my Mother is dead – I was born at Oakridge Lynch in the Parish of Bisley in the County of Gloucester as I have heard and believe. Soon after I was born my Mother went to live with me at the parish of Minchinhampton in the said County and until I was twelve years of age the parish Officers of Bisley aforesaid allowed my Mother One shilling a week towards my support – and during the whole of these years, I was residing in the said parish of Minchinhampton – When I was about nineteen years of age I was still residing in the said Parish of Minchinhampton and my Mother was examined as to my Settlement – I was removed by order of Removal to the said Parish of Bisley and received into the Workhouse there where I remained for one month – the said Order was not appealed against – About nineteen or twenty years ago I went to the Workhouse there again – they received me there – For several years up to the time of the Union being formed in Bisley aforesaid the Parish Officers of Bisley aforesaid relieved me at different periods with sometimes Six pence a week and sometimes a Shilling a week when I had got no work – About Seven years ago I was residing in the said Parish of Cheltenham and applied to the Overseers of the said Parish of Bisley for relief – they allowed me Ten shillings while I still resided in the said Parish of Cheltenham – At last Christmas I went again from Cheltenham to the said Parish of Bisley and was immediately admitted into the Workhouse there where I remained – I have do[ne] no Act to gain a Settlement in my own right – I am now actually chargeable to the said Parish of Cheltenham [mark]

1846: *removed to Bisley (birth)*: see **47011RO** *(MH: 15 Feb 1847) for further information.* [PS/CH/RA/2/8:15 (copy at PS/CH/RA/2/7:257). Note: "Mary Hill" delivered to Bisley 16 Apr 1846 by Charles Maisey.]

46020RO: Sat 28 Mar 1846 – **Ann Bradley**, singlewoman: About the year 1831, when I was unmarried and without Child or Children I was hired into the Parish of Saint Nicholas in the City of Gloucester by Charles Cooke of that Parish Plumber & Glazier to serve him for One Year from the time of my said hiring at the Wages of Five pounds a Year – Accordingly I went into the Service of the said Charles Cooke and continued in the same service under the same hiring for the space of one whole Year thence ensuing and received my said years wages. I resided and slept during the whole of the said year's service at the House of my said Master situate in the said Parish of Saint Nicholas – After I had completed my said year's service and being still unmarried and without Child or Children I was hired again to serve my said Master in the said Parish of Saint Nicholas for One year – Accordingly I continued in his Service a second year and resided and slept in the said Parish of Saint Nicholas during the last mentioned year's service – I have never done an Act to gain a Settlement since – I am now actually chargeable to the said Parish of Cheltenham and am an Inmate of the Union Workhouse there – [signed]

1846: *removed to St Nicholas, Gloucester (hiring and service)*: see **47003RO** *(AB: 12 Jan 1847) for further information.* [PS/CH/RA/2/8:16 (copy at PS/CH/RA/2/7:258). Note: "Ann Bradley" delivered to St Nicholas, Gloucester 22 Apr 1846 by Charles Maisey.]

46021RO: Mon 2 Apr 1846 (examinations on 29 Mar and 2 Apr) – **Norah** (also **Hanora**, **Honora**, **Anora**, **Nora**) **Hampton**, wife of Charles Hampton, soldier, and three children **Ann**, **Harriet**, and **Elizabeth**; also Elizabeth Hampton, widow, residing in Tewkesbury, mother-in-law of Norah Hampton. *Elizabeth Hampton*: I am the Widow of William Hampton deceased, he died about twenty one years ago – I was married to him At Tewkesbury in the said County about Fifty years ago by whom I had my Son Charles the husband of Norah Hampton now present - He is in the Army abroad and I have not seen him for three years – At the time I married my said Husband he rented of M^r. Simmonds of Tewkesbury aforesaid Whitesmith a Tenement consisting of a House and Shop situate in Barton Street in the said Parish of Tewkesbury being of the value of Sixteen pounds a Year. I resided with my said husband during his said tenancy in the said tenement for about Ten years after my said Marriage – About Forty years ago my said husband acquired by purchase for about One Hundred pounds an Estate consisting of a Freehold house situate in Barton Street in the said parish of Tewkesbury – My said husband took possession of the said Estate immediately on his acquisition thereof and continued in such possession from thence until the time of his death – During the time he so possessed the said Estate, he resided uninterruptedly in the said parish of Tewkesbury. My said Son Charles was born in the said parish of Tewkesbury about twenty seven years ago

He lived at Tewkesbury until he was about eighteen or nineteen years of age when he enlisted for a Soldier and has continued in the Army from that time up to the present time – I am now receiving relief from the said parish of Tewkesbury – [mark]

Norah Hampton: I was married to Charles Hampton a private in the Sixteenth Regiment of Foot Seven years ago at Cork in Ireland by whom I have three Children now living with me namely Ann aged Six years – Harriet aged two years and Elizabeth aged Two Months – My said husband is the Son of Elizabeth Hampton of Tewkesbury Widow – My husband is now abroad at Gibraltar in the Army. I and my said Children are now actually chargeable to the said Parish of Cheltenham – My said husband never did an Act to my knowledge to gain a Settlement [mark]

1846: *daughter Elizabeth baptised at Cork, Ireland 11 Jan, aged 8 days, where Charles Hampton had been serving with 16th Regiment of Foot; **removed to Tewkesbury (husband's settlement).** **1861:** the family lived at 19 Lower Hospital St Court, Birmingham: Charles Hampton (aged 44; labourer, born Tewkesbury), (H)anora (43; born Cork), Harriet (16; described as "brick-maker", born Dublin), Mary (12; born Birmingham); Elizabeth (10; button-maker), and Charles (7; born Birmingham) (RG9/2162/13/20). **1869:** (RETURNED) death of NH, aged 57 (buried 27 Apr at Cheltenham). **1871:** husband Charles lived in Aston, Birmingham with new wife (RG10/3147/10/14).* [PS/CH/RA/2/8:17 (copies at PS/CH/RA/2/7:259-60). Note: "Nora Hampton & Two Children" delivered to Tewkesbury 30 Apr 1846 by Charles Maisey.]

46022RO: Sat 18 Apr 1846 – **Hannah White**, widow; also Thomas Boodle, assistant overseer, of Cheltenham, relating to the settlement of Hannah White. *Thomas Boodle*: [confirms removal order of William White and wife Hannah of 20 Dec 1830]

Hannah White: About twenty five years ago I was married to my late husband William White in the said Parish of Cheltenham – he died about fifteen years ago – I and my said late husband are the persons named in the Order of Removal now produced by Thomas Boodle the Assistant Overseer. We were removed by virtue of the said Order About the time it bears date from the said Parish of Cheltenham to the Parish of Upper Swell in the said County by Henry Butt of Cheltenham who is now dead – We were delivered to M^r. Cook the then Overseer of the said parish of Upper Swell – I have done no act to gain a Settlement since – I am now actually chargeable to the said parish of Cheltenham – The said Order of Removal was not appealed against or superseded. [mark]

1846: *removed to Upper Swell (late husband's settlement).* **1846-8:** *(RETURNED) from 3Q 1846 until 1Q 1848 HW (aged 62) received parish relief from Stow-on-the-Wold as a non-settled resident of Cheltenham (G/CH/9d/1).* [PS/CH/RA/2/8:18 (copies at PS/CH/RA/2/7:262-3). Note: "Hannah White" delivered to to Upper Swell 18 May 1846 by Charles Maisey. See Gray **638** (husband William White: 8 June 1826).]

46023RO: 18 Apr 1846 – **Lydia Cotterell** (also **Cotterall**, **Cotterel**), widow: I am now about Seventy two years of age, when I was about Seventeen years of age unmarried and without Child or Children I was hired into the Parish of Ampney Saint Peter otherwise Eastington in the County of Gloucester and about three miles from Cirencester by Jonathan Chapple of that parish Farmer to serve him for one year from the time of my said hiring at the wages of Four pounds a year –

Accordingly I went into the service of the said Jonathan Chapple and continued in the same service under the said hiring for the space of one whole year thence ensuing and received my said years wages – I resided and slept during the whole of my said years service at the house of my said Master situate in the said Parish of Ampney Saint Peter otherwise Eastington – When I was about twenty four years of age I was married to my late husband James Cotterell at the said Parish of Ampney Saint Peter otherwise Eastington – that was his parish – he gained his Parish there by living servant to the said Jonathan Chapple for more than a twelve month before his marriage

About twenty two years ago – I was living with my said Husband in the parish of Rodborough in the said County, and he was taken from thence to the Gloucester Infirmary at Gloucester where he remained for nearly twelve months – I applied to the Overseers of the said Parish of Ampney Saint Peter otherwise Eastington for relief for him – Accordingly the Overseers of that parish allowed me Five shillings a week which I received for the whole time my said husband remained in the said Infirmary as aforesaid and while I and my Children resided in the said parish of Rodborough – At another time and about four years before my said husband's death which happened about Eighteen years ago – and while he resided with me and our Children in the said parish of Rodborough I again applied to the Overseers of the said parish of Ampney Saint Peter otherwise Eastington for relief. – They gave me on that occasion an allowance of Five shillings a week which they continued almost uninterruptedly to the time of my said Husband's death and during the whole of the time we received such last mentioned relief we resided constantly in the said Parish of Rodborough and my said husband died there – I am now actually chargeable to the said parish of Cheltenham [mark]

1841: *LC (aged 65; laundress) lived with son John (23; miller) in Rodborough (HO107/362/67/13).* **1846: removed to Eastington (Ampney St Peter) (Cirencester Union) (husband's settlement). 1847:** *death of LC (buried, aged 73, 28 Nov at Rodborough).* [PS/CH/RA/2/8:19 (copy at PS/CH/RA/2/7:261). Note: "Lydia Cotterall" delivered to Ampney St Peter (otherwise Eastington) 15 May 1846 by Charles Maisey.]

46024RO: Sat 25 Apr 1846 (examinations on 23 Apr) – **Mary Ann Cook** (also **Cooke**), single woman; also Edmund Edginton, maltster, residing in Stow-on-the-Wold, relating to the settlement of Mary Ann Cook.

Edmund Edginton: [confirms that MAC was removed from Stow-on-the-Wold to Lyneham, Oxon by order of 11 Dec 1845, and that the order was not appealed against]

Mary Ann Cook: I am an Inmate of the Cheltenham Union Workhouse and actually Chargeable to the said parish of Cheltenham   I am the person described in the Order of Removal now produced by Edmund Edginton and therein called Mary Cook. I was removed by him in last January to Lyneham in Chipping Norton Union, and was received and maintained at the expence of the said Hamlet of Lyneham – [mark]

1846: *MAC treated in Cheltenham Workhouse for syphilis Mar; the medical officer stated that "she might and ought to have been removed"* (Cheltenham Chron. 26 Mar); **removed to Lyneham, Oxon (previously established as her settlement).** [PS/CH/RA/2/8:20 (copies at PS/CH/RA/2/7:264-5). Note: "Mary Ann Cooke" delivered to Lyneham, Oxon 21 May 1846 by Charles Maisey.]

46025RO: 25 Apr 1846 – **Esther Hardiman**, single woman, and illegitimate daughter **Jane Elizabeth**: At Michaelmas 1832, being unmarried and without Child or Children I was hired into the Parish of Winchcomb [= Winchcombe] in the said County by M^{rs}. Swinborne [= Swinburne] of Corndean in the said Parish of Winchcomb Widow to serve her for one Year from the time of my said hiring at the Wages of Ten pounds a year –

Accordingly at the Michaelmas I have mentioned I went into the said M^{rs}. Swinborne's service and continued in the same service under the said yearly hiring for the space of one whole year thence ensuing. I resided and slept during the whole of my said years service at the house of my

Mistress situate at Corndean aforesaid in the said Parish of Winchcomb and received my said years wages – I have never done an Act to gain a Settlement since –

About four years ago last Christmas I was delivered of an illegitimate female Child named Jane Elizabeth at the Parish of Pinnock in the said County – I and my said Child are now actually chargeable to the said Parish of Cheltenham – [mark]

1842: *baptism of Jane Elizabeth Hardiman 22 May at Temple Guiting,"natural daughter" of Esther, who lived in Broadwater, Didbrook.* **1846: removed to Winchcombe (hiring and service), for Jane Elizabeth until aged sixteen (order quashed on appeal).** **1851:** *(RETURNED) EH (aged 45; charwoman, born Pinnock) lived with daughter Jane Elizabeth (9; scholar, born Pinnock) at house of mother Jane Hardiman (85; pauper and formerly charwoman, born Winchcombe) in Sherborne St, Cheltenham (HO107/1973/153/47).* **1888:** *death of EH in Sherborne St, Cheltenham (buried 12 Nov, aged 85).* "Order quashed on the merits at Glos Trinity Sessions July 1846. The pauper swore that the hiring was two days after Michaelmas day <u>until</u> the next Michaelmas day, which would not be a hiring for a year. – She dishonestly stated to me over and over again that the hiring was for a twelvemonth and only changed her statement upon examination in Court. It appeared afterwards that she had expressed herself uncomfortable in the Winchcomb Workhouse – and knew from the Governor of the House what she had to say." [PS/CH/RA/2/8:21 (copy at PS/CH/RA/2/7:266). Note: "Esther Hardiman & Child" delivered to Winchcombe 28 May by Charles Maisey.]

46026RO: 25 Apr 1846 – **Hannah Fisher**, single woman; also her sister Pamela Fisher, single woman, residing in Sherborne St, Cheltenham, relating to the settlement of sister Hannah Fisher.

Pamela Fisher: The said Hannah Fisher now present is my Sister –

Our Father and Mother Nathaniel and Mary Fisher were Parishioners of Kings Stanley [= King's Stanley] in the said County. They lived in the said Parish of Kings Stanley from the time I can first recollect until my Father died there about twenty three years ago – My Mother continued to live there until she came to Cheltenham about seven years ago – she died in Cheltenham last Christmas – I am some Years older than my said Sister Hannah, and was at home when she was born – She was born in the said Parish of Kings Stanley about twenty four years ago and lived in that parish with my said Mother until she came to Cheltenham about seven years ago – When my Mother came to Cheltenham my said Sister Hannah was sent by the Overseers of the said parish of Kings Stanley to the Stroud Union Workhouse in the said County and was there about two years – My said Sister came from the Stroud Workhouse to my said Mother at Cheltenham and lived with her there – this was about Five Years ago – My said Mother had relief from the said parish of Kings Stanley for as much as two years before she died at first Eighteen pence a week then half a Crown a week and afterwards eighteen pence a week and during the whole of the time she so received the relief she lived in the said parish of Cheltenham [mark]

Hannah Fisher: I am the Sister of Pamla [*sic*] Fisher now present – I am now an Inmate in the Cheltenham Union Workhouse – I have never done an Act to gain a Settlement in my own right [mark]

1820: *baptism of HF (father not mentioned in King's Stanley baptism register; similarly for Pamela in 1810).* **1845-6:** *from 1Q 1845 until 2Q 1846 HF (aged 23) received parish relief from Stroud as a non-settled resident of Cheltenham (G/CH/9d/1).* **1846: removed to King's Stanley (Stroud Union) (birth and/or mother's settlement).** **1851:** *HF (aged 37; "Idiot", born King's Stanley) was an inmate of Stroud Workhouse (HO107/1965/296/5).* [PS/CH/RA/2/8:22 (copies at PS/CH/RA/2/7:267-8). Note: "Hannah Fisher" delivered to King's Stanley 22 May 1846 by Charles Maisey.]

46027RO: Mon 4 May 1846 – **Margaret** (also **Margarett**) **Norris**, single woman, and illegitimate daughter **Linda**; also father Matthew Norris, labourer, residing in Tidenham, relating to the settlement of daughter Margaret.

Matthew Norris: About the year One thousand seven hundred and ninety six being then unmarried and without Child or Children I was hired into the Parish of Tidenham in the County of Gloucester by Farmer Prior of Wallop Farm in the parish of Tidenham to serve him for a Year from the time of my said hiring – My Master was to find me Victuals and Clothes – I was hired at Michaelmas – Accordingly at the Michaelmas, I went into the said Farmer Prior's service under the said yearly hiring and continued in the same Service for the space of one whole year from thence next ensuing. During the whole of my said years Service and for the last Forty days thereof I resided and slept at the house of my said Master in the parish of Tidenham aforesaid – When I had served the first year, I continued in my said Master's Service for two more years under the same terms as his yearly Servant and resided and slept during the whole of the said two years at my said Master's house in the said parish of Tidenham.

About the Year One thousand eight hundred and ten I was married to my Wife Margarett in a Church in the City of Dublin in the Kingdom of Ireland – We were married by Banns - Margarett Norris the Pauper who is now chargeable to the Parish of Cheltenham and now present is my daughter by my said Wife – She was born about Twenty six years ago in a house in which I was then lodging called Cross Hill in the Parish of Tidenham aforesaid – I saw my said Wife Margarett confined of my said daughter and was present in the Room at the time and brought the midwife. - I am not aware that my said daughter has ever done any act to gain a Settlement in her own right [mark]

Margaret Norris: I have never been married – About a fortnight ago I was delivered of a Female Bastard Child named Linda – I and my said Child are now actually chargeable to the said parish of Cheltenham – I have never done any Act to gain a Settlement in my own right. – [mark]

1846: *removed to Tidenham (father's settlement), for Linda until aged sixteen; Linda Norris was baptised at Cheltenham on day of mother's examination; both then resided at Union Workhouse in Cheltenham.* [PS/CH/RA/2/8:23 (copies at PS/CH/RA/2/7:269-70). Note: "Margaret Norris and Child" delivered to Tidenham 30 May 1846 by Charles Maisey.]

46028RO: Sat 16 May 1846 (examination on 12 May) – **Thomas Wilkins**, labourer, and wife **Susan**: About twenty four years ago being then unmarried and having no Child or Children I was hired into the parish of Haresfield in the said County by M^r. Chamberlain of Haresfield Mount in the said parish of Haresfield Farmer to serve him in that parish as a Husbandry servant for a year at the wages of Seven pounds. I entered into such service and continued therein under the said hiring for the space of one whole year and received my years wages and resided and slept in my said Master's house at Haresfield Mount in the said parish of Haresfield the whole time – at the expiration of such year I was again hired (being then unmarried and having no Child or Children) by the said M^r. Chamberlain to serve him in the said parish of Haresfield for another year at the same Wages – which year I also served and received my years wages and resided and slept in my said Master's house at Haresfield Mount aforesaid the whole year – I have never done any act since to gain a settlement – About twenty years ago I was married to my present Wife Susan in the parish Church of Cheltenham aforesaid – About fourteen or fifteen years ago being being then residing in the parish of Cheltenham I was relieved by the parish Officers of Haresfield aforesaid for about three or four weeks with about six or seven shillings in money – I am now actually chargeable to the said parish of Cheltenham. [mark]

1846: *removed to Haresfield (hiring and service): see* **49021RO** *(TW: 24 Mar 1849) for further information.* [PS/CH/RA/2/8:24 (copy at PS/CH/RA/2/7:271). Note: "Thos. Wilkins & Wife" delivered to Haresfield 9 June 1846 by Charles Maisey.]

46029RO: Sat 30 May/4 June 1846 (examinations on 30 May) – **Sarah Gilding**, widow, and five children **William**, **Mary Ann**, **Elizabeth**, **Charles**, and **James**; also Joseph Gilding, carpenter, residing in Westbury-upon-Severn, relating to the settlement of daughter-in-law Sarah Gilding. *Joseph Gilding*: The said Sarah Gilding is my daughter in law, she married my son Joseph Gilding at Cheltenham about twenty years ago – and he was forty two years of age when he died. He was born in the said parish of Westbury upon Severn about forty two years ago, at the house there were I then lived. I was at home at the time of his birth and recollect it – I have lived in Westbury upon Severn aforesaid all my life time except about Eleven years – About Fifty Years ago when I was about Twenty Years of age I was bound Apprentice to Thomas Grassing of the said parish of Westbury upon Severn, Carpenter and Wheelwright for Five years – I served the said term with my said Master residing all the time in my Master's house in the said parish of Westbury upon Severn – About two years before my said son's Marriage and while he lived at home with me I acquired by purchase of Richard Hawkes of Westbury upon Severn aforesaid Apple Merchant for the sum of Two hundred pounds a Freehold Estate consisting of a House Garden little Orchard and a piece of Land in the common Fields All situate in the parish of Westbury upon Severn aforesaid and now in my occupation   I took possession of the said Estate immediately on my acquisition thereof and continued in such possession from thence up to the present time, and during the whole of that time except about a year that I was in Cheltenham, I have resided uninterruptedly in the said parish of Westbury upon Severn – Before my said Son's Marriage he resided with me upon the said Estate uninterruptedly for as much as a twelve month – [signed]

Sarah Gilding: I am the Widow of Joseph Gilding late of Cheltenham aforesaid Carpenter deceased the Son of Joseph Gilding of Westbury upon Severn in the said County Carpenter now present – I was married to my said late husband at the parish Church of Cheltenham aforesaid in the year 1826, by whom I had my said five Children namely William aged sixteen Years – Mary Ann aged twelve Years, Elizabeth aged ten years – Charles aged six years, and James aged two Years – My said husband never did an act since our marriage to gain a settlement – I always understood his Settlement was in the said parish of Westbury upon Severn – None of my said Children have done an act to gain a settlement in their own right – they have always lived at home with me – I and my said Five Children are now actually chargeable to the said parish of Cheltenham – [signed]

1846: *removed to Westbury-upon-Severn (husband's settlement)*: see **47009RO** *(SG: 6 Feb 1847) for further information.* [PS/CH/RA/2/8:25 (copies at PS/CH/RA/2/7:272-3). Removal expenses for "Gilding" to Westbury-upon-Severn 17/- (3Q 1846: D4178). Overseers' records show removal expenses relating to a Gilding to Westbury in 1841: Gilding for Westbury-upon-Severn £1/8/- (2Q 1841: D4178) (no examination found).]

46030RO: Sat 13 June 1846 – **Henry Bennett**, labourer, wife **Mary** (**Jane**) and child **Henry**; also father John Bennett, gardener, residing in Stow-on-the-Wold, and Charles Maisey, magistrates' office and cabinet-maker, relating to the settlement of Henry Bennett. *John Bennett*: I am about Fifty four years of age   about thirty three years ago being then unmarried and without Child or Children I was hired by M^r. Brooks of the said parish of Stow on the Wold Solicitor to serve him in that parish for a year   accordingly I entered into M^r. Brooks' service, and served him the whole of the year under the said yearly hiring and resided and slept during the whole of the said year at the house of my said Master situate in the said parish of Stow on the Wold – I have never since done an act to gain a settlement – About thirty one Years ago I was married to my present Wife Mary in the parish Church of Stow on the Wold aforesaid by whom I had my said Son Henry now present who has lived at home with me until the last two years and has never done an act to my knowledge to gain a Settlement in his own right – About two years ago I was removed from the said Parish of Cheltenham to the said Parish of Stow on the Wold by Charles Maisey now present by virtue of the order of Removal now produced by him – The order of Removal was not appealed against [mark]

Charles Maisey: [confirms removal of John Bennett, wife and two children to Stow-on-the-Wold under order of 11 Jan 1844]

Henry Bennett: I am the Son of John Bennett now present. I am about Twenty two years of age. I have never done an act to gain a Settlement in my own right. I was married to my said Wife Mary at the parish Church of Cheltenham aforesaid at the latter end of last year by who I have one Child named Henry aged about five weeks. I and my said Wife and Child are now actually chargeable to the said Parish of Cheltenham [signed] Henry Bennett

1846: *removed to Stow-on-the-Wold (father's settlement)*: see **51019RO** *(HB: 6 Dec 1851) for further information.* [PS/CH/RA/2/8:26 (copies at PS/CH/RA/2/7:278-80). Removal expenses for "Bennett" to Stow-on-the-Wold £1/6/- (3Q 1846: D4178).]

46031RO: 13 June 1846 – **Hannah Weger** (more commonly **Wager**), single woman; also Charles Griffiths, magistrates' office, relating to the settlement of Hannah Weger.
Charles Griffiths: [produces and confirms removal order of 26 Apr 38 for Hannah Weger]
Hannah Weger: I am now in my Sixty third Year – About thirty two years [ago] being then unmarried and without Child or Children – I was hired into the Parish of Painswick in the said County by M^rs. Loveday of that parish to serve her for one year from the said time of my hiring at the wages of Five Pounds a Year – Accordingly I went into the said service of M^rs. Loveday and continued in the same service under the said yearly hiring for the space of one whole year thence ensuing – I resided and slept during the whole of my said years service at the house of my said Mistress situate in the said parish of Painswick and received my years wages – I lived in this service two years – I have never done an act to gain a Settlement since. – About eight years ago I was chargeable to the said parish of Cheltenham and my examination was taken before two Magistrates there as to my Settlement – I was removed by virtue of the order of Removal now produced by Charles Griffiths from the said parish of Cheltenham in the said parish of Painswick – The parish officers of Painswick aforesaid gave me Five shillings – I am now actually chargeable to the said parish of Cheltenham. [mark]
1831: *probably the HW convicted of damaging hedge of Mr Loveday, yeoman of Painswick, Mar (Q/PC/2/50/B/40).* **1838:** *removed to Painswick (see **38033RO:** HW: 26 Apr) (RETURNED).* **1841:** *HW (aged 55) servant living in Church St, Cheltenham (HO107/353/15/6/6).* **1846:** *removed to Painswick (hiring and service).* **1847:** *death of HW at Painswick Workhouse (buried at Painswick 3 Apr, aged 63).* [PS/CH/RA/2/8:27 (copies at PS/CH/RA/2/7:276-7). Removal expenses for "Weger" to Painswick 10/6 (3Q 1846: D4178).]

46032RO: Tues 7/17 July 1846 (examinations on 6 July) – **John Cook** (also **Cooke**), labourer; also Edward Lloyd Griffiths, solicitor, and Esther Hillman, residing in Painswick, relating to the settlement of John Cook. *John Cook*: I was born in the parish of Painswick in the said County about forty three years ago as I have always heard and believe – My Mother Mary Cook was never married and died when I was about three years of age – I was then taken to by Ann Wood who received two shillings a week for my maintenance from the Parish Officers of Painswick aforesaid from that time until I was fifteen or sixteen years of age – I then left her and was taken into the Workhouse of Painswick aforesaid and continued there for about a twelvemonth afterwards – About the years 1827 or 1828 I was living in the parish of Stroud in the said County and whilst residing there applied to Mr Baylis the then Overseer of Painswick aforesaid for relief – He had me examined before a Magistrate as to my settlement and after such examination relieved me with two or three shillings in money and a new pair of boots and at the time of receiving such relief I was residing in the said Parish of Stroud. I have never done an act to gain a Settlement in my own right – I am now actually chargeable to the said parish of Cheltenham and am an Inmate of the Union Workhouse there [mark]
Edward Lloyd Griffiths: [produces extract of Painswick register confirming baptism of John, son of Mary Cook on 24 Apr 1803]
Esther Hillman: I am the Wife of Thomas Hillman who lives at Tibuel [= Tibbiwell] Lane in the said parish of Painswick – I know John Cook the person now present – he is the illegitimate Son of Mary Cook who died about forty years ago – I remember the said Mary Cook – she came to live with my Mother Ann Wood when her said Son was very young – soon after his birth – and continued to live with my said Mother until he was grown up – he was born in the said parish of Painswick about forty three years ago – My said Mother Ann Wood received two shillings a week I believe from the parish officers of Painswick aforesaid for the maintenance of the said John Cook – My Mother has been dead several years – thirty two years [mark]
1846: *removed to Painswick (presumed) (birth).* **1851:** *(RETURNED) JC (aged 48; agricultural labourer receiving parish relief) lodged in Bath Rd, Cheltenham (HO107/1973/875/8).* [PS/CH/RA/2/8:28 (copies at PS/CH/RA/2/7:274-5a). Removal expenses for "Cooke" to Painswick 12/6 (3Q 1846: D4178).]

46033RO: [blank] July 1846 – **George Best**, and wife **Ann:** About seven years ago I rented from year to year at the rent of Sixteen pounds a year a tenement consisting of a separate and distinct dwelling house situate and being Number 7 Deans Walk in the Parish of [blank] in the City of Gloucester. I actually occupied the said premises under the said yearly renting in the said Parish from the said commencement of my tenancy unto about last November being for a period of nearly seven years. I paid the said yearly rent for the whole of the time I occupied the said premises as aforesaid. During the whole of my said tenancy I resided uninterruptedly in the said Parish of [blank] – I was charged and assessed to the poor rates of the said Parish of [blank] in respect to the said tenement there situate for the whole of my said tenancy and paid the same. I have never done an act to gain a settlement since. I was married to my wife Ann at the Parish of Evesham in the County of Worcester about twenty five years ago. I and my said wife are now actually chargeable to the said Parish of Cheltenham, and are in receipt of bread from Peter Butt the Relieving Officer of that Parish.
1846: *removal uncertain: examination form incomplete.* **1851:** *GB (aged 42, cabinet-maker, born Evesham, Worcs) lived with wife Ann (36; born Clifton, Som) and nephew Frederick Skerrett (4; born Cheltenham) at 9 Beaufort Buildings, Cheltenham (HO107/1973/93/8).* [PS/CH/RA/2/7:281.]

46034RO: Mon 20 July 1846 (examinations on 16 July) – **Henry Webb**, labourer, wife **Mary** and son **James**; also mother Mary Welch, residing in Swindon, relating to the settlement of son Henry. *Mary Welch*: The said Henry Web the person now present is my Son – He was born illegitimate at the said Parish of Swindon about twenty one years ago – he has lived at Swindon nearly the whole of his life time and has never done an act to gain a settlement – he was born in the same house, where I am now living – My maiden name was Webb. [signed]
Henry Webb: I am the illegitimate Son of Mary Welch now present and I am twenty one years of age – I was born at that Parish of Swindon in the said County – I have never done an act to gain a settlement in my own right – I was married at the Parish Church of Cheltenham about a twelve month ago to my Wife Mary Ann by whom I have one child named James aged seven months [mark]
1846: *removed to Swindon (birth).* **1851:** *HW (aged 26; agricultural labourer, born Swindon) lived in Swindon with wife Mary Ann (25; born Cheltenham) and son James (5; scholar, born Cheltenham) (HO107/1972/18/10).* [PS/CH/RA/2/8:29 (copies at PS/CH/RA/2/7:282-3). Note: "Henry Webb Wife & Child" delivered to Swindon 15 Aug 1846 by Charles Maisey.]

46035RO: Thurs 30 July 1846 – **Mary Bradley**, widow: I am the Widow of John Bradley and was married to him at the parish of Lower Slaughter in the said County about thirty six years ago – My said husband was settled there by living in the service of M^r. Collett of that parish for about eight years before I was married to him – About three years before my said Marriage with the said John Bradley being then unmarried and without Child or Children I was hired into the said Parish of Lower Slaughter by Mr Bryan of that Parish to serve him for one year from the time of my said hiring at the wages of five pounds a year – Accordingly I went forthwith into the service of M^r. Bryan and served him under the said yearly hiring for the space of three years thence next ensuing and was married from his service – I resided and slept during the whole of my said service with the said M^r. Bryan at his house situate in the said Parish of Lower Slaughter and received all my wages – I am now actually chargeable to the said Parish of Cheltenham [signed]
1841: *John Bradley (aged 63; labourer) lived at 2 Victoria Place, Bath Rd, Cheltenham with wife Mary (50) and niece Mary Fluke (6) (HO107/353/12/25/44).* **1843:** *death of John Bradley in Cheltenham (buried at New Burial Ground 20 Oct, aged 71).* **1846:** *removed to Lower Slaughter (Stow-on-the-Wold Union) (husband's settlement); (RETURNED) from 3Q until 4Q MB received parish relief from Stow-on-the-Wold as a non-settled resident of Cheltenham (G/CH/9d/1).* **1851:** *MB (64; widow and milk woman, born Dowdeswell) lodged in Union St, Cheltenham at home of James Hobbs, shoemaker (HO107/1973/895/49).* [PS/CH/RA/2/8:30 (copy at PS/CH/RA/2/7:284). Note: "Mary Bradley" delivered to Lower Slaughter 24 Aug 1846 by Charles Maisey.]

46036RO: Thurs 13 Aug 1846 – **Elizabeth Long**, single woman, residing near Crescent Terrace in Cheltenham: About fifteen years ago being then unmarried and having no child or children I

was hired into the parish of All Saints Evesham in the County of Worcester by Mr Daniel Edge of that Parish to serve him in that Parish for a year at the wages of ten pounds – I entered into such service and continued therein for the space of one whole year and received my years wages and resided and slept in my said Masters house in the said Parish of All Saints Evesham the whole year I continued in such service for four years afterwards and resided and slept in my said Master's house at All Saints Evesham the whole time – I have done no act since to gain a settlement – I am now in receipt of relief from the Relieving Officer of Cheltenham aforesaid [signed]
1846: *removed to All Saints, Evesham, Worcs (hiring and service).* [PS/CH/RA/2/8:31 (copy at PS/CH/RA/2/7:285).]

46037SE: [blank] Aug 1846 – **George Seal** (also **Sale**, **Seale**; also **Sele**, **Serl**), mason, wife **Charlotte**, and daughter **Sarah:** My Settlement is in the Parish of Bidford in the County of Warwick where my Father William Seal who is dead was legally settled. He was a Shoemaker and lived there all his life time and I was born there as I have heard and believe about fifty years ago last March. I lived at Bidford aforesaid until I was about nineteen years of age. – I have never done an act to gain a Settlement in my own right. About fourteen years ago I was residing in the said Parish of Cheltenham and was taken ill. Accordingly I went over to Bidford and applied to the Parish officers there for relief. They gave me two sovereigns in the whole at two different times and at the times I received such relief I was still residing in the said Parish of Cheltenham. For the last nineteen Years I have received from the Overseer of the said Parish of Bidford a sum of money yearly sometimes seven shillings and sometimes nine shillings called the Dudley Tole [for "Dole"] Money – a charitable contribution left by a Lady [Alicia, Duchess Dudley] to be given to poor persons belonging to Bidford who do not receive relief from the Parish and during the whole of these nineteen years I have resided in the said Parish of Cheltenham. I was married to my said wife Charlotte about twenty six years ago at the Parish Church in Cheltenham aforesaid by whom I have one child named Sarah aged twelve years. I and my said Wife and child are now actually chargeable to the said Parish of Cheltenham. When I was about fifteen years of age being then unmarried and without child or children I was hired into the said Parish of Bidford by Mr Wilks, who kept the Masons Arms to serve him for a twelvemonth. Accordingly I entered into the service of Mr Wilks and served him under the said yearly hiring for the space of two years thence next ensuing and resided and slept during the whole of my said two years service at the house of my said Master situate in the said Parish of Bidford –
[PS/CH/RA/2/7:286. Replaced by **46038RO** (GS: 22 Aug 1846).]

46038RO: Sat 22 Aug 1846 – **George Seal** (also **Sale**, **Seale**; also **Sele**, **Serl**), wife **Charlotte**, and daughter **Sarah**: I am about Fifty years of age. When I was about fifteen years of age being then unmarried and having no Child or Children I was hired into the Parish of Bidford in the County of Warwick by M^r. Smith of the Masons Arms in the said Parish of Bidford to serve him in that Parish for a year at the wages of Three pounds   I entered into such Service and continued therein under the said hiring for the space of two whole years and received my wages and resided and slept in my said Masters House at Bidford aforesaid the whole time – I have done no act since to gain a settlement – About twenty three years ago I was married to my present Wife Charlotte in the parish Church of Cheltenham aforesaid by whom I have one child named Sarah aged twelve years – I and my said Wife and Child are now actually chargeable to the said parish of Cheltenham – [mark]
1846: *removed to Bidford, Warks (hiring and service).* **1850:** *(RETURNED) death of GS in Cheltenham (buried at New Burial Ground 17 July, aged 56).* **1862:** *death of wife Charlotte, aged 66 (buried 13 June at New Burial Ground, Cheltenham).* [PS/CH/RA/2/8:32 (copy at PS/CH/RA/2/7:287). Replaces **46037SE** (GS: Aug 1846), which is substantially different in places.]

46039RO: Thurs 20 Aug 1846 – **(Mary) Ann Dyke** (also **Dike**), single woman, and her unnamed son [William]; also mother Mary Dyke, widow, residing in St James, Gloucester, relating to the settlement of Mary Ann Dyke. *Mary Dyke*: I was married to my late Husband David Dyke about twenty eight years ago in the parish Church of Tewkesbury by whom I had my said Daughter Mary

Ann now aged about Eighteen years – About six years ago my said husband rented a separate and distinct tenement consisting of a House and Garden situate in Cricklade Street in the parish of Cirencester in the said County of Mr Mullings at Eleven Guineas a Year for a year – We continued to reside and slept in such House for about three years and paid all the rent for the same.

My said husband was duly rated to all the Poor Rates made for the said parish of Cirencester during the time he occupied such House in respect of such House and all such Rates were duly paid – I paid part of the Rent and the Rates myself – My husband has been dead six months – My said Daughter – Mary Ann resided with us as part of the family the whole of the time we lived in Cirencester – My husband never done any act after he left Cirencester to gain a settlement that I have done no act since his Death [signed]

Mary Ann Dyke: I have never done any act to gain a settlement in my own right. I am actually chargeable to the said parish of Cheltenham and an Inmate of the Union Workhouse there – I was delivered of a Male bastard Child on the eighteenth day of July last [mark]

1841: *MAD (aged 13) lived with father David Dyke (41; tailor), his wife Mary (41), and eight other children in Cricklade St, Cirencester (HO107/380/1/36/18).* **1846:** *David Dyke died 20 Feb at Gloucester "after and long and painful illness" (Cheltenham Chron. 12 Mar) (buried 27 Feb 1846, aged 46); the family had apparently moved to Gloucester, perhaps to be near David's brother Daniel, also tailor; (18 July) birth of illegitimate son William at Cheltenham Workhouse;* **removed to Cirencester (father's settlement);** *son William died at Gloucester in 1847, buried 24 Sept at St Mary de Lode church.* **1851:** *MAD (51; housekeeper) and six children (but not Mary Ann) lived in Aberystruth, Monm (HO107/2447/292/38).* [PS/CH/RA/2/8:33 (copies at PS/CH/RA/2/7:288-9). Note: "Mary Ann Dyke and Child" delivered to Cirencester Workhouse 22 Sept 1846 by Thomas Griffiths".]

46040RO: 22 Aug 1846 – **Philip Janes**, and wife **Sarah**: In the year One thousand seven hundred and ninety one being then unmarried and having no child or children I was hired into the Parish of Llanwinnio [= Llanwinio] in the County of Carmarthen by William Davis Esquire of that parish to serve him in that parish as a Servant for a year at the wages of eight Guineas. I entered into such service and continued therein under the said hiring for the space of two whole years and received all my wages and resided and slept in my said Masters house in the said Parish of Llanwinnio the whole time. I have done no act since to gain a settlement – About forty six years ago I was married to my present Wife Sarah at Edinburgh – I am now actually chargeable to the said Parish of Cheltenham [mark]

1846: *removed to Llanwinio, Carmarthenshire (renting).* **1848:** *(RETURNED) death of PJ in Cheltenham (buried at New Burial Ground 17 Jan, aged 74).* [PS/CH/RA/2/8:34 (copy at PS/CH/RA/2/7:290).]

46041RO: Thurs 1 Oct 1846 (examinations on 26 Sept and 1 Oct) – Ann Phipps, wife of Charles Phipps, beer-seller, residing in Moreton-in-March, and Mary Castle, wife of Jesse Castle, relating to the settlement of **William**, **Henry**, and **Charles Petty**. *Ann Phipps*: I produce an Indenture of Apprenticeship signed by John Petty, William Cornbill and my husband the said Charles Phipps – The John Petty named in the said Indenture is the Son of my said husband and I knew him – I recollect his being apprenticed to the said William Cornbill – he was brought to our house when he was apprenticed – I remember his living with William Cornbill as an apprentice from the time the Indenture bears date namely 27th January 1824 for about three Years – he then went to serve the remainder of his seven years term of apprenticeship with William Coling of Blockley in the County of Worcester Cordwainer - he called at our house several times while he was living with Mr. Cowling [*sic*] – I know that he served the remainder of his apprenticeship with Mr. Cowling and was with him rather better than four years   he resided with his said Master at the said Parish of Blockley during the whole time he served as such apprentice as aforesaid [signed]

Mary Castle: The said William Petty is of the age of twelve years – the said Henry Petty is of the age of ten years and Charles Petty is of the age of eight years – they are the three children of my Son John Petty referred to in the annexed examination of Ann Phipps – I have not heard of the said John Petty for the last 3 years – he left Cheltenham about three years ago and his said three children have been since that time and now are in the Cheltenham Union Workhouse actually chargeable to the said Parish of Cheltenham. Their Mother Ann Petty died in Cheltenham just before her husband left – I remember my said Son being apprenticed to William Cornbill of Stow Shoemaker about twenty three years ago – His Master M^r. Cornbill failed and he served the last five years I believe of his apprenticeship with M^r. Coling of Blockley in the County of Worcester Cordwainer. I have been at Blockley during the time he served there under his apprenticeship and know that he lived in the House of M^r. Coling situate in the said Parish of Blockley during the time of his service as aforesaid –My said Son never did an act to gain a settlement afterwards – The Children are now present – they have done no act to gain a Settlement. [signed]

1843: *wife Ann Petty buried at New Burial Ground, Cheltenham 13 June, aged 29.* **1846: removed to Blockley, Worcs (father's settlement). 1851:** *(RETURNED) youngest son Charles (aged 12; born Cheltenham, baptised Winchcombe) was a pauper inmate of Cheltenham Union Workhouse (HO107/1973/1096/12); Henry (15; born Winchcombe, baptised Blockley, Worcs) was tailor's apprentice, living and working at 428 High St, Cheltenham (HO107/1973/784/4); William (age given as 14; born Cheltenham) was groom lodging in Aldermaston, Berks (HO107/1691/245/3).* [PS/CH/RA/2/8:35 (copies at PS/CH/RA/2/7:291-2).]

46042SE: Sat 24 and [blank] Oct 1846 – **Esther** (also **Hester**) **Smith**, single woman; also father William Smith, labourer, residing in Stroud, relating to daughter's settlement: [incomplete – no text.]
1846: *removal uncertain: examination form incomplete.* **1849:** *ES admitted to Cheltenham Workhouse 25 Aug, and again on 24 Sept, ill and with infant (G/CH/60/6).* [PS/CH/RA/2/7:293 (pages 294-5 blank).]

46043RO: Thurs 24 Dec 1846 (examinations on 19 and 24 Oct) – **Robert Ford**, labourer, and wife **Grace**; also Mary English, wife of Joseph English, residing in Leigh, Wilts, relating to the settlement of brother Robert Ford. *Mary English*: I am the Daughter of William Ford and Mary his Wife who are both dead   they resided at the parish of Brinkworth in the County of Wilts as long as I can remember – My said Father resided in a House of his own at Brinkworth aforesaid for many years – My said brother was born in such house about fifty three years ago – I remember it well – I lived in the same house at the time. [mark]
Robert Ford: The first place I remember myself was residing with my Father William Ford and Mary his Wife in the parish of Brinkworth in the County of Wilts – My said Father resided in a house at Brinkworth aforesaid for several years   About six years ago I was sent by orders of removal from the parish of Minchinhampton to the said Parish of Brinkworth together with my wife and delivered to the Overseer who received us and relieved asked for several weeks – such orders were not appealed against – I was married to my said Wife Grace about twenty nine years ago at Brinkworth aforesaid – I have done no act to gain a settlement in my own right – I am now in the receipt of relief from the relieving Officer of Cheltenham aforesaid. [mark]
1847: *removed to Brinkworth, Wilts (apparently parents' settlement).* **1851:** *RF (aged 59; agricultural labourer, born Brinkworth, Wilts) lived with wife Grace (61; also born Brinkworth), and granddaughter Lucy (5) in St Mary Westport, Malmesbury, Wilts (HO107/1835/348/18).* [PS/CH/RA/2/8:36 (copies at PS/CH/RA/2/7:297-8). Note: "Robert Ford & Grace his wife" delivered to Brinkworth, Wilts 16 Jan 1847 by Thomas Griffiths.]

1847

47001RO: Fri 9 Jan 1847 – **Emanuel Bridges**, stonemason, wife **Rose**, and seven children **Ann**, **William**, **Rosina** (also **Rosanna**), **Mary**, **Prudence**, **Elizabeth**, and **Jane**; also Edward James Boodle, magistrates' office, relating to the settlement of Emanuel Bridges and family. *Emanuel Bridges*: The first place I remember myself was in the parish of Chedworth in the said County – About eighteen years ago I was married to my present wife Rose in the parish Church of Chedworth aforesaid by whom I have seven children namely Ann aged 15 years William aged 13 years Rosina aged 11 years – Mary aged 8 years Prudence aged 7 years Elizabeth aged 5 years and Jane aged 3 years – About five years and two months ago I and my said wife and my first named six Children were sent by orders of removal from the said Parish of Cheltenham unto the said Parish of Chedworth and delivered to the Overseer there who received us – such orders were not appealed against – In the month of February last I myself Wife and Family became Inmates of the Union Workhouse at Northleach and chargeable to the said Parish of Chedworth, w[h]ere we resided for about five weeks at the expense of the said parish of Chedworth – The Assistant Overseer of the said parish of Chedworth at the expiration of such five weeks gave the Governor of the said Union Workhouse at Northleach in my presence the sum of twenty shillings to give me for me and my wife and Family to leave the said workhouse which I received from the said Governor [signed]
Edward James Boodle: [confirming that Emanuel Bridges, wife, and six children were removed to Chedworth under order of 7 Oct 1841, and that the removal was not appealed against]
1841: *EB (aged 50; stonemason) lived with wife Rose (30; née Crook) and children Ann (11), William (8), Rosanna (6), Mary (4), and Prudence (2) in Grove St, Cheltenham (HO107/353/16/33/26-7); removed to Chedworth (father's settlement): see* **41061RO** *(EB: 7 Oct) (RETURNED).* **1844:** *(24 Jan) daughter Jane born at 7 Bath Terrace, Cheltenham.* **1847:** *removed to Chedworth (father's settlement).* **1851:** *EB buried 29 Nov at Leckhampton; widow Rose (43; laundress) lived with five children at 39 Norwood St, Leckhampton (HO107/1972/223/12).* **1861:** *daughter Rosanna (26) lived with husband Walter Selley (24; mason) and three children at 42 Norwood St, Leckhampton; her sisters Elizabeth (19) and Jane (18) were visitors (RG9/1795/72/10), while mother Rose (53; widow) worked as servant at 22 Montpellier Villas, Cheltenham (RG9/1803/107/27).* [PS/CH/RA/2/8:37 (copies at PS/CH/RA/2/7:299-300). Note: "Emanuel Bridges Wife & Children" delivered to Chedworth 5 Feb 1847 by Charles Maisey.]

47002RO: 9 Jan 1847 – **Joseph Casey**, labourer, and wife **Elizabeth**; also Edward James Boodle, magistrates' office, relating to the settlement of Joseph Casey. *Joseph Casey*: The first place I remember myself was in the parish of Minchinhampton in the said County where I resided until I was upwards of twenty years of age – About forty two years ago I was married to my present wife Elizabeth in the Parish Church of Horsley – About five years ago I was removed by orders of Removal from the said Parish of Cheltenham unto the said Parish of Minchinhampton and delivered to the Overseer there who received me – such order was not appealed against [mark]
Edward James Boodle: [confirms removal of Joseph Casey and wife to Minchinhampton under order of 21 Dec 1841]
1841: *JC (aged 65; labourer) lived with family in Shelborne St, Cheltenham: Joseph (30; plasterer), Thomas (25; labourer), Elizabeth (20; servant), and Ann (1) (Elizabeth Casey absent from home on census night) (HO107/353/6/10/14-10/15); removed to Minchinhampton (father's apparent settlement): see* **41082RO** *(JC: 21 Dec) (RETURNED).* **1847:** *removed to Minchinhampton (father's apparent settlement).* **1848:** *(RETURNED) JC and wife admitted to and discharged from Cheltenham Workhouse June (G/CH/60/5/6).* **1851:** *the couple lived at 60 Sherborne St, Cheltenham: JC (75; cloth worker, born Minchinhampton), Elizabeth (74) (HO107/1973/154/48).* [PS/CH/RA/2/8:38 (copies at PS/CH/RA/2/7:301-2). Notes: "Joseph Casey Casey & Elizabeth his Wife" delivered to Stroud Union 11 Mar 1847 by Charles Maisey; removal expenses to Minchinhampton 11/6 (4Q 1846/1Q 1847: D4178).]

47003RO: Tues 12 Jan 1847 – **Ann Bradley**, single woman, and daughter **Fanny**; also Charles Maisey, magistrates' office, relating to the settlement of Ann Bradley. *Ann Bradley*: About the year 1831 being then unmarried and having no child or children I was hired into the Parish of Saint Nicholas in the City of Gloucester by Charles Cooke of that Parish Plumber and Glazier to serve him for one year from the time of my said hiring at the wages of Five pounds a Year – Accordingly I went into the service of the said Charles Cooke and continued in the same service under the said hiring for the space of one whole year thence ensuing and received my years wages – I resided and slept during the whole of the said years service in the house of my said Master situate in the said Parish of Saint Nicholas – In the month of April last year I was removed by orders of removal from the said Parish of Cheltenham unto the said Parish of Saint Nicholas and delivered to the Overseer there who received me – I was delivered of an illegitimate child named Fanny about six years ago [signed]

Charles Maisey: [confirms removal of Ann Bradley to St Nicholas, Gloucester under order of 28 Mar 1846, and that the removal was not appealed against]

1846: *removed to St Nicholas, Gloucester (hiring and service): see* **46020RO** *(AB: 28 Mar) (RETURNED).* **1847:** *removed to St Nicholas, Gloucester (hiring and service); at examination AB was accompanied by six-year-old illegitimate child; AB died at Gloucester Workhouse (buried at St Nicholas, Gloucester 28 Dec, aged 36).* [PS/CH/RA/2/8:39 (copies at PS/CH/RA/2/7:303-4). Notes: "Ann Bradley & Child" delivered to Gloucester Workhouse 5 Jan 1847; removal expenses to St Nicholas, Gloucester 15/- (4Q 1846/1Q 1847: D4178).]

47004RO: Sat 30 Jan 1847 – **Ann Dix**, single woman, inmate of Cheltenham Union Workhouse; also Charles Maisey, yeoman, magistrates' office, relating to the settlement of Ann Dix. *Ann Dix*: I am about twenty One Years of Age   I am the Daughter of Joseph and Elizabeth Dix – About two years ago I was removed by orders of removal from the said Parish of Cheltenham to the Hamlet of Highnam in the Parish of Churcham in the said County and delivered to the Overseer there who received me and sent me to the Union Workhouse at Gloucester where I remained for about six months at the expence of the said Hamlet of Highnam [mark]

Charles Maisey: [confirms that Ann Dix was removed to Highnam, Churcham under order of 3 Dec 1844, and that the removal was not appealed against]

1844: *removed to Highnam, Churcham (father's settlement): see* **44058SE** *(AD: 2 Dec 1844) (RETURNED).* **1847:** *removed to Highnam, Churcham (father's settlement).* [PS/CH/RA/2/8:40 (copies at PS/CH/RA/2/7:305-6). Notes: "Ann Dix" delivered to Gloucester Union 27 Feb 1847 by Charles Maisey; removal expenses to Highnam (and Hill to Bisley) 9/2 (4Q 1846/1Q 1847: D4178).]

47005RO: 30 Jan 1847 – **Maria Hill**, single woman, inmate of Cheltenham Union Workhouse, and daughter **Emily**; also Charles Maisey, yeoman, magistrates' office, relating to the settlement of Maria Hill. *Maria Hill*: About the Month of July 1845 I was removed by orders of Removal from the said Parish of Cheltenham to the Parish of Bisley in the said County and delivered to the Overseer there   such orders were not appealed against

I was delivered of an illegitimate Child named Emily about sixteen Months ago [mark]

Charles Maisey: [confirms removal of Maria Hill to Bisley under order of 3 July 1845, and that the removal was not appealed against]

1845: *removed to Bisley (birth): see* **45037SE** *(MH: 26 June); birth of illegitimate daughter Amelia Ann [= "Emily"] at Cheltenham Workhouse 2 Sept (RETURNED).* **1847:** *removed to Bisley (birth); death of baby Amelia Ann at Stroud Workhouse, aged 2 (buried at Bisley 5 Apr); (RETURNED) mother probably the MH who died at Cheltenham, aged 25 (buried at New Burial Ground 3 Aug).* [PS/CH/RA/2/8:41 (copies at PS/CH/RA/2/7:307-8). Notes: "Maria Hill & Child" delivered to the Stroud Union 27 Feb 1847   by Charles Maisey; removal expenses to Bisley (and Dix to Highnam) 9/2 (4Q 1846/1Q 1847: D4178).]

47006RO: 30 Jan 1847 – **Elizabeth Staite**, widow, and three children **John, Patience**, and **Mary Ann**; also Charles Maisey, yeoman, magistrates' office, relating to the settlement of Elizabeth Staite. *Elizabeth State*: I was married to my late husband Richard Staite in the Parish Church of Cheltenham about sixteen years ago by whom I have three Children namely John aged twelve years Patience aged seven Years and Mary Ann aged five Years. My said Husband died last November twelve months   about twelve months ago I and my said three Children were Removed by orders of Removal from the said Parish of Cheltenham unto the Hamlet of Gretton in the Parish of Winchcomb [= Winchcombe] in the said County and delivered to the Overseer there, such orders were not appealed against

I returned to Cheltenham in about a week afterwards where I have been residing ever since and have been relieved by the Parish Officer of Gretton from the time I so returned to Cheltenham until about nine weeks ago [signed]

Charles Maisey: [confirms removal of Elizabeth Staite and three children to Gretton, Winchcombe under order of 20 Dec 1845, and that the removal was not appealed against]

1847: *removed to Gretton, Winchcombe (husband's settlement): see* **47016RO** *(ES: 12 Mar 1847) for further information.* [PS/CH/RA/2/8:42 (copies at PS/CH/RA/2/7:309-10).]

47007RO: 30 Jan 1847 – **Joseph Scrivens**, labourer, and two children **Caroline** and **Henry**; also George Wilson, yeoman, relating to the settlement of Joseph Scrivens. *Joseph Scrivens*: About twenty five years ago being then unmarried and having no Child or Children I was hired into the into the Parish of Withington in the said County by Mr Commeline of that Parish for a Year at the wages of Nine Guineas   I served the whole year and resided and slept in my said Masters House at Withington aforesaid the whole time

I have two Children namely Caroline aged twelve Years and Henry aged ten years both born in lawful Wedlock

About Five years ago I and my said two Children with another Child were Removed by orders of Removal from the said Parish of Cheltenham unto the said Parish of Withington and delivered to the Overseer there who Received us   such orders were not appealed against   I have been several times relieved by the Parish Officers of Withington aforesaid since my said Removal and in the month of August last I was relieved by them for three weeks [mark]

George Wilson: [confirms removal of Joseph Scrivens and three children to Withington under order of 12 Jan 1841, and that the removal was not appealed against]

1831: *removed to Withington (presumed) (hiring and service): see* **31116SE** *(JS: 28 Oct).* **1832:** *(RETURNED) daughter Martha baptised at Cheltenham 22 Jan.* **1837:** *daughter Caroline and son Henry baptised at Cheltenham 14 May.* **1838:** *wife Ann buried at Cheltenham at New Burial Ground 24 Dec, aged 48.* **1841:** *removed to Withington (hiring and service): see* **41005SE** *(JS: 12 Jan); JS (aged 50; labourer) lived with children in Green's Place, Cheltenham (HO107/353/5/53/28).* **1847:** *removed to Withington (hiring and service).* **1851:** *JS (74; pauper, born Shipton Oliffe) lodged at 6 Park St, Charlton Kings with Edward Stevens (20; labourer), who married daughter Martha in Charlton Kings 26 Sept 1852 (HO107/1972/79/17); Caroline Scrivens (17) worked as house servant at 7 Gt Norwood St, Cheltenham (HO107/1973/907/2) and Henry Scrivens worked as agricultural labourer in Withington (HO107/1969/293/9).* [PS/CH/RA/2/8:43 (copies at PS/CH/RA/2/7:311-12). Note: "Joseph Scrivens & two Children" delivered to Withington 2 Mar 1847 by Charles Maisey.]

47008RO: Mon 1 Feb 1847 – **Charlotte Hancocks** (also **Hancock**, **Hancox**), single woman; also mother Ann Hancocks, residing in Longhope, relating to the settlement of Charlotte Hancocks. *Ann Hancocks*: About forty five Years ago I was married to my husband Thomas Hancocks in the parish Church of Lenton [= Linton] in the County of Hereford by whom I had my said Daughter Charlotte who was born in the said Parish of Longhope about twenty four Years ago   I and my said husband have been residing in the said Parish of Longhope for the last forty four years during which time we have received relief from the Officers of that Parish a great many times [mark]

Charlotte Hancocks: I am the Daughter of Thomas Hancocks and Ann his Wife and resided with them in the parish of Longhope in the said County until I was about thirteen years of age   I have done no Act to gain a settlement in my own right [signed]

1841: *CH (aged 15) lived with parents and seven brothers and sisters in Longhope (HO107/361/4/5/5).* **1847:** *removed to Longhope (settlement indicated by earlier provision of relief); examination presumably instigated by pregnancy, as illegitimate son Frederick baptised at Longhope 18 July.* **1851:** *Charlotte (aged 26; house servant, born Longhope) lived at lodging-house in Gt Malvern, Worcs (HO107/2043/148/45); son Frederick (3) lived with uncle Richard Beard's family in Longhope (HO107/1959/584/22).* [PS/CH/RA/2/8:44 (copies at PS/CH/RA/2/7:313-14). Notes: "Charlotte Hancocks" delivered to the Union 1

Mar 1847 by Charles Maisey; removal expenses to Longhope (and Gilding to Westbury on Severn)   18/6
(4Q 1846/1Q 1847: D4178).]

47009RO: Sat 6 Feb 1847 – **Sarah Gilding**, widow, and four children **Mary Ann**, **Elizabeth**, **Charles**, and **James**; also Charles Maisey, yeoman, magistrates' office, relating to the settlement of Sarah Gilding. *Sarah Gilding*: I was married to my late Husband Joseph Gilding at the Parish Church of Cheltenham in the year 1826 by whom I have four Children namely Mary Ann Aged 12 years Elizabeth aged 10 Years Charles aged six Years and James aged two years   My said husband died About 9 months ago – About six months ago I and my said Children were Removed by orders of Removal from the said Parish of Cheltenham unto the Parish of Westbury upon the Severn in the said County and delivered to the Overseer there who Received us   such orders were not appealed against

I and my said Children immediately afterwards returned to Cheltenham and have Resided there ever since and have been Relieved by the Parish Officer of Westbury upon Severn aforesaid from that time until the 23 of January last with three shillings a week [signed]
Charles Maisey: [confirms removal of Sarah Gilding and five children (including William, aged 16) to Westbury-upon-Severn under order of 30 May 1846, and that the removal was not appealed against]
1846: *death of Joseph Gilding at 7 White Hart St, Cheltenham in May (buried at New Burial Ground, Cheltenham 27 May); SG removed to Westbury-upon-Severn (husband's settlement): see* **46029RO** *(SG: 30 May) (RETURNED).* **1847:** *removed to Westbury-upon-Severn (husband's settlement); (RETURNED) SG and family returned to Cheltenham immediately after removal, while receiving relief from Westbury.* **1851:** *the family lived at 7 White Hart St, Cheltenham: SG (44; laundress), William (21; porter, born Westbury-upon-Severn), Elizabeth (15; dressmaker), Charles (11; errand boy), and James (7; scholar) (all but William born Cheltenham) (HO107/1973/442/2).* [PS/CH/RA/2/8:45 (copies at PS/CH/RA/2/7:315-16). Notes: "Sarah Gilding & Family" delivered to the Westbury-upon-Severn Union 1 Mar 1847 by Charles Maisey; removal expenses for Gilding to Westbury-upon-Severn (and Hancocks to Longhope) 18/6 (4Q 1846/1Q 1847: D4178).]

47010RO: Sat 6 Mar 1847 – **Elizabeth Davis**, widow, and two children **Alfred** and **Susannah**; also Charles Maisey, yeoman, magistrates' office, relating to the settlement of Elizabeth Davis. *Elizabeth Davies*: I am the Widow of Daniel Davis by whom I have two Children namely Alfred aged fifteen years and Susannah aged ten Years. I and my said two Children were last June twelvemonth removed by Orders of removal from the said Parish of Cheltenham to the Parish of Kings Stanley [= King's Stanley] in the said County and delivered to the Overseers there   such orders were not appealed against

I returned to Cheltenham soon afterwards and have been relieved by the Parish Officers of Kings Stanley aforesaid from that time until October last during all which time I continued to reside in Cheltenham aforesaid [mark]
Charles Maisey: [confirms removal of Elizabth Davis and two children to King's Stanley under order of 12 June 1845]
1837: *family removed to King's Stanley: see* **37023RO** *(Daniel Davis: 1 Apr 1837) (RETURNED); daughter Susanna baptised at Cheltenham 6 Aug.* **1841:** *Daniel Davis (aged 60; out-pensioner of Greenwich), wife Elizabeth (49), son Alfred (11), and daughter Susanna (4) lived in Bath Terrace, Cheltenham (HO107/353/12/13/21).* **1845:** *death of Daniel Davis at Cheltenham 8 May (buried at New Burial Ground 14 May, aged 65); ED and children removed to King's Stanley (45032SE: 31 May).* **1845-6:** *(RETURNED) from 3Q 1845 until 4Q 1846 ED and two children received parish relief from Stroud as non-settled residents of Cheltenham (G/CH/9d/1).* **1847:** *removed to King's Stanley (husband's presumed settlement).* **1851:** *ED (50; clothworker from Paganhill, Stroud, and widow) lived with daughter Susannah (15; clothworker) in Bread St, Stroud (HO107/1965/270/23).* [PS/CH/RA/2/8:46 (copies at PS/CH/RA/2/7:317-8). Note: "Ellen [*sic*] Davis and Two Children" to King's Stanley 19 Mar 1847 by Charles Maisey.]

47011RO: Mon 15 Feb 1847 – **Mary Hill**, single woman; also Charles Maisey, yeoman, magistrates' office, relating to the settlement of Mary Hill. *Mary Hill*: About ten months ago I

was removed by orders of removal from the said Parish of Cheltenham unto the Parish of Bisley in the said County and delivered to the Overseer there by Charles Maisey. [mark]
Charles Maisey: [confirms removal of Mary Hill to Bisley under order of 19 Mar 1846, and that the removal was not appealed against]
1846: *removed to Bisley (birth): see* **46019RO** *(MH: 19 Mar) (RETURNED).* **1847:** *removed to Bisley (birth).* **1854:** *(perhaps RETURNED) perhaps the MH who died at Sherborne St, Cheltenham, aged 72 (Gloucestershire Chron. 30 Dec).* [PS/CH/RA/2/8:47 (copies at PS/CH/RA/2/7:319-20. Note: "Mary Hill" delivered to Bisley 15 Mar 1847 by Charles Maisey. See perhaps **36025RO** (MH: 8 Aug 1836).]

47012RO: Sat 20/26 Feb 1847 (examinations on 20 Feb) – **John Blackmore**, wife **Mary**, and daughter **Sarah**; also Charles Maisey, yeoman, magistrates' office, relating to the settlement of John Blackmore. *John Blackmore*: I am about Sixty three years of Age   when I was about Seventeen years of Age being then unmarried and having no Child or Children I was hired by Mr Hart of Sinkley [*i.e.* St Looe's] School in the Parish of Minchinhampton in the said County for a Year as general Servant at the wages of three pounds a Year   I served the whole year under such hiring and resided and slept in my Masters house at Minchinhampton aforesaid the whole time and received my years wages   I have since been relieved by the Parish officers of Minchinhampton aforesaid for three or four years at a time whilst I was residing in Stroud   I was married to my Wife Mary about forty years ago in the parish Church of Hasfield by whom I have one Child named Sarah aged fifteen years   near four Years ago I was removed by orders of removal from the said Parish of Cheltenham to the said Parish of Minchinhampton with my Wife and family and delivered to the Overseer there
   Such orders were not appealed against [mark]
Charles Maisey: [confirms removal of John Blackmore, wife, and three children (also Mary Ann 15 and James 14) to Minchinhampton under order of 24 Apr 1843, and that the removal was not appealed against]
1841: *JB (aged 55; carpenter) lived with wife Mary (50) and children Mary (15), James (13), and Sarah (11) in Stanhope St, Cheltenham (HO107/353/9/53/6-7).* **1843:** *removed to Minchinhampton (hiring and service): see* **43036RO** *(JB: 24 Apr) (RETURNED).* **1847:** *removed to Minchinhampton (hiring and service).* **1851:** *(RETURNED) the family lived in Cheltenham, at Rowanfield, Alstone: JB (78; carpenter, born Horsley), and Mary (61; born Corse).* [PS/CH/RA/2/8:48 (copies at PS/CH/RA/2/7:321-2). Note: "John Blackmore Wife & Daughter" delivered to Minchinhampton 19 Mar 1847 by Charles Maisey.]

47013RO: [blank] Feb 1847 – **William Cook** (also **Cooke**), wife **Mary**, [and two children **Susan** and **John**]; also Charles Maisey, yeoman, magistrates' office, relating to the settlement of William Cook. *William Cooke*: About twelve months ago I and my Wife Mary and my two Children namely Susan then aged fifteen Years and John aged thirteen years were Removed by orders of Removal from the said Parish of Cheltenham unto the Parish of Painswick in the said County and delivered to the overseer there   such orders were not appealed against [incomplete]
Charles Maisey: [confirms removal of William Cook, wife, and two children to Painswick under order of 15 Jan 1846, and that the removal was not appealed against]
1847: *removed to Painswick (Stroud Union) (apprenticeship): see* **48031RO** *for further information on WC and family.* [PS/CH/RA/2/8:49 (examinations transcribed from PS/CH/RA/2/7:323-4).]

47014RO: Sat 20 Mar 1847 – James Hopkins, boots, relating to the settlement of brother **Henry Hopkins**: I am 24 Years of Age and the Son of Thomas Hopkins and Rebecca his Wife who did as long as I can remember reside in the parish of Saint Clement in the City of Worcester   my said Father Resided in a House of his own in that Parish   I remember my said brother who is now about thirteen Years of Age being born in the said Parish of Saint Clement and Resided there with his Parents for more than 12 Years   My said Father and Mother are both dead. [signed]
1846: *death of father Thomas at St Clement's, Worcester July.* **1847:** *removed to St Clement's, Worcester, Worcs (presumed) (parents' settlement).* **1871:** *HH (aged 38; ostler, born Worcester) probably lived at 3 Cheapside, Birmingham with wife Mary Ann (33) (RG10/3107/4/4).* [PS/CH/RA/2/8:50 (copy at

PS/CH/RA/2/7:326). Note: "Henry Hopkins" delivered to St Clement's, Worcester 17 Apr 1847 by Charles Maisey.]

47015RO: 20 Mar 1847 – **William Pimble** (also **Pymble**), labourer, and wife **Ann**; also Charles Maisey, yeoman, magistrates' office, relating to the settlement of William Pimble. *William Pimble*: In the month of August one thousand Eight hundred and forty five I was Removed by orders of Removal from the said parish of Cheltenham unto the Parish of Dymock in the said County and delivered to the Overseer there – about twenty seven years ago I was married to my present Wife Ann in the Parish Church of Cheltenham [mark]
Charles Maisey: [confirms removal of William Pimble, wife, and child (Robert, aged 13) to Dymock under order of 17 July 1845, and that the removal was not appealed against]
1841: *WP (aged 60; labourer) lived with wife Ann (40) and children William (13) and Robert (9) in Elm St, Cheltenham (HO107/353/9/62/24-5).* **1842:** *death of son Willliam Pimble at Cheltenham, aged 16 (buried at New Burial Ground 7 Jan).* **1845:** *removed to Dymock (settlement as indicated by earlier removals): see* **45041SE** *(WP: 10 July).* **1846:** *(RETURNED) from 3Q 1846 until 4Q WP and wife Ann received parish relief from Newent as non-settled residents of Cheltenham (G/CH/9d/1).* **1847:** *removed to Dymock (Newent Union) (settlement as indicated by earlier removals).* **1850:** *(RETURNED) death of WP (buried at New Burial Ground, Cheltenham 24 July, aged 73); marriage of son Robert to Caroline Hayward at Leckhampton 3 Sept, when both he and father WP described as gardeners.* **1851:** *Ann Pimble (52; fruiterer and widow, born Monmouth) lived in Hermitage Place, Cheltenham (HO107/1973/862/28); son Robert (19; gardener) lodged with wife Caroline at 17 Sandford St, Cheltenham (HO107/1973/801/38).* [PS/CH/RA/2/8:51 (copies at PS/CH/RA/2/7:327-8). Notes: "W^m. Pimble & Wife" delivered to the Newent Union 20 Apr 1847 by Charles Maisey; removal expenses to Dymock 15/2 (2Q 1847: D4178). See also 1827 removal order to Dymock (P125 OV 3/3/6).]

47016RO: Fri 12 Mar 1847 – **Elizabeth Staite**, widow, and three children **John**, **Patience**, and **Mary Ann**; also Charles Maisey, yeoman, magistrates' office, relating to the settlement of Elizabeth Staite.
Elizabeth Staite: I was married to my late Husband Richard Staite in the Parish Church of Cheltenham About sixteen years ago by whom I have three Children Namely John Aged twelve years Patience aged seven Years and Mary Ann aged four Years   My said husband died last November twelvemonth   I was Removed by orders of Removal from the said Parish of Cheltenham unto the Parish of Winchcomb [= Winchcombe], in the said County About Fourteen months ago and delivered to the Overseer there   such orders were not appealed against
   I returned to Cheltenham in about a week afterwards and was Relieved by the Overseers of Winchcomb aforesaid from that time until October last during the whole of which time I continued to reside in Cheltenham [signed]
Charles Maisey: [confirms removal of Elizabeth Staite and three children to Winchcombe under order of 20 Dec 1845, and that the removal was not appealed against]
1845: *removed to Gretton (husband's settlement): see* **45068SE** *(ES: 18/25 Dec) (RETURNED).* **1847:** *removed to Winchcombe (husband's settlement): see also* **47006RO** *(ES: 30 Jan).* **1851:** *John Staite (aged 16; born Cheltenham) stayed with maternal grandfather Charles James (63; both travellers and waggoners, born Guiting) at the King's Head Inn, Evesham, Worcs on census night (HO107/2044/129/26).* **1856:** *(RETURNED) marriage of daughter Patience to Henry Carr in Cheltenham 14 Apr.* **1861:** *ES (45) lived with mother Hannah James (75; both laundresses and widows, born Cheltenham) at the Back of 21 York St, Cheltenham (RG9/1798/43/31).* [PS/CH/RA/2/8:52 (copies at PS/CH/RA/2/7:329-30). Note: "Elizabeth Staite & 2 Children" delivered to Winchcombe Union 7 July 1847 by Charles Maisey.]

47017RO: 12 Mar 1847 – **Sarah Sears**, widow, and six children **Elizabeth**, **Charlotte**, **Thomas**, **William**, **Sarah**, and **John**; also Charles Maisey, yeoman, magistrates' office, relating to the settlement of Sarah Sears. *Sarah Sears*: I was married to my late Husband John Sears in the Parish Church of Cheltenham about fourteen Years ago by whom I have six Children namely Elizabeth aged 13 years Charlotte aged 11 years Thomas aged nine Years William aged Eight years Sarah aged Seven years and John aged about four years and nine months   My said husband died in November 1842 – I and my said Children were removed by orders of removal from the said Parish of Cheltenham unto the parish of Saint Lawrence Evesham in the County of Worcester about the month of May 1844 and delivered to the Overseer there   such orders were not appealed against – I returned to Cheltenham the following day and have Remained there ever since   I have been relieved by the Parish Officers of Saint Lawrence aforesaid from that time until about four months ago [signed]

Charles Maisey: [confirms removal of Sarah Sears and six children to St Lawrence, Evesham, Worcs under order of 4 May 1844, and that the removal was not appealed against]

1841: *SS (aged 35) lived in Evesham with husband John (44; shopkeeper), and children Charlotte (4), Thomas (3), William (1), and Sarah (6 mo) (HO107/1207/7/33/8).* **1842:** *death of John Sears in Cheltenham Nov.* **1844:** *removed to St Lawrence, Evesham, Worcs (husband's settlement): see* **44032SE** *(SS: 4 May 1844).* **1845-6:** *(RETURNED) from 2Q 1845 until 4Q 1846 SS and four children received parish relief from Evesham as non-settled residents of Cheltenham (G/CH/9d/1).* **1847:** ***removed to St Lawrence, Evesham, Worcs (husband's settlement).*** **1851:** *SS (44; charwoman and widow, born Brewood, Staffs) lived in Evesham, Worcs with children Elizabeth (16; servant), Charlotte (14; servant), Thomas (13; scholar), William (11; scholar), Sarah (10; scholar: all born Evesham), and John (birth registered 4Q 1842 at Cheltenham) (HO107/2044/108/25).* [PS/CH/RA/2/8:53 (copies at PS/CH/RA/2/7:331-2). Note: "Sarah Sears & 6 Children" delivered to Evesham 10 Apr 1847.]

47018RO: Sat 15 May 1847 – **Richard Sisom** (also **Sisam, Sissum, Sisum**), wife **Mary Ann**, and two children **Alfred** and **Ann**; also Charles Maisey, yeoman, magistrates' office, relating to the settlement of Richard Sisom. *Richard Sisom*: In the month of July One thousand eight hundred and forty three I and my wife Mary Ann and my Child Alfred were removed by orders of removal from the parish of Cheltenham in the said County to the parish of Sevenhampton in the said County as the place of my last legal settlement and delivered to the Overseers there who received us – I have another Child by my said Wife named Ann now aged about one year and a half. [mark]

Charles Maisey: [confirms removal of Richard Sisom, wife and son to Sevenhampton under order of 10 June 1843, and that the removal was not appealed against]

1841: *RS (aged 30; agricultural labourer) lived with wife (Mary) Ann (30) and son Alfred (1) at 20 Park St, Cheltenham (HO107/353/16/50/16).* **1843:** *removed to Sevenhampton (father's settlement): see* **43044RO** *(RS: 10 June) (RETURNED).* **1844:** *baptism of son James 19 Aug in Cheltenham; death of James in Cheltenham 3Q.* **c1846:** *daughter Ann born at Cheltenham.* **1847:** ***removed to Sevenhampton (father's settlement).*** **1851:** *(RETURNED) the family lived at 44 Stanhope St, Cheltenham: RS (42; agricultural labourer, born Gatton, Surrey), Maryann (29), Alfred (11; scholar), and Ann (5) (HO107/1973/501/22).* [PS/CH/RA/2/8:54 (copies at PS/CH/RA/2/7:333-4). Note: "R^d. Sisom Wife & two Children" delivered to Sevenhampton 10 May 1847 by Charles Maisey.]

47019RO: Sat 15 May 1847 – **Priscilla Sollis** (also **Sallis, Sollice**), single woman; also Charles Maisey, yeoman, magistrates' office, relating to the settlement of Priscilla Sollis. *Priscilla Sollis*: About two months ago last February I was removed by orders of removal from the Parish of Cheltenham aforesaid unto the parish of Hawling in the said County and delivered to the Overseer there – such order was not appealed against – I was in the Union Workhouse at Winchcomb [= Winchcombe] for eight weeks after the said removal at the Expence of the said Parish of Hawling – I have done no act to gain a settlement there [mark]

Charles Maisey: [confirms removal of Priscilla Sollis and mother Jane to Hawling under order of 25 Jan 1845, and that the removal was not appealed against]

1841: *PS (aged 12) lived with mother Jane Sollis (50) and sister Judith (28; sempstress) in Queen's Place, Cheltenham (HO107/353/10/26/19).* **1845:** *removed to Hawling with mother (father's settlement): see* **45005SE** *(Jane Sollis: 25 Jan) (RETURNED).* **1847:** ***removed to Hawling (Winchcombe Union) (father's settlement).*** **1851:** *(RETURNED) the family lived at 4 Bloomsbury Place, Lower High St, Cheltenham: Jane Sollis (65; nurse and widow, born Dowdeswell), daughters Julia (39; sempstress, born at Hawling before Jane's marriage) and Priscilla (21; born Hawling), along with two of PS's nieces, Anne Turner (7) and Harriet Hardman (13; both born Cheltenham) (HO107/1973/611/48).* [PS/CH/RA/2/8:55 (copies at

PS/CH/RA/2/7:335-6). Notes: "Priscilla Sollis" delivered to Winchcombe Union 10 May 1847 by Charles Maisey; removal expenses "Solles [*sic*]" to Hawling 5/- (2Q 1847: D4178).]

47020RO: Mon 24 May 1847 – **Ann Williams**, wife of Samuel Shipton Williams, and five children **Sarah**, **Henry**, **Jesse**, **Samuel**, **Maria**; also mother-in-law, Sarah Williams, relating to settlement of Ann Williams. *Sarah Williams*: My said Son is an illegitimate child of mine and was born in the parish of Newington Bagpath in the County of Gloucester about forty one years ago – he lived with me until he was married about Eighteen years ago – he never done any act to gain a settlement in his own right – I do not know where my said Son now is [mark]

Ann Williams: I was married to my husband Samuel Shipton Williams about Eighteen years ago in the parish Church of Horsley in the said County by whom I have five Children namely Sarah aged twelve years Henry aged ten years Jesse aged six years Samuel aged three years and Maria aged one year nine months – My said husband has never done any act to gain a settlement since our Marriage – He left me about seven months ago and I have heard nothing of him since nor do I know where he now is – [mark]

1847: *removed to Newington Bagpath (husband's settlement).* **1848:** *daughter Louisa baptised by reunited family in Horsley 11 Mar, with elder daughter Maria; an AW was an inmate of Cheltenham Workhouse Sept (and again, with infant child Feb 1849) (G/CH/60/6).* **1851:** *the family lived in Hay Lane, Horsley (all members born Horsley): Samuel (aged 44; agricultural labourer), Ann (39), George (18; agricultural labourer), Sarah (16; spinner working in cloth factory), Henry (14), Jesse (12; both agricultural labourers), Samuel (8), Maria (5; both scholars), Louisa (2), and Ellen (5 mo) (HO107/1966/274/5-275/6).* [PS/CH/RA/2/8:56 (copies at PS/CH/RA/2/7:337-8). Notes: "Ann Williams & 5 Children" delivered to Tetbury Union 8 June 1847 by Charles Maisey; removal expenses to Newington Bagpath £1/6/6 (2Q 1847: D4178).]

47021RO: Sat 5 June 1847 – **Hannah Stratford**, widow: I was married to my late husband John Stratford about fifty six years ago in the parish Church of Treddington [= Tredington; "Chipping Norton" struck out] in the County of Warwick ["Oxford" struck out] – My said husband died about seventeen years ago and was buried at Miserdine [= Miserden] – in the County of Gloucester as I have heard and believes [*sic*] and never done any act to my knowledge to gain a settlement – I have been receiving relief from the Overseers of Miserdine aforesaid for the last seven years until about three Months ago during the whole of which time I have been residing in Cheltenham [mark]

1847: *removed to Miserden (late husband's birth and apparent settlement).* **1851:** *(RETURNED) Hannah Stratford died at Cheltenham (buried 23 Feb, aged 85, at Miserden).* [PS/CH/RA/2/8:57 (copy at PS/CH/RA/2/7:339). Removal expenses for "Stratford" to Miserden 6/3 (3Q 1847: D4178).]

47022RO: 5 June 1847 – Hannah Williams, widow, relating to settlement of grandson **William Stratford**: I was married to my late husband John Stratford about fifty six years ago in the parish Church of Treddington [= Tredington; "Chipping Norton" struck out] in the County of Warwick ["Oxford" struck out] – My said husband died about seventeen years ago and was buried at Miserdine –

My said husband was born in the parish of Miserdine [= Miserden] in the County of Gloucester as I have heard and believes [*sic*] and never done any act to my knowledge to gain a settlement

I have been receiving relief from the Overseers of Miserdine aforesaid for the last seven years until about three months ago during the whole of which time I have been residing in Cheltenham – I was delivered of a Son named John about forty years ago who was married to his Wife Ann at Winchcomb [= Winchcombe] about twenty one years ago – they are both dead – My said Son John had his said Son William by his said Wife about Eleven years ago – My said Son John never done any act to gain a settlement in his own right – Two children of my said Son John are now in the Stroud Union Workhouse and chargeable to the said Parish of Miserdine – [mark]

1836: *WS removed as an unnamed infant of five weeks with his parents John and Ann, and four other children Thomas (8), John (6), Hannah (4), and Emma (2) from Leckhampton to Miserden 22 July (P198a OV/3/2/19): see* **36024RO** *(John Stratford).* **1847:** *removed to Miserden (late father's apparent settlement): see* **49065RO** *(William Niblett for WS) for further information.* [PS/CH/RA/2/8:58 (copy at PS/CH/RA/2/7:340).]

47023RO: Sat 12 June 1847 – **John Stone**, labourer, wife **Eleanor**, and six children **William**, **Henry**, **Edward**, **John**, **Jane**, and **Elizabeth**; also John Sheldon, magistrates' office, relating to the settlement of John Stone. *John Stone*: That I was married to my said wife Eleanor about fourteen years ago at the Parish of Churchdown in the said County by whom I have my six children now living with me namely William aged thirteen years Henry aged ten years Edward aged eight years John aged seven years Jane aged four years and Elizabeth aged three years – I and my said wife and said children are now actually chargeable to the said Parish of Cheltenham. – At the latter end of the year 1844 I and my said wife and said children were duly removed by orders of removal now produced from the said parish of Cheltenham to the Parish of Barnwood in the said County as the place of my last legal settlement – I acquired my Settlement by apprenticeship there to Joseph Lane of that Parish Cordwainer – We were taken to the Overseer of the said Parish of Barnwood by John Sheldon now present – there was no appeal against the same orders of removal – I and my said wife and Children came back to Cheltenham soon after John Sheldon left us at Barnwood as aforesaid and have been constantly relieved with money by the Parish officers of Barnwood from that time until the present time and whilst we resided in the said Parish of Cheltenham

I have done no act to gain a settlement since my said removal to Barnwood – [signed]

John Sheldon: [confirms removal of John Stone, wife, and six children to Barnwood under order of 2 Nov 1844, and that the removal was not appealed against]

1841: *JS (aged 25; clock-maker) lived in Coach Rd, Cheltenham, with wife Eleanor (Helena Rosina) (30), and four children (in 1830s JS had been shoemaker) (HO107/353/10/21/8).* **1844** *JS removed to Barnwood (apprenticeship): see* **44055SE** *(JS: 2 Nov).* **1845-7:** *(RETURNED) from 3Q 1845 until 2Q 1847 JS, wife Eleanor, and six children received parish relief from Gloucester as non-settled residents of Cheltenham (G/CH/9d/1).* **1847:** *removed to Barnwood (Gloucester Union) (apprenticeship).* **1851:** *(RETURNED) the family lived at 1 White Hart St, Cheltenham: JS (38; watchmaker, born Tuffley), Eleanor (41; born Wotton, baptised Gloucester), William (17; no occupation), Henry (13; scholar), Edward (11; scholar), Jane (8), Elizabeth (7), Alfred (3), and Mary (6 mo; all children born Cheltenham) (HO107/1973/441/1).* [PS/CH/RA/2/8:59 (copies at PS/CH/RA/2/7:341-2). Notes: "John Stone & Family" delivered to Gloucester Union 10 July 1847 by Charles Maisey; removal expenses to Barnwood [amount omitted] (3Q 1847: D4178).]

47024RO: 12 June 1847 – **Hannah Collins**, widow; also Charles Maisey, magistrates' office, relating to the settlement of Hannah Collins. *Hannah Collins*: I am the Widow of William Collins who died in Cheltenham in September 1845 – I was married to my said husband about thirty two years ago last April at the Parish Church of All Saints in the City of Hereford – I have done no act to gain a Settlement since my said husband's death – I am now actually chargeable to the said Parish of Cheltenham – My husband's parish was at Linton in the County of Hereford – I was removed to the said Parish of Linton by Charles Maisey by virtue of the order of removal he now produces in October 1845 – The order was suspended and my husband died – and after his death I was removed and delivered to the Overseer of the said parish of Linton – The order was not appealed against [mark]

Charles Maisey: [confirms removal of William Collins and wife to Linton, Heref under order of 16 Aug 1845]

1845: *husband William Collins, carpenter, died soon after his examination Aug, at 19 Fairview St, Cheltenham (Cheltenham Chron. 2 Oct) (buried at New Burial Ground, Cheltenham 26 Sept, aged 53): see* **45049SE** *(William Collins: 11 Aug); HC was removed to Linton, Heref (RETURNED).* **1847:** *removed to Linton, Heref (husband's settlement).* [PS/CH/RA/2/8:60 (copies at PS/CH/RA/2/7:343-4); the blank entry was previously filled out ready for HC's examination, on page 325. Note: "Hannah Collins" delivered to the Newent Union, Parish of Linton Heref 12 July 1847 by Charles Maisey.]

47025RO: 12 June 1847 – **Edwin Belcher**, labourer, wife **Ann**, and children **Mary Ann**, **Agnes**, **Adelaide**, **Jesse**, **Eleanor**, and an unnamed female child [**Hannah Elizabeth**]; also Jesse Castle, magistrates' office, relating to the settlement of Edwin Belcher. *Edwin Belcher*: About twenty one years ago being then unmarried and without child or children I was hired into the parish of Churchdown in the said County to M^r. Beckett of that Parish to serve him for a year – I entered into his Service and served him the whole year under the said hiring and resided and slept during the whole of such my Service in the said Parish of Churchtown – I have done no act to gain a Settlement since – About fifteen years ago I was married to my said Wife Ann at the parish of S^t. Mary de lode in the City of Gloucester by whom I have six children namely Mary Ann aged fourteen years Agnes aged twelve Years Adelaide aged ten years Jesse aged seven years Eleanor aged three years and a female child born on the seventh Instant and not named – I and my said Wife and children are now actually chargeable to the said Parish of Cheltenham – About the beginning of the year 1841 I and my said Wife and my said four children Mary Ann, Agnes, Adelaide and Jesse were removed by the order of removal now produced by Jesse Castle from the said parish of Cheltenham to the said parish of Churchdown – The order was not appealed against – We returned to Cheltenham soon after and have lived here ever since and from the time of our return up to within a month of the present time we have constantly been relieved with money from the said Parish of Churchdown whilst residing in the said Parish of Cheltenham [mark]

Jesse Castle: [confirms removal of Edwin Belcher and wife to Churchdown under order of 3 Dec 1840]

1840: *death of son Jesse (buried at New Burial Ground, Cheltenham, 15 Sept, aged 2); EB removed to Churchdown (hiring and service): see* **40108SE** *(EB: 3 Dec).* **1841:** *(RETURNED) EB (aged 30; agricultural labourer) lived with wife Ann (30), and children Mary (8), Agnes (7), Adelaide (5) and Jesse (8 mo) in Lower Alstone, Cheltenham (HO107/353/10/48/2).* **1845-7:** *from 3Q 1845 until 2Q 1847 EB, wife Ann, and four children received parish relief from Gloucester as non-settled residents of Cheltenham (G/CH/9d/1).* **1847:** *removed to Churchdown (Gloucester Union) (hiring and service); (RETURNED) unnamed daughter was Hannah Elizabeth, baptised at Cheltenham 8 Aug, when family lived in Alstone.* **1850:** *EB apparently buried at Cheltenham 1 May, aged 40.* **1851:** *widow Ann (42; charwoman receiving relief, born Bishop's Cleeve) lived with children Jesse (18), Eleanor (6), and Elizabeth (3; all three scholars and born Alstone, Cheltenham) (HO107/1973/572/4) in Alstone Rd, Alstone, Cheltenham; sisters Adelaide (14) and Agnes (16) lived and worked in Cheltenham (7 Lansdown Rd; HO107/1973/1008/26) and Leckhampton (HO107/1972/202/7) respectively.* [PS/CH/RA/2/8:61 (copies at PS/CH/RA/2/7:345-6). Notes: "Edwin Belcher & Family" delivered to Gloucester Union 10 July 10 1847 by Charles Maisey; removal expenses to Churchdown 10/6 (3Q 1847: D4178).]

47026RO: 12 June 1847 – **Elizabeth Bullock**, single woman; also Charles Maisey, magistrates' office, relating to the settlement of Elizabeth Bullock. *Elizabeth Bullock*: About six years ago I went over to Gloucester to the Overseers of the parish of S^t. Catharine in the City of Gloucester the place of my Settlement and applied to them for relief – They allowed me a shilling a week from that time for the four succeeding weeks and during the time I was living in the said parish of Cheltenham – About March 1846 I was removed by virtue of the orders of removal now produced from the said Parish of Cheltenham to the said Parish of S^t. Catharine - such order was not appealed against – I have received relief from the Parish officers of S^t. Catharine from the time up to about four months ago and have uninterruptedly during that time resided in the said parish of Cheltenham – [mark]

Charles Maisey: [confirms removal of Elizabeth Bullock to St Catharine, Gloucester under order of 12 Feb 1846]

1841: *perhaps the EB (aged 59; plain sewer) who lived in Burton St, Cheltenham (HO107/353/16/25/11).* **1846:** *EB removed to St Catharine's, Gloucester (father's settlement): see* **46007RO** *(EB: 14/19 Feb).* **1846-7:** *(RETURNED) from 2Q 1846 until 2Q 1847 EB (63) received parish relief from Gloucester as a non-settled resident of Cheltenham (G/CH/9d/1).* **1847:** *removed to St Catharine, Gloucester (father's settlement).* **1851:** *(probably RETURNED) an EB (aged 71, born Gloucester, though listed as annuitant) lodged in boarding-house at 3 Warwick Buildings, Winchcombe St, Cheltenham (HO107/1973/199/32), at which address she died several months later (buried at New Burial Ground, Cheltenham 30 Oct).* [PS/CH/RA/2/8:62 (copies at PS/CH/RA/2/7:347-8). Removal expenses for "Bullock" to Gloucester 2/4 (4Q 1847: D4178).]

47027RO: Sat 26 June 1847 – **George Smith**, cordwainer, wife **Emma**, and three children **Sidney**, **Emma**, and **Henry**; also James Evans, tailor, currently residing in Northleach, relating to the settlement of George Smith. *George Smith*: When I was about fourteen years old at Northleach in the County of Gloucester on the fourth day of November One thousand eight hundred and thirty one I was bound apprentice to Richard Andrews of Stow on the Wold in the County of Gloucester for the term of Seven years by Deed dated the fourth day of November One thousand eight hundred and thirty one which deed is executed by me and which I produce – At the time I was so bound my Father and Mother were both dead. the premium paid to my Master was paid out of a Public Charity fund – I served for the whole of the said term with my said Master residing all the time in my Masters house in the parish of Stow on the Wold aforesaid – After I was out of my time viz: on the twentieth day of October One thousand eight hundred and forty I was married to my Wife Emma at the parish Church of Cheltenham in the County of Gloucester by Banns – I have three children now living with me by my said wife viz: Sidney aged six Years Emma aged five years and Henry aged two years – I have been residing at Cheltenham aforesaid with my said wife and children for the last Eighteen months only, previously to that time I resided at Stow on the Wold aforesaid [signed]

James Evans: [produces and confirms details of indenture binding George Smith, son of Ralph Smith, to Richard Andrews, cordwainer, of 2 Nov 1831, and that the premium was paid by the Townsend charity fund]

1841: *GS (aged 20; shoemaker) lived with wife Emma (30) and son George (8 mo) in Sheep St, Stow-on-the-Wold (HO107/366/21/16/26).* **1847: removed to Stow-on-the-Wold (apprenticeship). 1848:** *daughter Ellen baptised at Stow-on-the-Wold 2 Jan, when the family resided at Stow Workhouse.* **1851:** *the family lived in Sheep St, Stow, but George Smith and son Henry had both died: Emma (45), Sidney (10), Emma (9), and Ellen (3; all three children "at home"; all surviving family born Stow) (HO107/1970/244/31).* [PS/CH/RA/2/8:63 (copies at PS/CH/RA/2/7:349-50). Note: "Geo Smith & Family" delivered to Stow-on-the-Wold 10 Aug 1847 by Charles Maisey. See **47030RO** (wife Emma Smith for children William and Eliza, by first marriage: 1 July 1847).]

47028RO: [blank] July 1847 (examination on 1 July 1847) - **Jane Townsend**, widow, and two children **George** and **Sarah**; also Charles Maisey, yeoman, magistrates' office, relating to the settlement of Jane Townsend. *Jane Townsend*: I am the Widow of George Townsend deceased. I was married to my said late husband at the Parish Church of S^t. Mary de Lode in the City of Gloucester about twenty seven years ago. I have two children by my said husband now living with me namely George aged about seventeen years and Sarah aged about twelve years. About six years ago I and my said late husband and said two children were residing at the said Parish of Cheltenham and in consequence of illness we were relieved by the Overseers of that Parish and were removed by the orders of removal now produced from Cheltenham aforesaid to the Parish of S^t. Mary de lode aforesaid and which is within the Gloucester Poor Law Union. We remained in that Parish for about a month and then returned to Cheltenham where my said husband died in April 1845 – He did no act after his said removal to gain a Settlement. About ten months after his death I applied to the overseers of the said Parish of St Mary de lode for relief and received from them two shillings and sixpence weekly from that time up to about three weeks since & during all the time I received such relief I resided uninterruptedly in the said Parish of Cheltenham. I and my said two children are now actually chargeable to the said Parish of Cheltenham.

Charles Maisey, on [blank] July 1847: [confirms removal of George Townsend, wife and two children Joseph (14) and Sarah (7) to St Mary de Lode, Gloucester under order of 3 May 1841, and that it was not appealed against]

1834: *JT removed to St Mary de Lode; apparently pregnant at time of examination: see* **34048SE** *(JT: 2 Sept 1834); daughter Sarah baptised at St Mary's, Cheltenham 12 Nov.* **1841:** *(RETURNED) the family appears to be dispersed (though probably lived in Cheltenham, with Jacob at St George's Place).* **1843:** *George Townsend ("trunkmaker") died at Sandford St, Cheltenham 20 Apr, aged 31 (Cheltenham Chron. 27 Apr).* **1845-7:** *from 2Q 1845 until 2Q 1847 Jane and two children received parish relief from Gloucester as non-settled residents in Cheltenham (G/CH/9d/1).* **1847: removed to St Mary de Lode, Gloucester (husband's settlement);** *they returned to Cheltenham soon after removal to Gloucester (RETURNED); Sarah's father George variously described as "Trunk Maker" and "carpenter".* **1851:** *JT (aged 48; plain sewer, born Hereford) lived with daughter Sarah in Victoria St, Fairview, Cheltenham (HO107/1973/119/62).*

[PS/CH/RA/2/8:64 (removal order lacks examinations, transcribed from PS/CH/RA/2/7:351-2. See **41033SE** (husband George Townsend: 3 May 1841).]

47029RO: Mon 5 July 1847 – **Mary Ann Daniels**, widow: I am the Widow of James Daniels deceased. I was married to my said late husband at the Parish Church of Bisley in the said County about fifteen years ago last Christmas –

My said husband died in Cheltenham aforesaid five years ago last January – he lived at Stroud when I married him – In Cheltenham I applied to the Overseers of the Parish of Stroud in the said County for parochial relief and received from them one shilling a week from that time until nine months ago – I resided uninterruptedly at the said parish of Cheltenham the whole time I received such parochial relief as aforesaid – My said husband never to my knowledge did an act to gain a settlement – I have never done an act to gain a settlement in my own right – I am now actually chargeable to the said Parish of Cheltenham – [mark]

1845-6: *from 4Q 1845 until 4Q 1846 MAD (66) received parish relief from Stroud as non-settled resident of Cheltenham (G/CH/9d/1).* **1847: *removed to Stroud (presumed) (husband's settlement).*** **1850:** *(RETURNED) MAD née Cambridge (twice-widowed, living in Fairview St, Cheltenham) married John Ivin in Cheltenham 21 Oct.* **1858:** *probably the Mrs. Mary Ivin who died 14 Oct at Union Workhouse, Cheltenham, aged 82 (*Cheltenham Chron. *19 Oct).* [PS/CH/RA/2/8:65 (copy at PS/CH/RA/2/7:353). Note: "Mary Ann Daniels" delivered to Stroud 13 Aug 1847 by Charles Maisey.]

47030RO: 5 July 1847 – Emma Smith, relating to the settlement of children **William** and **Eliza Meadows**: I am the wife of George Smith at present residing in the said parish of Cheltenham – Before I was married to the said George Smith I was the Widow of John Meadows then deceased – I was married to the said John Meadows at the parish Church of Stow on the Wold in the said County about twenty four years ago – I lived with my said husband John Meadows at Stow on the Wold aforesaid from the time of our Marriage until his Death about Eleven Years ago last May –

I had five Children by the said John Meadows two of whom are now living with me and are dependant [*sic*] upon me for support namely William aged about sixteen Years and Eliza aged about thirteen Years – About twenty years ago my said late husband John Meadows hired for a year four acres of land situate in Mauge[r]sbury in the said parish of Stow on the Wold of his brother William Meadows at the rent of Twelve pounds a Year – My said husband occupied the said land under the said Yearly hiring from the time of his hiring it as aforesaid for one year and upwards and paid the whole rent for the same and during the said one year of his said occupancy and paying rent he resided in the said parish of Stow on the Wold. [signed]

1841: *WM (aged 10) and Eliza (7) lived with stepfather George Smith's family in Sheep St, Stow-on-the-Wold (HO107/366/21/16/26).* **1847: *removed to Stow-on-the-Wold (father's settlement).*** **1851:** *EM (18; born Stow-on–the-Wold) was house servant living in Bourton-on-the-Hill (HO107/207/273/5).* **1852:** *death of EM (buried, aged 20, at Stow 15 June.* **1856:** *WM (boot-maker, living in Park St, St Pancras; father John Meadows "dead") married Elizabeth Williams 11 Aug at Old Church, St Pancras, Middlesex.* **1861:** *the couple lived in Leybourne Rd, St Pancras: WM (29; cordwainer, born Stow-on-the-Wold) and Elizabeth (28; born Kentish Town, Middlesex).* [PS/CH/RA/2/8:66 (copy at PS/CH/RA/2/7:354). Note: "W^m. & Eliza Meadows" delivered to Stow-on-the-Wold 10 Aug 1847 by Charles Maisey. See **47027RO** (George Smith: 26 June 1847.]

47031RO: 5 July 1847 – **Catharine Jones**, and two children **Joseph** and **Rosina**; also Charles Maisey, yeoman, magistrates' office, relating to the settlement of Catharine Jones. *Catharine Jones*: I was married to Benjamin Jones by Banns at the parish Church of Monmouth About fourteen years ago – I lived with my said husband for several years after our said Marriage and had by him two children namely Joseph aged about eleven Years and Rosina aged about seven years now living with me – About seven years ago my husband was in custody for assaulting me and since that time I have not seen him or heard from him.

I believe he is dead – About four years ago I and my said two Children came to reside at Cheltenham aforesaid – About two years ago I applied to the Overseers of the said Parish of Cheltenham for relief for myself and my said two children – I received such relief from the said Overseers and was removed by the orders of Removal now produced from the said parish of

Cheltenham unto the parish of Dinastow [= Dingestow, Monm] – I have done no act to gain a Settlement in my own right – I and my said two children are now actually Chargeable to the said Parish of Cheltenham [mark]

Charles Maisey: [confirms removal of Catharine Jones and two children to Dingestow, Monm under order of 16 Aug 1845, and that it was not appealed against]

1845: *removed to Dingestow, Monm; RETURNED.* **1847:** *removed to Dingestow, Monm (husband's presumed settlement).* [PS/CH/RA/2/8:67 (copies at PS/CH/RA/2/7:355-6). Notes: "Catherine [*sic*] Jones & her two Children" delivered to Monmouth Union 11 Aug 1847 by Charles Maisey; removal expenses to Dinestow £1/19/- (3Q 1847: D4178).]

47032RO: 5 July 1847 – **George Sterry**, labourer; also Charles Maisey, yeoman, magistrates' office, relating to the settlement of George Sterry. *George Sterry*: I was removed under orders of removal from Cheltenham to the parish of Barnwood in the Gloucester Union in this County twelve months ago last March – I remained there about a week

The Guardians of the Poor of the Gloucester Union allowed me two shillings and six pence a week and I came to Cheltenham [mark]

Charles Maisey: [confirms removal of George Sterry to Barnwood under order of 26 Feb 1846, and that it was not appealed against]

1846: *GS removed to Barnwood (hiring and service): see* **46011RO** *(GS: 26/28 Feb).* **1846-7:** *(RETURNED) GS received relief from Gloucester Union allowing him to return to Cheltenham immediately (from 2Q 1846 until 2Q 1847: G/CH/9d/1).* **1847:** *removed to Barnwood (hiring and service).* **1848:** *GS admitted to Gloucester Asylum 31 Jan.* **1849:** *GS died at Gloucester Asylum 28 Dec.* [PS/CH/RA/2/8:68 (copies at PS/CH/RA/2/7:357-8). Note: "George Sterry" delivered to Barnwood 13 Aug 1847 by Charles Maisey.]

47033RO: Wed 14 July 1847 – **Joseph Cooke** (also **Cook**) the younger, labourer, residing in Glos, wife **Louisa** and children **Elizabeth**, **Charlotte**, and **Maria**; also Joseph Cooke the elder, cloth-worker, residing in Rodborough, relating to the settlement of son Joseph Cooke. *Joseph Cooke the elder*: I am a Cloth worker residing at Rodborough in the County of Gloucester – I was married to my present Wife Hannah at the parish Church of Stroud in the County of Gloucester – On the 25th. day of December. 1817   Joseph Cook the pauper is my Son by my said Wife – he was born on the 11th. day of April 1819 at Stroud aforesaid – I had always resided at Stroud aforesaid previously to that time. [signed]

Joseph Cook the younger: I have done no act to gain a settlement in my own right – About eight years ago I was married to my present wife Louisa in the parish of Stroud in the said County by whom I have three Children namely Elizabeth aged seven years Charlotte aged five years and Maria aged three years –

I am now actually chargeable to the said Parish of Cheltenham [signed]

1847: *removed to Stroud (birth or parents' settlement); birth of son Joseph (baptised 16 Dec in Stroud), when family resided at Stroud Workhouse.* **1851:** *the family lived in Rodborough, in hamlet of Rubble Hole: JC (31; woollen-cloth worker, born Stroud), Louisa (31; born Minchinhampton), Elizabeth (11; born Stroud), Charlotte (9), Maria (both scholars, born Minchinhampton), Joseph (3; born Stroud), and Hannah (3 mo; born Rodborough) (HO107/1965/441/21-22).* [PS/CH/RA/2/8:69 (copies at PS/CH/RA/2/7:359-60). Note: "Joseph Cooke Wife and two Children" delivered to Stroud 11 Sept 1847 by Peter Vines.]

47034RO: Wed 1 Sept 1847 – **Esther Bevan**, widow: About fifty six years ago I was married to my late husband George Bevan in the parish Church of Tibberton in the said County – My said husband died in Tibberton about six months ago and was buried at that Parish's Expence – I lived in Tibberton the whole time I was married until about two months ago when I came to Cheltenham – Since I have been in Cheltenham I have received relief from the Parish Officers of Tibberton aforesaid

About two years before I was married I was hired by William Smith of the said Parish of Tibberton for a year at the wages of Four pounds – I served the whole year under such hiring and slept in my Masters house at Tibberton aforesaid the whole time – I have then never been married and had no Child or Children [mark]

1846: *burial of husband George Bevan at Tibberton 18 Dec, aged 74.* **1847:** *removed to Tibberton (presumed) (husband's settlement).* **1851:** *widow EB was licensee of Ten Bells at 115 Westgate St, Gloucester, where daughter Esther Jones was manager; the family lived at the public house: Esther (aged 84; born Upton St Leonards), daughter Esther Jones (34; born Tibberton), and her children Julia Esther (17; at home, born Tibberton), and William Jones (13; grocer's apprentice, born Gloucester City) (HO107/1961/297/7).* [PS/CH/RA/2/8:70 (copy at PS/CH/RA/2/7:361). Note: "Esther Bevans" delivered to Tibberton 11 Oct 1847 by Charles Maisey.]

47035SE: [blank] Sept 1847 – Thomas Saunders, residing in St Nicholas, Gloucester, relating to the settlement of wife **Dorothy Saunders**: That on the twenty sixth day of November 1821 I was married to my said Wife in the parish Church of Cheltenham   In the year 1837 I rented a separate and distinct tenement consisting of a Public house called the Crown and thistle situate in Barton Street in the Hamlet of Barton St Michael in the County of Gloucester at the Yearly rent of thirty five pounds. I continued in the occupation of the said House for the term of three Years at such Yearly rent and paid all the rent

I was duly rated to all poor rates made in the said Hamlet in respect of such house during the said three years and paid the whole of such rates. I have done no act since to gain a settlement [signed]
1841: *DS (aged 40) lived at 68 St George's Place, Cheltenham under maiden name Lambert, with father Robert Lambert (75; independent), daughter Elizabeth Saunders (15), and sister Elizabeth Green (35) (HO107/353/15/40/22); husband Thomas Saunders (50; tailor) lived separately in St Aldate St, Gloucester (HO107/379/1/9/11).* **1847:** *removal uncertain: evidence appears inconclusive and no removal order in register.* **1851:** *DS (57; born Cheltenham), lived with father Robert Lambert (89; widower and annuitant, born Durham) and daughter Elizabeth Ann Saunders (26; schoolmistress, born Gloucester) in St George's Place, Cheltenham (HO107/1973/639/1), while Thomas Saunders (63; tailor, born St Nicholas, Gloucester) was Master of St Bartholomew's Hospital in Gloucester (HO107/1961/281/65).* [PS/CH/RA/2/7:362.]

47036RO: Sat 11 Sept 1847 – **Mary Smith**, widow, residing at 55 Sherborne St, Cheltenham; also Jesse Castle, magistrates' office, relating to the settlement of Mary Smith.
Mary Smith: I am the Widow of William Smith deceased and was married to my said late husband at the Parish of Kings Stanley [= King's Stanley] in the said County about twenty five years ago – About five years ago and after my said husband's death I was unable to maintain myself and applied to the Parish Officers of Cheltenham aforesaid for relief – I was actually chargeable to the said Parish of Cheltenham and removed therefrom by virtue of the order of Removal now produced by Jesse Castle within a short period after the date of the said order – and taken to the Overseers of the said Parish of Kings Stanley who relieved me with eighteen pence a week from that time – the said order of Removal was not appealed against – I have done no act since to gain a Settlement – I am now actually chargeable to the said Parish of Cheltenham and am in receipt of relief from Peter Butt the relieving officer of that parish. [mark]
Jesse Castle: [confirms removal of Mary Smith to King's Stanley under order of 15 July 1842]
1841: *William Smith (50; labourer) and Mary (60) lived with daughter Margaret (15) in Commercial St, Cheltenham (HO107/353/12/21/36); death of William Smith (buried at New Burial Ground, Cheltenham 25 Nov, aged 51).* **1842:** *MS removed to King's Stanley (father's settlement): see* **42030RO** *(MS: 4 Apr).* **1847:** *removed to King's Stanley (father's settlement).* **1863:** *examination exhibited to Cheltenham magistrates, suggesting MS still alive (and in Cheltenham).* [PS/CH/RA/2/8:71 (copies at PS/CH/RA/2/7:363-4), indicating that MS originally and mistakenly thought husband's parish was Leonard Stanley. Note: "Mary Smith" delivered to King's Stanley 18 Oct 1847 by Charles Maisey. See **42060RO** (MS: 15 July 1842).]

47037SE: 11 Sept 1847 – **Thomas Augustus Eustace**, labourer, residing at 22 Corpus St, Cheltenham, with wife **Sarah**: I was married to my said Wife Sarah at the Parish Church of [blank] about the year [blank] I and my said wife are now actually chargeable to the said Parish of Cheltenham. About seventeen years ago I hired and rented of Mr Hyde for the term of one year at the rent of twenty two pounds a year a tenement consisting of a separate and distinct dwellinghouse and premises situate in the Parish of Bishops Cleeve [= Bishop's Cleeve] in the said County and called or known as the Crown and Harp Inn. I occupied the said premises under

the said taking for the said term of one year and upwards and the said yearly rent of twenty two pounds was actually paid by me for the said term of one year   During my said tenancy I resided uninterruptedly at the said Parish of Bishops Cleeve. I have never done an act since to gain a Settlement.
1847: *removal uncertain: evidence appears inconclusive and no removal order in register.* **1851**: *(RETURNED) TAE (aged 59; born Dublin) was porter living at bath-keeper's at 61 High St, Cheltenham (HO107/1973/229/38); wife Sarah (49; born Cheltenham) was servant at Royal Hotel, 97 High St, Cheltenham.* [PS/CH/RA/2/7:365.]

47038RO: Thurs 16 Sept 1847 – **Hannah Driver**, single woman; also Charles Maisey, yeoman, magistrates' office, relating to the settlement of Hannah Driver.
Hannah Driver: I resided with my Father and Mother Nathan and Hannah Driver at Painswick in the said County from the time I can first recollect until I was about twenty six [years] of age – I have never done an act to gain a settlement in my own right – About nine years ago I was residing in the Parish of Walcot in the City of Bath and became chargeable to that Parish and was duly removed from thence by orders of removal to the said Parish of Painswick and was received there by M^r. Constable the then Overseer – Such orders of removal were not appealed against – About a week after such removal I returned to the said Parish of Walcot and resided there for about twelve months then next following – During such my residence in the said Parish of Walcot I was constantly relieved by the Parish officers of Painswick aforesaid on account of their parish with one shilling a week – About two years and a half ago I was residing in the said Parish of Cheltenham and became chargeable to that Parish and was duly removed by virtue of the order of removal now produced by Charles Maisey from thence to the said Parish of Painswick and delivered by him to [the] then Overseer of Painswick. Such order of removal was not appealed against – I am now actually chargeable to the said Parish of Cheltenham – [signed]
Charles Maisey: [confirms removal of Hannah Driver to Painswick under order of 29 May 1845]
1835: *HD removed from Walcot, Bath to Painswick (P244 OV 3/3/4/6) (RETURNED).* **1845**: *HD removed to Painswick (father's presumed settlement): see* **45031SE** *(HD: 29 May) (RETURNED).* **1847**: *removed to Painswick (father's presumed settlement).* **1851**: *(RETURNED) HD (aged 67; living as widow, born Painswick) lived at 28 Swindon Place, Cheltenham with daughter Martha Webber (41; dressmaker, born Bath) and grandson William Webber (8; later also Parker) (HO107/1973/425/16).* **1861**: *the family lived in Park St, Cheltenham (RG9/1800/74/46).* **1865**: *death of HD 15 Dec at 4 Park Place, Cheltenham (Cheltenham Chron. 19 Dec).* [PS/CH/RA/2/8:72 (copies at PS/CH/RA/2/7:366-7). Note: "Hannah Driver" delivered to Painswick 11 Oct 1847 by Charles Maisey. See **49047RO** (daughter Martha Webber: 22 Sept 1849).]

47039RO: Mon 20 Sept 1847 – **Ann Hale**, widow: I am the Widow of John Hale who died at the parish of Charlton Kings about twelve years ago – I was married to him at the Parish Church of Leckhampton in the said County about sixty years ago – My said husband was settled in the parish of Shurdington in the said County as I have heard and believe by hiring and service with M^r. Sadler of that Parish before we were married – I recollect his living in such service for three whole years and I know that he resided in M^r. Sadler's house at Shurdington aforesaid during such three years service – He was unmarried and had no child or children at the time of his going into M^r. Sadler's service – he was serving M^r. Sadler at the time we were married – M^r. Sadler is dead – About thirty years ago I and my said husband were residing in the said Parish of Charlton Kings and being unable to pay our Rent applied to the Overseers of Shurdington aforesaid for relief – they relieved us with payment of the half of our rent namely in the payment of three pounds a Year from that time for the four following years and during the whole time of our receiving such Relief we were residing in the said Parish of Charlton Kings in houses belonging to M^r. Whithorne who is dead – the one situate in the Blind Lane near the Church and the other by the Prinns Arms Inn – About twenty years ago while we were still residing in Charlton Kings aforesaid my husband was taken ill with the typhus fever and I applied to the said Overseers of Shurdington for relief – they relieved me with ten shillings and by paying the Doctors Expences – About six years ago I was chargeable to the said parish of Charlton Kings and duly removed thence by orders of removal to the said Parish of

Shurdington and delivered to the Overseers of that Parish – such orders were not appealed against – I am now actually chargeable to the said Parish of Cheltenham – [mark]

1841: *AH (aged 65; laundress) lived in Little Herbert, Charlton Kings with grandchildren Eliza (25), Sarah (20), and Thomas (15) (HO107/353/2/31/3).* **1847: removed to Shurdington (husband's settlement). 1850:** *death of AH (buried at Charlton Kings 8 Jan, aged 75).* [PS/CH/RA/2/8:73 (copy at PS/CH/RA/2/7:368). Note: "Ann Hale" delivered to Shurdington 18 Oct 1847 by Charles Maisey.]

47040RO: Thurs 4 Nov 1847 – (examinations on 14 Oct and 4 Nov respectively) **John Stevens** (also **Stephens**), labourer, residing at 10 Worcester St, Cheltenham, wife **Eliza**, and five children **Charles**, **Sophia**, **Ann**, **William**, and **Alfred**; also Mary Mansell, currently residing in Alderton, relating to the settlement of John Stevens. *Mary Mansell*: My said Brother John is an illegitimate Son of my late mother Mother Elizabeth Stevens who has been dead a great many years – I remember my said Brother being born in the parish of Charlton Abbotts [= Charlton Abbots] in the said County about forty two years ago in which parish my said Mother resided until her death – I produce an Extract from the register of Baptisms of the parish of Charlton Abbotts as follows –

> "Daughter of Elizabeth Stevens / Mary baptized 1797 Septr. 10th. / John baptized 1805 August 21st. / Extracted from Charlton Abbotts Church / August 3rd. 1847   John Tucker Perpetual Curate"

I examined the extract with the Register and it is true   My said Mother died about 40 years ago [signed]

John Stevens: I was married to my wife Eliza about Eleven Years ago at the parish of Swindon by whom I have five children namely Charles aged about ten years Sophia aged about eight years Ann aged about six years William aged about four years and Alfred aged about two months – they are all living at home with me – I am about forty one years of age and the Son [*sic*] of Mary Mansell – I have never done an act to gain a Settlement in my own right – I and my said Wife and children are now actually chargeable to the said parish. [mark]

1847: removed to Charlton Abbots (birth). 1850: *birth of daughter Elizabeth (baptised at Charlton Abbots 9 June).* **1851:** *the family lived in Charlton Abbots: JS (aged 47; agricultural labourer, born Charlton Abbots), Eliza (29; born Cheltenham); Charles (13), Sophia (11), Ann (9), William (8; all four born Swindon), Alfred (5; born Cheltenham), and Elizabeth (10 months; born Charlton Abbots) (HO107/1971/77/5-6).* [PS/CH/RA/2/8:74 (copies at PS/CH/RA/2/7:369-70). Notes: "John Stevens & Family" delivered to the Winchcombe Union 30 Nov 1847; removal expenses to Charlton Abbotts 8/6 (4Q 1847: D4178).]

47041RO: Mon 22 Nov 1847 – **Maria Underwood**, widow, and daughter **Rosina**; also Charles Maisey, yeoman, magistrates' office, relating to the settlement of Maria Underwood.

Maria Underwood: I was married to my late Husband Charles Underwood in the parish Church of Saint Mary de lode in the City of Gloucester about the year 1822 by whom I have one child named Rosina now aged nearly twelve years – My husband died about twelve months [ago] – In the month of February 1846 I and my said Husband with my said child were removed by orders of removal from the said Parish of Cheltenham into the Hamlet of Hucclecott [= Hucclecote] in the said County and delivered to the Overseer there – [signed]

Charles Maisey: [confirms removal of George Underwood, his Maria, and two children George (20) and Rosina (10) to Hucclecote under order of 15 Jan 1846, and that the removal was not appealed against]

1841: *Charles Underwood (aged 45; smith) lived in Lower Gas Green, Cheltenham with wife Maria (45) and children George (15; smith) and Rosina (5) (HO107/353/10/20/6).* **1846:** *CU and Maria removed to Hucclecote (renting): see* **46002SE:** *(Charles Underwood: 15 Jan); (RETURNED) from 1Q 1846 until 4Q 1846 the family received parish relief from Gloucester as non-settled residents of Cheltenham (G/CH/9d/1); death of Charles Underwood (baptised at Churchdown 3 Aug 1794) at 37 Milsom St, Cheltenham (Cheltenham Chron. 26 Nov) (buried, aged 52, at New Burial Ground, Cheltenham on 19 Nov).* **1847: removed to Hucclecote (Gloucester Union) (late husband's settlement). 1851:** *(RETURNED) MU (57; charwoman, born Tewkesbury) lived at 15 Swindon Place, Cheltenham with children George (24; blacksmith) and Rosina (15; occasional servant; both children born Cheltenham) (HO107/1973/423/13).*

[PS/CH/RA/2/8:75 (copies at PS/CH/RA/2/7:374-5). Note: "Maria Underwood & her Child and Rosina" to Gloucester Overseer for Hucclecote 18 Dec 1847.]

47042RO: Thurs 9 Dec 1847 – **Mary Turner**, single woman; also Sarah Champion, relating to the settlement of sister Mary Turner. *Sarah Champion*: I am the wife of John Champion of Cheltenham Gardener   the said Mary Turner is my Sister – I well remember my said Sister being born in the Parish of Charlton Kings in the said County about sixty four years [ago] and lived with my Father Edward Turner and Mary his Wife – My said Sister has lived in Charlton Kings aforesaid all her life time until six months ago – The person now present is my said Sister. [mark] *Mary Turner*: The first place I remember myself was living with my Father and Mother Edward Turner and Mary his Wife in the Parish of Charlton Kings in the said County – My Father and Mother have both been long since dead – I have never done any act to gain a Settlement – I am now actually chargeable to the said Parish of Cheltenham and receiving two shillings a week from the Relieving officer – I have resided in Charlton Kings aforesaid all my life time until about six months ago – [mark]
1848: *removed to Charlton Kings (presumed) (birth).* **1851:** *(RETURNED) MT (aged 64; born Charlton Kings) was an "Out door pauper" lodging at 13 Kingston Place, Cheltenham (HO107/1973/71/10).* [PS/CH/RA/2/8:77 (copies at PS/CH/RA/2/7:376, 378). Note: "Mary Turner" delivered Charlton Kings 5 Jan 1848 by Thomas Griffiths.]

47043SE: Tues 7 Dec 1847 – William Dyer, labourer, residing in Charlton Kings, relating to the settlement of son **Samuel Dyer** with his wife **Jane** and three children **Elizabeth**, **Walter**, and **Samuel**: About the year 1811 I was married to my late wife Ann at the Parish Church in Cheltenham aforesaid by whom I had my said Son Samuel now aged about twenty nine years. He lived at home with me at Charlton Kings aforesaid until he was about fourteen or fifteen years of age.
1847: *removal unlikely as incomplete form struck through.* **1848:** *death of SD (buried at Cheltenham 27 May, aged 31).* **1851:** *widow Jane (32; laundress, born Gloucester) lived at 11 Windsor Terrace, Cheltenham with four children Elizabeth (9; born Cheltenham), Walter (7; born Charlton Kings), Samuel (5; born Cheltenham), and Frances (2; born Charlton Kings) (HO107/1973/71/11).* [PS/CH/RA/2/7:377.]

47044RO: Thurs 16 Dec 1847 – **Ann Hackford**, single woman: About Nineteen Years ago being then unmarried and having no Child or Children I was hired into the Parish of Fownhope in the County of Hereford by M[r] Morgan of that Parish Surgeon to serve him for one whole year At the wages of Three Guineas. I entered into such service and continued therein under such hiring for one whole year and resided and slept in my said Masters house at Fownhope aforesaid the whole Year and received my Years wages   About three years ago I was taken by orders of Removal from the City of Hereford to the said Parish of Fownhope and delivered to the Overseer there. I am now actually chargeable to the said Parish of Cheltenham [mark]
1847: *removed to Fownhope, Heref (presumed) (hiring and service); AH (suffering from "debility") was an inmate of Cheltenham Workhouse in 4Q (absconded 20 Jan 1848) (G/CH/60/5).* **1851:** *AH (aged 35; born Lugwardine, Heref) worked as cook in Stainton with Hellaby, in Yorkshire (HO107/2346/1/7/6).* **1853:** *AH lived in Prestbury where, aged 42 and spinster, she married widower George Slatter (50; labourer living in Prestbury).* [PS/CH/RA/2/8:78 (not in removals register; transcribed from PS/CH/RA/2/7:379).]

1848

48001RO: Mon 3 Jan 1848 – **Ann Loveday**, widow: About forty four years ago I was married to my late husband William Loveday in the parish Church of Coln S^t. Dennis in this County, My said Husband died about twelve Years ago in the Gloucester Infirmary

Near four years ago I was taken to the Union Workhouse at Tewkesbury by Neighbour Tombs the then Overseer of the Parish of Boddington in the said County where I remained about nine months and was relieved by the Overseer of Boddington All that time   I then came to Cheltenham where I have been residing ever since and for two years of that time I was relieved by the Relieving officer of the Said Parish of Boddington with a loaf of Bread and Six pence a week. I am now actually chargeable to the said Parish of Cheltenham [mark]

1848: *removed to Boddington (presumed) (husband's settlement): see* **50009RO** *(AL: 16 Mar) for further information about the family.* [PS/CH/RA/2/8:79 (copy at PS/CH/RA/2/7:380). Note: "Ann Loveday" delivered to Boddington 9 Feb 1848 by Thomas Griffiths.]

48002RO: Mon 17 Jan 1848 – **Richard Barrett**, residing at 15 St Paul's St South, Cheltenham, and wife **Martha**: About five years ago I rented a seperate [*sic*] and distinct tenement consisting of a House and Shop of M^r. Conner [also Connor] situate on the Uxbridge Road in the Parish of Ealing in the County of Middlesex by the year at the yearly rent of fifteen pounds. I resided in such house for upwards of one year under such taken [= taking] and paid a whole years rent for the same. I was duly rated to all poor rates made for the said Parish of Ealing in respect of such house and Shop for such year and paid the whole of such rates – I was married to my present wife Martha in the Parish Church of Shipperton [= Shepperton] in the County of Middlesex in the year 1824 [signed]

1848: *removed to Ealing, Middlesex (renting).* [PS/CH/RA/2/8:76 (copy at PS/CH/RA/2/7:373). Note: "R^d. Barrett & wife" delivered to Ealing, Middlesex 17 Feb 1848.]

48003RO: [blank] Jan 1848 – **Mary Davis**, single woman: About twenty five Years ago being then unmarried and having no Child or Children I was hired by William Whitehead Esquire of the Parish of Tirley [= Turleigh] in the County of Wilts for a Year at the Yearly wages of Twelve pounds   I continued in such service for two Years under such hiring in the said Parish of Tirley and then went with my said Master to the Parish of Walcot Bath in the County of Somerset where I resided with my said Master for three years under such hiring and received my wages and slept in my Masters house there

I have done no act since to gain a settlement

1848: *removed to Walcot, Bath, Som (hiring and service).* [PS/CH/RA/2/8:80 (not in removal register, so transcribed from PS/CH/RA/2/7:381). Removal expenses for "Davis" to Bath £1/5/6 (3Q 1848: D4178).]

48004RO: Sat 22 Jan 1848 – **Thomas Hooper**, labourer, wife **Martha**, and son **John**; also Daniel Hooper, also relating to the settlement of son Thomas. *Daniel Hooper:* About thirty six years ago being then unmarried and having no Child or Children I was hired into the Parish of the Leigh in the said County by the late Mr J^{no}. Higgs of that Parish for a year at the wages of Twelve Guineas   I served the whole year under such hiring and resided and slept in my said Masters house at the Leigh aforesaid the whole year and received all my wages   about Thirty three years ago I was married to my present wife Maria at the said Parish of the Leigh by whom I had my said Son Thomas who is now about twenty five years of age   The person present is my said Son [mark]

Thomas Hooper: About two years ago I was [married] to my wife Martha at the Parish Church of Saint Mary de lode in the City of Gloucester by whom I have one Child named John aged one year. I have done no act to gain a settlement in my own right   I am now actually chargeable to the said Parish of Cheltenham where I have been living nearly two years and no more [mark]

1848: *removed to The Leigh (father's settlement).* **1849:** *(RETURNED) daughter Sarah Ann baptised at Cheltenham 22 July, when family lived in Worcester St.* **1851:** *the family lived at 5 (back), Malvern Place,*

Cheltenham: TH (30; labourer, born The Leigh), Martha (28; born Sandhurst), John (5), born Gloucester and baptised The Leigh), and Sarah Ann (1) (HO107/1973/525/29). [PS/CH/RA/2/8:81 (copies at PS/CH/RA/2/7:382-3). Note: "Thos. Hooper Wife and Child" delivered to The Leigh 15 Feb 1848.]

48005RO: [blank] Jan 1848 – Elizabeth Vaughan, residing in Upton St Leonards, relating to the settlement of son **Charles Vaughan** (also **Vaughn**) and his wife **Mary Ann**: The said Charles Vaughan is an illegitimate Child of mine and was born in the said Parish of Upton Saint Leonards in the said County about thirty years ago. I have been living in the said Parish of Upton Saint Leonards about forty years and have been several times relieved by the Overseer of that Parish [mark]
1848: *son Alfred born at Bristol 3Q, and was perhaps living with grandparents in Bristol;* **removed to Upton St Leonards (presumed) (birth).** **1849:** *daughter Rosina born at Bristol 1Q (baptised at St James, Bristol 8 Apr).* **1851:** *CV (aged 32; victualler, born Upton St Leonards) lived at the Ship, Steep St, St Michael's, Bristol with wife Mary Ann (35), children Alfred (3) and Rosina (2), and parents-in-law Robert (60; formerly carpenter) and Mary Barrow (55; all five born Bristol) (HO107/1951/54/46).* [PS/CH/RA/2/7:384.]

48006RO: Thurs 27 Jan 1848 – **Mary Glover**, widow and inmate of Union Workhouse, Cheltenham: I have resided in Cheltenham Parish   I was married to my late husband William Glover in or about the year one thousand eight hundred and four at the Parish Church of Chedworth in the County of Gloucester by Banns – I lived with my said husband at Chedworth aforesaid from that time until his death which happened on the 27th day of September 1844. My husband never did any act to gain a settlement whilst I knew him. About twenty eight years ago whilst I and my husband lived at Chedworth we and our children were afflicted with Typhus Fever   we made application to the Overseers of the Parish of Cirencester in the County of Gloucester for Parish relief and we received relief from them in money and medical attendance whilst we received such relief from Cirencester we resided at Chedworth aforesaid

We received such relief for about three or four weeks and I think it was ten shillings a week [signed]
1841: *husband William Glover (60; shopkeeper, died 1844) lived in Chedworth with wife Mary (60), and two children John (15; agricultural labourer) and Henry (2) (HO107/363/9/22/6).* **1847:** *MG (68; suffering from effects of old age, houseless and destitute) was admitted to Cheltenham Workhouse late in year (discharged 29 Feb 1848) (G/CH/60/5).* **1848:** **removed to Cirencester (late husband's presumed settlement).** **1850:** *(RETURNED) death of MG at Fountain Inn, Bath Rd, Cheltenham 3 Apr, aged 71 (Cheltenham Chron. 11 Apr) (buried three days later at Chedworth).* [PS/CH/RA/2/8:82 (copy at PS/CH/RA/2/7:385). Note: "Mary Glover" delivered to Cirencester Union Workhouse 26 Feb 1848 by Thomas Griffiths.]

48007RO: Mon 7 Feb 1848 – **John Jeffries** (also **Jefferies**), labourer, wife **Catharine**, and son **George**: About twenty two years and a half ago I rented a seperate [*sic*] and distinct tenement consisting of the dwelling house situate in Bridewell Lane in the Parish of Saint Peter and Saint Paul in the City of Bath of Mr. Hewitt for a year at the yearly rent of thirteen pounds. I resided and slept in such house for four successive years and a half at that rent and paid all the rent for the same. I have done no act to gain a settlement since. Thirty four years ago last August I was married to my present wife Catharine at the Parish Church of St Stephens Bristol by whom I have one child named George aged eleven years [mark]
1848: *the Jeffries were frequent inmates of Cheltenham Workhouse: John (60; labourer, suffering from effects of age), Catherine (50; charwoman, ill health), and George (12); George absconded 11 Jan (G/CH/60/5);* **removed to St Peter and St Paul, Bath, Som (renting).** **1851:** *JJ (aged 64; sawyer) lived in Rackhay, Bristol with wife Catharine (58; both born St Stephen's, Bristol), and son George (15; plasterer, born St Augustine's, Bristol) (HO107/1948/69/39).* [PS/CH/RA/2/8:83 (copy at PS/CH/RA/2/7:387). Note: "John Jefferis Wife & Son" delivered to St Peter and St Paul, Bath 6 Mar 1848.]

48008RO: 7 Feb 1848 – **Caroline Darke** (also **Dark**), widow and inmate of Union Workhouse, Cheltenham, and daughter **Sarah Ann**: also William Darke, relating to the settlement of son, John Darke. *Caroline Darke*: I am a Widow. I was married to my late husband John Darke at Cheltenham about ten years ago. I have no child living by my said husband   My said husband died in the month of May one thousand eight hundred and forty four and was buried in the Parish of Bishops Cleeve

I have resided at Cheltenham ever since the death of my husband but previously to and up to his death we resided at Stoke Orchard. My husband never did any act to gain a settlement during the time I knew him   Since my said husbands death namely on the twenty eighth of June one thousand eight hundred and forty seven I have been delivered of a female bastard child named Sarah Ann who is now living with me in the Cheltenham Union Workhouse [mark]

William Darke: About forty five years ago I was married to my present wife Elizabeth in the Parish Church of Bishops Cleeve by whom I had my said Son John who was born in the Hamlet of Stoke Orchard aforesaid about thirty two years ago

About forty eight years ago being then unmarried and having no child or children I was hired by M[r]. Thomas White of the Parish of Twyning in that County of Gloucester for a year at the yearly wage of seven pounds. I served the whole year under such hiring and slept in my said masters house at Twyning aforesaid the whole year [mark]

1848: *removed to Twyning (late husband's settlement): see* **50024RO** *(second husband William Bartlett: 13 July 1850) for further information on the family.* [PS/CH/RA/2/8:82 (copies at PS/CH/RA/2/7:388-9). Removal expenses for "Darke" to Twyning 4/6 (1Q 1848: D4178).]

48009RO: Sat 12 Feb 1848 – **Jane Harding**, widow: About forty years ago I was married to my late Husband Uriah Harding at Stonehouse in the said County   My said Husband died about nine years ago in the Union Workhouse at Dursley in which Workhouse he resided for about two years before his death and was all that time chargeable to the Parish of North Nibley in the said County   In about twelve months after I was married my said Husband went into the Militia and I was living in the Parish of Randwick in the said County   I applied to the Overseers of North Nibley aforesaid for relief and was relieved by them with two shillings a week for about two years during the whole of which time I resided at Randwick aforesaid   I have on many other occasions received relief from the Overseers of North Nibley aforesaid [mark]

1848: *removed to North Nibley (Dursley Union) (late husband's settlement).* **1851:** *JH (aged 65; laundress, born Randwick) lived in Loose, Kent, at house of daughter and son-in-law Sarah (37; laundress, born Randwick) and Thomas Palmer (25; gardener), and daughter Emma (6 mo; both born Loose, Kent) (HO107/1610/453/6).* [PS/CH/RA/2/8:85 (copy at PS/CH/RA/2/7:390). Note: "Jane Harding" delivered to Dursley Union 14 Mar 1848 by Charles Maisey; removal expenses to North Nibley 9/8 (1Q 1848: D4178).]

48010RO: Thurs 17 Feb 1848 – **Edward Morris**: That I am about sixty six years of age   About thirty four years ago I was hired as a Footman by the Marquis [properly, Marquess] of Salisbury for a year   I continued in that service under such hiring for about six years and received all my wages during the whole time of such hiring and service   I was a Singleman without Children For the last three months of the time I lived in the said service I resided and slept at my said Masters House at Hatfield in the County of Herts   Since I left the Marquis of Salisburys service I have never done any act whereby to gain a settlement   I have been residing in the Parish of Cheltenham for twelve months last past and no more

Before coming to reside in Cheltenham I resided at Leckhampton in this County [signed]

c1814: *EM hired as footman to James Brownlow William Gascoyne-Cecil, 2nd Marquess of Salisbury (1791–1868).* **1847:** *EM (67; servant and widower) admitted as an inmate of Cheltenham Workhouse 31 Dec, suffering from ill health (G/CH/60/5).* **1848:** *removed to Hatfield, Herts (hiring and service).* **1851:** *(RETURNED) EM was an inmate of Cheltenham Workhouse: Edward Morris (aged 70; widower and gentleman's servant, born Berkeley) (HO107/1973/1093/6).* [PS/CH/RA/2/8:86 (order suspended as EM unfit to travel; suspension not lifted) (copy at PS/CH/RA/2/7:386).]

48011RO: 17 Feb 1848 – **Jane Scrivens**, and three children, **Emma**, **Ellen**, and **William**: I was married to my husband Edward Scrivens in the Parish Church of Hempstead [= Hempsted] in the said County about twenty two years ago by whom I have three children living with me namely Emma aged fourteen years Ellen aged ten years and William aged seven years. My said husband deserted me about seven years ago and I have not seen or heard of him since. About five years ago I was sent to the Union Workhouse at Cheltenham by the Relieving Officer of the Parish of Cubberley [= Coberley] in the said County and was there relieved at the expence of the said Parish of Cubberley for upwards of twelve months   I have since been relieved several times by the relieving Officer of Cubberley aforesaid during which time I have been living in Cheltenham   they gave me four loaves of bread and two shillings a week for three or four weeks. My Parish is Cubberley. My husband gained his Parish there by living at service with M^r. Day. The years before my said marriage and while I was unmarried and without child or children I was hired by M^r. Day of the said Parish of Cubberley for a twelvemonth – Immediately after such hiring I went into Mr Days service and served him the whole twelvemonth at Cubberley and resided in his house there during such service [mark]

1841: *the three children of Edward and Jane Scrivens were inmates of Charlton Kings Workhouse for children: James (11), Emma (6), and Ellen (4) (HO107/353/2/53/1).* **1843:** *JS was an inmate of Cheltenham Workhouse (G/CH/60/4).* **1848: removed to Coberley (Cheltenham Union) (husband's settlement).** **1850:** *(RETURNED) death of JS (buried at Cheltenham 26 June, aged 46).* **1851:** *children dispersed at census: Emma (18) lived as servant at 29 North Place, Cheltenham (HO107/1973/282/34); William (9; pauper, born Coberley) was apparently an inmate of Cheltenham Workhouse (HO107/1973/1103/26). [PS/CH/RA/2/8:87 (copy at PS/CH/RA/2/7:391).]*

48012RO: Sat 11 Mar 1848 – **Charles Simons** (also **Simonds**, **Symonds**), labourer, residing at 2 Elm St, Cheltenham, wife **Susan**, and six children **Rhoda**, **Charles**, **William**, **Henry**, **Margaret**, and **Ann**; also Sarah Mann, residing at 1 Elm St, Cheltenham, relating to the settlement of son Charles Simons. *Charles Simons:* I am about forty years of age   I have a Wife named Susan now living. I was married to her by banns at Redmarley Church in this County about fourteen years ago – I have six children by my said Wife now living with me namely Rhoda aged 13 years Charles aged 11 years William aged 10 years, Henry aged 7 years Margaret aged five years and Ann aged between two and three years   About seven or eight years ago whilst I was residing at Tewkesbury in this County with my family I had a lame hand and could not work. I went to the Board of Guardians of the Union of Upton upon Severn in the County of Worcester and applied to them for relief as a Parishioner of Longdon in the County of Worcester and in the Upton upon Severn Union   I was relieved by them with as much as two shillings and six pence a week for about five or six weeks and during the whole of this time I resided uninterruptedly at Tewkesbury aforesaid. I have never done an act to gain a settlement in my own right. I and my said wife and said children are now actually chargeable to the said Parish of Cheltenham. My mother Sarah Mann is the person now present [mark] *Sarah Mann:* The said Charles Simons now present is my son - he is illegitimate   he was born in the Parish of Longdon in the County of Worcester about forty years ago [mark of "Susan" Mann]

1841: *CS (aged 30; brickmaker) lived with wife Susan (28) and four children in Tewkesbury (HO107/380/7/3/1).* **1848: removed to Longdon, Worcs (Upton-upon-Severn Union) (birth).** **1848-51**: *(RETURNED) birth of two children Joseph and Nicholas, both at Cheltenham.* **1851:** *the family lived at 14 Elm St, Cheltenham: Charles (40; labourer), Susan (45; washerwoman, both born Tewkesbury), Rhoda (17; washerwoman), Charles (15), William (12; both labourers), Henry (6), Margaret (6), Ann (5), Joseph (2; all four listed as scholars), and Nicholas (2) (all children apparently born Cheltenham) (HO107/1973/516/11-12). [PS/CH/RA/2/8:88 (copies at PS/CH/RA/2/7:371-2 and (repeated) 392-3). Note: "Charles Simons Wife & Seven Children" delivered to Longdon, Worcs 19 June 1848 by Charles Maisey.]*

48013RO: Sat 7 Oct 1848 – **Eliza Slade**, and son, **Edwin**, aged five. [No examination included with removal order.]

1841: *ES (aged 24) lived with wife Eliza (25) and daughter Elizabeth (5 mo) in Vicarage Lane, Painswick (HO107/349/8/33/9).* **1848:** *ES (32; labourer, ill health) entered Cheltenham Workhouse with wife Eliza (32; charwoman, ill health), and son Edwin (3); amongst other admissions to workhouse, Eliza Slade was an inmate from 3 Oct 1848 (deserted by husband) and removed 13 Nov (G/CH/60/5/6); **removed to Painswick.** **1851:** (RETURNED) ES (aged 36; hawker, married to Edwin Slade and presumably separated) and son Edwin (7; both born Painswick) lodged at 2 Burton St, Cheltenham (HO107/1973/596/19). **1858:** death of ES at 6 Lypiatt St, Cheltenham (buried 14 Aug, aged 46) (Cheltenham Chron. 17 Aug). **1861:** Edwin Slade*

(17) was carpenter's apprentice living with uncle and aunt Adam and Mary Ann Brewer at 14 Lypiatt St, Cheltenham (RG9/1802/76/35). [PS/CH/RA/2/8:89.]

48014RO: 7 Oct 1848 – **John Thomas Hopgood**. [No examination included with removal order.]
1848: *John "Hapgood" recorded as an inmate of Cheltenham Workhouse from 2 Oct – 13 Dec 1848; removed to St James, Westminster.* **1850:** *(perhaps RETURNED) a John Hopgood, 14th Light Dragoons, died at 9 Jersey Place, Cheltenham on 23 Jan, aged 30; buried 26 Jan at Cheltenham. Note: "Thomas Draper"; another (unnamed) person also made deposition about JH's settlement.* [PS/CH/RA/2/8:90.]

48015RO: Mon 23 Oct 1848 – **Emma Price**, and three children, **Oliver** aged nine, **Martha** aged three, and **Thomas** aged 18 months. [No examination included with removal order.]
1848: *removed to Stoke-on-Trent, Staffs: see* **49066RO** *(EP: 3 Dec 1849) for further information.* [PS/CH/RA/2/8:91; deposition under oath by James Aidney. Note: "Emma Price and three Children" delivered to Stoke-on-Trent 20 Nov 1848 by Jesse Castle.]

48016RO: Sat 4 Nov 1848 – **Ambrose Dance**, wife **Hannah**, and son **Daniel**, aged about eleven. [No examination included with removal order.]
1848: *removed to Beckford: see* **50038RO** *(AD: 24 Dec 1850) for further information on AD and family.* [PS/CH/RA/2/8:92.]

48017RO: Mon 13 Nov 1848 – **Sarah Woolley** (also **Wooly**), inmate of Cheltenham Workhouse; also Thomas Woolley, relating to the settlement of Sarah Woolley. [No examinations included with removal order.]
1848: *removed to Meysey Hampton (presumably father's settlement); SW discharged from Cheltenham Workhouse 12 Dec (G/CH/60/5/6).* [PS/CH/RA/2/8:93.]

48018RO: Sat 18 Nov 1848 – **Solomon Ivin** (also **Iuens, Ivein, Ivens, Iving, Ivins**). [No examination included with removal order.]
1841: *SI (aged 50; labourer) lived with wife Charlotte (45) and children Mary (15), James (13), and Hannah (10) with eldest son John and his family in Cricklade, Wilts (HO107/1178/6/4/1): see* **41048SE** *(John Ivin: 9 Aug).* **1842:** *removed to Acton Turville (hiring and service): see* **42019RO** *(SI: 17 Feb) (RETURNED).* **1848:** *Charlotte Ivin died at Cheltenham (buried there 21 Mar); removed to Acton Turville (Chipping Sodbury Union); SI and children James and Hannah ("houseless & destitute") admitted to Cheltenham Workhouse 10 Dec (G/CH/60/6).* **1861:** *SI (73; brickmaker and widower, born Quenington) lived alone in Rodborough (RG9/1776/130/15).* [PS/CH/RA/2/8:94. Note: "Solomon Ivings" delivered to Chipping Sodbury 23 Dec 1848 by Jesse Castle.]

48019RO: 18 Nov 1848 – **Henry Ivin** (also **Iuens, Ivein, Ivens, Iving, Ivins**), wife **Mary**, and two children, **Sarah Ann**, aged about eight years, and unbaptised female infant of about five months. [No examination included with removal order.]
1820: *birth of HI, son of Solomon and Charlotte Ivin 25 Jan.* **1847-8:** *HI and family frequent residents in Cheltenham Workhouse, once citing "bad eyes" and "ill health", and once with an "infant" (G/CH/60/5 16 Oct 1847, etc).* **1848:** *birth of daughter Jane registered at Cheltenham 3Q; removed to Acton Turville (Chipping Sodbury Union) (father's settlement).* **1849:** *death of daughter Jane registered at Chipping Sodbury (1Q).* **1850:** *(RETURNED) birth of Thomas Ivin, registered at Cheltenham 3Q.* **1851:** *HI (aged 31; pauper and agricultural labourer, born Cheltenham) lived at 4 Cox's Row, Lower Alstone, Cheltenham, with wife Mary (33; pauper, born Shurdington), children (Sarah) Ann (10; born Leckhampton) and Thomas (8 months; born Alstone, Cheltenham), and Mary's younger brother and sister Joseph and Ann Harper (HO107/1973/556/2).* [PS/CH/RA/2/8:95.]

48020RO: 18 Nov 1848 – **George Ivin** (also **Iuens, Ivein, Ivens, Iving, Ivins**), and wife **Ann**. [No examination included with removal order.]
1848: *GI ("houseless & destitute") entered Cheltenham Workhouse 17 Oct (G/CH/60/6); removed to Acton Turville (Chipping Sodbury Union) (father's settlement); birth of daughter Harriet at Cheltenham 4Q; (family was removed 23 Dec).* **1851:** *GI (aged 30; brickmaker, born Glos) lived with railway brick-making gang in Westby, Lincs (HO107/2102/126/15), while wife Ann and small daughter lived with Ann Ivin's widowed mother and brother in Uffculme, Devon: Mary Searle (69; pauper, agricultural labourer), William (33; errand man), Ann Ivin (27; factory worker (wool), both born Uffculme), and Harriet Ivin (2; born*

Cheltenham) (HO107/1888/427/23). [PS/CH/RA/2/8:96. Note: "George Ivens Wife and Ann" delivered to Chipping Sodbury Union 23 Dec 1848 by Jesse Castle.]

48021RO: 18 Nov 1848 – **James Ivin** (also **Iuens, Iving, Ivins, Ivein, Ivens**). [No examination included with removal order.]
1828: *JI, son of Solomon and Charlotte Ivin, baptised at Cheltenham 3 Aug, when family lived in Charlton Kings.* **1841:** *JI removed with family to Acton Turville: see* **48028RO** *(John Ivin: 29 Nov 1848) (RETURNED).* **1842:** *removed to Acton Turville (hiring and service): see* **42019RO** *(SI: 17 Feb).* **1848:** *(RETURNED) JI was an inmate of Cheltenham Workhouse from 17 Nov 1848, aged 21;* ***removed to Acton Turville (Chipping Sodbury Union) (father's settlement).*** **1851:** *JI lodged in Lydney (aged 20; mason; born Hatherley) (HO107/2443/558/10).* **1854:** *(RETURNED) JI married for the first time, to Eliza Price 29 Jan: both lived in Rutland Place, Cheltenham.* Note: "James Ivins" delivered to Chipping Sodbury Union 23 Dec 1848 by Jesse Castle. [PS/CH/RA/2/8:97.]

48022RO: 18 Nov 1848 – **Hannah Ivin** (also **Iuens, Iving, Ivins, Ivein, Ivens**). [No examination included with removal order.]
1832: *baptism of HI, daughter of Solomon and Charlotte Ivin, at Norton 25 Mar.* **1841:** *HI removed with family to Acton Turville: see* **48028RO** *(John Ivin: 29 Nov 1848).* **1842:** *(RETURNED) removed to Acton Turville (hiring and service): see* **42019RO** *(SI: 17 Feb).* **1848:** *(RETURNED) HI admitted to Cheltenham Workhouse 12 Sept (G/CH/60/6);* ***removed to Acton Turville (Chipping Sodbury Union (father's settlement).*** [PS/CH/RA/2/8:98. Note: "Hannah Ivins" delivered to Chipping Sodbury Union 23 Dec 1848 by Jesse Castle.]

48023RO: 18 Nov 1848 – **Ann Haskins**, inmate of Cheltenham Workhouse. [No examination included with removal order.]
1848: ***removed to Taynton.*** **1851:** *AH (aged 26; unmarried, born Taynton) was resident "Magdalen(e)" (i.e. former prostitute), along with eleven other young women, in Magdalene Asylum, St Mary's Square, St Mary de Lode, Gloucester (HO107/1961/357/52).* [PS/CH/RA/2/8:99; G/CH/60/5 12 Nov–19 Dec 1848.]

48024RO: Thurs 23 Nov 1848 – **Jane Trew**. [No examination included with removal order.]
1848: *JT admitted to Cheltenham Workhouse late in year (discharged to Leckhampton 24 Dec);* ***removed to Leckhampton (Cheltenham Union).*** **1849:** *(RETURNED) birth of son Thomas William Feb at Cheltenham Workhouse; both remained at workhouse until 20 July (G/CH/60/6).* **1851:** *perhaps the JT (aged 26; unmarried, born Weston-super-Mare, Som) who worked as live-in house servant for Sarah Bingham, gentlewoman, at 4 Park Place, Cheltenham (HO107/1973/913/14); son Thomas (2) lodged with Mary Dowd (73) in York St, Cheltenham (HO107/1973/148/36).* [PS/CH/RA/2/8:100. Note: order of removal delivered to Cheltenham Workhouse 18 Dec 1848 by Thomas Boodle.]

48025RO: Sat 25 Nov 1848 – **James Dominey** (also **Domany, Domeny, Domney**), wife **Jane**, and five children, **James** aged fifteen years, **Emma** aged eleven years, **William** aged six years, **Ellen** aged five years, and **Joseph** aged three years. [No examination included with removal order.]
1841: *JD (aged 50; labourer) lived in Sidney St, Cheltenham with wife Jane (39; charwoman), and children Louisa (14), Amelia (10), James (7), Joshua (4), Emma (2), and William (aged 6 mo) (HO107/353/3/16/27).* **1845:** *removed to Uley (father's settlement): see* **48025RO** *(JD: 25 Nov 1848) for further information (RETURNED).* **1848:** ***removed to Uley (Dursley Union).*** **1851:** *JD (aged 71; born Uley) was an inmate of Dursley Workhouse, with children Emma (13) and William (10; both born Cheltenham) (HO107/1958/414/42).* **1858:** *(RETURNED) death of JD, aged 78, at 10 Clare Place, Cheltenham (buried at New Burial Ground 10 July) (Cheltenham Chron. 13 July).* **1861:** *widow Jane (57; bootmaker, born Bermondsey, Surrey) lived with son Joseph (18; shoemaker, born Cheltenham) and granddaughter Louisa Jane Mathews (4; born Birmingham) at 118 High St, Aston, Birmingham, Warks (RG9/2174/7/7).* **1879:** *death of Jane 21 Jan, at 20 St George's St, Cheltenham, aged 77.* [PS/CH/RA/2/8:101.]

48026RO: Mon 27 Nov 1848 – **Thomas Denley**, wife **Phoebe**, and two children, **Alice** aged about three, and **Mary Ann** aged about 18 months. [No examination included with removal order.]
1848: ***removed to Dursley.*** **1850:** *(RETURNED) death of wife Phoebe in Cheltenham (buried at New Burial Ground, aged 24).* **1851:** *TD (aged 25; widower and shoemaker, born Dursley) lived with two daughters, (Selina) Alice (Ann) (5) and Mary Ann (4; both born Cheltenham) in Upper Bath St, Cheltenham (HO107/1973/872/2); death of Mary Ann in Cheltenham (buried at New Burial Ground 18 Nov, aged 4).*

1851: *remarriage of TD, to Martha Deacon, 21 Sept in Cheltenham, and the couple had several further children.* **1871:** *Alice Denley, from TD's first marriage, married William Ivin, son of Henry Ivin, 14 May: see* **48019RO** *(Henry Ivin: 18 Nov 1848).* [PS/CH/RA/2/8:102.]

48027RO: 27 Nov 1848 – **James Cook**, and wife **Ann**. [No examination included with removal order.]
1848: *removed to Stroud.* [PS/CH/RA/2/8:103.]

48028RO: Wed 29 Nov 1848 – **John Ivin**, wife **Ann**, and three children, **Charles** aged six, **Charlotte** aged four, and **Maria** aged two. [No examination included with removal order.]
1841: *JI (aged 21; labourer) lived with wife Ann (26) and children Piety (2) and Charles (four mo) in Cricklade, Wilts (HO107/1178/4/1); father Solomon Ivin (50; labourer) and his family (Charlotte, 45; Mary, 15; James, 13; and Hannah, 10) lived with him; removed to Acton Turville (father's settlement): see* **41048SE** *(JI: 9 Aug 1841).* **1842:** *(RETURNED) death of daughter Piety in Cheltenham.* **1843:** *death of son Charles in Cheltenham; birth of second son Charles (two younger children also born at Cheltenham).* **1848:** *Ann Ivin (34; charwoman) deserted by husband 1Q and, with Charles, Charlotte, and Maria, entered Cheltenham Workhouse (re-admitted 27 July 1848) (G/CH/60/5);* **removed to Acton Turville (Chipping Sodbury Union).** **1851:** *Maria died at Gloucester (buried 8 Feb); JI (36; labourer, born Cheltenham) lived with wife Ann (38) and children Charles (8), Charlotte (6), and Piety (2) in Deacon St, Gloucester (HO107/1961/347/32).* [PS/CH/RA/2/8:104. Note: "John Ivings Ann his wife and three Childrin" delivered to Chipping Sodbury Union 23 Dec 1848 by Jesse Castle.]

48029RO: Wed 6 Dec 1848 – **Joshua Matthews** (also **Mathews**). [No examination included with removal order.]
1841: *JM and family lived in Park St, Charlton Kings: Joshua (aged 53; labourer), Martha (50), Thomas (24), Samuel (22), Ann (16), Emanuel (15), and Elisha (12) (HO107/353/1/11/16).* **1844:** *death of wife Martha, when family lived in Cheltenham, though she was buried at Charlton Kings on 18 Dec, aged 58).* **1848:** *removed to Charlton Kings.* **1851:** *(RETURNED) JM (66; widower and "day labourer on the road", born Brimscombe near Stroud) lived at 18 Hewlett Rd, Cheltenham with daughter Ann (24; born Stroud) (HO107/1973/52/29).* [PS/CH/RA/2/8:105.]

48030RO: [blank] Dec 1848 – **Mary Jane Draper**. [No examination included with removal order.]
1838: *baptism of MJD at St Mary de Crypt, Gloucester 4 Mar, when parents William (house painter) and Mary Anne Draper lived in St Owen's, Gloucester.* **1848:** *removed to St Owen, Gloucester (as only ten, represented at examination by Elizabeth Gardner (who lived in Cheltenham in 1851: HO107/1973/256/41).* **1859:** *(RETURNED) marriage of MJD to first husband, Charles Frederick Gardner 1Q in Cheltenham.* [PS/CH/RA/2/8:106.]

48031RO: Mon 18 Dec 1848 – **William Cook** (also **Cooke**), and wife **Mary**. [No examination included with removal order.]
1834: *baptism of son John Cook in Painswick 31 Oct.* **1838:** *a WC (aged 40, from Painswick) imprisoned for three months (with hard labour) for stealing 14 poundsweight of lead, at Bristol City Sessions 10 July; he said in excuse that "his family was frequently without food for hours together" (Gloucestershire Chron. 4 Aug).* **1841:** *WC and family lived in Rutland St, Cheltenham: William (60; labourer), Mary (50), Elizabeth (18), Hannah (16), Susan (12), John (9) (HO107/353/7/55/15).* **1842:** *removed to Painswick (apprenticeship): see* **42008RO** *(WC: 20 Jan) (RETURNED).* **1845:** *removed to Painswick (apprenticeship): see* **45070SE** *(WC: 27 Dec) (RETURNED).* **1847:** *removed to Painswick (Stroud Union) (apprenticeship): see* **47013RO** *(WC: Feb) (RETURNED).* **1848:** *removed to Painswick.* **1851:** *(RETURNED) WC (67; broadcloth weaver, born Painswick) lived with wife Mary (60; charwoman, born Painswick) in passage off Sherborne St, Cheltenham (HO107/1973/154/48).* [PS/CH/RA/2/8:107.]

48032RO: Thurs 21 Dec 1848 – **Harriet Saunders** (also **Sanders**), single woman, inmate of Cheltenham Workhouse. [No examination included with removal order.]
1845: *removed to Randwick (father's settlement): see* **45054SE** *(HS: 25 Sept); HS pregnant at examination.* **1846:** *son Charles baptised at Stroud 26 Jan, when HS was an inmate of Stroud Workhouse.* **1848:** *(RETURNED) HS ("houseless & destitute") admitted to Cheltenham Workhouse 11 Dec.* **1849:** *removed to Painswick (Stroud Union).* **1851:** *HS (aged 30; servant and pauper, born Painswick) was an inmate of*

Stroud Workhouse, with son Charles (2) (HO107/1965/298/9). [PS/CH/RA/2/8:108; G/CH/60/5 11 Dec 1848. Note: "Harriet Sanders" delivered to Stroud Workhouse 12 Jan 1849 by Thomas Boodle.]

48033RO: Sat 30 Dec 1848 – **Sophia Gothard** (also **Goddard**), and two children, **Harriet** aged about three years, and **Hannah** aged about six weeks. [No examination included with removal order.]
1848: *removed to Islington, Middlesex (appealed): see* **49022RO** *(SG: Apr 1849) for further information.* [PS/CH/RA/2/8:109. Note: "Appeal".]

48034RO: 30 Dec 1848 – **Mary Ann Lewis**, and unnamed male child, about two weeks old. [No examination included with removal order.]
1848: *MAL admitted ("houseless & destitute") with child to Cheltenham Workhouse 16 Dec (G/CH/60/6); removed to Rodborough.* [PS/CH/RA/2/8:110.]

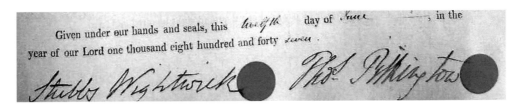

*Each Removal Order had to be authorized by two magistrates, who had also to affix their seal. In this case, Edwin Belcher, his wife, and their six children were removed to Churchdown (**47025RO**). They had previously been removed from Cheltenham to Churchdown in early 1841, after their examination in December 1840 (**40185SE**), but had returned immediately to Lower Alstone, Cheltenham. Between 1845 and 1847 they are recorded in Cheltenham as non-settled residents, paid regular relief from Gloucester (Churchdown was part of the Gloucester Union). Edwin Belcher apparently died in 1850, but the family had again returned to Cheltenham, and the 1851 national census finds them in Alstone Road. The magistrates here were both prominent citizen of Cheltenham, living in circumstances far removed from that of the paupers they examined: Thomas Pilkington had recently become a magistrate, and when he died in 1861 was Chair of the Bench of Cheltenham magistrates; Stubbs Wightwick was a magistrate and Deputy Lieutenant, who lived at Capel Court (now Malden Court), Pittville.*

1849

49001RO: Mon 1 Jan 1849 – **Robert Page**, wife **Hannah**, and daughter **Elizabeth** aged four months. [No examination included with removal order.]
1849: *removed to Leckhampton.* **1851:** *(RETURNED) the family lived at 5 Major's Row, Alstone, Cheltenham: RP (aged 23; labourer, Hannah (27; both born Charlton Kings), Elizabeth (2) and Susannah (4 mo; both born Cheltenham); birth of daughter registered at Cheltenham 1Q.* Note: "Robert Page" delivered to Cheltenham Workhouse 23 Jan 1849 by Thomas Boodle. [PS/CH/RA/2/8:111.]

49002RO: 1 Jan 1849 – **Thomas Baylis**, wife **Harriet**, and two children **Caroline** aged three years, and **Emma** aged five weeks. [No examination included with removal order.]
1847-9: *TB (47; labourer, suffering ill health, houseless and destitute) was a regular inmate of Cheltenham Workhouse with wife Harriet (33), and children Mary Ann (6) and Caroline (2) (G/CH/60/5 4Q 1847, etc).* **1849:** *removed to Lower Slaughter; TB received relief from Prestbury 2 Aug.* **1851:** *TB (aged 50; agricultural labourer, born Lower Slaughter) lived with wife Harriet (35; born Chosen [=Churchdown]), Mary Ann (9; born Cheltenham), Caroline (5; born Chosen), Emma (2; born Cheltenham, all three scholars), and Thomas's father John (79; pauper, born Lower Slaughter (HO107/1970/281/45) in Stow-on-the-Wold (registration district for Lower Slaughter).* [PS/CH/RA/2/8:112.]

49003RO: Sat 6 Jan 1849 – **George Hopcroft**, and wife **Ann**. [No examination included with removal order.]
1849: *removed to St Marylebone, Middlesex.* **1849:** *George and Ann Hopcroft (aged 61 and 60 respectively) admitted to Marylebone Workhouse 31 Jan "from Cheltenham" (discharged 10 Feb).* **1851:** *the couple lived at 11 Orchand Lane, Southampton, Hants: GH (63 labourer, born Westminster) and Ann (62; born Battersea, Surrey) (HO107/1669/590/30).* [PS/CH/RA/2/8:113.]

49004RO: Wed 10 Jan 1849 – **William Hilyer** (also **Helier**, **Hillyer**), wife **Maria**, and son **Robert** aged five months. [No examination included with removal order.]
1849: *removed to St Mary Magdalene, Taunton, Som.* **1850:** *(RETURNED) birth of daughter Sarah Maria registered at Cheltenham 2Q.* **1851:** *WH (aged 27; flyman, born Taunton, Som) lived with wife Maria (24; "at home", born Cheltenham), and children Robert (2; born Staffs) and (Sarah) Maria (11 months; born Cheltenham) "near Lansdown Crescent", Cheltenham (HO107/1973/1018/46).* **1861:** *the family lived at 1 Britannia Place, Fairview, Cheltenham (RG9/1798/72/40).* [PS/CH/RA/2/8:114.]

49005RO: Mon 15 Jan 1849 – **Joseph Tew,** and wife **Hannah**. [No examination included with removal order.]
1849: *removed to Middleton on the Hill, Heref.* **1851:** *(RETURNED) JT (aged 24; labourer, born Eastington, near Stroud) lived with wife Hannah (20; born Charlton Kings) at 4 Lawrence Court (or Passage), Exmouth St, Cheltenham (HO107/1973/854/13).* **1861:** *the couple lived at 6 Naunton Crescent, Cheltenham, as brickmaker and laundress respectively (RG9/1803/55/16).* [PS/CH/RA/2/8:115.]

49006RO: Tues 16 Jan 1849 – **Thomas Simmons** (also **Simmonds),** and wife **Ann**. [No examination included with removal order.]
1849: *removed to Topsham, Devon (stated settlement) (appealed): see* **50030RO** *(wife Ann Simmons: 2 Nov 1850) for further information on family.* [PS/CH/RA/2/8:116.]

49007RO: 16 Jan 1849 – **Rachel Thornton,** inmate of Cheltenham Workhouse. [No examination included with removal order.]
1841: *James Thornton (aged 40; ostler) lived with wife Rachel (35) in Mount Pleasant, Cheltenham (HO107/353/6/15/25).* **1849:** *removed to St Peter-in-the-East, Oxford, Oxon: 12 Feb (G/CH/60/6); death of RT in Headington, Oxford 4Q.* **1851:** *James Thornton (50; horse-keeper, born St-Peter-in-the-East, Oxford) lived at 17 King St, St Peter-in-the-East, Oxford, with mother, sister, brother-in-law, and nephew (HO107/1728/23/39).* **1855:** *death of James Thornton (buried at St Peter-in-'the-East, Oxford 20 July, aged 55).* [PS/CH/RA/2/8:117; G/CH/60/5 3 Dec. 1848.]

49008RO: Thurs 25 Jan 1849 – **John Davies** (also **Davis**)**,** wife **Ann**, and four children, **George** aged eight years, **William** aged five years, **Dinah** aged three years, and **Enos Walter** aged about four months. [No examination included with removal order.]
1849: *removed to Dumbleton (Winchcombe Union).* **1850:** *death of JD in Winchcombe Workhouse (buried at Dumbleton 6 May, aged 31); death of widow Ann at Dumbleton (buried there on 13 Dec, aged 29).* **1851:** *children George (9), William (6), and Dinah (4; all born Dumbleton) inmates of Winchcombe Union Workhouse.* [PS/CH/RA/2/8:118.]

49009RO: 25 Jan 1849 – **Eleanor Shadwell,** inmate of Cheltenham Workhouse. [No examination included with removal order.]
1849: *removed to Melksham, Wilts: 19 Feb.* **1851:** *ES (aged 19) worked as servant on farm in Melksham (HO107/1840/102/16).* [PS/CH/RA/2/8:119; G/CH/60/5 11 Jan 1849. Note: "Elin Shadwell" delivered to Melksham, Wilts 17 Feb 1849 by Jesse Castle.]

49010RO: 25 Jan 1849 – **Thomas Moss.** [No examination included with removal order.]
1849: *removed to Coberley (Cheltenham Union).* **1869:** *perhaps the TM, absent from Cheltenham for 1851 and 1861 censuses, who, as bachelor and labourer, married widow and laundress Eleanor Dix at Charlton Kings 5 Jan.* **1892:** *(RETURNED) TM died at Cheltenham Union Workhouse (buried 1 Mar, aged 79).* [PS/CH/RA/2/8:120.]

49011RO: Tues 30 Jan 1849 – **Reuben Yates** (also **Yeates**)**,** wife **Margaret**, and three children. [No examination included with removal order.]
1841: *RY (aged 30; journeyman shoemaker) lived with wife Margaret (35) and her three children from former marriage to carpenter William Gaze (buried 12 Jan 1834 at Churchdown, aged 30) in Exmouth St, Cheltenham (HO107/353/12/38/12); removed to Upton St Leonards (apprenticeship): see* **41047SE** *(RY: 2 Aug 1841) (RETURNED).* **1846:** *removed to Upton St Leonard's (apprenticeship): see* **46012RO** *(RY: 28/30 Feb 1846) (RETURNED).* **1849:** *removed to Upton St Leonards.* **1851:** *(RETURNED) the family lived in Gloucester Rd ("near the station"), Cheltenham: RY (44; cordwainer, born Churchdown), Margaret (52; born Hereford), Ann Gaze (20; servant), Martha Gaze (15; servant), as well as their own children Solomon (10) and Mary Ann (8) (HO107/1973/1004/18); Caroline Gaze (20) worked as servant to Robert Askwith, GP, in Montpellier Grove, Cheltenham (HO107/1973/1069/15) (both children born Cheltenham, and baptised from Exmouth St in 1852 and 1853 respectively); the children by Margaret Yates's former husband all born Churchdown.* [PS/CH/RA/2/8:121. See **46016RO** (wife Margaret Yates: 5/7 Mar 1846).]

49012RO: Sat 3 Feb 1849 – **Ann Patterson** (also **Paterson**)**.** [No examination included with removal order.]
1849: *removed to Tewkesbury: see* **50039RO** *(AP: 26 Dec 1850) for further information.* [PS/CH/RA/2/8:122.]

49013RO: Fri 2 Feb 1849 – **Charlotte Thackwell.** [No examination included with removal order.]
1841: *CT (age given as 50; shopkeeper) lived with son George Thackwell (27; watchmaker) and family in College St, St Nicholas, Gloucester (HO107/379/10/18/30).* **1849:** *removed to St Nicholas, Gloucester.* **1851:** *(RETURNED) George Thackwell (37; watchmaker, born Gloucester) lived with his family at 1 Grosvenor St, Cheltenham (HO107/1973/212/4).* [PS/CH/RA/2/8:123.]

49014RO: Mon 5 Feb 1849 – **Maria Vincent,** and child aged two years. [No examination included with removal order.]
1849: *removed to Christchurch, Hants.* [PS/CH/RA/2/8:124. Note: "Maria Vincent and Child" delivered to Christchurch, Hants 28 Feb 1849 by Jesse Castle.]

49015RO: Sat 10 Feb 1849 – **William Sparrow,** and wife **Sarah**. [No examination included with removal order.]
1849: *removed to Avening.* **1851:** *(RETURNED) WS (aged 55; labourer, born Avening) lived with wife Sarah (47; born Rodborough) at 5 Lawrence Court (or Passage), Exmouth St, Cheltenham, with Sarah's mother Judith Shelton (74; pauper) (HO107/1973/854/13).* [PS/CH/RA/2/8:125. See **43040RO** (mother-in-law Judith Shelton: 8 May 1843). The Sparrows lived next-door to the Tews (see **49005** Joseph Tew: 15 Jan 1849).]

49016RO: Fri 2 Mar 1849 – **Thomas Greening** (also **Grinning**), wife **Elizabeth** (also **Betty**), and four children **Maria** aged fourteen, **Eliza** aged eleven, **Charles** aged seven, and **Mary Ann** aged four. [No examination included with removal order.]
1849: *removed to Badgeworth.* **1850**: *(RETURNED) TG and wife Elizabeth ("destitute") admitted to Cheltenham Workhouse 3 Jan (discharged 10 Mar) (G/CH/60/6).* **1851**: *the family lived at 23 Commercial St, Cheltenham: TG (aged 45; labourer, born Withington), Elizabeth (50; born Old Sodbury), and children Maria (15; born Badgeworth), Eliza (13; born Cheltenham), Charles (9), and Mary Ann (5; four children "at home", last three "scholars"; last two born Leckhampton (HO107/1973/893/44).* [PS/CH/RA/2/8:126.]

49017RO: Wed 7 Mar 1849 – **Thomas Compton,** wife **Ann**, and six children, **Ann** aged twelve, **George** aged ten, **Jane** aged eight, **Thomas** aged five, **Eliza** aged two and **Emma** aged six months. [No examination included with removal order.]
1812: *baptism of TC at St Peter's, St Albans 13 Sept.* **1849**: *removed to St Peter, St Albans, Herts.* **1851**: *children George (12), Jane (10), Thomas (8), and Eliza (6; all scholars, born Cheltenham) were inmates of St Albans Union Workhouse (HO107/1713/528/3); father, widower, lived at 19 New Rd, Chelsea, London: TC (39; labourer, born St Albans) (HO107/1474/31/55).* [PS/CH/RA/2/8:127.]

49018RO: Mon 12 Mar 1849 – **Thomas Wilkins,** and wife **Susan**. [No examination included with removal order.]
1849: *removed to Hasfield (abandoned): see* **49021RO** *(TW: 24 Mar 1849) for further information.* [PS/CH/RA/2/8:128. Note: "Abandoned".]

49019RO: 12 Mar 1849 – **Martha Hayward.** [No examination included with removal order.]
1839: *removed to Nantmel, Radnorshire (hiring and service): see* **39016SE** *(MH: 12 Feb) for further information.* **1841**: *probably the MH (age recorded as 70) who lived in East St, Rhayader (nr Nantmel), Radnorshire (HO107/1458/12/4/3).* **1849**: *(RETURNED) removed to Nantmel, Radnorshire.* [PS/CH/RA/2/8:129.]

49020RO: Thurs 22 Mar 1849 – **Sophia Gothard,** and two children, **Harriet** aged about three, and **Hannah** aged about four months. [No examination included with removal order.]
1849: *removed to St Andrew Holborn above the Bars, Middlesex (previously appealed): see* **49022RO** *(SG: Apr 1849) for further information.* [PS/CH/RA/2/8:130.]

49021RO: Sat 24 Mar 1849 – **Thomas Wilkins,** and wife **Susan**. [No examination included with removal order.]
1846: *removed to Haresfield (hiring and service): see* **46028RO** *(TW: 16 May 1846) (RETURNED).* **1849**: *removed to Hasfield (abandoned): see* **49018RO** *(TW: 12 Mar); removed to Haresfield.* **1851**: *(probably RETURNED) a Susan Wilkins (45; labourer) lived in Gloucester St, Cheltenham (husband absent on census night) (HO107/1973/514/7).* **1852**: *a TW died at Cheltenham Workhouse (buried 20 Mar, aged 68) (Cheltenham Chron. 17 Mar).* [PS/CH/RA/2/8:131.]

49022RO: [blank] Apr 1849 – **Sophia Gothard,** inmate of Cheltenham Workhouse, and two children, **Harriet** aged about three years, and **Hannah** aged about four months. [No examination included with removal order.]
1841: *SG (aged 6) lived with parents Richard Gothard (28; cooper) and Sophia (29), and brother Richard (2) in Portland St, Walworth, Surrey (HO107/1064/5/47/42).* **1844**: *presumed death of mother Sophia Gothard in Poplar, Middlesex (buried there 17 Sept, aged 25).* **1845**: *daughter Harriet born at Newington, Surrey 3Q, when SG very young.* **1848**: *SG ("deserted by husband", though unmarried) and Harriet admitted to Cheltenham Workhouse 26 June; removed to Islington, Middlesex (appealed): see* **48033RO** *(SG: 30 Dec).* **1849**: *second daughter, Hannah, born at Cheltenham Workhouse Feb; removed to St Andrew Holborn above the Bars, Middlesex: see* **49020RO** *(SG: 22 Mar); removed to the Liberty of Saffron Hill, Hatton Garden and Ely Rents, Middlesex.* **1851**: *SG (17; born Newington, lived with widowed father Richard Gothard (38; wine cooper, born St Andrew's, Middlesex), brother Richard (12; brush maker) and daughter Harriet (4; scholar, both born Newington) in St Peter, Walworth, Surrey (HO107/1567/92/11).* **1853**: *SG married Samuel Priest at St Paul's, Hammersmith 28 July, giving age as 21.* **1861**: *father Richard (40; cellarman, born City of London) was patient in Guy's Hospital (RG9/316/155/8).* [PS/CH/RA/2/8:132; G/CH/60/5 2Q 1849.]

1849 – **Emma** and **Sarah Stratford.** [Only Emma Stratford was examined; no examination included with removal order.]
1836: *ES removed from Leckhampton to Miserden with father, John Stratford, and rest of family (see* PS/CH/RA/2/2:77 *Cheltenham Petty Sessions register).* **1841:** *the family lived in Leckhampton* (HO107/353/18/51/6). **1849:** *removed to Miserden (father's settlement).* **1851:** *(RETURNED) ES lived at 46 Stanhope St, Cheltenham (aged 16; house servant, born Leckhampton) (HO107/1973/502/24); sister Sarah likely to be the Sarah Stratford (12; born Glos) working in labourers' lodging-house in Barnstaple, Devon (HO107/1892/310/7).* [PS/CH/RA/2/8:133.]

49024RO: 26 Apr 1849 – **Charles Dodson,** and wife **Sarah**. [No examination included with removal order.]
1849: *removed to Brinkworth, Wilts.* **1851:** *(RETURNED) CD (aged 59; shoemaker, born Brinkworth, Wilts) lived with wife Sarah (29; shoe-binder, born Cricklade, Wilts) at 59 Sherborne St, Cheltenham (HO107/1973/153/46).* [PS/CH/RA/2/8:134.]

49025RO: Tues 1 May [written April] 1849 – **Elizabeth Wood,** inmate of Cheltenham Workhouse, and daughter, **Ellen** aged seven weeks. [No examination included with removal order.]
1849: *removed to Painswick: see* **50028RO** *(EW: 26 Aug) for further information.* [PS/CH/RA/2/8:135; G/CH/60/5.]

49026RO: Fri 4 May 1849 – **Ann Wood,** single woman. [No examination included with removal order.]
1849: *removed to Sevenhampton.* [PS/CH/RA/2/8:136.]

49027RO: Sat 12 May 1849 – **Sarah Browning,** single woman. [No examination included with removal order.]
1841: *SB (aged 50) lived with brother Moses Browning (55; gardener) at 4 York St, Cheltenham (HO107/353/5/47/17).* **1845:** *removed to Woodchester (father's presumed settlement): see* **45042SE** *(SB: 14 July 1845).* **1845-6:** *(RETURNED) from 3Q 1845 until 4Q 1846 SB (66) received parish relief from Stroud as a non-settled resident of Cheltenham (G/CH/9d/1).* **1849:** *removed to Woodchester (Stroud Union).* **1851:** *(RETURNED) SB (70; unmarried, washerwoman, born Woodchester) lived with brother Moses (75; gardener and widower) at same address in Cheltenham (HO107/1973/145/31).* [PS/CH/RA/2/8:137.]

49028RO: [blank] May 1849 – **Eliza Woodward,** and five children [not named]. [No examination included with removal order.]
1841: *EW lived with family in Hailes: John Woodward (aged 55; labourer), Eliza (34), Emma (14), Harriet (12), Charles (9; labourer), William (7), John (10 mo) (HO107/360/10/5/7).* **1849:** *removed to [blank]: removal uncertain.* **1851:** *EW (also Louisa) (46; born Blockley, Worcs) lived with husband John (70; pauper, born Stanton), and four children, Charles (18), William (16; both agricultural labourers), John (10), Charlotte (5; all born Hailes) in Gloucester St, Winchcombe (HO107/1971/105/45).* [PS/CH/RA/2/8:138. Note: Index to register includes "Woodward Jno wife & fam [Order No] 191, but order (dating to Feb or Mar 1850) cut out of register.]

49029RO: Thurs 17 May 1849 – **Robert Robbins** (also **Robins),** and wife **Mary**. [No examination included with removal order.]
1848: *probably Robert Robins, shoemaker, who married Mary Anne Smith at Cheltenham 3 Sept.* **1849:** *removed to Chedworth.* **1861-:** *(RETURNED) RR lived alone in St Paul's St South, Cheltenham from at least 1861 until 1881 (in 1861 place of birth "Chedworth") (RG9/1799/15/24), though in other censuses, including 1841, he is said to be Irish.* [PS/CH/RA/2/8:139. See **42069RO** (father Robert Robbins: 3 Sept 1842).]

49030RO: 17 May 1849 – **Emma Jones,** aged about sixteen years; also Rosetta Whiting, relating to the settlement of Emma Jones. [No examinations included with removal order.]
1849: *removed to St Mary, Lambeth, Surrey; Emma Jones admitted to Cheltenham Workhouse 18 May, aged 14, "houseless & destitute" (G/CH/60/5/6).* [PS/CH/RA/2/8:140.]

49031RO: Fri 8 June 1849 – **John Powers,** wife **Sarah**, and three children, **Thomas** aged twelve years, **James** aged eight and **William** aged four. [No examination included with removal order.]

1841: *baptism of son James 3 Jan, when family lived in Bath St, Cheltenham; removed to Brockworth (hiring and service): see* **49031RO** *(JP: 8 June); (6 June) the Powers family lived in Little Norwood St, Leckhampton: JP (aged 35; labourer), Sarah (30), Mary (11), George (7), Thomas (4), and James (1) (RETURNED).* **1849:** *removed to Brockworth (Gloucester Union).* **1851:** *JP (aged 56; agricultural labourer, born Luddington, Warks) lived with wife Sarah (50; born Brockworth), and children Thomas (13), James (10; both born Brockworth, and William (6; born Cheltenham) at "Cottage on Charlton Common", Charlton Kings (HO107/1972/175/11).* [PS/CH/RA/2/8:141. Note: "Wife and three Children of John Powers" delivered to Gloucester Union 20 Aug 1849 by Jesse Castle.]

49032RO: Sat 23 June 1849 – **Samuel Hall**, wife **Emma**, and three children, **William** aged ten, **Benjamin** aged six, and **Henry** aged three months. [No examination included with removal order.]
1849: *removed to Charlton Abbots.* **1851:** *SH (aged 39; slater and plasterer, born Charlton Abbots) lived with wife Emma (40; seamstress, born Prestbury) with children William (11; agricultural labourer, born Lower Guiting), Benjamin (7; born Hawling), and Henry (2; born Cheltenham; both "at home") in Prestbury (HO107/1972/63/23).* [PS/CH/RA/2/8:142. Note: "in respect of relief made necessary by sickness".]

49033RO: Thurs 5 July 1849 – **Thomas Simmons** (also **Simmonds**), and wife **Ann**. [No examination included with removal order.]
1849: *removed to Shaugh, Devon (father's settlement): see* **50030RO** *(wife Ann Simmons: 2 Nov 1850) for further information on family.* [PS/CH/RA/2/8:143. Note: "in respect of relief made necessary by the sickness of the said Thomas Simmons".]

49034RO: Thurs 19 July 1849 – **William Williams**, wife **Caroline**, and three children, **Caroline** aged about seventeen, **Frederick** aged about fourteen and **Clara** aged about six. [No examination included with removal order.]
1849: *removed to St Nicholas, Bristol.* **1851:** *(RETURNED) Caroline Williams (aged 41; born Thornbury) lived at 6 Berkeley Ave, Winchcombe St, Cheltenham with son Frederick (16; born Dursley) and daughter Clara (8; born Worcester) (HO107/1973/173/31); husband William absent on census night.* **1853:** *daughter Caroline married to Robert Bradshaw, receiver of taxes, at St Andrew, Clifton 22 June.* **1857:** *death of WW, aged 72, brewer, 18 Sept, at Kemble Berwery, Fairview St, Cheltenham, "after a protracted illness" (Cheltenham Mercury 19 Sept).* **1871:** *both daughters had married well, and widow Caroline Williams, living with Clara and son-in-law William Spencer in Birmingham, styled herself "annuitant" (RG10/3098/68/24).* [PS/CH/RA/2/8:144. Note: "in respect of relief made necessary by sickness of the said William Williams".]

49035RO: Thurs 2 Aug 1849 – **Elizabeth Bourne** (also **Bourn**), single woman, and son, **William** aged about six; also Thomas Bourne, relating to the settlement of [daughter] Elizabeth Bourne. [No examination included with removal order.]
1849: *EB and infant daughter removed to Ledbury, Heref (father's presumed settlement):* 23 Aug *(G/CH/60/6).* **1851:** *EB (aged 24; born Ledbury, Heref) worked as servant (without son) in Balsall Heath, Birmingham, Warks (HO107/2048/225/24); father Thomas Bourne lived in Birmingham with second wife and family (HO107/2048/202/42).* [PS/CH/RA/2/8:145.]

49036RO: Mon 6 Aug 1849 – **Frances Smith**, single woman. [To the Churchwardens and Overseers of Temple Guiting] Take notice that the Grounds of such Removal are, - That the said pauper Frances Smith is legally settled in your said parish of Temple Guiting by birth for that she the said Pauper was on or about the 11th December in the year 1799 born at Ford in your said parish of Temple Guiting in a house then rented and occupied by her father William Smith   That the said Frances Smith was the legitimate child of William Smith and which said William Smith at the time of her birth was legally settled at Temple Guiting aforesaid by being then and there the owner and occupier of freehold land at Ford aforesaid to the value of One hundred pounds and upwards

   That the said William Smith was at the same time legally settled in the said parish of Temple Guiting by renting and occupying a tenement in the same place consisting of a messuage and land of the Yearly value of Ten pounds and upwards and by residing upon the same tenement for Forty days and upwards after the birth of the said pauper – viz. until his death which happened in the year 1806   That the said pauper derives a settlement from her said father and has never done any Act to gain a legal settlement in her own right

1849: *removed to Temple Guiting (father's settlement).* **1851:** *(RETURNED) FS (aged 52; dressmaker, born Ford (near Temple Guiting) and lodged at 41 St James St, Cheltenham (HO107/1973/220/20).* [PS/CH/RA/2/8:146; text from Temple Guiting records at P157/OV3/3/1 (no examination included with Cheltenham removal order). Note: "Francis [*sic*] Smith" delivered to Winchcombe Union 28 Aug 1849 by Jesse Castle.]

49037RO: Thurs 16 Aug 1849 – **Edith Lewis**, widow. [No examination included with removal order.]
1849: *removed to Rodborough.* **1851:** *Edith Lewis (aged 71; widow, woollen-worker (spinner), and pauper, born Rodborough) lived alone in Butterrow, Rodborough (HO107/1965/436/11).* [PS/CH/RA/2/8:147.]

49038RO: 16 Aug 1849 – **(Sarah) Matilda Pimbery**, widow, inmate of Cheltenham Workhouse, and four children, **Anna Maria** (also **Hannah**) aged eight, **Emma** aged six, **Sarah** aged four, and **Charles** aged one and a half. [No examination included with removal order.]
1849: *removed to Rodborough (abandoned):* see **49044RO** *(SMP: 6 Sept 1849) for further information on SMP and family.* [PS/CH/RA/2/8:148; G/CH/60/5 31 July 1849. Note: "Order not made".]

49039RO: Sat 18 Aug 1849 – **James Wright**. [No examination included with removal order.]
1848: *JW (27; labourer, sick, houseless and destitute) admitted as an inmate of Cheltenham Workhouse with wife Mary (20) and child James (18 mo) 1Q (G/CH/60/5).* **1849:** *removed to St Philip and St Jacob, Bristol.* [PS/CH/RA/2/8:149.]

49040RO: Mon 27 Aug 1849 – **Mary Morfett** (also **Moffat**), and three children, **John** aged about 13, **Henry** aged about twelve, and **Jane** aged about four. [No examination included with removal order.]
1847: *MM (36; charwoman and widow, houseless and destitute) admitted to Cheltenham Workhouse with three children John (10), Henry (9), and Jane (2) late in year; she was removed to Gloucester Lunatic Asylum 18 Oct (G/CH/60/5).* **1849:** *removed to St Pancras, Middlesex (abandoned).* **1851:** *Mary Moffat (aged 44; widow and "house labourer", born Westerham, Kent) lived at 4 Taylor's Passage, Cheltenham with son Henry (13) and daughter Jane (6; both scholars) (HO107/1973/628/21).* [PS/CH/RA/2/8:150. Note: "Abandoned TG".]

49041RO: Tues 28 Aug 1849 – **Elizabeth Burdock**, single woman; also Lydia Tustin, in relation to the settlement of Elizabeth Burdock. [No examination included with removal order.]
1849: *removed to Painswick.* **1851:** *EB (aged 36; pauper, born Painswick) lodged in Pig St, Painswick (HO107/1964/186/4).* [PS/CH/RA/2/8:151. EB chargeable to Cheltenham through sickness.]

49042RO: 28 Aug 1849 – **Elizabeth King**. [No examination included with removal order.]
1849: *removed to Munsley, Heref; EK admitted to Cheltenham Workhouse 29 Aug, aged 17. (G/CH/60/5).* [PS/CH/RA/2/8:152.]

49043RO: Sat 1 Sept 1849 – **Fanny Kingsley**, and two children, **Mary Ann** aged about two, and **Fanny** aged about six months. [No examination included with removal order.]
1849: *husband William Kingsley (formerly shoemaker) held at Northleach House of Correction as army deserter 3 July "awaiting a route" (i.e. orders to travel to rejoin his regiment); removed to Malmesbury, Wilts.* **c1855:** *(RETURNED) birth of daughter Fanny at Cheltenham (as were two subsequent children).* **1860:** *death of Sergeant Kingsley (buried at Cheltenham 21 Jan).* **1861:** *FK (36; widow and dressmaker, born Malmesbury, Wilts) lived at 8 Union St, Cheltenham with mother Mary Russell (60; widow, born Bradford-on-Avon, Wilts) and five children Mary (Ann) (13; born Cirencester), Fanny (11), William (6), George (4), and John (2; all four born Cheltenham) (RG9/1803/104/21* [PS/CH/RA/2/8:153.]

49044RO: Thurs 6 Sept 1849 – **Sarah Matilda Pimbery**, inmate in Cheltenham Workhouse, and four children **Anna Maria** aged eight, **Emma** aged six, **Sarah** aged four, and **Charles** aged 18 months. [No examination included with removal order.]
1849: *SMP and four children admitted to Cheltenham Workhouse 31 July; removed to Rodborough (abandoned):* see **49038RO** *(SMP: 16 Aug 1849); removed to Rodborough (Stroud Union):* 1 Oct. **1851:** *SMP (aged 35; married, servant, born Bisley) was an inmate of Stroud Workhouse with children Hannah (9; born Rodborough), Emma (8; born Minchinhampton), Sarah (6; born Canterbury, Kent), and Charles (3; born Rodborough) (HO107/1965/300/13).* [PS/CH/RA/2/8:154; G/CH/60/5.]

49045RO: Thurs 20 Sept 1849 – **Jane Ball**, and two children, **Susan** aged about two and a half, and **William George** aged about three months; also Ann Paish, relating to the settlement of Jane Ball. [No examination included with removal order.]
1848: *husband William Ball (groom) killed when hit by Great Western engine from Gloucester at Hatherley Bridge Sept* (Gloucester Journal *23 Sept*) *(buried at Cheltenham 18 Sept, aged 26).* **1849:** *removed to Bisley.* **1851:** *JB (25; widow and agricultural labourer, on parish relief, born Edgeworth) lived with children Susanna (4) and William (1; both born Cheltenham) in Bisley (HO107/1964/352/8).* **1859:** *reviewed at subsequent examination in Cheltenham 9 Feb.* [PS/CH/RA/2/8:155.]

49046RO: 20 Sept 1849 – **Thomas Bright**, and wife **Mary Ann**. [No examination included with removal order.]
1849: *removed to St Peter and St Paul, Bath, Som.* **1850:** *perhaps the TB (French polisher) who died after suffering from "Consumption" for fifteen months, at Westgate Buildings in St Peter & St Paul, Bath on 9 June (buried 14 June, aged 49).* **1859:** *reviewed at subsequent examination in Cheltenham (perhaps indicating return of wife to Cheltenham).* [PS/CH/RA/2/8:156. Note: TB chargeable to Cheltenham through sickness.]

49047RO: Sat 22 Sept 1849 – **Martha Webber**, and son **William** aged six years. [No examination included with removal order.]
1841: *MW (aged 30; sempstress) lived with mother Hannah Driver (60; sempstress) in Witcombe Place, Cheltenham (HO107/353/4/29/22).* **1843:** *removed to St James, Bath (apprenticeship): see* **43010RO** *(MW: 6 Feb); illegitimate son William baptised at St James, Bath 26 July, while in St James's Place, Bath (though apparently born Cheltenham) (RETURNED).* **1849:** *removed to St James, Bath, Som.* **1851:** *(RETURNED) the family lived in Swindon Place, Cheltenham: Hannah Driver (67; born Painswick), Martha Webber (41; dressmaker, born Bath), and William Webber (8) (HO107/1973/425/16).* [PS/CH/RA/2/8:157. Note: "Martha Webber and her child" delivered to Bath 15 Dec 1849 by William Cole. See **47038RO** (mother Hannah Driver: 11 Sept 1847).]

49048RO: 22 Sept 1849 – **William Purnell**, and wife **Mary**. [No examination included with removal order.]
1849: *removed to Rodborough.* **1851:** *(RETURNED) WP (aged 78; in receipt of parish relief) lived with wife Mary (74; weaver; both born Stroud) in Commercial St, Cheltenham (HO107/1973/889/37).* [PS/CH/RA/2/8:158.]

49049RO: Thurs 4 Oct 1849 – **Frances Cockerill** (also **Cockerell**, **Cockrell**, **Cockrill**), and two children, **Martha** aged about 13, and **Fanny** aged about 11; also John Cockerill, relating to the settlement of sister-in-law, Frances Cockerell. [No examination included with removal order.]
1833: *marriage of Frances Fletcher to William Cockerill at All Saints & St John, Hertford, Herts 11 Mar.* **1849:** *removed to Hertingfordbury, Herts (husband's presumed settlement).* **1851:** *(RETURNED) FC (aged 42; married, and needleworker) lived with two daughters, Martha (17; attending as teacher at school), and Fanny (13; at school; all three born Cheltenham) at 17 Newman's Place, Cheltenham (HO107/1973/636/37).* [PS/CH/RA/2/8:159.]

49050RO: Sat 6 Oct 1849 – **Thomas Sadler**. [No examination included with removal order.]
1849: *removed to Uckington.* **1850:** *(RETURNED) death of TS in Cheltenham (buried at Elmstone Hardwicke 4 Apr, aged 78).* [PS/CH/RA/2/8:160.]

49051RO: Wed 10 Oct 1849 – **Caroline Moss**, single woman; also Henry Moss, relating to the settlement of daughter Caroline Moss. [No examination included with removal order.]
1840: *family removed to Painswick (father's settlement), including CM, aged 8: see* **40075SE** *(father Henry Moss: 11 July) (RETURNED).* **1849:** *CM ("houseless & destitute") admitted to Cheltenham Workhouse 11 Oct; removed to Painswick (Stroud Union) (father's settlement): 29 Nov (G/CH/60/6).* **1851:** *perhaps the CM (aged 22; unmarried, born "Wilts, Chelenham [sic]", an inmate of the Penitentiary at Lyncombe, Walcot, Bath, Som (HO107/1942/476/48).* [PS/CH/RA/2/8:161.]

49052RO: Thurs 11 Oct 1849 – **Elizabeth Pitt**; also John Pitt, relating to the settlement of Elizabeth Pitt. [No examination included with removal order.]
1849: *removed to Bagendon (father's presumed settlement).* [PS/CH/RA/2/8:162.]

49053RO: Sat 13 Oct 1849 – **Sarah Mason**. [No examination included with removal order.]
1849: *removed to Cowley.* **1851:** *(probably RETURNED) probably the SM (aged 31; born Cowley) who lived as housemaid at 25 Cambray, Cheltenham (HO107/1973/757/15).* [PS/CH/RA/2/8:163.]

49054RO: 13 Oct 1849 – **Mary Attwood**. [No examination included with removal order.]
1849: *removed to Uckington.* [PS/CH/RA/2/8:164.]

49055RO: 13 Oct 1849 – **Emma Hodges**, inmate of Cheltenham Workhouse; also Mary Ann Hodges, relating to the settlement of Emma Hodges. [No examination included with removal order.]
1849: *EH (aged 21) admitted to Cheltenham Workhouse 23 Sept;* **removed to Rodborough.** **1861:** *EH (28; woollen cloth worker, born Stroud) lived with parents in Rodborough (RG9/1776/103/20).* [PS/CH/RA/2/8:165; G/CH/60/5.]

49056RO: Wed 17 Oct 1849 – Ann Aldridge, relating to the settlement of niece **Emma Roberts**, single woman, inmate of Cheltenham Workhouse. [No examination included with removal order.]
1849: *removed to Churchdown (Gloucester Union).* **1851:** *ER (aged 23; servant, born Churchdown) was a pauper inmate of Gloucester Union Workhouse (HO107/1961/470/9).* [PS/CH/RA/2/8:166; G/CH/60/5 11 Oct 1849.]

49057RO: Sat 20 Oct 1849 – **Caroline Darke** (also **Dark**), widow, and daughter **Sarah Ann**; also William Darke, relating to the settlement of son, John Darke, late husband of Caroline Darke. [No examination included with removal order.]
1849: *removed to Stoke Orchard (husband's presumed settlement): see* **50024RO** *(second husband William Bartlett: 13 July 1850) for further information on the family.* [PS/CH/RA/2/8:167.]

490575RO: Mon 22 Oct 1849 – **Alice Kirby**, widow. [No examination included with removal order.]
1850: *removed to Stanley Pontlarge (Winchcombe Union).* **1855:** *an AK (aged 87) died at 11 Corpus Street, Cheltenham on 3 July (buried 6 July).* [PS/CH/RA/2/8:168.]

49058RO: Sat 27 Oct 1849 – **Hannah Marsden**. [No examination included with removal order.]
1849: *an Emma Marsden (aged 22) admitted to Cheltenham Workhouse 22 Oct and 4 Nov, when she gave birth to child.* **1850:** *removed to Churchdown: 12 Feb (G/CH/60/5/6).* [PS/CH/RA/2/8:169. Note: delivered to Gloucester Union on 9 Feb 1850 by Thomas Griffiths.]

49059RO: 27 Oct 1849 – **Jane Stephens**, and child, **Emma**, aged about seven weeks; also William Stephens, relating to the settlement of Jane Stephens. [No examination included with removal order.]
1849: *daughter Emma died at 8 weeks (buried at Cheltenham 9 Nov);* **removed to Orleton, Heref (father's presumed settlement).** [PS/CH/RA/2/8:170.]

49060RO: Sat 10 Nov 1849 – **Harriet Voules**, and five children, **Elizabeth** aged fourteen years, **Edward** aged ten years, **William** aged six years, **Harriet** aged four years, and **Eliza** aged three months. [No examination included with removal order.]
1849: *removed to All Souls, Bristol.* [PS/CH/RA/2/8:171. Note: "Voules and her five children" delivered to St Mary's Hospital, Bristol 7 December 1849 by Peter Vines.]

49061RO: Mon 12 Nov 1849 – **William Tovey**, the younger, wife **Mary**, and two children, **William** aged fifteen, and **Charles** aged ten. [No examination included with removal order.]
1849: *removed to Woodchester (Stroud Union).* **1851:** *(RETURNED) WT (aged 44; labourer, born Boddington) lived in Exmouth St, Cheltenham with wife (Mary) Anne (50; born Hereford), and children William (16; born Charlton Kings) and Charles (11; scholar) (HO107/1973/839/22-3).* [PS/CH/RA/2/8:172. Notes: WT chargeable through sickness to Cheltenham Union; "William Tovey, his Wife & two children" delivered to Stroud Union Workhouse 14 Dec 1849 by Peter Vines.]

49062RO: Wed 14 Nov 1849 – **Benjamin Tustin**, and wife **Elizabeth**. [No examination included with removal order.]

1828: *BT removed to Painswick: see P244 OV 3/3/3/2/14.* **1841:** *(RETURNED) BT (aged 60; labourer) lived with wife Elizabeth (50) and daughter Elizabeth (15) in Francis St, Cheltenham (HO107/353/12/41/19).* **1844:** *removed to Painswick (renting): see* **44054SE** *(BT: 2 Nov 1844) (RETURNED).* **1849:** *removed to Painswick (Stroud Union).* **1851:** *(RETURNED) BT (57; pensioner, Light Dragoons) and wife Elizabeth (55; charwoman, both born Cheltenham) lived in Leighton's Cottages, 57 New St, Cheltenham (HO107/1973/670/3).* **1860:** *death of BT (buried at New Burial Ground, Cheltenham 9 Jan, aged 88).* **1861:** *widow Elizabeth (74; born Bristol) remained lodger in New St, Cheltenham (39) (RG9/1800/89/21).* [PS/CH/RA/2/8:173. Note: "Benjaman Tustin and Elizabeth his Wife" delivered to Stroud Union Workhouse 8 Dec 1849 by Peter Vines.]

49063RO: Mon 26 Nov 1849 – **Selina Baldwin**, single woman; also Stephen Baldwin, relating to the settlement of daughter, Selina Baldwin. [No examination included with removal order.]
1849: *SB admitted to Cheltenham Workhouse 19 Nov, suffering from syphilis (G/CH/60/6);* **removed to Minsterworth (father's presumed settlement).** **1851:** *(RETURNED) SB (aged 17; seamstress, born Gloucester) lodged at 3 Elm St, Cheltenham (HO107/1973/629/22).* [PS/CH/RA/2/8:174. Note: "Selena Baldwin" delivered to Minsterworth 3 Jan 1850 by Thomas Griffiths.]

49064RO: Thurs 29 Nov 1849 – **Mary McCarthy**, single woman, inmate of Cheltenham Workhouse. [No examination included with removal order.]
1849: *MM (17) admitted to Cheltenham Workhouse 23 Nov, suffering from syphilis (G/CH/60/5/6);* **removed to St Giles, Middlesex** *(St Andrew, Holborn above the Bars crossed out).* [PS/CH/RA/2/8:175.]

49065RO: Mon 3 Dec 1849 – William Niblett, relating to the settlement of **William Stratford**. [No examination included with removal order.]
1841: *the family lived in Hill Cottages, Leckhampton: John Stratford (aged 35; agricultural labourer), wife Ann (35), and children Thomas (13), John (10), Hannah (9), Emma (7), William (5), and Sarah (3) (HO107/353/18/51/6).* **1843:** *death of mother Ann (buried at Leckhampton 30 July, aged 37).* **1847:** *father died (buried at Cheltenham 15 Mar, aged 42); removed to Miserden (late father's apparent settlement): see* **47022RO** *(Hannah Williams for grandson WS: 5 June) (RETURNED).* **1849:** *removed to Miserden (presumed) (late father's settlement).* [PS/CH/RA/2/8:176. See **49023RO** (sisters Emma and Sarah Stratford: 26 Apr 1849).]

49066RO: 3 Dec 1849 – Jesse Castle, relating to the settlement of **Emma Price**, and three children, **Oliver** aged ten, **Martha** aged four, and **Thomas** aged two and a half. [No examination included with removal order.]
Husband James may be the James Price imprisoned in Staffs on various occasions in the late 1840s. **1848:** *EP and children ("destitute") entered Cheltenham Workhouse 16 May, where they stayed several times; removed to Stoke-on-Trent, Staffs: see* **48015RO** *(EP: 23 Oct) (RETURNED).* **1849:** *EP and (at least) Thomas inmates of Cheltenham Workhouse from 2 Dec 1849.* **1850:** *removed to Stoke-on-Trent, Staffs: 5 Jan (G/CH/60/6); birth of Caleb William registered at Stoke 1Q (baptised at Penkhull, Stoke 15 Sept).* **1851:** *EP (29; servant, married but without husband, born Stoke-on-Trent) was a pauper inmate of Spittals Workhouse, Stoke-on-Trent with four children Oliver (12), Martha (4), Thomas (2), and Caleb (1) (but without husband) (HO107/2006/283/8).* [PS/CH/RA/2/8:177.]

49067RO: Sat 8 Dec 1849 – **Harriet Dunn**. [No examination included with removal order.]
1849: *removed to St Nicholas, Gloucester.* **1861:** *order reviewed at subsequent examination at Cheltenham 21 May.* [PS/CH/RA/2/8:178. Note: "Harriett Dunn" delivered to Gloucester Union Workhouse 3 Jan 1850 by Thomas Griffiths.]

49068RO: Sat 15 Dec 1849 – **Henry Austin**, wife **Margaret**, and child, **Linda** aged about three years. [No examination included with removal order.]
1849: *removed to Farmington (Northleach Union): see* **51013RO** *(Margaret Lucy Austin: 17 July 1851) for further information on the family.* [PS/CH/RA/2/8:179. Notes: "Margaret Austin & Child" delivered to Northleach Union 18 Jan 1850; "Removed: The Man H[enr]y Austin Promised to meet her at the Northleach Union but did not. Thomas Griffiths.]

49069RO: Mon 17 Dec 1849 – **Thomas Spragg**, wife **Charlotte**, and two children, **Charles** aged about four, and **Joseph** aged about 18 months. [No examination included with removal order.]

1849: *removed to Norton.* **1851:** *TS (aged 36; agricultural labourer, born Stoke Orchard) lived in Norton Lane, Norton with wife Charlotte (37; agricultural labourer, born Boddington), and sons Charles (6; born Norton) and Joseph (3; born Birmingham, Warks (HO107/1961/81/2).* [PS/CH/RA/2/8:180. Note: "Thomas Spragg Wife & 2 Children" delivered to Norton 15 Jan 1850 by Thomas Griffiths.]

49070RO: Tues 18 Dec 1849 – **Elizabeth Pearce**, and illegitimate daughter **Matilda** aged six. [No examination included with removal order.]
1850: *removed to Eastington:* *15 Mar (G/CH/60/6).* [PS/CH/RA/2/8:181.]

49071RO: Sat 22 Dec 1849 – **Deborah Nicholls**, inmate of Cheltenham Workhouse, and two children, **Charles Samuel** aged two years and four months, and **George Thomas** aged seven weeks. [No examination included with removal order.]
1839: *apparent emigration of husband Charles Nicholls's parents and other siblings as free settlers to Sydney, New South Wales.* **1841:** *Charles Nicholls (aged 25) worked as footman in Avening Court, Avening (HO107/362/1/3/1); wife DN (20) lived with father Samuel Alder and family four miles away, in Horsley (HO107/362/4/45/6); the couple had a daughter, Martha, soon after examination, baptised at Avening, where Charles remained a servant.* **1843:** *Charles and family apparently removed to Horsley (father's settlement): see* **43051SE** *(Charles Nicholls: 13 July).* **1847:** *(RETURNED) son (Samuel) Charles Nicholls baptised at Cheltenham 8 Aug 1847, when family lived in Bath Rd.* **1849:** *son George Thomas born at Cheltenham; DN ("Deserted by Husband") admitted with two children to Cheltenham Workhouse 29 Nov.* **1850:** *removed to Horsley:* *6 Feb, apparently with daughter Maria and infant (G/CH/60/5/6).* **1851:** *(RETURNED) DN (aged 30; married, and monthly nurse, born Horsley) lived with son George (1; born Cheltenham) and "nurse child" John Sims (9 mo) at "Back of Mount Pleasant", Cheltenham (HO107/1973/168/21); husband Charles Nicholls (26; groom, born Stratton, Som) apparently lodged at "beer house" at 5 Mount Pleasant, Cheltenham (HO107/1973/166/16); other son Charles (3; born Cheltenham) lived in Horsley with mother's parents Samuel and Tryphena ("Fanny") Alder (HO107/1966/394/14).* [PS/CH/RA/2/8:182.]

49072RO: Mon 24 Dec 1849 – **Richard Slatter**. [No examination included with removal order.]
1849: *RS admitted to Cheltenham Workhouse 22 Dec.* **1850:** *removed to St Margaret, Westminster, Middlesex:* *16 Jan (G/CH/60/6).* [PS/CH/RA/2/8:183.]

1850

50001RO: Mon 14 Jan 1850 – **John Bevan Hoskins**, wife **Lydia**, and eight children, **Edwin Joseph** aged 13, **Lydia** aged 11, **Clara** aged nine, **Esther** aged seven, **Alice** aged five, **John** aged three, **Arthur James** aged two, and **Julia** aged about nine months; also Hester Hoskins, relating to the settlement of John Bevan Hoskins. [No examination included with removal order.]
1841: *JBH (aged 25; shoemaker) lived with wife Lydia (25; born Som) in Walcot, Bath, Som with children Edwin (6; baptised Bristol), Lydia (3; born 1Q Cheltenham), and Clara (10 months; born 3Q 1840 Bristol) (HO107/970/6/21/34).* **1850:** *removed to St James, Bristol; after removal the family apparently sailed for Australia and then New Zealand: daughter Julia apparently died en route to Australia in Feb.* **1853/4:** *by* **1851** *JBH was established as boot and shoemaker on Lambton Quay, Wellington, New Zealand (Wellington Independent, 26 April 1851).* [PS/CH/RA/2/8:184.]

50002RO: Sat 5 Jan 1850 – **John Dix**, wife **Ann**, and five children, **Margaret** aged about 15, **Rhoda** aged about 13, **Emma** aged about six, **James** aged about four, and **Ann** aged about three. [No examination included with removal order.]
1840: *family removed from Badgeworth to Dowdeswell.* **1850** *removed to Badgeworth (Cheltenham Union); delivered to Dowdeswell.* **1851:** *JD (aged 42; an agricultural labourer, [born Dowdeswell]) lived at Cold Comfort, Dowdeswell with wife Ann (37; farmer's work-woman, born Donnington), and children Adelaide (19, "at home", born Dowdeswell), Rhoda (11; born Northleach), Emma (9; born Dowdeswell, both scholars), James (6), and Ann (5; both born Charlton Kings) (HO107/1969/304/5* [PS/CH/RA/2/8:185; see also P31 OV/3/2/44 (Badgeworth). Note: "John Dix Wife & family" delivered to Dowdeswell [Cheltenham Union] 27 Jan 1850 by Thomas Griffiths.]

50003RO: Thurs 17 Jan 1850 – **Thomas Long**, and son **Thomas**, aged nine. [No examination included with removal order.]
1850: *removed to Randwick (Stroud Union).* **1851:** *(RETURNED) TL (aged 58; gardener and widower, born Frocester) lodged with son Thomas (10; scholar, born Leckhampton) in Upper Bath St, Cheltenham (HO107/1973/873/4).* [PS/CH/RA/2/8:186. Note: "Thomas Long & Son" removed to Stroud Union 9 Feb 1850 by Thomas Griffiths.]

50004RO: Thurs 24 Jan 1850 – **William Kennett** (also **Kennet**), and wife **Elizabeth**. [No examination included with removal order.]
1850: *removed to Ripple, Worcs.* **1851:** *(RETURNED) WK (aged 71; whitesmith, born Beckford) lived at Woodbine Cottage, Alstone, Cheltenham with wife Elizabeth (72; born Malvern, Worcs) (HO107/1973/957/1).* [PS/CH/RA/2/8:187. Note: "Wᵐ Kennett & Elizabeth his Wife" delivered to Ripple, Worcs 16 Feb 1850 by Thomas Griffiths.]

50005RO: Thurs 14 Feb 1850 – **William Bartlett**, wife **Caroline**, and illegitimate daughter **Sarah Ann**, aged about two years; also John Bartlett, relating to the settlement of William Bartlett. [No examination included with removal order.]
1850: *removed to Stanton St John, Oxon: see* **50024RO** *(WB: 13 July 1850) for further information on WB and family.* [PS/CH/RA/2/8:188.]

50006RO: 14 Feb 1850 – **Emanuel** (also **Emmanuel**) **Stephens**, wife **Eve**, and six children **Eve**, **Adam**, **Robert**, **Ruth**, **Georgiana**, and **Sampson**. [No examination included with removal order.]
1850: *removed to Chedworth.* **1861:** *several of children appear in "List of Persons not in Houses" at Leonard Stanley: Sam[p]son Smith (aged 21; unmarried, brazier and tinman, born Haddington, Bucks [elsewhere: Stroud]), Eva Smith (22; wife of horse-dealer Gilroy Smith, place of place not stated [elsewhere: Bristol]), Adam Stephens (24; brushmaker, place of birth not stated [elsewhere: Chedworth]) (RG9/1771/119/36).* **1871:** *Emanuel Stephens (71; tinman and brazier, born Coleford) lived with wife Eve (75; born Cold Ashton) and son Robert (29; hawker, born Farnham, Surrey) in Hay Lane, Stroud (RG10/2640/5/2* [PS/CH/RA/2/8:189. Note: "Emanuel Stephens Eve his wife & their children" delivered to Chedworth 9 Mar 1850 by Thomas Griffiths.]

50007RO: 14 Feb 1850 – **Sarah Longford**. [No examination included with removal order.]
1850: *removed to St Mary, Pembroke, Pemb.* [PS/CH/RA/2/8:190. Order No 191 previously cut out of register.]

50008RO: Wed 6 Mar 1850 – **Henry Bishop**; also John Bishop, relating to the settlement of Henry Bishop. [No examination included with removal order.]
1850: *removed to Tetbury.* [PS/CH/RA/2/8:192. Note: "Henry Bishop" delivered to Tetbury Good Friday, 29 Mar 1850 by Thomas Griffiths.]

50009RO: Sat 16 Mar 1850 – **Ann Loveday**. [No examination included with removal order.]
1848: *removed to Boddington (presumed) (husband's settlement): see* **48001RO** *(AL: 3 Jan) (RETURNED).*
1850: *removed to Boddington (Tewkesbury Union) (presumed) (husband's settlement).* **1851:** *(RETURNED) AL (aged 67; laundress, born "Count Ends", Oxon (error for Coln St Aldwyns, Glos?]) lived with daughter Ann Daves (28; born Boddington) and son-in-law Edward Daves (30; labourer) at 23 Union St, Cheltenham (HO107/1973/135/11).* **1858:** *AL apparently died at Cheltenham Union Workhouse, aged 73 (buried 10 Sept) (Cheltenham Chron. 14 Sept).* [PS/CH/RA/2/8:193. Note: "Ann Loveday"delivered to Tewkesbury Union 6 Apr 1850 by Thomas Griffiths. See **41036SE** (AL: 13 May 1841).]

50010RO: Tues 19 Mar 1850 – **Ann Neal**. [No examination included with removal order.]
1850: *AN ("houseless & destitute") admitted to Cheltenham Workhouse on 9 Jan; removed to Stinchcombe (Dursley Union).* [PS/CH/RA/2/8:194. Note: "Ann Neal" delivered to Dursley Union 24 Apr 1850 by Thomas Griffiths. See **50032RO** (Hannah Neale to Stinchcombe: 14 Nov 1850).]

50011RO: 19 Mar 1850 – **Joseph Freeman**, wife **Susan**, and daughters **Mary Ann** aged ten, and **Hannah** aged twelve. [No examination included with removal order.]
1850: *removed to Hailes (Winchcombe Union).* **1851:** *JF (aged 61; labourer and pauper, born Oddington) lived in Gloucester St, Winchcombe with wife Susan (57; born Winchcombe) and daughters Mary Ann (17; born Winchcombe) and Hannah (13; born Hailes, both agricultural labourers) (HO107/1971/102/39).* [PS/CH/RA/2/8:195. Note: "Joseph Freeman Susan his Wife & their two Children viz Mary Ann & Hannah" delivered to Winchcombe Union 11 Apr 1850 by Thomas Griffiths.]

50012RO: Mon 8 Apr 1850 – **Charles Deane** (also **Dean**). [No examination included with removal order.]
1850: *CD admitted to Cheltenham Workhouse 31 Mar (G/CH/60/5); removed to St Helen's, Abingdon, Berks.* **1851:** *(RETURNED) CD (aged 35; unmarried and "navigator", construction labourer, born Bucks) was an inmate of Cheltenham Workhouse (HO107/1973/1097/15).* [PS/CH/RA/2/8:196. Note: CD chargeable to Cheltenham through sickness.]

50013RO: Thurs 25 Apr 1850 – **Sarah Stevens**. [No examination included with removal order.]
1850: *removed to Bisley: see* **52001RO** *(26 Jan 52) for further information.* [PS/CH/RA/2/8:197. Note: "Sarah Stevens" delivered to Bisley 17 May 1850 by Thomas Griffiths.]

50014RO: Mon 29 Apr 1850 – **Mary Coles**, and illegitimate son aged seven weeks. [No examination included with removal order.]
1850: *removed to Ledbury, Heref. MC and son discharged from Cheltenham Workhouse 4 July for removal "to her Parish" (G/CH/60/5).* [PS/CH/RA/2/8:198.]

50015RO: Fri 17 May 1850 – **Robert Beal** (also **Bale**, **Beale**). [No examination included with removal order.]
1850: *removed to Bourton-on-the-Water.* **1851:** *(RETURNED) RB (aged 64; unmarried and sawyer, born Bourton-on-the-Water) lodged at 3 Gore's Cottages, Gloucester Rd, Cheltenham (HO107/1973/613/52).* **1857:** *RB buried at Bourton-on-the-Water 5 Oct, aged 70.* [PS/CH/RA/2/8:199. Note: "Robert Beal" delivered to Bourton-on-the-Water 8 June 1850 by Thomas Griffiths.]

50016RO: Sat 25 May 1850 – **Mary Ann Shurmer** (also **Shermer**), single woman; also John Shurmer, relating to the settlement of Mary Ann Shurmer. [No examination included with removal order.]

1850: *ordered to be removed to Upton St Leonards but probably died before removal; MAS died at Cheltenham Workhouse 17 July (buried 22 July, aged 25).* [PS/CH/RA/2/8:200.]

50017RO: Mon 27 May 1850 – **John Marshall** the younger; also John Marshall the elder, relating to the settlement of John Marshall the younger. [No examination included with removal order.]
1850: *removed to Upper Guiting (Winchcombe Union).* [PS/CH/RA/2/8:201. Note: "John Marshall" delivered to Winchcombe Union 24 June 1850 by Peter Vines. See **38031RO** (JM: 23 Apr).]

50018RO: 27 May 1850 – **William Bromage**. [No examination included with removal order.]
1846: *death of wife Sarah in Cheltenham (buried 30 July), aged 76.* **1850:** *removed to Uckington (Cheltenham Union); (RETURNED) WB admitted to Cheltenham Workhouse 20 July, and at other times until at least mid 1851 (G/CH/60/5).* **1851:** *WB (aged 64; widower and labourer, born Uckington) was an inmate of Cheltenham Union Workhouse.* [PS/CH/RA/2/8:202.]

50019RO: Thurs 6 June 1850 – **Daniel Hooper**, and wife **Maria**. [No examination included with removal order.]
1850: *removed to The Leigh.* **1851:** *(RETURNED) DH (aged 59; agricultural labourer, born Elmore) lived at 24 Sun St, Cheltenham with wife Maria (59; born The Leigh) and daughter Priscilla Woods and family (see **50021RO** Joseph Wood: 30 June 1850) (HO107/1973/483/26).* [PS/CH/RA/2/8:203. Note: "Daniel Hooper and Wife" delivered to the Leigh 29 June 1850 by Peter Vines.]

50020RO: Sat 8 June 1850 – **Mary Cale**, and illegitimate child **Edwin**; also Benjamin Cale, relating to the settlement of daughter Mary Cale. [No examination included with removal order.]
1850: *birth of son Edwin 8 Mar; removed to Much Marcle, Heref (Ledbury Union).* **1851:** *MC (aged 26; unmarried, born Much Marcle, Heref) was an inmate of Ledbury Union Workhouse with son Edwin (10 [error for 1] (HO107/1975/121/54).* **1852:** *son Edwin baptised privately at St Nicholas, Gloucester 6 Dec; MC married John Hook (then waterman) 13 June, at St Nicholas, Gloucester.* **1861:** *the family lived in Oak Yard, St Nicholas, Gloucester: John Hook (35; corn porter, born St Nicholas, Gloucester), Mary (39; porter's wife, born Much Marcle, Heref), Edwin (11; born Cheltenham), Joseph (8), Henry (6; all three scholars), and Robert (1; the last three born St Nicholas, Gloucester) (RG9/1765/16/25).* [PS/CH/RA/2/8:204. Note: "Mary Cale & Child" delivered to Ledbury Union 2 July 1850 by Thomas Griffiths.]

50021RO: Thurs 13 June 1850 – **Joseph Wood** (also **Woods**), wife **Priscilla**, and five children, **William** aged nearly nine, **Amelia** aged about six, **Thomas** aged about four, **Mary Ann** aged about two, and **John** aged about 11 months. [No examination included with removal order.]
1850: *removed to Overbury, Worcs.* **1851:** *(RETURNED) the family lived at the same address as Daniel Hooper (head of household) and wife Maria, 24 Sun St, Cheltenham (see **50019** Daniel Hooper 6 June 1850): JW (28; son-in-law, agricultural labourer, born Teddington); Priscilla (26; laundress) William (10; both born The Leigh), Amelia (8; born Hardwicke), Thomas (6; both scholars), Mary Ann (4), John (2; all three born Elmstone Hardwicke) (HO107/1973/483/26).* [PS/CH/RA/2/8:205. Notes: chargeable to Cheltenham through the sickness of William Wood; "the within Paupers" delivered to Teddington [with Overbury part of Tewkesbury Union] 8 July 1850 by Peter Vines.]

50022RO: Mon 24 June 1850 – **Thomas Holloway**; also Betsy White, relating to the settlement of Thomas Holloway. [No examination included with removal order.]
1850: *removed to Rye, Sussex.* [PS/CH/RA/2/8:206. See **50023RO** (Betsy White: 24 June 1850).]

50023RO: 24 June 1850 – **Betsy White**. [No examination included with removal order.]
1850: *removed to Rye, Sussex.* [PS/CH/RA/2/8:207. See **50022RO** (Thomas Holloway: 24 June 1850).]

50024RO: Sat 13 July 1850 – **William Bartlett**, wife **Caroline**, illegitimate child **Sarah Ann** aged nearly three, and lawful child **John** aged about five months. [No examination included with removal order.]
1847: *wife-to-be Caroline Darke (aged 30; single, ill health) admitted to Cheltenham Workhouse Nov with 4-month-old illegitimate daughter Sarah Ann.* **1848:** *CD removed to Twyning (late husband's presumed settlement): see **48008RO** (Caroline Darke: 7 Feb) (RETURNED).* **1848-9:** *CD and daughter removed to Tewkesbury 4 Mar, but admitted to Cheltenham Workhouse again in 1849 (G/CH/60/5/6) (RETURNED).* **1849:** *CD removed to Stoke Orchard (late husband's presumed settlement): see **49057RO** (Caroline Darke:*

20 Oct). **1850:** *(RETURNED) WB (29; labourer, living in Stanhope St, Cheltenham) married Caroline Darke (aged 33; widow, also of Stanhope St) in Cheltenham 20 Jan; son John born at Cheltenham Workhouse 24 Apr;* **1850:** *WB and family removed to Stanton St John, Oxon: see* **50005RO** *(WB: 14 Feb);* ***removed to Gt Milton, Oxon.*** **1851:** *the family lived in Gt Milton, Oxon: WB (aged 29; labourer, born Stanton St John, Oxon), Caroline (33; "at home", born Uckington), Caroline's daughter Sarah (3), and John (11 months; both born Cheltenham) (HO107/1726/40/30).* [PS/CH/RA/2/8:208.]

50025RO: Tues 30 July 1850 – **Ellen Double**. [No examination included with removal order.]
1850: ***removed to St Matthew, Ipswich, Suffolk.*** **1851:** *ED (24; born Middlesex, London) lived with husband John Double (31; baker, born Haulton, Essex [Haughton, Suffolk]) and children John (8), James (7; both scholars, born Ipswich), and Ann Elizabeth (3; born Cheltenham) in Colchester, Essex (HO107/1781/40/5).* **1863:** *John Double charged with bigamy: the unsettled relationship between husband and wife relates to John Double's long-standing affair with Jane Simmonds: the* Chelmsford Chron. *(11 Dec) states that "John Double, aged 46, was charged with inter-marrying with Jane Simmonds, his former wife Ellen, being still alive"; the* Essex Standard *(18 Dec) adds that John Double had four children with Ellen Double née Pearman, whom he married at Ipswich Mar 1842; after 10 years they separated, he taking the children; "he afterwards became acquainted with one Jane Simmonds". Whatever the chronology, John Double married Jane Simmonds bigamously at Westminster 1Q 1859, having had a daughter, Ellen, with Jane in 1852. In 1861 John Double (41; foreman baker, born Haughton, Suffolk) lived with wife Jane (31; born Bath) and daughter Ellen (9; born Colchester) at 38 Sussex Rd, Lambeth, Surrey (RG9/364/103/21).* [PS/CH/RA/2/8:209. Note: "Ellen Double" delivered to Ipswich, Suffolk on Monday 26 August 1850 by Peter Vines.]

50026RO: Mon 12 Aug 1850 – **John Pixton**. [No examination included with removal order.]
1850: ***removed to Northfield, Worcs.*** **1851:** *JP buried 18 Dec at Cheltenham, aged 68.* [PS/CH/RA/2/8:210.]

50027RO: Sat 24 Aug 1850 – **Harriett Dean**. [No examination included with removal order.]
1850: ***removed to How Caple, Heref.*** [PS/CH/RA/2/8:211.]

50028RO: Mon 26 Aug 1850 – **Elizabeth Wood**, and illegitimate child **William**, aged six weeks. [No examination included with removal order.]
1849: *EW admitted into Cheltenham Workhouse aged 22 with child Ellen 22 Apr; removed to Painswick: see* **50028RO** *(EW: 26 Aug). (RETURNED) death of Ellen at 5 months (buried at Cheltenham 4 Sept).* **1850:** *EW readmitted to Cheltenham Workhouse 14 July and William Wood born at Cheltenham Workhouse same day; (both discharged 30 Sept) (G/CH/60/6);* ***removed to Painswick (Stroud Union).*** **1851:** *EW (aged 34; unmarried, born Horsley) was an inmate of Stroud Union Workhouse with son William (8 months; born Cheltenham) (HO107/1965/298/9).* [PS/CH/RA/2/8:212.]

50029RO: Fri 11 Oct 1850 – **Mary Gill**, single woman. [No examination included with removal order.]
1849-50: *MG ("houseless & destitute") admitted to Cheltenham Workhouse 11 Oct (and again by June 1850) (G/CH/60/5/6).* **1850:** ***removed to Kilmington, Devon.*** **1851:** *MG (aged 41; unmarried, born Kilmington, Devon) lodged at 16 Hatherley St, Cheltenham HO107/1973/942/10).* [PS/CH/RA/2/8:213. Notes: MG chargeable to Cheltenham through sickness; "Mary Gill" delivered to Axminster Union, Devonshire 1 Nov[r] 1850 by Thomas Griffiths.]

50030RO: Sat 2 Nov 1850 – **Ann Simmons** (also **Simmonds**), and son **Thomas**, aged about eleven months. [No examination included with removal order.]
1849: *removed to Topsham, Devon (stated settlement) (appealed): see* **49006RO** *(husband Thomas Simmons: 16 Jan); removed to Shaugh, Devon (husband's settlement): see* **49033RO** *(husband Thomas Simmons: 5 July) (order subject to appeal at Quarter Sessions in Oct: see* Cheltenham Chron. *25 Oct, where original order was confirmed); by then husband Thomas Simmons had died, at 7 Malvern St, Cheltenham, aged 37, leading to need to prepare replacement order.* **1850:** *(RETURNED) son Thomas baptised at Cheltenham 27 Jan, when family lived in Malvern St and father described as paper-maker; Thomas admitted to Cheltenham Workhouse 2 Apr (G/CH/60/5);* ***removed to Shaugh, Devon (late husband's settlement).*** **1851:** *(RETURNED) Ann (35; charwoman, born Gt Barrington) lived at 5 Cleveland Passage, Tewkesbury Rd, Cheltenham, with daughter Sarah (12; also born Gt Barrington), and son Thomas (1) (HO107/1973/470/1).* [PS/CH/RA/2/8:214.]

50031RO: Thurs 7 Nov 1850 – **Mary Guy**, widow, and daughter **Jane Maria** aged about one year and eleven months. [No examination included with removal order.]
1839: baptism of daughter Jane Maria in Cheltenham 23 May, when family lived in Union St; husband Thomas (bricklayer) died at Cheltenham (buried 9 Nov, aged 34). **1850: *removed to Frampton-upon-Severn.* 1851:** *(RETURNED) MG (23; widow and laundress) lived at 4 Jersey St, Cheltenham with daughter Jane Maria (2; both born Cheltenham) (HO107/1973/139/18); death of Jane Guy (buried at Cheltenham, aged two years and 9 months, 2 Sept).* [PS/CH/RA/2/8:215. Note: "Mary Guy & her child Jane Maria" delivered to Frampton-upon-Severn 28 Nov 1850 by Thomas Griffiths.]

50032RO: Thurs 14 Nov 1850 – **Hannah Neale**. [No examination included with removal order.]
1850: *removed to Stinchcombe (Dursley Union).* 1851: *an HN (aged 21; servant, born Nympsfield) was visitor at house of Mary Pegler (70; pauper) in Nympsfield [Dursley Union] (HO107/1959/255/5).* [PS/CH/RA/2/8:216. See **50010RO** (Ann Neal to Stinchcombe: 19 Mar 1850).]

50033RO: Mon 25 Nov 1850 – **Esther Smart**, and seven children, **Alfred** aged fourteen years, **Edmund** aged twelve, **Henry** aged nine, **George** aged seven, **Emily** aged five, **Baynham** aged three, and **Sarah Ann** aged five months. [No examination included with removal order.]
1841: Henry Smart (aged 35; sheriff's officer) lived in Barton St, Gloucester with wife Esther (32), and children Emma (7), Alfred (4), Edmund (3), and Henry (1) (HO107/355/17/8/11). **1850: *removed to St Nicholas, Gloucester*:** *it is not clear what prevented ES from supporting herself and family Nov.* **1851:** *the family was reunited, at 11 Loveday St, Birmingham, Warks, though Henry is now "labourer": Henry Smart (44; labourer; all born Gloucester except last child)), Hester (42), Alfred (15; printer), Edmund Henry (14), George Henry (11), Henry (12; all three labourers), Emily (9), Baynham (4), and Sarah Ann (nine mo, born Cheltenham) (HO107/2057/353/4).* [PS/CH/RA/2/8:217.]

50034RO: Thurs 5 Dec 1850 – **Edward** (also **Edwin**) **Orchard**, wife **Sarah**, and daughter **Caroline**, aged three. [No examination included with removal order.]
1850: *removed to St James, Bristol.* 1851: *EO and wife Sarah were inmates of Stapleton (Bristol) Asylum for the Poor: EO (aged 36; married, pauper and cordwainer, born Bristol) (HO107/1955/448/6), and Sarah (30; married, pauper and cap-maker, born Bristol) (HO107/1955/449/8).* **1861:** *the family were reunited at 2 East St, St Paul's, Bristol: EO (42; shoemaker), Sarah (38), Caroline (18; both milliners), and John Cook (six mo; nurse-child) (RG9/1719/66/16).* [PS/CH/RA/2/8:218.]

50035RO: Tues 10 Dec 1850 – **Mary Ann Baker**. [No examination included with removal order.]
1850: *removed to Walcot, Bath, Som.* [PS/CH/RA/2/8:219.]

50036RO: Sat 21 Dec 1850 – **Richard Ashwin**, and wife **Ann**. [No examination included with removal order.]
1850: *removed to St John, Gloucester.* [PS/CH/RA/2/8:220.]

50037RO: Tues 24 Dec 1850 – **Edward Jones**, wife **Eliza**, and nine children, **William** aged seventeen, **Betsy** aged fifteen, **Charles** aged thirteen, **Emily** aged eleven, **James** aged nine, **Sarah** aged seven, **Mary Ann** aged four, **Thomas** aged two, and infant aged about seven days. [No examination included with removal order.]
1848-9: an EJ admitted to Cheltenham Workhouse 7 Sept 1848 and again 17 May 1849 (G/CH/60/6). **1850: *removed to Hanley Castle, Worcs.* 1851:** *(RETURNED) EJ (44; agricultural labourer, born Birlingham, Worcs) lived at 77 Stanhope St, Cheltenham with wife Eliza (40; born Ripple, Worcs), and children William (17; agricultural labourer, born Birlingham, Worcs), Elizabeth (15; servant out of place), Emily (11; at home), Sarah (9), James (6), Mary Ann (4; last four born Hanley, Worcs), Thomas (4; all four scholars), and Eliza (three mo) (HO107/1973/503/27).* **1861:** *most of family lived in Blockhouse, Worcs (RG9/2093/15/26).* [PS/CH/RA/2/8:221.]

50038RO: 24 Dec 1850 – **Ambrose Dance**, wife **Hannah**, and son **Daniel**, aged about [blank] years. [No examination included with removal order.]
1841: AD (aged 45; agricultural labourer) lived in Staverton with wife Hannah (40) and three children (HO107/354/27/7/9). **1844: *removed to Beckford (hiring and service)*:** *see **44061SE** (AD: 21 Dec) (RETURNED).* **1848: *removed to Beckford*:** *see **48016RO** (AD: 24 Dec 1850) (RETURNED).* **1850: *removed to Beckford (Winchcombe Union).* 1851:** *AD (54; agricultural labourer, born Grafton, Beckford)*

was an inmate of Winchcombe Union Workhouse (HO107/1971/111/57); (RETURNED) his family lived in Gloucester Rd, Cheltenham: Hannah Dance (54; laundress, born Cranham), Diana A. (25; "poor idiot"), James (18; agricultural labourer), and Daniel (15; agricultural labourer; children all born Staverton) (HO107/1973/954/35). **1860:** *AD died (age unspecified) at Winchcombe Union Workhouse (buried at Beckford 5 Mar).* [PS/CH/RA/2/8:222.]

50039RO: Thurs 26 Dec 1850 – **Ann Patterson** (also **Paterson**), single woman, and illegitimate daughter **Sarah Ann**, aged two. [No examination included with removal order.]
1841: *AP (aged 11) was an inmate of Tewkesbury Union Workhouse (HO107/380/7/39/4).* **1849:** *AP admitted ("houseless & destitute" to Cheltenham Workhouse 2 Feb; removed to Tewkesbury: see* **49012RO** *(AP: 3 Feb); (RETURNED) AP re-admitted to Cheltenham Workhouse 2 July, aged 20 (G/CH/60/5).* **1850:** ***removed to Tewkesbury.*** **1851:** *birth of daughter at Cheltenham Union Workhouse 14 Jan, while she and daughter Sarah Ann were inmates (G/CH/60/6).* **1862:** *Sarah Ann imprisoned Aug for stealing money and other articles: her record of conviction at Gloucester Gaol states that her mother Ann was then "a charwoman at Cheltenham".* [PS/CH/RA/2/8:223.]

THE QUEEN V. SUSAN BARNETT. – Susan Barnett, the young woman who was tried on Tuesday last on a charge of murdering her infant, but convicted of manslaughter only, was this day brought up to receive judgment. It will be recollected that the body of the child, five weeks old, was found naked in a "carrier" running from a brook near Harford Bridge, on the road from Stow-on-the-Wold to Cheltenham.

Mr. Russell Gurney said, the only doubt in the case was as to whether the prisoner had not wilfully murdered the child. The jury, however, had taken a humane view of the case, and found her guilty of manslaughter only; still the crime of which she had been found guilty, that of recklessly abandoning her infant, which she had nursed for five weeks, so nearly approached that of murder that he (Mr. Gurney) was bound to pass upon her a severe sentence, which was that she be transported for the term of 20 years.

(*Cheltenham Chronicle,* 13 Apr 1854)

---

*In 1854, young Susan(nah) Barnett was convicted of the manslaughter of her infant son Alfred. She was sentenced to transportation for twenty years, and in the end served her sentence in England, was released on licence, married, and had a family. Three years before the death of her son, she had faced the magistrates in Cheltenham at a settlement examination (**51018RO**) in Cheltenham. The magistrates had removed her to her home village of Clapton, near Stow-on-the-Wold.*

1851

51001RO: Thurs 23 Jan 1851 – **Sarah Miller**, single woman. [No examination included with removal order.]
1850: *SM (aged 29) admitted to Cheltenham Workhouse 16 Dec (G/CH/60/5).* **1851:** *removed to St Marylebone, Middlesex: 9 Mar (G/CH/60/5).* [PS/CH/RA/2/8:224.]

51002RO: 25 Jan 1851 – **Mary Ann Jones**, single woman, and illegitimate son **Joseph**, aged 12; also Margaret Livesey, relating to the settlement of Mary Ann Jones. [No examination included with removal order.]
1851: *removed to Cirencester; on census night (30 Mar) MAJ (aged 31; labourer) was an inmate of Cirencester Union Workhouse, with son Joseph (12; scholar; both born Cirencester).* [PS/CH/RA/2/8:225.]

51003RO: Thurs 30 Jan 1851 – **Mary Hall,** wife of Robert Hall, in-pensioner at Greenwich Hospital in Kent, and two children **Joseph** and **Albert**. [No examination included with removal order.]
1851: *removed to Cirencester; (30 Mar) MH (aged 53; married, born Newbury, Berks) was visitor at West Mills, Newbury with younger son, Albert (9; scholar, born Reading) (HO107/1685/36/37); husband visiting nearby in Newbury, with other son, Joseph: Robert Hall (60; married, Greenwich Hospital, born Newbury, and blind), Joseph Hall (16; agricultural labourer, born Reading) (HO107/1685/222/1).* **1853:** *death of MH on 22 Jan at West Mills, Newbury, aged 55.* **1861:** *younger son, Albert (18) was whitesmith living in West Mills, Newbury (RG9/720/58/12).* **1865:** *Joseph Hall married Mary Ann Compton 16 Apr at St Mary's, Portsea, Hants.* **1871:** *his family lived at 11 Hobbs Court, Portsea, Hants: Joseph Hall (36; drayman, born Reading), Mary Ann (38; plain needlewoman, born Titchfield, Hants), Mary Alice (5), Joseph Albert (2; both scholars), and Charles Robert (four mo; all three born Portsea, Hants).* [PS/CH/RA/2/8:226. Notes: MH chargeable to Cheltenham through sickness; "the within named Paupers" delivered to Newbury[?] 22 Feb 1851 by Peter Vines.]

51004RO: 30 Jan 1851 – **Sarah Mason**, single woman, and four children **Elizabeth**, **George**, **Alfred**, and **Emil**y. [No examination included with removal order.]
1851: *removed to Bisley (Stroud Union); (30 Mar) SM (aged 40; servant, born like children at Chalford) was a pauper inmate of Stroud Workhouse, with George (7), Alfred (5), Emily (2), and Mary (one mo) (HO107/1965/297/7); eldest daughter presumably the Elizabeth Mason (15; house servant, born Bisley) who lived and worked at 3 Providence Terrace, Cheltenham (HO107/1973/900/59).* **1861:** *the family lived in Chalford Hill, Bisley: SM (49; charwoman living as widow), Elizabeth (23), Alfred (14; all three born Bisley), Emily (12), Mary (100, all four silk-workers, Emily and Mary born Cheltenham), Henry (6; a scholar, born Gloucester) (RG9/1773/94/7).* [PS/CH/RA/2/8:227.]

51005RO: Fri 31 Jan 1851 – **George Monk**. [No examination included with removal order.]
1851: *removed to Farmington (Northleach Union); GM discharged from Cheltenham Workhouse 6 Mar (G/CH/60/5); (30 Mar) GM (aged 42; unmarried, born Aldsworth) was a pauper inmate of Northleach Workhouse at Eastington (HO107/1969/132/16).* **1863:** *death of GM at Northleach Union Workhouse (buried at Farmington, aged 60, 9 Dec).* [PS/CH/RA/2/8:228. Note: GM chargeable to Cheltenham through sickness.]

51006RO: Tues 18 Feb 1851 – **Ann Milbourne** (also **Milbourn**, **Millbourne**), and illegitimate daughter **Emily**, aged about five months. [No examination included with removal order.]
1851: *AM admitted with daughter Emily to Cheltenham Workhouse 13 Jan (G/CH/60/5);* **removed to Blockley, Worcs;** *AM and daughter lived with widowed mother and family in Blockley: Mary Milbourne (aged 45; widow and agricultural labourer, born Blockley), Ann (20; servant, born Chipping Campden), George (17; agricultural labourer), Emma (14), Lucilla (12; both "Operative Silk Throwster"), Eliza (7; scholar), and Emily (6 mo; grand-daughter; last five born Blockley, Worcs) (HO107/2076/213/3).* **1852:** *death of daughter Emily at Blockley (buried 7 Oct, aged 2).* [PS/CH/RA/2/8:229.]

51007RO: Tues 25 Feb 1851 – **Elizabeth Welch**, widow, and two children, **Jane** about ten, and **Caroline** about four. [No examination included with removal order.]
1851: *removed to Tibberton.* [PS/CH/RA/2/8:230. See **51012RO** (Jane Welch: 26 June).]

51008RO: Sat 1 Mar 1851 – **Elizabeth Tovey**, single woman. [No examination included with removal order.]

1851: *ET was pregnant when admitted to Cheltenham Workhouse 27 Feb (G/CH/60/5);* **removed to Woodchester (Stroud Union);** *(30 Mar) ET (aged 30; unmarried and servant, born Rodborough) was a pauper inmate of Stroud Union Workhouse with daughter Ann (five days) (HO107/1965/301/14).* **1852:** *(RETURNED) death of daughter Ann in Cheltenham (buried 6 Feb, aged ten months).* **1854:** *death of ET (laundress, living in Sherborne St) in Cheltenham (buried 16 Aug, aged 36).* [PS/CH/RA/2/8:231. Note: "Elizabeth Tovey" delivered to Woodchester 25 Mar 1851 by Peter Vines.]

51009RO: Mon 24 Mar 1851 – **Thomas Heming** (also **Hemming**). [No examination included with removal order.]

1851: *removed to Pershore, Worcs (presumably appealed): see* **51011RO** *(TH: 17 Apr 1851).* [PS/CH/RA/2/8:232.]

51010RO: Sat 29 Mar 1851 – **Ann Howells** (also **Howell**). [No examination included with removal order.]

1851: *removed to Peterchurch, Heref; (30 Mar) one day after examination AH (aged 39; laundress, born Cheltenham) was a pauper inmate of Cheltenham Union Workhouse (HO107/1973/1100/21).* [PS/CH/RA/2/8:233. Notes: AH chargeable to Cheltenham through sickness; "the within named Pauper" delivered to Peterchurch, Heref 27 June 1851 by Peter Vines.]

51011RO: Thurs 17 Apr 1851 – **Thomas Heming** (also **Hemming**). [No examination included with removal order.]

1851: *ordered to be removed to Pershore, Worcs (presumably appealed): see* **51009RO** *(TH: 24 Mar 1851); (30 Mar) TH (aged 55; unmarried and stableman, born Charlton Kings) was a pauper inmate of Cheltenham Workhouse (HO107/1973/1101/22);* **removed to St Andrew, Pershore, Worcs.** **1861:** *(perhaps (RETURNED) perhaps the Thomas Hemming (64; unmarried, sale porter, born Cheltenham) who lived with niece Maria Mason at 17 Portland St, Cheltenham (RG9/1798/81/7).* **1874:** *death of that Thomas Hemming, aged 78 (porter), at 22 Sidney St, Cheltenham (buried 14 Mar).* [PS/CH/RA/2/8:234.]

51012RO: Mon 26 June 1851 – **Jane Welch**, aged about ten, and **Caroline Welch**, aged about four; also Thomas Boodle, magistrate's office, relating to the settlement of Jane and Caroline Welch. [No examination included with removal order.]

1851: *removed to Tibberton.* [PS/CH/RA/2/8:235. The circumstances under which new removal order required for children are unclear: see **51007RO** (Elizabeth Welch: 25 Feb 1851).]

51013RO: Thurs 17 July 1851 – **Margaret Lucy Austin**, and daughter **Linda** aged about five. [No examination included with removal order.]

1849: *removed to Farmington: see* **49068RO** *(Henry Austin: 15 Dec).* **1851:** *(RETURNED) MLA (aged 25; servant) lodged with daughter "E. Austin" (6; scholar, both born "England") at house of Robert Davis, groom, in St Paul's St, Cheltenham (HO107/1973/397/27);* **removed to Farmington.** **1857:** *MLA and daughter admitted to St Pancras Workhouse (Middlesex) 4 Aug: Lucy Austin (31) and Linda (10; both no place of residence, servant, referred by police); death of MLA at St Pancras Workhouse (Ward 27) Nov (buried at St Pancras Parish Chapel 12 Nov); Linda Austin subsequently discharged from workhouse "to Forest Gate" 12 Dec.* [PS/CH/RA/2/8:236.]

51014RO: Tues 5 Aug 1851 – **Honora Greening**. [No examination included with removal order.]

1851: *Honora Ryan married Private Charles Greening (60th King's Royal Rifle Regiment, born Cheltenham c1817) in Thurles, Co. Tipperary 31 Jan; Charles's regiment then left for Cape of Good Hope, where he received medal during 3rd Xhosa/Kaffir War 1850-3; HG pregnant during examination;* **removed to Boddington (Tewkesbury Union).** **1852:** *son Charles baptised 4 Mar, when HG resided at Tewkesbury Union Workhouse; son Charles died at Union Workhouse (buried 24 Apr, aged three months).* **1857:** *husband returned from South Africa, having received serious eye injury July 1856, which (despite several earlier convictions for desertion) resulted in him being admitted as pensioner to Royal Hospital at Greenwich, Kent.* [PS/CH/RA/2/8:237. See **37044RO** (father-in-law John Greeening 13 July 1837).]

51015RO: Tues 26 Aug 1851 – **Job Ring**; also Sarah Harwood, relating to the settlement of Job Ring. [No examination included with removal order.]
1851: *removed to Holton, Oxon.* [PS/CH/RA/2/8:238.]

51016RO: Thurs 11 Sept 1851 – **Hannah Payne**. [No examination included with removal order.]
1851: *(30 Mar) HP (aged 66; unmarried and servant of all work, born Oaksey, Wilts) lived at 52 St George's St, Cheltenham (HO107/1973/392/17); removed to Chippenham, Wilts.* **1861:** *HP lived in London Rd, Chippenham, Wilts: Hannah Payne (70; unmarried, and lodging-house keeper, born Oaksey, Wilts) (RG9/1283/109/22).* [PS/CH/RA/2/8:239.]

51017RO: Sat 13 Dec 1851 – **Mary Ann Tinson** (also **Tinsey**). [No examination included with removal order.]
1851: *(30 Mar) MAT (aged 19) lived at Cumberland House, lodging-house on Grove St, Cheltenham, with sister Charlotte (21; both unmarried, of "no business) and Charlotte's daughter Jane (1; all born Lower Guiting) (HO107/1973/633/31); removed to Lower Guiting (Winchcombe Union).* **1853:** *death of MAT (baptised and buried as "Tinsey") "in [the] "Union" at Winchcombe" (buried at Guiting Power 22 July).* [PS/CH/RA/2/8:240.]

51018RO: 13 Dec 1851 – **Susannah** (also **Susan**) **Barnett**. [No examination included with removal order.]
1851: *removed to Clapton (Stow-on-the-Wold Union).* **1854:** *SB charged at Gloucester Assizes with murder of five-month-old son Henry Albert Barnett, born at Stow Workhouse and found by labourer beside brook on Cheltenham Rd from Stow; SB found guilty of manslaughter (not murder) and sentenced to twenty years' transportation* (Cheltenham Chron. *9 Mar, 13 Apr, etc: see also Michael Halsted's* Cheltenham Book of Days *(2012; entry for 11 Feb); SB not transported, but served sentence in England, eventually at Fulham Refuge, a women's prison then under enlightened management, which prepared girls and women for re-entry into society on release: "S. B." (33; prisoner 626, unmarried, servant, born "Coapham, Gloucestershire") (RG9/29/118/4).* **1862:** *SB's licence to go "at large" signed 31 Mar; SB married Joseph Werrett (also Wherrek) 3Q, with whom she had several children, one named after first child, Henry Albert Werrett.* **1871:** *the family lived in Staverton: Joseph Werrett (aged 30; agricultural labourer, born Boddington), Susannah (41, born Clapham), Elizabeth (7; a scholar, born Staverton), and Henry Albert (5; born Cheltenham) (RG10/2662/52/10).* [PS/CH/RA/2/8:[241].]

51019RO: Sat 6 Dec 1851 – **Henry Bennett**, wife **Mary (Jane)**, and child **Elizabeth** aged about two. [No examination included with removal order.]
1846: *removed to Stow-on-the-Wold (father's settlement): see* **46030RO** *(HB: 13 June); death of son Henry, aged three months (buried at New Burial Ground, Cheltenham 21 Aug).* **1849:** *(RETURNED) baptism of daughter Elizabeth at Cheltenham 25 Dec, when family lived in Stanhope St.* **1851:** *(30 Mar) HB (aged 26; agricultural labourer, born Stow) lived at 70 Stanhope St, Cheltenham, with wife Mary Jane (25), and daughter Elizabeth (1; both born Cheltenham) (HO107/1973/503/26); removed to Stow-on-the-Wold.* **1852:** *death of HB at Lower Swell, aged 27 (buried 18 Apr at Stow-on-the-Wold).* **1853:** *(RETURNED) widow Mary Jane remarried in Cheltenham 20 Nov, to John Faulkner (sawyer, both of 32 St James St).* **1861:** *the family lived at 66 Queen St, Cheltenham: John Faulkner (53; timber sawyer), Mary (38), Elizabeth Bennett (12; scholar), and Ann Faulkner (John's mother, 73; widow, all four born Cheltenham) (RG9/1799/139/18).* [PS/CH/RA/2/8:[242]. Note: HB chargeable to Cheltenham on account of sickness. See **44004SE** (father John Bennett: 11 Jan 1844) for further information on HB and family.]

51020RO: Sat 27 Dec 1851 – **Lucy Hirons**, and four children, **William** aged about four, **James** aged about three, **Joseph** aged about one, and **Thomas** aged about ten weeks. [No examination included with removal order.]
1851: *removed to Rugby, Warks: see* **52004RO** *(LH: 4 Mar 1852) for further information.* [PS/CH/RA/2/8:[243]. Note: "This order was on the 4th. March 1852 abandoned & the Pauper removed to Stretton Fields".]

1852

52001RO: Mon 26 Jan 1852 – **Sarah Stevens**. [No examination included with removal order.]
1837: *husband James buried at St Mary's, Cheltenham 13 Feb, aged 69; SS removed to Bisley:* **37015RO** *(2 Mar 1837) (RETURNED).* **1845:** *SS removed to Bisley: see* **45035SE** *(SS/William Cole: 25 June 1845) (RETURNED).* **1850:** *SS removed to Bisley: see* **50013RO** *(SS: 25 Apr 1850) (RETURNED).* **1852: *removed to Bisley (Stroud Union).*** **1860:** *perhaps the Sarah Stevens who died at Stroud Workhouse (buried at Bisley, aged 81, 16 Feb).* [PS/CH/RA/2/8:[244]. See **34039SE** (James Stevens: 10 June 1834).]

52002RO: 26 Jan 1852 – **James Strange**, wife **Elizabeth**, and five children **Rhoda Ann** aged ten, **George** aged seven, **Charles** aged three, **Eliza** aged two, and **Henry** aged five months. [No examination included with removal order.]
1841: *JS (aged 20; agricultural labourer) lived with wife Elizabeth (20) at home of parents Daniel Strange (60; agricultural labourer) and Maria (60) at Poole Keynes, Wilts (HO107/1181/30/6/5).* **1845:** *removed to Poole Keynes, Wilts (father's settlement): see* **45012SE** *(JS: 20 Feb 1845); son George baptised at Poole Keynes 13 Apr.* **1848:** *(RETURNED) son Charles baptised 2 Feb, when family lived at 4 Andover Retreat, Cheltenham.* **1851:** *JS (32; no occupation given, born Poole Keynes, Wilts) lived with wife Elizabeth (31; born Cirencester) and children Rhoda (9; born Poole Keynes), George (6), Charles (3; both born Cheltenham), and Eliza (1; born Cirencester) in Andover Retreat, Cheltenham (HO107/1973/932/52).* **1852: *removed to Poole Keynes, Wilts (father's settlement).*** **1853:** *(RETURNED) son James baptised at Cheltenham 18 Sept.* **1861:** *the family lived at 9 Francis St, Cheltenham: JS (42; plasterer, born Poole, Wilts), Elizabeth (41; dressmaker, born Cirencester), George (16; brickmaker), Charles (12; both born Cheltenham), Eliza (11; born Cirencester), James (6; born Cheltenham), Henry B. (3; all four scholars), Alfred W. (ten mo; last three born Cheltenham) (RG9/1803/60/26).* [PS/CH/RA/2/8:[245].]

52003RO: Fri 6 Feb 1852 – **Hannah Scott**, single woman, and three illegitimate children, **John** aged four and a half, **Mary** aged two, and **Eliza** aged four months. [No examination included with removal order.]
1852: *removed to Bradford-on-Avon, Wilts.* [PS/CH/RA/2/8:[246].]

52004RO: Thurs 4 Mar 1852 – **Lucy Hirons**, and four children, **William** aged about four, **James** aged about three, **Joseph** aged about one year and nine months, and **Thomas** aged about four months; also Martha Hirons, relating to the settlement of daughter-in-law Lucy Hirons. [No examination included with removal order.]
1851: *James Hirons (aged 30; waiter, born Rugby, Warks) lived with wife Lucy (30; born Minchinhampton), and children William (3), James (1), and Joseph (11 months; all born Cheltenham) at 9 Lypiatt St, Cheltenham (HO107/1973/938/3); James may have deserted family later in year (no deaths registered, though possible later marriages: see also RG9/1315/17/34 Fisherton Anger, Salisbury, Wilts in 1861), leading to LH's inability to support herself and children.* **1852: *removed to Stretton Fields, Warks.*** **1860:** *(RETURNED) LH (widow, of Hatherley St, Cheltenham) married labourer Thomas Lewis in Cheltenham 14 May.* **1861:** *the family lived at 1 Hatherley Cottage, Cheltenham: Thomas Lewis (33; labourer, born Malmesbury, Wilts), Lucy (41; cook), and her children James (12), Joseph (11), and Thomas (9; all three scholars, born Cheltenham) (RG9/1802/77/38).* [PS/CH/RA/2/8:[247]. See **51020RO** (LH: 27 Dec 1851).]

52005RO: Wed 28 Apr 1852 – **Emily Harding**. [No examination included with removal order.]
1831: *EH baptised at St Mary de Lode, Gloucester 6 Feb, illegitimate daughter of Emma Harding (servant, living in Wootton St Mary, Gloucester).* **1852: *removed to St Mary de Lode, Gloucester.*** [PS/CH/RA/2/8:[248].]

52006RO: Thurs 20 May 1852 – **Sarah Baylis**. [No examination included with removal order.]
1850: *an SB discharged from Cheltenham Workhouse 11 Dec (G/CH/60/5).* **1852: *removed to Dilling* [*prob. = Dilwyn*]*, Heref.*** [PS/CH/RA/2/8:[249].]

52007RO: Sat 19 June 1852 – **Theophilus Lewis**, and son **George**, aged about 12; also James Lewis, relating to the settlement of Theophilus Lewis. [No examination included with removal order.]
1841: *TL (aged 28; journeyman maltster [baptised Eardisley, Heref]) lived in Corpus St, Cheltenham with wife Elizabeth (20), and children Amelia (5) and George (1).* **1850:** *wife Elizabeth died at 44 Queen Street, Cheltenham on 18 Oct, aged 44 (buried 22 Oct).* **1852:** *removed to Eardisley, Heref.* [PS/CH/RA/2/8:[250].]

[Illustration over]
*The Removal Order for Lucy Hirons (**52004RO**). She had been living with her husband James in Lypiatt Street, Cheltenham in 1851, but the following year she and and her four children were left destitute (probably through desertion) and removed to Rugby, her husband's place of birth. But Rugby would not accept her, and she and her children were sent back to Cheltenham, whose authorities then removed them to Stretton Fields, Warks in March 1852. This Removal Order shows the reduced form, not including a transcript of the settlement examination, in use from October 1848.*

G. E. WILLIAMS,
Public Office, Cheltenham,
Clerk to the Justices.

County of Gloucester, to wit. To the Churchwardens and Overseers of the Poor of the Parish of Cheltenham, in the County of Gloucester, and to the Churchwardens and Overseers of the Parish of or Township of *Stretton fields* in the County of *Warwick* and to each of them.

Whereas, Complaint hath been made, by the Churchwardens and Overseers of the Poor of the Parish of Cheltenham aforesaid, unto us, whose names are hereunder set and seals affixed, being two of Her Majesty's Justices of the Peace, acting in and for the said County of Gloucester, one of us being of the Quorum, and acting together in Petty session at Cheltenham aforesaid, that *Lucy Hivons and her four Children namely William aged about four years James aged about three years Joseph aged about one year and nine months and Thomas aged about four months*

have ~~hath~~ come to inhabit and now are inhabiting in the said Parish of Cheltenham, without having gained any legal Settlement there, and without having produced a Certificate of Settlement elsewhere. And further, that the said *Lucy Hivons and her said Children* have ~~hath~~ become, and now is, actually chargeable to the said Parish of Cheltenham. Now we, the said Justices, upon due proof thereof, and upon examination of witnesses upon oath, do hereby adjudge the premises to be severally true ; and we do likewise adjudge, as well upon examination upon oath *of Martha Hivons* as otherwise that the last legal Settlement of the said *Lucy Hivons and her said Children* is in the Parish of Township of *Stretton fields* in the County of *Warwick*

THESE are therefore to require you, the said Churchwardens and Overseers of the Poor of the said Parish of Cheltenham, in Her Majesty's name, forthwith to send unto the Churchwardens and Overseers of the said Parish of or *Township of Stretton fields* a notice, in writing, stating that the said *Lucy Hivons and her said Children* are so chargeable as aforesaid, together with a copy or counterpart of this Order, and to require you to remove and convey the said *Lucy Hivons and her said Children* from and out of the said Parish of Cheltenham unto the said Parish of or *Township of Stretton fields* , and there deliver, together with this our order, or a true copy thereof, unto the Churchwardens and Overseers, or one of them, of the Poor of the said Parish of or *Township of Stretton fields* according to law. And the said Churchwardens or Overseers of the Poor of the said Parish of *Township of Stretton fields* are hereby required to receive and provide for the said *Lucy Hivons and her said Children* according to law

Given under our hands and seals this *fourth* day of *March* in the year of our Lord, one thousand eight hundred and *fifty two*

INDEX OF PEOPLE

Bold page numbers are used to indicate examinants and dependants included in settlement examinations. Other people (principally relations, employers and landlords) have non-bold page numbers. An indexed name may appear more than once on the indicated page or in the relevant entry.

Tarlton, Charles l, **85;** Elizabeth **85**; Mary 85

Taylor, Agnes 66; Charles 241; Francis 335; Hannah 207; John 66; Margaret 241; Mary 66; Mr 213; Sarah 84, **241**, 335; Sarah Ann 242; Thomas 29; William **66**, 241, 335

Teakle (also Takel, Teacle, Teakkel), Ann, Charles, Edward, Elizabeth **285**; Ellen 285; James, Sophia, Thomas **285**

Teal(e), Teil: see Tale

Tennant, David 194

Tew, Hannah **385**; Joseph **385**, 386

Thackwell, Charlotte **386**; George 386

Thayer, Sarah 156

Theyer, Daniel 141, 220

Thomas, David **193, 194**; Grace **105**, 118; Henry **193, 194**; Isabella **105**, **118**; Jacob 97; James 105, 118; John 63, 118; Joseph, Josiah 218; Maria 187; Mary 106, **193, 194**; Mary Ann 218; Sarah **193, 194**

Thompson, Edward 340; Henry 162, 173; Judith 162; Pearson 173

Thornton, Colonel 99; James 385; Miss 126; Rachel **385**; William **140**

Thurston, Frances**,** Thomas **196**

Tibbs, Mr 63

Tiley, Ruth 347

Tilley, Mary Ann 119

Timbrell, Mr 115, 178

Tincombe, Jane 76

Tinkler, Elizabeth **198**

Tinsey: see Tinson

Tinson (also Tinsey), Charlotte, Jane 403; Mary Ann **403**

Tipper, Abraham 309; Elizabeth 226; James 309; Jane **308**; Richard, Thomas **226**

Tippetts, Mrs 37

Tipton, Elizabeth, Thomas 62

Tocknell, Mary 162

Togwell, William 253

Toleman, Benjamin **88**

Tombs, Hannah **91**; John 91; Mr 233; Neighbour 377; Richard 91

Tomlin, James **214**

Tottle, James 33, 65

Tovey, Ann 402; Charles 392; Elizabeth **402**; Mary **392**; William 326, **392**

Townsend, Ann 201; Charles 106, **201**; Elizabeth **40**; Emanuel 40; George **209**; George 36, **72, 370;** Henry **27**; Jacob **209**; Jacob **72**, 370; Jane **72**, **209**, **370**; Louisa 135; Lucy 27; Mr 75; Mrs 196; Richard **33**; Robert 201; Sarah **209**, **370**; Thomas **72**

Trew (also Treu, True), Charles 224; Elizabeth, Harriet **223**; Jane **382**; Mary Ann 224; Sarah **223**; Thomas William 382; William **223**, 224

Trigg, Elizabeth, Ellen **29**; Jemima 29; Mary, Mary Ann, Thomas **29**

Trinder, Henry Green 163; John 294;Mr 37; Priscilla **294**, **319**

Trotman, John 41

Troughton (also Troutton), John **300**; Margaret 188; Mary, Sarah **300**

True: see Trew

Tucker, Elizabeth 240; John 375; Major 58; Miss 176; Mrs 58; Samuel 87

Turk, Elizabeth **255**; George 256; Jane, Matilda, Susannah, Thomas 255; William 272

Turnberrow, Mr 225

Turner, Ann **57**, 366; Charlotte 144; David 238; Edward 376; Eliza xlix, **55**; Evan 11; George **57**; Mary 145, **238**, **376**, 376; Mrs 11; Priscilla **144**; Richard 344; Samuel 145; William **57**

Tustin, Benjamin **302**, **392**; Elizabeth **302**, **392, 393**; George 36; Grace 302; Jane **36**; Jonathan 302; Lydia 390; William 302

Twining (also Twyning), Esther 96; Job **65**, **96**; Samuel 96

Tyler, Caroline, John 129; Sophia, Thomas **129**

Tysoe, Charles 341

UNDERDOWN, Mr 65

Underwood, Charles 284, **340**, 375; George **340**, 375; James Joseph, Louisa **284**; Maria **340**, **375**; Mary Ann **284**; Rosina **340**, 375; Thomas 284; William **284**

Ursell, Charlotte, John **211**

VAISEY (also Vasey, Veisy, Vesey), Rufus 297; Thomas **291**, **296**; William 297

Vandeleur, Misses 27

Vasey: see Vaisey

Vaughan (also Vaughn), Alfred 378; Charles **378**; Elizabeth 378; Mary Ann **378**; Rosina 378; Thomas 158

Veisy: see Vaisey

Verrier, Charlotte, Elizabeth, George, John Lovadon**,** Joseph, Livinia, Rachael **208**

Verrinder, William 90

Vesey: see Vaisey

Vicary, William 208

Vickers, Christian, John 96; Sarah 169

Vincent, Ann, Henry **267**; Maria **386**

INDEX OF PLACES

Places are in Gloucestershire unless otherwise stated: in cases of ambiguity "Glos" may be added. The page numbers of parishes to which paupers were removed (or were perhaps removed) after their settlement examination in Cheltenham are marked in **bold**. Streets are indexed, but not individual street numbers. County abbreviations denote historical counties, not necessarily present-day ones. A place-name indexed here may appear more than once on the indicated page or in the relevant entry.

INDEX OF OCCUPATIONS

The very frequent terms "labourer" and "servant" are not indexed unless qualified by another word.

INDEX OF SELECTED TOPICS